AutoCAD's Entity Association Sublists (Rel...

(ENTITIES IN THE UNDERLYING DATABASE)

ADDITIONAL GROUP CODES FOR INDIVIDUAL ENTITY SUBLISTS ARE AS FOLLO...

7	.	Text Style Name
10	.	Text Starting point
11	.	Text Insertion Point (if not left-justified)
40	.	Text Height
41	.	Scale Factor
50	.	Text Rotation (in radians)
51	.	Obliquing Angle (in radians)
70	.	Text Flag (1 = invisible, 2 = constant, 4 = verify, 8 = preset)
71	.	Text Generation Flag (1 = mirrored, 2 = upside-down)
72	.	Text Justification Code (0 = left, 1 = centered along baseline, 2 = right, 3 = aligned, 4 = centered, 5 = fit between two points)
74	.	Vertical Alignment Codes (0 = baseline, 1 = bottom, 2 = middle, 3 = top)
0	.	"CIRCLE"
10	.	Center Point
40	.	Radius
0	.	"DIMENSION"
1	.	Dimension Text (if not default)
2	.	Pseudo-block Name
3	.	Dimension Style
10	.	Dimension Line Starting Point
11	.	Middle Point
12	.	Baseline Continue Point
13	.	Linear/Angle First Definition Point
14	.	Linear/Angle Second Definition Point
15	.	Diameter/Radius/Angle Definition Point
16	.	Dimension Arc Definition Point
40	.	Leader Length
50	.	Dimension Angle (in radians)
51	.	Angle between UCS and Dimensioned Entity X-Axis (in radians)
52	.	Differential angle for obliquing lines
53	.	Differential angle for rotated text

70	.	Dimension Type Flag (0 = horizontal or vertical, 1 = aligned, 2 = angular, 3 = diameter, 4 = radius, 5 = angular 3-point, 6 = ordinate, 64 = X-type ordinate; +128 = user-defined text location, +1 = user-supplied text)
0	.	"INSERT"
2	.	Block Name
10	.	Insertion point
41	.	X-scale Factor
42	.	Y-scale Factor
43	.	Z-scale Factor
44	.	Column Spacing (Minsert)
45	.	Row Spacing (Minsert)
50	.	Rotation Angle (in radians)
66	.	Attributes Flag (1 = attributes present)
70	.	Number of Columns (Minsert)
71	.	Number of Rows (Minsert)
0	.	"LINE"
10	.	Starting Point
11	.	Ending Point
0	.	"POINT"
10	.	Point Location
50	.	Angle of UCS X-axis when point was drawn (in radians)
0	.	"POLYLINE"
10	.	Entity Base point (0,0 + z-elevation)
40	.	Starting Width
41	.	Ending Width
66	.	Vertex Flag (1 = vertices follow)
70	.	PLINE Flag (1 = closed, 2 = fit curve, 4 = spline curve, 8 = 3D polyline, 16 = 3D mesh, 32 = closed 3D mesh, 64 = polyface mesh)
71	.	Polygon Mesh "M" Count (polyface mesh = number of vertices)
72	.	Polygon Mesh "N" Count (polyface mesh = number of faces)
73	.	Smooth Mesh "M" Density
74	.	Smooth Mesh "N" Density

		5 = quadratic B-spline, 6 = cubic B-spline, 8 = Bezier)
0	.	"SEQEND" (flag for end of vertices or attributes)
−2	.	Parent Entity Name
0	.	"SHAPE"
2	.	Shape Name
10	.	Insertion Point
40	.	Size
41	.	Scale Factor
50	.	Rotation Angle (in radians)
51	.	Obliquing Angle (in radians)
0	.	"SOLID"
10	.	First Point
11	.	Second Point
12	.	Third Point
13	.	Fourth Point (= third point if 3-sided)
0	.	"TEXT"
1	.	Text String
7	.	Style Name
10	.	Start Point
11	.	Insertion Point (if not left-justified)
40	.	Height
41	.	Width Factor
50	.	Rotation Angle (in radians)
51	.	Obliquing Angle (in radians)
71	.	Generation Flag (2 = mirrored, 4 = upside-down)
72	.	Horizontal Alignment Code (0 = left, 1 = centered along baseline, 2 = right, 3 = aligned, 4 = centered, 5 = fit between two points)
73	.	Vertical Alignment Codes (0 = baseline, 1 = bottom, 2 = middle, 3 = top)
0	.	"TRACE"
10	.	Starting Point (first corner)
11	.	Starting Point (second corner)
12	.	Ending Point (first corner)
13	.	Ending Point (second corner)
0	.	"VERTEX"
10	.	Vertex Point
40	.	Starting Width
41	.	Ending Width

Table continues at back of book.

Computer users are not all alike.
Neither are SYBEX books.

We know our customers have a variety of needs. They've told us so. And because we've listened, we've developed several distinct types of books to meet the needs of each of our customers. What are you looking for in computer help?

If you're looking for the basics, try the **ABC's** series. You'll find short, unintimidating tutorials and helpful illustrations. For a more visual approach, select **Teach Yourself**, featuring screen-by-screen illustrations of how to use your latest software purchase.

Mastering and **Understanding** titles offer you a step-by-step introduction, plus an in-depth examination of intermediate-level features, to use as you progress.

Our **Up & Running** series is designed for computer-literate consumers who want a no-nonsense overview of new programs. Just 20 basic lessons, and you're on your way.

We also publish two types of reference books. Our **Instant References** provide quick access to each of a program's commands and functions. SYBEX **Encyclopedias** provide a *comprehensive reference* and explanation of all of the commands, features and functions of the subject software.

Sometimes a subject requires a special treatment that our standard series doesn't provide. So you'll find we have titles like **Advanced Techniques, Handbooks, Tips & Tricks**, and others that are specifically tailored to satisfy a unique need.

We carefully select our authors for their in-depth understanding of the software they're writing about, as well as their ability to write clearly and communicate effectively. Each manuscript is thoroughly reviewed by our technical staff to ensure its complete accuracy. Our production department makes sure it's easy to use. All of this adds up to the highest quality books available, consistently appearing on best seller charts worldwide.

You'll find SYBEX publishes a variety of books on every popular software package. Looking for computer help? Help Yourself to SYBEX.

For a complete catalog of our publications:

SYBEX Inc.
2021 Challenger Drive, Alameda, CA 94501
Tel: (415) 523-8233/(800) 227-2346 Telex: 336311
SYBEX Fax: (415) 523-2373

SYBEX is committed to using natural resources wisely to preserve and improve our environment. As a leader in the computer book publishing industry, we are aware that over 40% of America's solid waste is paper. This is why we have been printing the text of books like this one on recycled paper since 1982.

This year our use of recycled paper will result in the saving of more than 15,300 trees. We will lower air pollution effluents by 54,000 pounds, save 6,300,000 gallons of water, and reduce landfill by 2,700 cubic yards.

In choosing a SYBEX book you are not only making a choice for the best in skills and information, you are also choosing to enhance the quality of life for all of us.

ENCYCLOPEDIA
AutoCAD
Release 11

ENCYCLOPEDIA
AutoCAD®
Release 11

Robert M. Thomas

SYBEX®

San Francisco • Paris • Düsseldorf • Soest

Acquisitions Editor: Dianne King
Series Editor: James A. Compton
Editor: David Krassner
Technical Editor: Ken Morgan
Word Processors: Donna Behrens, Scott Campbell, Ann Dunn, and Lisa Mitchell
Layout Artist: Helen Bruno
Screen Graphics: Delia Brown
Typesetter: Stephanie Hollier
Proofreader: Barbara Dahl
Book Designer: Thomas Ingalls + Associates
Cover Designer: Archer Design
Screen reproductions produced by XenoFont.

Library of Congress Card Number: 90-72080
ISBN: 0-89588-734-7

Manufactured in the United States of America
10 9 8 7 6 5 4 3 2 1

To my parents,
Lawrence E. and Helen F. Rayel,
in gratitude and fond remembrance

TABLE OF CONTENTS

PREFACE

T he *AutoCAD Desktop Companion* is designed to be used as a single, comprehensive source of immediate assistance while you are using AutoCAD. If a command sequence isn't working out as planned, or you are at a loss trying to correct or make changes to an AutoLISP routine, or perhaps you just aren't sure how to approach the production of a particular object in your drawing, this book contains valuable information that will help you find the solution and quickly return to productive drawing.

This book is not just a source of in-depth information on AutoCAD's many features and how they relate to one another. It is a complete toolbox that can provide answers to questions, alternative solutions, tips, tricks, and pitfalls to avoid. The format is nontechnical and intended to benefit all levels of users. Whether you are a brand-new or experienced AutoCAD user, this book can supplement the fundamentals you found in your tutorial or fill in any gaps that may remain from your training, offer new approaches to problems you may experience, warn you about areas in which problems are likely to occur, and offer examples and illustrations of AutoCAD's underdocumented features.

The commands and features herein are arranged according to broad categories of purpose. Thus, you will find chapters on such topics as commands that create entities, commands that edit entities, commands that control the computerized drawing environment within which these entities reside, AutoLISP functions, and system variables. Within the discussions of each command, all of the applicable command options are listed and explained.

SCOPE OF THE BOOK

This book is a complete reference that covers all aspects of using AutoCAD on the IBM PC and compatibles, under DOS. It encompasses all versions of the program, with emphasis on Version 2.1 through Release 11. Command discussions include references to the versions of the software in which the commands are available. If a command is handled differently in different versions, this is noted and explained as part of the command discussion.

ORGANIZATION AND LAYOUT

Part I contains information to use when setting up AutoCAD, before you actually begin to produce drawings. Chapters 1 and 2 contain a general overview of AutoCAD's abilities, differences between the versions, and hardware requirements and options. Chapters 3 and 4 offer detailed instructions for installing various peripheral hardware devices and configuring your computer's operating system for optimized AutoCAD performance.

Part II covers the computerized drawing environment created in memory by AutoCAD, and explains how you can take advantage of this environment to maximize drawing efficiency. Chapter 5 is a discussion of the structural components of the drawing environment. Chapters 6 and 7 introduce you to the tools provided by AutoCAD for controlling this drawing environment.

Part III covers the fundamental drawing entities you can create using Auto-CAD, and how they can be combined into more complex entities. Chapters 8 and 9 are a reference guide to the commands and command options at your disposal for creating a wide variety of drawing entities, from simple lines and arcs to complex polylines, blocks, and text-based entities.

Part IV discusses how drawing entities may be edited, modified, and arranged, and shows you how to create accurate hard-copy output of your finished drawing. Chapters 10 and 11 provide detailed explanations of Auto-CAD's various standard editing commands and the variety of optional approaches to making changes in your drawing. Chapter 12 combines a step-by-step description of the plotting process with a discussion of special techniques you can use to produce clear, precise hard-copy output as efficiently as possible.

Part V discusses how you may customize the AutoCAD program for maximum efficiency in your application. Chapter 13 contains a thorough listing of AutoCAD's system variables and their relationship to program operation. Chapter 14 demonstrates how you can redesign AutoCAD's screen, tablet, and pull-down menus. Chapter 15 describes the tools and techniques you can use to create library files of frequently used symbols and shapes, as well as custom text fonts.

Part VI introduces AutoLISP, AutoCAD's internal programming language. Chapter 16 examines the fundamental concepts of AutoLISP programming: procedures, conditional branching, and looping control structures. Chapter 17 is a list of predefined AutoLISP functions, with working examples of each one.

Part VII reveals user-accessible structures in AutoCAD's underlying database, and shows you techniques for manipulating that database to further maximize your productivity. Chapter 18 is a discussion of block attributes and a reference guide to the commands used to manipulate them. Chapter 19 lists and describes AutoLISP functions that access the underlying database. Chapter 20 teaches you how to create, read, and edit Drawing Interchange files for communication with other graphics software.

Part VIII covers special features of AutoCAD. Chapter 21 acquaints you with automatic and associative dimensioning commands, custom linetypes and hatch patterns, command scripts, slide files, freehand sketching, data-inquiry commands, and techniques for modifying standard commands. Chapter 22 lists examples of various types of add-on software products designed to be used with AutoCAD; particular attention is paid to AME, Autodesk's program for solid modeling and analysis.

Each discussion of an AutoCAD command is organized into sections: versions in which the command operates, command options, usage, special tips and warnings, related commands and system variables, and sample dialog you may recreate to learn more about how the command works. Other sections throughout the book include discussions of general techniques and approaches that apply to the various commands under discussion. You need not read the more explanatory material to obtain the information you require about a particular command; on the other hand, if your inquiry is more general—for example, if you are interested in learning how to draw the particular object you have in mind— you will find within the broader discussions an approach for discovering the assortment of AutoCAD commands, functions, and features you require. Where necessary, you may then turn to the more specific discussions of those commands, functions, and features with which you may not be familiar.

Also included are two valuable tools to help speed you through your Auto-CAD tasks. The first is a handy function-key template that fits directly onto your keyboard. The second is a Quick Reference Card of AutoCAD commands. Both are on a punch-out card at the back of the book.

Using This Book to Create Better Drawings Faster

As you look up specific information in this book, concentrate on what you intend to accomplish. Most of the time, the command is given a name relating to its goal. For example, commands that create things are nouns indicating what they create (Arc, Circle, Line, Polygon). Commands that change things are verbs (Copy, Erase, Hide, Move, Zoom).

Some commands (Aperture, Attdef, Block, Shape, Trace) have names that are peculiar to AutoCAD and whose meaning is therefore not so immediately obvious. These commands become meaningful through practice, experimentation, and familiarity with the program. Take time to find out about these commands before you actually need to use them.

If you are "stuck" regarding how to accomplish something, focus as specifically as you can on the fundamental tasks you intend to perform. In general, commands are arranged in this book according to broad categories of purpose: creating entities, changing entities, producing output, customizing, and so forth.

For example, suppose you want to enlarge a room in a floor plan. You won't find a command called "Enlarge the Room" (unless you have used AutoCAD's AutoLISP feature to create such a custom command!). But you will find a section on commands that change drawing entities.

Think first about *how* you are going to enlarge the room. By moving a wall line? Look up the Move command. By erasing and drawing new wall lines? Look up the Erase and Line commands. By stretching the wall lines? Look up the Stretch command. By enlarging the entire room by a certain scale? Look up the Scale command.

Even so, in some cases you may have to search more deeply than in others. The purpose of a command like Erase, after all, is obvious and self-explanatory. But what about a command like UCS? And the Trace command doesn't trace anything; it draws wide line segments.

To help you in those cases where the appropriate AutoCAD command name is not immediately obvious, AutoCAD commands and functions are detailed in three ways in this book:

- A quick statement of the purpose of the command.
- A more detailed explanation of the command's mechanics and its various options and subcommands.
- A simple command dialog that demonstrates the command and leads to a specific graphic result.

Thus, if you are really stuck, you can "browse" through the command discussions in this book to get a quick overview of what each command does. When you find the command whose purpose addresses your problem, you can read the Command Options and Usage sections for details.

If you are not using Release 11 of AutoCAD, be sure to read the Versions sections, which describe (where applicable) how different releases of AutoCAD implement certain commands.

Whenever appropriate, special notes, tips, and warnings will present useful shortcuts and work-arounds, and will alert you to troublesome situations that should be avoided.

You can enter the sample dialog yourself. Thus you can practice with the command in a general way, see what it is intended to do, and use the sample dialog as a basis for experimentation and further understanding. Before using the sample dialog, be sure to read the next section, "Conventions for Sample Dialogs."

CONVENTIONS FOR SAMPLE DIALOGS

The following typographical conventions apply to the sample command dialogs in this book:

- AutoCAD prompts and messages are shown in normal type:

  Command:
  From point:
  To point:

- User input from the keyboard is shown in **boldface** type:

  Command: **Line**
  From point: **0,0**
  To point: **5,5**

  It is assumed that all user input is followed by a press of the Enter key (or the space bar).

- If the user is required to perform an action rather than input data, this action is described in **boldface** type within parentheses:

  Command: **Erase**
  Select objects: **(pick a drawing entity to erase)**
  Select objects: **(press Enter)**
  Command:

  You do not follow an action of this type with a press of the Enter key unless you are specifically instructed to do so.

- In many cases, you have a choice between typing data from the keyboard and picking points on the screen using the pointing device. Optional input methods are listed in the Command Options section of the command discussions. The sample dialogs in this book use keyboard input. Once you have tested the sample dialog using keyboard input, you may wish to try it with the optional input methods.

- Most AutoCAD prompts offer default responses that you may enter simply by pressing the Enter key. They appear within angle brackets (< >) as part of the prompt; for example:

  Set new layer <current>:

  These default responses differ from system to system, and often from one drawing session to the next. For this reason, default responses are left out of the sample dialogs except when required for the sake of understanding.

OTHER TYPOGRAPHICAL CONVENTIONS

The following typographical conventions apply to other commands, prompts, and software references in this book:

- AutoCAD commands begin with a capital letter.

  Line
  Arc
  Insert

- AutoLISP functions are capitalized in the ordinary text:

    Redraw function

    They are lowercase in the sample listings:

    (redraw)

- AutoCAD system variables are in all uppercase:

    CMDECHO
    DIMZIN
    FLATLAND

- File names, including subdirectory path names, are displayed in all uppercase:

    COLUMBIA.DWG
    C:\ACAD\ACAD.PGP

ACKNOWLEDGMENTS

This ambitious project is the result of a lot of very hard work from many good people. Special thanks to David Krassner, whose outstanding editing produced a clear and concise text from the original manuscript. Also my sincere appreciation to Ken Morgan, Technical Editor, for his candid and knowledgeable insights. Thanks also to Jim Compton, Series Editor; Dianne King, Acquisitions Editor; Donna Behrens, Scott Campbell, Ann Dunn, and Lisa Mitchell, word processing; Helen Bruno, chapter art; Delia Brown, screen graphics; Stephanie Hollier, typesetting; Barbara Dahl, proofreader; Thomas Ingalls + Associates, book design; and Archer Design, cover design.

Thanks also to Duff Kurland of Autodesk for helpful advice and information. My thanks once again to Francia Friendlich and Rich Teich of the Aquarian Age Computer Center in San Francisco, who generously provided necessary hardware and technical support. Special thanks to my wonderful wife, Krista, for her infinite tolerance.

Finally, as always, thanks to Roscoe and Elaine for their inspiration and spiritual guidance, and for locating lost objects of my desire.

- RMT
1/30/91

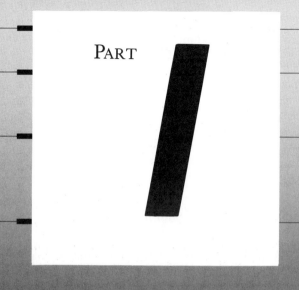

PART

1

PRELIMINARY CONSIDERATIONS

Using the extraordinary power of AutoCAD to maximum advantage involves more than just learning how its various commands work. It also involves understanding the computerized environment within which AutoCAD functions. This environment includes such elements as the computer's operating system, and the hardware devices (such as display devices, digitizers, printers, and plotters) with which AutoCAD must interact. Part I presents a general overview of AutoCAD and of the various ways to create a computerized environment that will allow you to run AutoCAD as efficiently and productively as possible.

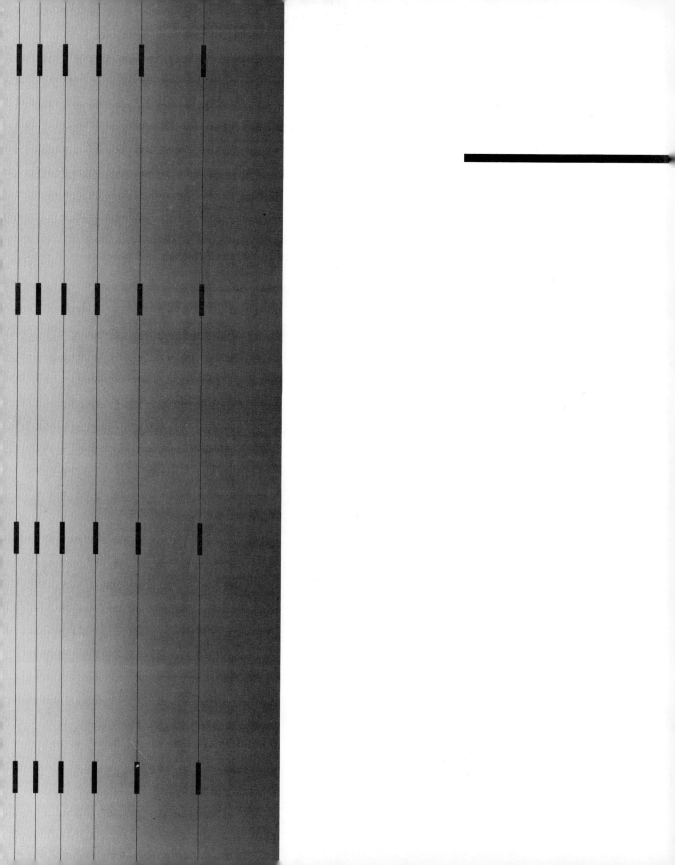

CHAPTER 1

AN OVERVIEW OF AUTOCAD

AN OVERVIEW OF AUTOCAD

AutoCAD is a full-featured collection of software tools designed to perform computer-aided drafting (CAD), including 3-D graphic modeling, from a desktop computer workstation. It was developed by Autodesk, Inc., a software-development firm located in Sausalito, California, and it was first released in December, 1982. Since its initial release, AutoCAD has seen many significant additions, enhancements, and revisions.

AutoCAD's development since its original release has been dramatic. Autodesk has developed its product in direct response to the needs and wishes of its users. Many new commands and features have been added, and many have been enhanced with several internal options. AutoCAD's numerous features, commands, and program options have become highly interrelated as additional refinements and enhancements have been made to successive versions of the program.

Today, AutoCAD is the most widely used microcomputer CAD application, and one of the most powerful and flexible desktop computer programs of any type to be found in the commercial software market. Because of its widespread acceptance, AutoCAD has become the standard desktop CAD program against which all other CAD programs are evaluated.

Microcomputer-based CAD, and AutoCAD in particular, have revolutionized the production of graphic information in the same way that word processing and desktop publishing have revolutionized the production of printed information. In the future, these CAD systems will continue to create powerful new features and achieve new levels of performance, enabling people to develop more sophisticated forms of visual communication.

APPLICATIONS FOR AUTOCAD

Autodesk understands the marketing value of developing its product to meet the needs of the widest possible variety of drafters. AutoCAD drawings can be found in such diverse fields as mechanical engineering, architectural design, software engineering, facilities planning and management, mapping, technical illustrating, business graphics, graphic design, and project planning.

No matter what the application, AutoCAD users appreciate the high degree of precision with which drawings can be produced, and the ease with which drawings may be subsequently copied, edited, modified, and transferred to other formats. AutoCAD has eased the burden of repetitive drawing, automated the creation of complex drawing entities, and brought new organizational capabilities to businesses that manage graphic information.

AutoCAD Features

AutoCAD does more than provide tools for the creation and manipulation of graphic entities. Many additional features allow you to organize and view a drawing in ways that are not possible in manual drafting. For example, you can:

- Group related parts of the drawing together and turn their display on and off at will.

- Manipulate drawing entities separately, or in groups as though they were a single drawing entity.

- Produce drawings using entity properties such as different colors, thicknesses, elevations in 3-D space, and noncontinuous linetype specifications, and change any of these properties at will.

- Use AutoCAD to store various kinds of nongraphic information—such as part numbers, materials specifications, costs, dimensions, labor and time requirements, and just about any conceivable text-based detail—and then associate this information with individual graphic entities in the drawing, update it as the drawing is changed, and export the data for analysis by a spreadsheet or database.

- Create an unlimited library of custom-made drawing entities and symbols, and insert them into different drawings at will. You change their color and linetype specifications, and proportionally scale them at insertion time. You can create, edit, and store these entities at any time during a drawing session.

- Add dimension information to your drawing easily by selecting relevant points on a drawing entity. AutoCAD automatically draws the dimension lines, leader lines, tick marks, and/or dimension text to your predefined specifications.

- Automate AutoCAD by means of command scripts that execute a series of computer commands in sequence, or by programming AutoCAD, with the internal AutoLISP programming language, to execute complex routines that create, edit, or modify the drawing or its display according to your instructions.

- Create drawings that can be exported and used in other graphics software programs.

- Construct 3-D wire-frame models of objects at any orientation in 3-D space and view them from any angle, with true perspective or parallel realizations, and with either suppression or realization of hidden lines. This capability appeared first in AutoCAD Release 10.

- Create sectional views of 3-D entities automatically by using an Auto-CAD feature called *clipping planes* to temporarily block out selected portions of the drawing. This capability too appeared with AutoCAD Release 10.

LEARNING THE PROGRAM

AutoCAD's extraordinary power and flexibility are its greatest assets. They are also its greatest liability, for all of that raw computing power comes at a price. Not only is AutoCAD one of the more expensive drafting software packages—Release 11's list price is $3,500—but its vast array of features also requires that users make an investment of time to fully understand the program and to acquire enough experience to use it effectively.

Autodesk, in recognition of the need for high-quality training, has developed a large number of Authorized Training Centers that provide high-quality training in all aspects of AutoCAD and AutoCAD-related software.

If a drafter intends to make serious use of AutoCAD, the necessary first step is to acquire some form of training. Training may be acquired formally from an Authorized Training Center, or informally from one or more of the dozens of AutoCAD tutorials and training aids that have come onto the software-learning market.

Many different fields of endeavor depend on accurate drafting; each has its own specific requirements and specifications. In addition, there are about as many different drafting styles as there are drafters. Sooner or later, a drafter's application of AutoCAD is likely to become personalized to a greater or lesser extent. Some individuals have developed unique and unanticipated new uses for AutoCAD. Because of this wide variety of applications, Autodesk designed AutoCAD with considerable flexibility—a basic CAD "toolbox" that can be organized and manipulated to suit as many different drafting needs as possible. Thus, once an individual has been trained in AutoCAD's fundamental program concepts and features, he or she may then determine the most efficient and productive combination of AutoCAD features and program techniques for the individual application.

This final stage in the attainment of AutoCAD mastery is usually accomplished through practice, trial and error, patient sifting through the extensive program documentation, and sharing of information and experience with other AutoCAD users. All these methods will be necessary and effective at one time or another, but the most important of them may well be the sharing of information and experience with others. There are many AutoCAD user groups, and membership in a nearby user group is highly recommended as a low-cost and extremely effective supplement to whatever training the user acquires.

COMPATIBILITY BETWEEN VERSIONS

AutoCAD drawings created with previous versions of the software can be edited using later versions as well. In general, the reverse is not true; that is, a drawing created or modified with a later version of the software cannot be edited using an earlier version. For this reason, we say that AutoCAD drawings are "upwardly compatible."

If a drawing was created using one of AutoCAD's earliest versions (specifically, versions prior to Version 2.0), AutoCAD will perform an automatic conversion of the underlying database format in order to make the drawing compatible with the later release. If you intend to insert one of these early-version drawings into a later drawing, you must either convert the drawing using Main Menu option number 8 or load the old drawing into the new version of Auto-CAD and then save it.

With each new release of AutoCAD, new commands and features are added, along with some subtle and not-so-subtle changes to existing commands. Experienced users normally face a short learning curve as they acclimate themselves to the new features. In all cases, this investment of time is well worth it, since each release brings significant new gains in drawing productivity.

Major changes to AutoCAD, beginning with Version 2.1, are summarized below:

Version 2.1   Three-dimensional visualization of lines with elevation and thickness; hidden-line removal (see Chapter 11); filleting polylines (Chapter 10); freezing layers to speed up regeneration (Chapter 6); printer-plotter output (Chapter 12); creation of memory variables and arithmetic expressions to use in response to AutoCAD prompts (Chapter 16).

Version 2.18   Introduction of the AutoLISP programming language (see Chapters 16 and 17).

Version 2.5   Introduction of the virtual screen to speed up zooming and panning (see Chapter 11); support for expanded and extended memory (Chapter 3); dynamic zoom (Chapter 11); context-sensitive help (Chapter 7); command Undo feature (Chapter 10); compiled menus (Chapter 14); Explode command to convert complex entities to simpler components (Chapter 10); new editing commands: Divide, Measure, Offset, Rotate, Scale, Stretch, and Trim (Chapter 10).

Version 2.6   3-D lines and 3-D faces (opaque planes) in a true XYZ coordinate system (see Chapter 8); associative dimensioning (Chapter 21); transparent Pan, Redraw, View, and Zoom commands (Chapter 11).

Release 9   Math coprocessor now required (see Chapter 2); Advanced User Interface to allow for pull-down menus, icon menus, and dialog boxes on certain display devices (Chapter 5); object snap enhanced for use with 3-D entities (Chapter 6).

Release 10   Full 3-D capability with user-selected coordinate systems oriented anywhere in 3-D space (see Chapters 5 and 6); multiple viewports allowing different simultaneous views of a drawing (Chapter 11); spline curves fitted to polylines (Chapter 10); polygon mesh commands (Chapter 9); perspective viewing of 3-D models (Chapter 11); use of AutoLISP in extended memory (Chapter 5).

Release 11   Network file locking (see Chapter 2); recovery and reconstruction of damaged drawing files (Chapter 3); fractional values, alternative angular units, cylindrical and spherical coordinates may be entered in response to Auto-CAD prompts, and improved dialog boxes (Chapter 5); improved contextual help (Chapter 7); multiple-view plotting in model and paper space (Chapter 12); extended entity data (Chapter 19); command aliasing, new dimensioning options, and external reference files (Chapter 21); the AutoCAD Development System (ADS), a C-language programming environment (Chapter 22).

If you are a registered owner of the program and desire an upgrade, Autodesk will charge you the difference in price between your current version and the latest version. Of course, if you are satisfied with your current version and see no reason to avail yourself of the latest features, you can still find considerable support for your old version among the training centers, user groups, and printed materials available on the subject.

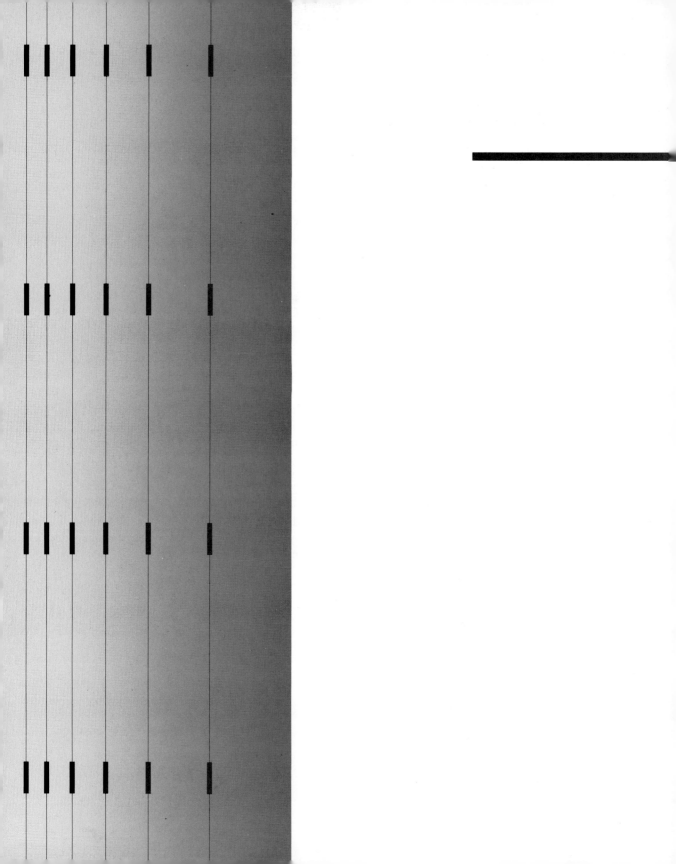

CHAPTER 2

HARDWARE REQUIREMENTS AND OPTIONS

HARDWARE REQUIREMENTS AND OPTIONS

A wide variety of drafting disciplines can benefit from using AutoCAD. The hardware requirements of one AutoCAD application may be completely different from the requirements of another. Therefore, AutoCAD supports an exceptionally large number of hardware devices. One or more combinations of these devices may be best for you, depending on the unique demands of your own application. Once you have decided to use the AutoCAD software, it is important that you take the time to critically examine the available hardware options in order to determine what particular setup will maximize your productivity.

LEARNING ABOUT HARDWARE

If you are new to desktop CAD, you have available a variety of resources to find out about the hardware you need. These include books and tutorials, user groups, hardware dealers, and professional consultants.

Books and Tutorials

A great many books on computer hardware and CAD in general can be found in bookstores or in the public library. They can provide you with in-depth information regarding available hardware options. It is easy to spend an afternoon browsing in the computer section of your local bookstore, picking up a considerable amount of valuable information. This method has the advantage of being inexpensive, leisurely, and pressure-free. However, if you are completely unfamiliar with some of the more technical aspects of computer hardware, sampling all of the many books available simply to find the right one can be a hit-or-miss proposition.

User Groups

You can receive much valuable advice—most of it free—from other CAD users. If you don't know other users, you can find them by attending a meeting of a *user group* in your area. Members of a user group tend to be enthusiastic and sincere. Most are eager to share their experiences, offer advice, and answer questions. You may find that their experiences and the quality of their information vary widely. Some are quite knowledgeable and objective; others may be "true believers," proselytizing their own pet system. Always maintain your objectivity. Bear in mind that someone else's solution, while seemingly attractive, may not be the best solution for you.

User groups promote themselves in local computer-oriented periodicals. Also, you can find a worldwide list of known AutoCAD user groups in each issue of Cadalyst magazine. Contact Cadalyst at 314 E. Holly, #106, Bellingham, WA 98225 for more information.

Dealers

A knowledgeable and responsible hardware dealer can help you analyze your CAD requirements and demonstrate a variety of possible hardware solutions that match your needs and budget. Beware of hardware dealers that do not take the time to understand your needs fully, or attempt to sell you a particular solution without offering alternatives. No matter how sincere and responsible a dealer may appear to be, you should visit as many as you can. This will acquaint you with the numerous possibilities in hardware systems for desktop CAD.

While investigating possibilities with dealers, bear in mind that the time they can afford to spend educating prospective customers is limited. You will be doing yourself and the dealer a favor if you learn as much of the basics as you can before walking into the showroom. When you finally make the purchase, buy from the dealer that took the time to understand your needs fully. This dealer will be the most cost-efficient in the long run.

Professional Consultants

You may also wish to secure the advice of a *professional consultant*. A good professional consultant can educate you, analyze your needs more thoroughly, and offer objective advice regarding any proposed CAD system. A consultant's time is expensive. The more you learn independently before obtaining a consultant's services, the less consulting time you will need. Consultants advertise their services in trade periodicals and newsletters, and sometimes through dealers. Many offer a free initial evaluative visit. Be sure to check your consultant's references carefully before paying for his or her advice.

REQUIRED HARDWARE

All versions of AutoCAD require a basic computer hardware setup that includes the following: a central processing unit (CPU) with sufficient random-access memory (RAM); disk storage; a display device; a keyboard; and operating-system software. Each of these devices will be explained momentarily.

If you are running AutoCAD Release 9 or later and using a CPU based on the Intel 8086 family of microprocessors (which includes all IBM and IBM-compatible machines), a *numeric coprocessor* is also required. If you are using an Intel 80486 CPU, the numeric coprocessor is built into the main processor.

Strictly speaking, a *hard-copy output device* is not required to run AutoCAD. However, most applications will require some form of hard-copy output, so a device of this type is required in most cases. Likewise, using a *digitizing input device* is almost always a significant improvement over entering drawing commands solely from the keyboard; therefore, this device may be considered a requirement for many applications as well.

The CPU

The *central processing unit,* or CPU, consists of a *microprocessor* and accompanying electronic circuitry required to process data and move it between various *peripheral devices* (such as the display monitor, keyboard, printer, or plotter). The microprocessor is the "brains" of the system, a complex set of miniature electronic switches etched onto a thin wafer of silicon. AutoCAD supports several different kinds of microprocessors. Table 2.1 shows the different hardware platforms that are available for AutoCAD.

THE INTEL 8086 FAMILY

In IBM and IBM-compatible computers, the CPU is based on the *Intel 8086 family* of microprocessors. At the time of this writing, the Intel microprocessors used for AutoCAD are the 80286, 80386, and 80486. The 8086 and 8088 microprocessors can be used only with versions of AutoCAD prior to Release 11.

The IBM AT, IBM PS/2 Models 30, 40, and 50, and computers advertised as compatible with these IBM systems use the Intel 80286. IBM PS/2 Models 70 and 80 and their compatibles use the Intel 80386 microprocessor. The IBM PC and older IBM XTs, as well as compatible non-IBM versions of these computers, use the Intel 8086 or 8088.

To the user who's not technically minded, the differences between these Intel microprocessors are in the number of processing features they support, the price,

RELEASE 11 VERSION	OPERATING SYSTEM
Standard	DOS 2.0 +
386	DOS 3.3 +
OS/2	OS/2
Apollo	Aegis 9.7 +
DEC 3100	Ultrix
DEC VAX	VMS 4.0
Macintosh	System 6.0.3 +
Sun 386i	Sun 4.0 +
Sun 3	Sun 4.0 +
Sun SPARC	Sun 4.0 +
Xenix	Xenix

DOS 3.1 or later is required to use AutoCAD on a network. DOS 2.0 or later and Macintosh System 6.0.3 platforms do not currently support Advanced Modeling Extension (AME). The VAX/VMS platform does not currently support the Advanced Development System (ADS).

Table 2.1: AutoCAD's Supported Operating System Platforms

and the speed with which they process data. The processing speed of a CPU, measured in *megahertz,* is defined by the maximum number of instructions the microprocessor can process per second. In theory, the higher the number of megahertz, the faster the speed of the microprocessor. A standard IBM PC/XT, using an Intel 8088, processes at 4.77 megahertz. An IBM PC/AT, using an Intel 80286, processes from 6 to 20 megahertz. Computers based on the Intel 80386 process from 12 to 25 megahertz. The intel 80486 processes from 25 to 33 megahertz. Megahertz is not the only factor that determines the actual processing speed of your system, however. Other factors include such things as the speed of your hard disk. Refer to the section on hard disks just ahead for more details regarding this.

The 80286, 80386, and 80486 microprocessors are more fully featured, capable of supporting larger amounts of RAM, multitasking, and advanced operating-system software. The faster and more fully featured the microprocessor, the more expensive it is, the more expensive will be the accompanying circuitry in the CPU, and the more expensive you can expect your overall CAD system to be.

Graphics programs such as AutoCAD require a blinding array of complex mathematical calculations to generate even relatively simple graphic information. Because of this, the first-time user may be tempted to buy the fastest microprocessor available. However, depending on how you intend to use AutoCAD, you may not need that much raw speed. Before investing in hardware that may be more powerful and expensive than you require, have a dealer or other Auto-CAD users demonstrate AutoCAD on different systems, using drawings similar to those you intend to produce. (AutoCAD comes with a variety of sample drawings that can be helpful in this regard.) Depending on the complexity of your drawings, the kind of graphic entities they contain, and your need for advanced computing features, you may find that a slower, less expensive CPU will perform adequately for you.

THE 80386

Generalizations about hardware platforms are difficult to make, because of the tremendous differences in individual user's requirements. You should carefully assess your personal needs before investing in any hardware or peripherals. However, the Intel 80386 processor is emerging as a good practical choice for general-purpose AutoCAD work.

An 80386-based microcomputer is a better platform than an 80286-based computer because the 80386 executes programs more quickly and can run software (such as AutoShade 386) that will not run on earlier processors.

Autodesk intends to release more software specifically developed to take advantage of the speed, memory, and high performance of the 80386. A program written for the 80386 usually will run faster than the same program written for the 80286, because of hardware limitations of the 80286 chip.

AutoCAD users can benefit from extended memory in both 80386 and 80286 computers today. However, an 80386-based system provides a clear upgrade path for future versions of AutoCAD under different operating systems, such as SCO XENIX 386 and Microsoft OS/2, as well as AutoCAD 386, a version of AutoCAD designed to take full advantage of the 80386's unique capabilities.

THE 80486

In spite of problems with its early versions, the Intel 80486 CPU is emerging as the appropriate choice for high-performance CAD work. For AutoCAD users, the required math coprocessor has always been an important cost factor. Because the 80486 includes the numeric coprocessor, it is no longer an added expense. The cost difference between an 80386 plus numeric processor and the 80486 alone is only a couple of hundred dollars; in return, the user gets CAD throughput processing up to 50% faster with the 80486—even if the two chips are rated at the same processing speed (e.g., 25 megahertz). As faster versions of this chip are developed, the cost of older 80486-based computers may decrease.

The Numeric Coprocessor

AutoCAD's graphic processing is based on *floating-point mathematics,* with as many as 16 digits of decimal precision. Floating-point math enables AutoCAD to achieve its extremely high degree of graphic precision, but it is memory-intensive and relatively slow. AutoCAD's processing speed can be noticeably improved by a *numeric coprocessor.* The numeric coprocessor is a special supplementary microprocessor specifically designed to process floating-point calculations in an Intel-based CPU. If you are using an Intel-based CPU with a version of AutoCAD earlier than Release 9, the use of the numeric coprocessor is optional. If you are using AutoCAD Release 9 or later, the numeric coprocessor is required. Unless you are on a very tight budget, chances are you will benefit significantly by installing a numeric coprocessor, even if it is not required.

Random-Access Memory (RAM)

Random-access memory (RAM) is that part of a CPU where data resides temporarily during processing. In all computer systems, data is first copied from the disk storage device to RAM, where processing takes place; then the newly processed data is written back to the disk storage device. Normally the user has the option of either *overwriting* the previous version of the data (replacing the old version with the new), or copying the processed data back to a new location on the disk, retaining the original version for reference, backup, or other purposes.

RAM is often measured in *kilobytes.* A kilobyte is equal to 1024 *bytes,* a byte being equal to a group of 8 *data bits,* and the data bit being the smallest unit of information a computer can process. Large amounts of RAM are measured in *megabytes.* A megabyte is equal to 1,024,000 bytes.

AutoCAD requires a minimum of 512K (512 kilobytes, or about 524,000 bytes) of RAM. If you intend to use AutoCAD's AutoLISP feature, a minimum of 640K is required. This is only a minimum RAM requirement; AutoCAD is capable of using up to 4 megabytes of RAM for its processing.

Large amounts of RAM enable AutoCAD to run more efficiently. With lesser amounts of RAM, AutoCAD employs a programming technique called *bank switching* to run in the smaller available memory.

If you have installed additional RAM beyond 640K, AutoCAD will detect this additional memory, load more of itself into RAM, store a larger portion of the drawing database in RAM, and thereby access the hard disk less often. Thus, large amounts of RAM and/or a very fast hard disk can perceptibly improve AutoCAD's performance.

Intel-based systems using the MS-DOS or PC-DOS operating system can directly address only 640K of RAM. To use larger amounts of RAM with MS-DOS or PC-DOS, you must employ either *extended* or *expanded* memory. These two types of extra memory differ in their technical specifications and in the hardware required to operate them.

Systems based on the 80286 and 80386 can use both extended and expanded memory. 8088 systems can use only expanded memory. AutoCAD automatically recognizes and makes use of both types of extra RAM. Except for the increase in operating efficiency, the effect of extended or expanded RAM on AutoCAD installation and performance is usually invisible to the user. However, if you are using this additional RAM for other programs in addition to Auto-CAD (such as RAM disks or special memory-resident utilities), you may have to specifically tell AutoCAD which area of additional RAM is available for its use. See the section in Chapter 4 entitled "Using More Than 640K" for instructions on how to do this.

Some users confuse RAM and disk storage. The two are not the same. Data processing only takes place in RAM; data is never processed directly on the disk storage device. Conversely, data is never stored permanently in RAM; when the computer is turned off, all data in RAM is irretrievably lost. Therefore, it is important that all data in RAM be copied to the disk storage device before you end a drawing session. AutoCAD does this automatically whenever you issue the Save or End command.

Hard Disk Storage

It is theoretically possible to run AutoCAD Release 9 and earlier from floppy disks, switching disks in the floppy-disk drive as the program requires during processing. But this has never been considered a practical method for operating such a large and complex program. For all practical purposes, you must use a *hard disk* to store your AutoCAD program and drawing files.

Two factors to consider when selecting a hard disk for your system are its *storage capacity* and its *access time*. Hard disks are designed to hold so much data that their storage capacity is measured in megabytes. A 20-megabyte hard disk, for example, holds about the same amount of data as fifty-six 5.25" double-density MS-DOS floppy disks, or about twenty-seven 720K 3.5" disks.

The practical minimum hard-disk size for the average AutoCAD application is 20 to 40 megabytes. AutoCAD's program files total about 4 megabytes; various support files, such as shape and text-font files, slides and slide-library files, hatch patterns, linetypes, and so forth, can occupy even more space. In addition, the drawing files generated by AutoCAD, even for relatively simple drawings, tend to become quite large. All this takes up a large amount of disk storage space. If you intend to use other application programs in addition to AutoCAD, you will need to reserve adequate storage space for them as well. If you have a 20-megabyte hard disk, you can expect to "clean house" fairly often, backing up old drawing files to floppy disks to make room on your hard disk for new drawing files. If you need to store many large drawings on your hard disk, or if you use many other application programs, you may need a larger hard disk.

A hard disk's access time is the speed with which it can store and retrieve data. Access time is measured in *milliseconds*; a millisecond equals one one-thousandth of a second. An access time of 40 milliseconds is about average and will work well in Intel 8088-based systems. An access time of 28 milliseconds is fairly fast. Consider a disk with this speed when purchasing an Intel 80286 or 80386 system.

It is not a good idea to couple a fast microprocessor with a slow hard disk. Depending on the size of your computer's random-access memory, AutoCAD may need to access the hard disk frequently. Even when you're using a fast CPU, a slow hard disk can noticeably slow down AutoCAD. Of course, faster hard disks are more expensive.

Monitor

The monitor will display your drawing while you are creating and editing it. AutoCAD requires both *graphic* and *text* display. With some monitors you can display both text and graphics on a single screen by switching between the two when necessary. In other AutoCAD systems, two monitors are used, one exclusively for text, and the other for graphics.

GRAPHICS DISPLAY

The graphics display contains the visualization of the drawing. It also includes some optional display features: the on-screen menu of AutoCAD commands; the line prompt area, which echoes command prompts; and the status line, which contains handy information: the current drawing layer, the coordinate location of the crosshairs, and whether any of AutoCAD's special drawing aids are currently active.

TEXT DISPLAY

AutoCAD's text display includes the program prompts, user-selected commands and command options, and other text-based output that may be required during the drawing session. This "running dialog" of user commands and responses can be extremely helpful in monitoring the progress of a drawing session. If you are using a system with a single monitor, this information will appear in a three-line *line prompt area* at the bottom of the monitor screen. A special function key, called the Flip Screen key, switches between graphic displays and a full-screen text display so that you can review your most recent set of commands or read lengthy text responses from AutoCAD.

CHOOSING THE RIGHT DISPLAY

In addition to choosing between a system with one or two screens, there are other factors to consider when deciding which display device is best for your system. These include whether to use a color or monochrome display, the size of the monitor, and the degree of resolution.

Most AutoCAD users prefer color displays, and with good reason. As drawings become more complex, assigning a specific color to related lines or pen sizes in the drawing can help you see the drawing better. Like any hardware that makes AutoCAD easier and more effective, color monitors are more expensive. Monochrome monitors, although displaying only a single color (usually green, amber, or white on a dark background) are a great bargain. For this reason they are usually used for the text display on two-screen systems. A monochrome graphics display will represent a worthwhile savings of money only if your drawings are simple and relatively uncluttered, and if color will not be of that much help.

You should determine the correct size for your graphics display screen based on the size of your drawings and the amount of detail they contain; also consider whether most of your drawing or only a small portion of it needs to be displayed on the screen at any given time. Large CAD drawings with a lot of detail displayed in full will benefit from the largest monitor screen you can afford. Monitors with a diagonal screen measurement of 19 inches are common for this purpose. Many users find that a 13-inch screen is adequate for their needs.

The *resolution* of your monitor is another important consideration when selecting a graphics display for AutoCAD. Resolution is a measurement of the accuracy with which the graphics display renders the details of a drawing. It is determined by counting the number of *pixels* your monitor is capable of displaying. A pixel is the smallest possible unit of visual information the graphic device is capable of displaying. If your monitor were to display only a single pixel, it would appear on the screen as a tiny pinpoint of light. If you were to examine it very closely, you would find that it is rectangular.

Pixel display is expressed both vertically and horizontally. The higher the number of vertical and horizontal pixels relative to the size of your screen, the better your monitor's resolution, and the more accurately it will display the details of your drawing. Also, monitors with higher resolution are easier on the eyes—an important consideration if you intend to spend long periods of time editing your drawings. For example, a 13-inch monitor with 640×350 resolution (640 horizontal pixels by 350 vertical pixels) is adequate for the average architectural AutoCAD application in which the monitor is not used for presentation purposes. Precision-engineering applications, or applications using Auto-CAD as a presentation device, will benefit from a higher resolution than this.

In order for a monitor to display drawings at the greatest possible resolution, it must be connected to the CPU via a *graphics card*. The graphics card is an electronic device that controls the flow of data to your monitor. There are a number of different types of graphics cards available. The graphics card you select must match the specifications of your particular monitor. Many monitors can use more than one type of graphics card, but not all possible combinations of monitor and card will produce the best screen appearance. Some color graphics cards are capable of displaying only a limited number of different colors or a low resolution. Other cards can display hundreds or even thousands of different color mixtures and hues at an extremely high resolution.

For example, if you are using an IBM-compatible computer with a color monitor, you can choose from three basic types of color graphics cards: a *color graphics adapter* (CGA), an *enhanced graphics adapter* (EGA), or a *video graphics array* (VGA). The CGA card will give you color, but not much resolution—its real province is game software. Acceptable screen appearance is possible using an EGA graphics card, which produces about 640×350 resolution and 16 colors. A VGA card and compatible monitor will produce somewhat better resolution (640×480, 800×600, or 1024×768 and from 16 to 256 colors at once). If screen appearance is important and your other hardware is compatible with the VGA card, it represents a good buy in relatively high resolution displays. If color is not important, you can save money by purchasing a monochrome monitor and graphics card. Hercules graphics cards are standard for this type of display; they display 720×348 resolution.

Many different hardware manufacturers produce monitors and graphics cards that deliver a variety of high-resolution displays and large numbers of colors in a wide range of prices. In the final analysis, there is a strong measure of subjectivity in monitor selection. Before making your purchase, try to see as many different displays as you can, and study them for as long as you can. Try to negotiate a reasonable "try-out" period with your dealer, during which time you can return the monitor and card for exchange credit if you find that it is not as comfortable as you anticipated.

AutoCAD drawings maintain a virtually infinite degree of precise drawing detail regardless of the resolution of the associated hardware. The resolution of any device reflects only the ability of that device to display an AutoCAD drawing.

I/O Ports

The various hardware devices are connected to your computer's CPU by means of cables attached to various *I/O ports*. I/O stands for input/output, meaning that data can be transferred to and from the hardware device. The I/O port is a receptacle for the cable, and is usually found on the back of the CPU. Most computers are equipped with at least one I/O port, generally for connection to a printer. Many CAD workstations have additional I/O ports for a digitizing device and one or more pen plotters. The monitor and keyboard have their own dedicated I/O ports.

The transfer of data between the CPU and peripheral device can take the form of *parallel* or *serial* communication. In parallel communication, data is transferred in groups of 16 data bits. It is a fast means of sending and receiving data, but it is only possible over short distances, usually 25 feet or less. In serial communication, data is sent bit by bit. This is slower, but the distances involved can be much longer.

Parallel I/O ports, because of their traditional connection to line-printing devices, are usually named LPT*n,* where *n* is a number from 1 to 4. Serial I/O ports, traditionally used for communication devices such as modems, are named COM*n,* where again *n* is a number from 1 to 4.

More recently developed hardware devices offer the user a choice between the two types of communication. When a peripheral device offers both types of connection, the choice of parallel or serial communication depends on such considerations as the distance between the device and the CPU, the speed with which the CPU can send and receive data, and the available I/O ports.

There is little standardization in the wiring of cables to the various hardware devices. While some manufacturers adhere to a standard, "straight through" wiring design, many cables have to be wired for a specific connection between a particular CPU and peripheral.

> *Tip:* Whenever you experience trouble with any hardware device, check the cable first. Many hardware problems are really cable problems. Keep a backup cable handy for both troubleshooting and replacement.

Data-Entry Devices

Entering AutoCAD commands, editing drawings, saving and copying your drawing-data files, and producing hard-copy output are all accomplished by means of a *data-entry device.* Most AutoCAD applications use a *keyboard* and *digitizing tablet* for data entry. Some users find that the less expensive *mouse* serves their purposes adequately.

KEYBOARD

Most, if not all, desktop computers require a keyboard to function, and Auto-CAD requires one as well. Although it is possible to edit drawings without touching the keyboard, most AutoCAD users develop a data-entry technique that combines both a keyboard and a digitizing device. A keyboard is especially handy for entering text into a drawing or, when a mathematical degree of precision is required, for entering graphic information as well.

Many CPU's are packaged with compatible keyboards, but some hardware manufacturers have developed add-on keyboards that provide advantages over the standard designs (for example, separate numeric and cursor keypads, extra function keys, or programmable keys). If you intend to make frequent use of your keyboard in AutoCAD, it is worthwhile to investigate alternatives.

Get the best keyboard you can afford, and test it before buying it. High-quality keyboards have *tactile key switches*—each key will resist a bit at first, then quickly descend with a bit more pressure, and pop back immediately upon release. A comfortable, high-quality keyboard will help you maximize your overall computing productivity. Bear in mind that the difference in price between a good keyboard and a bad keyboard—about 25 dollars—is not significant when included in the overall cost of a CAD workstation.

DIGITIZING TABLET

A *digitizing tablet* is the most flexible means of entering and editing drawing data. It consists of a flat surface and a pointing device, usually a puck or stylus equipped with one or more buttons. As you move the pointing device across the tablet's surface, the movement is matched by the movement of crosshairs in AutoCAD's drawing editor. You can also use the digitizing tablet to highlight commands in AutoCAD's screen menu. Coordinate point entry is accomplished by the push of a button on the puck or stylus. Additional buttons on the pointing device may be used to invoke frequently issued commands.

The tablet may be used for more than this, however. Up to four separate rectangular sections of the tablet may be reserved for *tablet menus*. Tablet menus are in turn divided into small rectangular boxes that can be configured to correspond to Auto-CAD commands, macros, responses to prompts, and the like. Picking the appropriate box on the tablet menu is the equivalent of typing out an AutoCAD command at the keyboard. Even a long preprogrammed string of commands and responses can be executed by a single pick; this can save enormous amounts of time. Refer to Chapter 14 for details on how to configure tablet menus.

You may also configure a tablet to match the coordinate system used by a particular drawing. When the tablet is configured in this fashion, you may digitize an existing paper drawing into AutoCAD by using the tablet pointing device to trace over it. For details on how to configure a tablet, see the section entitled "Configuring the Tablet" in Chapter 3.

AutoCAD supports many digitizing tablets, but not all. Your best choice is one of the tablets supported by AutoCAD, since tablets can be a bit tricky to install, often requiring some technical expertise and experience. Before purchasing any tablet not on AutoCAD's list of supported devices, be sure to see it demonstrated with AutoCAD, and see how it is installed as well.

Many tablets are equipped with a set of small switches that control the flow of data to and from the CPU. Consult your tablet's documentation for instructions regarding what switch settings are correct for your tablet, and how to connect it to your CPU. If the tablet is supported by AutoCAD, additional instructions may be found in the AutoCAD installation documentation.

MOUSE

The *mouse* is a simpler data-entry device, consisting of a palm-sized puck connected to the CPU by a long, insulated wire. When the mouse is moved across a flat surface, the movement is tracked by the crosshairs displayed in the Auto-CAD drawing editor. The user can highlight various commands by moving the crosshairs into the screen-menu area. Coordinate point selection is accomplished by moving the crosshairs to the desired location and pushing a button on the mouse. You can use the mouse's additional buttons, if any, to invoke frequently used AutoCAD commands. There are many different brands of mice on the market; some require a special surface on which to move.

A mouse is less expensive than a tablet, but it lacks some of the tablet's advantages. A mouse cannot be configured for menu selection as a tablet can, nor is a mouse effective as a tracing device. Still, you can devise an AutoCAD screen menu system that works effectively with a mouse, thereby creating a reasonably efficient and inexpensive data-entry system.

Pen Plotter

The *pen plotter,* usually referred to simply as the "plotter," is the hardware device of choice for producing hard-copy output of AutoCAD-generated drawings. A plotter consists of a frame that holds paper securely while a system of bars, pulleys, and rollers pulls a pen across the paper's surface. Many plotters augment the movement of the pen by moving the paper as well as the pen. Also, many plotters allow for the use of multiple pens, programmable pen speed and pressure, various paper sizes, automatic sheet feeding, automatic scaling, and configurable communications parameters, so that the plotter can be connected to as many different systems as possible.

If you are not technically minded, make sure your dealer is capable of fully supporting your chosen plotter, for all of a plotter's various features and options can make it a challenge to install and maintain. A plotter must be configured to match the format of the data coming from the CPU, and no two plotters tackle this configuration problem in exactly the same way. Plotters may connect to the serial port or to the parallel printer port, or they may require special connection hardware of their own. They may require standard cables or special custom cables. Plotters are usually equipped with a variety of switches that control how they receive data from the CPU, and how that data is translated into the correct pen-and-paper selection and movements.

Some plotters trade off speed against plot quality; be certain that your chosen plotter plots at a quality and speed you can live with. Plotter speed is measured in inches per second, or *ips*; that is, the number of inches the pen is capable of traveling in a straight, continuous line for one second. A very slow speed is 1 ips, while 32 ips is quite fast. A plotter's pen speed may differ depending on whether the pen is up (not drawing) or down (creating a line). Some plotters allow you to adjust the pen speed in either or both positions, so that you may set the fastest possible pen speed consistent with the speed of the ink flow and precise up-and-down pen movements.

Since plotter pens normally change direction frequently, the actual time spent plotting your drawings may be longer than brochures and advertisements would lead you to believe. If your drawings contain lots of small lines or text, for instance, expect that your plots will take longer. Also, even high-speed plotters may require slower speeds on drawings in which detail is fine, pen ink flows too slowly, or plot quality is paramount.

A plotter's resolution is an indication of the fineness of detail capable of being represented. Many plotter manufacturers express resolution in terms of the smallest pen movements, or "steps," the plotter can make. Small movements of fractions of a millimeter are standard; the smaller the movement, the higher the resolution and the greater the capacity for rendering detail.

When determining your need for a high-quality plotter, take into account your intended volume of output. If you intend a moderately high output (five to ten plots per day), you should seriously consider investing in a high-performance plotter.

The *electrostatic plotter* is a more recent development in plotter technology, producing high-quality plotted output. It tends to be faster, quieter, and more expensive than the traditional pen plotter. If you generate 50 to 100 plots a week, the higher cost may be justified in operator-time savings.

When evaluating a plotter, be certain to see it demonstrated using AutoCAD. Have it plot one of your own AutoCAD drawings, or a sample drawing that is similar to your own. By all means get a demonstration on your own intended plot medium, be it paper, vellum, or whatever. Bring the medium to the dealer if necessary. Check for clean line quality, well-defined text characters, smooth arcs and circles. Do diagonal lines show small, jagged edges? Plot some narrowly concentric circles at a variety of diameters. Determine the price, general availability, and reliability of the pens the plotter uses. Plot a complex drawing with a single pen—does it clog or run out of ink too quickly? Does the plotter have features that can help restore a drawing when pens dry up or clog?

Printer Plotter

A *printer plotter* is a printing device with graphics output capability. Printer plotters do not produce the kind of high-quality output you expect from an expensive, high-performance pen plotter. They are generally used as printers for other applications, and called upon to produce AutoCAD drawings in special situations where quality is not paramount and the pen plotter is not available.

Printer plotters create a graphic image composed of tiny dots printed on the paper. This results in an image resolution similar to that of a computer screen. Printer resolution is measured in dots per inch, or *dpi*: the maximum number of dots the printer uses for a 1-inch solid square. A good resolution is 300 × 300 dpi, while 200 × 72 dpi is about average.

AutoCAD automatically sends all printer-plotter output to the CPU's primary *printer device*. On most IBM and compatible systems, the primary printer device is the first parallel printer port, called LPT1. If you wish to direct the output to another port (such as the serial communications port), you must redirect the output from your operating system. For further details on how to redirect AutoCAD's output, consult your operating system's documentation.

AUTOCAD ON A NETWORK

Release 11 is the first version of AutoCAD designed to support network access. If you intend to use AutoCAD on a network, you must purchase a separate software license from AutoCAD for each user. Refer to Chapter 3 for additional information about installing AutoCAD on a network.

File Locking

When running on a network, AutoCAD implements a system of *automatic file locking* to prevent multiple users from simultaneously accessing the same drawing file. When a user attempts to access a drawing file that is already in use, Auto-CAD displays the following message:

Waiting for file: (dwgfile name)
The file (dwgfile name) was locked by (user name) at (lock time) on (lock date)
Press Control C to cancel.

If the user does not press Control C, AutoCAD will make twelve attempts to access the file. If the file remains locked, AutoCAD displays:

Access denied: (dwgfile name) is in use.
Press Return to continue:

AutoCAD will also lock drawing files that are called as external reference files; refer to Chapter 21 for more information on external reference files. AutoCAD support files, such as shape files, font files, etc., will be locked if a user on the network is modifying or compiling them.

If you unlock and modify an external reference file that is already in use, the changes you make will not appear to the other user until he or she either recalls the external reference file or saves and re-loads the drawing. Likewise, if one user's drawing references a support file, changes made to the support file by another user may not be reflected in the drawing until it is reloaded into the drawing editor.

If an AutoCAD file is locked, but you are certain that it is not in use, you may cancel the file lock with the Unlock Files option in the Files command. Refer to Chapter 7 for details regarding the Files command.

It is possible to implement file locking in single-user systems to prevent files from being edited accidentally. If you are using AutoCAD on a single-user system and receive a message that a file has been locked, you can use the Files command to unlock it.

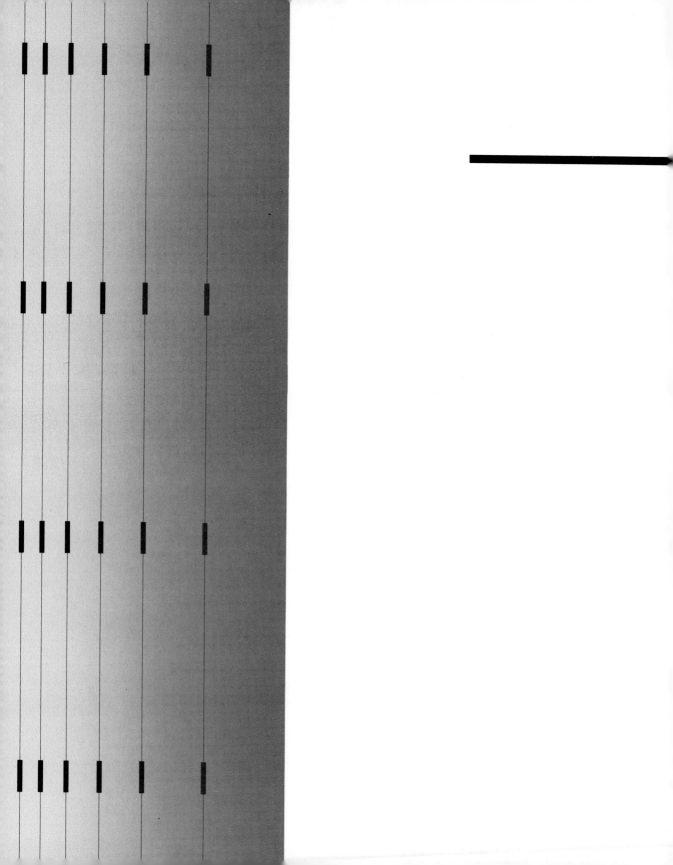

CHAPTER 3

INSTALLING AND CONFIGURING AUTOCAD

INSTALLING AND
CONFIGURING AUTOCAD

Although AutoCAD is complex, it is a relatively easy program for the average user to install and configure. You can accomplish most of the software installation and configuration by selecting your chosen hardware from a menu of devices supported by AutoCAD.

After selecting the appropriate hardware, you can optimize AutoCAD's performance using the techniques explained in Chapter 4. Even if you have only a little technical computer knowledge, it is easy to learn the techniques described in this chapter and to use them in developing your own ideal AutoCAD installation.

Before attempting to configure AutoCAD, take a few moments to read through the *documentation*—the instruction manuals and other printed explanatory material—for the hardware device. Even if all of the documentation isn't particularly clear to you the first time around, having at least a familiarity with it will make it easier to find answers later, when you have acquired more experience with the device. Whenever you configure or reconfigure AutoCAD, have the hardware documentation nearby; from time to time it may be necessary to refer to it in order to reply to questions and prompts that are displayed during the configuration process.

THE FIRST STEP: BACKING UP

AutoCAD is supplied on a set of floppy diskettes, either 5.25" 360K double-density, 5.25" 1.2Mb high-density, or 3.5" 720K standard. Never use these disks, which are called *master disks,* to run or install the AutoCAD program. Use them only as source disks for making backups. Your first step in any installation procedure is to make copies of each of these disks and store the originals in a secure location.

Copying using DOS

You can make copies of AutoCAD diskettes using the DISKCOPY command in DOS. Be certain that you have a blank disk for each master disk, and make sure that the blank disks have the same data-storage specifications as the master disks. It is not necessary to format the disks first; the DISKCOPY command will format disks while copying, if necessary. Label each blank disk with the information found on the label of a corresponding master disk and keep them together in pairs. Check to be certain that the DOS program file DISKCOPY.COM (or DISKCOPY.EXE) is on your default drive.

COPYING WITH TWO DISK DRIVES

If you have two floppy-disk drives, both of which support the data storage specification of your AutoCAD master disks, enter the following command at the DOS prompt:

DISKCOPY A: B:

(If your floppy-drive letters are not A and B, substitute the correct drive letters for A and B.)
DOS responds with:

Place SOURCE diskette in drive A:
Place TARGET diskette in drive B:
Press any key when ready...

Place an AutoCAD master disk (the source disk) in drive A, place a blank disk (the target disk) in drive B, and press Enter. DOS will make a copy of the disk. If the source disk has not been formatted, DOS will display the message "Formatting while copying." When the copy is complete, you will receive a message similar to the following:

Copy another disk (Y/N)?

Press **Y** (on some systems, followed by Enter) and you will be prompted to place new disks in the appropriate drives. Continue this process until all the master disks have been copied.

COPYING WITH ONLY ONE DISK DRIVE

If you have only a single floppy drive, enter the following command at the DOS prompt:

DISKCOPY A: A:

(If your floppy-drive letter is not A, substitute the correct drive letter for A.)
DOS responds with:

Place SOURCE diskette in drive A:
Press any key when ready...

Place an AutoCAD master disk (the source disk) in drive A and press Enter. In a few moments, DOS responds with:

```
Place TARGET diskette in drive A:
Press any key when ready...
```

Place a blank disk (the target disk) in drive A and press Enter. Depending on the size of your computer's memory and the storage capacity of your disks, it may be necessary to switch source and target diskettes more than once before a complete copy is made. When DOS has copied the entire disk, you will receive a message similar to the following:

```
Copy another disk (Y/N)?
```

Press **Y** and you will be prompted to place a new source diskette in the drive. Continue this process until all the master disks have been copied. Then store the master disks in a secure location.

README.DOC

After copies of the AutoCAD master disks have been made, the next step in installing the program is to read the file README.DOC. This file is an ASCII file containing supplementary information not included in AutoCAD's printed documentation. Depending on what hardware you have chosen, it may contain information that affects how you install and configure AutoCAD, so do not neglect to read it. Autodesk supplies a printout of this file with the program materials, but if you cannot find it or want to check the disk version as well, there are a number of ways to do so.

README.DOC is normally stored on the AutoCAD system disk labeled Drivers. Check the directory of this disk to see if README.DOC is there. You do this by placing the disk in drive A and entering the following command:

```
DIR A:README.DOC
```

If you have more than one disk labeled Drivers, first check the directory of driver disk number 1.

If the file exists on the disk in drive A, you will receive a directory listing containing that file's name. If DOS cannot find the file, you will receive the message "File not found." If DOS does not find the file, check your command syntax, or try another disk.

Once you have located README.DOC, you can read it in one of several ways. You can cause it to scroll across the screen with the following DOS command:

```
TYPE A:README.DOC
```

You can interrupt the scrolling by pressing Ctrl-S, and you can resume the scrolling with Ctrl-Q.

If the DOS file MORE.COM is present and DOS can locate it, you can enter the following command instead:

    MORE < A:README.DOC

This command will cause the scrolling to stop automatically each time the screen is filled. Pressing the space bar will cause a new screen of information to appear.

You can print out the file from the DOS prompt with the following command:

    COPY A:README.DOC PRN

This command copies the file to the computer's primary printing device. If your printer is on-line but does not respond, it may be connected to a port other than the one used as the primary printing device. If this is the case, you can substitute the correct printer port for PRN in the above example. Some examples of valid printer ports are LPT1 through LPT4 and COM1 through COM4. Substitute the correct printer port for PRN in the above example and issue the command again.

You can also read and print the file using a word processor, or a text editor with printing capability. If you use this method, take special care not to inadvertently erase or edit any portion of the file, as you may need to refer to it at various times when using AutoCAD.

INSTALLING AUTOCAD

Before installing AutoCAD, read through the introductory chapters of the *Installation and Performance Guide,* which contain a lot of useful information about installing and configuring the program. This guide can probably answer most of the questions you will have during installation.

Prior to Release 11, you could install AutoCAD on your hard disk by copying all its files into the appropriate subdirectories. However, AutoCAD Release 11 requires that you use an automatic installation procedure the first time you place it on your hard disk. To start the installation, place disk number 1 in drive A and enter:

    A:install

After a few seconds you should see the following prompts:

    Complete the following information:
    Name:

Company:
Dealer Name:
Dealer's Telephone Number:

You must enter at least four characters in each field in order to continue the installation prompt. You may move between fields by pressing the Tab key or the arrow keys. Enter the information carefully and check it for accuracy—this information is recorded permanently in AutoCAD's executable system file and may be required if you request technical support.

Next, you can specify the drive and directories where you want to install AutoCAD's system and support files. You may install both in the same subdirectory if you wish, but this is not recommended, because a large number of files in a single subdirectory can slow down the operating system. For more information on subdirectories, refer to the next section, Organization of Files in Subdirectories.

If you are upgrading from a previous version of AutoCAD, install AutoCAD 11 on a directory different from where your current version resides. For example, you could install the latest version on a subdirectory named ACAD11. This way, you will prevent any accidental overwriting of customized files from the old version. When you enter a subdirectory name, if the subdirectory does not already exist on the hard disk, AutoCAD creates it for you. For more information about these files, refer to the section Upgrading from a Previous Version later in this chapter.

Later on, when you have the new version up and running, you can move your customized AutoCAD files over to the directory containing the latest version. When you are satisfied that all custom files are intact, you may then safely erase the old version.

Alternately, you can choose to copy only selected parts of the software. Each screen of the installation program offers a choice and a default response; to accept the default, press Enter. Otherwise, type another response. You can correct a response by pressing the backspace key. Pressing the ESC key at any time cancels the installation and returns you to the operating system.

AutoCAD prompts you to enter the other master disks as needed. At the conclusion of the installation, AutoCAD checks the contents of two files on your system's root directory: AUTOEXEC.BAT and CONFIG.SYS. The program then offers to edit these files as necessary, to accommodate the installation of its files. You can choose not to edit the files at this time if you wish to reedit them later for some special configuration.

When the installation program is completed, you are ready to configure AutoCAD for your hardware devices. Store the Master Disks in a secure location and your backup copies in a separate location.

Copying Files on the Hard Disk

If you are using a version of AutoCAD prior to Release 11, or you intend to reorganize AutoCAD's system files for your own purposes, you will need to use the file-copy commands of your chosen operating system to move the files to their appropriate subdirectory locations. For information regarding file copying, refer to your operating system's documentation or contact your AutoCAD dealer.

ORGANIZATION OF FILES IN SUBDIRECTORIES

A hard disk is capable of holding thousands of different files. Because the storage capacity of the hard disk is so vast, it is convenient to organize files using a system of *subdirectories* to group related files together. Organizing related files in this way makes the operating system more efficient by speeding up searches for a particular file. It can also help the user by making particular data and program files easier to find.

For example, many AutoCAD users create a subdirectory named ACAD and store their AutoCAD program files there. When they wish to work with AutoCAD, they can log onto the ACAD subdirectory, and the operating system will ignore all the non-AutoCAD files stored elsewhere. Similarly, they may develop systems in which several different subdirectories are used to store drawing files, thus simplifying the process of managing these files by dealing with only a particular subset of the drawing files on the disk.

You may have as many subdirectories as you wish—just so you have space on your hard disk to accommodate them and the files they contain. You may create additional subdirectories within subdirectories, and continue to create subdirectories-within-subdirectories to whatever level suits your needs. (Most users don't go beyond two or three levels, however.)

All subdirectory schemes begin with a single *root directory*. This is the main directory that contains the first level of subdirectories, and may contain some data and program files as well. The root directory of a well-organized hard disk will contain only those files that must be located there. For example, if you boot your computer from the hard disk and intend to use the operating-system configuration file CONFIG.SYS, that file should be located in the root directory. If you intend to use the automatic batch execution file AUTOEXEC.BAT, this file should also be located in the root directory. Details regarding these files are presented later in this chapter.

You may place the operating-system file COMMAND.COM in the root directory, unless you have included special instructions regarding the location of this file in CONFIG.SYS.

Other program and data files will be stored in subdirectories. To create a subdirectory, enter the command **MD** followed by the name of the subdirectory you wish to create. For example, to create the subdirectory ACAD, enter the following command:

MD ACAD

Once the subdirectory is created, you can make that subdirectory the default current location from which to do your computer work. To make a subdirectory current, enter the command **CD** followed by the subdirectory name. For example, to make ACAD the current subdirectory, enter the following command:

CD ACAD

To the user, it appears that the hard disk is subdivided into separate physical locations where related files are stored. While it is useful to conceptualize a subdirectory system in this way, in actual practice subdirectories do not reserve a fixed amount of physical space on the hard disk. What actually occurs is that the operating system stores all data and program files in the first available hard-disk space it finds, and relates those files under a subdirectory name, as the user instructs via the operating system.

Thus, a subdirectory expands and contracts to accommodate changes to the number of files it contains. And as files are copied to and from RAM, it is possible for a subdirectory's files to become scattered all over the disk. Even individual files can be broken up and stored in several different physical locations, only to be reassembled when they are called into RAM. To the user it appears that the files are all sorted next to one another.

A hard disk with files broken up in this manner is said to be *fragmented.* Fragmentation reduces the efficiency of the operating system's searches for particular files. Several commercially available software utilities will rearrange the files and subdirectories on a hard disk, relocating them next to each other for fastest possible access.

Organizing Your AutoCAD Subdirectories

The following example should serve as a good general-purpose starting point for organizing your AutoCAD files into subdirectories. This subdirectory system relies on commands (which require DOS 3.3 or later) that must be added to the CONFIG.SYS. and AUTOEXEC.BAT files. The necessary file statements are used as examples in the sections covering these files:

- Copy files with the extension EXE into the subdirectory C:\ACAD.
- If you intend to use a RAM disk for AutoCAD program files, copy files with the extension OVL into the subdirectory C:\ACAD\OVERLAY. If you do not intend to use a RAM disk for program files, copy the OVL

files into the subdirectory C:\ACAD. (Four OVL files are exceptions to this rule. These configuration overlay files are listed below.)

- If you are configuring AutoCAD for the first time, or reconfiguring for different hardware, copy the files with the extension DRV or DVP into the subdirectory C:\ACAD. (You will erase these files when the configuration process is finished.)
- Copy files with the following extensions into the subdirectory C:\ACAD \SUPPORT: HLP; HDX; LIN; LSP; MNX; MSG; PAT; PGP; SHX; SLB; SLD.
- Copy files with the extensions MNU or SHP into the subdirectory C:\ACAD\SOURCE.
- If you have already configured AutoCAD, copy the following files into the C:\ACAD\CFG subdirectory: ACAD.CFG; ACADDG.OVL; ACADDS.OVL, ACADPL.OVL; ACADPP.OVL. If you intend to maintain multiple configurations of AutoCAD, you will need to create a separate configuration subdirectory for each one. These are described in detail later in this chapter.
- Copy your drawing files into your own chosen system of subdirectories. Above all, design a system that helps you keep the drawing files well organized. For example, you may want to put all the drawing files into a single subdirectory named C:\ACAD\DWGS.

An ACAD11.BAT file you could use to log onto the above drawing directory and to run Extended AutoLISP and AutoCAD is:

```
c:
cd \acad\dwgs
set acadcfg = c:\acad\cfg
set acad = c:\acad\support
extlisp
acad
remlisp
set acadcfg =
set acad =
```

This batch file sets C:\ACAD\DWGS as the current subdirectory, initializes C:\ACAD\CFG as the subdirectory where AutoCAD's configuration files can be found, initializes Extended AutoLISP, and runs AutoCAD. At the conclusion of AutoCAD, Extended AutoLISP is removed from memory, as is the setting for the configuration files. You can write similar files for different drawing subdirectories and configuration subdirectories.

The DOS PATH Command

Normally the operating system can only find program and data files in whatever subdirectory has been made current using the CD command. This can be inconvenient at times; for example, the user may require a program file found in a noncurrent (or "foreign") subdirectory but also need to use a data file found in the current subdirectory. DOS has a special command, PATH, that allows the operating system to find program files that are not in the current subdirectory. Using PATH, it is possible to specify a "search path" of various subdirectories that the operating system can follow when it does not find a requested program file in the current subdirectory. For example, the following command places the subdirectory ACAD on the search path:

```
PATH = C:\ACAD
```

Having issued this command, you may log onto any other subdirectory—one containing drawing files, for instance—and start the AutoCAD program files that are contained in the ACAD subdirectory.

The PATH command can reference several subdirectories in its search path. Each subdirectory in the list is separated from the others by a semicolon. For example, the following search path can be used to access two subdirectories:

```
PATH = C:\DOS;C:\ACAD
```

Using this PATH command, you can access the files in both the operating-system subdirectory (DOS) and AutoCAD, regardless of which subdirectory is current, while retaining the advantages of storing the files separately from each other.

CONFIG.SYS

CONFIG.SYS is an optional file containing various operating-system configuration parameters, and/or loading instructions for additional software. It is possible to use CONFIG.SYS to make changes to the operating-system environment that enable AutoCAD to run with the greatest possible efficiency. This file should be placed on the root directory of your hard disk or, if you boot your computer from a floppy disk, on the boot diskette.

The CONFIG.SYS file may contain lines like the following:

```
shell = c:\command.com c:\ /e:512 /p
files = 40
buffers = 35
```

The first line in this example enlarges the DOS environment space to 512 bytes. DOS will use this space to hold variable information useful to AutoCAD. Refer to

Chapter 4 for more information about DOS environment variables. The line FILES = 40 increases the number of files the operating system is capable of accessing simultaneously. DOS normally defaults to 8 files open at once, but this is far too few for AutoCAD. A value of FILES = 40 ensures that AutoCAD's system files plus a fairly large number of support files (shapes, fonts, AutoLISP, and so forth) can remain open and accessible at the same time, providing faster operation.

The line BUFFERS = 35 will set aside 35 blocks of RAM, each of 512 bytes, as temporary storage space for data that is frequently read from disk storage. If requested data is found in a buffer, the operating system can access it faster than it could by reading it repeatedly from disk. The optimal number of buffers is dependent on the overall performance of your system and on how you use Auto-CAD. It will require some experimentation to determine the best value for you. A value of 35 works well on most high-speed systems, but feel free to experiment with higher or lower settings.

If this line is not included in CONFIG.SYS, DOS will supply only two buffers—not nearly enough to run AutoCAD. In any event, do not set the number of buffers less than ten.

AUTOEXEC.BAT

AUTOEXEC.BAT is an optional file containing DOS commands that can be automatically executed in sequence when the operating system is loaded. Following is an example AUTOEXEC.BAT to work with the above example system:

```
path c:\;c:\acad
prompt $p$g
```

In the above example, the PROMPT statement causes the name of the current subdirectory to appear as part of the DOS prompt. The SET ACAD statement tells AutoCAD where the support files are.

If you intend to use AutoCAD with a RAM disk, add the RAM disk's drive letter to the PATH statement. For example, if the RAM disk is drive D, use the following:

```
path c:\;c:\acad;d:\
```

To copy the OVL files to the RAM disk, add the following statement to AUTOEXEC.BAT:

```
xcopy c:\acad\overlay\*.* d:\*.*
```

Upgrading from a Previous Version

If you are upgrading from a previous version of AutoCAD, be certain that you have an up-to-date backup of all current AutoCAD program and support files before installing the new version. Also be certain that you back up all current drawing files. If you experience a problem with your new version—a hardware driver file may not work properly, for example—you may wish to return to the old version as the problem is solved. Having a handy backup of your drawing files from the time of the upgrade will make the temporary return to the old version as painless as possible.

In particular, if you have altered or modified any of the following files in any way, be certain that you have an up-to-date backup of each:

ACAD.DWG	AutoCAD's prototype drawing file.
ACAD.HDX	Index file for AutoCAD's Help feature. Back it up if you have modified AutoCAD's Help file.
ACAD.HLP	AutoCAD's Help file.
ACAD.LIN	AutoCAD's linetype (noncontinuous line specification) library file.
ACAD.LSP	AutoCAD's auto-loading AutoLISP file.
ACAD.MNU	The source code for AutoCAD's on-screen menu.
ACAD.MSG	A file that displays an optional message at startup.
ACAD.PAT	AutoCAD's hatch pattern file.
ACAD.PGP	AutoCAD's external command library file.

You should make backups if you have modified AutoCAD's standard shape files, slide files, and AutoLISP files as well. If any of these files are overwritten by AutoCAD's standard versions during the installation process, the only way to restore them is by copying them from backup, thus overwriting the standard versions, or by combining new with old using a text editor.

Configuring Supported Hardware

After the AutoCAD system files are copied onto the hard disk, AutoCAD may be configured to respond correctly to various *peripheral hardware devices* such as video displays, digitizers, and hard-copy output devices. AutoCAD makes use of a special program file called a *device driver* to send and receive data in the appropriate format for the peripheral device. Generally, each peripheral device requires its own unique device driver. (In rare cases, hardware devices function similarly enough that they may both use the same device driver.)

AutoCAD is supplied with dozens of device drivers for various graphics displays, plotters, digitizers, and printer plotters. When AutoCAD furnishes the device driver for a particular hardware device, that device is said to be *supported* by AutoCAD.

When your peripheral hardware has been connected to your CPU and all the connections have been tested, you are ready to configure AutoCAD by linking the appropriate device drivers to the AutoCAD program files. If your hardware is supported by AutoCAD, this step is the easiest: AutoCAD will display a numbered list of devices. Simply enter the number for each device and answer a few questions (for example, about the particular make and model number). Most of the questions you are asked include common responses as default answers. Default responses can be selected by pressing Enter.

If you are configuring AutoCAD for the first time, you will be automatically presented with these lists of hardware devices before you use the program. If you are reconfiguring the program—for example, if you are upgrading to new hardware—you can invoke this process from a special Configuration menu and configure only those particular device drivers requiring it, or change some device options, such as a particular make and model number, associated with previously configured hardware.

Enter the information carefully. When in doubt about the answer to a particular question, consult the printed documentation supplied with your hardware device, or the *Installation and Performance Guide* supplied with AutoCAD.

As you respond to the various menu options and prompts, do not be overly concerned if you accidentally enter the wrong information. Although AutoCAD does not permit you to "back up" through the configuration process, you can repeat parts of the process as many times as you want. If you enter the wrong information, simply continue with the process, answering the remaining questions. When you are finished, reselect the hardware device where the problem occurred and enter the correct information.

Configuring for the First Time

To configure AutoCAD for the first time, log onto the AutoCAD system subdirectory and enter the command **ACAD** at the DOS prompt. You will see the following message:

AutoCAD is not yet configured.

In a few seconds, AutoCAD will display numbered lists of all the hardware devices for which it can find driver files on the hard disk. If it cannot find any driver files, it will display a message similar to the following:

> In order to interface to a device, AutoCAD needs the
> control program for that device, called a device driver.
> The device drivers are files with a type of .DRV.
>
> You must tell AutoCAD the disk drive or directory in
> which the device drivers are located. If you specify a
> disk drive, you must include the colon, as in A:
>
> Enter drive or directory containing the Display device drivers:

If you have stored your driver files on a separate subdirectory or on a floppy disk, enter the subdirectory name (preceded by the path and/or the floppy-drive letter, followed by a colon).

The Display Device

The first menu contains a numbered list of display devices. Find your display device and enter the correct number at the "Select device number or ? to repeat list:" prompt.

After you have selected your display device, you may be asked a series of questions regarding that device. These questions usually relate to optional features, such as colors for background, foreground, drawing, menus, and the like. If you are not sure which answer to give, accept the default answer for now. You can always change it later when you have had a chance to view the default configuration.

In particular, however, notice the following message:

> If you have previously measured the height and width of
> a "square" on your graphics screen, you may use these
> measurements to correct the aspect ratio.
>
> Would you like to do so? <N>

Since you have not already drawn a square in the AutoCAD drawing editor, answer this prompt with the default **N** for No. For details on calibration, see the section entitled "Calibrating Your Hardware" later in this chapter.

The Digitizer

Next, AutoCAD displays a list of supported digitizing devices. As before, locate your device and enter its number at the prompt. You may be asked various questions regarding the device—for example, the correct model number. If you're configuring a digitizing tablet, you may also be asked if you are using a puck or a stylus.

If you intend to use the keyboard as your only data-entry device, you many select device number 1, None, as your digitizing device.

The Pen Plotter

AutoCAD then displays a list of supported pen plotters. After you select the plotter from the list, you may be asked a number of questions regarding your selection—model number, how many pens, whether to change pens during plotting, and so forth. In particular, notice the calibration message, similar to the one you saw during display-device configuration:

> If you have previously measured the lengths of a horizontal
> and a vertical line that were plotted to a specific scale,
> you may use these measurements to calibrate your plotter.
>
> Would you like to calibrate your plotter? <N>

Unless you have already drawn a square in AutoCAD and plotted it, and are now using the measurements of that square to calibrate your plotter, answer this prompt with the default **N** for No. For details on calibration, see the section entitled "Calibrating Your Hardware" later in this chapter.

Next, you will be asked a series of questions regarding your intended plot specifications. The answers you give now to these questions will become the default responses to the same questions that will be repeated at plot time. The questions and what they mean are as follows:

Write the plot to a file? *<N>*   If you answer **Y** to this question, your plotting data will not be directed to the plotter, but rather to a file on disk, called a *plot file*. This can be useful if you have special plotting software that can direct the plot file to the plotter while other programs, i.e., AutoCAD, are running in the foreground. If you normally have no reason to send plotting data to a file, answer with the default **N**; plot data will then be sent directly to the plotter.

Size units (Inches or Millimeters) *<I>:*   If you normally measure the size of your plots in inches, answer with the default, **I**. If you measure plot sizes in millimeters, however, answer this question with **M**. How you answer this question will affect the subsequent display of other prompts and plotter questions, and in some cases, how you should answer them.

Plot origin in Inches <0.00,0.00>: In this case, the default response of **0.00,0.00** stands for the default starting position of the plotter, normally the lower-left corner of the drawing and the point relative to which other objects will be located on the paper. If you would like the plotter to position plots relative to a different point on the paper, enter those coordinates here. For example, if the plotter normally started just 0.5 inch from the bottom margin and 0.5 inch from the left margin, and you prefer to start the plot 2 inches from the bottom and 2 inches from the left, answer this question with **1.5",1.5"** representing 0.5 inch for the margin left by the plotter, and 1.5 additional inches so that the total paper margin adds up to 2 inches.

Standard values for plotting size; Enter the Size or Width,Height: If your plotter supports different standard plotting sizes, they will be listed here and you may pick one as the default plot size. For example, you may respond by entering **D** for D-size drawings. You may also answer the question by entering **MAX**, and your plotter's maximum plot size will be the default. If you prefer, you may enter any dimensions of width and height as the default. They will be added, along with the label USER, to the list of available plot sizes. If you enter a user-defined plotting size, be certain that your plotter is capable of plotting at those dimensions; otherwise, your plots may be distorted or may run off the paper. Notice that if you designated inches as the size unit in response to the second question, you must enter your plot size in inches here as well. Otherwise, enter the plot size in millimeters.

Rotate 2D plots 90 degrees clockwise? <N> Many plotters automatically plot in *landscape* orientation; that is, with the longer edge horizontal. If you wish to plot with the shorter edge horizontal, answer **Y** to this question in order to "rotate" the plot 90 degrees. Rotating the plot will also change the location of the plot's origin point on the paper.

> *Release 10 and later Note:* Plots are rotated automatically only when they are of the plan view in the world coordinate system. To rotate 3-D views, rotate the display to the desired viewing angle and plot that view. See Chapter 11 of this book for details on the use of the Dview command to rotate the display.

Pen width <0.010>: You may enter the exact width of your plotter pen here or accept the default. This question refers to the appearance of filled wide lines and filled solids. AutoCAD uses this pen-width figure to calculate the pen motion required to generate such figures.

Adjust area fill boundaries for pen width? <N> In applications requiring extreme accuracy of filled solids and wide lines, answer **Y** to this question and

AutoCAD will reduce the outer boundaries of solid filled areas by one-half of the pen width specified earlier. In many cases, the differences caused by this adjustment are not significant.

Remove hidden lines? <N>   If you answer **Y** to this question, 3-D plots will be plotted with hidden lines removed. All such removals are calculation-intensive, and as such will take a considerable amount of time. If you make hidden-line removal the default, be certain to override the default when plotting in 2-D; otherwise, you will be wasting a lot of time on 2-D plots.

Specify scale by entering: Plotted Inches = Drawing Units or Fit or ? <F>:   Normally, AutoCAD drawings are drawn "life-size" and scaled down to fit the hard copy at plot time. For example, if you normally plot at a scale of ⅛ inch to the foot, you could specify that ⅛ of a plotted inch equals 12 drawing inches, or **⅛" = 12"**. Several factors govern how you respond to this question. If you entered millimeters as your size unit, the prompt will appear as "Plotted Millimeters" and you should enter the plotted units accordingly. "Drawing Units," on the other hand, indicates the default drawing unit you use for your AutoCAD drawings. For example, suppose you chose millimeters as your size unit, decimal units as your drawing unit, and a single decimal drawing unit as equal to 1 kilometer. A scale of 2 = 1 would indicate that 2 plotted millimeters equals 1 kilometer (one drawing unit). Alternatively, you may enter the letter **F** in response to this prompt. AutoCAD will plot your drawings at whatever scale is necessary to fit the plot into your selected drawing size. If you enter a question mark in response to this prompt, you will receive a brief summary of these scaling options.

Your answers to any of these questions do not limit your plotting abilities in any way. You are only establishing defaults. These plot-specification questions are repeated each time you start a plot. At plot time you may enter different parameters for all these defaults, or change any that you wish.

If you do not intend to use a pen plotter, you may select device number 1, None, as your plotting device.

The Printer Plotter

AutoCAD will display a list of supported printer plotters. After selecting your device, you will be asked a series of questions regarding your printer plotter. You will also be given the option to calibrate your printer plotter, just as you were given that option with your pen plotter and display device. Do so only if you have plotted a square and are ready to enter the plotted measurements. Otherwise, enter the default **N**. For details regarding calibration, see the section entitled "Calibrating Your Hardware" later in this chapter.

After you have answered the questions regarding your make and model of printer plotter, you will be asked a series of questions similar to the ones listed for the pen plotter. Refer to the previous section for an explanation of these questions.

If you do not intend to use a printer plotter, you may select device number 1, None, as your printer plotting device.

Completing the Basic Configuration

After you have chosen your various hardware devices, AutoCAD will display a list of your choices. Be sure to check that the correct peripheral devices were selected, and that each device is configured for the correct I/O port. Press Enter. You will be returned to the AutoCAD Configuration menu (Figure 3.1).

If you accidentally selected the wrong hardware device or entered any erroneous information, you may reconfigure any particular device by selecting it from the menu and answering the associated series of configuration questions. For example, if you wish to reconfigure your plotter, select option number 5. Your current plotter configuration is displayed, and the prompt, "Install a different one?" appears. If you wish to configure a different plotter, answer **Y**. After Auto-CAD locates the device drivers, it will present you with the list of available plotter driver files. If you only wish to reenter some of the plotter's optional parameters, answer **N**. AutoCAD will then display the series of questions relating to the optional parameters of the current plotter. Your previous answers to these questions are shown as the default responses. You may accept the defaults by pressing the Enter key, or enter new information to overwrite the old.

```
              A U T O C A D (R)
       Copyright (c) 1982-90  Autodesk, Inc.  All Rights Reserved.
       Release Z.0.8B (7/23/90) 386 DOS Extender
       Serial Number:  198-10000550
       Licensed to:    Bob Thomas, Thomas Enterprises
       Obtained from:  Autodesk, Inc. - 1-415-331-0356

       Configuration menu

          0.  Exit to Main Menu
          1.  Show current configuration
          2.  Allow detailed configuration

          3.  Configure video display
          4.  Configure digitizer
          5.  Configure plotter
          6.  Configure printer plotter
          7.  Configure system console
          8.  Configure operating parameters

       Enter selection <0>:
```

FIGURE 3.1: AutoCAD's Configuration menu. This menu displays the various options available when configuring AutoCAD to communicate with your hardware. To configure a hardware device, enter the number that matches your device type as listed in the menu.

Changing the I/O Port Configuration

If you are configuring a version of AutoCAD earlier than Release 10 and you are not certain that the I/O ports are correct for your hardware, or if available I/O ports were not displayed during configuration, select Configuration menu option 2, "Allow I/O port configuration," followed by option 1, "Show current configuration." Review the I/O port information shown on your display screen. If necessary, reconfigure whichever device drivers were in error. This time, you will be asked to specify the exact I/O ports for your hardware. In selecting I/O ports, standard names such as LPT1 and COM1 are appropriate responses. AutoCAD supplies default I/O ports that are common for the particular hardware device. If you are uncertain which hardware device is connected to which I/O port, check your CPU's documentation or consult with your dealer.

Release 10 and later Note: As of Release 10, I/O port configuration is no longer optional. Whenever you configure or reconfigure AutoCAD Release 10, you will be asked to specify I/O ports for all hardware devices. I/O ports are always included in the display of the current configuration for Release 10.

Detailed Configuration

Certain hardware devices allow you to fine-tune their parameters by making adjustments to the driver files. Normally, these fine-tuning procedures are of little interest to the average user, and in addition they may require special technical knowledge. In a normal AutoCAD configuration routine, the prompts for these adjustments are suppressed. However, if you would like to take advantage of these additional fine-tuning parameters, you may select option number 2, "Allow detailed configuration," from the Configuration menu. (In versions prior to Release 10, this option was called "Allow I/O port configuration.")

For example, if you allow detailed configuration, many of AutoCAD's plotter drivers will allow you to specify the degree of *pen motion optimization* you desire. The degree of pen motion optimization refers to the amount of additional calculating AutoCAD will perform at plot time, to plot the entities in such a way as to minimize wasted pen motion. Most users prefer the maximum degree of pen motion optimization, as this reduces the amount of time spent plotting. However, for those applications where extra pen motion is not an issue or optimization affects the quality of the final plot, the user may specify a lesser degree of optimization.

The specifications required for detailed configuration vary among hardware devices. If you are curious about detailed configuration, you may select it and review the extra options afforded you. If you're unsure of your response, select the default that is offered. Bear in mind that if you choose to experiment with various fine-tuning options, you may cause unintended results and be forced to reconfigure your device from scratch.

Saving the Configuration

After you have entered all the correct device information, you will return to the Configuration menu. Enter **0** and you will receive the following message:

```
if you answer N to the following question, all configuration
changes you have just made will be discarded.

Keep configuration changes? <Y>
```

Enter **Y** (the default) or press Enter, and AutoCAD will save your configuration in a file called ACAD.CFG. When the configuration is saved, AutoCAD displays the program's Main Menu. It is possible to configure a single copy of AutoCAD for several different combinations of hardware devices, and then switch between them. For details and instructions, see the section entitled "Maintaining Multiple Configurations" in Chapter 4.

Testing the Configuration

After saving your configuration, you can test the hardware devices by displaying and plotting one of AutoCAD's sample drawings. Log onto the subdirectory containing the file COLORWH.DWG and begin AUTOCAD. From the Auto-CAD Main Menu, select option 2, "Edit an existing drawing," followed by the drawing name, COLORWH. If the chart of standard AutoCAD colors appears on your monitor screen, you know that your display device is working. Test your digitizing device by selecting the Line command from the screen menu followed by two different points on the screen. If AutoCAD draws a line between them, your digitizing device is working. Enter Ctrl-C followed by the Fill command. Turn the fill off, and enter the Plot command. Accept the default answers to the plot parameter questions by pressing Enter in response to each one. If you have installed a printer plotter, test it using the Prplot command, again accepting the default printer parameters.

Solving Problems

If one of your hardware devices is not working, try the following:

- Check the cable connection. Are you using the correct cable for your device? Is the cable connected to the correct port? Is the cable connected firmly on both ends?

- Check the power supply to your hardware device. Is the device receiving electrical power?
- Check the documentation for the particular device. Look for any special troubleshooting guidelines, or for instructions regarding AutoCAD.
- Check the switch settings and any of the device's other adjustable features. Are they all set properly? Does AutoCAD require that you change some switch settings? If the device has a self-test feature, use it.
- Check the AutoCAD configuration. Is AutoCAD configured for the correct device? Have you configured all the correct options for the device—for instance, the correct make and model number? Consult the AutoCAD *Installation and Performance Guide* for details regarding your hardware.
- Check to see if you are running any memory-resident software, RAM disks, or other programs that utilize your computer's memory in ways that might conflict with AutoCAD. Try using the device when these programs are not installed.
- If the problem seems intermittent, attempt to discern a pattern of circumstances under which the problem occurs. If you can detect such a pattern, try to isolate and change those factors that cause the problem.

If your hardware appears to be functioning properly but AutoCAD is still not working (e.g., system crashes, odd messages on the screen, etc.), the problem may be due to conflicts between AutoCAD and either RAM disks or programs such as memory-resident utilities (TSRs), extended-memory managers, and the like. The first step to take in diagnosing these kinds of problems is to try running AutoCAD in the simplest, most basic system possible—in other words, with no other programs in memory and no additional settings in the operating system beside those essential for AutoCAD to function.

If you cannot get AutoCAD to run in a minimal, no-frills configuration, consult your dealer about your hardware. If you are able to get AutoCAD to run in a basic configuration, begin to add your other programs one by one, starting with those you deem most important. Continue adding programs until a problem occurs. Some programs, such as TSRs and memory managers, allow you to change settings via the CONFIG.SYS or AUTOEXEC.BAT files. So when you discover a program that conflicts with AutoCAD, refer to its documentation to determine if an alternate setting will eliminate the trouble. Once a problematic program is running smoothly with AutoCAD, move onto the next one, until all are added and you have determined which ones are absolutely incompatible.

If you are unable to solve the problem after trying the troubleshooting steps outlined above, consult your dealer for assistance. When consulting your dealer, you will greatly enhance your chances for success if you supply the following information:

- Make, model number, any optional accessories, cable, and warranty information for the troublesome device.
- Make, model, and memory size for the computer you are using, as well as similar information on all of its peripheral devices and other optional equipment.
- Operating system and version number, plus any other software you are using. Make special note of any memory-resident utility programs, public-domain software, RAM-disk software, or software that requires special settings in the CONFIG.SYS or AUTOEXEC.BAT file.
- The serial number from your AutoCAD master disks.
- A description—as complete as you can make it—of the circumstances under which you experience the problem. Try to avoid jargon and diagnostic guesswork. Stick to the facts as you observe them.
- A copy of the files ACAD.CFG and (if it exists) ACAD.ERR.
- Any output that helps describe the problem. This includes all hard-copy output and screen dumps. If you cannot produce screen dumps, handwritten copies of error messages can be helpful.

Deleting the Driver Files

Once you have configured AutoCAD for your particular combination of hardware devices, you may safely delete the driver files from your hard disk. These driver files take up a lot of room and are no longer needed once AutoCAD creates the file ACAD.CFG. To delete the driver files, enter the following command:

```
DEL C:\ACAD\*.DRV
```

If you ever have to reconfigure AutoCAD, these driver files will be needed once more. In such a case, you may either copy the driver files from the floppy disk to the AutoCAD system-files subdirectory, or specify the location of the driver files (for example, on a floppy disk in drive A) at the start of the configuration process.

Configuring the Operating Parameters

If you wish, you may configure some additional operating parameters that will help you get the most from AutoCAD. To configure the operating parameters, select option 8, "Configure operating parameters," from the Configuration menu. When you select this option, the menu shown in Figure 3.2 is displayed.

```
              A U T O C A D (R)
Copyright (c) 1982-90  Autodesk, Inc.  All Rights Reserved.
Release Z.0.8B (7/23/90) 386 DOS Extender
Serial Number:  198-10000550
Licensed to:    Bob Thomas, Thomas Enterprises
Obtained from:  Autodesk, Inc. - 1-415-331-0356


Operating parameter menu


   0.  Exit to configuration menu
   1.  Alarm on error
   2.  Initial drawing setup
   3.  Default plot file name
   4.  Plot spooler directory
   5.  Placement of temporary files
   6.  Network node name
   7.  AutoLISP feature
   8.  Full-time CRC validation
   9.  Automatic Audit after IGESIN, DXFIN, or DXBIN
  10.  Login name
  11.  Server authorization and file locking

Enter selection <0>:
```

FIGURE 3.2: AutoCAD's Operating Parameter menu. You will see this menu when you select option 8 from the Configuration menu (Figure 3.1). This menu allows you to configure optional features of the AutoCAD program that apply to all hardware configurations.

Following is a brief description of each of these options:

Alarm on error   Enabling this feature will cause AutoCAD to sound a tone each time an error occurs. This can get annoying at times and is not recommended except under special circumstances. AutoCAD is supplied with this feature disabled.

Initial drawing setup   AutoCAD normally begins each new drawing with whatever settings are contained in the file ACAD.DWG. This drawing is called the *prototype drawing.* If you wish, you may select an existing drawing of your choice as the prototype by entering its name here. Before selecting a new prototype drawing, remember that it isn't always necessary. AutoCAD allows you to make whatever changes you like to ACAD.DWG by simply editing it in the drawing editor; and regardless of this setting, you may specify any existing drawing you wish to be the prototype whenever you begin a new drawing.

Default plot file name   This feature is of interest only if you intend to create plot files. Normally, when you request that plotter output be sent to a file, AutoCAD supplies a default plot-file name that is the same as the current drawing, except that the plot file's extension is PLT. If you would prefer that a different default name be used, you can specify that name here. This is useful for certain plotter buffer devices that expect to see a specific plot file each time. Regardless of the default, you are permitted to select a different plot-file name whenever plotting. You can also choose AUTOSPOOL as the default. Using this name has an effect on the following feature. (Refer to Chapter 12 for more information regarding plot files.)

Plot spooler directory This feature is of interest only if you intend to use plot spoolers or plot files. If you choose AUTOSPOOL as the name of your plot file, AutoCAD will direct the output not to a disk file, but instead to a background spooling program of your choice. Use this feature to tell AutoCAD where to find your spooling program. (You must install and configure your spooler separately, to recognize input from AutoCAD.) AutoCAD automatically assigns a file name for its output to a spooling program. These files always begin with $V (for spooling plot files) or $R (for spooling printer-plot files). When AutoCAD is finished writing these spooling files, it removes the dollar sign from the beginning of the spooling file's name. For safety's sake, configure your spooler program to ignore all files beginning with $V or $R.

Placement of temporary files As an editing session progresses, AutoCAD creates several files, called *temporary work files,* that hold parts of the drawing that are too large to fit in the available random-access memory. Normally, temporary work files are stored on the same drive and subdirectory as the current drawing, and deleted at the completion of each editing session. Placing these files on a different drive or subdirectory will have little impact on AutoCAD's overall performance, but you can improve AutoCAD's performance slightly if you instruct it to place these temporary work files on a RAM disk. To do so, select this option and supply the RAM disk's drive and, if applicable, its subdirectory name here.

Some temporary files—for example, files with the extension $A—are always stored in the same drive and subdirectory as the drawing file, even if you have indicated another drive and directory here.

Bear in mind that if you name a RAM disk drive and/or subdirectory (if applicable) here, you must initialize it before AutoCAD is initialized. You usually accomplish this by adding the appropriate lines to CONFIG.SYS and AUTOEX-EC.BAT. If you do not initialize the correct RAM disk drive and subdirectory, AutoCAD will display a warning message at start-up and will place the temporary files on the same subdirectory as the drawing file.

Make certain that your RAM disk space is at least large enough to accommodate your largest possible drawing file, with extra space if your editing sessions are long and many drawing entities are created or changed. If you run out of space for AutoCAD's temporary work files, AutoCAD will bring an early end to your drawing session with a disk-full error message. Fortunately, AutoCAD includes safety mechanisms so that under such disk-full conditions, the changes you have made to the drawing will be saved. In the event that the disk-full message is the symptom of a more serious hardware failure, AutoCAD may not be able to save the changes. In such an event, AutoCAD displays a message to that effect.

Tip: RAM disks are usually much smaller than hard disks, and therefore are more likely to develop disk-full error conditions. Whenever using a RAM disk to store temporary files, save the drawing to disk as often as practical, using the End command. When you use the End command to save a drawing, you release RAM disk space occupied by the "audit trail" of Undo or Redo commands. Alternatively, if you have no need for AutoCAD's Undo feature, you can disable the Undo command, or set the feature to Undo One, which also will conserve RAM-disk space.

Network node name This feature allows you to select a prefix, up to three characters long, that will be added onto the beginning of AutoCAD's temporary work file names. This is required when several AutoCAD users on a network edit different drawings that are located in the same subdirectory of a shared hard disk; unless the temporary files are distinguishable from each other, one user's file could easily be overwritten by another's. The prefix, called the *network node name,* must be unique to each user's configuration, and must contain only characters that are valid for use as DOS files names. Combinations of letters and numbers that identify each workstation usually work well, and allow for the addition of new network terminals without confusion.

AutoLISP feature AutoCAD is supplied with the AutoLISP feature enabled. If you do not intend to use AutoLISP, you can disable it, thereby allowing the RAM normally used by AutoLISP to be used instead for other AutoCAD processing. Answer **N** to the prompt:

> Do you want AutoLISP enabled?

in order to turn off the AutoLISP feature. If you are using AutoCAD with less than 640K of RAM, AutoLISP may be disabled automatically. When there is insufficient RAM, AutoCAD disables AutoLISP at start-up and displays the message:

> AutoLISP disabled.

Disabling AutoLISP here will suppress that message.

Release 10 and later Note: If you are using more than 512K of extended (not expanded) memory on an Intel 80286 system, you can enable a special version of AutoLISP called *Extended AutoLISP.* To do so, enable regular AutoLISP by answering **Y** to the prompt:

> Do you want AutoLISP enabled?

You will then be prompted:

Do you want to use Extended AutoLISP?

Answer **Y** to this prompt as well.

Even after you enable the Extended AutoLISP feature, you still must run the program EXTLISP.EXE each time you turn on or reboot your computer, before initializing AutoCAD. One fairly convenient way to do this is by placing EXTLISP.EXE in a subdirectory on your operating system's search path, and including the command EXTLISP in the AUTOEXEC.BAT file on the root directory. See the section entitled "Using More than 640K" in Chapter 4 for details and additional instructions on how to install Extended AutoLISP.

Full-time CRC validation AutoCAD is supplied with its full-time *cyclic redundancy check* feature disabled. A cyclic redundancy check is an diagnostic error-detection mechanism that verifies the integrity of the entire drawing file by immediately double-checking all data as it is stored. The feature is useful in cases where you suspect your hardware of corrupting the data it should be saving, but can slow down performance somewhat. If AutoCAD discovers that drawing data is not stored correctly, it will mark the drawing file as damaged, requiring you to take recovery steps (and hopefully isolate and solve the problem) before you re-edit the drawing file. To enable CRC validation, enter **Y** in response to the prompt:

Do you want full-time CRC validation?

Automatic audit after IGESIN, DXFIN, or DXBIN This feature provides an error-checking mechanism that examines the drawing database each time it imports an AutoCAD drawing interchange file. AutoCAD is supplied with this feature turned off. To turn it on, answer **Y** in response to the prompt

Do you want an automatic audit after IGESIN, DXFIN, or DXBIN?

For more information regarding drawing interchange files, see Chapter 20. For information regarding audits, refer to the discussion of the Audit command in Chapter 7.

Login name In network-configured AutoCAD, the default login name is assigned during the initial installation of each node. The login name is used by the system administrator to monitor simultaneous use of the system and check on locked files. Generally, the name of the individual user on each node is the login name. If no default name is used, AutoCAD will prompt you to enter a name each time you start AutoCAD. You may use this option to change the default login name. AutoCAD prompts:

Enter default login name or . for none <current name>:

Enter the new default name, or if you want no default, enter a period.

Server authorization and file locking   This option allows you to revise your network to include more users. In order to make any changes, you must apply for and receive a new server authorization code as part of an upgrade package from your dealer.

Warning: Make changes to the server authorization only when no one is using AutoCAD.

Upon selecting this option, AutoCAD prompts:

Your maximum number of users is *n*
Do you wish to change it?

In this message, *n* equals the maximum number of AutoCAD nodes on your system. If you intend to make changes, type **Y**. AutoCAD responds:

Enter the maximum number of users for this package:

Enter the new number carefully. AutoCAD responds:

Enter server authorization code or this package:

Enter the server authorization code carefully. Double-check this code before pressing Enter. AutoCAD then prompts:

Do you wish to run the executable from a read-only directory?

Respond either **Y** or **N**, depending on whether your network configuration requires running executable files from a read-only directory. (For example, 3com is a network that requires this.) If you answer **Y**, AutoCAD responds:

Specify a sharable directory for server temporary files:

AutoCAD normally uses the executable file directory to store temporary files. Since you are indicating that the executable directory is read-only, AutoCAD now needs an alternate directory for these files. Enter the name of a write-enabled directory for server files.

AutoCAD's last prompt is:

Enter a password to restrict unauthorized changes to the server authorization or . for none:

If you want a password for your system manager, enter it here. Otherwise, enter a period. If you enter a password, you must verify it by retyping it.

If you are the only user of a network-based version of AutoCAD, you have the option of turning off file locking. When you select this feature, AutoCAD begins its series of prompts, as described earlier. After you indicate the maximum number of users to be 1, AutoCAD responds:

Do you wish to enable file-locking?

Answer **Y** if you want file-locking enabled, **N** if you want it disabled. On a single-user networked system, you may marginally improve performance if you disable file locking. You cannot disable file locking on a multi-user system.

CONFIGURING NONSUPPORTED HARDWARE

Although AutoCAD supports many different hardware devices, it does not support them all. It is possible to use AutoCAD with nonsupported hardware devices, provided that the manufacturer of the device supplies a device driver for AutoCAD and is willing to provide any necessary technical assistance to help you configure and use the device. Autodesk cannot help you if you have problems with a nonsupported hardware device.

Despite this warning, there is usually nothing wrong with using AutoCAD along with many of the available nonsupported hardware devices; many of these devices work well. If you are considering the purchase of a nonsupported hardware device for any reason, be certain that the manufacturer is also supplying an AutoCAD device driver, along with complete and clearly written instructions on how to install, configure, and use the device with AutoCAD. If possible, get a demonstration of the device using AutoCAD before purchasing it.

The following is general information regarding the use of nonsupported hardware devices. It will help you understand the various factors involved before selecting and using nonsupported hardware.

Installing Third-Party Drivers

If the hardware manufacturer has supplied a complete, AutoCAD-compatible device driver, the installation should be fairly simple. Just copy the driver file to the AutoCAD system subdirectory. During the standard configuration process, the name of the hardware device will appear on the numbered list of devices. Select the device and answer any questions that are asked.

Installing ADI Drivers

Even in cases where AutoCAD does not directly support a specific manufacturer's product, many manufacturers, mindful of AutoCAD's popularity, design their products to work with AutoCAD and provide the necessary software.

Many hardware manufacturers supply a device driver that will work together with AutoCAD's special "generic" driver file called the *ADI device interface.* In effect, two drivers are used when you configure AutoCAD using the ADI device interface; AutoCAD must be configured for the ADI device interface, and the manufacturer's ADI driver must be installed as well. The ADI drivers supplied by hardware manufacturers may be installed in a variety of ways. Some are installed by invoking a special memory-resident program from the DOS prompt; others are installed by adding a command to the CONFIG.SYS file; some may require a special batch file for installation. You must consult the documentation supplied with your particular device to learn how to install your manufacturer's ADI driver. It is a good idea to read the documentation before you purchase the product. If the documentation seems too technical or unclear, you may wish to investigate alternatives.

AutoCAD's ADI device interface is included on the numbered list of supported hardware devices. There is a separate ADI device interface for graphics display, digitizer, pen plotter, and printer plotter. It is entirely possible to combine the ADI device interface for one peripheral device with an AutoCAD-supported driver for another.

To configure AutoCAD for the ADI device interface, enter the number for the ADI device interface from the list of supported device drivers. After you have selected the ADI device interface, you will be asked a series of questions, depending on what type of hardware device you intend to configure.

In order to configure the ADI device interface, you must understand two concepts that relate to how a computer manages its memory: *interrupts* and *hexadecimal numbers.*

INTERRUPTS AND HEXADECIMAL NUMBERS

When you're configuring AutoCAD for the ADI device interface, one piece of information you will be asked to provide is which *interrupt* your ADI device will use. An interrupt is a specific place in the computer's random-access memory that is set aside as a control point to manage the flow of information between the CPU and a peripheral device. Only a limited number of these interrupts are available; they tend to get used up fairly quickly. When you configure AutoCAD for an ADI device, it is particularly important that you know which interrupts are in use by other devices and which are available for use by the ADI device. Assigning two devices to the same interrupt can create a conflict, causing nonsensical information to appear or preventing the computer from operating at all.

The location of an interrupt in RAM is identified by means of a hexadecimal number. A hexadecimal number is a number that is based on a repeating cycle of 16 (as opposed to decimal numbers, which are based on a repeating cycle of 10).

Imagine counting in a hexadecimal numbering system: It begins, as does the decimal system, with 0, 1, 2, 3, etc., through 9. However, the next six hexadecimal numbers after 9 are expressed as A, B, C, D, E, and F, before continuing on with 10, 11, 12, etc., through 19. Hexadecimal numbers after 19 are expressed 1A, 1B, 1C, 1D, 1E, and 1F, before continuing on with 20 through 29 and then 2A through 2F. Table 3.1 shows equivalent values of decimal and hexadecimal numbering systems.

DEC.	HEX.	DEC.	HEX.	DEC.	HEX.	DEC.	HEX.
0	0	50	32	100	64	150	96
1	1	51	33	101	65	151	97
2	2	52	34	102	66	152	98
3	3	53	35	103	67	153	99
4	4	54	36	104	68	154	9A
5	5	55	37	105	69	155	9B
6	6	56	38	106	6A	156	9C
7	7	57	39	107	6B	157	9D
8	8	58	3A	108	6C	158	9E
9	9	59	3B	109	6D	159	9F
10	A	60	3C	110	6E	160	A0
11	B	61	3D	111	6F	161	A1
12	C	62	3E	112	70	162	A2
13	D	63	3F	113	71	163	A3
14	E	64	40	114	72	164	A4
15	F	65	41	115	73	165	A5
16	10	66	42	116	74	166	A6
17	11	67	43	117	75	167	A7
18	12	68	44	118	76	168	A8
19	13	69	45	119	77	169	A9
20	14	70	46	120	78	170	AA
21	15	71	47	121	79	171	AB
22	16	72	48	122	7A	172	AC
23	17	73	49	123	7B	173	AD
24	18	74	4A	124	7C	174	AE
25	19	75	4B	125	7D	175	AF
26	1A	76	4C	126	7E	176	B0
27	1B	77	4D	127	7F	177	B1
28	1C	78	4E	128	80	178	B2
29	1D	79	4F	129	81	179	B3
30	1E	80	50	130	82	180	B4
31	1F	81	51	131	83	181	B5
32	20	82	52	132	84	182	B6
33	21	83	53	133	85	183	B7
34	22	84	54	134	86	184	B8
35	23	85	55	135	87	185	B9

TABLE 3.1: Decimal/Hexadecimal Conversion Chart

DEC.	HEX.	DEC.	HEX.	DEC.	HEX.	DEC.	HEX.
36	24	86	56	136	88	186	BA
37	25	87	57	137	89	187	BB
38	26	88	58	138	8A	188	BC
39	27	89	59	139	8B	189	BD
40	28	90	5A	140	8C	190	BE
41	29	91	5B	141	8D	191	BF
42	2A	92	5C	142	8E	192	C0
43	2B	93	5D	143	8F	193	C1
44	2C	94	5E	144	90	194	C2
45	2D	95	5F	145	91	195	C3
46	2E	96	60	146	92	196	C4
47	2F	97	61	147	93	197	C5
48	30	98	62	148	94	198	C6
49	31	99	63	149	95	199	C7
							...etc.

TABLE 3.1: Decimal/Hexadecimal Conversion Chart (continued)

Hexadecimal numbers are used because computers process *binary code,* made up of electronic data bits processed in groups of 16. A hexadecimal numbering system is the most efficient means of expressing how these groups of 16 data bits are stored, altered, and moved about while in memory. Thus, when a specific place in RAM is assigned to be used as the control point for the flow of information to and from a peripheral device, that place is identified by means of a hexadecimal number.

GETTING HELP WITH AN ADI DRIVER

Autodesk does not provide support for ADI devices. When you purchase an ADI device, it is extremely important that you choose a reputable dealer—one that can provide a reasonable level of technical support. In addition, it is prudent to determine before the purchase that the manufacturer will provide technical support in addition to the dealer.

The manufacturer of the ADI device should provide you with documentation that includes all the technical details necessary to install and configure the device. This includes adequate technical information, such as which interrupts they use. Unfortunately, some manufacturers are remiss in this regard. If you cannot find the answers to AutoCAD's configuration questions in the documentation supplied with the ADI device, try accepting AutoCAD's default response. If a hardware conflict occurs anyway and you cannot solve the problem from the documentation, you may have no choice but to contact either the dealer or the manufacturer's technical support department.

CONFIGURING THE ADI GRAPHICS-DISPLAY INTERFACE

To configure AutoCAD's ADI graphics-display interface, select it from Auto-CAD's list of display options. You are prompted only to enter the interrupt location used by the ADI graphics-display driver you will be installing. Enter the code as a hexadecimal number, or accept AutoCAD's default by pressing Enter.

CONFIGURING THE ADI DIGITIZER INTERFACE

To configure AutoCAD's ADI digitizer interface, select it from AutoCAD's list of digitizer options. You are prompted only to enter the interrupt location to be used by the ADI digitizer driver you will be installing. Enter the code as a hexadecimal number, or accept AutoCAD's default by pressing Enter.

CONFIGURING THE ADI PEN-PLOTTER INTERFACE

To configure AutoCAD's ADI plotter interface, select it from AutoCAD's list of plotter options. You will be asked a series of general questions regarding the plotter you will be using. The answers to these questions should be found in the documentation for the plotter you intend to use; some manufacturers even provide the exact sequence of prompts and correct responses for their product. Be sure to study the manufacturer's documentation carefully before attempting to install an ADI plotter.

The ADI plotter driver can produce one of three possible plot file formats, or it can communicate with a special plotter driver file supplied by your plotter's manufacturer. A plot file is a disk file containing the plotter commands required to produce a drawing. If your plotter requires a special plot file, you must specify the format of that file. Following is a brief explanation of each of the three possible plot-file formats:

ASCII file   This format contains the plotter commands required to produce the drawing, coded as a series of decimal numbers. Each plotter command appears on a separate line in the file. It is possible to read this file using a text editor, in which case it will appear as a long series of numbers separated by commas. It is also possible to edit this file in a text editor, provided that you know the plotter commands represented by the numbers in the file. However, the practice of editing ASCII plot files requires considerable expertise and is not recommended—it is much easier to edit the drawing in AutoCAD and create a new plot file.

Binary file   This format, like the ASCII file format, contains plotter commands, in this case coded as binary numbers. It is not practical to read or edit this file, although there are some utility programs that can translate the binary numbers into hexadecimal numbers.

DXB file   This format is a unique binary format generated by the AutoCAD ADI plotter driver, or by a third-party software application such as AutoShade. It has the advantage of being a compact format that can be generated quickly.

If your plotter has its own driver file that works with the ADI driver file, you will be asked to specify the interrupt location used by your plotter's driver. This code must be supplied to you by your plotter's manufacturer. After you select the interrupt location, you will be asked a series of questions regarding your plotter's capabilities. These include the number of pens your plotter uses, the number of line styles, the pen speed, the maximum plot size, and the number of steps per inch. After you have entered this general information, the questions on the plotter defaults appear, and you may supply default answers as in the supported-plotter configuration process.

CONFIGURING THE ADI PRINTER-PLOTTER INTERFACE

You can configure the ADI printer plotter to produce a data file that can be sent to the printer plotter, or you can configure it to communicate directly with a separate driver supplied by the plotter's manufacturer.

To configure the ADI printer-plotter driver, select it from the list of supported drivers displayed by AutoCAD. You must first specify the maximum paper size and the resolution of your printer plotter in terms of the number of horizontal and vertical dots per inch that the printer plotter is capable of producing. This information is supplied to you in the plotter's documentation.

Next, you must specify the output format for your configuration. You may choose to have the ADI driver produce a binary data file or to have it communicate with a special driver supplied by the manufacturer.

If you choose to have AutoCAD's ADI driver communicate with a hardware driver supplied by your manufacturer, you must specify the correct interrupt location to be used by that driver. This information must be supplied to you in the documentation for your printer plotter.

After you have answered the ADI driver configuration questions, you will be asked the normal series of configuration questions, as is done with a supported device driver. The answers to these questions will be the default responses when you issue the Prplot command. Refer to Chapter 12 for more information regarding the Prplot command.

CALIBRATING YOUR HARDWARE

After AutoCAD has been configured to communicate with your various hardware devices, you may, if necessary, calibrate these devices to ensure that the commands and graphic information are communicated accurately.

Calibrating the Output Devices

The process of calibrating your output hardware consists of drawing a square and measuring its sides with a ruler after it is generated by the device. If the sides of the square are not reproduced with exactly the same length, you may enter the current measurements in response to AutoCAD's prompts, and AutoCAD will correct the information sent to the devices so that the display is produced accurately.

For example, following are the steps necessary to calibrate your monitor:

1. From AutoCAD's main menu, select task number 1, "Begin a NEW drawing."

2. When prompted for the name of the drawing, enter:

   CALTEST -

3. Using AutoCAD's Line command, draw a large square. The square should consist of horizontal and vertical lines, and it should be large enough that you can comfortably and accurately measure its sides with a ruler, tape measure, or similar measuring device. Since you have not yet calibrated your display device, it is possible that the square you have drawn will appear as a rectangle; therefore, do not rely on appearance alone to guide you when drawing the square. The following sequence will draw a square with sides that are 6 drawing units long:

   Command: **Line**
   From point: **1,1**
   To point: **6,1**
   To point: **6,6**
   To point: **1,6**
   To point: **C**

4. Measure the square that appears on the screen using a tape measure, ruler, or other measuring device.

5. If the horizontal and vertical dimensions are equal, there is no need to calibrate your display device. Invoke the Quit command, and confirm your intention to quit by pressing **Y**.

6. If the horizontal and vertical dimensions of the square are not equal, make a note of them. Be sure to note which dimension is vertical and which is horizontal.

7. After measuring, invoke AutoCAD's End command to store the drawing on disk.

8. When AutoCAD's Main Menu reappears, select option 5, "Configure AutoCAD," and press Enter. AutoCAD will display the current configuration.

9. Press Enter, and select option 3, "Configure video display." AutoCAD will ask you if you wish to select a new device driver.

10. Press **N.** You will then be asked the standard configuration questions for display drivers. When you see the following message press **Y**:

> If you have previously measured the height and width of
> a "square" on your graphics screen, you may use these
> measurements to correct the aspect ratio.
>
> Would you like to do so? <N>

11. AutoCAD then asks for the width and height of the square you just measured. Enter the horizontal measurement for the width and the vertical measurement for the height.

12. Select default responses for any other display configuration questions.

13. When the Configuration menu reappears, select option 0, "Exit to Main Menu," and press **Y** when asked to save your configuration changes.

14. When the Main Menu reappears, select option number 2 and edit the drawing CALTEST.

15. Check the measurements of the square. The horizontal and vertical dimensions should now be equal. If they are not, make a note of the new dimensions and repeat steps 3 through 15.

When calibrating, you do not need to perform any scaling or corrections to the measurements taken from the screen; enter them exactly as measured, using whatever format has been set up by means of the Units command. AutoCAD calibrates your display device by calculating and adjusting its display information according to the horizontal-to-vertical ratio that you measured. Refer to Chapter 6 for details regarding the Units command.

Pen and printer plotters can be calibrated using the same method. Measure the plotted output of the CALTEST drawing and repeat the above method to calibrate the pen plotter or printer plotter if necessary. If you have not plotted a drawing before and aren't sure of the orientation of the plotted output, you may wish to include a small amount of text in the CALTEST drawing, or draw an arrow or other mark to help you determine the orientation of the plotted square.

Configuring the Tablet

Configuring your digitizing tablet involves marking the areas to be used for tablet menu commands and the pointing area for coordinates on the screen. AutoCAD is supplied with a standard 12" × 12" tablet template; the default responses to the tablet configuration routine correspond to the settings for this standard tablet. If you have purchased a third-party tablet, consult the manufacturer's documentation to determine the correct responses to AutoCAD's configuration prompts. If you are configuring your own custom template, try practicing the procedure using AutoCAD's standard template first. In addition, the following general information will help.

AutoCAD allows up to four separate rectangular areas of the tablet to be used for menus of AutoCAD commands. Each of these rectangular menu areas is divided into a user-specified number of vertical columns and horizontal rows. The intersections of these columns and rows form boxes within the menu area; thus, the greater the number of columns and rows, the smaller the boxes will be.

AutoCAD's menu file can be customized so that commands or macros—or for that matter, just about any information that can be entered from the keyboard—can be entered simply by picking the corresponding command box with the tablet's puck or stylus. A carefully laid-out tablet menu system can dramatically improve AutoCAD's productivity. For more information on customizing tablet menus, refer to Chapter 14.

Follow these steps to configure a tablet:

1. Secure your tablet template firmly to the tablet.
2. From AutoCAD's Main Menu, select option 2, "Edit an EXISTING drawing."
3. When prompted for the name of the drawing, enter **ACAD** (or the name of your prototype drawing if different).
4. When the AutoCAD Command prompt appears, enter:

    TABLET CFG

    You will see the following prompt:

    Enter the number of tablet menus desired (0-4):

5. Enter the number of rectangular menu areas you intend to place on your tablet. If you are using AutoCAD's standard menu, enter **4**.

6. You are then asked to mark the tablet menu areas. You do this by picking the upper-left corner, lower-left corner, and lower-right corner of each menu area. These three points must form a 90-degree angle or AutoCAD will not accept them.

7. Each time you mark a tablet menu area, you are then asked to enter the number of vertical columns and the number of horizontal rows. The product of these two figures will be the number of command boxes available in that tablet menu area.

8. Repeat steps 6 and 7 for each menu area you desire.

9. After you have configured the tablet menu areas, you will be prompted to select the screen pointing area. To do this, pick the lower-left and upper-right corners of the area of the tablet to be used for screen pointing.

10. Save the drawing using the End command. AutoCAD will save the configuration information for subsequent editing sessions.

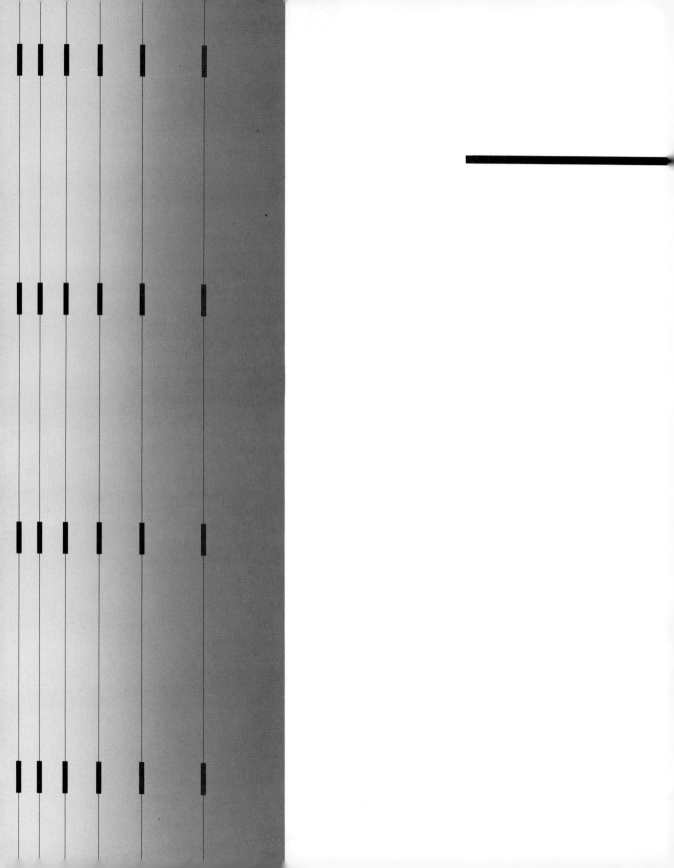

CHAPTER 4

OPTIMIZING AUTOCAD'S PERFORMANCE

OPTIMIZING
AUTOCAD'S PERFORMANCE

Different hardware devices and computer operating systems will have different effects on AutoCAD's performance. In many cases, you will be able to significantly enhance that performance by making adjustments to AutoCAD or to its operating environment. This chapter explains those techniques.

This chapter is based on the assumption that you have installed and configured a basic AutoCAD system under DOS. Once you have installed and configured the program, you may enhance AutoCAD's performance by setting specific values for variables that affect the operating environment, installing and managing additional random-access memory, and controlling the operating environment by means of batch files.

DOS ENVIRONMENT VARIABLES

A DOS *environment variable* is a small portion of RAM that is set aside and given a specific name. A value of some sort, either a number or a character string, is associated with that name and stored in RAM.

PATH is one such environment-variable name. You can associate PATH with a list of subdirectories by entering a command like the following at the DOS prompt:

    SET PATH = C:\DOS;C:\ACAD

When the name PATH is associated with subdirectories, DOS extends its search for executable program files whenever you enter a command at the DOS prompt. If DOS cannot find the program file on the currently logged subdirectory, it will search each subdirectory on the PATH list until it either encounters an executable program file or runs out of subdirectories.

AutoCAD has the ability to search RAM for certain environment-variable names and to read the values associated with them. AutoCAD's performance will then be affected by those values it finds.

THE SET COMMAND

It is possible for DOS to contain any number of different environment variables, depending on the amount of RAM space that is made available for them. Normally those variables are simply stored in RAM until an application program needs to make use of their associated values.

The SET command is used to create an environment variable and to associate a value with it. It is also used to display a list of all current environment variables and their associated values. For example, to see what environment variables are currently set in your system, enter the following at the DOS prompt:

    SET

You may see a list similar to the following:

    COMSPEC = C:\COMMAND.COM
    PROMPT = PG
    PATH = C:\DOS;C:\ACAD

COMSPEC is a DOS environment variable that tells the operating system where to find the file containing the system commands. The PROMPT environment variable tells the operating system how to display the DOS system prompt. The PATH environment variable contains names of hard-disk subdirectories where DOS may search for program files if it cannot find the correct program file on the currently logged subdirectory. (Refer to your DOS manual for details regarding these and other environment variables used by DOS.) You may find different or additional environment variables on the list, depending on the configuration of your computer's operating system.

When an environment variable is created using the SET command, the name of the environment variable follows SET, and the value associated with it is separated from the name with an equal sign. No spaces are used around the equal sign. You can invoke this command by entering it from the keyboard at the DOS system prompt.

DOS VARIABLES THAT AFFECT AUTOCAD

When AutoCAD is initialized—that is, when you enter **ACAD** at the DOS prompt—it will look for and accept values associated with certain special DOS environment variables, provided those variables have previously been set either at the DOS prompt or by means of commands placed in a batch file. AutoCAD can use the values contained in these special environment variables to manage the way it allocates RAM for various kinds of processing, chooses from among optional configurations, or searches for files on disk.

ACAD: Changing the Search Path

The ACAD environment variable contains the name of a drive and subdirectory where AutoCAD can locate its various support files—such as overlay files, shape files, AutoLISP files, drawings, and so forth—if it cannot find them anywhere using its *default search path*. AutoCAD's default search path includes the currently logged subdirectory followed by the subdirectory ACAD, if it exists. After looking in these two subdirectories, AutoCAD will search the subdirectories stored in the PATH environment variable, unless you have set the ACAD environment variable. If the ACAD environment variable has been set, Auto-CAD will limit further searching to the subdirectories stored in this variable. For example, if you have stored AutoCAD's support files in a subdirectory named C:\AUTOCAD, you can store the drive letter and subdirectory name to the ACAD environment variable as follows:

```
SET ACAD = C:\AUTOCAD
```

This can be helpful if you intend to limit AutoCAD's file search to a shorter search path than was set using PATH. However, if you have stored different types of support files in different subdirectories—LISP files separate from shape and font files, for example—you must be sure that the ACAD environment variable is set to find them all.

Alternate solutions may be simpler. For example, many AutoCAD users store unique support files for different clients in separate subdirectories. To find each client's support files quickly and easily, store AutoCAD's system files and in-common support files in subdirectories on the DOS search path (set using the PATH environment variable). Then, when editing a client's drawings, log onto the client subdirectory before invoking AutoCAD. This avoids the necessity of returning to DOS and resetting the ACAD environment variable each time you want to change to a new client.

When the search path is organized in this way, you can use AutoCAD's Shell or Sh command (Chapter 7) to switch to a different client subdirectory while still inside the drawing editor. When you end the drawing session, AutoCAD will save the current drawing in its original subdirectory, regardless of what subdirectory is currently logged. You can, of course, specifically request that the drawing be saved in any subdirectory of your choosing, by using the Save command and explicitly stating the subdirectory location as part of the file name.

ACADFREERAM: How AutoCAD Uses Memory

The DOS environment variable ACADFREERAM controls the amount of memory AutoCAD uses to store the results of its intermediate internal processing and variables. This memory is referred to as AutoCAD's *free RAM,* or *working storage space.* If the ACADFREERAM environment variable is not set, Auto-CAD will reserve 24K for its free RAM. In some applications, less space than this is needed. For example, if you rarely use the commands Hide, Offset, or Trim, you might like to release some memory usually set aside for those commands to be used as I/O page space instead; this would slightly improve Auto-CAD's performance. The following command will set ACADFREERAM to 20K:

```
SET ACADFREERAM = 20
```

Notice how, in the above example, the integer 20 expresses 20 kilobytes of data space in RAM. Integers are the only valid type of value for this environment variable.

The minimum value of ACADFREERAM is 5, although it is doubtful that you will be able to set its value that low in actual practice. If you set the value too low, AutoCAD will fail to load or function, but this will not hurt your system or AutoCAD. It simply means that you must reset ACADFREERAM to a higher value before using the program.

In most AutoCAD configurations, the default value of 24K is adequate. If AutoCAD runs out of free RAM during processing, it will display a message indicating that you must increase the value of ACADFREERAM. The maximum value for ACADFREERAM is 30.

If you are so inclined, you can experiment with this environment variable to determine whether a smaller value improves your system's performance. Set a small value for ACADFREERAM and test AutoCAD by asking it to load and perform a hidden-line removal on your largest drawing. If AutoCAD aborts or displays an error message, set ACADFREERAM to the next higher value and try again.

In general, if you set ACADFREERAM at all, set it to the smallest value with which you can safely edit all your drawings.

ACADCFG: Maintaining Multiple Configurations

The ACADCFG environment variable will help you maintain different combinations of hardware and different configuration options for a single set of Auto-CAD program files.

Normally, all of AutoCAD's configuration information is stored in the file ACAD.CFG, which is in turn stored in the same subdirectory as the AutoCAD system files. However, if you wish you may store this file in a separate subdirectory and store that subdirectory name in the environment variable ACADCFG. By configuring AutoCAD several times and storing each version of ACAD.CFG in its own subdirectory, you can maintain several different configurations simply by changing this environment variable's value before invoking AutoCAD.

For example, you may occasionally wish to use a special AutoCAD configuration that displays drawings without the accompanying screen menus and prompt areas, thereby allowing AutoCAD to be used as a presentation device. To accomplish this, begin by creating two subdirectories named WORKCFG and PRESCFG with the following DOS commands:

```
MD WORKCFG
MD PRESCFG
```

After creating these subdirectories, log onto your AutoCAD system subdirectory and copy your current configuration files to the subdirectory WORKCFG with the following command:

```
COPY ACAD.CFG \WORKCFG
```

DOS will respond with the message:

```
1 file(s) copied
```

If you don't receive this message, check to see that you are logged onto the AutoCAD system subdirectory and that you entered the COPY command correctly.

If you are using 80286-based DOS AutoCAD, after the ACAD.CFG file is copied, enter the following command to copy the system-driver files to the WORKCFG subdirectory:

```
COPY ACADD?.OVL C:\WORKCFG
```

DOS will respond:

```
ACADDG.OVL
ACADDS.OVL
2 File(s) copied
```

Next, enter the following command:

```
COPY ACADP?.OVL C:\WORKCFG
```

DOS will respond:

```
ACADPL.OVL
ACADPP.OVL
2 File(s) copied
```

After the ACAD.CFG file is copied, rename the current ACAD.CFG file to ACAD.OLD with the following command:

```
REN ACAD.CFG ACAD.OLD
```

Next, set the value of ACADCFG as follows:

SET ACADCFG = \WORKCFG

Finally, enter AutoCAD and edit a drawing. If AutoCAD responds normally, then it is able to find the configuration information in the subdirectory WORKCFG.

If you receive the message:

AutoCAD is not configured

press Ctrl-C, exit to DOS, and log onto the AutoCAD system subdirectory. Rename ACAD.OLD back to ACAD.CFG. Then try again to copy the configuration file to the WORKCFG subdirectory.

When AutoCAD is working correctly, reset the value of ACADCFG as follows:

SET ACADCFG = \PRESCFG

Log onto the AutoCAD system subdirectory and enter **ACAD**. You should soon see the message:

AutoCAD is not configured

because the subdirectory PRESCFG is empty.

Reconfigure AutoCAD for a display without on-screen menus or prompt areas. This configuration information will be stored in the file ACAD.CFG on the PRESCFG subdirectory. Enter the drawing editor to check that the display is as you intended. Even without a screen menu display, AutoCAD will respond to keyboard command entries, tablet menus, and script files.

Test your multiple configurations by setting the value of ACADCFG and entering AutoCAD. You should now have two different configurations of Auto-CAD available—without keeping multiple copies of the AutoCAD system files, and without reconfiguring AutoCAD each time you want to switch between them. Each time you wish to use one of the saved configurations, set the value of ACADCFG accordingly, prior to invoking AutoCAD. For extra convenience, you can write simple batch files to set the value of ACADCFG and to invoke AutoCAD from a single command at the DOS prompt. Here is an example that sets the value of ACADCFG to the subdirectory PRESCFG:

```
ECHO OFF
SET ACADCFG = \PRESCFG
ACAD
```

Refer to your DOS documentation for more information regarding batch files.

This technique can be used to accommodate different plotters, digitizers, and tablet configurations, or any set of hardware options you choose.

ACADALTMENU: Alternate Tablet Menu

If you have used AutoCAD's standard tablet menu to configure AutoCAD Release 11 or later for a digitizing tablet, you may alternate between the standard menu and a menu of your choosing by picking the Change Template option. This environment variable tells AutoCAD where to find a custom tablet menu. Assume, for example, that your own CUSTOM.MNU file is in the ACAD\SUPPORT subdirectory. To alternate between AutoCAD's standard menu and your CUSTOM.MNU file, enter the following at the DOS command prompt:

SET ACADALTMENU = C:\ACAD\SUPPORT\CUSTOM.MNU

Include the full name of the uncompiled menu, including the MNU file extension—this will allow AutoCAD to recompile the menu into an MNX file if you make changes. Be sure that your custom menu (or any third-party software) allows you to switch back to AutoCAD's standard menu. Refer to Chapter 14 for more details regarding custom menus.

ACADMAXMEM: Reducing the Amount of Available Memory

Normally, AutoCAD will use all the RAM it finds in your system. If you need to limit AutoCAD's use of memory, set this variable to the exact number of bytes you want it to use. For example, if you have a system with 4 megabytes of RAM but would like AutoCAD to find only 2, enter the following:

SET ACADMAXMEM = 2048000

Lowering the amount of memory AutoCAD may use will degrade overall performance. Do not use this variable unless you have a compelling reason to do so.

ACADPAGEDIR: Placement of Temporary Files

Setting this variable serves the same purpose that configuring AutoCAD's operating parameters for placement of temporary files did, as discussed in Chapter 3. In cases where a change in your hardware configuration renders the usual area for temporary file storage unavailable (e.g., a RAM disk is temporarily not configured), you may set a drive letter and directory in this variable to override the previous configuration setting. For example, to place temporary files on the root directory of drive D, enter the following at the DOS command prompt:

SET ACADPAGEDIR = D:\

To disable this directory, enter the following:

```
SET ACADPAGEDIR =
```

ACADMAXPAGE: Adjusting the Amount of Data in the First Page File

AutoCAD uses a system of *paging files* to store data that cannot be contained in RAM. The default size of the first page file is about 400K. AutoCAD fills this file with data before creating a second, smaller file. If you like, you can use this variable to instruct AutoCAD to create the second file before the first is completely full. For example, to instruct AutoCAD to create the second page file after 200K, enter the following at the DOS command prompt:

```
SET ACADMAXPAGE = 200000
```

To revert to the default size, enter the following:

```
SET ACADMAXPAGE =
```

ACADPLCMD and ACADPPCMD: Background Plotting and Printing

These variables allow you to configure AutoCAD Release 11 to plot or print in the background by means of an external shell command. Background printing allows you to continue working in AutoCAD while producing hard-copy output. If you would like to enable background plotting, you must use the following:

- A current Autodesk-supported Release 11 plotting or printing driver, or a third-party driver that supports this feature—consult your plotter dealer for information regarding a supported driver for your plotter.
- An external shell command (such as the DOS PRINT utility) that can support plot files sent to your plotter.

To set up this routine, perform the following steps:

1. Add the external shell command to the ACAD.PGP file. See Chapter 21 for details on how to edit ACAD.PGP.

2. Set the appropriate environment variable, using the external shell command name, followed by one space and %s. For example, using DOS PRINT as the external shell, the environment variable for plotting would be:

```
SET ACADPLCMD = PRINT %s
```

The variable for printing would be:

SET ACADPPCMD = PRINT %s

These SET commands should be added to a batch file such as AUTOEX-EC.BAT. They must be invoked before running AutoCAD.

3. Configure AutoCAD's operating parameters, as described in Chapter 3. Enter the default plot file name AUTOSPOOL, and assign an existing directory on your hard disk as the plot spooler directory.

If you have followed these instructions carefully, AutoCAD will respond to plotting and printing commands by creating a plot file and then returning you to AutoCAD while sending the file to the output device via your external shell program.

LISPHEAP and LISPSTACK: Controlling AutoLISP Memory

AutoLISP is a subset of the LISP programming language. AutoCAD users employ AutoLISP to customize the program and simplify the drawing process. For details regarding AutoLISP, refer to Chapters 16 and 17.

When AutoCAD is opened, it reserves a portion of RAM for AutoLISP. This area is divided into two separate areas, called the *heap space* and the *stack space.* AutoLISP uses the heap space to store AutoLISP memory variables and their values, user-defined functions, and character strings. The stack space is similar to AutoCAD's working memory, storing intermediate processing results.

In AutoCAD versions for DOS prior to Release 10, the default sizes for heap and stack space were 5K each. AutoCAD Releases 10 and later (not 80386-specific) reserve 40K for heap space and 3K for stack space. These default values may be changed by means of the DOS LISPHEAP and LISPSTACK environment variables.

For example, to change the AutoLISP heap space to 35K, enter the following at the DOS command prompt:

SET LISPHEAP = 35000

To set the AutoLISP stack space to 10K, enter the following command:

SET LISPSTACK = 10000

Notice that, unlike the environment variable ACADFREERAM, the number of bytes is represented literally. Normally, the combined total of heap and stack space cannot exceed 45K.

If you are using AutoCAD 386, you need not be as concerned with specific environment settings for heap and stack space. AutoCAD 386 handles memory requirements for AutoLISP automatically. However, the FILES statement in CONFIG.SYS limits the number of AutoLISP files you may have open at one time. A good working minimum would be FILES = 40. Refer to Chapter 3 for details regarding the contents of CONFIG.SYS. AutoCAD 386 permits you to set LISPHEAP and LISPSTACK settings if you need them to accommodate certain third-party memory-management software. They may in this case exceed the normal limit of 45K.

In general, the setting for LISPHEAP will be the larger of the two, as Auto-LISP depends on numerous memory variables and user-defined functions that can become quite complex, requiring large amounts of heap space. If the value of LISPHEAP is too small, AutoCAD will display the message:

Insufficient node space

If the value of LISPSTACK is too small, AutoCAD displays the message:

Lispstack overflow

If your version is earlier than Release 10, you will very likely want to increase the default values of LISPHEAP and LISPSTACK. When experimenting with different values, try to determine the smallest possible setting for LISPSTACK, allocating the remaining space for LISPHEAP.

USING MORE THAN 640K

Although DOS imposes a limit of 640K RAM for any of its application programs, it is possible for programs to make use of larger amounts of memory than this. There are two types of RAM that go beyond the 640K limit: *extended memory* and *expanded memory*.

AutoCAD can use up to 4 megabytes of either type of extra memory to augment its *I/O page space*. AutoCAD uses I/O page space to hold files that it normally stores on disk. By holding these files in extra RAM, AutoCAD can access the information much faster, thereby improving its speed and performance.

Extended Memory

Extended memory is used by IBM PC/AT computers (and their compatibles) equipped with processors that can run in a special mode called *protected mode*. Protected mode allows the microprocessor to access memory found between 1 megabyte and 16 megabytes. Programs must be written specifically for protected-mode operations in order to use this memory. AutoCAD is capable of accessing certain protected-mode operations in order to make use of extended memory. You'll learn more about this in a moment.

Expanded Memory

Expanded memory can be used by DOS programs that are written to access it and take advantage of it. Special software allows a DOS application to access the extra memory in 16K portions, using a technique similar to bank switching of program files to disk. There are two standard specifications for expanded memory: the Lotus/Intel/Microsoft Expanded Memory Specification (LIM-EMS) and the AST/Quadram/Ashton-Tate Enhanced Expanded Memory Specification (EEMS).

AutoCAD and Extra Memory

A good way to handle extra memory is simply running AutoCAD and letting it find and allocate the extra memory automatically. Each time you invoke AutoCAD, it will check for both extended and expanded memory and determine whether any portion of that memory is available for its use. Free memory includes any not currently being used for memory-resident software programs or RAM disks. AutoCAD then automatically configures whatever available extra memory it finds as additional I/O page space.

Alternatively, AutoCAD can make use of DOS environment variables to control how it allocates memory above the 640K DOS limit. This may be necessary in some situations where AutoCAD is not able to recognize when extra memory is being used by other software programs. For example, certain RAM disks may be "invisible" to AutoCAD, causing AutoCAD to overwrite them and the data they contain.

RAM disks that conform to the specifications of IBM's VDISK.SYS or MICROSOFTS RAMDISK.SYS will not present problems. If you are using a RAM disk with a different specification from that used by VDISK.SYS, or if you are not sure, the easiest way to find out is to just try it and see. To do so, first initialize the RAM disk, making note of its size. Then place some files there, start AutoCAD, and edit a drawing. Finally, exit AutoCAD and check to see if your RAM disk has become corrupted—that is, if files are missing or damaged, or if the size has changed. In those cases where AutoCAD's automatic memory-management system has problems, you must explicitly tell AutoCAD—by means of DOS environment variables—which areas of extended or expanded memory are available. The following sections explain how to do this.

ACADXMEM: PC/AT-STYLE EXTENDED MEMORY

If your computer has PC/AT-style extended memory, you can use the ACADXMEM environment variable to control the exact starting address and size of this memory available to AutoCAD.

If ACADXMEM contains a single value, that value is assumed to be the starting address where AutoCAD can begin its search for any available extended memory. If AutoCAD finds unavailable memory (such as a RAM disk) at or above this address, it will not use it.

The default starting address for all extended memory is 1024K; this is where AutoCAD begins its search for available memory. You cannot use a starting address lower than this figure. For example, assume that a system has 2 megabytes of extended memory configured with a 512K RAM disk. To enable Auto-CAD to bypass the first 512K of extended memory, enter the following command at the DOS prompt:

```
SET ACADXMEM = 1536K
```

Notice how adding 512K to the default starting address of 1024K gives you the correct starting address for AutoCAD's extended memory, 1536K.

ACADXMEM can contain a second value, separated from the first value by a comma. If the second value is present, it is assumed to be the maximum amount of extended memory AutoCAD may consider, even if there is more memory in the system beyond this maximum size.

For example, given a system with 2 megabytes of extended memory, the following command will cause AutoCAD to bypass the first 512K of extended memory and consider only the next 1 megabyte after that:

```
SET ACADXMEM = 1536K,1024K
```

With ACADXMEM set to this value, AutoCAD ignores the first and last 512K of extended memory.

If you wish, you may set ACADXMEM for only the maximum amount of memory to consider, starting at the default address. To do this, place a comma before the value of ACADXMEM, as in the following example:

```
SET ACADXMEM = ,512K
```

This will cause AutoCAD to use only the available memory it finds in the first 512K of extended memory, starting at the default 1024K address.

The following command instructs AutoCAD to ignore all the extended memory in your system:

```
SET ACADXMEM = NONE
```

ACADLIMEM: LOTUS/INTEL EXPANDED MEMORY

The use of some RAM disks and memory-resident software in Lotus/Intel expanded memory also may cause problems for AutoCAD. In those cases where it may be necessary to control AutoCAD's use of expanded memory, use the environment variable ACADLIMEM.

ACADLIMEM is set to a single value, indicating the maximum amount of expanded memory AutoCAD may use for additional I/O page space. For example, the following SET command will allow up to 512K of available expanded memory to be used by AutoCAD:

    SET ACADLIMEM = 512K

Expanded memory is normally available in 16K segments. ACADLIMEM may also be set to equal the maximum number of available memory segments to be used by AutoCAD. For example, the following command will set the value of ACADLIMEM equal to 32 segments, or 512K, of expanded memory:

    SET ACADLIMEM = 32

Both of the above commands allow only a maximum of 512K of expanded memory to be used by AutoCAD.

When you set ACADLIMEM to equal a given number of expanded-memory segments, it is possible to use negative numbers. When you specify a negative segment value, AutoCAD will use all available expanded memory except that number of segments. For example, the following command will allow all available expanded memory except for 32 segments (512K) to be used by AutoCAD:

    SET ACADLIMEM = − 32

LISPXMEM: Extended Memory Used by AutoLISP

If you are using 80286-based DOS AutoCAD Release 10 or later, and have configured the program to make use of the Extended AutoLISP feature, you may use the LISPXMEM environment variable to set the starting address and size of the extended memory to be used by Extended AutoLISP.

Only extended memory is available for Extended AutoLISP—expanded memory will not work. Do not attempt to install Extended AutoLISP unless your computer is equipped with at least 512K of PC/AT-style extended memory.

You activate Extended AutoLISP by running the program EXTLISP.EXE. You must set values for LISPXMEM before running this program. If no setting is given for LISPXMEM, Extended AutoLISP will use any available extended memory it finds.

The command syntax for LISPXMEM is similar to that for ACADXMEM. That is, the environment variable may be given up to two values. The first value is assumed to be the starting address where Extended AutoLISP can begin its search for any available extended memory. If Extended AutoLISP finds unavailable memory (such as a RAM disk) at or above this address, it will not use it.

The default starting address for all extended memory is 1024K; this is the default starting address where AutoCAD begins its search for available memory.

You cannot use a starting address lower than this figure. For example, assume that a system has 2 megabytes of extended memory configured with a 512K RAM disk, that AutoCAD is using the next megabyte (1024K) for its I/O page space, and that the remaining 512K is free to be used by Extended AutoLISP. To enable Extended AutoLISP to bypass the first 1536K of extended memory, enter the following command at the DOS prompt:

    SET LISPXMEM = 2560K

You find the correct starting address by adding the amount of memory to bypass (1536K) to the starting address (1024K) for a total of 2560K.

LISPXMEM can contain a second value, separated from the first value by a comma. If the second value is present, it is assumed to be the maximum amount of extended memory that Extended AutoLISP is to consider, even if there is more memory in the system beyond this maximum size.

For example, given a system with 3 megabytes of extended memory, the following command will cause Extended AutoLISP to bypass the first 1536K of extended memory and to consider only the next 512K after that:

    SET LISPXMEM = 2560K,512K

With ACADXMEM set to this value, Extended AutoLISP ignores the last 1280K of extended memory.

If you wish, you may set LISPXMEM for only the maximum amount of memory to consider, starting at the default address. To do this, place a comma before the value of LISPXMEM, as in the following example:

    SET LISPXMEM = ,512K

This will cause Extended AutoLISP to use only the available memory it finds in the first 512K of extended memory, starting at the default 1024K address.

Unlike ACADXMEM, LISPXMEM cannot be set to a value of NONE. If you do not wish to use extended memory with AutoLISP, simply do not run the program EXTLISP.EXE.

At the end of an AutoCAD session, you can, if necessary, reclaim the memory space occupied by EXTLISP.EXE (about 30K) by running REMLISP.EXE, a utility program supplied with AutoCAD.

USING AN EXPANDED MEMORY MANAGER

An *expanded memory manager*, or EMS manager, is a special software program that allows standard MS-DOS applications to address memory beyond the normal 640K limit. Most require at least an 80386 processor to function effectively. If you have installed an expanded memory manager on your machine and intend to use it with AutoCAD, you may need to consider the following.

First, check the documentation for your EMS manager to ascertain whether it conforms to the Virtual Control Program Interface (VCPI) specification. Using AutoCAD with an EMS manager that does not conform to this specification is possible, but not recommended.

If your EMS manager does not meet the VCPI specification, allocate all memory as *extended memory* before running AutoCAD. If you allocate any available RAM as expanded, AutoCAD will not find it. Use the ACADXMEM and LISPXMEM environment variables to allocate memory, as described earlier in this chapter.

If you *do* have a VCPI-compatible EMS simulator, you should allocate all available RAM as *expanded*; then AutoCAD will not see any extended memory. Even in this case, you may use some DOS-environment variables for managing extended memory. Different settings will work, depending on your version of AutoCAD.

If you are using Release 10c2a with Extended AutoLISP, try the following:

```
SET ACADLIMEM = , <size of RAM for I/O paging>
SET ACADXMEM = none
```

AutoCAD should then use any expanded memory that is not taken up by ACADLIMEM as extended memory for Extended AutoLISP. Be sure to run EXTLISP before running AutoCAD.

If you are using Release 10c7 and later with Extended AutoLISP and a VCPI-compliant EMS manager, set up all available RAM as expanded and try the following settings:

```
SET LISPXMEM = , <size of RAM for Extended AutoLISP>
SET ACADXMEM = none
```

AutoCAD will then use the remaining expanded memory for its I/O paging.

These settings may not work with all EMS managers. If these settings do not work for you, contact your Authorized AutoCAD dealer for additional assistance.

PART

II

MANAGING AN AUTOCAD DRAWING

Computer-aided drafting is more than simply using a computer to produce line drawings. The power and flexibility of computerized drafting lies largely in the fact that it enables the drafter to manipulate drawing entities in ways that are not possible using manual methods. When properly understood and managed, the drawing environment is your ally, guiding and supporting your efforts as you move from initial concept to finished drawing. Part II explains the structure of AutoCAD's computerized drafting environment, introduces the tools at your disposal for manipulating that environment to maximum advantage, and shows you additional tools that allow you to use the environment to accelerate the drawing process.

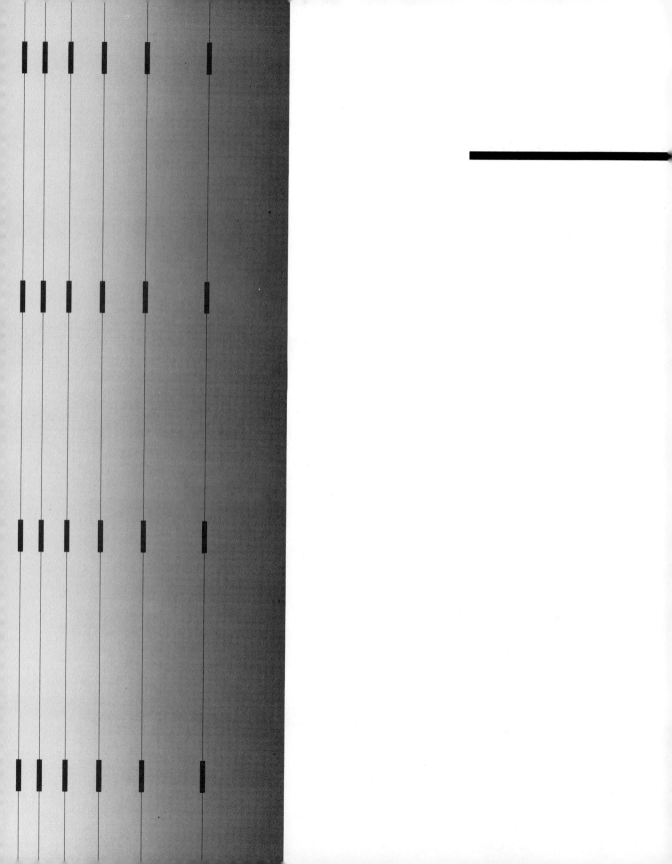

CHAPTER 5

The Drawing Environment

THE DRAWING ENVIRONMENT

AutoCAD presents an enormous variety of options and features to accommodate all kinds of drafters. Every detail regarding any particular entry is important, and the computer will take nothing for granted. Colors, linetypes, location, orientation, distances, angles, thickness, and offsets must be specified.

While this sheer number of features and options can make AutoCAD appear daunting to the neophyte, in fact, AutoCAD's wealth of commands and features, once fully understood, can greatly simplify the process of computer drafting. Part of this process is understanding the *drawing environment* in which entities are created and edited. This environment includes such staples as:

- Coordinate points in 2-D and 3-D space.
- Entity properties, such as colors and linetype specifications.
- Drawing layers that group related entities together.
- Conventional command dialog.
- Graphic entity values.

This chapter explains what is included in AutoCAD's drawing environment, and how that environment can be used to simplify the CAD process.

TWO-DIMENSIONAL COORDINATE SYSTEM

AutoCAD's drawing environment is based on the *Cartesian coordinate system,* which is used to locate points in space. In a two-dimensional Cartesian coordinate system, two infinitely long axes are placed at right angles in a single plane, as shown in Figure 5.1. The horizontal axis is called the *x-axis* and the vertical axis is called the *y-axis.* The plane that contains these axes is called the *X-Y plane.* Because this system is two-dimensional, only this single X-Y plane can exist within it, and all points must lie somewhere on the plane.

The x-axis and y-axis intersect at a single point, called the *origin.* Equidistant points, called *coordinates,* are placed along these two axes. Points on the x-axis to the right of the origin are positive in value, and increase as they move farther from the origin. Points on the x-axis to the left of the origin are negative in value and decrease as they become more distant from the origin. Similarly, coordinate points on the y-axis are positive above the origin and negative below the origin. The origin point itself is given x-y coordinates of zero.

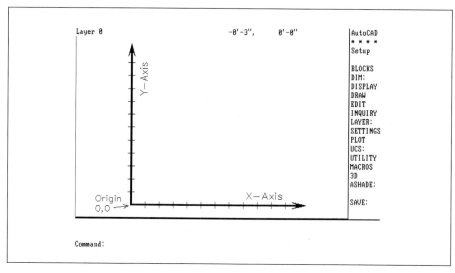

FIGURE 5.1: Two-dimensional Cartesian coordinate system. On many systems, the default orientation of the x- and y-axes is used—the positive x-axis is horizontal with coordinates incrementing to the right, and the positive y-axis is vertical with coordinate locations incrementing as it ascends. In the default configuration, angle zero degrees corresponds to the orientation of the positive x-axis.

We can identify any point by associating it with an x and y coordinate-point pair relative to the x- and y-axes, as shown in Figure 5.2. Imagine a point not located on either the x- or y-axis. By extending a line from that point perpendicular to the x-axis, you obtain an x coordinate value. Extending a line perpendicular to the y-axis will obtain a y coordinate point. This combination of x and y coordinates is unique to that point, and any point in the plane can be identified and located in this fashion.

Lines, arcs, circles, and other two-dimensional drawing entities can be placed anywhere on the plane, and their specific location can be obtained by determining the minimum set of coordinate points necessary to define them. For example, a straight line segment is defined by two coordinate points, the segment's endpoints. An arc can be defined by three points—for example, two endpoints and a center point. These relationships are illustrated in Figure 5.3.

THREE-DIMENSIONAL COORDINATE SYSTEM

A third dimension can be added to the cartesian coordinate system by introducing a third axis, called the *z-axis*. This axis extends through the origin point, perpendicular to the X-Y plane, as shown in Figure 5.4. Points on the z-axis

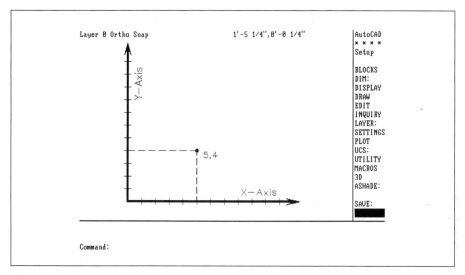

FIGURE 5.2: Locating a point in the Cartesian coordinate system. In this figure, the point 5,4 is located. Coordinates along the x- and y-axes are placed at equal intervals. The x coordinate of the selected point is 5, aligned with the fifth coordinate along the x-axis; the y coordinate is 4, aligned with the fourth coordinate along the y-axis. In this manner, any coordinate location in the X-Y plane can be identified by a unique set of x and y coordinate points.

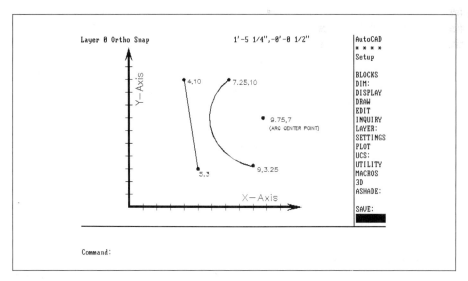

FIGURE 5.3: A line and an arc defined in the Cartesian coordinate system. In the X-Y plane, drawing entities can be created by specifying the coordinate points needed to define them. The line on the left requires two endpoints, 4,10 and 5,3. The arc requires three points: the endpoints, 7.25,10 and 9,3.5, plus the arc's center point, 9.75,7. AutoCAD stores both the entity type and its coordinate definition points in the underlying database, and translates this information into graphic images on the display screen and in hard-copy output.

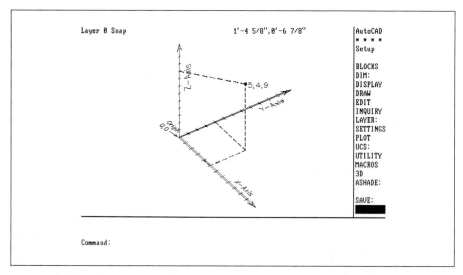

FIGURE 5.4: Three-dimensional Cartesian coordinate system. For drawing in 3-D, AutoCAD begins with a third axis: the z-axis. In this example, the point 5,4,9 is found in space by applying a z coordinate, 9, to the point 5,4. Point 5,4,9 is therefore elevated nine coordinates above point 5,4. Using the 3-D coordinate system, it is possible to identify every point in 3-D space with a unique set of three coordinate points.

above the X-Y plane are positive in value and increase as they become more distant from the origin. Points below the X-Y plane are negative in value and decrease as they become more distant from the X-Y plane.

Using a three-dimensional coordinate system, it is possible to locate any point anywhere in space by specifying its location relative to all three axes; that is, by supplying x, y, and z coordinate points, defined by drawing a perpendicular line from the point to each of the three axes, as shown in Figure 5.4.

Coordinate Planes in a Three-Dimensional System

The three-dimensional Cartesian coordinate system includes three fundamental planes formed in space by its three major axes: the X-Y plane found in the standard two-dimensional system, an X-Z plane, and a Y-Z plane. Portions of these planes are illustrated in Figure 5.5. A three-dimensional system can encompass an infinite number of additional planes in an infinite number of orientations. Any three points in space, including at least one point not located on any axis, will define a new plane. This is illustrated in Figure 5.6.

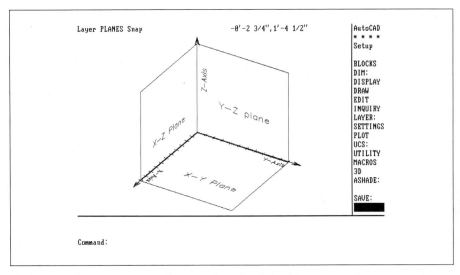

FIGURE 5.5: Fundamental drawing planes in a three-dimensional Cartesian coordinate system. A drawing plane is a 2-D surface extruded from a pair of intersecting lines, parallel to which 2-D drawing entities may be placed. In the above example, the intersecting lines happen to be the axes of a 3-D coordinate system, and the drawing planes are named after the intersecting axes that have defined them. The Y-Z plane, for example, is defined by the y- and z-axes.

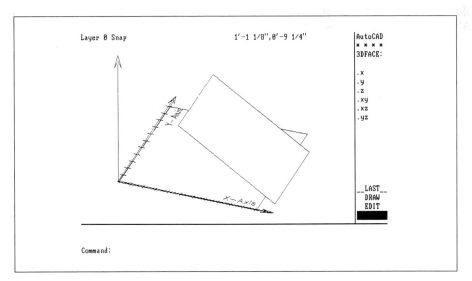

FIGURE 5.6: A drawing plane oriented in 3-D space. A drawing plane need not be aligned with the x-, y-, or z-axis. It can be tilted in any direction in 3-D space. In the above example, a drawing plane has been oriented at an angle to the X-Y plane.

AutoCAD 3-D Before Release 10

In Versions 2.1 through 2.5, AutoCAD provided for the visualization of certain entities in 3-D space by allowing entities to be elevated above or below the X-Y plane, as well as extruded into a new elevation. This process gave entities a third dimension, thickness. An example of elevation and extrusion is shown in Figure 5.7. Although these techniques made it possible to draw very rudimentary 3-D entities, they did not allow for certain other basic types of three-dimensional entities, such as diagonal lines and polygons drawn at any orientation in space.

In Version 2.6 and Release 9, AutoCAD enhanced its 3-D visualization process, making it possible to draw straight lines and polygons anywhere in three-dimensional space by entering the exact x-y-z coordinate points needed to define them. This made possible more detailed 3-D representations, but was cumbersome and slow for all but the simplest of drawings. Furthermore, it did not allow the generation of curved lines in three-dimensional space.

Release 10 3-D

With Release 10 and later, AutoCAD has simplified and generalized the production of 3-D entities, allowing you to define a *construction plane* at any

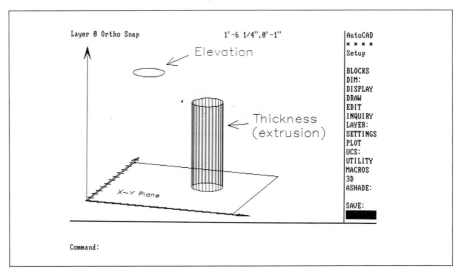

FIGURE 5.7: Elevation and extrusion. In the above figure, the circles were created as copies of each other, but they have had some of their entity properties changed. The circle on the left has been given an elevation, meaning that it now "floats" a specified distance above the X-Y plane. If the same circle had been given a negative elevation, it would be "floating" below the X-Y plane. The circle on the right has been given a thickness, meaning that it continues to remain in the X-Y plane, but has been extruded into a tube-like figure.

orientation in space, and to draw any AutoCAD entity on that plane. You may also give any entity an elevation and thickness relative to its construction plane. Alternatively, you may define entities in space using absolute x-y-z coordinate points.

The foundation for Release 10's three-dimensional drawing is the *world coordinate system,* the coordinate system formed by the Cartesian x-, y-, and z-axes, which are fixed and available at all times. Construction planes are defined by selecting three points relative to the world coordinate system. Figure 5.8 shows two circles drawn on two construction planes within the world coordinate system.

AutoCAD also simplifies the definition of construction planes by allowing you to define them in a variety of ways: rotating the current construction plane along one or more axes, moving the construction plane's origin point, using existing entities to orient the construction plane, changing the drawing's viewpoint and aligning the construction plane to it, or entering any three x-y-z coordinate points. You may store the locations of any number of construction planes with the drawing, and recall them by name.

Construction planes are formed within, and made relative to, a coordinate system called the *user coordinate system,* or UCS for short. When the default elevation is set to zero, the UCS and construction planes are the same. When the default elevation is given a value, however, the construction plane "floats" parallel to the UCS. For details on managing user coordinate systems, refer to the

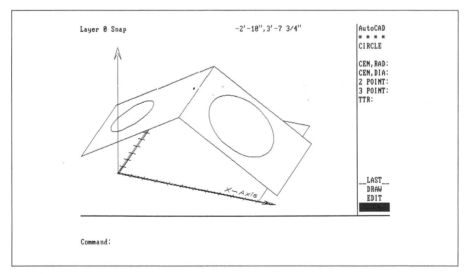

FIGURE 5.8: Two circles drawn on construction planes. Any entity drawn on a construction plane is oriented parallel to that plane, as the circles are in this drawing. They appear as ellipses because the viewing angle to these planes is from one side, not directly above.

UCS command in Chapter 6. For information on how to change the default elevation, refer to the Elev command in Chapter 6, as well as to the ELEVATION system variable in Chapter 13.

With a little practice, you can use construction planes to create complex three-dimensional drawings and view them from any conceivable angle, including perspective views.

DRAWING ENTITIES

AutoCAD drawings, despite their apparent complexity, can be broken down into a relatively small set of fundamental drawing elements, or *entities*. Drawing entities can be either *simple*, meaning that they are basic pieces of graphic information, created or modified as an indivisible unit, or *complex*, meaning that they are composed of more than one simple entity, but treated as a single drawing element.

Examples of simple entities are points, line segments, arcs, traces, and circles, as illustrated in Figure 5.9. Examples of complex entities include blocks, doughnuts, ellipses, polygons, polylines, solids, shapes, and text. They are illustrated in Figure 5.10.

If you are a new AutoCAD user who is experienced in manual drafting, you may not be accustomed to thinking in terms of drawing entities. The ability to

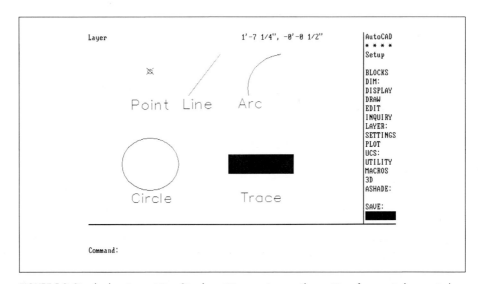

FIGURE 5.9: Simple drawing entities. Simple entities require no other entity reference to be created. They include the point (drawn by inputting a single point); line (drawn by inputting two points); arc (drawn by inputting three points); circle (drawn by entering a center point and a radius); and trace (a wide line drawn by entering a line width and two points).

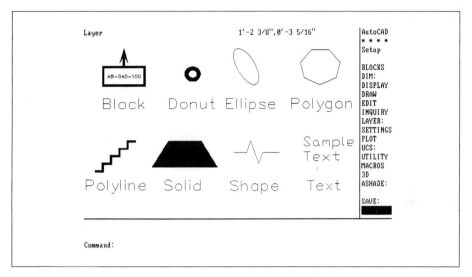

FIGURE 5.10: Complex drawing entities. Complex entities are created using other, simpler entities. The block is formed of any group of entities, inserted into a drawing as a single entity where appropriate. The polyline is composed of several line segments. The doughnut, ellipse, and polygon are all variations of polylines. The solid is a filled area of a drawing defined by three or more points. Shapes are composed of curved and straight line segments based on numerical descriptions in a separate shape file. Text is similar to shapes, based on numerical descriptions in a separate text-font file.

adjust your thinking in terms of manipulating entities as opposed to drawing and erasing lines is critical when you're first approaching AutoCAD. For example, a line segment in an AutoCAD drawing is less a line segment than a unique entity that may be moved, rotated, scaled, broken, or otherwise altered in a virtually limitless number of ways beyond simple erasure. Using AutoCAD, you may assemble several lines in one area of the drawing and, when ready, move or copy them into several different areas. This ability to manipulate entities in space gives you a great deal of flexibility in your drafting.

In addition, AutoCAD gives you the power to create and save complex, custom-made entities in the form of *blocks* and *shapes* that can be replicated and moved between drawings at will. The ability to remember and reuse entities in different drawings means that you no longer have to "reinvent the wheel" each time you begin a new drawing. The more you use AutoCAD, the more productive you become.

With Release 11, AutoCAD gives you the power to create *external reference files,* which are entire drawing files that can be included in other drawings. You can include many external files in a single drawing or reference a single external file in several different drawings. If you update an external drawing file, all drawings referencing that file will automatically reflect the changes you have made. Refer to Chapter 21 for details regarding external reference files.

Layers

AutoCAD allows you to create an unlimited number of layers for each drawing. These layers are analogous to the transparent overlays often used in manual drafting. When a layer is created, it is given a unique identifying name. Related entities can be placed on a layer, and the layer can be "turned off" and "turned on" at will in order to isolate portions of the drawing or to view different portions in combination with others. AutoCAD layers are in precise alignment; a point on one layer will always align perfectly with the same point on any other layer.

Each layer can be assigned its own unique combination of *color* and *linetype,* and entities placed upon it will be rendered with the color and linetype associated with that layer.

Colors

Standard color graphics displays normally allow the display of either 8, 16, or 256 different colors. There are eight standard color hues in AutoCAD; they are assigned numbers that are standard to all AutoCAD configurations. Auto-CAD's standard colors and their numbers are shown in Table 5.1. Sixteen-color

COLOR NUMBER	NAME
1	Red
2	Yellow
3	Green
4	Cyan
5	Blue
6	Magenta
7	Black
8	Gray
9	Bright Red
10	Bright Yellow
11	Bright Green
12	Bright Cyan
13	Bright Blue
14	Bright Magenta
15	Bright Grey

TABLE 5.1: AutoCAD's Standard Colors

displays use AutoCAD's standard colors, plus intensified versions of these colors. Displays with 256 colors allow you to mix colors by assigning color hues and brightness to numbers 10 and above, as shown in Table 5.2.

COLOR NAME	NUMBER	HUE	NUMBER	LIGHT-SATURATION
Red	10	Brightest	11	Brightest Pastel
	12	Bright	13	Bright Pastel
	14	Medium	15	Medium Pastel
	16	Dim	17	Dim Pastel
	18	Dimmest	19	Dimmest Pastel
Red-Orange	20	Brightest	21	Brightest Pastel
	22	Bright	23	Bright Pastel
	24	Medium	25	Medium Pastel
	26	Dim	27	Dim Pastel
	28	Dimmest	29	Dimmest Pastel
Orange	30	Brightest	31	Brightest Pastel
	32	Bright	33	Bright Pastel
	34	Medium	35	Medium Pastel
	36	Dim	37	Dim Pastel
	38	Dimmest	39	Dimmest Pastel
Yellow-Orange	40	Brightest	41	Brightest Pastel
	42	Bright	43	Bright Pastel
	44	Medium	45	Medium Pastel
	46	Dim	47	Dim Pastel
	48	Dimmest	49	Dimmest Pastel
Yellow	50	Brightest	51	Brightest Pastel
	52	Bright	53	Bright Pastel
	54	Medium	55	Medium Pastel
	56	Dim	57	Dim Pastel
	58	Dimmest	59	Dimmest Pastel

TABLE 5.2: AutoCAD Color Hues and Brightness

COLOR NAME	NUMBER	HUE	NUMBER	LIGHT-SATURATION
Light Yellow-Green	60	Brightest	61	Brightest Pastel
	62	Bright	63	Bright Pastel
	64	Medium	65	Medium Pastel
	66	Dim	67	Dim Pastel
	68	Dimmest	69	Dimmest Pastel
Yellow-Green	70	Brightest	71	Brightest Pastel
	72	Bright	73	Bright Pastel
	74	Medium	75	Medium Pastel
	76	Dim	77	Dim Pastel
	78	Dimmest	79	Dimmest Pastel
Yellow-Dark Green	80	Brightest	81	Brightest Pastel
	82	Bright	83	Bright Pastel
	84	Medium	85	Medium Pastel
	86	Dim	87	Dim Pastel
	88	Dimmest	89	Dimmest Pastel
Green	90	Brightest	91	Brightest Pastel
	92	Bright	93	Bright Pastel
	94	Medium	95	Medium Pastel
	96	Dim	97	Dim Pastel
	98	Dimmest	99	Dimmest Pastel
Green-Yellow	100	Brightest	101	Brightest Pastel
	102	Bright	103	Bright Pastel
	104	Medium	105	Medium Pastel
	106	Dim	107	Dim Pastel
	108	Dimmest	109	Dimmest Pastel
Aquamarine	110	Brightest	111	Brightest Pastel
	112	Bright	113	Bright Pastel
	114	Medium	115	Medium Pastel
	116	Dim	117	Dim Pastel
	118	Dimmest	119	Dimmest Pastel

TABLE 5.2: AutoCAD Color Hues and Brightness (continued)

COLOR NAME	NUMBER	HUE	NUMBER	LIGHT-SATURATION
Dark Aquamarine	120	Brightest	121	Brightest Pastel
	122	Bright	123	Bright Pastel
	124	Medium	125	Medium Pastel
	126	Dim	127	Dim Pastel
	128	Dimmest	129	Dimmest Pastel
Cyan	130	Brightest	131	Brightest Pastel
	132	Bright	133	Bright Pastel
	134	Medium	135	Medium Pastel
	136	Dim	137	Dim Pastel
	138	Dimmest	139	Dimmest Pastel
Cyan-Blue	140	Brightest	141	Brightest Pastel
	142	Bright	143	Bright Pastel
	144	Medium	145	Medium Pastel
	146	Dim	147	Dim Pastel
	148	Dimmest	149	Dimmest Pastel
Turquoise	150	Brightest	151	Brightest Pastel
	152	Bright	153	Bright Pastel
	154	Medium	155	Medium Pastel
	156	Dim	157	Dim Pastel
	158	Dimmest	159	Dimmest Pastel
Turquoise-Blue	160	Brightest	161	Brightest Pastel
	162	Bright	163	Bright Pastel
	164	Medium	165	Medium Pastel
	166	Dim	167	Dim Pastel
	168	Dimmest	169	Dimmest Pastel
Blue	170	Brightest	171	Brightest Pastel
	172	Bright	173	Bright Pastel
	174	Medium	175	Medium Pastel
	176	Dim	177	Dim Pastel
	178	Dimmest	179	Dimmest Pastel

TABLE 5.2: AutoCAD Color Hues and Brightness (continued)

COLOR NAME	NUMBER	HUE	NUMBER	LIGHT-SATURATION
Blue-Purple	180	Brightest	181	Brightest Pastel
	182	Bright	183	Bright Pastel
	184	Medium	185	Medium Pastel
	186	Dim	187	Dim Pastel
	188	Dimmest	189	Dimmest Pastel
Purple	190	Brightest	191	Brightest Pastel
	192	Bright	193	Bright Pastel
	194	Medium	195	Medium Pastel
	196	Dim	197	Dim Pastel
	198	Dimmest	199	Dimmest Pastel
Red-Purple	200	Brightest	201	Brightest Pastel
	202	Bright	203	Bright Pastel
	204	Medium	205	Medium Pastel
	206	Dim	207	Dim Pastel
	208	Dimmest	209	Dimmest Pastel
Magenta	210	Brightest	211	Brightest Pastel
	212	Bright	213	Bright Pastel
	214	Medium	215	Medium Pastel
	216	Dim	217	Dim Pastel
	218	Dimmest	219	Dimmest Pastel
Dark Magenta	220	Brightest	221	Brightest Pastel
	222	Bright	223	Bright Pastel
	224	Medium	225	Medium Pastel
	226	Dim	227	Dim Pastel
	228	Dimmest	229	Dimmest Pastel
Maroon	230	Brightest	231	Brightest Pastel
	232	Bright	233	Bright Pastel
	234	Medium	235	Medium Pastel
	236	Dim	237	Dim Pastel
	238	Dimmest	239	Dimmest Pastel

TABLE 5.2: AutoCAD Color Hues and Brightness (continued)

COLOR NAME	NUMBER	HUE	NUMBER	LIGHT-SATURATION
Red-Maroon	240	Brightest	241	Brightest Pastel
	242	Bright	243	Bright Pastel
	244	Medium	245	Medium Pastel
	246	Dim	247	Dim Pastel
	248	Dimmest	249	Dimmest Pastel

TABLE 5.2: AutoCAD Color Hues and Brightness (continued)

Each entity you create may be assigned a specific color; also, entity colors may be edited and changed at any time. Many users follow the convention required in earlier releases of AutoCAD, wherein all entities on a specific layer were assigned a color, and each separate color used in a drawing required its own layer. Later versions of AutoCAD, beginning with Version 2.5, allow you to place entities with different colors on the same layer, although this should be done carefully, as mixing several colors on a single layer can make a drawing difficult to view and edit.

Linetypes

In its default configuration, AutoCAD draws all entities using continuous, unbroken lines. However, you may define any number of noncontinuous line-types containing dashes, dots, and spaces. AutoCAD will use these linetypes to create entities that contain lines—specifically, line segments, two-dimensional polylines, arcs, circles, and blocks containing these entities.

Each entity you create may be assigned a specific linetype, and you may change the linetype of any entity at will. In earlier versions of AutoCAD (prior to Version 2.5), each linetype was assigned to a separate layer, and entities drawn using that linetype were drawn on or moved to the associated layer. Many users continue to follow that convention. Later versions of AutoCAD allow you to place entities with different linetypes on the same layer.

COMMAND CONVENTIONS

AutoCAD commands fall into a few broad categories:

Commands That Create Entities These commands are invoked by entering the *name* of the entity you wish to create—Line, Arc, Block, Circle, Text, and so forth. You can find detailed descriptions of these commands in Chapter 8.

Commands That Change Entities   These commands are invoked by entering the *action* you wish to take—Trim, Fillet, Break, Explode, Erase, and so forth. You can find detailed descriptions of these commands in Chapter 9.

Commands That Manage the Drawing Environment   These commands are usually invoked by entering the *aspect* of the drawing environment you wish to change—Aperture, Axis, Grid, Linetype, Snap, and so forth. Occasionally these commands imply a form of action, such as End, Save, Purge, or Undo. You can find detailed descriptions of these commands in Chapter 7.

Commands That Affect the Screen Display of the Drawing   These commands are invoked by entering the type of *display change* that you desire—Fill, Zoom, Pan, Regen, Redraw, Vpoint, and so forth. You can find detailed descriptions of these commands in Chapter 11.

Commands That Affect AutoCAD's Special Features   These commands are usually invoked by entering the name of the special feature you wish to utilize—Attdef, Shell, Dxfin, Dxfout, Vslide, Script, and so forth. You can find detailed descriptions of these commands in Chapters 18, 20, and 21.

AutoCAD is ready to receive a command when the word

    Command:

appears in the prompt-line area of the screen display. This is referred to as the AutoCAD *Command prompt.*

Entering Commands

You can assemble AutoCAD drawings by entering commands via the keyboard, screen menus, tablet menus, or buttons on your pointing device. The most cumbersome method of entering commands is via the keyboard: Type the command and press Enter or the space bar. AutoCAD will respond with the various options associated with the chosen command. If your desired command is visible in the on-screen menu area, AutoCAD will highlight it as you type, doing a search of the on-screen menu to highlight the command that matches your keystrokes. Once the command you desire is highlighted, you can press the menu select key—on most IBM-compatible systems, this is the Insert key—and the highlighted command will be invoked. This feature can save a few keystrokes.

Commands are more easily entered by means of the on-screen or tablet menu. To select an on-screen command, use your pointing device to move the crosshairs into the on-screen menu area. When you enter the menu area, the crosshairs disappear from the screen. At that point, moving the pointing device up and down causes the visible menu items to be highlighted. When the desired command is highlighted, you pick it the way you would pick coordinate points in the drawing area, by pressing the pointing device's pick button. This will execute the command, and the various options for the command will appear in the Command-prompt area just as though you had typed the command at the keyboard.

There is one exception to this: If you select the Help command and immediately select an on-screen AutoCAD command, AutoCAD will display a brief description of that command in the text-display area, rather than executing the command.

Not everything that appears in the on-screen menu area is an AutoCAD command. Some of the words that appear are *keywords* that trigger the display of other menus.

AutoCAD follows certain conventions when displaying words in the on-screen menu area:

- Words in uppercase and followed by a colon (e.g., ERASE:) are AutoCAD commands that will be executed when picked. In some cases, they will also cause the display of submenus.

- Words in uppercase but not followed by a colon (e.g., EDIT) are not AutoCAD commands and will only cause the display of submenus.

- Words in lowercase or mixed case (e.g., window, eXit) are command options, which are valid only when the correct accompanying command has been previously picked. When displayed using mixed case, these command options can be invoked by entering only the uppercase letter or letters at the keyboard.

The *pull-down menu* is another form of the on-screen menu. AutoCAD's pull-down menu is a feature available to users whose graphics display supports a special AutoCAD feature called the *Advanced User Interface,* and who have AutoCAD Release 9 or later. If your hardware supports this special feature and you have configured your display with a status line, moving the crosshairs into the status line will change the display into a *menu bar.* You may then highlight and pick one of the keywords displayed in the menu bar, causing the appearance of a pull-down menu, as illustrated in Figure 5.11. You can then highlight command options as displayed in this menu, in a manner similar to highlighting commands in AutoCAD's standard on-screen menu.

Picking certain AutoCAD commands that offer a large number of options can trigger the appearance of an *icon menu,* as illustrated in Figure 5.12. Icon menus display a group of options that are illustrated with small slides, called *icons,* to clarify precisely what options are available. You may select an option by highlighting a small box to the left of each icon.

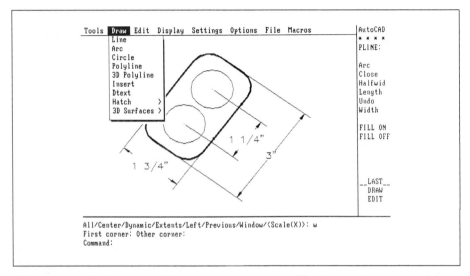

FIGURE 5.11: A pull-down menu. After zooming in on a portion of the drawing, the user moved the crosshairs to the uppermost line of the screen, and the menu bar appeared. Moving the pointing device, the user highlighted the word *DRAW* in the menu bar and pressed the pick button. The Draw pull-down menu is temporarily superimposed on the drawing, offering the user a selection of entity draw commands. Moving the pointing device downward will highlight whichever command the user intends to select. The graphics display must support the Advanced User Interface (AUI) to use pull-down menus.

Selecting AutoCAD commands that affect drawing settings may cause the appearance of a *dialog box*, which contains various options that can be entered interactively using both the pointing device and the keyboard as required. A dialog box is illustrated in Figure 5.13. Specific standard screen-menu displays, icon menus, and dialog boxes are illustrated throughout this book in the sections dealing with the commands that cause their appearance.

Canceling Commands

You can cancel an AutoCAD command in progress at any time by pressing Ctrl-C from the keyboard. Commands can also be canceled by highlighting and picking *CANCEL* from an on-screen menu, or by picking CANCEL from a tablet menu. If you have entered an incorrect response to a prompt but don't wish to cancel the command, you may cancel only the pending response by pressing Ctrl-X before pressing the Enter key or the space bar. If the response is short, you may prefer to "back up over it" using the Backspace key or Ctrl-H.

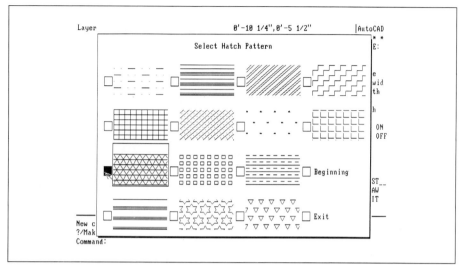

FIGURE 5.12: An icon menu. This typical icon menu is one of a series that appears when the user selects the Hatch command from the pull-down menu shown in Figure 5.11. The user moves the small arrow until it points to one of the small boxes in the icon menu. The selected box changes to a filled solid, and a rectangle appears around the selected hatch pattern (in this case, NET3). Pressing the pick button will select this hatch pattern. The box marked BEGINNING indicates that there is another hatch-pattern icon menu that may be selected by picking that box. The box marked EXIT may be selected to remove the icon menu without selecting any pattern. The graphics display must support the Advanced User Interface to use icon menus.

Transparent Commands

Some AutoCAD commands may be invoked while other AutoCAD commands are in progress. These *transparent commands* are Ddemodes, Ddlmodes, Ddrmodes, Graphscr, Help, Pan, Redraw, Redrawall, Resume, Setvar, Textscr, View, and Zoom. When entered during another AutoCAD command, these commands must be preceded by an apostrophe character ('). AutoCAD will pause execution of the current command, display all appropriate prompts and options for the transparent command, and resume the current command when the transparent command has completed functioning.

Most of these commands cause changes to the screen display of the drawing. Ddemodes will change the drawing environment setting, Ddlmodes changes layer properties, and Ddrmodes changes drawing aids. Setvar changes the settings of certain internal system variables affecting AutoCAD, but some of the changes made with Setvar will not go into effect until the end of the current command.

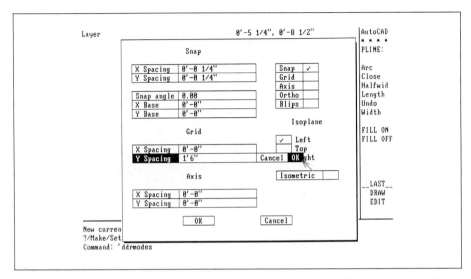

FIGURE 5.13: A dialog box. A dialog box presents to the user a number of different options, which may be selected in any order. In the above figure, the user has changed the Y spacing by moving the arrow to the indicated box. The box is highlighted, and the user entered **1'6"** as the new Y spacing. Next the user moves the arrow to the box marked OK to confirm the selection. When the desired options in the dialog box are set, the user will move the arrow to the box labeled OK and press the pick button. All requested changes will be implemented. The graphics display must support the Advanced User Interface to use dialog boxes.

Any transparent command may be entered as a stand-alone command whenever the Command prompt is displayed. When you enter these commands at the Command prompt, the apostrophe is not used.

Repeating Commands

You may repeat an AutoCAD command that has processed through to a normal completion any number of times by pressing the Enter key or the space bar. This has the same effect as typing or picking the command again. In some cases, repeated commands will repeat command options as default responses. Refer to the individual command description in this book for details on how a particular command behaves when it repeats.

Beginning with AutoCAD Release 9, you may also repeat a command by preceding the first invocation of the command with the word *Multiple,* as in Multiple Erase. When a command is preceded by the modifier Multiple, it will automatically repeat each time it concludes processing, until you enter Ctrl-C or select *CANCEL* in response to a prompt.

When composing custom menus, you may include the special syntax *^C^C to cause a command to repeat automatically until Ctrl-C is pressed. Refer to Chapter 14 for details.

SELECTING COORDINATE POINTS

AutoCAD provides several different methods for selecting coordinate point information. As you develop your own drafting style, you will undoubtedly use one or two favorite methods. However, it is best to become familiar with them all. For example, if you usually create line segments by picking their endpoints, you may sometimes be in a situation where you know the length of the line but not the location of its endpoint. In the latter situation, it would be easier to use polar coordinates to create the line. AutoCAD's various point-selection methods are explained in the upcoming sections.

Picking Coordinates with the Pointing Device

The simplest and most direct means of entering coordinate point information is by moving the intersection of the screen crosshairs to the desired coordinate point and pressing the pointing device's pick button. You may respond in this manner to any command prompt that requests coordinate information.

Absolute Coordinates

Coordinate point information may also be entered from the keyboard in the form of numbers separated by commas, as in the following dialog from Auto-CAD Release 11:

> Command: **Line**
> From point: **5,4 (entering 2-D coordinate point x = 5, y = 4)**
> To point: **6,7,12 (entering 3-D coordinate point x = 6, y = 7, z = 12)**
> To point: **(press Enter)**

The result of the above dialog is illustrated in Figure 5.14.

Coordinate points entered in this manner are called *absolute coordinates*. 2-D points require two numbers, x and y coordinates, with the x coordinate always supplied first. When you enter 3-D points, three numbers are required; Auto-CAD assumes that they are x, y, and z coordinates, in that order.

In AutoCAD Release 10 and later, 3-D points entered using absolute coordinates will be positioned relative to the current construction plane. Figure 5.15

shows how the dialog just shown will position a point in a construction plane that is not parallel to the world coordinate system.

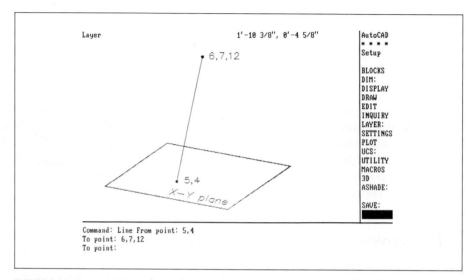

FIGURE 5.14: Drawing a line with absolute coordinate entry. In the above example, a 3-D line is located in space by using the keyboard to enter the coordinates of the line's starting point (5,4) and ending point (6,7,12). When the z coordinate is omitted, AutoCAD assumes that the z coordinate is that of the current construction plane. In this figure, the current construction plane is the same as the X-Y plane.

Polar Coordinates

Another common method for entering coordinate information from the keyboard uses *polar coordinates*. Polar coordinates specify both a distance and an angle from the last point specified, using the following syntax:

@ distance < angle

Here is an example of how this syntax is used:

Command: **Line**
From point: **5,4 (entering 2-D coordinate point x = 5, y = 4)**
To point: **@6.25<45**
To point: **(press Enter)**

In the above example, the response to the first "To point:" prompt indicates a distance of 6.25 drawing units from the last specified point (5,4) at an angle of 45 degrees. Figure 5.16 illustrates the line segment created using this dialog.

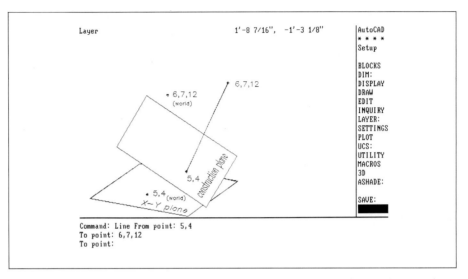

FIGURE 5.15: Drawing a line: absolute coordinate entry in a 3-D construction plane. In this example from AutoCAD Release 10, the construction plane has been oriented in 3-D space by defining it as a user coordinate system. Notice the location of points 5,4 and 6,7,12 in the never-changing world coordinate system. However, these points are now located relative to the current construction plane; a line drawn between them will appear in a different location from the line drawn in Figure 5.14.

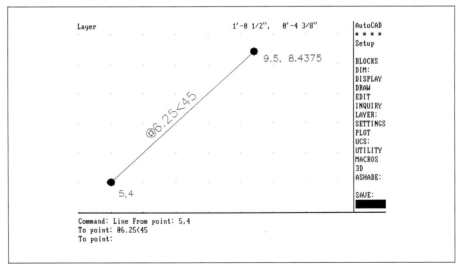

FIGURE 5.16: Drawing a line: polar coordinate entry. The line in the above example was drawn by entering the starting point (5,4) followed by a polar coordinate entry (@6.25<45). AutoCAD extends the line at the given distance and angle; it computes the opposite endpoint of the line by projecting the line onto the x- and y-axes.

Angle and distance information will be accepted in the format defined for the drawing with the Units command. For details regarding the possible formats for distance and angle information, refer to the Units command in Chapter 6.

In AutoCAD Release 9 and earlier, polar coordinates are used to enter 2-D points only. They can be positioned above or below the X-Y plane according to the value of the ELEVATION system variable. Refer to Chapter 13 for information on how to change the value of the ELEVATION system variable. In Release 10 and later, polar coordinates are subject to the same rules, but they are positioned relative to the current construction plane.

Spherical Coordinates

Release 11 and later releases offer a means to specify polar coordinates in 3-D space, called *spherical coordinates*. You may specify spherical coordinates from the keyboard using the following syntax:

> distance < angle in X-Y plane < angle above X-Y plane

Here is an example of how this syntax is used:

> Command: **LINE**
> From point: **5,4**
> To point: @**6.25**<**45**<**50**
> To point: **(press Enter)**

In the above example, the response to the "To point:" prompt indicates a distance of 6.25 drawing units from the last specified point (5,4) at an angle of 45 degrees measured from the x-axis in the X-Y plane of the current User Coordinate System (UCS), at a 50 degree angle above the X-Y plane of the current UCS. Figure 5.17 illustrates the line segment created using this dialog.

Cylindrical Coordinates

Release 11 and later releases also provide an alternate means of specifying polar coordinates in 3-D space, called *cylindrical coordinates*. You may specify cylindrical coordinates from the keyboard using the following syntax:

> distance < angle in X-Y plane , distance above X-Y plane

Here is an example of how this syntax is used:

> Command: **LINE**
> From point: **5,4**
> To point: @**6.25**<**45,50**
> To point: **(press Enter)**

The above example indicates a distance of 6.25 drawing units from the last point specified, at an angle of 45 degrees from the x-axis in the X-Y plane of the current UCS, at a perpendicular distance of 50 drawing units above the X-Y plane of the current UCS. Notice that the substitution of a comma for the second "<" symbol is all that distinguishes cylindrical from spherical coordinate syntax. Figure 5.18 illustrates the line segment created using this dialog.

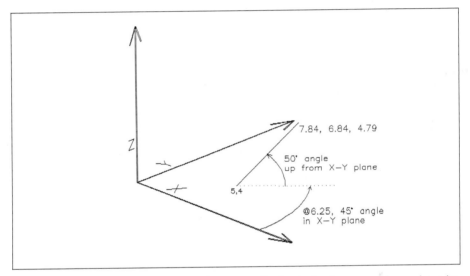

Figure 5.17: Drawing a line—spherical coordinate entry. The line in the above example was drawn by entering the starting point (5,4) followed by a spherical polar coordinate entry (@6.25<45<50). As in polar coordinate entry, AutoCAD discovers a new endpoint by first projecting a point at the given distance and angle of 45 degrees in the current construction plane; it then elevates the endpoint of the line by an angle of 50 degrees above the X-Y plane (using 5,4 as the angle vertex) to locate the new endpoint at xx,yy,zz.

Last Point Entered: The @ Symbol

AutoCAD always stores and "remembers" the last set of coordinate points entered, whether by keyboard or by on-screen point pick. You may quickly reselect this point by entering the symbol @ in response to any prompt that accepts coordinate point information.

In AutoCAD Release 10 and later, this point is stored as a 3-D point. If @ is supplied to a prompt requesting 2-D coordinate information, the stored z coordinate is ignored. Versions earlier than Release 10 and later store this point as a 2-D point.

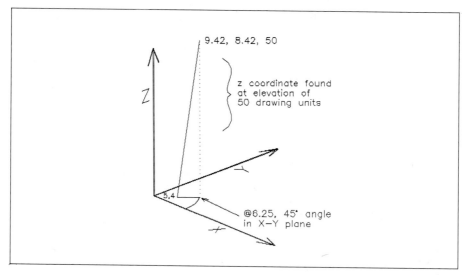

Figure 5.18: Drawing a line—cylindrical coordinate entry. Similar to spherical coordinate point entry, AutoCAD uses cylindrical coordinate point entry to find a coordinate point relative to the last selected point (5,4), at a distance of 6.25 units and angle of 45 degrees in the current construction plane. Then AutoCAD measures a distance of 50 drawing units above the X-Y plane to arrive at the new line end-point of xx,yy,zz.

Relative Coordinate Points

The @ symbol can be combined with coordinate points to specify a new point relative to the last point picked. For example, imagine that the last point picked was 5,4. A new point located 6 units farther along the x-axis and 8 units farther along the y-axis from this point may be entered with the following syntax:

   @6,8

This has the same effect as selecting point 11,12.

In AutoCAD Release 10 and later, you may use this relative-coordinate method to supply 3-D points. As with the x and y coordinates, the z coordinate will be calculated relative to the z coordinate of the last point picked.

Point Filters

Point filters assist you when entering points in those cases when it is easiest to enter x, y, and z coordinates separately rather than all at once. To use a point filter, enter a period (.) followed by one or two coordinates that you intend to enter next, as in the following example:

> Command: **Line**
> From point: **.XY**

This indicates to AutoCAD that only the x and y coordinates need to be considered from the next point selection. Continuing with the dialog, AutoCAD prompts:

> Command: **Line**
> From point: **.XY** of

At this point, you may supply coordinate information in any normal manner. The z coordinate, if included, will be ignored. AutoCAD then prompts:

> Command: **Line**
> From point: **.XY** of **(select point 5,4,5)**
> (need Z) **(select point 0,0,10)**

Here you may enter a point with the required z coordinate using any normal method of point selection. The z coordinate of this point (10) will be used with the x and y coordinates of the previous point (5,4) to create the line's starting point (5,4,10).

If you choose, you may enter only a numeric value for the z coordinate, as follows:

> Command: **Line**
> From point: **.XY** of **(select point 5,4,5)**
> (need Z) **(enter 10)**

This has the same effect of selecting point 5,4,10.

You can filter for single coordinates if you like. Consider the following dialog, which assumes that the current elevation is 10:

> Command: **Line**
> From point: **.x** of **(pick point 0,0,10)**
> (need YZ) **.y** of **(pick point 5,4,10)**
> (need Z) **5**
> To point: **(again pick point 5,4,10)**
> To point: **(press Enter)**

The above dialog will draw a line from point 0,4,5 to point 5,4,10.

The following dialog for Release 11 combines different methods of point selection to construct a vertical isosceles triangle. Current elevation is 0.

> Command: **Line**
> From point: **5,4**
> To point: **@10<90**
> To point: **.xy**

of **mid**
of @
(need Z) **10**
To point: *c*

World Coordinates

In AutoCAD Release 10 and later, it is possible to enter absolute coordinates in the world coordinate system, regardless of the current construction plane. To do so, precede them with an asterisk, as follows:

*5,4,0

This will position a point at 5,4 in the world X-Y plane.

Relative input may be specified for the world coordinate system as well. For example, the following dialog will draw a line 10 units long starting from world 5,4 in the world X-Y plane:

Command: **Line**
From point: ***5,4,0**
To point: **@*10<90**
To point: **(press Enter)**

In the above example, notice that the @ symbol will return the absolute world coordinate system information as selected in response to the previous prompt. The asterisk following this symbol indicates that the distance and direction are to be measured in the world coordinate system.

Relative coordinates can also be expressed in the world coordinate system. The following dialog draws the same line as the previous dialog:

Command: **Line**
From point: ***5,4,0**
To point: ***0,10,0**
To point: **(press Enter)**

SELECTING AutoCAD ENTITIES

Once entities are drawn, they may be edited in a variety of ways. The process of making changes to an AutoCAD drawing always begins by selecting the entity or entities to be edited. AutoCAD provides a standard selection process that includes a number of optional selection mechanisms to offer maximum flexibility in isolating only those desired entities.

When you select a command that will cause changes to one or more entities, AutoCAD first prompts:

Select objects:

The AutoCAD prompts generally refer to drawing entities as *objects* when the prompt relates to selecting entities from the display, as this one does. In other contexts, such as extracting entities or entity properties from the drawing database, AutoCAD uses the term *entities*. Both terms refer to the same thing: the entities found in AutoCAD's drawing database. (For consistency's sake, this book uses the term *entities* throughout.)

Each time you select an entity (or group of entities) using one of the available selection options, the above prompt will repeat, permitting you to select additional entities. On most graphic displays, AutoCAD *highlights* the selected entities by changing their appearance slightly. AutoCAD refers to the entities you have selected as a *selection set*.

You can repeat any combination of different selection methods to add more entities to the selection set. You may also remove any entities that were unintentionally selected. (Refer to "Removing Entities" later in this chapter for details.) Entities must be visible on the screen in order to be selected.

Once you have selected all the entities you intend to edit, respond to this prompt by pressing the space bar or the Enter key. AutoCAD then continues with the editing command, using the selection set you have created.

THE SELECT COMMAND

It is also possible to create a selection set without invoking an editing command, by means of the Select command. The Select command creates a selection set using all the options described below. The selection set created using this command can then be reselected during other editing commands.

Selection Options

Following are various optional methods for building a selection set:

Object Pointing   When the "Select objects:" prompt appears, AutoCAD replaces the screen crosshairs with a small *pickbox*. The simplest and most direct means of selecting entities is to position the pickbox on the entity you wish to select and press the pick button. (When selecting wide lines or solids, position the pickbox over one of the entity's edges.) AutoCAD searches the drawing database until it finds an entity that crosses this point.

AutoCAD searches the database starting with the most recently added entity and continuing to the first entity. In cases where two or more entities overlap the selection point, AutoCAD will find the most recently added entity. To select a previously added entity, use one or more of the other selection options below.

Multiple Object Pointing   If you wish to select several entities by pointing to them, you can speed up the process by selecting the Multiple option. To do this, enter the letter **M** in response to the "Select objects:" prompt. AutoCAD repeats the prompt while you select the entities you wish to edit. After you have selected the entities, press Enter. AutoCAD then searches the database and highlights the entities you selected.

When using the Multiple option, if two entities overlap the same selection point, you can select them both by selecting the point twice. This technique will work only when you're using the Multiple option.

Window Selection   You can select several entities as a group by means of the Window option. The Window option allows you to select entities by placing a rectangular "window" around them. All entities that are completely enclosed within the window will be selected. Entities that touch the window boundaries but are otherwise completely enclosed will be included in the selection set. There is one exception to this rule regarding windowing entities: If an entity is only partially visible on the screen, and therefore capable of being only partially enclosed within the window, it will still be included in the selection set.

To use the Window option, enter **W** in response to the "Select objects:" prompt. AutoCAD responds:

First corner:

Respond to this prompt by entering the coordinate points of one corner of the rectangular window. Any method of coordinate point entry is acceptable, but most users prefer to use the screen crosshairs to pick the point. After the first corner is selected, AutoCAD prompts:

Other corner:

Respond to this prompt by entering the coordinates of the corner of the rectangular window opposite the first. If you are using the screen crosshairs to indicate the coordinates, AutoCAD will draw an expandable box to help you visualize the location of the window and the entities that will be included.

After you have selected the other corner, the window disappears, the entities completely enclosed within the window are highlighted, and the "Select objects:" prompt repeats, allowing you to continue building the selection set.

Crossing Window Selection   The Crossing Window option is similar to the regular Window option, except that entities that are only partially enclosed in the crossing window will be included in the selection set. Because of this, you can use the Crossing Window option to select entities that are not fully visible on the screen.

To use this option, enter **C** in response to the "Select objects:" prompt. The dialog is the same as for the Window option above. On many displays, the crossing window will appear slightly different from the regular window.

Box Window Selection   The Box Window option allows you to select entities via either a regular or crossing window, depending on how you enter the points for the window's corners. After selecting the first corner, you can create a regular window by entering the second point to the right of the first. If you enter the second point to the left of the first, you will create a crossing window.

To use this option, enter **BOX** in response to the "Select objects:" prompt. All other dialog is the same as for windowing. The Box option is especially useful when included in custom menus. Refer to Chapter 14 for details on creating custom menus.

Automatic Selection   The Automatic Selection option allows you to combine the object and window selection mechanisms. After selecting this option, you select a point on the display screen. AutoCAD searches the database as with regular point selection. If no entity is found, AutoCAD automatically switches to the box selection mechanism, allowing you to create either a regular or crossing window, depending on where you position the second point, as with the Box option above.

After entities are selected, the "Select objects:" prompt repeats. Automatic selection remains active through all subsequent point picks, even if another option is chosen.

To activate this option, enter **AU** in response to the "Select objects:" prompt. The Automatic option is especially useful in custom menus. Refer to Chapter 14 for details on creating custom menus.

Selecting the Last Entity   The Last option allows you to immediately select the most recently added entity currently on the screen without pointing, windowing, or entering coordinate information. This option will only select the most recent visible entity; selecting it repeatedly has no other effect than to select the same entity again.

To use this option, enter **L** in response to the "Select objects:" prompt. The most recent entity is immediately selected and the "Select objects:" prompt repeats.

Selecting the Previous Selection Set   AutoCAD stores and "remembers" the last selection set. If you wish to perform a series of editing options on the same selection set, the Previous option allows you to reselect the last selection set you created.

To use this option, enter **P** in response to the "Select objects:" prompt. The entities in the previous selection set are automatically selected and highlighted. If you erase the entities in a selection set, the set is emptied and cannot be reselected with this option. If no previous selection set exists, AutoCAD will respond with the following error message:

No previous selection set.

Using Only One Option   The Single option disables the repetition of the "Select objects:" prompt. This option helps speed things along a bit by causing the editing command to continue immediately after you have selected one entity or set of entities.

To use this option, enter **SI** at the "Select objects:" prompt. The prompt will repeat and you may use a single selection option of your choice. The Single option is especially useful in custom menus. Refer to Chapter 14 for details on creating custom menus.

Undo Selection   The Undo option allows you to remove the entity or group of entities you most recently added to the selection set. If you selected a single entity, that entity will be removed. If you selected a group of entities using a windowing option, the entire group will be removed. If you repeat the Undo option, you can step back through the selection set, removing entities in reverse order until the selection set is empty.

To use this option, enter **U** in response to the "Select objects:" prompt. Entities are automatically removed and the "Select objects:" prompt repeats.

Removing Entities   The Remove option allows you to interactively remove entities from the selection set. After selecting this option, you may continue to use all the other selection mechanisms, but instead of adding entities to the selection set, the selection mechanisms will now remove them. This option allows you to pick and choose specific entities that you do not want to edit. For example, a common practice is to select a large group of entities using a window, and then use the Remove option to eliminate a few that you did not wish to include.

To use this option, enter **R** in response to the "Select objects:" prompt. The "Select objects:" prompt changes to a "Remove objects:" prompt. Dialog for various selection mechanisms continues to function normally for entity removal.

Adding Selections   The Add option allows you to change from the "Remove objects:" prompt to the "Select objects:" prompt, thereafter adding additional entities to the selection set. The dialog for other selection mechanisms remains unchanged. You may switch back and forth between the Add and Remove options as many times as necessary to build your selection set.

To use this option, enter **A** in response to the "Remove objects:" prompt. The "Remove objects:" prompt changes back to a "Select objects:" prompt.

Canceling the Selection Process   At any time, you may terminate the entire selection process, along with the active editing command, by entering Ctrl-C in response to any prompt. After you enter Ctrl-C, the selection set is abandoned and the AutoCAD Command prompt returns.

Commands That Restrict the Selection Set Process

Certain AutoCAD commands, such as Stretch, require that entities be selected by specific selection options. Where a command requires a particular selection mechanism, it is noted in the individual command description in this book.

SELECTING VALUES

In the course of creating and editing a drawing, you will find it necessary from time to time to enter certain specific numeric values, such as measurements of distances, angles, displacements, number of copies, and so forth. As with coordinate points and entity selection, AutoCAD provides several optional methods for entering values associated with drawing entities.

Options available to you include the type of format in which you may enter values, as well as a few optional techniques for making the entries.

The format of numeric input is controlled by AutoCAD's Units command. Auto-CAD offers a choice of several numeric formats, some of which may be combined: scientific notation, decimal units, feet and inches, and fractional. When entering angle information, you may choose decimal degrees, minutes and seconds, grads, radians, and surveyor's units.Prior to AutoCAD Release 11, the valid format for numeric input was governed by settings in the Units command. In Release 11 and later, AutoCAD accepts any appropriate numeric input format regardless of the current Units setting. Refer to the description of the Units command in Chapter 6 for details regarding the selection and entry of different format values. You may choose to enter numeric values by either typing them directly from the keyboard, picking numbers off of a menu or tablet, or entering points to represent measurements.

Distance and Angle

You can assign measures of angle and distance by typing the correct value and pressing Enter. This will work at any prompts that ask for a measurement (e.g., height, width, radius, chord length, angle of rotation, and so forth).

Alternatively, you can "show" AutoCAD the correct value by entering two points. AutoCAD will accept the distance or angle between the points as the response to the prompt.

In AutoCAD's standard configuration, angle measurements follow the orientation illustrated in Figure 5.19; that is, angles increase in a counterclockwise direction from zero degrees, which is oriented horizontally to the right.

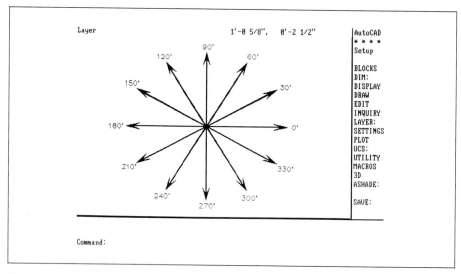

Figure 5.19: AutoCAD's standard angle-measurement system

For new entities, AutoCAD uses this technique to accept values from a default point. For example, when you draw a circle, AutoCAD prompts for a center point. After you assign the center point, AutoCAD prompts for a radius value. If you move the crosshairs away from the center point, you will see a line rubberbanding from the chosen center point. When you pick a second point in response to the prompt for a radius value, AutoCAD assumes that the distance from the center point to the selected point is the radius you want. Refer to the description of the circle command in Chapter 8 for an illustration of this technique.

Displacement

Displacement refers to the amount and direction of movement made when entities are copied or relocated in the drawing, or when the entire drawing itself is reoriented within the drawing editor.

Displacements are usually entered by selecting two points. The first selected point becomes the *base point,* or anchor point, for the subsequent displacement. The second selected point determines the amount and angle of displacement. When entering displacements via point picks, notice that the base point may be selected somewhat arbitrarily, because it is the relationship between these two points, not their specific coordinate locations, that determines the amount and direction of movement.

For example, imagine a circle such as the one shown in Figure 5.20. Assume that you wish to make a copy of this circle. After you invoke the Copy command and select the circle, AutoCAD prompts you for a base point. The selected base point is located to one side of the circle. The second point is selected 5 drawing units away, at an orientation of 53.13 degrees. Figure 5.20 illustrates the result. After the second point is selected, the copy of the circle is drawn at a distance of 5 drawing units and an angle of 53.13 degrees from the first. Notice that the relationship between the second circle and the second selected point is the same as the relationship between the first circle and the base point.

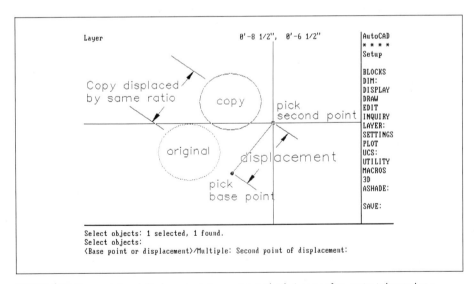

FIGURE 5.20: Base point and displacement: two-point method. A copy of an entity is located at a specific distance and absolute angle from the original. This distance and angle may be specified by entering two points. AutoCAD calculates the distance and absolute angle formed by these two points, and uses them to relocate the copy. The same process is used when moving entities.

If you choose, you can enter displacements from the keyboard using absolute or relative coordinates. For example, to move the circle illustrated in Figure 5.20, you could enter the following dialog:

Command: **Copy**
Select objects: **(select the circle)**
Select objects: **(press Enter)**
Base point or displacement: **0,0**
Second point of displacement: **3,4**

This dialog specifies a base point located at 0,0 and a second point at 3,4. The distance between these points is 5 drawing units, and the angle is 53.13 degrees; the copy of the circle would be drawn at this orientation. Likewise, if a point had been previously selected anywhere in the drawing, you could enter the following:

Command: **Copy**
Select objects: **(select the circle)**
Select objects: **(press Enter)**
Base point or displacement: **@5<53.13**
Second point of displacement: **(press Enter)**

In AutoCAD Releases 9 and later, the Copy and Move commands allow displacements in 3-D space, using 3-D coordinates. The Pan command allows only 2-D displacements. Refer to the descriptions of the Copy and Move commands in Chapter 10, and the Pan command in Chapter 11, for details regarding their syntax.

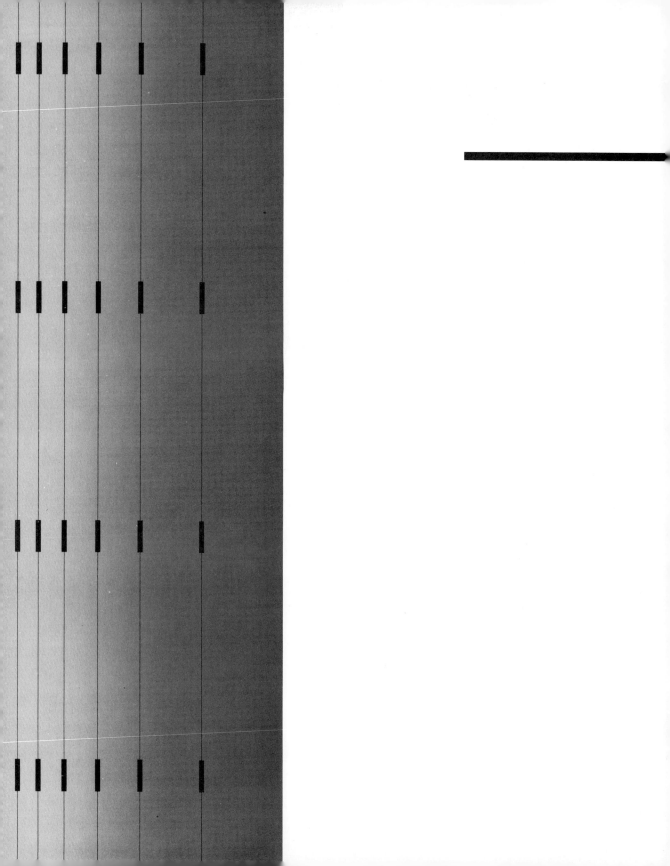

CHAPTER 6

CONTROLLING THE DRAWING PROCESS

CONTROLLING THE DRAWING PROCESS

he commands presented in this chapter act upon the properties of drawing entities by making changes to the environment in which those entities are drawn. You can use these commands to:

- Determine the layer upon which entities will reside and the default entity properties for any particular layer.
- Specify entity linetypes, colors, elevations, extrusion thicknesses, and construction planes.
- Set the maximum drawing size and set AutoCAD to accept only entities that fall within certain area limits.
- Control the way in which entities are referenced in the drawing database, and the configuration of the digitizing tablet if you are using one.
- Report on the status of AutoCAD's installation in your hardware.

None of the commands presented in this chapter actually produce drawing entities, but they make the process of drawing with AutoCAD much more intuitive and efficient. These commands provide a handy means to control several of AutoCAD's *system variables* (special memory variables that determine environment parameters). In some cases, if you need to make a change to a single aspect of the environment, or if you wish to make an environment change while in the middle of another command, you can do so by changing the value of the system variable. This can save time by avoiding the display of menus or additional environmental options you may not need. Refer to Chapter 13 for details on the system variables.

COLOR

Sets the color for all subsequently drawn entities.

VERSIONS

2.5 and later.

COMMAND OPTIONS

Color Number, Color Name, Byblock, Bylayer.

USAGE

The Color command allows you to draw entities of a specific color regardless of other factors that might normally affect color, such as the default color assigned to a particular layer.

If you're changing the colors frequently, consider customizing the AutoCAD screen or tablet menus to speed up the changes. Use macros to draw a single entity with a special color and reset the Color command to Bylayer.

Beware when combining entities of different colors into blocks with Byblock. Results are unpredictable when inserting or changing the color of such blocks.

RELATED COMMANDS

Change, Layer.

RELATED SYSTEM VARIABLES

CECOLOR (current entity color).

SAMPLE DIALOG

The following sample dialog turns the entity color to red, draws a short line, and returns the entity color to Bylayer:

```
Command: Color
New Entity Color <BYLAYER>: Red
Command: Line
From point: 0,0
To point: 5,5
To point: (press Enter)
Command: Color
New entity color <Red>: Bylayer
Command:
```

DDEMODES

Uses a dialog box to interactively access selected features of the Color, Elev, Layer, and Linetype commands.

VERSIONS

Release 9 and later, with AutoCAD's display device configured for the Advanced User Interface.

COMMAND OPTIONS

All Ddemodes options are contained within the dialog box. They include setting the current entity color, setting the current layer, setting the current text-style, and setting the current entity linetype, elevation, and thickness.

USAGE

Ddemodes places the most frequently accessed entity-change features within a single dialog box that graphically represents these features and allows for interactive access and multiple changes from a single command. Refer to Figure 6.1 for an illustration of a typical dialog box using Ddemodes.

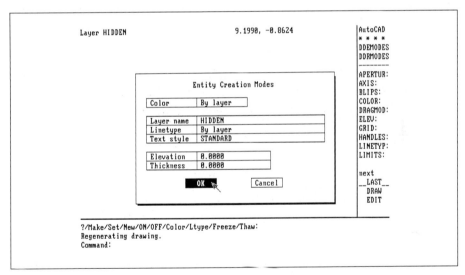

FIGURE 6.1: A sample dialog box using Ddemodes. This figure illustrates how the Ddemodes dialog box is used to set properties for new entities. When the user presses the pick button, the entity properties will be activated and the dialog box will disappear from the screen.

The Ddemodes command is convenient and requires minimal knowledge of command syntax. This makes it an especially useful command for beginning users. If you have more experience with AutoCAD command syntax, you may prefer to avail yourself of some alternatives to the Ddemodes dialog box:

- The individual commands used to change entity properties can be faster, especially when generated with macros.
- All settings changed with Ddemodes can also be changed by using the Setvar command to change system variables. When you're changing only a single entity property, especially within another command, this method can be faster.
- Standard entity-property settings can be quickly established using dedicated layers.

When you use Ddemodes as a transparent command, the changes you implement are not implemented until the conclusion of the active command. To make the changes take effect immediately, invoke Ddemodes from the Command prompt. Refer to Chapter 21 for details regarding transparent commands.

RELATED COMMANDS

Color, Elev, Layer, Linetype, Setvar.

RELATED SYSTEM VARIABLES

CLAYER (current layer), CECOLOR (current color), CELTYPE (current linetype), ELEVATION (current elevation), THICKNESS (current thickness), POPUPS (availability of dialog boxes).

SAMPLE DIALOG

Figure 6.1 illustrates how Ddemodes can be used to change the entity color to green, the current layer to Walls, the linetype to Continuous, the elevation to 15 drawing units, and the thickness to 8 drawing units.

To change the entity color to green, move the arrow to the box showing the current entity color and press the pick button. AutoCAD displays a list of currently available colors. Move the arrow to the desired color and press the pick button.

To change the current layer, move the arrow to the box showing the current layer name and press the pick button. AutoCAD responds by displaying a list of current layer names.

To scroll through the list of layers, move the arrow to the boxes labeled Page Up or Page Down and press the pick button. To scroll more slowly, move the arrow to the box marked Up or Down and press the pick button.

To select the new current layer, move the arrow to the box containing the layer name Walls, and press the pick button.

To change the elevation to 15 drawing units, move the arrow to the box containing the current elevation and press the pick button. Type the new elevation and press the Enter key.

To change the thickness to 8 drawing units, move the arrow to the box containing the current thickness and press the pick button. Type the new thickness and press Enter.

After the changes are made, move the arrow to the box labeled OK, and press the pick button. The dialog box disappears and the changes are implemented. To cancel all the changes, move the arrow to the box labeled Cancel, and press the pick button. You can also cancel the changes and the dialog box by pressing Ctrl-C from the keyboard.

DDLMODES

Uses a dialog box to interactively access the features of the Layer command.

VERSIONS

Release 9 and later, with display device configured for the Advanced User Interface.

COMMAND OPTIONS

All Ddlmodes options are contained within the dialog box. They include listing layer data, creating new layers, setting a layer current, turning layers on and off, freezing and thawing layers, and changing a layer's default color and linetype settings.

To scroll through the list of layers, move your mouse pointer to the small box in the vertical scroll bar to the right of the linetype names. Press the pick button and move the small box up and down to view all available names or pick the up or down arrows to scroll through the list. If you are using AutoCAD Release 9 or 10, there is no scroll bar. You may use the boxes marked Page Up and Page Down, or simply Up and Down, to scroll through the list of names.

AutoCAD's Layer command presents a wide variety of options, which must be selected individually in command-line fashion. The Ddlmodes command opens a dialog box that is a graphic representation of Layer's various options. See Figure 6.2 for an illustration of a typical dialog box using Ddlmodes.

Two columns, each with two check boxes, control the visiblity of layers.

The column marked Global controls layer visibility in all viewport configurations. This column includes two check boxes, labeled On and Frz (Freeze), for each layer. You may toggle each check box on or off by moving the mouse pointer into the box and pressing the pick button.

If you click the On box, the layer is visible (unless frozen). If the On box is empty, entities on the layer will not be displayed. If you click the Freeze box, the layer is frozen. If empty, the layer is thawed. Refer to the discussion of the Layer command later in this chapter for more details regarding frozen and thawed layers.

Release 11 and later versions introduce another column of check boxes, labeled VP Frz (for Viewport Freeze). This column includes two check boxes for each layer, labeled Cur (Current) and New, which give you the ability to freeze and thaw layers in individual viewports. The meaning of the Current box changes, depending on whether you are in model or paper space. In model space, if you click the Current box, the selected layer is frozen in the current viewport. If you are in paper space, clicking the Current column freezes the layer in all viewports and overrides the global settings. If you click the New column, all new viewports will show the selected layer as frozen. Refer to the discussion of the Vplayer command later in this chapter for more details on controlling layer visibility on a per-viewport basis.

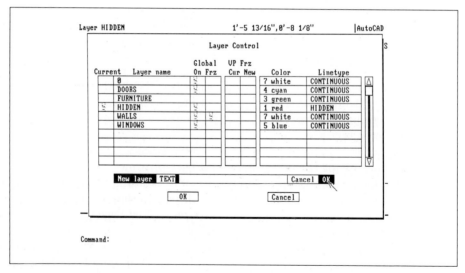

FIGURE 6.2: A sample dialog box using Ddlmodes. This figure illustrates how the Ddlmodes dialog box is used. The marks that appear in the small boxes indicate which features are currently activated. The pointing-device arrow has been moved to the box labeled OK on the same line as the new layer information. When the pick button is pressed, the new layer will be added to the list of layers. Moving the pointing-device arrow to the box labeled OK near the bottom of the dialog box and pressing the pick button activates the layer changes; the dialog box then disappears from the screen.

USAGE

Ddlmodes is an improvement over the Layer command when changing layer properties or making multiple changes to layer settings; but if you simply wish to move between existing layers, consider using macros on the screen or tablet menu for greater speed. Refer to Chapter 14 for details on creating macros.

When you use Ddlmodes as a transparent command, thawing layers, changing colors, and changing linetypes are not immediately visible on the screen. To make the changes visible, regenerate the drawing. Refer to Chapter 21 for details on transparent commands.

RELATED COMMANDS

Layer.

RELATED SYSTEM VARIABLES

CLAYER (current layer), POPUPS (availability of dialog boxes).

SAMPLE DIALOG

Figure 6.1 illustrates how Ddlmodes can be used to add a new layer named Text, make Hidden the current layer, change its default color to red and its linetype to Dashed, freeze the Walls layer, and turn off the Furniture layer.

To add the new layer, move the arrow to the New Layer box and press the pick button. Type the name of the new layer, **TEXT**, and press Enter.

To make the Hidden layer current, move the arrow to the box to the right of the layer name, in the column headed Current, and press the pick button.

To change the color of the Hidden layer to red, move the arrow to the box on the same line as Hidden, in the column labeled Color, and press the pick button. Enter the color **Red**.

To change the linetype of the Hidden layer to dashed, move the arrow to the box on the same line as Hidden, in the column labeled Linetype, and press the pick button. Enter the linetype **Dashed**. (Be sure that the linetype was previously loaded; refer to the discussion of the Linetype command for details.)

To freeze the Walls layer, move the arrow to the box on the same line as Walls, in the column labeled Frozen, and press the pick button. Layers are frozen when a check mark appears in the box, and thawed when the box is empty.

To turn off the Furniture layer, move the arrow to the box on the same line as Furniture, in the column labeled On, and press the pick button. Layers are on when a mark appears in the box, and off when the box is empty.

After the changes are made, move the arrow to the box labeled OK, and press the pick button. The dialog box disappears and the changes are implemented. To cancel all the changes, move the arrow to the box labeled Cancel, and press the pick button. You can also cancel the changes and the dialog box by pressing Ctrl-C from the keyboard.

Dducs

Uses two dialog boxes to interactively access features of the UCS command.

VERSIONS

Release 10 and later, with a display driver that supports the Advanced User Interface (ADI).

COMMAND OPTIONS

After invoking Dducs, you are presented with the first dialog box (Figure 6.3), which allows you to recall named UCS's, up to the last ten UCS's used during the current drawing session, or the WCS. If you wish to create a brand-new UCS, select the box labeled "Define a new current UCS." This causes the second dialog box (Figure 6.4) to appear. Using this dialog box, you can enter a new name for the current UCS, or rotate, move, or align a new UCS. Refer to the UCS command in this chapter for details regarding user coordinate systems and how they are manipulated.

USAGE

Unlike other dialog-box commands, Dducs cannot be used as a transparent command.

RELATED COMMANDS

UCS.

RELATED SYSTEM VARIABLES

UCSFOLLOW (always display UCS plan view), UCSNAME (current UCS name, if named), UCSORG (UCS origin point), UCSXDIR (UCS x-axis orientation), UCSYDIR (UCS y-axis orientation), WORLDUCS (UCS equal or not equal to WCS). All system variables are read-only except UCSFOLLOW. If UCS-FOLLOW is set to a value of 1, AutoCAD will automatically display each new UCS in plan view. If UCSFOLLOW is set to 0, changing the UCS does not change the display. If you are using multiple viewports, you can set UCSFOLLOW separately for each viewport.

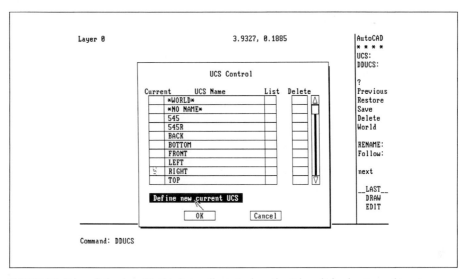

FIGURE 6.3: Dducs dialog box #1. This figure illustrates how the Dducs dialog box is used to set properties for user coordinate systems. In the above dialog box, a list of named user coordinate systems is presented. The mark that appears in the small box to the left of the UCS name indicates that it is current. The user has moved the pointing-device arrow to the box for defining a new UCS. Pressing the pick button now will display the dialog box pictured in Figure 6.4.

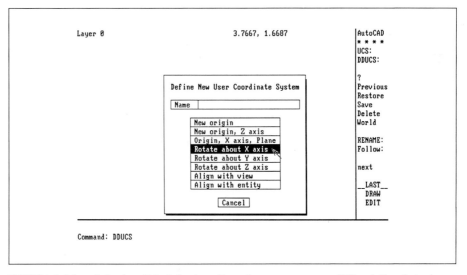

FIGURE 6.4: Dducs dialog box. This dialog box allows the user to set a new UCS and, if so desired, give it a name for fast recall later. Highlighting the box labeled OK and pressing the pick button will cause the selected changes to take effect and the dialog box to disappear from the screen.

SAMPLE DIALOG

Figure 6.4 illustrates how you can use the dialog box to name a new UCS by supplying a unique name and rotating the current UCS counterclockwise around the x-axis.

ELEV

Changes the settings for the current entity elevation and extrusion thickness.

VERSIONS

Version 2.18 and later.

COMMAND OPTIONS

New current elevation Enter the new elevation from the keyboard or tablet, or "show" AutoCAD the new elevation by entering two coordinate points. AutoCAD will accept the distance between the two points as the value of the new elevation.

New current thickness Enter the new thickness using the same techniques described above.

USAGE

The Elev command works by assigning new values to the ELEVATION and THICKNESS system variables.

With Release 10 and later, there are better alternatives to the Elev command. Elevation can and should be controlled using construction planes; refer to the discussion of the UCS command later in this chapter for details. Thickness can be controlled by using the Setvar command to change the THICKNESS system variable. Elev is scheduled to be eliminated in future releases of AutoCAD.

In AutoCAD versions that support them, 3-D faces, 3-D polylines, and 3-D meshes cannot be given a thickness. These entities ignore the current setting of the THICKNESS system variable. Text entities are always generated with a thickness of zero, but you can give them a thickness using the Change command.

Tip: When using AutoCAD Version 2.18 through Release 9, you can draw a line parallel to the z-axis by applying a thickness value to a point entity.

RELATED COMMANDS

Change, Setvar.

RELATED SYSTEM VARIABLES

ELEVATION (current elevation), THICKNESS (current thickness).

SAMPLE DIALOG

The following sample dialog changes the current setting of the ELEVATION and THICKNESS system variables from zero to 15 and 8 drawing units, respectively. The first value is entered from the keyboard, while the second is entered using two points. In actual practice, you may enter values for elevation or thickness using either the keyboard or the two-point method.

```
Command: Elev
New current elevation <0'0">: 15
New current thickness <0'0">: (pick a point)
Second point: (pick a second point 8 units away)
Command:
```

FILL

Controls the display of wide polylines, traces, and solids by toggling fill mode on and off.

VERSIONS

All.

COMMAND OPTIONS

On   Enter **ON** to toggle fill mode on. When fill mode is on, wide lines and solids will be displayed on the screen as filled-in solid entities.

Off   Enter **OFF** to toggle fill mode off. When fill mode is off, only the outlines of wide lines and solids will be displayed on the screen.

USAGE

AutoCAD provides the option of turning *fill mode* on and off for the sake of speed when redrawing and regenerating drawings. When fill mode is on, wide lines and solids are displayed accurately, but take longer to regenerate. Outlines of wide lines and solids can be displayed much more quickly. Figure 8.23 in Chapter 8 illustrates a solid as it would be displayed in both outline and filled-in mode.

When you turn fill mode on or off, the changes to your drawing display are not immediate. The changes will be displayed the next time a drawing regeneration is performed, by invoking either the Regen command or another AutoCAD display command that requires a drawing regeneration, such as Zoom All. Refer to Chapter 11 for details regarding these and other display commands.

RELATED SYSTEM VARIABLES

FILLMODE (controls whether fill mode is on or off).

SAMPLE DIALOG

> Command: **Fill**
> ON/OFF <On>: **OFF**
> Command: **Regen (Drawing is regenerated with wide lines and solids in outline form.)**
>
> Command: **Fill**
> ON/OFF <On>: **ON**
> Command: **Regen (Drawing is regenerated with wide lines and solids filled in.)**

GRAPHSCR

Forces the display of the graphics screen on single-screen systems.

VERSIONS

All.

COMMAND OPTIONS

None.

USAGE

AutoCAD uses two types of display, text and graphics. The graphics display includes the representation of all drawing-entity information in the AutoCAD drawing database—in other words, the drawing itself. The text display is a "running history" of all commands, prompts, responses, and text-based input.

On systems employing a single monitor, only one of these displays is visible at a time. The Graphscr command forces the display of the graphic entities in the drawing editor.

On most single-screen systems, text and graphics can be conveniently toggled back and forth with a function key, usually F1. The Graphscr command is most useful with command macros in which the graphics display must be forced regardless of the display's current status.

RELATED COMMANDS

Textscr.

SAMPLE DIALOG

Command: **Graphscr (Graphics screen is displayed.)**
Command: **Textscr or press Flip Screen key (Text screen is displayed.)**
Command: **Graphscr or press Flip Screen key (Graphics screen is displayed.)**
Command:

HANDLES

Assigns a unique hexadecimal number, called a *handle,* to every entity in the drawing. Via the Destroy option, the Handles command can also take away all the handle numbers in the drawing.

VERSIONS

Release 10 and later.

COMMAND OPTIONS

On   Enter **ON** to assign entity handles to all entities in the drawing. AutoCAD will display the message ''Handles are enabled'' whenever the Handles command is subsequently invoked.

Destroy   Enter **Destroy** to delete all handles from the drawing. When you select this option, AutoCAD displays the following message:

Completing this command will destroy ALL
database handle information in the drawing.
Once destroyed, links to the drawing from
external database files cannot be made.
If you really want to destroy the database
handle information, please confirm this by

> entering <*PASSWORD*> to proceed or "NO"
> to abort the command.
> Proceed with handle destruction <NO>:

This message is a safety device; it is designed to prevent accidental erasure of entity handles. Upon receiving this message, if you are certain that you want to destroy entity handles, enter the special password. Entering anything else aborts the command.

USAGE

Some third-party software developers and AutoLISP programmers find it useful to extract drawing entities from AutoCAD's underlying drawing database. An entity may be accessed either by means of its *entity name,* or, in Release 10 and later, by means of its *entity handle.* Entity names are assigned during each editing session and can change from one session to the next, but the entity handle is stored on disk and remains associated with that entity throughout its existence. Entity handles allow developers a more reliable means of extracting specific entities from the drawing database between editing sessions.

Database handles are required only if you are using or developing an application that requires consistent links to external data files. Using the Handles command significantly increases the size of your drawing file. Turn on handles only if it is required.

Once handles are enabled, the only reason to destroy them is to decrease the size of the drawing file. It is generally not wise to destroy handles once they have been created. If you do elect to destroy handles, make a backup of the original drawing file first.

Note: Regardless of whether handles are enabled, drawing files created using the Wblock command have no handles.

RELATED SYSTEM VARIABLES

HANDLES (entity handles enabled/disabled).

SAMPLE DIALOG

The following sample dialog enables handles:

> Command: **Handles**
> Handles are off
> ON/DESTROY: **ON**
> Handles are enabled
> Command:

LAYER

Manages AutoCAD's transparent overlay system.

VERSIONS

All. The Make option is available only in Version 2.5 and later.

COMMAND OPTIONS

? Enter a question mark to display a list of all layers currently defined for the drawing. AutoCAD responds with the following prompt:

Layer name(s) for listing <*>:

Enter the layer name or names you wish to include in the list. Wild-card characters (? and *) are acceptable. Following are some examples of valid uses of wild-card characters:

L*	All layers beginning with the letter *L*.
??2*	All layers with *2* appearing as the third character in the layer name.
F???-FPLAN	All layers beginning with *F* and ending with the characters *-FPLAN*, with any three characters in between. A single asterisk (*) is the default response, the asterisk being a wild-card character for all layer names in the data file.

Refer to Chapter 21 for a more detailed discussion of wild-card characters.

After you enter the layer names or press Enter, AutoCAD responds with a list of currently defined layers. This list includes:

- the layer name;
- whether it is on, off, frozen, or thawed;
- the color; and
- the linetype.

Make Enter **M** or **Make** to create a new layer and set it as current at the same time. AutoCAD responds:

New current layer <*current layer*>:

Enter the name of the layer you wish to create and/or make current. If the layer name is already defined, the layer is set current only. Wild-card characters cannot be used; enter one layer name only.

Set   Enter **S** or **Set** to set a previously defined layer as the current layer. AutoCAD responds:

> New current layer <*current layer*>:

Enter the name of the layer you wish to set current. If the layer name is not already defined, it cannot be made current; use the Make option instead.

New   Enter **N** or **New** to create new layers without making any of them current. AutoCAD responds:

> New layer name(s) <*current layer*>:

Enter the name or names of the new layers you wish to create. If entering more than one layer name, separate the names with commas. Wild-card characters cannot be used to name new layers.

ON   Enter **ON** to turn on layers that were previously turned off; that is, to make the entities on those layers visible. If a layer is already on, this option has no effect. You may use wild cards or a series of layer names separated by commas. Layers that were frozen as well as turned off must be thawed before they can be turned back on.

OFF   Enter **OFF** to turn layers off; that is, to make the entities on those layers invisible. AutoCAD responds:

> Layer name(s) to turn off:

You may respond with wild cards or with a series of layer names separated by commas. If a layer is already turned off, this option has no effect. If you elect to turn off the current layer, either by entering its name or (as is more likely) because of a wild-card entry, AutoCAD prompts:

> Really want layer <*current layer*> (the CURRENT layer) off? <N>

If you type **N** or press Enter, AutoCAD will turn off all requested layers except the current layer. If you enter **Y** in response to this prompt, AutoCAD will turn off the current layer, but all newly created entities will be invisible until this layer is turned back on again.

Color   Enter **C** or **Color** to change the default color for all entities placed on a layer (or layers). AutoCAD responds:

> Color:

Enter a color name or number that is valid for your display. (Refer to the section on colors in Chapter 3 for details on how to determine available colors for your display.)

When you assign a color to a layer, AutoCAD will automatically turn the layer on. If you intend to assign a color to a layer and turn the layer off (or keep it off), enter the color name or number preceded by a minus sign. If a layer is frozen, you may change its color, but it will not be thawed.

AutoCAD responds:

> Layer name(s) for color <*current layer*>:

Enter the name or names of layers to be assigned the default color. You may use wild-card characters or enter a list of layer names separated by commas.

Ltype   Enter **L** or **Ltype** to change the default linetype for all entities placed on a layer (or layers). AutoCAD responds:

> Linetype (or ?) <CONTINUOUS>:

Enter a linetype name that either has been previously loaded or is present in the ACAD.LIN file. Refer to the discussion of the Linetype command in this chapter for details regarding linetypes and the ACAD.LIN file. Alternatively, you may enter a question mark in response to this prompt. AutoCAD then displays a list of all currently loaded linetypes. After you enter a layer name, AutoCAD responds:

> Layer name(s) for linetype <*current layer*>:

Enter the name or names of the layers to be assigned the default linetype. You may use wild-card characters or enter a list of layer names separated by commas.

Freeze   Enter **F** or **Freeze** to turn off selected layers; AutoCAD will disregard the entities located on frozen layers when regenerating or redrawing. AutoCAD responds:

> Layer name(s) to freeze:

Enter the name or names of the layers you wish to freeze. You may use wild-card characters or enter a list of layer names separated by commas. If you enter the name of the current layer, either directly or as part of a wild-card character group, AutoCAD responds:

Cannot freeze layer <current layer>. It is the CURRENT layer.

AutoCAD will then freeze all requested layers except the current layer.

Thaw Enter **T** or **Thaw** to unfreeze previously frozen layers. AutoCAD responds:

Layer name(s) to thaw:

Enter the name or names of the previously frozen layers you wish to unfreeze. You may use wild-card characters or enter a list of layer names separated by commas. If a layer is not frozen, this option has no effect.

USAGE

Each AutoCAD drawing may include an unlimited number of *layers,* which are analogous to the transparent overlays often used in manual drafting. As in manual drafting, you group related entities by placing them on a layer. AutoCAD layers are in precise alignment; a point on one layer will always align perfectly with the same point on any other layer. Newly created entities are always placed on the layer that is set as current using this command.

When assigning default colors to layers, if you precede the color name or number with a minus sign, AutoCAD will assign the color to the layers of your choice and turn them off at the same time. This can save you a little time if this is your intention, especially if you are working with several layers at once.

Freezing layers, as opposed to simply turning them off, can speed up subsequent panning, zooming, and regeneration. This is because AutoCAD completely disregards the frozen entities during editing operations. However, thawing these layers will require a drawing regeneration before the entities become visible again.

Turning layers off will not speed up zooming, panning, and regeneration because AutoCAD *does* regenerate these entities—it simply doesn't display them. When a layer is turned back on, the faster redraw is all that is required to make the entities visible again.

The layer-options prompt reappears after each layer option is selected, allowing you to make several different changes before returning to the Command prompt. The changes go into effect after you press Enter in response to the layer-options prompt.

If a layer is turned off, it is turned back on automatically when you set it current.

Warning: Frozen layers cannot be set current. You must thaw them first.

RELATED COMMANDS

Ddemodes, Ddlmodes, Vplayer.

RELATED SYSTEM VARIABLES

CLAYER (current layer).

SAMPLE DIALOG

The following sample dialog will create five new layers, make layer Hidden current, set the default color of the Hidden layer to red and its linetype to Dashed, and turn it off. Then, all layers whose names begin with *F1* are given blue default color. The layer F112-WINDOWS is set current, and all other layers whose names begin with *F1* are turned off, except the current layer and the layer F112-FPLAN:

```
Command: Layer
?/Make/Set/New/ON/OFF/Color/Ltype/Freeze/Thaw: N
New layer name(s): F112-FPLAN,F113-FPLAN,F112- WINDOWS,F113-
WINDOWS
?/Make/Set/New/ON/OFF/Color/Ltype/Freeze/Thaw: M
New current layer <0>: HIDDEN
?/Make/Set/New/ON/OFF/Color/Ltype/Freeze/Thaw: L
Linetype (or ?) <CONTINUOUS>: Dashed
Layer name(s) for linetype DASHED <HIDDEN>: (press Enter)
?/Make/Set/New/ON/OFF/Color/Ltype/Freeze/Thaw: C
Color: -Red
Layer name(s) for color -RED <HIDDEN>: (press Enter)
Really want layer HIDDEN (the current layer) off? <N> Y
?/Make/Set/New/ON/OFF/Color/Ltype/Freeze/Thaw: C
Color: Blue
Layer name(s) for color BLUE <HIDDEN>: F1*
?/Make/Set/New/ON/OFF/Color/Ltype/Freeze/Thaw: S
New current layer <HIDDEN>: F112-WINDOWS
?/Make/Set/New/ON/OFF/Color/Ltype/Freeze/Thaw: OFF
Layer name(s) to turn Off: F1*
Really want layer F112-WINDOWS (the CURRENT layer) off? <N> N
?/Make/Set/New/ON/OFF/Color/Ltype/Freeze/Thaw: ON
Layer name(s) to turn On: F112-FPLAN
?/Make/Set/New/ON/OFF/Color/Ltype/Freeze/Thaw: (press Enter)
Command:
```

LIMITS

Controls the area within which drawing entities are normally created.

VERSIONS

All. In AutoCAD Release 10 and later, limits are only defined in the world coordinate system. There is no z-axis limit in any version of AutoCAD.

COMMAND OPTIONS

ON   This option turns on the limits error-checking. When limits are on, Auto-CAD does not allow you to construct or move entities using coordinate points that fall outside the defined limits.

OFF   This option turns off the limits error-checking, allowing you to place entities anywhere.

Point pick   AutoCAD accepts any input of coordinate point information as the new lower-left corner of the drawing limits. You may also respond by pressing Enter, and the current default will be accepted. After a valid point is entered, AutoCAD prompts:

> Upper right corner <*current upper right*>:

AutoCAD then accepts coordinate point input as the new upper-right corner of the drawing limits. You may also respond by pressing Enter, and again the current default will be accepted.

USAGE

AutoCAD's drawing environment is virtually unlimited, allowing you to place entities on any set of coordinate points. The Limits command allows you to define a given portion of the drawing area that will contain all the drawing entities. Figure 6.5 illustrates a drawing with limits set to match a 36" × 48" plotting surface. If entities fall entirely within the drawing limits, the Zoom All command will display the drawing limits on the monitor screen. The on-screen drawing grid is displayed only within the drawing limits.

The drawing limits are set using a 2-D rectangular plane, defined using two coordinate points, a lower left and an upper right. Many AutoCAD users define the lower-left coordinate point to be 0,0 and the upper-right point to accommodate the real-world dimensions of the object they are drawing.

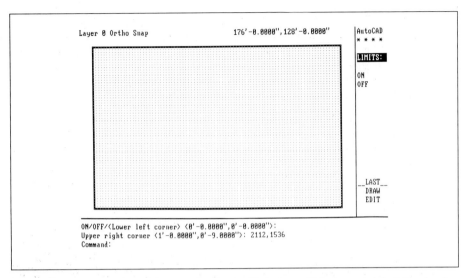

FIGURE 6.5: Drawing editor with limits set for 36″ × 48″ plotting at ¼ inch equals 1 foot. The drawing limits in this figure have been set based on the assumption that the plotter will produce drawings on paper measuring 48 inches wide (along the x-axis) by 36 inches high (along the y-axis), with a margin of 2 inches all around. Therefore, the available plotting area is actually 44 inches wide by 32 inches high. The drawing will be plotted at a scale of ¼ inch to 1 foot; therefore, the real-world dimensions of the available plotting area are 2,112 inches wide by 1,536 inches high. Accordingly, the drawing limits are set as follows: lower-left corner, 0,0; upper-right corner, 2112,1536.

AutoCAD allows *limits-checking* as an error-prevention device. Once the drawing limits are defined, you can instruct AutoCAD to allow new entities to be placed in the drawing only when their construction points fall within the drawing limits. (Refer to the LIMCHECK system variable, Chapter 13, for details.)

Tip: Limits are best set in the prototype drawing. It is possible to have different prototype drawings for different drawing limits. Refer to Chapters 3 and 21 for further information on prototype drawings.

Set your drawing limits to the real-world dimensions of your drawing, rather than to the actual dimensions of your plotting or printing surface. This will make it possible for you to use AutoCAD's automatic dimensioning feature and create your drawing in a real-world context. At plot time, you may scale down the drawing by whatever scale factor you desire in order to fit the dimensions of your hard-copy surface.

To determine the correct drawing limits for real-world drawings, multiply the dimensions of your hard-copy surface by a scaling factor equal to the drawing scale ratio. For example, if you intend to plot at a scale of ¼ inch to 1 foot, the scaling factor would be 48 (12 inches divided by ¼ inch).

If you intend to plot on paper measuring 36 inches by 48 inches, multiply your paper dimensions by 48; allowing for 2-inch margins on the plotting paper, this would yield real-world dimensions of 1,536 inches (128 feet) by 2,112 inches (176 feet). If you intend to plot at a scale of 1/8 inch to 1 foot, the scaling factor will be 96 (12 inches divided by 1/8 inch), and your real-world dimensions would be 3,072 inches (256 feet) by 4,224 inches (352 feet), assuming the same paper margins.

You can quickly and easily control AutoCAD's drawing limits by changing the values of the system variables LIMMIN (the lower-left corner) and LIMMAX (the upper-right corner). Likewise, the system variable LIM-CHECK will control whether AutoCAD's limits-checking is enabled or disabled. These system variables may be changed using the Setvar command, AutoLISP, or macros.

Warning: Even when AutoCAD's limits-checking mechanism is turned on, it is possible to inadvertently place entities outside the drawing limits. For example, when you define a polygon or circle close to the edge of the defined limits, a portion of the figure may fall outside. If you do this, you may considerably slow down zooming. To check if entities are outside the drawing limits, invoke Zoom All and turn the grid on.

Beware of changing the drawing limits with layers off or frozen. When layers are off, all entities may appear to be inside the limits, but zooming and panning will achieve undesired results. For safety's sake, consider changing limits with all layers on.

RELATED COMMANDS

Setvar.

RELATED SYSTEM VARIABLES

LIMMIN (lower-left coordinate limits), LIMMAX (upper-right coordinate limits), LIMCHECK (limits-checking enabled/disabled).

SAMPLE DIALOG

The following sample dialog turns on limits-checking and sets the drawing limits to equal 2,304 by 1,728 drawing units. These drawing limits will fit on a drawing sheet measuring 36 inches high by 48 inches wide when plotted at a scale of 1/4 inch to 1 foot:

```
Command: Limits
ON/OFF/<Lower left coordinate point>: ON
Command: (press Enter)
LIMITS
```

ON/OFF/<Lower left coordinate point>: **0,0**
Upper right corner <12,9>: **2304,1728**
Command:

LINETYPE

Allows you to draw lines composed of any pattern of dots and dashes, to store a variety of patterns within a drawing, or to create new patterns as desired.

VERSIONS

2.0 and later.

COMMAND OPTIONS

?   Enter a question mark when you wish to see what linetypes are available to be loaded into the drawing. AutoCAD responds:

File to list <ACAD>:

Enter the name of the linetype library file you wish to list, or press Enter to list the file ACAD.LIN. You need not type the file extension; the extension LIN is assumed. When AutoCAD finds the requested file, it displays all linetype definitions it finds within.

Create   Enter **C** to create a new linetype definition and to store it in a linetype library file (usually ACAD.LIN). AutoCAD responds:

Name of linetype to create:

Enter a descriptive name for the linetype pattern you are creating. AutoCAD responds:

File for storage of linetype <ACAD>:

Enter the name of the linetype library file in which the linetype definition is to be stored. Do not include the file extension; an extension of LIN is assumed. You may press Enter to accept the default linetype library file name (usually ACAD).

AutoCAD then checks the hard disk for the file you requested, and checks to see if a linetype by that name already exists. If it finds a preexisting linetype definition, it responds:

Name already exists in this file. Current definition is:

This is followed by a description of the linetype. AutoCAD then asks:

Overwrite (Y/N)<N>?

If you do not wish to replace the current linetype description with your new line-type description, type **N** or press Enter. Otherwise, press **Y**. AutoCAD responds:

Descriptive text:

Enter a series of periods and underline characters that approximates how your line-type will look in the drawing editor. For example, you could enter the following:

— — — — — — . — — — . — — — — — — . — — — . — — — — — —

The above descriptive text consists of underline characters, spaces, and periods that represent an alternating series of long and short dashes separated by dots. This descriptive text should occupy only one line. It need not represent your final linetype with pinpoint precision; a close approximation, enough to distinguish it from other stored linetypes, is sufficient. AutoCAD responds:

Enter pattern (on next line):A,

Enter a series of numbers separated by commas, indicating to AutoCAD how the line is to be drawn. The relationships between these numbers will deter-mine the length of dashes and spaces, as well as the placement of the dots in the linetype's pattern. Dashes are represented by positive numbers, spaces by nega-tive numbers, and dots by zeroes. For example, the descriptive text just shown can be represented to AutoCAD as follows:

A,.6, − .2,0, − .2,.3, − .2

In this example, the first number, .6, indicates a dash, because the number is positive and represents a value other than zero. The second number, − .2, repre-sents a space, because it is negative and represents a value other than zero. The length of the space will be one-third the length of the dash, because .2 is one-third of .6. The third number is zero, so a dot will be drawn. The next number, − .2, represents a space equal in length to the first space. It is followed by .3, represent-ing a dash half as long as the first dash. Finally, the pattern is completed with another space, − .2. AutoCAD will repeat this pattern over and over when draw-ing lines using this linetype.

All linetype descriptions must begin with the letter *A* followed by a comma. In addition, the first number in the pattern definition must be either a dash speci-fication or a zero; do not begin the description with a negative number, as this will cause unacceptable displays.

When the pattern definition is entered, AutoCAD stores the linetype descrip-tion in the file and loads the linetype into the drawing. If you wish to create all subsequent entities with this linetype, use the Set option, which will be explained in a moment. If you wish to assign this linetype to a particular layer, use the Layer Ltype option, explained earlier in this chapter.

Load Enter **L** to load a previously defined linetype into the drawing. AutoCAD responds:

> Linetype(s) to load:

Enter the name of the linetype you wish to load. You may load several linetypes from a single linetype library by entering all their names, separated by commas. You may also use wild-card characters. To load all the linetypes in the library file, enter a single asterisk (*). AutoCAD responds:

> File to search <ACAD>:

Enter the name of the linetype library file in which the definitions can be found. Enter only the name of the file, not the extension; an extension of LIN is assumed. Press Enter if you wish to accept the default file name (usually ACAD).

AutoCAD then searches the named file for the named linetype definitions and loads them. If a linetype definition is not found, AutoCAD displays the following error message:

> Linetype not found. Use the LOAD option to load it.

If a named linetype definition was previously loaded, AutoCAD displays the following message:

> Linetype already loaded. Reload it <Y>?

Type **Y** or press Enter if you wish to reload the linetype definition. Enter **N** if you do not wish to reload the linetype.

Set Enter **S** to indicate that all subsequent entities are to be drawn using a particular linetype definition. AutoCAD responds:

> New entity linetype (or ?) <BYLAYER>:

The name of the current linetype is displayed as part of the prompt. Press Enter to keep the current linetype. If you enter the name of another linetype, all subsequent lines, arcs, circles, and 2-D polylines will be drawn using that linetype. To change linetypes, you must invoke the Linetype Set option again.

If you respond to AutoCAD's prompt by entering a question mark, AutoCAD will display all linetype definitions currently loaded in the drawing. Notice that AutoCAD does not search a library file for this display.

If the requested linetype is not loaded, AutoCAD will automatically search the file ACAD.LIN, and if the definition is found there, AutoCAD will load it and make it current. If AutoCAD does not find the requested definition in ACAD.LIN, it will display the following message:

Linetype not found. Use the LOAD option to load it.

In this case, invoke Linetype Load, and specify the linetype library file where the definition can be found.

USAGE

AutoCAD entities composed of lines, circles, arcs, or 2-D polylines are normally displayed using continuous lines. However, if you wish, you may draw these lines using patterns of dots and dashes. For example, many drafters use broken lines to illustrate hidden lines in isometric drawings, as illustrated in Figure 6.6.

To create entities using an alternate linetype, you must first create (or have available) a *linetype definition*—data that identifies a particular pattern of dots and dashes. The linetype definition is stored in an ASCII file called a *linetype library file*.

Linetype library files always have the extension LIN. They are normally stored in the same subdirectory as AutoCAD's system files, so that AutoCAD may easily find them. AutoCAD is supplied with a library file of standard linetypes, called ACAD.LIN. The linetypes stored in ACAD.LIN are illustrated in Figure 6.7.

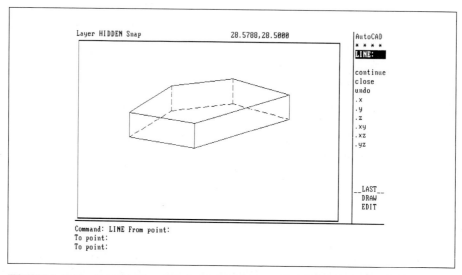

FIGURE 6.6: Hidden lines in an isometric drawing. An isometric drawing of an irregularly shaped object is made easier to visualize by means of hidden lines. The Hidden layer is set to a default dashed linetype, and the hidden lines are drawn upon that layer. Another layer is set to a default continuous linetype, and the nonhidden lines are drawn upon that layer.

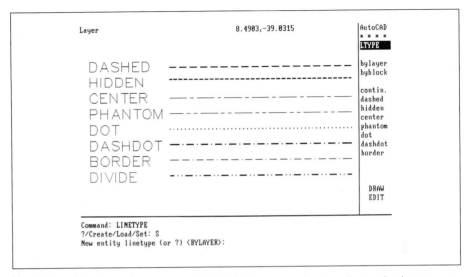

FIGURE 6.7: AutoCAD standard linetypes. This figure illustrates the linetypes that can be drawn using the eight standard noncontinuous linetypes supplied with AutoCAD. Using the Linetype command, you can load any of these linetypes into the drawing, set any of them as the default linetype for new entities, or create additional linetypes of your own and add them to AutoCAD's linetype file, ACAD.LIN. Release 11 and later releases offer additional scaled versions of these standard linestyles, at 1/2 and double scale.

In order to use a particular linetype, you must first *load* that linetype into the drawing, using the Linetype Load option. Once a linetype has been loaded, you may indicate to AutoCAD that you wish all subsequent entities to be drawn using that linetype, or you may assign that linetype to a particular layer, causing all lines drawn on that layer to be rendered using that linetype.

There is no limit to the number of linetype descriptions in a linetype library file; unless you have an exceptionally large number of linetypes that require a sophisticated system of organization, consider placing all linetype descriptions in the file ACAD.LIN. This makes accessing them as easy as possible.

It is advisable to write linetype descriptions so that they appear visually correct in drawings that are not scaled; that is, at a scale of one to one. Usually this means writing the linetype description with values of 1 drawing unit or less. This will give you the greatest degree of flexibility when using different linetypes in different drawings at different scales. Refer to the Ltscale command just ahead for details on scaling linetype descriptions.

Warning: Reloading a linetype will cause a drawing regeneration; this can waste time. The only occasion to reload a linetype is when you have changed the linetype definition. If a linetype definition has not been changed, do not reload the linetype definition.

RELATED COMMANDS

Load, Ltscale.

SAMPLE DIALOG

Command: **Linetype**
?/Create/Load/Set: **L**
Linetype(s) to load: **DASHED,DASHDOT**
File to search <ACAD>: **(press Enter)**
Linetype DASHED,DASHDOT loaded

LTSCALE

Changes the scale of linetypes relative to the scale of the current drawing by applying a *scale factor* to the original linetype description.

VERSIONS

All.

COMMAND OPTIONS

New scale factor   Enter a number by which the linetype description should be multiplied. You can increase the linetype scale by entering a factor greater than 1. Reduce the scale by entering a number less than 1 but greater than 0. Negative numbers are not allowed.

USAGE

Since you may be called upon to draw at different scales and with different units of measurement from time to time, Ltscale allows you to supply a multiplication factor to your linetype descriptions. For example, if you wish to use a linetype with dashes originally set at ¼ drawing unit, applying a scale factor of 4 with Ltscale will cause the dashes to be drawn at a length of 1 drawing unit.

If the original linetype description has a simple one-to-one drawing scale, you can easily rescale the linetype by applying a multiplication factor that matches the scale of the current drawing.

For example, suppose the current drawing will be plotted at a scale of ⅛ inch to 1 foot. Since 1 foot divided by ⅛ inch equals 96, you can be assured of reasonable line appearance using a linetype scale factor of 96.

Tip: For convenience, set the linetype scale factor in each of your prototype drawings.

Note: An alternate method for setting the linetype scale factor is changing the value of the LTSCALE system variable.

Warning: The linetype scale factor is global, affecting all linetypes in the drawing. Keep your original linetype descriptions at a consistent one-to-one scale so that they respond predictably to the scale factor.

RELATED COMMANDS

Linetype, Setvar.

RELATED SYSTEM VARIABLES

LTSCALE (current linetype scale).

SAMPLE DIALOG

```
Command: Ltscale
New scale factor <1>: 96
Command:
```

PURGE

Reduces the size of the drawing by eliminating block names, shape-file names, layer names, linetype names, and text-style names, in cases where those names are not referenced by any entity in the drawing.

VERSIONS

All.

COMMAND OPTIONS

Blocks   Enter **B** to step through all unused block names. Respond to each by pressing either **Y** (yes, delete) or **N** (no, keep).

LAyers   Enter **LA** to step through all unused layer names. Respond to each by pressing either **Y** (yes, delete) or **N** (no, keep).

LTypes   Enter **LT** to step through all unused linetype descriptions. Respond to each by pressing either **Y** (yes, delete) or **N** (no, keep).

SHapes   Enter **SH** to step through all unused shape-file names. Respond to each by pressing either **Y** (yes, delete) or **N** (no, keep).

STyles   Enter **ST** to step through all unused text-style names. Respond to each by pressing either **Y** (yes, delete) or **N** (no, keep).

All   Enter **A** to step through all unused named entities. Respond to each by pressing either **Y** (yes, delete) or **N** (no, keep).

USAGE

As drawings are edited and reedited, certain named entities often build up even though they do not reference any entity in the drawing. For example, layers have all their entities deleted, blocks are replaced by other blocks, shapes are removed, and text styles are changed. AutoCAD retains global information regarding each of these "unused" named entities; large numbers of them can increase the time it takes to load the drawing. The Purge command permanently deletes these unused named entities from the drawing database, in some cases significantly reducing drawing-file size and loading time.

Versions earlier than Release 10 require that Purge be the *first* command invoked in any particular drawing session. Once any other command is invoked, Purge can no longer be invoked unless the drawing session is ended and the drawing file is reentered. Starting with Release 10, you may invoke the Purge command anytime before you make a change to the drawing database (for example, by drawing or editing an entity). This permits you to view a drawing prior to purging it.

You may invoke only one Purge command per drawing session. If you use a lot of nested blocks, however, you may have to invoke Purge several times, as the unused nested block names are not automatically purged with the parent block. To repeat the Purge command, first save the drawing with End, and then reenter and invoke Purge again. If your drawings are really complex, you can save a little time by writing a script file. Refer to Chapter 14 for details regarding script files.

Warning: Purge a drawing only when the number of unused named entities is large enough to make it worthwhile. Once a named entity is purged, it must be reloaded to be used again. Purging only a few unnamed entities (as in the following sample dialog, which is for demonstration purposes) will not significantly reduce drawing size or loading time.

SAMPLE DIALOG

Command: **Purge**
Purge unused Blocks/LAyers/LTypes/SHapes/STyles/All: **A**

Purge Block OLD – PART <N>? **Y**
Purge Block XBOX <N>? **Y**
Purge Layer SCRATCH <N>? **(press Enter)**
Purge Linetype HIDDEN <N>? **(press Enter)**
No unreferenced shapes found
No unreferenced styles found
Command:

RENAME

Allows you to change the name of specific named entities.

VERSIONS

All. Named user coordinate systems and viewports are features of AutoCAD Release 10 and later. Earlier versions accept **V** as a response to change the name of a drawing view.

COMMAND OPTIONS

First enter the type of named entity whose name you wish to change. In each case, AutoCAD responds with the following prompts, referencing the chosen named entity:

Old entity name:
New entity name:

For example, if you enter **B** or **Block**, AutoCAD responds:

Old block name:

Enter the current block name and AutoCAD responds:

New block name:

Enter the new block name.

Block   Enter **B** to change the name of a block.

LAyer   Enter **LA** to change the name of a layer.

LType   Enter **LT** to change the name of a linetype description.

Style   Enter **S** to change the name of a text style.

Ucs   Enter **U** to change the name of a user coordinate system.

VIew   Enter **VI** to change the name of a drawing view.

VPort   Enter **VP** to change the name of a viewport configuration.

USAGE

The Rename command allows you to change your mind regarding the names of certain complex named entities without having to rebuild such entities from the beginning. A named entity is any entity that is accessible by a unique name, as opposed to coordinate point picks. The added flexibility of the Rename command is especially useful if you find that you must alter your overall drawing-file organization as your drawing evolves. Entities affected by Rename include blocks, layers, linetypes, text styles, user coordinate systems, views, and viewports.

You cannot change a shape name with the Rename command. This is because shape names reside in a separate file of shape descriptions on the hard disk. Shape names can be changed by editing the source-code (SHP) file, and reinserted into the drawing using the Shape command. Refer to Chapter 15 for details.

RELATED COMMANDS

Purge.

SAMPLE DIALOG

```
Command: Rename
Block/LAyer/LType/Style/Ucs/VIew/VPort: LA
Old Layer name: Scratch
New Layer name: Inner-Walls
Command:
```

STATUS

Displays current statistics related to the drawing environment and entities therein.

VERSIONS

All.

COMMAND OPTIONS

None.

USAGE

The Status command permits you to receive a quick summary of the condition of your drawing, available disk space, available RAM, and I/O page space. It is often used as the first step in troubleshooting. A typical output of the Status command is listed in Figure 6.8.

RELATED SYSTEM VARIABLES

Status reads and displays the contents of the following: AXISMODE, CE-COLOR, CELTYPE, CLAYER, ELEVATION, FILLMODE, GRIDMODE, GRIDUNIT, INSBASE, LIMCHECK, LIMMAX, LIMMIN, ORTHO-MODE, OSMODE, QTEXTMODE, SNAPMODE, SNAPUNIT, and THICKNESS. See to Chapter 13 for details regarding the values stored in these variables.

SAMPLE DIALOG

The following command produces a screen similar to the one pictured in Figure 6.8:

Command: **Status**

TABLET

Toggles the digitizing tablet's tablet mode on and off, configures the tablet for menus and pointing area, and calibrates the tablet for absolute coordinate input.

VERSIONS

All.

COMMAND OPTIONS

ON   Enter **ON** to toggle the tablet to *tablet mode.* In this mode, you can use the tablet to trace manual hard-copy drawings into AutoCAD.

```
Command: Status
322 entities in CHAP6
Model space limits are X:     0.0000   Y:     0.0000  (Off)  (World)
                       X:    14.0000   Y:    11.0000
Model space uses       X:    -5.0915   Y:    -2.7286 **Over
                       X:     6.7542   Y:     6.0408
Display shows          X:    -6.2166   Y:    -3.4164
                       X:     7.5802   Y:     8.2598
Insertion base is      X:    -5.0000   Y:    -4.0000   Z:     0.0000
Snap resolution is     X:     1.0000   Y:     1.0000
Grid spacing is        X:     0.0000   Y:     0.0000

Current space:         Model space
Current layer:         0 (Off)
Current color:         BYLAYER -- 7 (white)
Current linetype:      BYLAYER -- CONTINUOUS
Current elevation:     0.0000  thickness:      0.0000
Axis off  Fill on  Grid off  Ortho off  Qtext off  Snap off  Tablet off
Object snap modes:     None

Free disk (dwg/temp): 13109248/8269824 bytes
Virtual memory allocated to program: 2552K
Amount of program in physical memory/Total (virtual) program size: 100%
Total conventional memory: 384K       Total extended memory: 5116K
Swap file size: 388K bytes
Page faults: 0     Swap writes: 0       Swap reclaims: 0
Command:
```

FIGURE 6.8: Statistical report using the Status command. This figure illustrates a typical display that results when you invoke the Status command. Included are the drawing limits and extents; current viewport dimensions; base point; snap-resolution and grid-display settings; the current layer, color, linetype, thickness, and elevation; the current setting of the drawing aids and object-snap modes; free RAM, disk space, and I/O page space; and available extended memory.

OFF   Enter **OFF** to toggle off *relative mode,* returning the tablet to normal screen pointing and menu picks.

CAL   Enter **CAL** to calibrate your tablet in absolute mode. In order to trace existing manual drawings, AutoCAD must know the drawing's coordinate system. This is easily accomplished by entering any two points on the manual drawing whose coordinate points are known and fall on the sensitive area of the tablet. Before calibrating, secure the manual drawing to the digitizing tablet. It is important that the drawing not move during tracing, but the actual orientation of the drawing is immaterial. AutoCAD will calculate the coordinate system based on the point entry you make when calibrating.

After you enter **CAL**, AutoCAD responds:

> Digitize first known point:

Pick a point on the drawing whose coordinates are known to you. AutoCAD responds:

> Enter coordinates for first point:

Enter the coordinates for the point you just picked. AutoCAD responds:

> Digitize second known point:

TABLE —— **167**

Pick a different known coordinate point on the manual drawing. AutoCAD responds:

Enter coordinates for second point:

Enter the coordinates for the point you just picked.

Once your tablet is calibrated, you may enter whatever AutoCAD commands are required to create the entities on your manual drawing, picking the appropriate entity coordinate points from the manual drawing. AutoCAD enters the exact coordinate locations based on the calibration information you entered.

It is possible to digitize drawings that are larger than the tablet. Each time you move a new section of the drawing over the tablet, simply recalibrate using two more known coordinate points. When finished tracing, remember to turn off absolute mode if you intend to use your tablet as a menu and pointing device.

CFG   Enter **CFG** if you wish to configure your tablet for menu and screen pointing areas. Refer to Chapter 3 for details on how to use the Tablet Cfg command.

USAGE

The digitizing tablet serves as a pointing device, a command menu, and a coordinate digitizer. The Tablet command allows you to manage the purposes to which you intend to put the tablet. You can configure the tablet to act as a mouse, furnish the tablet with commands and macros that can be invoked with a single pick, or use the tablet to precisely digitize coordinate information into the drawing. This last application is especially useful if you are attempting to transfer manual drawings into computerized format.

When using your tablet in tablet mode, it is a good idea to set limits-checking off, so that any coordinate on the manual drawing that happens to fall outside the drawing limits will still be entered by AutoCAD. After the drawing is completely entered, you can reset new limits or turn limits-checking back on. Refer to the discussion of the Limits command earlier in this chapter for more details.

Absolute tablet mode may be quickly toggled on and off with Ctrl-T.

SAMPLE DIALOG

Command: **Tablet**
ON/OFF/CAL/CFG **CFG**
Enter number of menu areas desired (0-4) <2>: **2**
Do you want to realign tablet menu areas? <N> **Y**
Digitize upper left corner of menu area 1: **(pick point)**
Digitize lower left corner of menu area 1: **(pick point)**
Digitize lower right corner of menu area 1: **(pick point)**
Enter the number of columns for menu area 1: **25**

Enter the number of rows for menu area 1: **9**
Digitize upper left corner of menu area 2: **(pick point)**
Digitize lower left corner of menu area 2: **(pick point)**
Digitize lower right corner of menu area 2: **(pick point)**
Enter the number of columns for menu area 2: **25**
Enter the number of rows for menu area 2: **9**
Do you want to respecify the screen pointing area? <N> **Y**
Digitize lower left corner of screen pointing area: **(pick point)**
Digitize upper right corner of screen pointing area: **(pick point)**
Command:

TEXTSCR

Forces the display of the text screen on single-screen systems.

VERSIONS

All.

COMMAND OPTIONS

None.

USAGE

AutoCAD uses two types of display, text and graphics. The graphics display includes the representation of all drawing-entity information in AutoCAD's drawing database—in other words, the drawing itself. The text display is a "running history" of all commands, prompts, responses, and text-based input.

On systems employing a single monitor, only one of these displays is visible at a time. The Textscr command will force the display of the text-based input, commands, and responses.

On most systems, the text display can be toggled with the graphics display using a Flip Screen function key, often F1. The Textscr command is most useful with command macros in which the text display must be forced regardless of the display's current status.

Beginning with Release 11, you can toggle on the text screen and clear it as well, using AutoLISP's Textpage function. Refer to Chapter 17 for details regarding this function.

RELATED COMMANDS

Graphscr.

SAMPLE DIALOG

Command: **Textscr (Text screen is displayed.)**
Command: **Graphscr or press Flip Screen key (Graphics screen is displayed.)**
Command: **Textscr or press Flip Screen key (Text screen is displayed.)**
Command:

UCS

Manages and controls the orientation of the current user coordinate system (UCS).

VERSIONS

Release 10 and later.

COMMAND OPTIONS

Origin   Enter **O** to change the origin point of the current UCS. The new UCS will maintain the current axis orientation, but will move to the new origin point. After you enter **O**, AutoCAD responds:

Origin point:

Enter a 2-D or 3-D point in the current UCS. This point becomes the new UCS's origin point.

ZAxis   Enter **ZA** to rotate the current UCS by specifying a new orientation for the z-axis. In effect, you are "tilting" the z-axis, and the UCS is tilted in the same direction, to remain perpendicular with the z-axis. The following dialog uses the ZAxis option to reorient the UCS:

Command: **UCS**
Origin/ZAxis/3point/Entity/View/X/Y/Z/Prev/Restore/Save/Del/?/
<World>: **ZA**
Origin point <0,0,0>: **(press Enter)**
Point on positive portion of the Z axis: **0, –3,10**

AutoCAD responds by reorienting the UCS as shown in Figure 6.9.

3point   Enter **3** to create a new UCS by entering three nonlinear, coplanar points (in the current UCS) that will intersect it. The first point is the origin point, the second point will fall on the positive portion of the new UCS's x-axis, and the third point will fall anywhere within the new UCS's X-Y plane. For example, assuming

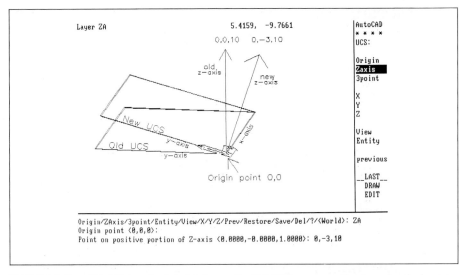

FIGURE 6.9: New UCS (ZAxis option). In this figure, the UCS ZAxis command has been invoked, rotating the current UCS by realigning its z-axis. The default origin point is accepted, and a point that the new z-axis will intersect is entered; in this example, the point is 0, −3,10. Selecting this point rotates the z-axis clockwise in the Y-Z plane, and the current UCS is rotated by an equal amount, to remain perpendicular with the z-axis.

that the world coordinate system is the current UCS, a new UCS can be made current using the following dialog:

> Command: **UCS**
> Origin/ZAxis/3point/Entity/View/X/Y/Z/Prev/Restore/Save/Del/?/
> <World>: **3**
> Origin point <0,0,0>: **5,4,0**
> Point on positive portion of the X axis: **10,2,0**
> Point on the positive Y portion of the UCS X-Y plane: **10,2,1**

AutoCAD responds by making a new UCS current, as shown in Figure 6.10.

If you wish, you can use Osnap overrides to find the points that define the new UCS, thus creating a UCS to match existing entities. The following option allows AutoCAD to calculate a new UCS based on an existing entity.

Entity   Enter **E** to select an existing entity whose orientation will be the basis for the new current UCS. For example, Figure 6.11 shows a 3-D face in an orientation not parallel to the WCS. To use that orientation of this 3-D face as the new UCS, enter **E**. AutoCAD responds:

> Entity:

Pick the 3-D face (using Osnap to help if you wish). AutoCAD immediately creates the new UCS parallel to that entity, as illustrated in Figure 6.12.

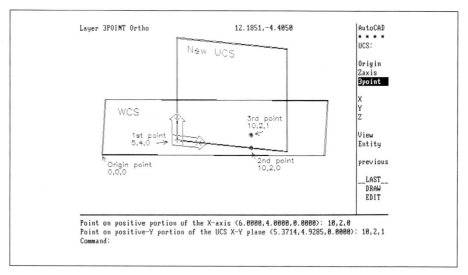

```
Layer 3POINT Ortho                    12.1851,-4.4050    AutoCAD
                                                         * * * *
                                                         UCS:

                  New  UCS                               Origin
                                                         Zaxis
                                                         3point

                                                         X
                                                         Y
         WCS                                             Z
                              3rd point
                              10,2,1                     View
    1st point                   ⊛ ←                      Entity
    5,4,0  →
                                                         previous

     Origin point            2nd point                   __LAST__
     0,0,0                    10,2,0                       DRAW
                                                           EDIT

Point on positive portion of the X-axis <6.0000,4.0000,0.0000>: 10,2,0
Point on positive-Y portion of the UCS X-Y plane <5.3714,4.9285,0.0000>: 10,2,1
Command:
```

FIGURE 6.10: New UCS (3point option). In this figure, a new UCS is established by selecting three points in the current WCS. The first point selected is WCS point 5,4,0. This point will be the origin point for the new UCS. Next, WCS point 10,2,0 is selected as a point that will fall on the positive x-axis of the new UCS. The final point can be any WCS point that falls in the positive X-Y plane of the new UCS. In this figure, WCS point 10,2,1 was chosen. The new UCS is now established, oriented so that the three selected WCS points are coplanar.

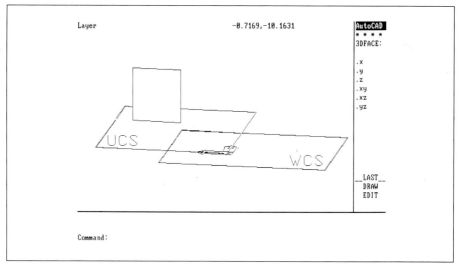

```
Layer                             -0.7169,-10.1631    AutoCAD
                                                      * * * *
                                                      3DFACE:

                                                      .x
                                                      .y
                                                      .z
                                                      .xy
                                                      .xz
                                                      .yz

      UCS

                                      WCS
                                                      __LAST__
                                                       DRAW
                                                       EDIT

Command:
```

FIGURE 6.11: A 3-D face in the current UCS. In this figure, a 3-D face has been drawn perpendicular to the current UCS. Since the UCS is parallel to and floating above the WCS, the 3-D face is also floating above the WCS. Drawing a 3-D face with this orientation is a little easier using an elevated UCS; only one z coordinate outside of the current construction plane needs to be considered, rather than two.

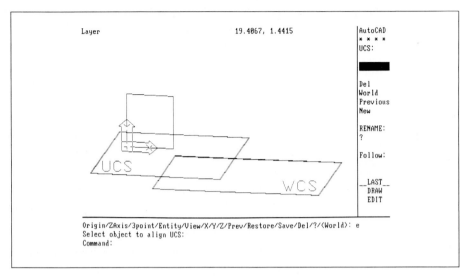

FIGURE 6.12: New UCS (Entity option). The 3-D face in Figure 6.11 can be used to align a new UCS quickly, using the UCS Entity command. Different entities follow different rules when used to establish a new UCS; refer to the discussion of the UCS command in this chapter for details.

3-D polylines and meshes cannot be used to create a new UCS. The new UCS will be calculated as follows, depending on the entity picked:

2-D polyline	Origin is the polyline's starting point. The x-axis extends from the starting point to the first vertex. The z-axis is determined by the polyline's current orientation, so if the polyline rests in the WCS X-Y plane, the z-axis will be parallel to the WCS z-axis.
3-D face	Origin is the 3-D face's first point, the x-axis is taken from the second point, and the y-axis from the first and fourth points. A 3-D face with only three edges cannot be used to create a new UCS.
Arc	Origin is the arc center point. The x-axis passes through the arc endpoint that appears closest to the pick point. The z-axis is determined by the arc's current angle of orientation relative to its center and endpoints.
Block	Origin is the insertion point. The x-axis is the same as the entity's angle of rotation. The z-axis is taken from its orientation in space.
Circle	Origin is the circle center point. The x-axis passes through the pick point. The z-axis is determined by the circle's current angle of orientation.

Dimension	Origin is the midpoint of the dimension text. The x-axis is parallel to the x-axis of the dimension's original orientation.
Line	Origin is the line endpoint nearest to the pick point. The x-axis and y-axis are oriented so that the line's opposite endpoint has a y coordinate of zero. The line always falls on the X-Z plane of the new UCS.
Solid	Origin is the solid's first point. The x-axis extends from the first point to the second point. The z-axis is determined by the current orientation.
Text	Same as Block.
Trace	Origin is the trace's "from point." The x-axis extends through the trace's center line. The z-axis is determined by the trace's orientation.

View Enter **V** to establish the current UCS as the current view of the drawing. The origin point remains the same.

X Enter **X** to rotate the current UCS around the x-axis. AutoCAD responds:

Rotation angle around the X axis:

Enter the amount of rotation, specifying an angle using the format set by the Units command. Positive numbers will cause the UCS to rotate counterclockwise (when looking directly at the origin point down the x-axis). Negative numbers will cause clockwise rotation.

Y Enter **Y** to rotate the current UCS around the y-axis. AutoCAD responds:

Rotation angle around the Y axis:

Enter the amount of rotation, specifying an angle using the format set by the Units command. Positive numbers will cause the UCS to rotate counterclockwise (when looking directly at the origin point down the y-axis). Negative numbers will cause clockwise rotation.

Z Enter **Z** to rotate the current UCS around the z-axis. AutoCAD responds:

Rotation angle around the Z axis:

Enter the amount of rotation, specifying an angle using the format set by the Units command. Positive numbers will cause the UCS to rotate counterclockwise (when looking directly at the origin point down the z-axis—i.e., in plan view). Negative numbers will cause clockwise rotation.

Previous   Enter **P** to restore the previous UCS. AutoCAD stores up to the last ten UCS's, and you may step back through them by repeating this option.

Restore   Enter **R** to recall a named UCS that was saved using the Save option. AutoCAD responds:

> Name of UCS to restore:

Enter the name of a saved UCS.

Save   Enter **S** to save the current UCS under a unique name. AutoCAD responds:

> UCS Name:

Enter a unique name for the current UCS. The name can have up to 31 characters.

Delete   Enter **D** to delete named UCS's. For example, after you enter **D**, Auto-CAD responds:

> Name of UCS to Delete:

When naming UCS's to delete, you may use wild-card characters (* and ?), or you may enter several UCS names separated by commas. The name of the current UCS can be deleted, but you will not be able to restore it unless you resave it.

?   Enter the question mark to display a list of all saved UCS names. The origin, x-axis, y-axis, and z-axis are shown relative to the current UCS, not the WCS.

World   Enter **W** to make the current UCS the same as the WCS.

USAGE

AutoCAD Release 10 works within a 3-D Cartesian coordinate system called the *world coordinate system,* or WCS. A *user coordinate system* (UCS) is a plane that can be oriented at any location within the WCS. Once a UCS is established, drawing entities may be created based on coordinate points found within that UCS. Figure 6.13 illustrates a UCS located above and at a slight angle to the X-Y plane of the WCS. When this UCS is made current using the UCS command, entities can be created in that coordinate system just as they might be created on the X-Y plane.

The UCS command can create any number of user coordinate systems, move them, rotate them, remember them under unique names, recall them, and delete them. Your success in using AutoCAD's 3-D features depends in large measure on how well you can organize and manage user coordinate systems.

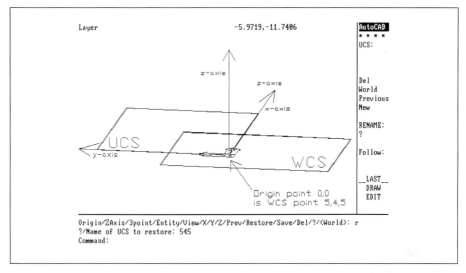

```
Layer                           -5.9719,-11.7406    │AutoCAD│
                                                     * * * *
                                                    UCS:


                     z-axis          z-axis         Del
                                                    World
                                                    Previous
                                       x-axis       New

                                                    RENAME:
                                                    ?
         UCS
              y-axis                    WCS          Follow:


                                                    __LAST__
                                                    DRAW
                              Origin point 0,0      EDIT
                              is WCS point 5,4,5

Origin/ZAxis/3point/Entity/View/X/Y/Z/Prev/Restore/Save/Del/?/<World>: r
?/Name of UCS to restore: 545
Command:
```

FIGURE 6.13: World coordinate system and user coordinate system, with UCS icon at origin. In this figure, a new user coordinate system has been set with its origin point at world coordinate system point 5,4,5. This new UCS is floating above and parallel to the world coordinate system. New entities will default to this construction plane while this UCS remains current and the ELEVATION system variable is set to zero.

Tip: When working with even a few named UCS's, use the Dducs command to display a dialog box of UCS options. See the discussion of the Dducs command earlier in this chapter for details.

Naming and saving user coordinate systems can save a lot of time when working in 3-D. If possible, develop some standard user coordinate systems and save them on your prototype drawings. If you have dozens of prototype drawings, use a script file to create and name them for each drawing. See Chapter 14 for more information regarding script files.

RELATED COMMANDS

Dducs, Ucsicon.

RELATED SYSTEM VARIABLES

UCSFOLLOW (always display UCS plan view), UCSNAME (current UCS name, if any), UCSORG (UCS origin point), UCSXDIR (UCS x-axis orientation), UCSYDIR (UCS y-axis orientation), WORLDUCS (UCS equal/not equal to WCS). All system variables are read-only except UCSFOLLOW. If UCSFOLLOW is set to a value of 1, AutoCAD will automatically display each new UCS in plan view. If UCSFOLLOW is set to 0, changing the UCS does not change the display. If you are using multiple viewports, you can set UCSFOLLOW separately for each viewport.

SAMPLE DIALOG

Refer to the Command Options section for sample dialog and illustrations of this command.

UCSICON

Controls the display of the *user coordinate system icon,* a small icon that informs you of the orientation of the current UCS.

VERSIONS

Release 10 and later.

COMMAND OPTIONS

ON   Enter **ON** to turn on the display of the UCS icon.

OFF   Enter **OFF** to turn off the display of the UCS icon.

All   If multiple viewports are displayed, enter **A** when making changes to the UCS icon display that are to apply to all viewports. If you do not enter **A** before making changes, the changes will apply to the current viewport only. Refer to the discussion of the Vport command in Chapter 11 for more information regarding viewports.

Noorigin   Enter **N** to force the display of the UCS icon (when display is enabled) away from the origin point of the current UCS. When you pick **N**, AutoCAD displays the UCS icon only in the lower-left corner of the viewport, regardless of the UCS's origin point. However, the UCS icon will continue to show the orientation of the x-axis and y-axis relative to the current viewpoint.

ORigin   Enter **OR** to force the display of the UCS icon to appear at the origin point of the current UCS. If the origin point is not displayed or is too close to the edges of the viewport, AutoCAD displays the icon in the lower-left corner of the viewport until the origin point is displayed in an area that will allow the UCS icon to be positioned there.

USAGE

The various forms of the UCS icon are illustrated in Figure 6.14. Normally, the UCS icon displays the orientation of the x-axis and y-axis. In addition, the UCS icon will show a small + symbol when it is positioned at the origin of the current UCS, and the letter *W* when the UCS is also the WCS. When your drawing viewpoint is such that it is impossible to distinguish between x and y coordinate points or to pick coordinate points with the pointing device—for example, when looking at the UCS "edge on"—the UCS icon becomes the "broken pencil" illustrated in Figure 6.14.

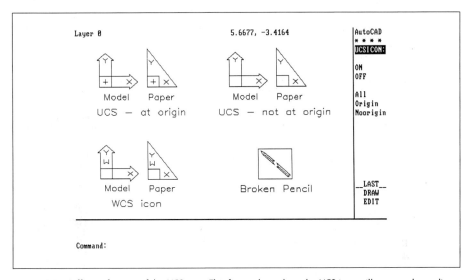

Figure 6.14: Different formats of the UCS icon. This figure shows how the UCS icon will appear, depending on whether the current UCS is in model or paper space. When the icon is at the origin of the UCS, a small cross appears at the intersection of the axis markers. When it is not at the origin, only the axis markers are displayed. When the world coordinate system is current, a *W* appears in the y-axis marker. When the current viewing angle is such that entities cannot be edited (e.g., if the construction plane is being viewed from the edge, appearing as a line), the Broken Pencil icon appears: entities may not be edited until the viewing angle is changed slightly. On some monitors, the X and Y symbols will disappear if the viewing angle is from the negative z-axis (i.e., underneath the drawing, looking up).

Note: The UCS icon display is also controlled by the value of the UCSICON system variable. Each viewport may have its own value for UCSICON. The Setvar command will allow you to make changes in the UCS icon display while in the middle of other command sequences.

RELATED COMMANDS

Setvar.

RELATED SYSTEM VARIABLES

UCSICON (icon on/off, origin display).

SAMPLE DIALOG

```
Command: Ucsicon
ON/OFF/All/Noorigin/ORigin: OR
Command: (press Enter)
UCSICON
ON/OFF/All/Noorigin/ORigin: ON
Command:
```

UNITS

Allows you to interactively control the numeric format used to enter and display linear values, angular values, and coordinate points.

VERSIONS

All. Fractional units are not available in AutoCAD Version 2.5 and earlier.

COMMAND OPTIONS

When you invoke Units, AutoCAD displays a menu of options, as shown in Figure 6.15. The examples shown in the figure indicate how each format displays fifteen and one-half drawing units.

Select the appropriate linear value format by number. For example, to choose decimal units, enter **2**. This format will be used to display and enter linear values, such as lengths, distances, and displacements.

The format you select will also control the display of coordinate points in the status line, and, to a lesser extent, the format for entering coordinate points from the keyboard.

If you have chosen engineering (3) or architectural (4) units, AutoCAD assumes that the basic drawing units are inches. If you enter coordinate points or distances without specifying the units, AutoCAD records the numeric input as inches. To specify feet, use an apostrophe ('). To specify inches, use a quotation character (").

The scientific (1), decimal (2), and fractional (5) formats make no assumptions regarding units. In these formats, a drawing unit can represent whatever unit of measurement you like; however, the symbols for feet and inches are not valid in these formats.

```
                                                              <
                                                              <
                                                              <
    Command: Units                                            <
    Systems of units:      (Examples)                         <
                                                              <
       1.   Scientific      1.55E+01                          <
       2.   Decimal         15.50                             <
       3.   Engineering     1'-3.50"                          <
       4.   Architectural   1'-3 1/2"                         <
       5.   Fractional      15 1/2                            <
                                                              <
    With the exception of Engineering and Architectural modes, <
    these modes can be used with any basic unit of measurement. <
    For example, Decimal mode is perfect for metric units as well <
    as decimal English units.                                 <
                                                              <
    Enter choice, 1 to 5 <4>:                                 <
                                                              <
                                                              <
                                                              <
                                                              <
                                                              <
```

FIGURE 6.15: The Units command—systems of units. This figure illustrates the menu of units formats displayed when you invoke the Units command. Fractional units are available starting with AutoCAD Version 2.6. The examples, first included with Release 10, show how each format will display fifteen and one-half drawing units.

After you select the desired units, AutoCAD prompts for the degree of precision. If you selected scientific, decimal, or engineering units, you will see the following prompt:

Number of digits to right of decimal point (0 to 8):

Simply enter the number of decimal places you desire, to a maximum of eight. This setting only affects the display of decimal places; you may continue to enter values from the keyboard with up to 16 significant digits of precision.

If you selected architectural or fractional units, you will see the following prompt:

Denominator of smallest fraction to display
(1, 2, 4, 8, 16, 32, or 64):

Enter the largest denominator desired. For example, to display values accurate to the nearest $1/4$ inch, enter **4**; for the nearest $1/16$ inch, enter **16**.

AutoCAD next displays a menu of available angular units formats, as shown in Figure 6.16. Select the appropriate format for angular units by number. For example, to use decimal degrees, enter **1**.

The examples shown in Figure 6.16 indicate how each format displays a 45-degree angle.

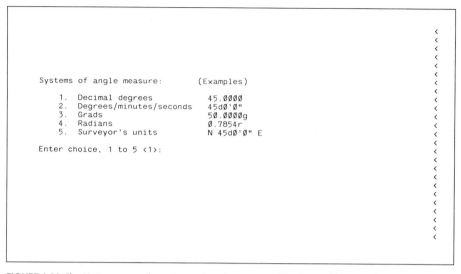

```
Systems of angle measure:        (Examples)

     1.  Decimal degrees          45.0000
     2.  Degrees/minutes/seconds  45d0'0"
     3.  Grads                     50.0000g
     4.  Radians                   0.7854r
     5.  Surveyor's units          N 45d0'0" E

Enter choice, 1 to 5 <1>:
```

FIGURE 6.16: The Units command—systems of angle measure. This figure illustrates the menu of angle-measurement formats displayed when you invoke the Units command. Surveyor's units became available in AutoCAD Version 2.5. The examples, first included with AutoCAD Release 10, show how each format will display exactly 45 degrees.

The following conventions apply to the display of the various angular units formats:

Decimal degrees	Displayed as numbers only, no special symbols.
Degrees/minutes/ seconds	Degrees are followed by a lowercase *d,* minutes by an apostrophe ('), and seconds by a quotation mark (").
Grads	Displayed as numbers followed by a lowercase *g.*
Radians	Displayed as numbers followed by a lowercase *r.*
Surveyor's units	Displayed as a bearing point, either north or south, and the number of degrees away from the bearing point, in the degrees/minutes/seconds format, followed by the bearing direction, either east (E) or west (W).

If the angle is precisely north, south, east, or west, it can be expressed by a single uppercase letter—N, S, E, or W respectively. The menu example, N 45d0'0" E, indicates "Facing north, bearing 45 degrees, zero minutes, zero seconds east."

Using surveyor's units, angles that cannot be expressed as bearings are expressed using absolute degrees/minutes/seconds format.

Using polar coordinates to indicate a line twenty-six drawing units long at an absolute angle of 62.5 degrees would appear in each format as follows:

Using decimal degrees:	@26<62.5
Using degrees/minutes/seconds:	@26<62d30'00''
Using grads:	@26<69.4444
Using radians:	@26<1.0908
Using surveyor's units:	@26<N27d30'00''E

After you select your desired format for angular units, AutoCAD prompts:

Number of fractional places for display of angles (0 to 8):

Although the prompt says "fractional," AutoCAD is actually asking for the number of decimal places of precision (for decimal degrees, grads, or radians). You may enter up to eight decimal places of precision.

If you have selected degrees/minutes/seconds or surveyor's units as your format for angle measure, the number of decimal places controls the display of minutes and seconds as follows:

SELECT:	AutoCAD WILL DISPLAY:
0	Degrees only (62d)
1	Degrees and minutes only (62d30')
2	Degrees and minutes only (62d30')
3	Degrees, minutes, whole seconds (62d30'00'')
4	Degrees, minutes, whole seconds (62d30'00'')
5	Degrees, minutes, seconds—1 decimal place (62d30'00.0'')
6	Degrees, minutes, seconds—2 decimal places (62d30'00.00'')
7	Degrees, minutes, seconds—3 decimal places (62d30'00.000'')
8	Degrees, minutes, seconds—4 decimal places (62d30'00.0000'')

After you select the appropriate angular-units precision, AutoCAD prompts:

Direction for angle 0:
East	3 o'clock	=	0d
North	12 o'clock	=	90d
West	9 o'clock	=	180d
South	6 o'clock	=	270d

Enter direction for angle 0 <0d>:

AutoCAD will supply angle values in the menu in whatever angular units format was just selected.

AutoCAD's standard orientation for angles is illustrated in Chapter 5, Figure 5.19. This standard assumes that absolute angle zero, when viewed from a point directly overhead, is directed horizontally and to the right ("east" or "three o'clock").

You may, if you wish, orient angle zero in whatever direction you choose, by supplying an absolute angle that will then become the orientation for angle zero. All other angles are oriented accordingly.

For example, to orient angle zero so that it is directed horizontally to the left, enter 180 degrees (in your chosen angle format).

After you have entered the orientation for angle zero, AutoCAD prompts:

> Do you want angles measured clockwise? <N>

AutoCAD normally increments angles counterclockwise beginning with angle zero. You may reverse this, incrementing angles in a clockwise direction instead, by entering **Y** in response to this prompt.

In its standard angle-measurement system, AutoCAD defaults to counterclockwise when utilizing angle-dependent mechanisms (such as drawing arcs or rotating entities). A positive value for included angles is measured counterclockwise; a negative value is measured clockwise.

However, if you have indicated here that angles are to be measured clockwise, this situation is reversed. Positive values are now clockwise, negative values counterclockwise.

Once you have selected the desired formats, AutoCAD will display your responses as defaults the next time you invoke the Units command. This makes subsequent editing of selected formats a little easier.

USAGE

You can change units at any time during a drawing session. If you wish to change only a single aspect of the current units format, you can do so quickly by instead using the Setvar command to change the value of the applicable system variable. These system variables are listed just ahead.

Regardless of your chosen numeric format, you can always enter numeric values in decimal units or scientific notation. When you do so, AutoCAD assumes that the values entered represent the basic drawing unit for the current format—that is, inches when the current format is architectural or engineering, and drawing units for all others.

Starting with Release 11, AutoCAD accepts fractional input even if the selected coordinate and distance format is decimal. Prior to Release 11, fractional input was not accepted if decimal units were the chosen format.

You may enter absolute angle values using decimal numbers in any current angle format. AutoCAD assumes that any decimal angle measure entered from the keyboard is in the currently selected format. If you have selected grads or radians as your angle format, decimal number entry is assumed to be the chosen format. If you have selected degrees/minutes/seconds or surveyor's units as your format, decimal entry is accepted as fractional degrees.

However, you may always enter angle information from the keyboard using any of AutoCAD's angle formats. If you have not selected radians format with the Units command, but wish to use it for angle input, include the suffix *r* behind the angle measure. For example:

@26<1.0908r

Likewise, you can use grads for angle input by including the suffix *g* behind the angle measure. For example:

@26<69.4444g

To input angle information in degrees/minutes/seconds or surveyor's units, select these formats with the Units command. If you have changed the orientation of angle zero or the counterclockwise increment of angles, these entries will be affected accordingly.

It is possible to temporarily override any changes made to AutoCAD's zero angle orientation and counterclockwise measurements, and to use AutoCAD's standard angle orientation instead. To do so, you must precede the angle value by << to indicate an absolute AutoCAD standard angle. For example, the syntax

@2.5<<45

indicates a distance of 2.5 drawing units at AutoCAD's standard 45-degree orientation, regardless of whatever current angle orientation has been set.

Warning: In Release 10 and 11, the examples shown in the menu for engineering, architectural, and fractional units are not quite correct. If you attempt to enter some of these sample values exactly as they are displayed in the menu, you will get an error message. In architectural, engineering, or fractional units format, values for feet and inches are not separated by a hyphen; rather, there should be no space between feet and inches at all. Fractions, however, are separated from whole numbers by a hyphen. The correct format for the examples shown in the menu is:

3. Engineering	1'3.50"
4. Architectural	1'3-1/2"
5. Fractional	15-1/2

Some third-party software and AutoLISP programs may be affected by clockwise measurement of angles. If you select clockwise angle measurement, you may have to edit your AutoLISP routines or switch back to counterclockwise angle measurement to use a third-party program. To avoid problems, use the absolute angle indicator (<< as mentioned earlier) when writing AutoLISP routines.

RELATED SYSTEM VARIABLES

LUNITS (numeric values for linear units), LUPREC (linear unit precision), AUNITS (angular units), AUPREC (angular precision), ANGBASE (direction of angle zero), ANGDIR (clockwise/counterclockwise measurement of angles).

SAMPLE DIALOG

The following dialog will set AutoCAD for engineering units, six decimal places of precision, angles measured in radians with six decimal places of precision, angle zero pointing north (i.e., twelve o'clock), and angles incremented in a counterclockwise direction.

```
Command: Units
Systems of units: (Examples)
Enter choice, 1 to 5 <2>: 3
Number of digits to right of decimal point (0 to 8): 6
Systems of angle measure: (Examples)
Enter choice, 1 to 5 <2>: 4
Number of fractional places for display of angles (0 to 8) <6>: 6
Enter direction for angle 0.000000r <0.000000r>: 1.570796
Do you want angles measured clockwise? <N> N
```

VPLAYER

Controls the visibility of layers in individual viewports.

VERSIONS

Release 11 and later.

COMMAND OPTIONS

?   Enter a question mark to obtain a list of the frozen layers in a single viewport. If you are working in model space, AutoCAD switches to paper space, then responds:

Select a viewport:

Pick a viewport with the pointing device. AutoCAD lists the names of layers frozen in that particular viewport. If you began in model space, AutoCAD returns to model space after displaying the list. Refer to Chapter 12 for details regarding model and paper space.

Freeze Enter **F** to freeze layers in one or more viewports. AutoCAD responds:

> Layer(s) to Freeze:

You may enter layer names using the syntax described in the Layer command, discussed earlier in this chapter. After you have entered the layer names, Auto-CAD prompts:

> All/Select/<Current>:

You may select the currently active viewport by typing **C** or pressing Enter. To select other viewports, enter **S**. AutoCAD responds:

> Select objects:

You may select viewports by picking them with the pointing device or windowing them. Refer to Chapter 5 for details regarding AutoCAD's selection mechanisms.

To select all viewports, enter **A**. Viewports that are not currently visible will be included. Refer to the discussion of the Mview command in Chapter 11 for details regarding the visibility of viewports.

Thaw Enter **T** to thaw layers that were previously frozen in one or more viewports with this command's Freeze option. AutoCAD responds:

> Layer(s) to Thaw:

You may enter layer names using the syntax described in the Layer command, discussed earlier in this chapter. If you have frozen layers using the Layer command, you will not be able to thaw them using this command. Use Layer Thaw instead.

After you have entered the layer names, AutoCAD prompts:

> All/Select/<Current>:

Respond to this prompt as described in the Freeze option for this command.

Reset Enter **R** to reset the default visibility settings of layers in selected viewports. AutoCAD responds:

> Layer(s) to Reset:

Enter layer names following the syntax described in the discussion of the Layer command earlier in this chapter. AutoCAD prompts:

All/Select/<Current>:

Respond to this prompt as described in the Freeze option for this command.

Newfrz   Enter **N** to create a new frozen layer. AutoCAD prompts:

New viewport frozen layer name(s):

Enter layer names using the syntax described in the discussion of the Layer command earlier in this chapter. AutoCAD will freeze the selected layers in all viewports.

Vpvisdflt   Enter **V** to set the default visibility state for layers. Layers will adopt this default visibility state in any new viewports you create with the Mview command (discussed in Chapter 11). AutoCAD prompts:

Layer name(s) to change default viewport visibility:

Enter layer names following the syntax described in the discussion of the Layer command earlier in this chapter. AutoCAD responds:

Change default visibility to Frozen/<Thawed>:

Type **T** or press Enter to set the default to Thawed. Enter **F** to set the default to Frozen.

USAGE

Vplayer is similar to the Layer command, discussed in detail earlier in this chapter. If you understand the Layer command and are experienced with it, you will find it much easier to learn and understand Vplayer.

Vplayer can be invoked only when the TILEMODE system variable is set to either zero or "off," which allows AutoCAD to treat viewports as entities. The default visibility setting provides some consistency in the behavior of layers when you create new viewports using Mview; thus, unless you specify otherwise, a layer is assumed to be thawed in new viewports.

If you have frozen layers using the Layer command, they will appear frozen in new viewports, regardless of any default setting you apply using Vplayer. Furthermore, you will be unable to thaw these layers using Vplayer Thaw. Vplayer can change the visibility only of layers that are set On and Thawed using the Layer command.

When using Vplayer New, a newly created layer is frozen in all viewports. This makes it easy to thaw it in a single viewport. Use the Layer command, discussed earlier in this chapter, to create a new layer that is thawed in all viewports.

RELATED COMMANDS

Layer.

RELATED SYSTEM VARIABLES

TILEMODE (allows for Viewport manipulation in paper space), MAXACTVP (controls the maximum number of visible viewports).

SAMPLE DIALOG

The following sample dialog sets the default state of the Hidden Layer as frozen, and thaws it in the currently selected viewport:

```
Command: Vplayer
?/Freeze/Thaw/Reset/Newfrz/Vpvisdflt: V
Layer name(s) to change default viewport visibility: HIDDEN
Change default visibility to Frozen/<Thawed>: F
?/Freeze/Thaw/Reset/Newfrz/Vpvisdflt: T
Layer(s) to Thaw: HIDDEN
All/Select/<Current>: (press Enter)
?/Freeze/Thaw/Reset/Newfrz/Vpvisdflt: (press Enter)
Command:
```

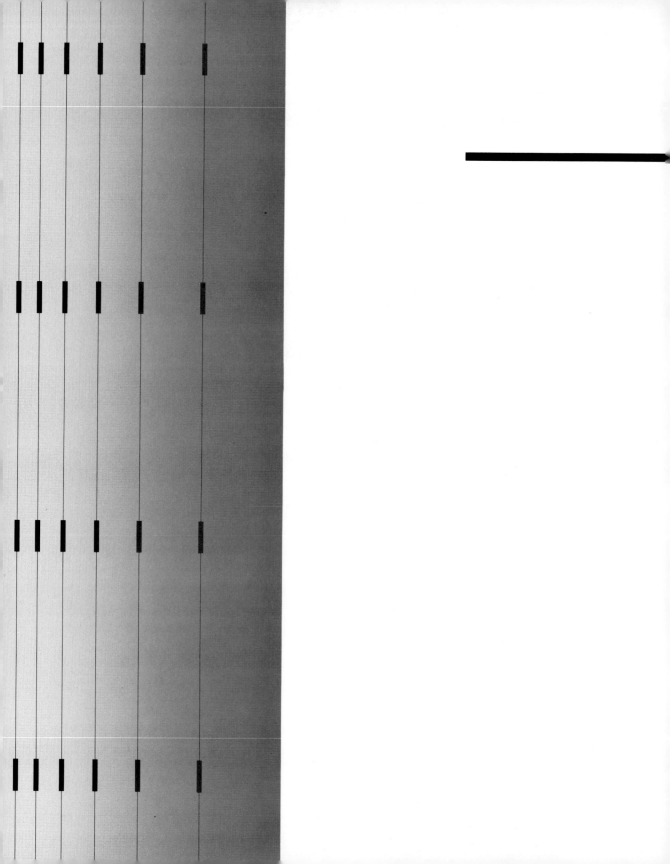

CHAPTER 7

ACCELERATING THE DRAWING PROCESS

ACCELERATING
THE DRAWING PROCESS

AutoCAD drawings are extremely precise, requiring that each drawing entity be associated with a specific set of coordinate points that determine its exact location in the drawing. This process is different from manual drafting, which is usually more flexible. Manual drafters can draw entities on paper in relation to each other without thinking about their absolute Cartesian coordinate locations.

AutoCAD provides a number of useful software tools that help the drafter manage the process of creating and editing drawing entities in AutoCAD's ultra-precise environment. For example, AutoCAD allows you to limit possible coordinate locations to an adjustable grid of *snap points*; this speeds up the process of drawing, copying, moving, and scaling entities. You can make all or only some of these snap points visible or invisible on the display screen. Other tools include *object snap* (finding coordinate locations by using previously drawn entities) and *dynamic dragging* (a process that allows you to preview changes to drawing entities before those changes become final).

A drafter using a computer must carefully manage drawing files on disk as well—making backups often, copying files when needed, and deleting old files when they are no longer needed.

AutoCAD provides file-management tools that can be used while inside the drawing editor. Included are tools to copy, rename, and delete drawing files; you can even leave the drawing editor temporarily, access other programs, and return to the drawing editor without reloading the AutoCAD program or the current drawing file.

AutoCAD also provides on-screen help for its many commands. By entering a question mark at the Command prompt, followed by a command name, the user is given a short summary of that command's features, and a reference to the section of AutoCAD's documentation where the features are covered in more detail. Beginning with Version 2.5, this Help feature can be accessed while in the middle of a command sequence, interrupting a command immediately to give you a quick summary of its features, and continuing from the point of interruption.

By themselves, none of the tools listed in this chapter actually create or modify drawing entities; but if you become familiar with them, you will create and manage your AutoCAD drawings far more productively than would be possible without them.

APERTURE

Adjusts the size of the object-snap aperture, as illustrated in Figure 7.1. Refer to the discussion of the Osnap command in this chapter for details regarding the use of object snap.

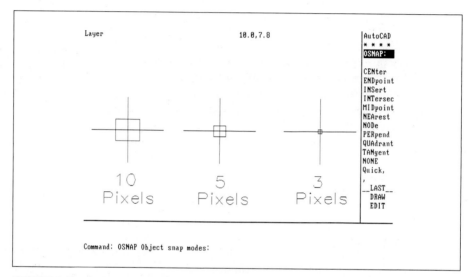

FIGURE 7.1: The object-snap aperture at 10, 5, and 3 pixels. This figure illustrates the relative sizes of the object-snap aperture when set to 10 pixels (AutoCAD's default), 5 pixels, and 3 pixels, by means of the Aperture command. A smaller aperture requires that entity construction points be closer to the intersection of the crosshairs, but can help if many entities are very close together in the display, or if several applicable construction points fall within a larger aperture.

VERSIONS

All.

COMMAND OPTIONS

The Aperture command prompts only for the size of the aperture, in pixels. See the sample dialog.

USAGE

The object-snap aperture is a small rectangular box surrounding the intersection of the crosshairs used by the screen pointing device. The aperture is used to find construction points on existing entities in a drawing, without having to locate those points precisely with the intersection of the crosshairs. As long as the requested construction point falls within the aperture, AutoCAD will locate it for the purposes of object snap.

The size of the aperture is measured by the number of pixels from the intersection to the side of the box. The minimum size is 1 pixel; the maximum is 50 pixels. The default size of the aperture is 10 pixels, as illustrated in Figure 7.1. Refer to Chapter 2 for a discussion of screen pixels.

An aperture that is too large may locate the wrong construction point. For example, if you are attempting to snap to an intersection and more than one intersection falls within the box, AutoCAD will only snap to one—usually the one closest to the intersection of the crosshairs. If you are working with a drawing in which a lot of entities are close together, you may wish to reduce the size of the aperture to create a more precise degree of object selection.

The size of the aperture is stored in the APERTURE system variable, which can be changed with the Setvar command. Use Setvar to change the aperture while in other commands, or when changing the aperture within AutoLISP.

Tip: Certain AutoLISP programs can make use of object-selection mechanisms to identify or select drawing entities. In these cases, the AutoLISP routine may temporarily reduce the aperture size for purposes of precision, since a human hand is not manipulating the aperture.

Warning: The aperture is not the same as the pickbox. The pickbox is a small rectangle used to select entities for editing purposes. Remember that the aperture relates exclusively to object snap. You can adjust the size of the pickbox by changing the value of the PICKBOX system variable. Refer to Chapter 13 for details.

RELATED COMMANDS

Osnap, Setvar.

RELATED SYSTEM VARIABLES

Aperture.

SAMPLE DIALOG

The following dialog changes the aperture size from its default of 10 pixels to 8 pixels:

```
Command: Aperture
Object snap target height (1-50 pixels): 8
Command:
```

AUDIT

Examines the current drawing file for errors, optionally fixing errors that it finds, and produces a separate report on disk showing what was done.

VERSIONS

Release 11 and later.

COMMAND OPTIONS

Fix any errors detected? Enter **Y** if you would like AutoCAD to attempt to correct the errors that it finds in the drawing database. Enter **N** or press Enter if you would like AutoCAD to produce an audit report without correcting errors.

USAGE

The Audit command is nearly automatic, requiring only that you specify whether AutoCAD should attempt to correct errors in the current drawing database. Audit produces an ASCII file containing information about the drawing database. This file uses the name of the current drawing, followed by the extension .ADT. You can view this file by sending it to the printer or screen, or by displaying it with a text editor or word processor.

SAMPLE DIALOG

```
Command: Audit
Fix any errors detected? <N> Y
```

AXIS

Displays "tick marks" along the edge of the drawing editor.

VERSIONS

All. The Snap option is not available in AutoCAD Version 2.18 and earlier; in these versions, set the axis value to zero if you want it set equal to the current snap resolution. In Release 10 and later, the axis is only displayed in the plan view of the world coordinate system, when a single viewport is active.

COMMAND OPTIONS

Tick spacing   Enter the distance between tick marks that you would like to see displayed. This value should be entered in the current units format. Entering zero will set the tick spacing equal to the snap value. If you enter a number followed by **X**, AutoCAD will set the tick spacing as a multiple of the current snap resolution. For example, entering **4X** sets the tick spacing to equal four times the snap resolution.

ON   Enter **ON** to turn on the display of the tick marks.

OFF   Enter **OFF** to turn off the display of the tick marks.

Snap   Enter **S** or **Snap** to set the tick spacing equal to the snap value.

Aspect   Enter **A** or **Aspect** to set different values for horizontal and vertical tick spacing. AutoCAD displays the following prompts:

>   Horizontal spacing(X):
>   Vertical spacing(X):

You may respond to these prompts by entering values for horizontal or vertical tick spacing, or by entering a number followed by **X**, to set either tick spacing as a multiple of the current snap resolution. The Aspect option is not available if the snap style is Isometric.

USAGE

The Axis command displays tick marks as an alternative or adjunct to the Grid command, which displays grid points throughout the drawing editor, and the Snap command, which causes the crosshairs to snap to specified coordinate points. It is useful in those cases where grid points interfere with good visualization of the drawing, where a measurement scale on the screen can aid the drawing process, or where you desire an alternate measurement system along with the grid. Alternatively, it is possible to set the tick spacing as a multiple of the snap resolution, in cases where the resolution is set to such a fine scale that the tick spacing is too dense to be displayed.

When possible, set the tick marks to equal the snap resolution or a multiple of the snap resolution. When you change the snap resolution, the axes will automatically change to reflect the new resolution.

Tip: Axis is most useful when Units is set to Architectural or Engineering. With these units set, the axis displays longer tick lines to mark whole inches or feet.

Warning: When snap resolution is fine, AutoCAD may suppress the display of tick marks when zooming out. Set tick spacing wide enough to be seen at any zoom level.

RELATED COMMANDS

Grid, Snap.

RELATED SYSTEM VARIABLES

AXISMODE (controls axis display), AXISUNIT (controls axis spacing).

SAMPLE DIALOG

The following dialog assumes a current snap value of ½ drawing unit. It will set the tick spacing to 2 drawing units and turn on the display. Figure 7.2 illustrates the result of this dialog.

```
Command: Axis
Tick spacing(X) or ON/OFF/Snap/Aspect <.5>: 4X
Command:
```

DDRMODES

Uses a dialog box to interactively access selected features of the Axis, Grid, Isoplane, and Snap commands.

VERSIONS

Release 9 and later. Ddrmodes requires that AutoCAD's display device be configured for the Advanced User Interface.

COMMAND OPTIONS

All Ddrmodes options are contained within the dialog box. They include setting the x and y spacing for snap, grid, and axis; snap rotation angle and base point; toggles for snap, grid, axis, ortho, and blips; current isoplane orientation; and snap grid style (Isometric or Standard).

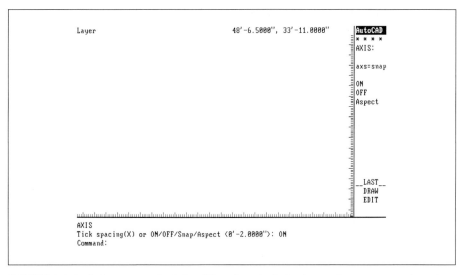

Layer   48'-6.5000", 33'-11.0000"

FIGURE 7.2: Axis display per sample dialog. When the axis display is turned on or set to a value using the Axis command, tick marks will appear along the border of the graphics-display area. When Auto-CAD's units format is set to architectural or engineering units, inches are displayed with shorter tick marks, while feet are represented with longer tick marks. If the magnification permits, fractions of inches may be represented with shorter tick marks, while whole inches are represented with longer tick marks. As shown above, short tick marks appear every 2 inches, and longer tick marks appear every foot.

USAGE

Ddrmodes places the most frequently accessed drawing aids within a single dialog box that graphically represents these features and allows for interactive access and multiple changes from a single command. Refer to Figure 7.3 for an illustration of a typical dialog box.

Tip: Ddrmodes can be used as a transparent command. Refer to Chapter 21 for details regarding transparent commands.

Ddrmodes is convenient and easy, requiring minimal knowledge of command syntax, but there are effective alternatives to the Ddrmodes command:

- The individual commands used to change entity properties can be faster, especially when generated with macros.
- All settings changed using Ddrmodes can also be changed by changing system variables.

RELATED COMMANDS

Axis, Blipmode, Grid, Isoplane, Ortho, Snap.

RELATED SYSTEM VARIABLES

Several system variables control the values that can be changed with this dialog box. They are:

AXISMODE	Axis display enabled/disabled
AXISUNIT	Axis-point spacing in x and y orientations
BLIPMODE	Blip display enabled/disabled
GRIDMODE	Grid display enabled/disabled
GRIDUNIT	Grid-point spacing in x and y orientations
ORTHOMODE	Ortho mode enabled/disabled
SNAPANG	Rotation angle
SNAPBASE	Base point for origin and rotation of snap points
SNAPISOPAIR	Current isometric plane (top, right, or left)
SNAPMODE	Snap enabled/disabled
SNAPSTYL	Snap style, either standard or isometric
SNAPUNIT	Snap-point spacing in x and y orientations

SAMPLE DIALOG

Figure 7.3 illustrates how Ddrmodes can be used to change the snap X spacing to 1 drawing unit and Y spacing to $1/2$ drawing unit, and to enable the display of the grid and ortho mode. Notice that since the box marked Isometric is not selected and marked with an AutoCAD check mark, the snap style is Standard. To change the x and y spacing for either snap, grid, or axis, move the arrow to the appropriate box and select it. The box containing the value will be highlighted, and two new boxes will appear on the same line, one labeled Cancel, the other labeled OK. Enter the new spacing value, and then move the arrow to the box labeled OK and select it.

To return to the drawing editor, select the box labeled OK in the lower part of the dialog box; all changes made will be implemented. To cancel all changes, move the arrow to the box labeled Cancel, and press the pick button. You can also cancel the changes as well as the dialog box by pressing Ctrl-C from the keyboard.

DRAGMODE

Enables and disables AutoCAD's dynamic dragging feature.

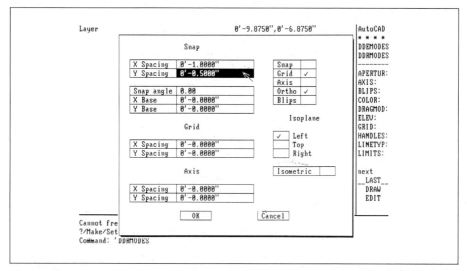

FIGURE 7.3: A sample dialog box using Ddrmodes. The illustrated dialog box will appear when you select the Ddrmodes command (if your display is configured for the Advanced User Interface). Dialog boxes allow you to change several different options with a single command, rather than invoking a series of AutoCAD commands. In the pictured dialog box, the pointing-device arrow has been moved into the box containing the current y-axis snap value. That box is highlighted. Select the box with the pick button and enter the new value using the keyboard. When all changes are complete, move the arrow to the box labeled OK and press the pick button. The dialog box disappears, and the new changes are enabled.

VERSIONS

All. The Auto option was added in AutoCAD Version 2.5; in earlier versions, dynamic dragging was by request only.

COMMAND OPTIONS

ON   Enter **ON** if you wish for AutoCAD to enable dynamic dragging by request. When dynamic dragging is enabled, AutoCAD will implement the feature when you enter the keyword **Drag** at appropriate points in command processing—for example, after selecting a center point for a circle, or after entering a base point for displacement when moving an object.

OFF   Enter **OFF** when you wish for AutoCAD to ignore all requests for dynamic dragging, disabling this feature altogether.

Auto   Enter **A** if you wish for AutoCAD to use dynamic dragging automatically whenever possible. If you select this option, it is not necessary to specifically request dynamic dragging as an option within commands; AutoCAD will always respond as if the request had been made. This is the default state for this feature.

USAGE

Dynamic dragging is a feature that allows you to preview the results of certain commands before you have completed them, by displaying intermediate versions of entities as you move the crosshairs. Depending on the command, entities will enlarge, contract, or otherwise move about the screen as you move your pointing device. For example, if you are drawing a circle and have selected a center point, AutoCAD shows a highlighted circle that expands and contracts as you move the crosshairs farther from or nearer to the selected center point, before you actually select or enter a radius value. Likewise, if you are moving an entity and have selected a base point for displacement, AutoCAD will show you a highlighted version of the entity moving around the screen as you move the crosshairs, before you actually select the second point of displacement.

In some displays, the dragging feature slows down processing, as AutoCAD must continually update and redraw the intermediate display of particular entities. If the dynamic dragging feature slows you down, or if you wish to disable it temporarily for any reason, this command will allow you to toggle back and forth between enabled and disabled dynamic dragging.

If you would like to use dynamic dragging but it is too slow for your display device, you can "smooth out" the dynamic dragging feature by setting snap mode on with a small snap value. In many cases this will reduce the number of times AutoCAD attempts to generate the highlighted figure.

If you are dragging a complex set of entities such as a block, AutoCAD will only generate part of the selection set before checking the location of the crosshairs to see if they have changed. If they have, AutoCAD starts all over at the new location. You can control how often AutoCAD checks the crosshairs for a new location (and thus how much of the entity it can generate) by changing the values of the DRAGP1 and DRAGP2 system variables.

The default value for DRAGP1 is 10; the default for DRAGP2 is 25. If you wish to experiment with different settings for these variables, begin with DRAGP2; on most systems, the value of this variable will make a more visible difference. To regenerate less of the intermediate entity, use the Setvar command to reduce the value of DRAGP2—for example, try reducing it by half, to 12. To generate more of the entity, increase the value of DRAGP2. If you do not get the results you want after working with DRAGP2, then try experimenting in the same way with DRAGP1. Refer to Chapter 13 for details on the Setvar command.

RELATED COMMANDS

Setvar.

RELATED SYSTEM VARIABLES

DRAGMODE, DRAGP1, DRAGP2.

SAMPLE DIALOG

The following sample dialog will disable the dynamic dragging feature:

```
Command: Dragmode
ON/OFF/Auto: OFF
Command:
```

END

Saves the current drawing to disk and returns you to AutoCAD's Main Menu.

VERSIONS

All.

COMMAND OPTIONS

None. However, if you select this command from the on-screen menu, you will be asked to confirm your selection.

USAGE

Use the End command when you are finished with the drawing session. Only one other command, Save, will update the current drawing file, but Save assumes that you intend to continue editing, and thus leaves you in the drawing editor. You can end the drawing session without updating the current drawing file by means of the Quit command.

Warning: If you are working from a RAM disk, be certain that the End command saves your drawing file to the hard disk, not to the RAM disk. Drawing files on a RAM disk are lost when the computer is turned off or rebooted. The easiest way to be sure of this is to run the AutoCAD program from the RAM disk, but always load drawing files directly from the hard disk by including the drive letter with the file name. Refer to Chapter 4 for details regarding AutoCAD and RAM disks.

RELATED COMMANDS

Quit, Save.

FILES

Allows you to perform disk-file maintenance operations while inside the drawing editor. You can access this command from AutoCAD's Main Menu as well.

VERSIONS

All.

COMMAND OPTIONS

When you invoke the Files command, the File Utility menu appears, with the following options:

```
0. Exit File Utility Menu
1. List Drawing files
2. List user specified files
3. Delete files
4. Rename files
5. Copy file
```

- Enter **0** (or press Enter) to return to the drawing editor (or to the Main Menu, if you started from there.)
- Enter **1** to list all drawing files (that is, files with the extension DWG). AutoCAD responds:

    Enter drive or directory:

    If you wish to list files on the currently logged subdirectory, you may respond to this prompt by pressing Enter. Otherwise, enter the drive letter followed by a colon (followed by any subdirectory names, if different from the currently logged subdirectory), as in the following example:

    C:\acad\dwgs

    If AutoCAD finds any drawing files on the specified directory, it will list their names and the total number of files found. After reviewing the names of the files found by AutoCAD, press Enter.

- Enter **2** to list all files according to a specification of your choosing. Wild cards are allowed. After you enter **2**, AutoCAD responds:

  Enter file search specification:

  Using wild-card characters, enter the specification for the file types you wish to list. For example, to list all compiled shape files on the currently logged subdirectory, enter the following:

  *.shx

  In the above example, AutoCAD will list only those files with the SHX file extension. You may see a list similar to the following:

  SIMPLEX.SHX   TXT.SHX   COMPLEX.SHX   ITALIC.SHX
  4 files
  Press RETURN to continue:

  After reviewing the names of the files found by AutoCAD, press Enter. AutoCAD will redisplay the File Utility menu.

- Enter **3** to delete specific files. Wild cards are allowed. After you enter **3**, AutoCAD responds:

  Enter file deletion specification:

  To delete a single file, enter the name and extension (if any) of that file. To delete several files with similar names, use wild-card characters. For example, you could enter the following:

  *.bak

  AutoCAD responds by asking you to confirm the deletion of each file it finds that matches your specification. For example, you may see messages such as the following:

  Delete ACAD.BAK? <N>
  Delete OFFICE.BAK? <N>
  Delete NOZZLE.BAK? <N>
  Delete COLUMBIA.BAK? <N>

  Each time AutoCAD displays a name of a file, press **Y** to delete the file, or **N** or Enter to keep it.

  After AutoCAD displays all the files that match your specification, it displays the following message:

  n files deleted.
  Press RETURN to continue:

In the above example, *n* is the number of files that you elected to delete. Press Enter to complete the command and return to the File Utility menu.

- Enter **4** to rename a specific file. Wild cards are not allowed. After you enter **4**, AutoCAD responds:

    Enter current filename:

Enter the exact name and extension (if any) of the file you wish to rename. AutoCAD responds:

    Enter new filename:

Enter the new name of the file; the file is then renamed. If AutoCAD cannot find the requested file, or if the file name contains illegal characters (such as wild cards), you may see the following message:

    Rename not successful
    Press RETURN to continue:

If the file was renamed, however, AutoCAD responds:

    File renamed.
    Press RETURN to continue:

Press Enter to complete the command and return to the File Utility menu.

- Enter **5** to copy a specific file. Wild cards are not allowed. After you enter **5**, AutoCAD responds:

    Enter name of source file:

Enter the exact name of the file you wish to copy (the source file). You may include other drive letters or subdirectories if the source file is not on the currently logged subdirectory. When AutoCAD finds the source file, it responds:

    Enter name of destination file:

Enter the name and extension of the new duplicate file. Again, you may include drive letters and subdirectory names if you wish. After AutoCAD has copied the file, it displays the following message:

    Copied *nnnnn* bytes.
    Press RETURN to continue:

In the above example *nnnnn* is the number of bytes in the file you copied. Press Enter to complete the command and return to the File Utility menu.

If your file name contains illegal characters (such as wild cards), AutoCAD will display a message to that effect and will not copy the file.

USAGE

Disk-file maintenance is an important part of CAD. Using the Files command, you can list, delete, rename, or copy files.

Be careful when copying files. There is no request for confirmation if the destination file you specify already exists. If you copy a file and name an existing file as the destination, the source file will overwrite the preexisting file of the same name.

Warning: There is no recovery from deleted files using this command. Once you confirm that a file is to be deleted, you should consider it to be deleted permanently. You may be able to restore from a backup copy.

SAMPLE DIALOG

See the command options for samples of dialog using this command.

GRID

Displays a regularly spaced series of dots in the drawing editor, within the current drawing limits.

VERSIONS

All. The Snap option is not available in AutoCAD Version 2.18 and earlier; in these versions, set the grid value to zero if you want the grid spacing to equal the current snap resolution.

In versions of AutoCAD that support 3-D, the display of the grid is rotated to reflect the current 3-D viewpoint. In some cases, this will render the grid too dense to be displayed.

In versions prior to Release 10 and later, the display of the grid always matches the drawing limits. In AutoCAD Release 10 and later, the grid matches the drawing limits if the current construction plane matches the world coordinate system. If you are not in a world construction plane, the grid extends throughout the viewport.

COMMAND OPTIONS

Grid spacing   Enter the distance between grid marks that you would like to see displayed. Entering zero will set the grid spacing equal to the snap value.

If you enter a number followed by **X**, AutoCAD will set the grid spacing as a multiple of the current snap resolution. For example, **8X** sets the grid spacing to equal eight times the snap resolution.

ON   Enter **ON** to turn on the display of the grid marks.

OFF   Enter **OFF** to turn off the display of the grid marks.

Snap   Enter **S** or **Snap** to set the grid spacing equal to the snap value.

Aspect   Enter **A** or **Aspect** to set different values for horizontal and vertical grid spacing. AutoCAD displays the following prompts:

Horizontal spacing(X):
Vertical spacing(X):

You may respond to these prompts by entering values for horizontal or vertical grid-point spacing, or by entering a number followed by **X**, to set either grid-point spacing as a multiple of the current snap resolution.

USAGE

The drawing grid is a drawing aid employed when a measurement scale on the screen can aid the process of creating entities; it is not part of the drawing and will not be plotted. It is frequently used along with the Snap command, causing the crosshairs to snap to specified grid points. In cases where the snap resolution is set to such a fine scale that AutoCAD cannot display the grid-point spacing, it is possible to set the spacing between the grid points as a multiple of the snap resolution.

When possible, set the grid to equal a multiple of the snap resolution. When you change the snap resolution, the grid will automatically change to reflect the new resolution.

The grid always matches the rotation and isometric style of the snap resolution. Refer to the discussion of the Snap command in this chapter for details.

You can quickly turn the grid off and on by pressing Ctrl-G or a function key (F6 on most systems).

Warning: When snap resolution is fine, AutoCAD may suppress the display of grid points when zooming out.

The Aspect option is not available if the snap style is Isometric.

RELATED COMMANDS

Axis, Ddrmode, Setvar, Snap.

RELATED SYSTEM VARIABLES

GRIDMODE (controls grid display), GRIDUNIT (controls grid spacing).

SAMPLE DIALOG

The following dialog assumes a snap value of ½ drawing unit. It will set the horizontal grid-point spacing to 2 drawing units (four times snap) and the vertical spacing to 1 drawing unit (two times snap), and will turn on the display. The resulting display appears in Figure 7.4.

```
Command: Grid
Grid spacing(X) or ON/OFF/Snap/Aspect <.5>: A
Horizontal spacing(X) <.5>: 4X
Vertical spacing(X) <.5>: 2X
Command:
```

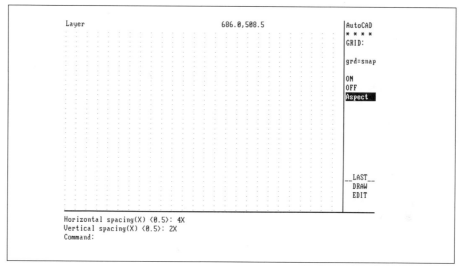

FIGURE 7.4: Grid display per sample dialog. This figure illustrates the grid display that results when the grid spacing is set to different multiples of the snap spacing. Rather than being evenly spaced apart, the grid marks appear every fourth snap point in the x-axis direction, and every other snap point in the y-axis direction. If you change the snap spacing, the grid spacing will retain the same multiples of the new snap resolution.

HELP OR ?

Provides context-sensitive assistance for AutoCAD commands.

VERSIONS

All. The Help command may be accessed as a transparent command beginning with Version 2.5. When you use the Help command in this fashion, it must be preceded with a leading apostrophe.

COMMAND OPTIONS

?   At the Command prompt, the question mark equals the **Help** command.

Command Name   After accessing the help system, you may enter a specific command for which you desire an explanation or a referral to the AutoCAD documentation. If you press the Enter key in response to this prompt, Auto-CAD displays a list of all available commands.

Press Return   If you press Enter (Return) after invoking Help from the Command prompt, AutoCAD displays a list of commands, valid formats for keyboard input, and entity-selection options, along with referrals to the appropriate sections of the AutoCAD documentation.

USAGE

If you use the Help command transparently, AutoCAD will assume that you want help with the command in progress. If you are being prompted for an optional response within a command, AutoCAD displays a short explanation of the current command prompt, followed by:

>>Do you want more help for the <*command*>? <N>

If you respond by typing **Y**, more detailed information appears, along with a reference to the section in the AutoCAD documentation where you can find still more information. If you respond by typing **N** or pressing Enter, AutoCAD continues with the command.

> *Tip:* The Help command uses an ASCII text file named ACAD.HLP. You can customize this file with a text editor to include any additional help messages of your own; or, if you create your own commands using AutoLISP, you can include help messages for them as well. Refer to Chapter 14 for details.

SAMPLE DIALOG

The sample dialog is Figure 7.5 accesses the Help command during the Grid command.

ISOPLANE

Selects one of three special snap ratios and axis orientations that can be used to create isometric drawings.

```
Command: Grid                                                                 <
Grid spacing(X) or ON/OFF/Snap/Aspect <0.0000>: '?                           <
The  GRID  command controls the display of a grid of alignment dots to assist <
in the placement of objects in the drawing.                                   <
                                                                              <
Format:     GRID  Grid spacing(X) or ON/OFF/Snap/Aspect <current>:           <
                                                                              <
The various options are described below.                                      <
                                                                              <
     Spacing(X)  - A simple number sets grid spacing in drawing              <
                   units.  A number followed by "X" (e.g., "2X")             <
                   sets the grid spacing to a multiple of the current        <
                   Snap resolution.  A value of zero locks the grid          <
                   spacing to the current Snap resolution.                   <
     ON          - Turns grid on with previous spacing.                      <
     OFF         - Turns grid off.                                           <
     Snap        - Locks the grid spacing to the current Snap                <
                   resolution (same as a spacing value of zero).             <
     Aspect      - Permits a grid with different                             <
                   horizontal and vertical spacing.                          <
                                                                              <
See also:   Section 8.2 of the Reference Manual.                            <
Press RETURN to resume GRID command.                                         <
Resuming GRID command.                                                       <
Grid spacing(X) or ON/OFF/Snap/Aspect <0.0000>:                             <
```

FIGURE 7.5: Context-sensitive help during the Grid command. Beginning with AutoCAD Version 2.5, you can use the Help command transparently by entering an apostrophe followed by a question mark at most AutoCAD prompts. The above figure shows the screen that appears when accessing Help during the Grid command. After reading the summary of Grid command features, press Enter to resume the Grid command at the point of interruption.

VERSIONS

All.

COMMAND OPTIONS

Left   Enter **L** to select the "left" isometric plane, which uses the axes oriented at 90 (vertical) and 150 (horizontal) degrees.

Top   Enter **T** to select the "top" isometric plane, which uses the axes oriented at 30 (vertical) and 150 (horizontal) degrees.

Right   Enter **R** to select the "right" isometric plane, which uses the axes oriented at 90 (vertical) and 30 (horizontal) degrees.

Toggle   You may press Enter or the space bar, and AutoCAD will toggle between the three isometric planes in the following order: left, top, and right.

USAGE

Isometric drawings are two-dimensional drawings that represent 3-D objects. They are not true 3-D drawings. The isometric snap ratio, as illustrated in Figure 7.6, has three axes instead of two, oriented at 30, 90, and 150 degrees. The Isoplane command selects any two of these axes and adjusts snap mode, ortho mode, and cursor-key movement accordingly.

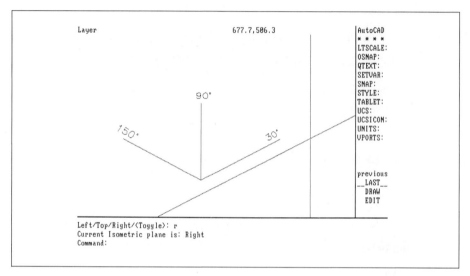

FIGURE 7.6: Isometric snap ratio. This figure illustrates the appearance of the crosshairs when Isometric snap is enabled and the isometric plane is toggled to Right. The three basic isometric angles, 30, 90, and 150 degrees, are also displayed. This special snap grid allows you to create 2-D drawings that give the appearance of 3-D (see Figure 7.15).

It is possible to draw in any of the isometric planes, regardless of the orientation of the crosshairs, when snap is active. Keep the grid visible to assist yourself when drawing along the "foreign" axis—for example, when drawing vertical lines with the isoplane set for "top."

You can quickly toggle between isometric planes, even during commands, by pressing Ctrl-E.

Ortho mode always follows the axes of the current isometric plane, regardless of whether snap is turned on or off. Alternatively, the isometric plane can quickly be set using Setvar or macros.

Warning: Isoplane will not work unless the snap style has been previously set to Isometric. The cursor-movement keys are affected by the isoplane only when snap mode is turned on.

RELATED COMMANDS

Setvar, Snap.

RELATED SYSTEM VARIABLES

SNAPISOPAIR (current isometric view), SNAPSTYL (current snap style).

SAMPLE DIALOG

The following dialog changes the current isometric plane to right:

```
Command: Isoplane
Left/Top/Right/(Top): R
Command:
```

ORTHO

Toggles AutoCAD's orthogonal mode on and off.

VERSIONS

All. In AutoCAD Release 10 and later, orthogonal mode always applies to the orientation of the crosshairs in the current construction plane.

COMMAND OPTIONS

Enter **ON** to toggle orthogonal mode on; enter **OFF** to toggle it off again.

USAGE

Orthogonal mode causes AutoCAD to generate new entities using points parallel to the orientation of the crosshairs. Figure 7.7 illustrates a rubberband line moving parallel to the horizontal crosshairs during a Line command in orthogonal mode.

By eliminating the possibility of erroneous diagonals, orthogonal mode is useful if you are generating a series of horizontal or vertical lines. However, since AutoCAD's orthogonal mode sees horizontal and vertical in relation to the current setting of the snap grid, you may also use orthogonal mode to force diagonal line drawing, by rotating the snap grid to a desired angle. Figure 7.8 depicts how orthogonal mode appears when the snap grid is rotated 45 degrees. Refer to the discussion of the Snap command for details on rotating the snap grid. If you are

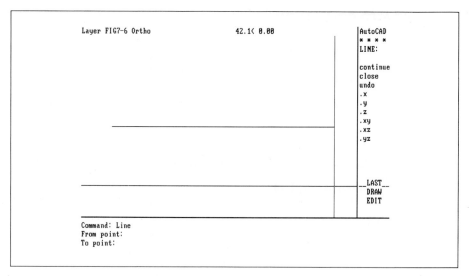

FIGURE 7.7: Rubberband line in orthogonal mode. When AutoCAD's orthogonal mode is enabled, the rubberband line behaves differently. Rather than extending from the selected point to the intersection of the crosshairs, the line extends from the selected point to a point perpendicular to one of the crosshair lines. As you move the pointing device, AutoCAD will snap the rubberband line from one crosshair line to the other, always maintaining the perpendicular aspect. With only a little practice, you will find it easy to control the rubberband line when in orthogonal mode. This is a big help when drawing parallel and perpendicular lines.

using an isometric snap grid, othogonal mode will follow the isometric orientation of the current snap setting.

Orthogonal mode will affect other values entered using the pointing device. For example, if entering angle information while orthogonal mode is on, you will only be able to enter angle values of 0, 90, 180, or 270 degrees (unless you first rotate the snap grid) or use object-snap overrides (see Osnap, this chapter). Since the endpoint of the rubberband line does not necessarily meet the intersection of the crosshairs, distance values entered using two points may be affected as well.

If you attempt to move, copy, rotate, or otherwise change the orientation of your drawing's entities, othogonal mode will force the entity movement or rotation to remain parallel with the crosshairs.

AutoCAD selects the horizontal or vertical angles of orientation automatically. As you move the crosshairs around in orthogonal mode, the rubberband line will jump back and forth from one orientation to the other.

Tip: Ortho's most practical purpose is for use within command macros, where it can force orthogonal mode on or off, regardless of its current status. Refer to Chapter 14 for details regarding macro construction.

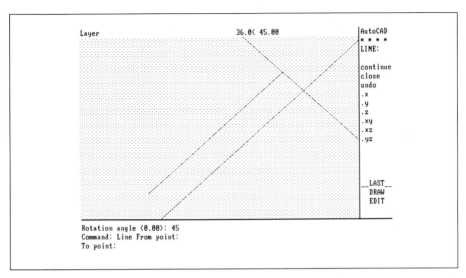

FIGURE 7.8: Rubberband line in orthogonal mode, with snap rotated 45 degrees. Although the normal orientation of the crosshairs is horizontal and vertical, it is possible to use orthogonal mode to draw diagonal lines as well. In this figure, the snap grid is rotated 45 degrees using the Snap Rotate command. When the snap is rotated, the crosshairs are rotated as well, and orthogonal mode is now set to a 45-degree orientation. Diagonal lines drawn using this technique maintain their orientation when the horizontal-vertical snap is restored.

There are plenty of alternatives to the Ortho command, which is usually the least efficient means of toggling othogonal mode when working from the Command prompt. On most systems, a special function key (usually F8) will toggle orthogonal mode on and off, even while in the middle of another command sequence. Ctrl-O is another convenient toggle for orthogonal mode at any time during or between commands.

You can also turn orthogonal mode on and off by using the Setvar command to change the value of the ORTHOMODE system variable. Refer to Chapter 13 for details on the values for ORTHOMODE.

RELATED COMMANDS

Setvar.

RELATED SYSTEM VARIABLES

ORTHOMODE.

SAMPLE DIALOG

> Command: **Ortho**
> ON/OFF: **ON**
> Command:

OSNAP

Sets default object-snap modes for subsequent coordinate point picks.

VERSIONS

2.0 and later. In versions prior to Release 9, object snap did not work intuitively when not in plan view. As of Release 9, it became possible to use object snap to find construction points in 3-D space when outside of plan view. For example, you can use midpoint and endpoint modes on all four visible edges created by an extruded line segment. In Release 10 and later, arcs and circles must be parallel to the current UCS in order to be found using object snap.

COMMAND OPTIONS

There are several object-snap modes available:

Center   Enter **Cen** to snap to the center point of circles and arcs. If using Release 10, first set the current UCS parallel to the circle or arc.

Endpoint   Enter **End** to snap to endpoints of lines.

Insert   Enter **Ins** if you wish to snap to insertion points of blocks, attributes, text, and shapes.

Intersection   Enter **Int** to snap to intersection points between entities. AutoCAD will not find an intersection if one only appears to exist because of the angle of the current viewpoint. Intersections must actually exist in 3-D space for AutoCAD to find them.

Midpoint   Enter **Mid** to snap to midpoints of line segments and arcs.

Nearest   Enter **Near** to snap to the entity point within the aperture that appears nearest to the intersection of the crosshairs in the current viewing angle.

Node   Enter **Node** to snap to point entities.

Perpendicular   Enter **Per** to snap to a point that is perpendicular to the previously selected point.

Quadrant   Enter **Quad** to snap to the horizontal and vertical extents of an arc or a circle.

Quick   Enter **Quick** to change the manner in which AutoCAD picks construction points. Normally, AutoCAD finds all construction points within the aperture that match the chosen object-snap modes, and picks the construction point closest to the crosshairs. However, if you select Quick mode, AutoCAD will search the aperture until it finds the first construction point matching one of the modes, select that point, and stop searching. This is useful if many entities cross the aperture, but you know that only a single construction point will be found. Intersection mode is an exception to this. Quick mode does not work when AutoCAD is looking for intersection points.

Tangent   Enter **Tan** to snap to a point that will create a tangent to an arc or a circle.

None   Enter **None** to disable the global object-snap mechanism. If using a temporary object-snap override, enter **None** as an option in addition to other options. If AutoCAD cannot find the selected construction point, it will choose the intersection of the screen crosshairs instead.

USAGE

AutoCAD's *object-snap mechanism* is a powerful selection tool that permits you to find specific entity construction points quickly while creating and modifying drawings. This process is illustrated in Figure 7.9, using object snap for intersections. The object-snap mechanism can be accessed in two ways:

Global Object Snap   To use global object snap, invoke the Osnap command, followed by the types of construction points to which you intend to snap. An *aperture,* a small box used to find these points, will surround the intersection of the screen crosshairs. Thereafter, you may select these construction points when selecting coordinate points for creating or modifying entities. To do so, position the crosshairs so that the desired point falls anywhere within the aperture; AutoCAD will automatically find the desired point.

When global object snap is invoked, the aperture will remain displayed, and object snap will remain in effect, until you reinvoke the command and reset the selection mechanism to another object-snap mode or to "none," meaning that object snap is disabled.

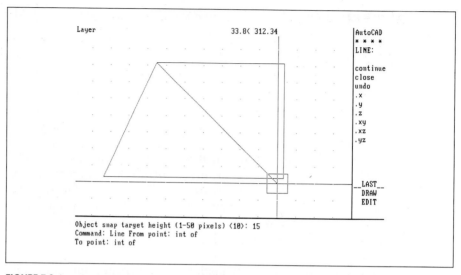

FIGURE 7.9: Locating intersections using Osnap. When object snap is enabled (by means of object-snap overrides or the Osnap command), AutoCAD will snap to specified entity construction points. For example, this figure illustrates a line being drawn that will connect two intersections not coinciding with any of the current snap points. If you set object snap to Intersection, AutoCAD will snap to intersection points when the pick button is pressed, as long as the intersection point falls within the aperture, as shown above. As you move the crosshairs, however, AutoCAD still snaps only to the snap points, as long as snap mode is enabled.

Temporary Object-Snap Override   To use *object-snap override*, enter the specific object-snap mode desired at any AutoCAD prompt that requests a point. (Refer to the sample dialog.) AutoCAD will respond by enabling the object-snap mechanism for that point selection only, and will return to the previous mode as soon as a valid point is found. If no object-snap point is found within the aperture, AutoCAD will display an error message to that effect in the Command-prompt area.

Tip: If the aperture is on the screen and you do not want it there, invoke Osnap None to remove it. If necessary, edit your prototype drawing and invoke Osnap None there as well.

Warning: The object-snap End option is not the same as the End command. The End command ends the drawing session when invoked from the Command prompt.

RELATED SYSTEM VARIABLES

OSMODE (bit-code for current object-snap mode).

SAMPLE DIALOG

The following sample dialog produces the line segment shown in Figure 7.10. Two versions of the sample dialog are shown. The first uses global object snap; the second uses temporary object snap overrides.

```
Command: Osnap
Object snap modes: quad,tan
Command: Line
From point: (pick point #1 near large circle)
To point: (pick point #2 near small circle)
To point: (press Enter)
Command: Osnap
Object snap modes: none
Command:

Command: Line
From point: quad
of (pick point #1 near large circle)
To point: tan
to (pick point #2 near small circle)
To point: (press Enter)
Command:
```

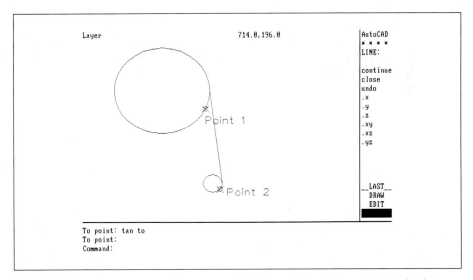

FIGURE 7.10: Drawing a line using Osnap per sample dialog. This figure shows a line that has been drawn tangent to two circles. The object-snap override was set to Tangent before both endpoints were selected, and then the Line command was ended by simply pressing Enter in response to the last "To point:" prompt. The points on the circles that were actually selected are marked. Notice how the endpoints of the line are clearly different from the points selected. The key to using object snap successfully is to select an entity as close to the desired points as you can estimate.

QUIT

Ends the drawing session without saving any changes.

VERSIONS

All.

COMMAND OPTIONS

Because the Quit command carries with it the potential to eliminate hours of editing work, Quit provides a Yes/No prompt to confirm that you really intend to end the session without saving any changes. See the sample dialog.

USAGE

The Quit command provides a means to terminate a drawing session gone awry, or to leave a drawing after making changes you do not intend to save.

Use Quit sparingly. Remember that when you save your changes with the End command, AutoCAD stores the previous version of your drawing file on disk using the drawing file's name with the file extension BAK. Thus, it is always possible to retrieve the drawing file that existed just prior to your latest changes. To retrieve the file, rename the BAK file to another name, and change the file extension from BAK to DWG. Refer to the discussion of the Files command earlier in this chapter for details on renaming files while inside AutoCAD; or, rename the file from the DOS prompt. After renaming the file and changing its extension to DWG, you can edit or view it normally using AutoCAD.

RELATED COMMANDS

End, Save.

SAMPLE DIALOG

The following sample dialog is the only way possible to end a drawing session without saving your changes:

    Command: **Quit**
    Really want to discard all changes to drawing? **Y**

SAVE

Saves the drawing's current changes to disk and continues the editing session.

VERSIONS

All.

COMMAND OPTIONS

File name   The current name of the drawing file is displayed as the default, and if you press Enter in response to this prompt, the file is saved under the current name. The previous version of the file is retained on disk, its file extension changed to BAK. Alternatively, you may save the drawing under a different name by entering that name in response to this prompt. If you do so, you will create a new drawing file containing all drawing information in the current file up to that point. The disk version of the current drawing file is left unchanged. If you respond to this prompt with the name of a drawing file already on disk, AutoCAD responds:

> A drawing with this name already exists.
> Do you want to replace it <N>

Enter **Y** if you wish to overwrite the existing file with the current file. Enter **N** if you do not wish to overwrite the file, in which case the Save command is then canceled.

USAGE

The Save command is useful and powerful, and should be invoked as often as possible. Save is just like End, except that instead of returning you to Auto-CAD's Main Menu, it leaves you in the drawing editor. The Save command is your first line of defense against unexpected circumstances (such as power failures or hardware problems) that can cause the computer to crash. If you save the drawing file often, you will not run the risk of losing hours of drafting work to the unexpected hazards of modern computer technology.

> *Warning:* If you save the current file under another name and in so doing overwrite an existing file on disk, no BAK file for the existing file is created. Overwriting files in this manner is permanent; you cannot recover the overwritten file unless you have another backup copy on a subdirectory or a floppy disk.

Many computer users (including some notable experts in the field) have marveled at how those who back up their data regularly also seem to have a lower rate of hardware and software foul-ups, glitches, and data-destroying problems. Perhaps this is merely a folk adage similar to the notion that if you carry your umbrella on a cloudy day, there's less chance that it will rain. Whether such unscientific observations are valid or not, regularly backing up your work is self-evidently a good thing to do.

RELATED COMMANDS

End, Quit.

SAMPLE DIALOG

The following sample dialog saves the current drawing:

```
Command: Save
File name <C:\acad10\chap7>: (press Enter)
Command:
```

Sн

Allows access to commands while inside the drawing editor. The Sh command is a version of the Shell command.

VERSIONS

All.

COMMAND OPTIONS

OS command   Enter the name of the operating system command you wish to use. When the command has completed processing, you will return to the Command prompt. On single-screen systems, it may be necessary to press the Flip Screen key or to invoke the Graphscr command to return the display to the drawing editor.

Press enter   If you press Enter in response to the "OS command" prompt, AutoCAD will display an operating system prompt similar to the one you see before invoking AutoCAD.

When you see this prompt, you can enter a series of operating system commands, just as if you were at the original operating system prompt. When you are ready to return to the drawing editor, enter **exit** and normal AutoCAD processing will return.

USAGE

The Sh command is used to access the operating system as opposed to application programs.

It is functionally the same as the Shell command. Its advantage over the Shell command is that it allows for a faster return to the drawing editor when the operating system command is completed. Sh allocates a small amount of memory, 27Kb, for its functions.

Although Sh is intended for internal operating system commands, any command that uses 27K or less of memory can be accessed with Sh. Since Sh reloads the drawing editor more quickly upon completion, Sh should be the command of choice for running small utility-type programs. If you attempt to use the Sh command and receive a message indicating that the program is too big to fit in memory, try using the Shell command instead.

Note: You can increase the amount of memory used by Sh if you so desire. Refer to Chapter 14 for details.

Warning: Do not use Sh to load memory-resident utilities or other programs that load themselves into RAM and do not leave RAM entirely upon completion. Doing so may cause AutoCAD to crash. Load memory-resident software before running AutoCAD.

RELATED COMMANDS

Shell.

SAMPLE DIALOG

The following sample dialog copies a BAK file to a DWG file while inside the drawing editor, thus saving the BAK file from being overwritten during subsequent Save commands:

```
Command: Sh
DOS command: COPY CURRFILE.BAK OLDFILE.DWG
1 file(s) copied
Command:
```

SHELL

Allows access to other software commands while inside the drawing editor.

VERSIONS

All.

COMMAND OPTIONS

OS command   Enter the name of the external application program. When the application has completed processing, you will return to the Command prompt. On single-screen systems, it may be necessary to press the Flip Screen key or to invoke the Graphscr command to return the display to the drawing editor when Shell is finished processing.

Press Enter   If you press Enter in response to the "OS command" prompt, AutoCAD will display an operating system prompt similar to the one you see before invoking AutoCAD.

When you see this prompt, you can enter a series of operating system commands, just as if you were at the original operating system prompt. When you are ready to return to the drawing editor, enter **exit** and normal AutoCAD processing will return.

USAGE

The Shell command can be used to access other programs, such as a word processor, spreadsheet, or database, while inside the AutoCAD drawing editor. It does this by moving a portion of its program files from RAM to disk temporarily, releasing the vacated RAM for use by the outside application. When the application has completed its processing, AutoCAD restores the program files and resumes normal processing.

Shell uses about 127K of memory for its external processing. You can change this amount by editing the file ACAD.PGP with a text editor. Refer to Chapter 14 for details on editing ACAD.PGP. The maximum amount of RAM available to Shell depends on both the amount of RAM in your system and your version of AutoCAD. If you are using AutoCAD 386, you will not be able to allocate as much RAM for Shell functions as you would with other versions. Always experiment first with an empty drawing file when testing new changes to ACAD.PGP, to ensure against loss of important data.

> *Warning:* Do not use Shell to load memory-resident utilities or other programs that load themselves into RAM and do not leave RAM entirely upon completion. Doing so may cause AutoCAD to crash. Load memory-resident software from the original operating system prompt only, before running AutoCAD.

RELATED COMMANDS

Sh.

SAMPLE DIALOG

The following sample dialog enters a word-processing and database program while inside the drawing editor, using DOS AutoCAD:

```
Command: Shell
OS command: (press Enter)
Type EXIT to return to AutoCAD.
C>> (enter word-processing commands)
C>> (enter database commands)
C>> EXIT
Command:
```

SNAP

Allows you to enter points precisely, by forcing AutoCAD to pick only those points that fall on an imaginary grid of snap points. You can also use Snap to control the spacing and orientation of the snap points, and to enable or disable point snapping at any time, even while executing other commands.

VERSIONS

All. In Release 10 and later, snap is disabled when the drawing is viewed in perspective.

COMMAND OPTIONS

Snap spacing   To set snap points at regular intervals, enter the distance between the snap points. Figure 7.11 illustrates a snap value of one drawing unit. You make the snap points visible in the drawing editor by enabling the drawing grid. Refer to the discussion of the Grid command earlier in this chapter for details. When snap is enabled, the crosshairs can only find points 1 drawing unit apart.

Figure 7.12 shows the same set of snap points when viewed from a non-plan orientation in 3-D space. Notice how the crosshairs are affected. Since the construction plane remains the same, all entities will continue to fall on that plane, even when created from this orientation.

ON   Enter **ON** to enable point snapping. Alternate methods for enabling point snapping are outlined in the Usage section ahead.

OFF   Enter **OFF** to disable point snapping. Alternate methods for disabling point snapping are outlined in the Usage section ahead.

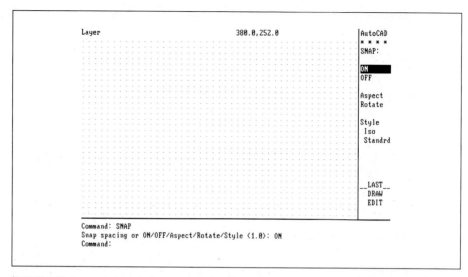

FIGURE 7.11: Snap spacing—1 drawing unit. This figure shows a typical snap spacing and visible grid, 1 drawing unit apart along both the x- and y-axes, with drawing limits set so that the grid fills the screen display. In plan view, this appears as a regularly spaced series of tiny dots. Compare this plan-view appearance of the grid to the non-plan view in Figure 7.12.

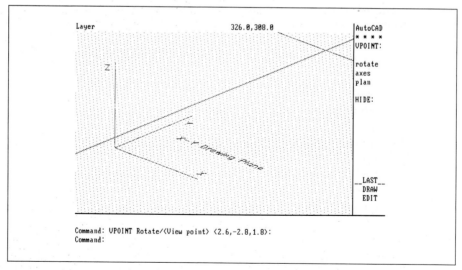

FIGURE 7.12: Snap spacing in non-plan view. In non-plan view, the visible snap points appear out of alignment, resulting from a combination of the new viewing angle and the resolution of the monitor. The three axes are added to show you the new orientation of the current drawing plane. Notice also how the crosshairs appear to be lying flat upon the drawing plane. They will remain in this orientation as you move them around the drawing editor with the pointing device.

Aspect   Enter **A** if you desire snap points that are not equally spaced—i.e., farther apart along either the x-axis or the y-axis. Figure 7.13 illustrates how the Aspect option is used to create snap points that are ½ drawing unit apart along the x-axis and 1 drawing unit apart along the y-axis.

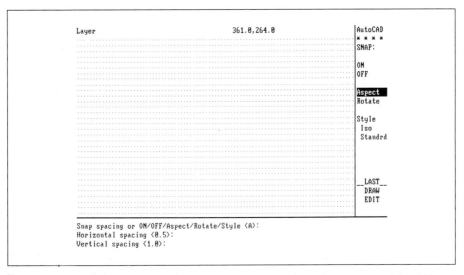

FIGURE 7.13: Snap spacing—Aspect option. In this figure, the grid points are again spaced at different intervals. (Compare to the spacing in Figure 7.4.) The difference here is that the grid display has been set to zero (or in Version 2.5 and later, to Snap). With this grid setting, a grid point will appear for each snap point in the display. The snap points, however, have been irregularly spaced in this figure, using the Snap Aspect command.

When you enter **A**, AutoCAD responds:

   Horizontal spacing:

Enter the distance between the snap points along the x-axis—in this case, *.5*. AutoCAD responds:

   Vertical spacing:

Enter the distance between the snap points along the y-axis, **1**.

Rotate   Enter **R** if you wish to align the snap points in other than the usual horizontal/vertical orientation. When the snap points are rotated and snap is enabled, the crosshairs are rotated as well. Figure 7.14 illustrates rotated snap points that are also set to the aspect mentioned above.

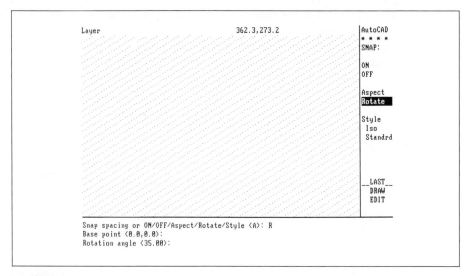

FIGURE 7.14: Snap spacing—Aspect and Rotate options. In this figure, the snap points are set to different spacing in the x and y directions, and then rotated 35 degrees. By combining features of the Grid and Snap commands, including aspect spacing, multiple spacing, rotation, and style, you have virtually unlimited flexibility in setting up the precise combination of grid display and snap resolution to serve your drawing needs.

When rotating the snap points, you are asked for a base point around which the rotation will take place, and an angle of rotation. Any of AutoCAD's standard data-entry mechanisms is acceptable here. You may, for example, "show" AutoCAD the angle of rotation by entering two points, or by using object snap to align the rotation of the snap points with an existing entity on the screen.

Style Enter **S** to enable one of two possible snap-point "styles," either *Standard* or *Isometric*. Standard style refers to the regular spacing of snap points along the x-axis and y-axis, even when this spacing is not equal. Isometric style is a special orientation of snap points that permits you to draw 2-D entities in such a way as to provide the illusion of three dimensions. When you enter **S**, AutoCAD responds:

Standard/Isometric:

Enter **S** for Standard, **I** for Isometric. When you enter **I**, AutoCAD responds:

Vertical spacing:

Vertical spacing in isometric grids is analogous to the snap spacing of standard grids; that is, the grid points will be spaced in such a way as to appear equidistant along the vertical spacing, but at an "angle" that provides the 3-D illusion. Note that this is not the same as AutoCAD's 3-D feature; isometric entities are drawn on a 2-D plane, as illustrated in Figure 7.15.

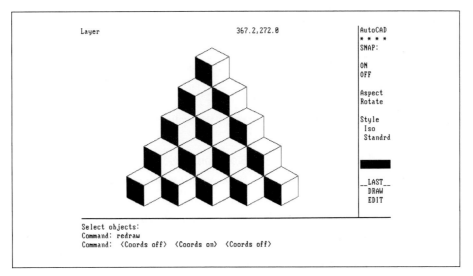

FIGURE 7.15: Isometric 2-D drawing. The above 3-D illusion is a 2-D drawing created using Isometric snap. The top, left, and right Isometric snap styles were used to create the faces of one cube, which was then copied to produce the final illusion. Even in AutoCAD Release 10, which includes true 3-D modeling capability, there is still a place for isometric drawing. For example, solids are not filled when viewed from a non-plan viewing angle. This makes the Isometric feature indispensable if you want to draw filled solids that appear to be angled in 3-D space.

USAGE

AutoCAD's extremely high level of drawing precision can sometimes get in the way. Point snapping allows you to draw with a high degree of accuracy in those cases where relationships between most entities in the drawing are fixed at some level of tolerance. For example, in rendering certain architectural drawings, accuracy to within an inch or more might be acceptable. When snap is on, the movement of the crosshairs will be confined to points found on a two-dimensional rectangular grid, skipping all points in between. Although the grid is always rectangular, you have a number of options regarding the relationships between the snap points, as explained in the command options.

Remember to use two different commands when employing the Isometric snap feature: Snap S I followed by Isoplane. Remember also that while the snap points are set in Isometric mode, Ctrl-E will toggle between the three isometric angles. Refer to the discussion of the Isoplane command in this chapter for details.

Point snapping can be enabled and disabled at any time, even while in the middle of another command. On most systems, the F9 function key toggles point snapping. Ctrl-B does so as well.

RELATED COMMANDS

Grid, Setvar.

RELATED SYSTEM VARIABLES

Several system variables control the values associated with point snapping. They are:

SNAPANG	Rotation angle
SNAPBASE	Base point for origin and rotation of snap points
SNAPISOPAIR	Current isometric plane (top, right, or left)
SNAPMODE	Snap enabled or disabled
SNAPSTYLE	Snap style, either Standard or Isometric
SNAPUNIT	Snap-point spacing in x and y orientations

Refer to Chapter 13 for details regarding these variables and the values they contain.

SAMPLE DIALOG

The result of the following sample dialog can be seen in Figure 7.16.

```
Command: Snap
Snap spacing or ON/OFF/Aspect/Rotate/Style: S
Standard/Isometric: I
Vertical spacing: .5
Command: (press Enter)
Snap spacing or ON/OFF/Aspect/Rotate/Style: R
Base point <0,0>: (press Enter)
Rotation angle <0>: 30
Command: (press Enter)
Snap spacing or ON/OFF/Aspect/Rotate/Style: ON
Command:
```

TIME

Allows you to access a special timer that indicates dates and times spent editing the current drawing.

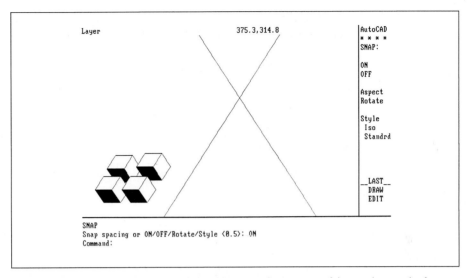

FIGURE 7.16: Snap spacing per sample dialog. The unusual orientation of the crosshairs in this figure is the result of rotating the snap points while they are set to Isometric snap style. The cubes in the lower left indicate how the snap points were rotated. This, of course, is a 2-D drawing—the hidden-line illusion was created in a matter of seconds using the Trim command to remove portions of lines, and complex solids to create the appearance of hidden portions of the solid faces.

VERSIONS

2.5 and later.

COMMAND OPTIONS

When you first invoke the Time command, AutoCAD displays statistics as seen in Figure 7.17.

The first line, "Current time," indicates the status of the internal system clock when the Time command was invoked. The second line, "Drawing created," indicates the date and time the drawing was first created; this line never changes. The third line, "Drawing last updated," indicates the last date and time the drawing file was saved with the End or Save command. All times are expressed in 24-hour format, where, for example, "16:36" equals 4:36 P.M.

The fourth line, "Time in drawing editor," indicates the total time of all editing sessions on this drawing to date. The fifth line, "Elapsed timer," indicates the total time spent during the current drawing session (or since the timer was reset). The final line, "Timer on(off)," indicates whether or not the internal timer is currently accumulating time.

```
Command: TIME

Current time:          15 Mar 1991 at 01:32:47.020
Drawing created:       05 Jan 1989 at 08:43:14.420
Drawing last updated:  30 Aug 1990 at 01:21:59.510
Time in drawing editor: 0 days 01:58:10.990
Elapsed timer:          0 days 00:10:23.240
Timer on.
Display/ON/OFF/Reset: R
Timer reset.
Display/ON/OFF/Reset: D

Current time:          15 Mar 1991 at 01:32:49.880
Drawing created:       05 Jan 1989 at 08:43:14.420
Drawing last updated:  30 Aug 1990 at 01:21:59.510
Time in drawing editor: 0 days 01:58:13.850
Elapsed timer:          0 days 00:00:01.370
Timer on.
Display/ON/OFF/Reset:

Command:
```

FIGURE 7.17: Statistics displayed using the Time command. Invoking the Time command produces a short statistical report indicating the amount of time spent in the drawing editor during the current drawing session, and the amount of time spent editing the drawing since it was created. In the above figure, AutoCAD's drawing timer is reset. Notice the difference between the "Elapsed timer" line before and after the Reset option. Times displayed are in military format; the current time displayed is 4:36 P.M.

After the display of time statistics, AutoCAD displays the following prompt:

Display/ON/OFF/Reset:

Display   Enter **D** to repeat the display of the time statistics, showing accumulations since the last display.

ON   Enter **ON** to turn the internal timer on, if it was previously turned off.

OFF   Enter **OFF** to stop the timer and prevent any further accumulation of time—for example, if you are taking a break while the drawing editor remains on the screen.

Reset   Enter **R** if you wish to reset the current timer to zero; total accumulations of time will remain unchanged.

USAGE

AutoCAD uses the computer's internal system clock to record the date and time a drawing was created and last edited, the total amount of time spent in the drawing editor since the drawing was created, and the total amount of time spent so far during the current drawing session.

So that the Time command can return meaningful statistics, your operating system's internal clock must be accurately set for the correct date and time before you enter AutoCAD's drawing editor.

To set the current date and time accurately, you must use whatever internal clock mechanisms are available in your particular hardware and operating-system configuration. Many users must enter the current date and time whenever they turn on the computer. Some hardware systems are equipped with battery-operated internal clocks and special software that automatically enters this information, setting the operating system's internal clock when you boot up the computer.

> *Warning:* Add-on hardware clocks are not always accurate in computers that operate at certain speeds. If using a battery-operated clock or other automatic hardware clock mechanism, check it often for accuracy.

RELATED SYSTEM VARIABLES

CDATE (current date/time), DATE (date in Julian format), TDCREATE (date and time the drawing was created), TDINDWG (time spent in this drawing session), TDUPDATE (date and time of last update using Save or End command), TDUSERTIMER (elapsed time in this drawing session, or since last reset). All these system variables are read-only. Those values that can be changed may be changed only by means of the Time command.

SAMPLE DIALOG

The sample dialog shown in Figure 7.17 resets the internal timer to zero. Note the change in "Elapsed timer," while "Time in drawing editor" continues to accumulate.

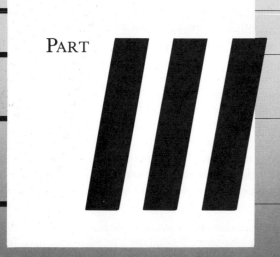

PART

III

AutoCAD's Drawing Tools

AutoCAD drawings are based fundamentally on combinations of simple drawing entities: long and short straight-line segments, arcs, circles, and various solid-filled polygon shapes. Likewise, the foundation of AutoCAD is the set of commands used to produce these basic drawing entities. Auto-CAD does not stop there, however. In addition to the tools provided to produce fundamental drawing entities, AutoCAD provides a set of sophisticated commands that produce more complex entity types: poly-lines, blocks, shapes, ellipses, polygon meshes, and so on. The more you understand the various drawing tools at your disposal, the better you are able to pick and choose between them, selecting the right tool for any situation. Part III introduces AutoCAD's simple and complex drawing entities, and the tools used to create and reproduce them.

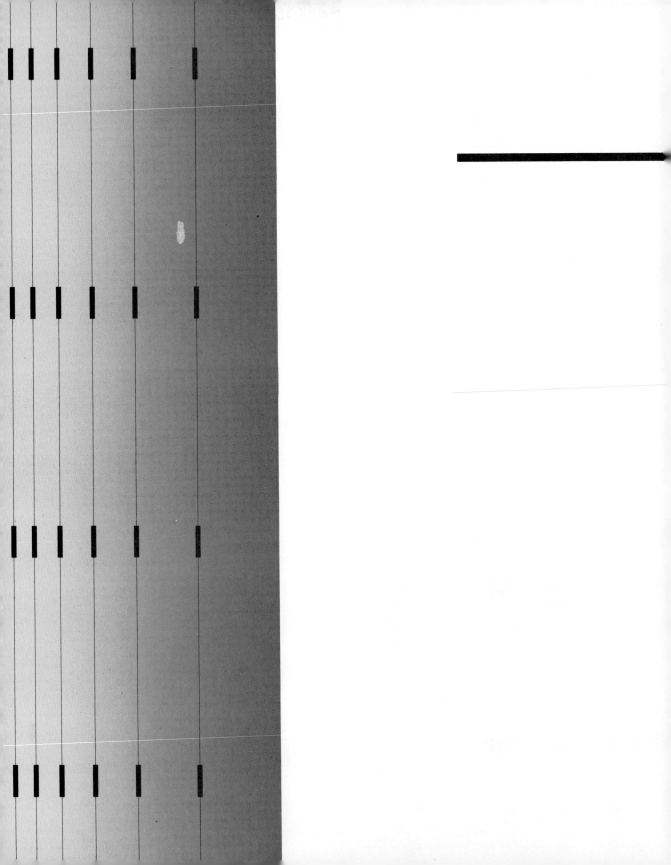

CHAPTER 8

CREATING SIMPLE ENTITIES

CREATING SIMPLE ENTITIES

A simple entity is an AutoCAD drawing entity consisting of a single, irreducible unit of graphic information. Examples of simple entities are 2-D and 3-D line segments, arcs, circles, faces, points, solids, and traces. You can create a simple entity by entering a minimal amount of coordinate point information as required by AutoCAD to display it on the screen or to produce hard-copy output. For example, to create a line segment, you must provide two coordinate points that indicate the endpoints of the line. AutoCAD then draws the line between the two specified points.

Often there is more than one set of coordinate points that can be used to generate a given entity. Because of this, AutoCAD provides various optional methods of producing the same result. In addition, as was discussed in Chapter 5, there are several methods for entering coordinate information. For the neophyte Auto-CAD user, these entity-creation options may produce an illusion of complexity where none really exists.

For example, you can create the same circle by entering a center point and a radius, by entering the endpoints of the circle's diameter, or by selecting three points and having AutoCAD draw a circle that joins them. For another example, consider the arc; there are a dozen optional methods for creating this simple entity!

When simple entities can be created by various means, you can be certain that each method has its own distinct advantages, depending on the drafting situation. You can choose the method that suits you best, based on such considerations as your own particular drawing style, or the existence of other entities whose construction points can be used to help you generate new entities—for example, placing the endpoint of a line at an intersection using Osnap.

In AutoCAD Release 10 and earlier, the format for keyboard entry of coordinate points and distance values is controlled by the default drawing-units format. You may refer to Chapter 6 for a detailed discussion of the Units command, which defines the format for keyboard entry of these values.

ENTERING COORDINATE POINTS

The information in this chapter outlines the various options for generating simple entities in AutoCAD. You may wish to refer to Chapter 5 for a detailed presentation of the methods for entering coordinate point information. For quick reference, however, that information is briefly summarized here:

Absolute Coordinates   Entered as real numbers separated by commas; for example:

   2,2.25,5.875

Relative Coordinates   Entered as above, but preceded by the @ symbol, indicating that the coordinate information is relative to the previously selected point; for example:

   @1.25,2,12

Polar Coordinates   Entered using a distance and absolute angle value, relative to the last point picked. For example,

   @2.25<90

indicates a distance of 2.25 drawing units from the previously selected point, at an angle of 90 degrees.

Pointing-Device Pick   Entered by moving the crosshairs to the desired point on the screen (often assisted by Snap or Osnap) and selecting the point with the pick button on the pointing device. This method is used to enter the x and y coordinates in the current construction plane; to enter a point in 3-D space using the crosshairs, you must either use point filters or set a nonzero value for the ELEVATION system variable.

3DFACE

Draws 2-D planes at any orientation in 3-D space.

VERSIONS

Version 2.6 and later. Starting with Release 10, any of a 3-D face's edges can be made invisible.

COMMAND OPTIONS

First point   Select the first endpoint of the 3-D face's beginning edge. You may use any of AutoCAD's standard methods for entering 3-D points.

Second point   Enter the opposite endpoint of the 3-D face's starting edge.

Third point   Enter the endpoint of the next edge of the 3-D face. If you are drawing a triangular plane, press Enter after entering this point; AutoCAD then displays the constructed triangular 3-D face.

Fourth point   If constructing a quadrilateral 3-D face, enter the endpoint of the 3-D face's third edge. The fourth edge is automatically constructed from this point and the original starting point.

Complex planes   After you enter the fourth point, AutoCAD repeats the "Third point" prompt. If you press Enter in response to this prompt, AutoCAD constructs the quadrilateral plane. If you enter another point, AutoCAD builds another plane section, beginning with the edge formed by the previously selected point and the currently selected point. After you select this point, AutoCAD repeats the "Fourth point" prompt. If you press Enter in response to this prompt, AutoCAD constructs a triangular plane section formed by the last three selected points, and repeats the "Third point" prompt. When you press Enter in response to this prompt, AutoCAD ends the command.

If, however, you select another point in response to the "Fourth point" prompt, AutoCAD constructs another quadrilateral plane section using the last four selected points, and repeats the "Third point" prompt. When you press Enter in response to this prompt, AutoCAD ends the command.

This continues until you press Enter rather than picking a point at the "Third point" prompt.

USAGE

The 3-D face is an "opaque" plane section—opaque because it will obstruct entities that are positioned behind it during a Hide command. 3-D faces can be combined to construct complex 3-D shapes and surfaces.

3-D faces can be constructed as quadrilateral or triangular plane sections, or as combinations of the two.

Figure 8.1 illustrates triangular, quadrilateral, and complex planes, and the order in which the points were entered to produce them. In order to become comfortable with the process, you may wish to practice building complex 3-D faces in the current construction plane.

Invisible edges (available in Release 10 and later) allow a set of 3-D faces to appear as a single plane having many sides, as illustrated in Figure 8.2. The process of making some edges of a series of 3-D faces invisible is best learned after you have practiced and acquired some experience building 3-D faces.

To make an edge invisible, you must inform AutoCAD that you intend for the edge to be invisible before you enter the first point of that edge. To inform AutoCAD that an upcoming edge is invisible, type **I** before selecting that edge's first

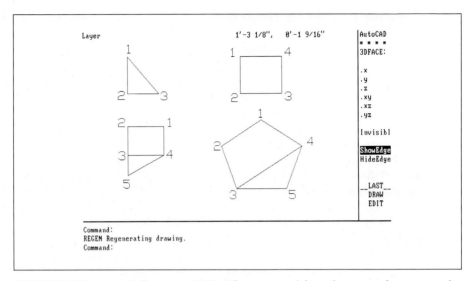

FIGURE 8.1: 3-D faces. In this figure, AutoCAD's 3Dface command draws three-point, four-point, and five-point planes in plan view. All edges are visible. The numbers indicate the order of entry for the corner points. By entering points carefully, you can build relatively complex planes such as the five-sided plane in the lower right.

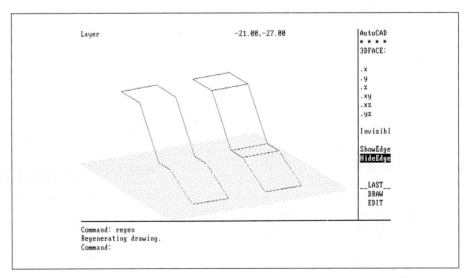

FIGURE 8.2: 3-D faces with invisible and visible edges. The 3-D faces on the left use invisible edges to give the appearance of a single plane that has been "bent" in 3-D space. The copy of this entity on the right reveals the invisible edges that do not appear in the figure on the left. The figure on the left may be entered using the sample dialog found in this reference entry.

point. The *I* must also be entered before using any other point-selection aids, such as Osnap or point filters, to indicate the edge's first point. The sample dialog contains examples of how and when to enter the *I* that makes an upcoming edge invisible.

If you are new to the process of constructing a series of 3-D faces, making some edges invisible may not seem particularly intuitive, since you must enter the *I* for the upcoming edge, before you have entered the point that will complete the current edge. Practice and patience are your best allies when acquiring expertise in building complex 3-D faces. Try variations on the sample dialog in order to get a feel for how it is done.

Tip: In Release 10 and later, the easiest way to construct a series of coplanar 3-D faces is to first change the current UCS to align with the faces you intend to construct. If there is no current entity that can be used to align the UCS, draw the first face using absolute world coordinates; then use it to align the UCS, switch to plan view, and construct the remainder. Also in Release 10 and later, complex surfaces that behave as if constructed from 3-D faces can be quickly constructed using a *polygon mesh,* as described in Chapter 9.

Warning: It is possible to create 3-D faces with corners that are not coplanar. Such 3-D faces may appear "folded" or impossible to view accurately from any angle. They will not be opaque; that is, entities that lie behind them will remain visible when a Hide command is invoked.

RELATED COMMANDS

Solid.

SAMPLE DIALOG

The following sample dialog constructs the 3-D faces illustrated in Figure 8.2. For clarity, absolute world coordinates are used to indicate the endpoints of the edges. To construct the faces without invisible edges, omit the *I* responses before entering coordinate points.

```
Command: 3Dface
First point: 1,5,10
Second point: 1,10,10
Third point: I 6,10,10
Fourth point: 6,5,10
Third point: I 11,5,3
Fourth point: 11,10,3
Third point: I 14,10,3
Fourth point: 14,5,3
Third point: 20,5,0
```

Fourth point: **20,10,0**
Third point: **(press Enter)**
Command:

ARC

Draws simple arcs in the current construction plane using a variety of options.

VERSIONS

All.

COMMAND OPTIONS

The command options are explained below and include sample dialogs. As shown, absolute coordinate points are entered using the keyboard, but they may be selected just as easily using any of AutoCAD's standard point-selection methods and drawing aids.

Three-point arc   The *three-point arc* is perhaps the simplest arc to draw. Select any three coplanar points and AutoCAD will draw the arc required to connect them. The first selected point is considered the arc's starting point, and the arc is drawn counterclockwise, connecting the remaining two points. (If you have configured AutoCAD to measure angles clockwise, arcs will be drawn clockwise instead of counterclockwise.)

After the first two points are selected, AutoCAD displays a rubberband arc connecting the selected points and the intersection of the crosshairs as it moves about on the screen. Figure 8.3 illustrates a typical three-point arc connecting some previously drawn intersections.

The command dialog for a three-point arc is as follows:

Command: **Arc**
Center/<Start point>: **1,1**
Center/End/<Second point>: **5,4**
End point: **9,1**
Command:

Start, Center, Endpoint (S,C,E)   The *start, center, endpoint arc* also uses three coordinate points; the second point defines the center point of the circle of which the arc is a part. Such an arc is illustrated in Figure 8.4.

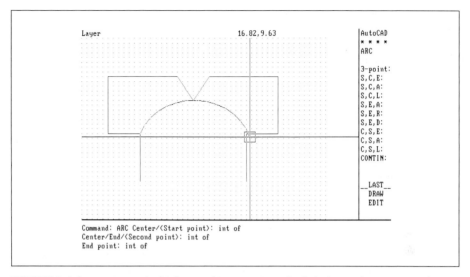

FIGURE 8.3: A three-point arc. In this figure, object snap is used to help draw a three-point arc, by selecting intersection points for each of the arc's required three points. The first two intersections have been found, and the final intersection point is within the aperture. AutoCAD previews the resulting arc as a curved rubberband line, extending through the first two selection points and ending at the current intersection of the crosshairs (not the point that AutoCAD will snap to when the user presses the pick button).

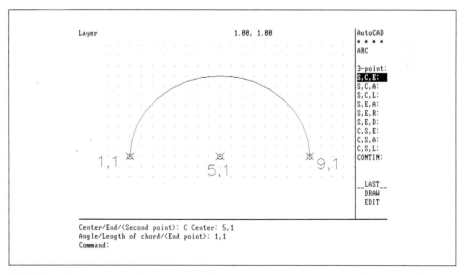

FIGURE 8.4: Start, center, endpoint arc. In this figure, the user has again selected three points, but has indicated to AutoCAD that the second point is the center of the arc. The selected points are, in order, 9,1; 5,1; and 1,1.

If the specified endpoint does not intersect an arc with the selected starting point and center point, AutoCAD draws an arc anyway, using the selected starting point and center point, and ends the arc at a point that is collinear with the starting and ending point, as illustrated in Figure 8.5. The command dialog of a start, center, endpoint arc is as follows:

Command: **Arc**
Center/<Start point>: **9,1**
Center/End/<Second point>: **C** Center: **5,1**
Angle/Length of chord/<End point>: **1,1**
Command:

Center, Start, Endpoint (C,S,E) The *center, start, endpoint arc* is similar to the start, center, endpoint arc just explained. In this case, however, the center point is entered first, followed by the arc's starting point. In all other respects it follows the same rules. Notice the slight difference in the command dialog shown below:

Command: **Arc**
Center/<Start point>: **C** Center: **5,1**
Start point: **9,1**

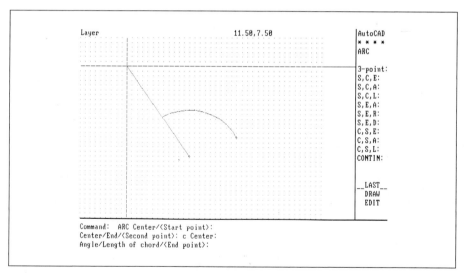

FIGURE 8.5: Start, center, endpoint arc—collinear endpoint. In this figure, the user has entered a start and center point for an arc using the pointing device. Because an arc with the requested starting and center point cannot pass through the current intersection of the crosshairs, AutoCAD does the next best thing, placing the endpoint on a rubberband line that extends between the arc's center point and the intersection of the crosshairs, as illustrated. This is also a rubberband arc, meaning that it will change as the crosshairs are moved, until a point is selected. When the point is selected, AutoCAD draws the arc.

Angle/Length of chord/<End point>: **1,1**
Command:

Start, Endpoint, Center Point (S,C,E) The *start, endpoint, center point arc* is similar to the other three-point arcs just described, except for the order in which the points are entered. The included angle of the arc and its resulting "bulge" are determined by the location of the arc's center point, which must be oriented so that an arc is possible.

When the location of the arc's center point is such that an arc cannot be drawn between the two selected points, AutoCAD will draw the arc from the starting point to a point that is collinear with the center point and the selected endpoint. Such an arc is illustrated in Figure 8.6. The command dialog that produces this arc is listed below:

Command: **Arc**
Center/<Start point>: **5,1**
Center/End/<Second point>: **E**
End point: **5,4**
Angle/Direction/Radius/<Center point>: **4,3**
Command:

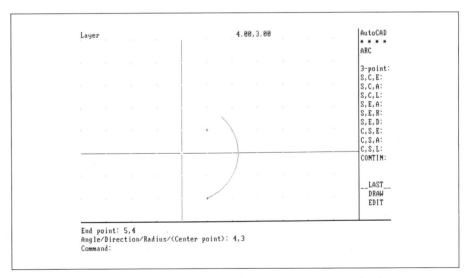

FIGURE 8.6: Start, endpoint, center point arc. In this figure, the arc's starting and ending points are drawn first—notice the small blips on the screen—and AutoCAD prompts for the center point. As in the previous figure, an arc with the indicated start, end, and center point will not end exactly at the chosen endpoint, so AutoCAD places the arc endpoint on an imaginary line that extends through the selected endpoint and center point.

Start, Center, Included Angle (S,C,A)   The *start, center, included angle arc* is constructed from two coordinate points and from the arc's included angle from the starting point. Arcs generated using this option are normally drawn counterclockwise. There are two ways to draw the arc clockwise. One is to change AutoCAD's default angle-measurement configuration from counterclockwise to clockwise. The other is to enter the included angle as a negative number. Entering angles as negative numbers always causes them to be drawn in the reverse direction of the current configuration. The following sample dialog produces the arc shown in Figure 8.7:

```
Command: Arc
Center/<Start point>: 5,1
Center/End/<Second point>: C Center: 3,3
Angle/Length of chord/<End point>: A
Included angle: 270
Command:
```

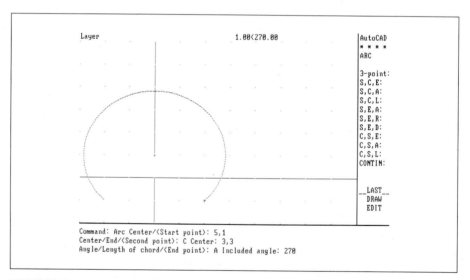

FIGURE 8.7: Start, center, included angle arc. In this figure, the user entered the arc's starting point and center, and is now indicating the included angle of the arc by means of the pointing device. The current position of the crosshairs is 270 degrees from the last point referenced (the arc's center point), and AutoCAD displays a rubberband 270-degree arc with the indicated center point. In addition to the rubberband arc, a rubberband line extends from the arc's center point to the current location of the crosshairs, "erasing" the congruent portion of the crosshair line.

Center, Start, Included Angle (C,S,A)   The *center, start, included angle arc* is similar to the start, center, included angle arc just described, except that the center point is entered first, followed by the starting point and the included-angle value. This necessitates a slight change in the command dialog, as shown below:

Command: **Arc**
Center/<Start point>: **C** Center: **3,3**
Start point: **5,1**
Angle/Length of chord/<End point>: **A**
Included angle: **270**
Command:

Start, End, Included Angle (S,E,A) The *start, end, included angle arc* is generated by entering the arc's endpoints first, followed by the included angle of the arc that joins them. The included angle will determine the radius of the resulting arc, as well as its location in the construction plane relative to the arc's endpoints. Figure 8.8 illustrates two such arcs. In both examples, the endpoints are equally spaced, but the included-angle value causes a significant difference in the location of each arc's center point.

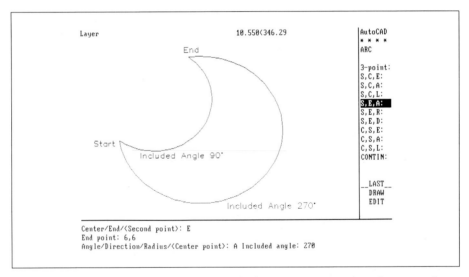

FIGURE 8.8: Two start, end, included angle arcs. In this figure, two arcs were drawn by entering the same start and end points, followed by different included angles. In this case, the angles were entered using the keyboard. The difference in the arcs' included angles accounts for the difference in their size. Because the arcs' endpoints are fixed, AutoCAD must adjust the center point and radius of each arc so that each arc may start and end at the requested points.

When AutoCAD's angle-measurement system is set to the default, arcs will be drawn counterclockwise unless the included angle is entered as a negative number. If the angle-measurement system is reconfigured to clockwise, the reverse is true.

The following sample dialog generates a start, end, included angle arc:

```
Command: Arc
Center/<Start point>: 1,1
Center/End/<Second point>: E
End point: 5,4
Angle/Direction/Radius/<Center point>: A
Included angle: 90
Command:
```

Start, Center, Length of Chord (S,C,L)   The *start, center, length of chord arc* is constructed of two coordinate points and a value—the length of the *arc chord*. The arc chord is the straight line, perpendicular to the line joining the arc's center and midpoint, that connects the arc's endpoints. Such an arc is illustrated in Figure 8.9.

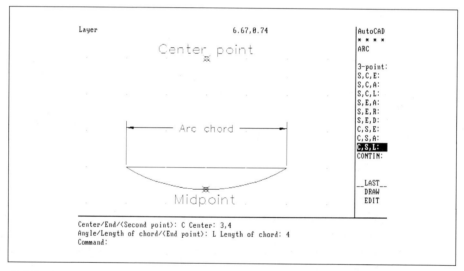

FIGURE 8.9: Start, center, length of chord arc. This arc is drawn by entering the starting point, the center point, and the length of the arc's chord. The arc's chord is the straight line connecting the start and endpoint of the arc; it is always perpendicular to, and bisected by, an imaginary line drawn between the arc's center point and midpoint. The length of the chord, as it extends from the starting point, will determine the location of the arc's endpoint as well.

AutoCAD always draws this type of arc counterclockwise, regardless of the default setting for angle measurement. Also, AutoCAD will draw a minor arc (less than 180 degrees) when the value for the chord length is positive. Entering a negative value for the length of the chord will cause a major arc (greater than 180 degrees) to be drawn.

The command dialog for drawing a start, center, length of chord arc is as follows:

```
Command: Arc
Center/<Start point>: 1,1
Center/End/<Second point>: C Center: 3,4
Angle/Length of chord/<End point>: L
Length of chord: 4
Command:
```

Center, Start, Length of Chord (C,S,L)   The *center, start, length of chord arc* is a variation on the arc just described; the difference is that the center point is entered
first, followed by the starting point. The command dialog is therefore slightly
different, as in the following example:

```
Command: Arc
Center/<Start point>: C
Center: 3,4
Start point: 1,1
Angle/Length of chord/<End point>: L
Length of chord: 4
Command:
```

Start, End, Length of Radius (S,E,R)   The *start, end, length of radius arc* is generated by entering a start point, an endpoint, and the length of the arc's radius.
The length of the radius will determine the location of the arc's center point and
the amount of "bulge" of the arc. AutoCAD always draws this type of arc counterclockwise, regardless of the default setting for angle measurement. Also,
AutoCAD will draw a minor arc (less than 180 degrees) when the radius value is
positive. Entering a negative value for the radius will cause a major arc (greater
than 180 degrees) to be drawn.

AutoCAD will signal if an impossible radius value is entered—that is, if the
length of the radius is less than half the distance between the two endpoints. In
such an event, the Arc command is canceled, and you must reenter the arc endpoints and radius value.

The following sample dialog produces an arc like the one illustrated in
Figure 8.10:

```
Command: Arc
Center/<Start point>: 1,1
Center/End/<Second point>: E
End point: 10,1
Angle/Direction/Radius/<Center point>: R
Radius: 6
Command:
```

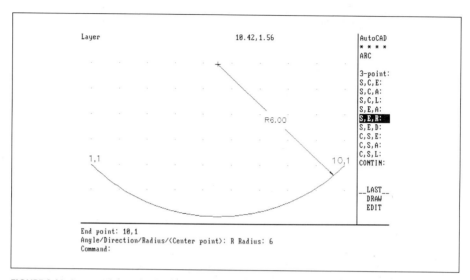

FIGURE 8.10: Start, end, length of radius arc. This arc was drawn by entering a starting point of 1,1, an ending point of 10,1, and a radius of 6. AutoCAD calculates the location of the arc's center point and its included angle based on these three parameters. Because the arc's radius was entered as a positive number, AutoCAD located the center point so that the resulting arc is less than 180 degrees. It is possible to draw an arc greater than 180 degrees using these parameters; AutoCAD would have drawn that arc instead if the radius had been entered as a negative number.

Arc Continuation   This form of an arc can be used when you wish to create an arc that begins tangent to the last line or arc drawn. When you respond to the first prompt by pressing Enter, AutoCAD takes the starting point from the last arc or line endpoint, and its direction from the orientation of the last arc or line. You may then select the endpoint, and the arc is drawn. An example of this arc is illustrated in Figure 8.11. The following sample dialog generates this type of arc, tangent to the endpoint of a previously drawn line:

> Command: **Line**
> From point: **1,1**
> To point: **5,5**
> To point: **(press Enter)**
> Command: **Arc**
> Center/<Start point>: **(press Enter)**
> End point: **3,7**
> Command:

Start, End, Starting Direction (S,E,D)   The *start, end, starting direction arc* is generated by entering a starting and ending point, followed by an angle direction in which AutoCAD is to begin drawing the arc. The starting direction determines the location of the arc's center point, its radius, and the amount of

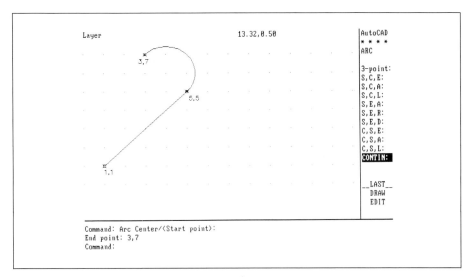

FIGURE 8.11: Arc continuation from line endpoint. When a line is drawn, AutoCAD remembers its endpoint and angle of orientation. In the above figure, the user has pressed Enter in response to the prompt for the arc's starting point. AutoCAD interprets this response to mean that the arc is to be drawn tangent to the line segment. AutoCAD uses the line's endpoint as the arc's starting point, and the line's orientation as the arc's starting angle. All that is needed to draw the arc is an endpoint. The center point, radius, and included angle will be calculated so as to draw the arc with the requested starting angle to the selected endpoint.

"bulge" in the arc. This method is helpful when you wish to draw an arc that is tangent to a previously drawn entity, and you can no longer access that entity by simply pressing Enter at the prompt for a starting point.

An arc of this type is illustrated in Figure 8.12. Here is the command dialog that generates this type of arc:

Command: **Arc**
Center/<Start point>: **END** of **(pick endpoint of line)**
Center/End/<Second point>: **E**
End point: **(pick arc endpoint)**
Angle/Direction/Radius/<Center point>: **D**
Direction from start point: **@1<45**
Command:

USAGE

The Arc command constructs a simple arc based on three selected coordinate points, or two coordinate points and a value that makes construction of an arc possible. Coordinate points may be the arc's endpoints, its midpoint, or the center point of the circle of which the arc is a part. The selected coordinate points

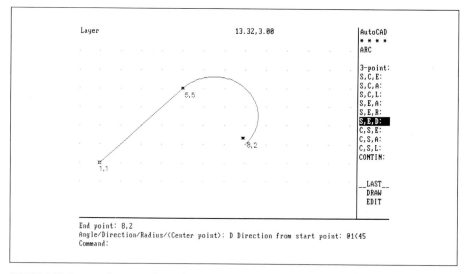

```
Layer                          13.32,3.00          AutoCAD
                                                   * * * *
                                                   ARC

                                                   3-point:
                                                   S,C,E:
                                                   S,C,A:
                  5,5                              S,C,L:
                                                   S,E,A:
                                                   S,E,R:
                                                   S,E,D:
                                                   C,S,E:
                              8,2                  C,S,A:
                                                   C,S,L:
                                                   CONTIN:

         1,1                                       __LAST__
                                                   DRAW
                                                   EDIT


End point: 8,2
Angle/Direction/Radius/<Center point>: D Direction from start point: @1<45
Command:
```

FIGURE 8.12: Start, end, starting direction arc. In the above figure, the user indicates that the arc is to begin at the endpoint of the line by selecting it with the pointing device, instead of pressing Enter. Picking the point allows the user to draw the arc with a starting angle that is not tangent to the line. The user next picks the arc endpoint (8,2) using the pointing device. Finally, the user indicates the starting angle for the arc. AutoCAD draws the requested arc using the requested points and angle. Even though an arc with these parameters cannot fall exactly on the requested endpoint, AutoCAD draws the arc, letting the arc end as close to the requested endpoint as possible.

must lie within the current construction plane; absolute entry of 3-D points is not allowed.

If you're constructing an arc using coordinate points plus a value, the required value may be the arc's included angle, length of chord, radius, or arc direction. Any combination of points and values that makes construction of an arc possible is permitted, but they must be entered in a specific sequence, as described in the Command Options section.

When you enter coordinate points for arcs, all of AutoCAD's standard point-entry methods are valid. When entering distance and angle values, you may supply the values by picking a point on the screen. AutoCAD will extend a rubberband line from the last selected point to the intersection of the crosshairs. In the case of distance values, AutoCAD will supply the distance between the two points as the entered value. When you provide angle values, AutoCAD will supply the absolute angle formed by the two points on the screen, using the current angle-measurement system (set with the Units command).

Warning: On some systems using AutoCAD Version 2.5 and later, curved lines may not appear as smooth curves, but rather as a series of short line segments. This is because of the current setting of the drawing view resolution, which may be changed using the Viewres command. Refer to Chapter 11 for more details on this command.

SAMPLE DIALOG

The Command Options section of this reference entry contains sample dialog for each of AutoCAD's arc options.

CIRCLE

Draws full circles in the current construction plane.

VERSIONS

All.

COMMAND OPTIONS

3P Enter **3P** if you wish to draw a three-point circle. AutoCAD responds by prompting for three coordinate points in turn, and then drawing a circle that intersects them. Figure 8.13 illustrates such a circle. The command sequence that creates the illustrated circle is as follows:

```
Command: Circle
3P/2P/TTR/<Center point>: 3P
First point: 5,4
Second point: 7,4
Third point: 6,8
Command:
```

2P Enter **2P** if you wish to draw a two-point circle. AutoCAD responds by prompting for two coordinate points and drawing a circle that intersects them. The two points you select will form the endpoints of the circle's diameter, and the orientation of these points will determine the location of the circle's center point. Figure 8.14 illustrates a two-point circle. The command sequence that creates the illustrated circle is as follows:

```
Command: Circle
3P/2P/TTR/<Center point>: 2P
First point on diameter: 5,4
Second point on diameter: @4<180
Command:
```

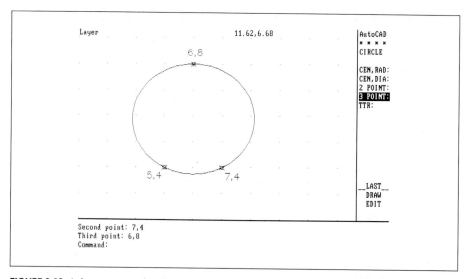

FIGURE 8.13: A three-point circle. The three-point circle illustrated in this figure is drawn by invoking the Circle command, entering **3P**, and entering three points that are parallel to the current construction plane. The three points can be entered in any order. In Release 10, the three points must have equal z coordinates in the current construction plane, or AutoCAD will not draw the circle.

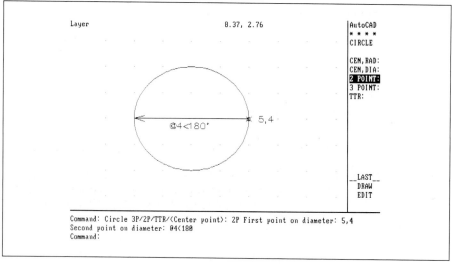

FIGURE 8.14: A two-point circle. Two-point circles are especially useful when the diameter of the circle is known, but not the center point. The above circle was drawn by invoking the Circle command, entering **2P** followed by coordinates for a point on the circle's circumference (5,4), and referencing the second point by means of polar coordinates, using the circle's diameter as the length parameter. This can be more convenient than stopping to calculate the circle's center point (which in this case would be point 3,4).

TTR   Enter **TTR** if you wish to draw a circle tangent to two other line entities. Select the two line entities—the tangent object-snap override is automatically enabled—and enter a specified radius. AutoCAD will draw the resulting circle tangent to the chosen entities, with the tangent points as close as possible to the points used to select the entities. The value of the radius will determine the circle's center point and resulting orientation. Figure 8.15 illustrates this type of circle. The command sequence that creates the illustrated circle is as follows:

Command: **Circle**
3P/2P/TTR/<Center point>: **TTR**
Enter Tangent spec: **(pick first circle)**
Enter second Tangent spec: **(pick second circle)**
Radius: **.25**
Command:

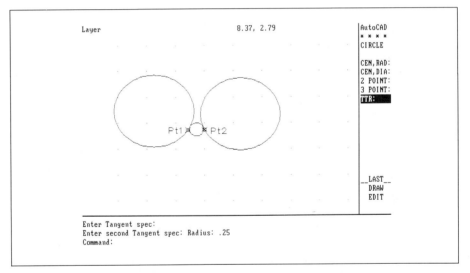

FIGURE 8.15: A circle tangent to two other circles. In this figure, a small circle with a known radius is drawn tangent to two larger circles, using the Circle TTR command. After the user invokes the circle command and enters **TTR**, AutoCAD prompts for two tangent points. (The tangent object-snap override is automatically enabled.) After the tangent points are entered, AutoCAD prompts for the radius. These parameters are used to determine the exact location of the requested circle. If the circle could not have been drawn, AutoCAD would have displayed the error message, "Circle does not exist."

Center point   You may also draw a circle by first specifying its center point. AutoCAD then responds by prompting for a diameter or radius. Such a circle is illustrated in Figure 8.16. Two methods for drawing this circle are listed in the following sample dialog:

> Command: **Circle**
> 3P/2P/TTR/<Center point>: **2,9**
> Diameter/<Radius>: **@3<90**
> Command:
>
> Command: **Circle**
> 3P/2P/TTR/<Center point>: **2,9**
> Diameter/<Radius>: **D**
> Diameter: **6**
> Command:

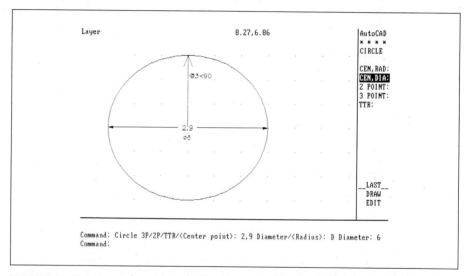

FIGURE 8.16: A center and radius (or diameter) circle. If the center point of the circle is known, you may create it by invoking the Circle command and entering the center point, followed by either the circle's diameter or its radius. You may enter the radius using the pointing device; or you may enter it from the keyboard, either by entering the radius value, or by referencing a point from the center point using polar coordinates. Alternatively, you may enter **D** followed by the diameter of the circle, as shown in the above Command-prompt area.

USAGE

The Circle command includes several options for drawing circles in a variety of situations. Circles may be drawn using two or three coordinate points, or a single coordinate point plus a value for either the radius or the diameter.

Tip: Polar coordinates make drawing and orienting circles easier. Refer to the sample dialogs for two-point and center-point circles to see examples of how polar coordinates can be used to define the radius and diameter of circles.

The Circle command will draw circles with only a standard line thickness of "zero." If you wish to draw circles using thick or weighted lines, or filled circles that are displayed and plotted as solids, use either the Donut command or the PLine command with the Arc option. Refer to Chapter 9 for details on using these commands to draw thick or filled circles.

On some systems using AutoCAD Version 2.5 and later, curved lines may appear not as smooth curves, but rather as a series of short line segments. This is because of the current setting of the drawing view resolution, which may be changed using the Viewres command. Refer to Chapter 11 for more details regarding this command.

If you attempt to create a circle using parameters that make drawing the circle impossible—for example, a circle tangent to two parallel lines with a radius less than half the distance between them—AutoCAD responds:

Circle does not exist.

and cancels the command.

Circles may only be drawn parallel to the *current* construction plane, or using 3-D points that have equal z coordinates. To draw circles in 3-D space, first change the construction plane, and then draw the circle and reset the previous construction plane. If you attempt to create a circle outside of the current construction plane, you will receive the following message:

Invalid 2nd Point

AutoCAD will repeat the circle prompt until it receives correct coordinate point and/or value information.

SAMPLE DIALOG

The Command Options section contains a sample dialog for each of Auto-CAD's arc options.

LINE

Creates continuous line segments between user-specified endpoints, either in the current construction plane, or (with Release 10) in 3-D space.

VERSIONS

All. Only 2-D lines are available in releases prior to Release 9. If your version is Release 9, you must use 3Dline to enter lines in 3-D space.

COMMAND OPTIONS

From point   After you invoke the Line command, AutoCAD responds by prompting for the starting point of the line. Enter the desired coordinate location of the line's starting point.

To point   After you enter the starting point, AutoCAD prompts for the endpoint of the line segment. When you move the pointing device, AutoCAD "previews" the line segment by displaying a rubberband line between the starting point and the intersection of the crosshairs. When the second point is entered, AutoCAD draws a line segment between the two points.

   Each time you enter an endpoint, AutoCAD assumes it to be the starting point for another line segment as well, and thus repeats the "To point:" prompt and the rubberband-line sample. When you are finished constructing additional continuous line segments, press Enter in response to the "To point:" prompt.

U   If you change your mind for any reason after selecting a line's endpoint, you may enter **U** (for "undo") in response to the "To point:" prompt. AutoCAD will then erase the previous line segment and show a new rubberband line extending from the previous starting point. You may continue to enter **U** and AutoCAD will continue to "back up" through the current Line command until all line segments are undone.

C   If the line segments are to form a polygon, you may draw the last line segment by entering **C** (for "close"). This option will draw a line segment from the last selected point to the original starting point—the point that was entered in response to the "From point:" prompt.

Press Return   The Enter (Return) key has two functions within the Line command. When you press Enter in response to the "From point:" prompt, AutoCAD will begin drawing line segments from the last endpoint selected during the previous Line or Arc command, if any. When you press Enter in response to the"To Point:" prompt, AutoCAD ends the Line command and redisplays the Command prompt.

USAGE

   Use the Line command to draw a single line segment or continuous, joined line segments that can be edited individually. To create line segments, sequentially pick the coordinate points that mark the line segment's endpoints, as illustrated in Figure 8.17. Coordinate points may be entered using any of AutoCAD's standard methods.

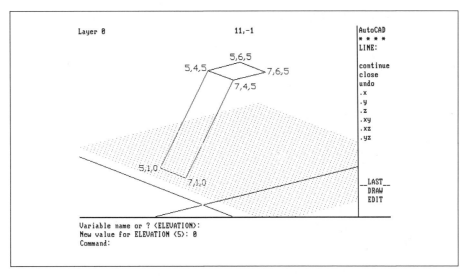

```
Layer 0                            11,-1              AutoCAD
                                                     * * * *
                                                     LINE:

                        5,6,5                        continue
              5,4,5                    7,6,5          close
                                                     undo
                              7,4,5                  .x
                                                     .y
                                                     .z
                                                     .xy
                                                     .xz
                                                     .yz

         5,1,0
              7,1,0                                 __LAST__
                                                     DRAW
                                                     EDIT

 Variable name or ? <ELEVATION>:
 New value for ELEVATION <5>: 0
 Command:
```

Figure 8.17: Line segments with the line command. These line segments were created using the sample dialog listed in the Line command section of this chapter. The viewing angle has been rotated to help you better visualize the relationships between the lines (notice the position of the grid and crosshairs). Although the sample dialog uses point filters and elevation changes to produce these lines, you could enter the same lines by referencing absolute 3-D coordinates. Refer to Chapter 5 for details about various means of coordinate-point entry.

In AutoCAD Release 9 and earlier, the Line command is used to create lines using x and y coordinate points only. In Version 2.18 and later, however, you may use the Line command to draw line segments in 3-D space that are parallel to the x-y construction plane, by changing the value of the ELEVATION system variable. Refer to Chapter 13 for details regarding system variables. You may draw lines parallel to the z-axis by entering points and giving them a thickness.

With Release 10 and later, *point filters* can be effectively used to enter the z coordinates of 3-D line endpoints when entering the x and y coordinates with the pointing device. Refer to Chapter 5 for details on point filters.

The Line command will draw line segments with only a standard line thickness of "zero." If you wish to draw line segments using thick or weighted lines, use the PLine or Trace command. Refer to Chapter 9 for details on using PLine. Details on the Trace command can be found later in this chapter.

Warning: If you draw a line segment or arc and subsequently erase it, that entity's endpoint is remembered by AutoCAD. If you then begin to draw another line segment and press Enter in response to the "From point:" prompt, AutoCAD will begin the current line segment at the erased entity's endpoint. In such a case, enter Ctrl-C to cancel the command, and use Osnap Endp to snap to the desired visible endpoint—unless, of course, the erased entity's endpoint is where you would like to begin!

When you wish to draw a line tangent from the endpoint of an arc and you press Enter in response to the "From point:" prompt, AutoCAD prompts only for the length of the line, since its orientation is already determined by the arc. In such a case, the rubberband line will not extend to the intersection of the crosshairs but instead will extend in the direction of the arc's tangent angle, showing a length equal to the distance between the starting point and the intersection of the crosshairs. Such a line is illustrated in Figure 8.18.

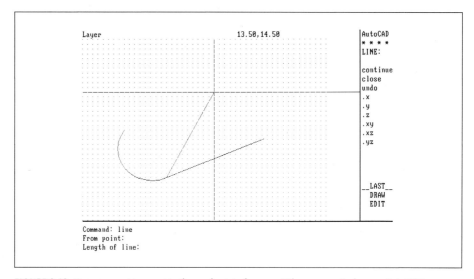

FIGURE 8.18: Line segment tangent to the endpoint of an arc. When an arc is drawn, AutoCAD remembers both its endpoints and its ending angle. If you invoke the line command and press Enter instead of picking a starting point, AutoCAD assume that you want to draw a line from the arc's endpoint, and at the same angle (i.e., a line tangment to the endpoint). Under these circumstances, the relative position of the crosshair is irrelevent, since the orientation of the line is already known. But the distance between the crosshairs and the arc endpoint is still very important, as AutoCAD uses that distance to determine the length of the line. (If you perfer you could enter the length of the keyboard.)

RELATED COMMANDS

PLine.

SAMPLE DIALOG

The following sample dialog produces the line segments illustrated in Figure 8.18. Coordinate points are shown as keyboard entry, but may be selected using the pointing device, or with polar or relative coordinates.

```
Command: LINE
From point: .xy of 5,4 (need Z) 5
To point: 5,1
To point: 7,1
To point: 'setvar
Variable name or ?: ELEVATION
New value for ELEVATION <0>: 5
Resuming LINE Command.
To point: 7,4
To point: 7,6
To point: 5,6
To point: 5,4
To point: 7,4
To point: (press Return)
Command: SETVAR
Variable name or ? <ELEVATION>: (press Return)
New value for ELEVATION <5>: 0
Command:
```

POINT

Places a point at a desired location in a drawing.

VERSIONS

All. In AutoCAD Version 2.6 and later, 3-D coordinates may be entered as locations for the Point command.

COMMAND OPTIONS

None. When you invoke the Point command, AutoCAD responds with the prompt "Point:". Enter the coordinates for the point location; AutoCAD places the point symbol, if any, at that location.

USAGE

Use the Point command to place a point symbol at any coordinate location in the drawing. You have the option of allowing the point symbols to remain absolute (enlarging as you zoom in, shrinking as you zoom out) or relative (staying the same size as you zoom in and out). In those cases where you intend to use the point as a "node" for Osnap, you may also choose to place no visible symbol at all.

Two system variables, PDMODE and PDSIZE, control the display of the point. PDMODE contains an integer value from 0 to 4 that represents a particular symbol for the point, as illustrated in Figure 8.20. You may add to this value either 32, 64, or 96, in order to draw a second symbol around the base symbol. If you add 32 to the base integer value, AutoCAD will draw a circle around the base symbol. Adding 64 causes AutoCAD to draw a square around the base symbol. Adding 96 causes AutoCAD to draw both a circle and a square around the base symbol, as illustrated in Figure 8.19.

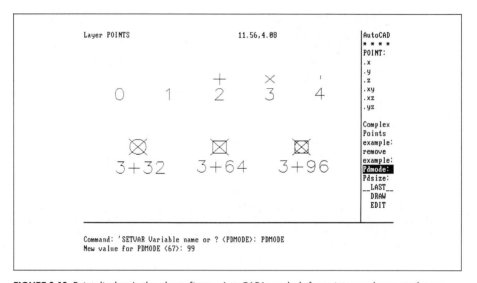

FIGURE 8.19: Point display. In the above figure, AutoCAD's symbols for points are shown on the top line, with the required integer setting for PDMODE underneath. Setting PDMODE to a value of 1 will suppress the display of points, but they may still be found by Osnap. In the above Command-prompt area, the point symbol is being changed from 67 (an X with a square, or 3 + 64) to 99 (an X with both circle and square, or 3 + 96). Once PDMODE has been set, regenerating the drawing will cause all points to be drawn using the same symbol.

The PDSIZE system variable controls the size of the point symbol specified with PDMODE. Relative sizes of the point symbols based on different values of PDSIZE are illustrated in Figure 8.20.

PDSIZE may also contain negative values. If so, the point symbols will be drawn relative to the screen size only, and thus will maintain the same size regardless of the current zoom factor of the drawing.

Warning: If you change the value of the PDMODE and PDSIZE system variables, points already entered in the drawing will not change in appearance until a regen is performed. If you have enabled "Fast Zoom mode" using the Viewres command and set the value of PDSIZE to a negative number, the point symbol may enlarge anyway when you zoom in. In these cases, in order to maintain the correct relative size of the point symbol, either set ''fast zooms'' off or perform a regen.

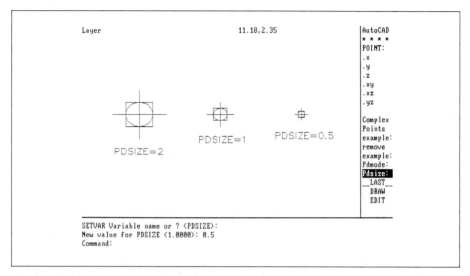

FIGURE 8.20: Different sizes for the point symbol—PDMODE = 98. In the above figure, the point symbol is established by setting the PDMODE system variable to 98 (2 for the cross, plus 96 to include a small circle and square). The PDSIZE system variable will adjust the size of the point symbol, shown here at relative sizes of 2, 1, and ½ drawing unit. Once PDSIZE is set, regenerating the drawing will cause all point symbols to be drawn at the same size.

RELATED SYSTEM VARIABLES

PDMODE, PDSIZE.

SAMPLE DIALOG

The following command sequence will place an *X* with a circle around it at the requested coordinate location:

Command: **Setvar**
Variable name or ?: **PDMODE**
New value for PDMODE: **35**
Command: **Point**
Point: **5,4**
Command:

SOLID

Draws 2-D filled quadrilateral or triangular solids.

VERSIONS

All.

COMMAND OPTIONS

First point   Select the first endpoint of the solid's beginning edge. You may use any of AutoCAD's standard methods for entering points.

Second point   Enter the opposite endpoint of the solid's starting edge.

Third point   If the solid is triangular, enter the final endpoint that will define the solid, and press Enter to complete the command. AutoCAD will then render the constructed solid. If, however, you are constructing a quadrilateral solid, enter the starting endpoint of the edge opposite (that is, not intersecting) the solid's starting edge. Refer to Figure 8.21 for an illustration of the relative position of the solid's third point.

Fourth point   If constructing a quadrilateral solid, enter the endpoint of the edge opposite the solid's starting edge. AutoCAD then constructs the solid, and if fill mode is on, fills the solid using the direction and length of the two edges you entered.

Complex solids   After you enter the fourth point, AutoCAD repeats the "Third point:" prompt. If you press Enter in response to this prompt, AutoCAD ends the command. You may enter another point, however. If you intend to construct another quadrilateral solid adjacent to the first, this point should be the starting endpoint of the edge opposite the previous edge. AutoCAD then repeats the "Fourth point:" prompt. If you press Enter in response to this prompt, AutoCAD constructs a triangular solid using the last three selected points, and repeats the "Third point:" prompt. If you press Enter in response to this prompt, AutoCAD ends the command. If, however, you select another point in response to the "Fourth point:" prompt, AutoCAD will fill in another quadrilateral section, using the last four selected points. AutoCAD then repeats the "Third point:" prompt, starting the process all over again. If you press Enter in response to this prompt, AutoCAD ends the command.

Figure 8.22 (presented with the sample dialog) illustrates the process of building a complex solid entity and the order in which points must be entered to achieve the desired result.

USAGE

To construct a filled solid entity, invoke the Solid command. AutoCAD then prompts for the corner points of the solid you intend to construct.

How you enter the corner points is as important as entering the points themselves, because AutoCAD uses the order in which you select the corner points to determine how the solid is to be filled. Figure 8.21 illustrates the order in which the corner points of a rectangular solid must be entered to achieve a correctly filled solid.

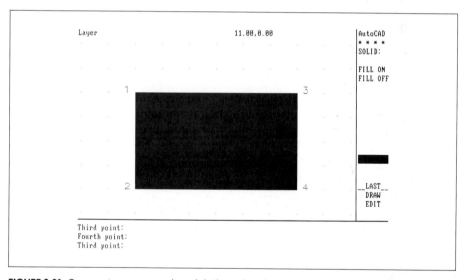

FIGURE 8.21: Constructing a rectangular solid. The order of point entry for solids is slightly different from the order of point entry for 3-D faces. When you enter a solid, AutoCAD needs to know not only the solid's corner points, but also how to fill the solid area. In the above figure, the coordinate points are entered first from top to bottom on the left (1 and 2), and then from top to bottom on the right (3 and 4). AutoCAD then draws the solid by filling the area from top to bottom, as indicated by the order of point entry.

Solids appear as unfilled outlines when AutoCAD's fill mode is off. You may toggle fill mode on and off by using the Fill command, or by changing the values of the FILLMODE system variable. Refer to Chapter 6 for details regarding the Fill command, and to Chapter 13 for details on FILLMODE.

When you're constructing a complex series of solids, it is helpful to draw an outline first, using a polyline. The vertex points of the polyline can then be used, along with Osnap Int, to construct the complex solid. To erase the polyline after the solid is complete, use Erase, window both entities, and then remove the solid from the selection set with a point pick. Alternatively, you may place the polyline on a separate layer and freeze it, thus preserving it for later editing if necessary.

Warning: If you enter a quadrilateral solid's points in a circular direction, Auto-CAD will fill the solid using opposite edges in reverse directions to each other. The result is a "bow tie" rather than a filled quadrilateral.

RELATED COMMANDS

3Dface.

RELATED SYSTEM VARIABLES

FILLMODE (governs whether solids appear filled or not).

SAMPLE DIALOG

The following sample dialog constructs the solid illustrated in Figure 8.22:

Command: **Solid**
First point: **11,19.5**
Second point: **15.75,16.25**
Third point: **13.25,16.75**
Fourth point: **13.25,15.75**
Third point: **15.75,16.25**
Fourth point: **11,13**
Third point: **(press Enter)**
Command:

TRACE

Draws continuous line segments at a specified width.

VERSIONS

All.

COMMAND OPTIONS

Trace width The Trace command always prompts first for the trace width, offering the last specified width as the default. Enter the width of the trace using any of AutoCAD's standard value-entry mechanisms.

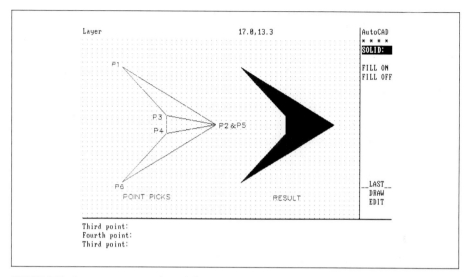

FIGURE 8.22: Constructing a complex solid. Four-point and three-point solids may be built adjacent to one another using a single Solid command, although the technique may require a little practice. The trick is to remember that you are telling AutoCAD how to fill the solid as well as the solid's area. In this figure, a fairly complex solid shape is built from six point picks, the order of which is shown in the outline version on the left. Notice how the second and fifth selection points are the same. This fills the solid first between lines 1-2 and 3-4, and then between lines 3-4 and 5-6.

From point   After you enter the trace width, AutoCAD responds by prompting for the starting point of the wide line. Simply enter the desired coordinate location of the line's starting point.

To point   After the starting point is entered, AutoCAD prompts for the endpoint of the wide line segment. When you move the pointing device, AutoCAD "samples" the line segment by displaying a rubberband line between the starting point and the intersection of the crosshairs.

When the second point is entered, AutoCAD does not immediately draw a line segment between the two points. Instead, AutoCAD waits until the next endpoint, if any, is entered. By waiting in this fashion, AutoCAD is able to miter an even bevel between the two wide line segments without erasing and redrawing the previous segment. Thus, as a series of wide line segments is drawn, Auto-CAD always seems to lag one segment behind. This is normal.

Each time an endpoint is entered, AutoCAD assumes it to be the starting point for another wide line segment, and thus repeats the "To point:" prompt and the rubberband-line sample. When you are finished constructing continuous wide line segments, press Enter in response to the "To point:" prompt; AutoCAD then displays the complete entity.

USAGE

The Trace command prompts for a specified width, and subsequently prompts for a series of line-segment endpoints. The selected endpoints are assumed to lie on the center line of the wide line segments. The Trace command miters the line segments as they are created; thus, the display of the wide lines is always delayed by one line segment, while AutoCAD waits for the next line segment, in order to determine the correct angle of mitering. An example of the type of lines created using Trace is shown in Figure 8.23. The wide line segments drawn using Trace can be edited individually.

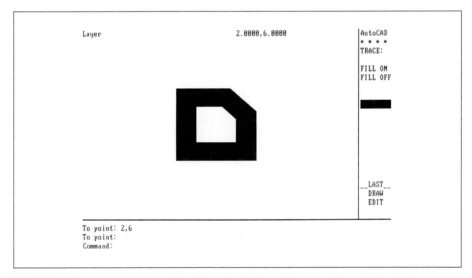

FIGURE 8.23: Line segments created using Trace. In the above figure, a polygon (with all of its corners correctly mitered) is drawn using the sample dialog listed in the Trace command entry of this chapter. If you had begun this sequence at one of the corners, the last corner would not have been mitered correctly. (The Trace command has no Close option, as does PLine.) Often, the trick isn't all that obvious to the beginner: To miter all the corners, begin and end the Trace command at the midpoint of one of the sides, rather than at one of the corners.

To create Trace line segments, sequentially pick the coordinate points that mark the line segment's endpoints on the centerline, as illustrated in Figure 8.23. Coordinate points may be entered using any of AutoCAD's standard methods.

The wide lines generated with the Trace command will be displayed as filled solids unless AutoCAD's fill mode is turned off. To turn off the fill mode, use the Fill command, details for which can be found in Chapter 6.

Note: The Trace command is functionally similar to the Line command, but Trace does not have an Undo or Close option.

Tip: Trace will miter all intersections as a series of line segments is drawn, but if you are drawing a closed figure, it will not miter an intersection formed by the original starting point and final endpoint. To draw a closed figure using Trace, begin the figure at the midpoint of a line segment, select all intersections, and end with the same line segment's midpoint. This will result in a smooth closed figure. The sample dialog ahead is an example of this technique.

You cannot use Setvar to change the width of the line segments while in the middle of the Trace command. The new value will not become effective until the current Trace command is concluded.

The value of the line width stored in the TRACEWID system variable is never less than what is possible using the maximum number of decimal places (or the lowest fractional denominator) as specified with the Units command. See Chapter 13 for details on the TRACEWID system variable, and Chapter 6 for details regarding the Units command.

RELATED COMMANDS

Fill, Line.

RELATED SYSTEM VARIABLES

FILLMODE (solid fill display on or off), TRACEWID (default trace line width).

SAMPLE DIALOG

The following sample dialog produces the wide line segments illustrated in Figure 8.23:

```
Command: Trace
Trace width <0.0625>: 1
From point: 2,6
To point: 2,8
To point: 4,8
To point: 5,7
To point: 5,5
To point: 2,5
To point: 2,6
To point: (press Enter)
Command:
```

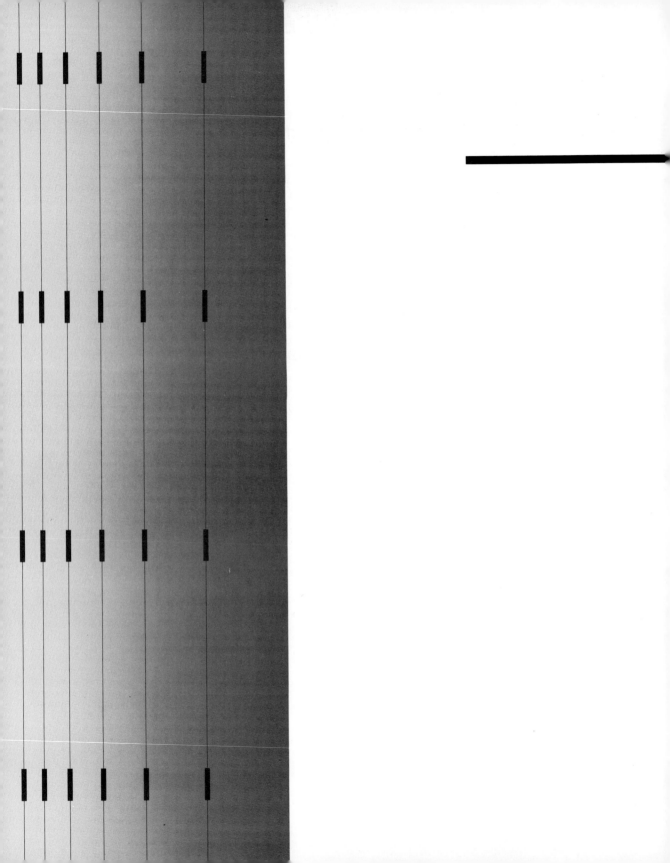

CHAPTER 9

CREATING COMPLEX ENTITIES

CREATING COMPLEX ENTITIES

A complex entity is an AutoCAD drawing entity that, while composed of more than one simple entity, can still be selected and modified as though it were a single unit of graphic information. Examples of complex entities include 2-D and 3-D polylines, blocks, doughnuts, ellipses, polygons, solids, shapes, and text.

A complex entity requires its own set of parameters, such as endpoints, insertion points, scaling factors, diameters, axes, and numbers of sides. AutoCAD prompts for the necessary parameters after you enter the name of the complex entity you wish to generate. For example, to enter a polyline, you invoke the command PLine, after which you must specify the coordinate location of each vertex along the line, plus other variations such as line widths and curved segments. As you will see, entities such as doughnuts, ellipses, and polygons are really just variations and simplifications of the PLine command. As you become more experienced in generating complex entities, you will find that many different variations and subcommands are often available. Once the underlying principles of the complex entity are understood, its variations and subcommands are much easier to understand as well.

Each variation and optional subcommand has its own advantage and purpose, depending on the drafting situation. You can choose whatever variation suits you best, based on such considerations as your particular drawing style, your personal preference, or the existence of other entities whose construction points can be used to help generate new entities—for example, placing the vertex of a polyline at an intersection using Osnap.

ENTERING CONSTRUCTION DATA

The format for keyboard entry of construction data is controlled by the default drawing-units format. You may refer to Chapter 6 for a detailed discussion of the Units command, which defines the format for keyboard data entry.

The information in this chapter outlines the various options for generating complex entities in AutoCAD. You may wish to refer to Chapter 5 for a detailed presentation of the various methods for entering coordinate point information. For quick reference, however, that information is briefly summarized here:

Absolute Coordinates   Entered as real numbers separated by commas, as in

2,2.25,5.875

Relative Coordinates Entered as above but preceded by the @ symbol, indicating that the coordinate information is relative to the previously selected point, as in

   @1.25,2,12

Polar Coordinates Entered using a distance and absolute angle value, relative to the last point picked, as in

   @2.25<90

(This example indicates a distance of 2.25 drawing units from the previously selected point, at an angle of 90 degrees.) With polar coordinates, the distance and angle are always measured in the current construction plane (that is, the current user coordinate system, including any value for elevation as contained in the ELEVATION system variable).

Pointing-Device Pick Entered by moving the crosshairs to the desired point on the screen (often assisted by Snap or Osnap) and selecting the point using the pick button on the pointing device. This method is used to enter the x and y coordinates in the current construction plane; to enter a point in 3-D space, you must either use point filters or set a nonzero value for the ELEVATION system variable.

3DMESH

Allows you to create a polygon mesh by individually entering each vertex (intersection) of the mesh.

VERSIONS

Release 10 and later.

COMMAND OPTIONS

Mesh M size Enter the number of vertices that will lie in the M direction of the polygon mesh.

Mesh N size Enter the number of vertices that will lie in the N direction of the polygon mesh.

Vertex (M,N) Enter the coordinate locations of each vertex in the polygon mesh. AutoCAD supplies a prompt indicating the M and N address of each vertex beginning with vertex 0,0, followed by vertex 0,1, and so forth until all vertices have been supplied in the N direction. Then AutoCAD prompts for the vertices in the N direction starting with M + 1. Refer to Figure 9.1 to see the order in which vertices are supplied in the sample mesh.

The total number of vertices required to generate the mesh is equal to the M size times the N size. Unfortunately, AutoCAD does not display the 3-D mesh until all vertices have been supplied in both the M and N directions.

USAGE

A *polygon mesh* is a matrix of crisscrossing lines that define a surface. The lines that form the matrix divide the surface into columns and rows. These columns and rows are constructed along opposing directions. AutoCAD labels the directions of these columns and rows as the *M* and *N* directions. A simple polygon mesh with four rows in the M direction and four rows in the N direction is shown in Figure 9.1.

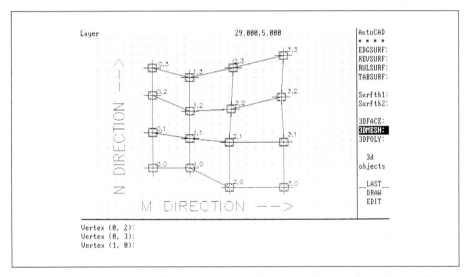

FIGURE 9.1: A simple polygon mesh. A simple 4 × 4 polygon mesh defining a flat surface can be generated fairly quickly using the 3Dmesh command. In the illustrated mesh, the coordinate locations of vertices are entered individually, starting in the lower-left corner and moving in the N direction. The next four vertices begin one column to the right, starting at the lowest point (to the right of the initial vertex) and again moving in the N direction. After four vertices are entered, the next vertex is again located one column to the right at the lowest point, and so on to the final vertex in the upper-right corner.

Once generated, a polygon mesh can be edited like any polyline. Each intersection of lines in the mesh is a polyline vertex with a specific M and N location. This vertex can be moved in any direction in 3-D space.

Figure 9.1 illustrates a 4 × 4 polygon mesh defining a flat surface. It contains a total of 16 vertices. The M and N directions are specified, as is the order in which the vertices will be entered. Notice that the vertices are entered beginning with the N direction, and the mesh is then built up along the M direction. Refer to the sample dialog, which will construct the simple mesh illustrated in Figure 9.2.

Tip: 3Dmesh can be used effectively in creating extremely simple meshes and smoothing the polygon mesh surface with the PEdit command. Refer to Chapter 10 for details regarding the PEdit command and its use with polygon meshes.

3Dmesh is, quite simply, a long and tedious method for building meshes. It has more practical value when called from within AutoLISP routines, where mesh vertex points can be calculated within controlled loops. (Refer to Chapters 16 and 17 for details regarding AutoLISP.) Avoid using it unless the mesh is extremely simple. Try the Edgesurf, Revsurf, Rulesurf, and Tabsurf commands for faster and simpler mesh construction.

SAMPLE DIALOG

The following sample dialog rotates the drawing viewpoint and creates the 3-D mesh illustrated in Figure 9.2:

Command: **Vpoint**
Rotate/<View point> <0,0,1>:**1.1,−1.1,.65**

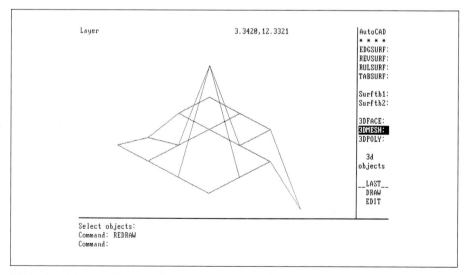

FIGURE 9.2: A 3-D polygon mesh. This mesh, generated with the 3Dmesh command, uses 3-D points to establish key vertices in 3-D space. A simple mesh such as this can be used as a framework for smooth-surface meshes, or the vertex points can be used to create more complex meshes. This mesh can be built using the sample dialog in the 3Dmesh command.

```
Command: 3Dmesh
Mesh M size: 4
Mesh N size: 4
Vertex (0, 0): 2,6
Vertex (0, 1): 2,7, − .25
Vertex (0, 2): 2,8
Vertex (0, 3): 2,9
Vertex (1, 0): 3,6
Vertex (1, 1): 3,7
Vertex (1, 2): 3,8
Vertex (1, 3): 3,9
Vertex (2, 0): 4,6
Vertex (2, 1): 4,7,3
Vertex (2, 2): 4,8
Vertex (2, 3): 4,9
Vertex (3, 0): 5,6
Vertex (3, 1): 5,7
Vertex (3, 2): 5,8
Vertex (3, 3): 5,9, − 2
Command:
```

3Dpoly

Creates polylines in 3-D space using XYZ coordinates.

VERSIONS

Release 10 and later.

COMMAND OPTIONS

From point   After you invoke the 3Dpoly command, AutoCAD prompts for the starting point. You may use any of AutoCAD's standard methods for entering 3-D points. You may also enter a 2-D point (x and y coordinates only). When 2-D pointsare entered, AutoCAD uses the value of the ELEVATION system variable as the z coordinate.

Endpoint   In response to AutoCAD's prompt for endpoints, you may repeatedly supply endpoints of additional line segments. As you move the pointing device, AutoCAD displays a rubberband line from the last point entered to the intersection of the crosshairs. Each time you select a new endpoint, AutoCAD draws the line segment from the previously selected point to the currently selected point and repeats the prompt. When the 3-D polyline is complete, press

Enter in response to the endpoint prompt. AutoCAD then redisplays the Command prompt.

Close Enter **C** to close the 3-D polyline. AutoCAD responds by drawing a straight line segment from the previously selected endpoint to the original starting point of the 3-D polyline. If you intend to draw a closed polygon figure, wherein the start and end points are just another vertex in the closed polyline, use the Close option to draw the last segment, as opposed to simply picking the original starting point. AutoCAD will react differently to a closed polyline when curve-fitting, filleting, chamfering, and so forth.

Undo If the line segment just created is not correct, you may enter **U** to have the line segment erased. If you wish, you can continue to step back through the polyline until you arrive at the original starting point.

USAGE

The 3Dpoly command is a convenient way to enter polylines in 3-D space using XYZ coordinate points, as opposed to the more general PLine command, which may require several changes to the UCS and may only be able construct several connected polylines in 3-D space.

3-D polylines constructed using 3Dpoly can consist of straight line segments with zero width only—no arc segments are possible. However, you may curve-fit a 3-D polyline. Also, you may edit its vertices using PEdit. (Refer to Chapter 10 for details regarding the PEdit command.)

The 3Dpoly command functions in a manner similar to the Line command in Release 10 and later; the difference is that the segments in a 3-D polyline are joined into a single entity.

RELATED COMMANDS

PLine.

SAMPLE DIALOG

The following sample dialog produces a 3-D polyline similar in appearance to the 3-D lines in Chapter 8, Figure 8.3:

```
Command: 3Dpoly
From point: 5,4,5
To point: 5,1,0
To point: 7,1,0
To point: 7,4,5
```

To point: **7,6,5**
To point: **5,6,5**
To point: **5,4,5**
To point: **7,4,5**
To point: **(press Enter)**
Command:

BLOCK

Allows you to define a group of entities in a drawing as a single unified entity, which you may then replicate or modify as you see fit using other AutoCAD commands.

VERSIONS

All.

COMMAND OPTIONS

Block Name   Enter a unique name for the group of entities you wish to collect into a block. For example, imagine that you have drawn a special symbol of a window and you intend to replicate it throughout the drawing, as in Figure 9.3. You could then enter **Window** as the block name.

Block names may be as long as 31 characters. In addition to letters and numbers, you may use the dollar sign ($), hyphen (-), and underscore character (_) in your block names.

If you enter the name of a previously named block, AutoCAD responds:

Block already exists. Redefine it? <N>

If you reply by entering **N** or pressing Enter, AutoCAD cancels the Block command. If you enter **Y**, AutoCAD continues with the Block command, overwriting the current block definition with the new block definition you are creating. You may then select whatever entities you choose (including other block references) to include in the redefined block.

Bear in mind, however, that you cannot select the block reference that is currently using this name as an entity to include in the redefined block. To do so would create a *circular block reference,* wherein a block would be endlessly referencing itself. However, if you wish to include some or all of a block's entities in its redefinition, there is a technique to accomplish this. First, you must insert the block using the asterisk option (as explained in the section on the Insert command later in this chapter) so that the block entities are inserted without creating

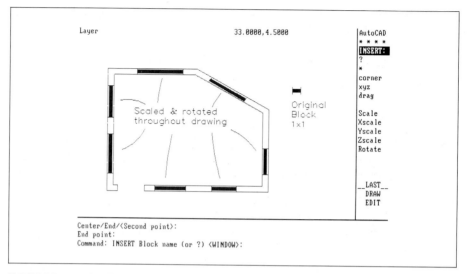

FIGURE 9.3: A window block replicated in several parts of a drawing. In this figure, a block named Window, measuring 1 drawing unit by 1 drawing unit, is scaled to various lengths and rotation angles and inserted between wall lines on the left. The 1-by-1 dimensions give this block a great deal of flexibility.

a block reference. Then you may select these entities for inclusion in the redefined block. Alternatively, if you are using AutoCAD Version 2.5 or later, you may use the Explode command to change a block reference into its component entities, and then select them for inclusion in the redefined block.

?   If you enter a question mark instead of a block name, AutoCAD responds by listing all the blocks currently named in the drawing. If you are using AutoCAD Release 10 or later, refer to the discussion of wild-card characters in Chapter 21.

Insertion base point   After you enter a block name, AutoCAD prompts for an insertion base point for the block. The insertion base point is a point relative to which the block's component entities are drawn. In the illustration in Figure 9.3, the insertion point chosen is the lower-left corner of the window symbol. However, the insertion point could have been located elsewhere; AutoCAD can use any insertion point as a reference point by which it generates a block's component entities.

The principle behind the insertion point is this: A block functions as a kind of "mini-drawing" within the larger overall drawing. The block insertion point, therefore, is this mini-drawing's origin point—in other words, its own point 0,0. In fact, if you subsequently write a block to a disk file—refer to the discussion of the Wblock command for details—an AutoCAD drawing file is created and the base insertion point is used as the new drawing's 0,0 origin point.

When selecting an insertion point, remember to choose a point that will make intuitive sense when you insert the block back into drawings, and also will allow for a logical means of scaling and rotating the block. Inserting, scaling, and rotating are all done relative to the insertion point. In the example in Figure 9.3, the insertion point was chosen so that changes to the x and y scaling parameters would allow for proportional changes to the dimensions of the window symbol. Also, if necessary, the window symbol could be easily rotated to fit into any angled wall because of the location of its insertion point. Refer to the Insert command for details on inserting, scaling, and rotating a block.

Select objects   Once you have entered the block's name and insertion point, you may select the specific entities you wish to include in its definition. If necessary, you may refer to Chapter 5 for details on AutoCAD's various entity-selection mechanisms.

After selecting all appropriate entities, press Enter. The block is now defined (or redefined), and the selected entities have disappeared from the drawing. You may cause them to return by invoking either the Oops command (which will cause the component entities to return, but not as a block reference) or the Insert command (which will insert a block reference into the drawing).

USAGE

When you invoke the Block command, you are asked to enter a unique *block name,* after which you select the block's *insertion point* and the entities that are to be joined together to form the block. When you have thus defined the block, the selected entities disappear from the screen. They may be recalled using the Oops, Undo, or Insert command. (Oops and Undo are explained in Chapter 10; Insert is explained later in this chapter.)

Blocks have several distinct advantages over simple copying of entities within the drawing file. For instance, a block may be "written out" to a separate drawing file on disk, and thereafter inserted into other drawings. This feature allows blocks to be passed from drawing to drawing; you needn't "reinvent the wheel" each time you need to use a block in a new drawing. In fact, a significant part of the time savings you can realize with AutoCAD comes from its ability to develop a library of frequently used custom symbols that are quickly inserted into several drawings.

Unlike the Copy and Move commands, which reproduce and relocate entities within a drawing, the Block command permits the scaling of blocks along their x-, y-, and z-axes and the rotation of blocks around their insertion points as they are inserted into a drawing. Refer to the discussion of the Insert command later in this chapter for details.

If the parameters of a block change later on, you need only redefine the block; all occurrences of the block in that drawing are automatically updated as well.

Blocks may be assigned certain *attributes,* such as materials and price specifications, which can be extracted from the drawing for use in a bill of materials or a database program. Thus, in addition to making your drafting easier, AutoCAD can help you organize the materials aspects of your drawings. Refer to Chapter 18 for details regarding this powerful capability.

Blocks save disk space. A block definition is only stored once in the drawing. Thereafter, AutoCAD need only store the insertion points and scaling factors of the block, rather than replicating each entity definition over and over again.

Special Features

Certain entity attributes affect how blocks are defined and how they will be inserted. Entity linetypes, colors, and layers may be fixed or variable, depending on how they are defined at the time a block containing them is defined.

VARIABLE BLOCKS

The fundamental technique for defining a variable block is to begin by placing all of its entities on layer 0. Be certain that the current linetype and color for all entities are set to Bylayer or Byblock, using the Linetype and Color commands respectively. (Refer to Chapter 6 for details regarding these commands.)

When entities composing a block are placed on layer 0 with these color and linetype settings, the resulting block will "adopt" the layer, color, and linetype settings of the layer on which it is inserted in any drawing. In early versions of AutoCAD, which did not have the Color and Linetype commands, this was the only means by which a block's layer, color, and linetype could be changed after the block was defined. It is still a good technique to be as flexible as possible when designing a block.

You may also define the color and linetype of specific entities to be Byblock. When a block's entity colors and linetypes are thus defined, the block will adopt the current settings for color and linetype at the time it is inserted.

For example, suppose that you have defined a block whose entity colors are Byblock, and that the current entity color setting is Bylayer. If you insert that block on a layer whose default color is blue, the block will adopt the current entity color setting and thus will appear blue. If, however, you change the current color setting to Green and insert the same block on the same layer, the block will continue to adopt the current entity color setting, and thus will appear green instead of blue.

Block entities with colors and linetypes defined as Bylayer will adopt the colors and linetypes of the layer on which they reside when the block is inserted. If the block's entities reside on a named layer, they will be inserted on that layer each time the block is inserted, adopting that layer's color and linetype characteristics as well. If the block is inserted into a new drawing and the named layer does not yet exist, the layer, including its default linetype and color, is created.

FIXED BLOCKS

If you intend for the layers, colors, and/or linetypes of a block to be fixed— that is, unchanging regardless of the layer on which the block is inserted—define all entity layers, colors, and linetypes outright before gathering the entities into a block. This will produce a block whose entity properties do not change.

Notice that entities positioned on a specific named layer will retain that layer specification when inserted into another drawing. If the layer does not exist, AutoCAD will create it.

MIXED BLOCKS

You may freely combine variable entities with entities having fixed layers, colors, and linetypes in the same block. Block entities may exist on multiple layers.

Blocks may also contain other blocks. Such blocks-within-blocks are called *nested blocks*. Blocks that are nested within other blocks and contain variable entities will adopt the entity colors and linetypes of the outer block. For example if a block containing entities drawn on layer 0 with color Byblock is nested within a block whose entity colors are defined explicitly as Red, the nested block will appear red when inserted.

In most cases, colors, linetypes, and layers of nested blocks should be either defined explicitly or drawn on layer 0 with Bylayer or Byblock entity attributes, to minimize confusion.

Notes on Using the Block Command

It is possible to define 3-D blocks in Version 2.6 and later, but the process is a little tricky, and it may require some practice for you to develop proficiency. For best results if you have Release 10 or later, keep the following in mind:

- The 3-D coordinate system of a newly created block is the same as the UCS in effect at the time the block is created. As with any block, the insertion point becomes the block's origin—in other words, point 0,0,0 for that block. If the block's entities are elevated and the insertion point is not elevated, the block will always be elevated when you insert it.
- When a block is inserted, its defined 3-D coordinate system aligns with the UCS in effect at insertion time.

Thus, to minimize confusion, always be certain that the current coordinate system is aligned properly to a block's entities before you define the block, and check the setting for the ELEVATION system variable to be certain that the block will be aligned properly along its z-axis. Otherwise, you may wind up with a peculiarly aligned block that will not scale or rotate properly.

Like 2-D blocks, 3-D blocks will rotate only around the z-axis of their insertion point. In Release 10 and later, however, you are free to assign a new UCS and to rescale or rotate an inserted block as you wish.

Blocks are most useful when they can be used as templates; that is, inserted into a wide variety of drawings. When creating a block that you intend to use as a template, construct a small model in "1 by 1" drawing unit scale, as illustrated by the window symbol in Figure 9.3 and by the 25-tooth gear in Figure 9.4. When a block is drawn at a scale of 1 to 1, the x and y scaling factors can be used to insert the block in the widest variety of situations. Of course, when constructing 3-D blocks, use a z scale of 1 unit as well.

When redefining a block, always write the new definition out to disk using Wblock. Later, if you find you must redefine the same block in other drawings, you can insert the new definition using the asterisk option of the Insert command, and quickly redefine the block, updating all occurrences of that block in the drawing. (See the discussion of the Insert command later in this chapter for details on using the asterisk option.)

As discussed in Chapter 5, starting with AutoCAD Release 11, you can create *external reference files*—entire drawings that can be included in other drawings. These files can be a very useful alternative to inserting entire drawing files as blocks. For example, when you update an external reference drawing, the changes will be reflected automatically in any drawings that reference it. For more details regarding external references and Release 11's Xref command, refer to Chapter 21.

If you use entities from an old drawing to create a block, first invoke the List command for those entities in order to double-check their entity properties. You may want to change some colors, layers, or linetypes now and save yourself a lot of time later.

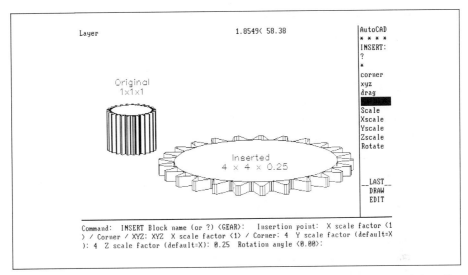

FIGURE 9.4: A 1 × 1 × 1 block of a gear in 3-D. In this figure, a 1 × 1 × 1 3-D block is scaled on all three axes using the XYZ option. The scale along each axis may be entered individually; the default is always equal to the scale for the x-axis, making it easy to scale equally in all three directions. In this figure, a 3-D block of a gear is scaled to 4 units along the x- and y-axes, and ¼ unit along the z-axis.

If an inserted block contains colors or linetypes that are incorrect but cannot be changed, often the fastest and simplest course of action is to change the block into its component entities using the Explode command, or erase it and reinsert it using the asterisk option, and then edit the stubborn entities.

RELATED COMMANDS

Insert, Wblock, Xref.

SAMPLE DIALOG

The following sample dialog would create a block named Window (such as the symbol shown in Figure 9.3). Its entities are drawn in 1 × 1 scale, and the origin is at point 5,4 in the drawing.

```
Command: Block
Block name (or ?): Window
Insertion point: 5,4
Select objects: W
First corner: 4,3
Other corner: 7,6
Select objects: (press Enter)
Command:
```

DONUT (OR DOUGHNUT)

Creates circles and ring shapes using wide polylines. It can also be used to generate solid filled circles.

VERSIONS

Version 2.5 and later.

COMMAND OPTIONS

Inside diameter   Enter the value of the doughnut's inner diameter (or zero if drawing a filled circle). You may enter a value by typing it from the keyboard or by picking two points on the screen. AutoCAD accepts the distance between the two points as the value for the inner diameter.

Outside diameter   Enter the value of the doughnut's outer diameter. This value should, of course, be greater than the inner diameter. You may enter a value by typing it from the keyboard or by picking two points on the screen. AutoCAD accepts the distance between the two points as the value for the outer diameter.

Center of doughnut   Pick the center point using any of AutoCAD's standard point-entry methods. AutoCAD automatically repeats this prompt, allowing you to select any number of locations for copies of the ring or filled circle. When finished, press Enter in response to this prompt.

USAGE

The Donut command simplifies what was in earlier versions of AutoCAD a cumbersome polyline technique. To draw a ring or a filled circle, invoke Donut (or the alternate form, Doughnut), enter an inner and outer diameter for the ring, and pick the ring's center point. For a filled circle, specify an inner diameter of zero. The most recently entered diameters are stored as default responses.

RELATED COMMANDS

PLine.

SAMPLE DIALOG

The following sample dialog creates a pair of ring shapes as illustrated in Figure 9.5:

Command: **Donut**
Inside diameter <0.5>: **1**
Outside diameter <1>: **2**
Center of doughnut: **5,4**
Center of doughnut: **8,4**
Center of doughnut: **(press Enter)**
Command:

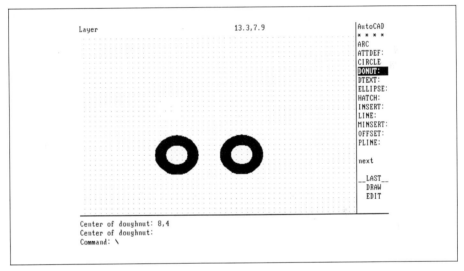

FIGURE 9.5: Two filled rings using the Donut command. Two simple donuts (curved wide polylines) are created using the Donut command, as per the sample dialog for this command. The inner diameters are 1 drawing unit, and the outer diameters are 2 drawing units.

DTEXT

Displays text on the screen as it is being entered. Dtext is a variation on the Text command. The prompts and options are the same as for Text.

VERSIONS

Version 2.5 and later.

COMMAND OPTIONS

Refer to the Text command for details regarding the command options, as they are the same for both commands.

USAGE

The Dtext command is useful in situations where a display of text in the drawing is needed as the text is being entered. For example, you may wish to preview the appearance of the text before actually including it in the drawing.

Dtext is also handy when entering several lines of text. Unlike the Text command, Dtext repeats the text-entry prompt for additional lines of text without requiring you to repeat the Text command and bypass the text-options prompt. Dtext also permits you to select a point at the text-entry prompt; AutoCAD will move the cursor to that point, allowing you to place subsequent lines of text anywhere within the drawing.

Dtext always displays its preview text left-justified. When all text has been entered, AutoCAD redraws the entered text. If you are entering text that is not left-justified, Dtext redraws the text in the correct orientation.

You can enter special characters like underscore and overscore toggles using Dtext, but they are displayed literally (as in %%u or %%o) until all text has been entered. When redrawn, special characters are replaced by their respective symbols. Refer to the discussion of the Text command for details regarding special characters.

An example of Dtext is presented in Figure 9.6. Notice how the text being entered is echoed in the Command-prompt area.

Before the Dtext command is concluded, you can edit the text only by backspacing through everything you have typed so far, deleting as you do so. You cannot move the cursor to a particular place within the text except by backspacing.

To end the Dtext command, press Enter in response to the text-entry prompt. You may cancel the Dtext command at any time by pressing Ctrl-C.

SAMPLE DIALOG

The following sample dialog inserts the text that appears in Figure 9.6. Compare this dialog to that of the Text command; notice how much easier it is to enter multiple lines of text using Dtext rather than Text.

```
Command: DText
Justify/Style/<Start point>: 2,7
Height <0.125>: 0.2
Rotation angle <0.00>: (press Enter)
Text: Text sample - (press Enter)
```

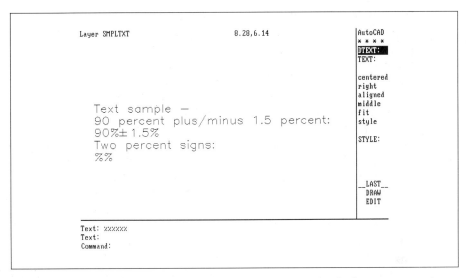

FIGURE 9.6: Text entered using the Dtext command. The text generated in this figure was entered using the sample dialog for the Dtext command. The third line contains extra percent signs to indicate to AutoCAD that a percent sign in the generated text is followed by a special plus/minus character.

Text: **90 percent plus/minus 1.5 percent: (press Enter)**
Text: **90%%%%p1.5% (press Enter)**
Text: **Two percent signs: (press Enter)**
Text: **%%%%% (press Enter)**
Command:

EDGESURF

Constructs a coons surface patch bounded by four lines, arcs, or 2-D or 3-D polylines that are joined at their endpoints to form a four-sided surface boundary, as illustrated in Figure 9.7.

VERSIONS

Release 10 and later.

COMMAND OPTIONS

Select edge 1   Select the first edge by picking it with the pointing device or by entering a coordinate point that it intersects. This first edge determines the M

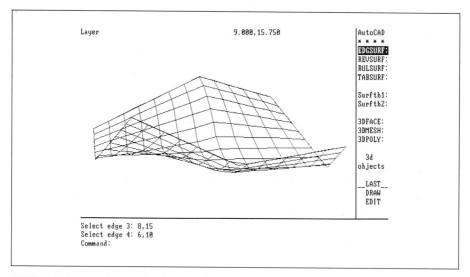

```
Layer                         9.000,15.750          │AutoCAD
                                                     │* * * *
                                                     │EDGSURF:
                                                     │REVSURF:
                                                     │RULSURF:
                                                     │TABSURF:
                                                     │
                                                     │Surftb1:
                                                     │Surftb2:
                                                     │
                                                     │3DFACE:
                                                     │3DMESH:
                                                     │3DPOLY:
                                                     │
                                                     │   3d
                                                     │objects
                                                     │
                                                     │__LAST__
                                                     │ DRAW
                                                     │ EDIT


   Select edge 3: 8,15
   Select edge 4: 6,10
   Command:
```

FIGURE 9.7: Coons surface patch using Edgesurf. This polygon mesh was generated using the sample dialog for the Edgesurf command. Edgesurf uses four 3-D polylines whose endpoints must be connected, forming the boundaries of a surface in 3-D space. Selecting these polylines by point pick divides the surface into a grid. The number of vertices in each direction is determined by the settings for the SURFTAB1 and SURFTAB2 system variables.

direction for the surface polygon mesh, starting with the endpoint closest to your selection point.

Select edge 2,3,4   The other three edges may be selected in any order. The N direction is determined by the two edges that touch the endpoints of the first edge. After the edges are selected, mesh generation is automatic.

USAGE

The Edgesurf command creates a polygon mesh using existing geometry, calculating all vertices in the M and N directions based on the geometry of the edges and the setting of two system variables, SURFTAB1 and SURFTAB2. The SURFTAB1 system variable contains the number of vertices in the M direction, while SURFTAB2 contains the number of vertices in the N direction. These values can be set using the Setvar command. Refer to Chapter 13 for details regarding the Setvar command. Refer to the 3Dmesh entry in this chapter for a description of a polygon mesh.

The higher the values of SURFTAB1 and SURFTAB2, the finer the resolution of the resulting mesh. However, bear in mind that meshes with very fine resolution take longer to regenerate, and greatly enlarge the size of the drawing file.

Tip: Set the values of SURFTAB1 and SURFTAB2 as low as possible while still generating an acceptable mesh. Remember that surfaces generated using Edgesurf can be smoothed using the PEdit command.

RELATED SYSTEM VARIABLES

SURFTAB1 (number of tabulations in the M direction), SURFTAB2 (number of tabulations in the N direction).

SAMPLE DIALOG

The following dialog sets new values for SURFTAB1 and SURFTAB2, changes the drawing viewpoint, draws four 3-D polylines, and constructs a coons surface patch using them, as illustrated in Figure 9.7:

```
Command: Setvar
Variable name or ?: SURFTAB1
New value for SURFTAB1 <6>: 12
Command: Setvar
Variable name or ? <SURFTAB1>: SURFTAB2
New value for SURFTAB2 <6>: 12
Command: Vpoint
Rotate/<View point> <0,0,1>: 1, − .45,.35
Regenerating drawing.
Command: 3Dpoly
From point: 4,11,0
Close/Undo/<Endpoint of line>: 4,14,1
Close/Undo/<Endpoint of line>: 4,16,0
Close/Undo/<Endpoint of line>: (press Enter)
Command: 3Dpoly
From point: 4,16,0
Close/Undo/<Endpoint of line>: 7,16, − 1
Close/Undo/<Endpoint of line>: 8,16,0
Close/Undo/<Endpoint of line>: (press Enter)
Command: 3Dpoly
From point: 8,16,0
Close/Undo/<Endpoint of line>: 8,13,0
Close/Undo/<Endpoint of line>: 8,10,2
Close/Undo/<Endpoint of line>: (press Enter)
Command: 3Dpoly
From point: 8,10,2
Close/Undo/<Endpoint of line>: 6,10,0
Close/Undo/<Endpoint of line>: 4,11,0
Close/Undo/<Endpoint of line>: (press Enter)
Command: Edgesurf
```

```
Select edge 1: 4,14,1
Select edge 2: 4,16
Select edge 3: 8,15
Select edge 4: 6,10
Command:
```

ELLIPSE

Creates elliptical shapes composed of short polyline segments. It can also be used to quickly draw isometric representations of circles in 2-D drawings.

VERSIONS

Version 2.5 and later.

COMMAND OPTIONS

Axis endpoint ellipse   You may construct an ellipse by entering the endpoints of the ellipse's major and minor axes. After you invoke the Ellipse command, AutoCAD responds with the following prompt:

<Axis endpoint 1>/Center:

Enter the first endpoint of either the major axis or the minor axis of the intended ellipse. AutoCAD responds:

Axis endpoint 2:

Enter the coordinates of the other axis endpoint. The orientation of this axis will determine the orientation of the final ellipse. Also, the midpoint of this axis will be the center point of the ellipse. AutoCAD responds by drawing a circle on the screen and prompting:

<Other axis distance>/Rotation:

Enter the coordinate points that correspond to the endpoint of the second ellipse axis. The distance of this axis is measured as a perpendicular line from the midpoint of the first axis to a point on the circumference of the ellipse. If you move the pointing device, AutoCAD will display a rubberband version of the final ellipse as well as a rubberband line indicating the other axis distance. This process is illustrated in Figure 9.8.

Axis, rotation ellipse   You may construct an ellipse by entering the diameter of a circle and rotating that circle by a factor of 0 to 89.4 degrees. To construct such

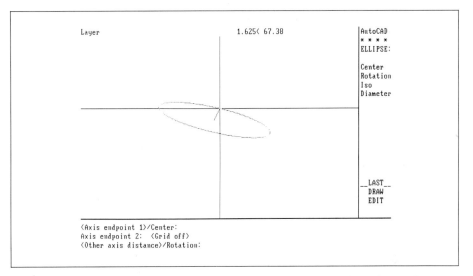

FIGURE 9.8: Axis endpoint ellipse. To enter an axis endpoint ellipse, indicate the endpoints of two perpendicular endpoints that intersect the quadrant of the ellipse. In this figure, the endpoints of the first axis have been entered.

an ellipse, invoke the Ellipse command. AutoCAD prompts:

<Axis endpoint 1>/Center:

Pick the first endpoint of the ellipse's major axis. AutoCAD responds:

Axis endpoint 2:

Pick the other endpoint of the ellipse's major axis. AutoCAD responds by drawing a circle on the screen and prompting:

<Other axis distance>/Rotation:

Enter **R** in response to this prompt. AutoCAD responds:

Rotation around major axis:

You may enter an angle value corresponding to the number of degrees of rotation that AutoCAD will use to rotate the circle around the axis you just specified. If you move the pointing device, AutoCAD will display the angle of rotation on the screen, expressed as a rubberband line from the axis midpoint to the intersection of the crosshairs, at the current angle of rotation using AutoCAD's angle-measurement system. In addition, a rubberband ellipse is displayed showing the ellipse resulting from the current angle of rotation. When you select a point, the rotated circle is projected onto the drawing plane and the resulting ellipse is drawn. This process is illustrated in Figure 9.9.

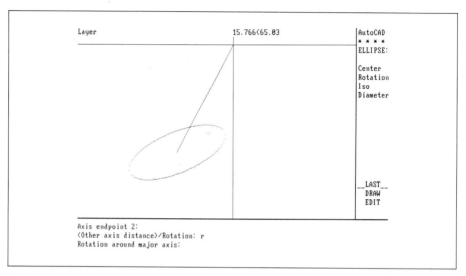

```
Layer                              15.766<65.03        AutoCAD
                                                       * * * *
                                                       ELLIPSE:

                                                       Center
                                                       Rotation
                                                       Iso
                                                       Diameter




                                                       __LAST__
                                                       DRAW
                                                       EDIT

Axis endpoint 2:
<Other axis distance>/Rotation: r
Rotation around major axis:
```

FIGURE 9.9: Axis, rotation ellipse. To enter an axis, rotation ellipse, enter the endpoints of a line that AutoCAD will use for the major (longer) axis of the ellipse. AutoCAD also uses this line as the diameter of a circle being rotated in 3-D space. As the circle is rotated, it is projected onto the 2-D construction plane, forming an ellipse.

Center, axis endpoint ellipse You may also construct an ellipse by entering the center point, followed by a coordinate point for the endpoint of the first axis and a value for the length of the second axis. To construct this type of ellipse, invoke the Ellipse command. AutoCAD will prompt:

<Axis endpoint 1>/Center:

Enter **C** in response and AutoCAD will prompt:

Center of ellipse:

Select a coordinate location for the ellipse's center point. AutoCAD responds:

Axis endpoint:

If you move the pointing device, AutoCAD will draw a rubberband line from the selected point to the intersection of the crosshairs, indicating both the length of the first axis and its orientation. Remember that the length of the rubberband axis, extending as it does from the ellipse's center point, represents only half of the axis that will be used to draw the final product.

After you select the endpoint of the first axis, AutoCAD responds:

<Other axis distance>/Rotation:

AutoCAD now displays a second rubberband line extending from the ellipse's center point. This line represents the distance of the second axis from the midpoint to the ellipse's circumference, but does not necessarily indicate its orientation, since the orientation of the second axis is fixed—that is, perpendicular to the first axis. After you enter the second axis endpoint, AutoCAD draws the resulting ellipse. This type of ellipse is illustrated in Figure 9.10.

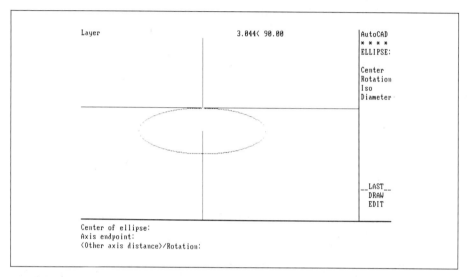

Layer   3.044< 90.00   AutoCAD
                                                                    * * * *
                                                                    ELLIPSE:

                                                                    Center
                                                                    Rotation
                                                                    Iso
                                                                    Diameter

                                                                    __LAST__
                                                                    DRAW
                                                                    EDIT

Center of ellipse:
Axis endpoint:
<Other axis distance>/Rotation:

FIGURE 9.10: Center, axis endpoint ellipse. In this figure, the center of the ellipse is entered first, followed by the endpoint of the first axis, either major or minor. The orientation of the first axis is determined by the center point and endpoint, and the length of the axis will be double the distance between the center point and endpoint. All that remains is to pick the endpoint of the second axis, or enter a value for its length.

Center, endpoint, rotation ellipse   This variation on the center point ellipse offers the option of entering a center point, first axis length, and degree of rotation around the first axis—similar to the axis, rotation ellipse described earlier. To construct this type of ellipse, invoke the Ellipse command. AutoCAD responds:

>   <Axis endpoint 1>/Center:

Enter **C** in response, and AutoCAD will prompt:

>   Center of ellipse:

Select a coordinate location for the ellipse's center point. AutoCAD responds:

>   Axis endpoint:

If you move the pointing device, AutoCAD will draw a rubberband line from the selected point to the intersection of the crosshairs, indicating both the length of the first axis and its orientation. Remember that the length of the rubberband axis, extending as it does from the ellipse's center point, represents only half of the axis that will be used to draw the final product. After you select the axis endpoint, AutoCAD draws a circle using your center point and axis endpoint to define that circle's radius.

After you have selected the endpoint of the first axis, AutoCAD responds:

<Other axis distance>/Rotation:

Enter **R** in response to this prompt. AutoCAD responds:

Rotation around major axis:

You may enter an angle value corresponding to the number of degrees of rotation that AutoCAD will use to rotate the circle around the axis you just specified. If you move the pointing device, AutoCAD will display the angle of rotation on the screen—expressed as a rubberband line from the axis midpoint to the intersection of the crosshairs—at the current angle of rotation using AutoCAD's angle-measurement system. In addition, a rubberband ellipse is displayed with the resulting ellipse as the current angle of rotation. When you select a point, the rotated circle is projected onto the drawing plane, and the resulting ellipse is drawn. This process is illustrated in Figure 9.11.

Isometric circles   If you have set AutoCAD's snap style to Isometric, the Ellipse command offers an option that will allow you to quickly draw ellipses that appear as circles on isometric planes in 2-D drawings. To construct such an isometric circle, first set AutoCAD's snap style to Isometric, and then invoke the Ellipse command. AutoCAD responds:

<Axis endpoint 1>/Center/Isocircle:

Enter **I** in response, and AutoCAD will prompt for an isometric circle:

Center of circle:

Select the coordinate points for the center of the isometric circle. AutoCAD then prompts:

<Circle radius>/Diameter:

You may either enter a value for the circle radius, or select coordinate points. If you select coordinate points, AutoCAD will accept the distance between them and the center of the circle as the length of the radius. AutoCAD draws the ellipse that represents a circle of the specified parameters drawn in the current isometric plane.

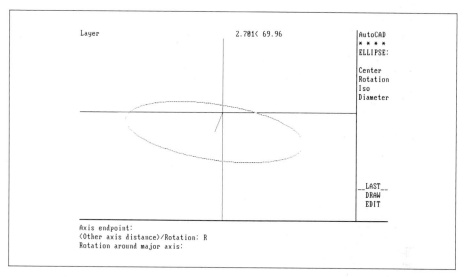

FIGURE 9.11: Center, endpoint, rotation ellipse. The center, endpoint, rotation ellipse is similar to the axis, rotation ellipse illustrated in Figure 9.9. In this figure, the length and orientation of the first axis are entered by picking a center point and axis endpoint. AutoCAD calculates the full length of the axis and then rotates a circle in space, projecting it onto the current construction plane. Entering the degree of rotation finishes the ellipse.

Alternatively, you may enter **D** in response to the above prompt, and Auto-CAD will respond with the following:

Circle diameter:

Enter the diameter of the circle; AutoCAD will construct the ellipse that represents this circle in the current isometric plane.

USAGE

In the above options, the orientation of the first axis also determines the orientation of the resulting ellipse. However, you may enter either the major axis or the minor axis as the first.

The isocircle is similar to the rotated circle just described, but the degree of rotation defaults to standard isometric degrees. AutoCAD produces the isocircle by projecting a circle drawn in the current isometric plane setting onto the 2-D drawing plane.

If you are using Release 10 and later, bear in mind that the Ellipse command draws only ellipses, and does not construct circles in 3-D space. If you wish to draw circles in 3-D space, first set the appropriate UCS, and then invoke the Circle command.

SAMPLE DIALOG

The following sample dialog constructs two ellipses, both represented in Figure 9.12. The first ellipse is drawn using the two-axis method. The second is an isometric circle. Notice how the snap style must be changed to draw the isometric circle.

```
Command: Ellipse
<Axis endpoint 1>/Center: 1,6
Axis endpoint 2: @4<0
<Other axis distance>/Rotation: 1
Command: Snap
Snap spacing or ON/OFF/Aspect/Rotate/Style <0.25>: S
Standard/Isometric <S>: I
Vertical spacing <0.25>: (press Enter)
Command: Ellipse
<Axis endpoint 1>/Center/Isocircle: I
Center of circle: 8,6
<Circle radius>/Diameter: 1.5
Command: Snap
Snap spacing or ON/OFF/Rotate/Style <0.25>: S
Standard/Isometric <I>: S
```

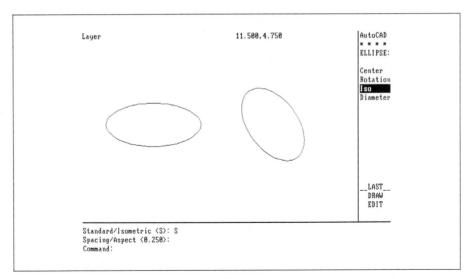

FIGURE 9.12: Ellipses per sample dialog. When the snap style is Isometric, you can draw "isometric circles" that are actually ellipses in the current construction plane. After you select the Isocircle option, AutoCAD prompts for a center point, plus your choice of either a diameter or a radius. The resulting circle is rotated according to the isoplane setting (top, right, or left) and projected onto the current construction plane, forming an ellipse.

Spacing/Aspect <0.25>: (press Enter)
Command:

INSERT

Inserts previously defined blocks into the drawing.

VERSIONS

All. Version 2.6 and later allow you to control the z scale factor of blocks containing 3-D entities.

COMMAND OPTIONS

Block name   AutoCAD first prompts for the name of a block to insert. After you have supplied a name in response to this prompt, AutoCAD searches the drawing database for a block of the requested name.

If AutoCAD does not find a block with the requested name in the drawing database, it will begin a search along its designated *search path* for a drawing file with the requested name. AutoCAD's search path is as follows:

1. The currently logged subdirectory.
2. The subdirectory named from the ACAD environment variable (if any).
3. AutoCAD's system subdirectory.

If a drawing file with this name is found, AutoCAD loads the file into the current drawing as a block and saves it as a block definition within the current drawing's database. If no drawing file is found with this name, AutoCAD displays the following prompt:

Can't open file
in (*current directory*)
or (*ACAD environment variable subdirectory, if any*)
or (*system subdirectory*)
Invalid

In such an instance, you may repeat the Insert command by pressing Enter and entering another name.

In Release 11 and later, if your graphics display supports the Advanced User Interface, you can respond to the "Block name" prompt by typing a *tilde* (~). Auto-CAD will display a dialog box containing the names of the defined blocks in the drawing. You may select a block name from the list or select the "Type it in" box to enter an external drawing name not on the list.

? If you respond to the "Block name" prompt by entering a question mark, AutoCAD responds by listing all the named blocks in the drawing database. It will not list drawing files along the search path, however. After you have read the list of block names, you may repeat the Insert command by pressing Enter.

* The *asterisk option* is a special feature at your disposal when entering names of blocks to insert. When the block name is preceded by an asterisk, it is not inserted as a block at all, but rather as a series of entities that are added to the drawing database. The result is not a block reference; entities may be modified separately, as if drawn from scratch.

Some block features are not available when you enter a block's entities in this fashion:

- You are not allowed separate x, y, and z scale factors. You may, however, enter an overall scale factor using any of AutoCAD's standard value-entry methods. All entities are enlarged or reduced by the scale factor you enter.

- Dynamic dragging is not enabled when you use the asterisk option.

- You may not use the scaling and rotation angle presets described later in this reference entry.

Despite these drawbacks, insertion using the asterisk option is quite useful. If you have a version of AutoCAD earlier than Version 2.5, it is your only substitute for the Explode command. It is a handy way to redefine complex blocks if only a few entities therein need to be modified. It is also a valuable alternative to drawing entities from scratch in situations where a block reference is not required or desired—for example, if only one reference occurs in a particular drawing.

Insertion point When you have entered a valid block name, AutoCAD next prompts for the block insertion point. You may enter the insertion point using any of AutoCAD's coordinate-point entry methods. On many AutoCAD configurations, a temporary image of the block will appear to move across the screen as you move the pointing device. This allows you to "preview" the position of the block if you were to pick the current intersection of the crosshairs as the block's insertion point. This AutoCAD feature, referred to as *dynamic dragging,* is illustrated in Figure 9.13.

In addition, you may respond to the "Insertion point" prompt by presetting the block's scaling and rotation angle factors. Refer ahead for details.

X scale factor After you select the insertion point, AutoCAD prompts for the block's x scale factor. If you respond with an integer greater than 1, AutoCAD will enlarge the block along its own x-axis by multiplying its current x-axis dimension by the factor you entered. For example, if you enter an x scale factor

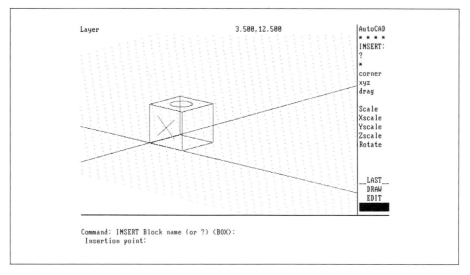

Layer · · · · · · · · · · · 3.500,12.500 · · · · · · AutoCAD
* * * *
INSERT:
?
*
corner
xyz
drag

Scale
Xscale
Yscale
Zscale
Rotate

__LAST__
DRAW
EDIT

Command: INSERT Block name (or ?) <BOX>:
    Insertion point:

FIGURE 9.13: Inserting a block. In this figure, the viewing angle has been rotated, and a 3-D block named Box is being inserted. The insertion point is the lower-left corner of the block; the block's dimensions are 1 drawing unit by 1 drawing unit. As you move the pointing device, the preview image of the block follows the corresponding movement of the crosshairs.

of 2, AutoCAD will double all of the block's x-axis dimensions. If you enter an x scale factor of 0.5, AutoCAD will cut the x-axis dimensions in half.

Y scale factor   After you enter the x scale factor, AutoCAD prompts you to enter the y scale factor. The y scale factor works the same as the x scale factor, except that it multiplies the block's y-axis dimensions.

Scaling point pick   You may, if you choose, respond to the "X scale factor" prompt by selecting a scaling point. If you pick a scaling point, AutoCAD calculates this point's x-axis and y-axis from the insertion point and uses these distance values as the x and y scale factors. If you move the pointing device before selecting this point, AutoCAD will scale the block's temporary image on the screen so that you may preview the resulting image of the block if you were to pick the current intersection of the crosshairs as the scaling point. This process is illustrated in Figure 9.14.

When inserting 3-D blocks and scaling by point pick, as in Figures 9.13 and 9.14, AutoCAD takes the z scale factor from the x scale factor. To enter a separate z scale factor, use the XYZ option, explained just ahead.

Corner   You may, if you choose, respond to the x scale factor prompt by entering **C**. This explicitly tells AutoCAD that you intend to select x and y scaling

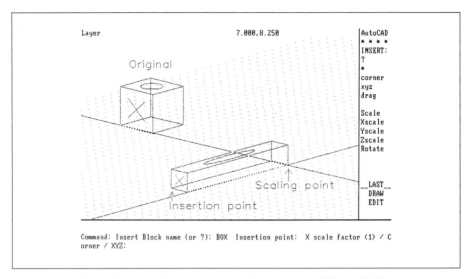

FIGURE 9.14: Scaling a block by picking a point. In this figure, a copy of the Box block is being inserted near the original, shown in the top left. The insertion point has been selected, and the block is now being scaled along the x- and y-axes by moving the crosshairs relative to the insertion point.

factors by picking a coordinate point. AutoCAD prompts for a corner point, and you may enter one using any of AutoCAD's standard point-entry methods. If dynamic dragging is in effect, you may move the pointing device and preview the resulting block image on the screen.

XYZ If you are entering 3-D blocks and desire separate x, y, and z scale factors, respond to the "X scale factor" prompt by entering **XYZ**. AutoCAD responds by prompting in turn for x, y, and z scale factors. You may enter values using any of AutoCAD's standard value-entry methods.

Rotation angle After you have entered the scaling factors for the block, AutoCAD prompts for the desired rotation angle. The block will be rotated around its insertion point by the angle value you enter in response to this prompt. If dynamic dragging is enabled, AutoCAD will display a temporary image of the scaled block rotating around the insertion point as you move the pointing device. You may enter the angle of rotation using any of AutoCAD's standard angle-entry methods.

AutoCAD Release 9 and later allow you to *preset* scaling factors and the rotation angle before inserting the block. With dynamic dragging enabled, this feature allows you to preview the image of the block in its final (or near-final) orientation before you select the insertion point, rather than afterward. The following preset options are available:

Scale If you wish to scale the block by the same factor in the x-, y-, and z-axes, respond to the "Insertion point" prompt by entering **S**. AutoCAD then prompts for a scale factor, and the preview image is redisplayed at the new scale. This process is illustrated in Figure 9.15.

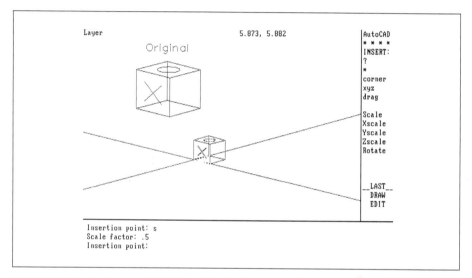

FIGURE 9.15: Previewing a scaled block with the Scale option. In this figure, the Box block has been preset to an overall scale of ½ drawing unit. Once the scale preset has been established, the preview image appears at the selected scale, allowing you to see how the scaled block will appear before it is inserted. After insertion, AutoCAD will prompt for the rotation angle as usual.

Xscale If you wish to scale the block along its x-axis, enter **X** in response to the "Insertion point" prompt. AutoCAD prompts for an x scale factor. The preview image is then redisplayed at the new scale, and the "Insertion point" prompt repeats.

Yscale If you wish to scale the block along its y-axis, enter **Y** in response to the "Insertion point" prompt. AutoCAD prompts for a y scale factor. The preview image is then redisplayed at the new scale, and the "Insertion point" prompt repeats.

Zscale As with the x and y scaling prompts just described, you enter **Z** in response to the "Insertion point" prompt if you wish to scale the block along its z-axis. AutoCAD prompts for a z scale factor. The preview image is then redisplayed at the new scale, and the "Insertion point" prompt repeats.

Rotate   If you wish to preset the block's rotation angle, enter **R** in response to the "Insertion point" prompt. AutoCAD prompts for a rotation angle, and the preview image is then redisplayed at the new angle.

PScale   PScale is a temporary scaling preset similar to Scale. If you enter **PS** in response to the "Insertion point" prompt, AutoCAD prompts for a scale factor and draws the temporary preview image at the desired scale, but prompts for an additional scale factor after the insertion point is picked. This allows you to "fine-tune" the scaling factor after you have inserted the block.

PXscale   PXscale is a temporary scaling preset similar to PScale. If you enter **PX** in response to the "Insertion point" prompt, AutoCAD prompts you for an x scale factor and draws the temporary preview image at the desired scale, but prompts for an additional x scale factor after the insertion point is picked.

PYscale   PYscale works like PXscale and PScale, but affects the y scale factor only. To use this option, enter **PY** in response to the "Insertion point" prompt.

PZscale   PZscale works like PXscale and PScale, but affects the z scale factor only. To use this option, enter **PZ** in response to the "Insertion point" prompt.

PRotate   PRotate works like the Rotate option described earlier, but causes AutoCAD to prompt again for a new rotation angle after the block is inserted.
As noted, presets may be either permanent or temporary. If the presets are permanent, the block is inserted according to the preset values. If the presets are temporary, you are prompted for additional scaling factors and rotation angles after you enter the insertion point, as in the standard Insert command.
All the preset options are entered in response to the "Insertion point" prompt. Each time you enter a preset option, you are reprompted for the insertion point. You may enter as many preset options as you like, in any order or combination.
In general, you may mix temporary and permanent preset options. You will be prompted again for options not preset or options only temporarily preset. The one exception to this is the temporary preset for z scale factors. If you wish to enter such a preset, enter temporary presets or no presets for the x and y scale factors, and use the XYZ option when prompted to do so.
If you enter values more than once for the same preset option, the latest response is used. In most cases, the scaling factor and rotation angle will be visible on the screen immediately after you enter a preset value.

USAGE

If you do not see any of the block's preview images, try entering the keyword **Drag** at the insertion point; you could also try scaling the block or responding to rotation-angle prompts. This should cause the temporary image to appear. If you still do not see the preview image, it may be that the insertion point is so far removed from the block's entities that the image cannot appear on the screen, or that the DRAGMODE system variable has been set to zero. If DRAGMODE is set to a value of zero, AutoCAD's dynamic dragging feature is disabled, and these preview images will not appear. Use the Setvar command to set DRAGMODE to a value of 2. Refer to Chapter 13 for details regarding DRAGMODE.

If some or all of a block's entities have been defined for a layer other than zero, and those layers are frozen or off at insertion time, you may not see any of the block. You may see only the part of the block that has entities on visible layers. Check layer visibility if you cannot see an inserted block—refer to Chapter 6 for details regarding the Layer command.

The location of the block's insertion point, relative to the block's entities, will control the appearance and location of the block after scaling and rotating. At times, you may not see the block's preview image because the combination of scale factors, the rotation angle, or the current zoom magnification causes the block to be located off the screen, relative to the insertion point.

If the location of the insertion point is a problem, cancel the Insert command with Ctrl-C, zoom out so that more of the drawing area is visible, and then reinsert the block. If necessary, insert the block using the asterisk option and redefine it with a new insertion point.

RELATED SYSTEM VARIABLES

DRAGMODE (enables or disables dynamic dragging).

SAMPLE DIALOG

The following sample dialog inserts the block named Window as illustrated in Figure 9.16, using presets for x, y, and z scale factors and rotating the block after it is inserted:

```
Command: Insert
Block name (or ?): Window
Insertion point: (pick a point)
X scale factor <1> / Corner / XYZ: XYZ
X scale factor <1> / Corner: 36
Y scale factor (default = X): 8
Z scale factor (default = X): 36
```

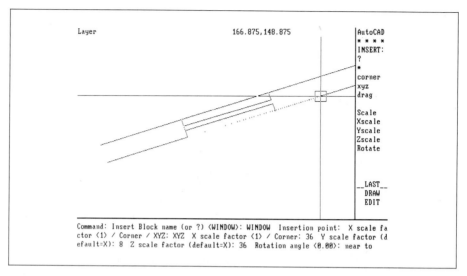

FIGURE 9.16: Inserting a window block per sample dialog. In this figure, the Window block has been preset to an x-axis scale of 36, a y-axis scale of 8, and a z-axis scale of 36. This represents a 36-by-36-inch window in an 8-inch wall. The Window block is previewed at this scale and inserted between the wall lines, and is now being rotated into position using the wall line to help pinpoint the rotation angle.

Rotation angle <0.00>: **NEAR** to **(pick a point on the wall)**Command:
Command:

Minsert

Allows multiple insertions of a block by combining features of the Insert and Array commands.

VERSIONS

Versions 2.5 and later.

COMMAND OPTIONS

Minsert first prompts for a block name, insertion point, scaling factors, and rotation angle. The prompt sequence for entering this data is detailed in the Command Options section of the Insert command. There is one difference when using Minsert, however: you are not permitted to use an asterisk in front of a block name.

After you have entered the necessary information for inserting the block, AutoCAD prompts for multiple copies of the block in a manner similar to the rectangular Array command:

> Number of rows (---):

Respond to this prompt by entering an integer to indicate the number of rows of blocks in the array. After you enter the number of rows, AutoCAD prompts for the number of columns:

> Number of columns (¦ ¦ ¦):

Again, respond to this prompt by entering an integer, indicating the number of columns (the number of blocks in each row).

AutoCAD then prompts for the distance between the columns and rows of the array:

> Unit cell or distance between rows (---):
> Distance between columns (¦ ¦ ¦):

This distance is measured from the insertion point of the original block to the insertion point of the block in the adjacent column or row at the rotation angle previously supplied. It is *not* the spacing between the objects in the array.

If you enter positive distances, AutoCAD makes copies in rows from bottom to top and in columns from left to right. If you enter negative distances, Auto-CAD copies in the reverse direction. You may enter a positive distance for the one and a negative distance for the other, if you wish, thus controlling the direction of the resulting array.

Refer to Figure 10.2 for an illustration of distances between rows and columns in a rectangular array. Refer to the discussion of the Array command in Chapter 10 for more details regarding the creation of rectangular arrays.

USAGE

The Minsert command can be duplicated by invoking the Insert command followed by the Array command. Unlike these two commands, however, the Minsert command results in an array that is considered a single object for selection and editing purposes. Polar arrays cannot be created using the Minsert command.

RELATED COMMANDS

Insert, Array

RELATED SYSTEM VARIABLES

DRAGMODE (enables or disables dynamic dragging)

SAMPLE DIALOG

The following sample dialog assumes the existence in the drawing of a block named "Box," with default measurements of 1 × 1 drawing units:

```
Command: MINSERT
Block name (or ?): BOX
Insertion point: 7,7
X scale factor <1> / Corner / XYZ: (press Enter)
Y scale factor (default = X): (press Enter)
Rotation angle <0.00>: (press Enter)
Number of rows (---) <1>: 6
Number of columns (¦ ¦ ¦) <1>: 6
Unit cell or distance between rows (---): 2
Distance between columns (¦ ¦ ¦): 2
```

PFACE

Allows construction of a complex polygon mesh, called a *polyface mesh* or *ratmesh,* with non-rectangular 3-D faces.

VERSIONS

Release 11 and later.

COMMAND OPTIONS

Vertex (#)   Enter the coordinate locations of each vertex in the mesh you intend to create. Make special note of the vertex locations and the order in which you enter them, as you will use the number of each vertex to construct the faces in the mesh.

Face (#), vertex (#)   You must construct each face individually, which you do by entering the numbers of all its vertices and then pressing Enter. When you finish each face, AutoCAD will prompt for the next face in the mesh. When all faces have been constructed, press Enter, and AutoCAD will construct the mesh.

If you desire an invisible edge for any of the faces, enter a negative vertex number for the beginning vertex of the invisible edge.

You may change the color of individual faces by entering **COLOR** in response to the vertex number prompt. When you enter **COLOR**, AutoCAD responds:

```
New color <current>:
```

Respond with a valid color number or name for your system. Refer to Chapter 5 for details regarding AutoCAD's coloring system.

USAGE

The Pface command is designed for meshes with non-rectangular faces or meshes that cannot be generated using the Edgesurf, Revsurf, Rulesurf, or Tabsurf commands. The primary purpose of the command is for use in AutoLISP and Advanced Development System programs, where the process of building such meshes can be automated.

Polyface meshes cannot be edited using the Pedit command. In other words, you cannot smooth them or edit individual vertices. You can, however, use any 3Dface editing command.

The process of building meshes manually with the Pface command can quickly become tedious. If you must use Pface from the command prompt, though, the following steps will help make the process a little easier:

- First, construct a representation of the mesh on a separate layer reserved for this purpose, using line entities. This will help you visualize the mesh you are trying to create. Design the mesh to be small and simple, as you can expand the finished mesh afterwards using the Array, Move, and Copy commands.

- Use the Dtext command to enter reference numbers for easy recall. Number each intersection, starting with 1, and number each face, again starting at 1.

- Set the layer for the mesh as the current layer and set global object snap to *intersection* using the Osnap command.

- Invoke Pface and pick each vertex coordinate using the pointing device. Select them in numerical order, as shown by the reference numbers on the screen.

- Construct each face with the vertex numbers, using the reference numbers for faces that you have entered on the screen.

- Return to the layer with the reference entities and erase the scratch lines and reference text.

RELATED COMMANDS

3Dface

SAMPLE DIALOG

The following sample dialog will produce the polyface mesh illustrated in Figure 9.17:

```
Command: PFACE
Vertex 1:INSERT 9D
 6,2,1
Vertex 2: 6,4,1
Vertex 3:  6,6,1
Vertex 4: 7,3,2
Vertex 5: 7,5,2
Vertex 6:8,2,1
Vertex 7: 8,4,0
Vertex 8: 8,6,1
Vertex 9: (press Enter)
Face 1, vertex 1: 1
Face 1, vertex 2: 4
Face 1, vertex 3: 6
Face 1, vertex 4: (press Enter)
Face 2, vertex 1: 1
Face 2, vertex 2: 2
Face 2, vertex 3: 4
Face 2, vertex 4: (press Enter)
Face 3, vertex 1: 2
Face 3, vertex 2: 3
Face 3, vertex 3: 5
Face 3, vertex 4: (press Enter)
Face 4, vertex 1: 3
Face 4, vertex 2: 5
Face 4, vertex 3: 8
Face 4, vertex 4: (press Enter)
Face 5, vertex 1: 3
Face 5, vertex 2: 6
Face 5, vertex 3: 7
Face 5, vertex 4: (press Enter)
Face 6, vertex 1: 2
Face 6, vertex 2: 7
Face 6, vertex 3: 8
Face 6, vertex 4: (press Enter)
Face 7, vertex 1: 2
Face 7, vertex 2: 5
Face 7, vertex 3: 8
Face 7, vertex 4:  (press Enter)
Face 8, vertex 1: 2
Face 8, vertex 2: 4
```

Face 8, vertex 3: **6**
Face 8, vertex 4: **(press Enter)**
Face 9, vertex 1: **(press Enter)**
Command: **MIRROR**
Select objects: **L**
1 found
Select objects: **(press Enter)**
First point of mirror line: **8,2**
Second point: **8,3**
Delete old objects? <N> **(press Enter)**
Command: **VPOINT**
Rotate/<View point> <0.000,0.000,1.000>: **.65, −3,1**
Regenerating drawing.
Command: **SHADE**
Command:

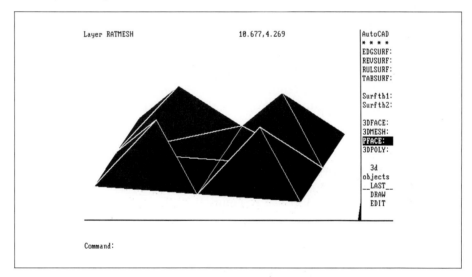

Figure 9.17: A shaded polyface mesh. This relatively simple ratmesh was generated with the sample dialog for the Pface command and then shaded. To generate a ratmesh, it is necessary to designate all the vertices in the mesh, as well as all the resulting faces. This mesh has eight vertices and eight faces—the resulting mesh is mirrored to achieve the object you see here.

POLYGON

Constructs a closed polygon with 3 to 1024 sides.

VERSIONS

Version 2.5 and later.

COMMAND OPTIONS

Number of sides   After you invoke the Polygon command, AutoCAD first prompts for the number of sides. Enter an integer from 3 to 1024. The integer must be entered from the keyboard or picked from a screen or tablet menu.

Edge   Enter **E** to specify the endpoints of one of the polygon's sides, or "edges." AutoCAD prompts:

> First endpoint of edge:

Select an endpoint of one of the polygon's sides using any standard point-selection method. AutoCAD responds:

> Second endpoint of edge:

A rubberband line appears from the first endpoint to the intersection of the cross-hairs. Select the second endpoint of the polygon's side, and AutoCAD completes construction of the polygon.

Center of polygon   Alternatively, you may enter the polygon's center point using any of AutoCAD's standard point-selection methods. If you enter a point instead of selecting the Edge option, AutoCAD prompts:

> Inscribed in circle/Circumscribed about circle

You may respond to this prompt by entering either **I** or **C**. If you enter **I**, you are indicating that the vertices of the polygon will intersect the circumference of a cir-cle whose radius you will provide. In other words, the polygon will fit exactly within a circle, as illustrated in Figure 9.18. If you enter **C**, you are indicating that the midpoint of each of the polygon's sides will lie tangent to the circumfer-ence of a circle whose radius you will provide, as illustrated in Figure 9.18. After you select one of these options, AutoCAD prompts:

> Radius of circle:

Enter the radius of the circle about which the polygon will be drawn. AutoCAD then constructs the requested polygon.

You may enter the radius by picking a point. AutoCAD displays a rubber-band line extending from the selected center point to the intersection of the cross-hairs. As you move the crosshairs, AutoCAD displays a preview image of the polygon that will result if the current intersection of the crosshairs is picked.

If you enter the radius by typing it at the keyboard or by selecting a number from a menu, AutoCAD draws the polygon with its lowermost side parallel to

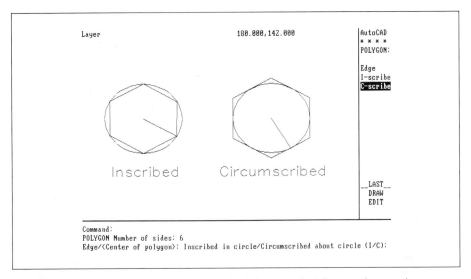

FIGURE 9.18: Polygons inscribed in and circumscribed about a circle. When you draw a polygon, AutoCAD prompts for a polygon that is either inscribed in or circumscribed about a circle. This figure illustrates the difference. The polygon on the left is inscribed in a circle, meaning that its vertices will intersect the circumference. The polygon on the right is circumscribed; the midpoints of all its sides intersect the circumference of the circle.

the current snap angle. If you have not rotated the snap angle, this line will be horizontal.

USAGE

The Polygon command simplifies the construction of closed polygons by prompting for the number of sides and the length of a side. It then draws a closed polyline representing the requested polygon.

A polygon is actually a polyline. You may use the Explode command to edit its sides individually if you choose. You may also edit it using the PEdit command. Refer to Chapter 10 for details regarding the Explode and PEdit commands.

Although the Polygon command will not draw polygons with wide lines, you may change the width of the polygon's line by using the PEdit command after the polygon is drawn. If you need to draw many wide-line polygons, simplify the process by combining these two commands into a macro, or (if you draw only a few types of polygons) create a block library of standard polygon shapes.

RELATED COMMANDS

PLine.

SAMPLE DIALOG

The following sample dialog creates a nine-sided polygon, as illustrated in Figure 9.19:

Command: **Polygon**
Number of sides: **9**
Edge/<Center of polygon>: **E**
First endpoint of edge: **(pick a point)**
Second endpoint of edge: **(pick a point)**
Command:

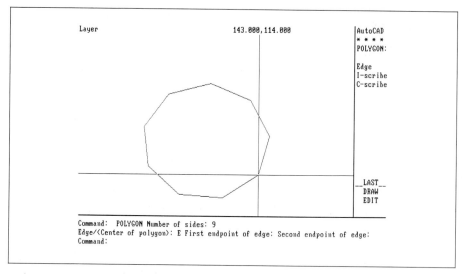

FIGURE 9.19: Nine-sided polygon per sample dialog. The Polygon command greatly simplifies the process of generating complex polygons. In this figure, a nine-sided polygon is generated after you enter the number of sides and the endpoints of one of those sides.

PLINE

Creates 2-D AutoCAD polylines, a special entity type.

VERSIONS

All.

COMMAND OPTIONS

From point   All polylines begin with this prompt. After invoking PLine, you must enter a starting point, using any of AutoCAD's standard coordinate-point entry methods.

Once you have entered a starting point, AutoCAD responds:

Current line-width is:

This prompt will indicate the line width as established either in the prototype drawing or as a result of changing it during a previous PLine command. Auto-CAD always remembers the last line width used for a polyline and uses that as the default for subsequent polylines. If the line width is not correct, you must change it by means of the Width option. Otherwise, you may proceed to construct your polyline.

Straight Line Segments

AutoCAD initially expects that polylines will consist of straight line segments, and thus displays a prompt of options that are available in *straight-line mode:*

Arc/Close/Halfwidth/Length/Undo/Width/ <Endpoint of line >:

Endpoint   If you enter a second coordinate point, AutoCAD draws a segment of the polyline from the previously selected point to the currently selected point, and repeats the prompt. You may continue to add straight line segments by supplying additional endpoints. When the polyline is complete, press Enter in response to this prompt. The command is then complete and AutoCAD's Command prompt reappears.

Arc   Enter **A** to switch to *arc mode,* described in detail in the next section, "Arc Segments."

Close   Enter **C** to close the polyline. AutoCAD responds by drawing a straight line segment from the previously selected endpoint to the original starting point of the polyline. If you desire a closed polygon figure, wherein the starting and ending points are the same vertex in the closed polyline, use the Close option to draw the last segment, as opposed to simply picking the original starting point. AutoCAD will react differently to a closed polyline when curve-fitting, filleting, or chamfering.

Halfwidth   Enter **H** to indicate to AutoCAD that you intend to specify the half-width of the next polyline segment; that is, the measurement from the polyline's center line to its edge. AutoCAD responds by prompting:

Starting half-width:

Enter the half-width of the polyline segment at its starting point. You will notice as you move the pointing device that a rubberband line appears, extending from the previously selected point to the intersection of the crosshairs. If you choose, you may pick a point, and AutoCAD will accept the length of the rubberband line as the half-width of the polyline. Alternatively, you may enter a value from the keyboard. AutoCAD then prompts:

Ending half-width:

The value of the starting half-width becomes the default value for the ending half-width, and you may specify this value simply by pressing Enter. If you wish for the ending half-width to be different, producing a tapered segment, enter what you wish the half-width of the polyline to be at the endpoint of the next segment.

AutoCAD then repeats the polyline options; you may enter other options, or the endpoint of the next segment.

Length   Enter **L** to draw a line segment at the same angle as the previous line segment (or tangent to the previous arc segment). AutoCAD responds:

Length of line:

As you move the pointing device, AutoCAD displays a rubberband line from the previously selected point to the intersection of the crosshairs. When you pick a second point, AutoCAD accepts the distance between the previous endpoint and the currently selected point as the length of the next line segment. It then draws the line segment at the same angle as the previous line segment. This will not necessarily be the same angle as the rubberband line. Alternatively, you may simply enter the length of the line segment from the keyboard.

Undo   If the line or arc segment just created is not correct, you may enter **U** to have the line segment erased. If you wish, you can continue to step back through the polyline until you arrive at the original starting point.

Width   Enter **W** to indicate to AutoCAD that you intend to specify the width of the next polyline segment—that is, the perpendicular measurement from the polyline's edge to its opposite edge. AutoCAD responds by prompting:

Starting width:

Enter the width of the polyline segment at its starting point. You will notice as you move the pointing device that a rubberband line appears, extending from the previously selected point to the intersection of the crosshairs. If you choose, you may pick a point, and AutoCAD will accept the length of the rubberband line as the width of the polyline.

This may be slightly misleading, since the endpoints of a wide polyline are at its center line, not at the edge. You may prefer to use the Halfwidth option just described. Alternatively, you may simply enter a value for the width from the keyboard.

AutoCAD then prompts:

Ending width:

The value of the starting width becomes the default value for the ending width, and you may enter this value simply by pressing Enter. If you wish for the ending width to be different, producing a tapered segment, enter what you wish the width of the polyline to be at the endpoint of the next segment.

AutoCAD then repeats the polyline options; you may enter other options, or the endpoint of the next polyline segment.

Arc Segments

When you enter **A** from the list of polyline options, you indicate to AutoCAD that the next line segment in the polyline will be an arc. AutoCAD switches to *arc mode* and displays the options available when drawing arc segments, as follows:

Angle/CEnter/CLose/Direction/Halfwidth/Line/Radius/Second pt/Undo/
Width/Endpoint

Each of these options is explained below.

Endpoint of arc   You may respond to the arc options by selecting the endpoint of the arc segment you intend to draw. As you move the crosshairs, AutoCAD displays a rubberband arc, starting tangent to the last polyline segment drawn, and ending at the intersection of the crosshairs. If the arc is the first segment of the polyline, AutoCAD will use the direction of the last arc, line, or polyline drawn as the starting direction of the arc. The arc segment's center point and included angle are calculated automatically based on the starting point, direction, and selected endpoint.

Angle   Enter **A** to indicate to AutoCAD that you wish to enter the included angle of the arc segment. AutoCAD prompts:

Included angle:

Enter the included angle of the arc. You may use any of AutoCAD's standard methods for entry of angle values. AutoCAD then prompts:

Center/Radius/Endpoint:

If you enter an endpoint, AutoCAD draws the arc beginning at the endpoint of the last polyline segment (or starting point). The center point of the arc is calculated automatically, so that an arc with the included angle you specified is drawn between the two endpoints. Normally, the arc is drawn counterclockwise between these two points. If you want the arc drawn clockwise, thus changing the location of the center point, enter a negative value for the included angle. After the arc endpoint is entered, AutoCAD redisplays the arc options. You may continue to draw arc segments using any of the options.

If you enter **C** in response to the above prompt, AutoCAD responds:

Center point:

Enter the center point of the arc using any standard point-selection method. AutoCAD draws the arc segment encompassing the included angle. The radius of the arc is the distance between the previously selected polyline vertex and the selected center point.

If you enter **R** in response to the "Center/Radius/Endpoint:" prompt, Auto-CAD responds:

Radius:

Enter the radius of the arc segment either by typing it from the keyboard or by selecting two points on the screen. AutoCAD uses the distance between these points as the radius of the arc segment. Next, AutoCAD prompts:

Direction of chord:

If dynamic dragging is enabled, AutoCAD displays a preview image of the resulting arc along with a rubberband line representing its included chord. As you move the pointing device, you will be able to see the arc segment that will result from picking a point in response to this prompt. AutoCAD uses the angle between the last polyline vertex and the intersection of the crosshairs as the angle of orientation for the chord of the arc, which is fixed in length now that you have entered the included angle and radius.

You may also enter the angle of orientation from the keyboard. Or, you may press Enter to accept the default, which is the ending angle of the last polyline arc segment, as stored in the LASTANGLE system variable.

After the arc segment is drawn, AutoCAD redisplays the arc options.

CEnter You may specify the center point of the arc segment by entering **CE** from the arc options. AutoCAD responds:

> Center point:

Enter the arc segment's center point using any of AutoCAD's standard point-entry methods. AutoCAD responds:

> Angle/Length/End point:

If you enter an endpoint now, AutoCAD draws the arc from the last segment's endpoint, using the selected center point and endpoint. If the selected endpoint does not intersect the arc, AutoCAD draws the arc so that its endpoint is collinear with the arc's center point and the selected endpoint, as shown in Figure 9.20.

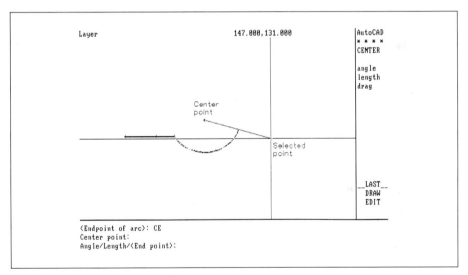

FIGURE 9.20: Adding an arc to a polyline—center, endpoint. In this figure, after the first straight segment of a polyline was entered, the Arc Segment option was chosen, followed by a center point for the arc. Now AutoCAD prompts for an arc endpoint. As you move the pointing device, a rubberband line extends from the chosen center point, and a rubberband arc extends from the last polyline vertex.

If you enter **A**, AutoCAD responds:

> Included angle:

Enter the arc's included angle; AutoCAD draws the arc from the last segment's endpoint, using the selected center point and included angle.

If you enter **L**, AutoCAD responds:

Length of chord:

Enter the length of the arc segment's chord; AutoCAD draws the arc resulting from these selected parameters.

CLose If the endpoint of the arc segment is the original starting point of the polyline, you may enter **CL**. AutoCAD will close the polyline with an arc segment. The center point and included angle of the arc segment are calculated automatically, based on the direction and endpoint of the previous segment.

Direction If you do not wish to use the direction of the previous segment as the starting direction of the arc segment, you may enter **D** to specify another starting direction. AutoCAD responds:

Direction from starting point:

Enter the absolute angle of direction using any of AutoCAD's standard methods for entering angle values. For example, you may enter angle degrees from the keyboard, or enter two coordinate points using the pointing device. AutoCAD will accept the angle formed by the two points as the new starting direction of the arc segment. After you enter the new starting direction, the arc options repeat.

Halfwidth This option is the same as the Halfwidth option in straight-line mode, described earlier.

Line When you are finished drawing arc segments and wish to draw a straight line segment, enter **L**. AutoCAD responds by switching back to standard straight-line mode and displaying the original straight-line options.

Radius You may draw the arc segment by entering the arc radii, followed by either the included angle or the arc endpoint. AutoCAD first prompts:

Radius:

Enter the radius of the arc segment. You may also enter the radius by picking any two coordinate points on the screen. AutoCAD accepts the distance between these two points as the radius of the arc segment. AutoCAD then prompts:

Angle/End point:

If you enter a coordinate point in response to this prompt, AutoCAD draws the arc segment using the selected radius from the endpoint of the last segment to the selected endpoint. The center point and included angle are calculated automatically.

If you wish to indicate the included angle of the arc segment instead, enter **A** in response to this prompt. AutoCAD responds:

Included angle:

Enter the arc's included angle using any of the standard angle-entry methods. AutoCAD responds:

Direction of chord:

The length of the chord is already established from the included angle and radius. AutoCAD only needs to know the angle of direction of the chord. You may enter an angle value or pick a point. AutoCAD uses the angle formed by the previous segment's endpoint and the selected point as the angle of direction for the chord. Before this point is entered, AutoCAD displays a rubberband line and a preview of the resulting arc on the screen. After you enter an angle of direction, AutoCAD draws the arc.

Second pt Enter **S** if you wish to draw the arc segment as a three-point arc. Since the starting point is the same as the endpoint of the previous segment, AutoCAD prompts:

Second point:

Enter the second point of the arc using any of AutoCAD's standard point-entry methods. AutoCAD responds:

End point:

Enter the endpoint of the arc. AutoCAD draws the arc through the three selected points.

Undo This option is the same as in straight-line mode, described earlier.

Width This option is the same as the Width option in straight-line mode, described earlier.

USAGE

A *polyline* is a special line composed of one or more straight and/or curved line segments and vertices that are treated as a single drawing entity. Polylines have many special features:

- They can be made up of any combination of straight and curved line segments.

- Each segment in a 2-D polyline can be drawn at varying widths, including "tapered" segments that have different widths at their starting and ending points. Refer to the Width option for details.

- All intersections of a single polyline or only specific vertices can be filleted or chamfered with a single command. Refer to Chapter 10 for details regarding the Fillet and Chamfer commands.

- Polylines can be curve-fit or spline-fit to create smooth curved lines. Refer to Chapter 10 for details on curve-fitting for polylines.

Tip: Regardless of the version, the PLine command can only draw polylines in a single 2-D plane. Release 10 and later allows you to draw 3-D polylines using the 3Dpoly command; however, 3Dpoly only draws straight line segments at zero width. If you are using Release 10 and later, you may take advantage of some of PLine's options in 3-D space by changing the UCS and continuing a new polyline from the endpoint of the previous one. However, such polylines are likely to appear distorted from different viewing angles.

RELATED COMMANDS

3Dpoly.

SAMPLE DIALOG

The following sample dialog produces the polyline pictured in Figure 9.21:

```
Command: PLine
From point: 1,6
Current line-width is 0.00
Arc/Close/Halfwidth/Length/Undo/Width/<Endpoint of line>: W
Starting width <0.0>: 0.05
Ending width <0.05>: (press Enter)
Arc/Close/Halfwidth/Length/Undo/Width/<Endpoint of line>: @2<0
Arc/Close/Halfwidth/Length/Undo/Width/<Endpoint of line>: A
Angle/CEnter/CLose/Direction/Halfwidth/Line/Radius/Secondpt/Undo/
Width/<Endpoint of arc>: CE
Center point: @1<0
Angle/Length/<End point>: @1<0
Angle/CEnter/CLose/Direction/Halfwidth/Line/Radius/Secondpt/Undo/
Width/<Endpoint of arc>: L
Arc/Close/Halfwidth/Length/Undo/Width/<Endpoint of line>: @2<0
Arc/Close/Halfwidth/Length/Undo/Width/<Endpoint of line>: @3<90
Arc/Close/Halfwidth/Length/Undo/Width/<Endpoint of line>: @2<180
Arc/Close/Halfwidth/Length/Undo/Width/<Endpoint of line>: A
Angle/CEnter/CLose/Direction/Halfwidth/Line/Radius/Secondpt/Undo/
Width/<Endpoint of arc>: CE
```

Center point: @**1**<**180**
Angle/Length/<End point>: **A**
Included angle: **−180**
Angle/CEnter/CLose/Direction/Halfwidth/Line/Radius/Secondpt/Undo/
Width/<Endpoint of arc>: **L**
Arc/Close/Halfwidth/Length/Undo/Width/<Endpoint of line>: @**2**<**180**
Arc/Close/Halfwidth/Length/Undo/Width/<Endpoint of line>: **C**
Command:

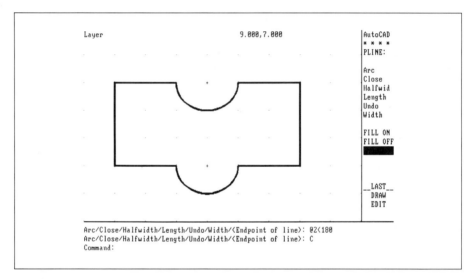

FIGURE 9.21: Polyline created per sample dialog. It combines several polyline drawing options, including adjusting the width, combining arc segments with straight segments, drawing clockwise and counterclockwise arc segments, and closing the polyline.

REVSURF

Creates a polygon mesh by rotating a line entity (called a path curve) around an axis.

VERSIONS

Release 10 and later.

COMMAND OPTIONS

Select path curve With any of AutoCAD's standard entity-selection methods, select the line entity you wish to use as a path curve. Only a single line entity can be selected.

Select axis of revolution   Select the open line entity you intend to use as the axis of revolution. An example is pictured in Figure 9.22. The result of full-circle and half-circle revolution is pictured in Figure 9.23.

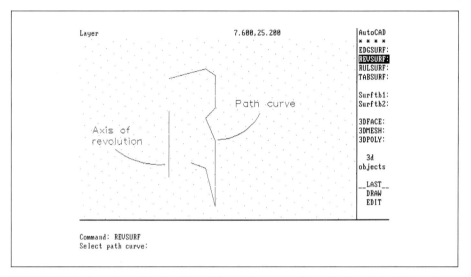

FIGURE 9.22: The basic Revsurf tools: a 3-D polyline path curve and an axis of revolution. The path curve will be rotated around the axis, generating a polygon mesh as it goes. The number of vertices in the mesh is controlled by the SURFTAB1 and SURFTAB2 system variables. Two possible meshes generated by this path curve and axis are illustrated in Figure 9.22.

Start angle   If you would like the mesh generation to begin at the location of the path curve, enter a start angle of zero. Otherwise, you can begin the polygon mesh at an angle offset from the path curve, along the revolution path.

Included angle   The included angle of revolution can be any number of degrees up to 360, a full circle. For example, entering an included angle of 90 degrees will produce a polygon mesh created by rotating the path curve one quarter of a circle around the axis of revolution.

The direction of the revolution angle is determined by the point with which you pick the axis of revolution. That is, if you look down the axis of revolution with the pick point farthest away from you on the line, the direction of the revolution will appear to be counterclockwise. This is illustrated in Figure 9.24.

USAGE

The Revsurf command first prompts you to select a *path curve*, or profile, and then rotates it around an axis. Both the path curve and the axis must be existing

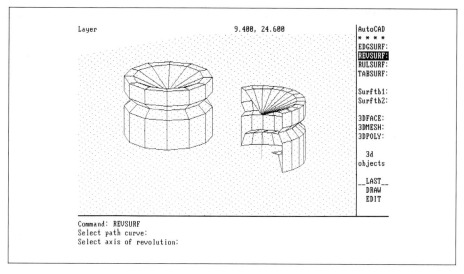

FIGURE 9.23: Revsurf: full-circle and half-circle. This hidden-line rendering illustrates two possible polygon meshes generated using the path curve and axis of revolution illustrated in Figure 9.21. The mesh on the left is a full-circle mesh. The mesh on the right is a half-circle mesh. Notice that the same number of vertices is used for each; in the half-circle mesh, they must necessarily be closer together.

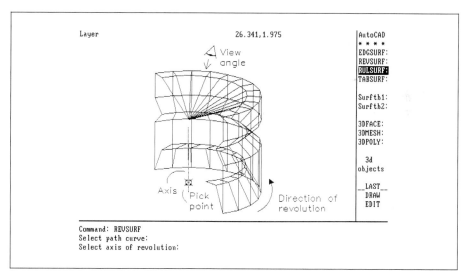

FIGURE 9.24: Revsurf: picking the axis of revolution. When you use the Revsurf command, the point by which you pick the axis of revolution is critical in determining the direction in which the path curve is rotated. The rule is as follows: As you look down the axis of revolution from a point in line (or nearly in line) with the endpoints, so that the pick point is nearest to the more distant endpoint, the direction of revolution will appear to be counterclockwise. In this figure, the viewing angle is from the top and the pick point is near the bottom, resulting in the illustrated direction of revolution.

entities in the drawing. The path curve can be any line entity—arc, circle, line, or 2-D or 3-D polyline. It defines the N direction of the polygon mesh. (Refer to the description of the 3Dmesh command in this chapter for a definition of a polygon mesh.) The axis, which determines the M direction of the polygon mesh, can be any open line or polyline. If a polyline is chosen, the axis is considered to be a straight line drawn between the polyline's starting and ending points.

You may generate the polygon mesh beginning with the path curve, or you may specify a start angle, which will cause the polygon mesh to begin at the specified angle of rotation along the revolution path, away from the path curve. You may rotate a full circle or only a portion of the full circle.

The mesh resolution is determined by the values of two system variables, SURFTAB1 and SURFTAB2. The SURFTAB1 system variable contains the number of vertices in the M direction (along the angle of revolution), while SURFTAB2 contains the number of vertices in the N direction (along the path curve). These values can be set using the Setvar command. Refer to Chapter 13 for details regarding Setvar.

The higher the values of SURFTAB1 and SURFTAB2, the finer the resolution of the resulting mesh. Bear in mind, however, that meshes with very fine degrees of resolution take longer to regenerate, and greatly enlarge the size of the drawing file.

Tip: Set the values of SURFTAB1 and SURFTAB2 as low as possible while still generating an acceptable mesh. Remember that surfaces generated using Revsurf can be smoothed with the PEdit command.

RELATED SYSTEM VARIABLES

SURFTAB1 (number of tabulations in the M direction), SURFTAB2 (number of tabulations in the N direction).

SAMPLE DIALOG

The following dialog sets new values for SURFTAB1 and SURFTAB2, changes the drawing viewpoint, draws two 3-D polylines, and uses them to create a full-circle Revsurf mesh:

```
Command: Setvar
Variable name or ?: SURFTAB1
New value for SURFTAB1 <6>: 12
Command: Setvar
Variable name or ? <SURFTAB1>: SURFTAB2
New value for SURFTAB2 <6>: 12
Command: Vpoint
```

```
Rotate/<View point> <0,0,1>: 1.4375, − .75,.675
Regenerating drawing.
Command: 3Dpoly
From point: 7,20,1
Close/Undo/<Endpoint of line>: 8,20,.5
Close/Undo/<Endpoint of line>: 8.25,20,0
Close/Undo/<Endpoint of line>: 8.25,20,1
Close/Undo/<Endpoint of line>: 8,20,1.25
Close/Undo/<Endpoint of line>: 8.25,20,1.5
Close/Undo/<Endpoint of line>: 8.25,20,2
Close/Undo/<Endpoint of line>: 8,20,2
Close/Undo/<Endpoint of line>: 7,20,1.5
Close/Undo/<Endpoint of line>: (press Enter)
Command: 3Dpoly
From point: 7,20,0
Close/Undo/<Endpoint of line>: 7,20,1
Close/Undo/<Endpoint of line>: (press Enter)
Command: Revsurf
Select path curve: 8,20,2
Select axis of revolution: 7,20,0
Start angle <0>: (press Enter)
Included angle ( + = ccw, − = cw) <Full circle>: (press Enter)
Command:
```

RULESURF

Generates a ruled surface between two selected line entities.

VERSIONS

Release 10 and later.

COMMAND OPTIONS

Select first defining curve   Point to the line entity you intend to use for the first defining curve. If the defining curve is open, it is a good idea to pick that entity using a point as close as possible to one of its endpoints; AutoCAD will begin generating the ruled surface lines at the endpoint nearest your selection point. If you prefer, you may use Osnap Endp to select the entity precisely at its endpoint.

Select second defining curve   Point to the line entity you intend to use for the second defining curve. As is the case with the first defining curve, if it is open, it is a good idea to pick that entity using a point as close as possible to one of its endpoints—in most cases, the point you pick should be as close as possible to the previous selection point. If you prefer, you may use Osnap Endp to select the second entity precisely at its endpoint. This is because AutoCAD uses the endpoints closest to your selection points to construct the first line of the ruled surface. If opposing endpoints are used, the result may be a "folded surface" as the ruled surface lines intersect. Therefore, it is important to select the entities with points that "show" AutoCAD how to orient the ruled surface lines.

Figure 9.25 illustrates two ruled surfaces that can result from different point picks on the same two defining curves. In one case, the arcs were selected incorrectly, resulting in a "folded" ruled surface.

If your ruled surface lines intersect, use the Undo command to delete the mesh. Then try again, changing only one of your point picks. If your defining curves are closed, the location of the point pick does not matter.

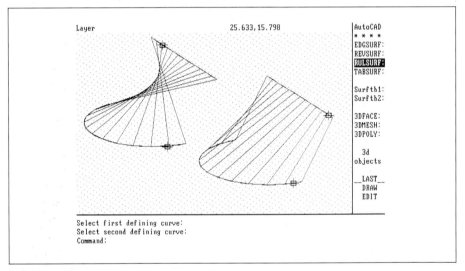

FIGURE 9.25: Rulesurf: correct and incorrect point picks. This figure uses copies of the same two defining curves to illustrate the importance of correct pick points when selecting open defining curves. In addition to picking the curves, you are also showing AutoCAD at which end of each line entity to begin the mesh. The rule of thumb is to pick the curves using points close to the endpoints that are nearest to each other, not farthest apart.

USAGE

A *ruled surface* is a type of polygon mesh consisting of a series of lines whose endpoints are spaced at equal intervals along two other line entities in space. (Refer to the description of the 3Dmesh command in this chapter for a definition of a polygon mesh.) The line entities, also called *defining curves,* may be lines, polylines, arcs, or circles. One of the defining curves may be a point, but not both. (If both were points, a ruled surface using them would appear only as a line.)

The number of lines representing the ruled surface is controlled by the value of the SURFTAB1 system variable. AutoCAD constructs the ruled surface by drawing lines that join the two defining curves at equal intervals, beginning with the endpoints of the defining curves that are nearest to the points you used to select them. Figure 9.26 illustrates ruled surfaces generated between an arc and a line, and between a circle and an octagon.

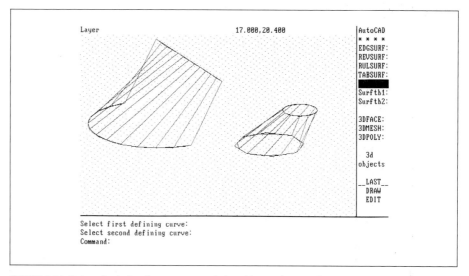

FIGURE 9.26: Rulesurf ruled surfaces: open and closed lines. These surfaces were generated using the sample dialog for the Rulesurf command. The ruled surface on the left was generated between two open "defining curves," a line segment and an arc, while the rule surface on the right was generated using closed "defining curves"—two circles.

If the endpoints of a defining curve are the same—for example, a polygon or circle—it is said to be *closed*. If the endpoints of a defining curve are not the same—for example, a line or arc—it is said to be *open*. In generating a ruled surface, if one defining curve is closed, the other must be closed as well, or it must be a point. If one defining curve is open, the other must be open as well, or it must be a point.

In a ruled surface, only the N direction is used. No lines are generated in the M direction, and the value of the SURFTAB2 system variable is not used.

Tip: When possible, use Osnap Endp to select your defining curves precisely at the endpoints where the first ruled surface line is to be drawn. This gives you the greatest possible control over how your ruled surface is generated.

If you are having trouble generating an acceptable ruled surface between two closed entities (a circle and a polygon, for example), try mirroring one of the entities "in place" with the Mirror command and responding **Y** to the prompt "delete old entities." Then try generating the ruled surface using the mirrored entity.

RELATED SYSTEM VARIABLES

SURFTAB1 (controls the number of lines generated along the defining curves, also called the *N direction*).

SAMPLE DIALOG

The following sample dialog sets the value of the SURFTAB1 system variable, changes the drawing viewpoint, and constructs the entities required to generate the ruled surfaces pictured in Figure 9.25:

```
Command: Setvar
Variable name or ?: SURFTAB1
New value for SURFTAB1 <6>: 12
Command: Vpoint
Rotate/<View point> <0,0,1>:1, − .45,.35
Regenerating drawing.
Command: Arc
Center/<Start point>: 15,14
Center/End/<Second point>: C
Center: 17,14
Angle/Length of chord/<End point>: 19,14
Command: Line
From point: 15,15,2
To point: 19,15,2
To point: (press Enter)
Command: Polygon
Number of sides: 8
Edge/<Center of polygon>: 20,16
Inscribed in circle/Circumscribed about circle (I/C): C
Radius of circle: @1<0
Command: Circle
3P/2P/TTR/<Center point>: 20,17,1
Diameter/<Radius>: @.5<0
Command: Rulesurf
Select first defining curve: 15,15,2
Select second defining curve: 15,14
Command: Rulesurf
```

Select first defining curve: **20.5,17,1**
Select second defining curve: **19,16**
Command:

SHAPE

Inserts predefined shapes from a shape file into a drawing.

VERSIONS

All.

COMMAND OPTIONS

Shape name   Enter the name of the shape you wish to insert into the drawing. A shape file containing this shape name must have been previously loaded into the drawing using the Load command. (Refer to Chapter 15 for details on the Load command.)

?   Enter a question mark if you wish to see a list of all currently loaded shape names. AutoCAD responds by listing the shape names and the files that contain them. After all the shape names are listed, AutoCAD repeats the Command prompt. You may then press Enter to repeat the Shape command, if desired.

Starting point   Enter the insertion point of the shape using any of AutoCAD's standard coordinate-point entry methods. As you move the pointing device, a preview image of the shape moves about on the screen. The intersection of the crosshairs indicates the shape's insertion point.

Height   Enter the height of the shape. This value is used as the scaling value for the shape. For example, if the original shape was scaled as 1 drawing unit by 1 drawing unit, a shape height of 2 will double the size of the shape, a shape height of 3 will triple it, and so on. The actual result of the shape scaling value depends on the relationship between the original shape scale and the current scale of the drawing.

   To allow the greatest degree of flexibility at insertion time, most shapes should be defined as one-by-one shapes.

Rotation angle   After the shape is inserted and scaled, it may be rotated around its insertion point. As you move the crosshairs, a preview image of the scaled shape is rotated on the screen. When you select a point, the angle referenced by the insertion point and the selected point becomes the angle of rotation. Alternatively, you may enter the value of the rotation angle from the keyboard or from a menu.

USAGE

Shapes are special entities similar in function to blocks. They are composed of lines, circles, and arcs. To insert a shape into a drawing, you must first load a special disk file, called a *shape definition file,* into the drawing. Shape definition files have the extension SHX. They may contain up to 255 separate *shape definitions,* which are special numerical sequences used by AutoCAD to recreate the given shape.

Like blocks, shapes are placed at an insertion point, and then scaled and rotated. Unlike blocks, shapes cannot be defined "on the fly" from existing entities in a drawing, nor can they contain complex entities (although a shape can subreference another shape). Shapes, therefore, are less flexible and harder to define than blocks; on the other hand, they take up less space and can be drawn faster than blocks.

Use shapes when they are simple in structure and you wish to save as much time and disk space as you can. Otherwise, blocks will better serve your purposes.

Warning: When a drawing contains shapes, AutoCAD must always be able to find the referenced shape definition file along its search path. Always have backups of your shape files handy in case the shape files on your hard disk are accidentally erased or destroyed.

For details regarding shape definitions and instructions for loading shape files into a drawing, refer to Chapter 15.

RELATED COMMANDS

Insert.

SAMPLE DIALOG

The following dialog inserts a shape called Edge into a drawing, as illustrated in Figure 9.27. Refer to Chapter 15 for the definition of this shape.

```
Command: Shape
Shape name (or ?): Edge
Starting point: 3,7
Height <1>: 8
Rotation angle <0.00>: 90
Command:
```

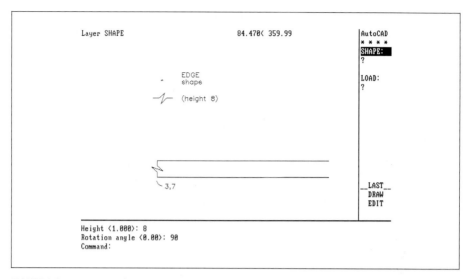

FIGURE 9.27: Inserting a shape into a drawing. In this figure, a single shape called Edge is inserted into a drawing to "cap" two lines that are 8 drawing units apart. The original shape is 1 × 1; the original and enlarged versions of the shape are shown in the upper left.

TABSURF

Generates a ruled surface by extruding a line entity (called a path curve) according to the direction and length of a second line entity (called a direction vector).

VERSIONS

Release 10 and later.

COMMAND OPTIONS

Select path curve   Pick the line entity you wish to use as a path curve.

Select direction vector   Pick the open line entity you wish to use as a direction vector. The direction vector will indicate the length and direction of the path curve's extrusion, starting from the endpoint closest to your pick point. Thus, the point you use to select the direction vector has a direct bearing on how the path curve will be extruded.

If the path curve is extruded in the wrong direction, use the Undo command to delete the polygon mesh. Then select the entities again, this time selecting the direction vector using a point near the opposite endpoint.

USAGE

The Tabsurf command prompts you to select a line entity to use as a path curve (or *profile*) and extrudes it a specific length and direction equal to the length and direction of a second selected line entity, the direction vector. Both path curve and direction vector must be existing entities in the drawing. The path curve can be any line entity—an arc, circle, line, or 2-D or 3-D polyline. It may be open or closed. It defines the N direction of the polygon mesh. (Refer to the description of the 3Dmesh command in this chapter for a definition of a polygon mesh.) The axis determines the M direction of the polygon mesh. The direction vector can be a line or polyline, but it must be open. If a polyline is chosen, the direction vector is considered to be a straight line drawn between the polyline's starting and ending points; intermediate vertices are ignored.

The direction vector need not be located near the path curve, although it is more convenient if it is. The direction vector gives AutoCAD its "instructions" on how to extrude the path curve into a ruled surface. The angle of direction and the length of the direction vector, beginning with the endpoint closest to the point you use to select it, will equal the direction and length of the path curve's extrusion. The process is illustrated in Figure 9.28.

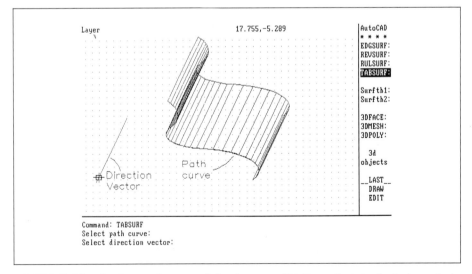

FIGURE 9.28: Tabsurf tools—a path curve and direction vector. This figure illustrates the tools required by the Tabsurf command: a path curve and direction vector. The path curve is the curved polyline that forms the lower edge of the ruled surface. The direction vector is a nearby line entity.

The number of lines used to generate the ruled surface is controlled by the SURFTAB1 system variable. The higher the value of SURFTAB1, the greater the number of lines used to generate the ruled surface. Lines are generated in one direction only. The value of SURFTAB2 is irrelevant when using Tabsurf.

Tip: When possible, use Osnap Endp to select the direction vector. This gives you the greatest possible control over the direction of the resulting ruled surface.

RELATED SYSTEM VARIABLES

SURFTAB1 (number of tabulations in the ruled surface).

SAMPLE DIALOG

The following dialog sets a new value for SURFTAB1, changes the drawing viewpoint, draws a polyline and a line, and generates the ruled surface shown in Figure 9.28:

```
Command: Setvar
Variable name or ?: SURFTAB1
New value for SURFTAB1 <6>: 12
Command: Vpoint
Rotate/<View point> <0,0,1>: 1, − .45,.35
Regenerating drawing.
Command: PLine
From point: 15,6
Current line-width is 0'-0"
Arc/Close/Halfwidth/Length/Undo/Width/ <Endpoint of line>: A
Angle/CEnter/CLose/Direction/Halfwidth/Line/Radius/Second pt/Undo/
Width/ <Endpoint of arc>: 17,5
Angle/CEnter/CLose/Direction/Halfwidth/Line/Radius/Second pt/Undo/
Width/ <Endpoint of arc>: 19,5
Angle/CEnter/CLose/Direction/Halfwidth/Line/Radius/Second pt/Undo/
Width/ <Endpoint of arc>: 22,5
Angle/CEnter/CLose/Direction/Halfwidth/Line/Radius/Second pt/Undo/
Width/ <Endpoint of arc>: (press Enter)
Command: Line
From point: 20,1,0
To point: 20,2,2
To point: (press Enter)
Command: Tabsurf
Select path curve: 15,6
Select direction vector: 20,1
Command:
```

STYLE

Creates text styles, or defines the current text style from those available.

VERSIONS

All.

COMMAND OPTIONS

Text style name   First enter the name of a new style, or a current style. Auto-CAD indicates whether the style name is new or preexisting, and supplies prompts (along with default responses) for the various style parameters. If it is an existing style, the default responses will be the stored parameters for that particular style. For a new style, the default responses are those for the Standard text style.

Next, in Release 11 and later, if your display device supports the Advanced User Interface, AutoCAD will display a dialog box containing all the shape files that it finds, including font files. You may select a font file from the list, or pick the "Type it in" box to enter a font file name from the keyboard. Refer to the discussion of dialog boxes in Chapter 5 for details.

?   Enter a question mark to list all the currently loaded text styles.

Height   Enter a value for the height of the text characters. Entering the value will cause all text using this style to be generated at the same height. Auto-CAD will not prompt for a text height when using the Text command with this style. A style of this type is called a *fixed-height style*. Alternatively, you may enter **0** as the height. A text style with a height of zero is called a *variable-height style*. Auto-CAD will prompt for the text height when using the Text command with this style, and can adjust the height of the text characters when using the Aligned text option. (Refer to the discussion of the Text command for details.)

Width factor   Normally, the width of the text characters is determined automatically—first by their definition in the font file, and then as a function of the style height. However, if you prefer, you may enter a width factor that will compress or expand the characters relative to their height. For example, a width factor of 2 means that the characters will be generated twice as wide as they would be normally. A width factor of 0.5 means that characters will be generated half as wide as they would be normally. A width factor of 1 generates characters with normal width.

Obliquing angle   Text characters are normally generated upright, with an obliquing angle of zero degrees. If you prefer, you can apply a slant to the text characters by entering a value for the obliquing angle. Such a value will cause the characters to slant from their normal upright orientation. Figure 9.29 illustrates characters with a significant 35-degree obliquing angle. A positive obliquing angle produces a forward slant; a negative obliquing angle produces a backward slant.

Backwards   You may answer this prompt either **Y** or **N** . A response of **Y** generates text as mirror-text—that is, backwards. If you enter **N** , text is generated in normal orientation.

Upside-down   You may answer this prompt either **Y** or **N** . A response of **Y** generates text upside down. If you enter **N**, text is generated in normal orientation.

Vertical   This prompt will appear if the selected font file is capable of producing text that is vertically oriented, as demonstrated in Figure 9.28. If you desire vertical text, answer **Y** . If you desire ordinary horizontal text, enter **N** .

USAGE

The *text font* defines a consistent general shape of the text characters. Some frequently used AutoCAD text fonts are roman, italic, and simple line characters.

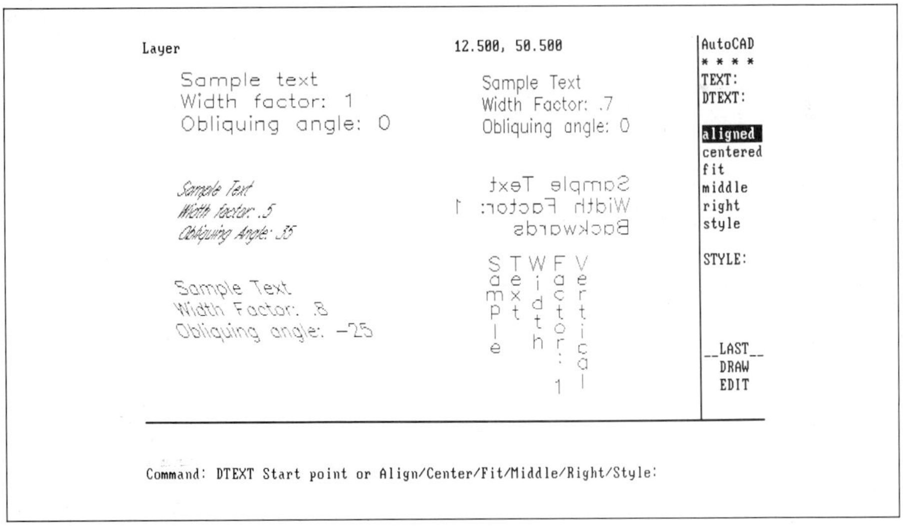

FIGURE 9.29: Roman simplex using different text parameters. This figure illustrates how a single text font can be made to appear different by means of different text parameters set using the Style command: obliquing angle, width factor, and orientation.

Text fonts are contained in *font files,* special disk files that contain the definitions for drawing text characters. Font files are similar to shape files in that they also contain numerical descriptions of drawing entities. They also have the extension SHX. Font files usually contain numerical descriptions for all the letters of the alphabet, numbers, punctuation marks, and other special symbols used in generating text. AutoCAD supplies several such font files.

All AutoCAD drawings contain at least one default text style, named Standard. It is an extremely simple, single-line font with nonfixed height, a width factor of 1, no obliquing angle, and a normal orientation: forward, upright, and horizontal. It uses a font file named TXT.SHX.

Several different text styles may use the same font file, changing parameters other than the font for each individual style. A single drawing may contain several different text styles, with as many fonts as there are font files to define them.

To define a new text style, invoke the Style command. AutoCAD prompts for the name of the font file, and all necessary parameters to use when generating text characters. After you have answered all the prompts, the style you named becomes the current style. You can make any existing style the current style by invoking the Style command, entering the name of an existing style, and answering all the parameter prompts by pressing Enter to accept the default responses.

Unless you change it with the Style option, the Text command will generate text using the current named text style.

Prior to Release 9, AutoCAD was supplied with four font files. They were:

TXT	Simple, straight-line font
SIMPLEX	Simple, curved-line font
COMPLEX	Multistroke, roman, serif font
ITALIC	Multistroke, italic, serif font

As of Release 9, twenty new font files were added:

CYRILLIC	Cyrillic alphabet, alphabetical
CYRILTLC	Cyrillic alphabet, transliteration
GOTHICE	English gothic
GOTHICG	German gothic
GOTHICI	Italian gothic
GREEKC	Double-stroke greek alphabet
GREEKS	Single-stroke greek alphabet
ITALICC	Double-stroke italic (replaces old ITALIC)
ITALICT	Triple stroke italic
MONOTXT	Non-proportional, straight line font, like TXT

ROMANC	Double-stroke roman serif (replaces old COMPLEX)
ROMAND	Double-stroke roman sans serif
ROMANS	Single-stroke roman sans serif (replaces old SIMPLEX)
ROMANT	Triple-stroke roman serif
SCRIPTC	Double-stroke script (handwriting simulator)
SCRIPTS	Single-stroke script (handwriting simulator)
SYASTRO	Symbols, astrological
SYMAP	Symbols, mapping
SYMATH	Symbols, mathematical
SYMETEO	Symbols, meteorological
SYMUSIC	Symbols, music

Refer to Chapter 15 for detail regarding the modification and customization of shape and text-font files.

RELATED COMMANDS

Dtext, Text.

RELATED SYSTEM VARIABLES

TEXTSTYLE (current text style).

SAMPLE DIALOG

The following dialog creates a text style named Italic, using the ITALIC.SHX font file. It is a variable-height style with slightly compressed characters and normal orientation.

```
Command: Style
Text style name (or ?) <STANDARD>: Italic
New style.
Font file <txt>: ITALIC
Height <0' – 0">: (press Enter)
Width factor <1.00>: 0.85
Obliquing angle <0.00>: (press Enter)
Backwards? <N> (press Enter)
Upside-down? <N> (press Enter)
Vertical? <N> (press Enter)
ITALIC is now the current text style.
Command:
```

TEXT

Inserts textual information into a drawing, allowing you to select the text style, the alignment of the text, and its size.

VERSIONS

All.

COMMAND OPTIONS

Start point   If you wish to enter left-justified text in the currently loaded text style, enter a point. AutoCAD responds by prompting for other text parameters, as follows:

- Height. If you have defined the current text style with a text height of zero (indicating nonfixed text height—refer to the Style command in this chapter for details), you will receive this prompt. Enter the height of the text. If you move the crosshairs, you will see a rubberband line extending from the text starting point to the intersection of the crosshairs. This line represents the height of the text if you select the current point as displayed. Alternatively, you may enter a value for the text height from the keyboard or from a menu, if available.

  If your drawing is to be plotted at a particular scale, you may have to multiply your text height by the drawing scale factor, since the text is really a drawing entity and will be scaled as well. For example, suppose you are drawing at a scale of ¼ inch to 1 foot. If you want the text on your plotted drawing to appear ¼ inch high, enter the text at a height of 1 foot. For text ⅛ inch high, enter it at a height of ½ foot.

- Rotation angle. Enter the rotation angle for the text baseline. Often, this angle is zero, for horizontal text. You can enter text at any angle you choose. You can enter the angle from the keyboard, or you can visually display the angle by selecting a point. As with similar commands, a rubberband line will stretch from the text starting point to the current location of the crosshairs' intersection. Selecting the point selects the displayed angle of orientation.

Text   After selecting the starting point, height, and rotation angle, enter the text by typing it at the keyboard. AutoCAD handles spaces differently in this particular case. Although AutoCAD usually interprets a press of the space bar the same as a press of the Enter key, you may enter spaces in response to this prompt and they will be treated as spaces in the text line. When you press Enter, AutoCAD draws the entered text.

After the text is drawn, AutoCAD redisplays the Command prompt. You may enter subsequent lines of text by pressing Enter to repeat the Text command, and pressing Enter again to bypass the options. AutoCAD then displays the text prompt, and you may immediately enter another line of text, which will be displayed underneath the previous line. You may repeat this sequence until all text is entered.

You need not repeat the Text command immediately to avail yourself of this feature. Whenever you repeat Text (or Dtext), the last line of text entered during the current drawing session is highlighted. You may accept the style, height, and orientation of the highlighted text as the default for the additional text by pressing Enter; the text that you enter will be aligned underneath the highlighted text. If the last line of text was erased, this feature will not be available.

In Release 11 and later, the first prompt you see after entering the Text command is:

Justify/Style/<start point>:

If you do not enter a point, you may select one of the following options:

Style Enter **S** to change the current text style to another loaded style. AutoCAD responds:

Style name (or ?):

Enter the name of a previously defined text style. This style becomes the current style for subsequent text entry, and the text options prompt is redisplayed. You may enter the desired responses to subsequent prompts for text options. To review a list of all currently loaded text styles, enter a question mark in response to this prompt. After listing the styles, AutoCAD repeats the text options prompt. If you wish to load one of the listed styles, press **S** again and enter the style name.

Justify Enter J to make changes to the current alignment setting of the text. You have the following alignment options:

Align Enter **A** if you want AutoCAD to adjust the text so that it will fit between two specified points. The first point you assign will be the starting point for the text; the second point will determine both text height and orientation. AutoCAD will adjust the height of the text so whatever you type fits between the two points. When text is aligned in this manner, the insertion point is the leftmost point.

After you have chosen the alignment points, AutoCAD prompts for text, as above. Enter the text you wish to include in the drawing, and then AutoCAD will return you to the command prompt.

Fit Enter **F** if you wish the text to be fitted between two points. AutoCAD Release 11 and later releases also prompt for the height of the text, offering the current height as the default. AutoCAD will make the text characters as narrow or wide as necessary to fit the text the amount of space you specify, while maintaining the requested height. The two points you enter will also determine the orientation of the text.

If you enter additional lines of text, they will appear below the previous lines. Characters in these lines will also be made as narrow or wide as needed to fit into the dimensions of the specified baseline.

You may not use the fit option with vertical text fonts.

Center Enter **C** to align the text baseline along a center point. AutoCAD prompts:

Center point:

Assign a center point using any of AutoCAD's standard coordinate-entry methods, and AutoCAD will center the text around it. AutoCAD also prompts for a text height and rotation angle. If you want to enter another line of text, you can press Return in response to the text options prompt. AutoCAD will then center the next line of text below the previous line.

Middle Enter **M** to center the text along its baseline and center the baseline through the middle of the text. AutoCAD prompts:

Middle point:

As with the Center option, AutoCAD will center all text along the middle point you specify. After choosing the middle point, you are prompted for height, rotation angle, and text content, as described above.

Right Enter **R** to right-justify text. After you have selected this option, it works the same as the other examples given above, except that the text will be right-justified instead of left-justified.

The following options are available in Release 11 and later. They are all followed by additional prompts for height and rotation angle, offering the current settings as default. None of these options may be used with vertical text fonts.

TL (Baseline Top Left) Enter **TL** to left-justify text below the baseline.

TC   (Baseline Top Center) Enter **TC** to center text below the baseline.

TR   (Baseline Top Right) Enter **TR** to right-justify text below the baseline.

ML   (Baseline Middle Left) Enter **ML** to left-justify text through the baseline.

MC   (Baseline Middle Center) Enter **MC** to center text though the baseline.

MR   (Baseline Middle Right) Enter **MR** to right-justify text through the baseline.

BL   (Baseline Bottom Left) Enter **BL** to left-justify text over the baseline. If there are any descenders (that is, letters that extend below the baseline such as g, p, or y), the text will be raised in relation to the baseline, until these letters descend to it but not below it.

BC   (Baseline Bottom Center) Enter **BC** to center text over the baseline. Again, descenders will force the text higher, so that they extend only to the baseline.

BR   (Baseline Bottom Right) Enter **BR** to right-justify text over the baseline. As with the previous two options, all letters will extend to the baseline, but not below it.

If you wish to enter more text, press Return to repeat the Text command and then press Return again to bypass the text options prompt. AutoCAD will redisplay the text prompt, allowing you to type more text. This text will be below the previous line of text amd set at the same height, orientation, and relationship to its insertion point.

USAGE

Refer to Figure 9.30 for illustrations of how each alignment option of the Text command changes the relationship between the entered text and its associated baseline.

Special Characters

The standard text fonts supplied with AutoCAD contain certain special symbols that do not normally appear on a keyboard. These include the degree symbol, the plus/minus symbol, underscores, and overscores.

Special characters can be introduced into text strings with the % % symbol. For example, to include a plus/minus symbol, enter the following text string:

    90% %p

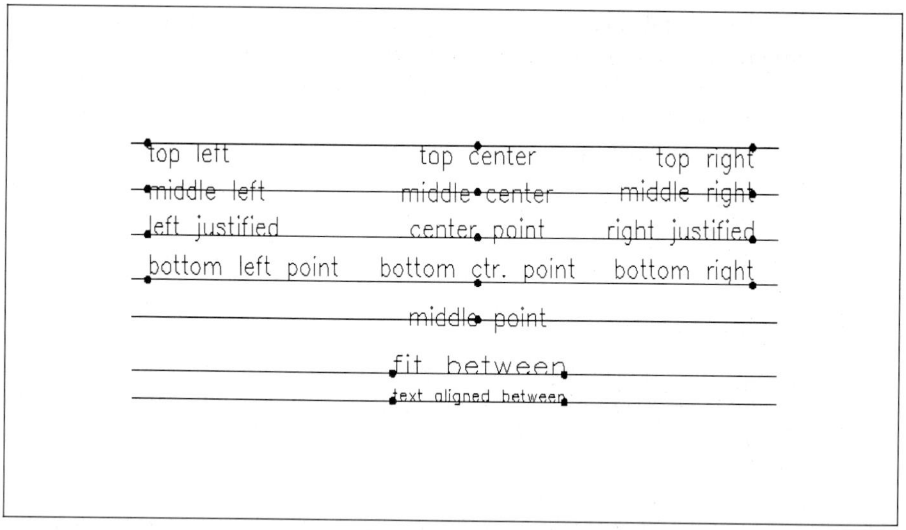

FIGURE 9.30: Text alignment options. This figure illustrates the various text orientations and alignments available at the time text is inserted. The points used to orient the text are highlighted. Note how the baseline is lower for "bottom" options than for normal left- or right-justified text. This is because the descenders in the text force the baseline down. Also, notice how the text height changes for aligned text, whereas the text width changes for fitted text.

In this example, AutoCAD will understand that the string % %p is not to be represented literally, and will replace it with the plus/minus symbol. Such text was illustrated in Figure 9.6.

The special characters include:

% %c	Circle diameter symbol
% %d	Degree symbol
% %o	Following text is overscored (or if currently overscored, turns overscoring off)
% %p	Plus/minus symbol
% %u	Following text is underscored (or if currently underscored, turns underscoring off)
% % %	Single percent sign
% %*nnn*	Special ASCII character (where *nnn* is the character number, starting at 130)

Under most circumstances, the single percent sign is typed normally. However, if you need to type a percent sign followed by a special character, enter three percent signs (to force a single percent sign) followed by two more percent signs and the special character code. If you need to enter two percent signs, you must type three percent signs twice, for a total of six!

For example, the following sample text includes a percent sign followed by the plus/minus symbol, and two percent signs next to each other. The results when entering these strings in AutoCAD were shown in Figure 9.6.

```
Text sample -
90 percent plus/minus 1.5 percent:
90%%%%%p1.5%
Two percent signs:
%%%%%%
```

Release 10 and earlier Tip: Use the AutoLISP program CHGTEXT.LSP (supplied with AutoCAD) to edit a large amount of text after it has been entered in the drawing. CHGTEXT allows you to select a line of text and correct its contents, while retaining all the other text attributes.

Unless you have loaded CHGTEXT.LSP or another AutoLISP routine that helps make changes to text, the only way to make such changes to text is to invoke the Change command and retype the entire line. Be very careful when entering text. If you are prone to typographical errors, consider entering text using the Dtext command, which will at least allow you to view the text in the drawing as you enter it, and will allow you to back up (erasing as you go) through the text that you have entered, in order to correct an error before the text is actually drawn.

If text was entered using the Aligned option, it may be difficult to respecify the exact text height later on. You can find out the height of a line of text by invoking the List command and selecting the text line in question. In order to simplify the process of making subsequent text changes, use a consistent standard text height whenever possible.

RELATED COMMANDS

Dtext, Style.

RELATED SYSTEM VARIABLES

TEXTEVAL (allows AutoLISP expressions during text input), TEXTSIZE (default text height), TEXTSTYLE (current text-style name).

SAMPLE DIALOG

The following sample dialog inserts the text that appeared in Figure 9.6:

```
Command: TEXT
Justify/Style/<Start point>: 2,7
```

```
Height <0.125>: 0.2
Rotation angle <0.00>: (press Enter)
Text: Text Sample - (press Enter)
Command: (press Enter)
TEXT Justify/Style/<Start point>: (press Enter)
Text: 90 percent plus/minus 1.5 percent: (press Enter)
Command: (press Enter)
TEXT Justify/Style/<Start point>: (press Enter)
Text: 90%%%%p1.5% (press Enter)
Command: (press Enter)
TEXT Justify/Style/<Start point>: (press Enter)
Text: Two percent signs: (press Enter)
Command: (press Enter)
TEXT Justify/Style/<Start point>: (press Enter)
Text: %%%%% (press Enter)
Command:
```

WBLOCK

Takes an existing block definition and writes it to a separate drawing file on disk.

VERSIONS

All.

COMMAND OPTIONS

File name   Enter the name of the drawing file that is to hold the block definition. It is a common practice to give the drawing file the same name as the block; this prevents confusion when passing blocks between drawings.

If a drawing file of the same name is found on disk, AutoCAD prompts:

```
A drawing with this name already exists.
Do you want to replace it? <N>
```

Enter **Y** if you wish to overwrite the existing file; otherwise, enter **N** to cancel the command.

Block name   Enter the name of the block that is to be written into the drawing file.

Equal sign option   If the drawing file and block have the same name, you may enter an equal sign (=) in place of the block name. This saves a little typing effort.

Asterisk option   If you wish to write the entire drawing into the file, rather than just a block, enter an asterisk (*) for the block name. This is functionally the same as the Save command; however, certain references that are specific to the drawing will not be included when a file is written this way: named views, viewports, UCS's, and unreferenced symbols.

No-block option   You may also use Wblock to write specific entities to a drawing file without creating a block definition. Press Enter when prompted for a block name. AutoCAD then prompts:

Insertion base point:

Select a coordinate point that will serve as the origin point (0,0,0) in the drawing file to be written. When the point is selected, AutoCAD prompts:

Select objects:

You may select the entities you wish to write to disk by means of AutoCAD's standard entity-selection methods. When you have selected all the entities you wish to write to disk, press Enter to have the drawing file written. The selected entities disappear from the screen; however, the Oops command will restore them.

USAGE

The Wblock command allows you to transfer block definitions between drawings; this means that you do not have to create the same block definition from scratch each time you begin a new drawing. The Wblock command is fully automatic. Enter the name of the new drawing file followed by the name of the block, and the drawing file is created automatically.

Wblock works in concert with the Block and Insert commands. Usually, you will have defined a block with the Block command before using Wblock. The Insert command will scan any drawing for a selected block name, and if it does not find the block, it will look along AutoCAD's search path for a drawing file with the selected name. (Refer to Chapter 4 for details regarding AutoCAD's search path.) If it finds a drawing file with the selected name, it inserts the drawing file as a block definition in the current drawing.

Wblock is functionally the same in all versions of AutoCAD. In Release 10 and later, however, the existence of different user coordinate systems makes the process of writing blocks and/or drawing entities to disk files a little trickier.

Whenever a block is created in Release 10 and later, the UCS that is in effect at the time becomes that block's own "world coordinate system." Each time the block is inserted into a drawing, its own world coordinate system aligns with the current UCS. Likewise, when a block is written to a drawing file, its own world coordinate system will align with the world coordinate system of the new drawing file. This process allows all blocks to be rotated and scaled consistently when they are inserted into other drawings.

Therefore, before defining blocks or writing entities out to disk files, check to be sure that the current UCS is the correct UCS, and that you will be creating a properly oriented block or drawing file on disk.

Tip: If you are using a version earlier than Release 10, or if you no longer require named views, viewports, or UCS's in your drawing, Wblock with the asterisk option is an effective substitute for the Purge command. Depending on the number of unreferenced or unneeded entities, this technique will produce a smaller drawing file, leaving all drawing entities intact. Once you are satisfied that the new file meets your needs, you can reclaim disk space by erasing the old file. Using Wblock with the asterisk option instead of Purge saves time by eliminating the requirement to end the drawing session and reload the drawing in order to make the Purge command available. However, Purge offers the option to retain named views, viewports, UCS's, and specific unreferenced entities as necessary.

RELATED COMMANDS

Block, Insert, Save.

SAMPLE DIALOG

The following sample dialog writes the WINDOW block out to an external disk file:

```
Command: Wblock
File name: WINDOW
Block name: =
Command:
```

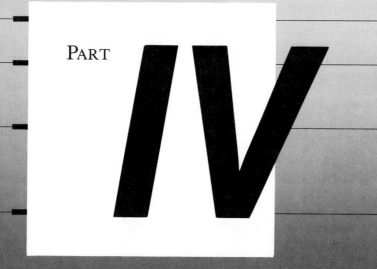

PART

IV

EDITING AND PLOTTING DRAWINGS

Once a drawing has been created, it often must be revised. In manual drafting, this process is accomplished by erasing and redrawing a portion (or in some cases, all) of the drawing. In drafting with AutoCAD, revisions can take many different timesaving forms: stretching, moving, rotating, scaling, and instantly changing colors, linetypes, elevations, and so on. In addition, AutoCAD can be used to display selected portions of the drawing, or to display a 3-D drawing from many different perspectives. Once the drawing is completed precisely as you like it, AutoCAD will instruct your plotting device to reproduce it on paper with a level of precision and accuracy unmatched by manual methods. Part IV discusses the tools for revising drawings in AutoCAD, introduces the methods for changing the display, and outlines the means of producing hard-copy output of your finished drawings.

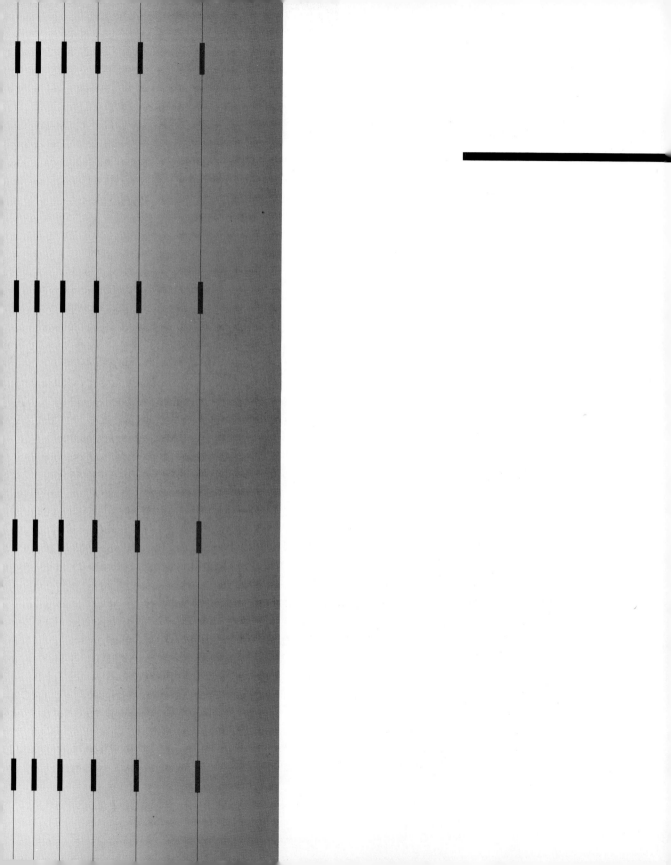

EDITING ENTITIES

EDITING ENTITIES

As an AutoCAD drawing progresses from its opening stages to its final plot, it is often necessary to make changes to its component entities. AutoCAD provides several commands that effect a number of different alterations to drawing entities. For example, there are AutoCAD commands to erase entities in whole or in part, rotate them, scale them to new sizes, copy them, move them to new locations, change their color or linetype, change complex entities into their component simple entities, or reverse the effects of changes you have made.

The syntax for most editing commands follows the same general pattern. First, invoke the command, usually a verb indicating the type of change you wish to make—for example, Erase, Copy, or Move. Next, select the entity or entities upon which you wish to perform the changes. If any further information is required in order to make the changes, AutoCAD will prompt you for it after all the entities have been selected. Finally, AutoCAD makes the requested changes, updating the display of the drawing on the screen.

For example, you can erase a line by invoking the Erase command and selecting the line. You can move the line to a new location by invoking the Move command, selecting the line, and then selecting two points that indicate to AutoCAD the length and direction of the line's movement.

Some editing commands contain a number of options. For example, there are two types of arrays, polar and rectangular. There are many different options for the PEdit command, which makes changes to polylines. When an editing command has several options, you can be certain that each option has its own distinct purpose or advantages, depending on the drafting situation. You can choose whatever method suits you best, based on such considerations as your own particular drawing style, or the existence of entities whose construction points can be used to help you edit.

Many entities can be selected for editing by picking a coordinate point on the entity. In most cases, the selection point can fall anywhere on the entity, but in a few cases, the location of this point also controls how the desired change is to be made. You may enter the coordinates of the selection point by moving the pointing device so that the intersection of the crosshairs touches a point on the entity, and then pressing the select button. Alternatively, you may select the entity by entering the selection point from the keyboard.

In those cases where an editing command allows it, several entities may be selected together and edited as a group. Groups of entities may be selected individually by picking a point on each one; or they may be selected together as a group by "windowing"—drawing a special rectangle around the entities and selecting them all at once.

An entity or group of entities you select for editing is called a *selection set.* The command descriptions in this chapter assume that you are already familiar with the various optional means of selecting entities and producing a selection set. If necessary, refer to Chapter 5 for details regarding AutoCAD's standard entity- and point-selection methods.

The format for keyboard entry of coordinate points and distance values is controlled by the default drawing-units format. Refer to Chapter 6 for a detailed discussion of the Units command, which defines the format for keyboard entry of these values.

ARRAY

Produces an array (multiple copies) of selected drawing entities, either in a circle (a polar array) or in a selected number of columns and rows (a rectangular array).

VERSIONS

All.

COMMAND OPTIONS

Rectangular array   After selecting the objects to include in the array, enter **R** to indicate that you want to create a rectangular array. An example of a rectangular array is illustrated in Figure 10.1. AutoCAD responds:

Number of rows (---):

Respond to this prompt by entering an integer that indicates the number of rows in the array. In an array, a row is horizontal, as indicated by the hyphens contained within parentheses in the prompt.

Each row in the array may include one or more copies of the selected entities. Since the intended array will be in a rectangular pattern, the number of copies in each row will be the same as the number of columns in the array.

After you enter the number of rows, AutoCAD prompts for the number of columns:

Number of columns (¦ ¦ ¦):

Again, respond to this prompt by entering an integer that indicates the number of columns in the array. Columns in an array are vertical, as indicated by the bar symbols within parentheses in the prompt.

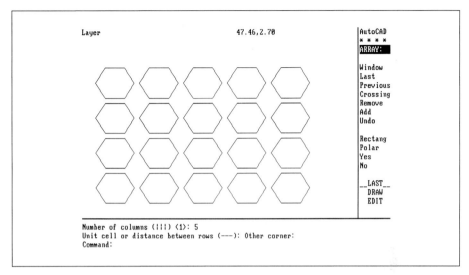

Layer   47.46,2.78   AutoCAD
                                                             * * * *
                                                             ARRAY:

                                                             Window
                                                             Last
                                                             Previous
                                                             Crossing
                                                             Remove
                                                             Add
                                                             Undo

                                                             Rectang
                                                             Polar
                                                             Yes
                                                             No

                                                             __LAST__
                                                                DRAW
                                                                EDIT

Number of columns (¦¦¦) ⟨1⟩: 5
Unit cell or distance between rows (---): Other corner:
Command:

FIGURE 10.1: A rectangular array. The original hexagon is positioned in the lower left. The array consists of four horizontal rows by five vertical columns. The array is actually a form of multiple copying, with copies all made in a precise mathematical relationship to each other.

Each column in the array may include one or more copies of the selected entities. Since the array is a rectangular pattern, the number of copies in each column will be the same as the number of rows in the array.

AutoCAD then prompts for the distance between the columns and rows of the array:

Unit cell or distance between rows (---):
Distance between columns (¦ ¦ ¦):

These distances are measured from the starting point of each column or row to the starting point of the next column or row. They are *not* the spacing between the objects in the array. Refer to Figure 10.2 for an illustration of distances between rows and columns in a rectangular array.

If you enter positive distances, AutoCAD makes copies in rows from bottom to top, and in columns from left to right. If you enter negative distances, Auto-CAD copies in the reverse direction. If you wish, you may enter a positive distance for one measure and a negative distance for the other, thus controlling the direction of the resulting array.

Alternatively, you may enter a point in response to the "Distance between rows" prompt. If you do, AutoCAD responds:

Other corner:

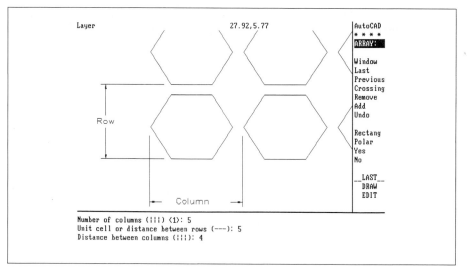

FIGURE 10.2: Distances between rows and columns in a rectangular array. This figure illustrates how rows and columns are measured in a rectangular array: All measurements are parallel to the current snap angle. The distance between columns is measured horizontally from the leftmost point of the original entity to the leftmost point of its nearest copy on the right. The distance between rows is measured from the lowest point of the original to the lowest point of its nearest copy above. Entering negative distance values reverses the direction in which the copies are made.

AutoCAD is prompting for the opposite corner of a window, represented by a small rubberband box on the screen. AutoCAD will use the vertical dimension of the small box as the distance between rows and the horizontal dimension of the box as the distance between columns. Enter a second point that indicates the correct vertical and horizontal dimensions. AutoCAD then creates the array.

Polar array   After selecting the objects to include in the array, enter **P** to create a polar, or circular, array. AutoCAD responds:

> Center point of array:

Indicate the coordinates of the array's center point. AutoCAD will generate the array around this point, using a reference point for each of the entities you have included in the item. (Refer to the Usage section for a warning regarding the reference points for various entities.) AutoCAD then prompts:

> Number of items:

In an array, an *item* is the same as the selection set you created when you selected entities for the array. In other words, AutoCAD is prompting for the number of times you would like the group of selected entities to be reproduced. This number includes the original item.

If you know the number of times you wish the entities to be reproduced, respond to this prompt with a positive integer. If you are not sure how many items will be in the array, you may press Enter in response to this prompt. AutoCAD responds:

Angle to fill:

Indicate the included angle of the array. For example, if the array is to be a full circle, enter **360**, for 360 degrees (or their equivalent in the current units format). If the array is to be a half-circle, enter **180** degrees. If a quarter-circle, enter **90** degrees, and so forth. If you press Enter in response to this prompt, AutoCAD assumes that you want to array the items in a full circle.

If you enter a positive number in response to this prompt, AutoCAD will generate the array counterclockwise. If you enter a negative number, AutoCAD will generate the array clockwise. If you have changed the default for AutoCAD's angle-measurement system, this process will be reversed.

If you pressed Enter in response to the "Number of items" prompt, AutoCAD displays another prompt:

Angle between items:

You must specify an angle between items if you have not indicated the number of items. Enter the angle between the copies of the items you selected to array. AutoCAD repeats this prompt until a number is entered or you cancel the command with Ctrl-C.

You may respond with a positive or negative number. A positive number will cause AutoCAD to generate the array counterclockwise; a negative number will generate the array clockwise. If you have changed AutoCAD's default angle-measurement system, the reverse will be true.

After you have responded to the above, AutoCAD prompts:

Rotate objects as they are copied <Y>?

Respond to this prompt by entering either **Y** (the default) or **N**. If you enter **Y**, AutoCAD adjusts the angle of orientation of each entity in the array so that it maintains the same aspect, relative to the array's center point, as the original entity. If you enter **N**, all the entities in the array maintain the same angle of orientation as the original entities.

For example, if you made a polar array of an arrow shape that was pointing at the array's center point, and indicated that the arrow was to be rotated as it was copied, then all the arrows in the array would point at the center point. If you indicated that the arrow was not to be rotated as it was copied, all the arrow copies would point in the same direction.

Polar arrays with nonrotated entities can produce surprising results if the entities are not gathered into a block first. Refer to the warning ahead for details.

An example of a polar array is illustrated in Figure 10.3.

```
Layer                           14.31,7.27        AutoCAD
                                                  * * * *
                                                  ARRAY:

                                                  Window
                                                  Last
                                                  Previous
                                                  Crossing
                                                  Remove
                                                  Add
                                                  Undo

                                                  Rectang
                                                  Polar
                                                  Yes
                                                  No

                                                  __LAST__
                                                    DRAW
                                                    EDIT

Number of items: 8
Angle to fill (+=ccw, -=cw) <360>:
Rotate objects as they are copied? <Y>
```

FIGURE 10.3: A polar array. Although the most common application of the Array command is making multiple copies, it can be used in other ways as well—for example, to construct a complex geometric pattern using the Polar Array feature. The original hexagon used in the figure is located in the six o'clock position. An array of eight hexagons was produced using the sample dialog for the Array command.

USAGE

AutoCAD aligns the array's rows and columns with the current orientation of the crosshairs. Thus, you may also control the orientation of the array by changing the snap rotation angle, thereby changing the orientation of the crosshairs. After the array is created, you may realign the crosshairs; the array will remain in its original orientation. Refer to Chapter 7 for details regarding the Snap command.

Entities in an array may be edited individually using AutoCAD's editing commands.

In AutoCAD versions earlier than 2.5, the polar array was called the *circular* array. You were prompted for the center point and the angle between items, and were then asked to choose either the number of items or the angle to fill. If you entered the angle to fill, it had to be a negative number; positive numbers were assumed to be the number of items.

You can still see this sequence of prompts in later versions if you enter **C** in response to the Rectangular/Polar prompt. However, there is no advantage to this, and it may be quite confusing as well. (It is too easy to generate an array with 360 items instead of a full-circle array!) Therefore, the C option is not recommended, or even documented, in Version 2.5 and later.

Warning: When generating polar arrays without rotating objects, you may get unpredicted results. This is because AutoCAD uses different reference points for objects when determining their distance from the center point of the array. This is especially noticeable if your arrays include closed polylines such as those generated with the Polygon command. If your arrays do not appear as planned, gather the entities into a block first, with the insertion point as close to the center of the selection set as possible. After generating the array, you may explode the entities if you like.

RELATED COMMANDS

Minsert.

SAMPLE DIALOG

The following sample dialog generates the array illustrated in Figure 10.3:

```
Command: Polygon
Number of sides: 6
Edge/<Center of polygon>: 7,2
Inscribed in circle/Circumscribed about circle (I/C): C
Radius of circle: 2
Command: Array
Select objects: L
1 found.
Select objects: (press Enter)
Rectangular or Polar array (R/P): P
Center point of array: 7,4
Number of items: 8
Angle to fill ( + =ccw, − =cw) <360>: (press Enter)
Rotate objects as they are copied? <Y> (press Enter)
Command:
```

BREAK

Partially erases an arc, circle, line, polyline, or trace.

VERSIONS

All.

COMMAND OPTIONS

Enter first point   You will receive this prompt if you have selected the entity to be broken by means other than picking it with the pointing device. Enter the first break point in response to this prompt.

Enter second point   You will receive this prompt after you enter the first break point. AutoCAD expects you to enter a second break point on the entity, after which the entity is erased between the two selected points.

Enter second point (or F)   If you have selected the entity to be broken by picking it with the pointing device, AutoCAD assumes that the point you used to select the entity is the same as its first break point. If this is so, simply enter the second break point. If this is not so, enter **F**. AutoCAD then displays the "Enter first point" prompt, and the selection of break points continues as described above.

USAGE

You may select the entity to be broken using any of AutoCAD's standard entity-selection methods, but only one entity may be selected at a time for the Break command. If you select the entity using the Window or Last Selection option, two break points are required.

When an entity is partially erased, it is split into two entities of the same type.

Tip: When breaking a line entity between two intersection points, try to select the line using a small "crossing" window, and then use Osnap Int to select the two points. This method is usually the fastest.

Note: If you are breaking a line entity and the second break point is beyond the endpoint of the line, the line will be erased from the first break point to the endpoint. If the second break point does not fall on the entity, the entity will be broken at the point nearest to the selected point.

Warning: After you break a curve-fit polyline, the remaining polylines cannot be decurved.

When you break a circle, the order in which the points are selected is important. Circles are always broken counterclockwise from the first break point to the second. Refer to the sample dialog.

RELATED COMMANDS

Fillet, Trim.

SAMPLE DIALOG

The following dialog draws and breaks entities as illustrated in Figure 10.4:

Command: **Circle**
3P/2P/TTR/<Center point>: **7,7**
Diameter/<Radius>: **4**
Command: **Line**
From point: **4,11**
To point: **4,3**
To point: **(press Enter)**
Command: **Line**
From point: **10,11**
To point: **10,3**
To point: **(press Enter)**
Command: **Break**
Select object: **W**
First corner: **3,2**
Other corner: **5,12**
Enter first point: **int** of **4,9.5**
Enter second point: **int** of **4,4.5**
Command: **Break**
Select object: **(pick circle)**

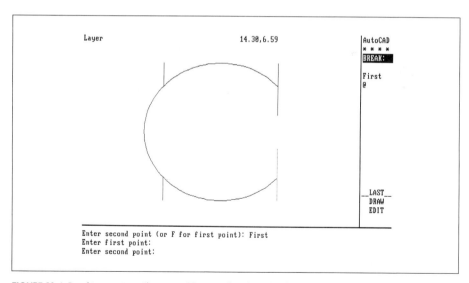

FIGURE 10.4: Breaking entities. The vertical lines and circle in this figure have been partially erased using the sample dialog for the Break command. Any line entity can be broken using this command. In this figure, the Osnap override Int was employed to locate break points at intersections. In AutoCAD Version 2.5 and later, the Trim command simplifies the process of breaking entities between intersections.

Enter second point (or F for first point): **F**
Enter first point: **int** of **10,4.5**
Enter second point: **int** of **10,9.5**
Command: **Break**
Select object: **10,6**
Enter second point (or F for first point): **10,8**

CHAMFER

Trims two nonparallel lines through a process illustrated in Figure 10.5.

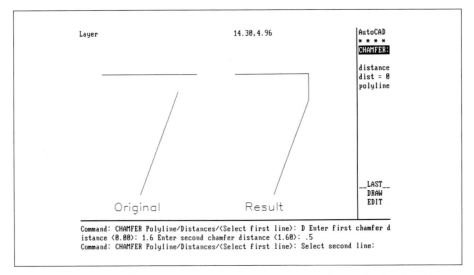

FIGURE 10.5: Chamfer of two lines. In this figure, the two lines on the left are to be chamfered using the Chamfer command. The chamfer distances are entered first; the first distance is 1.6 and the second is .5. After you select the lines to be chamfered, AutoCAD extends the lines until they intersect, trims the first selected line from the intersection point by the first distance, trims the second line from the intersection point by the second distance, and finally connects the two line endpoints with a straight line. The result is shown on the right.

VERSIONS

All.

COMMAND OPTIONS

Distance Type **D** to enter values for the first and second chamfer distances. AutoCAD responds:

Enter first chamfer distance:

Enter the value for the first chamfer distance using any of AutoCAD's standard methods for entering distance values. AutoCAD then prompts:

Enter second chamfer distance:

Enter the value for the second chamfer distance.

Polyline   Type **P** to chamfer all the vertices of a polyline. If the chamfer distance is currently zero, the straight line segments of the polyline will remain unchanged. Arc segments in the polyline will be removed, however.

After you select this option, AutoCAD prompts:

Select polyline:

Pick the polyline you intend to chamfer. AutoCAD will begin at the starting point of the polyline, trimming the first segment by the first chamfer distance, and trimming the second segment by the second chamfer distance. It then moves to the second segment, trimming its other end by the first chamfer distance, and trimming the adjacent segment by the second chamfer distance. It continues stepwise in this fashion until it reaches the end of the polyline.

When AutoCAD chamfers a polyline, it places a chamfer line at each vertex of the polyline. If two straight line segments are separated by an arc segment, the arc segment is deleted and replaced with a chamfer line. The chamfer lines connecting the chamfered endpoints of the polyline segments are added to the polyline as additional segments, and are therefore subject to other polyline editing commands.

Some vertices of the polyline may not be possible to chamfer—for example, if a segment is shorter than the chamfer distance. When performing a chamfer on a polyline, AutoCAD always displays the result of the Chamfer command in the Command-prompt area. Any of the following messages may appear if they apply to the selected polyline:

MESSAGE	MEANING
N lines were chamfered	The number of chamfer lines added
N lines were parallel	No chamfer possible on parallel lines separated by an arc segment
N lines were out of limits	Limits-checking was on; chamfer line would have fallen outside the drawing limits
N lines were too short	Polyline segment was shorter than chamfer distance

MESSAGE	MEANING
N lines were divergent	Two line segments separated by an arc segment diverge as they approach the arc segment; segments themselves therefore do not intersect so as to be chamfered

Select first line   If you have entered chamfer distances, you may select any two lines (or adjacent polyline segments) to chamfer. The first line selected will be trimmed by the first chamfer distance.

Select second line   After you have entered the first line, you may select the second line or adjacent polyline segment to chamfer. The first line selected will be trimmed by the first chamfer distance, and the second by the second chamfer distance.

USAGE

The Chamfer command trims two nonparallel lines by first extending them until they intersect (if they do not intersect already). Next, it trims the first line from the intersection point by a predetermined distance, and the second line from the intersection point by a second predetermined distance. It then connects the two line endpoints with a straight line.

The Chamfer command requires two distance values. These values can be zero or any positive number. If the values are zero, the Chamfer command will trim two nonparallel lines until they meet at an intersection point. The intersection point is the point that is closest to the points used to select the lines. If the chamfer distances are not zero, AutoCAD trims back the first selected line by the first distance, and the second selected line by the second distance.

When you specify chamfer distances that are not the same, bear in mind that the order in which you select lines to be chamfered will determine which line is chamfered by which distance. As you acquire more experience, you may find it worthwhile to be consistent in entering the shorter distance first and the longer second, or vice versa.

If you have just begun the Chamfer command, you may change the values of the chamfer distances by using the Setvar command transparently to change the values of the CHAMFERA and CHAMFERB system variables. Refer to Chapter 13 for details.

If you wish to chamfer all the intersections of a closed polyline, be sure you have closed it (using the C option or PEdit). If you do not close it this way, Auto-CAD will not chamfer the intersection between the start and end points.

You cannot chamfer two polylines or curved simple line entities such as arcs. You can, however, achieve the same results using Fillet, Change, or Trim on these entities. Refer to the descriptions of those commands for details.

RELATED COMMANDS

Fillet, Trim.

RELATED SYSTEM VARIABLES

CHAMFERA (first chamfer distance), CHAMFERB (second distance).

SAMPLE DIALOG

The following sample dialog draws two lines, sets distances, and chamfers the lines. The result of this dialog is illustrated in Figure 10.5.

```
Command: Line
From point: 2,10
To point: 7,10
To point: (press Enter)
Command: (press Enter)
LINE From point: 6,9
To point: 4,3
To point: (press Enter)
Command: Chamfer
Polyline/Distances/<Select first line>: D
Enter first chamfer distance <0.00>: 1.6
Enter second chamfer distance <1.60>: .5
Command: (press Enter)
CHAMFER Polyline/Distances/<Select first line>: 6,9
Select second line: 7,10
```

CHANGE

Allows you to change specific properties of selected entities.

VERSIONS

All. Version 2.5 and later have the Property Change option. In AutoCAD versions prior to Version 2.5, the Change command changed only the change point, elevation, layer, and thickness. In versions of AutoCAD through Release 10, it is possible to mimic the earlier syntax by responding to the "Change point" prompt with **L** (for layer) or **E** (for elevation). If you respond by entering **E,**

AutoCAD will prompt for both a new elevation and a new thickness. As of Release 11, however, this syntax is no longer possible. Scripts and AuotLISP files must use the current syntax described in this section.

COMMAND OPTIONS

Properties   Enter **P** if you wish to change specific entity properties. When you enter **P**, AutoCAD displays the following prompt:

Change what property (Color/LAyer/LType/Thickness) ?

After you select the entity property you intend to change, AutoCAD will redisplay this prompt, allowing you to change other properties. To end the command and cause the changes to take place, press Enter in response to this prompt.

The available entity options are:

- **Color.** Enter **C** to change the color. AutoCAD prompts:

  New color:

  Enter the new color name or color number. AutoCAD will change the color of all the entities in the selection set you have chosen, except for blocks that contain entities with fixed colors. (Refer to the Block command for details regarding block colors.) If you want to keep the current color, press Enter.

- **LAyer.** Enter **LA** to change the current layer. AutoCAD prompts:

  New layer:

  Enter the name of an existing layer, or press Enter if you choose not to change any layers. AutoCAD will change the layer of all the entities in the selection set, except for blocks that contain entities with fixed layers.

- **LType.** Enter **LT** to change the current linetype. AutoCAD prompts:

  New linetype:

  Enter the name of a previously loaded linetype or of a linetype found in ACAD.LIN, or press Enter if you choose not to change any linetypes. AutoCAD will change the linetype of all the entities in the selection set except for blocks that contain entities with fixed linetypes.

- **Thickness.** Enter **T** to change the current thickness. AutoCAD prompts:

  New thickness:

  Enter a value for the new thickness. If you wish, you may enter two points; AutoCAD will accept the distance between these two points as the new thickness value. AutoCAD will change the thickness of all the entities in the selection set, except for blocks that contain entities with fixed thickness. If you want to keep the current thickness, press Enter.

Change point   Enter a point if you intend to change the geometry or location of entities. The change that takes place depends both on the location of the change point and on the type of entity you have selected to change. The list that follows indicates how selecting a change point will modify different types of entities. If you are changing a selection set with many entities, AutoCAD will prompt you for a series of entity change points. Refer to the sample dialog and to Figures 10.6 and 10.7 for illustrations of how entering a change point affects different entities.

- **Attribute.** The change point becomes the new text location point for the attribute. AutoCAD then prompts for a new text style, height, rotation angle, attribute tag, prompt, and default value.
- **Blocks.** The change point becomes the new insertion point for the block. AutoCAD also prompts for a new rotation angle.
- **Circles.** The distance between the change point and the circle's current center point becomes the new radius for the circle.
- **Lines.** All line endpoints in the selection set closest to the change point will converge on the change point. However, if AutoCAD is in Ortho mode, lines will be redrawn perpendicular to either the horizontal or vertical crosshairs as they intersect the insertion point, depending on which is closer to the line endpoint.
- **Text.** The change point becomes the new insertion point for the text. AutoCAD then prompts for a new text style, height, rotation angle, and text string.

USAGE

The Change command is a convenient substitute for erasing and redrawing entities when only one or two entity attributes need to be changed. The attributes you can change include:

- The endpoints of line segments, by entering a new endpoint.
- The radius of a circle, by entering a value or a point.
- The location of text and blocks, by entering a new location point.
- The style, height, rotation angle, and contents of text lines, by entering the new information in response to a series of prompts.
- The rotation angle of blocks, by entering a new angle or a point indicating the new angle.

- The color, elevation, layer, linetype, and thickness of drawing entities, by entering new values.
- The default value, prompt, tag, and text properties of an attribute definition that is not yet part of a block, or that is released from a block via the Explode command.

If you build a selection set containing several different kinds of entities, bear in mind that attributes, blocks, circles, and text will be changed one at a time by means of change points. If you build a selection set including more than one of these entities and enter a change point, the change point is temporarily ignored; AutoCAD prompts for new change points for each entity in the selection set. If line entities are also in the selection set, the lines will converge on the initial change point as AutoCAD reaches each line in the selection set.

However, entity properties such as color, elevation, layer, linetype, and thickness may be changed globally using a selection set composed of several different entity types.

Blocks containing entities with fixed linetypes, colors, layers, thicknesses, or elevations cannot have these properties changed using the Change command. To change these properties, first explode the block using the Explode command. (Refer to the Block command in Chapter 9 for details regarding blocks.)

> *Tip:* If making global changes of entity layer, linetype, thickness, and/or color properties in AutoCAD Release 10 or later, use the Chprop command instead of Change. It is a faster, simplified version of Change.

The Change P command is a good option to use if you intend to change a group of entities with varying properties to entities having a single property in common. However, AutoCAD will not change the properties of blocks having fixed entity properties. To change the entities in a block, explode the block first.

AutoCAD versions prior to Release 11 allowed you to use the Change command to change the elevation of entities. As of Release 11, this is no longer a legal option. To change the elevation of entities in Release 11, use the Move command, as discussed later in this chapter.

RELATED COMMANDS

Chprop.

SAMPLE DIALOG

The following dialog takes the entities shown in Figure 10.6 and changes them to the entities shown in Figure 10.7. Notice that the first change point entered becomes the change point for the lines in the drawing, even though AutoCAD displays the message

Change point ignored

This allows AutoCAD to "pick up" all the entities as it moves through the selection set. Text entities were not included in the selection set in this example. The order of the prompts may change, depending on the order of the entities in the selection set.

Command: **Change**
Select objects: **W**
First corner: **(pick point)**
Other corner: **(pick point)**
7 found.
Select objects: **(press Enter)**
Properties/<Change point>: **14,7**
Change point ignored
Enter block insertion point: **2,7 (block O moved)**
New rotation angle <0.00>: **(press Enter)**
Change point ignored
Enter block insertion point: **2,4 (block X moved)**
New rotation angle <0.00>: **45**

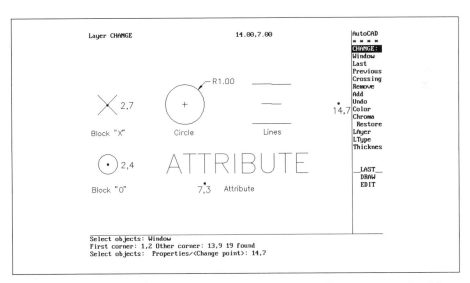

FIGURE 10.6: Various entities to be changed. This figure, along with Figure 10.7, illustrates five different entity types and how the Change command will interact with each one when the Change Point option is used. In this figure, the entities are selected by means of a window, and the first change point (14,7) is entered. AutoCAD will step through each entity as change points are entered. The results are pictured in Figure 10.7.

Change point ignored
Enter text insertion point: **7,3 (attribute moved)**
Text style: STANDARD
New style or RETURN for no change: **(press Enter)**
New height <1.00>: **.5**
New rotation angle <0.00>: **(press Enter)**
New tag <ATTRIBUTE>: **NEW-ATT**
New prompt <Attribute value>: **(press Enter)**
New default value <0>: **(press Enter)**
Change point ignored
Enter circle radius: **2 (circle changed, lines changed to point 14,7)**
Command:

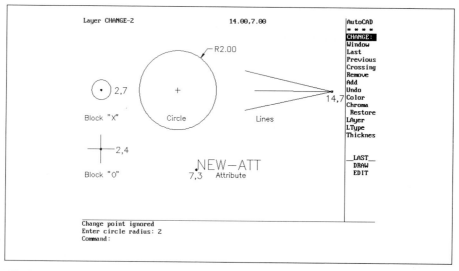

FIGURE 10.7: Entities changed per sample dialog. The result of the sample dialog on the entities pictured in Figure 10.6 is shown here. The X and O blocks are moved to new positions, and the X block has also been rotated 45 degrees. The radius of the circle has been enlarged, the attribute tag and its height have been changed, and at the conclusion of the command, the three lines have converged on the original change point, 14,7.

CHPROP

Allows you to change entity properties. A streamlined version of the Change command, Chprop does not allow the use of a change point, but it will change the color, layer, linetype, and thickness of any entity. Chprop is easier to use than the Change command when you're changing these properties globally in a selection set of different entity types.

EARLIEST VERSIONS

Release 10.

COMMAND OPTIONS

The options for the Chprop command follow the same rules as the similar options described under the Change command earlier in this chapter. Review the Change command for option descriptions and additional sample dialog.

USAGE

To use Chprop, first invoke the command name, and then select the entities you wish to change and the properties of the selected entities you intend to change.

After you select an entity property and enter its new value, the Chprop prompt continues to repeat, allowing you to globally change any of the other available attributes. When you press Enter in response to the prompt, the Chprop command is executed.

RELATED COMMANDS

Change.

SAMPLE DIALOG

The following dialog changes the color and thickness of the entities shown in Figure 10.6 using the Chprop command:

```
Command: Chprop
Select objects: W
First corner: (pick point)
Other corner: (pick point)
12 found.
Select objects: (press Enter)
Change what property (Color/LAyer/LType/Thickness) ? C
New color <BYLAYER>: Red
Change what property (Color/LAyer/LType/Thickness) ? T
New thickness <0.00>: 12
Change what property (Color/LAyer/LType/Thickness) ? (press Enter)
Command:
```

COPY

Makes copies of selected entities at selected locations in the drawing.

VERSIONS

All. AutoCAD versions earlier than 2.5 do not include the Multiple option. In these versions, it is necessary to repeat the Copy command in order to make multiple copies.

COMMAND OPTIONS

Base point or displacement After you select the objects you wish to copy, Auto-CAD first prompts for either a base point or a displacement. Both take the same form, an x and y coordinate value separated by a comma, but they will be interpreted differently based on how you respond to the second prompt.

For example, suppose you intend to make a copy of the hexagon pictured in Figure 10.8. After you select the entity and press Enter, AutoCAD prompts for the base point or displacement. If you enter

    7,6

either by typing it at the keyboard or by picking point 7,6 with the pointing device, AutoCAD will at first assume that your response is a base point, as will be explained momentarily.

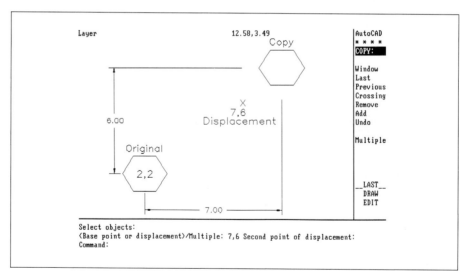

FIGURE 10.8: Copying an entity using the Copy command, Displacement option. The original hexagon is in the lower left of the drawing, and has been selected for copying. After you select the hexagon and press Enter, AutoCAD prompts for a displacement. You may pick point 7,6 or enter **7,6** from the keyboard. AutoCAD prompts for a second point of displacement, but you press Enter instead. AutoCAD then locates the copy of the hexagon 7 units along the x-axis and 6 units along the y-axis from the original.

However, if you respond to the next prompt, "Second point of displacement," by pressing Enter, AutoCAD will interpret your initial input of 7,6 as a *displacement,* or an instruction to place the copy 7 drawing units along the x-axis and 6 drawing units along the y-axis, as illustrated in Figure 10.8. Notice that Auto-CAD will accept the displacement values even if entered with the pointing device, because the displacement value has the same syntax structure as an x-y coordinate point.

Second point of displacement As mentioned above, if you press Enter in response to this prompt, AutoCAD interprets your response to the previous prompt as an x-y displacement, and immediately makes the copy at the designated location.

However, if you respond by entering another x-y coordinate point, AutoCAD interprets the response to the first prompt as a *base point*; that is, a point relative to which the selected objects can be copied. The second point entered therefore becomes the *point of displacement*; that is, the means to measure the angle and direction from the original to the location of the copy, using the distance and angle between the two selected points.

For example, if you entered **7,6** in response to the first prompt and **9,8** in response to the second prompt, AutoCAD would make a copy of the original at a point found 2 units along the x-axis and 2 units along the y-axis from the base point; in other words, at the same distance and angle as exists between points 7,6 and 9,8. An illustration of this type of displacement is seen in Figure 10.9. Notice that, while the response to the "Base point or displacement" prompt is the same as in Figure 10.8, the point response to the second prompt produces a far different result.

Multiple Enter **M** in response to the "Base point or displacement" prompt if you intend to make multiple copies of the selection set. AutoCAD responds:

Base point:

A displacement value is not allowed when making multiple copies. Therefore, respond to this prompt by entering a base point only. You may enter the base point using any of AutoCAD's standard point-entry methods. AutoCAD then prompts:

Second point of displacement:

Respond to this prompt only by entering another point. AutoCAD copies the objects at the same distance and angle as exists between the base point and the second point of displacement. This time, because you selected the Multiple option, AutoCAD repeats the prompt, allowing you to select a new second point, and thus a new angle and distance relationship between the original base point and the new

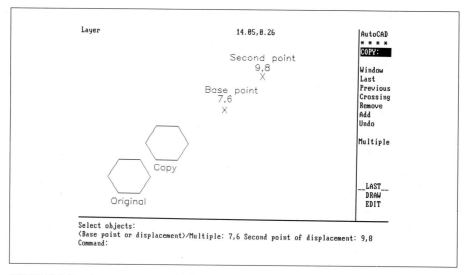

FIGURE 10.9: Copying an entity using the Copy command, Base Point and Second Point option. Select the hexagon in the lower left of the drawing for copying. After you select the hexagon and press Enter, AutoCAD prompts for a base point or displacement. Pick point 7,6 (or enter **7,6** from the keyboard). AutoCAD prompts for a second point of displacement; pick or enter point 9,8. AutoCAD then locates the copy at the distance and orientation indicated by the two selected points. Each point on the copy is the same distance from the corresponding point on the original.

second point. This process repeats until you press Enter in response to the prompt, whereupon AutoCAD ends the command.

USAGE

Be careful when using a pointing device that has both a Return button and a pick button. When using such a pointing device to select displacement points, be sure not to press Return when you intend to select a point. For example, if you entered point **1000,1000** as the base point, moved the crosshairs, and accidentally pressed the Return button instead of the pick button, the objects would be copied in a remote part of the drawing instead of the intended point. It may appear on the screen as if no copy was made at all. Other effects could be a surprise second regeneration of the drawing when zooming or panning, because of a change in the drawing extents. If you select a second point of displacement on the screen and the copied entities do not appear, undo the Copy command before trying again. Refer to the Undo and U commands in this chapter for details.

Tip: If making multiple copies, consider entering **0,0** as the base point. When 0,0 is the base point, you can then enter x-y displacements as the second point, using different displacement values for each copy.

RELATED COMMANDS

Move.

SAMPLE DIALOG

The following dialog draws a small hexagonal polygon and copies it in four locations in the drawing, as seen in Figure 10.10:

> Command: **Polygon**
> Number of sides: **6**
> Edge/<Center of polygon>: **2,2**
> Inscribed in circle/Circumscribed about circle (I/C): **C**
> Radius of circle: **1**
> Command: **Copy**
> Select objects: **L**
> 1 found.
> Select objects: **(press Enter)**
> <Base point or displacement>/Multiple: **M**
> Base point: **7,6**
> Second point of displacement: **9,8**
> Second point of displacement: **17,8**

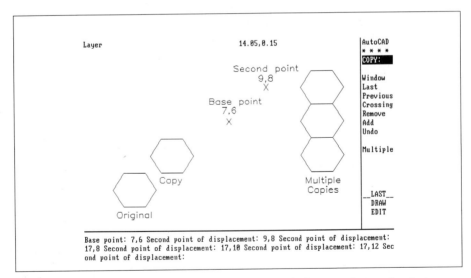

FIGURE 10.10: Copying an entity using the Copy command, Multiple option. Again, select the hexagon in the lower left of the drawing for copying. After you select the hexagon and press Enter, AutoCAD prompts for a base point or displacement. Enter **M** for the Multiple option. AutoCAD prompts for a base point. Enter or pick point 7,6. AutoCAD prompts for a second point of displacement. Each time you enter a new point of displacement, AutoCAD locates the copy according to the distance and angle between the original base point and the second point of displacement.

Second point of displacement: **17,10**
Second point of displacement: **17,12**
Second point of displacement: (**press Enter**)
Command:

DDEDIT

Allows interactive editing of Text entities or attributes by means of a dialog box.

VERSIONS

Release 11 and later, with displays that support the Advanced User Interface.

COMMAND OPTIONS

Select text or Attdef object   Pick either a single visible attribute or a single line of text on the screen. You may use point selection (via pointing device or keyboard) or select Last if the desired entity was the last one entered. No other selection mechanism is allowed.

For details regarding text entities, refer to the discussion of the Text command in Chapter 9. If you select a line of text, a dialog window appears containing the text. Pick the displayed line using the pointing device, or move the pointing device onto the text and press the space bar or any character, and the whole line will be deleted, leaving only the typed character. You can move the cursor within the line to add or delete characters. When you are finished, press Enter or pick the box marked OK. To cancel your edits, pick the box marked Cancel or press Ctrl-C. Once you have made a selection, the dialog box will disappear. Refer to Figure 10.11 for an illustration of this technique.

For details on block attributes, refer to Chapter 18. If you select an attribute instead of a line, a different dialog box appears. You may edit the tag, prompt, or default value of the attribute, but not the current value.

As you complete each edit, the prompt reappears, allowing you either to select another entity or press Enter to conclude the command.

Undo   Enter **U** to restore the original text or attribute settings after completing the edit but before concluding the command.

USAGE

Ddedit is intended to provide a flexible means of changing text-based entities. You will have to re-enter the text or use the Change command discussed earlier

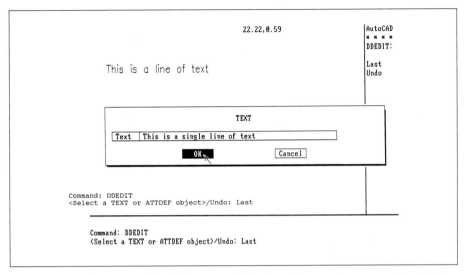

FIGURE 10.11: Editing text with the Ddedit command. This figure illustrates how text may be edited in the Ddedit dialog box. Notice that the text in the dialog box has been altered. When the OK box is selected, the dialog box will disappear and the text will be changed in the drawing.

in this chapter, though, if your display device does not support the Advanced User Interface. If your edits are extensive, it might be simpler just to use the Change command and re-enter the entire text line. This will retain the original text style.

The Attedit command provides an alternate but less intuitive means of changing an attribute's tag, prompt, and default, as well as an its current value. Refer to Chapter 18 for details.

You can step back through the changes you have made, reversing them one by one, by pressing **U**. Use **U** with caution, though. If you enter **U** after concluding the command, you are invoking the Undo command, and you will reverse *all* text and attribute changes you made with Ddedit.

RELATED COMMANDS

Attedit, Change, Dtext, Text.

SAMPLE DIALOG

The following sample dialog inserts a line of text and edits it, as illustrated in Figure 10.11:

Command: **TEXT**
Justify/Style/<Start point>: **1,6**
Height <0.32>: **.5**

Rotation angle <0.00>: **(press Enter)**
Text: **This is a line of text**
Command: **Ddedit**
<Select a TEXT or ATTDEF object>/Undo: **L**
<Select a TEXT or ATTDEF object>/Undo: **(press Enter)**
Command:

DIVIDE

Draws point or block entities (called nodes) at equally spaced intervals along a single line entity.

VERSIONS

Version 2.5 and later.

COMMAND OPTIONS

Number of segments   Enter the number of segments into which you intend to divide the entity. Enter an integer; the minimum value is 2, the maximum is 32767. AutoCAD responds by placing point entities at the intersections of each segment. Notice that the entity is not actually cut into separate segments; the point entities are drawn at equally spaced intervals only. Once drawn, these points are easy to select using Osnap Node or Ins.

Block   If you would prefer that a predefined block be placed along the entity instead of point entities, enter **B**. AutoCAD responds:

Block name to insert:

Enter the name of a block that has been predefined in the drawing. The block *must* be predefined; AutoCAD will not look for drawing files on disk during the Divide command. AutoCAD then prompts:

Align block with object?

If you respond by entering **Y**, AutoCAD will rotate the block so that its insertion angle is always tangent to the line entity. This can be especially useful when using this command on a curved entity, as in Figure 10.12. Finally, AutoCAD prompts:

Number of segments:

Enter an integer from 2 to 32767 indicating the number of segments in which you intend to divide the entity. AutoCAD responds by inserting the block at the

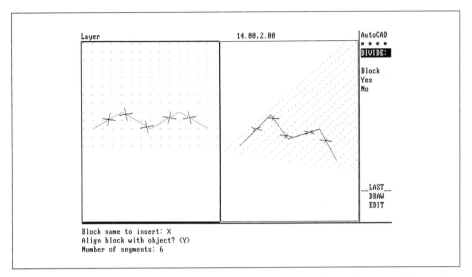

FIGURE 10.12: The Divide command used on a polyline. In this figure, the Divide command is used to divide a 3-D polyline into six segments. A block named X has been used as the marker symbol on the polyline. Since the polyline's vertices are in 3-D space, the viewing angle on the left shows how the marker points are actually placed on the 3-D line—at different elevations relative to the current construction plane.

intersections of each segment. Once drawn, these points are easy to select using Osnap Ins.

USAGE

You may use the Divide command to draw equally-spaced nodes along entities (polylines, arcs, lines, or circles). Select only one line entity using point selection—either enter a coordinate from the keyboard or point to the entity using your pointing device. Crossing, Last, and Window selection are not allowed.

If you do not specify a block name to insert, AutoCAD draws point entities at the intersections of equal sized segments along the line entity, using the current setting of the PDMODE and PDSIZE system variables. Entities are not placed at the endpoints of the line entity.

Although a block must be predefined to be used by this command, it needn't actually be referenced within the drawing. In other words, you may define a block for this purpose and not restore it using Insert or Oops. Alternatively, you may insert a block (using a drawing file on disk) and immediately erase it, and AutoCAD will still be able to use it as a marker in the divide command. Another alternative is to include such an unreferenced block in the prototype drawing. (Be careful not to accidentally delete it when using the purge command, however.)

RELATED COMMANDS

Measure.

SAMPLE DIALOG

The following dialog constructs a 3-D polyline and draws a block named X at ten equally spaced segments. The result of this dialog is illustrated in two viewpoints in Figure 10.12.

```
Command: 3Dpoly
From point: 1,2
Close/Undo/<Endpoint of line>: 4,4,4
Close/Undo/<Endpoint of line>: 7,2,2
Close/Undo/<Endpoint of line>: 10,4,3
Close/Undo/<Endpoint of line>: 13,2
Close/Undo/<Endpoint of line>: (press Enter)
Command: Divide
Select object to divide: 13,2
<Number of segments>/Block: B
Block name to insert: X
Align block with object? <Y> Y
Number of segments: 6
Command:
```

ERASE

Deletes entire entities from the drawing database.

VERSIONS

All.

COMMAND OPTIONS

Select objects   There are no options per se within the Erase command—just AutoCAD's different entity-selection methods for specifying the entities you intend to erase. Refer to Chapter 5 for a detailed presentation of AutoCAD's entity-selection methods.

Create the selection set you intend to erase, and then press Enter. The entities are removed from the screen.

USAGE

If you accidentally erase an entity and want it restored, you can invoke the Oops command, restoring all entities removed during the most recent Erase command. If you want to restore entities erased earlier than that, you must use the Undo command to back up through the current sequence of AutoCAD commands until the desired Erase command is undone.

Although Erase and Oops are available in all versions, the Undo command is only available in Version 2.5 and later. In versions prior to Version 2.5, only the most recently erased entities can be restored, using the Oops command.

You may restore erased entities during the current drawing session only. When you end the drawing session using End or Quit, erased entities are deleted permanently and cannot be restored thereafter.

Tip: When you are selecting the most recent entity to erase (in the case of a mistake, for example), the Last option is most useful and can be effectively included in a small screen- or tablet-menu macro, as follows:

```
[Erase-L]^C^CErase;L;;
```

Refer to Chapter 14 for details on macros and how they are used. Simply selecting this macro will cause the most recently entered entity to be removed. You can also create a tiny but handy "erase last" command using AutoLISP:

```
(defun C:EL( )
   (command "Erase" "L" "")
)
```

Add the above to the file ACAD.LSP, and thereafter you can quickly remove the most recently drawn entity by invoking the command EL. Refer to Chapters 16 and 17 for details regarding AutoLISP and its use in creating new AutoCAD commands.

RELATED COMMANDS

Oops.

SAMPLE DIALOG

The following sample dialog draws a circle, erases it, and restores it again:

```
Command: Circle
3P/2P/TTR/<Center point>: 5,5
```

Diameter/<Radius>: **5**
Command: **Erase**
Select objects: **L**
Select objects: **(press Enter)**
Command: **Oops**

EXPLODE

Changes a complex entity into its component simple entities.

VERSIONS

Version 2.5 and later. In Version 2.6 and later, you may also explode associative dimension entities into lines, solids, and text. Dimension entities, when exploded, are always placed on layer 0 and given a color and linetype of Byblock. In AutoCAD Release 10 and later, you may also explode a polygon mesh, which is then replaced with 3-D face entities.

COMMAND OPTIONS

Select block reference, polyline, dimension, or mesh You may select the desired block or polyline using point selection or the Last option; Window and Crossing options are not allowed. Only one entity may be selected at a time.

Once an entity to explode has been selected, AutoCAD replaces it with copies of the simple entities used in its construction. There are exceptions to this, however; refer to the warning ahead.

USAGE

Warning: In most cases, the screen appearance of an entity before and after conversion will remain the same. There are exceptions, however. If the entity is a wide polyline, exploding the polyline will replace it with lines and arcs, which have a width of zero. Likewise, if an exploded block contains the color and linetype attribute Byblock, the colors and linetypes of these entities may change.

If you explode a block containing attributes, the attribute definitions may reappear on the screen. Attribute values are lost.

If you explode a block containing complex entities, these entities are not exploded. However, you may reinvoke the Explode command and explode the complex entities separately if you wish.

Entities existing in either model or paper space can be exploded. The component simple entities will remain in the same space as the original complex entity. Refer to Chapter 12 for a discussion of model and paper space.

SAMPLE DIALOG

The following dialog creates a 2-D polyline and explodes it into simple line segments:

```
Command: PLine
From point: 1,2
Close/Undo/<Endpoint of line>: 4,4
Close/Undo/<Endpoint of line>: 7,2
Close/Undo/<Endpoint of line>: 10,4
Close/Undo/<Endpoint of line>: 13,2
Close/Undo/<Endpoint of line>: (press Enter)
Command: Explode
Select block reference, polyline, dimension, or mesh: L
Command:
```

EXTEND

Increases the length of selected line entities until they intersect a selected boundary edge.

VERSIONS

Version 2.5 and later.

COMMAND OPTIONS

Select boundary edges   Boundary edges are selected using any of AutoCAD's standard entity-selection methods. You may have any number of boundary edges. When all boundary edges are selected, press Enter.

The following entities may be used as boundary edges: lines and polylines (both open and closed, 3-D and 2-D), sketch lines, circles, and arcs. The following may not be used as boundary edges: blocks, points, shapes, solids, text, 3-D faces, and traces.

Select object to extend   entities to extend must be selected by point pick. The entity is extended starting with the endpoint nearest the pick point, and moving outward to the nearest boundary edge. If the pick point used to select an entity is too close to the endpoint opposite the boundary edge, the entity will not extend at all. To achieve predictable results, pick entities as close as possible to the endpoint that is nearest the boundary edge. Reselecting the same entity will cause it to extend to the next boundary edge, and so on until the entity can intersect no more boundary edges. AutoCAD repeats the "Select object to extend" prompt until you press Enter, whereupon the Extend command ends.

The following entities may be extended using the Extended command: arcs, lines, and open 2-D polylines. The following entities may not be extended; blocks, circles, closed lines and polylines, points, shapes, solids, texts, 3-D entities, and traces.

USAGE

You may select any number of entities to extend, but you must select them individually using point picks, not as a group using Window options. The command ends when you press Enter in response to the entity-selection prompt.

There are many ways to defeat the Extend command. If you select invalid boundary edges, AutoCAD responds:

> No edges selected

If you select invalid entities to extend, AutoCAD responds with one of the following:

> Cannot extend this entity.
> Cannot extend a closed polyline.

If the selected entity will not intersect an edge, AutoCAD may respond with one of the following:

> Entity does not intersect an edge.
> No edge in that direction.

If the entity you want to extend cannot be extended parallel to the current construction plane, AutoCAD prompts:

> The entity is not parallel to the UCS.

To extend the entity, use the Ucs command with the Entity option to move the User Coordinate System parallel to the entity. Next invoke Extend and select the boundary edges and the entity. Finally, invoke UCS Previous. Refer to Chapter 6 for a detailed discussion of the Ucs command.

Things can get somewhat confusing when you select multiple boundary edges, especially when using the Window or Crossing option. AutoCAD highlights all entities selected, whether they are valid boundary edges or not. Furthermore, the selected boundary edges remain highlighted throughout the command as you select the entities you wish to extend. If you select an entity to extend and it does not, or if it extends to meet an edge other than the one you intended, chances are that you have attempted to extend the chosen entity to an invalid edge. In such a case, your only recourse is to terminate the Extend command, undo the command (if that's what you want), and reedit the entity—possible methods include drawing a scratch line for the correct boundary edge, editing the entity using commands like Trim, Change, and Erase, redrawing the entity altogether or changing the current UCS.

RELATED COMMANDS

Fillet, Chamfer.

SAMPLE DIALOG

The following sample dialog draws a diagonal line, offsets it, and extends the offset line to meet a common line. The result of this dialog is illustrated in Figure 10.13.

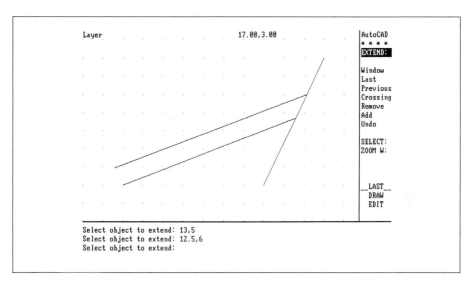

FIGURE 10.13: Extend command per sample dialog. In this figure, two lines are extended to a third boundary edge. When extending lines and arcs, be sure to select the entity to extend as close as possible to the endpoint nearest the boundary edge. If the endpoints in the lower left had been picked, the lines would not have extended at all.

```
Command: Line
From point: 13,2
To point: 16,9
To point: (press Enter)
Command: (press Enter)
LINE From point: 6,2
To point: 13,5
```

To point: **(press Enter)**
Command: **Offset**
Offset distance or Through <Through>: **1**
Select object to offset: **6,2**
Side to offset? @**1**<**90**
Select object to offset: **(press Enter)**
Command: **Extend**
Select boundary edge(s)...
Select objects: **13,2**
1 selected, 1 found.
Select objects: **(press Enter)**
Select object to extend: **13,5**
Select object to extend: **12.25,5.75**
Select object to extend: **(press Enter)**
Command:

FILLET

Trims two nonparallel lines, extending them until they intersect, if necessary, or trimming them at the point of intersection. The Fillet command also enables you to specify a fillet radius so that subsequent Fillet commands will join the lines using a smooth arc with the specified radius when possible, as illustrated in Figures 10.14 and 10.15. You may also use the Fillet command to fillet all the vertices of a polyline at once, as illustrated in Figure 10.16.

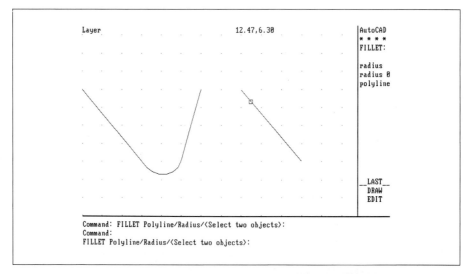

FIGURE 10.14: Filleting line entities. In this figure, the two line segments on the left have been filleted to a curved intersection (fillet radius not zero). The Fillet command is repeated, and the straight line segments in the middle and on the right will be selected for filleting. The result is shown in Figure 10.15.

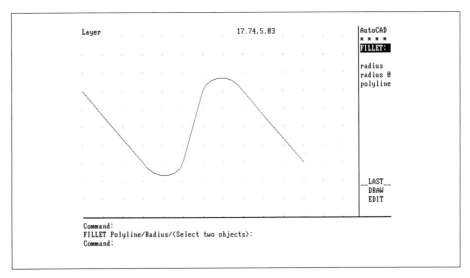

FIGURE 10.15: The results of filleting line entities. The fillet is applied to the endpoints of the selected lines, resulting in a single line consisting of line and arc segments. Since the original lines did not intersect, AutoCAD calculated the intersection point as though the lines were to be extended infinitely, and filleted them accordingly.

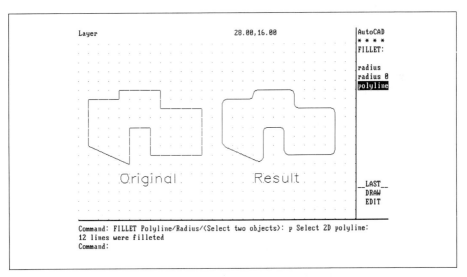

FIGURE 10.16: Filleting a polyline. This figure illustrates the effect of filleting a closed polyline. Although the polyline was selected with a single point pick, all of its vertices were filleted. If a fillet had not been possible at one or more of the vertices, AutoCAD would have filleted those that were possible, and ignored those that were impossible.

VERSIONS

All.

COMMAND OPTIONS

Polyline   Enter **P** to fillet all the vertices of a polyline. AutoCAD prompts:

Select polyline:

Select the polyline by means of a point pick, or with the Window or Crossing option. If more than one polyline is selected, AutoCAD will fillet the polyline most recently added to the drawing database.

When AutoCAD fillets a polyline, it places a fillet at each vertex of the polyline. If two straight line segments are separated by an arc segment, the arc segment is deleted and replaced with a fillet.

Some vertices of the polyline may not be possible to fillet. When performing a fillet on a polyline, AutoCAD always displays the result of the Fillet command in the Command-prompt area. Any of the following messages may appear if they apply to the selected polyline:

N lines were filleted	Indicates the number of fillets added.
N lines were parallel	No fillet is possible on parallel line segments separated by an arc segment.
N lines were out of limits	Limits-checking was on and the fillet would have fallen outside the drawing limits.
N lines were too short	The polyline segment was shorter than the fillet radius.
N lines were divergent	Two line segments, separated by an arc segment, diverge as they approach the arc segment, and therefore do not intersect such that a fillet can be placed between them.

Radius   Enter **R** to change the value of the fillet radius. AutoCAD prompts:

Enter fillet radius:

Enter the value of the fillet radius from the keyboard, or pick two points on the screen. Changing the value of the fillet radius will not change fillets that have already been drawn. To change the value of a previously drawn fillet radius, you must erase it and refillet the two lines.

Select two lines As described above, select the two line entities you intend to fillet, and AutoCAD will perform the necessary alterations automatically.

USAGE

If using Window or Crossing to select lines, be careful to include only the lines you intend to fillet. If you include more than two lines, AutoCAD will fillet those that were most recently added to the drawing database. Once the lines are selected, the fillet is performed automatically.

You can fillet two lines to an intersection by setting the fillet radius to zero.

In AutoCAD Version 2.5 and later, the Fillet command will fillet arcs and circles, as illustrated in Figure 10.17. Unlike straight lines, curved lines may be selected only by point pick. AutoCAD will place the fillet as close as possible to the location of the pick points used to select the circles or arcs. In many cases, you will only be able to approximate the correct pick points, since the fillet is not visible yet. If you fillet a line and arc and do not get the intended result, use the U command to reverse the effect of the Fillet command, and try again with two points that are closer to the fillet location.

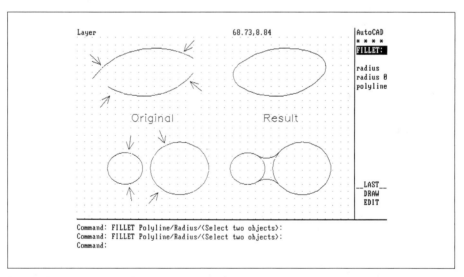

FIGURE 10.17: Filleting circles and arcs in AutoCAD Version 2.5 and later. AutoCAD treats the points used to pick the entities as reference points when filleting. AutoCAD will attempt to fillet the curved line entities as close to the pick points as possible. In this figure, arrows indicate valid pick points in the entities on the left. The results are shown on the right.

In AutoCAD Release 10 and later, the Fillet command works only with line entities that are parallel to the current construction plane. In other words, the z coordinates of all the endpoints of the lines must be the same in the current UCS. In some cases, this may be accomplished by invoking the UCS command with the Entity option to move the UCS parallel to the lines. In other cases, the lines may appear acceptable, but in fact are oriented in a way that makes a fillet impossible. If you attempt to fillet lines without success, check the location of the UCS or change the viewpoint to be certain that a fillet is possible.

Tip: You may change the value of the fillet radius at any time by invoking the Setvar command and changing the value of the FILLETRAD system variable. Refer to Chapter 13 for details.

Filleting of open lines and polylines that already intersect will be performed according to the following priorities:

- AutoCAD will first attempt to fillet from the endpoints of the lines that are closest to the intersection.
- If this is not possible, AutoCAD will fillet so as to keep the lines' starting points on the screen.

If you find that you are getting unwanted results when filleting intersecting lines, try creating the fillet using the Trim command. You can construct a fillet arc by first drawing a circle tangent to both lines. Refer to the discussion of the Trim command for details. The fillet arc, if any, is drawn on the same layer as the lines being filleted. If the lines are on different layers, the fillet arc is drawn on the current layer.

You cannot fillet solids, traces, text, 3-D faces, or lines in 3-D space.

RELATED COMMANDS

Chamfer.

RELATED SYSTEM VARIABLES

FILLETRAD (current fillet radius).

SAMPLE DIALOG

The following dialog draws the lines in Figure 10.14 and fillets them with a 1-unit radius, so they appear as in Figure 10.15:

```
Command: Line
From point: 4,7
To point: 7,3
To point: (press Enter)
Command: (press Enter)
LINE From point: 9,3
To point: 10,7
```

To point: **(press Enter)**
Command: **(press Enter)**
LINE From point: **12,7**
To point: **15,3**
To point: **(press Enter)**
Command: **Fillet**
Polyline/Radius/<Select two objects>: **R**
Enter fillet radius <0.00>: **1**
Command: **(press Enter)**
Fillet Polyline/Radius/<Select two objects>: **7,3; 9,3**
Command: **(press Enter)**
Fillet Polyline/Radius/<Select two objects>: **10,7; 12,7**
Command:

MEASURE

Draws point or block entities (called "nodes") at equally spaced intervals along a single line entity.

VERSIONS

Version 2.5 and later.

COMMAND OPTIONS

Segment length   Enter the length of the segments into which you intend to divide the entity. AutoCAD responds by placing point entities at the intersections of each segment. Notice that the entity is not actually cut into separate segments; the point entities are simply drawn at equally spaced intervals. Once drawn, these points are easy to select using Osnap Node or Ins.

Block   If you would prefer that a predefined block be placed along the entity instead of point entities, type **B** in response to the "Segment length/Block" prompt. AutoCAD responds:

Block name to insert:

Enter the name of a block that has been predefined in the drawing. The block *must* be predefined; AutoCAD will not look for drawing files on disk with the same name during the Measure command. AutoCAD then prompts:

Align block with object?

If you respond by entering **Y**, AutoCAD will rotate the block so that its insertion angle is always tangent to the line entity. This can be especially useful when using the Measure command on a curved entity, as in Figure 10.18. Finally, Auto-CAD prompts:

Segment length:

Enter the segment length. AutoCAD responds by inserting the block at the intersections of each segment. Once drawn, these points are easy to select using Osnap Ins.

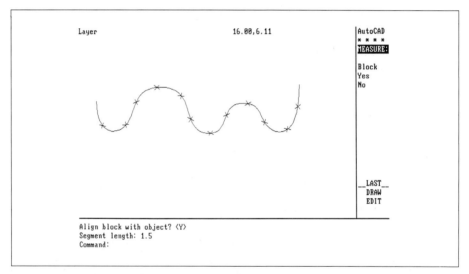

FIGURE 10.18: The Measure command, Block option. In this figure, the Measure command is used to place a block at equally spaced intervals along a curved polyline. The block used is an X-shaped block, and it has been aligned so as to be tangent to the line at the point of insertion. This option is the default; if you specify that the block not be aligned, it will be inserted at each point at its original angle of rotation.

USAGE

If you do not specify a block name, AutoCAD draws point entities using the current settings of the PDMODE and PDSIZE system variables. AutoCAD will place these entities along the line entity until it reaches or exceeds the opposite endpoint. In the case of circles, AutoCAD places these entities along the circumference of the circle beginning at angle 0 from the center point. This process is illustrated in Figure 10.19.

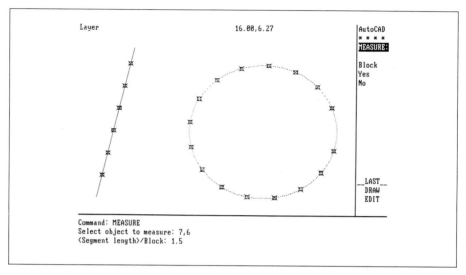

Layer   16.00,6.27   AutoCAD
                                                          * * * *
                                                          MEASURE:

                                                          Block
                                                          Yes
                                                          No

                                                          __LAST__
                                                          DRAW
                                                          EDIT

Command: MEASURE
Select object to measure: 7,6
<Segment length>/Block: 1.5

FIGURE 10.19: The Measure command. This figure illustrates the results of using the Measure command on a line and a circle. Both have had point markers drawn on them at intervals of 1.5 drawing units. In the case of the line segment, AutoCAD places the markers at intervals beginning from the endpoint closest to the point used to pick the entity. In the case of the circle, AutoCAD places markers starting with a point from angle zero and moving clockwise. Notice that no marker is placed on the starting point.

Tip: Although a block must be predefined to be used by this command, it needn't actually be referenced within the drawing. In other words, you may define a block for this purpose and not restore it using Insert or Oops. Alternatively, you may insert a block using a drawing file on disk, and immediately erase it; Auto-CAD will still be able to use it as a marker in the Measure command. Another alternative is to include such an unreferenced block in the prototype drawing. (Be careful not to accidentally delete it when using the Purge command, however.)

RELATED COMMANDS

Divide.

SAMPLE DIALOG

The following dialog sets the value of the PDMODE and PDSIZE system variables, draws a 3-D line and a circle, and then places point entities on them at equally spaced segments of 1.5 drawing units. The result of this dialog is illustrated in Figure 10.19. Notice how points are spaced along the circumference of the circle: AutoCAD begins at angle zero and continues until it has completed the circumference. No attempt is made to place a marker at the starting or ending point on either entity.

Command: **Setvar**
Variable name or ?: **PDMODE**
New value for PDMODE <0>: **67**
Command: **Setvar**
Variable name or ? <PDMODE>: **PDSIZE**
New value for PDSIZE <0.00>: **.3**
Command: **3Dline**
From point: **2,2,0**
To point: **4,11,4**
To point: **(press Enter)**
Command: **Circle**
3P/2P/TTR/<Center point>: **11,6**
Diameter/<Radius>: **4**
Command: **Measure**
Select object to measure: **2,2**
<Segment length>/Block: **1.5**
Command: **(press Enter)**
Measure
Select object to measure: **7,6**
<Segment length>/Block: **1.5**
Command:

MIRROR

Creates a reverse-image copy of selected entities.

VERSIONS

All.

COMMAND OPTIONS

First point of mirror line   After you select the entities you wish to copy, AutoCAD prompts for the first endpoint of the mirror line. This point may be located anywhere in the drawing. Figure 10.20 demonstrates how the location and orientation of the mirror line affect the location of the copied objects.

Second point   After you enter the first endpoint of the mirror line, AutoCAD requests the second point. If dynamic dragging is enabled, you will see a preview image of the copied entities moving on the screen as you move the crosshairs. If the entities are not visible, enter the word **Drag** in response to this prompt. If the preview image is still not visible, the DRAGMODE system variable may be set to zero, or the location of the mirror line may be such that the copied entities will fall outside of the display area.

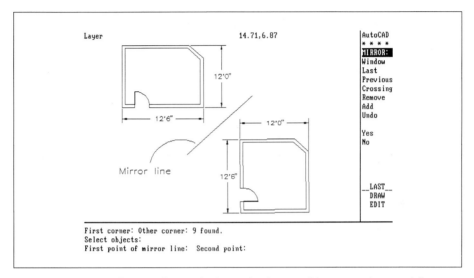

FIGURE 10.20: Locating the mirror line. In this figure, the drawing of the room in the upper left is being mirrored. The first point of the mirror line has been selected, and as the pointing device is moved, a rubberband line appears, and a preview of the resulting mirrored copy can be seen. Notice how the orientation of the room changes, but the orientation of the dimension text does not.

Delete old objects   If you intend to keep the original entities, respond to this prompt by entering **N**. If you intend to delete the original entities, enter **Y**. After you respond to this prompt, AutoCAD creates a mirrored copy of the selected entities. A mirrored copy made using this command is illustrated in Figure 10.21.

USAGE

If you are using the Mirror command to create reverse-image copies that include text, you may set the value of the MIRRTEXT system variable to 1, making text entities immune to mirroring. When MIRRTEXT is set to 1, text is located in its mirrored position, but maintains normal readability. If MIRRTEXT is 0, text is reversed like any other entity.

Tip: By drawing the mirror line across the selected entities and answering **Y** to the "Delete old objects" prompt, you can use the Mirror command as a means to "flip" entities in a drawing, rather than copying and/or moving them.

Warning: Although the MIRRTEXT system variable controls the readability of mirrored text, it does not control the orientation of multiple lines of text. If you attempt to mirror such text entities using a horizontal mirror line, the multiple lines of text may appear in reverse order. Figures 10.22 and 10.23 illustrate this—notice the effect of the Mirror command on the words *Mirror Line.* Therefore, leave out multiple lines of text when mirroring horizontally, and copy the text instead. Alternatively, you may mirror the text again, answering **Y** to the "Delete old objects" prompt.

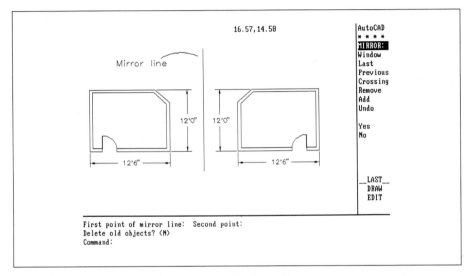

FIGURE 10.21: The results of the Mirror command. This figure illustrates the sort of reversal that occurs when mirroring objects. Notice that not only are the wall orientations reversed, but also the orientation of the door, and its relative position in the wall. The text is still readable however, because the MIRRTEXT system variable has been set to a value of zero.

RELATED COMMANDS

Copy, Move.

RELATED SYSTEM VARIABLES

MIRRTEXT (controls readability of mirrored text).

SAMPLE DIALOG

The following dialog sets the value of the MIRRTEXT system variable to zero, and then uses the Mirror command to reverse the entities in Figure 10.22 along their horizontal midpoint axis. The result is shown in Figure 10.23.

    Command: **Mirror**
    Select objects: **W**

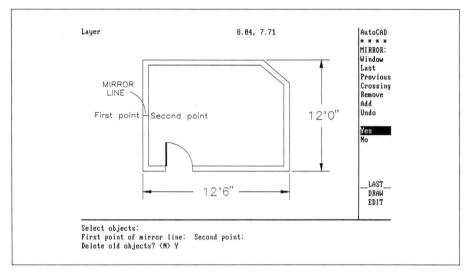

FIGURE 10.22: The Mirror command—mirroring text. The mirror line need not be long; only its angle of orientation is significant. In this figure, the drawing of the room is about to be "flipped"; that is, mirrored along a center axis. Original entities will be deleted in this case, since the goal is not to produce a copy, but rather to reorient the existing entities. Notice the two lines of text, *Mirror Line,* on the left. Compare them to the result of this command in Figure 10.23.

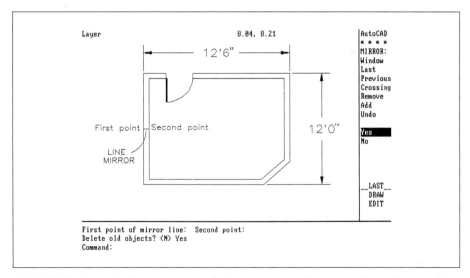

FIGURE 10.23: The result of mirroring text. In this figure, the room drawing has "flipped" as intended, and the text remains readable, but *Mirror Line* has become *Line Mirror.* While AutoCAD will maintain the readability of individual lines of text when mirroring (provided that the MIRRTEXT system variable is set to zero), it will not prevent the reversal of multiple text lines if you are mirroring with a horizontal mirror line. The solution is to move the text instead, or remirror it.

First corner: **(pick the first window corner)**
Other corner: **(pick the second window corner)**
9 found.
Select objects: **(press Enter)**
First point of mirror line: **Mid**
of **(pick vertical line midpoint as shown)**
Second point: **Mid**
of **(pick second vertical line midpoint as shown)**
Delete old objects? <N> **Y**
Command: **Redraw**

MOVE

Allows you to change the location of selected entities within the current construction plane.

VERSIONS

All.

COMMAND OPTIONS

Base point or displacement   After you select the objects you wish to move, AutoCAD prompts for either a base point or a displacement. Both take the same form, an x and y coordinate value separated by a comma, but they will be interpreted differently based on how you respond to the second prompt.

For example, suppose you intend to move the rectangle labeled Table in Figure 10.24. After you select the entity and press Enter, AutoCAD prompts for the base point or displacement. You enter

7,6

either by typing it at the keyboard or by picking point 7,6 with the pointing device. AutoCAD at first assumes that your response is a base point, as will be explained shortly.

However, if you respond to the next prompt, "Second point of displacement," by pressing Enter, AutoCAD then interprets this initial input as a *displacement*; that is, an instruction to move the entities 7 drawing units along the x-axis and 6 drawing units along the y-axis, as illustrated in Figure 10.25. Notice that AutoCAD will accept the displacement values even if entered using the pointing device, because the displacement value has the same syntax structure as an x-y coordinate point.

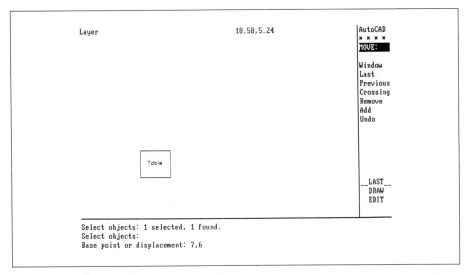

FIGURE 10.24: Moving an entity with the Move command. The displacement principles illustrated in Figures 10.8 and 10.9 apply to the Move command as they do to the Copy command. In this figure, a small table shape is being moved using the Displacement option. The result is seen in Figure 10.25.

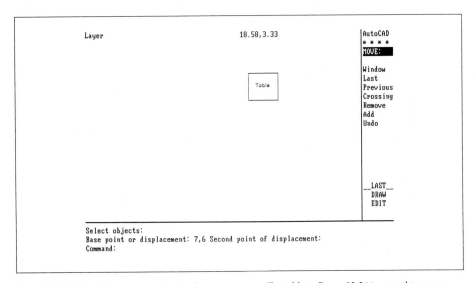

FIGURE 10.25: The Move command—Displacement option. The table in Figure 10.24 is moved to a new location using the displacement option. Compare this to the hexagon that was copied in Figure 10.8. Move and Copy function in the same way, but in the case of the Move command, the original entity does not remain in the drawing.

Second point of displacement As explained, if you press Enter in response to this prompt, AutoCAD interprets your response to the first prompt, "Base point or displacement," as an x-y displacement, and immediately moves the entities to the new location.

However, if you respond to this prompt by entering another x-y coordinate point, AutoCAD reinterprets the response to the previous prompt to be a *base point*; that is, a point relative to which the selected entities are to be moved. The second point entered therefore becomes the *point of displacement*; that is, the means to measure the angle and direction of movement using the coordinate relationship between the two selected points.

For example, if you entered **7,6** in response to the first prompt and **9,8** in response to the second prompt, AutoCAD would move the entities to a point found 2 units along the x-axis and 2 units along the y-axis from the base point; in other words, at the same distance and angle as exists between points 7,6 and 9,8. An illustration of this type of displacement is seen in Figure 10.26, where the base point is 7,6 and the second point of displacement is 9,8. Notice that, while the response to the first prompt is the same as in Figure 10.25, the point response to the second prompt produces a far different result.

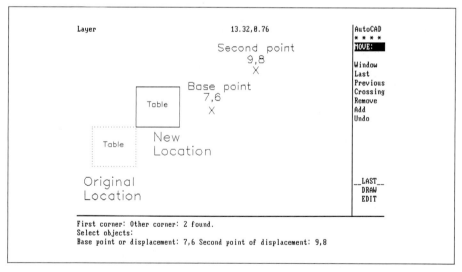

FIGURE 10.26: The Move command—Base Point/Displacement option. The Base Point/Displacement Point option in the Move command duplicates the Copy command, except that no original remains at the conclusion of the command. In this figure, the base and displacement points are marked in the upper part of the drawing; the old and new locations of the table are shown in the lower left. Compare to the Copy command in Figure 10.9.

USAGE

Be careful when using a pointing device that has both a Return button and a pick button. When using such a pointing device to select displacement points, be sure not to press Return if you intend to select a point. For example, if you entered point **1000,1000** as the base point, moved the crosshairs, and accidentally pressed the Return button instead of the pick button, the objects would likely be moved to a remote part of the drawing instead of the intended point. The entities on the screen may seem to disappear altogether. Other effects could be a surprise second regeneration of the drawing when zooming or panning, because of a change in the drawing extents. If you select a second point of displacement on the screen and the entities do not move there, undo the Move command before trying again. Refer to the discussion of the Undo command for details.

RELATED COMMANDS

Copy.

SAMPLE DIALOG

The following dialog draws a square and moves it to a new location:

```
Command: Polygon
Number of sides: 4
Edge/<Center of polygon>: 5,4
Inscribed in circle/Circumscribed about circle (I/C): C
Radius of circle: @1<90
Command: Move
Select objects: L
1 selected, 1 found.
Select objects: (press Enter)
Base point or displacement: 5,4
Second point of displacement: (press Enter)
Command:
```

OFFSET

Offsets a line entity—copies it parallel to itself—at a distance you select.

VERSIONS

Version 2.5 and later.

COMMAND OPTIONS

Offset distance   Enter the distance between the original entity and the copy you intend to create, using any of AutoCAD's standard methods for entering such values. If you are offsetting a wide polyline, the offset distance is measured between the center lines of the original and the copy.

Through   Enter **T** if you prefer to indicate the amount of offset by using a single point instead of specifying a distance. AutoCAD will generate the offset copy so that it intersects a point you select.

Select object to offset   Select the entity to offset by means of a point pick. Do not use the Window, Crossing, or Last options, since AutoCAD will offset only one entity at a time.

Side to offset   This prompt appears if you entered an offset distance. Respond by picking a point on either side of the original entity. AutoCAD then generates the copy of that entity at the selected distance on the selected side.

The point you select can be located anywhere in the drawing, as long as it is clearly to one side or the other of the original entity. Avoid selecting points that are too close to the original, as this may lead to an offset copy generated on the wrong side.

If the original entity is an arc or a circle, or if it contains curved segments, be certain that the offset distance is close enough to generate a parallel entity. If the offset distance is too large to generate an offset copy, you will see the following prompt:

No parallel at that offset

Through point   This prompt appears if you entered **T** in response to the "Offset distance" prompt. AutoCAD now prompts for a single point. When you pick the point, AutoCAD generates the copy so that it intersects the selected point.

If you are working in 3-D and offsetting an entity that is not in the current UCS, you may not get the results you intended. This is because the viewing perspective is misleading when you're selecting offset points. For example, if Auto-CAD cannot draw an offset because the point you selected is already intersecting the original, AutoCAD responds:

Invalid through point

Try using a plan view of the entity and reselecting the offset point.

USAGE

You may only offset the following line entities: arcs, circles, lines, 2-D and 3-D polylines, and traces. Use the Copy command on other entities.

Offset is especially powerful as a means to create parallel polylines and arcs, as it will shorten or lengthen arcs or polyline segments as necessary to generate the offset copy. Refer to the sample dialog for an example of Offset used to generate parallel polylines containing arc segments.

If the entity you want to offset cannot be copied parallel to the current construction plane, AutoCAD prompts:

> That entity is not parallel to the UCS.

To offset the entity, use the Ucs command with the Entity option to move the UCS parallel to the entity. Then invoke Offset, followed by UCS Previous. Refer to Chapter 6 for a detailed discussion of the Ucs command.

The Offset command has been known to generate results other than what you intended. If the offset does not appear correct, try one of the following:

- Undo the command and try again, using different points to pick the entity, or choosing another through point.
- If you're offsetting a polyline, undo the command and explode the polyline. Then try to offset the segments individually. Alternatively, you may use the PEdit command to change specific attributes of the polyline copy.

Note: Using Offset on tapered polylines can produce inexact copies, especially if arc segments are involved. Use PEdit to clean up the copy if necessary.

RELATED COMMANDS

Copy.

SAMPLE DIALOG

The following dialog produces the parallel polylines shown in Figure 10.27:

```
Command: PLine
From point: 4,10
Current line-width is 0.00
Arc/Close/Halfwidth/Length/Undo/Width/<Endpoint of line>: 11,10
Arc/Close/Halfwidth/Length/Undo/Width/<Endpoint of line>: A
Angle/CEnter/CLose/Direction/Halfwidth/Line/Radius/Second   pt/Undo/
Width/<Endpoint of arc>: 11,3
Angle/CEnter/CLose/Direction/Halfwidth/Line/Radius/Second   pt/Undo/
```

Width/<Endpoint of arc>: **L**
Arc/Close/Halfwidth/Length/Undo/Width/<Endpoint of line>: **4,3**
Arc/Close/Halfwidth/Length/Undo/Width/<Endpoint of line>: **(press
Enter)**
Command: **Offset**
Offset distance or Through: **1**
Select object to offset: **4,3**
Side to offset? **4,4**
Select object to offset: **4,4**
Side to offset? **4,5**
Select object to offset: **4,5**
Side to offset? **4,6**
Select object to offset:
Command:

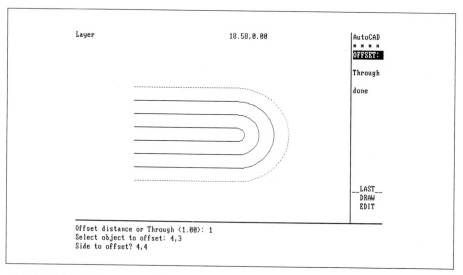

FIGURE 10.27: The Offset command per sample dialog. A series of evenly spaced, parallel lines and arcs can be generated quickly using the Offset command. The original entity selected to offset is highlighted in this drawing; once the offset distance and entity are entered, you can quickly generate the copies of the original polyline by repeatedly picking the same side of the original entity.

Oops

Restores the most recently erased selection set.

VERSIONS

All.

COMMAND OPTIONS

None.

USAGE

To recover the most recently erased selection set, invoke the Oops command. No options are available. The selection set is redisplayed and the entities are added to the drawing database once more.

Oops can be used after defining a block with the Block command, or after writing entities directly to disk using the Wblock command. It restores the entities erased by these commands.

Warning: Oops will restore only the previously erased selection set. Use U or Undo to recover beyond the previous erasure.

RELATED COMMANDS

U, Undo.

SAMPLE DIALOG

The following dialog draws, erases, and recovers a line:

```
Command: Line
From point: 1,1
To point: 8,8
To point: (press Enter)
Command: Erase
Select objects: L
Select objects: (press Enter)
Command: Oops
```

PEDIT

Enables you to add new vertices to a polyline, move existing vertices, remove selected vertices, close or open a polyline, change its width, join line entities into a single polyline, break a polyline into two polylines, or fit a continuous curved polyline to the vertices of a straight-segment polyline.

VERSIONS

All.

COMMAND OPTIONS

Select polyline   PEdit always begins with this prompt. In response, select one polyline using any of AutoCAD's standard entity-selection methods. If you select a line entity that is not a polyline or mesh, AutoCAD responds:

> Entity selected is not a polyline
> Do you want to turn it into one?

Enter **Y** if you want the selected entity to become a polyline. Otherwise, enter **N** and AutoCAD cancels the PEdit command.

Options for 2-D Polylines

The command syntax for editing 3-D polylines and meshes is based on the general syntax for editing 2-D polylines. When learning to edit polylines and meshes, begin by understanding 2-D polylines first. Learning to edit the other forms of polylines will be much easier if you learn to edit 2-D polylines first. Editing options for 3-D polylines and polygon meshes are available in Release 10 and later.

GENERAL 2-D POLYLINE EDITING

Close   Enter **C** to close an open polyline. If the starting and ending points of the polyline are not the same, a straight polyline segment is added to join them.

If the polyline is open but the starting and ending points are the same, closing the polyline will not change the display of the polyline on the screen. Chamfer, Fillet, and curve-fitting will behave differently, however. Closing a polyline has a significant effect on how it reacts to curve-fitting, fillets, and chamfers. These commands have no effect on the endpoints of open polylines, even if they are the same point, but will apply to all vertices of a closed polyline.

Join   Enter **J** to select other polylines, lines, or arcs and connect them, together with the currently selected polyline, into a single polyline. AutoCAD responds:

> Select objects:

Select the entities to be joined to the polyline using any of AutoCAD's standard entity-selection methods. Selected entities must meet at the endpoints, and at least one must meet an endpoint of the selected polyline; otherwise, AutoCAD ignores them.

After AutoCAD has joined all the entities it can, you may determine the status of the new polyline by exiting the PEdit command, invoking the Select command, and then selecting the new polyline. The polyline will be highlighted, indicating its new configuration. Press Ctrl-C to avoid creating a new selection set, or press Enter.

Width Enter **W** to change the width of the polyline. AutoCAD responds:

Enter new width for all segments

Enter a new width by using the keyboard, or by picking two points on the screen. If you pick two points, AutoCAD uses the distance between them as the new polyline width.

Fit curve Enter **F** to fit a curved polyline to the vertices of a straight-segment polyline. AutoCAD replaces each segment with two arcs joining the vertices, as illustrated in Figure 10.28.

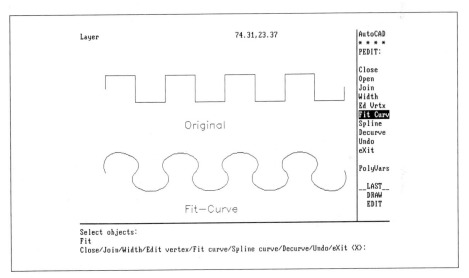

FIGURE 10.28: Polyline with curve fitted. The Fit Curve option is the most radical means of applying curves to the vertices of a polyline. The fit-curve is generated by joining the vertices with a pair of arcs. The original polyline and the fit curve of the same line are illustrated in this figure. Once the fit curve has been applied to the polyline, individual arc segments may be changed by means of the Tangent suboption within the Edit Vertex option. Refer to the PEdit command for details.

Often, when using the Fit Curve option, the results are not as intended. PEdit includes a Tangent option (described ahead under "Editing Polyline Vertices") to allow you to specify exact tangent directions for arcs where they intersect the vertices of the straight-segment polyline. Also, refer to the Decurve option, which reverses the Fit Curve option.

Spline curve Enter **S** to fit a different type of curve to the polyline. The *spline curve* is usually a smoother curved line than the one generated by the Fit Curve option. The Spline Curve option treats the polyline as a frame for either a quadratic or cubic B-spline curve, as illustrated in Figure 10.29. These curves are in fact approximations of curved lines, composed of a series of short line segments.

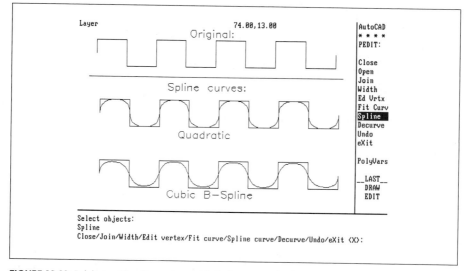

FIGURE 10.29: Polyline with spline curves added. This figure illustrates the two types of spline curves that can be fit to a polyline frame using the Spline Curve option. The quadratic spline curve is generated when the SPLINETYPE system variable is set to a value of 5. The cubic-B spline curve is fit to the polyline when this system variable has been set to a value of 6.

The type of spline curve, quadratic or cubic, is controlled by the SPLINETYPE system variable. If SPLINETYPE has a value of 5, a quadratic spline curve is generated. If SPLINETYPE has a value of 6, a cubic spline curve is generated.

Other system variables affect spline curves as well. The SPLFRAME system variable controls whether the spline curve frame (the original straight-segment polyline) remains visible on the screen. If set to 1, the frame is displayed; if set to 0, the frame is not displayed. The SPLINESEGS system variable controls the number of segments drawn between each vertex of the spline frame. The higher the number of spline segments, the finer the resolution of the spline curve, but the longer it will take to regenerate, and the more disk space it will occupy. The default value is 8, which renders a good approximation in most cases.

If you prefer, you can generate a curve that is a combination of spline and fit curves by using a negative integer for the SPLINESEGS system variable. If the value of SPLINESEGS is negative, the spline curve is generated, and the segments of the spline curve are then treated as a polyline to which the Fit Curve option is applied. The result is an approximation of the spline curve using arcs rather than short line segments.

Changing the value of these system variables will cause the appearance of the curved polylines to change when the drawing is regenerated.

Decurve Enter **D** to remove any curve-fitting and thus restore the original straight-segment polyline frame. If you have exploded the polyline, it can no longer be decurved. You may use the Undo option to restore the curve-fit polyline if you explode it during the current editing session.

Undo Enter **U** to reverse the previous polyline editing request. You can enter **U** repeatedly and "back up" to the beginning of the current editing session.

eXit This is the default response. When the general polyline editing prompt is displayed, type **X** or press Enter to end the PEdit command and return to the AutoCAD Command prompt.

EDITING POLYLINE VERTICES

Edit vertex When the general polyline editing prompt is displayed, entering **E** causes a new prompt of vertex-editing options to appear:

Next/Previous/Break/Insert/Move/Regen/Straighten/Tangent/Width/
eXit<N>:

In addition, a small *X* symbol, the *vertex marker*, appears at the first vertex of the polyline, indicating that this vertex is the current vertex and may be edited individually using one of the displayed options. Figure 10.30 shows the vertex marker.

After each editing option is entered and the editing process is completed, AutoCAD redisplays the Edit Vertex options, until you enter **X**. At that point, AutoCAD redisplays the general polyline editing prompt.

Next This is the default response. Enter **N** or press Enter to move the vertex marker sequentially to the next vertex in the polyline.

Previous Enter **P** to move the vertex marker sequentially to the preceding vertex. When you enter **P**, it becomes the default response until you enter **N** again.

The vertex marker can only be moved forward or backward, one vertex at a time (except with polygon meshes). It cannot jump from the last vertex to the first, even if the polyline is closed.

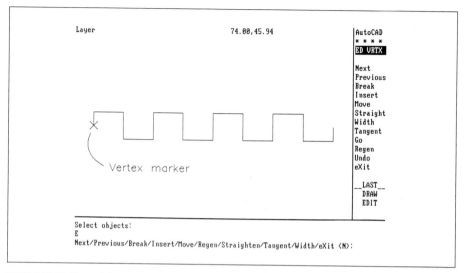

FIGURE 10.30: The polyline vertex marker. When you edit individual vertices of a polyline, a small *X* appears at each vertex indicating which vertex may be edited. Entering **N** will move the marker from the polyline's starting point to its ending point. Entering **P** reverses the movement of the marker. Once entered, N or P becomes the default response to this prompt.

Break Enter **B** to break the polyline by deleting segments between two chosen vertices, or simply by separating the polyline at one of its vertex points. Figure 10.31 shows an example. When you enter **B**, AutoCAD stores the location of the current vertex and displays the following prompt:

> Next/Previous/Go/eXit

Press **N** or Enter to move the vertex marker forward along the polyline. Enter **P** to reverse its direction. When the vertex marker is located at the desired second vertex, type **G.** The segments between the two vertices are deleted, and the polyline becomes two polylines.

If you press **G** without moving the vertex marker, the polyline is split at the current vertex point. The screen display will not change, but the resulting polylines may be edited separately.

After breaking the polyline, AutoCAD redisplays the Edit Vertex options. If you decide not to break the polyline, press **X** to have the Edit Vertex options redisplayed.

Insert Enter **I** to insert a new vertex into the polyline, as shown in Figure 10.32. AutoCAD responds:

> Enter location of new vertex:

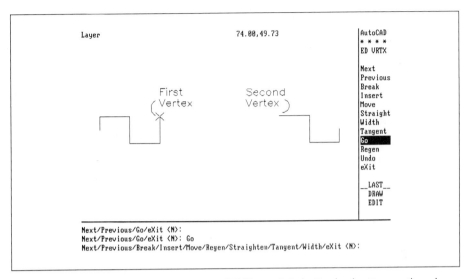

FIGURE 10.31: Breaking a polyline. Prior to AutoCAD Version 2.5, the Break suboption was the only means of partially erasing a polyline. When Break is selected, the current location of the vertex marker is stored in memory. You may then move the vertex marker along the polyline until you arrive at the second break point. Entering **G** (for "Go") erases the polyline between the two vertices, resulting in two polylines; the vertex marker then returns to the original vertex. In Version 2.5 and later, the Break command can be used for polylines, and is usually a faster and easier method.

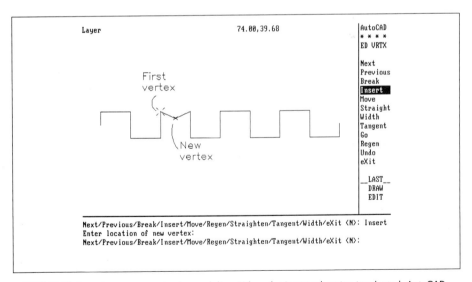

FIGURE 10.32: Inserting a new vertex in a polyline. When the Insert suboption is selected, AutoCAD prompts for a new vertex location, placing that vertex immediately following the current one. After a new vertex is inserted, entering **N** will move the vertex marker to that vertex.

Select a point using any of AutoCAD's standard point-selection methods. The new vertex is added at that point, and the surrounding polyline segments are adjusted. The new vertex is always positioned after the current vertex.

Move Enter **M** to change the location of the current vertex, as shown in Figure 10.33. AutoCAD responds:

Enter new location:

Select a point using using any of AutoCAD's standard point-selection methods. The current vertex is relocated to that point, and the surrounding polyline segments are adjusted accordingly.

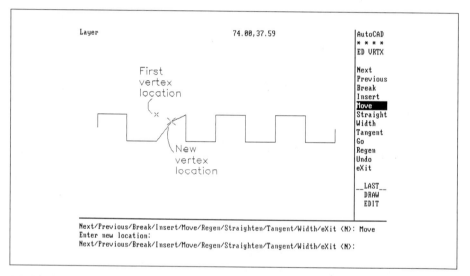

FIGURE 10.33: Moving a polyline vertex. When the Move suboption of the Edit Vertex option is selected, AutoCAD prompts for a new location of the current vertex. If you move the pointing device, a rubberband line will appear, extending from the current vertex to the intersection of the crosshairs. Selecting a point, as shown in the figure above, changes the location of the vertex.

Regen Enter **R** to regenerate the selected polyline.

Straighten Enter **S** to remove all vertices between two selected vertices. AutoCAD responds:

Next/Previous/Go/eXit

Press **N** or Enter to move the vertex marker forward along the polyline. Enter **P** to reverse its direction. When the vertex mark is located at the desired second vertex, enter **G.** The vertices between the two vertices are deleted, and all segments are replaced by a single straight line segment. Figure 10.34 shows an example.

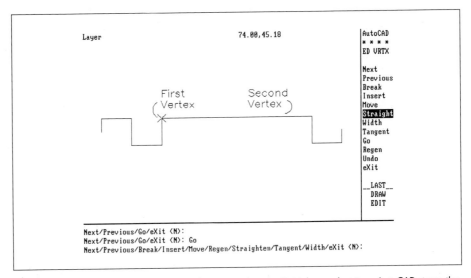

FIGURE 10.34: Straightening a polyline. When you select the Straighten suboption, AutoCAD stores the current location of the vertex marker. You may then move the vertex marker to another vertex. When you enter **G** (for "Go"), AutoCAD replaces all segments between the two vertices with a straight segment joining them, as illustrated in this figure. After straightening, the vertex marker returns to the original vertex.

You can replace a single arc segment with a straight line segment using this option. Position the vertex marker at the starting vertex of the arc segment and type **G.** The arc will be replaced by a straight line.

If you decide not to straighten any of the polyline's segments, type **X** to redisplay the Edit Vertex options.

Tangent This option is used with the Fit Curve option to control the starting direction of curve-fit arcs from the current vertex. It has no effect on spline curves. To change the starting direction of a curve-fit arc, move the vertex marker to the desired vertex and enter **T.** AutoCAD responds:

Direction of tangent:

Enter the starting direction of the curve-fit arc by using the keyboard or by entering a point. If you enter a point, AutoCAD uses the angle formed by the current vertex and the selected point as the starting direction of the curve-fit arc.

Width   Enter **W** to change the starting and ending width of the polyline segment beginning at the current vertex. AutoCAD responds:

Enter starting width:

Enter the starting width of the segment by using the keyboard or by entering a point. If you enter a point, AutoCAD uses the distance between the current vertex and the selected point as the new starting width. AutoCAD then prompts:

Enter ending width:

Enter the ending width of the segment by using the keyboard or by entering a point. If you enter a point, AutoCAD uses the distance between the current vertex and the selected point as the new ending width. If the ending width is the same as the starting width, you may simply press Enter.

AutoCAD will display the new widths when you exit from the Edit Vertex options, or when you enter **R** for Regen.

eXit   When the Edit Vertex options are displayed, enter **X** to return to the general polyline editing prompt.

Editing Options for Polygon Meshes

PEdit is used to edit 3-D polylines in Release 10 and later. Editing 3-D polylines is the same as editing 2-D polylines, except that the width-changing options—3-D polylines always have zero width—and the tangent options are not available. (3-D polylines may be spline-fit or curve-fit only.) Editing results are displayed in three dimensions, and editing prompts accept 3-D points.

In AutoCAD Release 11, polyface meshes cannot be edited using PEdit. Refer to the discussion of the Pface command in Chapter 9 for details about polyface meshes. Other polygon meshes (which are available in Release 10 and later) are treated as polylines for editing purposes—each intersection of the mesh is considered a polyline vertex. Refer to the discussion of the 3dmesh, Edgesurf, Revsurf, Rulesurf, and Tabsurf commands in Chapter 9 for details regarding the construction of polygon meshes.

When you invoke the PEdit command and select a polygon mesh, the following general mesh options are displayed:

Edit vertex/Smooth surface/Desmooth/Mclose/Nclose/Undo/eXit <X>:

EDITING MESH VERTICES

Edit vertex   When the general polyline editing prompt is displayed, entering **E** causes the vertex marker to appear at vertex 0,0 and a new prompt of vertex editing options to appear:

Next/Previous/Left/Right/Up/Down/Move/REgen/eXit <N>:

Next This option, which is the default response, advances the vertex marker to the next vertex in the mesh when you press **N.** The vertex marker advances along the N direction first, then advances one vertex in the M direction, again advances through the vertices in the N direction, advances one vertex in the M direction, and so on. Figure 10.35 illustrates the order in which the vertex marker advances through the vertices of a simple mesh.

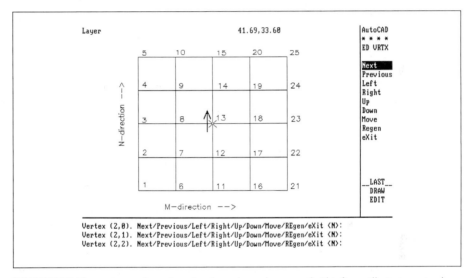

FIGURE 10.35: The vertex marker advancing through a polygon mesh. This figure illustrates a simple five-by-five flat-surface polygon mesh. Like polylines, each vertex of a mesh may be individually edited. The vertex numbers in this figure indicate the order in which the vertex marker will advance through the mesh vertices. This order is the same order in which the 3Dmesh command accepts coordinate points when creating polygon meshes.

Previous Enter **P** to reverse the stepwise direction of the vertex marker through the mesh. When you enter **P,** it becomes the default response until you enter **N** again.

Left Enter **L** to move the vertex marker one vertex back in the N direction. This is the same as Previous, except that the Left option never moves the marker in the M direction.

Right   Enter **R** to move the vertex marker one vertex forward in the N direction. This is the same as Next, except that the Right option never moves the marker in the M direction.

Down   Enter **D** to move the vertex marker one vertex back in the M direction.

Up   Enter **U** to move the vertex marker one vertex forward in the M direction.

Move   Enter **M** to move the current vertex to a new point in 3-D space. You may select the new point using any of AutoCAD's standard point-selection methods.

REgen   Enter **RE** to regenerate the mesh on the screen.

eXit   Enter **X** to return to the general mesh editing prompt.

GENERAL POLYGON-MESH EDITING

The general mesh editing prompt allows you to generate a smooth surface from a polygon mesh, or undo the effects of smooth-surface editing, as well as open or close the mesh in either the M or N direction.

Smooth surface   Enter **S** to smooth the mesh surface. When you select this option, AutoCAD treats the mesh as a three-dimensional frame to which it applies a curve in both the M and N directions, similar to the spline curves that are applied to 3-D polylines. Three types of smooth surfaces can be fit to a polygon mesh; they are controlled by the SURFTYPE system variable. The surface types are:

- **Quadratic B-spline surface.** This is the least smooth surface. It requires a minimum of three vertices in each direction. It will be produced when SURFTYPE is set to 5. This surface is illustrated in Figure 10.36.

- **Cubic B-spline surface.** This surface will appear smoother than the quadratic when fit to meshes having relatively few vertices at extreme angles. It will be produced when SURFTYPE is set to a value of 6. This surface is illustrated in Figure 10.37.

- **Bezier surface.** This surface is the most rounded of the three types. It will be produced when SURFTYPE is set to a value of 8. This surface is illustrated in Figure 10.38.

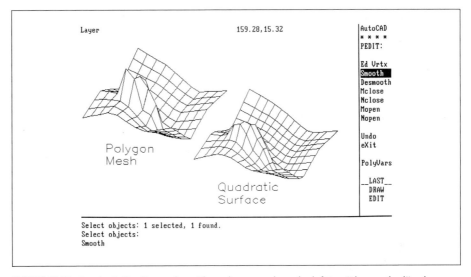

FIGURE 10.36: Quadratic B-spline surface. The polygon mesh on the left is a "desmoothed" polygon mesh. A copy of the mesh on the right has been fitted with a quadratic B-spline smooth surface. Notice that the vertices that have been drawn up in the z-axis are less radically differentiated when the smooth surface is applied.

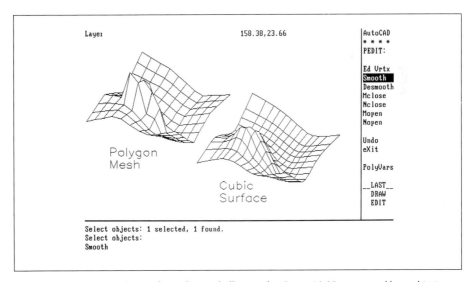

FIGURE 10.37: Cubic B-spline surface. The mesh illustrated in Figure 10.35 is repeated here, this time fitted with a cubic B-spline surface. This surface is slightly smoother than the quadratic smooth surface. It tends to be more effective with vertices at more extreme angles of separation.

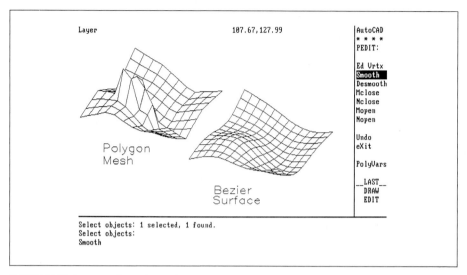

FIGURE 10.38: Bezier surface. The mesh in Figures 10.36 and 10.37 is fitted with a Bezier smooth surface in this figure. The Bezier surface is the "smoothest" of the smooth surfaces. It can only be fitted to meshes having no more than eleven vertices each in the M and N directions.

Desmooth Enter **D** to remove the smooth surface produced by the Smooth option, restoring the original mesh.

Mclose Enter **M** to close an open mesh in the M direction.

Mopen When a mesh is closed in the M direction, enter **M** to open it.

Nclose Enter **N** to close an open mesh in the N direction.

Nopen When a mesh is closed in the N direction, enter **N** to open it.

Undo As with other forms of polyline editing, enter **U** to reverse the effect of the previous editing request. You can enter **U** repeatedly and "back up" to the beginning of the current editing session.

eXit When the general mesh editing prompt is displayed, enter **X** to end the PEdit command.

USAGE

If you need to keep different types of smooth surfaces in the same drawing, use the Explode command to explode a polygon mesh after fitting the smooth surface to it. This replaces the mesh with 3-D faces and makes it no longer subject to the value of the SURFTYPE system variable. However, you can no longer decurve the mesh.

If you break, explode or trim a curve-fit polyline, the original polyline frame is deleted, and the curve-fit polyline becomes permanent. If you need to restore the original polyline, you must use the Undo command. When you explode a polygon mesh to which a smooth surface has been fit, it is replaced by 3-D faces. The original mesh is deleted. To restore it, use the Undo command.

Using Offset on a curve-fit polyline will copy only the curve-fit, not the original frame. The copy cannot be decurved, although the original can. The Join option automatically decurves a curve-fit polyline. However, you can curve-fit the new polyline after joining other lines to it.

Using the Edit Vertex option, you can only edit the vertices of a curve-fit polyline's frame, not the curve itself—unless you first use an editing command such as Offset that deletes the frame and makes the curve-fit permanent. Object snap, on the other hand, does not see the frame, only the curve.

When you smooth a polygon mesh with SPLFRAME set to 1, the original mesh is displayed instead of the curve. If SPLFRAME is set to 0, only the smooth curve surface is displayed. There is no provision for displaying both surfaces at the same time. You can, however, copy the mesh, smooth one surface, and then move the two together.

RELATED SYSTEM VARIABLES

SPLFRAME (controls display of original polyline to which spline curves are fit); SPLINESEGS (controls number of segments used in spline curves); SPLINETYPE (controls spline curves fit to polylines); SURFTYPE (controls the type of smooth surface generated); SURFU (controls number of segments in smooth surface M direction); SURFV (controls number of segments in smooth surface N direction).

SAMPLE DIALOG

The following dialog draws and edits the polyline illustrated in Figure 10.39. The results of this dialog are pictured in Figure 10.40.

```
Command: PLine
From point: 5,6
Current line-width is 0.00
Arc/Close/Halfwidth/Length/Undo/Width/<Endpoint of line>: W
Starting width <0.0>: .25
Ending width <0.25>: (press Enter)
Arc/Close/Halfwidth/Length/Undo/Width/<Endpoint of line>: 9,10
```

Arc/Close/Halfwidth/Length/Undo/Width/ <Endpoint of line>: **14,10**
Arc/Close/Halfwidth/Length/Undo/Width/ <Endpoint of line>: **18,6**
Arc/Close/Halfwidth/Length/Undo/Width/ <Endpoint of line>: **26,6**
Arc/Close/Halfwidth/Length/Undo/Width/ <Endpoint of line >: **(press Enter)**
Command: **PEdit**
Select polyline: **26,6**
Close/Join/Width/Edit vertex/Fit curve/Spline curve/Decurve/Undo/eXit
<X>: **E**
Next/Previous/Break/Insert/Move/Regen/Straighten/Tangent/Width/
eXit <N>: **(press Enter)**
Next/Previous/Break/Insert/Move/Regen/Straighten/Tangent/Width/
eXit <N>: **(press Enter)**
Next/Previous/Break/Insert/Move/Regen/Straighten/Tangent/Width/
eXit <N>: **(press Enter)**
Next/Previous/Break/Insert/Move/Regen/Straighten/Tangent/Width/
eXit <N>: **M**
Enter new location: **18,4**
Next/Previous/Break/Insert/Move/Regen/Straighten/Tangent/Width/
eXit <N>: **I**
Enter location of new vertex: **21,8**
Next/Previous/Break/Insert/Move/Regen/Straighten/Tangent/Width/

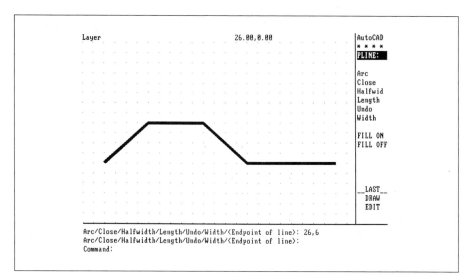

FIGURE 10.39: Polyline per sample dialog. This figure illustrates a typical wide polyline with five vertices, drawn and then edited according to the sample dialog from the PEdit command in this chapter. The fourth vertex is moved, a new vertex is inserted after it, the SPLINETYPE system variable is set to 2, and the polyline is fitted with a quadratic spline curve. The results of the editing process are shown in Figure 10.40.

eXit <N>: **X**
Close/Join/Width/Edit vertex/Fit curve/Spline curve/Decurve/Undo/eXit
<X>: **'Setvar**
>>Variable name or ?: **SPLINETYPE**
>>New value for SPLINETYPE <5>: **2**
Resuming PEDIT command.
Close/Join/Width/Edit vertex/Fit curve/Spline curve/Decurve/Undo/eXit
<X>: **S**
Close/Join/Width/Edit vertex/Fit curve/Spline curve/Decurve/Undo/eXit
<X>: **(press Enter)**
Command:

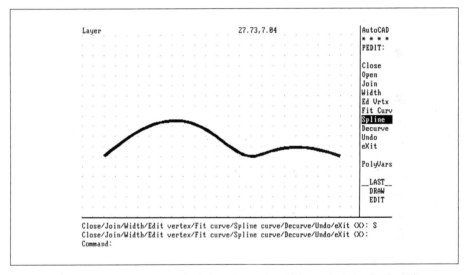

FIGURE 10.40: Polyline edited per sample dialog. The results of the sample dialog for the PEdit command should look like this figure. This figure and the previous figure suggest the extraordinary flexibility and drawing potential of polylines.

REDO

Reverses the effects of an Undo or U command, restoring the drawing to its state at the time the Undo or U command was invoked.

VERSIONS

Version 2.5 and later.

COMMAND OPTIONS

None.

USAGE

To reverse the Undo command, simply invoke the Redo command. The effects of Undo are automatically reversed.

Warning: Redo can only be used immediately following the Undo command. If any other command is invoked between Undo and Redo, the Undo can no longer be reversed.

RELATED COMMANDS

Undo.

SAMPLE DIALOG

The following dialog draws two lines, executes the Undo command to delete the lines, and then invokes the Redo command, restoring the lines on the screen:

```
Command: Line
From point: 2,16
To point: 14,26
To point: (press Enter)
Command: Line
From point: 2,26
To point: 14,16
To point: (press Enter)
Command: Undo
Auto/Back/Control/End/Group/Mark/<number>: (press Enter)
LINE
Command: Redo
Command: Undo
Auto/Back/Control/End/Group/Mark/<number>: 2
LINE LINE
Command: Redo
Command:
```

ROTATE

Rotates a selected group of entities around a designated base point.

VERSIONS

Version 2.5 and later. In versions prior to Version 2.5, the Rotate command could be simulated by turning the entities into a block, and then reinserting and rotating the block using the asterisk option. Refer to the Block command for details if using a version prior to Version 2.5.

COMMAND OPTIONS

Base point   Select the base point for rotation using any of AutoCAD's standard point-selection methods. The base point may be located anywhere; its location relative to the selected entities will determine their resulting new orientation. For example, a centrally located base point, as illustrated in Figure 10.41, will cause the entities to rotate in place, while a base point located away from the chosen entities will cause them to turn in a circle, as illustrated in Figure 10.42.

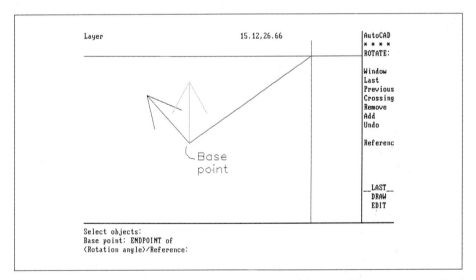

FIGURE 10.41: The Rotate command—central base point. In this illustration of the Rotate command, the arrow has been selected and the base point is placed at the arrow's endpoint, found by using object snap. Next, the rotation angle may be entered from the keyboard or by picking a point. As you move the pointing device, a rubberband line extends from the base point to the intersection of the crosshairs, indicating the angle of rotation if you were to pick the current point. Also, a preview image of the arrow appears, showing you how the arrow would be oriented at the current angle of rotation.

Rotation angle   After selecting the base point, select the angle of rotation. If an exact angle of rotation is known, you may enter it from the keyboard. Alternatively, you may indicate the angle of rotation by moving the crosshairs and picking a point.

As you move the crosshairs, you will notice a rubberband line extending from the base point. The absolute angle of this line, as measured using AutoCAD's angle-measurement system, will be the angle of rotation. If dynamic dragging is enabled, a preview image of the rotated entities will appear on the screen, indicating how the currently displayed angle of rotation will affect them. As soon as you pick a point, the entities are rotated.

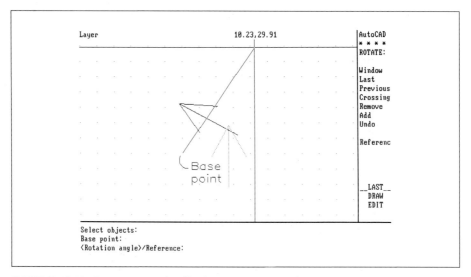

FIGURE 10.42: The Rotate command—offset base point. In using the Rotate command, the placement of the base point can have a significant effect on how the selected entities are to be relocated. In this figure, the arrow maintains its orientation in relation to the base point as it moves in a circle around it. The illustrated angle is about 55 degrees.

Reference angle You may also determine the angle of rotation by entering **R,** and then indicating the entities' current angle of orientation and the desired ending angle of orientation. This method is convenient when the current and ending orientation angles are known, but the exact angle of rotation would be cumbersome to calculate.

To use this option, enter **R** in response to the "Rotation angle" prompt. Auto-CAD responds:

    Reference angle:

Enter the current orientation angle of the selected entities. You can enter the reference angle from the keyboard if it is known, or you may "show" AutoCAD the reference angle by picking two points—for example, by picking the endpoints of a line oriented at the reference angle, by means of object snap. AutoCAD responds:

New angle:

Enter the new orientation angle. AutoCAD uses these two angles to calculate the degree of rotation that is necessary to orient the entities at the new angle. An example of this process is illustrated in Figure 10.43.

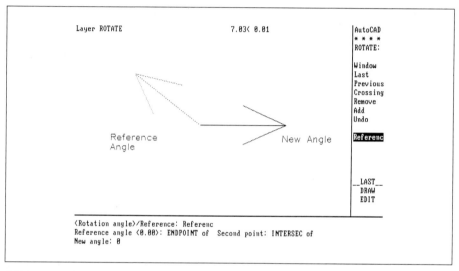

FIGURE 10.43: The Rotate command—Reference Angle option. If you know the finishing angle of rotation but not the current angle of rotation, you can have AutoCAD calculate the correct amount of rotation for you.

SAMPLE DIALOG

The following dialog draws a simple arrow and rotates it 135 degrees:

Command: **Line**
From point: **8,21**
To point: **8,25**
To point: **7,23**
To point: **(press Enter)**
Command: **Line**
From point: **8,25**
To point: **9,23**
To point: **(press Enter)**
Command: **Rotate**
Select objects: **9,23**

```
1 selected, 1 found.
Select objects: 7,23
1 selected, 1 found.
Select objects: 8,21
1 selected, 1 found.
Select objects: (press Enter)
Base point: 8,21
<Rotation angle>/Reference: 135
Command:
```

SCALE

Enlarges or reduces the size of entities by a specified scale. Scale factors greater than 1 enlarge the entities; scale factors between 0 and 1 shrink the entities.

VERSIONS

Version 2.5 and later. In earlier versions of AutoCAD, the Scale command was also emulated by means of the Block command. Unlike the Scale command, which scales along both the x- and y-axes by the same amount, the Block command is a bit more flexible, because it can scale the x and y factors independently.

COMMAND OPTIONS

Base point After selecting the entities you wish to enlarge or reduce, select the base point for scaling by using any of AutoCAD's standard point-selection methods. Bear in mind that the entities may change location while the scaling is taking place. To prevent this, scale entities individually, and select a base point that intersects an entity you wish to remain in place.

Scale factor Enter the scale factor by which you intend to enlarge or reduce the selected entities. For example, to double the size of the entities, enter a scale factor of **2** or move the crosshairs 2 drawing units in any direction. To reduce the size of the entities to one-half their original size, enter **0.5** or move the crosshairs ½ drawing unit in any direction.

Reference If you would like AutoCAD to calculate the exact scale factor for you, enter **R**. AutoCAD responds:

Reference length:

Enter a known dimension for the selected entities. Any known dimension will suffice, as long as you also know what the new length of that dimension will be at the conclusion of the command. AutoCAD then responds:

New length:

Enter the desired new length of the indicated dimension. AutoCAD then scales all the entities according to the same ratio you entered.

USAGE

You may enter a scale factor either by typing it from the keyboard or by using the pointing device to extend a rubberband line from the base point to the current location of the crosshairs. AutoCAD will use the length of the line, measured in drawing units, as the scale factor. If dynamic dragging is enabled, you will see a preview image of the entities growing and shrinking as you move the crosshairs farther from or closer to the base point.

Alternatively, using the reference option, you can enter the current size and ending size of the selected entities, thus allowing AutoCAD to do your scaling calculations for you.

Warning: The Scale command will only change scaling factors equally along both the x- and y-axes. It will not scale these factors separately. In the case of 3-D entities, scaling will take place by the same factor along the z-axis as well.

SAMPLE DIALOG

The following dialog draws a rectangle and scales it to three quarters of its original size. Because the base point is located on the rectangle's horizontal line, that line remains in place after scaling. (Try scaling the same rectangle using different base points, and observe how the location of the lines changes.)

```
Command: PLine
From point: 7,20
Current line-width is 0.00
Arc/Close/Halfwidth/Length/Undo/Width/<Endpoint of line>: 7,24
Arc/Close/Halfwidth/Length/Undo/Width/<Endpoint of line>: 17,24
Arc/Close/Halfwidth/Length/Undo/Width/<Endpoint of line>: 17,20
Arc/Close/Halfwidth/Length/Undo/Width/<Endpoint of line>: C
Command: Scale
Select objects: L
1 found.
Select objects: (press Enter)
Base point: 12,20
<Scale factor>/Reference: .75
Command:
```

STRETCH

Allows you to selectively move portions of entities within the drawing, while maintaining connections to points that remain in place.

VERSIONS

Version 2.5 and later. In AutoCAD Release 10 and later, 2-D entities (arcs and 2-D polylines) may only be moved or stretched parallel to their own construction plane. You may stretch a 3-D entity by changing the current UCS so that it is parallel to the direction in which you intend to stretch the entity.

COMMAND OPTIONS

After invoking the Stretch command, you must select the entities you intend to stretch. This must be done with at least one Crossing window. Refer ahead to Usage section for details on how entities must be selected for this command.

Base point   After you select the objects you wish to move, AutoCAD prompts for a base point. You may enter this point by using the keyboard or by picking a point with the pointing device. The base point is a point relative to which the selected entities are to be moved.

New point   AutoCAD then prompts for a new point. The relationship between this second point and the first point indicates the angle and direction that those entities falling within the selection window are to be moved. For example, if you entered **7,6** in response to the first prompt and **9,8** in response to the second prompt, AutoCAD would move the entities to a point found 2 units along the x-axis and 2 units along the y-axis from the base point.

All entities falling partially within the window are then stretched so that those portions falling within the selection window maintain their current relationship with the moved entities. This process is illustrated in Figures 10.44 and 10.45.

USAGE

When you invoke the Stretch command, AutoCAD prompts you to select entities by means of a "crossing" window. If the crossing window includes entities that you do not intend to stretch, you may remove them from the selection set by entering **R** in response to the "Select objects:" prompt and selecting them by means of point picks. Do not attempt to remove them by means of Window or Crossing options, as this will adversely affect the results of the Stretch command.

Those entities that lie entirely within the selecting window will move in their entirety. Those entities that lie only partially inside the window will stretch; that

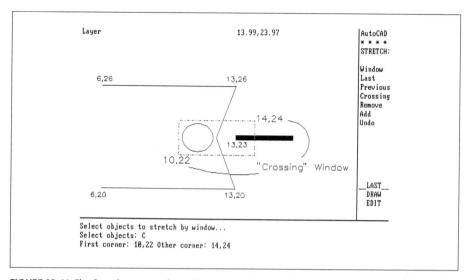

FIGURE 10.44: The Stretch command—entities to stretch. In this figure, a crossing window is used to select a specific portion of the drawing to be stretched using the Stretch command. Only the two thin horizontal lines on the left are not selected. The only entity completely selected is the small circle.

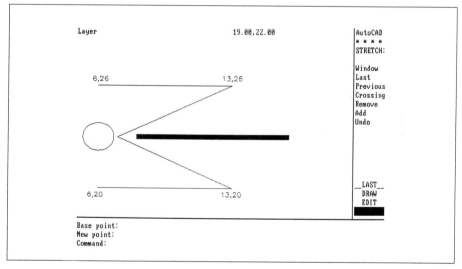

FIGURE 10.45: The Stretch command, after stretching per sample dialog. This figure illustrates the results of moving the selected vertices a specific distance to the left, as per the sample dialog for the Stretch command.

is, the endpoints and vertices inside the window will move while the endpoints outside the window will remain in place.

Blocks, circles, points, shapes, and text are never stretched; they are either moved in their entirety (just like the Move command would move them) or left alone. They will be moved if they are selected and their *entity reference point* is located within the selection window. Entity reference points are as follows:

Block	The insertion point
Circle	The center point
Shape	The insertion point
Text	The leftmost baseline point

Think of the Stretch command as a combination of the Move and Change commands. It is critical that you select entities carefully in order for this command to give you the results you intended. Use dynamic dragging to preview the entities you select to stretch.

Note: Polygons, doughnuts, and ellipses are actually polylines, and can therefore be edited using Stretch.

RELATED COMMANDS

Change, Move.

SAMPLE DIALOG

The following dialog will stretch the entities shown in Figures 10.44 and 10.45:

```
Command: Stretch
Select objects to stretch by window...
Select objects: C
First corner: 10,22
Other corner: 14,24
3 found.
Select objects: (press Enter)
Base point: 11,18
New point: 6,18
Command:
```

TRIM

Allows you to partially erase entities at points of intersection with line entities (arcs, circles, lines, and polylines).

VERSIONS

Version 2.5 and later.

COMMAND OPTIONS

Select cutting edges   After you invoke the Trim command, AutoCAD responds by prompting for the cutting edges you intend to use as boundary lines for trimming. You may use any of AutoCAD's standard entity-selection methods to select the cutting edges. An entity can be both a cutting edge and an entity to be trimmed, as illustrated in Figure 10.46.

After all cutting edges are chosen, press Enter to indicate to AutoCAD that this part of the selection process is complete.

Select object to trim   Once cutting edges are chosen, AutoCAD prompts for entities to trim. Select entities to trim by point picks only; no Window or Last options are allowed. The part of the entity you use to select will be the part that is erased.

AutoCAD repeats this prompt, allowing you to select additional entities for trimming. When all entities are trimmed, press Enter to end the command and return to the Command prompt.

USAGE

The Trim command is related to the Break and Fillet commands. Trim allows you to partially erase existing entities by first selecting "cutting edges"—that is, existing line entities that serve as boundary points for the partial erasure. After you select the cutting edges, select the entities that are to be trimmed; these entities are then partially erased.

If you have selected multiple cutting edges, and have chosen the entity to be trimmed by means of a point on the entity located between those cutting edges, the chosen entity is erased between the cutting edges. If you pick a single cutting edge, or choose an entity to be trimmed by picking a point between its endpoint and the cutting edge, the part of the entity you use to select is the part that is erased. This process is illustrated in Figures 10.46 and 10.47.

> *Warning:* When a curve-fit polyline is trimmed, it is changed into ordinary polylines containing arc segments, and can no longer be decurved. To retain curve-fit information, decurve the polyline before trimming, and recurve it afterward.

The entity you want to trim must be parallel to the current construction plane. If not, AutoCAD prompts:

That entity is not parallel to the UCS.

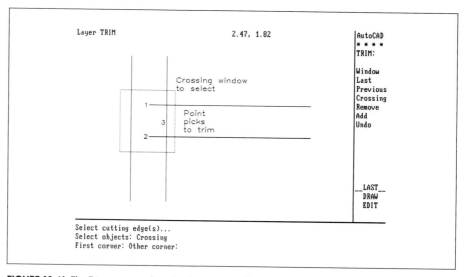

FIGURE 10.46: The Trim command—selecting entities. This figure selects all the lines as cutting edges with a crossing window, and picks the indicated points as the lines to trim. The result is shown in Figure 10.47.

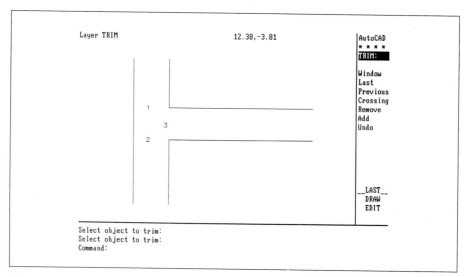

FIGURE 10.47: The Trim command—results per sample dialog. This figure illustrates the open-T intersection cleared out using the Trim command. While Trim is much easier to use than Break in situations like these, this process can be streamlined a little bit further by means of a custom menu macro. Refer to Chapter 14 for details regarding menu macros.

To trim such an entity, use the Ucs command with the Entity option to move the UCS parallel to the entity. Next invoke Trim and select the cutting edge(s) and the entity to trim. Finally, invoke UCS Previous. Refer to Chapter 6 for a detailed discussion of the Ucs command.

RELATED COMMANDS

Break, Fillet.

SAMPLE DIALOG

This dialog draws four lines and trims them to an open-T intersection:

```
Command: Line
From point: 7,18
To point: 7,27
To point: (press Enter)
Command: Line
From point: 9,18
To point: 9,27
To point: (press Enter)
Command: Line
From point: 8,24
To point: 17,24
To point: (press Enter)
Command: Line
From point: 8,22
To point: 17,22
To point: (press Enter)
Command: Trim
Select cutting edge(s)...
Select objects: C
First corner: 6,21
Other corner: 10,25
4 found.
Select objects: (press Enter)
Select object to trim: 8,24
Select object to trim: 8,22
Select object to trim: 9,23
Select object to trim: (press Enter)
Command:
```

U

Reverses the effect of the previous command. The U command is the same as Undo 1, but is faster and easier to type.

VERSIONS

Version 2.5 and later.

COMMAND OPTIONS

None. The U command is automatic. If you undo a command by mistake and want to invoke it again, issue the Redo command immediately.

USAGE

If you continue to repeat the U command, AutoCAD will step backward through the drawing session, undoing each command in turn until it reaches the beginning of the drawing session. As AutoCAD undoes commands, it displays the command name in the Command-prompt area.

If the Auto option of the Undo command has been engaged, command macros invoked from AutoCAD's standard screen or tablet menu are reversed as though they were a single command.

Many of the settings for the Undo command will affect the U command as well. Refer to the discussion of the Undo command for details on options that are available. Every option described in the Undo section, insofar as it applies to the Undo 1 command, will apply to the U command as well.

Note: When used to restore an erased entity, the U command looks a lot like the Oops command, but it is more complete. For example, Oops will restore a block's erased entities after a block is defined, but Undo will restore the entities and undefine the block at the same time. The U command, however, only works on the previous command; Oops restores the last erased entity even if other commands have been invoked between the Erase and Oops commands.

RELATED COMMANDS

Redo, Undo.

SAMPLE DIALOG

This dialog draws a line and then invokes the U command to delete it:

    Command: **Line**
    From point: **1,1**
    To point: **12,12**
    To point: (**press Enter**)
    Command: **U**

```
LINE
Command:
```

UNDO

Selectively backs up through the commands invoked during the current drawing session, reversing their effects.

VERSIONS

Version 2.5 and later.

COMMAND OPTIONS

Number   You may enter an integer indicating the number of commands you intend to undo. For example, enter **3** to undo the last three commands, enter **4** to undo the last four commands, and so on. If you undo too many commands, use Redo to restore all of them, and then undo a smaller number.

When undoing a specific number of commands, Undo always stops if it encounters an *undo mark* on the audit trail. Refer ahead to the Mark option for details on how these marks are placed along the audit trail.

Auto   Enter **A** to enable the Undo Auto option. AutoCAD prompts:

    ON/OFF

Enter **ON** or **OFF** as appropriate. When Undo Auto is enabled, menu macros and command sequences selected from screen and tablet menus are to be considered a single command for purposes of undoing them. This is AutoCAD's default Undo state. If Undo Auto is off, all command macros and sequences must be undone individually.

Undo Auto works by automatically invoking Undo Group and Undo End markers along the audit trail at the start and completion of each menu sequence. See the End and Group options for details.

Back   Enter **B** to undo a series of commands back through the current drawing session, until either the beginning of the drawing session or an undo mark is encountered. If AutoCAD finds that it is about to undo all commands to the beginning of the drawing session, it displays the following message:

    This will undo everything. OK <Y>

Enter **Y** if your intent is to undo back to the start of the drawing session. Otherwise, enter N.

Undo Back always stops if it encounters an undo mark on the audit trail. Refer ahead to the Mark option for details on how these marks are placed along the audit trail.

Control   Enter **C** to control the extent of the Undo command's abilities. Auto-CAD responds:

    All/None/One:

Enter **A** to enable the full Undo feature. This is the default condition. When Undo Control All is invoked, AutoCAD maintains a complete audit trail for purposes of undoing commands. Enter **N** to disable the Undo feature completely. When Undo Control None is invoked, the Undo command will not undo anything. If an audit trail already exists, it is discarded. You may want to disable Undo in order to save the disk space taken up by the audit trail. AutoCAD automatically deletes the audit trail's file at the end of each drawing session, but if the current drawing session is long, the file can become excessively large. If Auto-CAD displays

    disk almost full!

messages during a drawing session, invoke Undo Control None to recover some additional space. After you invoke the Undo Control None option, the Undo prompt is changed to the following:

    All/None/One:

These are the only options available when Undo has been disabled. To reenable the full Undo command, enter **A.**

Enter **O** to limit Undo to reversing the previous command only. This allows you to correct mistakes, but will not allow you to step back through earlier commands in the drawing session. It is functionally the same as limiting Undo to the Undo 1 option. (The U command will also continue to work normally.) If an audit trail exists when this option is invoked, it is deleted.

When you invoke the Undo Control One option, the Undo prompt becomes:

    Control/<1>:

This prompt indicates that the Control option is the only option available, and only the previous command can be undone.

End   Enter **E** to indicate the end of a group of commands that are to be treated as a single command for Undo purposes. This option is used along with the Group option, and will have an effect only if the Group option has been previously invoked.

Group   Enter **G** to indicate the start of a group of commands that are to be treated as a single command for Undo purposes. After invoking the Undo Group option, you may continue to enter commands. After entering the last command in the intended group, invoke the Undo End option. When you undo past this point, all commands identified as being in the group are undone at once, rather than individually.

When a group of commands is undone, AutoCAD does not display each command name in the Command-prompt area. Instead, it displays the word *GROUP.*

With the Undo Auto option enabled, picking a menu command automatically invokes Undo Group before the menu commands are invoked, and Undo End at the conclusion of the menu command sequence. This is why you will see the word *GROUP* appear in the Command-prompt area from time to time even though you haven't set this option manually.

Mark   Enter **M** to place a mark along the audit trail. When you invoke the Undo Back option, or undo any specific number of commands, the Undo process stops upon encountering the mark. You must then invoke another Undo option for the process to continue.

USAGE

As you enter commands, AutoCAD maintains an *audit trail* of commands and their options. The Undo command reads this audit trail in order to reverse the effects of previous commands. AutoCAD cannot skip to various points along this audit trail, but must back through it sequentially, reversing commands as it goes.

When AutoCAD can no longer continue to undo commands, it will display the following message:

Everything has been undone

Some commands, such as Shell and Plot, cannot be undone. If AutoCAD encounters one of these commands, it will display the command name only.

Tip: Whenever possible, undo a number of commands at once rather than repeating the Undo or U command a certain number of times. Each time you invoke Undo or U, the command being reversed may redraw or (worse yet) regenerate the screen. To avoid doing this multiple times, enter the number of commands you want to undo, or use Undo Mark and Back to reverse a sequence of commands. This ensures only one screen regeneration or redraw, regardless of the number of undone commands.

Warning: When you disable or limit Undo, reenabling the full Undo feature does not restore the audit trail. A deleted audit trail is deleted permanently.

After you invoke the Undo Group option (but before you invoke the Undo End option), the group of commands is called an *unterminated group*. The Undo or U command will continue to reverse commands normally through the commands in an unterminated group, but will never proceed past the initial Undo Group marker. If you find that you cannot undo commands because you are at the start of an unterminated group, invoke the Undo End option. Then, you may undo the terminated group (even though there are no longer any commands in it), and Undo will continue.

RELATED COMMANDS

Redo, U.

SAMPLE DIALOG

The following dialog draws three lines, and then invokes the Undo 2 command to delete the last two:

```
Command: Line
From point: 1,1
To point: 12,12
To point: (press Enter)
Command: Line
From point: 2,1
To point: 13,12
To point: (press Enter)
Command: Line
From point: 3,1
To point: 14,12
To point: (press Enter)
Command: Undo 2
LINE LINE
Command:
```

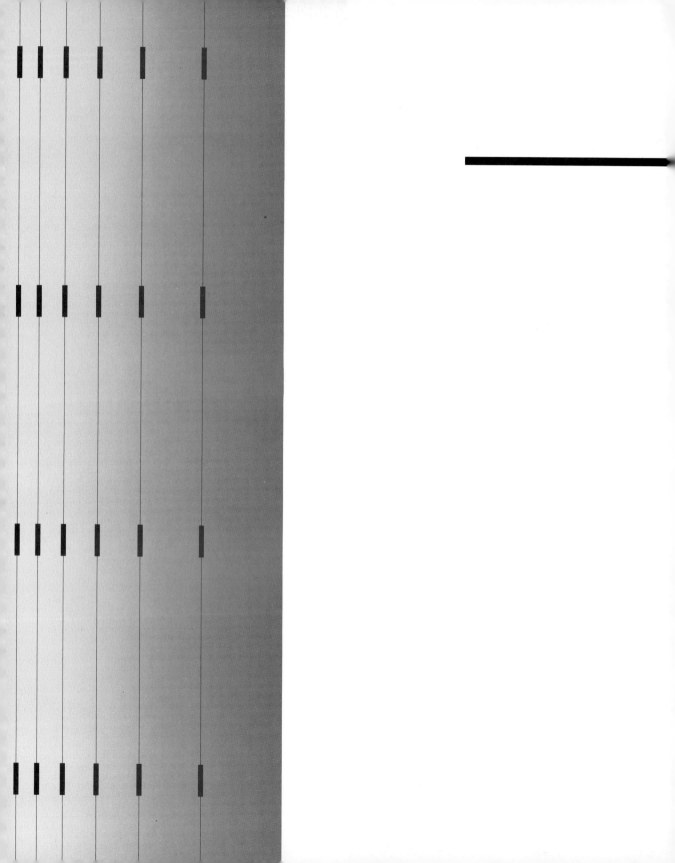

CHAPTER 11

CHANGING THE DRAWING DISPLAY

CHANGING THE DRAWING DISPLAY

AutoCAD stores graphic information at an extremely high level of detail and mathematical precision. Even the most sophisticated display devices will not reproduce this level of detail perfectly. The subtler details of your drawing may not appear accurately when the entire drawing is reproduced on the screen.

Even a simple AutoCAD drawing may contain a considerable number of individual drawing entities, and as drawings become more complex, it takes increasing amounts of time for drawing entities to be generated and displayed on the screen.

To solve the problem of displaying highly detailed graphic images as quickly as possible, AutoCAD provides you with a variety of commands that help control the drawing display. For example, AutoCAD permits you to display and edit portions of the drawing, enlarged so as to reveal smaller details. You can also control the degree of precision with which AutoCAD displays curved lines, text, and filled entities. In versions that support 3-D, AutoCAD also provides several methods for controlling the viewing perspective of 3-D drawings.

These various display-control options are described in this chapter. As you practice and acquire understanding of them, undoubtedly you will develop a personal style of managing the screen display—a style suited to the type of drawings you create and to your preferences regarding the best means to generate and edit drawing entities.

You will become a more efficient AutoCAD user when you have understood and practiced with all of the display commands and their options. Then you may readily call upon the most efficient option in any given situation.

In order to help you understand the various display commands as fully as possible, the following sections present general background information, and define the terms you need to know in managing AutoCAD's screen display.

HOW AUTOCAD MANAGES THE SCREEN DISPLAY

AutoCAD stores all graphic information in a special database that includes the type of entities contained in the drawing, along with the Cartesian coordinate information that will locate each entity precisely in space. Each entity in the drawing database may also include certain attribute information, such as color, linetype, and layer upon which the entity resides. The drawing database also contains general information regarding the drawing's size, layering structure, block definitions, associated shape and text-font files, default screen or tablet menu, and so on.

AutoCAD also remembers specific information regarding the computer and display devices being used. This information was supplied to AutoCAD when you configured the program. When you load an existing drawing, AutoCAD reads all the records in the drawing database, and uses the configuration information to translate those records into graphic representations on your computer screen. If you have instructed AutoCAD to display only a portion of the drawing, only that portion is displayed, even though the entire database is scanned. If you are beginning a new drawing, AutoCAD scans the information in a prototype drawing database, usually named ACAD.DWG, and uses the information it finds there as defaults for the display of the new drawing.

Floating-Point and Integer Values

The mathematical information in the drawing database is stored as *floating-point values*. A floating-point value is a mathematical expression—a coordinate point, for example—that is accurate to 16 decimal places.

Each floating-point value in AutoCAD's drawing database need not have the maximum number of decimal places. AutoCAD will use as many decimal places as required to express the value precisely, up to 16. Since different values may contain different numbers of decimal places, the decimal point is said to "float" to its proper precision for each numeric value. A floating-point system allows for the highest degree of precision when storing graphic information in a disk file, while at the same time keeping disk files from becoming larger than necessary.

Unfortunately, floating-point calculations on a computer are relatively slow compared to other available means. For example, AutoCAD could calculate much more quickly if it used *integers*. Integers, for our purposes, are whole numbers within the range -32768 to $+32767$. When a mathematical expression can be calculated using whole numbers within this range, integers are markedly faster. Since decimal values and numbers outside the given range are not allowed, the accuracy of the drawing suffers in any application that requires a higher degree of mathematical precision than integers can provide.

The mathematics of graphic images is quite complex. Using floating-point mathematics to translate the drawing database into its graphic representation on the screen would be unacceptably slow, undercutting all the advantages of using a computer to create and edit drawings. Fortunately, the number of pixels in a monitor screen is relatively limited, and the highest degree of screen resolution can be managed successfully using integer-based mathematics. Thus, when AutoCAD is called upon to display graphic information on the screen, it converts the floating-point values in the drawing database to integer-based approximations on the display screen, allowing much faster screen display than would otherwise be possible.

When you add a single new entity or edit a relatively small group of entities on the screen, the changes to the current display will appear to be immediate, or at least nearly so. However, things tend to slow down when you invoke a command that requires AutoCAD to refresh the entire screen display—for example, if you elect to magnify a small portion of the drawing, change the display from one portion of the drawing to another, or change from displaying a portion of the drawing to displaying the entire drawing. Under these circumstances, scanning the entire database each time you intended to refresh the screen would be quite time-consuming, even if the drawing was only moderately large.

The Virtual Screen

Beginning with Version 2.5, each time AutoCAD scans the drawing database, it holds integer-based screen-display information in memory, referring to this information as the *virtual screen*. All or part of the virtual screen may actually appear on the monitor at any given time. The part of the drawing that appears on the monitor is called the *viewport*. Beginning with Release 10, it is possible to split the viewing area into several parts and display more than one viewport at the same time.

When AutoCAD receives instructions that require a change in the viewport, it first checks to see if all the necessary information is stored in the virtual screen. If so, it will change the location of the viewport and quickly refresh the graphic image that appears on the monitor. If the required information is not available in the current virtual screen, AutoCAD will rescan and recalculate the values in the drawing database, automatically creating a new virtual screen and viewport that make the requested display possible.

When no rescanning is involved, AutoCAD updates the display by performing a *redraw*. If AutoCAD must rescan the drawing database, it performs a *drawing regeneration* (or *regen* for short). Redraws are much faster than regens, since no rescanning is involved.

Generally speaking, AutoCAD performs a regeneration when the requested display is outside the virtual screen, or when the requested magnification of the drawing is very large, relative to the fineness of detail in the drawing.

All experienced AutoCAD users look for ways to make display changes as fast as possible. The trick to doing this is to create a situation in which the virtual screen is large enough to contain all the information you need to accommodate all subsequent changes in the display. Many of AutoCAD's display commands were implemented to facilitate this.

The benefits of the virtual screen are most effectively demonstrated when you use the Zoom command with the Dynamic option. This option displays the virtual screen and the current viewing area at the same time. Refer to the Zoom command in this chapter for details.

Other Display Techniques

In addition to managing the virtual screen, other fast-display tricks are available to users who are familiar with the various display commands. These include:

- Making curved lines appear as short line segments instead of smooth curves. (Refer to the Viewres command.)
- Turning fill off. (Refer to Chapter 6 for details on the Fill command.)
- Using Qtext to display text temporarily as rectangles instead of character strings. (Refer to the Qtext command.)
- Using the Zoom Dynamic option to ensure that no unnecessary regens are performed. (Refer to the Zoom command.)
- Using the View and Vports commands to save and recall specific viewports during current and subsequent editing sessions. (Refer to the View and Vports commands.)
- Turning the grid off whenever possible. (Refer to Chapter 7 for details regarding the Grid command.)

Dview

Allows you to make changes to the viewing angle of 3-D drawings. If you like, you can make these changes dynamically, previewing the results by displaying a graphic representation of the viewing angle as you change it.

VERSIONS

Release 10 and later.

COMMAND OPTIONS

Select objects   AutoCAD begins the Dview process by prompting you to select entities. Select those entities that will compose a good representative sampling of all the entities currently visible on the screen. You may use any standard entity-selection method to choose some, all, or none of the entities if you wish. The entities you select will change their orientation on the screen relative to the viewing angles you enter, as you enter them. By using only selected entities, you speed up the preview process considerably, allowing AutoCAD to sample only a few entities to preview on the screen. This process is illustrated in Figure 11.1.

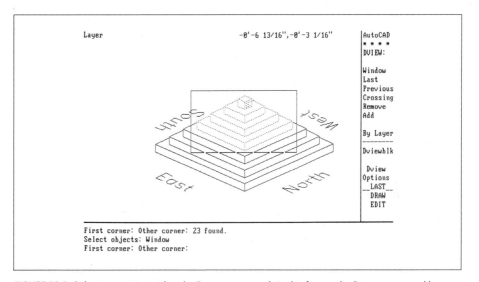

FIGURE 11.1: Selecting entities within the Dview command. In this figure, the Dview command has been invoked and AutoCAD prompts to select objects. Since the pyramid's orientation will be effectively represented using only a portion of the entities on the screen, those entities are selected, using the Window option. The selected entities will be the only ones dynamically reproduced during the Dview command processing.

Alternatively, you may respond to the prompt by selecting no objects at all. AutoCAD will provide a special preview image consisting of an elementary 3-D sketch of a house. You may use this sketch to preview the results of the new viewing angle.

If the small house does not appeal to you, you may create a 3-D block of your own with the name DVIEWBLOCK. If you have such a block defined in the current drawing, AutoCAD will display it instead of the little house.

Regardless of which entities you select for previewing, the entire drawing will be reoriented to the new viewing angle at the conclusion of Dview.

After you have selected the entities you wish to use for previewing, press Enter. AutoCAD then presents the Dview options.

CAmera   Enter **CA** to change the viewing position relative to the target point. AutoCAD responds:

Enter angle from X-Y plane:

As you change the angle from the X-Y plane, you will rotate the camera to a point above or below the current construction plane. This angle determines both the camera's elevation and—because it is always pointed toward the target point from the same distance—its orientation in 3-D space as well.

When AutoCAD displays this prompt, a *slider* appears in the right side of the screen, as illustrated in Figure 11.2. The slider shows a scale from 90 degrees to – 90 degrees. In this case, 90 degrees is the same as a plan view of the current UCS (looking directly down), and – 90 degrees is the opposite view angle (looking directly up). Thus, an orientation of zero degrees would view the current construction plane horizontally, making it appear as a straight line. These angles are illustrated in Figures 11.3 and 11.4.

You may enter the desired viewing angle by using the keyboard or by moving the diamond-shaped pointer within the slider. The pointer will appear when you position the crosshairs within the slider. As you move the pointing device, the pointer will follow, and the selected entities will appear to rotate. It is important to remember that you are not actually rotating the entities; rather, AutoCAD is attempting to display the entities as they will appear if you select the camera's current viewing angle. To select a new angle, press the pick button when the entities appear to be viewed from the proper elevation.

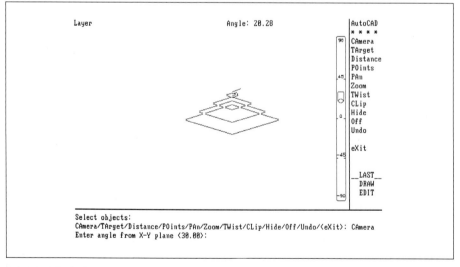

FIGURE 11.2: The Dview command showing the camera slider bar. The slider bar to the right of the display indicates the degree to which the camera is rotated around the target point, either above or below the X-Y plane. The diamond-shaped pointer is currently at angle 20.28 (as indicated in the status line). Two lines extend from the original angle of rotation, 30 degrees, to the location of the pointer. As you move the crosshairs to change the location of the pointer, the screen display reflects the current camera position.

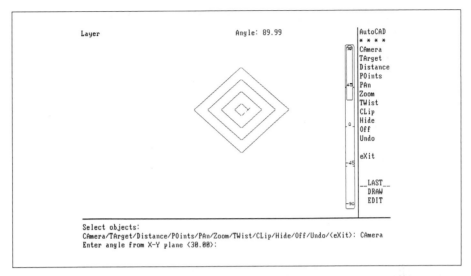

FIGURE 11.3: The Dview command, with the camera reoriented to angle 89.99, or nearly plan view. In this figure, the diamond pointer is moved to the top of the slider bar, and the display shows the appearance of the pyramid in plan view—in other words, with the camera directly above and looking down at the target point, which is currently the center of the pyramid's base.

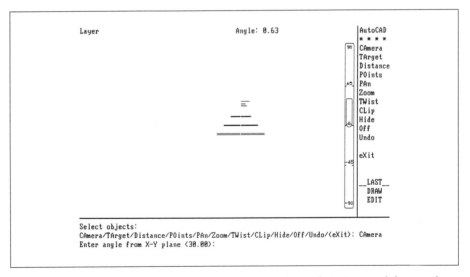

FIGURE 11.4: The Dview command, with the camera reoriented to angle 0.63, or nearly horizontal view. In this figure, the diamond pointer is moved to near zero in the slider bar, and the display shows the appearance of the pyramid in horizontal elevation view—in other words, with the camera viewpoint parallel to the X-Y plane.

The pointer's starting position within the slider is equal to the current viewing angle of the camera. For example, if you selected this option while in plan view, the pointer's starting position would be at 90, indicating that the camera is looking straight down from directly above the target point. As you move the pointer, a pair of rubberband lines extends from the starting location to the pointer's current location. The appearance of the selected entities changes as you bring the camera closer to zero, where you will be viewing the entities from an elevation viewpoint. Figure 11.5 illustrates this camera/target metaphor, showing how the camera's motion would appear if you were able to step back and observe this motion from a distant point. As the viewing angle increases from zero (elevation angle), the camera moves in a circle around the target point. What you see on the screen is how the entities would appear when you view them through the lens of this imaginary camera.

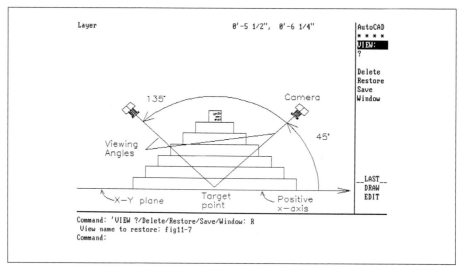

FIGURE 11.5: Another look at the camera's position relative to the X-Y plane. If you were to look at the pyramid in horizontal elevation view and watch the rotation of the camera around the target point, it would appear something like this figure. As the angle of rotation increases, the camera moves farther above the X-Y plane, until it passes 90 degrees (directly overhead). Then it descends toward the X-Y plane from the opposite side.

After you enter the angle from the X-Y plane, AutoCAD prompts:

Enter angle in X-Y plane from X axis:

As this angle is changed, you will rotate the camera around the target point, parallel to the current construction plane. The angle determines both the camera's position and its orientation in space. It is measured relative to the x-axis of the current construction plane. For example, if you enter an angle of zero, Auto-CAD points the camera toward the target point parallel to the x-axis, oriented in such a way that if the camera were actually on the x-axis, it would be looking down toward the origin (from right to left in plan view). An angle of 90 degrees would point the camera parallel to the y-axis, again looking toward the camera's origin (from top to bottom in plan view). An angle of 180 degrees would point the camera parallel to the x-axis, but this time oriented so that it was looking away from the origin (from left to right in plan view). These angles are illustrated in Figure 11.6. Notice how the camera is always directed at the target point as you change its angle in the X-Y plane.

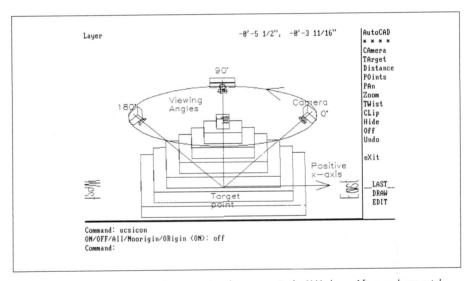

FIGURE 11.6: The Dview command—positioning the camera in the X-Y plane. After you have established the desired elevation of the camera, you are prompted to move the camera parallel to the X-Y plane, at the selected elevation. If you were to view this manipulation of the camera from a distance, you might see something like this figure. At zero degrees, the camera is positioned above the positive x-axis; as the angle increases, the camera moves counterclockwise around the target point, always maintaining the same elevation, and always pointed at the target point.

TArget   Enter **TA** to change the location of the target point. Moving the target point will not change the location of the camera in space, but it will change the camera's orientation, since the camera is always pointed toward the target point. This process is illustrated in Figure 11.7. When you enter **TA**, AutoCAD responds:

    Enter angle from X-Y plane:

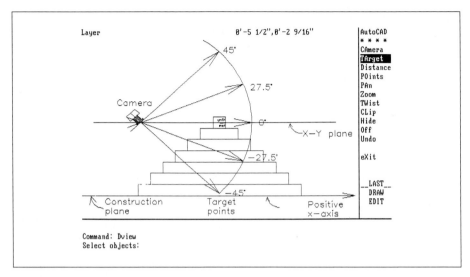

FIGURE 11.7: The Dview command—moving the target point above or below the X-Y plane. When the camera is located in the correct position relative to the entities being viewed, you may adjust its orientation by moving the target point. In the above figure, the target point is being rotated around the camera position in a plane perpendicular to the X-Y plane.

As you change this angle, you will be moving the target point to a new location above or below the current construction plane. As you move the target point, the camera "follows" it, allowing different parts of the drawing to come into view.

As is also the case when using the Camera option, a slider appears to the right, allowing you to change the angle while watching the resulting appearance of the screen display. You may select a new angle by entering it from the keyboard or by moving the diamond-shaped pointer and pressing the pick button when you reach the desired angle and/or preview display.

Beginning users sometimes have trouble understanding the relationship between the target point's angle from the X-Y plane and what appears in the preview display. Remember that AutoCAD displays the viewing angle from the point of view of the camera while you move the target point; in other words, changing the target point is the same as changing the camera orientation without changing its position in space.

After you enter the first angle, AutoCAD prompts:

> Enter angle in X-Y plane from X axis:

When you enter an angle in response to this prompt, you will move the target point around the camera parallel to the current construction plane, at whatever distance and angle you specified as the result of your previous angle entry. As you move the target point, the camera follows it, allowing you to view different parts of the drawing. This is illustrated in Figure 11.8.

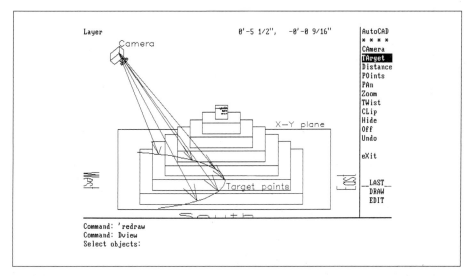

FIGURE 11.8: The Dview command—moving the target point within the X-Y plane. When the target point is located in the correct position relative to the X-Y plane, you may further adjust the camera's orientation by moving the target point parallel to the X-Y plane. In the above figure, the target point is being rotated around the camera position in a plane parallel to the X-Y plane. Angle zero would place the target point parallel to the positive x-axis. Increasing the angle will rotate the target point counterclockwise.

Distance　After you have established the correct viewing angle, you may move the camera back and forth along the viewing angle. This option allows you to move in close to detailed parts of the drawing, or move back to include more of the drawing entities in the display. This process is illustrated in Figure 11.9.

To invoke the Distance option, enter **D**. AutoCAD responds:

> New camera/target distance:

The current distance between the camera and the target is displayed as the default answer. To accept this distance, thereby not changing anything, press Enter. Otherwise, enter a distance you prefer.

A slider also appears at the top of the screen when you invoke the Distance option. This slider is labeled 0x through 16x, indicating that the distance between camera and target can be increased by as much as 16 times the original distance. If you move the pointer to the part of the slider between 0x and 1x, you will decrease the distance between camera and target. For example, if you locate the pointer exactly midway between 0x and 1x, you will multiply the current distance between camera and target by a factor of .5, or one-half the current distance, thereby bringing them closer together. As you move the pointer, Auto-CAD displays a preview of the selected entities on the screen.

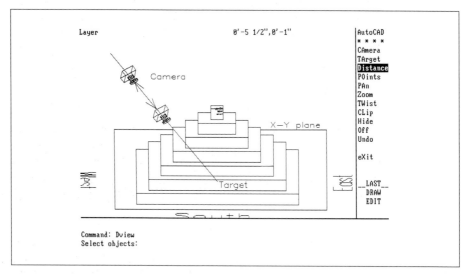

FIGURE 11.9: The Dview command—adjusting the camera distance. When the viewing angle is established, you may use Dview's Distance option to move the camera closer to the target point, thus magnifying the display, or farther from the target point, shrinking the display. This option also enables perspective viewing.

Since the Distance option works as a multiple of the current distance, the closer you bring the camera to the target, the less change in position you will see as you move the slider. When the camera is farther away from the target, the changes using the Distance option are much more perceptible.

The Distance option also turns on perspective view mode. When perspective view mode is turned on, entities are scaled so as to appear smaller the farther they are from the camera. By typing **D** and pressing Enter in response to the prompt for a distance, you can turn on perspective view mode without changing the distance if you like.

While the Distance option allows you to move close to the entities in the drawing, thereby increasing their magnification, it also distorts the perspective. If you intend to magnify a portion of the drawing to work on it in detail, turn perspective mode off using the Off option, and use the Dview Zoom option to magnify the drawing.

POints   Enter **PO** if you prefer to define the camera and target points by entering absolute x, y, and z coordinates rather than relative angles. If perspective view is on when you select this option, AutoCAD temporarily turns it off, as points selected using the pointing device must be selected in standard view mode. However, you may select the new points using any of AutoCAD's standard coordinate-point selection methods. AutoCAD prompts:

Enter target point:

After you select the target point, AutoCAD prompts:

Enter camera point:

Here again, enter the location of the camera using any of AutoCAD's standard point-selection methods.

PAn Enter **PA** to shift the position of the camera without changing the viewing angle or the level of magnification. This command is functionally the same as AutoCAD's Pan command, except that in these circumstances, you may pan while in perspective view mode. Refer to the discussion of the Pan command in this chapter for details regarding Pan.

After you enter **PA**, AutoCAD responds:

Displacement base point:

As with the Pan command, AutoCAD is asking for a base point, or anchor point, which can be used as the starting point for determining the angle and distance of the camera's movement. You may select any point in the current viewing area or, if you are not in perspective view mode, you may enter specific coordinate points from the keyboard. After you enter the base point, AutoCAD responds:

Second point:

Enter the second point using the pointing device or, if not in perspective view mode, the keyboard. AutoCAD calculates the distance and angle between the selected points in the current viewing plane, and moves the camera location by those values. This process is illustrated in Figure 11.10.

Zoom Enter **Z** to increase or decrease the magnification, and thereby the level of visible detail, in the drawing. Unlike AutoCAD's Zoom command, which allows for several optional methods of zooming, Dview allows only two Zoom options, one for perspective view mode and one for standard view mode.

If perspective view mode is on, AutoCAD prompts for changes in the camera's "lens length":

Adjust lens length:

The metaphor of lens length follows the same viewing principles as a real-world camera lens, in which a shorter lens length will widen the field of view, allowing more of the drawing to fit on the screen (zooming out), while a longer lens length will narrow the field of view, bringing entities closer to the viewing plane (zooming in). The default lens length is 50 millimeters. To demonstrate this feature to

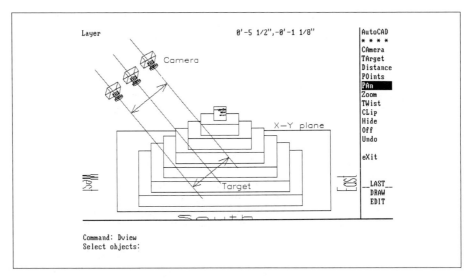

FIGURE 11.10: The Dview command—panning the camera. When the camera's viewing angle and distance are established, you may "scroll" the screen display using the Pan option. This causes the camera to move across the display without changing the viewing angle or distance. If perspective viewing is enabled, this option will cause changes in the perspective view as well.

yourself, try editing AutoCAD's Office sample drawing, using perspective view mode with lens lengths of 50, 35, and 150 millimeters. Notice also the differences in appearance between standard and perspective view modes.

TWist Enter **TW** to rotate the camera using the line between camera and target as the axis. The camera is rotated counterclockwise as you increment the angle of rotation, starting with angle zero. AutoCAD prompts:

New view twist:

You may enter a rotation angle from the keyboard or select a point on the screen. As you move the pointing device, a rubberband line extends from the center of the viewing plane to the intersection of the crosshairs. When you pick a point, the angle of this line in the viewing plane will be used by AutoCAD as the angle of camera rotation.

CLip Enter **CL** to place special *clipping planes* in the current view of your drawing. Clipping planes are useful when you wish to isolate only a portion of your drawing for viewing. They act as invisible walls that allow only those portions of entities falling between them to be displayed. Clipping planes are always perpendicular to the viewing angle.

When you enable perspective view mode, the front clipping plane is automatically enabled at the camera location, obscuring those portions of entities that fall behind the camera. This usually results in a clearer display. Front clipping is always on in perspective view mode, although you may position the front clipping plane anywhere you like. You may enable or disable the back clipping plane according to your preference.

You can enable, disable, and relocate both the front and back clipping planes while in standard view mode.

After you enter **CL**, AutoCAD prompts:

    Back/Front/<Off>:

Your options are as follows:

- Enter **B** to enable the back clipping plane. AutoCAD responds:

    ON/OFF/<Distance from target>:

    Enter a value for the distance between the target point and the back clipping plane. AutoCAD positions the clipping plane perpendicular to the viewing angle at the specified distance, and turns it on, thereby obscuring all portions of entities that fall behind it. Enter **OFF** if you want to disable the clipping plane, allowing entities behind it to become visible again. Enter **ON** to enable the back clipping plane at the current distance.

- Enter **F** to enable the front clipping plane. If perspective view mode is enabled, AutoCAD responds:

    Eye/<Distance from target>:

    If standard view mode is enabled, AutoCAD responds:

    Eye/ON/OFF/<Distance from target>:

    Enter **E** to enable the front clipping plane at the current camera position.

    If you want the front clipping plane at a location other than the current camera position, enter the distance between the front clipping plane and the target point. AutoCAD positions the clipping plane perpendicular to the viewing angle, between the camera and target point at the specified distance, and turns it on, thereby obscuring all portions of entities that fall in front of it.

    If you are currently using standard view mode, you may enter **ON** to enable the front clipping plane at the current distance, or **OFF** to disable the front clipping plane at the current distance. In perspective view mode, these options are not available, as front clipping is always on.

Hide Enter **H** to suppress the hidden lines in the preview display. This option is automatic, like AutoCAD's Hide command. (Refer to the Hide command in this chapter for details regarding hidden-line suppression.) Unlike the Hide command, however, the Dview Hide option will work only on those entities you selected for Dview; this can make it faster than the Hide command, which will work on the entire display.

The hidden-line display generated by this option is applicable to the current viewing angle only; AutoCAD will erase the hidden-line display and generate a normal wire-frame representation when you change the viewing angle or exit Dview.

Off Enter **O** to turn off perspective view mode if you have previously turned it on using the Distance option.

Undo Enter **U** to reverse the effects of the previous Dview option. You can enter **U** repeatedly and "back up" through the current series of options until you have reversed them all.

eXit The Dview options will repeat after you select each option and enter the required data. To end the command and display the complete drawing at the new viewing angle, enter **X** or press Enter. AutoCAD responds by displaying the drawing at the new viewing angle and returning you to the Command prompt.

USAGE

Although Dview can be used on any AutoCAD drawing, its primary purpose is to represent changes in perspective when viewing 3-D models. Figure 11.11 illustrates a plan view of one such model. Figure 11.12 illustrates a 3-D view of the same model.

To change the viewing angle dynamically, invoke the Dview command. AutoCAD prompts you to select any of several methods for changing the viewing angle in 3-D space, as explained in the Command Options section. After making the desired changes to the viewing angle and perspective, press Enter or type **X**. AutoCAD redraws the display to reflect your new viewing angle.

To help visualize the changes that can be made using Dview, AutoCAD prompts for the various command options using a *camera/target* metaphor. Imagine looking at a 3-D drawing through the range finder of a camera that is focused on a specific point (the *target point*) in the drawing. A line drawn from the center of the camera lens to the point of focus determines the *viewing angle*. When using Dview, you determine a viewing angle by positioning imaginary camera and target points relative to the entities in the drawing. When the camera and target points have been established, you may move the camera back to include a

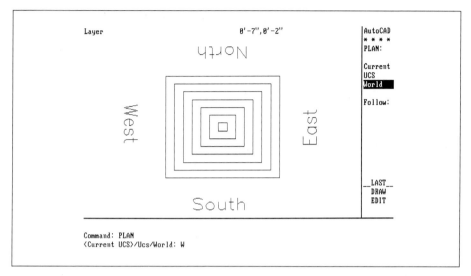

FIGURE 11.11: A model of a 3-D pyramid displayed in plan view. The pyramid measures 4″ × 4″, with a center point at 0,0. Compare this viewing angle to that in Figure 11.12, where the z-axis dimensions of the pyramid are readily apparent.

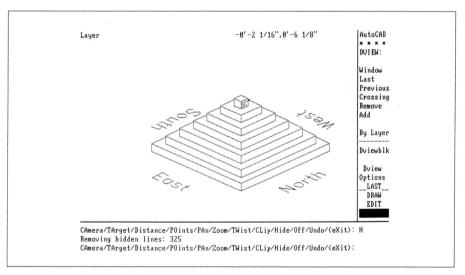

FIGURE 11.12: A model of a 3-D pyramid from a 3-D viewing angle. Because the viewing angle has changed, the z-axis dimensions are now visible. Compare the orientation of the words *North, South, East,* and *West* to their orientation in AutoCAD's plan view.

greater amount of the drawing in the display, move the camera forward to magnify detail, or move the camera from side to side to display different parts of the drawing at the same viewing angle.

The camera may be repositioned relative to the target point, or the target point may be repositioned relative to the camera. This relationship was illustrated in Figures 11.1 through 11.10.

Any number of viewing angles, including those selected using Dview, can be stored and recalled using the View command. Thus, Dview need only be used once to create a viewing angle, and thereafter restored with View. Refer to the View command in this chapter for details. Clipping planes and perspective view mode may be enabled either by using Dview, or by setting new values for the system variables BACKZ, FRONTZ, and VIEWMODE, and regenerating the drawing. Refer to Chapter 13 for details regarding system variables.

Tip: You will have better control of the Camera and Target options if you turn snap mode off before using Dview.

When you enter the viewing angle, and especially when you use sliders to preview the display, the preview entities will appear to rotate on the screen. Keep in mind, however, that it's not the entities that are rotating, but rather the viewing position. Thus, moving the target point from left to right causes the display to shift in the opposite direction. Moving the camera likewise causes the display to appear to rotate in the opposite direction.

On the other hand, the Distance, Pan, and Twist options work literally; that is, the dynamic display matches the movement of the crosshairs, and the resulting camera position is only interpolated relative to the display.

To use Dview effectively and avoid confusion about what is happening, keep the camera/target metaphor in mind when selecting new viewing angles, and be certain that you have selected enough entities to generate a representative dynamic display. As you practice using this command, it will become easier.

If the world coordinate system is not the current UCS when you begin using Dview, AutoCAD will normally make it the current UCS, and return you to your previous UCS when you exit Dview. This is because the camera and target will change position relative to the current UCS, and that can be very confusing if the current UCS is not the world coordinate system.

You can disable this automatic change to the world coordinate system by setting the WORLDVIEW system variable to 0. You may want to do this if you are using the Points option and entering absolute camera and target points relative to the current UCS, or if you just want to see what happens when Dview works from a non-world coordinate system. Otherwise, keep this system variable set to 1. Refer to Chapter 5 to learn about the world and user coordinate systems, and to Chapter 13 for details regarding system variables.

RELATED COMMANDS

View, Vpoint.

RELATED SYSTEM VARIABLES

BACKZ (location of back clipping plane); FRONTZ (location of front clipping plane); LENSLENGTH (focal length of camera lens); TARGET (location of target point); VIEWCTR (center of view); VIEWDIR (viewing direction); VIEWMODE (current viewing mode); VIEWSIZE (current viewing height); VIEWTWIST (current camera orientation angle along the viewing-angle axis). These system variables cannot be modified with the Setvar command; you can change their settings by changing the display using Dview. Also, the WORLD-VIEW system variable controls the active coordinate system during Dview. Refer to Chapter 13 for details regarding system variables.

SAMPLE DIALOG

The following dialog uses the 3-D pyramid shown in Figures 11.11 and 11.12. Beginning with the plan view in Figure 11.11, this dialog will create the 3-D view in Figure 11.12.

```
Command: Dview
Select objects: W
First corner: 0,0 Other corner: 15,11
39 found.
Select objects: (press Enter)
CAmera/TArget/Distance/POints/PAn/Zoom/TWist/CLip/Hide/Off/
Undo/<eXit>: CA
Enter angle from X-Y plane: 30
Enter angle in X-Y plane from X axis: 45
CAmera/TArget/Distance/POints/PAn/Zoom/TWist/CLip/Hide/Off/
Undo/<eXit>: H
Removing hidden lines: 300
CAmera/TArget/Distance/POints/PAn/Zoom/TWist/CLip/Hide/Off/
Undo/<eXit>: X
Command:
```

HIDE

Generates a screen display of 3-D entities with hidden lines removed.

VERSIONS

Version 2.17 and later. The reliability of the Hide command has increased in later versions. Release 9 and later include special 3-D entity types—3-D lines and faces, and polygon meshes in later releases—that work well with the Hide command.

COMMAND OPTIONS

The Hide command is fully automatic. However, if you select the command from the screen menu or the standard tablet menu, you are prompted to confirm it by entering either Yes or No.

You can force the display of hidden lines in a different color if you prefer. To do so, use the Layer command to create new layers with the prefix *Hidden* in the layer name. (Refer to Chapter 5 for details regarding the Layer command.) For example, if your 3-D drawing consists of entities on layers named Walls, Doors, and Windows, create new layers named Hiddenwalls, Hiddendoors, and Hiddenwindows. You may assign whatever default colors you like to these new layers, or turn them off or freeze them if you prefer.

When you invoke the Hide command, AutoCAD will generate hidden lines using the color of the named layer with the prefix *Hidden*. If the Hidden layer is turned off or frozen, the corresponding lines will not be visible.

Thus, you may use several different colors for hidden lines, or selectively render certain hidden lines invisible. However, you cannot use this technique to control the linetypes of hidden lines. AutoCAD ignores the default linetype of Hidden layers when displaying hidden lines, using instead the linetype of the entity's current layer.

Layers with the prefix *Hidden* are just like any other layer; you may place entities upon them if you want.

USAGE

Normally, AutoCAD's 3-D drawings are displayed in a *wire-frame* representation, meaning that all entities are displayed regardless of their relative location within the viewport.

A "hidden line" is a line entity that, from the current viewing perspective, is located behind another entity. If these entities were viewed in the real world, the hidden line would not be visible.

The Hide command produces a visualization of solid 3-D objects as they might appear in the real world. When a 3-D drawing is complex, involving many lines and faces, this visualization is much clearer and more comprehensible.

Tip: There is no point in going to the trouble of generating a hidden-line display more than once. After you have created an acceptable hidden-line display, use the Mslide command to create an AutoCAD slide file from it. The next time you want to display your drawing with hidden lines removed, use the Vslide command to recall the hidden-line display. Vslide can make hidden-line displays appear nearly instantaneously. Refer to Chapter 21 for details regarding Mslide and Vslide.

The Hide command works differently depending on the entity type. The following guidelines will help you generate correct visualizations of hidden-line drawings:

Text and Attributes   Text information is ignored by the Hide command. To leave text out of a hidden-line display, place it on a separate layer, and then freeze or turn off that layer.

Circles and Arcs   AutoCAD renders circles that have an extruded thickness as solid objects, not hollow tubes. If you intend to display a hollow tube, draw a circle from two semicircular arcs—or use the Donut command, explained in Chapter 9—and extrude the arcs or doughnut. If part of a circle is hidden from view, however, it will be displayed as hollow, not solid. Figure 11.13 illustrates this.

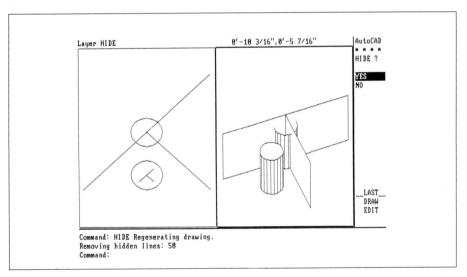

FIGURE 11.13: The Hide command—circles with extruded thicknesses. The entities on the left are in plan view. The two circles have extruded thicknesses. One circle is intersected by two lines, and the other circle encloses two lines. When viewed in 3-D with hidden lines removed, the circle enclosing the lines appears solid, hiding the lines. The circle intersected by two lines appears hollow, however, because it is only partially visible from this angle.

Closed Polylines A closed polyline with an extruded thickness is considered hollow. To render it as a solid object, "cap" it with a 3-D face at the appropriate elevation.

3-D Faces and Polygon Meshes 3-D faces and polygon meshes are always considered opaque and will hide portions of any entity that falls behind them (except text and attributes). All edges of 3-D faces not hidden by another opaque entity will be visible in a hidden-line display. When creating polygons from 3-D faces, use invisible edges for all but the outer edges.

Points and Lines Points and lines with extruded thicknesses will sometimes produce inaccurate hidden-line drawings when they intersect or touch each other. For example, Figure 11.14 shows two extruded lines intersecting. Notice how the point of intersection is not displayed in the hidden-line rendering. However, if one of the lines is broken at the point of intersection, the intersection line is revealed, as illustrated in Figure 11.15.

The Hide command is quite calculation-intensive, meaning that it is usually slow on all but the simplest of drawings. To speed up the Hide command, remove all unnecessary detail first.

- Freeze all layers containing entities that are not required for the display. Do not simply turn the layers off; entities on layers that are turned off will

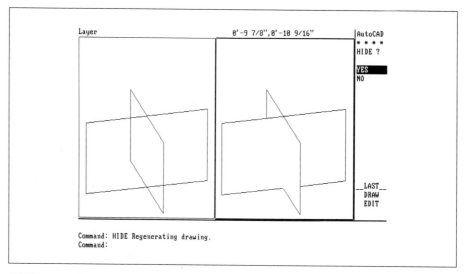

FIGURE 11.14: The Hide command—intersecting lines with extruded thicknesses. In this figure, two lines are given extruded thicknesses and viewed from a 3-D angle. When hidden lines are removed, no intersection line appears. This effect may be desirable at times. Compare with Figure 11.15.

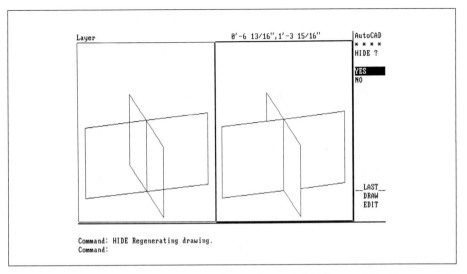

Command: HIDE Regenerating drawing.
Command:

FIGURE 11.15: The Hide command—intersecting lines with extruded thicknesses. In this figure, one of the lines is broken at the point of intersection (using AutoCAD's Break command), making a total of three lines. When hidden lines are removed, a line of intersection is visible. Compare this to the previous figure, which uses only two intersecting lines.

still be considered by the Hide command and may obstruct other entities even while not displaying themselves. This may result in figures with portions mysteriously removed, as illustrated in Figure 11.16.

- Entities that do not affect the final result, such as text and lines without extruded thicknesses, can be placed on separate layers, frozen, and then thawed after the hidden-line process is complete. This gives AutoCAD fewer entities to consider, thus speeding up the process.

- Zoom in to the greatest level of magnification you can. The less detail in the drawing, the faster the Hide command will work. When a hidden-line display is active, zooming and panning will *always* force a regeneration of the drawing, so invoke all necessary Zoom and Pan commands before invoking Hide.

- Once a hidden-line display is complete, it will remain that way until entities are regenerated. This means that you can add new entities, edit existing ones, and perform redraws while retaining the hidden-line display, as long as the commands you execute do not require that any hidden entities or the drawing itself be regenerated. (Breaking and/or moving lines, for example, will often cause a regeneration of the selected entities, while leaving the other entities alone.)

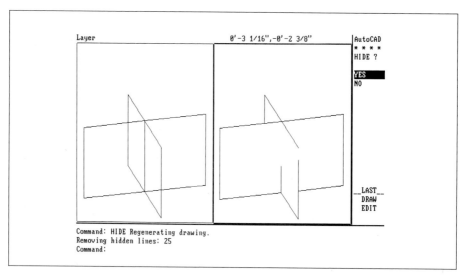

FIGURE 11.16: The Hide command—portions mysteriously removed. In this figure, the hidden-line removal appears to have malfunctioned. Actually, the extra lines were removed because a layer containing a 3-D face was turned off. When performing a hidden-line removal, AutoCAD will use entities on layers that are off, and will hide entities that are positioned behind them. To keep such entities from interfering with the hidden-line removal, freeze the layer containing them.

SAMPLE DIALOG

The following sample dialog creates an array of 3-D faces, selects a viewpoint, and hides the display, as shown in Figure 11.17:

```
Command: 3Dface
First point: 11,9,0
Second point: 11,9,6
Third point: 16,14,6
Fourth point: 16,14,0
Third point: (press Enter)
Command: Array
Select objects: L
1 found.
Select objects: (press Enter)
Rectangular or Polar array (R/P): R
Number of rows (---): 1
Number of columns ( | | | ): 5
Distance between columns ( | | | ): 2
Command: Vpoint
Rotate/<View point> <0'−0'',0'−0'',0'−1''>: 2.75,−1,3
```

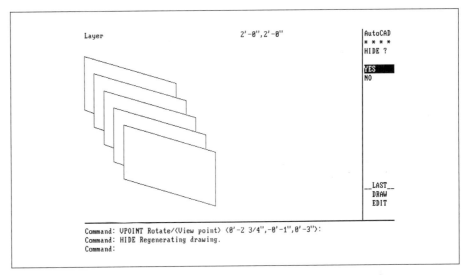

```
         Layer                            2'-0",2'-0"               AutoCAD
                                                                    * * * *
                                                                    HIDE ?

                                                                    YES
                                                                    NO




                                                                    __LAST__
                                                                     DRAW
                                                                     EDIT

         Command: UPOINT Rotate/<View point> <0'-2 3/4",-0'-1",0'-3">:
         Command: HIDE Regenerating drawing.
         Command:
```

FIGURE 11.17: The Hide command—a series of 3-D faces. This figure illustrates a simple hidden-line removal of a series of 3-D faces, as per the sample dialog in the section on the Hide command in this chapter. Compare the results of the sample dialog with this figure.

Regenerating drawing.
Command: **Hide**
Regenerating drawing.

MSPACE

Changes the setting of the current viewport from paper space to model space. Refer to Chapter 12 for a detailed discussion of model and paper space.

VERSIONS

Release 11 and later.

COMMAND OPTIONS

When you invoke the Mspace command, one of the displayed paper-space viewports is made active for editing in model space. You cannot use this command until you have created viewports in paper space using the Mview command. Refer to the discussion of the Mview command further on for details.

This command can be invoked only when the value of the TILEMODE system variable is set to zero. Refer to Chapter 13 for details about the use of TILEMODE.

USAGE

To use drawing editor commands in individual viewports created in paper space, use the Mspace command. When you invoke the Mspace command, one of the currently displayed viewports (usually the last active one) is made current for editing in model space. You can determine which viewport is active by observing the display of the screen crosshairs: AutoCAD's normal display of the screen crosshairs appears only within the currently active viewport, and the viewport border is highlighted. If you wish to make a different viewport active, point the small selection arrow at any point in the desired viewport and press the pick button. The screen crosshairs will then appear within your selected viewport.

Once you have selected your viewport, you may use whatever AutoCAD commands you like to change entities or their display within that viewport. Updates to entities in the active viewport will be reflected in other viewports that display the same entities.

RELATED COMMANDS

Pspace.

RELATED SYSTEM VARIABLES

TILEMODE (determines the availability of paper space.)

SAMPLE DIALOG

The following series of commands will allow you to create two viewports in paper space and make one active for model space editing:

Command: **TILEMODE**
New value for TILEMODE <1>: **0**
Entering Paper space. Use MVIEW to insert Model space viewports.
Regenerating drawing.
Command: **MVIEW**
ON/OFF/Hideplot/Fit/2/3/4/Restore/<First Point>: **2**
Horizontal/<Vertical>: **(press Enter)**
Fit/<first point>: **F**
Regenerating drawing.
Command: **MSPACE** (One viewport becomes active—move pointing device between viewports and observe display)

Mview

Creates rectangular viewing ports in paper space.

VERSIONS

Release 11 and later.

COMMAND OPTIONS

Pick points   To create a single viewport in the graphics display area, pick two opposite corner endpoints with the pointing device. This is similar to windowing objects. When you pick the corner points, the current model-space display will appear in the viewport. All paper-space viewports can be treated as AutoCAD drawing entities: you can scale them, move them, copy them, rotate them, and so forth. You cannot select or edit the entities you see in the viewports, however. To do that, first switch to model space using the Mspace command and then select the appropriate viewport. Refer to the discussion of the Mspace command earlier in this chapter.

ON   Enter **ON** to enable the display of entities within a viewport. To display a viewport's entities, choose one of its borders with the pointing device.

OFF   Enter **OFF** to disable the display of entities within a viewport. When you pick a viewport border using the pointing device, the entity display within the viewport is turned off and the viewport appears empty.

Hideplot   Enter **H** to instruct AutoCAD to perform a hidden-line removal on one or more paper-space viewports when plotting. After you select this option, AutoCAD prompts:

ON/OFF:

Enter **ON** to enable automatic hidden-line removal, enter **OFF** to disable automatic hidden-line removal. After you choose your option, AutoCAD prompts:

Select objects:

Select the desired viewports using any of AutoCAD's standard entity-selection methods (point pick, windowing, removal, and so forth—refer to Chapter 5 for details regarding entity selection).

The default status for paper-space viewports is OFF.

Fit   Enter **F** to create a new viewport that fills the current graphics screen. This viewport automatically becomes the new active viewport. If you are zoomed in on a portion of the total paper space, the resulting viewport will fit only that portion of paper space displayed on screen. Thus, you could zoom out after creating such a viewport and find that it is quite small.

2,3,4   These number options create multiple viewports similar to the Vports command. If you select **2**, AutoCAD prompts for the correct division:

    Horizontal/<Vertical>:

If you choose **3**, AutoCAD prompts:

    Horizontal/Vertical/Above/Below/Left/Right:

If you enter **H**, the three viewports will be arranged horizontally; if **V**, they will be arranged vertically. The other options prompt you to place a single window relative to two smaller windows: either above, below, to the left, or to the right. If you choose **4**, AutoCAD will create four equal-sized viewports.

After you choose the number of windows you want, AutoCAD prompts:

    Fit/<first point>:

If you enter **F**, AutoCAD draws the viewports to fit the current magnification of the graphics display, as described under the Fit option earlier. Alternatively, you can instruct AutoCAD to create the viewports within the dimensions of a rectangle; select the rectangle by picking its opposite corners with the pointing device.

Restore   Enter **R** if you wish to create paper-space viewports using a viewport configuration saved with the Vports command. Refer to the discussion of the Vports command later on in this chapter for details on saving such viewport configurations. AutoCAD will prompt:

    ?/Name of window configuration to insert:

Enter the name of the configuration or **?** to see a list of currently named configurations. After entering the name of the configuration, AutoCAD prompts for the overall size of the viewports, as before:

    Fit/<first point>:

If you enter **F**, AutoCAD draws the viewports to fit the current magnification of the graphics display, as described under the Fit option earlier. Alternatively,

AutoCAD will create the viewports within the dimensions of a rectangle selected by picking its opposite corners.

USAGE

You may invoke the Mview command only while in paper space. If you are editing a viewport in model space, AutoCAD will switch automatically to paper space, and return you to model space at the conclusion of the command. As with other commands that apply to paper space, the TILEMODE system variable must be set to zero, or OFF.

Tip: Newly created viewports adopt the current entity display, with one exception. You can create multiple views of the drawing with the Vports command and name the resulting configuration. Use the Restore option of Mview to recreate the same named configuration in paper space. The drawing viewpoints in the named configuration will be retained when AutoCAD draws the paper-space viewports. Once the configuration has been created in paper space, you can move and resize it at will. Finally, be sure to use the View command in paper space and name the paper-space view.

RELATED COMMANDS

Mspace, Pspace, Vports (when TILEMODE is on).

RELATED SYSTEM VARIABLES

TILEMODE (controls access to this command; it must be set to zero or OFF); MAXACTVP (determines the maximum number of viewports that may be visible at one time).

SAMPLE DIALOG

The following dialog produces three viewports in paper space, similar to the configuration shown in Figure 11.18:

```
Command: MVIEW
ON/OFF/Hideplot/Fit/2/3/4/Restore/<First Point>: 3
Horizontal/Vertical/Above/Below/Left/<Right>: L
Fit/<first point>: (pick lower-left point)
Second point: (pick upper-right point)
Regenerating drawing.
Command:
```

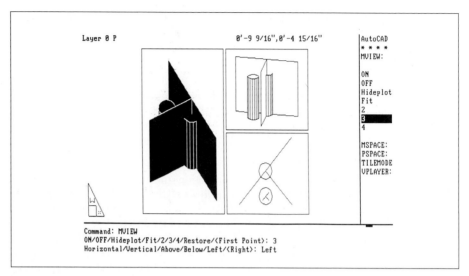

```
Layer 0 P                            0'-9 9/16",0'-4 15/16"      AutoCAD
                                                                * * * *
                                                                MVIEW:

                                                                ON
                                                                OFF
                                                                Hideplot
                                                                Fit
                                                                2
                                                                3
                                                                4

                                                                MSPACE:
                                                                PSPACE:
                                                                TILEMODE
                                                                VPLAYER:




Command: MVIEW
ON/OFF/Hideplot/Fit/2/3/4/Restore/<First Point>: 3
Horizontal/Vertical/Above/Below/Left/<Right>: Left
```

FIGURE 11.18: Multiple viewports in paper space. This paper-space viewport configuration was created using the Mview command, the 3 option, and Left—as in the sample dialog. After the viewports were created with Mview, the spaces between them were made with the Move and Stretch commands. Viewports in paper space can be treated as entities.

PAN

Allows you to scroll across the drawing in any direction, while maintaining the same viewing angle and magnification.

VERSIONS

All.

COMMAND OPTIONS

Base point or displacement After you invoke Pan, AutoCAD prompts for either a base point or a displacement. Both take the same form, an x and y coordinate value separated by a comma, but they will be interpreted differently based on how you respond to the next prompt.

For example, suppose you intend to move the drawing 7 units to the right and 6 units up. In response to the "Base point or displacement" prompt, enter:

7,6

You may enter this by typing it at the keyboard or by picking point 7,6 with the pointing device.

AutoCAD at first assumes that your response is a base point, as will be explained shortly. However, if you respond to the next prompt, "Second point of displacement," by pressing Enter, AutoCAD then interprets the input to the "Base point or displacement" prompt as a *displacement*; that is, an instruction to move the drawing 7 units along the positive x-axis and 6 units along the positive y-axis. Because the displacement value has the same syntax structure as an x-y coordinate point, AutoCAD will accept a displacement value even if entered using the pointing device.

Second point of displacement   As explained, if you press Enter in response to this prompt, AutoCAD interprets your response to the "Base point or displacement" prompt as an x-y displacement, and immediately relocates the drawing.

However, if you respond to this prompt by entering another x-y coordinate point, AutoCAD interprets the response to the previous prompt to be a *base point* and the second point to be the *point of displacement*. AutoCAD moves the drawing by the angle and distance formed between these two points.

For example, if you entered **7,6** in response to the first prompt and **9,8** in response to the second prompt, AutoCAD would move the drawing 2 units along the positive x-axis and 2 units along the positive y-axis; in other words, the drawing would move by the same distance and angle as exists between points 7,6 and 9,8.

USAGE

Warning: Be careful when using a pointing device that has both a Return button and a pick button. When using such a pointing device to select displacement points, be sure not to press Return if you intend to select a point. For example, if you picked point 1000,1000 as the base point, moved the crosshairs, and accidentally pressed the Return button instead of the pick button, the drawing might very likely disappear from the screen! Other unwanted effects could include an unnecessary regeneration of the drawing, resulting from the radical shift in viewport position, and a second regeneration when you recover from the first with the U or Undo command. (Refer to Chapter 10 for details regarding U and Undo.)

As of Version 2.6, the Pan command can be used *transparently*; that is, while in the middle of the command dialog for another command. To use Pan transparently, invoke the Pan command preceded by an apostrophe, as follows:

    'Pan

AutoCAD indicates that Pan is being used transparently by preceding all prompts with the following symbol:

> >

When you have responded to the Pan command options, AutoCAD displays a message indicating that the original command is resumed. The dialog then continues normally.

The ability to use the Pan command transparently can be a big help when drawing entities with construction points that fall outside the current viewport. Simply begin drawing the entity, and as required invoke a transparent Pan command to move the drawing to a location where the next construction point falls within the current viewport.

If you intend to use Pan transparently, or frequently, use the Zoom command first to set a reasonably sized virtual screen. If your virtual screen is large enough to encompass all your intended construction points, you will be able to invoke the Pan command at much greater speeds, bypassing the need for a complete regeneration of the drawing file.

If you must regenerate, you can terminate a full regeneration by pressing Ctrl-C. This saves time when other entities in the drawing need not be displayed in order to invoke current commands.

Pan will regenerate the drawing automatically if you move outside the boundaries of the virtual screen and automatic regeneration is turned on using the Regenauto command. If you turn automatic regeneration off, AutoCAD will display a warning message before performing the regeneration. This allows you to cancel the Pan command and select a different displacement, ideally one that won't require a regeneration.

In general, you may find it more useful to turn automatic regeneration off in the prototype drawing rather than leave it on. Refer to the discussion of the Regenauto command in this chapter for details.

The Pan command will perform drawing regenerations instead of redraws if "Fast Zoom mode" is turned off. Refer to the Viewres command in this chapter for details.

> *Tip:* The View command can be used to quickly pan to areas of the drawing that you address repeatedly, often without forcing an unnecessary regeneration. Refer to the View command in this chapter for details.

RELATED COMMANDS

Zoom.

SAMPLE DIALOG

The following dialog will pan to a new location in the drawing file, as illustrated in Figures 11.19 and 11.20:

```
Command: Circle
3P/2P/TTR/<Center point>: 7,6
Diameter/Radius: 10,6
Command: Line
From point: (pick point 10,6)
To point: 'Pan
>>Displacement: (pick point 10,6)
>> Second point: (pick point 16,10)
Resuming LINE command.
To point: (pick point 4,0)
To point: (press Enter)
Command:
```

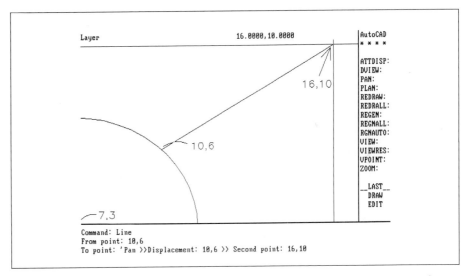

FIGURE 11.19: The Pan command—entering the points of displacement. After the starting point for a line is entered, the Line command is interrupted by a transparent Pan command, in order to find a second point not currently on the display screen. AutoCAD suspends the Line command and prompts for the points of displacement for the transparent Pan.

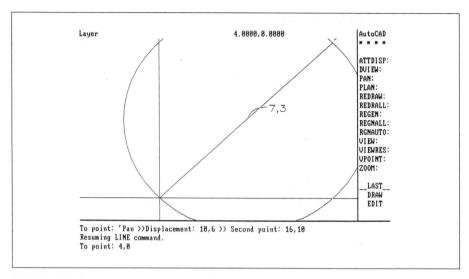

FIGURE 11.20: The Pan command—the new display. After the points of displacement for a transparent Pan command are entered, AutoCAD changes the display and resumes the Line command. The location of the endpoint of the line is now visible, and the line segment is drawn.

PLAN

Quickly restores the plan view of either the current UCS, a named UCS, or the world coordinate system. In Release 11, the Plan command may be used only in model space.

VERSIONS

Release 10 and later.

COMMAND OPTIONS

Current UCS   Enter **C** to change to the plan view of the current UCS. This is the default option, and can also be entered by pressing Enter.

Ucs   Enter **U** to specify a named UCS for which you would like a plan view. AutoCAD responds:

> ?/Name of UCS:

Enter the name of the UCS, or enter a question mark. If you enter a question mark, AutoCAD displays a list of the named user coordinate systems and repeats the prompt. If you press Enter in response to this prompt, AutoCAD cancels the Plan command.

World   Enter **W** to display a plan view of the world coordinate system.

USAGE

To quickly restore a plan view of a particular UCS, invoke the Plan command. AutoCAD prompts for the UCS whose plan view you desire, and automatically changes the display. If multiple viewports are active, the display is changed only in the currently active viewport. Refer to Chapter 5 for details regarding user coordinate systems.

> *Tip:* The UCSFOLLOW system variable can be used to combine the effects of the UCS and Plan commands. If UCSFOLLOW is set to a value of 1, a plan view is generated whenever you specify a new UCS; if set to 0, no plan view is generated when the UCS is changed. If multiple viewports are active, UCSFOLLOW can be set for each viewport, allowing for automatic plan views in some but not in others. Refer to Chapter 13 for details regarding UCSFOLLOW.

> *Note:* Although the Plan command will display a plan view of any saved UCS, it never changes the current UCS. If you wish to change the current UCS as well, invoke the UCS command, followed by the Plan command.

RELATED COMMANDS

UCS.

RELATED SYSTEM VARIABLES

UCSFOLLOW.

SAMPLE DIALOG

The following dialog assumes a UCS named ISOVIEW, and changes to that UCS from the world coordinate system:

```
Command: Plan
< Current UCS >/Ucs/World: U
?/Name of UCS: Isoview
Regenerating drawing.
Command:
```

PSPACE

Activates paper space; changes the setting of the current view from model space to paper space. Refer to Chapter 12 for details about the differences between model and paper space.

VERSIONS

Release 11 and later.

COMMAND OPTIONS

This command can be invoked only when the value of TILEMODE is set to zero. Refer to Chapter 13 for details on the use of TILEMODE.

When you invoke the Pspace command, AutoCAD switches from model space to paper space. Paper space is a special drawing environment that allows you to create multiple viewports of a drawing. Unlike viewports created in model space, you may treat paper-space viewports as drawing entities: copying, moving, and scaling them at will. You may plot paper space as if it were the drawing, thereby plotting multiple viewing angles of the same drawing on a single page with a single plot command.

USAGE

In general, use paper space to set up multiple displays of a single drawing file for display on the screen or for plotted output.

You can create entities in paper space using standard AutoCAD drawing commands. These entities can be included in plots made when paper space is active. If you switch to model space or set TILEMODE to 1, you will not be able to access entities you have created in paper space. Likewise, while in paper space, you cannot edit entities created in model space. You can, however, jump back and forth between model and paper space as often as necessary to achieve the results you want.

RELATED COMMANDS

Mspace

RELATED SYSTEM VARIABLES

TILEMODE (determines the availability of paper space).

SAMPLE DIALOG

The following series of commands will switch you to paper space and create two viewports:

> Command: **TILEMODE**
> New value for TILEMODE <1>: **0**
> Entering paper space. Use MVIEW to insert model space viewports.
> Regenerating drawing.
> Command: **MVIEW**
> ON/OFF/Hideplot/Fit/2/3/4/Restore/<First Point>: **2**
> Horizontal/<Vertical>: **(Press Return)**
> Fit/<First Point>: **F**
> Regenerating drawing.
> Command: **MSPACE** (AutoCAD switches to model space).
> Command: **PSPACE** (AutoCAD switches back to paper space).

QTEXT

Toggles the display of text between normal text characters and a rectangular outline showing the approximate location and height of the text entities (quick-text mode). When the rectangular outline is displayed, redraws and regenerations are much faster.

VERSIONS

All.

COMMAND OPTIONS

ON Enter **ON** to turn quick-text mode on. When Qtext is first turned on, no changes will become apparent until the drawing is next regenerated. At that time, text will be replaced with rectangles indicating the space occupied by the text.

When Qtext is on, text that you enter continues to be displayed normally, so that you can confirm its appearance, spelling, and so forth. Subsequent regeneration of the drawing will change the text characters to rectangles.

OFF Enter **OFF** to restore the display of text to normal characters. No change will be apparent until the next regeneration is performed.

USAGE

To speed up the display of drawings containing text, invoke the Qtext command. AutoCAD prompts you to turn quick-text mode on or off. To display text as simple rectangles, turn Qtext on; to display it as text characters, turn Qtext off.

Qtext works in situations where you must redraw or regenerate often, and at the same time need to be aware of the location of text in the drawing. If the space occupied by text does not concern you, you can save even more time by placing the text on a separate layer and freezing it.

Note: Redraw does not change the display of text after you turn Qtext on or off. To change the display, you must regenerate the drawing, either by invoking the Regen command or by changing the display in such a way as to cause a regeneration.

RELATED SYSTEM VARIABLES

QTEXTMODE (quick-text mode on or off).

SAMPLE DIALOG

The following dialog creates the display changes illustrated in Figures 11.21 and 11.22:

```
Command: Qtext
ON/OFF <Off>: On
Command: Regen
Regenerating drawing.
Command: Qtext
ON/OFF <On>: Off
Command: Regen
Regenerating drawing.
Command:
```

REDRAW

Refreshes the current screen display without scanning the entire drawing database.

VERSIONS

All.

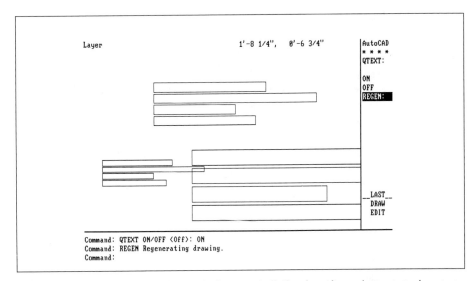

FIGURE 11.21: The Qtext command—text display turned off. The above figure demonstrates how text appears when Qtext is turned on. Compare this figure with the text that appears in Figure 11.22. Notice how the boxes representing text are accurate in representing the text height, but can be a little misleading when representing the length of the text lines.

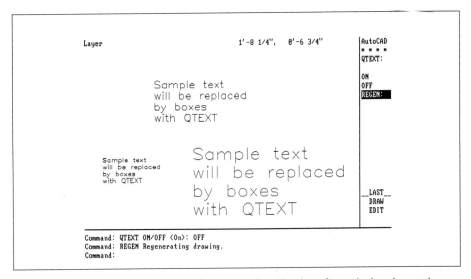

FIGURE 11.22: The Qtext command—text display turned on. The above figure displays the text that was hidden in Figure 11.21. Notice how the lines of text compare to the Qtext boxes in Figure 11.21. The text height is represented accurately, as is the relative length of the text lines, but the absolute length of the text lines appears greater than the actual text.

COMMAND OPTIONS

None. Redraw is automatic. You can, however, terminate redraw by pressing Ctrl-C. When a redraw is terminated, those parts of the drawing database not yet redrawn will remain invisible until a full redraw is performed. Furthermore, you will not be able to select those entities yet to be redrawn.

USAGE

The primary purpose of Redraw is to restore a display that is incorrect because of erased entities, cluttered blip markers, and so forth. This command is internally invoked by AutoCAD during many commands that cause changes to the screen display. To save time, the Redraw command is used instead of the Regen command in later versions of AutoCAD when panning and zooming within the virtual screen. For details regarding the virtual screen, refer to "The Virtual Screen" earlier in this chapter.

In AutoCAD Version 2.6 and later, the Redraw command can be invoked *transparently*; that is, while other commands are in progress. To invoke Redraw transparently, enter the command preceded by an apostrophe in response to any AutoCAD command or option prompt (except for those prompts that request text):

'Redraw

AutoCAD will interrupt the command in progress, refresh the screen display, and when finished, display a message indicating that it is resuming the original command.

In Release 10 and later, AutoCAD allows the display of multiple viewports. Redraw will affect the display of the current viewport only. Refer to the Vports command in this chapter for details.

> *Tip:* Several commands automatically redraw the screen. If you are not using a digitizing tablet, the Redraw command itself is inconvenient to type, and it never seems to be handy on the screen menu when you need it. You can get the same effect by pressing the Grid On/Off function key twice.

If you are about to invoke several commands that redraw the screen—for example, a layer change followed by Zoom or Pan—use Ctrl-C to terminate the redraws and save time. When the command sequence is completed, you can let the last redraw run to its conclusion.

RELATED COMMANDS

Redrawall.

REDRAWALL

Performs a redraw in all viewports (as opposed to Redraw, which performs a redraw in the currently active viewport only).

VERSIONS

Release 10 and later.

COMMAND OPTIONS

None. Redrawall is automatic.

USAGE

To redraw all viewports, invoke the Redrawall command. In all other respects, Redrawall is the same as Redraw. Refer to the discussion of the Redraw command for details.

RELATED COMMANDS

Redraw.

REGEN

Scans the entire drawing database and calculates the correct screen display for the current viewport. This process is called a *regeneration*.

VERSIONS

All. Prior to Version 2.5, most AutoCAD commands that changed the drawing display caused a regeneration as well.

COMMAND OPTIONS

None; Regen is automatic. You can, however, terminate the regeneration with Ctrl-C. When a regeneration is terminated, those parts of the drawing database not yet scanned will not become visible until a full regeneration is performed. Furthermore, you will not be able to select those entities yet to be regenerated.

USAGE

The Regen command is internally invoked by AutoCAD whenever the screen display changes to such an extent that a simple redraw will not generate an accurate display—for example, when zooming to an exceptionally large magnification, or when zooming or panning outside of the current virtual screen. (For details regarding the virtual screen, refer to "The Virtual Screen" earlier in this chapter.)

Avoid regenerating the drawing whenever possible. Use the Zoom Dynamic option to preview whether a regeneration will be necessary when either zooming or panning. Often a slight adjustment in zoom magnification or panning displacement will mean the difference between a regeneration and the much faster redraw. Refer to the Zoom command in this chapter for details.

Tip: Set Regenauto off to prevent being surprised by an unnecessary regeneration. Refer to the Regenauto command for details.

Drawing regenerations are best avoided by setting an adequate size for AutoCAD's virtual screen. For details on how to manage the size of AutoCAD's virtual screen, refer to the Zoom Dynamic option in the discussion of the Zoom command later in this chapter.

RELATED COMMANDS

Regenall.

REGENALL

Performs a regeneration in all viewports (as opposed to Regen, which performs a regeneration in the currently active viewport only).

VERSIONS

Release 10 and later.

COMMAND OPTIONS

None; Regenall is automatic.

USAGE

To regenerate a drawing simultaneously in all viewports, invoke the Regenall command. In all other respects, Regenall is the same as Regen. Refer to the discussion of the Regen command for details.

RELATED COMMANDS

Regen.

REGENAUTO

Enables or disables automatic drawing regenerations during commands that cause significant changes to the screen display.

VERSIONS

Version 2.5 and later.

COMMAND OPTIONS

ON   Enter **ON** if you want AutoCAD to perform automatic drawing regenerations without warning you first.

OFF   Enter **OFF** to disable automatic drawing regeneration, causing AutoCAD to issue a warning before regeneration.

USAGE

If you turn Regenauto off, AutoCAD will display the following warning message before performing automatic drawing regenerations:

About to regen, proceed? <Y>

If you answer **Y**, AutoCAD regenerates the drawing and continues with the command. If you type **N**, AutoCAD terminates the command.

Drawing regenerations are necessary but slow and annoying for all but the simplest of drawings. The following steps will help avoid unnecessary regenerations:

- Turn on "Fast Zoom mode" using the Viewres command.
- Turn Regenauto off.
- Use the Zoom Dynamic option to set up a sufficiently large virtual screen.

Details on these commands can be found in this chapter.

Warning: If Fast Zoom mode is disabled, automatic regenerations will be performed regardless of the setting of Regenauto.

Turning Regenauto on will cause AutoCAD to regenerate the drawing.

RELATED COMMANDS

Regen.

RELATED SYSTEM VARIABLES

REGENMODE (automatic regeneration status, either on or off).

SHADE

Produces a solid-filled rendering of the current screen display.

VERSIONS

Release 11 and later.

COMMAND OPTIONS

The Shade command is fully automatic. When you invoke Shade, AutoCAD blanks the screen, calculates the shaded rendering, and displays a message in the command prompt area indicating the progress of the command as a percentage completed. When the necessary calculations are finished, AutoCAD displays the shaded image.

The style of shaded rendering is affected by the current settings of the SHADEDGE and SHADEDIF system variables. SHADEDGE may contain a value from 0 to 3, as summarized below:

0   Faces are filled in and shaded but edges are not highlighted.

1   Faces are filled in and shaded, and edges are highlighted using the background screen color.

2   Faces are not filled in or shaded but will hide entities behind them. Edges are highlighted using their defined color properties. This effect is similar to a hidden-line rendering using the Hide command.

3   Faces are filled in but not shaded. Edges are highlighted using the background screen color. The effect of different settings of the SHADEDGE variable can be seen in Figure 11.23.

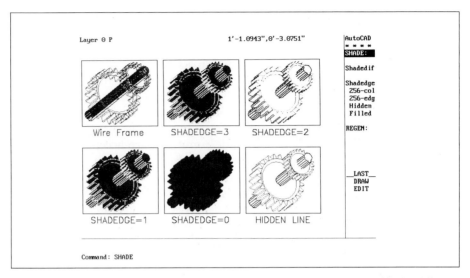

Figure 11.23: Various options using the Shade command. This figure illustrates the effect that different settings of the SHADEDGE variable have on the same drawing. This illustration is typical of the results on a 16-color or monochrome display. More striking differences may be seen on a 256-color display. Compare the difference in results between the shading when SHADEDGE = 2 and the hidden-line rendering using the Hide command.

AutoCAD determines the degree to which faces should be shaded by assuming a single, directed light source from the current viewing angle and an ambient light source surrounding the entities. The SHADEDIF system variable controls the relative intensity of these two light sources by specifying the percentage of ambient light; the higher the percentage of ambient light, the less direct light, and thus the less the contrast between faces. A value of 100 means that all light is ambient. Zero indicates that all light is directed. A value of 70 (the default) indicates that 70% of the light is ambient, while 30% is directed.

USAGE

The Shade command is capable of producing some striking screen displays. Although it is not as flexible or powerful as AutoShade (a separate rendering utility by Autodesk), it allows you to preview the appearance of more detailed shaded renderings and dress up the screen display of 3-D models. It is fairly fast, given the intensity of the math involved. The speed of the Shade command depends on the complexity of your drawing, the amount of RAM you have available, and the overall speed of your hardware.

Shade works best on polygon meshes and 3-D faces. It may have trouble with extruded line entities and intersecting entities on separate construction planes. Freeze as many layers as possible before invoking Shade; use the minimum number of entities to produce an acceptable shaded image.

When the SHADEDGE system variable is set to a value of 2, the Shade command produces results similar to the Hide command. It can be faster than the Hide command, but may not be as thorough; the Shade command might miss details in the drawing that the Hide command would understand.

If the results of the Shade command are acceptable, by all means use the Mslide command to record the rendered image to a slide file. A slide file can display images much faster than the Shade command can. For details regarding slide files, refer to the discussion of the Mslide and Vslide commands in Chapter 21. AutoCAD can only display shaded images on screen; working alone, it cannot produce hard-copy output of a shaded image. However, some third-party screen-capture utilities are capable of sending AutoCAD's graphics screen or the contents of a slide file to a graphics-capable printer; talk to your dealer about these if you are interested.

RELATED SYSTEM VARIABLES

SHADEDGE (Determines shading style); SHADEDIF (determines lighting effects for shading faces).

SAMPLE DIALOG

The following sample dialog sets an even distribution of ambient and direct light and allows for full shading before invoking the Shade command:

```
Command: SHADEDIF
New value for SHADEDIF <70>: 50
Command: SHADEDGE
New value for SHADEDGE <2>: 1
Command: SHADE
Shading complete.
```

VIEW

Saves views (viewing angles, orientations, and magnifications) as part of the drawing file, and recalls them at the user's request. The View command can also delete saved views that are no longer needed.

VERSIONS

All. The View Window option was introduced in AutoCAD Version 2.17. Release 11 and later save views in both model and paper space. Refer to the discussion of model and paper space in Chapter 12 for details.

COMMAND OPTIONS

Named views created in paper space save the current displayed configuration of paper-space viewports. Views created in model space save the current viewing angle and magnification.

?   Enter the question mark to display a list of view names and their coordinate locations in the current drawing. After AutoCAD displays the list, it repeats the View command prompt so that you may select a view name.

Delete   Enter **D** to delete a named view. AutoCAD prompts:

View name to delete:

Enter the name of the view you wish to delete. AutoCAD automatically deletes that view from the list of named views.

Restore   Enter **R** to restore a named view. AutoCAD prompts:

View name to restore:

Enter the name of the view you wish to restore. AutoCAD automatically restores that view.

The restoration may be performed without a drawing regeneration, depending on whether the named view is parallel to the current view's viewing plane, at a moderate level of magnification, and within the current virtual screen. If you are changing the viewing angle in 3-D space, magnifying to a level greater than approximately 50 to 1, or moving outside the current virtual screen, AutoCAD will perform a drawing regeneration to restore the named view. Refer to the Zoom Dynamic option of the Zoom command later in this chapter for details on how to manage the virtual screen.

Views created in model space may be restored in paper space, and vice versa. If you are in paper space and attempt to restore a view originally created in model space, AutoCAD first switches to model space and prompts you to select the viewport in which to restore the view. Similarly, if you are in model space and attempt to restore a view created in paper space, AutoCAD first switches to paper space, then restores the view. If you wish to return to the original space set-ting after restoring the view, you must invoke the Mspace or Pspace commands as appropriate, both of which are detailed in this chapter.

Save   Enter **S** to save the current view under a unique view name. AutoCAD prompts:

> View name to save:

Enter a unique name under which you intend to save the current view. The view name is saved, and AutoCAD returns to the Command prompt. View names can be up to 31 characters long. They can be composed of letters or numbers, but no punctuation marks, except for the dollar sign ($), hyphen (-), and underscore (_).

Window   Enter **W** to save a portion of the current display as a named view. Auto-CAD responds by prompting you to enter the opposite corners of a rectangular win-dow that will enclose the named view:

> First corner:
> Other corner:

Enter the coordinate points of opposite corners of the window using any of Auto-CAD's standard methods for coordinate entry. After you enter the first corner point, AutoCAD displays a rubberband rectangle, allowing you to visualize the size and area of the proposed named view.

Entering views using the Window option is a convenient way of saving views without sitting through a regeneration or redraw in order to make the proposed view current. It is the only case in which AutoCAD will save a noncurrent view. Notice that the Window option is only good for views that are parallel to the cur-rent viewing plane.

USAGE

In Release 10 and earlier, as well as in Release 11 model space, a named *view* is a combination of *viewing angle* and *magnification*. A viewing angle is established by means of a relationship between a *target point* and a *viewing point*. In versions of AutoCAD that support 3-D, target and viewing points are 3-D coordinate points that may be located anywhere in 3-D space. These points are established using the Vpoint and Dview commands, described in this chapter.

In Release 11 and later, named views created in paper space include the cur-rently displayed configuration of paper-space viewports. Restoring a paper-space view restores the entire configuration. Refer to the discussion in Chapter 12 for more details regarding the features of paper space.

In earlier 2-D versions of AutoCAD, the target and viewing point always shared the same z-axis, changing location only in the x-y construction plane. Target and viewpoint would default to the center of the screen, and would be relocated using the Pan and Zoom commands. This maintained a constant plan view of various portions of the 2-D drawing.

Magnification is a factor that controls the scale of drawing entities relative to the size of the monitor screen. A higher magnification will display less of the drawing, but the displayed portion appears "closer" and in much greater detail. AutoCAD can magnify a portion of a drawing by as much as a trillion times its original size (though it is difficult to imagine circumstances in which such an extreme amount of magnification would be practical). All versions of AutoCAD control magnification by means of the Zoom command, described later in this chapter.

Beginning with Version 2.6, you can use the View command transparently— that is, while other commands are in progress. To use View transparently, enter an apostrophe followed by **View** in response to another AutoCAD command prompt, as follows:

'View

AutoCAD will interrupt the command in progress and display the view prompt. The View command functions normally, except that restoring views that require a drawing regeneration is not allowed. When the new viewport is displayed, AutoCAD will display a message indicating that it is resuming the original command, and will repeat the prompt at which the transparent View command was invoked. Transparent View cannot be invoked during the Dview, Pan, Vpoint, or Zoom commands, or during another View command.

In addition to recalling named 3-D views, the View command can be an effective substitute for the Zoom and Pan commands when working with 2-D standard or isometric drawings. The following is an easy-to-implement system for 2-D drawings, using named views that will speed up zooming and panning by substituting the View command and eliminating most unwanted drawing regenerations:

1. Edit your prototype drawing to include a series of contiguous named views, as illustrated in Figure 11.24. The views in Figure 11.24 are named using compass points, but you may use any naming system you prefer—numbers, letters, abbreviations, etc.

2. Use the Zoom All option to display a view of the drawing limits. Name this view as well, using "ALL" or some similar name.

3. Make sure that "Fast Zoom mode" is turned on using the Viewres command (described later in this chapter).

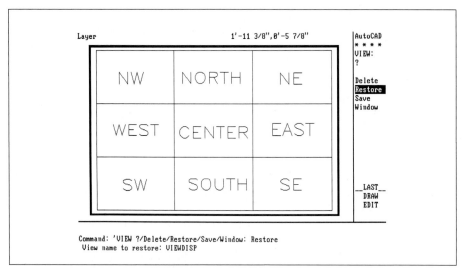

FIGURE 11.24: The View command—a set of contiguous named views. In this figure, the dark outer line represents the drawing limits, while the inner lines indicate the boundaries of nine named views. Once you have set up these contiguous views and named the view of the drawing limits, you can quickly move between them using only a redraw.

4. Save the prototype drawing. Now, whenever you edit a new drawing, the virtual screen will default to the size of the drawing limits, and you can quickly jump from view to view without performing a drawing regeneration. These views can be displayed transparently as well, since no regeneration is required. To quickly zoom to the drawing limits, invoke View Restore All rather than Zoom All, or in Release 11 and later, use Zoom Vmax.

5. To further enhance this system, consider placing the view names in a custom screen or tablet menu. If they are placed in a tablet menu, arrange the command boxes in the same relative position on the tablet as the named views in the prototype drawing; this provides a convenient visual representation of the prototype drawing's named-view configuration.

You can also add this named view system to existing drawings.

Whenever you save the drawing, always invoke View Restore All first, to maintain the size of the virtual screen.

Note: Unfortunately, changing the viewport in 3-D space always regenerates the drawing. However, if you are zooming and panning within the same 3-D viewport, these techniques can be applied within that viewport as well.

Warning: If you save a view using an existing view name, the previous view is overwritten. No warning message is given. Therefore, when saving views, be sure that your chosen view name is unique, unless overwriting a previous view is your intention.

RELATED COMMANDS

Dview, Pan, Vpoint, Zoom.

RELATED SYSTEM VARIABLES

VIEWCTR (current viewport center point), VIEWDIR (current viewport viewing angle), VIEWSIZE (current viewport height). These system variables are "read-only," meaning that they are not modifiable by means of the Setvar command. The values of these variables can only be changed indirectly by means of commands that change the current viewport: View, Dview, Pan, Vpoint, and Zoom. Refer to the command description in this chapter for details.

VIEWPORTS (OR VPORTS)

Controls the number and location of multiple viewports on the screen. In addition, Vports can be uscd to save, restore, and delete named viewport configurations, or to display the names and coordinate locations of saved viewport configurations.

VERSIONS

Release 10 and later. In Release 11 and later, this command works only when TILEMODE is set to zero. See Chapter 13 for details regarding the TILE-MODE system variable.

COMMAND OPTIONS

Save Enter **S** to save the current viewport configuration under a unique name. AutoCAD prompts:

> ?/Name for new viewport configuration:

Enter a unique name under which you intend to save the current viewport configuration. The configuration is saved, and AutoCAD returns to the Command prompt.

Viewport configuration names can be up to 31 characters long. They can be composed of letters or numbers, but no punctuation marks except for the dollar sign ($), hyphen (-), and underscore (_).

AutoCAD saves the identification number and location of each viewport in the viewport configuration. Each viewport in a configuration is automatically assigned a unique identification number by AutoCAD. These numbers increase sequentially as new viewport configurations are added and saved. You can determine the identification numbers of viewports for the currently active viewport configuration by entering a question mark, as will be explained shortly.

When multiple viewports are displayed on the screen, the screen graphics area is arbitrarily assigned a special display grid wherein the lower-left corner is coordinate 0,0 and the upper-right corner is coordinate 1,1. AutoCAD remembers viewport locations by storing the relative coordinates of each lower-left and upper-right corner.

Thus, a viewport covering the left half of the graphics area would extend from coordinate 0,0 (the lower-left corner of the graphics screen) to coordinate 0.5,1 (the upper midpoint of the screen). The right half viewport would extend from point 0.5,0 (the lower midpoint of the graphics screen) to point 1,1 (the upper-right corner).

Figure 11.25 illustrates the coordinate locations of a standard four-viewport configuration.

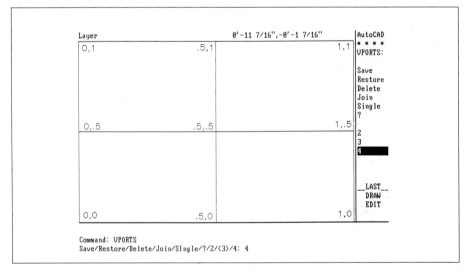

FIGURE 11.25: The Vports command—four viewports, showing coordinate locations. Multiple viewports are created using a special set of coordinate points that range from 0 to 1 along the x- and y-axes of the graphics display screen. Splitting the screen into four viewports, as shown above, creates viewports with x and y dimensions equal to one-half of each axis. The exact coordinate points of the corners of each viewport are illustrated above.

In addition to the viewport locations, AutoCAD remembers the viewing angle and magnification of each viewport at the time the configuration is saved.

Alternatively, you may enter a question mark in response to this prompt. AutoCAD responds by displaying a list of all named viewport configurations and their coordinate locations. Viewport numbers are displayed for the active configuration only.

If you enter the name of a previously saved viewport configuration, AutoCAD responds:

> That viewport configuration already exists. Replace it? <N>

Respond by entering **Y** if you intend to overwrite the previous configuration information with the current information. If you decide not to overwrite the previous configuration, type **N** or press Enter.

Restore   Enter **R** to restore a previously named viewport configuration. AutoCAD prompts:

> ?/Name of viewport configuration to restore:

Enter a valid viewport configuration name. AutoCAD restores the named viewport configuration. Alternatively, you may enter a question mark, and AutoCAD will then display all named viewport configurations and their coordinate locations. Viewport numbers are displayed for the active configuration only.

Delete   Enter **D** to delete a named viewport configuration that is no longer needed. AutoCAD responds:

> ?/Name of viewport configuration to delete:

Enter a valid viewport configuration name, and AutoCAD will delete it. Alternatively, you may enter a question mark, and AutoCAD will display all named viewport configurations and their coordinate locations.

If you wish to restore a deleted viewport configuration, use the U or Undo command. Refer to Chapter 10 for details regarding these commands.

Join   Enter **J** to join two viewports into one. AutoCAD prompts:

> Select dominant viewport <current>:

Of the two viewports you intend to join, pick the one that contains the settings you intend to keep in the new viewport after joining. This is the dominant viewport. If the current viewport is dominant, you may press Enter. If the current viewport is not the viewport you intend to make dominant, move the pointing device so that the small arrow is located in the desired viewport, and then press the pick button. This makes the selected viewport current, and thus dominant. After you select the dominant viewport, AutoCAD prompts:

Select viewport to join:

Select the second viewport, and AutoCAD will join the two together.

Viewports cannot be joined unless they are fully adjacent; that is, they must have one boundary entirely in common. Thus, viewports you intend to join may only result in a new viewport that is rectangular in shape.

SIngle   Enter **SI** to return to a single viewport display. The settings of the single viewport are automatically taken from the settings of the current viewport.

?   Enter a question mark to display a list of all named viewport configurations and their coordinate locations. Viewport numbers are displayed for the active configuration only. Figure 11.26 shows a typical viewport configuration listing that AutoCAD provides when you select this option.

The configuration named SIMPLE is illustrated in Figure 11.27. The configuration named COMPLEX is illustrated in Figure 11.28. The configuration named *LAST is the configuration that was in effect prior to the current configuration. This configuration is not accessible using the Vports command and is displayed for information purposes only.

```
Current configuration:
id# 1
    corners: 0.5000,0.0000 1.0000,1.0000
id# 3
    corners: 0.0000,0.0000 0.5000,1.0000

Configuration *LAST:
    0.0000,0.0000 1.0000,1.0000

Configuration COMPLEX:
    0.0000,0.0000 0.5000,0.6667
    0.0000,0.6667 0.2500,1.0000
    0.5000,0.0000 1.0000,1.0000
    0.2500,0.6667 0.5000,1.0000

Configuration SIMPLE:
    0.5000,0.0000 1.0000,1.0000
    0.0000,0.0000 0.5000,1.0000
```

FIGURE 11.26: A viewport configuration listing. This is a typical listing similar to the listing you might see when you select the Vports ? command. The numbers following the configuration names indicate what portions of the screen are occupied by the viewports in each configuration.

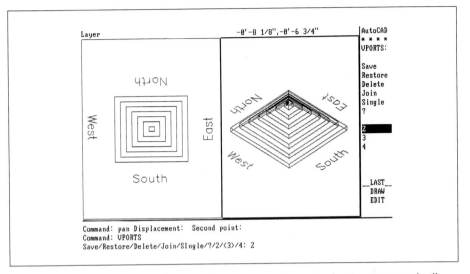

FIGURE 11.27: The Vports command—division into two equal viewports. The Vports command will quickly split the display in two, either horizontally or vertically—in this case, vertically. This feature allows you to display two viewing angles of the same drawing simultaneously.

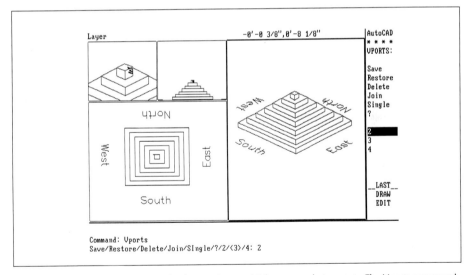

FIGURE 11.28: The Vports command—division into multiple, unequal viewports. The Vports command can create a number of interesting multiple-viewing configurations. The above viewport configuration can be created using the sample dialog found in the Vports section of this chapter.

2   Enter **2** to split the current viewport into two viewports. AutoCAD prompts:

Horizontal/Vertical:

Enter **H** to split the current viewport using a horizontal boundary. Enter **V** to split it using a vertical boundary.

3   Enter **3** to split the viewport into three viewports. AutoCAD prompts:

Horizontal/Vertical/Above/Below/Left/<Right>:

Enter **H** to split the current viewport using two horizontal boundaries. Enter **V** to split the current viewport using two vertical boundaries.

Alternatively, you may elect to create three viewports by first splitting the current viewport in half, and then splitting one of the new viewports in half again. The remaining options indicate the location of the larger viewport relative to the two smaller ones. Enter **A** if you want the larger viewport above the smaller viewports, **B** if you want it below the smaller viewports, **L** if you want it to the left, or **R** (or press Enter) to place it to the right of the smaller viewports.

4   Enter **4** to split the current viewport into four equally sized viewports.

USAGE

If your hardware supports the Advanced User Interface, you can access a dialog box containing several viewport configurations from the Settings pull-down menu, as illustrated in Figure 11.29. Refer to Chapter 5 for details regarding dialog boxes and pull-down menus.

RELATED SYSTEM VARIABLES

CVPORT (identification number of the currently active viewport).

SAMPLE DIALOG

The following dialog creates the viewport configuration illustrated in Figure 11.28:

```
Command: Vports
Save/Restore/Delete/Join/SIngle/?/2/<3>/4: 2
Horizontal/<Vertical>: V
Regenerating drawing.
Command: (pick left viewport, making it current)
Command: Vports
Save/Restore/Delete/Join/SIngle/?/2/<3>/4: 3
```

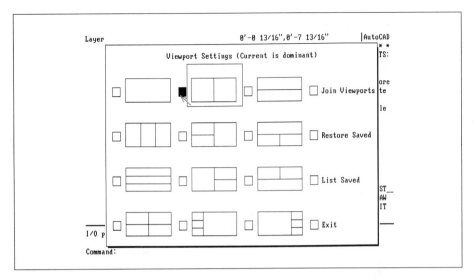

FIGURE 11.29: The Vports command—sample viewport configurations displayed in an icon menu. This icon menu appears when you select "Set viewports" from the Display pull-down menu, in AutoCAD configurations that support the Advanced User Interface. In this figure, the icon indicating two vertical viewports is being selected—notice the solid filled box with the arrow pointing to it, and the rectangle that surrounds the nearby icon. When the icon is thus selected, AutoCAD will execute a macro that invokes the Vports command and splits the screen display as requested.

Horizontal/Vertical/Above/Below/Left/<Right>: **H**
Regenerating drawing.
Command: **Vports**
Save/Restore/Delete/Join/SIngle/?/2/<3>/4: **J**
Select dominant viewport <current>: **(pick lowest of the three on the left)**
Select viewport to join: **(pick viewport immediately above)**
Regenerating drawing.
Command: **(pick upper-third viewport)**
Command: **Vports**
Save/Restore/Delete/Join/SIngle/?/2/<3>/4: **2**
Horizontal/<Vertical>: **V**
Regenerating drawing.
Command:

VIEWRES

Allows you to control the speed with which AutoCAD regenerates drawings, by controlling the resolution of curved lines as viewed on the screen. In addition, the Viewres command is used to turn on and off Fast Zoom mode, which determines whether zooming and panning are performed using drawing regeneration, or using redraws whenever possible.

VERSIONS

Version 2.5 and later. In AutoCAD Release 10 and later, the circle zoom percent can be set separately for each viewport.

COMMAND OPTIONS

Do you want fast zooms?   Enter **Y** if you want AutoCAD to perform zooms and pans within the context of a virtual screen, thus increasing speed, but not changing the display resolution as it zooms in and out. Remember that the trade-off is speed versus screen appearance. If appearance is paramount and speed is of little consequence, enter **N** to turn Fast Zoom mode off. When Fast Zoom mode is off, the circle zoom percent is irrelevant, since most display changes will regenerate the drawing.

Enter circle zoom percent   Enter a percentage equal to or less than the percentage of magnification you generally use when zooming in or out. If you normally zoom to 10 times the initial drawing size, enter 1000 or less; if 20 times the initial drawing size, enter 2000 or less, and so on.

USAGE

To control the display of curved lines and Fast Zoom mode, invoke the Viewres command. AutoCAD first prompts you to choose whether or not to enable Fast Zoom mode, and then prompts you to enter a zoom percent for curved lines.

Fast Zoom Mode   When enabled, Fast Zoom mode allows AutoCAD to generate a large virtual screen. For a more detailed presentation of the virtual screen, refer to the discussion under "The Virtual Screen" at the beginning of this chapter.

Zooming and panning within the boundaries of the virtual screen are usually faster because AutoCAD can refresh the screen display using virtual-screen data, rather than refreshing the screen display by regenerating it using the drawing database.

AutoCAD automatically adjusts the size of the virtual screen to be as large as possible relative to the current level of magnification. When you invoke the Zoom All option, AutoCAD regenerates the screen and sets the virtual screen to the same size as the drawing limits.

AutoCAD will regenerate the drawing, and thus recalculate the virtual screen, whenever you do any of the following:

- Change the viewing angle in 3-D space.
- Pan outside the boundaries of the current virtual screen.
- Zoom in or out to a level of magnification that cannot be supported by the current integer-based data in the virtual screen—on the average system, about a 50-to-1 zoom ratio.
- Perform an explicit regeneration using the Regen command.
- Invoke any command that changes the screen display when Fast Zoom mode is turned off.

Circle Zoom Percent   AutoCAD never displays curved lines as true curves; the resolution of computer display screens is not high enough to make such a time-consuming display necessary. In fact, AutoCAD draws curved lines as a series of tiny line segments called *vectors,* so small and close together as to make the line appear curved when viewed on the screen.

Each time AutoCAD regenerates the drawing, it calculates the number of vectors required to display curved lines as smooth curves, using the current level of magnification. The greater the magnification, the larger the number of vectors.

The more vectors used to display a curved line, the longer AutoCAD will take to redraw and regenerate the drawing. Conversely, the fewer vectors required, the faster the drawing will be regenerated.

However, if you have enabled Fast Zoom mode, AutoCAD may not regenerate the drawing each time you zoom to higher levels of magnification. Thus, enlarging details of the drawing with Fast Zoom mode enabled may cause circles to appear as polygons, and arcs to appear as straight line segments, as illustrated in Figure 11.30.

You can force AutoCAD to use more vectors than normal by adjusting the *circle zoom percent.* When the circle zoom percent is set to 100 (the default), AutoCAD generates curved lines using enough vectors to display them as smooth curves at the current level of magnification, whatever that may be.

If you adjust the circle zoom percent to 200, AutoCAD will generate arcs and circles using twice as many vectors. Thus, you will be able to increase the magnification of the drawing by twice as much before the individual vectors become visible. If you adjust the circle zoom percent to 300, three times as many vectors will be drawn, and you will be able to magnify the current display by a factor of three before individual vectors become visible.

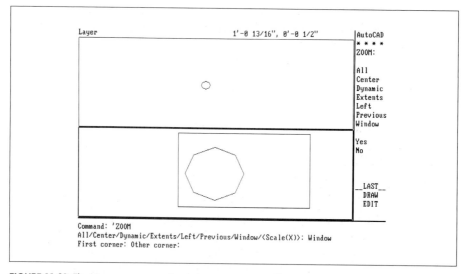

FIGURE 11.30: The Viewres command—circle zoom percent. The two viewports in this figure show the relationship between a circle as displayed after it has been drawn, and as subsequently magnified using the Zoom Window command. Because the circle zoom percent has been set to 100 using the Viewres command, the enlarged circle does not appear as a circle but rather as an eight-sided polygon. If the lower viewport is regenerated, however, the enlarged entity will appear as a circle again.

Adjusting the circle zoom percent therefore becomes a trade-off between three factors:

1. The degree to which you magnify the drawing.
2. The speed with which AutoCAD redraws all those vectors.
3. The appearance of curved lines at higher levels of magnification.

If you don't magnify your drawing to more than five times its initial magnification, except perhaps on rare occasions, you will gain no significant improvement in the appearance of curved lines by setting the circle zoom percent to 20,000 (the maximum setting). AutoCAD never draws more vectors than necessary to display smooth curves at the current magnification, but you may slow down performance considerably in those cases where you first zoom in for greater levels of detail, and then zoom out again, thereby forcing AutoCAD to redraw more vectors than may actually be required. For the sake of improved speed, it is often preferable to live with circles that from time to time are displayed as many-sided polygons. Thus if you zoom to five times the initial magnification, try setting the circle zoom percent to no more than 500—and perhaps less.

The appearance of curved lines on the monitor bears no relationship whatsoever to how they are plotted or printed. AutoCAD uses a different algorithm when plotting; curved lines are always plotted with the ideal number of vectors regardless of the drawing magnification or the circle zoom percent.

If screen appearance is immaterial, you can increase the speed of redraws and regenerations by setting the circle zoom percent to less than 100. This forces AutoCAD to draw fewer vectors than necessary, thus increasing redraw and regeneration speed. For example, a circle zoom percent of 50 will force Auto-CAD to regenerate curves with half the required number of vectors for the current level of magnification. AutoCAD never draws a circle with fewer than eight vectors, however.

> *Tip:* You can usually find a nice balance point between speed and screen appearance. Bear in mind that each increase in the circle zoom percent carries with it the possibility that you may at some time, when zooming beyond your usual levels of magnification, force AutoCAD to draw curves with more vectors than necessary. It's better to start conservative and inch your way up rather than enter an overly large circle zoom percent and complain that AutoCAD is too slow.

Maintaining a virtual screen actually slows down AutoCAD by a small amount, as the memory used by the virtual screen is a little less memory available for AutoCAD processing. The theory is that for most drawings, you more than make up for that slight performance loss with considerably faster zooms and pans. However, if your drawings are exceptionally large (several megabytes in size) and your computer memory is limited, maintaining a virtual screen may reach a point of diminishing returns, as AutoCAD regenerates your drawing and stores an exceptionally large virtual screen as well, cutting off significant amounts of memory that could be used for other processes.

If your drawings are that big, or if your drawing style is such that even a virtual screen just doesn't help, turn off Fast Zoom mode. In your case, an extremely fast computer with multiple megabytes of memory and a multitasking operating system may be the only real solution. If you cannot afford such a high-priced alternative, remember that no law says you must be sitting at your computer, computing, every minute of every day in order to be productive. Use the regeneration time to answer calls, rest your eyes (really—that is *most* important), or develop new and more creative design ideas in your imagination (the ultimate CAD workstation). Remember that AutoCAD's floating-point mathematics (the culprit) is indispensable to the precision and accuracy of your drawings.

VPOINT

Allows you to adjust the viewing angle of the current viewport, by defining a relationship between a target point and a viewing point. The Vpoint command is usually used on 3-D drawings, but it may be used on 2-D drawings as well.

VERSIONS

Version 2.1 and later. In Release 11 and later, the Vpoint command works only in model space. Refer to Chapter 12 for a detailed discussion of model space.

COMMAND OPTIONS

Rotate Enter **R** to establish the viewing angle by entering two angles. AutoCAD responds:

> Enter angle in X-Y plane from X axis:

AutoCAD expects an absolute angle measured counterclockwise from angle zero (the positive x-axis) in the current construction plane. This angle is similar to the angle measurements used when entering polar coordinates to draw entities. In other words, if you were looking at the current construction plane in plan view, 90 degrees would be pointing straight up, 180 degrees would be to the left, 270 degrees would be pointing straight down, and so on. This first angle therefore orients the viewpoint on the X-Y plane, on the circumference of a circle with the target point at the center. (The radius of the circle is immaterial, since the distance between the target and the viewing point is not considered in measuring the viewing angle.)

After you have entered this angle, AutoCAD prompts:

> Enter angle from X-Y plane:

In response to this prompt, AutoCAD expects another angle, this one measured in a plane that is perpendicular to the current construction plane, and oriented in space according to the previously entered angle. Within this perpendicular plane, AutoCAD measures the angle counterclockwise, using the line of intersection of the two planes as angle zero. Increasing the second angle "tilts" the viewing angle up from the X-Y plane, in a circular orientation, again using the target point as the center. This process is illustrated in Figures 11.31 and 11.32.

When the second angle is entered, AutoCAD displays the drawing extents as viewed from the selected angle.

View point By entering numbers for the x, y, and z coordinates separated by commas, you may enter the coordinates of a viewpoint directly. The distance between the selected viewing point and target point does not matter; what matters is the angle between them in 3-D space. Points close to the target or far away may be chosen. AutoCAD always displays the full extents of the drawing when generating a viewing point using the Vpoint command. For example, the same

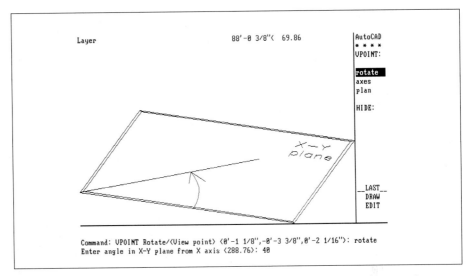

FIGURE 11.31: The Vpoint command—entering an angle in the X-Y plane. Using the Vpoint Rotate option, you must first enter the viewing angle parallel to the current construction plane. This angle is measured counterclockwise from the positive x-axis using the target point (default 0,0) as the origin. This figure illustrates an angle of 40 degrees in the X-Y plane. (The target point is changed by setting the TARGET system variable; refer to Chapter 13 for details.)

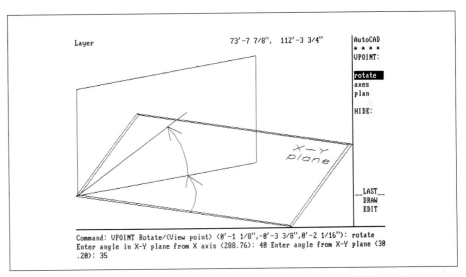

FIGURE 11.32: The Vpoint command—entering an angle perpendicular to the X-Y plane. Once the viewing angle in the X-Y plane is established, you are prompted to enter an elevation angle; this angle is measured counterclockwise around the origin point, perpendicular to the X-Y plane, using the first angle as the positive x-axis. This is illustrated above. The distance from the target is computed automatically; AutoCAD will display the entity extents from the selected viewing angle.

plan view of the drawing may be selected by entering point 0,0,1 or point 0,0,20. The same viewing angle will be displayed after entering point 1,1,1 or point 2,2,2. This process is illustrated in Figure 11.33.

Axes (press Return)   Press Enter (Return) to select the viewing point dynamically, by means of a rotating set of x, y, and z coordinates. After you press Enter, Auto-CAD responds by temporarily overriding the current display with the display of an *axis tripod* and a *2-D globe*. Also displayed is a small marker that moves as the pointing device is moved.

The axis tripod represents the x-, y-, and z-axes of the current construction plane. The 2-D globe represents a spherical surface, with the current target point as the center, that has been exploded, stretched, and flattened into a circular surface. The intersection of the straight lines is the top pole of the globe's axis, equivalent to a plan view of the current drawing. The small inner circle is the globe's "equator," which represents the current X-Y plane. The larger, outer circle actually represents a single point, namely the bottom pole of the sphere, which has been stretched outward and upward, thus flattening the globe into a circle and making all points on it accessible to the marker.

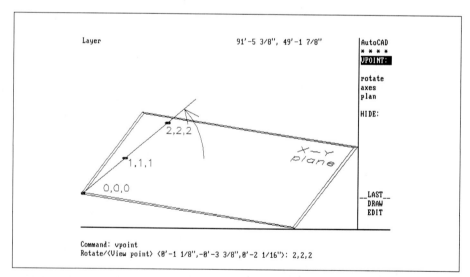

FIGURE 11.33: The Vpoint command—entering a point to establish the viewing angle. You may establish the viewing angle by entering a single point. AutoCAD will compute the viewing angle from the relationship between the selected point and the target point. The distance between the selected point and the target point does not matter; AutoCAD always displays the drawing extents from the selected viewing angle.

The axis tripod will rotate as the marker is moved inside the boundaries of the 2-D globe, reflecting their appearance from the current viewing angle as indicated by the location of the marker on the sphere. For example, placing the marker inside the smaller circle and closing the intersection of the lines will generate a viewing angle close to plan view. Placing the marker close to the inner circle will generate a horizontal, or elevation view. Placing the marker between the inner and outer circles will produce the effect of looking at the drawing from underneath the current construction plane.

This process is illustrated in Figure 11.34.

USAGE

To change the viewing angle of a drawing, invoke the Vpoint command. Auto CAD prompts for a 3-D viewing point. When the point is entered, AutoCAD calculates the new viewing angle based on the angle between the viewing point and the current target point. (The default target point is 0,0,0.) The drawing display is scaled so that the drawing extents fit within the current viewport.

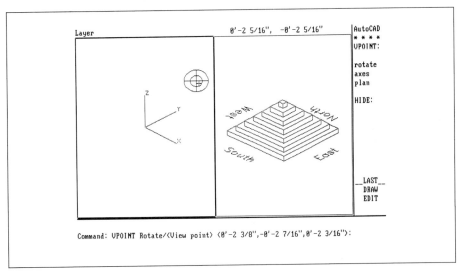

FIGURE 11.34: The Vpoint command—entering a viewing angle using the Axes option. The left viewport displays the Vpoint Axes option screen: a representation of the x-, y-, and z-axes and a globe that has been flattened into two dimensions. The outer circumference of the globe is its "south pole," the center point is its "north pole," and the inner circumference is its "equator." Moving the small cross around the globe will change the relative orientation of the axes. The viewport on the right shows what the drawing display will be after the view angle illustrated on the left is selected.

Once the drawing is regenerated with the new viewing angle, you may draw or edit entities, or zoom or pan throughout the display at will. Hidden-line displays will remain intact as long as another drawing regeneration is not performed.

Alternatively, you may enter the viewing angle by specifying two angles—the first in relation to the x-axis within the current construction plane, and the second in relation to a plane perpendicular to the current construction plane, using the first angle as a base.

A third method may be used to enter the new viewing angle. When you press Enter in response to the viewing-angle prompt, AutoCAD displays an icon that can be used to visualize the relationship between the x-, y-, and z-axes in the current construction plane. By moving the pointing device, you may rotate these three axes on the screen until you have displayed the desired viewing angle. Pressing the pick button then regenerates the drawing using the selected viewing angle.

These methods are illustrated in Figures 11.31, 11.32, 11.33, and 11.34.

Note: Prior to Release 10, the Vpoint command always used point 0,0,0 as the target point. As of Release 10, you may change the location of the target point for Vpoint by means of the Dview Target command. You cannot generate perspective views using Vpoint; use Dview instead.

A precise and pleasing viewing angle can require some trial and error to achieve. When a good angle has been found, use the View command to save 3-D views that you may want to recreate.

A 3-D view may appear more pleasing after you perform a hidden-line removal with the Hide command. After the hidden-line removal is performed, use the Mslide command to create an AutoCAD slide file of the result. Auto-CAD can display a slide file inside any drawing much more quickly than the Hide command can repeat a hidden-line removal.

Changes to the 3-D viewing angle are always accompanied by a drawing regeneration. If experimenting to find a perfect viewing angle, freeze most of the drawing's layers, visualizing only the minimum number of entities required to evaluate the correct viewing angle. Be especially sure to freeze those containing filled lines, curved lines, and text. This makes the regeneration of the remaining entities much faster. After the correct viewing angle is found, thaw the appropriate layers. If using AutoCAD Release 10 and later, try Dview instead.

If you intend to perform a hidden-line removal, let the drawing regenerate fully first. Refer to the Hide command in this chapter for tips and warnings regarding Hide.

RELATED COMMANDS

Dview.

RELATED SYSTEM VARIABLES

BACKZ (location of back clipping plane); FRONTZ (location of front clipping plane); LENSLENGTH (focal length of camera lens); TARGET (location of target point); VIEWCTR (center of view); VIEWDIR (viewing direction); VIEW-MODE (current viewing mode); VIEWSIZE (current viewing height); VIEWTWIST (current camera orientation angle along the viewing-angle axis). These system variables are not modifiable using the Setvar command; you can change their settings indirectly by changing the display with Dview.

SAMPLE DIALOG

The following dialog will result in the viewing angle pictured in Figure 11.35:

```
Command: Vpoint
Rotate/<View point>: R
Enter angle in X-Y plane from X axis: 225
Enter angle from X-Y plane: 45
Regenerating drawing.
Command:
```

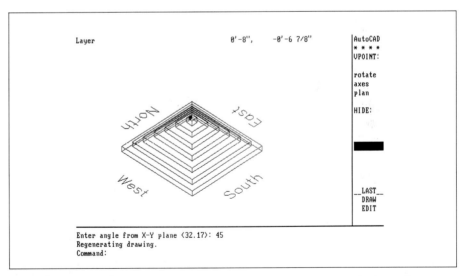

FIGURE 11.35: The Vpoint command—entering an angle via the Rotate option. This figure illustrates the display that results from rotating the plan view of the pyramid 225 degrees in the X-Y plane, as per the sample dialog in the Vpoint section of this chapter.

ZOOM

Allows you to magnify portions of your drawing, enlarging the display to permit finer degrees of detail in drawing and editing entities.

VERSIONS

All.

COMMAND OPTIONS

All   Enter **A** to shrink the size of a plan-view drawing to include the drawing's defined limits, which were set using the Limits command (described in Chapter 6). Zoom All always forces a drawing regeneration.

Some changes made to the drawing will affect the drawing *extents*—that is, the size of the drawing based on the entities it contains, not the defined limits. If you add drawing entities that extend beyond the drawing limits, and a Zoom All command is invoked, the drawing display will be further shrunk to include those entities as well. When the overall size of the drawing extents is reduced, either by erasing or by moving entities, the Zoom All command may again be affected.

When viewing a drawing from a non-plan viewpoint, there is no difference between the Zoom All and Zoom Extents options. Zoom All always zooms according to the boundaries of the drawing extents in non-plan views.

Center   Enter **C** to indicate to AutoCAD that you intend to pick a new center point for the display. AutoCAD responds by prompting:

Center point:

Enter the new center point either by picking it with the pointing device or by entering coordinates from the keyboard. Only x-y coordinates in the current construction plane can be used for this purpose. After you have entered the new center point, AutoCAD prompts:

Magnification or Height:

You may respond to this prompt by pressing Enter, in which case AutoCAD will not change the current magnification, but will move the selected center point to the center of the current display. The effect of using Zoom Center in this way is similar to the Pan command (described earlier in this chapter). However, if you enter a number, AutoCAD assumes that the number is the height of the new display. For example, if you enter **10**, AutoCAD moves the center point to the center of the display and draws the display 10 drawing units high.

If you enter a number followed by an *X* (for example, **10X**), AutoCAD assumes that the number is a magnification factor based on the current drawing magnification. Thus, if you enter **10X**, AutoCAD moves the center point to the center of the display and draws the display at ten times the current magnification.

In AutoCAD Release 11 and later, if TILEMODE is set to zero and you are working in model space, you may enter a magnification factor relative to paper space. To do so, follow the magnification factor with the letters **XP**. This option is useful when you are setting up multiple views of a drawing in paper space for plotting. Refer to the Scale Factor option of this command for details.

Dynamic   Enter **D** to enable AutoCAD's *dynamic zoom* feature. Dynamic zoom allows you to visualize the current drawing limits and extents, current viewport, current size of the virtual screen, and projected size and location of the new viewport. In so doing, AutoCAD provides a means to tell if your intended zoom will cause a drawing regeneration or not.

After you enter **D**, AutoCAD clears the screen and presents a special screen of information relating to the proposed zoom, as illustrated in Figure 11.36. The current drawing extents are displayed as a rectangle filling most of the display area. Another rectangle, formed by short lines that indicate only the rectangle's corners, indicates the boundaries of the current virtual screen, the area within

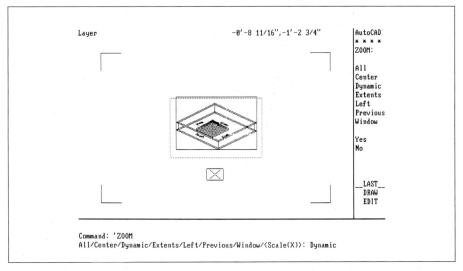

FIGURE 11.36: The Zoom Dynamic command. This figure illustrates the information that is available under the Zoom Dynamic option. The four right-angle lines in the corners of the screen indicate the dimensions of the current virtual screen. The dotted rectangle near the center of the screen indicates the current viewport. The solid rectangle that appears to be overlapping the viewport is the current drawing extents. The small rectangle with the *X* in the middle is the currently selected view.

which zooming and panning may be done without forcing a drawing regeneration. A highlighted rectangle appears within the virtual screen, indicating the size and location of the current view. Finally, a rectangle with an *X* in the center indicates the size and location of the proposed new view. This rectangle is called the *view box*.

As you move the pointing device, the view box will follow the movement around the display. If you press the pick button, the *X* disappears and is replaced by a small arrow pointing to the right side of the view box. Moving the pointing device now enlarges and reduces the size of the view box, while it remains in place. Pressing the pick button again toggles back to the *X* display, and the view box will again move about the display while retaining its current size. You can toggle back and forth, changing the size and location of the pick box until it conforms to the size and location of the new view.

If you move the view box outside the boundaries of the virtual screen, or if you reduce its size considerably, a small hourglass figure appears in the lower-left corner of the display, as illustrated in Figure 11.37. This symbol indicates that the current size and/or location of the proposed new viewport will force a drawing regeneration. Enlarging the view box or changing its location to a point fully within the virtual screen boundaries will cause the hourglass symbol to disappear, indicating that the size and location of the new view is sufficient to be displayed using the faster redraw.

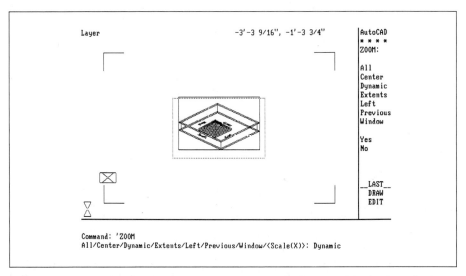

FIGURE 11.37: The Zoom Dynamic command—drawing regeneration required. In the above figure, the selected viewport has been moved just outside the area of the virtual screen. In the process, a small hourglass figure has appeared in the lower-left corner of the display. This indicates that displaying this view will require a drawing regeneration instead of a redraw.

While you are moving and adjusting the size of the view box, AutoCAD generates those entities that occupy the virtual screen. You need not wait for these entities to be generated completely in order to select a size and location for the new view. AutoCAD generates these entities for your convenience, but you may ignore them if you already know what part of the drawing you intend to enlarge.

Extents   Enter **E** to display the largest possible magnification of all entities in the drawing. When you invoke Zoom Extents, AutoCAD ignores the drawing limits and instead uses the boundaries formed by the drawing entities to determine the size of the display. If entities occupy only a small portion of the available drawing limits, this will result in a much larger display of those than will Zoom All.

Zoom Extents displays the drawing entities at the largest possible magnification. This often means that entities on the very edge of the screen will be hard to visualize or select. Under such circumstances, repeat the zoom and reduce the size of the display by a small factor. (Refer to the Zoom Scale option ahead.)

Left   Enter **L** to indicate to AutoCAD that you intend to pick a new lower-left corner point for the display. AutoCAD responds by prompting:

Lower left corner point:

Enter the new point either by picking it with the pointing device or by entering coordinates from the keyboard. Only x-y coordinates in the current construction plane can be used for this purpose. After you have entered the new lower-left point, AutoCAD prompts:

Magnification or Height:

You may respond to this prompt by pressing Enter; AutoCAD will not change the current magnification, but will move the selected corner point to the lower left of the current display. The effect of using Zoom Left in this way is similar to the Pan command (described earlier in this chapter). However, if you enter a number, AutoCAD assumes that the number is the height of the new display. For example, if you enter **10**, AutoCAD moves the selected point to the lower left of the display and draws the display 10 drawing units high.

If you enter a number followed by an *X* (for example, **10X**), AutoCAD assumes that the number entered is a magnification factor based on the current drawing magnification. Thus, if you enter **10X**, AutoCAD moves the selected point to the lower left of the display and draws the display at ten times the current magnification.

In AutoCAD Release 11 and later, if TILEMODE is set to zero and you are working in model space, you may enter a magnification factor relative to paper space. To do so, follow the magnification factor with the letters **XP**. This option is useful when you are setting up multiple views of a drawing in paper space for plotting. Refer to the Scale Factor option of this command for details.

Previous   Enter **P** to restore the previous view. Zoom P will restore the previous view whether or not it was selected using the Zoom command. Views created using Dview, Plan, Restore, View, Vpoint, or Zoom will be restored by this option. Successive Zoom Previous commands will "back up" through additional previously saved views, to the limits allowed by your version of AutoCAD.

Vmax   Enter **V** to zoom to the limits of the current virtual screen. This is the largest possible drawing area that can be displayed without forcing a time-consuming drawing regeneration. This option will work only if you have enabled Fast Zooms using the Viewres command, described earlier in this chapter.

Window   Enter **W** to specify the exact area of the drawing display you wish to enlarge, by picking opposite corners of a rectangular window corresponding to the desired view. AutoCAD prompts:

First corner:

Enter one corner of the intended view. AutoCAD responds:

Other corner:

Enter the opposite corner of the intended view. As you move the pointing device, a rubberband window appears on the screen to assist you in visualizing the intended new view.

Depending on the size and location of the new view, and on whether Fast Zoom mode is enabled, AutoCAD may display the new view using only a redraw, or if necessary, using a drawing regeneration.

Scale Factor   You may enter a number in response to this prompt, and AutoCAD will interpret it as a magnification factor relative to the full view of the entire drawing. For example, a scale factor of 1 displays the entire drawing. A scale factor of 2 magnifies the drawing two times, a scale factor of 3.5 magnifies the drawing 3.5 times, and so on. As the scale factor increases, the drawing entities will appear larger, and less of the whole drawing will fit on the screen.

Scale factors between 0 and 1 will reduce the size of the drawing entities. For example, a scale factor of 0.5 will cause the entities to appear half as large as they would when the full drawing was displayed.

The current center point of the display remains unchanged as you enlarge or reduce entities using this option.

You can also enter a scale factor relative to the current zoom magnification, rather than relative to the entire drawing. To do so, enter **X** after the scale factor—for example, **2X**. This causes entities on the screen to appear twice as large as their current magnification. If you enter **0.5X**, entities will appear half as large as their current magnification. As before, the center point of the display remains unchanged.

In AutoCAD Release 11 and later, if you have paper space On, and are working in model space within a viewport, you may enter a magnification scale factor that is relative to overall paper space rather than to just the current magnification of the drawing in the viewport. To do so, follow the magnification factor with the letters **XP**. This option is useful when setting up multiple views of a drawing in paper space for plotting. It has no effect, however, when TILEMODE is set to a value other than zero (meaning that model space is the default). Figure 11.38 illustrates how zoom factors may differ when relative to paper and model space. For a detailed discussion of paper space and model space, refer to Chapter 12.

USAGE

By enlarging portions of the drawing, the Zoom command permits a higher degree of accuracy than would be possible otherwise, given the relatively low resolution of a monitor screen.

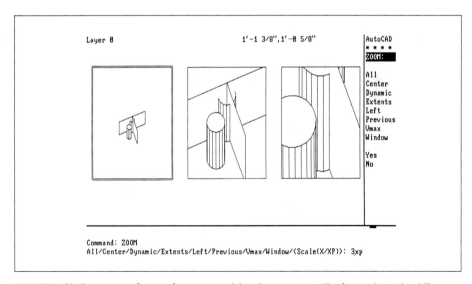

FIGURE 11.38: Zoom magnification factors in model and paper space. This figure shows the difference between the resulting displays of zoom magnification, depending on whether the scale factor is relative to model space or paper space. From left to right, the scale factors are: Zoom All; Zoom 3x (relative to model space); and Zoom 3xp (relative to paper space).

In AutoCAD Release 10 and later, a maximum of ten previous views are saved; you can access them by using successive Zoom Previous commands to "back up" through the remembered views. In versions prior to Release 10, only five previous views are saved. In Release 11 and later, 10 views are saved in model and paper space—20 in all.

As of Version 2.6, the Zoom command can be invoked transparently—that is, while other commands are in progress. To use Zoom transparently, enter an apostrophe followed by **Zoom** in response to another AutoCAD command prompt:

'Zoom

AutoCAD will interrupt the command in progress and display a prompt of available Zoom command options, as follows:

Center/Dynamic/Left/Previous/Window/Scale Factor:

The Zoom All and Zoom Extents options are not available when using Zoom transparently, because these options always perform a regeneration. Zoom Dynamic will not work if you specify a view that requires a regeneration. However, the other options will operate normally. Transparent Zoom cannot be invoked during the Dview, Pan, View, or Vpoint commands, or during another Zoom command.

When the new view is displayed, AutoCAD will inform you that it is resuming the original command, and will repeat the prompt at which the transparent command was invoked.

Tip: To make the Zoom command as fast and efficient as possible, enable Fast Zoom mode using the Viewres command (described earlier in this chapter). This will allow most normal zooming to be performed without a drawing regeneration, saving significant amounts of time.

Use the View command to save a view of the drawing's limits. Name this view "ALL," or some similar name. Then, instead of using Zoom All, use View Restore All. If the virtual screen includes the drawing limits, you will avoid a regeneration, in addition to being able to use this command transparently. Refer to the View command earlier in this chapter for details.

The Zoom All and Zoom Extents commands read the current settings of the drawing limits and extents—as reported by the LIMMAX, LIMMIN, EXTMAX, and EXTMIN system variables—to determine the degree of magnification necessary to display the entire drawing. (Refer to Chapter 13 for details regarding system variables.) Because they do not change the current display, editing commands that cause a reduction in the drawing extents will not update the values found in these system variables.

Zoom All and Zoom Extents will update these system variable settings. If these commands change the settings of EXTMIN and EXTMAX, AutoCAD may need to repeat the Zoom command to account for these new changes. When this happens, AutoCAD displays the following message:

Redisplay caused by change in drawing extents

You can avoid double regenerations of the drawing by Zoom All if you have set drawing limits large enough that drawing entities will not be likely to exceed them, ensuring that Zoom All will regenerate the drawing only once. You can also set limits-checking on (via the LIMCHECK system variable—refer to Chapter 13 for details) so that no entity may be placed outside the current drawing limits.

Avoiding the problem of double regenerations using Zoom Extents is more difficult. A compromise solution might be to draw a rectangle that represents a constant drawing-extents boundary on a separate layer, and turn the layer off. Changes to entities within this boundary will have no effect on Zoom Extents, since this option will always zoom to the boundary. Alternatively, you can simply not use Zoom Extents or Zoom All and instead use other, more predictable display-change commands, such as View Restore or Zoom Vmax.

RELATED SYSTEM VARIABLES

EXTMAX (upper-right corner of the area of drawing extents), EXTMIN (lower-left corner of the area of drawing extents), LIMMAX (upper-right corner of the drawing limits), LIMMIN (lower-left corner of the drawing limits).

SAMPLE DIALOG

The following dialog demonstrates several Zoom command options. It will create the screen illustrated in Figure 11.39, starting with the pyramid drawing illustrated in Figure 11.12.

```
Command: Vports
Save/Restore/Delete/Join/SIngle/?/2/<3>/4: 4
Regenerating drawing.
Command: (pick lower-right viewport)
Command: Zoom
All/Center/Dynamic/Extents/Left/Previous/Window/<Scale(X)>: 2X
Command: (pick upper-right viewport)
Command: Zoom
All/Center/Dynamic/Extents/Left/Previous/Window/<Scale(X)>: C
Center point: 9,8
Magnification or Height: 3
Command: (pick upper-left viewport)
Command: Zoom
```

All/Center/Dynamic/Extents/Left/Previous/Window/<Scale(X)>: **W**
First corner: **4,1**
Other corner: **10,1**
Command: **(pick lower-left viewport)**
Command: **Zoom**
All/Center/Dynamic/Extents/Left/Previous/Window/<Scale(X)>: **0.5x**
Command:

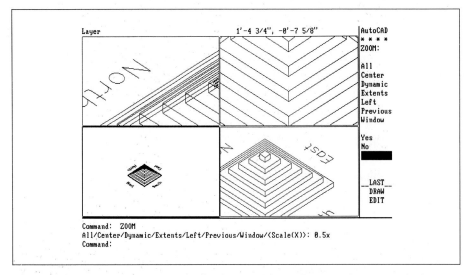

FIGURE 11.39: The Zoom command—various options producing different results. Using multiple viewports, the effects of different Zoom command options on the same drawing can be observed. These various magnifications were established using the sample dialog found in the Zoom section of this chapter.

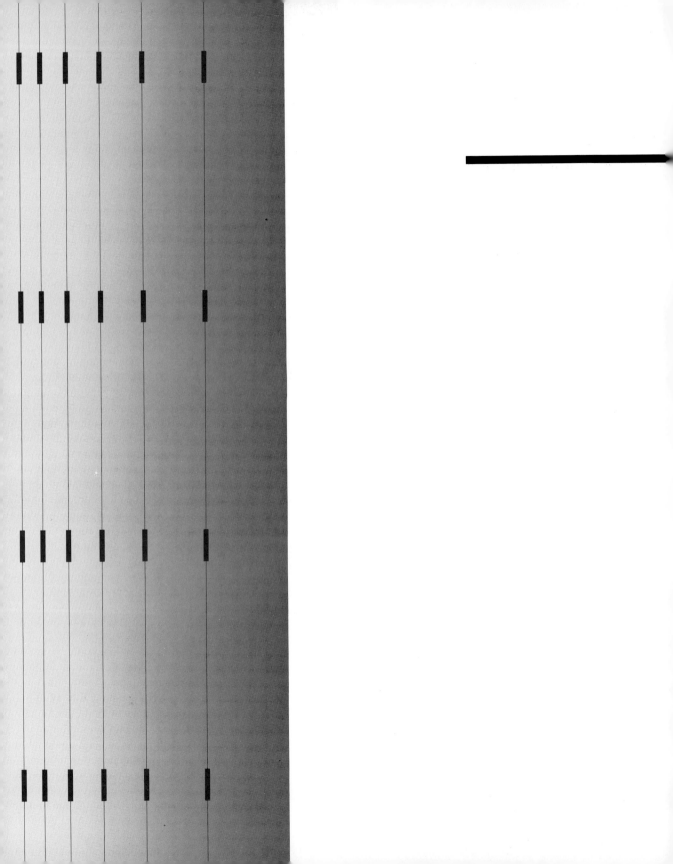

CHAPTER 12

PRINTING AND PLOTTING

Printing and Plotting

I n most AutoCAD applications, the ultimate goal is the production of *hardcopy output*—usable working drawings on a *drawing surface* such as paper, film, or vellum.

AutoCAD can generate two forms of hard-copy output:

- A *plotted drawing,* which is produced using a *pen plotter,* a device that holds (and often moves) a drawing surface while moving a pen or a series of pens across it, recreating each entity in the drawing database.

- A *printed drawing,* which is produced using a *printer plotter,* a device such as a dot-matrix printer or laser printer that reproduces a drawing by means of a series of horizontal lines made up of tiny dots, in a manner similar to the way the computer displays your drawing on the monitor screen.

AutoCAD Version 2.5 and later releases will generate a third type of output: a *plot file.* AutoCAD creates a plot file when the instructions it normally sends to the pen plotter or printer plotter are redirected to a disk file instead. The plot file can be copied like any other disk file; the plotting instructions contained within it can then be sent to the plotter at a later time, or the plot file can be moved to a different computer for plotting elsewhere.

Plot files usually require a special software program to send them to a plotting device, or special hardware that is dedicated to sending plot files to the device. AutoCAD does not supply such software or hardware; it must be purchased separately. Hardware and software dealers can usually demonstrate and recommend several options.

Many printer plotters can process a plot file copied directly to the I/O port to which they are connected; check the documentation of your plotting device to see if it can handle this type of output.

Managing Computer Time

All forms of hard-copy output take time. Given a drawing of average size and complexity, a pen plotter takes the most time, but it produces the highest-quality output. A printer plotter takes about the same amount of time regardless of the complexity of the drawing, but produces a lower-quality output. Laser printers generally work faster than dot-matrix printers and produce higher-quality plots as well.

Because of the time constraints involved, it is usually best to save the pen plotter for production of final drawings, and use the printer plotter for intermediate check plots while the drawing is under development. If the intended check plot contains relatively few drawing entities, however, the pen plotter could be faster, since the printer plotter will not produce simple drawings any faster than complex ones.

You can produce a plot file for the pen plotter and it will take less time than direct output to the device, allowing you to return to your computer sooner. However, you still must send the plot file to the plotter at some point. Therefore, the plot file is really a time-deferral device, suitable when plots can be generated at a later time or on another computer—perhaps during off-hours, or by someone not as familiar with AutoCAD, or by an outside plotting service.

Plotter Buffers

Because plotters and printers are mechanical devices that translate electronic data into hard-copy output, they work much more slowly than a computer can send information to them. Therefore, output devices generally work with a *buffer,* a special built-in amount of memory that is reserved to hold information sent from the computer while the plotting device is still processing prior information. Without a buffer, an output device would work in stops and starts, first receiving and processing some information, then making the mechanical moves required to produce a portion of the hard copy, then receiving and processing the next amount of information, and so on. The buffer keeps the plotter working smoothly, holding processed information and sending it to the plotter's mechanical output mechanism at a speed the device can handle.

If buffers are large enough, they can quickly receive and store all of the plotting information sent from the computer, send it to the plotter at the correct speed, and return control of the computer to you while the plotter continues to plot. This can be a great timesaving device. Unfortunately, the buffers built into most plotters are not large enough to store an entire drawing.

A number of commercially available buffers can serve this purpose. Most are hardware devices that are connected between the computer and the output device. Some software products for this purpose exist as well, but should be used with additional RAM beyond the 640K DOS limit, since AutoCAD requires virtually all this memory.

Another form of buffer is the *dedicated plot file server,* a separate hardware device—actually a small computer—whose only purpose is to send plot files to the plotting device. This type of device is useful in high-volume plotting situations where plotting is more efficiently managed away from the CAD workstation, and where the quantity of plots makes it an economical alternative to a third-party plotting service.

INITIATING THE PLOT

You may plot any drawing using the pen plotter by selecting option 3, "Plot a drawing," from AutoCAD's Main Menu. AutoCAD prompts:

Enter NAME of drawing:

Enter the name of the drawing you wish to plot. AutoCAD will then prompt for the plotting parameters.

If you are inside the drawing editor, you may initiate a plot of the current drawing by invoking the Plot command. AutoCAD assumes that you intend to plot the current drawing, and prompts you for the plotting parameters.

To plot a drawing using the printer plotter, select option 4, "Printer Plot a drawing," from AutoCAD's Main Menu. AutoCAD prompts:

Enter NAME of drawing:

Enter the name of the drawing you wish to plot. AutoCAD will then prompt for the plotting parameters, as will be explained shortly. If you are inside the drawing editor, you may printer-plot the current drawing by invoking the Prplot command.

Whichever device you have chosen, you will be offered the option to produce a plot file as one of the plotting parameters.

PLOTTING A PORTION OF THE DRAWING

AutoCAD begins by offering you the choice of plotting all or part of the drawing. If you initiated the plot from the Main Menu, AutoCAD prompts:

Specify the part of the drawing to be plotted by entering:
Display, Extents, Limits, View, or Window:

If you initiated the plot from within the drawing editor, the prompt is similar but abbreviated:

What to plot -- Display, Extents, Limits, View, or Window:

Each of these options is explained below:

Display   Enter **D** to plot the current viewport. If you initiated the plot from the Main Menu, this option will plot the viewport that was current when the drawing was last saved to disk. If you are inside the drawing editor, this option will plot the currently displayed viewport.

Extents   Enter **E** to plot the drawing extents. If you select this option, Auto-CAD will plot a rectangular area that is just large enough to contain all the current entities in the drawing. When drawings are plotted in plan view, this area may not be the same as the drawing limits, which indicate the maximum drawing size regardless of the relative location of drawing entities.

AutoCAD determines the drawing extents by reading the current settings of the EXTMAX and EXTMIN system variables, and uses the coordinate points found therein to determine the degree of magnification necessary to plot the drawing entities. (Refer to Chapter 13 for details regarding system variables.) The settings of these system variables are updated during drawing regenerations. Because they do not regenerate the drawing, many AutoCAD editing commands, even when they change the drawing extents, will not update the values found in these system variables.

Because of this, the plotted output of 2-D or plan-view drawings may appear smaller that you expected if you edited entities that reduced the drawing extents and are now selecting the Extents plotting option. This applies even if you have ended the drawing session and are plotting from the Main Menu. To plot a plan-view drawing reliably using the Extents option, invoke Zoom Extents or Zoom All first. Refer to Chapter 11 for details regarding the Zoom command.

Limits   Enter **L** to match the plotted area of a plan-view drawing with the current drawing-limits settings. If you are not plotting a drawing in plan view, the settings for drawing limits are ignored, and this option is the same as the Extents option.

View   Enter **V** to plot a named view within the drawing. AutoCAD prompts:

   View name:

Enter the name of the view you intend to plot.

Window   Enter **W** to indicate directly to AutoCAD which portion of the drawing you wish to plot. If you are inside the drawing editor, AutoCAD prompts for opposite corners of a rectangular window marking the plotted portion of the drawing:

   First corner:
   Other corner:

You may use the pointing device to indicate the opposite corners of the window. If you are plotting from the Main Menu, AutoCAD prompts:

   First point:
   Second point:

You must enter the coordinate points using the keyboard.

You may not use the Window option if perspective view mode is active.

DEFAULT PLOT SPECIFICATIONS

When producing either hard-copy output or plot files, you have several different options and considerations to keep in mind. Many of these options apply whether you intend to generate plotted drawings, printed drawings, or plot files; for example, you must specify the drawing's size and overall scale, its location and orientation on the drawing surface, and whether to suppress hidden lines, if they exist. For the sake of convenience, since many parameters apply to each form of output, AutoCAD always refers to the production of plotted drawings, printed drawings, and plot files as *plotting,* and to the resulting output as a *plot,* regardless of the output device chosen.

Each time you invoke a command to produce a plot, AutoCAD provides a series of prompts that enable you to set up whatever parameters are necessary to produce your intended results. The prompts for these parameters include default responses, so that when they remain consistent, you need not reset them each time. In fact, when you first configured AutoCAD to recognize your plotting devices, you answered a series of questions that became the default responses to these plotting prompts. These prompts and their responses are summarized later in this chapter; refer to Chapter 3 for information regarding the installation of output devices, and for more detailed information about the answers to these prompts.

Whenever you change one of these parameters, the new response becomes the default response for the next time. AutoCAD presents these standard default plotting parameters in a single screenful of prompts, similar to the following:

```
Plot will NOT be written to a selected file
Sizes are in Inches
Plot origin is at (0.00,0.00)
Plotting area is 10.00 wide by 7.35 high (MAX size)
Plot is rotated 90 degrees clockwise
Pen width is 0.010
Area fill will NOT be adjusted for pen width
Hidden lines will NOT be removed
Plot will be scaled to fit available area

Do you want to change anything? <N>
```

These lines indicate the current setting for the standard plotting parameters (with the exception of pen numbers and speeds, as explained in the next section). They include any changes you may have made the last time you produced a plot. If you type **N** or press Enter, AutoCAD prepares to plot your drawing.

If you answer by typing **Y,** however, AutoCAD will present a series of prompts for each of the parameters, as described in the upcoming sections.

Changing Pen Assignments

If you are using a pen plotter that allows you to configure multiple pens, user-controllable pen speeds, or built-in, noncontinuous linetypes, AutoCAD begins the sequence of parameter prompts by displaying a screen similar to the one shown in Figure 12.1. This screen indicates the current status of your plotter's configuration for whatever multiple pens, varying linetypes, and pen speeds are supported.

AutoCAD then displays the following prompt:

Do you want to change any of the above parameters? <N>

If the current setting for pen numbers, speeds, and linetypes is correct, type **N** or press Enter. AutoCAD will then continue with the prompt sequence for default plotting parameters.

If you wish to change the setting for one or more of your plotter's pens, enter **Y**. AutoCAD responds:

```
Enter values, blank = Next value, Cn = Color n, S = Show current values,
X = Exit
        Layer         Pen  Line  Pen
        Color         No.  Type  Speed
        1 (red)        1    0    36        Pen number <1>: 2
```

```
    Entity      Pen  Line  Pen          Entity      Pen  Line  Pen                    <
    Color       No.  Type  Speed        Color       No.  Type  Speed                  <
                                                                                       <
    1 (red)      1    0    36           9            1    0    36                      <
    2 (yellow)   2    0    36           10           1    0    36                      <
    3 (green)    3    0    36           11           1    0    36                      <
    4 (cyan)     4    0    36           12           1    0    36                      <
    5 (blue)     5    0    36           13           1    0    36                      <
    6 (magenta)  6    0    36           14           1    0    36                      <
    7 (white)    7    0    36           15           1    0    36                      <
    8            8    0    36                                                          <
                                                                                       <
    Line types   0  = continuous line                                                 <
                 1  = ..............................                                   <
                 2  = ----    ----    ----    ----                                     <
                 3  = -----    -----    -----    -----                                 <
                 4  = ------.  ------.  ------.  ------.                                <
                 5  = ---- -   ---- -   ---- -   ---- -                                 <
                 6  = --- - -  --- - -  --- - -  --- - -                               <
                                                                                       <
                                                                                       <
                                                                                       <
                                                                                       <
                                                                                       <
```

FIGURE 12.1: A typical initial display of plotting parameters for a multi-pen plotter. This plotter uses eight pens and includes seven different linetypes, installed on a system configured for AutoCAD's standard color numbers.

At this point, AutoCAD will loop through the current settings for each color, up to a maximum of 15, beginning with color number 1. If you are using fewer than 15 colors, you need not be concerned with the settings for the unused colors. Simply leave the default settings for these colors alone.

PEN NUMBERS

If your plotter supports multiple pens, AutoCAD first prompts for the pen number to assign to the indicated color. Enter your plotter's pen number for the color displayed in the prompt. In the above example, you would enter the pen number for the color red. If that pen number happens to be 1, you may accept the default response by pressing Enter. In the example, the user has responded by entering pen number 2.

You can configure some single-pen plotters to use multiple pens. If you do so, AutoCAD will pause when plotting, and will prompt you to change pens manually whenever necessary. In this case, you may assign pen numbers of your choosing to the colors, but you should be certain that each color with which you intend to plot has a unique pen number, so that AutoCAD will pause the plot and prompt you to make the switch.

LINETYPE

Next, if your plotter supports built-in noncontinuous linetypes, AutoCAD prompts you to enter the number corresponding to one of those linetypes:

Layer Color	Pen No.	Line Type	Pen Speed	
1 (red)	2	0	36	Line type <0>: 4

Notice that as you enter responses, AutoCAD changes the prompt to reflect the values that you have entered. If the current setting is correct, press Enter. Otherwise, enter the appropriate value. The linetypes supported by your plotter, along with their corresponding numbers, are displayed in the initial screen of settings. In the sample prompt, the user has responded by entering linetype number 4.

A plotter's built-in, noncontinuous linetypes are not the same as AutoCAD's noncontinuous linetypes. You cannot mix AutoCAD's linetypes with the linetypes supported by your plotter. To do so would yield unpredictable results. Use AutoCAD's Continuous linetype in order to produce your plotter's built-in, noncontinuous linetypes at plot time.

PEN SPEED

After you have entered the number of the linetype, AutoCAD prompts you for the pen speed, if variable pen speeds are supported by your plotter:

| 1 (red) | 1 | 4 | 36 | Pen speed <36>: |

Normally, AutoCAD automatically assigns the fastest possible pen speed as the default speed, but for some pens this may be too fast—for example, if the ink cannot flow evenly at the current speed. You may need to experiment somewhat with different pen speeds to find the optimal speed for your particular pen type.

After you assign the pen number, linetype, and speed, AutoCAD loops to the next color number on the list, prompting again for pen number, linetype, and speed. This process continues through color number 15, and then begins anew with color number 1.

Type **X** to end the process of selecting pen assignments.

FASTER SELECTION OF PEN SETTINGS

You can speed up the process of assigning pen parameters with some special responses to the pen setting prompts:

C<number> Enter **C** followed by a color number to skip directly to that color. For example if you enter **C3** in response to any pen setting prompt, AutoCAD skips to color number 3.

*<value> If you would like the value you enter to apply to the current color as well as all the colors that follow, you can enter an asterisk before the value. For example, if you want 18 to be the pen speed for the current pen assignment as well as for all the pen assignments that follow, enter ***18** in response to the prompt for pen speed.

X You may enter **X** at any time to end the pen assignment prompts and continue with the default plot setting prompts.

Plotting to a File

AutoCAD next prompts for the first of the displayed plotting defaults:

Write the plot to a file?

If you wish to create a plot file, enter **Y.** If you want the output to go directly to the plotter, enter **N.**

If you enter **Y,** AutoCAD responds:

Enter file name for plot:

You may enter whatever legal file name you like, within the confines of legal file names for the operating system. DOS imposes a maximum of eight alphanumeric characters (A–Z, 0–9), and no punctuation marks except the dollar sign ($), hyphen (-), and underscore (_). If you like, you may add a three-character file extension, separated from the file name by a period.

If you do not specify a file extension, the default extension PLT is automatically added for pen-plotter files, and LST is added for printer-plotter files. The default file name is the same as the current drawing. You may, if you choose, include existing disk subdirectories in the file name, separating them from the file name and each other with backslashes. You may also include a drive letter, followed by a colon.

Plotting Size Units

AutoCAD next prompts you to indicate the size units you intend to use for the plot size specifications you are about to be asked to enter:

Size units (Inches or Millimeters):

If you intend to measure your plots in inches, enter **I.** If you intend to measure your plots in millimeters, enter **M.** This will affect the default responses and prompts that follow.

Plotting Origin

If you are using a pen plotter, the plotted output is normally positioned on the paper with the lower-left corner of the drawing as near as possible to the lower-left corner of the paper. This point is the *plot origin point*—referred to as the "plot origin." AutoCAD assumes this point to be coordinate point 0,0 on the plotting surface. (It need not be the same as point 0,0 in your drawing file.) Figure 12.2 illustrates this.

You can relocate your drawing on the paper by changing this origin point relative to the current origin point. AutoCAD prompts for a new origin point as follows:

Plot origin in (*inches or millimeters*):

AutoCAD prompts for either inches or millimeters depending on your response to the prompt for plotting size units.

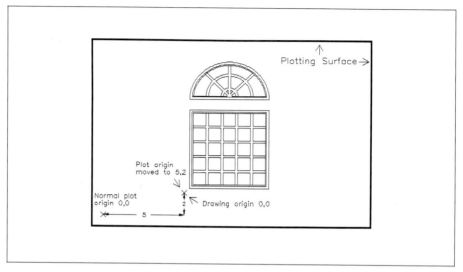

FIGURE 12.2: Plot origin point compared to the drawing origin point. In this figure, a pen plot of a drawing of a window, which was offset only slightly from the drawing origin point, is centered on the plotting surface by indicating to AutoCAD that the pen-plot origin point is 5,2. This has the effect of moving the plot origin point 5 units to the right and 2 units up.

For example, assume that you have configured AutoCAD for engineering drawing units (inches and feet), and that the current plot origin point is 0,0. If you enter **1,1** as the new plot origin, you will move the plot origin 1 inch to the right and 1 inch upward. This has the effect of "shifting" the plot on the paper in the same direction by the same distance. As you might expect, if you shift the plot origin too far, some of your drawing may not fit on the plotting paper.

Some pen plotters have wide default margins and will allow you to shift the plot origin to the right and downward by a modest amount, by using negative numbers in response to the above prompt. Consult your device documentation to see if your plotter will allow you to do this.

If you are using a printer plotter, the plot origin is usually located in the upper-right corner, although a few models may place the origin elsewhere. Consult your printer documentation if you are not sure. As with pen plotters, AutoCAD calls this point 0,0. Also as with pen plotters, you may move this origin point by entering new coordinates relative to point 0,0. For example, again assuming feet and inches as the current units format, if you want to shift the printer-plotter output 1 inch to the right and 1 inch down, enter **1, −1.**

Notice that the response to this prompt is always relative to point 0,0; it is not relative to the current origin point.

Plot Size

When you configure your plotting device, AutoCAD stores one or more standard plot sizes for your particular device, labeling them A, B, C, and so on. Also, AutoCAD stores a plot size named Max, which is the maximum allowable size for your plotter.

AutoCAD displays these sizes on a screen similar to the one shown in Figure 12.3.

```
Standard values for plotting size

Size    Width    Height
A       10.50     8.00
B       16.00    10.00
C       21.00    16.00
D       33.00    21.00
E       43.00    33.00
MAX     44.72    35.31

Enter the Size or Width,Height <MAX>:
```

FIGURE 12.3: Typical default sizes for a plotter that is capable of plotting in five standard sizes, plus a maximum size. You indicate the desired plot size by entering the letter for the size, or Max. The size you enter is displayed as the default the next time you plot.

AutoCAD remembers the last size chosen, and presents that size as the default. You may select the default by pressing Enter. Alternatively, you may select one of the displayed standard sizes by entering the letter corresponding to that size, or you may enter **Max** to indicate that you want the plot to be the maximum size.

If none of the displayed sizes is correct for this particular plot, you may enter your own plotting size dimensions by entering the plot width and height (using either inches or millimeters, as indicated earlier). Enter the values for width and height separated by a comma, as in the following example, which sets a plot size of 14 inches wide by 11 inches high:

Enter the Size or Width,Height (in INCHES): **14,11**

The plot size entered using these values is stored as the User size; it is remembered as the default, and it will be included in the next display:

Size	Width	Height
A	10.50	8.00
B	16.00	10.00
C	21.00	16.00
D	33.00	21.00
E	43.00	33.00
MAX	44.72	35.31
USER	14.00	11.00

Enter the Size or Width,Height (in INCHES) <USER>:

Only one User plot size is stored by AutoCAD. You may change the User size by entering new width and height values at the prompt. Once AutoCAD has stored a User size, you may select it by entering **User** at the prompt.

You may also enter a plot size that is larger than the listed maximum. AutoCAD will appear to accept whatever plot size you enter, and just before plotting, it will display the following message:

Plotting area exceeds plotter maximum

Nonetheless, AutoCAD will attempt to plot at the size you have entered. If your size is too large for the plotter, the plotted output will appear enlarged, and if some entities are thus located beyond the maximum plot size, they will not be plotted.

Rotating Plan-View Plots

If you are plotting or printing a plan view of your drawing, AutoCAD will allow you to change the orientation of the plot. This can be helpful if your plotter normally plots in portrait (upright) orientation, and you wish to plot in landscape (horizontal) orientation, or vice versa.

Prior to Release 11, 3-D views could not be rotated. However, you could use the Dview command to change the rotation of the display and then plot the display.

Beginning with Release 11, this restriction is removed; both 3-D and 2-D plots can be rotated. In addition, you can rotate plots at angles of 90, 180, or 270 degrees by entering the desired angle of rotation. If you do not wish to rotate the plot, enter a rotation angle of zero. The old responses of **Y** for "Rotate the plot 90 degrees" and **N** for "not rotated" will work in Release 11, just as they did in earlier versions.

Pen Width

AutoCAD expects that all pens will have a uniform width. In order to "fill" wide lines and solid filled areas, it will adjust for wide lines and solid-filled entities by moving the pen back and forth in a series of stepwise motions. In order to accomplish this accurately, AutoCAD prompts for the width of the pen you are using:

Pen width <0.010>:

It uses the width of the pen to calculate its stepwise increases in motion. If you enter a pen width that is larger than the actual pen width, AutoCAD may not lift the pen between entities, believing that the pen is so wide that an up-motion command is unnecessary.

If your pens are in millimeters and you have selected inches as your plot dialog units, you must convert your metric pen width to inches in order to respond to this prompt.

Area Fill Boundaries

With a pen plotter, AutoCAD normally draws wide polylines, traces, and filled solids as outlines, and fills them in using back-and-forth pen strokes. Because AutoCAD normally moves the pen along the outer boundaries of the entity, the line of ink actually extends one-half of a pen width on either side of the entity boundary. In most drawings, this distance is so slight as to be negligible. However, certain applications must adhere to extremely close tolerances. In these applications, AutoCAD can pull in the pen one-half of the pen width, so that the line of ink extends just to the boundary edge. To adjust the area fill boundaries, enter **Y** in response to the following prompt:

Adjust area fill boundaries for pen width?

If you must adjust area fill boundaries, be sure that you have entered the exact pen width.

If your plot includes filled circles (created using the Donut command with the inner diameter set to zero—refer to Chapter 9 for details), you may find that answering **Y** to this prompt causes filled circles to be drawn with a small open area in the center.

If your solid-filled circles are left open because of the area fill setting, try drawing a point or small series of concentric circles at the center of the solid-filled circle. If the filled circle is very small, you may wish to substitute a series of concentric circles to produce the filled circle, instead of using the Donut command. This has the added advantage of plotting much faster than filled circles created using Donut, in addition to solving the problem of that tiny open space.

Plotting with Hidden Lines Removed

If you are plotting a 3-D view of a drawing, you can generate the plot with hidden lines suppressed. AutoCAD prompts:

Remove hidden lines?

If you respond **Y,** AutoCAD will suppress the hidden lines in your drawing. This process is similar to the process of generating a screen display of your drawing with hidden lines suppressed; if the drawing is relatively complex, the plot will take considerably more time than a plot including hidden lines. Refer to the Hide command in Chapter 11 for details, tips, and warnings regarding hidden-line suppression.

Scaling the Plot

AutoCAD drawings are usually constructed "life-size"—that is, in real-world scale. Later, when it is time to plot, they are scaled to whatever proportions are appropriate to produce the final plotted drawing. This system allows for greater ease and flexibility, but can take a little time to get used to at first, especially if you are accustomed to calculating scale while drawing.

For example, when drawing a line representing a wall that is 20 feet long, the following dialog will do the trick. (In this example, AutoCAD's units are assumed to be feet and inches.)

Command: **Line**
From point: **1,1**
To point: **@20'<0**
To point: **(press Enter)**

Refer to Chapter 8 for details regarding the Line command, and Chapter 5 for details regarding drawing units and coordinate entry methods.

The line is now stored in AutoCAD's drawing database as a 20-foot-long line. Among other things, this makes it possible to use AutoCAD's automatic dimensioning feature to add dimension text and leader lines, and to scale the drawing to whatever scale ratio you choose at plot time.

This method works well enough until you add text-based entities, such as explanatory text, leaders, and dimensions, to the drawing. At this point, you must again think in terms of scale while drawing. For example, if you intend to plot at a scale of ¼" to the foot, and you would like your text to appear ¼" high in the plotted output, the text in your drawing should be drawn one foot high to ensure it is scaled back down to the correct height at plot time.

AutoCAD will scale a plotted drawing by automatically calculating the plotted length of lines according to the scale parameters you specify. You enter these parameters by indicating to AutoCAD the desired ratio of *plotted inches*—or *millimeters,* if you have chosen to use millimeters—to *drawing units.*

AutoCAD prompts for the scale factor as follows:

Specify scale by entering:
Plotted Inches = Drawing Units or Fit or ?:

If your intention was to plot the 20-foot wall line at a scale of ¼ inch to 1 foot, you could enter any of the following responses to the above prompt:

1/4″ = 1′
1/4″ = 12
0.25 = 12

All of the above express the scale ratio of ¼ inch to 1 foot. Having entered the above scale, you can then expect the wall line to be 5 inches long when AutoCAD plots it.

You may enter the scale ratio in the current format set with AutoCAD's Units command, or in decimal drawing units regardless of the current units format.

Here are a few common plotting scales that could be entered using decimal drawing units:

1 = 1	Real-world scale; one to one
0.5 = 1	Half scale
0.25 = 1	Quarter scale
0.25 = 12	¼ inch to 1 foot, or current equivalent
0.125 = 12	⅛ inch to 1 foot, or current equivalent
0.0625 = 12	1/16 inch to 1 foot, or current equivalent
1 = 48	Same as ¼ inch to 1 foot, multiplied out to whole numbers
1 = 96	Same as ⅛ inch to 1 foot, multiplied out to whole numbers

You may also specify the scale by typing **F.** If you do, AutoCAD will "fit" the plotted output; that is, AutoCAD will scale it to whatever scale is required to fit it within the chosen drawing size.

Some scaling inaccuracies may occur if your plotter needs to be *calibrated.* If necessary, refer to Chapter 3 for details on how to calibrate your plotter to reflect scale ratios accurately.

Effective Plotting Area

After all the plotting parameters have been set up, AutoCAD displays a message similar to the following, indicating the actual size of the plot:

Effective plotting area: 8.00 wide by 11.00 high

This message indicates what rectangular area of the plotting surface will be encompassed by the plot.

If you have indicated a specific plot scale parameter, the actual plot may be too large for the drawing surface. In such a case, AutoCAD will plot from the drawing origin point and include whatever part of the drawing will fit on the drawing surface, leaving out lines that extend beyond the plotter's maximum plot area. Conversely, the specified scale may result in a plot that is much smaller than the plotting surface, leaving unused space.

Pen-Plotter Setup

Immediately following the "Effective plotting area" prompt, if you are using a pen plotter, AutoCAD prompts you to prepare the plotter:

Position paper in plotter.
Press RETURN to continue or S to Stop for hardware setup

If you need to connect the plotter to a shared I/O port or load paper into the plotter, you may do so now; when the plotter is ready, press the Enter key to have AutoCAD begin plotting the drawing. If you enter **S**, AutoCAD displays the following message:

Do hardware setup now.
Press RETURN to continue:

At first glance, entering **S** may seem like an unnecessary extra step, since AutoCAD is already paused and you can load paper and ready the plotter while the first message is displayed on the screen. However, AutoCAD provides the S option because it always begins a plot by sending a reset code to the plotter. This reset code may disable any special controls you have set up using your plotter's control panel. If you type **S**, AutoCAD sends the reset code to the plotter and then pauses. Now you may adjust your plotter using the control panel if you like, and then press Enter to begin the plot.

If you are using a printer plotter, AutoCAD does not include the S option, but will pause with the following message:

Position paper in plotter.
Press RETURN to continue:

AutoCAD assumes that the printer plotter is connected to the I/O port for the computer's primary list device (called LPT1 on most systems). If your printer plotter is not connected to this port, you may redirect the output to another port when you configure AutoCAD, or you may redirect it by using the operating system's MODE command just before initializing AutoCAD. Refer to Chapter 3 for details regarding AutoCAD installation and configuration, and consult your operating system's documentation for more information on redirecting the output.

You may begin the printer plot by pressing Enter.

Canceling the Plot

At any time during the plot setup or the plotting process, you may cancel the operation by pressing Ctrl-C. AutoCAD displays the message

```
Plot canceled.
Press RETURN to continue:
```

if you are using a pen plotter, or

```
Printer Plot canceled.
Press RETURN to continue:
```

if you are using a printer plotter.

When this message appears, you may press Enter. After doing so, you will return to the drawing editor or the Main Menu, depending on where you were when you began the plotting process.

If you cancel a plot after AutoCAD has already begun sending information to the plotting device, the plot may not stop immediately. This happens if your plotting device is connected to a hardware buffer, is using a software buffer, or has a large built-in buffer. Some buffers and plotting devices allow you to clear the buffer from the computer keyboard or control panel. If you are not sure that you can do this, consult your hardware documentation or ask your dealer.

How AutoCAD Plots

When sending output to the printer plotter, AutoCAD scans the drawing in thin horizontal lines, converting each line to a series of dots that represent that portion of the drawing. Each line is sent to the printer plotter and the drawing is constructed from top to bottom.

When using a pen plotter, the process is more complex. AutoCAD scans the drawing database and translates drawing-entity information into pen motions (or a combination of pen and paper motions).

In order to reduce the time spent plotting with a pen plotter, AutoCAD will calculate *pen-motion optimization,* which reduces unnecessary pen motion between entities when the pen is in the "up" position. This process is internal and completely automatic. However, if you watch your pen plotter closely while it is plotting, you may see what appear to be odd pen motions, such as entities that are drawn before previous entities are completed, or entities drawn in ways that do not relate to the way they were created in the drawing editor.

If you so desire, when you configure AutoCAD for your plotter, you can control the amount of pen-motion optimization AutoCAD uses. Refer to Chapter 3 for details.

Plotting with Release 10 and later

When plotting with Release 10 and later, change the UCS to the world coordinate system before plotting. This makes it easier to position the plot exactly where you would like it on the plotting surface. If you name the current UCS, you can easily return to it after plotting, using the UCS Restore command. Refer to Chapter 5 for details regarding coordinate systems and to Chapter 6 for details on the UCS command.

PAPER SPACE

Release 11 introduces a new display and plotting feature to AutoCAD: *paper space.* Paper space is similar to AutoCAD's multi-viewport display feature but adds some important new options and restrictions.

In Release 11, AutoCAD's traditional drawing environment is referred to as *model space* in order to distinguish it from paper space. Paper space allows you to display several different viewpoints of the same drawing on the screen. Unlike traditional viewports in model space, you can move, scale, overlap, and otherwise arrange the location and size of paper-space viewports as you like. In addition, when you are working in paper space, these multiple viewports can be plotted just as they are displayed on the screen.

Paper space offers considerably more display options for the imaginative AutoCAD user. Its primary purpose is to allow you to produce multiple views of various parts of a drawing on a single hard-copy plot. Since most users will avail themselves of paper-space features for producing plotted output, a general description of paper space is taken up here. Details on display commands specific to paper space are discussed in Chapter 11.

Figure 12.4 illustrates how multiple views of a single drawing may be arranged and subsequently plotted using paper space.

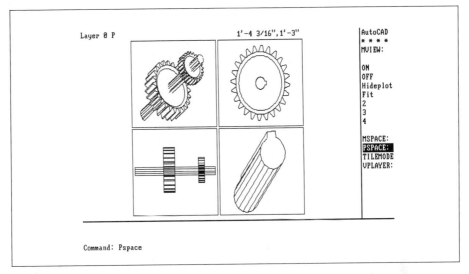

Figure 12.4: Different drawing views in paper space. This figure illustrates a typical paper-space configuration. Four viewports were created in paper space using the Mview command. Each viewport was then scaled slightly with the Scale command to create the small space between them. Switching to model space, the viewing angle was changed and selected layers were frozen in each viewport, arriving at the display shown.

Establishing Paper Space

To enter paper space from the standard AutoCAD drawing environment, set the value of the TILEMODE system variable to zero or off. The value of TILE-MODE may be changed by invoking Tilemode from the Command prompt. When AutoCAD prompts for a new value for TILEMODE, enter **0** to turn it off, or **1** to turn TILEMODE on.

When TILEMODE is zero, AutoCAD enters paper space—this means you may now create *non-tiled* (overlapping) viewports. To leave paper space and return to model space, set TILEMODE to 1—this means that you may now create only *tiled* (non-overlapping) viewports.

When you first enter paper space, the drawing editor appears blank. You cannot view any of the drawing's entities until you first create a paper-space viewport for them. To create viewports in paper space, use the Mview command, discussed in detail in Chapter 11. The Mview command creates paper-space viewports using command options similar to AutoCAD's Vports command, also discussed in Chapter 11.

For example, to create a single viewport in paper space, invoke the Mview command and pick two points to designate the opposite corners of a rectangle.

When you create viewports in paper space, the current model-space view of the drawing appears in each viewport. Viewports are always quadrilateral. The maximum number of viewports you may display simultaneously is limited by your hardware configuration. You can determine this maximum by viewing the setting of the MAXACTVP system variable.

Once you have created the paper-space viewports, you may edit them as you would any AutoCAD entity, although while in paper space, you may not edit the drawing entities displayed within those viewports. You may move, copy, erase, rotate, and stretch paper-space viewports. You may also change the entity properties associated with the viewports, such as color, linetype, and layer location, until the appearance of each is to your liking. Paper-space viewports respond to normal AutoCAD editing commands.

You turn individual viewports on or off with the Mview command, and you can selectively control the visibility of layers in each viewport using the Vplayer command. You may plot with hidden lines removed in one viewport and not in others. Refer to Chapter 11 for details regarding these commands and individual viewport settings.

When you have constructed a satisfactory configuration of paper-space viewports, name and save the configuration using the View Save command. Thereafter, you may use the View Restore option from either model or paper space to return to this configuration. When restoring a paper space configuration from model space, you are switched automatically to paper space.

You can also create new entities—for example, polylines and text—in paper space. The entities you create in paper space are visible only in paper space, and you may select, edit, and plot them only when you are in paper space.

You cannot use the Dview, Plan, or Vpoint commands while editing in paper space.

Editing Entities in Paper Space

It is possible to edit your drawing's entities while the current paper space configuration remains on screen. To do so, invoke the Mspace command to switch to model space temporarily. AutoCAD will highlight one of the visible viewports, and you may edit entities within that viewport as if you were in the drawing editor. Figure 12.5 illustrates this.

You may use any of the paper-space viewports to edit entities after invoking the Mspace command; however, only one paper-space viewport is available, or *active*, at any one time when editing in model space. AutoCAD indicates the available viewport by displaying a highlighted box around it. You may change the active viewport

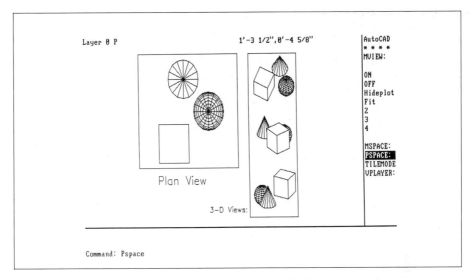

FIGURE 12.5: Editing entities in model space and paper space. This figure contains four viewports in paper space, each with a different viewing angle on the drawing. Note, though, that it appears as if there were only two viewports, with one showing three viewing angles. The borders of the three viewports on the right were suppressed by assigning the viewports to a frozen layer. Although this hid the viewport border, the drawing entities themselves remained visible. Finally, a large border was drawn in paper space around all three, using the Pline command. The text was also added in paper space.

by moving the pointing device cursor—a small arrow—into the desired viewport and pressing the pick button. If you have trouble selecting a viewport with the pointing device, type Ctrl-V. Each time you type Ctrl-V, AutoCAD will highlight viewports in turn until you reach the one you want.

When you are editing in model space, changes made to entities in one viewport will be reflected in other visible viewports as well.

Plotting in Paper Space

To plot in paper space, either save the drawing while in paper space and plot from the main menu, or invoke the Plot or Prplot command while in the drawing editor.

Plotting options available in paper space are the same as those in model space, as described earlier in this chapter. Exercise caution if you select the Extents or Window options, as the coordinates used are relative to paper space only, which may be different from the same coordinates applied to model space.

Tips for Using Paper Space

When editing paper-space viewports:

- To change the size and area of a paper-space viewport, invoke the Stretch command and use a crossing window to select one or two corners of the viewport.

- When you freeze a paper-space viewport's layer, the entities within that viewport remain visible but the viewport outline disappears. Thus, to make the outline of a paper-space viewport invisible, invoke the Chprop command and move the viewport to a frozen layer, or use the Layer command to freeze the viewport's layer. You cannot freeze the current layer, however.

- If you want to edit the viewport later, you must first thaw its layer in order to select it for editing.

When creating multiple viewports:

- Establish a flexible view of the drawing in model space first, to reduce editing time after the viewports are created.

- Using Mview's Fit option can make multiple viewports difficult to select afterward. Consider using the two-point option if you know that you will be moving or resizing the viewports after you create them.

- The Copy Multiple command, as well as the Array command, are useful tools when constructing multiple viewports. Copying viewports also copies their default display states, such as Hideplot. Refer to the discussion of the Mview command in chapter 11 for details regarding default display states.

When switching to model space:

- You may move between viewports during editing commands, while building a selection set of entities to edit or selecting displacement points. However, certain display commands will not allow you to move between viewports until the command has completed its processing; these are: Dview, Grid, Pan, Snap, Vplayer, Vpoint, and Zoom.

- To display paper-space viewports with hidden lines removed, switch to model space and invoke the Hide command for each viewport. Afterwards, use the Mslide command to record the hidden-line display for faster recall later.

- If you are using the keyboard, the following command aliases in the standard version of ACAD.PGP will simplify switching between model and paper space: **MS** for model space and **PS** for paper space.

When plotting in paper space:

- Although you are limited in the number of viewports you may see on the screen at once, you are not limited in the number of viewports you can actually plot. If you have created more viewports than your hardware can can display, you must turn off some viewports in order to see others. Alternatively, you can explicitly turn on some viewports, and AutoCAD will arbitrarily turn off others as necessary.

- When you are ready to plot, turn all desired viewports on. Even though some may not be visible on the screen, they will still plot.

- If you have edited entities in model space, be sure you switch back to paper space before you start your plot. Otherwise, you will be plotting only the current viewport, not the paper space display.

- AutoCAD will *not* plot paper-space viewports that have been explicitly turned off.

- Do not answer **Y** to the hidden-line option of the plot command. This option applies only to plots made from model space. To produce a hidden-line plot in paper space, invoke the Mview command, select the desired viewports, and use the Hideplot option to indicate that hidden lines are to be removed when plotting.

PART **V**

CUSTOMIZING AUTOCAD

The real power of AutoCAD lies in its ability to adapt. Rather than forcing you to change your drafting style to conform to its specifications, Auto-CAD allows you to change its specifications to suit your drafting style. Chapter 13 describes the numerous system variables AutoCAD provides; many of these variables can be changed during the drawing session, or even during the execution of commands, offering you a great deal of flexibility while creating or revising drawings. Chapter 14 explains how to create customized screen, tablet, pull-down, or icon menus that can display and execute any set of individual AutoCAD commands, arranged and organized as you see fit. In addition, Chapter 14 explains how to create custom command macros that allow you to invoke several commands in sequence, further simplifying and speeding up your drafting session. Chapter 15 shows you how to create shape files for storing and inserting frequently used symbols into your drawings, as well as how to create customized text fonts.

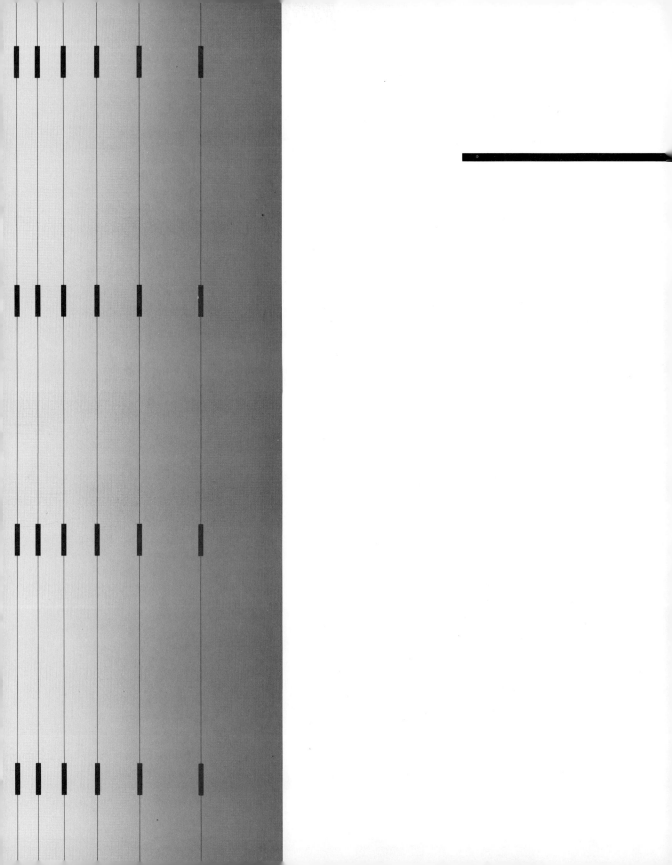

Managing Variables

MANAGING VARIABLES

AutoCAD uses a large set of *system variables* that keep track of many default settings for its features. A system variable is a named portion of memory that stores data affecting an aspect of AutoCAD's functioning. System variables keep AutoCAD as flexible as possible, making it useful in the widest possible variety of applications.

The names of system variables are standard and always remain the same; the data they contain will change, sometimes from one user's application to another, or sometimes from one drawing session to another.

PURPOSES OF SYSTEM VARIABLES

Using system variables, it is possible to set up a variety of different default drawing environments. This allows you to choose an optimal setting for producing any given drawing.

For example, some system variables control whether drawing aids are currently in effect. Other system variables store data that directly affects the performance of AutoCAD commands—for example, how text is copied when using the Mirror command, the density of polygon meshes, or the visibility of block attribute information. Still other system variables store more general information: the amount of time spent in the drawing, or the subdirectory location of the drawing on the hard disk.

HOW SYSTEM VARIABLES ARE CHANGED

In AutoCAD Version 2.5 and later, the data in most system variables can be changed directly using AutoCAD's Setvar command (described later in this chapter). This allows the user maximum control over AutoCAD's functioning, so that AutoCAD itself will be as helpful as possible for a particular application. The Setvar command is also *transparent,* meaning that you can temporarily suspend another AutoCAD command, change the data in a system variable to something more useful, and resume the suspended command at the point of interruption.

Beginning with Release 11, it is possible to change the values of non-read-only system variables by typing the variable name at the command prompt. The one exception to this is the UCSICON variable. The Ucsicon command makes changes to the UCSICON variable but displays a variety of options unacceptable to the variable. To change UCSICON directly, use the Setvar command.

System variable names cannot be entered transparently from the command prompt.

This degree of flexibility in controlling AutoCAD's functioning carries with it certain destructive capabilities as well, since a change to some system variables at the wrong time could bring AutoCAD to a complete standstill. AutoCAD prevents this by declaring some system variables to be *read-only,* meaning that the data they contain cannot be changed directly by the operator. However, this data can usually be changed safely by invoking AutoCAD commands. For example, the lower-left and upper-right corners of the drawing limits are stored in the read-only system variables named LIMMIN and LIMMAX. You cannot change their data using Setvar; you can, however, change their data by invoking the nontransparent Limits command and setting new drawing limits.

The data contained in system variables that are not read-only may also be changed using the Setvar function in AutoLISP. Another AutoLISP function, Getvar, will retrieve data stored in system variables (including those declared read-only); the data can then be saved to separate memory variables for whatever further processing you intend to do. You can change the data in many read-only system variables by using AutoLISP's Setvar function, then invoking the AutoCAD command that updates them from inside the routine. Refer to Chapters 16 and 17 for details regarding AutoLISP and its interaction with system variables.

The data in some system variables may be updated repeatedly as certain AutoCAD commands are invoked. For example, during a drawing session, AutoCAD always stores the coordinates of the last selected point. As you can imagine, the data held in this particular system variable is updated constantly.

System variables beginning with the letters *DIM* are also called *dimension variables,* because their values affect the performance of AutoCAD's automatic dimensioning feature. Prior to Version 2.6, you could change their values only by entering the variable name at the "Dim:" prompt after invoking AutoCAD's Dim command. Beginning with Version 2.6, you can access dimension variables like other system variables.

DATA TYPES IN SYSTEM VARIABLES

Different system variables accept different types of data, but each system variable accepts only one type of data. System variables accept the following types of data:

Integers   These are whole numbers within a limited range. System variables using integers convey special meanings to AutoCAD. For example, some system variables control whether certain AutoCAD features, such as grid display and dynamic dragging, are active. A value of 1 indicates that the program feature is active. A value of 0 disables the feature.

Many dimension variables accept only integer values of 0 and 1. When the Setvar command is used to enter values for these dimension variables, either 0 or 1 may be supplied. Alternatively, you may enter **on** (for 1) or **off** (for zero).

Integer Bit-Codes Some integer system variables accept *bit-code* data. Bit-code integers have meanings that can be combined by adding the integer values together.

For example, the OSMODE system variable controls which object-snap modes are currently active. When object snap is set using the OSMODE system variable, each object-snap mode is assigned an integer: 1 for endpoint, 2 for midpoint, 4 for center point, 8 for node point, and so on.

However, object-snap modes may be active in any combination. Thus, you may activate more than one object-snap mode by setting the value of OSMODE to equal the total of one or more of the valid object-snap integers; for example, 3 for endpoint/midpoint, 6 for midpoint/center point, 15 for endpoint/midpoint/center point/node point, and so on.

If you attempt to set OSMODE to an integer that does not total some combination of valid object-snap integers, AutoCAD will ignore it. For more details regarding OSMODE, refer to the summary of system variables later in this chapter.

Coordinate Points This is a list of two or three real numbers (depending on whether the point is 2-D or 3-D), separated by commas. Point data is normally displayed in the numeric format set by the Units command (see Chapter 6).

Real Numbers These are numbers that contain decimal points. System variables that contain real numbers will accept integers, but will convert them to their decimal equivalents.

Strings A string is any series of alphanumeric characters, including punctuation and spaces, that will not be used for computational purposes. String data is displayed within in quotation marks. All AutoCAD system variables that contain string data are read-only.

This chapter summarizes all of AutoCAD's system variables, what data is valid for each, by what means their data may be changed, and how changes to their data affect AutoCAD's performance. Following is a brief discussion of the Setvar command, through which you control the data in most system variables.

SETVAR

Changes the data contained in AutoCAD's system variables, except those declared read-only.

VERSIONS

Version 2.5 and later. Whenever the Setvar command is mentioned in this chapter, AutoCAD Version 2.5 or later is assumed.

Versions prior to 2.5 use AutoLISP's Setvar function. Refer to Chapter 17 for details regarding AutoLISP functions.

The availability of different system variables varies from version to version of AutoCAD. To find out what system variables are available for your version, print the list of system variables that is displayed in response to the Setvar ? command, or consult the summary of system variables in this chapter.

In Release 11 and later, the Setvar command is useful when performing transparent changes to system variables that are not read-only while other commands are in progress. When you want to make a change at the command prompt, simply enter the variable name and the new setting. Setvar can be used with the ? option to list all variables, and Wildcard characters can be used to narrow the scope of the listing.

COMMAND OPTIONS

? Enter a question mark to receive a list of the system variables that are available for your version of AutoCAD. The list will also show the current data contained in each variable, and whether the variable is read-only. If you like, you can toggle the printer echo on (press Ctrl-Q) and send the list to your printing device for later reference. Be sure to toggle the printer echo off—press Ctrl-Q again—after the list is complete.

Variable Name Enter the name of the system variable whose data you wish to change, followed by the new data.

USAGE

To change the value of a system variable, invoke the Setvar command. Auto-CAD will prompt for the name of the system variable whose data you intend to change, and the new data:

Variable Name or ?:

If Setvar was invoked previously during the drawing session, the name of the previously selected system variable is presented as the default response the next time you invoke the Setvar command. This makes short-term, temporary changes to system-variable data a little more convenient.

After you enter the name of the system variable, AutoCAD prompts:

New value for (*chosen system variable*):

The currently stored data is presented as the default response. After you enter the new data (or press Enter to keep the current data), AutoCAD updates the system variable and returns to the Command prompt. The stored data and the name of the system variable are remembered and presented as the default response the next time you invoke Setvar during the drawing session.

If you attempt to enter incorrect data, such as a real number for a system variable that requires an integer, AutoCAD will reject the data with an error message and not update the system variable.

You can update some system variables while in the middle of other AutoCAD commands. To do so, invoke the Setvar command preceded by an apostrophe, as follows:

'Setvar

AutoCAD will temporarily suspend the current command and display the normal prompt sequence for the Setvar command. After the Setvar command has completed processing, AutoCAD returns you to the original command at the point of departure.

If you invoke the Setvar command and enter the name of any read-only system variable, AutoCAD will display the data but will not allow you to make any changes.

> *Warning:* When you use the Setvar command transparently, some changes to system variables will not be reflected in the display until the conclusion of the command. Other changes to system variables, such as changes to the grid display, require a redraw or regen before they are reflected in the display. Where such anomalies occur, they are mentioned in the system variable summary in this chapter.

SAMPLE DIALOG

The following dialog uses the Setvar command to interrupt the Line command and turn off the display of point-marker blips, by changing the value of the BLIPMODE system variable from 1 to 0. Notice that while the same thing can be accomplished using the Blipmode command, Setvar is transparent, while Blipmode is not.

Command: **Line**
From point: **'Setvar**
>>Variable name or ?: **BLIPMODE**
>>New value for BLIPMODE <1>: **0**
Resuming LINE command.
From point:

SYSTEM VARIABLE SUMMARY

The following entries summarize all AutoCAD system variables through Release 11. Each entry includes the earliest version in which the variable appears (with modifications made to later versions noted), the type of data it accepts, the effect of the variable on AutoCAD, the range of valid data it may contain, the default (if applicable), and whether the variable is read-only. They are arranged here according to broad categories of purpose.

BLOCK ATTRIBUTE DEFAULTS

Block attributes have many different configurable parameters, such as visibility, preset data, and verification, controllable by means of the Attdef command. (Refer to Chapter 18 for details regarding block attributes.) The following system variables provide an alternate means for controlling those features as well as other features—whether attribute data is requested at all, and how AutoCAD will prompt for attribute data.

AFLAGS

Controls the block attribute parameters used by the Attdef command (Chapter 18).

When stored in AFLAGS, the following integers set the indicated block attribute parameter to Y:

1 = Invisible
2 = Constant
4 = Verify
8 = Preset (Release 9 and later)

More than one parameter may be set to Y by adding the appropriate integers together; for example:

3 = Invisible/Constant
5 = Invisible/Verify

6 = Constant/Verify
7 = Invisible/Constant/Verify
9 = Invisible/Preset

EARLIEST VERSION

2.0

DATA TYPE

Integer bit-code

DEFAULT

0

READ-ONLY

No

ATTDIA

Controls whether block attribute entry is made via a series of prompts on the command line, or a dialog box.

When stored in ATTDIA, the following integers set the indicated features:

0 = Attribute data dialog via command-line prompts
1 = Attribute data entry via dialog box

EARLIEST VERSION

Release 9. Requires Advanced User Interface.

DATA TYPE

Integer

DEFAULT

0

READ-ONLY

No

ATTMODE

Controls the visible display of block attributes, allowing you to turn them all on or off, or to display them according to their individual attribute flags.

When stored in ATTMODE, the following integers set the indicated features:

0 = All attributes invisible
1 = Attributes display according to the attribute flags set when they were created
2 = All attributes visible

Other integers will be stored, but AutoCAD will ignore them.

EARLIEST VERSION

2.0

DATA TYPE

Integer

DEFAULT

1

READ-ONLY

No

ATTREQ

Enables or disables requests for block attribute data when inserting blocks with attributes. If disabled, all attributes will be given default values as supplied when they were defined.

When stored in ATTREQ, the following integers set the indicated features:

0 = Disable requests for attribute data
1 = Enable prompts (or dialog box; see ATTDIA system variable) for attribute data

EARLIEST VERSION

Release 9

DATA TYPE

Integer

DEFAULT

1

READ-ONLY

No

CONFIGURATION DEFAULTS

These system variables store data related to many of AutoCAD's configurable drawing defaults, such as drawing limits, that are normally set using AutoCAD commands. Some of these system variables are read-only, while others may be changed using Setvar and AutoLISP. Each is noted accordingly.

EXPERT

Suppresses the extra confirmation prompts ("Are you sure?") for commands that can produce unusual situations or overwrite existing data; for example, if EXPERT is set to 1, the prompt

Do you really want to turn the current layer off?

is suppressed. When suppressed, the command behaves as if Y were given in response to the prompt.

The following integers set the indicated features:

0 = All extra confirmation prompts are issued

1 = Suppress prompts in Layer command and all "About to regen, Proceed?" prompts

2 = Suppress the above, plus the safety prompts in the Block, Wblock, and Save commands, when previously stored data is about to be overwritten

3 = (Version 2.6 +) Suppress the above, plus safety prompts in the Linetype command when previously loaded linetypes are about to be overwritten

4 = (Release 10 +) Suppress the above, plus safety prompts in the UCS and Vports commands when previously saved UCS's and named viewport configurations are about to be overwritten

5 = (Release 11 +) Suppress the above, plus safety prompts that relate to dimensioning styles, when overwriting existing styles using Dim Save or when overriding dimensioning variables, will override existing dimension styles. Refer to associative dimensioning in Chapter 21 for details regarding dimension styles.

EARLIEST VERSION

2.1

DATA TYPE

Integer

DEFAULT

0

READ-ONLY

No

EXTMAX

Stores the coordinate location of the upper-right corner of the drawing extents (the smallest possible rectangle that encloses all existing entities in the drawing). The value of this system variable is used when zooming or plotting the current drawing extents.

These numbers are displayed in AutoCAD's current units format. (Refer to the Units command in Chapter 6 for details.)

EXTMAX is updated whenever the drawing extents are enlarged, or when the Zoom All or Zoom Extents command (Chapter 11) is invoked.

EARLIEST VERSION

All

DATA TYPE

A 2-D coordinate point, or in AutoCAD Release 10 and later, a 3-D point

READ-ONLY

Yes

EXTMIN

Stores the coordinate location of the lower-left corner of the drawing extents (the smallest possible rectangle that encloses all existing entities in the drawing). The value of this system variable is used when zooming or plotting the current drawing extents.

These numbers are displayed in AutoCAD's current units format. (Refer to the Units command in Chapter 6 for details.)

EXTMIN is updated whenever the drawing extents are enlarged, or when the Zoom All or Zoom Extents command (Chapter 11) is invoked.

EARLIEST VERSION

All

DATA TYPE

Coordinate point

READ-ONLY

Yes

FILEDIA

Controls whether command options that manipulate files—such as Mslide and Vslide—are made via command line prompts or a dialogue box.

When stored in FILEDIA, the following integers set the indicated features:

0 = File data dialogue via command line prompts
1 = File data entry via dialogue box.

EARLIEST VERSION

Release 11. Requires Advanced User Interface.

DATA TYPE

Integer

DEFAULT

1

READ-ONLY

No

FLATLAND

Controls the implementation of Release 10's 3-D features. If FLATLAND is enabled, AutoCAD Release 10 performs with only a subset of 3-D features, thus becoming functionally identical to Release 9. If FLATLAND is not enabled, Release 10's 3-D features are fully implemented.

FLATLAND exists because there are a few cases in which changes made to AutoCAD commands, AutoLISP functions, system variables, and DXF file output in Release 10 may cause compatibility problems with some macros, AutoLISP routines, and other third-party software written for Release 9. Enabling FLATLAND allows these third-party applications to work.

However, the functional changes between Releases 9 and 10 are minimal, and if you do experience compatibility problems with third-party software, you should update these applications as soon as possible. FLATLAND is available in Release 11, but may be set only to zero. All other changes are ignored.

When stored in FLATLAND, the following integers set the indicated features:

0 = Enable full implementation of Release 10's 3-D features
1 = Disable Release 10 implementation; act like Release 9

EARLIEST VERSION

Release 10

DATA TYPE

Integer

DEFAULT

0

READ-ONLY

No

INSBASE

Stores the location of the insertion base point, which is used when the drawing file is inserted into another drawing.

In Release 10 and later, this system variable may contain a 3-D point. The values are displayed and may be entered using the current units format as set with AutoCAD's Units command (Chapter 6).

EARLIEST VERSION

All

DATA TYPE

Coordinate point

DEFAULT

0,0,0

READ-ONLY

No

LIMCHECK

Controls AutoCAD's drawing limits checking; when limits-checking is enabled, AutoCAD will not allow drawing entities to be created outside the boundaries set by the drawing limits. Refer to the system variables LIMMAX and LIMMIN, and the Limits command in Chapter 6, for details regarding the drawing limits.

When stored in LIMCHECK, the following integers set the indicated features:

0 = Limits-checking disabled; entities may be created outside the drawing limits
1 = Limits-checking enabled; entities may not be created outside the drawing limits

EARLIEST VERSION

All

DATA TYPE

Integer

DEFAULT

0

READ-ONLY

No

LIMMAX

Stores the 2-D coordinate location of the upper-right corner of the drawing limits (the rectangle that defines the outermost boundaries of the drawing). The value of this system variable is used when invoking the Zoom All command (Chapter 11) or when plotting the current drawing limits (Chapter 12).

These numbers are displayed in AutoCAD's current units format for coordinate points. (Refer to the Units command in Chapter 6 for details.)

EARLIEST VERSION

All

DATA TYPE

Coordinate point

DEFAULT

12.0,9.0

READ-ONLY

Yes

LIMMIN

Stores the 2-D coordinate location of the lower-left corner of the drawing limits (the rectangle that defines the outermost boundaries of the drawing). The value of this system variable is used when invoking the Zoom All command (Chapter 11) or when plotting the current drawing limits (Chapter 12).

These numbers are displayed in AutoCAD's current units format for coordinate points. (Refer to the Units command in Chapter 6 for details.)

EARLIEST VERSION

All

DATA TYPE

Coordinate point

DEFAULT

0,0

READ-ONLY

No

LTSCALE

Contains a factor by which the sizes of noncontinuous-linetype definitions—that is, the lengths of dashes and spaces—are multiplied to remain proportional to the rest of the drawing.

The dashes and spaces in noncontinuous linetypes are usually defined so as to be comfortably readable in a drawing plotted at one-to-one scale. The value of LTSCALE is adjusted to accommodate the actual scale of the drawing.

For example, assume that you intend to plot a drawing at a scale of $1/4$ inch to 1 foot, and you have entered lines in real-world scale in AutoCAD. The program is therefore storing information that is 48 times as large as the final plotted output (12" $\div$ $1/4$" = 48).

If LTSCALE is set to a value of 1 under these circumstances, the dashes and spaces would be so small that the line would appear continuous. However, if you change the value of LTSCALE to 48, the line is scaled so as to render the dashes and spaces visible.

Bear in mind that LTSCALE does not change the linetype definitions or the settings of any other system variable; rather, it simply multiplies the linetype definitions loaded into the drawing.

A DIMSCALE value of 1 produces no changes to linetype definitions. LT-SCALE values greater than 1 increase the size of dashes and spaces, while values between 0 and 1 reduce those sizes.

Any positive real number may be used.

EARLIEST VERSION

2.0

DATA TYPE

Real number

DEFAULT

1 (no scaling; multiply by 1)

READ-ONLY

No

MAXACTVP

Indicates the maximum number of viewports that can simultaneously display entities on the screen.

The maximum number of entity-visible viewports depends on your display-hardware configuration. This variable is set to the legal maximum when you configure your display device. You can set this variable to a lower figure, but you may not set it to a number higher than your display configuration allows. For example, VGA-based display systems can support a maximum of sixteen entity-visible viewports at one time; you can therefore reset this variable to 15, but not to 17.

In paper space, you can create more viewports than the maximum, but any viewports created after the maximum has been reached will not show entities. They will still plot, however, as long as the viewport is turned on. Refer to the Mview command in Chapter 11 for details.

EARLIEST VERSION

Release 11

DATA TYPE

Integer

DEFAULT

Available maximum number of entity-visible viewports, as determined by display-hardware configuration

READ-ONLY

No

MAXSORT

Indicates the maximum number of named items (files, layers, blocks, views, and so forth) that AutoCAD will sort before they are displayed. If the number of named items is greater than this variable, sorting will not take place. MAX-SORT will store a value from zero (no sorting) to 32767. Values greater than this are not allowed; negative numbers are converted to their absolute value.

EARLIEST VERSION

Release 11

DATA TYPE

Integer

DEFAULT

200

READ-ONLY

No

MENUECHO

Controls the display of AutoCAD prompts and responses in the Command-prompt area, when commands and responses are invoked from a menu rather than from the keyboard.

The ^P symbol may be placed in a menu macro to enable the display of menu items and prompts when they have been suppressed.

In AutoCAD Version 2.5 and earlier, the following integers set the indicated features, when stored in MENUECHO:

0 = All AutoCAD commands, prompts, and user responses are displayed in the Command-prompt area when selected from menus
1 = Suppress the prompt-area display of items selected from menus
2 = Menu items are suppressed, and AutoCAD system prompts are suppressed when selected items and responses are both coming from the menu; responses are displayed
3 = Menu items, as well as AutoCAD system prompts and responses, are suppressed when coming from the menu

In Version 2.6 and later, this system variable was revised to accept bit-code data, using the following integer values:

1 = Suppress the prompt-area display of items selected using menus
2 = Suppress the display of items selected from menus, and suppress AutoCAD system prompts when responses come from a menu macro; responses are displayed
4 = Suppress ^P toggling of Command-prompt display

You may combine any of these values by adding them together. For example, to enable all of the above, set MENUECHO to 7.

In all versions of AutoCAD, you may force the display of all menu items, system prompts, and responses by setting MENUECHO to 0.

EARLIEST VERSION

All

DATA TYPE

Integer

DEFAULT

1

READ-ONLY

No

MENUNAME

Stores the name of the active screen/tablet menu. The current menu name is the only valid data for this system variable. The value may be read and stored to AutoLISP memory variables by means of AutoLISP's Getvar function. You can change it by calling the Menu command (Chapter 17).

EARLIEST VERSION

All

DATA TYPE

String

DEFAULT

"acad"

READ-ONLY

Yes

PFACEVMAX

Indicates the maximum number of vertices that may be entered before a 3-D face is created.

A 3-D face entity can have either three or four coplanar vertices. When you invoke the Pface command, AutoCAD prompts for a series of vertices. You may enter as many vertices as you like, but AutoCAD "builds" a series of three- and four-sided faces for you as you enter them. This system variable influences the face-construction mechanism; however, it is read-only and unchangeable in Release 11.

EARLIEST VERSION

Release 11

DATA TYPE

Integer

DEFAULT

4

READ-ONLY

Yes

PLATFORM

Records the current operating system configuration of AutoCAD. Platform is intended for use by AutoLISP and ADS developers whose applications must behave differently under different platforms. This variable allows the same program to choose between several functions by analyzing the strings they contain. AutoCAD may store the following strings in PLATFORM:

386 DOS Extender	Apollo Domain
Apple Macintosh	DEC VAXstation
DECstation	DOS
Sun 3	Sun 386i
Sun 4/SPARCstation	XENIX 386

EARLIEST VERSION

Release 11

DATA TYPE

String

DEFAULT

Dependent on the operating system configuration

READ-ONLY

Yes

POPUPS

Controls whether the menu bar, pull-down menus, icon menus, and dialog boxes are enabled, in display configurations that support the Advanced User

Interface. AutoCAD must be configured for a display driver that supports the Advanced User Interface (Chapter 3). POPUPS is set during the AutoCAD configuration process, and remains at that setting until the program is reconfigured for another display device (Chapter 3).

When stored in POPUPS, the following integers set the indicated features:

0 = Advanced User Interface features disabled
1 = Advanced User Interface features enabled

EARLIEST VERSION

Release 9

DATA TYPE

Integer

READ-ONLY

Yes

SCREENSIZE

Stores the horizontal and vertical pixel size of the graphics display screen, or the current viewport in Release 10 and later.

Data is stored in a coordinate point format. The first number represents the pixel size of the screen along the x-axis; the second, along the y-axis.

EARLIEST VERSION

All

DATA TYPE

Coordinate point

READ-ONLY

Yes

SHADEDGE

Controls the display of faces shaded with the Shade command. When stored in SHADEDGE, the following integers set the indicated features:

0 = Faces are filled in and shaded, edges are not highlighted. This produces a smoother looking surface but requires monitors with a 256-color display.

1 = Faces are filled in and shaded, edges are highlighted using the background screen color. This allows the visible portion of the wireframe model to be seen clearly. This also requires a 256-color display.

2 = Faces are not filled in or shaded, but will hide entities behind them. Edges are highlighted using their defined color properties. The effect is similar to hidden-line rendering with the Hide command. It will produce results more quickly than the Hide command, but some details may be lost. It is the preferred Shade setting for monochrome monitors. The effect of different settings of the SHADEDGE variable on a monochrome monitor can be seen in Chapter 11, Figure 11.23.

3 = Faces are filled in using their entity color, but are not shaded. Edges are highlighted using the background screen color. This will produce a filled-in rendering on color monitors that do not have 256-color display.

EARLIEST VERSION

Release 11

DATA TYPE

Integer

DEFAULT

Dependent on display configuration

READ-ONLY

No

SHADEDIF

Controls the degree of contrast in shaded renderings, using the Shade command. In order to provide shaded renderings on 256-color displays, AutoCAD assumes two default light sources: an ambient, overall light source and a diffused light aimed at the display from the current viewing angle. Although you cannot change the location of these default light sources, you can control their relative intensity by means of the SHADEDIF system variable. This variable accepts an integer from zero to 100 to represent the relative percentage of diffused light, with ambient light taking the remainder. As the the number in SHADEDIF gets higher, the contrast between lighter and darker portions of the drawing will be greater and the drawing surfaces will appear more reflective.

This variable has no effect if SHADEDGE is set to 2 or 3.

EARLIEST VERSION

Release 11

DATA TYPE

Integer

DEFAULT

70

READ-ONLY

No

TILEMODE

Controls access to AutoCAD's paper space. Refer to Chapter 12 for a detailed discussion of the features available in paper space. When stored in TILE-MODE, the following integers set the indicated features:

0 = Paper space is enabled. Viewports can be adjusted to any size and may overlap. Model space can be accessed within individual viewports using the Mspace command.

1 = Paper space is disabled. Only model space is accessible; viewports are *tiled,* that is, they fill the display screen and may not overlap.

EARLIEST VERSION

Release 11

DATA TYPE

Integer

DEFAULT

1

READ-ONLY

No

UNITMODE

Controls the display of numeric values. When stored in UNITMODE, the following integers set the indicated features:

0 = Displays fractional, feet-and-inches, and surveyor's units in standard AutoCAD format. For example, fifteen-and-a-half units will be displayed as: **15 ½**.

1 = Displays fractional, feet-and-inches, and surveyor's units in the same format used to input these values. At this setting, fifteen-and-a-half units will be displayed as: **15-½**.

To better observe the differences between these display formats, invoke the Units command with UNITMODE set to 1 and then to 0, and note the differences in the display of the format examples.

EARLIEST VERSION

Release 11

DATA TYPE

Integer

DEFAULT

0

READ-ONLY

No

CURVE AND MESH DEFAULTS

The following system variables control various default options for AutoCAD's special curve fitting and mesh features.

SPLFRAME

Controls whether the spline-curve frame (the original straight-segment polyline) remains visible on the screen. In Release 10 and later, SPLFRAME also controls the visibility of the original defining mesh of a fit-curve polygon mesh and the visibility of the invisible edges of 3-D faces. For details regarding polylines and polygon meshes, refer to Chapter 9, and to the PEdit command in Chapter 10.

When stored in SPLFRAME, the following integers set the indicated features:

0 = Do not display the original defining polylines and meshes, or the invisible edges of 3-D faces

1 = Display the original defining polylines and meshes, and the invisible edges of 3-D faces

Changing the value of these system variables will cause the appearance of the curved polylines to change when the drawing is regenerated.

EARLIEST VERSION

Release 9

DATA TYPE

Integer

DEFAULT

0

READ ONLY

No

SPLINESEGS

Controls the number of segments drawn between each vertex of a fit-curve spline frame. For details regarding spline frames, refer to the PEdit Spline command in Chapter 10.

If the value of SPLINESEGS is negative, then the spline curve is generated, and the segments of the spline curve are then treated as a polyline to which the Fit Curve option is applied. The result is an approximation of the spline curve using arcs rather than short line segments.

Any positive integer is valid, but the higher the integer, the higher the number of spline segments. This will make the resolution of the spline curve finer, but it will take longer to regenerate, and will occupy larger amounts of disk space. Therefore, set SPLINESEGS to the minimum value required to produce an acceptable curved line on your configuration.

Changing the value of SPLINESEGS will cause the appearance of the curved polylines to change when the drawing is regenerated.

EARLIEST VERSION

Release 9

DATA TYPE

Integer

DEFAULT

8

READ ONLY

No

SPLINETYPE

Controls the type of spline curve generated by the PEdit Spline command (Chapter 10).

When stored in SPLINETYPE, the following integers set the indicated features:

5 = Generate a quadratic B-spline curve
6 = Generate a cubic B-spline curve

Changing the value of this system variable will cause the appearance of the curved polylines to change when the drawing is regenerated.

EARLIEST VERSION

Release 10

DATA TYPE

Integer

DEFAULT

6

READ ONLY

No

SURFTAB1

Controls the number of tabulations along the edges of ruled surfaces. Specifically, this system variable controls:

- The number of lines connecting the two defining curves used in the Rulesurf command (Chapter 9).
- The number of vertices used in the M direction when generating polygon meshes with the Edgesurf and Revsurf commands (Chapter 9).
- The number of lines used to generate the ruled surface with the Tabsurf command (Chapter 9).

Any positive integer is valid. However, the higher the value of SURFTAB1, the finer the resolution of the resulting mesh or ruled surface. Meshes with very fine degrees of resolution take longer to regenerate, and greatly enlarge the size of the drawing file. Therefore, set SURFTAB1 to the minimum value required to generate an acceptable mesh for your application.

EARLIEST VERSION

Release 10

DATA TYPE

Integer

DEFAULT

6

READ-ONLY

No

SURFTAB2

Controls the number of vertices used in the N direction when generating polygon meshes with the Edgesurf and Revsurf commands (Chapter 9).

Any positive integer is valid. However, the higher the value of SURFTAB2, the finer the resolution of the resulting polygon mesh. Meshes with very fine degrees of resolution take longer to regenerate, and greatly enlarge the size of the drawing file. Therefore, as with SURFTAB1, set SURFTAB2 to the minimum value required to generate an acceptable mesh for your application.

EARLIEST VERSION

Release 10

DATA TYPE

Integer

DEFAULT

6

READ-ONLY

No

SURFTYPE

Controls the type of smooth surface to be fitted to a polygon mesh using the PEdit Smooth command (Chapter 10).

When stored in SURFTYPE, the following integers set the indicated features:

5 = Generate a quadratic B-spline surface
6 = Generate a cubic B-spline surface
8 = Generate a Bezier surface

Changing the value of these system variables will cause the appearance of smoothed surfaces to change when the drawing is regenerated.

EARLIEST VERSION

Release 10

DATA TYPE

Integer

DEFAULT

6

READ-ONLY

No

SURFU

Controls the number of segments drawn in the M direction between each vertex of a smooth surface fit to a polygon mesh. For details regarding polygon-mesh editing, refer to the PEdit Smooth command in Chapter 10.

Any positive integer is valid, but the higher the integer, the higher the number of segments. This will make the resolution of the smoothed surface finer, but it will take longer to regenerate, and will occupy larger amounts of disk space.

Changing the value of SURFU will cause the appearance of the smoothed surface to change when the drawing is regenerated.

EARLIEST VERSION

Release 10

DATA TYPE

Integer

DEFAULT

6

READ-ONLY

No

SURFV

Controls the number of segments drawn in the N direction between each vertex of a smooth surface fit to a polygon mesh. For details regarding polygon-mesh editing, refer to the PEdit Smooth command in Chapter 10.

Any positive integer is valid, but the higher the integer, the higher the number of segments. This will make the resolution of the smoothed surface finer, but it will take longer to regenerate, and will occupy larger amounts of disk space.

Changing the value of SURFV will cause the appearance of the smoothed surface to change when the drawing is regenerated.

EARLIEST VERSION

Release 10

DATA TYPE

Integer

DEFAULT

6

READ-ONLY

No

Date and Time Data

The following system variables control various date and time statistics relating to the current drawing—for example, the date and time the drawing was created, the total time spent editing the drawing, and the amount of time spent in the current editing session. These system variables have no real default settings; they read the computer's system clock and are updated each time they are called by either the Setvar or Time command, or by AutoLISP's Getvar function. They are all read-only; AutoLISP routines can read them and process the data they contain, but they cannot be updated except by subsequent readings of the computer's system clock.

CDATE

Stores the current system date as a real number, always with eight places to the left of the decimal point and nine places to the right. CDATE accepts the date and time returned by the computer's system clock.

For example, if CDATE were read at precisely 3:30 P.M. on November 15, 1991, it would return the following real number:

19911115.153000000

From left to right, these numbers represent:

- The year (first four places, 1991).
- The month (next two places, 11).
- The day (last two places, 15).
- The decimal point.
- The number of hours past midnight (first two places after decimal point; expressed in "military time"; for example, 3:00 P.M. equals 15).
- The number of minutes past the hour (next two decimal places, 30).
- The number of seconds past the minute (next two decimal places, 00).
- The number of milliseconds past the second (last three decimal places, 000).

While the number returned by CDATE is easy to read and interpret, arithmetic expressions with dates are difficult because of the irregular format of the calendar represented by the data. To perform arithmetic expressions with dates, use the DATE system variable, explained next.

You can change the value of CDATE by causing it to be read, either with the Setvar or Time command, or with the Getvar function in AutoLISP.

EARLIEST VERSION

All

DATA TYPE

Real number

DEFAULT

The value of CDATE is updated from the system clock each time it is read.

READ-ONLY

Yes

DATE

Stores the current system date as a real number, always with seven places to the left of the decimal point and eight places to the right. The number to the left of the decimal point expresses the current system date as a Julian date, so that arithmetic expressions may be performed using it.

The number to the left of the decimal point represents the elapsed fraction of the current day, and may be converted to hours, minutes, and seconds using Julian date-conversion math. For example, if DATE were read at precisely 3:00 P.M. on March 15, 1992, it would return the following real number:

2448697.62500000

The number returned by DATE is in *Julian date* format, a special means of counting dates that allows you to perform accurate date math. The seven-digit number to the left of the decimal point is the Julian date. The numbers to the right of the decimal point indicate the elapsed fraction of the current day. In the above example, exactly 15 hours have elapsed.

The accuracy of the DATE system variable depends on the setting of your computer's system clock, which must be set to UTC Greenwich mean time. Some system clocks are set differently; if yours is among them, DATE will not return a true Julian date.

The Julian date returned by this system variable can be converted to the calendar date using special math. An AutoLISP program that will perform this conversion is used as a sample routine in Chapter 16.

DATE reads the date and time stored in the computer's system clock. You can change the value of DATE by causing it to be read, either with the Setvar or Time command, or with the Getvar function in AutoLISP.

EARLIEST VERSION

All

DATA TYPE

Real number

DEFAULT

The value of DATE is updated from the system clock each time it is read.

READ-ONLY

Yes

TDCREATE

Stores as a real number the date and time that the drawing file was created, always with seven places to the left of the decimal point and eight places to the right. The number to the left of the decimal point expresses the current system date as a Julian date, so that arithmetic expressions may be performed using it.

The number to the left of the decimal point represents the elapsed fraction of the current day, and may be converted to hours, minutes, and seconds using Julian date-conversion math. For details, refer to the DATE system variable explained earlier, and to Chapter 16.

The accuracy of the TDCREATE system variable depends on the setting of your computer's system clock, which must be set to UTC Greenwich mean time. Some system clocks are set differently; if yours is among them, TDCREATE will not return a true Julian date. The value stored in TDCREATE cannot be changed.

EARLIEST VERSION

All

DATA TYPE

Real number

DEFAULT

The date and time the drawing was created

READ-ONLY

Yes

TDINDWG

Stores the total editing time spent in the drawing from the time the drawing file was created. This time is incremented with each drawing session. The time is stored as a real number, with as many as seven places to the left of the decimal point and nine places to the right.

This number represents the total number of days spent on the drawing, expressed as a real number. For example, if you have spent exactly two-and-a-half days working on this drawing, TDINDWG would return:

2.500000

TDINDWG calculates the cumulative total editing time by reading the date and time returned by the computer's system clock and the value stored in the TDUPDATE system variable.

You can change the value of TDINDWG by causing it to be read, either with the Setvar or Time command, or with the Getvar function in AutoLISP.

EARLIEST VERSION

All

DATA TYPE

Real number

DEFAULT

The value of TDINDWG is updated each time it is read.

READ-ONLY

Yes

TDUPDATE

Stores the date and time the drawing file was last saved to disk. The date is stored as a real number, always with seven places to the left of the decimal point and eight places to the right. The number to the left of the decimal point expresses the current system date as a Julian date, so that arithmetic expressions may be performed using it.

The number to the left of the decimal point represents the elapsed fraction of the current day, and may be converted to hours, minutes, and seconds using standard math. For details, refer to the DATE system variable explained earlier.

The accuracy of the TDUPDATE system variable depends on the setting of your computer's system clock, which must be set to UTC Greenwich mean time. Some system clocks are set differently; if yours is among them, TDUPDATE will not return a true Julian date.

You can change the value of TDUPDATE by invoking the Save or End command.

EARLIEST VERSION

All

DATA TYPE

Real number

DEFAULT

The value of TDUPDATE is updated each time the drawing file is saved to disk.

READ-ONLY

Yes

TDUSRTIMER

Stores the total editing time spent in the drawing during the current drawing session. The time is stored as a real number, with as many as seven places to the left of the decimal point and eight places to the right.

This number represents the total amount of time you have spent on this drawing, as a real number. For example, if it has been exactly six hours since you entered the drawing editor, TDUSRTIMER would return:

0.2500000

TDUSRTIMER calculates the cumulative total editing time by reading the date and time returned by the computer's system clock.

You can change the value of TDUSRTIMER by invoking the Save or End command.

EARLIEST VERSION

All

DATA TYPE

Real number

DEFAULT

The value of TDUSRTIMER is updated each time the drawing file is saved to disk.

READ-ONLY

Yes

DIMENSIONING DEFAULTS

The following system variables, whose names are explained in Table 13.1, control the many different default settings that apply to AutoCAD's automatic dimensioning feature. Many of these system variables interact with one another, and it is noted where this is so. None of these variables are read-only; all may be changed by means of the Dim or Dim1 command. Select the variable name at the command prompt or the "Dim:" prompt, and AutoCAD will ask for the new data. Refer to Chapter 21 for details regarding automatic dimensioning.

These system variables may also be changed using AutoLISP's Setvar function. Starting in Version 2.6, you may also use the Setvar command to change any of these variables.

Many dimensioning system variables accept only 1 or 0 as valid data, to toggle a specific dimensioning feature on and off. When updating these variables using the Setvar command, AutoLISP function, or comand prompt, enter **1** or **0**; when updating these variables at the "Dim:" prompt, enter either **ON** (instead of 1) or **OFF** (instead of 0).

Dimension variables that accept color information allow you to enter the name of the color (red, blue, etc.) when you enter the variable name at the "Dim:" prompt. If you enter the name at the Command Prompt, you must use a valid color number instead. Refer to Chapter 5 for details regarding Auto-CAD's handling of color information.

DIMALT

Enables and disables alternate dimensions. If DIMALT is enabled, AutoCAD creates dimension entities with the dimension values displayed in two formats: the default units format, and that value multiplied by a given factor for the alternate

DIMENSIONING VARIABLE	MEANING
DIMALT	Alternate units selected
DIMALTD	Alternate unit decimal places
DIMALTF	Alternate unit scale factor
DIMAPOST	Default suffix for alternate text
DIMASO	Create associative dimensions
DIMASZ	Arrow size
DIMBLK	Arrow block name
DIMBLK1	First arrow block name
DIMBLK2	Second arrow block name
DIMCEN	Center mark size
DIMCLRD	Dimension lines, arrowheads, leaders color
DIMCLRE	Extension lines color
DIMCLRT	Dimension text color
DIMDLE	Dimension line extension
DIMDLI	Dimension line increment for continuation
DIMEXE	Extension above dimension line
DIMEXO	Extension line origin offset
DIMGAP	The gap between the dimension line text when the text is inside it or minimum visible dimension line
DIMLFAC	Linear unit scale factor
DIMLIM	Generate dimension limits
DIMPOST	Default suffix for dimension text
DIMRND	Rounding value
DIMSAH	Separate arrow blocks
DIMSCALE	Overall scale factor
DIMSE1	Suppress the first extension line
DIMSE2	Suppress the second extension line
DIMSHO	Update dimensions while dragging
DIMSOXD	Suppress outside extension dimension
DIMSTYLE	Named dimension variable settings
DIMTAD	Place text above the dimension line
DIMTFAC	Scale factor for tolerence text height
DIMTIH	Text inside extensions is horizontal
DIMTIX	Place text inside extensions
DIMTM	Minus tolerance
DIMTOFL	Force line inside extension lines
DIMTOH	Text outside extensions is horizontal
DIMTOL	Generate dimension tolerances
DIMTP	Plus tolerance
DIMTSZ	Tick size
DIMTVP	Text vertical position
DIMTXT	Text height
DIMZIN	Zero suppression

TABLE 13.1: The Dimensioning Variables

dimension. For example, regular dimensions can be expressed in inches, while alternate dimensions are expressed in millimeters (inches multiplied by 25.4). If alternate dimensions are enabled using DIMALT, you must also store values in the system variables DIMALTF (alternate dimension multiplier factor) and DIMALTD (number of decimal places for alternate dimensions).

Alternate dimensions are always displayed in decimal format within square brackets, [ ].

When stored in DIMALT, the following integers set the indicated features:

0 = Alternate dimension display disabled
1 = Alternate dimension display enabled

EARLIEST VERSION

2.1

DATA TYPE

Integer

DEFAULT

0

DIMALTD

Controls the number of decimal places in the alternate dimension display. For DIMALTD to have any effect, you must have enabled alternate dimensioning by setting the DIMALT system variable to 1.

EARLIEST VERSION

2.1

DATA TYPE

Integer

DEFAULT

2

DIMALTF

Stores the factor by which a dimension value is multiplied in order to arrive at the alternate dimension value. For example, if regular dimensions are expressed in inches, you may have alternate dimensions expressed in millimeters by setting DIMALTF to 25.4.

EARLIEST VERSION

2.1

DATA TYPE

Real number

DEFAULT

25.4 (to change inches to millimeters)

DIMAPOST

Stores a string value added to alternate-dimension strings when alternate dimensioning is set using the DIMALT, DIMALTF, and DIMALTD system variables. For example, if the value of DIMAPOST is set to mm and the alternate dimension is 25.4, the alternate-dimension string would appear as [25.4mm].

Valid data includes any meaningful series of alphanumeric characters except a single period, which will reset the value of DIMAPOST to no value.

In Release 11, the value of DIMAPOST must be changed from the "Dim:" prompt.

EARLIEST VERSION

2.6

DATA TYPE

String

DEFAULT

No value

DIMASO

Controls whether AutoCAD's automatic dimensions are associative. Refer to Chapter 21 for details regarding associative dimensioning.

When stored in DIMASO, the following integers set the indicated features:

0 = Associative dimensioning disabled
1 = Associative dimensioning enabled

EARLIEST VERSION

2.6

DATA TYPE

Integer

DEFAULT

1

DIMASZ

Controls the size of the arrows at the endpoints of the dimension line. The value in this system variable represents the length of the arrow in drawing units from its tip to the point where it intersects the dimension line. AutoCAD uses the arrow size as the base factor for determining where to align dimension lines and text (inside or outside of extension lines).

If the DIMBLK system variable is set to contain the name of a block to be used instead of arrows, the setting of the DIMASZ variable will be used to scale the named block. Refer to DIMBLK for details.

Valid data includes any real number that represents a pleasing dimension-arrow size. The value is displayed in the current units format, and you may change it by entering a new value in that format or in decimal drawing units. If DIMASZ is set to zero, arrows will not be drawn. This size of dimension arrows will be affected if the overall dimensioning scale is changed using the DIM-SCALE system variable.

EARLIEST VERSION

All

DATA TYPE

Real number

DEFAULT

0.18 (or $^3/_{16}$")

DIMBLK

Controls whether dimensioning arrows are replaced by an AutoCAD block of your choosing.

AutoCAD provides three types of default symbols for the endpoints of dimension lines: the arrow, the tick mark, and the "dot" (filled circle). If DIMBLK is set to the name of an existing block, the named block will replace AutoCAD's defaults at the endpoints of dimension lines.

The block's insertion point is placed at the dimension line's endpoints. The block is oriented according to the angle of the dimension line at the rightmost endpoint, and rotated 180 degrees for insertion at the opposite endpoint.

The block used should be drawn within dimensions of 1 drawing unit by 1 drawing unit, as its size will be factored by the setting of DIMASZ (times DIM-SCALE, if not zero). This allows you to use the same basic block at any drawing scale. Refer to DIMASZ and DIMSCALE for further information on how these system variables scale block sizes.

If your block measures less than 1 drawing unit horizontally, it may "float" off of the dimension line's endpoint. To connect it to the dimension line, add a short horizontal line to your block, from the insertion point extending to the left, until the horizontal width of the block plus the line total 1 drawing unit.

In Release 11, the value of DIMBLK must be changed from the "Dim:" prompt.

If you wish to use the dot dimension-line endpoint, set DIMBLK to "dot". To use the arrow, set DIMBLK to equal a period (which empties it of any string), and DIMTSZ to zero. To use tick marks, refer to the discussion of the DIMTSZ system variable.

EARLIEST VERSION

2.5

DATA TYPE

String

DEFAULT

No value

DIMBLK1

Works like DIMBLK, except that it will insert the named block on the right-most dimension-line endpoint only. However, in order for DIMBLK1 to work at all, DIMSAH must be set to 1.

In Release 11, the value of DIMBLK1 must be set from the "Dim:" prompt.

EARLIEST VERSION

Release 10

DATA TYPE

String

DEFAULT

No value

DIMBLK2

Works like DIMBLK, except that it will insert the named block on the leftmost dimension-line endpoint only. However, in order for DIMBLK2 to work at all, DIMSAH must be set to 1.

In Release 11, the value of DIMBLK2 must be set from the "Dim:" prompt.

EARLIEST VERSION

Release 10

DATA TYPE

String

DEFAULT

No value

DIMCEN

Controls whether center marks are drawn when dimensioning circles and arcs. If the value of DIMCEN is greater than zero, a center mark is drawn; its length from the arc or circle center point is determined by the value of DIM-CEN. If DIMCEN is zero, no center mark is drawn. If DIMCEN is less than zero, the center mark will be drawn along with center lines. The center mark will be drawn using the absolute value of DIMCEN, and the center lines will be offset from the center mark by the absolute value of DIMCEN.

The size of the center mark will be changed if the overall dimensioning scale is changed using the DIMSCALE system variable.

EARLIEST VERSION

2.1

DATA TYPE

Real number

DEFAULT

0.09 ($^3/_{32}$'')

DIMCLRD

Stores the current default color for dimension lines, leaders, and arrowheads. If you change this variable from the "Dim:" prompt, you may enter a color name, BYLAYER, or BYBLOCK. If you change DIMCLRD from the Command Prompt, you must enter an integer corresponding to the desired color, zero for BYBLOCK, or 256 for BYLAYER. Refer to Chapter 5 for details regarding color numbers.

EARLIEST VERSION

Release 11

DATA TYPE

Integer

DEFAULT

0 (BYBLOCK)

DIMCLRE

Stores the current default color for dimension extension lines. Refer to the description of DIMCLRD for rules regarding assignment of colors.

EARLIEST VERSION

Release 11

DATA TYPE

Integer

DEFAULT

0 (BYBLOCK)

DIMCLRT

Stores the current default color for dimension text. Refer to the description of DIMCLRD for rules regarding assignment of colors.

EARLIEST VERSION

Release 11

DATA TYPE

Integer

DEFAULT

0 (BYBLOCK)

DIMDLE

Controls how far the dimension line extends past the extension lines. This system variable will have an effect only if the DIMTSZ system variable (enabling tick marks) is not set to zero.

The degree of extension will be changed if the overall dimensioning scale is changed using the DIMSCALE system variable.

EARLIEST VERSION

2.1

DATA TYPE

Real number

DEFAULT

0

DIMDLI

Controls the amount of offset of successive dimension lines when using the Baseline and Continue options of the Dim command. (Refer to Chapter 21 for details.)

The offset for successive dimension lines will be changed if the overall dimensioning scale is changed using the DIMSCALE system variable.

EARLIEST VERSION

2.1

DATA TYPE

Real number

DEFAULT

0.38

DIMEXE

Controls how far the extension line extends past the dimension line. The amount of extension will be changed if the overall dimensioning scale is changed using the DIMSCALE system variable.

EARLIEST VERSION

2.1

DATA TYPE

Real number

DEFAULT

0.18 ($^3/_{16}$'')

DIMEXO

Controls how far the extension lines are to be offset from the dimension points you select. This offset is changed if the overall dimensioning scale is changed using the DIMSCALE system variable.

EARLIEST VERSION

2.1

DATA TYPE

Real number

DEFAULT

0.0625 ($^1/_{16}$'')

DIMGAP

Stores the distance between the dimension line and dimension text when the dimension line is broken around the dimension text. When the dimension line is broken for text, AutoCAD places the text within the extension lines only if the remaining lengths of the dimension line are at least equal to this variable.

EARLIEST VERSION

Release 11

DATA TYPE

Real number.

DEFAULT

0.09

DIMLFAC

Stores a real number used as a multiplication factor of dimension lengths. The dimension length multiplied by this value is presented as the default dimension text. DIMLFAC is usually set to 1, but you may set it to other values when you are dimensioning drawings that have been scaled inside AutoCAD's drawing editor.

DIMLFAC has special meaning in paper space. You can use AutoCAD to calculate the scaling of model space to paper space by entering DIMLFAC at the "Dim:" prompt in paper space, followed by **V**. AutoCAD prompts:

Select viewport to set scale:

Pick one of the viewports on the screen, and AutoCAD assigns a scale factor that represents model space dimensions in paper space. This factor is stored in DIMLFAC as a negative number (to distinguish it from a model-space scale factor), but the absolute value of the number is used in paper space.

You can also assign a negative number to DIMLFAC at any time, to indicate a specific scaling factor for paper space.

When DIMLFAC is bound to a negative number, it is ignored when dimensioning in model space.

EARLIEST VERSION

2.1

DATA TYPE

Real number

DEFAULT

1.0

DIMLIM

Controls whether the dimension limits are added to the default text. Setting DIMLIM to 1 will have the effect of displaying the dimension twice; however, prefixes and suffixes will be displayed only once. Refer to the Dim command (Chapter 21) for details.

When stored in DIMLIM, the following integers set the indicated features:

0 = Do not display dimension limits with default text
1 = Display dimension limits with default text

EARLIEST VERSION

2.1

DATA TYPE

Integer

DEFAULT

0

DIMPOST

Stores a string value added to dimension text strings. For example, if the value of DIMPOST is set to "mm" and the dimension text is 100, the dimension text string would appear in the drawing as "100mm".

Valid data includes any meaningful series of alphanumeric characters—except a single period, which will reset the value of DIMPOST to no value.

In Release 11, DIMPOST may be changed only from the "Dim:" prompt.

EARLIEST VERSION

2.6

DATA TYPE

String

DEFAULT

No value

DIMRND

Controls the degree to which dimension values will be rounded off when displayed as dimension text. To round off to whole numbers, set DIMRND to 1; to the nearest half-unit, set it to 0.5; to the nearest quarter-unit, set it to 0.25; and so on.

DIMRND does not effect the default number of decimal places in dimension text. The number of decimal places is controlled by the Units command (Chapter 6).

EARLIEST VERSION

2.1

DATA TYPE

Real number

DEFAULT

0 (no rounding)

DIMSAH

Controls whether separate blocks are displayed at the endpoints of the dimension line. If DIMSAH is set to a value of 1 and DIMTSZ is set to 0, the block names found in the DIMBLK1 and DIMBLK2 system variables will be inserted at the endpoints of the dimension line. If DIMSAH is set to 0, the values of DIMBLK1 and DIMBLK2 are ignored, although a block name in the DIMBLK system variable, if present, will be used for both endpoints.

When stored in DIMSAH, the following integers set the indicated features:

0 = Disable separate endpoint blocks
1 = Enable separate endpoint blocks

EARLIEST VERSION

Release 10

DATA TYPE

Integer

DEFAULT

0

DIMSCALE

Stores a positive real number used as a factor by which the sizes of dimension entities—for example, dimension text, tick marks, line extensions, offset lengths, and arrowheads—are multiplied to remain proportional to the rest of the drawing.

Dimension size values are usually scaled so as to be readable in a drawing plotted at one-to-one scale, and the value of DIMSCALE is adjusted to accommodate whatever is the actual scale of the drawing.

For example, if you intend to plot a drawing at a scale of ¼ inch to 1 foot, and you have entered lines at real-world scale in AutoCAD, the program is storing information about a drawing that is 48 times as large as the final plotted output (12" ÷ ¼" = 48).

If DIMSCALE is set to a value of 1 under these circumstances, the dimension text, offsets, tick marks, and so forth would be too small to be of any practical value. However, if you change the value of DIMSCALE to 48, the dimensions are scaled so that these things are visible.

Bear in mind that DIMSCALE does not change the default dimension values or the settings of other dimension variables; rather, it simply multiplies those dimension entities whose readability benefits from being drawn at a larger scale.

A DIMSCALE value of 1 produces no changes to the default dimension-entity size. DIMSCALE values greater than 1 will increase the dimension-entity size; values between 0 and 1 will reduce the dimension-entity size.

EARLIEST VERSION

2.1

DATA TYPE

Real number

DEFAULT

1 (no scaling; multiply by one)

DIMSE1

Controls the display of the first dimension extension line (the one closest to the first dimension point entered).

When stored in DIMSE1, the following integers set the indicated features:

0 = Draw the first extension line
1 = Suppress the first extension line

EARLIEST VERSION

2.1

DATA TYPE

Integer

DEFAULT

0

DIMSE2

Controls the display of the second dimension extension line (the one closest to the second dimension point entered).

When stored in DIMSE2, the following integers set the indicated features:

0 = Draw the second extension line
1 = Suppress the second extension line

EARLIEST VERSION

2.1

DATA TYPE

Integer

DEFAULT

0

DIMSHO

Controls whether associative dimensions are updated while they are being dynamically changed on the display screen. (Refer to Chapter 21 for details regarding associative dimensioning.) If DIMSHO is set to a value of 1, associative dimensions are constantly updated while being dynamically changed; if set to 0, associative dimensions are not updated until they are set in place.

When stored in DIMSHO, the following integers set the indicated features:

0 = Disable dynamic updating of associative dimensions
1 = Enable dynamic updating of associative dimensions

EARLIEST VERSION

2.6

DATA TYPE

Integer

DEFAULT

1

DIMSOXD

Controls whether AutoCAD will draw dimension lines outside extension lines in those cases where there is no room between the extension lines for both dimension lines and text. If DIMSOXD and DIMTIX are set to a value of 1 and the dimension lines will not fit within the extension lines, AutoCAD will not draw the dimension lines at all. If DIMSOXD is set to zero, AutoCAD draws dimension lines outside the extension lines when necessary. DIMSOXD has no effect if DIMTIX is set to zero.

When stored in DIMSOXD, the following integers set the indicated features:

0 = Draw outside dimension lines when necessary
1 = Suppress the dimension line if it won't fit between the extension lines

EARLIEST VERSION

Release 10

DATA TYPE

Integer

DEFAULT

0

DIMSTYLE

Stores the name of the current *dimension style*. In Release 11 and later, Auto-CAD permits you to name and save current settings of dimension variables, except DIMSHO and DIMASO. You can maintain any number of these named dimension styles. New or updated dimensions adopt the settings associated with the current dimension style name in this variable. For details regarding saving and restoring named dimension styles, refer to Chapter 21.

This variable is read-only; it is changed whenever you save or restore a named dimension style. If you change any of the current dimension variable settings, this variable is bound to the special symbol *UNNAMED until you again restore or save a new named style.

EARLIEST VERSION

Release 11

DATA TYPE

String

DEFAULT

*UNNAMED

DIMTAD

Controls the placement of dimension text, either above the dimension line or centered within it. If DIMTAD is set to a value of 1, text is placed above the dimension line. Otherwise, text is centered within the line.

When stored in DIMTAD, the following integers set the indicated features:

0 = Center dimension text within the dimension line
1 = Place dimension text above the dimension line

EARLIEST VERSION

2.1

DATA TYPE

Integer

DEFAULT

0

DIMTFAC

Stores the scale factor that determines the size of text in dimension tolerance values. This variable has no effect unless either DIMLIN is on or DIMTOL is on and the value of DIMTM does not equal DIMTP.

EARLIEST VERSION

Release 11

DATA TYPE

Real Number

DEFAULT

1

DIMTIH

Controls the angle at which dimension text is drawn when that text is placed inside the extension lines. If DIMTIH is set to a value of 1, text is always drawn horizontally. If set to a value of 0, text is drawn at the same angle of orientation as the dimension line.

When stored in DIMTIH, the following integers set the indicated features:

0 = Align inside dimension text with the dimension line
1 = Align inside dimension text horizontally at all times

EARLIEST VERSION

2.1

DATA TYPE

Integer

DEFAULT

1

DIMTIX

Controls whether dimension text is drawn inside or outside the extension lines. If DIMTIX is set to a value of 1, AutoCAD will always draw dimension text inside the extension lines, even if the dimension lines are outside the extension lines or suppressed altogether. If DIMTIX is set to a value of 0, AutoCAD will place dimension text within the extension lines when it can fit both text and dimension lines there; otherwise, it will place text and dimension lines outside the dimension lines.

When stored in DIMTIX, the following integers set the indicated features:

    0 = Place text within dimension lines if there is room
    1 = Always place text within the extension lines

EARLIEST VERSION

Release 10

DATA TYPE

Integer

DEFAULT

0

DIMTM

Stores the value of minus tolerance for automatic dimensioning. If you intend to add tolerances to your dimensions, note that DIMTM will have no effect unless either the DIMTOL or DIMLIM system variable is set to 1.

DIMTM also works with DIMTP (see ahead).

Valid data includes any positive real number. AutoCAD will supply the minus sign when adding tolerances to dimension text.

EARLIEST VERSION

2.1

DATA TYPE

Real number

DEFAULT

0

DIMTOFL

Controls the placement of the dimension line. When DIMTOFL is set to a value of 1, a dimension line is always drawn between the extension lines, even if the text is placed outside the extension lines. If set to zero, the dimension line follows the placement of text.

When stored in DIMTOFL, the following integers set the indicated features:

0 = Dimension line follows text
1 = Dimension line always drawn between extension lines

EARLIEST VERSION

Release 10

DATA TYPE

Integer

DEFAULT

0

DIMTOH

Controls the angle at which dimension text is drawn when that text is placed outside the extension lines. If DIMTOH is set to a value of 1, text is always drawn horizontally. If set to a value of 0, text is drawn at the same angle of orientation as the dimension line.

When stored in DIMTOH, the following integers set the indicated features:

0 = Align outside dimension text with the dimension line
1 = Align outside dimension text horizontally at all times

EARLIEST VERSION

2.1

DATA TYPE

Integer

DEFAULT

1

DIMTOL

Controls whether tolerances are included in dimension text. If DIMTOL is set to 1, tolerances will be included, provided that values have been set for DIMTP and/or DIMTM. If DIMTOL is set to zero, tolerances are ignored.

When stored in DIMTOL, the following integers set the indicated features:

0 = Do not include tolerances in dimension text
1 = Include tolerances in dimension text

EARLIEST VERSION

2.1

DATA TYPE

Integer

DEFAULT

0

DIMTP

Stores the value of plus tolerance for automatic dimensioning. If you intend to add tolerances to your dimensions, note that DIMTP will have no effect unless either DIMTOL or DIMLIM is set to 1.

DIMTP also works with DIMTM.

EARLIEST VERSION

2.1

DATA TYPE

Real number

DEFAULT

0

DIMTSZ

Controls the size of dimensioning "tick marks," and whether they are displayed instead of arrowheads or endpoint blocks. If DIMTSZ is set to a value other than zero, AutoCAD will override all system variables relating to endpoint blocks and will draw tick marks instead. If DIMTSZ is set to zero, AutoCAD will use endpoint blocks as instructed by other system variables (refer to DIMBLK, DIMBLK1, DIMBLK2, DIMSAH, and DIMASZ above).

Setting DIMTSZ to zero will suppress tick marks; AutoCAD will draw arrowheads instead (unless DIMBLK, DIMBLK1, DIMBLK2, or DIMSAH has been set to a nondefault value). Tick marks will be scaled according to the DIMSCALE system variable.

EARLIEST VERSION

2.1

DATA TYPE

Real number

DEFAULT

0

DIMTVP

Controls the position of text above or below the dimension line by multiplying the value of DIMTVP by the value of DIMTXT. Text will be offset above the dimension line if DIMTVP is positive, or below the dimension line if DIMTVP is negative. If the text position is such that it crosses the dimension line, the line is split to accommodate it.

DIMTVP will have no effect if DIMTAD (text above dimension line) is set to 1. DIMTVP is subject to scaling by the DIMSCALE system variable.

EARLIEST VERSION

Release 10

DATA TYPE

Real number

DEFAULT

0 (text crosses dimension line)

DIMTXT

Controls the height of the dimension text. Dimension text defaults to the specified height, subject to the value found in the DIMSCALE system variable. However, AutoCAD draws dimension text using the current text style; if the current text style has a fixed height, AutoCAD will draw the dimension text using the fixed height rather than the value of DIMTXT.

EARLIEST VERSION

2.1

DATA TYPE

Real number

DEFAULT

0.18 ($^3/_{16}$'')

DIMZIN

Controls how zero feet and inches are displayed in dimension text. In Auto-CAD versions earlier than 2.5, only values of 1 (include zero feet and inches) and 0 (suppress zero feet and inches) were valid. As of Version 2.6, additional values for DIMZIN are 2 (suppress zero inches only) and 3 (suppress zero feet only).

Starting with Version 2.6, the value of DIMZIN will control the AutoLISP Rtos function, which converts real numbers to strings (see Chapter 17), the same way it affects the conversion of dimension values to text.

When stored in DIMZIN, the following integers set the indicated features:

    0 = Suppress zero feet and inches
    1 = Include zero feet and inches
    2 = Suppress zero inches only (Version 2.6+)
    3 = Suppress zero feet only (Version 2.6+)

EARLIEST VERSION

2.1

DATA TYPE

Integer

DEFAULT

0

DISK FILE DEFAULTS

These system variables relate to how AutoCAD manages files on disk, including placement of drawing files, locations of drawing and support files, and placement of temporary files. They are read-only; you change them either by reconfiguring AutoCAD or by changing DOS environment variables before running AutoCAD. They are also updated automatically when you begin each drawing session.

As with any read-only variable, the data these system variables contain may be read and stored to memory variables by means of AutoLISP's Getvar function (see Chapter 17). This can be useful in AutoLISP routines that make choices or look for other files based on the file locations and names stored in these variables.

The Setvar command will display the data in these system variables.

ACADPREFIX

Limits the search path used by AutoCAD to find its system and support files. AutoCAD will look for these files first on the currently logged subdirectory, then on the subdirectory containing AutoCAD's system files, and finally on the subdirectory listed in this system variable. If the DOS environment variable ACAD (see Chapter 4) is not set to any value before AutoCAD is initialized, AutoCAD will set ACADPREFIX equal to a null value, but it will include in its search path the currently logged subdirectory and the directory containing AutoCAD's system files. To change the value of ACADPREFIX, invoke the following command at the DOS prompt, prior to initializing AutoCAD:

SET ACAD = d:\subdirectory,

where *d* is the name of a disk drive letter, and *subdirectory* is the name of a subdirectory path.

EARLIEST VERSION

2.6

DATA TYPE

String

DEFAULT

The value of the DOS environment variable ACAD, if any

READ-ONLY

Yes

DWGNAME

Stores the name of the current drawing. This name is used as the default drawing name for the Save and End commands (Chapter 7). This system variable is never changed during a drawing session.

EARLIEST VERSION

All

DATA TYPE

String

DEFAULT

The name of the current drawing

READ-ONLY

Yes

DWGPREFIX

Stores the subdirectory location of the current drawing. To locate the current drawing when the drawing is updated on disk during the Save and End commands, this string is added to the current drawing name. This system variable is never changed during a drawing session.

EARLIEST VERSION

All

DATA TYPE

String

DEFAULT

The subdirectory location of the current drawing

READ-ONLY

Yes

TEMPPREFIX

Stores the directory and subdirectory path for placement of AutoCAD's temporary files, created during each drawing session. These files hold data used by AutoCAD throughout the drawing session, and are erased when the drawing session ends.

Valid data includes any valid drive/subdirectory path name, or the character string "DRAWING".

To change TEMPPREFIX, use AutoCAD's Configuration menu. Refer to Chapter 4 for details on how to specify to AutoCAD where to place its temporary files.

EARLIEST VERSION

2.6

DATA TYPE

String

DEFAULT

No data, or "DRAWING", indicating that temporary files are to be placed on the same subdirectory as the drawing file.

READ-ONLY

Yes

DISPLAY DEFAULTS

The following system variables control various display options in AutoCAD's drawing editor. Most of these system variables can be changed using either the Setvar command, AutoLISP's Setvar function, or special AutoCAD commands. Exceptions to this are noted—for example, when the system variable is read-only and may be changed only by means of a special AutoCAD command.

When these system variables are read-only, AutoLISP may retrieve their data using the Getvar function, or change them by calling the appropriate AutoCAD commands.

AXISMODE

Controls the display of axis tick marks on the display screen.

When stored in AXISMODE, the following integers set the indicated features:

0 = Axis ticks are invisible
1 = Axis ticks are visible

If you change the value of AXISMODE from the Command Prompt, with Setvar, or with AutoLISP, the results will not become visible until the next drawing regeneration. To make the results visible immediately, use the Axis command (Chapter 7) instead.

EARLIEST VERSION

All

DATA TYPE

Integer

DEFAULT

0

READ-ONLY

No

AXISUNIT

Controls the spacing of the axis tick marks, when visible. Data is entered and displayed in 2-D coordinate-point format. The first real number controls the x-axis spacing, and the second controls the y-axis spacing. If either number is set to zero, the corresponding axis spacing will equal the current snap value.

The numbers can be entered by means of decimal numbers or the current coordinate-point format as set with the Units command (Chapter 6).

If you change the value of AXISUNIT from the Command Prompt, with Set-var, or with AutoLISP, the results will not become visible until the next drawing regeneration. To make the results visible immediately, use the Axis command (Chapter 7) instead.

EARLIEST VERSION

All

DATA TYPE

2-D point

DEFAULT

0,0

READ-ONLY

No

BACKZ

Controls the distance between the back clipping plane and the target point. (Refer to the Dview command, Chapter 11.)

The data stored in BACKZ will be displayed in the current units format.

EARLIEST VERSION

Release 10

DATA TYPE

Real number

DEFAULT

0

READ-ONLY

Yes

BLIPMODE

Controls the display of coordinate-point marker "blips" on the screen.

When stored in BLIPMODE, the following integers set the indicated features:

0 = Marker blips are not displayed
1 = Marker blips are displayed

BLIPMODE is also an AutoCAD command that will change the value of this variable. When you invoke Blipmode from the Command Prompt, you are prompted to turn the blips **ON** or **OFF**. Integer values will not be accepted. The results are the same whether you use the command or reset the variable using Setvar or AutoLISP.

EARLIEST VERSION

All

DATA TYPE

Integer

DEFAULT

1

READ-ONLY

No

CECOLOR

Controls the color in which new entities are drawn.

Several different strings are valid data for this system variable:

- A string consisting of the current color number, a space, and the color name within parentheses; for example, "1 (red)".
- "BYLAYER"—indicating that the color of new entities will default to the entity color assigned to the layer upon which they are drawn, or to which they are moved.
- "BYBLOCK"—indicating that the color of new entities will be white until combined with other entities in a block, at which time they will adopt

the color in effect when the block is created (or inserted, if the block's entities reside on layer 0).

For further details regarding these strings and their meaning, refer to the Color command in Chapter 6. This variable may be changed only by means of the Color command.

EARLIEST VERSION

2.5

DATA TYPE

String

DEFAULT

"BYLAYER"

READ-ONLY

Yes

CELTYPE

Controls the linetype that new line-based entities use when drawn.

Valid data is a string consisting of the current linetype description, either "CONTINUOUS" (for continuous lines) or the name of a valid noncontinuous linetype definition loaded in the drawing or referenced in the file ACAD.LIN— for example, "DASHED". Other valid strings include:

- "CONTINUOUS"—indicating that new entities will be drawn using AutoCAD's internal continuous linetype.
- "BYLAYER"—indicating that the linetype of new entities will default to the linetype assigned to the layer upon which they are drawn or to which they are moved.
- "BYBLOCK"—indicating that the linetype of new entities will be continuous until combined with other entities in a block, at which time they will adopt the linetype in effect when the block is created.

For further details regarding these strings and their meaning, refer to the Linetype command in Chapter 6. This variable may be changed only by means of the Linetype command.

EARLIEST VERSION

2.5

DATA TYPE

String

DEFAULT

"BYLAYER"

READ-ONLY

Yes

CLAYER

Stores the name of the current drawing layer. This variable may be changed only by means of the Layer Set or Layer Make commands. Refer to Chapter 6 for details regarding the Layer command and its options.

EARLIEST VERSION

All

DATA TYPE

String

DEFAULT

The name of the current layer

READ-ONLY

Yes

CMDECHO

Controls the display of command prompts and responses in the Command-prompt area when AutoCAD commands are called from AutoLISP routines.

When stored in CMDECHO, the following integers set the indicated features:

0 = Command prompts and responses are not displayed
1 = Command prompts and responses are displayed

EARLIEST VERSION

All

DATA TYPE

Integer

DEFAULT

1

READ-ONLY

No

COORDS

Controls the display of coordinate information in AutoCAD's status line. When stored in COORDS, the following integers set the indicated features:

0 = Coordinate display is updated only when points are picked
1 = Coordinate display tracks the position of the crosshairs at all times
2 = Coordinate display tracks the position of the crosshairs, and displays angle and distance information when the rubberband line appears on the screen

EARLIEST VERSION

All

DATA TYPE

Integer

DEFAULT

2

READ-ONLY

No

CVPORT

Stores the identification number of the active viewport. When CVPORT is updated with a new valid identification number, the new viewport is made the active viewport.

The viewport whose identification number is used must be currently visible on the display screen. Other integers, or identification numbers of viewports not currently visible, are ignored. Refer to the Vports command, Chapter 11, for more details regarding viewports.

EARLIEST VERSION

Release 10

DATA TYPE

Integer

DEFAULT

1

READ-ONLY

No

DRAGMODE

Controls the behavior of AutoCAD's dynamic dragging feature. When DRAGMODE is set to 0, dynamic dragging is disabled; set to 1, dynamic dragging is enabled.

When dynamic dragging is enabled, AutoCAD will track the position of certain entities during intermediate stages of certain commands, expanding, contracting, or moving them on the display screen as you move the crosshairs. This allows you to preview the effects of commands before actually entering point or value data. Refer to the Dragmode command, Chapter 7, for details.

In AutoCAD versions prior to 2.5, you must specify the keyword **Drag** in response to command prompts that accept dynamic dragging. Examples of commands that use dynamic dragging include Circle (Chapter 8), Ellipse (Chapter 9), Change, Copy, Insert, Move, Scale, and Stretch (Chapter 10).

Beginning with Version 2.5, the value of DRAGMODE can be set to 2. This has the effect of enabling dynamic dragging automatically for all command prompts that accept it—in other words, without requiring that the user enter the keyword **drag.**

When stored in DRAGMODE, the following integers set the indicated features:

0 = Dynamic dragging disabled
1 = Dynamic dragging enabled, but only on request
2 = Dynamic dragging enabled automatically on all commands that make use of it

EARLIEST VERSION

All

DATA TYPE

Integer

DEFAULT

1 (before Version 2.5), 2 (Version 2.5 and later)

READ-ONLY

No

DRAGP1

Controls how often AutoCAD checks the location of the crosshairs and updates the preview image when you are using the dynamic dragging feature. Refer to the Dragmode command in Chapter 7 for details regarding dynamic dragging.

AutoCAD senses how quickly the crosshairs are being moved and uses either this system variable or DRAGP2 to regulate how often it checks the crosshairs' location. If you are moving the crosshairs slowly, DRAGP1 is used. If you are moving the crosshairs more quickly, DRAGP2 is used.

Larger integer values mean that more time will elapse between location checks, and more of the preview image will be drawn. Smaller values mean that the location is checked more often and that less of the image will be drawn as you move the pointing device, but the dynamic dragging effect will appear smoother.

EARLIEST VERSION

2.5

DATA TYPE

Integer

DEFAULT

10

READ-ONLY

No

DRAGP2

Controls how often AutoCAD checks the location of the crosshairs and updates the preview image when you are using the dynamic dragging feature. Refer to the Dragmode command in Chapter 7 for details regarding dynamic dragging.

AutoCAD senses how quickly the crosshairs are being moved and uses either this system variable or DRAGP1 to regulate how often it checks the crosshairs' location. If you are moving the crosshairs quickly, DRAGP2 is used. If you are moving the crosshairs more slowly, DRAGP1 is used. If you set larger values to this system variable, more time will elapse between location checks, and more of the preview image will be drawn, but the movement may not be as smooth. Smaller values mean that the location is checked more often and that less of the image will be drawn as you move the pointing device, but the dynamic dragging effect will appear smoother.

EARLIEST VERSION

2.5

DATA TYPE

Integer

DEFAULT

25

READ-ONLY

No

FILLMODE

Controls the screen display of filled solids, wide polylines, and traces.

When stored in FILLMODE, the following integers set the indicated features:

0 = Display wide lines and solids in outline format only
1 = Display wide lines and solids filled in.

If you change the value of FILLMODE from the Command Prompt, using Setvar, using the Fill command, or from within AutoLISP, the results will not become visible until the next drawing regeneration.

EARLIEST VERSION

All

DATA TYPE

Integer

DEFAULT

1

READ-ONLY

No

FRONTZ

Controls the distance between the front clipping plane and the target point. (Refer to the Dview command, Chapter 11.)

The number will be displayed in the current units format as set with the Units command (Chapter 6).

EARLIEST VERSION

Release 10

DATA TYPE

Real number

DEFAULT

0

READ-ONLY

Yes

HIGHLIGHT

Controls whether drawing entities are highlighted when they are selected for editing.

When stored in HIGHLIGHT, the following integers set the indicated features:

0 = Entities are not highlighted when selected
1 = Entities are highlighted when selected

EARLIEST VERSION

All

DATA TYPE

Integer

DEFAULT

1

READ-ONLY

No

LENSLENGTH

Stores the lens-length value, in millimeters, for zooming when perspective view mode is enabled. Refer to the Zoom option of the Dview command in Chapter 11 for details.

EARLIEST VERSION

Release 10

DATA TYPE

Real number

DEFAULT

50.0

READ-ONLY

Yes

MIRRTEXT

Controls how text is copied when mirrored. For details regarding the Mirror command, refer to Chapter 10.

When drawing entities are copied using the Mirror command, they are reversed as well. When text is mirrored, it can appear either reversed, as do the other drawing entities, or "unreversed"; that is, copied to the new mirrored location, but not actually reversed at that location, so that it remains readable.

When stored in MIRRTEXT, the following integers set the indicated features:

0 = Copied text is repositioned relative to the mirror line, but not reversed (remains readable)

1 = Copied text is fully mirrored—that is, both repositioned and reversed

Other values have the same effect as 1.

EARLIEST VERSION

2.5

DATA TYPE

Integer

DEFAULT

1

READ-ONLY

No

PDMODE

Controls how point entities are displayed and plotted. Point entities may be drawn using a variety of symbols (dot, cross, *X,* tick mark, or no symbol), and these symbols may be combined with two other special enhancement symbols (circle, square, or both) to create a variety of standard point-display styles.

When stored in PDMODE, the following integers set the indicated features:

0 = Point displayed as a dot (.)
1 = Point not displayed (but accessible via all standard entity-selection methods)
2 = Point displayed as a cross (+)
3 = Point displayed as an *X*
4 = Point displayed as a tick mark—a small vertical line extending upward from the point (in release 10 and later, relative to the current UCS)

In addition, you may add a circle, a square, or both, drawn around the point, by adding one of the following values to the integer selected from the above list:

+ 32 = draws a circle around the point
+ 64 = draws a square around the point
+ 96 = draws both circle and square around the point

EARLIEST VERSION

All

DATA TYPE

Integer

DEFAULT

0 (point displayed as plain dot)

READ-ONLY

No

PDSIZE

Stores a factor by which the size of the symbol used for point entities is multiplied to remain proportional to the rest of the drawing. The best size for point symbols will vary from display to display, and can be easily determined by a few moments of experimentation with your display device. The default is 0; try setting PDSIZE to 10, and then to 0.5, in order to get a possible range of sizes on your display device.

PDSIZE will accept negative numbers as well. When the value of PDSIZE is negative, AutoCAD displays point symbols as a percentage of the screen or plotted output size, and adjusts them as you zoom in and out of the drawing or indicate what portion of the display to plot.

When you change the value of PDSIZE, changes in the size of point symbols already on the screen will not be displayed until a drawing regeneration is performed.

EARLIEST VERSION

2.0

DATA TYPE

Real number

DEFAULT

0 (no scaling)

READ-ONLY

No

QTEXTMODE

Enables AutoCAD's quick-text mode, which forces lines of text to be drawn as rectangles, indicating the relative size and position of text entities without having to regenerate them completely each time a regen is performed. Refer to Chapter 9 for details regarding the Text and Qtext commands.

When stored in QTEXTMODE, the following integers set the indicated features:

0 = Quick-text mode not enabled
1 = Quick-text mode enabled

EARLIEST VERSION

All

DATA TYPE

Integer

DEFAULT

0

READ-ONLY

No

REGENMODE

Controls whether AutoCAD's automatic regeneration feature is enabled. If this system variable is set to 0, AutoCAD will prompt

About to Regen, Proceed?

before performing a drawing regeneration as part of another command such as Zoom or Pan, allowing the user to cancel the command before triggering a potentially time-wasting drawing regeneration. If REGENMODE is set to 1, AutoCAD performs the drawing regeneration whenever necessary without asking for confirmation.

When stored in REGENMODE, the following integers set the indicated features:

0 = Automatic regeneration disabled; AutoCAD prompts before regenerating
1 = Automatic regeneration enabled; AutoCAD performs all necessary drawing regenerations without prompting

EARLIEST VERSION

2.5

DATA TYPE

Integer

DEFAULT

1

READ-ONLY

No

TARGET

Stores the point toward which the viewing angle is oriented during the Vpoint and Dview commands. For details regarding the viewing angles and the camera/target metaphor in the Dview command, refer to Chapter 11.

Data is entered as a 3-D coordinate point. The point is displayed in the current units format. The target point is always expressed in terms of the current UCS. If multiple viewports are being used, each viewport may have its own target point.

You may change the point stored in this variable only by mens of the Vpoint and Dview commands. AutoLISP routines may read this variable and use the point value found therein; AutoLISP may change the variable by passing a point to the Dview Target command.

EARLIEST VERSION

Release 10

DATA TYPE

3-D coordinate point

DEFAULT

0,0,0

READ-ONLY

Yes

VIEWCTR

Stores the center point of the display in the current viewport. In Release 10, if multiple viewports are being used, this system variable may have different values for each viewport.

EARLIEST VERSION

All

DEFAULT

The center of the current viewport

DATA TYPE

Coordinate point. (In Release 10, a 3-D point is returned when FLATLAND equals zero.)

READ-ONLY

Yes

VIEWDIR

Stores the direction of the viewing angle (always in world coordinates, in relation to the point stored in the TARGET system variable).

For purposes of calculating the viewing angle, AutoCAD considers the TARGET point as if it were an origin point, and then stores in VIEWDIR a point that forms the correct viewing angle from the target point.

Refer to the Dview command, Chapter 11, for details regarding target points and viewing angles.

EARLIEST VERSION

Release 10

DATA TYPE

3-D coordinate point

DEFAULT

0,0,1 (plan view to the current target point)
The Dview and Vpoint commands.

READ-ONLY

Yes

VIEWMODE

Controls the status of the viewing mode, enabling perspective view mode and the front and back clipping planes, and reflecting the status of the UCSFOLLOW system variable.

Data in VIEWMODE may include any sum of the following integers, indicating which corresponding features are enabled:

0 = Standard viewing mode
1 = Perspective viewing mode
2 = Front clipping plane enabled
4 = Back clipping plane enabled
8 = UCSFOLLOW system variable is set to nonzero
16 = Front clipping plane is positioned using the FRONTZ system variable

Some of these integers interact. For example, VIEWMODE will never be set to 16, since the location of the front clipping plane is irrelevant if the front clipping plane is not enabled. If VIEWMODE is set to 2, the front clipping plane is enabled, but it defaults to the position of the camera, ignoring whatever value is contained in FRONTZ. When VIEWDIR is set to 18, the front clipping plane is enabled and located according to the FRONTZ system variable.

When UCSFOLLOW is set to nonzero, 8 is added to the total contained in VIEWMODE. This signals to AutoCAD that changes to the UCS will cancel the current viewing mode. If UCSFOLLOW is set to zero, changes to the UCS are possible while in perspective view.

EARLIEST VERSION

Release 10

DATA TYPE

Integer bit-code

DEFAULT

0

READ-ONLY

Yes

VIEWSIZE

Stores the height of the current display, in drawing units. This figure equals the number of vertical drawing units in the current viewing plane. The viewing plane is not necessarily parallel to the current UCS; thus, when you view 3-D drawings from non-plan viewing angles, the number of vertical drawing units in the viewing plane may be different from the number of drawing units visible on the screen.

When you invoke commands that change the viewing angle or magification AutoCAD uses the data in VIEWSIZE to measure the new magnification of the drawing display.

EARLIEST VERSION

All

DATA TYPE

Real number

DEFAULT

9 (same as AutoCAD's default y-axis drawing limits)

READ-ONLY

Yes

VIEWTWIST

Stores the camera's orientation around the viewing angle, as entered using the Dview Twist command (Chapter 11).

Data is expressed in the current angle-measurement format as defined using AutoCAD's Units command (Chapter 6).

EARLIEST VERSION

Release 10

DATA TYPE

Real number

DEFAULT

0 (the camera is not rotated around the viewing angle)

READ-ONLY

Yes

VISRETAIN

Sets visibility status (On or Off, Frozen or Thawed) for externally referenced drawing layers. When stored in VISRETAIN, the following integers control these layer's visibility:

0 = Use visibility status as preserved in the external reference drawing (reset on each Xref reload)
1 = Use visibility status as preserved in the layer table of current drawing

EARLIEST VERSION

Release 11

DATA TYPE

Integer

DEFAULT

0

READ-ONLY

No

VPOINTX, VPOINTY, VPOINTZ

Store the x, y, and z coordinates, respectively, of the 3-D point viewing angle (see VIEWDIR). Prior to Release 10, these three system variables were used together as the point by which the current 3-D viewing angle was calculated in relation to the drawing origin point.

Before Release 10, valid data for this system variable includes any real numbers that, taken together, represent a point that forms the current viewing angle when aligned with point 0,0,0.

As of Release 10, these system variables must correspond to the coordinate point stored in VIEWDIR.

These variables are no longer used in Release 11. Use VIEWDIR instead.

VERSIONS

2.5 through Release 10

DATA TYPE

Real numbers

DEFAULT

VPOINTX = 0.0
VPOINTY = 0.0
VPOINTZ = 1.0

READ-ONLY

Yes

VSMAX

Stores the coordinate location of the upper-right corner of the virtual screen, the area in which zooming and panning are permitted without requiring a drawing regeneration. Refer to the Zoom Dynamic command, Chapter 11, for details regarding the virtual screen.

Valid data for VSMAX is a 2-D coordinate point, displayed in AutoCAD's current units format.

VSMAX is updated whenever a drawing regeneration is performed. Its calculation is an internal process and is not subject to modification by the user.

EARLIEST VERSION

2.6

DATA TYPE

Coordinate point

DEFAULT

Not applicable

READ-ONLY

Yes

VSMIN

Stores the coordinate location of the lower-left corner of the virtual screen, the area in which zooming and panning are permitted without requiring a drawing regeneration. Refer to the Zoom Dynamic command, Chapter 11, for details regarding the virtual screen.

Valid data for VSMIN is a 2-D coordinate point, displayed in AutoCAD's current units format.

VSMIN is updated whenever a drawing regeneration is performed. Its calculation is an internal process and is not subject to modification by the user.

EARLIEST VERSION

2.6

DATA TYPE

Coordinate point

DEFAULT

Not applicable

READ-ONLY

Yes

WORLDVIEW

Controls the viewing angles set using the Dview or Vpoint command (Chapter 11).

If you are using these commands in a non–World Coordinate System, the Camera and Target options may produce confusing results. This is because the camera's angle of inclination is relative to the X-Y plane of the current UCS, which could be in any orientation relative to the current viewing angle.

If WORLDVIEW is set to 1, AutoCAD will automatically switch to the World Coordinate System when you invoke the Dview command, and will reset the original UCS when you are finished. This gives you a fixed plane of reference when setting up new viewing angles.

When stored in WORLDVIEW, the following integers set the indicated features:

0 = Camera and Target in Dview and Vpoint are relative to the current UCS

1 = UCS is automatically changed to WCS for Dview and Vpoint commands, and returns to previous UCS on exit

EARLIEST VERSION

Release 10

DATA TYPE

Integer

DEFAULT

1

READ-ONLY

No

Drawing Aid Defaults

The following system variables control various default options for AutoCAD's drawing aids. Most of these system variables can be changed using either the Setvar command, AutoLISP's Setvar function, or special AutoCAD commands. Exceptions to this are noted—for example, when the system variable is read-only and may be changed only by means of a special AutoCAD command. When these system variables are read-only, AutoLISP may retrieve their data using the Getvar function, or change them by calling the appropriate AutoCAD commands from within the AutoLISP routine.

APERTURE

Controls the size of the object-snap aperture box, which appears around the crosshairs when object-snap modes are enabled.

Valid data includes an integer representing the length, in pixels, of one side of the object-snap aperture.

EARLIEST VERSION

All

DATA TYPE

Integer

DEFAULT

10

READ-ONLY

No

ELEVATION

Stores the elevation above the current construction plane. This value becomes the default z coordinate when only x and y coordinates are entered. It is useful to change the value of the elevation when using the pointing device to enter a series of points at the same z coordinate.

In AutoCAD Release 10 and later, if you change the UCS, the elevation remains the same relative to the new UCS. Refer to the UCS command in Chapter 11 for details.

EARLIEST VERSION

2.1

DATA TYPE

Real number

DEFAULT

0

READ-ONLY

No

GRIDMODE

Controls the display of the drawing grid on the screen. Refer to the Grid command, Chapter 7, for details regarding the drawing grid.

When stored in GRIDMODE, the following integers set the indicated features:

0 = Drawing grid not displayed
1 = Drawing grid displayed

If you change the value of GRIDMODE from the Command Prompt, using Setvar, or from within AutoLISP, the results will not become visible until the next drawing regeneration or Redraw command. To turn the grid on or off immediately, use the Grid function key or the Grid command. Refer to Chapter 7 for details.

EARLIEST VERSION

All

DATA TYPE

Integer

DEFAULT

1

READ-ONLY

No

GRIDUNIT

Controls the x-y aspect spacing of the drawing grid. Refer to the Grid command, Chapter 7, for details on the drawing grid's aspect spacing. In setting values for GRIDUNIT, the x coordinate equals the grid's spacing along the x-axis, and the y coordinate equals the grid spacing along the y-axis.

The values are displayed using the current units format.

EARLIEST VERSION

All

DATA TYPE

2-D coordinate point

DEFAULT

0,0

READ-ONLY

No

ORTHOMODE

Enables AutoCAD's orthogonal mode, forcing lines to be drawn parallel to the crosshairs. Refer to the Ortho command, Chapter 7, for details regarding orthogonal mode.

When stored in ORTHOMODE, the following integers set the indicated features:

    0 = Orthogonal mode not enabled
    1 = Orthogonal mode enabled

EARLIEST VERSION

All

DATA TYPE

Integer

DEFAULT

1

READ-ONLY

No

OSMODE

Controls the setting of AutoCAD's object-snap feature, indicating to what types of construction points AutoCAD will force coordinate point entry. For details regarding object snap, refer to the Osnap command, Chapter 7.

OSMODE accepts a positive integer. It can be any sum of one or more of the following integers:

       0 = none
       1 = endpoints
       2 = midpoints
       4 = centers of circles and arcs
       8 = nodes (points added to line entities)
     16 = quadrants of circles and arcs
     32 = intersections
     64 = block or text insertion points
   128 = perpendicular points
   256 = tangent points
   512 = nearest entity point to crosshairs
 1024 = quick-Osnap mode

To set the value of OSMODE, first choose the entity construction points to which you would like AutoCAD to snap. Add the corresponding integers together and set the value of OSMODE to the total. You can also change the value of OSMODE by means of the Osnap command.

EARLIEST VERSION

2.0

DATA TYPE

Integer bit-codes

DEFAULT

0 (none)

READ-ONLY

No

PICKBOX

Controls the size of the entity-selection box, which appears when AutoCAD displays the "Select objects:" prompt. You may enlarge the box by setting PICKBOX to a higher integer, making the selection box larger. Setting PICK-BOX to a lower integer makes the selection box smaller, narrowing AutoCAD's range when selecting an entity to edit.

EARLIEST VERSION

All

DATA TYPE

Integer

DEFAULT

3

READ-ONLY

No

SKETCHINC

Stores the minimum distance (in drawing units) you must move the pointing device in order for AutoCAD to generate a line when using the Sketch command (Chapter 21). The smaller this number, the less movement of the pointing device is required, and the greater will be the resolution of the sketched line (which is actually made up of a series of very small lines).

While fine resolution in sketched lines is generally a good thing, the effect on the size of AutoCAD drawing files is considerable. The Sketch command can quickly add thousands of tiny lines to the drawing database, making the drawing file unwieldy for loading, regenerating, or even backing up to diskettes.

Therefore, if you are using the Sketch command, set this system variable to the largest amount you can consistent with your need for good resolution of sketched lines.

EARLIEST VERSION

All

DATA TYPE

Real number

DEFAULT

0.1

READ-ONLY

No

SKPOLY

Controls whether contiguous lines drawn using the Sketch command (Chapter 21) are drawn as individual line segments or as polylines. When SKPOLY is set to 0, sketched lines are generated as line segments. Otherwise, they are generated as polylines.

Generating sketched lines as polylines may reduce the size of the drawing file and speed up regenerations since, with polylines, each segment does not have to be stored as a unique drawing entity.

When stored in SKPOLY, the following integers set the indicated features:

0 = Sketched lines are generated as line segments
1 = Sketched lines are generated as polylines

EARLIEST VERSION

2.1

DATA TYPE

Integer

DEFAULT

0

READ-ONLY

No

SNAPANG

Controls the rotation of the snap grid and the crosshairs. Refer to the Snap command, Chapter 7, for details regarding the snap rotation angle. As of Release 10, the value of this system variable applies to the current UCS and the current viewport. When using multiple viewports, you may have a different snap angle for each viewport.

When you change the value of SNAPANG, the angle of the crosshairs will respond immediately, but the grid will not be displayed at the new angle until the next redraw or drawing regeneration. To change the appearance of the grid immediately, use the Snap Rotate command (Chapter 7), which forces a redraw.

EARLIEST VERSION

All

DATA TYPE

Real number

DEFAULT

0.0

READ-ONLY

No

SNAPBASE

Controls the location of the base point of the snap grid. AutoCAD uses this base point as the point around which it will rotate the snap grid if requested. As of Release 10, the value of this system variable applies to the current UCS as well as the current viewport. When using multiple viewports, you may have a different snap base point for each viewport.

EARLIEST VERSION

All

DATA TYPE

Coordinate point

DEFAULT

0,0

READ-ONLY

No

SNAPISOPAIR

Controls the display of the current isometric snap grid (see Chapter 7).

When stored in SNAPISOPAIR, the following integers set the indicated features:

0 = Snap grid is isometric left
1 = Snap grid is isometric top
2 = Snap grid is isometric right

When you change the value of SNAPISOPAIR, the angle of the crosshairs will respond immediately, but the grid will not be displayed at the new snap aspect until the next redraw or drawing regeneration. To change the appearance of the grid immediately, use the Isoplane command (Chapter 7), which forces a redraw.

EARLIEST VERSION

All

DATA TYPE

Integer

DEFAULT

0

READ-ONLY

No

SNAPMODE

Enables AutoCAD's snap mode, forcing coordinate points that are selected using the pointing device to fall on special "snap points." These snap points are configured using either the Snap command (Chapter 7) or the system variables whose names begin with *SNAP.*

When snap mode is enabled, it affects only points selected with the pointing device. Non-snap points may be selected from the keyboard at all times. Object-snap overrides supercede the setting of this variable.

When stored in SNAPMODE, the following integers set the indicated features:

0 = Snap mode not enabled (any coordinate point may be selected)
1 = Snap mode enabled (only snap points may be selected with the pointing device)

EARLIEST VERSION

All

DATA TYPE

Integer

DEFAULT

0

READ-ONLY

No

SNAPSTYL

Controls AutoCAD's snap grid style, allowing you to choose between Standard and Isometric snap styles. As of Release 10, snap styles apply to the current viewport. When using multiple viewports, you may have different snap styles in each viewport.

When stored in SNAPMODE, the following integers set the indicated features:

    0 = Snap style is Standard (2 axes set at 90 degrees)
    1 = Snap style is Isometric (3 axes at 30, 90, and 150 degrees)

EARLIEST VERSION

2.1

DATA TYPE

Integer

DEFAULT

0 (standard)

READ-ONLY

No

SNAPUNIT

Controls the x-y aspect spacing of the snap grid. Refer to the Snap command, Chapter 7, for details regarding the snap grid's aspect spacing. In setting values for SNAPUNIT, the x coordinate equals the snap grid spacing along the x-axis, and the y coordinate equals the snap grid spacing along the y-axis.

Valid data is displayed and may be entered using the current units format.

EARLIEST VERSION

All

DATA TYPE

2-D coordinate point

DEFAULT

1,1

READ-ONLY

No

THICKNESS

Stores the default extrusion distance of line entities. When THICKNESS is set to a nonzero value, line entities are extruded parallel to the z-axis by the stored amount. This provides a quick, convenient means to create vertical planes from lines and polylines, vertical cylinders from circles, vertical curved planes from arcs, and so on.

As of Release 10, entities are always extruded parallel to the z-axis of the current UCS at the time they are drawn. Entities always retain their extrusion orientation regardless of further changes to the UCS. If you change the UCS, however, the default thickness is retained, now relative to the new UCS. Refer to the UCS command in Chapter 11 for details.

If the number is positive, the extrusion is in the direction of the positive z-axis. A negative number will extrude entities in the opposite direction.

EARLIEST VERSION

2.1

DATA TYPE

Real number

DEFAULT

0 (no extrusion; draw line entities as 2-D lines)

READ-ONLY

No

TRACEWID

Stores the default width of traces (AutoCAD wide line segments). For details regarding traces, refer to the Trace command in Chapter 8.

The value stored in TRACEWID has no effect on the width of wide polylines.

EARLIEST VERSION

All

DATA TYPE

Real number

DEFAULT

0.05

READ-ONLY

No

TEXT DEFAULTS

The following system variables control various default settings related to the way AutoCAD handles text in a drawing.

TEXTEVAL

Controls the way in which AutoCAD interprets input to the prompt to enter text or attributes. Text and attribute data may be interpreted literally, meaning that all characters entered are considered to be part of the text string; or text may consist of input that begins with either an exclamation point, "!", or an open parenthesis, "(", and thus be considered an AutoLISP expression to be evaluated as such, rather than simply reproduced in the drawing as entered. TEXTEVAL allows you to store lengthy text strings in AutoLISP expressions and enter the expression instead of the actual text.

Note: TEXTEVAL has no effect on the Dtext command, which always interprets text input literally.

When calling the Text command from within an AutoLISP routine, you may input AutoLISP expressions in response to text prompts; the expression will then be evaluated, regardless of the setting of TEXTEVAL.

When stored in TEXTEVAL, the following integers set the indicated features:

0 = All text input is accepted literally; no AutoLISP expressions are allowed

1 = Text input beginning with either "!" or "(" is assumed to be an AutoLISP expression, and an attempt will be made to evaluate it

EARLIEST VERSION

2.6

DATA TYPE

Integer

DEFAULT

0

READ-ONLY

No

TEXTSIZE

Stores the default height for newly created text styles (in versions prior to Release 9). In AutoCAD Release 9 and later, this system variable stores the default height for new text entities using the current text style. If the current style is defined with a fixed height, the value of this system variable is ignored.

EARLIEST VERSION

All

DATA TYPE

Real number

DEFAULT

0.2

READ-ONLY

No

TEXTSTYLE

Stores the name of the current default text style.

You can change the value of TEXTSTYLE by creating a new style using the Style command, or by changing the current style using the Text or Dtext command.

EARLIEST VERSION

2.6

DATA TYPE

String

DEFAULT

"STANDARD"

READ-ONLY

Yes

UNITS FORMAT DEFAULTS

These system variables store data related to AutoCAD's units format, normally set using the Units command. None of these system variables are read-only. If you are making a quick or temporary change to only one of these features, you can save a little time by setting them individually rather than sifting through all of them when using the Units command.

ANGBASE

Controls the orientation of AutoCAD's angle zero. The default is horizontal, pointing to the right (positive x-axis). You may use any positive real number representing between 0 and 360 degrees (using the current format for angular units, as set using the Units command or the AUNITS system variable). A value of 0, for example, sets AutoCAD's angle zero to the default horizontal position. A value of 90 sets AutoCAD's angle zero pointing up.

The value for this variable should be entered in the current format for angle values. For example, if radians is the current angle format, 90 degrees would be entered as 1.57079.

After you change the format for angle units, rounding differences may affect the setting of ANGBASE slightly, if it is set to a value other than zero.

EARLIEST VERSION

Version 2.5. As of Release 10, the setting of ANGBASE is always applied to the current UCS.

DATA TYPE

Real number

DEFAULT

0

READ-ONLY

No

ANGDIR

Controls whether angles are incremented clockwise or counterclockwise. When stored in ANGDIR, the following integers set the indicated features:

0 = Angles incremented counterclockwise
1 = Angles incremented clockwise

EARLIEST VERSION

2.5

DATA TYPE

Integer

DEFAULT

0

READ-ONLY

No

AUNITS

Controls the format for angle values.
When stored in AUNITS, the following integers set the indicated features:

    0 = Decimal degrees
    1 = Degrees/minutes/seconds
    2 = Grads
    3 = Radians
    4 = Surveyor's units (in Version 2.5 and later)

EARLIEST VERSION

All

DATA TYPE

Integer

DEFAULT

0

READ-ONLY

No

AUPREC

Controls the number of decimal places of precision for angle units. Any integer from 1 to 8 may be used.

EARLIEST VERSION

All

DATA TYPE

Integer

DEFAULT

4

READ-ONLY

No

LUNITS

Stores the current linear-units format, as is usually set with AutoCAD's Units command.

When stored in LUNITS, the following integers set the indicated features:

SYSTEM OF UNITS	EXAMPLE
1 = Scientific	2.575E +01
2 = Decimal	25.75
3 = Engineering	2'-1.75"
4 = Architectural	2'-1 3/4"
5 = Fractional	25 3/4 (added in Version 2.6)

EARLIEST VERSION

All

DATA TYPE

Integer

DEFAULT

2 (decimal units)

READ-ONLY

No

LUPREC

Stores the number of decimal places of precision for the linear-units format, as is usually set using AutoCAD's Units command, which indicates that the maximum allowable number of decimal places of precision is 8. Refer to the Units command, Chapter 6, for details regarding AutoCAD's linear-units formats.

When LUPREC is set using the Setvar command, any positive integer may be used.

EARLIEST VERSION

All

DATA TYPE

Integer

DEFAULT

4

READ-ONLY

No

USER COORDINATE SYSTEM DEFAULTS

The following system variables control various default settings related to the way AutoCAD Release 10 and later manages user coordinates systems. Except for UCS-ICON and UCSFOLLOW, these system variables are read-only. When the variable is read-only, AutoLISP routines can read the data it contains using the Getvar function, and process it as required, but can only update it by calling the UCS command from within the routine. Refer to Chapters 16 and 17 for details regarding AutoLISP. Refer to the UCS command, Chapter 11, for details on user coordinate systems.

UCSFOLLOW

Controls how the UCS is displayed whenever it is changed or a new UCS is created.

When stored in UCSFOLLOW, the following integers set the indicated features:

0 = Display new UCS's using the current viewing angle
1 = Always display new UCS's in plan view

EARLIEST VERSION

Release 10

DATA TYPE

Integer

DEFAULT

0

READ-ONLY

No

UCSICON

Controls the display of AutoCAD's UCS icon. Refer to the Ucsicon command, Chapter 11, for details regarding the user coordinate system icon. If you are using multiple viewports, the value of UCSICON can be set separately for each viewport.

When stored in UCSICON, the following integers set the indicated features:

0 = UCS icon is not displayed
1 = UCS icon display is enabled, displayed in the lower-left corner of the viewport
2 = When the icon is displayed, it is displayed at the UCS origin point, provided that the icon fits completely on the screen when positioned there
3 = Combination of 1 and 2

EARLIEST VERSION

Release 10

DATA TYPE

Integer bit-code

DEFAULT

1

READ-ONLY

No

UCSNAME

Stores the name of the current UCS (if named).

EARLIEST VERSION

Release 10

DATA TYPE

String

DEFAULT

No data

READ-ONLY

Yes

UCSORG

Stores the origin point of the current UCS. If you are using multiple viewports, the values contained in this system variable may be different for each viewport.

EARLIEST VERSION

Release 10

DATA TYPE

3-D coordinate point

DEFAULT

0,0,0

READ-ONLY

Yes

UCSXDIR

Stores the direction of the x-axis of the current UCS (always in world coordinates, in relationship to world coordinate point 0,0,0). If you are using multiple viewports, the values contained in this system variable may be different for each viewport.

EARLIEST VERSION

Release 10

DATA TYPE

3-D coordinate point

DEFAULT

1,0,0 (parallel to WCS x-axis)

READ-ONLY

Yes

UCSYDIR

Stores the direction of the y-axis of the current UCS (always in world coordinates, in relationship to world coordinate point 0,0,0). If you are using multiple viewports, the values contained in this system variable may be different for each viewport.

No system variable exists for the direction of the UCS z-axis, because this axis is always perpendicular to the X-Y plane of the current UCS.

EARLIEST VERSION

Release 10

DATA TYPE

3-D coordinate point

DEFAULT

0,1,0 (parallel to WCS y-axis)

READ-ONLY

Yes

WORLDUCS

Stores an integer indicating to AutoCAD whether the current user coordinate system (UCS) is the same as the World Coordinate System (WCS).

When stored in WORLDUCS, the following integers indicate their respective conditions:

0 = UCS and WCS are different
1 = UCS and WCS are the same

The value of WORLDUCS is automatically changed to 0 when a non-WCS UCS is referenced, and automatically changed to 1 when the WCS is made the current UCS.

EARLIEST VERSION

Release 10

DATA TYPE

Integer

DEFAULT

1

READ-ONLY

Yes

MISCELLANEOUS SYSTEM VARIABLES

Following are system variables that control various unique aspects of Auto-CAD's performance. Some are read-only and unchangeable, some are changeable only by means of commands, while others are fully changeable, as noted.

ACADVER

Stores the release number for the current version of AutoCAD.

By itself, ACADVER has no effect on AutoCAD's performance. However, it can be read in AutoLISP functions and used as a version check to determine if certain command sequences and functions can be performed, thus allowing AutoLISP routines to be valid among several versions.

EARLIEST VERSION

Release 9

DATA TYPE

String

READ-ONLY

Yes

AREA

Stores the most recent area calculated using the Area command (Chapter 21). Its data can be extracted and used by AutoLISP routines that calculate areas.

EARLIEST VERSION

All

DATA TYPE

Real Number

READ-ONLY

Yes

CHAMFERA

Controls the first chamfer distance. The Chamfer command (Chapter 10) uses the data in this and the CHAMFERB system variable to create chamfered line intersections from existing lines or polylines.

If the number is too large to chamfer the selected lines, AutoCAD cancels the Chamfer command.

EARLIEST VERSION

All

DATA TYPE

Real number

DEFAULT

0 (no chamfering)

READ-ONLY

No

CHAMFERB

Controls the second chamfer distance. The Chamfer command (Chapter 10) uses the data in this and the CHAMFERA system variable to create chamfered line intersections from existing lines or polylines.

If the number stored in CHAMFERB is too large for a chamfer of the selected lines, AutoCAD cancels the Chamfer command.

When chamfering polylines, AutoCAD will chamfer those intersections it can, and ignore those it can't.

EARLIEST VERSION

All

DATA TYPE

Real number

DEFAULT

0 (no chamfering)

READ-ONLY

No

DIASTAT

Indicates how the operator exited from the most recently displayed dialog box. When stored in DIASTAT, the following integers indicate:

0 = The operator exited via the Cancel button
1 = The operator exited via the OK button

This variable is useful for AutoLISP and ADS applications that need to monitor the operator's response to dialog-box prompts.

EARLIEST VERSION

Release 11

DATA TYPE

Integer

DEFAULT

1

READ-ONLY

No

DISTANCE

Stores the most recent distance value calculated using the Dist command (Chapter 21). Its data can be extracted and used by AutoLISP routines that work with distances.

EARLIEST VERSION

All

DATA TYPE

Real number

READ-ONLY

Yes

_ERRNO

Contains an integer code corresponding to an error condition or other program feedback detected by AutoLISP or ADS applications. In Release 11, there are many error codes. For a complete listing of these codes and their meanings, refer to the AutoCAD Development System Programmer's Reference. Some common Release 11 codes that may be reported and stored in _ERRNO are:

2 = Entity processing function referenced an invalid entity name
3 = Ssget exceeded the maximum number of allowable selection sets
8 = Entnext reached the end of entity file
13 = Handent referenced invalid handle
14 = Handent was called when handles not enabled
20 = Setvar attempted to set a read-only variable
25 = Entmod referenced an invalid layer name
30 = Entmod referenced an invalid entity group code
47 = Entmake did not include a required group code sublist
52 = Entsel did not receive pick point(s)

_ERRNO provides a mechanism for immediate feedback on a program's performance for testing and debugging and other information useful to the program operator. However, _ERRNO may not be directly cleared or modified by either the AutoCAD operator or a program; rather, it retains its current value until a new condition causes AutoCAD to bind it to a new value. Therefore, read the contents of _ERRNO as soon as you suspect an error to have occurred. Be aware, though, that the number stored in _ERRNO may reflect some previous condition of the system.

EARLIEST VERSION

Release 11

DATA TYPE

Integer

DEFAULT

No data

READ-ONLY

Yes

FILLETRAD

Stores the current fillet radius. The Fillet command (Chapter 10) uses the data in this system variable to create line intersections from existing lines or polylines.

If the number stored in FILLETRAD is zero, the Fillet command causes lines to intersect to a point. Otherwise, they are joined by means of an arc with the stored radius. If the radius is too large to join the lines, AutoCAD cancels the Fillet command.

When filleting polylines, AutoCAD will fillet those intersections it can, and ignore those it can't.

EARLIEST VERSION

All

DATA TYPE

Real number

DEFAULT

0 (fillet to a point)

HOW TO CHANGE

The Setvar command, AutoLISP's Setvar function, or the Fillet command.

READ-ONLY

No

HANDLES

Controls whether entities in AutoCAD's drawing database are assigned *handles*—unique alphanumeric strings that remain constant for each entity from drawing session to drawing session.

Entity handles are useful when AutoLISP routines and macros must access the same drawing entities each time they are used. If these entities change location or are in close proximity to other entities in the drawing, it may be difficult if not impossible for AutoCAD to select them consistently via point pick. Entity handles are a reliable method of selecting the exact desired set of entities each time. Refer to the Handles command, Chapter 7, for details regarding entity handles.

When stored in HANDLES, the following integers set the indicated features:

0 = Entity handles are not used
1 = All entities are assigned unique handles

Entity handles may only be enabled or disabled using the Handles command. AutoLISP routines may read the value of the HANDLES system variable to determine if handles are enabled for a drawing, and call the Handles command to enable them if not. However, AutoLISP cannot disable entity handles once they are enabled, since this process requires manual entry of a random password (see Chapter 6).

EARLIEST VERSION

Release 10

DEFAULT

0

DATA TYPE

Integer

READ-ONLY

Yes

LASTANGLE

Stores the ending angle of the last arc entered. This angle is used to draw line segments tangent to the endpoints of arcs. Refer to the Arc and Line commands, Chapter 9, for details.

As of Release 10, the value of LASTANGLE will be displayed when you access it using the Setvar command, but only if the current UCS contains the last arc drawn. The value is displayed in the current units format. Whenever you attempt to draw a line segment from the endpoint of an arc by pressing Enter in response to the "From point" prompt, the line segment will be both tangent to the arc and in the same X-Y plane as the arc, regardless of the setting of the current UCS.

EARLIEST VERSION

All

DATA TYPE

Real number

DEFAULT

0.0

READ-ONLY

Yes

LASTPOINT

Stores the last set of coordinate points entered, except for the second point used to indicate an angle or distance.

As of Release 10, this system variable may contain three real numbers, the third of which represents the z coordinate. The value is displayed and may be updated using the current units format as set with AutoCAD's Units command (Chapter 6).

To reference the coordinates stored in LASTPOINT, enter @ in response to any prompt that requests a point.

If you are drawing a line segment or arc, you may do so starting from the endpoint of the last line or arc in the drawing database, regardless of the current setting of LASTPOINT; simply press Enter in response to the "From point:" prompt. AutoCAD starts the line segment or arc from the endpoint of the last arc or line segment in the database, even if that line segment or arc was previously erased. If you start a line segment or arc in this fashion, the starting point so selected becomes the new value for LASTPOINT.

The value of LASTPOINT is unchanged by the U and Undo commands. Use this variable instead of LASTP3D in Release 11 and later.

EARLIEST VERSION

All

DATA TYPE

Coordinate point

DEFAULT

Not applicable, as this variable is constantly updated throughout a drawing session

READ-ONLY

No

LASTPT3D

Behaves the same as LASTPOINT in AutoCAD Version 2.6 and Release 9. LASTPT3D contains a z coordinate, while LASTPOINT did not.

In Release 10 and later, this system variable is exactly the same as LASTPOINT when the FLATLAND system variable is set to zero. If you are using Release 10 and FLATLAND is zero, do not use LASTPT3D; use LASTPOINT instead. This feature was discontinued as of Release 11, LASTPOINT instead.

VERSIONS

2.6–10

DATA TYPE

Coordinate point

DEFAULT

Not applicable, as this variable is constantly updated throughout a drawing session

READ-ONLY

No

PERIMETER

Stores the most recent perimeter calculated using the Area command (Chapter 21). Its data can be extracted and used by AutoLISP routines that work with perimeter figures.

EARLIEST VERSION

All

DATA TYPE

Real number

DEFAULT

0.0

READ-ONLY

Yes

USERI1-USERI5; USERR1-USERR5

Allows users to store integer values. There are five USERI variables available for storage of integers and five USERR variables available for storage of real numbers. They are numbered 1 through 5 as part of the variable name—e.g., USERI1, USERI2, USERR1, USERR2, and so forth. They are most often used by AutoLISP and ADS programmers as safe storage for values that must be available from session to session.

If you intend to use these variables, it is prudent to read the variable before using its value to ensure it has not been bound to a different value by third-party software. For example, before binding USERR5 to a value, enter the following function:

(getvar "USERR5")

If the function returns nil, you may safely bind it to a value. Later, before using the value in USERR1, check it again to be certain that your third-party software has not changed its value.

EARLIEST VERSION

Release 10

DATA TYPE

Integers for USERI(x), and real numbers for USERR(x).

DEFAULT

No data

READ-ONLY

No

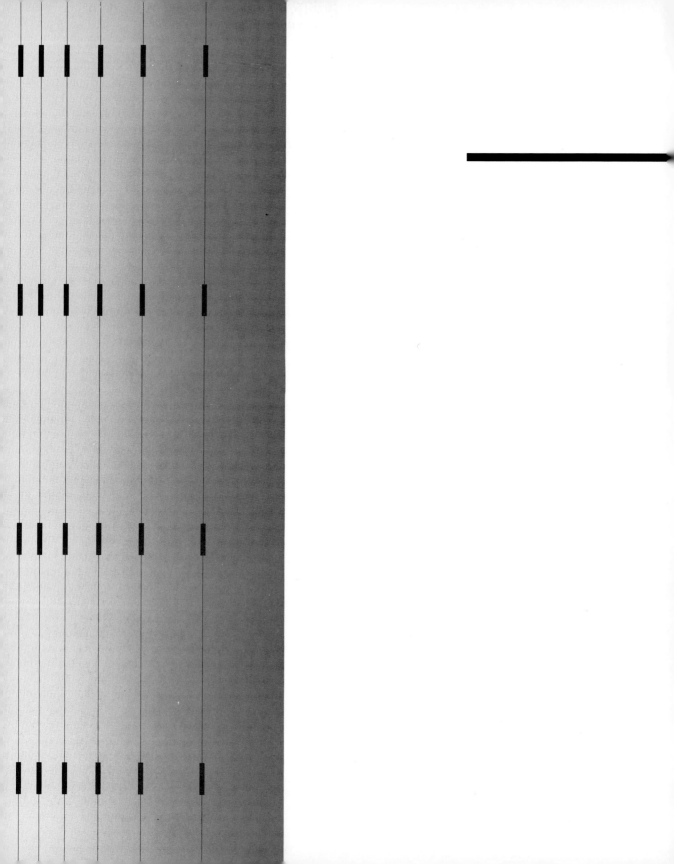

CHAPTER 14

CREATING CUSTOM MENUS AND COMMAND MACROS

CREATING CUSTOM MENUS AND COMMAND MACROS

The drafting tools provided in AutoCAD as it comes "off the shelf" are well-suited for general drafting requirements. However, your drafting situation may present its own unique challenges, for which the off-the-shelf AutoCAD tools won't work as well as you might like.

AutoCAD provides the means by which you may modify and customize its off-the-shelf tools so that they address your particular drafting needs more efficiently.

Custom menus and *command macros* are powerful tools at your disposal for improving your productivity. Custom menus enable you to eliminate unnecessary menu selection picks and repetitive keyboard entry. Command macros allow you to use AutoCAD more efficiently, by combining different commands into one, and automatically invoking preset command-option responses. This chapter explains how to modify the AutoCAD menu and create macros that will enhance your CAD abilities.

PURPOSES OF CUSTOM MENUS AND COMMAND MACROS

Custom menus are used for the following purposes:

- To group frequently used AutoCAD commands together on the screen or digitizing tablet, saving time by allowing you to move between them more quickly.
- To reduce the number of choices you need to make, by eliminating commands and features that are rarely (if ever) used.
- To combine several commands and features into a *macro,* wherein a single menu pick will execute a series of AutoCAD commands in sequence, eliminating the need to pick each command separately.

Custom menus and command macros can save many minutes of wasted effort—savings that quickly add up to hours of increased productivity. AutoCAD's menus are easy to modify, and the time taken to learn these modification techniques is an investment that will profit you handsomely.

AutoCAD can have as many different menus as you desire. They are stored on disk in separate files and loaded using the Menu command. Following is a summary of the Menu command's functions and features.

MENU

Loads AutoCAD menus from disk into the program, where they can be accessed and used.

VERSIONS

All. Starting with Version 2.5, AutoCAD menus are now *compiled* before they are loaded. Compiled menus can be loaded and executed much faster than non-compiled menus. The process of compiling the menu is automatic, and occurs only when you attempt to load a new (noncompiled) menu or make changes to an existing menu. In versions prior to 2.5, AutoCAD simply reads and loads the noncompiled menu.

COMMAND OPTIONS

Menu name   Enter the name of the menu you want AutoCAD to load. Auto-CAD will look on the search path for a menu file with that name, compile it if necessary, and load it.

.   Enter a period to load no menu at all. AutoCAD will not load a menu, but this option will disable you from entering commands using the pointing device. (You can still enter commands from the keyboard and use the pointing device for windowing, selecting coordinate points, and other input not related to selecting commands.)

Press Enter   If a default menu name appears in the menu prompt, you may press Enter to load it.

USAGE

Noncompiled menus must have the file extension MNU. Files with this extension are ASCII files that you can create and edit using your text editor. When AutoCAD compiles a menu, a new file is created, with the extension MNX. These MNX files are the ones actually used by AutoCAD to activate and display the menu.

AutoCAD is supplied with a single standard menu, in both compiled and non-compiled formats. In its compiled format, it is called ACAD.MNX, while in its noncompiled format, it is called ACAD.MNU.

AutoCAD needs only the compiled (MNX) file on disk in order to load the menu. If you make changes to the MNU file, however, it is a good idea to keep both files in the same subdirectory, so that AutoCAD can detect that changes were made and recompile the edited menu before loading it.

When entering menu names, do not include a file extension; the extension MNX is assumed. AutoCAD first looks for a file with the given name and the extension MNX. Next, it looks for a file with the same name and the extension MNU. If only an MNX file is found, AutoCAD loads the menu. If only an MNU file is found, AutoCAD compiles it, creating an MNX file, and then loads it.

If both files are found, AutoCAD compares the date and time that the files were created. If they were created at the same time, AutoCAD loads the MNX file. If not, AutoCAD assumes that changes were made to the MNU file. It then recompiles the MNU file, overwriting the old MNX file with a new one. Then it loads the MNX file.

When AutoCAD is compiling a menu, it displays a message to that effect. After compiling, AutoCAD updates the file directory, showing both files as having the same date and time.

RELATED SYSTEM VARIABLES

, MENUNAME (the name of the currently loaded menu; read-only).

SAMPLE DIALOG

Command: **Menu**
Menu file name or . for none: **ACAD**
Loaded menu C:\ACAD\ACAD.mnx
Command:

THE TEXT EDITOR

The text editor is the essential tool for all modifications to AutoCAD. This includes the menus, shape and font files (see Chapter 15), AutoLISP programs (see Chapters 16 and 17), linetypes, hatch patterns, and external command files (see Chapter 21). Text editors produce a special type of disk file, sometimes referred to as an *ASCII file*. (ASCII stands for American Standard Code for Information Interchange.) ASCII files contain only standard character codes, or

"ASCII codes," that represent alphanumeric characters (A–Z, 0–9) and standard punctuation marks (!, *, ;, etc.). Nonstandard codes are not permitted in these files; for example, no codes are used to designate underlining, boldfacing, automatic paragraph alignment, and so forth.

There are many different text editors on the market. DOS provides a text editor called EDLIN, and if you already know how to use it, you can use it right away to modify AutoCAD.

Users not already familiar with EDLIN may prefer one of the many commercial text editors that are available, some of them quite reasonably priced. PC-Write, for example, is a low-cost word-processing program that can produce ASCII files. Many DOS add-on utility programs, such as PC-Tools and Pathminder, include high-quality, easy-to-use text editors as one of their features. If you already own a commercial word-processing program, chances are good that you can use it as a text editor. For example, WordStar functions as a text editor by producing ASCII files in "nondocument mode." WordPerfect will save files to disk in ASCII format, calling them "DOS text files." You may have to study your word processor's documentation to find out how to use it as a text editor.

THE MODIFIABLE MENU FILE

You can create or modify an AutoCAD menu by editing a file with the extension MNU and placing valid menu commands and macros within it.

In general, if you can enter a command, a response to a prompt, a coordinate point, or other data using the keyboard, you can incorporate it into a custom menu or macro. Custom menus and macros will pause to permit you to make different inputs at times during processing, allowing a single menu or macro to be useful in a variety of situations.

To write an effective custom menu, you must have a good working knowledge of AutoCAD. All the characters, punctuation marks, and spaces in a menu are extremely important, and all count for something; there is no room for anything superfluous or overlooked. Without a working understanding of AutoCAD, you could write a custom menu that did not work and never figure out why. But, for more experienced AutoCAD users, there is a brighter side to the story: You need not be afraid to experiment, to try something out just to see what happens. Even if your custom menu does not work, you will not hurt AutoCAD or your computer. At worst, you may bring AutoCAD's processing to a halt, but even in this remote possibility, you can solve the problem simply by rebooting the computer and starting over. You can edit and reedit MNU files until they accomplish exactly what you intended.

AutoCAD's standard menu, ACAD.MNU, is a good model for study and practice in modifying menus. If you decide to use ACAD.MNU, by all means first make a copy of it with a different name—MY.MNU or CUSTOM.MNU, for example. If you work only with the copy, you can make whatever changes and perform whatever experiments you like, knowing that you can always revert back to the original if things should go too far awry. Standard menu examples in this book come from the Release 11 version of ACAD.MNU.

If ACAD.MNU is not currently on your hard disk, you can find it on the master disks supplied with the program. Look for the file on a disk labeled Support Disk or on a master-disk subdirectory named SOURCE.

THE SCREEN MENU STRUCTURE

In its noncompiled form, AutoCAD's standard menu is many lines long. When you first load the menu into your text editor, you will see a long list of AutoCAD commands, plus various symbols aligned on the leftmost column of the file.

Each line in a custom menu contains a specific *command sequence,* a series of one or more AutoCAD commands, command options, and whatever responses might be appropriate. Each sequence begins at the leftmost position, and can continue to the right indefinitely. (There is a special technique, presented later in this chapter, that you can use to ''wrap'' long command sequences onto several lines in the file, so that they are visible in their entirety on the screen.)

Command sequences are not case-sensitive; that is, they can be entered using either uppercase or lowercase characters; AutoCAD's standard menu generally uses uppercase characters for the portions of the menu file relating to the on-screen menus, tablet menus, and digitizing-button commands, and lowercase characters for the pull-down and icon menus; but exceptions are not uncommon.

AutoCAD menu files are divided into *major sections,* which can be further divided into *submenus.* The major sections are used to group related submenus or command sequences together; the submenus contain AutoCAD command sequences and macros. It is the submenus that are displayed on the screen in the form of pull-down menus, icon menus, or AutoCAD's more familiar standard screen-menu area.

Major Sections

The major sections of an AutoCAD menu are identified by specific *section labels.* Each major section contains either submenus or command sequences that relate to a particular hardware device or screen-display area. They are:

Comment   This section contains any text useful to a user reading the MNU file. There is no format requirement. A Comment section will not be displayed or made active and ends when another section begins.

Buttons   This section contains commands and functions that are invoked by pressing buttons on the pointing device.

Aux1   This section contains commands that are invoked by pressing the buttons on an *auxiliary function box,* an external hardware device with buttons that can be configured to invoke AutoCAD commands.

Pop1–Pop10   Sections labeled POP1 through POP10 contain submenus that will be displayed as *pull-down menus* if your hardware display supports the Advanced User Interface.

Icon   This section contains submenus that appear on the display as *icon menus,* if your hardware display device supports them.

Screen   This section contains submenus that appear in AutoCAD's standard screen-menu area.

Tablet1–Tablet4   Sections labeled TABLET1 through TABLET4 contain command sequences executed by touching specific areas of the digitizing tablet.

Major sections appear in the menu preceded by three asterisks—for example, ***BUTTONS or ***SCREEN. Major sections of the menu are not commands. A custom menu is not required to have all these major sections.

Submenus

Major sections of the menu may contain any number of *submenus.* This is especially evident in the Screen major section, whose many submenus determine which part of the menu appears in the screen-menu area at any given moment. Each submenu in the Screen section contains a list of the specific command sequences that will be executed when picked with the pointing device. These command sequences can include special commands that change the menu display.

Like the major sections, submenus are identified by specific *submenu labels.* These labels are preceded by two asterisks; for example, the first submenu in the Screen section of AutoCAD's standard menu is labeled **S.

ENTERING COMMANDS USING A CUSTOM MENU

The structure and contents of AutoCAD menus can range from the simplistic to the highly sophisticated. Figure 14.1 illustrates a simple AutoCAD custom menu in its most fundamental form: a single command sequence, invoking the Line command and no more.

FIGURE 14.1: A basic AutoCAD custom menu. The above lines are a valid AutoCAD screen menu, consisting of a Screen section, a submenu labeled S, and a single command. When AutoCAD's menu processor encounters a string of characters on a line in the menu file, it interprets them as keyboard input; in this case, selecting the lone command displayed by this menu is the same as entering the Line command from the keyboard.

The process of compiling, highlighting, and reading lines in a menu is handled by a part of the AutoCAD program called the *menu processor.* The following example demonstrates how the menu processor works:

1. Use your text editor to create a file called BASIC.MNU, and place the lines shown in Figure 14.1 within it. Load that menu into AutoCAD's drawing editor by invoking the Menu Basic command. The following should appear in the screen-menu area:

   line

   Notice that the lines containing labels, ***SCREEN and **S, are not displayed at all.

2. Highlight this line with your pointing device and press the pick button. AutoCAD will automatically invoke the Line command. You can then go on to pick endpoints for the lines.

From this example, you can see that in a custom menu's most fundamental form, the menu processor simply reads the characters that it finds on the selected menu line and returns them in response to AutoCAD's prompts, just as though you had typed them at the keyboard.

Notice that the menu processor makes no judgments about the characters it reads or the context in which menu items are selected. On the contrary, it reads them literally and enters them in sequence, right or wrong, exactly as you have typed them into the MNU file. For example, if you were to select the Line command as it appears in this menu, and immediately select it again, AutoCAD's menu processor would dutifully repeat the "line" command sequence in response to the "From point:" prompt, causing an error message!

You can reload the AutoCAD standard menu by invoking the command Menu Acad at the Command prompt.

The following sections show you how to improve upon this fundamental concept, making the menu more useful and less prone to error.

CONTROL CHARACTERS

AutoCAD menus use special punctuation marks called *control characters* as symbols to represent special keys on the computer's keyboard, or to control the behavior of menu command sequences. Following is a summary of AutoCAD's control characters.

Semicolon: ;

The semicolon is the most important menu control character. In a menu command sequence, it represents a press of the Enter key. Alternatively, you can use the space character to represent the Enter key in a command sequence, just as AutoCAD itself will accept a press of the space bar instead of the Enter key in most commands.

In this book, for the sake of clarity, only the semicolon is used to represent the Enter key.

To demonstrate how the semicolon is used in AutoCAD menus, reedit BASIC.MNU so that the command sequence appears as follows:

```
line;0,0;12,12;;
```

Exit the text editor, enter AutoCAD's drawing editor, and invoke the command Menu Basic. Again, the command sequence appears on the screen, this time slightly different:

line;0,0

These are the first eight characters of the command sequence you just entered. AutoCAD will display a maximum of the first eight characters of any command sequence in the screen-menu area.

Again highlight this command sequence and press the pick button. AutoCAD automatically draws a line from point 0,0 to point 12,12. This is what would have happened had you entered the same characters from the keyboard, using the Enter key in place of the semicolon.

AutoCAD includes an automatic Enter at the end of each command-sequence line, unless the line ends with a backslash, control character, plus sign, or semicolon. For the sake of consistency, a semicolon is included at the end of all example lines in this book, where AutoCAD would supply the Enter key anyway.

In the present example, two semicolons appear at the end of the command sequence. The first represents the Enter that is issued following entry of the coordinate point 12,12; the second represents the Enter that is pressed to end the Line command.

Be very careful when typing spaces or semicolons in menus. It is a common mistake among both beginners and experienced menu builders to leave one out or to add one too many, usually with the result that the command sequence will not work.

Backslash: \

The backslash character is used whenever the command sequence must pause to accept input from the user. The backslash can accept input that is either digitized or typed from the keyboard; for example:

[ZOOM IN] ZOOM;W;\\

This simple macro invokes the Zoom command, issues a return, invokes the Window option with the *W,* issues another return (as you would if you were typing these commands at the keyboard), and finally pauses twice to get the coordinates of the corners of the zoom window from the user. No semicolon follows the second backslash, as the Enter key is not normally pressed after the window corner picks.

Brackets: [ ]

You can begin any menu line with characters that are enclosed in brackets. AutoCAD will not consider the characters enclosed in brackets to be part of the command sequence, but instead will process the command sequence beginning with the character that immediately follows the brackets.

AutoCAD treats the characters between brackets differently, depending on which main section is currently active:

- In the Screen section, AutoCAD will display only the characters found within brackets in the screen-menu area, instead of the command sequence. A maximum of eight characters will be displayed; you may include fewer or more than eight if you choose. Observe the following example:

  [D-LINE:]^C^CLINE;0,0;12,12;;

Using the above example, AutoCAD would display

  D-LINE:

in the screen-menu area, and invoke the command sequence beginning with the double Ctrl-C that immediately follows the brackets.

AutoCAD's standard menu generally follows some traditional rules regarding characters between brackets for screen-menu displays:

1. If the command sequence invokes an AutoCAD command, the AutoCAD command appears within the brackets, in all upper-case characters, followed by a colon; for example:

   [LINE:]
   [COPY:]
   [VPOINT:]

2. If the command sequence does not invoke an AutoCAD command, but instead only displays another menu, the characters between brackets indicate the type of menu to be displayed, all in uppercase characters, but not followed by a colon; for example:

   [DRAW]
   [EDIT]
   [DISPLAY]

3. If the command sequence includes only the responses to a previously invoked AutoCAD command, the characters between brackets indicate the response, in lowercase characters. If the response could be entered from the keyboard using only one or two key characters, those key characters are displayed in uppercase; for example:

   [CENter]
   [ENDpoint]

[INSert]
[INTersec]

4. Some optional command responses that consist of a single word less than eight characters long dispense with brackets altogether; for example:

Window
Crossing
Last
Previous

Exceptions to these general rules can be found, and you are under no obligation to follow them.

- In the Aux, Buttons, and Tablet sections, characters between brackets are not displayed, and are therefore ignored, making brackets a useful means of adding comments to your menu file—indicating command-box locations on the tablet, identifying button numbers on the pointing device, or inserting general comments explaining what the command sequence does. Here are some examples:

[T-100]^C^CLINE;0,0;12,12;;
[Button #6]^C^CLINE;0,0;12,12;;
[Draws a line between 0,0 and 12,12]^C^CLINE;0,0;12,12;;

- In the Pop1 through Pop10 submenus, brackets serve two purposes.
  The first line after the menu-section label contains the pull-down *menu name,* which will appear in the menu bar; this menu name is bracketed. In the lines that follow, the brackets contain the menu items that are displayed in the pull-down menu when it is selected. Here is an example:

***POP4
[Display]
[Redraw]'redraw
[~--]
[Zoom Window]'zoom w
[Zoom Previous]'zoom p

Refer to the section on pull-down menus in this chapter for more details.

- In the Icon menu section, the first line after the submenu label contains the menu name enclosed in brackets. In the lines that follow, brackets enclose the names of the slide files that are displayed within the icon menu, followed by the command sequences that are invoked when the icon is selected; for example:

```
***icon
**ES
[Electrical Shapes]
[es(con1)]^C^CSHAPE;CON1;
[es(res)]^C^CSHAPE;RES;
```

Refer to the section on icon menus in this chapter for more details.

Asterisk: *

In Release 9 and later, if an asterisk plus a cancel sequence (*^C^C) follows the brackets in any menu command sequence, the selected command will repeat until the user either selects a new command from the menu or presses Ctrl-C to cancel the repeating command. Here is an example:

```
[ERASE]*^C^CERASE;\;;
```

This command sequence invokes the Erase command, allowing you to pick a single entity from the screen, whereupon it will disappear immediately. It then repeats the sequence, allowing you to select another, and repeating until you press Ctrl-C or pick another command sequence that begins with Ctrl-C. This can be handy when erasing individual entities scattered throughout a drawing.

AutoCAD's standard menu includes this asterisk syntax in pull-down menus, but not in the Screen section menus. However, it can be used in any menu section when you find it useful.

Caret: ^

Control keys, such as Ctrl-C or Ctrl-O, are represented in AutoCAD menus by typing a caret (^) before a letter. For example, you can enter Ctrl-C as follows:

```
^C
```

These two characters will be interpreted by AutoCAD's menu processor as a single press of Ctrl-C from the keyboard. Ctrl-C will cancel most AutoCAD commands in progress. Some commands, such as the Dim command, will not be canceled with a single Ctrl-C. You can invoke two Cancel commands in an Auto-CAD menu by entering Ctrl-C twice:

```
^C^C
```

As you study AutoCAD's standard menu, you will notice that most commands are preceded by a double Ctrl-C, as in the following example:

[LINE:]^C^CLINE;

This ensures that if a menu command sequence is selected while another command is in progress, the command in progress will be canceled first, preventing the selected command from being misinterpreted as a response to the in-progress command.

Also, notice that no space appears between the Ctrl-C and the Line command. If a space were typed there, the menu processor would interpret it as a press of the Enter key, and the results would not be as intended.

The exception to this principle would be in the case of AutoCAD's transparent commands, where no canceling effect would be intended. For example, consider the following command sequence:

[PAN:]'PAN;

In this example, the double Ctrl-C is replaced by an apostrophe, signaling to AutoCAD that the command is to be invoked transparently. In this case, you can invoke the transparent command while another command is in progress, or from the Command prompt as a standard command.

Plus Sign: +

AutoCAD menu command sequences begin in the first column of each command line, and can extend indefinitely to the right. However, to make a long command sequence easier to read, you may insert a plus sign at the end of a line in the file, and continue the command sequence on the next line, just as though the entire sequence were on the same line.

The plus sign can be inserted anywhere in the line, even in the middle of a word if necessary. It is invisible to the AutoCAD menu interpreter, and can make the menu much easier to read and edit by allowing a long sequence of commands to appear on several lines in the menu file. There is no limit to the length of a command sequence that uses this technique.

When a long command sequence occupies many lines in this fashion, it is said to be *wrapped around*. In a submenu that will be displayed on the screen, command sequences that are wrapped around do not reduce the maximum number of display lines available for use within that submenu. In other words, even though wrapped-around command sequences occupy several text lines in the menu file, the AutoCAD menu processor sees them as a single line. Thus, your maximum number of available display lines remains the same.

CONTROLLING SUBMENUS

AutoCAD menus use special syntax to define how and when submenus are *activated,* making accessible the command sequences they contain. The syntax that controls which submenu is activated takes the following form:

$<*key character*> = <*submenu label*>

When this special set of characters is encountered in the processing of any command sequence, it will cause the named submenu to be activated. For example, if you wished for the Erase submenu to appear on the screen, you would include the following characters at the appropriate point in the menu:

$S = ERASE

The letter *S* that appears after the dollar sign indicates that the Erase submenu is part of the Screen section. The *S* is the Screen section's *key character,* and is supplied between the dollar sign and the equal sign.

You can see from the above example that the command syntax for activating a Screen section submenu is $S = followed by the name of the submenu. As Screen section submenus are displayed, AutoCAD keeps track of them, to a maximum of eight (or ten in AutoCAD Release 10). It is possible to backtrack through these screen-menu references by means of the following syntax:

$S =

In this case, *S* is always used as the key character between the dollar sign and the semicolon. Each time these characters are encountered in a command sequence, AutoCAD will "recall" the previous submenu and display it, until the maximum of eight (or ten) have been recalled. Once it has backtracked through the previous eight submenus (or it runs out of previous submenus, whichever comes first), this syntax has no effect.

These other key characters are used for other major menu sections:

$A1 =	Aux1 section
$B =	Buttons section
$I =	Icon section
$P1 through $P10 =	Pop1 through Pop10
$T1 through $T4 =	Tablet1 through Tablet4

There are slight differences in the way each menu section handles the activation of its submenus. These differences are explained in the upcoming sections, which describe each main menu section in more detail.

CREATING SCREEN MENUS

This section will explain how Screen section submenus are displayed, and will demonstrate a technique you can employ to create a new submenu in the Screen section of AutoCAD's standard menu. You will do this by modifying a copy of AutoCAD's standard menu.

Activating Screen Section Submenus

When Screen section submenus are activated, they are immediately displayed in the screen-menu area. Normally, the submenu is displayed starting with the first line in the screen-menu area, and continuing through all the lines in the submenu, or until the screen-menu area is filled. Thus, submenus in the Screen section can contain as many command sequence lines as there are lines available in your monitor's screen-menu area. The number of available lines varies among different display configurations. Many monitors display 21 lines in the screen-menu area. If your monitor is like this, each submenu in your Screen section can be up to 21 lines long. If any submenu is longer than the maximum displayed on your monitor, the extra lines will not appear.

Submenus are not required to contain the maximum number of lines. When a submenu has fewer than its maximum number of lines, the lines in the submenu are displayed, and any previously displayed commands that are not overwritten by the new submenu will continue to appear on the screen. These previous commands will function normally if selected.

The submenu display can be further controlled by means of an optional number that follows the submenu label, instructing it to begin the display on a particular line in the screen-menu area. For example,

**S 3

would indicate that the S submenu begins on the third line of the screen-menu area, leaving the first two lines intact. Any command sequences found on these two lines will remain active and accessible to the pointing device after the S submenu is displayed.

Creating a New Screen Submenu

The submenu created in this section will be called Macros. You can use it to store the custom menu macros to be discussed later in this chapter.

Load a copy (not the original) of AutoCAD's standard menu into your text editor and locate the Screen section. (You will find the Screen section label, ***SCREEN, on approximately line 1379 of AutoCAD Release 11's standard

```
***COMMENT
    Copyright (C) 1986-1990 by Autodesk, Inc..   Version 1.1 for Release 11
***SCREEN
**S
[AutoCAD]^C^C^P$S=X $S=S (setq T_MENU 0)(princ) ^P$P1=POP1 $P2=P2DRAW +
$P4=P4DISP $P6=P6OPT $P8=POP8
[* * * *]$S=OSNAPB
[BLOCKS]$S=X $S=BL
[DIM:]$S=X $S=DIM ^C^CDIM
[DISPLAY]$S=X $S=DS
[DRAW]$S=X $S=DR
[EDIT]$S=X $S=ED
[INQUIRY]$S=X $S=INQ
[LAYER:]$S=X $S=LAYER ^C^CLAYER
[MVIEW]$S=X $S=MV
[PLOT]$S=X $S=PLOT
[SETTINGS]$S=X $S=SET
[SOLIDS]^C^C^P(progn(setq m:err *error*)(princ))+
(defun *error* (msg)(princ msg)(setq *error* m:err m:err nil f nil)(princ))+
(if (null c:solbox)(progn (menucmd "S=X")(menucmd "S=SOLLOAD"))+
(progn (menucmd "S=X")(menucmd "S=SOLIDS")))(princ);^P
[SURFACES]$S=X $S=3D
[UCS:]$S=X $S=UCS1 ^C^CUCS
[UTILITY]$S=X $S=UT
```

FIGURE 14.2: The opening lines of the Screen section of ACAD.MNU. The S submenu in AutoCAD Release 11's standard menu is more complicated than the menu in Figure 14.1. Most of the command sequences consist of references to other submenus ($S = *submenu label*). Line 19, Solids, invokes AutoLISP functions as though they were entered from the keyboard. DIM, LAYER, and UCS invoke commands as well as referencing other submenus; notice the colons that appear within the brackets on these lines, indicating that an AutoCAD command will be invoked if this line is picked.

menu.) The first few lines following this label are illustrated in Figure 14.2. All AutoCAD menus have an opening screen menu that looks something like this.

Notice that the section label is immediately followed by the label of the first submenu in the Screen section, the S submenu. This is the submenu that is displayed in the screen-menu area when you first load AutoCAD's standard menu.

Once you have found the S submenu, locate the cursor on any convenient blank line. (The line above the Save command sequence in the S submenu is usually blank. If it is, place the cursor there.) Once you are on a blank line in the S submenu, type in the following, beginning at the leftmost column position:

[MACROS]^C^C$S = X $S = MACROS

This command sequence will cause the word *MACROS* to appear on the screen. Next, a double cancel is invoked to cancel any command that might be active when *MACROS* is picked with the pointing device. Then, two submenu references are invoked: the X submenu followed by the Macros submenu.

The X submenu already exists in AutoCAD's standard menu. You will find it immediately following the S submenu. It is illustrated in Figure 14.3.

```
***Comment
        Copyright (C) 1986-1990 by Autodesk, Inc..
        Version 1.1 for Release 11

**X 3




[  LAST  ]$S= $S=
[  DRAW  ]^C^C$S=X $S=DR
[  EDIT  ]^C^C$S=X $S=ED
```

FIGURE 14.3: The X submenu in AutoCAD Release 11's standard menu. The X submenu is referenced first, before any other AutoCAD screen submenus are referenced. The submenu is displayed starting on line 3, leaving the previous lines 1 and 2 active; lines 3 through 17 are blank. These blank lines clear out command sequences from previous submenus and help prevent confusion. Finally, the X submenu displays three common command sequences on lines 18, 19, and 20. Provided that subsequently referenced submenus do not overwrite these lines (most do not), these command sequences become a "common denominator" for other submenus.

The next step is to create the Macros submenu. You can place the macros submenu anywhere in the Screen section, as long as it is just before or just after another submenu, so as not to interfere with the display of other submenus. You can create one such acceptable place for the new submenu label by adding a new line just above the X submenu label, and entering the following submenu label on that line:

**MACROS 3
**X 3

Notice also how the number 3 follows the **MACROS submenu label. As previously mentioned, this number will induce the Macros submenu to begin its display on the third line of the screen-menu area.

If you like, you can add additional blank lines, as many as 15, following the submenu label. (If you enter more than 15, you will interfere with the display of the X submenu, which begins on line 16.) The blank lines you enter will overwrite command sequences from previously displayed menus. Later, you can return to this submenu and place command sequences of your own on these blank lines.

If you would like to place command sequences on the Macros submenu right now, following are two simple but useful command sequences you might try:

```
[ZOOM-W]'ZOOM;W;\\
[ZOOM-P]'ZOOM;P;
```

These two command sequences will allow you to pick the Zoom Window and Zoom Previous commands from a single menu pick, rather than selecting Zoom followed by Window or Zoom followed by Previous. They are good examples of how simple command sequences in a custom menu make AutoCAD faster and easier.

Since Zoom is a transparent command, these command sequences do not begin with the double Ctrl-C, but rather with the apostrophe. This makes it possible to select this submenu and these commands while another command is in progress.

Now, save the new menu file, and your work is finished. Enter AutoCAD's drawing editor and load the copy of AutoCAD's standard menu. If everything has been entered correctly, you should be able to reference the Macros submenu as you would any other submenu.

CREATING TABLET MENUS

If you use a digitizing tablet as your input device, you can make the drawing process much more efficient by means of custom tablet menus. AutoCAD allows you to specify up to four separate areas of your tablet as menu areas, plus a remaining area to be used as the screen pointing area. These menu areas are rectangular, but they may be arranged on the tablet in any way you choose. With a well-organized set of tablet menus, you can bypass the hierarchical screen menu altogether.

Once each tablet menu area is defined, it may be partitioned to contain as many smaller rectangular boxes as you choose. The boxes within a tablet menu area are automatically numbered by AutoCAD, beginning with number one in the upper left, continuing horizontally, row by row, and ending with the box in the lower right. Each one of the boxes can be designated as a particular Auto-CAD command, setting, or macro.

The first step in creating a custom digitizing tablet is to design a model of your tablet menu areas, their location on the digitizing tablet, the number of boxes in each, and the location on the tablet of the screen pointing area.

Once you have settled on an arrangement of tablet menu areas and commands, you can use AutoCAD to create a *template,* a drawing of your arrangement. Label each box in the menu area with its intended AutoCAD command or command sequence. When your template design is satisfactory, plot it out at the correct scale. Then fasten the template onto the surface of your digitizing tablet.

The arrangement of commands on your template drawing should be made so that a minimum of motion is required to move from command to command. Related commands should be grouped together. Commands often used in sequence should be located near each other.

Tip: To prevent your template from wearing out too quickly, you may consider laminating it. If you don't want to laminate it, another trick is to use AutoCAD's Mirror command to "flip" the finished template, plotting it in reverse on sturdy clear vellum. Then reverse the vellum when fastening the template to your digitizing tablet.

When your template is in place, you are ready to configure AutoCAD to respond to your custom tablet menus, using the Tablet Cfg command. Refer to Chapter 4 for details regarding this command and how to use it to configure tablet menu areas.

Placing Custom Commands on the Digitizing Tablet

Once your digitizing tablet has been configured, you may assign AutoCAD commands, settings, macros, and so forth to the labeled menu-area boxes. This is done by adding command sequences to the Tablet1 through Tablet4 menu sections.

AutoCAD's standard menu has already assigned various AutoCAD commands and settings to Tablet sections 2, 3, and 4. These entries correspond to a standard template provided with AutoCAD. If you are using AutoCAD's standard template, only the Tablet1 section should be edited. Leave the others alone. If you are using your own template, the others can be overwritten.

In AutoCAD's standard menu, Tablet1 has room for as many as 200 user-definable commands. Figure 14.4 illustrates a considerably smaller tablet menu area with six columns and six rows. Boxes in this tablet menu are numbered from 1 to 36. Using this example, menu section Tablet1 would contain a total of only 36 lines. The first line corresponds to box number 1, the second line to box number 2, and so on through all the command boxes.

Figure 14.5 illustrates a possible arrangement of AutoCAD View command options, arranged so as to correspond to standard sections of the drawing, predefined as named views. (Refer to the View command, Chapter 11, for details on named views.)

In order to correspond to the illustrated menu area, the Tablet1 section of the menu file should appear as in Figure 14.6. Notice how some of the command boxes in the tablet menu were enlarged simply by repeating the same command in the corresponding boxes.

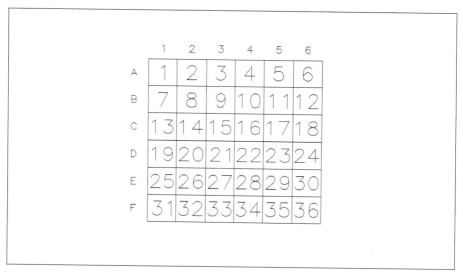

FIGURE 14.4: A small tablet menu area with numbered boxes. The above figure represents a user-configurable tablet menu area. It is a rectangle divided into six equally-spaced columns (1–6) and rows (A–F). The 36 command boxes that result will correspond to a line in one of the Tablet sections in the menu file. The Tablet section for this example will have 36 lines; the first line will be activated if the user selects box number 1, the second if the user selects box number 2, and so on through box number 36.

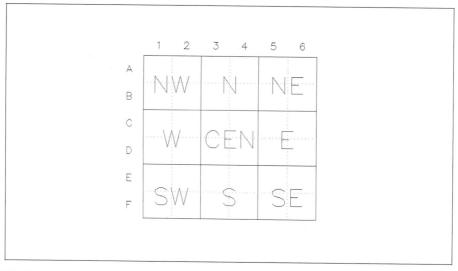

FIGURE 14.5: Tablet menu area used to call named views of a drawing. This figure takes the 6-by-6 tablet menu in Figure 14.4 and divides it up into nine larger command boxes. You may create a prototype drawing that has nine adjacent named views whose name and relationship to each other correspond to the layout of the tablet menu in this figure. Assuming that the virtual screen accommodates the drawing limits, you may quickly jump to any other portion of the drawing, transparently and usually without a regen, by picking the indicated box with the pointing device.

```
***TABLET1
[A1-box1]'VIEW;R;NW;
[A2-box2]'VIEW;R;NW;
[A3-box3]'VIEW;R;N;
[A4-box4]'VIEW;R;N;
[A5-box5]'VIEW;R;NE;
[A6-box6]'VIEW;R;NE;
[B1-box7]'VIEW;R;NW;
[B2-box8]'VIEW;R;NW;
[B3-box9]'VIEW;R;N;
[B4-box10]'VIEW;R;N;
[B5-box11]'VIEW;R;NE;
[B6-box12]'VIEW;R;NE;
[C1-box13]'VIEW;R;W;
[C2-box14]'VIEW;R;W;
[C3-box15]'VIEW;R;CEN;
[C4-box16]'VIEW;R;CEN;
[C5-box17]'VIEW;R;E;
[C6-box18]'VIEW;R;E;
[D1-box19]'VIEW;R;W;
[D2-box20]'VIEW;R;W;
[D3-box21]'VIEW;R;CEN;
[D4-box22]'VIEW;R;CEN;
[D5-box23]'VIEW;R;E;
[D6-box24]'VIEW;R;E;
[E1-box25]'VIEW;R;SE;
[E2-box26]'VIEW;R;SE;
[E3-box27]'VIEW;R;S;
[E4-box28]'VIEW;R;S;
[E5-box29]'VIEW;R;SW;
[E6-box30]'VIEW;R;SW;
[F1-box31]'VIEW;R;SE;
[F2-box32]'VIEW;R;SE;
[F3-box33]'VIEW;R;S;
[F4-box34]'VIEW;R;S;
[F5-box35]'VIEW;R;SW;
[F6-box36]'VIEW;R;SW;
```

FIGURE 14.6: Example of Tablet1 menu section. The listing in this figure shows how nine transparent View commands are placed in a tablet menu of 36 lines, so as to correspond to the tablet menu configuration pictured in Figure 14.5. Commands are repeated in boxes that are adjacent, so that the selectable command boxes are enlarged. Solid lines indicate the selectable boxes; dotted lines indicate the total number of command boxes available. If you so desired, you could further subdivide the named views into quadrants for a greater level of detail, all without causing a drawing regeneration.

Boxes in a tablet menu area can contain macros, such as the ones described later in this chapter. Long command sequences can be wrapped around several text lines for easier editing, and all custom menu syntax (such as wrapping lines using the plus sign, and submenu references) can be used where desired in the tablet sections of the custom menu file.

Multiple template designs are possible as well. The configuration of the digitizing tablet is stored as part of the drawing, so if you wish to use more than one template design, you will need a prototype drawing for each. If you use a consistent template design, you can change commands assigned to the boxes by referencing submenus within the Tablet menu sections, as described in the upcoming section.

Activating Tablet Submenus

The command sequences in the Tablet menu sections are not displayed on the screen, but may contain submenus that are activated by means of the syntax

$Tn = submenu label

where *n* is the number of the Tablet section, and *submenu label* is the submenu label within that section.

You would only need submenus in these sections if you wanted to use different sets of commands within the same tablet menu configuration. AutoCAD's standard menu, for example, includes a portion of the template with the heading Text. This portion of the template will work with either the Text or Dtext command, and Auto-CAD gives you the opportunity to switch between them. You can switch between Text and Dtext commands by selecting another command box labeled Text that you will find in the Settings portion of the template. Picking this box displays a submenu in the screen-menu area that will allow you to select either Text or Dtext as the command of choice for the Text portion of the template.

How this works is as follows: The Text command box in the Settings portion of the template is box number 146 in the Tablet4 section of AutoCAD's standard menu. On line number 146 in the Tablet4 section (line number 5,128 overall), you will find the following submenu references:

$S = X $S = TEXTSET

These references will cause the X and Textset submenus to appear in the screen-menu area. This submenu allows you to choose either the Text or the Dtext command:

```
**TEXTSET 5
[DTEXT]$S = X $S = DTEXT ^C^C$T4 = DTEXT1 $T4 = DTEXT2

[REG.TEXT]$S = X $S = TEXT ^C^C$T4 = TEXT1 $T4 = TEXT2

[STYLE:]$S = X $S = STYLE ^C^CSTYLE
```

In either case, additional submenu references are called. First, the screen submenu related to the chosen command is displayed in the screen-menu area. Next, tablet submenus are referenced. For example, imagine that you selected the DTEXT option from the screen menu. The following tablet submenus would be referenced:

$T4 = DTEXT1 $T4 = DTEXT2 $T4 = DTEXT3 $T4 = DTEXT4 $T4 = DTEXT5

This syntax indicates that, among others, the Dtext1 and Dtext2 submenus should be referenced in the Tablet4 section. These are small submenus, and can be found near the end of the *TABLET4* section.

```
**DTEXT1 110
^C^C$S = X $S = DTEXT DTEXT STYLE
**DTEXT2 133
^C^C$S = X $S = DTEXT DTEXT ALIGNED
^C^C$S = X $S = DTEXT DTEXT MIDDLE
^C^C$S = X $S = DTEXT DTEXT FIT
```

Notice the numbers that follow the submenu label. These numbers tell the menu processor the box number at which to begin the submenu's command sequences. In the above example, Dtext1 would begin at command box number 110, and Dtext2 would begin at box number 133. Each submenu affects only the beginning box number and overwrites a box for each line that follows up to the end of the new submenu. These command sequences are aligned perfectly for the Text portion of Auto-CAD's standard menu. They reference the appropriate screen menu and call the Dtext command with the selected option.

Note: If you had selected Text from the Textset screen submenu, a different set of tablet submenus would have been referenced, and these same command boxes would have invoked the Text screen submenus and Text command instead. Thus, a single portion of the standard template is capable of doing "double duty."

CREATING BUTTON MENUS

The Aux and Buttons menu sections are usually smaller than the other sections. The Aux menu section corresponds to the buttons of an auxiliary input device, a box with numbered buttons. Each line of the menu section coincides with a matching button—line one for button number one, line two for button number two, and so on.

The Buttons menu section works almost the same way, assigning command sequences of your choice to the buttons on a digitizing puck or mouse. There is one exception to this: The first button on the mouse or digitizing puck is always configured as the pick button. Thus, the lines in the Buttons section begin with the second button instead of the first.

Except as just noted, the rules for assigning command sequences to input buttons are the same as those for assigning command sequences to command boxes on the tablet template.

Activating Button Submenus

The Aux and Buttons menu sections are not displayed on the screen, but may contain submenus that are activated by means of this syntax. Because these menus are not displayed, the existence of submenus in these sections is less critical than in other sections, and you may prefer to use no submenus in these menu sections. The AutoCAD standard menu, for example, contains no submenus for these sections.

If you want to use subsections in these menus, however, you may. For example, imagine that you are using a three-button mouse as your pointing device. One button on the mouse is always the pick button; the other two may be configured. By configuring one button to toggle the other, using the Buttons menu listed in Figure 14.7, you could use submenus in the Buttons section to allow some degree of flexibility in the mouse commands.

```
***BUTTONS
**B1
;
$B=B2
**B2
'REDRAW
$B=B3
**B3
'ZOOM;W;\\
$B=B4
**B4
'ZOOM;P;
$B=B1
```

FIGURE 14.7: A custom Buttons menu section. The above submenu section illustrates how one button may be used to reference a submenu, and in so doing, change the commands that will be invoked by other buttons. In this menu, button 3 contains the submenu references, and button 2 is the button whose meaning is changed. Button 1 is always the pick button, so a line for this button is not even included in the menu file. Thus, the first line of each of these submenus applies to button number 2.

In the example, the third mouse button toggles the second by activating a new submenu each time it is pressed, cycling through four submenus in order. The second button becomes, in turn, the Enter key, a transparent redraw, a Zoom Window command, and a Zoom Previous command. If you aren't used to toggling your pointing-device buttons like this, it make take some getting used to.

You can get even fancier with this concept if you like. For example, you can use Screen section submenus to display the status of the mouse toggle button on the last line of the screen display, using the button menu and Screen section submenus listed in Figure 14.8.

```
***BUTTONS                                              <
**B1                                                    <
;                                                       <
$B=B2;$S=M2;                                            <
**B2                                                    <
'REDRAW                                                 <
$B=B3;$S=M3;                                            <
**B3                                                    <
'ZOOM;W;\\                                              <
$B=B4;$S=M4;                                            <
**B4                                                    <
'ZOOM;P;                                                <
$B=B1;$S=M1;                                            <
                                                        <
***SCREEN                                               <
**M1 21                                                 <
[Enter]                                                 <
**M2 21                                                 <
[REDRAW]                                                <
**M3 21                                                 <
[ZOOM-W]                                                <
**M4 21                                                 <
[ZOOM-P]^                                               <
                                                        <
```

FIGURE 14.8: A custom Buttons section with corresponding Screen section submenus. This is an example of how submenus in one menu section can be referenced from another. The above submenu system works like the one in Figure 14.7, with an important twist: Each time the meaning of button 2 is changed, the button's current meaning is displayed on line 21 of the on-screen menu.

In the custom menu shown in Figure 14.8, the third mouse button toggles the second by activating a new Buttons section submenu, and at the same time activating a screen submenu, which displays the current status of the second mouse button on the last line of the screen display (line 21 in this example).

CREATING NEW PULL-DOWN MENUS

If your display device is capable of supporting the Advanced User Interface, you have access to additional AutoCAD menus called *pull-down menus*. These menus are displayed on the screen when you activate AutoCAD's *menu bar*, as illustrated in Figure 14.9. In this figure, the user first moved the crosshairs into the top line of the screen, activating the horizontal menu bar. The user then highlighted the keyword *Assist*. When the user pushed the select button, the pull-down menu below that keyword appeared on the screen.

```
Assist  Draw  Modify  Display  Settings  Options  Utility  File  Solids
Help!                                                             * * * *
                                                                  BLOCKS
Cancel                                                            DIM:
                                                                  DISPLAY
Osnap: <mode>                                                     DRAW
CENter                                                            EDIT
ENDpoint                                                          INQUIRY
INSert                                                            LAYER:
INTersection                                                      MUIEW
MIDpoint                                                          PLOT
NEArest                                                           SETTINGS
NODe                                                              SOLIDS
PERpendicular                                                     SURFACES
QUAdrant                                                          UCS:
Quick,<mode>                                                      UTILITY
TANgent                                                           ASHADE
NONE                                                              RMAN
                                                                  BONUS
FILTERS      >                                                    SAVE:



Command:
```

FIGURE 14.9: AutoCAD's pull-down menu bar. Pull-down menus such as the one pictured here are a feature in display devices that support the Advanced User Interface. These menus are activated and displayed when you move the crosshairs into the top line of the screen display (normally AutoCAD's status line). In this figure, the user has highlighted the keyword *Assist* and pressed the pick button to reveal the pull-down menu below the keyword.

A pull-down menu remains in place until the user takes one of the following actions:

- Select a command or option from any of those displayed on the screen in any menu area.
- Select any point on the graphics screen.
- Type anything at the keyboard.
- Move the pointing device into the rightmost screen-menu area.

Any of these will cause the pull-down menu to disappear from the screen.

The lines in AutoCAD's standard menu that allow for the display of this pull-down menu are listed in Figure 14.10.

Although the appearance and behavior of the pull-down menu is different from the AutoCAD standard screen menu, the techniques for creating or modifying it are similar to the techniques for creating AutoCAD screen submenus.

You are allowed a maximum of ten pull-down menus. Each pull-down menu has its own menu section label, the word *Pop* followed by a number.

The first line after the menu section label contains the pull-down menu's *keyword* enclosed in brackets. AutoCAD places that word into the horizontal menu bar. When that word is selected by the user, the commands that follow it in the

```
***Comment
        Copyright (C) 1986-1990 by Autodesk, Inc..
        Version 1.1 for Release 11
***POP1
[Assist]
[Help!        ]'?
[---]
[Cancel       ]^C^C
[---]
[Osnap: <mode>]^C^C$p1= $p1=* OSNAP \
CENter
[ENDpoint     ]ENDP
INSert
[INTersection]INT
MIDpoint
NEArest
NODe
[PERpendicular]PER
QUAdrant
[Quick,<mode> ]QUICK,^Z$p1=*
TANgent
NONE
[---]
[FILTERS      >]$p1=filters $p1=*
```

FIGURE 14.10: The Assist pull-down menu section, Pop1. The menu lines in this figure correspond to the pull-down menu pictured in Figure 14.9. You can compare the two in order to see what command sequences would be invoked were you to highlight and pick one of the displayed options.

menu section are displayed in the form of a pull-down menu on the screen. If no menu commands appear below the keyword, the word will still appear, but the user will not be able to highlight or select it. Thus, in Figure 14.10, the keyword *Assist* appears in brackets just below the Pop1 section label, and in the menu bar when the user moves the crosshairs there.

The command sequences in pull-down menus are structured in the same way as commands in the screen menu. Words appearing in brackets will be displayed in the pull-down menu. You can have as many lines in a pull-down menu as you have lines in your display device to show them. When the user moves the cursor to highlight the display of one of these commands and then selects it, the command sequence following the brackets will be executed by AutoCAD, as though it had been typed at the keyboard. The command sequence can include submenu references in any other menu section.

Activating Pull-down Submenus

Submenus in pull-down menu sections Pop1 through Pop10 are activated by referencing the pull-down menu section number as part of the key character, as in

$Pn = submenu

where *n* is the number of the pull-down menu to be activated, and *submenu* is the name of the submenu label. For example, the AutoCAD standard menu includes a submenu named Filters in the Pop1 section. The Filters submenu contains its own keyword and command sequences. This submenu could be activated with the following syntax:

$P1 = filters;

However, the activated pull-down submenu will not automatically appear on the screen. To display the activated submenu, move the crosshairs to the menu bar and select the submenu with the pick button.

It is possible to force the display of any pull-down menu at almost any time, by means of the syntax

$P*n* = *;

in a custom menu, where *n* is the number of the pull-down menu to be activated. Thus, to activate submenu filters in the pull-down menu section Pop1, and display it at the same time, use the following syntax:

$P1 = filters;$P1 = *;

The display syntax for pull-down menus works well when it is included in pull-down menu command sequences. It will not work as well in screen-menu command sequences. If you try it, you will find that the presence of the crosshairs in the screen-menu area will cause the pull-down menu to appear and quickly disappear again.

You can have as many pull-down submenus as you like. Pull-down menu sections are always referenced by number, and you can change the display of any pull-down submenu from within any other submenu, simply by referencing the correct menu section number. Therefore, when building complex menu displays, be cautious that you display only what you intend to display at any given time. Note that only one pull-down menu can appear on the screen at any one time. When you create a pull-down submenu that is referenced from another in the same section, be sure that the submenu contains at least one reference activating the original; this will allow you to restore the original pull-down menu when desired.

Special Features of Pull-down Menus

Names of pull-down menus can be of any length, but they occupy space in the menu bar starting from the left and continuing to the right until there is no more room. If your pull-down menu names are too long, pull-down menus with higher numbers may not appear in the menu bar, and thus will be completely unavailable. If you use all ten pull-down menu keywords in your horizontal menu bar, the keywords should average no more than eight letters each in order to fit.

Unlike with screen menus, the size of a pull-down menu is adjusted automatically to accommodate the largest sequence of bracketed characters that it contains. This proves to be something of a mixed blessing, as you must learn to manage available screen space when editing them. Also, if a pull-down menu appearing to the right of the screen contains long sequences of bracketed characters, it may not appear on the screen as you intended. Your safest course of action is to keep all sequences of bracketed characters as concise as possible.

Two minor features are available to help with the appearance of your pull-down menus. The first is a symbol composed of two hyphens surrounded by brackets:

[--]

When this symbol occupies a line in a pull-down menu, it will cause the appearance of a line separating the items in the pull-down menu. You can choose to include a command sequence following this special symbol if you wish. In such a case, the command sequence will be executed if the line is highlighted and selected by the user. If no command sequence follows, the effect of selecting the line is to cause the pull-down menu to disappear from the screen.

Using the second feature, it is possible to adjust the display of the words within brackets. When any bracketed items are preceded by a tilde (~), the item will appear at a lower intensity than a normal bracketed item. This display technique can be used to identify short prompts or symbols that are not intended to represent commands, or for any other display purpose you wish. Except for their appearance on the screen, bracketed items preceded by a tilde will function as any other pull-down menu item.

CREATING ICON MENUS

Icon menus are available to users whose display devices can support the Advanced User Interface. They represent a significant improvement when selecting blocks, shapes, text styles, hatch patterns, or other forms of graphic input where names alone don't adequately convey the exact nature of the desired entities or command sequences.

An icon menu is a means to preview graphic input selections before actually inserting them into a drawing. When an icon menu is displayed on the screen, up to 16 graphic options can be presented to the user, along with a special "arrow" character that moves to select the desired option. In addition, icon menus can reference other icon menus, making it possible to review any number of options in sequence.

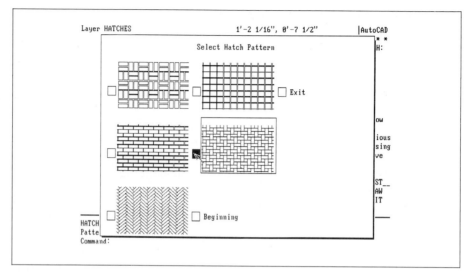

FIGURE 14.11: A hatch-pattern icon menu. The icon menu pictured here is not part of AutoCAD's standard menu. The hatch patterns are custom patterns, definitions for which can be found in Chapter 21. From the left, they are: Altbr (alternating bricks), Mbrick (mortar bricks), Parquet (parquet floor), Tile (grouted tile), and Weave (woven slats). The user has moved the pointing arrow into the rectangular button for the Weave pattern; at the same time, a rectangle appeared around the icon.

Figure 14.11 illustrates an icon menu for hatch patterns. Definitions for these hatch patterns can be found in Chapter 21.

There are three simple steps to creating an icon menu:

1. Create an AutoCAD slide file for each option to be displayed in the icon menu.
2. Optionally, use AutoCAD's SLIDELIB.EXE utility to combine the slides into a slide library file on the hard disk.
3. Add the syntax for displaying the icon menu to ACAD.MNU.

Once the slides are created and ACAD.MNU is changed, the display of the icon menu is handled automatically by AutoCAD. Fortunately, the icon menu syntax that must be added to ACAD.MNU is easy to learn, and in most respects follows conventions similar to other custom menu displays.

Each of the three steps just listed will be discussed in detail in the upcoming sections.

Creating the AutoCAD Slide Files

Slides to be used in icon menus are created the same way you would create any other AutoCAD slide—using the Mslide command (Chapter 21) and giving the slide file a unique name. Here are two tips to keep in mind:

- Keep the drawings as simple as you can. Don't use filled lines, solids, or complicated drawings. The resulting display of your icon slide will be very small, and tiny details will be lost anyway. The simpler the slides, the faster the display of the icon menu.
- When making the slide, enlarge the graphic image to fill the entire screen. If the image cannot fill the screen, center the drawing in the screen as much as possible.

Once the slide files are created, you are ready to incorporate them into an icon menu. However, in order for your icon menu to work, all the slides must be on disk and available to AutoCAD. If you create a lot of icon menus, the dozens (or even hundreds) of slides will take up space on the hard disk and be quite cumbersome to manage. Unfortunately, the problem of disk space is impossible to overcome at this time, but you can make it easier to manage groups of related slide files by combining them into a single disk file called a *slide library,* using a special utility, SLIDELIB.EXE.

Creating a Slide Library File

To create a slide library file, first use your text editor to create an ASCII file that contains a single-spaced list of the slide file names you intend to combine into the library file.

To create the library file used in the sample icon file, the following list of slide file names was entered into an ASCII file named HPNAMES:

```
C:\ACAD\ALTBR
C:\ACAD\GRILL
C:\ACAD\MBRICK
C:\ACAD\PARQUET
C:\ACAD\WEAVE
```

Notice that the file extension SLD is assumed for each of these slide file names. The subdirectory path name for each slide (in this example, C:\ACAD) is included, although the path name will not be saved in the library file. (Collecting the slides into a single library file makes individual slide path names unnecessary.)

If you wish, you can combine slides from several subdirectories into a single slide library file. Also, if you know that all the slides will be contained on the default subdirectory when you create the library file, you can safely omit the path name from the list.

The ASCII file containing the list of slide names was arbitrarily assigned the file name HPNAMES. You can name your own file anything you like.

Once the HPNAMES file was created, it had to be copied onto the same sub-directory as the file SLIDELIB.EXE, by logging onto that subdirectory and entering the following command at the operating-system prompt:

SLIDELIB HP < HPNAMES

The first word on this command line executes SLIDELIB.EXE. The next word is the name of the library file to create. In this case, the resulting library file is named HP, and is automatically given a file extension of SLB. You need not specify the file extension in the command line.

> *Note:* You may name your library files anything you like, but you will simplify subsequent typing by keeping the names short.

The third word on the command line is the file name of the list of slides to be combined into the library file. It is preceded by the < symbol to indicate to DOS that HPNAMES is to be used as input by SLIDELIB.EXE.

Alternatively, you may enter **SLIDELIB** followed by the name of the library file, at the operating-system prompt. The program will pause, allowing you to enter the slide file names that you intend to include in the slide library file.

Once SLIDELIB.EXE has completed execution, the library file HP.SLB, containing all the slides in the list, will be created. Once the library file has been created, you may copy the original slide files and the list of slide names onto a backup disk and erase them from the hard disk. This will open up some hard disk space for you.

Do not erase the slide files without backing them up first. If you wish to add slides to the library, you must create a brand-new slide library to replace the old one. Thus, you may need to use those original slide files and the list of names again. There is no procedure for simply adding slides to an existing library file, nor is there any procedure for deleting individual slides from the library file.

Slides may be viewed from the library in response to AutoCAD's Vslide command (Chapter 21). Simply reference the library as part of the slide name, as in the following example:

HP(WEAVE)

Note that the library name is followed by the slide name contained in parentheses. No spaces are used to separate the names. A path name can be included as well in response to the Vslide prompt:

C:\ACAD\SLIDES\HP(WEAVE)

Any slide that is part of a library may be referenced using the above *library (slide name)* syntax.

Creating the Icon Menu in AutoCAD's Standard Menu

After you have created your slides and placed them in a library file of your choosing, you are ready to modify ACAD.MNU to include a reference to the new icon menu.

All icon menus are contained within a single menu section labeled *Icon.* Each icon menu is a unique submenu within Icon. In AutoCAD's standard menu, the Icon menu section follows the Pop9 menu section (line 788 overall).

To add the new hatch-pattern icon menu to ACAD.MNU, first locate the Icon menu section. There are four hatch-pattern icon menus, labeled *hatch1, hatch2, hatch3, and hatch4.* Locate and insert the hatch4 submenu label (approximately line 1058 in Release 11), and move the last line in this subsection (approximately line 1074 in Release 11).

Two lines above this line is the following command sequence:

[Beginning]$i = hatch1 $i = *

This command sequence appears in the third hatch-pattern icon menu. It displays the word *Beginning* in the icon menu, and if selected, it will force the display of the first hatch-pattern menu. Since all the hatch-pattern menus contain a similar submenu reference for the next icon menu in the sequence, it is this particular command sequence that allows the user to redisplay the first, "looping" through them all.

There is no Beginning slide; but this is not a problem. The first character within the brackets is a space. When AutoCAD reads the initial space inside the brackets, it understands that there is no slide to be displayed, and the word within the brackets is displayed on the icon menu instead.

However, we are adding an extra hatch-pattern submenu, because it will be necessary to change this command sequence to the following:

[Next]$i = hatch4 $i = *

This will force the display of the new hatch-pattern submenu when the word *Next* is selected.

Skip down two lines and insert a new submenu label, **hatch5,* followed by command sequences, as illustrated in Figure 14.12.

```
[acad(triang)]^P(setq m:hp "triang")  ^P
[acad(zigzag)]^P(setq m:hp "zigzag")  ^P
[acad(angle)]^P(setq m:hp "angle")  ^P
[ Next]$I=hatch5 $I=*
[ Exit]




**hatch5
[Select Hatch Pattern]
[hp(altbr)]^C^Chatch;altbr;
[hp(mbrick)]^C^Chatch;mbrick;
[hp(parquet)]^C^Chatch;parquet;
[hp(tile)]^C^Chatch;tile;
[hp(weave)]^C^Chatch;weave;
[ Beginning]$I=hatch1 $I=*
[ Exit]




**hatchs
[Select Hatch Style]
[acad(hatchn)]^P(setq m:hs ",N")  ^P
[acad(hatcho)]^P(setq m:hs ",O")  ^P
```

FIGURE 14.12: A new hatch-pattern icon submenu. The lines in this figure show how AutoCAD's standard menu was changed to accommodate the extra hatch-pattern icon menu pictured in Figure 14.11.

Notice that the submenu label is preceded by two asterisks, to distinguish it
from the menu section label. An icon menu title has been added in brackets
below the submenu label:

[Select Hatch Pattern]

Each line that follows this title line begins with the name of a slide in brackets.
Following the name of each slide is the command sequence necessary to begin the
hatch pattern using that slide, as in the following example:

[hp(weave)]^C^CHATCH;WEAVE;

The second to last line of the new icon submenu contains the reference that previously was placed in the Hatch4 submenu:

[Beginning]$i = hatch1 $i = *

Finally, notice that the last line of the icon menu contains the word *Exit* in
brackets:

[Exit]

This will remove the display of the icon menu from the screen if the user has
selected it by accident. As before, a leading space indicates to the menu processor
that no slide exists, and *Exit* is displayed instead.

Activating and Displaying the Icon Submenu

Once the icon menu has been set up in ACAD.MNU, the only step that remains is to include the reference to display it in another command sequence of your choosing. The reference may be placed in a pull-down menu section, an original screen-menu section, or both. The following is a typical icon menu reference, using the Hatch1 icon submenu:

[Hatch...]^C^C$i = hatch1 $i = *

This line comes from the Pop2 section of AutoCAD's standard menu.

Notice the similarities to the pull-down menu references. In this case, the first reference causes the Hatch1 icon submenu to become active—i.e., capable of being displayed:

$i = hatch1

Notice that the letter *i* follows the dollar sign, and no number is used because there can be only one icon-menu section. An equal sign follows the letter *i*, followed by the name of a particular icon submenu—in this case, the Hatch1 submenu.

Usually, once an icon submenu is referenced, you will intend that it be displayed immediately on the screen. The reference that does this is similar to the pull-down menu reference for display:

$i = *

When AutoCAD reads this syntax, the active icon submenu is immediately displayed, and the user is free to choose one of its options.

Special Features of Icon Menus

- You can include up to 16 individual command sequences on a single icon menu.
- Pressing Ctrl-C at the keyboard causes the icon menu to disappear from the screen.
- Icon menus are flexible. You can combine different libraries of slides in the same icon menu, and slides that are not in library files with library-file slides. You can, if you choose, reference slide names with a full path name, as in the following examples:

```
[concrete]^C^CHATCH;CONCRETE;
[c:\acad\hatch\escher]^C^CHATCH;ESCHER;
[hp(grill)]^C^CHATCH;GRILL;
[hp(weave)]^C^CHATCH;WEAVE;
```

In these examples, slide files named CONCRETE.SLD (on the default subdirectory) and ESCHER.SLD (on the C:\ACAD\HATCH subdirectory) have been referenced along with slides that are part of the HP.SLB library file (also on the default subdirectory).

Remember that the command sequences following the slide names must be valid AutoCAD menu command sequences, and are subject to all the rules pertaining to custom menu commands and macros.

- Unfortunately, the individual slides that are displayed in the icon menus included in AutoCAD's standard menu are not included with AutoCAD's master program disks, but rather in the ACAD.SLB slide library file. Slide library files are not modifiable. If you wish to add to or modify the standard AutoCAD icon menus, you can do so using your own slide files or library files in combination with ACAD.SLB.

Custom Menu Macros

If it suits your purposes, you can place different command options and responses, or different AutoCAD commands, within the same command sequence. There is no limit to the strings of commands and responses you create, as long as the characters in the command sequence correspond to the same characters that you would enter at the keyboard (or simulate by means of control characters, such as a backslash for point picks).

Such a string of commands is called a *macro*. Macros are easy to create and are executed more quickly and efficiently than manual menu selections. Macros can be powerful devices for improving your AutoCAD efficiency and making your drawing process easier, especially if you find yourself repeating the same series of commands over and over.

Drawing

For example, consider the simple object, a curved arrow, shown on the top in Figure 14.13. This everyday symbol can be drawn by invoking the Arc and Line commands, or by using the following macro:

```
[ARROW-A:]^C^CARC;\\\LINE;@;\;MIRROR;L;;END;\\N;
```

From a single menu pick, this macro will prompt you to draw a three-point arc, prompt you to draw a line segment from the arc's ending point, and mirror the line segment at an angle of your choosing. Compare the time it takes to execute this command sequence with the time it takes to issue the same sequence of commands with AutoCAD's standard menu, and you will understand how macros can help you draw more efficiently.

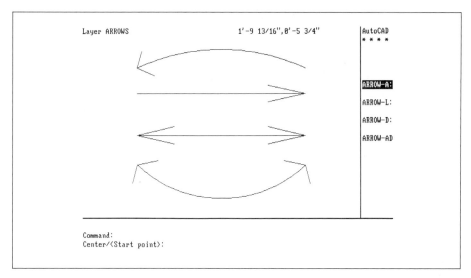

FIGURE 14.13: Simple arrow symbols drawn using macros. This figure depicts the four simple arrow figures that can be drawn from the macros in the accompanying text. Simple symbols like these, which may change slightly from insertion to insertion in a drawing, can't always be reproduced exactly using blocks or shapes. A macro will help create them quickly, with an equal or lesser number of point picks.

Variations on this theme are easy to imagine. Following is a straight-line arrow:

    [ARROW-L:]^C^CLINE;\\\;MIRROR;L;;END;\END;\N;

The following macro draws arrowheads on both endpoints of a straight line, essentially duplicating the sequence of the previous macro:

    [ARROW-D:]^C^CLINE;\\\;MIRROR;L;;END;\END;\N; +
    LINE;END;\\;MIRROR;L;;END;\END;\N;

The last arrow macro duplicates the curved arrow, but then selects one arrowhead line segment and prompts you to select the other. Two picks near the arc will then copy the arrowhead on the other side:

    [ARROW-AD]^C^CARC;\\\LINE;@;\;MIRROR;L;;END;\\N; +
    MIRROR;L;\;MID;\CEN;\N;

The following macro combines the 3Dface command with point filters to help draw four-sided planes in space (or in Release 10 and later, not aligned with the current UCS):

    [4SFACE:]^C^C3DFACE;.xy;\.xy;\.xy;\.xy;\;

With one hand on the pointing device and the other manipulating the numeric keypad, you can build four-sided planes quickly. This macro can be modified to build faces with any number of sides.

The following macro combines the Ellipse and PEdit commands, allowing you to quickly build ellipses with wide polylines. First, it prompts you to enter the ellipse axes; then it draws the ellipse and prompts for the width of the line. Finally, it redraws the ellipse with the specified wide polyline:

```
[W-ELLPSE]^C^CELLIPSE;\\\PEDIT;L;W;\X;
```

The following macro uses the same principle for polygons:

```
[W-PLYGON]^C^CPOLYGON;\\\\PEDIT;L;W;\X;
```

If you repeatedly draw the same kinds of ellipses and polygons, you can substitute fixed values for backslashes where appropriate in these macros.

Editing

The following macro combines the Move and Rotate commands. It prompts you to select entities by windowing them, and then prompts for a base point and displacement point. Then it rotates the entities around the last point picked:

```
[MOVE-R:]^C^CMOVE;W;\\;\\ROTATE;P;;@;\
```

An easy variation is the reverse of the above—first rotating, then moving:

```
[ROTATE-M]^C^CROTATE;W;\\;\\MOVE;P;;@;\
```

The following macro creates a rotated copy of windowed entities. It prompts you to select the entities, and then prompts for a rotation point. The original entities will not appear until you perform a redraw, so Redraw is included in the sample macro:

```
[COPY-R:]^C^CCOPY;W;\\;0,0;0,0;ROTATE;P;;\\REDRAW;
```

Combining editing commands into useful macros can be a lot of fun, even bordering on the fanciful. The following macro combines the Stretch, Scale, Move, and Rotate commands, all on the same set of selected entities:

```
[ST-SMR:]^C^CSTRETCH;C;\\;\\SCALE;P;;\\MOVE;P;;@;\ROTATE;P;;@;\
```

Macros need not be complicated to be useful, however. Even simple command sequences can be quite effective. In fact, you may find that the simplest ones are the ones you use the most often. The following command sequence will clean out an open-T intersection from intersecting pairs of lines in any orientation, as illustrated in Figure 14.14:

```
[OPEN-T:]^C^CTRIM;C;\\;\\\;
```

Display

The following macro quickly combines transparent Zoom and Pan, avoiding the additional point picks of dynamic zoom:

```
[Z-PAN:]'ZOOM;W;\\'PAN;\\
```

Since Zoom Previous following this macro will only recall the Pan command, the following replaces Zoom Previous when you've used the above macro and want to back up:

```
[BACKUP]'ZOOM;P;;P;
```

The following macros will rotate the UCS 10 degrees clockwise or counterclockwise along the requested axis. Repeated selection will increment the angle of rotation. You can substitute whatever angle of rotation you prefer.

```
[ROTATE]
[ UCS]
```

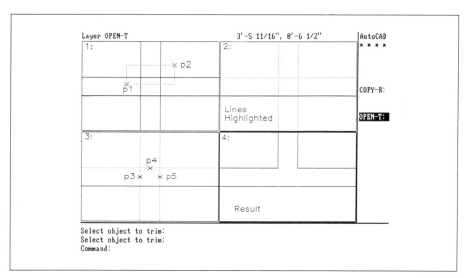

FIGURE 14.14: Cleaning out an open-T intersection with the Open-T macro. Cleaning out overlapping lines to an open-T intersection is an example of the kind of drawing operation that is done the same way each time. A handy macro in a custom menu that simply displays the operation to be performed and automates the "crossing window" selection will make the process easier and more accessible to the beginning user.

```
[X – 10d]^C^CUCS;X; – 10;
[X + 10d]^C^CUCS;X;10;

[Y – 10d]^C^CUCS;Y; – 10;
[Y + 10d]^C^CUCS;Y;10;

[Z – 10d]^C^CUCS;Z; – 10;
[Z + 10d]^C^CUCS;Z;10;
```

Utility

If you change system variables often, you can make the job faster and easier with macros. The Setvar submenu has room for several such macros. The Setvar submenu in the Screen section can be accessed with the following syntax:

```
[SETVAR:]$S = X;$S = SETVAR;
```

Following are examples of macros that change system variables. In most cases, these macros include submenu references back to the previous menus. Assuming that the Setvar submenu in the following example was referenced using the above syntax, the $S = submenu reference is repeated, once to reference back to the X submenu, and the second time to reference the menu that was displayed prior to the X submenu.

```
**SETVAR 3
['SETVAR:]'SETVAR;
?
[ELEV 0]'SETVAR;ELEVATION;0;$S = ;$S = ;
[ELEV ?]'SETVAR;ELEVATION;\$S = ;$S = ;
[BLIP ON]'SETVAR;BLIPMODE;0;$S = ;$S = ;
[BLIP OFF]'SETVAR;BLIPMODE;1;$S = ;$S = ;
[ICON]
[ ON]^C^CUCSICON;ON;$S = ;$S = ;
[ OFF]^C^CUCSICON;OFF;$S = ;$S = ;
[ ORIGIN]'SETVAR;UCSICON;3;$S = ;$S = ;
[ L-LEFT]'SETVAR;UCSICON;1;$S = ;$S = ;
[FILL]
[ ON]'SETVAR;FILLMODE;1;
[ OFF]'SETVAR;FILLMODE;0;
[ REGEN]^C^CREGEN;$S = ;$S = ;
```

In the case of the Fill On/Off macros, the automatic submenu reference was excluded, to allow the user to select the Regen option, which does include the submenu references. If the user does not want to regenerate the drawing after changing the status of filled display, the X submenu contains a macro, labeled Last, that will reference the prior menu.

Many system variables can be changed by means of AutoCAD commands. An advantage of the Setvar command is that it is transparent, and thus can change the values of some system variables while in the middle of other command sequences. This is especially useful with system variables such as ELEVATION and BLIPMODE.

In the case of the UCS icon macros, turning the icon on and off is accomplished by invoking the Ucsicon command, while the origin and lower-left display macros are handled with the Setvar command. The fact that the UCSICON system variable is a bit-code integer variable allows for a greater degree of flexibility in determining the icon display status. Refer to Chapter 13 for more information regarding this and other system variables.

TIPS FOR EDITING CUSTOM MENUS AND MACROS

It is an acceptable practice and frequently useful to change the on-screen menu display while an AutoCAD command sequence is in progress. You can do so freely; submenu references do not interrupt a command sequence in progress, and can be included within them. Follow each submenu reference with a space or semicolon.

To test your modified menu, go into AutoCAD's drawing editor and enter the command **Menu**, followed by your menu file name. AutoCAD will recompile your custom menu, and in a moment or so, your new menu will appear. Try selecting your new commands and see what happens. If things don't work out smoothly, enter your text editor and check to see that your command sequences were entered correctly. Then return to the drawing editor, invoke the Menu command, and try selecting your new commands again after AutoCAD recompiles your menu. To simplify the process of moving between AutoCAD and your text editor, refer to the section on modifying AutoCAD's external command file, ACAD.PGP, in Chapter 21.

Test and modify brand new command sequences in a separate, smaller menu file first; then, when you have them working, add them to your larger custom menus using your text editor. This makes the process of compiling virtually instantaneous as you move back and forth between AutoCAD and the text editor.

As you test your custom menu, you may discover that you have inadvertently created a submenu that offers no way to reference another needed submenu, or that does not allow you to return to the root menu. In this case, your only recourse is first to make a note of what happened, during what sequence of commands and menu picks, and what was displayed at the time, so you can find the problem area quickly and correct it using your text editor. Then, cancel the command sequence by pressing Ctrl-C, if necessary, or invoke the Menu command followed by either the default name of the current menu or a new menu. When the menu is reloaded, you will be at the top of the menu file again.

Other potential problems can be more subtle. Often, an extra space will be left inadvertently at the end of a line. This space will not be visible in your text editor, but it will be read by the menu processor as an additional press of the Enter key, causing unintended results.

Also, when editing tablet menus, remember that the menu box number for command sequences is determined by the lines in the tablet menu subsection; if you add an unintended carriage return in the subsection, or leave out a plus symbol at the end of a "wrap-around" line, you will cause subsequent command sequences to shift to the next command box. Under these circumstances, command boxes might produce entirely unpredictable command sequences.

Nevertheless, don't be afraid to experiment and make mistakes. Making mistakes is a positive experience and a powerful learning device. You cannot hurt AutoCAD with a custom menu. Although it is possible to write command sequences that don't operate as you anticipate, you can always return to Auto-CAD's standard menu by invoking the Menu Acad command at the keyboard.

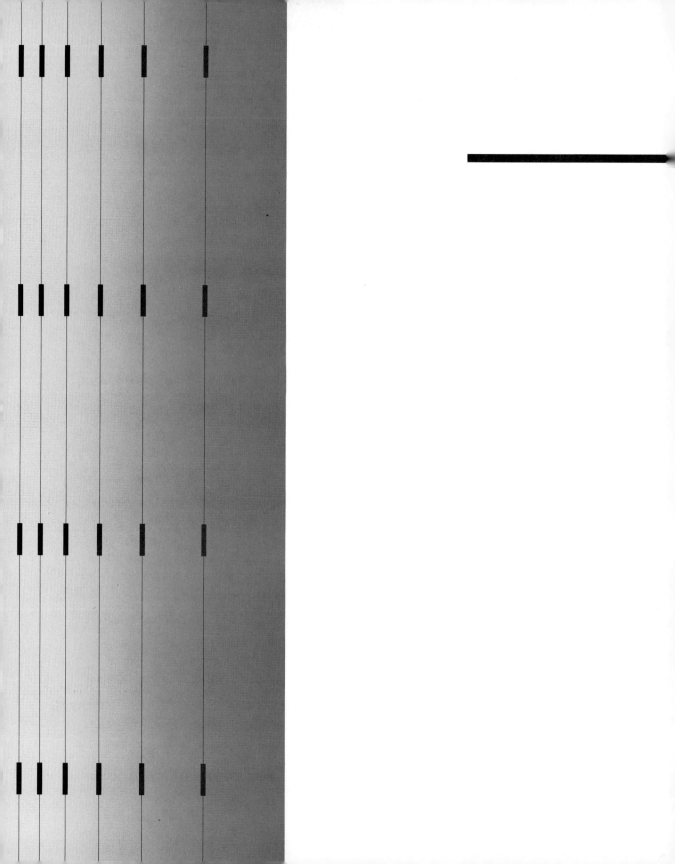

CHAPTER 15

DESIGNING SHAPES AND TEXT FONTS

DESIGNING SHAPES AND TEXT FONTS

A shape is a combination of arcs, circles, and lines that is treated as a single drawing entity. Shapes are used the way a manual drafter uses templates; that is, to insert repeatedly drawn symbols and other standard entities throughout a drawing. In this respect, they are similar to *blocks,* which also are used to replicate common entities throughout drawing files. Refer to Chapter 9 for details regarding blocks.

Shapes use less memory and hard disk space than blocks, and they are faster to regenerate. Shapes can be easier to manage on the hard disk as well, because many different shapes can be compiled into a single *shape file* that can be shared by any number of drawings. Shapes are usually used to represent drawing symbols that must be replicated often during a drawing session, and that are relatively uncomplicated: signs, pointers, connectors, balloons, valves, specification symbols, and so forth. Figure 15.1 illustrates several such shapes, the definitions for which will be found in this chapter. An AutoCAD drawing may contain any number of different shapes from any number of different shape files, up to the limit of your hard disk's storage capacity.

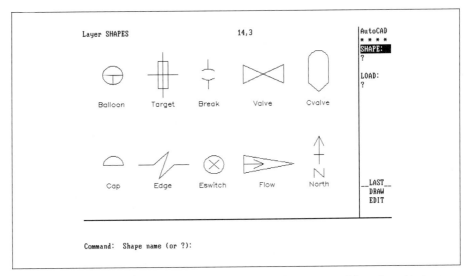

FIGURE 15.1: Sample shapes used in this chapter. The above shapes are used throughout this chapter as examples for demonstration and study. The name of each shape appears underneath. These shapes exemplify the fundamental elements of shape definitions. Notice that, unlike blocks, they are composed of only lines, arcs, and circles.

This chapter discusses how shapes are created, placed into shape files, compiled, and loaded into drawing files.

THE STRUCTURE OF SHAPE FILES

AutoCAD shape files are ASCII files with the file extension SHP. You can name them using any valid DOS file name. Shape files are edited using a text editor. If you are unfamiliar with text editors, refer to the brief explanation and summary of their use in Chapter 14.

The ASCII shape file contains a list of *shape definitions,* special sequences of characters and numbers that are the instructions AutoCAD uses to create the shape. A single shape file can contain from 1 to 255 individual shape definitions. Each shape definition in the file contains at least two lines of text. The first line is a *header line* containing general information about the shape. The lines following the header line contain a series of numbers, called *elements,* which are separated by commas.

A shape file must be *compiled* before it can be used in a drawing. When a shape file is compiled, a new file is created. This new file is a non-ASCII file identified by the original file name plus the extension SHX. The SHX file is the file used by AutoCAD during a drawing session.

Beginning with Release 11, AutoCAD has added two new features to the structure of ASCII shape files that make them easier to read:

- Shape files may contain blank lines, which allows you to separate the shape definitions within the ASCII file.

- Any information following a semicolon on a line will be ignored when the shape file is compiled. This allows you to add descriptive remarks and comments to a shape file. For an example, refer to the header line of the Valve shape just ahead, which includes a Release 11-style comment.

Shape-Definition Header Lines

The header line always begins with an asterisk, which indicates the start of a shape definition. Following the asterisk, the header line contains:

- A *shape number,* which must be a unique number associated with that shape.

- The exact *number of elements* in the following lines, which will be used to draw the shape.

- A *shape name,* which must be a unique name used by AutoCAD to locate the shape definition within the file, and which is always entered in uppercase letters.

Following is a typical header line for a shape:

*1,6,VALVE; Common butterfly valve symbol, 1x1 scale.

In this example, the shape number is 1, there are six elements in the shape definition, and the name of the shape is VALVE.

Elements of Shape Definitions

AutoCAD uses the shape elements (the numbers that follow the header line) to define the arcs, circles, and line segments that create the shape. Shape definition elements may be from one to three digits. Each element is followed by a comma.

The elements in a shape definition represent the movements of an imaginary pen that can be positioned *pen-down* (drawing visible lines) or *pen-up* (not drawing) and relocated while in either position. A shape is therefore defined by combining pen-up and pen-down positions with pen motions.

Some shape definitions require more than just pen movements. The relationships between the line segments of a more complex shape may require that the shape be drawn very large, and then scaled down in order to fit within a drawing. Scaling instructions are therefore part of many shape definitions.

A single shape definition may contain up to 2,000 elements. Because so many elements are allowed per shape, it is possible for the elements of a shape definition to occupy many lines of text in the shape file. No single line of text in a shape definition file can extend past 80 columns (the rightmost column on most computer screens). If any line in your shape file is longer than this, the file will not compile.

It is easy to continue a long list of elements onto multiple lines of text in the file. Simply end each line with the comma following an element, and continue normally on the next line.

Every line in a shape file must end with a carriage return. In files that contain multiple lines, this will happen naturally, except for the last line in the file, where it is easy to forget. Make sure the last line in all SHP files ends with a carriage return.

Hexadecimal Numbers

For the shape file to be processed as quickly as possible, it can use a *hexadecimal* number system in addition to the more common decimal counting system. While a decimal system is based on counting cycles of ten, a hexadecimal system is based on counting cycles of sixteen. Refer to Chapter 4 for a detailed explanation of hexadecimal numbers.

If shape definitions can use decimal numbers, why bother using hexadecimal numbers? The reason has to do with the way in which MS-DOS computers handle bits of data—normally in groups of 16, or in the case of 80386 systems, in groups of 32. A numbering system based on 16 uses memory more efficiently and increases computer speed, making the insertion of shapes as fast as possible and reducing the overall size of the AutoCAD drawing file.

When a shape definition uses hexadecimal numbers, the numbers include a leading zero—for example, 0A, 0B, 0C, 0D, 0E, 0F. Hexadecimal numbers larger than F are not used. Decimal numbers are not preceded by a leading zero.

Signal Elements

Certain elements in a shape definition have special meanings and are reserved for specific purposes. These numbers are called *signal elements*. They are as follows:

- **1** brings the imaginary pen down. Pen movements that follow this element produce visible lines. This is the default pen position at the start of each shape.

- **2** brings the pen up. Pen movements that follow this element will not produce visible lines. This allows for the production of shapes with separate line segments.

- **3** scales down (reduces) the overall size of the shape. This signal element must be followed by an additional element, a whole number by which all line lengths in the shape are divided. This allows for some additional flexibility while working with standard line lengths.

- **4** scales up (magnifies) the overall size of the shape. It must be followed by a single element, a whole number by which all line lengths in the shape are multiplied.

- **5** causes AutoCAD to store the current pen location in memory for quick recall later. Only one pen location at a time can be stored in this manner. If you wish that a second pen location be stored, you must first recall the previously stored location using signal element 6. Signal element 5 is often used for generating several line segments from a single reference point.

- **6** causes AutoCAD to recall a previously noted pen location, and position the pen there. Signal element 5 must have been previously issued.

- **7** causes AutoCAD to include another shape from the same shape file (called a *subshape*) in the current shape definition. It is followed by the unique shape number stored on that shape's header line. The additional shape will be drawn starting at the current pen location. The referenced shape must be a member of the same shape file. This is useful when several shapes share line configurations.

- **8** causes AutoCAD to draw a single nonstandard line segment. It is followed by two elements indicating movement parallel to an x-axis combined with movement parallel to a y-axis.

- **9** causes AutoCAD to draw a series of nonstandard line segments. It is followed by a series of pairs of elements, indicating pen movement parallel to an x-axis and a y-axis. The series is terminated with a special pair of elements: 0,0.

- **00A** causes AutoCAD to produce an octant arc. It is followed by two elements that define the radius of the arc, the arc length measured in octants, and whether the arc is clockwise or counterclockwise.

- **00B** causes AutoCAD to produce a nonstandard arc. It is followed by elements that define the starting point, ending point, starting angle, and length.

- **00C** causes AutoCAD to draw a different type of nonstandard arc called a *bulge arc*. It is followed by three elements that define the x-y movement of the pen, producing a straight line. It then adds a "bulge factor" that "bends" the line into an arc.

- **00D** causes AutoCAD to draw a series of bulge arcs. The series is terminated by the special element pair 0,0.

- **0** signals the end of the shape definition. All shape definitions end with a single zero.

Standard Line Lengths

Shape definitions utilize standard values to achieve maximum loading and drawing efficiency. AutoCAD shape definitions can use 15 standard lengths for straight lines. These line lengths are expressed as hexadecimal numbers ranging from 1 drawing unit (1) to 15 drawing units (F). Lines that have fractional lengths or lengths longer than 15 are considered nonstandard line lengths. It is possible to use such nonstandard lines, but they are not generated as quickly as standard lines. Nonstandard lines will be discussed shortly.

Standard Angles

AutoCAD shape files recognize 16 standard angles at which line segments may be drawn. These standard angles are illustrated in Figure 15.2.

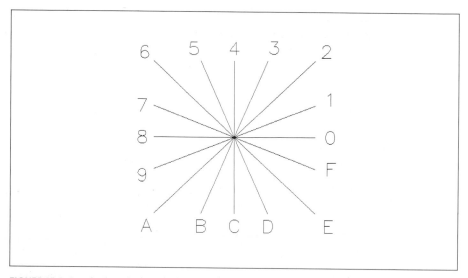

FIGURE 15.2: Standard angles. The fastest shapes are drawn using standard line lengths and angles. This figure illustrates how 1-unit shape lines would be drawn at AutoCad's 16 standard angles. The angles are numbered using a hexadecimal system, allowing each angle to be expressed as a single character, 0 to 9 and A to F.

You will notice that angle zero in Figure 15.2 is AutoCAD's standard orientation for angle zero. The angles increase in a counterclockwise direction, and are represented by hexadecimal numbers from 0 through F.

Examples of Standard Line-Angle Elements

You may draw standard line lengths at standard angles by combining the hexadecimal numbers for line length and angle. Following are some examples; notice that when you draw standard values, the elements must include a leading zero:

010   This element, in the absence of any signal element preceding it, indicates to AutoCAD that a 1-unit line is to be drawn at angle zero. The first digit is the leading zero, indicating that standard values are being used. The second digit represents the standard length of the line, 1 drawing unit, and the third digit represents the standard angle, zero.

02D   This element uses the same syntax to indicate that a 2-unit line is to be drawn at angle D.

0F4   This element indicates that a 15-unit line is to be drawn at angle 4.

The shape definition named VALVE, shown in Figure 15.1, uses standard line-angle elements combined with signal elements to move the pen up and down:

```
*1,6,VALVE; Common butterfly valve symbol, 1x1 scale.
1,014,02F,014,029,0
```

In this example, the signal element 1 indicates the pen-down position. The next element, 014, moves the pen 1 drawing unit at angle 4, producing a vertical line. The next element, 02F, moves the pen 2 units down and to the right. The fourth element, 014, again moves the pen 1 unit at angle 4. The fifth element, 029, moves the pen down and to the left. The sixth element, 2, indicates the pen-up position. The last element is 0, indicating the end of the shape definition.

Octant Arcs

Curved lines are added to shapes using standard arc segments, also known as *octant arcs*. An octant arc is a 45-degree arc. Larger arcs can be created by combining octant arcs. Eight octant arcs will form a full circle. You may combine octant arcs with line segments, scaling, and pen up/down motions to produce a wide variety of useful shapes. The radius of an octant arc may be any whole number from 1 to 255, and octant arcs may be drawn either clockwise or counterclockwise.

An octant arc begins at one of eight standard starting angles. These starting angles are numbered 0 through 7, beginning with AutoCAD's standard angle 0, and moving counterclockwise. They are called *octant angles*. These eight starting angles are illustrated in Figure 15.3. Notice that the numbers for octant angles are different from standard angles used to draw line segments.

Note: Octant arcs may span any number of 45-degree octants, as indicated by the shape definition elements that define them.

Octant arcs are preceded by the signal element 00A. When AutoCAD encounters signal element 00A in a shape definition, the next two elements will be used to define an octant arc. The first element following the signal element indicates the arc's radius, and the second element indicates whether the arc is to be drawn clockwise or counterclockwise, the arc's starting octant angle, and the number of octants it will span.

For example, the following fragment from a shape definition defines an octant arc that has a radius of 1 drawing unit, is drawn counterclockwise starting at octant angle 2, and spans two octants, or 90 degrees:

```
00A,1,022,
```

The first element is the signal element. The second element indicates the radius, 1 drawing unit. The third element indicates that the arc is to be drawn counterclockwise, by virtue of the fact that this element is expressed as a positive

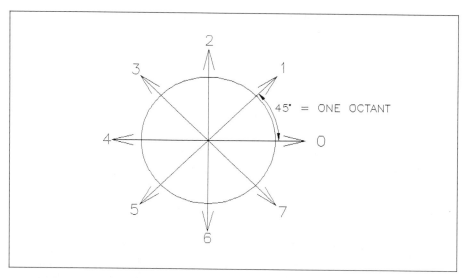

FIGURE 15.3: Standard octant arcs and starting angles. Octant arcs are drawn spanning a specified number of octants, from one through seven. Thus a semicircle spans four octants, and a quarter-circle spans two. They can begin at any octant angle, indicated here using numbered arrows. The arc with the arrowheads would be an octant arc starting at angle zero and spanning one octant. An octant arc spanning zero octants is a full circle.

number. If this second element were to be expressed as a negative number, the octant arc would be drawn clockwise. The first digit is a leading zero, required when using octant arcs. The second digit, 2, indicates that the starting angle is octant angle 2, and the third digit, also 2, indicates that the octant arc spans 2 octants, or 90 degrees.

To draw this same arc clockwise would require the following elements:

    00A,1,−022,

If the octant arc is beginning at angle zero, you can omit the leading zero and the starting angle digit, as follows:

    00A,1,−2,

This syntax would indicate an octant arc with a radius of 1 drawing unit, beginning at angle zero and spanning two octants, drawn clockwise. In all other cases, if you include the starting angle, include the leading zero as well.

You can draw a full circle in a shape definition by signaling an octant arc and indicating a span of 0 octants—not 8 as you might expect. The following shape definitions include octant arc elements for a half-circle and a full circle. They produce the Balloon and Cap shapes illustrated in Figure 15.1.

```
*2,12,BALLOON
2,010,1,00A,1,0,028,2,010,1,01C,0
*3,6,CAP
1,028,00A,1,-044,0
```

Parentheses in Shape Definitions

If you prefer, you may enclose groups of elements in parentheses in order to distinguish elements that work together. For example, it is a common practice to enclose the elements following a signal element in parentheses, as in the following example:

```
*2,12,BALLOON
2,010,1,00A,(1,0),028,2,010,1,01C,0
```

Parentheses may be included anywhere among the elements in a shape definition. They are a visual aid for your convenience only. AutoCAD disregards parentheses when compiling the shape file, and they are not included when you count the number of elements for the header line.

Scaling Shapes

The small number of standard line lengths, arcs, and angles may seem limiting, but there are techniques at your disposal to make them less so. One such technique is *shape scaling*. Shapes may be drawn large and then scaled down to a more manageable insertion size, using signal element 3. Conversely, you can enlarge small shapes by including the signal element 4.

Most shapes can be inserted comfortably in the largest variety of drawings when they are drawn to overall dimensions of 1 drawing unit by 1 drawing unit. This overall size makes it easy to rescale the shape at insertion time. When you use standard line lengths and angles, however, it may become necessary to draw shapes larger than this, so that all the relationships between the lines are correct. For example, consider the following shape definition, for the Eswitch shape illustrated in Figure 15.1:

```
*4,16,ESWITCH
2,020,1,00A,2,0,2,018,01C,1,026,2,02C,1,022,0
```

The octant circle has a radius of two drawing units, because after it is drawn, it is necessary to move the pen 1 drawing unit in from the circumference and 1 drawing unit down, in order to place it in the proper starting position to draw the X in the center. The X is then drawn, using lengths of 2 drawing units.

This works well, but the overall size of the completed shape is 4 drawing units by-4 drawing units (the diameter of the circle). To scale the shape back down to 1 by1, add the following elements to the beginning of the shape (italics added for emphasis only):

*4,18,ESWITCH
3,4,2,020,1,00A,2,0,2,018,01C,1,026,2,02C,1,022,0

Adding the scale-down factor of 4 will reduce the overall size of the shape to 1 drawing unit by 1 drawing unit.

You can start the scaling process anywhere within the shape, and all subsequent lines will be scaled accordingly. If you can indicate more than one scale factor within a shape, the new scale factor is multiplied by the previous scale factor. For example, if you scale a shape down by a factor of 4, and then indicate a second scale-down factor of 4 within the same shape definition, subsequent lines will be scaled down by a factor of 16. Normally, you will want to scale the shape only once. However, the problem of cumulative scaling may arise if you use subshapes. Refer to the section on subshapes in this chapter for more information.

You can reset the scaling factor within a shape by entering the opposite signal element followed by the current scaling factor. For example, if you have scaled a shape down by a factor of 4 and would like to return the scale factor to 1, enter the following elements:

4,4,

Although the mathematics of scale would not indicate that this is the correct scale factor, AutoCAD will understand that you intend to reverse the previous scaling factor.

It is possible to combine scale-down and scale-up codes to produce fractional scaling factors. For example, if you scale down by a factor of 4 and immediately scale back up by a factor of 3, the result is an overall scaling factor of ³/₄, or 0.75. Notice that in order to return to the original scale factor, you must reverse both scaling codes; in this case, scale down by 3, and back up by 4.

The scaling factor is automatically reset to 1 when a new shape is inserted or the Shape command is canceled.

Nonstandard Lines

AutoCAD shape files allow for nonstandard pen movement by means of a special signal element, 8, that instructs AutoCAD to move its pen to specific coordinate points. The coordinates are referenced by combining pen movements along the x-axis and y-axis.

If the value of movement along the x-axis is negative, the pen moves to the left. If positive, the pen moves to the right. Likewise, if the value of movement along the y-axis is negative, the pen moves down. If the value of movement along the y-axis is positive, the pen moves up. The range of pen movement for nonstandard lines is −127 to +127 drawing units.

For example, the following fragment from a shape definition defines a line drawn from the current pen position to a point 4 units to the right and 14 units up:

```
8,(4,14),
```

The first element following the signal element indicates the distance along the x-axis; the second element indicates the distance along the y-axis. The following syntax would move the pen the same distance to the left and down:

```
8,( − 4, − 14),
```

The following shape definition uses nonstandard lines to draw the shape named Edge in Figure 15.1:

```
*5,14,EDGE
1,030,8,(3,3),8,( − 2, − 6),8,(3,3),030,2,0
```

Connecting Nonstandard Lines

When a long series of nonstandard lines appears in a shape definition, it is possible to indicate the entire series to AutoCAD with a one signal element, 9. If your shape definition contains a long series of such lines, and your shape file is large and contains many such shape definitions, you can use this technique to save disk space by making the shape file that much smaller, and improve your loading, compiling, and drawing times slightly.

When you indicate a series of nonstandard lines with signal element 9, AutoCAD will treat each subsequent pair of elements as indicating x-y pen movement, until it encounters two consecutive zero elements.

For example, the shape named Flow in Figure 15.1 can be defined using a series of nonstandard lines as follows:

```
*6,27,FLOW
2,8,(2, − 1),1,9,(2,1),( − 4,0),(0, − 2),(10,2),( − 10,2),(0, − 2),(0,0),
2,040,1,8,( − 2,1),0
```

Element number 6 begins a series of six nonstandard lines, ending with elements 19 and 20, both zero. After the series of nonstandard lines, AutoCAD lifts the pen and finishes the shape.

Nonstandard Arcs

It is possible to create shape definitions including arcs that do not begin on an octant angle, or whose total degrees are not multiples of 45. There are two methods for doing this. One method creates an *offset arc,* and the other method creates a *bulge arc.*

Offset Arcs

An offset arc references the two nearest standard offset angles and draws the arc in relation to those angles. Offset arcs are signaled by element 00B, which is followed by five special elements that describe the offset arc.

The first three of these elements describe how the nonstandard arc is offset from the nearest standard arc. The last two elements are the standard arc-description elements we have seen before.

For example, here are the numerical elements that describe a small, nonstandard arc beginning at 52 degrees and ending at 127 degrees, with a radius of 5 drawing units, drawn counterclockwise:

    00B,(40,210,0,5,012)

The first element is 00B, signaling to AutoCAD that an offset arc is to be described. The next two elements indicate the *starting* and *ending offsets* for this arc. These elements are calculated using the following formula:

1. Determine the starting angle of the offset arc. In our example, this is 52 degrees.

2. Determine the next lowest standard octant angle from the starting angle of the offset arc. In this example, this would be octant angle 1, which is 45 degrees.

3. Determine the difference in degrees between the starting angle of the offset arc and the octant angle. In this case, the difference is 7 degrees, or 52 minus 45.

4. Multiply this difference by 256. In our example, this results in 1,792.

5. Divide the result by 45. In our example, this results in 40.82.

6. Round the result to a whole number. In our example, this is 40.

Therefore, the starting offset for our sample arc is 40. This is the numerical element that immediately follows element 00B.

The formula for calculating the offset for the endpoint of the arc is almost the same:

1. Determine the ending angle of the nonstandard arc. In our example, this is 127 degrees.

2. Determine the next lowest standard octant angle from the ending angle of the offset arc. In this example, this would be octant angle 2, 90 degrees.

3. Determine the difference in degrees between the ending angle of the offset arc and the octant angle. In this case, the difference is 37 degrees (127 minus 90).

4. Multiply this difference by 256. In our example, this results in 9,472.

5. Divide the result by 45. In our example, this results in 210.48.

6. Round the result to a whole number. In our example, this is 210.

Therefore, the ending offset for the offset arc is 210. This is the next element in the offset arc description.

The next element is always zero. This zero simply indicates that the radius of the offset arc is less than the maximum allowable 255 drawing units. If you attempt to use a radius greater than 255 drawing units, the shape file will not compile.

The fourth and fifth elements in the offset arc description are the same as if a standard arc were being drawn. In this case, the radius is 5 drawing units, so the fourth element is 5. The arc is drawn counterclockwise, it begins in octant 1, and it spans a total of 2 octants; so, the fifth element is 012.

Figure 15.1 includes a shape named Break, which contains this offset arc. Following is the complete shape definition for Break:

```
*7,33,BREAK
3,10,2,030,024,1,00B,(40,210,0,5,012),2,030,014,1,054,
2,0AC,038,1,00B,(40,210,0,5,052),2,038,01C,1,05C,0
```

Here is what the elements in this shape definition mean:

3,10,	This shape is scaled down by a factor of 10.
2,030,024,	The pen is lifted and moved 3 drawing units to the right, 2 drawing units up.
1,00B,(40,210,0,5,012),	The pen is lowered and the offset arc described above is drawn.
2,030,014,	The pen is lifted and moved 3 units to the right, 1 unit up.
1,054,	The pen is lowered and a line is drawn 5 units up.
2,0AC,038,	The pen is lifted and moved 10 units down (hexadecimal A = 10; C = angle C, straight down), then 3 units to the left.

1,00B,(40,210,0,5,052),	The pen is lowered and the offset arc described above is drawn. This time, however, it begins in octant 5. Otherwise, it is the same arc; calculating its starting and ending offsets yields the same results as the first arc.
2,038,01C,	The pen is lifted and moved 3 units to the right, 1 unit down.
1,05C,0	The pen is lowered, a line is drawn 5 units down, and the shape definition ends.

The secret to designing nonstandard shapes like this one is to use AutoCAD in the sketching and design process. In this example, the shape was quickly sketched in AutoCAD, and the arc's starting angle, ending angle, and radius were found using the List command (see Chapter 21). To visually represent the starting and ending angles and radius, the arc's endpoints and center point were connected with lines using Osnap. The radius of the arc is the distance between the center point and an endpoint. AutoCAD's angular dimensioning feature was used to determine its starting and ending angles. This design sketch is illustrated in Figure 15.4.

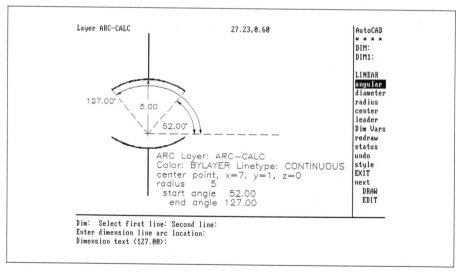

FIGURE 15.4: Determining arc values using AutoCAD. Calculating offset and bulge arcs begins by determining the starting and ending angle for the arc to be drawn. In this figure, the Osnap feature was used to draw angle lines, and automatic dimensioning indicates the starting and ending angles of the arc, as well as its radius. The text in the lower right is the output of the List command, referencing the same arc. Using these values, you can quickly calculate the elements of the offset arc.

When AutoCAD first measured the radius, starting angle, and ending angle of the arc, these measurements were fractional. However, for purposes of calculating offsets, these fractional dimensions were rounded to the nearest whole number without problem.

BULGE ARCS

If all this calculating of offset arcs seems daunting, there is an optional means of producing a nonstandard arc, if you have AutoCAD Version 2.5 or greater and your arc is 180 degrees or less. This second type of nonstandard arc is called a *bulge arc*.

The process of creating a bulge arc involves drawing a nonstandard straight line segment using x-y movement as we have seen before, and then "bulging" it from its center point. The signal element for a single bulge arc is 00C. The 00C element is followed by three elements: the x-axis pen movement, the y-axis pen movement, and the *bulge factor,* the amount of bulge to be applied to the line.

Following is an example:

```
00C,(5,5,60)
```

In this example, a new pen position is determined by moving the pen 5 drawing units to the right and 5 drawing units up. Then a bulge factor of 60 is applied to the line between the previous and current pen positions. Because the bulge factor is positive, the final arc will be drawn counterclockwise. If the bulge factor had been negative, the final arc would have been drawn clockwise.

You can apply a bulge factor within a range of –127 to +127. Using the maximum or minimum value will result in a 180-degree arc. An arc larger than 180 degrees has to be drawn as a standard arc, a nonstandard arc using offset calculations, or a series of bulge arcs.

Following is the shape definition of the Break shape again, drawn using bulge arcs instead of offset arcs. The bulge arc was drawn from a line 6 drawing units long, with an applied bulge factor of 50.

```
*7,29,BREAK
3,10,2,030,024,1,00C,( – 6,0,50),2,030,014,1,054,
2,0AC,038,1,00C,(6,0,50),2,038,01C,1,05C,0
```

Notice that because fewer elements were used to create the bulge arcs, the number of elements in the header line is reduced from 33 to 29.

Signal element 00D can be used to indicate a series of bulge arcs. Such a series is terminated by two zeros, as was the case with a series of nonstandard line segments. For example, the following fragment of a shape definition produces a series of bulge arcs:

00D,(10,10,60),(10,10, − 60),(3,14,120),(3,14, − 120),(0,0),

If you wish, you can apply a bulge factor of zero, which results in a straight line. This is very useful when connecting a continuous series of straight lines and bulge arcs into a continuous line. By using the zero bulge, you are spared the trouble of going back and forth between the various special elements to call non-standard lines and bulge arcs; for example:

00D,(5,5,60),(5,5, − 60),(5,0,0),(5,5,60),(5,5, − 60),(0,0),

Note how simply supplying a bulge factor of zero adds a straight line element (5,0,0) within the series of bulge arcs.

How to Calculate the Correct Bulge Factor

Once you have designed and dimensioned your shape, you can continue to use AutoCAD to determine the correct bulge factor. Here is the procedure to follow:

1. Determine the angle of your arc using AutoCAD, as illustrated in Figure 15.4.
2. Divide the arc angle by 180, and multiply the result by 127.

This yields the correct bulge factor.

If you choose to draw the arc clockwise, apply the bulge factor as a negative number; otherwise, apply the bulge factor as a positive number.

Subshapes

It is possible for a shape definition to reference another shape definition. This is useful if more than one shape in the shape file contains common elements. For example, consider these two shape definitions from a Release 11 shape file:

```
*7,33,BREAK   ; -- Note: This shape is referenced in #8, BREAKA:
3,10,2,030,024,1,00B,(40,210,0,5,012),2,030,014,1,054,
2,0AC,038,1,00B,(40,210,0,5,052),2,038,01C,1,05C,0

*8,18,BREAKA  ; -- Note: This shape references #7, BREAK:
7,7,2,064,028,1,8,(2,4),8,(2,-4),2,024,018,1,028,0
```

The second shape definition begins by referencing the first, with signal element 7 followed by the shape number of the Break shape, 7. AutoCAD will draw the Break shape as described, and then continue with the BreakA shape, which relocates the pen and draws a simple letter *A* in the middle of the shape.

Notice that because the Break shape was scaled down by a factor of 10, the BreakA shape, when it continues after referencing the Break shape, will also be scaled by a factor of 10. Scaling factors are not reset when you reference subshapes or return to the original shape definition. If you need to adjust the scaling factor while referencing subshapes, you must do so explicitly, using the 3 (scale down) and 4 (scale up) signal elements described earlier in this chapter.

Other Shape Definitions

For purposes of study, following are the shape definitions for the remaining shapes pictured in Figure 15.1:

```
*9,20,TARGET
3,4,2,038,1,060,2,038,05C,1,0A4,2,02C,1,010,06C,028,064,010,0
*10,10,CVALVE
3,4,022,054,00A,(2,4),05C,02E,0
*11,28,NORTH
3,9,2,05C,018,1,024,02E,024,2,016,1,064,8,(−1,−2),2,020,
1,8,(−1,2),2,04C,018,1,020,0
```

COMPILING A SHAPE FILE

As mentioned earlier, AutoCAD's modifiable shape files are ASCII files created using a text editor, and must have the extension SHP. These files contain a series of shape definitions that must use the syntax described in the previous sections.

After you have created a file containing shape definitions, the file must be compiled before being used by AutoCAD to generate shapes. To compile the file, follow this procedure:

1. Load AutoCAD, or if AutoCAD is already loaded, go to AutoCAD's Main Menu.

2. Select option 7, "Compile shape/font description file."

3. Enter the name of the file to compile. The file extension is not necessary; SHP is assumed. If the file is located on a drive or subdirectory other than the current default, include the drive letter and subdirectory path before the file name. AutoCAD responds:

   Compiling shape/font description file...

4. After compilation is complete, AutoCAD responds

> Compilation successful. Output file *name.*SHX contains *nnn* bytes.

where *name* is the file name you entered, and *nnn* is the size of the file in bytes.

5. If the shape file contains errors, AutoCAD will terminate the compilation process and display an error message. Common errors include such things as extending a line of elements too far to the right, failing to include a comma, entering an unknown signal element, failing to enter a signal element, and failing to enter the correct number of elements in the header line.

When the file is successfully compiled, enter AutoCAD's drawing editor, invoke the Load command, and enter the name of the SHX file. Once loaded, shapes in the file may be inserted using the Shape command.

If you have finished editing your SHP file and have compiled it into an SHX file, you may, if you choose, make a backup copy of the SHP file and delete it from your hard disk, in order to reclaim disk space. AutoCAD only reads the SHX file when working with shapes.

COMMANDS FOR LOADING AND USING SHAPES

The Load and Shape commands are used to load shape files and insert shapes in the drawing.

LOAD

Loads a compiled shape file into the drawing, making it possible to reference the shapes that the file contains.

VERSIONS

All. However, if you are creating a shape file in an AutoCAD version earlier than 2.5, the 00C (bulge arcs) and 00D (series of bulge arcs) shape definition elements are not available.

COMMAND OPTIONS

Name of shape file   Enter the name of the shape file you intend to load into the drawing. AutoCAD looks for the file along its subdirectory search path and loads it, making all the shapes it contains available for insertion into the drawing.

? Enter a question mark to receive a list of shape files that are already loaded into a drawing.

USAGE

AutoCAD must know where to look for shape names requested using the Shape command. Only files that are explicitly loaded into the drawing are searched for shapes. If you have several shape files on your hard disk, loading shape files enables AutoCAD to confine its search to those files where the shapes can be found.

If your shape files are on a separate disk drive or on a subdirectory not on AutoCAD's search path, you may include the drive letter and subdirectory name(s) before the file name; for example:

    D:\ACAD\SHAPES\SHXFILE

The file extension is never given; an extension of SHX (compiled shape file) is assumed.

RELATED COMMANDS

Style.

SAMPLE DIALOG

The following dialog loads a shape file named PC into the drawing, and requests a list containing the name of the loaded shape file:

    Command: **Load**
    Name of shape file to load (or ?): **PC**
    Command: **(press Enter)**
    LOAD Name of shape file to load (or ?): **?**
    Loaded shape files:
      PC

SHAPE

Inserts a shape from a loaded shape file into the drawing.

VERSIONS

All.

COMMAND OPTIONS

? Enter a question mark to receive a list of shape names from files that are loaded into a drawing.

Shape name Enter the name of the shape that you intend to insert.

Starting point Enter the point where you intend to insert the shape. You may enter the point using any of AutoCAD's standard coordinate-point entry methods (see Chapter 5). If you select the point using the pointing device, AutoCAD will display a preview image of the shape with its insertion point at the intersection of the crosshairs; the image will move as you move the pointing device. If you do not see the preview image, enter **Drag** in response to this prompt. If you still do not see the preview image, check the setting of the DRAGMODE system variable, which should be set to 1 or 2 in order to enable dynamic dragging. Refer to Chapter 13 for details regarding system variables.

Height Your response to this prompt determines the overall size of the shape. How the shape reacts to your response depends on how the shape was originally defined. See the Usage section for more information.

Rotation angle After you enter the insertion point and the height of the shape, AutoCAD prompts for the shape's rotation angle around the insertion point. You may enter an angle by typing it from the keyboard, or by entering a point. Auto-CAD assumes that the absolute angle referenced by the insertion point and selected point is the angle of rotation for the shape. If dynamic dragging is enabled and you move the crosshairs before selecting the angle, you will see a preview image of the shape rotating around the insertion point.

USAGE

The use of the Shape command is intuitive, except for the prompt to enter the height of the shape. AutoCAD scales shapes by adjusting their vertical dimension—their "height"—to the number of drawing units you indicate in response to the Height prompt. Their horizontal dimension is scaled accordingly.

For example, if you have defined your shape to overall dimensions of 1 drawing unit by 1 drawing unit, entering 1 drawing unit as the height of the shape will insert the shape at its original size. If you specify 2 drawing units as the height of the shape, the shape will double in size. Enter 3 drawing units and the shape triples in size, $1/2$ drawing unit and the shape will be half-size, and so on.

Shapes drawn at uneven scales, or at overall scales other than 1 drawing unit, will react less predictably. Fortunately, if you have enabled dynamic dragging, you can preview the size of all shapes before actually entering them, by moving the crosshairs before responding to the prompt for the shape height. AutoCAD assumes that the distance between the insertion point and the intersection of the crosshairs is the height of the shape, and scales the shape accordingly on the screen. Thus, you will see a preview image of the shape enlarge and contract as you move the crosshairs in relation to the insertion point.

If you are unable to scale the shape the way that you intend, redefine the shape and include signal elements for scaling that will reduce or enlarge the overall size of the shape to a manageable amount. See "Scaling Shapes" in this chapter for details.

If you are using Release 11 or later, shapes can be part of external reference drawings, displayed along with the other referenced entities. Refer to Chapter 21 for details about external reference files. While shapes in external reference drawings can be displayed in the current drawing, they cannot be inserted into it simply by invoking the Shape command. To include such shapes in your drawings, you must explicitly load their files; you then may invoke the Shape command to insert them.

RELATED COMMANDS

Insert.

SAMPLE DIALOG

The following sample dialog inserts a shape named Target at point 5,5 at its original size, and at an angle of 45 degrees:

    Command: **Shape**
    Shape name (or ?): **Target**
    Starting point: **5,5**
    Height <0′ – 1″>: **(press Enter)**
    Rotation angle <0.00>: **45**
        Command:

TEXT-FONT FILES

If you want to create text in AutoCAD using your own unique text font and you have some perseverance, you can do so by means of a special type of shape file called a *text-font file*. AutoCAD will read your custom text-font file and insert text with that font style into your drawings, using the same commands it uses to insert standard text.

The sections that follow relate to the development of text-font files only; refer to Chapter 9 for details regarding the commands used to enter text and determine text styles in AutoCAD.

Text-Font Files Compared with Shape Files

Text-font files are similar to ordinary shape files. Like shape files, they have the file extension SHP. They are created and edited using your text editor. They contain shape definitions of each letter of the alphabet, as well as numbers, punctuation marks, and any special characters that might be necessary to produce text in a drawing. These shape definitions use the same elements in the same way as ordinary shapes, with only a few exceptions:

- Text-font files contain certain special shape definitions that distinguish them from ordinary shape files. For instance, a text-font file must begin with a special shape definition that identifies the overall scaling, letter positioning, and orientation of the characters. This special shape definition is always the first shape definition in the file and always has the shape number zero. The header line contains the shape number, the number of elements in the shape (always 4), and the name of the text font. AutoCAD uses the numerical elements in this shape definition to determine the scaling and orientation of the font:

  1. The first element indicates the maximum number of drawing units that uppercase letters will extend above the baseline of the text. This number is also used to determine the overall scaling of the font.

  2. The second element indicates the maximum number of drawing units that lowercase letters will extend below the baseline of the text.

  3. The third element is the orientation mode element. This number is zero if the text font is only horizontal. If the font contains optional pen motions for vertical orientation, the mode element is 2. No other numbers are used in this position.

  4. The fourth element is the zero that finishes all shape definitions.

Following is an example of such a shape definition:

```
*0,4,sample
100,30,2,0
```

The elements in this shape definition for a font named Sample indicate that the uppercase characters will extend 100 drawing units above the baseline, the lowercase letters will extend 30 units below the baseline, and the text is dual-oriented; that is, it can be entered in both horizontal and vertical orientation.

Characters in a text-font file are often designed at a large scale, which allows complex characters to be created using the whole numbers that shape definitions require. When the text-font file is compiled and used, this shape definition will be used to scale the font down, so that the options regarding text height in the Style command will be applied consistently to all characters in the font file.

A text-font file must also contain a special shape definition for a line feed, instructing AutoCAD to move the pen a specific distance to a new line when entering repeated lines of text. This shape definition, which is always number 10, includes the pen-up signal element, followed by pen motion downward a specified distance; for example:

```
*10,5,lf
2,8,(0, − 140),0
```

This example raises the pen and moves it 140 units straight down.

- Unlike ordinary shape files, the numbering system in text-font files is standardized. In a text-font file, the shape numbers in the header line correspond to a set of standard number codes used to generate those text characters, called ASCII codes. Table 15.1 contains the ASCII codes for text characters. The use of these standard ASCII codes means that all text-font files are, in effect, prenumbered. For example, the shape number for an uppercase *A* is always 65.

- The header lines in a text-font file include shape names, but these names are entered in lowercase, as opposed to the uppercase names in ordinary shape files. This is because the standard numbering system in text-font files eliminates the need to name the shapes; when the text-font file is compiled, AutoCAD will ignore the lowercase shape names, thus conserving space in the compiled file. The only reason to include lowercase shape names is to make individual text characters easier to locate for subsequent editing.

It is useful to study the source code for the standard text-font files that come with AutoCAD. These files have been thoroughly tested, are extremely efficient in their use of shape definition elements, and are thus useful models for your own text-font files. Compare the shape definitions in these files to the characters that are generated on screen; this will help you understand the relationship between the definitions and the graphic output. You can find these files on the AutoCAD Support Files diskette, in a separate subdirectory named SOURCE. Copy these files onto your hard disk before attempting to read them or make any changes. Do not work with the original SHP files supplied by Autodesk.

32	(space)	64	@	96	' (rev. apostrophe)
33	!	65	A	97	a
34	"	66	B	98	b
35	#	67	C	99	c
36	$	68	D	100	d
37	%	69	E	101	e
38	&	70	F	102	f
39	'	71	G	103	g
40	(	72	H	104	h
41	)	73	I	105	i
42	*	74	J	106	j
43	+	75	K	107	k
44	,	76	L	108	l
45	–	77	M	109	m
46	.	78	N	110	n
47	/	79	O	111	o
48	0	80	P	112	p
49	1	81	Q	113	q
50	2	82	R	114	r
51	3	83	S	115	s
52	4	84	T	116	t
53	5	85	U	117	u
54	6	86	V	118	v
55	7	87	W	119	w
56	8	88	X	120	x
57	9	89	Y	121	y
58	:	90	Z	122	z
59	;	91	[	123	{
60	<	92	\	124	| (vertical bar)
61	=	93	]	125	}
62	>	94	^	126	~ (tilde)
63	?	95	_ (underscore)	127	° (degrees)

Table 15.1: ASCII Codes for Text Characters

Designing Character Shapes

The process of creating a text-font file from scratch is time-consuming. The first step is to create a shape definition for each letter, number, punctuation mark, and symbol to be used in the font. All the techniques you have seen so far may be used to generate these text-character shape definitions.

It is important that text characters be of consistent size. To help with this, create a template drawing of boxes into which you can draw your text characters. This template drawing should show you the maximum height and width of all the characters in the text-font file. Figure 15.5 shows one possibility for such a template.

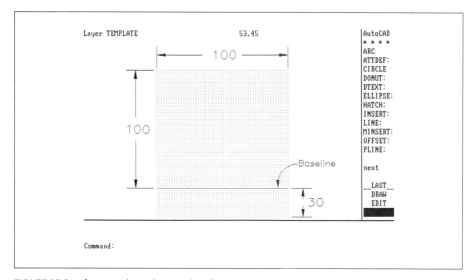

FIGURE 15.5: A font template. This template for designing text fonts was set up to measure 100 drawing units by 100 drawing units above the baseline, and 30 additional drawing units below the baseline. The grid has been set for 2 units—1 unit would not have been visible. Although this is a serviceable template for text fonts, it can be used to design any shape.

The template drawing has a snap value of 1 drawing unit, making it easier to draw characters that can be accurately dimensioned and translated into x-y pen movements using whole numbers. This example is not the only possibility for a template drawing. Feel free to experiment and develop the template that is just right for you. Figure 15.6 illustrates a lowercase *b* drawn in the sample template.

Following is the shape definition that will produce the lowercase *b*:

```
*98,26,lcb
1,8,(0,95),2,8,(0,−92),
1,00D,(36,8,59),(−5,41,45),(−31,0,53),(0,0),
2,8,(48,−51),0
```

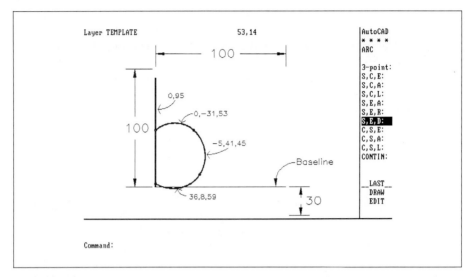

FIGURE 15.6: Designing a lowercase *b*. In this figure, a lowercase *b* has been drawn into the template shown in Figure 15.5. This character consists of a vertical line plus four bulge arcs. The vertical line is 95 drawing units long. The arc endpoints are marked with small dots to indicate their starting and ending points.

Notice that this shape definition is composed of one nonstandard line segment and three bulge arcs. The pen is lifted twice. The first time is to move it into position to draw the curve of the letter. The second time is to move the pen to its standard finishing position, which is the lower-right corner of the letter, plus an allowance of 18 drawing units of space between the *b* and whatever letter may follow it.

A good procedure for creating letters with curves is as follows:

1. Draw the letter.

2. Once the letter looks just the way you want it, mark all arc endpoints for later reference. A small circle or *x* can be useful for doing this. Use Auto-CAD's Osnap feature to make multiple copies of the mark at each arc endpoint.

3. Determine the bulge of each curved line in the character. Use the formula that was given in the section on bulge arcs in this chapter.

4. Make notes of the results and all the necessary shape definition elements.

5. Once the x-y pen movements and bulges have been determined, enter your text editor and type up all the necessary elements for this character.

Testing the Font Characters

As you design your font characters, place the shape definitions in a special shape file, not a text-font file, with the character name in uppercase. This will speed up the process of compiling the file, and you can enter the character as a shape to see if your shape definition is correct. Once the shape definition is correct, you can use your text editor to add it to the text-font file. Remember to convert the shape name in the header line to lowercase at this point.

Dual-Orientation Text-Font Files

Once each character's shape definition has been created and tested, you may add special signal elements to the description, allowing the font to be entered in either vertical or horizontal orientation. Text-font files that can be entered with either vertical or horizontal orientation are called *dual-orientation text-font files*.

In a dual-orientation text-font file, each shape definition contains special optional pen-motion elements. AutoCAD ignores these optional elements unless the user specifies vertical text orientation when the font file is loaded into the drawing. These optional pen-motion elements are usually found at the beginning and end of each shape definition. Their purpose is to lift and relocate the pen to the correct starting and finishing positions that orient the text vertically.

Figure 15.7 illustrates the extra pen motions necessary to adapt the lowercase *b* in Figure 15.6 to vertical orientation. These optional pen-motion elements are preceded by the special signal element 00E. The first element that follows this special signal element is processed by AutoCAD only in vertical orientation. Subsequent elements are processed normally.

There is no special signal element for a series of optional pen motions. If you need to use a series of optional elements, each optional element must be preceded by the code 00E.

Following is the shape definition for the lowercase *b* with optional vertical-orientation elements added. (Italics are included for emphasis only.) Notice that the total number of elements in the header line has been increased to account for these additional elements.

```
*98,38,lcb
00E,2,00E,8,( − 16, − 100),1,8,(0,95),2,8,(0, − 92),
1,00D,(36,8,59),( − 5,41,45),( − 31,0,53),(0,0),
2,8,(48,51),00E,2,00E,8,( − 32, − 30),0
```

At the end of this shape definition, more optional pen motions relocate the pen to the lowermost center position in the shape. Each shape definition in the text-font file

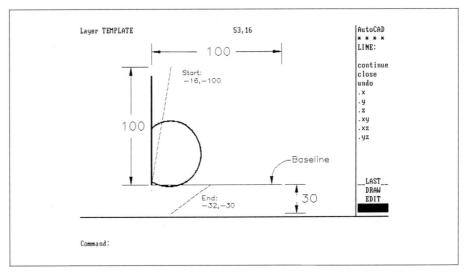

FIGURE 15.7: Adding vertical pen motions to lowercase *b*. To include the lowercase *b* as part of a dual-orientation text-font file, two extra pen-up motions were added, represented here by dashed lines. The starting pen motion assumes that, no matter what the previous character, the shape definition left the pen in the same position relative to the character. Thus, the optional motion lifts the pen and moves it down to the lower left to begin drawing the *b*. When finished, another optional pen motion lifts the pen from its normal finishing position and moves it to the ending position, where the following character can pick it up and continue generating more vertical text characters.

will begin, as this one does, with an optional pen motion straight down the center line of the character. This causes the characters to line up vertically.

The exact vertical pen motions you enter in your font file will depend on how you want your text characters to line up vertically—to the right, to the left, or along the center line.

Third-Party Font Files

There is no way to avoid it: Creating your own font files will take a lot of time and require a great deal of perseverance. Many third-party developers have produced a number of attractive font files for AutoCAD. Some of these ready-made font files are available in both SHP and SHX format; others are available in SHX format only, making them impossible for you to modify and edit. Still, in light of the time you can save, it is worth it to investigate the possibility of finding a third-party AutoCAD font that will fulfill your needs. Your dealer is a good place to start looking. Also, several developers now advertise their fonts in periodicals that are geared toward CAD.

PART

VI

AutoLISP

AutoLISP may be the single most powerful tool in AutoCAD. Using AutoLISP, you may create brand-new AutoCAD commands that display your own prompts and messages, make decisions, perform internal calculations, draw complex sets of entities, or modify existing AutoCAD commands to perform special operations. AutoLISP allows AutoCAD to perform repetitive and calculation-intensive aspects of the drafting process, thereby freeing you to focus on the more creative design aspects. AutoLISP is the ultimate tool for creating a CAD software application that is truly your own. Part VI introduces the AutoLISP function syntax and control structures, and details AutoLISP's set of predefined functions, which you can use to create custom AutoLISP functions of your own.

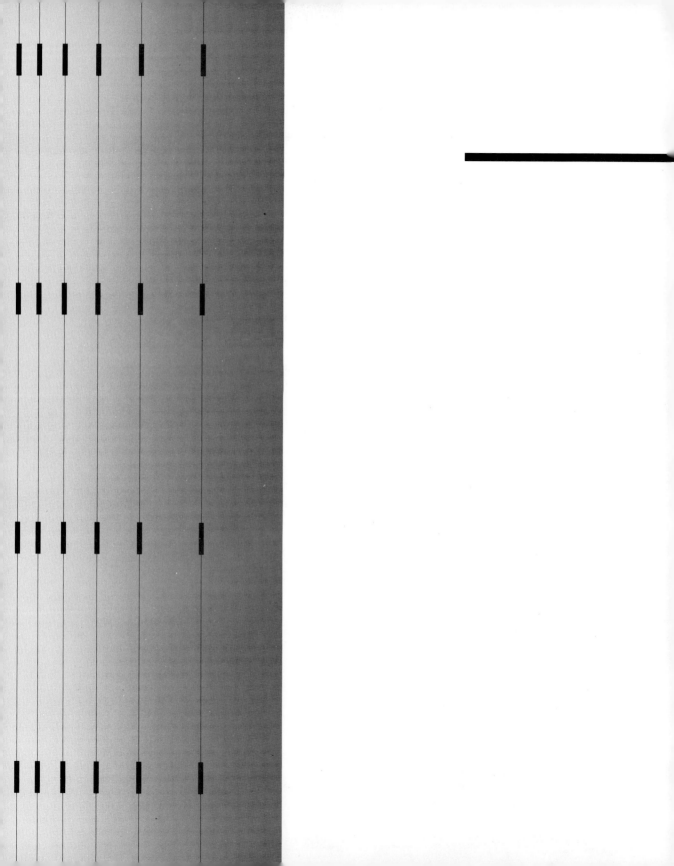

SYNTAX AND STRUCTURES

SYNTAX AND STRUCTURES

AutoLISP may be the most powerful AutoCAD tool at your disposal—a built-in set of predefined functions that can be used as a procedural programming language. When used with other AutoCAD features such as system variables and custom menus, AutoLISP enables you to customize Auto-CAD to your personal specifications, greatly enhancing the speed and ease with which you can create and edit complex drawings.

You can use AutoLISP to create new AutoCAD commands or redefine standard commands to your liking, to perform internal calculations and store formulas for solving common drafting problems, to develop intelligent macros that make logical and mathematical decisions, to interact with you to access variable graphic information parameters, or to access and modify AutoCAD's underlying database directly.

AutoLISP is an outgrowth of the "variables and expressions" feature introduced in Version 2.1. This feature was used to store data to memory variables within the computer's memory during the drawing session, and to retrieve it later for analysis, conditional operations, or responses to AutoCAD command prompts. This process was accomplished by entering functions at the keyboard, or in sequence by means of a script file. (Refer to Chapter 21 for details regarding script files.) Since the variables and expressions feature was underdocumented and a bit hard to manipulate, many users paid little attention to it.

Beginning with Version 2.18, AutoCAD introduced the full AutoLISP language, including an *AutoLISP interpreter.* This feature allowed users to create ASCII files called *AutoLISP files* (with the extension LSP). These files contained a series of functions that could be loaded into memory and evaluated in sequence. This process was more flexible, faster, more powerful, and easier to manage than the variables and expressions feature. Autodesk added special new functions that allowed these routines to be more interactive, prompting the user for information and displaying messages, making decisions based on conditional statements, and repeating special sequences of functions until conditional criteria were met.

Since the inception of AutoLISP, AutoCAD users have responded with an astonishing array of AutoLISP applications, ranging from the ingeniously simple to the highly specialized and complex. Many of these applications are in the public domain, posted on computer bulletin boards that cater to AutoCAD users. Some are available for purchase as commercial software. Some of Autodesk's own add-on software, such as AutoSketch, AEC Mechanical, and AEC Architectural, depend heavily on AutoLISP.

AutoLISP has continued to evolve; each new release of AutoCAD since Version 2.18 has included some refinements and enhancements to AutoLISP.

AutoLISP shares many of its functions and its overall syntax structure with Common LISP, its parent programming language. Common LISP is itself just one dialect of a programming language that has many different dialects—MacLISP, UCI LISP, InterLISP, and even Franz LISP. Although AutoLISP is a limited programming language, it uses many conventional control structures that are common to all programming languages. Readers with some experience in programming will immediately recognize such control structures as if-then-else statements and controlled loops.

Since AutoLISP is a small language, limited in scope, it is relatively easy for nonprogrammers to learn. Once you have learned AutoLISP's *vocabulary* (the predefined function names and what they accomplish) and *syntax* (the rules for arranging functions into working routines), AutoLISP routines are fairly easy to create and modify using your text editor.

Like any programming language, AutoLISP requires strict adherence to its rules of logic and syntax. The development of AutoLISP applications is often marked by a process of patiently moving between the drawing editor and the text editor until the routine functions smoothly. Although it may take time to develop a fully functional AutoLISP application, the time you invest in a well-planned application usually pays off handsomely in terms of greater productivity, ease of use, and reduced training time for new users.

This chapter summarizes the syntax and procedural rules of AutoLISP. Chapter 17 will discuss its fundamental vocabulary. In Part VII, Chapter 19 will introduce some advanced functions and show you how to use AutoLISP to access AutoCAD's underlying database.

LISTS

In AutoLISP, a *list* is any group of individual items of information, called *members,* enclosed within a matched set of parentheses and separated from each other by at least one space. Members of a list can be numbers, characters, or even other lists. They derive their meaning from the nature of their contents and/or the context in which they appear. The *length* of a list is the number of individual members it contains; lists can be of any length. The following are typical lists:

LIST	DESCRIPTION
(+ 1 2)	Three members: plus sign, 1, and 2
("A" "B")	Two members: "A" and "B"
(1 (2 3) 4 5)	Four members: 1, a list of two members, 4, and 5

Atoms

In AutoLISP, any data type that is not a list is called an *atom*. An atom is any unit of information that cannot be broken down into smaller components—i.e., anything that is not a list. Examples of atoms include numbers and symbols.

There is one exception to the mutual exclusivity of atoms and lists: the special symbol *nil,* which stands for a null value, or no-value—literally nothing at all. AutoLISP perceives nil both as an atom, because it is an irreducible symbol, and as an "empty list," making nil two data types in one.

Functions

The basic building block of AutoLISP is the *function.* A function is a list of data items that AutoCAD understands as an instruction to perform a specific type of process and return the result of that process. The list that makes up a function is always contained within a matching pair of parentheses that indicate the beginning and end of the list of data to be evaluated.

Unless explicitly told otherwise, the AutoLISP interpreter always assumes that a list is a function, and that the first member of the list is the *function operator*— a string of alphanumeric characters representing a command to evaluate the remaining data in some specific way.

For example, the following is a rudimentary AutoLISP function:

(+ 1 2)

This function is a list containing three members: the plus sign, and the integers 1 and 2. The plus sign is the function operator. The AutoLISP interpreter will read this function and add the numbers together, returning the result of 3.

The characters used for function operators are usually mnemonic strings or special symbols that indicate the function's purpose. For example, following are some examples of AutoLISP's basic math functions, details about which can be found in Chapter 17:

EXAMPLE	DESCRIPTION
(+ 36 9)	Addition; adds 9 to 36, returns 45
(– 36 9)	Subtraction; subtracts 9 from 36, returns 27
(* 36 9)	Multiplication; multiplies 36 by 9, returns 324
(/ 36 9)	Division; divides 36 by 9, returns 4

The data following the function operator comprises its *arguments.* In the examples just presented, each function has two arguments, 36 and 9, that are operated upon in different ways depending on the function.

AutoLISP functions may be entered at the Command prompt, and the result will be displayed in the Command-prompt area. Go into the drawing editor and try entering the above examples to see the results.

Nesting Functions

The results returned by functions can be used as the arguments of other functions, in a powerful AutoLISP technique called *nesting.* Proper arrangement of parentheses among nested functions is critical. For example, here is a valid AutoLISP function:

(* (+ 1 2) (+ 3 4))

In this function, two functions for addition are nested within a multiplication function. These combined functions return a value of 21.

The addition functions in this example are located on what is called the *second level* of nesting, because they are nested within one other function. Notice how the parentheses that surround the multiplication function also must enclose both addition functions, so that they are understood by the AutoLISP interpreter to be the arguments of the multiplication function. You can build very deep levels of functions-within-functions. The AutoLISP command interpreter can trace nested functions up to 100 levels deep.

The AutoLISP interpreter will evaluate nested functions beginning with the deepest level. Following is an example of an addition function nested three levels deep:

(– (* 2.36 (+ 1 3)) 2)

This function returns the value 7.44. This is the result of a three-level computation. First, the integer 1 is added to 3, returning 4. Next, 4 is multiplied by 2.36, returning 9.44. Finally, 2 is subtracted from 9.44, returning the final value, 7.44.

Notice how the parentheses are arranged in matched pairs surrounding functions, including all nested functions. Careful arrangement of these parentheses requires alertness and a little experience.

Data Lists

A list that is not a function—that is, a list of members that does not include a function operator— is called a *data list*. Data lists are frequently used to store coordinate point information. For example, a 2-D coordinate point can be expressed as a data list containing two numbers, the first number indicating the x coordinate, and the second indicating the y coordinate:

(6.75 2)

This data list can be used to represent point 6.75,2.

A 3-D point can be represented by a data list of three numbers; for example:

(6.75 2 12.0)

This data list includes the number 12.0 in the third position, representing the z coordinate.

Several AutoLISP functions return data lists, and such lists can be used as arguments for functions. You may also use data lists in your routines by entering them explicitly. When entered explicitly, data lists should be preceded by an *apostrophe,* as follows:

'(6.75 2.8 12)

The apostrophe is shorthand for a special AutoLISP function called the Quote function, which allows AutoLISP to read a data list without misinterpreting it as a bad function.

The *dotted pair* is a special form of data list. It contains two members, separated by a period. The dotted pair is frequently used to represent AutoCAD entity data in AutoLISP routines. It has special rules regarding its construction and manipulation; refer to Chapter 19 for details.

AUTOLISP FILES

AutoLISP files are ASCII files containing AutoLISP routines that always have the file extension LSP. They can be modified with a text editor and must be loaded into memory before AutoCAD can use the functions they contain. Details on loading AutoLISP files are given later in this chapter.

DATA TYPES

There are several different types of data in AutoLISP. Different function operators have different requirements for the types of data they will accept as arguments; for example, the math function operators in the previous section required that the arguments be numbers. Math functions will reject arguments that are not numbers, causing the AutoLISP interpreter to display an error message and cease processing.

Different data types for AutoLISP include entity names, file descriptors, integers, and real numbers.

Entity Names

Each AutoCAD entity is stored in a special underlying database, and is given a unique *entity name*. This entity name is associated with all the necessary coordinate and drawing-property information to reproduce it on the display monitor or hard-copy output device. The more complex an individual entity, the longer the list of information that will be associated with its entity name. The use of entity names is discussed in detail in Chapter 19.

File Descriptors

Special functions in AutoLISP can open a file on disk for storage of information, or read the information contained in disk files. When a file is opened under AutoLISP, it is assigned a special data type, called a *file descriptor,* that acts as a pointer to that file, keeping track of its physical location on the disk for storage and access, and distinguishing it from any other selected files.

Integers and Real Numbers

AutoLISP recognizes two forms of numbers: *integers* and *real numbers*. Integers can be processed quickly, but they are limited in that they are whole numbers only, and restricted in range. On 16-bit workstations, whole numbers from $-32,768$ to $+32,767$ are valid integers. On 32-bit workstations, valid integers range from $-2,147,483,648$ to $+2,147,483,647$. AutoLISP functions that move integers to and from AutoCAD are limited to the 16-bit range. Integers outside of the valid range are converted to real numbers whenever possible; in expressions that require integers, however, integers outside the range produce an error message. Integers never include a decimal point.

Real numbers always contain a decimal point. They are more flexible than integers, but are processed more slowly. AutoCAD allows real numbers with up to 16 significant digits.

The result of processing integers is also an integer. For example, here is a function using integers:

(+ 23 2)

The result returned by this function is 25.

Following is the same function using two real numbers instead of two integers:

(+ 23.0 2.0)

The result returned by this function is 25.0. It is a real number because the arguments were both real numbers.

You can combine real numbers and integers in functions that accept real numbers. When you do, the function returns a result that is also a real number; for example:

(+ 23 2.0)

In this case, because an integer (23) and a real number (2.0) were mixed, the result returned is a real number, 25.0.

If a real number has a value between −1.0 and +1.0, its decimal point is preceded by a leading zero. For example, this is a valid real number:

0.33

This is not a valid real number, because the leading zero is missing:

.33

Here is a good rule of thumb regarding integers and real numbers: Use integers when you are sure that you need only whole numbers in your processing, and that these numbers (as well as the results of calculations using them) will stay within the allowed range for integers. In all other cases, or when in doubt, use real numbers.

Most AutoLISP functions will accept integers even if they normally expect real numbers; the integer will be automatically converted to a whole real number. This is true, for example, in the case of data lists that represent coordinate point information. However, the reverse is not true. If a function requires an integer argument, it will reject a real number and return an AutoLISP error message.

MEMORY VARIABLES

Memory variables are the basic means by which a computer can organize, store, and recall information. All programming languages depend on the manipulation of memory variables.

When an AutoLISP memory variable is created, it is given a *variable name,* and is subsequently bound to a *value* (the specific piece of information that is associated with its name).

Memory-variable names are strings of alphanumeric characters. Any sequence of characters, numbers, or punctuation marks is valid, with the following exceptions:

- They may not be numbers, although they may include numbers.
- They may not include spaces or the punctuation marks ;' " ( ) and .
- They should not duplicate the names of any predefined AutoLISP function names or constants.

Memory-variable names may be as many characters long as you like, up to the limit of available memory space. However, processing of your AutoLISP routines will be faster and you will conserve computer memory space if you keep them short, preferably six characters or fewer; refer ahead to the section entitled "Memory Management," near the end of this chapter, for details.

Often, memory-variable names are mnemonic descriptions of the type of value they contain. For example, you might choose to store angle information in memory variables with names derived from *ang* (*ang1, ang2,* etc.). Likewise, you could store coordinate point information in memory variables with names derived from *pt* (*pt1, pt2,* etc.).

While a memory variable is bound to a value, subsequent functions can use the memory-variable name as an argument (provided the value represented is a valid argument to that function). As these functions are evaluated, whenever the memory variable's name is encountered, the AutoLISP interpreter substitutes the value of the memory variable for the name.

Note: It is common for a single memory variable to be bound to different values at different points in the processing of an AutoLISP routine.

Because of memory variables, one set of general instructions can be used on many different sets of data. Without memory variables, AutoLISP routines would have to be reedited each time the data changed.

AutoLISP uses a special function called Setq to create memory variables and bind them to values. Details on this function can be found in Chapter 17. Here is a brief example of how this function works:

```
(setq x 2)
```

The Setq function's first argument is the name of the memory variable. The second argument is the value to which the memory-variable name is bound. The function just shown creates memory variable x and binds it to the value 2.

Once the AutoLISP interpreter has evaluated the above function, the following function becomes valid:

```
(* 2.36 x)
```

AutoLISP will substitute 2 for x in this function, and will multiply 2.36 by 2, returning 4.72 as the result.

At the AutoCAD Command prompt, you can quickly find out the value of any memory variable by typing an exclamation point followed by the memory-variable name. For example, assume that you have assigned a value to the memory variable x. At the AutoCAD Command prompt, type:

```
!x
```

AutoCAD responds with the current value of the memory variable x.

Constants

A memory variable whose value never changes is called a *constant*. AutoLISP makes use of three constants:

Nil   The value of nil represents "False", or a no-data value. Nil is returned by functions that cannot or should not return a value. For example, the Redraw function redraws the current viewport, but returns no value, because no value is necessary; instead, it returns nil.

Nil is also returned by test functions that evaluate relationships between their arguments. For example, the following function tests to see if two arguments are equal:

```
(= 6 4)
```

They are not equal, so the function returns nil to signify the inequality.

Pi   The value of pi is approximately 3.1415926. The advantage of this constant is that *pi* is easier to type than 3.1415926, and because the actual value of pi computes to an infinite number of decimal places, using the constant is more accurate than explicitly stating a real number. Refer to the "Radians" section later in this chapter for an example of how this constant is used in functions.

T   The value of T represents "True," or the opposite of nil. This value is returned by functions that test relationships between arguments. For example, the following function tests to see if the first argument is greater in value than the second argument:

(> 6 4)

This is indeed the case, so the function returns T.

Strings

Strings are sequences of one or more alphanumeric characters, including spaces and punctuation marks, that do not require mathematical processing. A string is always surrounded by quotation marks. For instance, consider the following AutoLISP function:

(prompt "This is a string")

This function takes the sequence of characters *This is a string* and displays them in AutoCAD's Command-prompt area.

When creating strings, you can use a maximum of 100 characters (or 99 prior to Release 9) between any single set of quotation marks. You can create longer strings than this by joining two or more strings together; refer to the Strcat function in Chapter 17 for details.

Such joined strings can be of any length. The computer allocates memory for them as needed, up to the limits available. Notwithstanding, long strings use up a lot of computer memory and slow down processing; therefore, it is a good idea to keep them as short as possible.

Selection Sets

You can select entities in groups using AutoLISP. A group of entities can be given a name, called a *selection set,* and acted upon as a group. Manipulation of selection sets is demonstrated in Chapter 19.

Symbols

The term *symbol* is a general term used to describe a set of ASCII characters that stands for something else. For example, memory-variable names and function operators are symbols. A string is different from a symbol because it is literal, representing only itself. Likewise, a number is different from a symbol because it can only represent its own value.

The characters that make up a symbol can include any combination of ASCII letters, numbers, and punctuation marks except ' ( ) . " and ; which are reserved and have special meaning in AutoLISP. Refer to the upcoming section for details.

PUNCTUATION MARKS

A few special punctuation marks are extremely important in AutoLISP and are explained below.

Apostrophe

The apostrophe (') represents AutoLISP's Quote function, so that

'ABC

is the same as

(quote ABC)

The Quote function is discussed in detail in Chapter 17.

Parentheses

Parentheses were described earlier in this chapter as the means by which data lists and functions are defined and kept separate from each other; for example:

(+ 1 2)(− 12 4)

Period

The period (.) is used by the AutoLISP interpreter in two ways. Most commonly, it represents the decimal point in real numbers; for example:

(12.75, 6.3768)

In addition, the period separates data items in a special type of data list called the *dotted pair*. Dotted pairs are discussed in detail in Chapter 19.

Quotation Marks

Quotation marks (" ") delineate character strings; for example:

"ABCDE"

This would be understood by the AutoLISP interpreter to be the literal string of characters ABCDE. Because they are surrounded by double quotes, it would not mistake them for a symbol or function operator.

Semicolon

The semicolon (;) identifies *comment lines* in an AutoLISP file. Comment lines are lines of text that are ignored by the AutoLISP interpreter; you may use them to place notes to yourself or others in the AutoLISP file. When the AutoLISP interpreter encounters a semicolon, it disregards all text that follows on the same line; for example:

```
( + 1 2) ; "Add" function adding 1 plus 2...
```

If this line were encountered in an AutoLISP file, the AutoLISP interpreter would read and interpret the function, but ignore the semicolon and everything after it. It would begin looking for additional data on the following line.

As you would expect, if a semicolon appears as the first character in the line, the entire line is ignored.

Spaces and Line Feeds

Spaces keep individual items of data separate from each other within lists. In the examples you've seen, spaces are used to separate arguments from each other, as well as from the function operators.

However, once the members of a list are separated from each other by at least one space, you may add as many additional spaces as you like, in order to make the file more readable for you. The AutoLISP interpreter ignores extra spaces following a single space, and spaces that come between lists.

Line feeds are treated as spaces by the AutoLISP interpreter. That is, you may separate items by placing them on lines following one another, as well as by placing spaces between them. For example, the AutoLISP interpreter will have no trouble reading the following function:

```
( +
1
2
)
```

In this example, line feeds have replaced the spaces found in the previous example.

INDENTATION

When several functions are nested within each other, the program flow can become difficult to follow. One way to help sort things out is to arrange functions on consecutive lines within the AutoLISP file in such a way as to isolate specific functions. For example, following is a function presented earlier:

```
(− (* 2.36 (+ 1 3)) 2)
```

It could also be arranged in the following fashion:

```
(−
    (* 2.36
     (+ 1 3)
    )
    2
)
```

When arranged in this fashion, each nested function occupies a separate line in the file. The inner functions are indented, with deeper functions receiving the greater degree of indentation. The right parenthesis of each function—except for the deepest—is placed on a separate line, at the same level of indentation as its corresponding left mate. The deepest function is quite simple and its meaning readily understood, so it occupies a single line, along with both its parentheses, at the greatest amount of indentation. This layout helps the eye to isolate specific functions and their arguments, and to see which sets of parentheses belong together, by having mates share the same degree of indentation. If a parenthesis had been accidentally left out, it would be fairly easy to spot.

The AutoLISP interpreter has no trouble with this arrangement as long as the minimum of one space separates individual data items on any given text line.

This kind of arrangement of functions is optional and somewhat subjective. For example, you may not wish to indent your AutoLISP files rigorously unless the function is more than two or three levels deep or involves some special, complex analysis. The key issue here is to make the files as easy as possible for people to read. As you acquire more experience, you will undoubtedly settle on a layout method that works best for you.

Especially if your AutoLISP files are going to be read by someone else, you should make every possible effort to keep them clear.

Uppercase and Lowercase

Uppercase and lowercase characters may be used interchangeably within an AutoLISP routine. AutoLISP is not case-sensitive. The sample AutoLISP routines in this book use lowercase except for names of system variables.

Radians

AutoLISP uses *radians* to measure angles. Many AutoCAD users measure angles using degrees, so conversion between the two systems of angle measurement is often necessary.

Angle degrees can be converted to radians using simple math. To convert degrees to radians, divide the degrees by 180, and multiply the result by pi. In AutoLISP, the mathematics look like this:

    (* pi (/ angle 180))

Radians can be converted to degrees using the reverse mathematics: Divide the radians by pi, and multiply the result by 180. In AutoLISP, the mathematics look like this:

    (* (/ angle pi) 180.0)

Control Structures in Programming

AutoLISP routines accomplish programmed tasks by means of certain fundamental *control structures,* described in the sections ahead. These structures include interactive functions, sequences, branching, and looping.

Interactive Functions

Using AutoLISP, it is possible to create interactive programs that pause and prompt the user to input data; store the data received into memory variables; and implement a wide variety of programmed processing using that data, returning the results in the form of messages to the user, graphic information displayed on the screen, or information written to a file on disk.

Several predefined AutoLISP functions will pause and accept specific types of information from the user. These functions begin with the letters *G e t* and are therefore referred to as *Get functions.* Details about their use are presented in Chapter 17; they are summarized here:

FUNCTION NAME:	PAUSES FOR INPUT OF:
Getangle	Relative angles
Getcorner	Corners of rubberband rectangle (Version 2.5+)
Getdist	Distances
Getint	Integers

FUNCTION NAME:	PAUSES FOR INPUT OF:
Getkword	Keyword responses (Version 2.5+)
Getorient	Absolute angles of orientation (Version 2.5+)
Getpoint	Coordinate points
Getreal	Real numbers
Getstring	Character Strings

Each of these functions can display a custom-designed prompt in the Command-prompt area to remind the user of the specific data being requested. When appropriate, you may enter data from the keyboard, or by "showing" AutoCAD the correct value using the pointing device. For example, the following function pauses the routine and asks for distance information from the user:

```
(setq dist1
    (getdist "\nEnter two points to show the distance: ")
)
```

In this example, the Getdist function is nested within a Setq function. This nested function will cause the routine to pause, receive the distance information from the user, and store the information in a memory variable named *dist1*.

From the prompt, it appears that the user will enter the distance information by picking two points with the digitizing device. AutoLISP will automatically compute the distance between these points as the distance value to bind to *dist1*. However, this function would also allow the user to ignore the prompt and enter the distance information from the keyboard, using the current AutoCAD units format.

Sequences

Sequence structures are sets of functions that are performed one after another. When an AutoLISP file is loaded into memory (refer to "Loading Routines" ahead), the functions within are evaluated one after another, beginning with the first function in the file and continuing through to the last function. For example, the following are two functions that would be evaluated in sequence:

```
(getdist "Enter distance #1: ")
(getdist "Enter distance #2: ")
```

These function would be performed one after the other, prompting the user for the two distances.

When the AutoLISP interpreter encounters nested functions, the functions on the deepest level are evaluated first, followed by the next deepest level, and so on to the outermost level. The sequential execution resumes when the AutoLISP interpreter evaluates the outermost level of a function; for example:

```
(setq x (getdist "Enter distance #1: "))
(setq y (getdist "Enter distance #2: "))
```

In this example, the first Getdist function is evaluated, followed by the Setq x function, which stores the value returned by Getdist in the memory variable *x*. This completes the functioning of the nested functions, and the next function in the sequence is evaluated. This function is also nested; the Getdist function is evaluated first, followed by the Setq y function. This process is diagramed in Figure 16.1.

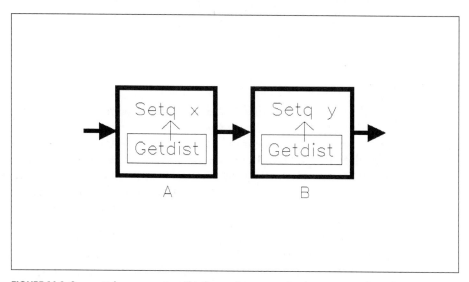

FIGURE 16.1: Sequential programming. This figure diagrams a simple sequence of two functions. The first function in the sequence contains a nested Getdist function, which is called, and the result is passed to the outer function, Setq, as its value argument to bind to the memory variable *x*. The AutoLISP interpreter moves on to the next function in the sequence, again processing a nested Getdist function and passing the result to a Setq function. The AutoLISP interpreter will then move on to the next function, or end processing if no more functions follow.

Branching

Either/or decision making by the computer is called *branching*. In this process, the AutoLISP interpreter is presented with a test function that returns either a value or nil. Other functions follow the test function, and are either ignored or processed based on the result returned by the test function. There are two Auto-LISP functions that perform branching operations, If and Cond. Both are described in detail in Chapter 17.

The If function is demonstrated in the following short user-defined function, which creates an AutoCAD command called Testif to compare two distances entered by the user:

```
(defun C:TESTIF( / x y)
    (setq x (getdist "Enter distance #1: "))
    (setq y (getdist "Enter distance #2: "))
    (if
        (= x y)
        (prompt "\nThey are equal")
        (prompt "\nThey are not equal")
    )
    (princ)
)
```

In this sequence, two distance values are entered by the user and stored to memory variables named *x* and *y*. The data in these two variables becomes the basis for an either/or decision made by AutoLISP.

The If function first evaluates the logical function (= x y), substituting the values that were entered by the user for x and y. This function returns T if the two values are equal, and nil otherwise. If the test function returns T, the first function following it will be evaluated, prompting the user that the values are equal. If the values are not equal, the second function is evaluated instead, displaying the other prompt. This process is illustrated in Figure 16.2.

Branching in AutoLISP need not always decide between two functions. The If function may choose between a function to perform if the test function returns a value, or nothing at all. For example, the If function structure is used in the following example to reset a distance value to 1 unit if the user has entered less than 1 unit:

```
(defun C:TESTIF( / x)
    (setq x (getdist "Enter a distance of at least 1 unit: "))
    (if (< x 1.0)
        (setq x 1.0)
    )
    (princ x)
    (princ)
)
```

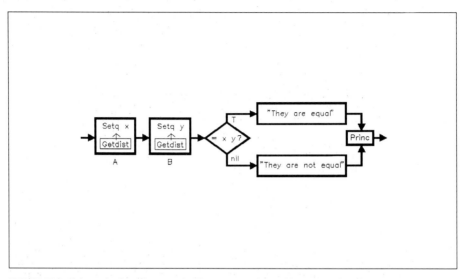

FIGURE 16.2: If-then-else branching. In this figure, a conditional branching function sequence is diagramed. The first two functions establish values for memory variables *x* and *y*. A test expression is then evaluated by the If function, testing if *x* is equal to *y*. If *x* is equal to *y*, the first function is evaluated, shown in the diagram as the top branch, or the do-if-true branch. If *x* does not equal *y*, the second branch—the do-if-nil branch, or "else" branch—is evaluated. Both branches return to the next function in the sequence, and processing ends.

In this example, after a distance value has been entered, the test function

$$(< x\ 1.0)$$

determines whether the value entered was less than 1. If so, the function returns T, and the value of the variable is reset to 1. Otherwise, because no alternate function is present within the If function, nothing happens, and the *x* variable remains bound to the value entered by the user. This process is illustrated in Figure 16.3.

The listing in Figure 16.4 illustrates a more practical application of sequential functions, using a series of Setq functions followed by an If function. The function being defined, named J2C, will convert the Julian period day number stored in AutoCAD's DATE, TDCREATE, and TDUPDATE system variables to strings containing the correct calendar date. To use J2C, enter the listing carefully into an AutoLISP file, load the file using the Load command, and enter the following at the AutoCAD Command prompt:

```
(j2c (getvar "TDCREATE"))
```

If you have recreated the listing in Figure 16.4 correctly, AutoCAD will return the date on which the drawing was created.

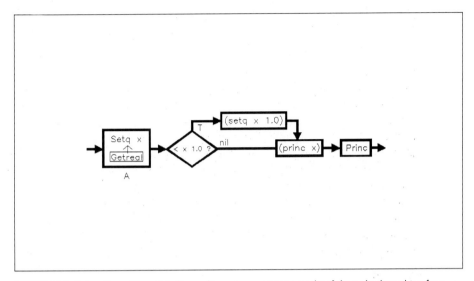

FIGURE 16.3: If-then branching. This figure diagrams a variation on the if-then-else branching function. The first function establishes a value for memory variable *x*. The test expression is then evaluated, testing whether *x* is less than 1. If *x* is less than 1, the branching function is evaluated. If *x* is not less than 1, the branching sequence is bypassed. The next functions in the sequence are evaluated, and processing ends.

```
(defun j2c (jpd)                                            <
    (setq jpd   (- (fix jpd) 1721119.0)                     <
          year  (fix (/ (1- (* 4 jpd)) 146097.0))           <
          jpd   (- (* jpd 4.0) 1.0 (* 146097.0 year))       <
          day   (fix (/ jpd 4.0))                           <
          jpd   (fix (/ (+ (* 4.0 day) 3.0) 1461.0))        <
          day   (- (+ (* 4.0 day) 3.0) (* 1461.0 jpd))      <
          day   (fix (/ (+ day 4.0) 4.0))                   <
          month (fix (/ (- (* 5.0 day) 3) 153.0))           <
          day   (- (* 5.0 day) 3.0 (* 153.0 month))         <
          day   (fix (/ (+ day 5.0) 5.0))                   <
          year  (+ (* 100.0 year) jpd)                      <
    )                                                       <
    (if (< month 10.0)                                      <
        (setq month (+ month 3))                            <
        (setq month (- month 9)                             <
              year (1+ year)                                <
        )                                                   <
    )                                                       <
    (strcat (itoa (fix month)) "/"                          <
            (itoa (fix day))    "/"                         <
            (itoa (fix year))                               <
    )                                                       <
)                                                           <
                                                            <
```

FIGURE 16.4: How a single Setq function can be used to process a series of memory variables in sequence. Each memory-variable name is followed by a function that calculates its value, and that value is bound to the variable. After the calculations of *month, day,* and *year,* a final branching condition reevaluates the value bound to *month,* and if necessary, updates *month* and *year.* The last function in the sequence concatenates a string of *month, day,* and *year.* This string is returned by the Defun function, because it is the result of the last function in the sequence.

The Cond function is another function used to perform either/or branching. The Cond function differs from the If function in that it is used to select a single process from more than two possibilities, as shown in the following example:

```
(defun C:TESTCOND( / x)
        (setq x (getint "\nEnter a positive 1: "))
        (cond
           ( (< x 0)
              (prompt "\nNegative value entered: ")
           )
           ( (< x 1)
              setq x 1)
           )
           ( (> x 1)
              (prompt "\nValue entered: ")
           )
        )
        (princ x)
        (princ)
)
```

In this example, after the user enters a value, which is then stored in the memory variable x, the Cond function will perform one of three possible processes, based on logical conditions it evaluates. Each logical condition is the first function in one of three lists presented as arguments to the Cond function.

Cond first tests to see if a negative value was entered, by testing whether the value of x is less than zero. If so, it evaluates the remaining functions in that list, displaying a message and the value entered. Having found a test function that returned a value, the Cond function now ignores all its remaining arguments.

If x is not less than zero, the Cond function moves on to the next test function, testing to see if the value of x is less than 1. If so, x is reset to 1, the number 1 is displayed in the Command-prompt area, and the remaining arguments are ignored.

If x is not less than 1, the third logical function is evaluated, testing to see if the value of x is greater than 1. If so, the routine displays a message along with the value that was entered. The Cond function may include any number of such lists, each one beginning with a test condition and the expressions to evaluate if that condition is the first one found to result in a value. Once a non-nil test expression is found, the remaining arguments to Cond are always ignored. This process is illustrated in Figure 16.5.

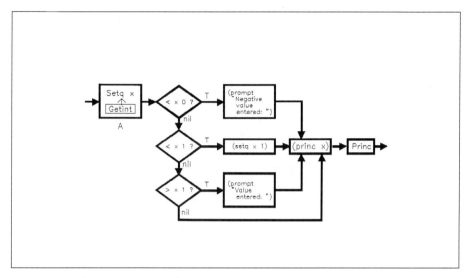

FIGURE 16.5: A diagram of the Cond function. The Cond function, like the If function, evaluates a test condition. Unlike the If function, Cond can evaluate a series of test expressions, moving onto the next test expression until it finds one that does not return nil. When a test expression returns a value, Cond processes the function sequence that follows the test function, and then returns to the main program sequence. Once one of the test functions returns a non-nil value, the Cond function skips the remaining test functions.

Controlled Looping

AutoLISP has three functions that control repetition, or *looping*: the Foreach function, the Repeat function, and the While function. All these functions will cause a sequence of functions to repeat until a given test condition is met, but the While function conveys the principle of controlled looping most clearly.

The While function begins by evaluating a test condition. As long as the test condition returns a value, the series of functions that follow will repeat until the test condition returns nil; for example:

```
(defun C:TESTWHILE( / x)
    (while (/ = x 1)
        (setq x (getint "\nEnter a positive 1: "))
        (prompt (strcat "\nYou entered " (itoa x)))
    )
    (princ)
)
```

In this example, the While function tests the value of *x*. As long as *x* does not equal 1, the sequence enclosed in the While function will repeat, displaying the value just entered and prompting again if 1 is not the entered value. This process is diagramed in Figure 16.6.

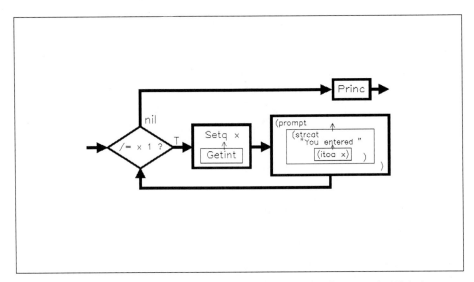

FIGURE 16.6: A diagram of the While function. Like the other branching functions, the While function evaluates a test function. As long as the test function returns T, the function sequence nested within the While function is evaluated. When the sequence is complete, the test function is reevaluated. When the test function finally returns nil, the AutoLISP interpreter breaks out of the loop and moves on to the next function in the sequence that follows the While function.

PLANNING AN AUTOLISP ROUTINE

The process of developing an AutoLISP routine is similar to the process of developing a custom menu macro. In one sense, an AutoLISP routine is really a more complex macro: The instructions contained in an AutoLISP routine are executed in sequence, and they build on each other, the results of previous instructions being used to carry out subsequent instructions.

A useful routine must be thought out in advance. The first step in writing any AutoLISP routine is to sit down with a pencil and paper and describe in plain English exactly what it is that you would like the routine to do. This exercise is extremely important as a timesaving and error-preventing device. It will help you organize your thoughts, and can keep you on track as you work out the actual function sequences. Programmers refer to this plain-English version of a routine as *pseudocode*. It's simply good organization; no other single step will save you more time or prevent more errors.

A good way to structure the routine is to break down its processes into a series of small, simple steps. When the time comes to translate the routine into Auto-LISP code, use the Defun function (see Chapter 17) to create small functions that accomplish these steps, and that are then called in sequence. There are good reasons for writing routines based on small functions:

- Defining functions results in better program organization, with a complex process broken down into simple steps, and with each step handled by a defined function.

- Small, general-purpose functions are "portable." Functions defined in one AutoLISP routine can be shared by other AutoLISP routines, saving node space when several routines are loaded.

- Problems are easier to locate, since small functions can be debugged individually. Once debugged, they can be reliably used in other processes.

After developing the pseudocode, try out various functions by entering them at the AutoCAD Command prompt. Start with the predefined functions, and build them into your own user-defined functions created with the Defun function. This pretesting procedure will help you spot problems early in the development process, and save you considerable time. Make notes of the steps you take, or turn on printer echo with Ctrl-Q, to monitor function entry and results.

As your function sequence takes shape, you can move to the text editor and start building an AutoLISP file containing your tested functions. As an aid to yourself for subsequent editing or debugging of the file, place plenty of comments in the Auto-LISP file to explain the meanings and operations of functions. There is no limit on the number of comments in an AutoLISP file, although they do enlarge the file and, if extensive, may slow the process of loading it by a few seconds. If you use a lot of comments, you may wish to keep two copies: one with extensive comments for editing, and one without comments for loading and executing.

LOADING ROUTINES

After creating an ASCII file containing your sequence of AutoLISP functions, you may enter AutoCAD's drawing editor and load the file into memory. The Load function, described in the upcoming section, brings a file of AutoLISP expressions into memory and evaluates those expressions. Load returns the result of evaluating the last expression in the file.

Load requires the name of a file, contained within quotes, with the extension LSP. The file extension is never used; LSP is assumed. The file name can include drive letters or subdirectory path names, separated by the forward slash (/); for example:

"c:/lspfiles/demo"

A single backslash character is not allowed, as the AutoLISP interpreter will mistake it for a control character. However, you may use two backslash characters to separate subdirectory names from file names; for example:

"c:\\lspfiles\\demo"

Load is the means by which ASCII files of AutoLISP routines are made usable by the AutoLISP interpreter. All AutoLISP files must be loaded with this function before they can be used (except ACAD.LSP, which is automatically loaded at the start of each drawing session).

In AutoCAD versions prior to Release 10, the Load function may only be executed from the Command prompt; that is, not from within another AutoLISP expression. If no drive letter or subdirectory is included as part of the file name, the AutoLISP file must be located on the current subdirectory, or in the subdirectory containing AutoCAD's system files.

Starting with Release 10, you may load AutoLISP files while another AutoLISP routine is running. If the AutoLISP file is not on the current subdirectory and no subdirectory path was specified, AutoCAD will look for the file along its search path, loading the routine when it locates the file.

If for any reason the loading process does not succeed, AutoCAD will display an error message. Common reasons for failure to load are:

- There is not enough node space.
- The AutoLISP file was not found. (It may have been misspelled.)
- The expressions in the file could not be properly evaluated (unbalanced parentheses, perhaps, or other syntax errors).

Starting with Release 10, if you are loading a file from within an AutoLISP routine, the display of the error message will cancel the routine that is running. If you do not want the routine in progress to be canceled when a Load operation fails, you may supply an optional string argument to the Load function after the file name. Then, if the Load operation fails, this string is returned by the Auto-LISP interpreter—to be stored in a memory variable for later testing, perhaps—and the current AutoLISP routine continues to function.

Note: The Load *function* is not the same as the Load *command,* which is used to load shape files. Refer to Chapter 15 for more information on the Load command.

Following are some examples that illustrate the use of the Load function:

(load "FILENAME")   Loads FILENAME.LSP into memory and returns the result of evaluating the last expression in the file. In Release 10 and later, Auto-CAD will look for FILENAME.LSP along AutoCAD's search path.

(load "FILENAME" "bad LISP file")   Loads FILENAME.LSP to memory and returns the result of evaluating the last expression in the file. If for any reason the file cannot be properly loaded, AutoCAD will display the message, "bad LISP file".

(load   "C:/ACAD/LSPFILES/FILENAME")   Looks   for   the   file FILENAME.LSP on the subdirectory ACAD/LSPFILES on drive C, and if the file is found, loads the file as in the previous example.

DEBUGGING AUTOLISP ROUTINES

Your completed AutoLISP routine may not function perfectly the very first time. The development of an AutoLISP routine is sometimes marked by a grinding process of *debugging,* methodically getting rid of problems that interfere with the routine's ability to achieve its intended results. Some problems are subtle, requiring good logic skills to locate and correct, and the solution to one problem can reveal another problem waiting underneath. A program may have to be tested several times before it runs correctly. This may necessitate several trips back and forth between the drawing editor and the text editor.

As you learn AutoLISP and acquire more experience, however, the number of "bugs" in your AutoLISP routines will certainly diminish, and the development of programs will take decreasing amounts of time. If you are a beginner, don't try an overly ambitious routine to start. Be satisfied with small routines that might be little more than menu macros at first. These build your confidence, help develop your thinking, and are often surprisingly useful.

Even after your AutoLISP routines seem to be working perfectly, keep a notebook handy to jot down any surprises that might pop up days or even weeks later—perhaps when a new user tries the same routine. Note when the problem occurred, under what circumstances, and what needs to be done to correct the problem. Don't rely on memory alone to guide you as you move between Auto-CAD and your text editor.

ACAD.LSP

It would be inconvenient to load frequently used AutoLISP files each time you enter the drawing editor. AutoCAD uses a special AutoLISP file named ACAD.LSP to remember frequently used new AutoCAD commands and Auto-LISP functions. ACAD.LSP may be edited using your text editor, as any other AutoLISP file. You may include frequently used custom commands and functions of your own in this file. Every time you enter the drawing editor, AutoCAD searches the system subdirectory for this file; if the file is found, AutoCAD loads it into memory and evaluates the functions it contains. Thereafter, it is available throughout that drawing session.

S::STARTUP

The AutoLISP interpreter cannot load additional AutoLISP files or evaluate user-defined functions until after the ACAD.LSP file has been completely loaded. If you are using AutoCAD Release 10 or later and would like to execute a user-defined function automatically at the start of every drawing session, you can define a special function, which must be named S::STARTUP (including the double colon), to include in ACAD.LSP. It will be called immediately after ACAD.LSP is loaded.

For example, the following sequence prompts for the user's name and stores it to a memory variable, while not allowing null input:

```
(initget 1)
(setq name (getstring T "\nPlease enter your name: "))
```

If you would like this prompt to appear at the start of each drawing session, include the following lines in the file ACAD.LSP:

```
(defun S::STARTUP( )
    (initget 1)
    (setq name (getstring T "\nPlease enter your name: "))
)
```

ABORTING AUTOLISP ROUTINES

In the middle of execution of a lengthy AutoLISP routine, it may happen that you wish to abort the process—for instance, if the routine is offering clearly incorrect or unintelligible results, or if it appears to stop processing altogether.

You can abort an AutoLISP routine by pressing Ctrl-C or Ctrl-Break. This will cause execution of the AutoLISP routine to cease after evaluation of the current function is complete. AutoCAD will also display the following message:

Error: Console Break

Once you have aborted an AutoLISP routine, you are returned to the AutoCAD Command prompt, where you may take any corrective action required.

THE UNBALANCED-FUNCTION PROMPT

There is a likelihood that, as you build increasingly complex functions with deeper levels of nesting, you may accidentally leave out a parenthesis or two. This will produce unpredictable results from your AutoLISP routine, as the command interpreter struggles to understand what's happening. In such an event, you may see the prompt

n>

where *n* is a number, in place of the familiar AutoCAD Command prompt. This number equals the number of right parentheses that are still needed to produce an equal number of left and right parentheses in the AutoLISP routine.

There is only one way to get rid of this prompt and return to AutoCAD's Command prompt: Enter that same number of right parentheses at the keyboard. It is unlikely that this will correct the functioning of your AutoLISP routine, since there is no way to predict which of the right parentheses were left out.

If you find that this prompt persists even after you have entered the correct number of right parentheses, the cause is probably a missing quotation mark. Once the AutoLISP interpreter encounters a quotation mark, everything that follows, including right parentheses, is treated as part of a string. This includes the parentheses that you type at the keyboard. The solution is to type a set of quotation marks followed by the correct number of right parentheses.

It will help if you keep the number of nesting levels low until you have the AutoLISP routine working consistently. Once the file is working, you can go back and nest functions to reduce the number of needed memory variables and use your LISPSTACK space more efficiently.

MEMORY MANAGEMENT

On computer systems using DOS, the common means of managing Auto-LISP memory are:

- Setting the LISPHEAP and LISPSTACK environment variables at the DOS prompt.

- Installing Extended AutoLISP (if you are using Release 10 or later and sufficient extended memory is available).
- Enabling virtual memory using the Vmon function.

LISPHEAP, LISPSTACK, and Extended AutoLISP are discussed in detail in Chapter 4. The Vmon function is discussed below.

The Vmon Function

Vmon enables virtual-memory addressing for AutoLISP. After you enable Vmon, AutoCAD will store user-defined functions on disk if they will not fit in the node space available for AutoLISP. When a function is needed, AutoLISP reads it into memory from the disk, overwriting a currently unneeded function as it does so. As AutoLISP processes routines, a function may have to be read from disk several times, or the same functions may continually overwrite each other. This slows down AutoLISP, but it allows AutoLISP's limited node space to accommodate more functions.

Only functions are stored to disk this way. Symbols, data lists, entity names, selection sets, and so forth are all stored in RAM. For Vmon to work most efficiently, it should be called before any of your user-defined functions are loaded. Functions loaded before Vmon are not subject to being read from disk. They remain in RAM and are called from there.

The list of AutoLISP subroutines and expressions is stored in a memory variable named *atomlist*. This list may be managed to conserve memory space; if virtual memory is activated with Vmon, *atomlist* is removed from your use, as manipulating *atomlist* after Vmon is enabled can lead to unpredicted results.

Once Vmon is called, it cannot be undone. To disable Vmon, end the drawing session.

Strings and Symbol Names

In addition, you will use memory more efficiently if you keep character strings in your routines as short as possible. This is not always easy if you are attempting to write clear and complete prompts to the user. Still, given the relatively limited amount of space for AutoLISP on a 640K DOS system, you are advised to find a balance between friendly prompts and space for processing.

If you use the same string constant more than once, you can save memory space by storing the string as a variable and using the variable instead.

Also, use memory-variable names that are no more than six characters in length. AutoCAD will use a single AutoLISP *memory node* (ten bytes on 16-bit systems, twelve bytes on 32-bit systems) to store a variable name that is up to six characters long, but a seven-character name will require two nodes. In other words, with long variable names, you will be using space for two names to store only one, wasting precious node space.

In general, you can make more efficient use of AutoLISP memory if you use *local* symbols rather than *global* symbols whenever possible. Refer to the discussion of AutoLISP's *Defun* function in Chapter 17 for details on the definition and use of local and global symbols.

A single Setq function can define more than one variable at a time. It is usually more efficient to write:

```
(setq a 1
      b 2
      c 3
      d 4
)
```

than to use four Setq functions:

```
(setq a 1)
(setq b 2)
(setq c 3)
(setq d 4)
```

Whenever possible, make your AutoLISP routines modular by breaking them down into smaller, more general-purpose functions. Then nest the smaller functions together to produce more complex routines. With this type of structure, identical small functions can be shared among many larger routines, saving both memory space and loading time.

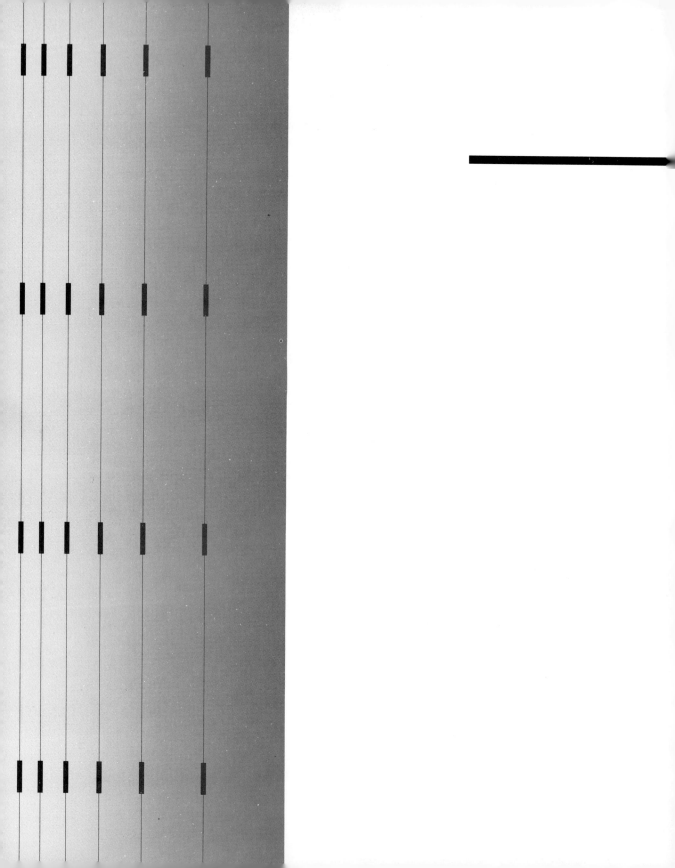

AUTOLISP FUNCTIONS

AutoLISP Functions

This chapter contains descriptions of fundamental predefined AutoLISP functions. Functions that are used with entity-association lists are described in detail in Chapter 19. The Load and Vmon functions are described in Chapter 16.

Included in each function description is a brief explanation of its usage, plus examples of how it is used. You may enter most of these examples at the Auto-CAD Command prompt to see the results for yourself. In the case of some of the longer examples, you will probably prefer to enter them in an AutoLISP file first, and then load the file using the Load function.

Most of these functions are available for all AutoCAD versions starting with Version 2.18. Exceptions are noted in the individual function descriptions under "Usage."

Many examples demonstrate a function's use within the context of other functions, so that you may better understand how the function is applied in practice. If you don't know the meaning of other predefined functions used in an example, you will find them described in detail elsewhere in this chapter, or in Chapter 16 or 19.

'

Returns the characters or list following it, without attempting to perform any evaluations. This function is shorthand for AutoLISP's Quote function.

REQUIRED ARGUMENTS

Any string of characters not including a space, or any single list of data enclosed in parentheses.

USAGE

When the apostrophe is used in place of the Quote function, it does not require a surrounding set of parentheses. It is the only function in AutoLISP that does not.

The Quote function is useful in situations where a data list, memory-variable name, function name, or other expression must be passed to the AutoLISP interpreter without evaluation. Examples of such usage are:

- When coordinate points must be passed as arguments to functions, in the form of a list of real numbers.
- When a memory-variable name, not the value it represents, is the argument of the function.
- When lists are being combined with other lists.
- When function names are the arguments of another function, but are not to be evaluated at the same time.

If you quote a list that contains other lists, the inner lists will not be evaluated. This version of the Quote function may be seen in many of the function examples in this chapter.

EXAMPLES

'(0 0 0)	Returns (0 0 0)
'(23 (a b))	Returns (23 (a b))
'a	Returns a

*

Multiplies a series of numbers, and returns the product.

REQUIRED ARGUMENTS

One or more numbers.

USAGE

The list of arguments may be of any length. If one number is supplied, it is multiplied by 1. If two are supplied, they are multiplied together. If more than two arguments are used, the first two are multiplied, the product is multiplied by the next, the new product is multiplied by the next, and so on until all arguments are multiplied together. If all the numbers are integers and the total is within the acceptable range for integers, an integer is returned. Otherwise, a real number is returned.

EXAMPLES

(* 43)	Returns 43
(* 43 2)	Returns 86

(* 43 2 2.5)   Returns 236.5
(* 43.0 −2)   Returns −86.0

Error

Executes a series of functions if an AutoLISP error condition occurs.

REQUIRED ARGUMENTS

You can define *Error* to accept a series of AutoLISP expressions of any length.

USAGE

AutoLISP's normal error-handling mechanism will display a trace-back of the code that caused the error, from nesting levels of up to 100 functions deep. In complex routines, this can cause seemingly interminable scrolling of long code sequences in the Command-prompt area. Others who are using your routines may find this annoying, especially if the user has only canceled the routine by pressing Ctrl-C.

If you intended that the routine make only temporary changes to system variables, these changes will remain in effect if the routine ends early because of an error condition or a Ctrl-C by the user, requiring that you manually reset the system variables.

By defining a function called *Error*, you can customize the error-handling mechanism to eliminate the trace-back, restore original system-variable values, and so forth. Use the Defun function to create a new function with this name, replacing AutoLISP's standard error-handling mechanism.

EXAMPLES

The following example serves as a model for temporarily redefining AutoCAD's standard error-handling routine, and then restoring it. Try pressing Ctrl-C at this routine's "Pick line:" prompt, and compare it with pressing Ctrl-C during other AutoLISP routines when AutoLISP's standard error-handling mechanism is in effect. Notice how Ctrl-C also restores the value of the PICKBOX system variable.

```
(defun C:testerr( )
  (setq olderr *error*)
    oldpic (getvar "pickbox")
  )
  (setvar "PICKBOX" 1)
```

```
(defun *error* (msg)
  (princ msg)
  (setvar "PICKBOX" oldpic)
  (setq *error* olderr)
  (princ)
)
(setq x (entsel "\nPick line: "))
(setvar "PICKBOX" oldpic)
(setq *error* olderr)
(princ)
)
```

+

Adds a series of numbers, and returns the total.

REQUIRED ARGUMENTS

One or more numbers—either integers or reals, or a combination.

USAGE

The list of numbers to be added may be of any length. If one number is supplied, zero is added. If all the numbers are integers and the total is within the acceptable range for integers, an integer is returned. Otherwise, a real number is returned. Negative numbers may be included in the list.

EXAMPLES

(+ 1)	Returns 1
(+ 1 2 3)	Returns 6
(+ 4.5 7 90.1)	Returns 101.6
(+ 4.5 −7 90.1)	Returns 87.6
(+ 32767 1)	Returns 32768.0

−

Subtracts a series of numbers, and returns the difference.

REQUIRED ARGUMENTS

One or more numbers—either integers or reals, or a combination.

USAGE

The list of arguments may be of any length. If one number is supplied, it is subtracted from zero. If two arguments are used, the right is subtracted from the left. If more than two arguments are given, the second through the last are summed, and the total is subtracted from the first argument. If all the numbers are integers and the total is within the acceptable range for integers, an integer is returned. Otherwise, a real number is returned. Negative numbers may be used.

EXAMPLES

(– 43)	Returns – 43
(– 43 2)	Returns 41
(– 43.0 1 1)	Returns 41
(– 43 2 – 43)	Returns 84
(– 43 (+ 2.0 3))	Returns 38.0

Performs a division, and returns the quotient.

REQUIRED ARGUMENTS

One or more numbers.

USAGE

The list of arguments may be of any length. If one number is supplied, it is divided by 1. If two arguments are used, the left is divided by the right. If more than two arguments are given, the second through the last are multiplied, and the first argument is divided by the product. If all the numbers are integers and the quotient is within the acceptable range for integers, the number is rounded to the nearest whole number and returned as an integer. Otherwise, a real number is returned. Negative numbers may be used.

EXAMPLES

(/ 43 2)	Returns 21
(/ 43.0 2)	Returns 21.5
(/ 430 – 2.0 4)	Returns 53.75
(/ 430 (– 2.0 4)	Returns – 215.0

/=

Tests to see if all members in the list are not numerically equal; returns T if they are not numerically equal, or nil otherwise.

REQUIRED ARGUMENTS

At least two, which can be numbers or strings.

USAGE

The list of arguments may be of any length. Strings are compared on the basis of their ASCII equivalents. Only the numerical equivalence is tested, not whether the arguments are evaluated to the same thing. All arguments must be equal for this function to return T; otherwise, it returns nil.

EXAMPLES

(/= "cat" "cat")	Returns nil
(/= "cat" "Cat")	Returns T
(/= "cat" cat)	Returns T
(/= 1 1.0)	Returns nil
(/= 4 4.0 (* 2 2))	Returns nil

1+

Increments its argument by 1, and returns the result.

REQUIRED ARGUMENTS

Only a single number, or a function returning a number. The number may be a real or an integer.

USAGE

This function is often used to count items (number of copies of an entity made, number of times a procedure is repeated, and so on).

EXAMPLES

(1+ 5)	Returns 6
(1+ 77.756)	Returns 78.756

1−

Subtracts 1 from its argument, and returns the result.

REQUIRED ARGUMENTS

Only a single number, or a function returning a number. The number may be a real or an integer.

USAGE

This function is often used to count items (number of copies of an entity remaining, number of times a procedure needs to be repeated, and so on).

EXAMPLES

(1− 5)	Returns 4
(1− 77.756)	Returns 76.756

<

Tests to see if each successive argument in the list is numerically less than the argument to its left; returns T if so, or nil otherwise.

REQUIRED ARGUMENTS

At least two, which can be numbers or strings.

USAGE

The list of arguments may be of any length. Strings are compared on the basis of their ASCII equivalents. Only the numerical relationship is tested. Each successive argument must be less than the argument to its right for this function to return T; otherwise, it returns nil.

EXAMPLES

(< 3 1 1)	Returns nil
(< "A" "b")	Returns T
(< "a" "B")	Returns nil
(< (* 4.34 6.7) (/ 265 8.6))	Returns T

<=

Tests to see if each successive argument in the list is numerically less than or equal to the argument to its left; returns T if so, or nil otherwise.

REQUIRED ARGUMENTS

At least two, which can be numbers or strings.

USAGE

The list of arguments may be of any length. Strings are compared on the basis of their ASCII equivalents. Only the numerical relationship is tested. Each successive argument must be less than or equal to the argument to its right for this function to return T; otherwise, it returns nil.

EXAMPLES

(<= 3 1 1)	Returns nil
(<= 1 1 3)	Returns T
(<= "A" "b")	Returns T
(<= "a" "B")	Returns nil
(<= "A" "A")	Returns T

=

Tests to see if all members in the list are numerically equal, and returns T if equal, or nil otherwise.

REQUIRED ARGUMENTS

At least two, which can be numbers or strings.

USAGE

The list of arguments may be of any length. Strings are compared on the basis of their ASCII equivalents. Only the numerical equivalence is tested, not whether the arguments are evaluated to the same thing. All arguments must be equal for this function to return T; otherwise, it returns nil.

EXAMPLES

(= "cat" "cat")	Returns T
(= "cat" "Cat")	Returns nil
(= "cat" cat)	Returns nil
(= 1 1.0)	Returns T
(= 4 4.0 (* 2 2))	Returns T

>

Tests to see if each successive argument in the list is numerically greater than the argument to its left; returns T if so, or nil otherwise.

REQUIRED ARGUMENTS

At least two, which can be numbers or strings.

USAGE

The list of arguments may be of any length. Strings are compared on the basis of their ASCII equivalents. Only the numerical relationship is tested. Each successive argument must be greater than the argument to its right for this function to return T; otherwise, it returns nil. Arguments that are equal will cause this function to return nil.

EXAMPLES

(> 3 2 1)	Returns T
(> "A" "b")	Returns nil

(> "a" "B")	Returns T
(> (* 4.34 6.7) (/ 225 8.6))	Returns T

>=

Tests to see if each successive argument in the list is numerically greater than or equal to the argument to its left; returns T if so, or nil otherwise.

REQUIRED ARGUMENTS

At least two, which can be numbers or strings.

USAGE

The list of arguments may be of any length. Strings are compared on the basis of their ASCII equivalents. Only the numerical relationship is tested. Each successive argument must be greater than or equal to the argument to its right for this function to return T; otherwise, it returns nil.

EXAMPLES

(>= 3 1 1)	Returns T
(>= 1 3 1)	Returns nil
(>= "A" "b")	Returns nil
(>= "a" "B")	Returns T
(>= "A" "A")	Returns T

~

Returns the integer complement.

REQUIRED ARGUMENTS

A single integer, or a function returning a single integer.

USAGE

This function returns the bitwise complement of the argument (which is not the same as zero minus the argument).

EXAMPLES

(˜ 0)	Returns − 1
(˜ 1)	Returns − 2
(˜ − 1)	Returns 0
(˜ 52)	Returns − 53
(˜ 32767)	Returns − 32768

ABS

Returns the absolute value of its argument.

REQUIRED ARGUMENTS

A single number, or a function returning a number. The number may be a real or an integer.

USAGE

This function converts negative values to positive. If the argument is positive, it is returned unchanged. If the argument is an integer, an integer is returned; otherwise, a real number is returned.

EXAMPLES

(abs − 17.89)	Returns 17.89
(abs 5)	Returns 5

ADS

Returns a list of all ADS functions loaded with the Xload function.

REQUIRED ARGUMENTS

None

USAGE

The Ads function is available in Release 11 and later. This function is useful both for determining which ADS functions have been loaded during the current drawing session and for locating the subdirectory of the original EXE files (or EXP files, if you are using AutoCAD 386). The function returns a list of strings containing the ADS file names and their original subdirectory locations.

EXAMPLES

Assume that you have two ADS programs on disk, called MAGNETS.EXP and GRAVITY.EXP, and that they are in the ADS subdirectory, which is on AutoCAD's file search path. Then:

(xload "magnets")
(xload "gravity")
(ads)   Returns ("C:\\ads\\magnets.exp"
                                  "C:\\ads\\gravity.exp")

And

Tests to see if all of a list of expressions are not evaluated to nil. Returns T if all are not nil; returns nil if any one is nil.

REQUIRED ARGUMENTS

A series of any number of valid expressions.

USAGE

This function is used to evaluate a series of expressions. In this way, an Auto-LISP routine can process if-then-else decisions, conditional decisions, and controlled loops based on complex criteria.

EXAMPLES

(and (= 1 1.0) (/= 2 3.0))	Returns T
(and (/= 1 1) (/= 2 3.0))	Returns nil
(setq x 0 y 1)	
(and x y)	Returns T
(setq x 0 y nil)	
(and x y)	Returns nil

ANGLE

Returns an absolute angle based on a line that is formed by two 2-D points, measured counterclockwise from the x-axis of the current construction plane.

REQUIRED ARGUMENTS

Two 2-D points. You may supply 3-D points, but they are projected onto the current construction plane.

USAGE

The points used as arguments to this function are assumed to lie in the current construction plane, and the angle is measured relative to the x-axis of that plane. A line need not exist in the drawing between these two points; AutoCAD returns the angle as if a line segment actually existed, starting with the first argument and ending at the second. The angle measurement is always returned in radians, regardless of the current setting of AutoCAD's angle units.

EXAMPLES

(angle '(0 0) '(5 5))   Returns 0.785398 (45 degrees)

(angle '(5 5) '(0 0))   Returns 3.92699 (225 degrees)

ANGTOS

Returns an angle value converted to a string.

REQUIRED ARGUMENTS

A number, which Angtos interprets to be a real number—an angle value as measured in radians. Following the number, two optional arguments are allowed. The first optional argument, an integer from 0 to 4, determines the angular-units format for the string. The second optional argument, an integer from 0 to 8, determines the number of decimal (or fractional, if appropriate) places of accuracy.

USAGE

The string returned by this expression is controlled by the system variables AUNITS, AUPREC, and DIMZIN. Unless the optional arguments are explicitly used, the units format of the string is determined by the settings of AUNITS and AUPREC; that is, by the default setting of AutoCAD's units format using the Units command.

The setting of DIMZIN controls whether zero units are to be included in the string if the angle is less than zero in the current format. Refer to Chapter 13 for details regarding DIMZIN.

EXAMPLES

(angtos 0.785398 0 0)	Returns " 45 "
(angtos 0.785398 0 2)	Returns " 45.00 "
(angtos 0.785398 1 2)	Returns " 45d0'0'' "
(angtos 0.785398 2 2)	Returns " 50.00g "
(angtos 0.785398 3 2)	Returns " 0.79r "
(angtos 0.785398 4 2)	Returns " N 45d0' E "

APPEND

Returns a single list from a series of lists.

REQUIRED ARGUMENTS

Lists only. The arguments cannot be expressions unless those expressions return lists; when you use an expression as an argument to Append, the Auto-LISP interpreter will evaluate it first and use the result, not the expression itself.

USAGE

Append is useful in cases where a repeated function or several functions are returning lists that must be condensed into one list. There are other more useful functions that combine numbers and strings into lists; refer to the Cons and List functions. Append can be used to add a z coordinate to a 2-D coordinate list, provided that the z coordinate is added in the format of a list containing a single number. Lists within lists to be combined are added as lists within the resulting list, as shown in the examples.

EXAMPLES

(append '(0 1) '(7))	Returns (0 1 7)
(append '(0 1 7) '(12))	Returns (0 1 7 12)
(append '(0 1 7 12) '((43 10) 5))	Returns (0 1 7 12 (43 10) 5)

APPLY

Takes any function, supplied as its first argument, and applies a list, supplied as its second argument, as arguments to the given function.

REQUIRED ARGUMENTS

A valid AutoLISP function, either predefined or user-created, and a list. The number of items in the list must be valid for the quoted function.

USAGE

The Apply function is used in situations where the arguments for a function have been gathered by other functions into a list, rather than memory variables that can be supplied directly to a function. It is a shortcut alternative to extracting the atoms from the list into memory variables. It can be used when node space is at a premium and the cost of creating memory variables is not justified.

EXAMPLES

(apply '/= '("cat" "Cat" "dog"))   Returns T
(apply 'angtos '(0.785398 0 4))   Returns "45.0000"

ASCII

Returns the first character in the string, converted to its equivalent ASCII character code.

REQUIRED ARGUMENTS

A single string of any length. Only the first character in the string is significant.

USAGE

The Ascii function can be used when ASCII codes are required—for instance, when sending printing codes to the printer—but only the character is known, or when the codes need to be extracted from strings supplied by other functions.

EXAMPLES

(ascii "C")   Returns 67
(ascii "Cat")   Returns 67
(ascii "c")   Returns 99

ATAN

Returns the arctangent of the number supplied as its argument.

REQUIRED ARGUMENTS

One or two numbers, either integers or reals. The Atan function always returns a real in the range of $-\pi$ to $+\pi$ radians.

USAGE

Atan is a general arctangent solving function for trigonometric problems. If one argument is supplied, the arctangent for that number is returned. If two arguments are supplied, the first is divided by the second, and the arctangent of the result is returned. If the first argument is positive and the second argument is zero, 1.570796 is returned. If the first argument is negative and the second is zero, -1.570796 is returned.

EXAMPLES

(atan 6)	Returns 1.40565
(atan 12 2.0)	Returns 1.40565
(atan 5.23329)	Returns 1.38199
(atan 12.45 2.379)	Returns 1.38199

ATOF

Converts a string to a real number, and returns the real number.

REQUIRED ARGUMENTS

A string in the form of numerals. A period can be included and will be interpreted as a decimal point. A minus sign can also be included, and the real number returned will be a negative number.

USAGE

Strings must be converted to numbers before calculations can be performed using their values. The strings may be supplied by the user or by other AutoLISP functions. Integers are never returned by this function; even if the string is a whole number within the valid range of integers, this function only returns real numbers. If alphabetical characters are used as the argument, this function returns zero.

EXAMPLES

(atof "1")	Returns 1.0
(atof "98.6")	Returns 98.6
(atof "12345E – 2")	Returns 123.45

ATOI

Converts a string to an integer, and returns the integer.

REQUIRED ARGUMENTS

A string in the form of whole numbers within the valid range for integers. A minus sign can also be included, and a negative integer is returned.

USAGE

Strings must be converted to numbers before calculations can be performed using their values. The strings may be supplied by the user or by other Auto-LISP functions. Real numbers are never returned by this function. If the string includes a decimal point, the fractional portion is omitted and an integer is returned. If alphabetical characters are used as the argument, this function returns zero.

EXAMPLES

(atoi " – 1")	Returns – 1
(atoi "98.6")	Returns 98
(atoi "12345E – 2")	Returns 12345
(atoi "big")	Returns 0

ATOM

Tests to see if the argument is an atom or a list. If an atom, returns T; otherwise, returns nil.

REQUIRED ARGUMENTS

Only a single argument. There are no restrictions on the argument type, only that it can be evaluated as either a list or an atom. If you use as the argument an expression or variable that is evaluated to nil, Atom will return T.

USAGE

The Atom function can be useful in checking the performance of list-constructing functions, and making decisions regarding which function may be applied to a particular argument.

EXAMPLES

(atom 1)	Returns T
(atom '(1 2 3 4))	Returns nil
(atom nil)	Returns T

BOOLE

Makes comparisons of the binary bits in integers, and returns the number of true comparisons made based on selectable criteria.

REQUIRED ARGUMENTS

At least three arguments, all integers. The first argument sets up the kind of comparisons to be made between the binary-code bits of the other arguments.

USAGE

The binary comparisons between the remaining arguments are made between the bits in the first position of each, then the bits in the second position, then the third, and so on. In each case, a *result bit* is created in the same position and set to either 0 or 1. When bits in each position have been compared, the result bits form a binary number. The integer equivalent of the resulting binary number is returned.

An integer between 1 and 15 may be used as the first argument to determine what bit values in the compared integers will set each result bit to 1. The following are the basic comparison values to which the first argument can be set:

1   Result bit set to 1 when both comparison bits are 1

2   Result bit set to 1 when first comparison bit is 1 and second is 0

4   Result bit set to 1 when first comparison bit is 0 and second is 1

8   Result bit set to 1 when both comparison bits are 0

You may combine these integers to make more complex comparisons; for example:

6   Result bit set to 1 when either the first or second comparison bit is 1, but not both; combination of 2 and 4

7   Result bit set to 1 if either of the comparison bits is 1, or if both are 1; combination of 1, 2, and 4

12   Result bit set to 1 when first comparison bit is 0 and second is either 1 or 0; combination of 8 and 4

EXAMPLES

(boole 6 12 24)	Returns 20
(boole 7 12 24)	Returns 28
(boole 12 12 24)	Returns −13

BOUNDP

Tests to see if an atom is bound to a value (i.e., is not nil). If the atom is bound to a value, this function returns T. Otherwise, it returns nil.

REQUIRED ARGUMENTS

An atom, preceded by the quote character or enclosed in the Quote function.

USAGE

Boundp is useful for evaluating memory variables before passing them to expressions as arguments, thereby avoiding situations where possible nil values could force error messages.

EXAMPLES

(setq x 0 y nil)	
(boundp 'x)	Returns T
(boundp 'y)	Returns nil

CAR

Returns the first member in a list.

REQUIRED ARGUMENTS

A list.

USAGE

Car is frequently used to isolate the x coordinate from a coordinate point list. However, it can be used to extract the first member from any list. Car will return nil if the list has no members.

EXAMPLES

(car '(1 2 3))	Returns 1
(car '((1 2) 3))	Returns (1 2)

CADR

Returns the second element in a list.

REQUIRED ARGUMENTS

A list of at least two members. If the list has fewer than two members, Cadr returns nil.

USAGE

Cadr is frequently used to isolate the y coordinate from a coordinate point list, but its use is not restricted to coordinate point lists; it may be used on any list. Cadr will not isolate the second element in a dotted pair, however. Use the Cdr function for dotted pairs instead.

EXAMPLES

(cadr '(1 2 3))	Returns 2
(cadr '((1 2) 3))	Returns 3

CADDR

Returns the third element in a list.

REQUIRED ARGUMENTS

A list of at least three members. If the list has two members or fewer, Caddr returns nil.

USAGE

Caddr is frequently used to isolate the z coordinate from a coordinate point list. However, you may use Caddr on any list of three or more members, where the third member is required.

EXAMPLES

(caddr '(1 2 3))	Returns 3
(cadr '((1 2) 3))	Returns nil

CHR

Reads an integer as an ASCII code and returns the ASCII character that corresponds to that code.

REQUIRED ARGUMENTS

A single integer.

USAGE

Chr is frequently used in concatenating strings, to prevent the AutoLISP interpreter from misinterpreting ASCII characters in the strings as control characters—for example, if you intend to use quotation marks within a prompt string.

EXAMPLES

(chr 34)	Returns "
(strcat "Do you wish to " (chr 34) "purge" (chr 34) " now?")	Returns "Do you wish to "purge" now?"

Close

Closes an open disk file and returns nil.

REQUIRED ARGUMENTS

A file descriptor stored in a memory variable. The file descriptor is a special data type created when a disk file is opened using the Open function.

USAGE

It is very important to close all open files when they are no longer needed for reading or writing data. The Close function is the only way to accomplish this. For example, if you leave files open and attempt to create node space by manipulating the atom list, you may lose data in the file, or create lost sectors on the disk, or both. Therefore, whenever you open a file using the Open function, be sure to include a corresponding Close function in your routine, to explicitly close the file as soon as it is no longer needed.

EXAMPLES

Assuming that the memory variable *x* holds a valid file descriptor,

```
(close x)
```

closes the file on disk, and if necessary, updates its contents. The file can no longer be accessed for either reading or writing until opened again using the Open function.

Command

Invokes an AutoCAD command while inside an AutoLISP routine, and returns nil.

REQUIRED ARGUMENTS

A valid AutoCAD command, followed by valid responses to the prompts issued by AutoCAD. You may use memory variables containing the correct responses as arguments. Most arguments should be strings; however, numeric data will be accepted if the option prompt accepts numbers—for example, the row and column prompts in the Array command.

USAGE

Any AutoCAD command and the necessary optional response(s) that can be invoked from the keyboard may be invoked from within AutoLISP by using the Command function. This function has many possible applications. For example, you may store a read-only system variable in an AutoLISP memory variable, and then invoke the AutoCAD command that changes the system variable. Later you can restore the original system-variable value by reinvoking the command and using the memory variable that stores the old value as the argument to the command. You may draw, edit, change the display, and generally automate the editing process with routines containing this function.

The AutoLISP interpreter assumes that all arguments of this function are data entered in response to AutoCAD prompts, and a press of the Enter key is assumed after each. If you wish to indicate a press of the Enter key explicitly—for example, to accept a default response or to indicate the end of a selection process—use two quotation marks with nothing between them as an argument to this function.

In AutoCAD Release 9 and later, you may use the pause symbol in the list of arguments for the Command function, and AutoCAD will pause and wait for user input before resuming the function. If you like, you may invoke transparent commands while a Command function is paused.

If your AutoLISP routine includes a pause for text entry, set the value of the TEXTEVAL system variable to 1, and do not use the Dtext command; use the Text command only. Refer to Chapter 9 for details regarding the Text and Dtext commands.

If you pause the Command function, you cannot enter an AutoLISP expression. You can select items from the screen, tablet, or pull-down menus as valid responses when the Command function is paused.

You may not use any function beginning with *Get* while inside the Command function. In general, use the pause symbol instead. If data must be stored, invoke the *Get* functions and store the data to memory variables, and then invoke the Command function and use the variables as arguments. Alternatively, it is possible to suspend the Command function before all the necessary arguments are supplied, perform other processing (including a Get function), and then resume the Command function where it left off. Both of these techniques are illustrated in the following examples. The first obtains two points, then displays the distance and draws a line segment between them:

```
(defun C:Segment( / x y)
    (setq x (getpoint "Line \nFirst point: ")
        y (getpoint x "\nTo point: ")
```

```
        )
        (prompt "\nLength of segment is: ")
        (princ (rtos (distance x y)))
        (command "Line" x y """")
        (princ)
    )
```

This second example does the same thing, except that it begins the Line command and stores the operator input while the command is in progress. It uses fewer memory variables and is slightly faster:

```
(defun C:Segment( / x)
    (command "Line" pause)
    (setq x (getvar "LASTPOINT"))
    (command pause """")
    (prompt "\nLength of segment is: ")
    (princ (rtos (distance x (getvar "LASTPOINT"))))
    (princ)
)
```

Even though AutoLISP functions require angle information expressed in radians, AutoCAD commands that prompt for angle information, even when called from inside AutoLISP, expect angle information expressed in the current angular-units format. This can require some conversion when passing angle information to AutoCAD commands inside AutoLISP. For example, consider a situation in which degrees is the current units format, and you have prompted the user for an angle using Getangle and stored that information to a memory variable:

```
(setq x (getangle "\nEnter an angle:"))
```

No matter how the user enters the angle information in response to this prompt, the memory variable x contains the information in radians. Later in processing, if you wanted to use this information as part of an AutoCAD Rotate command, the following syntax would *not* work:

```
(command "ROTATE" "L" """" '(0 0) x)
```

This would not work because the memory variable x is supplying information not to an AutoLISP function, but rather in response to an AutoCAD command prompt for the angle of rotation. In order for the value of x to be used in this case, it must be converted back to degrees. The following function will do the job:

```
(command "ROTATE" "L" """" '(0 0) (* (/ x pi) 180))
```

EXAMPLES

The following example assumes that the read-only system variables TARGET and VIEWDIR have been stored in AutoLISP memory variables *target* and *camera*:

```
(setq target (getvar "TARGET")
      camera (getvar "VIEWDIR")
)
```

Now the *dview* angle can be temporarily reset:

```
(command "dview" "" "points" "6,6,0" "10,3,10" "x")
```

And later, restored:

```
(command "dview" "" "points" target camera "x")
```

The following example draws two concentric circles, using the pause symbol. Notice how more than one command may be invoked in sequence using a single Command function call.

```
(command "circle" "6,4.5" pause "circle" "6,4.5" pause)
```

The following creates a 3-by-5 array from a windowed object:

```
(command "array" "w" pause pause "" "r" 5 3 pause pause)
```

The following examples create two-key Zoom command macros:

```
(defun C:ZW( )
  (command "zoom" "w" pause pause)
  (princ)
)
(defun C:ZP( )
  (command "zoom" "p")
  (princ)
)
(defun C:ZA( )
  (command "zoom" "a")
  (princ)
)
(defun C:ZC( )
  (command "zoom" "c" pause "")
  (princ)
)
```

Cond

Evaluates a series of lists containing AutoLISP expressions, and evaluates the expressions found in the first list it finds whose first expression is not evaluated to nil. After evaluating the expressions in this list, the Cond function ignores the remaining lists and returns the result of the last evaluated expression. If the first expression in every list is evaluated to nil, Cond returns nil as well.

REQUIRED ARGUMENTS

At least one list containing at least two AutoLISP expressions.

USAGE

Cond is AutoLISP's conditional-branching function. It is used to choose a particular series of expressions from a list of many, and to evaluate the chosen expressions while ignoring the others. In other words, the Cond function is a means to select a single choice from several alternatives; each alternative is a separate list of AutoLISP expressions.

Each argument list presented to Cond may contain any number of AutoLISP expressions, but must contain at least two. The Cond function steps through the argument lists presented to it, evaluating the first expression in each list. If the first expression is evaluated to nil, Cond ceases to evaluate expression in that list, and moves on to the next list, again evaluating the first expression.

When Cond finds an expression that is not evaluated to nil, it evaluates the remaining expressions in that list. It then returns the result of the last expression evaluated, and does not evaluate any more of its argument lists.

It is common for the last argument in the Cond function to be a list that begins with the symbol *T,* AutoLISP's logical "true" symbol. This symbol is never evaluated to nil, and if Cond goes through all the previous lists, this last one will always be evaluated. If all lists begin with an expression that is evaluated to nil, Cond returns nil.

Most of the time, the first expression in each of the arguments is a logical expression of some sort, but it doesn't have to be. As long as the first expression in the argument list is not evaluated to nil, Cond will evaluate all the other expressions found there.

EXAMPLES

This example assumes that you have entered a string naming an entity type (all in uppercase) and stored it in a memory variable named *et*:

```
(cond ( ( = et "LINE") (command "line" "0,0" "5,5" "") )
       ( ( = et "CIRCLE") (command "circle" "5,5" "5,0") )
       ( ( = et "SOLID") (command "solid" "0,5" "0,0" "5,5" "5,0" "") )
       ( ( = et "TRACE") (command "trace" "0.25" "5,5" "5,0" "") )
       ( T (prompt "\nEntity type not found by COND function.") )
)
```

Cons

Adds a new member to the beginning of a list.

REQUIRED ARGUMENTS

Two arguments. Depending on whether the second argument is an atom or a list, it returns two distinctly different types of list.

USAGE

If the second argument is a list, Cons takes the first argument and adds it to the beginning of the list presented as the second argument. If the first argument is a list, the list is added to the second as a list within the list.

If the second argument is an atom, the Cons function will create a special type of list called a *dotted pair*. Dotted pairs have only two members, separated by a period. They are more memory-efficient than ordinary lists of two members. (They cannot be used as coordinate point lists, however.) Dotted pairs are most frequently seen as sublists in entity-association lists (Chapter 19). This function is the only means by which you can create dotted pairs.

EXAMPLES

(cons '1 '(2 3 4))	Returns (1 2 3 4)
(cons '(1 2) '(3 4))	Returns ((1 2) 3 4)
(cons '0 "LINE")	Returns (0 . "LINE"), a dotted pair

Cos

Returns the cosine of its argument, assumed to be an angle.

REQUIRED ARGUMENTS

A single argument, which must be an angle expressed in radians. Integers are acceptable if a whole number is used as the argument; this function always returns a real number.

USAGE

The Cos function is the general cosine solving function for trigonometric problems. Angles expressed in degrees must be converted to radians before being passed to this function. The first example ahead includes a nested function that converts 45 degrees to radians; you may use this formula when such conversion is needed.

EXAMPLES

(cos (* pi (/ 45 180.0)))	Returns 0.707107
(cos 6.2)	Returns 0.996542
(cos 5)	Returns 0.283662

CVUNIT

Converts a number or list of numbers from one unit of measurement to another.

REQUIRED ARGUMENTS

The Cvunit function requires three arguments: a number or list of numbers, a string showing the current unit of measurement, and a second string specifying the new unit of measurement.

USAGE

The Cvunit function will use the first three numbers only as the first argument. Longer lists are not allowed in Release 11.

In 32-bit systems, if you want to use an integer outside of the 16-bit range (-32768 to $+32767$) as the first argument in this function, convert it to a real number first.

The strings representing valid units of measurement are stored in the ASCII file ACAD.UNT, which may be modified by the user. In most cases, singular and plural forms may be used interchangeably. ACAD.UNT includes approximately 150 standard units of measurement, including simple mathematical conversions. Refer to Chapter 21 for more details about the ACAD.UNT file.

The Cvunit function can be used to determine a scaling factor, which may be stored in a memory variable and applied to several subsequent values in a routine. This is usually more efficient than repeating this function and its string arguments several times in an AutoLISP file. This technique will not work, though, in cases where incremental offsets are applied to the base measurement—for example, when converting Fahrenheit to Celsius. In these cases, use the Defun function instead to define a separate conversion function. For example, here is a function that converts Fahrenheit to Celsius:

```
(defun f2c(x)
    (read (rtos (cvunit x "fahrenheit" "celsius") 2 6)))
```

Once defined as shown, (f2c 32.0) returns 0.0, and (f2c 64.0) returns 17.7778.

If a unit string cannot be found in ACAD.UNT, or if two incompatible units of measurement are chosen, Cvunit returns nil.

EXAMPLES

(cvunit 1 "gallon" "fluid_ounces")	Returns 128.0
(cvunit 1 "pound" "ounces")	Returns 16.0
(cvunit 1 "pound" "fluid_ounces")	Returns nil
(setq in2yds (cvunit 1 "inches" "yards"))	Returns 0.0277778
(* 72 in2yds)	Returns 2.0
(cvunit '(72 144 0) "inches" "feet")	Returns (6.0 12.0 0.0)

DEFUN

Returns a new function or AutoCAD command containing user-definable processes.

REQUIRED ARGUMENTS

The following arguments, in the following order:

1. The name of the function or command that is being created.
2. A list of arguments required by the function, and any memory variables local to that function.

3. A series of valid AutoLISP expressions to be evaluated when the new function is called.

USAGE

Defun is one of AutoLISP's most powerful functions. The first argument must be a character string. Although this character string is to be interpreted literally—that is, not evaluated on the spot as a function name or memory variable—you do not need to enclose it within the Quote function or precede it with an apostrophe. Defun assumes that the character string in the first argument position is the name of the function being defined.

The second argument is the *argument list,* a list of characters enclosed within a pair of parentheses. The characters in the argument list represent arguments that are required by the function (if any), plus any *local variables* used within the function (if any). Again, the list itself will not be evaluated, even though it is not enclosed in a Quote function, as Defun already understands its meaning from its position as the second argument.

Arguments and local variables in the list are separated by means of a forward slash. If the list contains no slash character, the members of the list are all assumed to be arguments.

For example, the following fragment from a Defun function indicates that a function named Newfunc is to be created, and will have two arguments:

```
(defun NEWFUNC (a b)
```

The data type of these arguments will be determined by the use of the symbols *a* and *b* in the series of AutoLISP expressions that follows. For example, suppose Newfunc were to double the first argument and divide the result by the second argument. The complete function would appear as follows:

```
(defun NEWFUNC (a b)
   (/ (* a 2) b)
)
```

Once the AutoLISP interpreter has evaluated this Defun function, you may treat Newfunc as any other AutoLISP function. Therefore,

```
(newfunc 12 3)
```

returns 8.

If you attempt to use Newfunc with fewer than two arguments, AutoCAD will display an error message. If you attempt to use strings instead of numbers, Auto-CAD will also display an error message, since the expressions in Newfunc require numbers.

If a slash character appears in the list following the function name, the Auto-LISP interpreter treats these as local variables. A local variable is used inside a function like any other memory variable, but when the function completes processing, the variable is reset to whatever value it had before the function began processing. For example, consider the following function:

```
(defun NEWFUNC (a b / x)
    (setq x (getint "\nFirst atom in list: "))
    (cons x (/ (* a 2) b))
)
```

This version of Newfunc performs the same calculation as before, but first it prompts you to enter an integer from the keyboard, and then it creates a dotted pair consisting of the integer you entered and the result of the math performed on the arguments. For example, once the AutoLISP interpreter has evaluated this Defun function, you can call Newfunc as follows:

```
(newfunc 12 3)
```

AutoLISP prompts:

First atom in list:

Enter an integer—for example, **6**. AutoLISP would return:

(6 . 8)

Since *x* was defined as a local variable in the argument list, it will not retain its value when the function is complete. If *x* did not exist before the function was called, or had a nil value, it will have a nil value when the function has completed its processing. If *x* had a different value—for example, 3—it will be reset to this value when the function completes its processing.

Notice that in the above example, two AutoLISP expressions follow the function name and argument list. These expressions were evaluated in sequence when the Newfunc function was called. You can have any number of AutoLISP expressions following the argument list, and you need not make them into a list (that is, you need not enclose them all within a set of parentheses). As long as they are valid AutoLISP expressions, the AutoLISP interpreter will evaluate them all in sequence, just as if you had entered them at the AutoCAD Command prompt.

If a variable in a function is not explicitly defined as local, it is assumed to be *global,* meaning that it will retain its current value when the function completes its processing. To define a variable as global, simply leave it out of the argument list.

Both global and local variables are useful in AutoLISP, depending on the context. If you use local variables wisely, you can get one variable name to do the work of several different variables, thereby conserving precious node space. You can also be sure that your memory variables are not carrying unneeded or incorrect data throughout your routine. On the other hand, global variables can be passed freely among functions and commands, always holding the data to which they were last bound.

It is possible to define a function with no arguments and no local variables, or one or the other, as the following examples indicate:

(defun (newfunc (a / x)   *a* is an argument, variable *x* is local

(defun (newfunc (/ x)   No arguments, and one local variable, *x*

(defun (newfunc ( )   No arguments and no local variables

There is a potentially more powerful application of the Defun function: to create brand-new AutoCAD commands. Creating new AutoCAD commands requires almost the same syntax as creating AutoLISP functions. You begin by using AutoLISP's Defun function, but you enter **C:** in front of the function name. This informs the AutoLISP interpreter that an AutoCAD command, not an AutoLISP function, is being created. In the following example, Newfunc has been transformed into an AutoCAD command:

```
(defun C:NEWFUNC (/ a b)
    (setq a (getreal "\nNumber to double: ")
          b (getreal "\nNumber to divide by: "))
    (/ (* a 2.0) b)
)
```

Since Newfunc is now defined as an AutoCAD command, the use of arguments is impractical (because all AutoCAD commands are strings of characters with no spaces in between). Therefore, instead of using arguments, all required data is requested by Get functions and bound to local memory variables.

Once the expression just presented has been evaluated by the AutoLISP interpreter, the following dialog is valid:

```
Command: Newfunc
Number to double: 12
Number to divide by: 3
8.0
Command:
```

EXAMPLES

The following functions demonstrate the Defun function by creating both functions and commands that convert radians to degrees and degrees to radians:

(defun dtr(a) (* pi (/ a 180.0)))   Returns DTR

(dtr 90)   Returns 1.5708

```
(defun rtd(a) (* (/ a pi) 180.0))                          Returns RTD
(rtd 1.570796)                                             Returns 90.0
(defun C:dtr(/ a)
      (setq a (getreal "\nEnter angle in degrees: "))
      (* pi (/ a 180.0)))
)                                                          Returns C:DTR
```

Sample dialog:

Command: **DTR**
Enter angle in degrees: **90**
1.5708

```
(defun C:rtd(/ a)
      (setq a (getangle "\nEnter angle in radians: "))
      (* (/ a pi) 180.0))
)                                                          Returns C:RTD
```

Sample dialog:

Command: **RTD**
Enter angle in radians: **1.570796**
90.0

DISTANCE

Returns a real number, which is the distance in drawing units between the two points supplied as its arguments.

REQUIRED ARGUMENTS

Two point lists, which can be 2-D (two real numbers), 3-D (three numbers), or a combination.

USAGE

In AutoCAD Release 10 and later, the distance returned by this function is the distance in 3-D space between the 3-D points supplied as its argument. However, if one or both of the point arguments is 2-D, or if the FLATLAND system variable is not zero, the distance returned is the distance between the points as projected onto the current construction plane. Release 9 ignores the z coordinate, and returns the 2-D distance between the points as projected onto the current construction plane. Versions prior to Release 9 require 2-D coordinate point information only.

EXAMPLES

(distance '(1 1) '(5 5))	Returns 5.65685
(distance '(1 1 0) '(5 5 5))	Returns 7.54983
(distance '(1 1) '(5 5 5))	Returns 5.65685 (when the WCS is the current construction plane)

EQ

Returns T if two arguments are bound to the exact same data.

REQUIRED ARGUMENTS

Two arguments. The Eq function will accept any data form, and evaluate it accordingly.

USAGE

Eq will only return T if the two arguments are bound to the exact same data, as opposed to merely identical data. It is frequently used to see if memory variables are duplicating each other's contents.

EXAMPLES

The following examples assume the following memory variable assignments:

```
(setq a '(1 2 3)
      b a
      c '(1 2 3)
)
```

Given the above, Eq returns the following:

(eq a b)	Returns T
(eq a c)	Returns nil, because *a* and *c* are only identical lists, not the exact same list

EQUAL

Returns T if two arguments are bound to identical data.

REQUIRED ARGUMENTS

Equal requires two arguments. It will accept any data form, and evaluate it accordingly.

A third argument, called the *fuzz factor,* is used when comparing numbers. The fuzz factor is a number that indicates the maximum allowable difference between the two arguments in order for them to be considered equal.

USAGE

Equal will return T when the two arguments are bound to identical data, including the exact same data. It is the function of choice for determining if two different expressions will be evaluated to the same thing.

The fuzz factor is handy because a computer may calculate slight differences between real numbers stored in its memory, depending on the method used to calculate or store them. The differences may be so small that the numbers, when displayed, appear equal even though they are stored in memory as unequal. Evaluating these apparently equal numbers will give surprising results. For example,

    (equal (sqrt 26) 5.09902)

returns nil, even though the arguments, if evaluated separately, appear to result in the same thing. Applying a fuzz factor to this expression will achieve the correct result of T:

    (equal (sqrt 26) 5.09902 0.00001)

EXAMPLES

These examples assume the following memory-variable assignments:

    (setq a '(1 2 3)
          b a
          c '(1 2 3)
)

Given the above, Equal returns the following:

(equal a b)	Returns T, since the same data must also be identical data
(equal a c)	Returns T, because the two lists are duplicates of each other
(equal (* 2.0 2.0) (+ 3 1))	Returns T, because both expressions will be evaluated to the same result

EVAL

Evaluates an AutoLISP expression and returns the result.

REQUIRED ARGUMENTS

A single argument in any valid data form.

USAGE

While this function may appear to be redundant, it comes in handy in Auto-LISP routines where data may not otherwise be evaluated as you intend. For example, if the following were the last expressions in a series, the series may return 5:

```
(setq x 2
      y 3
)
( + x y)
```

However, if you wanted the calculation to be performed, but the series itself to return nil, you could add the following expression:

```
(setq x 2
      y 3
)
( + x y)
(eval nil)
```

The Eval function will return what the evaluated data returns. This may cause a problem if you attempt to use the Eval function with the Quote function. For example,

```
(eval '(2 3))
```

returns an error message. This is because the Eval function attempts to evaluate both the Quote function and the list being quoted. Use the Quote function alone to return the desired list.

EXAMPLES

(eval 5)	Returns 5
(eval (+ 2 3))	Returns 5
(eval nil)	Returns nil

EXP

Returns the natural antilog of the argument, as a real number.

REQUIRED ARGUMENTS

A number, real or integer.

USAGE

Exp is a natural-antilog solving function for scientific and exponential calculations.

EXAMPLES

(exp 2)	Returns 7.38906
(exp pi)	Returns 23.1407
(exp 5)	Returns 148.413
(exp 10)	Returns 22026.5

EXPT

Returns a base number raised to a given power.

REQUIRED ARGUMENTS

Two arguments, both numbers. The first is the base, and the second is the power to which the base will be raised. If both numbers are integers, an integer is returned. (If the total exceeds the acceptable range for integers, however, an incorrect result is returned.) If one or both numbers are real numbers, a real number is returned.

USAGE

Expt is an exponential math solving function. For example, you use Expt to square and cube numbers.

EXAMPLES

(expt 5 2)	Returns 25
(expt 5.0 2)	Returns 25.0
(expt 2.0 3.0)	Returns 8.0

FINDFILE

Returns a string consisting of the name of the file used as its argument, including the file's subdirectory location.

REQUIRED ARGUMENTS

A string of valid file-name characters.

USAGE

The Findfile function is available in AutoCAD Release 10 and later. It can be used to search for files when the exact subdirectory location is not known. If you supply a file name as the argument of Findfile, the function will search Auto-CAD's search path for it. If it finds the file on the search path, it returns the full name of the file, including the subdirectory location, as a string that can then be passed to AutoLISP's other file-manipulation functions. Refer to Chapter 4 for details regarding AutoCAD's search path for files.

If the file name for which you are searching includes a file extension, you must include the file extension for AutoLISP to find the file. If AutoLISP does not find the file along the search path, it returns nil.

You may indicate a drive letter and subdirectory names in the argument. If a drive letter or subdirectory name is included in the file name, AutoLISP will not look for the file along the search path, but instead will confine its search for the file to the named drive or subdirectory, again returning nil if the file is not found, or the full name of the file if found.

When specifying subdirectories in AutoLISP, use the forward slash (/) rather than the backslash (\ ) to separate subdirectory names. AutoLISP reads the backslash character as a signal for control characters (see Chapter 16) rather than a path separator. If you cannot use the forward slash as part of your file-name string, you may use a double backslash (\\) instead.

EXAMPLES

The following examples assume a subdirectory structure and file locations as implied in the strings returned by the functions:

(findfile "acad.lsp")	Returns "acad/acad.lsp"
(findfile "acad")	Returns nil; therefore, all files named "acad" in this example must have file extensions as well
(findfile "c:/acad/acad.pat")	Returns "c:/acad/acad.pat"

FIX

Converts a real number into an integer, if possible. Returns the integer, or if an integer is not possible, converts the argument number to a whole real number, and returns the whole real number.

REQUIRED ARGUMENTS

A single number, real or integer.

USAGE

If an integer is supplied as the argument, it is simply returned. If a real number is supplied as the argument, the decimal portion is removed and the number is returned as an integer. If the real number is out of range for integers (– 32768 to + 32767, including 32-bit systems), the decimal portion is removed and the number is returned with a decimal value of zero.

EXAMPLES

(fix 256)	Returns 256
(fix 4096.123484)	Returns 4096
(fix 40123.75)	Returns 40123.0
(fix (* pi 2))	Returns 6

FLOAT

Converts an integer to a real (floating-point) whole number.

REQUIRED ARGUMENTS

A single number, real or integer.

USAGE

If the argument is a real number, it is simply returned by the function. If the argument is an integer, it is returned as a real number with a decimal value of zero.

EXAMPLES

(float 256)	Returns 256.0
(float 54.375)	Returns 54.375

FOREACH

Steps through a list of atoms and evaluates an expression for each.

REQUIRED ARGUMENTS

Three arguments, in the following order:

1. A memory-variable name.
2. A list of atoms.
3. An expression or series of expressions.

USAGE

Foreach is a looping function that will repeatedly execute a series of expressions. The first argument is the name of a memory variable. The memory variable need not be already bound to a value. Foreach will sequentially bind it to a value or values in the list supplied as its second argument. After binding the name to a memory variable, Foreach evaluates the series of functions. In most cases, the series will make use of the memory variable at some point, although it does not have to. The number of times Foreach evaluates the series of expressions is controlled by the number of atoms in the argument list. When Foreach runs out of atoms in the list, it stops evaluating the series of expressions and returns the result of the last expression evaluated.

The argument list could be created by a separate series of functions. For example, the atoms in the argument list can be returned by a series of functions, and the list assembled by means of the Cons or List function; the whole list could be stored to a memory variable as it is built up.

The series of expressions does not have to be enclosed in parentheses; in other words, it is not required that the series of expressions be a list of expressions.

EXAMPLES

The following series, which includes the Foreach function, will draw a series of line segments based on the points in the argument list stored in memory variable *y*:

```
(setq x '(6 1)
      y '((10 5) (8 7) (6 5) (6 1) (2 5) (4 7) (6 5))
)
(foreach pt y
    (command "line" x pt "")
    (setq x pt)
)
```

This series returns (6 5) and draws the lines.

GCD

Returns the greatest common denominator of two integers.

REQUIRED ARGUMENTS

Two integers.

USAGE

Gcd is a common-denominator solving function for a variety of mathematical problems.

EXAMPLES

(gcd 1920 2000)	Returns 80
(gcd 1920 2100)	Returns 60
(gcd 1920 100)	Returns 20

GETANGLE

Pauses for user input of an angle, and returns that angle in radians.

REQUIRED ARGUMENTS

None, but two optional arguments are allowed: a point and a string. Either one or both may be used; if both are used, they must appear in the following order:

1. A default "first point," when entering the angle by means of point picks.
2. A string that is displayed in the Command-prompt area as a prompt for the user.

USAGE

Getangle is one of two AutoLISP interactive mechanisms for retrieving angle information. (The other is Getorient, for Version 2.6 and later.) Getangle is frequently nested inside a Setq function, as the angle information is usually stored in memory for later processing.

You may enter the angle information directly from the keyboard. If entered from the keyboard, the data is accepted in the current angular-units format as defined by the Units command (Chapter 6), but the angle data returned by the function is always converted to radians, regardless of the input format.

AutoLISP always expresses angles based on AutoCAD's standard angle orientation—zero radians oriented horizontally and to the right in the current construction plane, and incremented clockwise.

If you have configured AutoCAD for its standard angle-orientation defaults using the Units command, the angle returned by Getangle is always the same as the angle entered, or its equivalent in radians. However, if you have changed AutoCAD's standard angle-orientation defaults, some conversion will be done so that the angle returned by this function is relative to AutoLISP's angle orientation.

Getangle ignores the currently set direction of angle zero, but obeys the direction of angle increment. Getangle is designed to return an AutoCAD standard angle (expressed in radians) that is found relative to standard angle zero. It will increment standard angle zero by the entered number of degrees—using the current direction for angle increment as set with the Units command—and return the AutoCAD standard angle that it finds.

For example, suppose you have set angle units as decimal degrees, angle zero oriented horizontally and pointing to the left (AutoCAD's standard 180 degrees), and angles incremented counterclockwise. Under these circumstances, if you specified 270 degrees in response to Getangle, the function would return 4.71239, which is AutoCAD's standard 270-degree angle expressed in radians. This is quite different from the current setting for 270 degrees, which is oriented in the opposite direction.

Getangle is useful when you need to input and store relative-angle information, such as a degree of rotation or an angle between items in a polar array—angle values that are independent of the current angle zero.

If you intend that absolute-angle information (for instance, the orientation of a baseline) be returned rather than a relative angle, use the Getorient function instead of Getangle. Using the same parameters, Getorient would return 1.5708, which is AutoCAD's standard 90-degree angle expressed in radians. AutoCAD's standard 90-degree angle is equal to the current angle setting for 270 degrees.

Alternatively, you may enter the angle data by picking two points on the screen. AutoCAD reads the angle formed by the two points and rotates standard angle zero by that number of degrees in the current angle-increment direction, returning the AutoCAD standard angle that it finds. If the optional point argument is present, AutoCAD takes that point as the first point entered. A rubber-band line will appear, extending from this point to the intersection of the crosshairs, and you may enter the second point.

Coordinate points may be entered from the keyboard in the standard fashion—as numbers separated by commas using the current units format or the decimal equivalent in drawing units. If you are using Release 10 and later, Getangle will accept 3-D point input, but the angle is always measured in the current construction plane; 3-D points not in the current construction plane will be projected onto that plane, and the angle measurement will then be taken.

Getangle's prompt argument can be any appropriate string of characters, as seen in the examples ahead. The prompt may also include control characters, the most frequent being the \n character, which inserts a line feed before the prompt, placing the prompt on its own line in the Command-prompt area. For clarity, you may want to end the prompt string with a space, as this will separate Auto-CAD's echo of your input from the prompt.

EXAMPLES

(getangle)	Pauses and will accept input without a prompt or default initial point. Returns the angle information in radians after it has been entered.
(getangle '(0 0) "\nEnter angle: ")	Returns "Enter angle: " and waits for angle information; rubberband line will extend from point 0,0 in the current construction plane. When angle information is entered, Getangle returns the angle information in radians.
(setq ang (getangle "\nEnter angle: "))	Functions as the previous example, but does not include the default initial point, and will store the angle information in the memory variable *ang*.

GETCORNER

Pauses for input of a point, and draws a rubberband rectangle on the screen as the user moves the pointing device.

REQUIRED ARGUMENTS

A point argument, which is the first corner of the rubberband rectangle it draws on the screen. The user supplies the opposite corner, and this point is returned by the function. You may also include an optional prompt string as a second argument to this function.

USAGE

Getcorner is used most frequently as a means by which AutoLISP can mimic AutoCAD's Windowing selection mechanism, in cases where selection sets are built outside of regular commands. However, it can easily be used in any other situation where the opposite corner points of a rectangle are needed.

Getcorner is available in AutoCAD Version 2.6 and later. In Release 10 or later, it will accept a 3-D point as its point argument, but the z coordinate will be ignored. The corner points are always assumed to be in the current construction plane. The z coordinate is taken from the setting of the ELEVATION system variable.

If you wish, you can use a nested Getpoint function to select the first corner point of the rectangle. The second example below shows how this is done.

EXAMPLES

The line

```
(getcorner '(0 0) "\nEnter opposite corner from point 0,0: ")
```

displays the indicated prompt and pauses for the user to enter a point, drawing a rubberband rectangle on the screen as the pointing device is moved. When the point is selected, the coordinates are returned.

```
(setq pt2 (getcorner
           (setq pt1 (getpoint "\nEnter first corner: "))
           "\nOther corner: "
      )
)
```

The above function displays the "Enter first corner:" prompt and pauses for the user to input a point. This point is stored in memory variable *pt1* and returned by the Setq function, taken as the point argument to the Getcorner function. Getcorner then displays the "Other corner:" prompt and pauses for input, drawing the rubberband rectangle anchored at the first point. When the second point is selected, it is stored in memory variable *pt2*. Thus, *pt1* and *pt2* may be used as opposite corner points for further processing.

GETDIST

Pauses for user input of a number and returns the number. Alternatively, the user may input two points, and the distance between them is returned. Getdist always returns a real number.

REQUIRED ARGUMENTS

None, but two optional arguments, an anchor point and a prompt string, may be used. You may use either one or both; if both are used, the anchor point must appear first, followed by the prompt string.

USAGE

The Getdist function is one of two AutoLISP interactive mechanisms for retrieving real numbers. (The other is Getreal, which accepts keyboard input only.) Getdist is often nested inside a Setq function, as the numeric information returned must frequently be stored in memory for later processing.

You may enter the numeric information directly from the keyboard. If entered from the keyboard, the data is accepted in the current angular-units format as defined by the Units command (Chapter 6), but the data returned by the function is always converted to a real decimal number, representing drawing units.

Alternatively, you may enter the numeric data by picking two points on the screen. AutoCAD measures the distance between the two points and returns that value. Thus, Getdist is used to obtain such information as the length of lines and the distance between construction points. After the first point is input, a rubberband line will appear, extending from this point to the intersection of the crosshairs.

If the optional anchor-point argument is provided, the AutoLISP interpreter assumes this to be the first point, and extends the rubberband line from this point. The user need only pick the second point. Coordinate points may be entered from the keyboard in the standard fashion, as numbers separated by commas using the current units format, or the decimal equivalent in drawing units. If you are using Release 10, Getdist returns the distance between the two points in 3-D space, unless the FLATLAND system variable is not set to zero. If FLATLAND is not set to zero, Getdist works as in previous versions of Auto-CAD, accepting 2-D points only, unless the Initget function is available and set to accept 3-D points. In Release 11 and later, Getdist accepts 3-D points.

Getdist's prompt argument can be any appropriate string of characters, as seen in the examples ahead. The prompt may also include control characters, the most frequent being the \n character, which places a line feed before the prompt, keeping the prompt on its own line in the Command-prompt area. For clarity, you may want to end the prompt string with a space, as this will separate Auto-CAD's echo of your input from the prompt.

EXAMPLES

(getdist)	Pauses and accepts input without a prompt or default initial point. Returns the numeric information after the user has input valid data.
(getdist '(0 0) "\nEnter distance from 0,0: ")	Displays the prompt string and waits for distance information; a rubberband line will extend from point 0,0 in the current construction plane. When the second point is entered, or a number is entered from the keyboard, Getdist returns the distance or the entered number.
(setq d (getdist "\nEnter distance: "))	Functions as the previous example, but does not include the default initial point, and will store the angle information in the memory variable *d*.

GETENV

Returns the setting of operating-system environment variables as a string. If an environment variable is not found or is not set, the function returns nil.

REQUIRED ARGUMENTS

A string representing the name of a valid operating-system environment variable.

USAGE

Getenv, which is available in AutoCAD Release 10 only or later, is useful in cases where the setting of an environment variable might be used to control AutoLISP's processing. For example, Getenv could be used to retrieve the name of a configuration subdirectory stored in ACADCFG, and thus be alerted to the hardware devices currently being used.

Getenv cannot change environment variables. Generally speaking, it is not advisable to attempt to change environment variables while inside AutoCAD.

EXAMPLES

(getenv "ACADCFG")   Returns "C:\ACAD\ALTCFG" or a similar path name, if one exists; otherwise, returns nil.

(getenv "LISPHEAP")   Returns the current setting of the LISPHEAP environment variable, or nil if not set.

GETINT

Pauses to accept input of an integer, and returns the integer.

REQUIRED ARGUMENTS

None, but an optional prompt string may be provided.

USAGE

Getint is used to obtain integer values from the user. Integers (whole numbers from -32768 to $+32767$ on both 16-bit and 32-bit systems) obtained by means of keyboard input or menu picks are the only allowable input. Points cannot be used to input integers when using Getint.

EXAMPLES

The line

```
(setq x (getint "\nEnter whole number from − 32768 to + 32767: "))
```

displays the prompt, pauses for integer input, and stores the input to memory variable *x*.

GETKWORD

Pauses to receive a string from the user. The string is tested for validity based on a list of valid keywords set using the Initget function.

REQUIRED ARGUMENTS

None, but an optional prompt string indicating which responses are valid is highly recommended.

USAGE

Getkword is used to elicit specific string information that will affect subsequent processing—for example, yes or no responses. If an invalid response is entered, Getkword will repeat until it receives a valid response.

The Initget function controls the testing for valid responses; therefore, this function is used in tandem with Initget. An example of the two functions is given ahead; refer to the discussion of the Initget function for more details on how Initget is used.

In other respects, Getkword operates in a manner similar to the Getstring function.

EXAMPLES

The lines

```
(initget "Yes No Quit")
(getkword "\nYes/No/Quit: ")
```

display the prompt and pause for valid user input, which may be one of the following in either uppercase or lowercase: Y, N, Q, Ye, Yes, No, Qu, Qui, or Quit. The corresponding keyword is returned, exactly as it appears in the string argument for the Initget function. For example, if you entered **q** in response to this example, Getkword would return "Quit".

GETORIENT

Pauses for user input of an angle, and returns that angle in radians.

REQUIRED ARGUMENTS

None, but two optional arguments, an anchor point and a prompt string, are allowed. If both are used, the anchor point must be the first argument.

USAGE

Getorient, which is available in AutoCAD Version 2.6 and later, is one of two AutoLISP interactive mechanisms for retrieving angle information. (The other is Getangle.) Getorient is frequently nested inside a Setq function, as the angle information returned is often stored in memory for subsequent processing.

You may enter the angle information directly from the keyboard. If entered from the keyboard, the data is accepted in the current angular-units format as defined by the Units command (Chapter 6), but the angle data returned by the function is always converted to radians, regardless of the input format.

Getorient returns angle information relative to both the currently set direction of angle zero and the direction of angle increment. Getorient returns an Auto-CAD standard angle (expressed in radians) that is found relative to the current angle zero. It will increment the current angle zero by the entered number of degrees, using the current direction for angle increment as set with the Units command, and will return the AutoCAD standard angle that it finds.

AutoLISP always expresses angles based on AutoCAD's standard angle orientation—zero radians oriented horizontally and to the right in the current construction plane, and incremented counterclockwise.

If you have configured AutoCAD for its standard angle-orientation defaults using the Units command, the angle returned by Getorient is always the same as the angle entered, or its equivalent in radians. However, if you have changed AutoCAD's standard angle-orientation defaults, some conversion will be done so that the angle returned by this function is relative to AutoLISP's consistent angle orientation.

For example, suppose you have set angle units as decimal degrees, angle zero oriented horizontally and pointing to the left (AutoCAD's standard 180 degrees), and angles to be incremented counterclockwise. Under these circumstances, if you entered 270 degrees in response to Getorient, the function would return 1.5708, which is 90 degrees expressed in radians. In the current units format, 90 degrees is AutoCAD's standard angle equivalent of 270 degrees.

Getorient is useful when you need to input and store absolute-angle information (i.e., any angle that is expressed relative to the current angle zero, such as a baseline).

If you intend that relative-angle information be returned—such as the angle between items in a polar array—rather than an absolute angle, use the Getangle function instead of Getorient. For example, using the same parameters, Getangle would return 4.71239, which is AutoCAD's standard 270-degree angle expressed in radians. Getangle found AutoCAD's standard 270-degree angle by rotating standard angle zero 270 degrees in the currently set direction.

Alternatively, you may enter the angle data by picking two points on the screen. AutoCAD reads the angle formed by the two points relative to the current setting for angle zero, and then increments angle zero by that number of degrees in the current angle increment direction, returning the AutoCAD standard angle that it finds. If the optional point argument is present, AutoCAD takes that point as the first point entered. A rubberband line will appear, extending from this point to the intersection of the crosshairs, and you may enter the second point.

Coordinate points may be entered from the keyboard in the standard fashion, as numbers separated by commas using the current units format or the decimal equivalent in drawing units. In Release 10 or later, Getorient will accept 3-D point input, but the angle is always measured in the current construction plane; 3-D points not in the current construction plane will be projected onto that plane, and the angle measurement will then be taken.

As seen in the examples ahead, Getorient's prompt argument can be any appropriate string of characters. The prompt may also include control characters, the most frequent being the \n character, which places a line feed before the prompt, displaying the prompt on its own line in the Command-prompt area. For clarity, you may want to end the prompt string with a space, as this will separate AutoCAD's echo of your input from the prompt.

EXAMPLES

(getorient)	Pauses and accepts input without a prompt or default initial point. Returns the angle information in radians after it has been entered.
(getorient '(0 0) "\nEnter angle: ")	Returns "Enter angle: " and waits for angle information; a rubberband line will extend from point 0,0 in the current construction plane. When angle information is entered, Getorient returns the angle information in radians.
(setq o_ang (getorient "\nEnter angle: "))	Operates as the previous example, but does not include the default initial point, and will store the angle information in the memory variable *o_ang*.

GETPOINT

Pauses for user input of a point, and returns the coordinates as a list of real numbers.

REQUIRED ARGUMENTS

None, but two optional arguments, an anchor point and a prompt string, may be used. You may use either one or both; if both are used, the anchor point must appear first, followed by the prompt string.

USAGE

Getpoint is AutoLISP's primary mechanism for receiving point data from the user. It is frequently nested inside a Setq function, as the point information is often stored in memory for subsequent processing.

Alternatively, you may enter the point by picking a point on the screen. If the optional anchor-point argument is provided, the AutoLISP interpreter extends a rubberband line from this point to the intersection of the crosshairs. The point the user picks is returned by the function.

The coordinate point may be entered from the keyboard in the standard fashion, as numbers separated by commas using the current units format, or the decimal equivalent in drawing units.

Getpoint can return either 2-D points or 3-D points, depending on which version of AutoCAD you are using and the settings of the Initget function and/or the FLATLAND system variable. 2-D points are returned as a list of two real numbers; 3-D points are returned as a list of three real numbers. In Release 10, Getpoint returns 3-D points, unless the FLATLAND system variable is not set to zero. If FLATLAND is not set to zero, Getpoint works as in previous versions of AutoCAD, returning 2-D points only, unless the Initget function is available and set to accept 3-D points. In Release 11 and later, Getpoint accepts 3-D points.

Getpoint's prompt argument can be any appropriate string of characters, as seen in the examples ahead. The prompt may also include control characters, the most frequent being the \n character, which places a line feed before the prompt, displaying the prompt on its own line in the Command-prompt area. For clarity, you may want to end the prompt string with a space, as this will separate Auto-CAD's echo of your input from the prompt.

EXAMPLES

(getpoint)	Pauses and accepts input with out a prompt or default initial point. Returns the point as a list of two real numbers after the user has input valid data. For example, if you enter point 5,5,10, this function returns (5.0 5.0 10.0).
(getpoint '(0 0) "\nEnter point: ")	Displays the prompt string and waits for point information; a rubberband line will extend from point 0,0 in the current construction plane.

	When the point is entered, or when coordinates are entered from the keyboard, Getpoint returns the selected point as a list of real numbers.
(setq pt (getpoint "\nEnter point: "))	Functions as the previous example, but does not include the default anchor point, and will store the coordinate list in memory variable *pt*.

GETREAL

Pauses for user input of a real number, and returns the number. If the user enters an integer, it is converted to a real number.

REQUIRED ARGUMENTS

None, but an optional prompt string may be used.

USAGE

Getreal is one of AutoLISP's two interactive mechanisms for retrieving real numbers. (The other is Getdist, which accepts either keyboard input or input by picking two points.)

You may enter the numeric information directly from the keyboard or from a menu; picking points is not allowed using Getreal. If entered from the keyboard, the data is accepted in the current units format as defined by the Units command (Chapter 6), but the data returned by the function is always converted to a real decimal number.

Getreal's prompt argument can be any appropriate string of characters, as seen in the examples ahead. The prompt may also include control characters, the most frequent being the \n character, which places a line feed before the prompt, displaying the prompt on its own line in the Command-prompt area. For clarity, you may want to end the prompt string with a space, as this will separate Auto-CAD's echo of your input from the prompt.

EXAMPLES

(getreal)	Pauses and accepts input without a prompt, and

	returns the numeric information after the user has input valid data.
(getreal "\nEnter a real number: ")	Displays the prompt string, and waits for a real number or integer.

(setq rn (getdist
      "\nEnter a real number: "
)
)
	Operates as the previous example, and stores the real number in the memory variable *rn*.

GETSTRING

Pauses for user input of a string of alphanumeric characters, and returns the string.

REQUIRED ARGUMENTS

None, but an argument for allowing spaces in the string and an optional prompt-string argument may be used. If both are used, the space-character argument must be the first.

USAGE

Getstring is one of AutoLISP's two interactive mechanisms for retrieving string data. (The other is Getkword, which tests the data for validity before accepting it.) Getstring does not automatically test the validity of the data that is entered by the user. Any valid string is accepted and returned.

You may enter the string information directly from the keyboard or from a menu. When the string is displayed, it is shown enclosed in quotation marks.

Normally AutoCAD treats a press of the space bar the same way it treats a press of the Enter key. This is also true when using the Getstring function. However, because spaces are often used in strings, the function provides a mechanism to allow you to enter space characters as part of the string. When a second argument is provided and is not evaluated to nil, the function will assume that space characters are part of the text. When this argument is present, the string may only be terminated with the Enter key.

There is a limit of 132 characters that can be accepted into any one string requested by this function. If you need to input longer strings, you can input them as several short strings and piece them together using the Strcat function.

Getstring's prompt argument can be any appropriate string of characters, as seen in the examples below. The prompt may also include control characters, the most frequent being the \n character, which places a line feed before the prompt, displaying the prompt on its own line in the Command-prompt area. For clarity, you may want to end the prompt string with a space, as this will separate Auto-CAD's echo of your input from the prompt.

EXAMPLES

(getstring)	Pauses and accepts input without a prompt, and returns the string characters entered. If numbers are entered, they are converted to string data. Press Enter or the space bar to end the input.
(getstring T "\nEnter some text: ")	Displays the prompt string and waits for a string to be entered. Because a non-nil argument (in this case, the symbol T) is present, spaces may be included in the entered string.

(setq str (getstring T
    "\nEnter some text: "
)
)
	Operates as the previous example, and will store the string in the memory variable *str*.

GETVAR

Returns the value stored in a system variable.

REQUIRED ARGUMENTS

The name of a system variable, entered as a string enclosed in quotes.

USAGE

Getvar will extract the current value of any system variable, including a read-only variable, for storage in memory variables and AutoLISP routines that make use of such values. It cannot change the value of a system variable; refer to the Setvar function for information on changing the value of system variables.

EXAMPLES

(getvar "CMDECHO")	Returns the current value of the CMDECHO system variable.
(getvar "LASTANGLE")	Returns the ending angle of the last arc entered. (LASTANGLE is a read-only system variable.)

GRAPHSCR

Forces display of the graphics screen on single-screen systems, and returns nil.

REQUIRED ARGUMENTS

None.

USAGE

Graphscr, along with Textscr and Textpage, allows you to control the single-screen display from within AutoLISP routines. It is functionally the same as the Graphscr command.

EXAMPLES

(graphscr)	Changes the display to the graphics screen. If the graphics screen is already displayed, this function has no effect other than to return nil.

GRCLEAR

Temporarily clears the current viewport.

REQUIRED ARGUMENTS

None.

USAGE

When called, Grclear blanks the display screen. In Release 10 and later, if multiple viewports are active, Grclear will blank the current viewport. The contents of the screen may be restored by invoking the Redraw command or calling the Redraw function without arguments.

EXAMPLES

(grclear)   Returns nil, and blanks the screen.

GRDRAW

Draws a temporary line that is not part of AutoCAD's drawing database.

REQUIRED ARGUMENTS

Three arguments in the following order:

1. A starting 2-D or 3-D coordinate point, as a list of either two or three real numbers.
2. An ending 2-D or 3-D coordinate point, also a list of real numbers. (If integers are used, they are interpreted as whole real numbers.)
3. An integer indicating the color of the line.

The third argument, color of the line, may be specified as −1 (in addition to integers corresponding to colors supported by your display device). A color of −1 indicates that the line will be the complementary color of all areas that it crosses, including other visible entities.

Grdraw may include an optional fourth argument, also an integer. If this argument is present and does not equal zero, the line will be drawn as a highlighted line, such as lines might appear when selected for inclusion in a selection set. This optional argument is useful only on display devices that support highlighting of lines.

USAGE

The lines drawn by the Grdraw function appear on the screen, but they are not part of AutoCAD's drawing database. They will be removed by any command or function that causes a redraw of the screen or a drawing regeneration; they cannot be included in selection sets, nor can their construction points be found with object-snap modes.

EXAMPLES

(grdraw '(0 0) '(10 10) 3)   Returns nil, and draws a green line between points 0,0 and 10,10.

(grdraw '(0 0 0) '(10 10 10) 1 1)   Returns nil, and draws a red line between points 0,0,0 and 10,10,10, in highlighted mode.

GRREAD

Pauses and returns a list based on the input from various AutoCAD input devices.

REQUIRED ARGUMENTS

None. However, you may optionally supply any AutoLISP expression that does not return nil. This will cause Grread to return a list of the current location of the intersection of the crosshairs.

USAGE

Grread is a means of determining the exact nature of the user's input, be it a coordinate point, a screen or tablet menu box, a keyboard character, or a pointing-device button number.

The list returned by Grread has two members: an integer indicating which input device was read, and a second member indicating the data that was read. These lists are summarized below:

CODE	DEVICE	DATA
2	Keyboard	ASCII character code for key
3	Pick button	Coordinate point list, in current UCS
4	Screen menu	Line number (top line: 0)
5	Crosshairs	Coordinate point list, in current UCS
6	Pointing-device buttons	Button number (pick button not included; first button after pick: 0)
7	Tablet menu 1	Menu box number
8	Tablet menu 2	Menu box number
9	Tablet menu 3	Menu box number
10	Tablet menu 4	Menu box number
11	Aux1 menu	Button number
12	Pointing-device buttons	Coordinates associated with button number, when the Grread function is called a second time, immediately after a button number was returned while the crosshairs were visible in the graphics screen.

Points returned by this function are 3-D points (in Release 10 only if the FLAT-LAND system variable is not zero) relative to the current UCS, if applicable.

The second element of the list returned by Grread may be extracted using the Cadr function.

Selecting a menu item with Grread returns the screen line number or tablet box number, but does not activate the command sequence for that menu line. Thus, if you have overwritten a screen-menu line using Grtext, you may use Grread to pick the line number.

EXAMPLES

The function

(grread)

called without arguments, pauses and waits for the user to input something. The following are examples of the lists returned by Grread when different forms of input are used:

(2 65)	Keyboard character input (uppercase A)
(4 0)	Screen-menu cell number 0 selected (top line of display)
(4 4)	Screen-menu cell number 4 selected (line 5 on display)
(4 6003)	Pull-down menu number 6 selected, line number 3
(3 (4.0 8.0 0.0))	Pick button selected, coordinates returned
(6 1)	Pointing-device button 0 selected (first button after the pick button)

The line

(grread T)

shows how the intersection of the crosshairs may be read. It returns a list like

(5 (4.0 8.0 0.0))

where the list is the current coordinate location of the crosshairs.

GRTEXT

Displays a text string in either the screen menu, the status line, or the coordinate display areas.

REQUIRED ARGUMENTS

Two arguments in the following order:

1. An integer specifying the location of the text to be displayed.
2. The text string to be displayed.

In addition, Grtext may be used with a third optional argument; an integer that, if positive and not zero, will display the text in highlighted characters on those displays that support such characters. If called with an argument of zero, it will de-highlight the box.

Grtext may be called without arguments. In such a case, it will restore the screen menu, status line, and coordinate display to their normal current status.

USAGE

Integer codes for available locations are as follows:

– 2	Text will be written in the coordinate display area.
– 1	Text will be written in the status display area.
0 and up	Text will be written on a line in the screen-menu area. Menu lines are numbered from top to bottom, beginning with zero for the top line.

Warning: Using the Grtext function can have unwanted side effects—for example, the appearance of random vectors in the display area—on certain display configurations. Still, Grtext does no lasting harm, and if unwanted side effects occur, the display screen can be restored by calling Grtext without arguments, and if necessary, calling the Redraw function without arguments as well.

If writing highlighted text into lines of the screen-menu area, first write the text without highlighting it, and then write the text again with the highlight code included in the function. This minimizes the chance of unwanted side effects in some drawing displays. Only one line may be highlighted at a time. If you highlight another line, the previously highlighted text is displayed normally.

Text displayed in these menu areas is invisible to AutoCAD; that is, it will be overwritten if any command updates the normal data display in these areas. In addition, if you use Grtext to overwrite a line in the screen-menu area, the command sequence for that line will still be activated if you pick that line. To pick the line without activating the command sequence, use the Grread function.

EXAMPLES

The following example creates a new AutoCAD command called Now, which will display the current system time in the coordinate display area. On most systems, the coordinate display will return when the crosshairs are moved, if coordinate tracking is on.

```
(defun c:now(/ x)
    (setq x (rtos (getvar "cdate") 2 6)
        x (strcat "Time: "
                (substr x 10 2) ":"
                (substr x 12 2) ":"
                (substr x 14 2)
            )
        )
    )
    (grtext −2 x)
    (princ)
)
```

If

Evaluates an AutoLISP expression based on whether an initial test expression is evaluated to nil; returns the value of the evaluated expression.

REQUIRED ARGUMENTS

Two AutoLISP expressions, with a third optional expression. The first expression is the test expression. The second expression is the "do-if-true" expression, evaluated only if the test expression does not return nil. A third expression, the "do-if-nil" expression, is evaluated only if the test expression returns nil.

USAGE

The If function enables the AutoLISP interpreter to make choices. When the If function contains only two argument expressions, it will choose to evaluate or skip the second expression, based on the results of evaluating the first expression; that is, if the first expression returns a value the second expression is evaluated. Otherwise, the second expression is ignored and the If function returns nil. When the If function contains three argument expressions, it chooses between the second and third based on the results of evaluating the first; that is, if the first expression returns a value, the second expression is evaluated and the third is ignored. However, if the first expression returns nil, the second expression is ignored and the third expression is evaluated.

Because the If function can only choose between two functions, its value would seem limited if you wanted it to evaluate or ignore a series of functions. However, the Progn function is often used to evaluate a series of functions as a single function, and can be used effectively inside the If function as either the "do-if-true" or "do-if-nil" function. Refer to the discussion of the Progn function for details.

EXAMPLES

```
(if ( = (getvar "CMDECHO") 1)
   (setvar "CMDECHO" 0)
)
```

In the above example, the Getvar function returns the current value of the CMDECHO system variable, and the = function evaluates whether the setting of the CMDECHO system variable is 1. The If function tests the result. If CMDECHO is set to 1, the test expression returns T, and the following expression is evaluated, setting CMDECHO to zero. Otherwise, the expression is ignored, leaving CMDECHO set to its current value.

```
(if ( = (getint "\nEnter a 1: ") 1)
   (prompt "\nCongratulations!")
   (prompt "\nNope.")
)
```

In the above example, the Getint function prompts you to enter a 1, and returns the integer you enter. The = function evaluates whether the integer returned by Getint equals 1. The If function tests the result returned by the = function. If you entered 1, the = function returns T, and the first Prompt function is evaluated, while the other Prompt function is ignored. If the = function returns nil, the first Prompt function is ignored, and the second one is evaluated instead.

INITGET

Controls the validity of responses to the first "Get" function that follows.

REQUIRED ARGUMENTS

At least one of the following arguments:

1. A control-bit integer indicating what data types are valid input for the next "Get" function.
2. A string containing valid keywords that will be accepted by the "Get" function, in addition to its usual form of input—for example, a special character or keyword in addition to numbers or points in response to the Getdist function.

USAGE

Initget is available in AutoCAD Version 2.6 and later.

The following are valid control-bit integer arguments to the Initget function:

1 Do not allow null input; that is, do not accept a press of the Enter key or space bar without a value.

2 Do not allow zero input.

4 Do not allow negative numbers.

8 Allow points to be selected outside the drawing limits. (This temporary override of limits-checking is needed only if limits-checking is currently set.)

16 Return points as 3-D points rather than 2-D points (for Auto-CAD versions prior to Release 10, or in Release 10 if the FLATLAND system variable is not set to zero). In Release 11 and later, functions that return points always return 3-D points.

32 Use a highlighted line for rubberband lines (if the display device controls the Advanced User Interface).

You may combine various validity checks by adding these integers together. For example, 48 will combine returning 3-D points with displaying a highlighted rubberband line. For clarity's sake when reading the AutoLISP routine, you may show what integers have been combined by specifying them within the + function. For example,

  (+ 1 8)

can be used as the control-bit argument. It returns integer 9, disallowing null input and accepting points outside the drawing limits.

Various Get functions will ignore certain control bits. Largely, this is a matter of common sense. (Getint, for instance, accepts only integers and ignores control bit 16, which returns point data as 3-D rather than 2-D points.) The control bits ignored by the different Get functions are summarized below:

- Getangle ignores 4 (do not accept negative numbers), 8 (override limits-checking), 16.

- Getcorner ignores 2 (do not allow zero), 4 (disallow negative numbers).

- Getdist ignores 8 (override limits-checking).

- Getint ignores 8 (override limits-checking), 16 (return 3-D points instead of 2-D), 32 (use highlighted rubberband line).

- Getkword ignores 2 (do not allow zero), 4 (do not accept negative numbers), 8 (override limits-checking), 16 (return 3-D points instead of 2-D), 32 (use highlighted rubberband line).

- Getorient ignores 4 (do not accept negative numbers), 8 (override limits-checking), 16 (return 3-D points instead of 2-D).
- Getpoint ignores 2 (do not allow zero), 4 (disallow negative numbers).
- Getreal ignores 8 (override limits-checking), 16 (return 3-D points instead of 2-D), 32 (use highlighted rubberband line).
- Getstring ignores all control bits.
- Getvar ignores all control bits.

The string of valid keywords contains optional responses that may be accepted by the Get function in addition to its regular form of input; for example:

```
(initget "Last Quit")
(setq angvar (getangle "\nLast/Quit/<angle>: "))
```

In this example, the Getangle function will accept all valid forms of input for angles (numbers or two points), and in addition will accept the keywords Last and Quit, storing whatever is returned by Getangle in the memory variable *angvar.* This memory variable can then be tested to perform alternate processing based on its contents. For instance, if *angvar* is equal to "Last", the AutoLISP routine might process based on the contents of the LASTANGLE system variable; or, if *angvar* is equal to "Quit", the AutoLISP routine might ignore further processing. It is up to you as the AutoLISP programmer to write the code that will manage the possibilities that result.

The individual keywords in a keyword string are separated by spaces. Thus, any number of keywords may be used in a single keyword string.

The use of uppercase and lowercase in the keyword string is important. When a keyword contains both uppercase and lowercase letters, as in the example just presented, the user may enter either the entire word or only that portion of the word that appears in uppercase in the keyword string. In the above example, therefore, the user may enter either **L** or **Last** for "Last", or **Q** or **Quit** for "Quit".

Notice that although case is important in determining valid keyword responses, the actual entry by the user is not case-sensitive. A keyword returned by the Get function will appear just as it does in the Initget function's keyword string. For instance, with the current example, the user could enter any of the following:

- Uppercase or lowercase **L**.
- The keyword **Last** using any combination of uppercase and lowercase letters.

Upon receiving this input, the Getangle function will always return "Last", just as it appears in the Initget function's keyword string. Thus, further processing to determine if a keyword was entered need only be based on how that keyword appears in the keyword-string argument, not on how the user may have selected it.

EXAMPLES

```
(defun C:DEMO ( / angvar)
   (initget ( + 1 32) "Last Quit")
   (setq angvar (getangle "\nLast/Quit/<angle>: "))
   (cond ( ( = angvar "Last")
            (prompt "\nValue of LASTANGLE: ")
            (princ (angtos (getvar "LASTANGLE")))
          )
          ( ( = angvar "Quit")
            (prompt "Quitting...")
          )
          ( T
            (prompt "\nAngle entered: ")
            (princ (angtos angvar))
          )
   )
   (princ)
)
```

The above example creates an AutoCAD command that demonstrates how the Initget function works and how the results returned by a Get function may be used when keywords are part of the valid input. In this AutoLISP-defined Demo command, the Cond function will evaluate one of three possible responses based on what is returned by Getangle: displaying the value of the LASTANGLE system variable, quitting, or displaying the angle that was entered. In real-world processing, the prompt functions inside the Cond function would be replaced by other, more practical functions that make use of the results returned by Getangle.

INTERS

Returns the intersection point of two lines formed by four points supplied as the arguments of the function.

REQUIRED ARGUMENTS

Four arguments that must be points. An optional fifth argument may be supplied. If the fifth argument is nil, the lines are extended infinitely in order to return the intersection point. In the absence of the fifth optional argument, or if the fifth argument is present and is not evaluated to nil, Inters returns the intersection point only if the line segments actually intersect. If not, the function returns nil.

USAGE

The Inters function can be used in a wide variety of routines, whenever line locations are known and the intersection point is needed. The first two arguments are the endpoints of one line segment; the second two arguments are the endpoints of the other line segment.

The endpoints of the line segments may be supplied as quoted lists of real numbers, or as the result of other functions that return points. The lines themselves do not have to be present in the drawing; that is, Inters will return an intersection point, if one exists, whenever four valid points are supplied as its arguments.

If a fifth argument is present and is evaluated to nil, both lines are considered infinite, and the intersection point is returned (unless they are parallel, in which case nil is returned).

In Release 10 and later, 3-D points may be supplied, and a 3-D point is returned. Earlier versions that support 3-D points will accept 3-D point arguments, but the lines formed are projected onto the current construction plane, and the intersection in the current construction plane is returned. This will also happen in Release 10 if the FLATLAND system variable is not set to zero.

EXAMPLES

(inters '(0 0 0) '(5 5 5) '(5 0 0) '(0 5 5))	Returns (2.5 2.5 2.5). If FLATLAND is not equal to zero, or if you are using AutoCAD Release 9 or earlier, this example returns (2.5 2.5).
(inters '(0 0 0) '(1 1 1) '(5 0 0) '(0 5 5))	Returns nil, because the line segments do not actually intersect.
(inters '(0 0 0) '(1 1 1) '(5 0 0) '(0 5 5) nil)	Returns (2.5 2.5 2.5), because the fifth nil argument indicates that the lines are infinite in length.

ITOA

Converts an integer to a string, and returns the string.

REQUIRED ARGUMENTS

An integer. If a real number is supplied, it will produce an error message.

USAGE

Itoa is useful when an integer must be handled as a string—for example, when combining an integer with other string data. Int will accept 16-bit and 32-bit integers, depending on the system you are using. Refer to Chapter 16 for details regarding integers.

EXAMPLES

The lines

```
(setq i (getint "\nInteger: "))
(strcat "\Integer entered: " (itoa i))
```

return ''Integer entered:'' plus the integer in memory variable *i*. In this example, the integer stored to memory variable *i* can only be combined with a string using the Strcat function after it has been converted to a string with the Itoa function.

LAMBDA

Applies a list of arguments to a series of expressions, and returns the result of the last expression.

REQUIRED ARGUMENTS

Two arguments, the first being a list of variables, and the second being a series of functions that use the variables in the list.

USAGE

The Lambda function is related to the Defun function, in that it creates a new function by evaluating a series of functions and returning a result. Unlike Defun, however, Lambda creates no function name, and thus does not store the function it creates in memory. Global and local variables are irrelevant, since the function itself is not stored anywhere. The function created by Lambda must be evaluated immediately to be useful; thus, a function created by Lambda is usually found within the Apply or Mapcar function, where the new function can be immediately applied to a given list of arguments.

Lambda is useful in situations where it would make sense to define a new function, but the function is only needed once in a long routine, node space is at a premium, and storing the new function isn't necessary.

EXAMPLES

The variables used in a function defined by Lambda must be consistent with the arguments to which Lambda's defined function will be applied. This example uses Lambda to define a function that multiplies three numbers together, nested inside a Mapcar function. The Mapcar function, therefore, supplies it with argument lists containing three numbers each.

```
(mapcar '(lambda (x y z)
        (* x y z)
     )
     '(1 2 3) '(4 5 6) '(7 8 9)
)
```

This example returns (28 80 162), a list of results obtained by applying the Lambda function to each of the argument lists.

LAST

Returns the last member of a list.

REQUIRED ARGUMENTS

A single list, which may contain other lists.

USAGE

The Last function is used when the last item in a list is desired. It is practical with general data lists when the meaning of the last member will be consistent. Last is not a useful function for returning coordinate information, since the coordinate point list may be 2-D, containing two members; or 3-D, containing three members; use the Cadr or Caddr function instead.

EXAMPLES

(last '(1 2 3 4))	Returns 4
(last '(1 2 (3 4)))	Returns (3 4)

LENGTH

Returns the number of members in a list, always an integer.

REQUIRED ARGUMENTS

A single list.

USAGE

The Length function is used as a means to determine how many members a list contains. For example, this information might be useful in determining the number of times a looping function must repeat when operating on the members of a data list that could be of any length.

EXAMPLES

(length '(1 7 9 31))	Returns 4
(length '((1 7) (9 31)))	Returns 2

LIST

Returns a list containing its arguments.

REQUIRED ARGUMENTS

At least one argument, which may be any valid AutoLISP expression or atom.

USAGE

List is often used to create coordinate point lists from two or three real numbers, but it can create any form of list, with the exception of dotted pairs. Use the Cons function (Chapter 19) to create dotted pairs.

EXAMPLES

(list 5.5 12.0 6.5)	Returns (5.5 12.0 6.5)
(list "dog" "cat")	Returns ("dog" "cat")
(list '(1 2) 3)	Returns ((1 2) 3)

LISTP

Tests to determine if its argument is a list; returns T if a list, or nil otherwise.

REQUIRED ARGUMENTS

One argument.

USAGE

The Listp function is often used to determine if the contents of a memory variable are a list, in situations where one form or another of processing will be used depending on whether a variable is a list or an atom.

An exception occurs with regard to the symbol nil. AutoLISP, like most forms of LISP, interprets nil as an empty list, as well as an atom. Thus, if a memory variable is bound to nil and passed as an argument to the Listp function, the function will return T.

EXAMPLES

(listp '(1 2 3))	Returns T
(listp 1)	Returns nil

LOAD

Loads an AutoLISP file into memory, evaluates the expressions in the file, and returns the result of the last expression.

REQUIRED ARGUMENTS

The name of a file with the extension LSP, contained within quotes. The file extension is never used; LSP is assumed. In Release 10 and later, a second optional argument may be provided: a string that will be displayed by AutoCAD if the loading process is unsuccessful for any reason.

USAGE

Load is the means by which ASCII files of AutoLISP routines are made usable by the AutoLISP interpreter. All AutoLISP files must be loaded with this function before they can be used (except ACAD.LSP, which is automatically loaded at the start of each drawing session). Refer to Chapter 16 for more details on this function.

EXAMPLES

(load "FILENAME")	Loads FILENAME.LSP into memory and returns the result of evaluating the last expression in the file. In Release 10 and later, AutoCAD will look for FILENA-ME.LSP along AutoCAD's search path.
(load "FILENAME" "bad LISP file")	Loads FILENAME.LSP to memory and returns the result of evaluating the last expression in the file. If for any reason the file cannot be properly loaded, AutoCAD will display the message, "bad LISP file".

Log

Returns the natural logarithm of a number.

REQUIRED ARGUMENTS

A single number.

USAGE

The Log function is used to compute natural logarithms in routines that require them.

EXAMPLES

(log 12)	Returns 2.48491
(log pi)	Returns 1.44473

Logand

Returns the integer resulting from a Boolean AND comparison of a series of integers.

REQUIRED ARGUMENTS

At least two integers. Real numbers are not allowed. The Logand function will accept and return 32-bit integers on 32-bit systems. Refer to Chapter 16 for more details about AutoLISP's integer handling.

USAGE

Refer to the Boole function for an explanation of bit comparisons of integers. Logand is the functional equivalent of the Boole function when Boole's first argument is 1; that is, each result bit is set to 1 when all corresponding bits in the arguments are also 1.

EXAMPLES

(logand 12 24)	Returns 8
(logand 6 24 96)	Returns 0

LOGIOR

Returns the integer resulting from a Boolean OR comparison of a series of integers.

REQUIRED ARGUMENTS

At least two integers. Real numbers are not allowed. The Logior function will accept and return 32-bit integers on 32-bit systems. Refer to Chapter 16 for more details on AutoLISP's integer handling.

USAGE

Refer to the Boole function for an explanation of bit comparisons of integers. Logior is the functional equivalent of the Boole function when Boole's first argument is 7; that is, each result bit is set to 1 if any one or all of the corresponding bits in the arguments are also 1.

EXAMPLES

(logior 12 24)	Returns 28
(logior 6 24 96)	Returns 126

LSH

Returns the integer that results from a bit-shift to the bits of an integer.

REQUIRED ARGUMENTS

The integer on which the bit-shift is to be performed, and the number of bit places that are shifted.

USAGE

If the second argument of Lsh is positive, the bits are shifted to the left. If the second argument is negative, the bits are shifted to the right. If the top bit changes (0 to 1, or 1 to 0), the sign of the integer changes.

EXAMPLES

(lsh 12 2)	Returns 48
(lsh 12 −2)	Returns 3
(lsh 12000 2)	Returns 48000
(lsh 12000 −2)	Returns 3000

Mapcar

Returns a list of results from applying a function to a given list of arguments.

REQUIRED ARGUMENTS

The name of a function and at least one list of arguments for that function.

USAGE

Mapcar is handy when a function must be used on several different sets of arguments. The number of argument lists supplied to Mapcar must equal the number of arguments required by the function. And the number of atoms in each list should be the same, so that Mapcar will apply the function consistently to the atoms in each argument list. The upcoming examples demonstrate this.

The functions passed to Mapcar as its first argument may be predefined Auto-LISP functions or user-defined functions. You may also create a function on the spot and use it as Mapcar's first argument, without bothering to define it separately with the Defun function; use the Lambda function to define a one-time custom function and pass it to Mapcar as its first argument. Refer to the Lambda function for an example of this.

EXAMPLES

(mapcar 'strcat '("A" "B" "C") '("1" "2" "3"))	Returns ("A1" "B2" "C3")

The following example uses Mapcar to update a 3-D coordinate point. It adds 1 unit along the x-axis and 2 units along the y-axis, and keeps the z-axis the same:

    (mapcar ' + '(12.5 7.75 8.75)   Returns (13.5 9.75 8.75)
    '(1 2 0))

MAX

Returns the largest of a series of numbers.

REQUIRED ARGUMENTS

Any number of arguments, but they must be real numbers or integers.

USAGE

Max is used in situations where maximum values must be obtained. Notice that the numbers supplied to Max are not contained in a list, but rather are a simple series of arguments separated by spaces.

EXAMPLES

    (max 1 7 2.5 4.75 3)   Returns 7
    (max 1 –7 2.5 4.75 3)   Returns 4.75

MEMBER

Searches a list for a given expression or atom, and returns a list beginning with the found expression plus any members of the original list that appear after the found member. If the member is not found, this function returns nil.

REQUIRED ARGUMENTS

A single list of data.

USAGE

Member is AutoLISP's list-searching function. It can determine whether a particular atom is found on a list, and in combination with the Car function it can help extract an atom from any position within a list. The upcoming examples demonstrate this.

EXAMPLES

(member '1 '(7 8 3 1 5 6 12))   Returns (1 5 6 12)

You can search for and (if found) extract a member from a list as follows:

(car (member '1 '(7 8 3 1 5 6 12)))   Returns 1

If the Member function does not find the given atom, both functions return nil, as follows:

(car (member '9 '(7 8 3 1 5 6 12)))   Returns nil

MENUCMD

Switches among the submenus of the currently active AutoCAD menu, and always returns nil.

REQUIRED ARGUMENTS

A string that consists of a main-section letter, an equal sign, and a submenu in the currently active menu. Only one string is allowed.

USAGE

Menucmd allows AutoLISP routines to display submenus that relate to responses required during any point in the processing. In other words, by using Menucmd, you can coordinate menus and AutoLISP routines.

The string argument required by Menucmd mimics the submenu reference syntax in the menu file, except that the leading dollar sign is not used. The submenu display syntax for Menucmd thus takes the form

MAIN = SUBMENU

where *MAIN* is a letter corresponding to one of AutoCAD's standard menu sections, and *SUBMENU* corresponds to a valid submenu name within the section.

The main section is referenced by a single letter, combined with a number where appropriate, as follows:

A1	Aux1 menu
B	Buttons menu
I	Icon menu
P1–P10	Pull-down menus 1 through 10
S	Screen menu
T1–T4	Tablet menus 1 through 4

The following examples demonstrate this syntax in use.

EXAMPLES

(menucmd "S=LINE")	Displays the Line submenu of the screen menu.
(menucmd "S=")	Displays the previously displayed screen submenu.
(menucmd "S=S")	Displays the AutoCAD root menu.

The following will work if your display supports the Advanced User Interface.

menucmd "P3=*")	Displays the pull-down menu number 3.
(menucmd "I=hatch3")	Activates the Hatch3 icon submenu.
(menucmd "I=*")	Displays the activated icon submenu.

MIN

Returns the smallest of a series of numbers.

REQUIRED ARGUMENTS

Any number of arguments, but they must be real numbers or integers.

USAGE

Min is used in situations where minimum values must be obtained. Notice that the numbers supplied to Min are not contained in a list, but rather are a simple series of arguments separated by spaces.

EXAMPLES

(min 1 7 2.5 4.75 3)	Returns 1
(min 1 –7 2.5 4.75 3)	Returns – 7

MINUSP

Tests to determine whether a number is negative (less than zero). Returns T if the number is negative, or nil otherwise.

REQUIRED ARGUMENTS

A single number, either real or integer.

USAGE

Minusp is used in situations where one form or another of processing will take place depending on whether a variable has a negative value or not.

EXAMPLES

(minusp – 1)	Returns T
(minusp 1)	Returns nil

Not

Evaluates an expression and returns T if the expression returns nil. Otherwise, this function returns nil.

REQUIRED ARGUMENTS

An AutoLISP expression.

USAGE

The Not function tests the validity of expressions that are expected to be evaluated as nil, or "not true." It is used within control functions, such as If and While, that make processing choices based on the results of evaluating test expressions.

EXAMPLES

(not (= "dog" "cat"))	Returns T
(not (= "dog" "dog"))	Returns nil

Nth

Returns the member of a list found in a specified position.

REQUIRED ARGUMENTS

An integer indicating the position number within the list, and a list from which a member is to be extracted.

USAGE

The Nth function can be used to extract a member of a list when the position of the member is known. Positions within a list are numbered from left to right starting with zero; that is, the first position is number 0, the second position is number 1, the third is 2, and so on. If the position number specified by the first argument of Nth is greater than the highest position number in the list, Nth returns nil.

EXAMPLES

(nth 5 '(1 2 3 4 5 6 7))	Returns 6
(nth 9 '(1 2 3 4 5 6 7))	Returns nil

NULL

Evaluates an expression and returns T if the expression returns nil. Otherwise, this function returns nil.

REQUIRED ARGUMENTS

An AutoLISP expression.

USAGE

Null is used to test the validity of expressions that are expected to be evaluated as nil. It is functionally the same as the Not function.

EXAMPLES

(null "dog")	Returns nil (because "dog" is a string constant, not a nil value)
(null (= "dog" "cat"))	Returns T
(null (= "dog" "dog"))	Returns nil
(null xyz)	Returns T, unless "xyz" is a memory variable bound to some value, in which case it returns nil

NUMBERP

Tests to determine whether an expression is a number; returns T if so, or nil otherwise.

REQUIRED ARGUMENTS

A single AutoLISP expression.

USAGE

The Numberp function is used in situations where one form or another of processing will take place depending on whether a variable has been bound to a string or number value. Numberp will return T if the expression is evaluated to either a real number or an integer.

EXAMPLES

(numberp – 1.3715)	Returns T
(numberp ''Last'')	Returns nil

OPEN

Opens a file on disk for reading the data it contains, or for storing data written to disk. If a file is successfully opened for either reading or writing, the file descriptor is returned. If for any reason a file cannot be opened, this function returns nil.

REQUIRED ARGUMENTS

A string containing the name of the file to be opened, and a string indicating how the file is to be used—for reading, for writing, or for adding to its contents.

USAGE

The file-name argument can be any valid file name. If a file extension is included, it is separated from the file name with a period. The name is enclosed within quotes; for example:

''filename.ext''

Subdirectory names and/or a drive letter may be included as part of the filename, separated from the file name by forward slashes; for example:

''c:/acad/files/filename.ext''

A single backslash (\) is not allowed, as the AutoLISP interpreter will mistake it for a control character; however, you may use two backslashes to separate subdirectory names from file names; for example:

"c:\\acad\\files\\filename.ext"

If no drive letter or subdirectory name is specified, the currently logged subdirectory will be used.

The second argument may be one of three lowercase letters, indicating the *file mode* (how the file will be used). These letters are also also enclosed in quotation marks:

"a"   If this argument follows the file name, the file is opened in *append mode.* Any data written to the file will be appended to the end of any data currently found there. If no file with the given name exists, the file is created with no data, and data may be written into it. This mode is available in AutoCAD Version 2.6 and later.

> *Warning:* Some DOS programs write files with a Control-Z or "end-of-file" character at the end. If you open one of these files in append mode, the data will be appended, but after the Control-Z character. Later, when such a file is read, the data after the Control-Z marker will not be found. You cannot append data to files ending with a Control-Z character unless you first strip away the character using a special utility designed to do that.

"r"   If this argument follows the file name, the file is opened in *read mode.* Data may be read from the file, but no data may be written to it. If the file is not found, the Open function returns nil.

"w"   If this argument follows the file name, the file is opened in *write mode.* Data may be written to the file; however, if the file already exists at the time the Open function is called, the previous data contained in the existing file is destroyed. The file descriptor returned by the Open function is a special data type and cannot be accessed directly by AutoLISP functions. It takes the form

<File #nnnnnnnn>

where *nnnnnnnn* is a number assigned internally by AutoCAD. In order to make use of the file after it has been opened, the file descriptor must be stored in a memory variable. Subsequent processing can then call the file by means of the memory-variable name, not by the file descriptor.

EXAMPLES

(setq file1 (open "file1.txt" "r"))   Returns the file descriptor for "file1.txt" and stores it in memory variable *file1.*

	"file1.txt" must be on the currently logged subdirectory, or nil will be returned. The data in this file may be read, but the file may not be written to.
(setq file2 (open "c:/acad/file2.txt" "w"))	Returns the file descriptor for "c:/acad/file2.txt" and stores it in memory variable *file2*. If the file already exists, it is completely overwritten. If not, it is created.
(setq file3 (open "c:file3.txt" "a"))	Returns the file descriptor for "c:file3.txt" on the currently logged subdirectory of drive C, and stores it in memory variable *file3*. If the file already exists, the data written to it is appended to the end of the current file. If the file is not found, it is created, and the data is added to it.

OR

Returns T if any of its expressions does not return nil. If all return nil, the Or function returns nil.

REQUIRED ARGUMENTS

A series of any number of valid expressions.

USAGE

The Or function is used to evaluate a series of expressions. In this way, an AutoLISP routine can process if-then-else decisions, conditional decisions, and controlled loops based on complex criteria.

EXAMPLES

(or (= 1 1.0) (/= 2 2))	Returns T, because one expression returns T

(or (= 1 2) (= 2 3))	Returns nil, because both expressions return nil
(or (= 1 2) (+ 1 1))	Returns T, because the expression (+ 1 1) does not return nil
(setq x 0 y nil)	
(or x y)	Returns T, because one expression is not nil.
(setq x nil y nil)	
(or x y)	Returns nil, because both expressions are nil.

OSNAP

Returns a point that results when a given object-snap override, or set of such overrides, is applied to a point supplied as an argument.

REQUIRED ARGUMENTS

A coordinate point followed by a string containing a list of valid object-snap overrides.

USAGE

Osnap is a means of applying object-snap overrides while in AutoLISP—for example, in situations where the coordinates of a construction point are needed but currently unknown. When you supply a set of known coordinates plus the desired object-snap mode to this function, the correct set of coordinates will be returned. Refer to Chapter 7 for details regarding object-snap overrides.

By including all desired object-snap modes in the string, separated by commas, you may use more than one object-snap mode at one time.

Note: In AutoCAD Releases 9 and 10, if a 3-D point is supplied as the first argument, a 3-D point is returned; if a 2-D point is supplied, a 2-D point is returned. In Release 11 and later, 3-D points are always returned.

The reliability of the Osnap function depends on a number of factors: the size of the object-snap aperture, the current 3-D view, the current value of the FLAT-LAND system variable (in Release 10), the presence of other entities nearby, and whether more than one construction point falls within range. In order for this function to work reliably, all these factors should be carefully controlled. Generally you will have more predictable results (but more programming work to do) if you calculate needed coordinate points by other means—the Polar function, the Inters function, or mathematical formulae. Use this function when all other means fail.

EXAMPLES

(osnap '(0 0 0) ''int'')	Returns the intersection point found nearest to point 0,0,0. If no intersection point is found, it returns nil.
(osnap '(1 1) ''end,mid,quad'')	Returns the endpoint nearest to point 1,1. If no endpoint is found, it returns the nearest midpoint. If no midpoint is found, it returns the nearest quadrant. If none of these construction points is found, it returns nil.

POLAR

Returns a coordinate point relative to a given reference point, at a given angle and a given distance.

REQUIRED ARGUMENTS

Three arguments in the following order:

1. A starting reference point.
2. A reference angle, expressed in radians.
3. A reference distance from the starting reference point.

USAGE

The first argument to this function, the starting reference point, may be a quoted list of numbers or a function returning a point. The next argument, the reference angle, must be expressed in radians. The last argument is a distance, which can be a number or a function returning a number. The point returned by the Polar function is a list of real numbers indicating the coordinate point located at the given angle and distance from the reference point.

In versions of AutoCAD that support 3-D, a 3-D point may be supplied as the first argument to this function.

In Release 10, the point returned by the Polar function is a 3-D point unless the FLATLAND system variable is not zero.

The angle argument is always assumed to be in the current construction plane, with angle zero as the positive x-axis, and increasing in a counterclockwise direction. The point returned, therefore, is always located in the current construction plane.

EXAMPLES

(polar '(0 0 0) 0.785398 7.07107) Returns (5.0 5.0 0), assuming that the current construction plane is the world coordinate system. Note that 0.785398 is 45 degrees in radians.

The following example uses Get functions to establish a point relative to the entered point:

```
(setq r_pt
  (polar
    (setq_ r_pt(getpoint "\Enter the base point: "))
    (getangle r_pt "\nEnter the reference angle: ")
    (getdist r_pt "\nEnter the offset distance: ")
  )
)
```

PRIN1

Print the AutoLISP expression supplied as its argument in the Command-prompt area, or writes it to a file; returns the expression.

REQUIRED ARGUMENTS

None, but an AutoLISP expression is usually supplied. An optional argument may be added following the expression: a memory variable, bound to a file descriptor of a disk file that has been opened for writing. Refer to the Open and Close functions for details on opening files.

USAGE

If the optional file argument is present, Prin1 writes the expression to the file just as it would appear on the screen.

If an expression is quoted, the exact expression is written; if the quoted expression is a list, the parentheses surrounding the list are included. If the expression is a string, the string is displayed on the screen and/or written to the file including its surrounding quotation marks.

Any control characters in a string will be interpreted literally; that is, they will not be evaluated. For example, "\n" in a string will appear on the screen and be written to a file as a backslash character followed by a lowercase *n*, not as a line feed.

EXAMPLES

The line

```
(prin1 "\nPrint this line")
```

returns "\nPrint this line" and displays "\nPrint this line" on the screen. Thus, the display in the Command-prompt area would appear as follows:

```
"\nPrint this line""\nPrint this line"
```

This is not particularly readable; the following function, which calls the Princ function after the Prin1 function, works better:

```
(defun ptest( )
    (prin1 "\nPrint this line")
    (princ)
)
```

This returns

```
"\nPrint this line"
```

Refer to the Princ function for more details on using Princ as the last function in a series.

The following example opens FILE1.TST in append mode on the currently logged subdirectory, writes "Print this line" to the file, and closes it:

```
(setq file1 (open "file1.tst" "a"))
(prin1 "Print this line" file1)
(close file1)
```

PRINC

Prints an expression supplied as its argument in the Command-prompt area or writes it to a file; returns the expression. Princ is like Prin1, except that it evaluates control characters.

REQUIRED ARGUMENTS

None, but Princ is often accompanied by at least one optional argument: an expression or string to be returned and either displayed in the Command-prompt area or written to a file. A second optional argument may be added following the expression: a memory variable, bound to a file descriptor of a disk file that has been opened for writing. Refer to the Open and Close functions for details on opening files.

USAGE

If the optional file argument is present, Princ writes the expression to the file just as it would appear on the screen.

If the expression is evaluated, the result of the expression is printed. If the expression is quoted, the exact expression is written; if the quoted expression is a list, the parentheses surrounding the list are included. If the expression is a string, the string is displayed on the screen and/or written to the file without including its surrounding quotation marks.

Any control characters in a string will be evaluated before they are displayed or written. For example, "\n" in a string will appear on the screen or be written to a file as a line feed, but the control character will appear in "\n" format in the string returned by the function.

Princ is often used without arguments as the last function in a series. When Princ is used without arguments, it will display a null character in the Command-prompt area. This is useful when a series of functions would otherwise display the result of the last function in the Command-prompt area.

EXAMPLES

The line

```
(princ "\nPrint this line")
```

displays a line feed followed by "Print this line" in the Command-prompt area of the screen, and returns "\nPrint this line". Thus, the display in the Command-prompt area would appear as follows:

```
Print this line"\nPrint this line"
```

This is not particularly readable; the following function works better:

```
(defun ptest( )
   (princ "\nPrint this line")
   (princ)
)
```

This returns:

```
Print this line
```

The following example opens FILE1.TST in append mode on the currently logged subdirectory, writes a line feed followed by "Print this line" to the file, and closes it:

```
(setq file1 (open "file1.tst" "a"))
(prin1 "\nPrint this line" file1)
(close file1)
```

PRINT

Displays a line feed, an AutoLISP expression supplied as its argument, and a space in the Command-prompt area; returns the expression. Alternatively, it may write the same sequence to file.

REQUIRED ARGUMENTS

None, in which case Print will return a single line feed. Print is usually provided with an AutoLISP expression. An optional memory-variable argument may be added following the expression; this memory variable must be bound to a file descriptor of a disk file that has been opened for writing. Refer to the Open and Close functions for details on opening files.

USAGE

If the optional file argument is present, Print writes the line-feed/expression/space sequence to the file just as it would appear on the screen. Print is therefore useful when writing a series of strings to separate lines in a file, without requiring that you explicitly indicate the line-feed or return character for each new line.

If the argument expression is a Quote function, the quoted argument is written; if it is a quoted list, the parentheses surrounding the list are written. If the expression is a string, the string is displayed on the screen and/or written to the file including its surrounding quotation marks.

Any control characters in a string will be interpreted literally; that is, they will not be evaluated. For example, "\n" in a string will appear on the screen or be written to a file as a backslash character followed by a lowercase *n*, not as a line feed.

EXAMPLES

The line

```
(print "Print this line")
```

returns "Print this line" and displays a line feed followed by "Print this line" plus an extra space on the screen. Thus, the display in the Command-prompt area would appear as follows:

"Print this line" "Print this line"

Obviously, this double display is not usually desirable; the following function, which calls the Princ function after the Print function, works better:

```
(defun ptest( )
    (print "Print this line")
    (princ)
)
```

This returns:

"Print this line"

Refer to the Princ function for more details on using Princ as the last function in a series.

The following example opens FILE1.TST in append mode on the currently logged subdirectory, writes a line feed followed by "Print this line" to the file, and closes it:

```
(setq file1 (open "file1.tst" "a"))
(print "Print this line" file1)
(close file1)
```

The following function will clear a 25-line text screen:

```
(repeat 25 (print))
```

PROGN

Evaluates a series of expressions and returns the last expression evaluated.

REQUIRED ARGUMENTS

Any number of valid AutoLISP expressions that are capable of being evaluated in sequence.

USAGE

Progn allows you to treat a series of expressions as if they were a single expression. For example, it is commonly used within an If function, which allows only a single expression to be evaluated after the test expression.

EXAMPLES

```
(setq a (getint "\nInteger 1: ")
     b getint "\nInteger 2: ")
)
(if ( = a b)
  (progn
    (prompt "\nThey are equal: ")
    (princ a)
    (princ " = ")
    (princ b)
  )
  (progn
    (prompt "\nThey are not equal: ")
    (princ a)
    (princ " / = ")
    (princ b)
  )
)
(princ)
```

PROMPT

Displays a string supplied as its argument in the Command-prompt area; returns nil.

REQUIRED ARGUMENTS

A string.

USAGE

Prompt does what it says—it displays prompts. It can be used any time you want to deliver a message to the user.

EXAMPLES

The line

```
(prompt "\nProcessing complete")
```

returns nil and displays ''Processing completenil'' in the Command-prompt area. When a prompt is the last function is a series, the word *nil* will be displayed on the screen following the prompt. To eliminate the display of *nil* following the prompt (or the unwanted display of data returned by any final function in a series), follow the function with the Princ function, as follows:

```
(defun ptest( )
    (prompt "\nProcessing complete")
    (princ)
)
```

Entering

```
(ptest)
```

returns "Processing complete" without the trailing *nil*.

QUOTE

Returns the expression supplied as its argument without attempting to evaluate it.

REQUIRED ARGUMENTS

Any string of characters or numbers not including a space, or any single list of data enclosed in parentheses.

USAGE

The Quote function is useful in situations where a list of data, memory-variable name, function name, or other expression must be passed to the AutoLISP interpreter without evaluation. Examples of such usage are:

- When coordinate points must be passed as arguments to functions in the form of a list of real numbers.
- When a memory-variable name, not the value it represents, is the argument of the function.
- When lists are being combined with other lists.
- When function names are the arguments of another function, but are not to be evaluated at the same time.

Note: The apostrophe character can be used as a shorthand version of this function. Refer to the ' function for examples.

If you are quoting a list that contains other lists, the inner lists will not be evaluated.

EXAMPLES

(quote (0 0 0))	Returns (0 0 0)
(quote (23 (a b)))	Returns (23 (a b))
(quote a)	Returns a

READ

Returns the first atom or list from a string of atoms or lists.

REQUIRED ARGUMENTS

A string.

USAGE

The Read function operates on strings the way the Car function operates on lists; that is, it returns the first atom it finds in any string. If the string contains lists, the first list is returned. If the string contains characters, the characters up to the first space are returned.

Character strings returned by Read are not surrounded by quotation marks. If you pass them as arguments to other functions, the AutoLISP interpreter will attempt to evaluate them as variable names.

A list returned by Read can serve as an argument in functions requiring lists.

EXAMPLES

(read "pi rho sigma tau")	Returns pi
(read "(0 0)(5 5)(12.5 2.65)")	Returns (0 0)

READ-CHAR

Returns the ASCII code for a single character read from either the keyboard buffer or a file.

REQUIRED ARGUMENTS

None, if characters are to be read from the keyboard buffer. If the character is to be read from a file, a memory variable containing a file descriptor of a file open for reading must be supplied.

USAGE

If the keyboard buffer is empty, Read-char pauses for keyboard input. Input can be terminated by pressing either the Enter key or the space bar. When input is made, the function returns the first character in the buffer. If the function is repeated, the next character is read, and so on until all characters are read.

If characters are read from a file open for reading, the first function call reads the first character, and subsequent calls read the following characters until the entire file is read. When Read-char reaches the end of the file, it returns nil.

EXAMPLES

Given the following:

```
(setq f2 (open "f2" "w"))
(prin1 "ABC" f2)
(close f2)
(setq f2 (open "f2" "r"))
```

the upcoming function uses Read-char within a repeating loop, ending the loop when the Read-char function returns nil:

```
(while (setq x (read-char f2))
        (prin1 x)
        (princ (chr 32))
)
```

This function displays

34 65 66 67 34

in the Command-prompt area and returns " ".

READ-LINE

Returns a string of characters read from the keyboard or from a file.

REQUIRED ARGUMENTS

None, if the string of characters is to be read from the keyboard buffer. If the character string is to be read from a file, a memory variable containing a file descriptor for a file open for reading must be supplied.

USAGE

If the keyboard buffer is empty, Read-line pauses for keyboard input. Input may be terminated with the Enter key; the space bar is considered part of the input. When input is made, the function returns the characters entered. When used in this fashion, Read-line works like Getstring with the T argument supplied; refer to the Getstring function for details.

If characters are read from a file open for reading, the first function call reads the first line of characters in the file, and returns that line. Subsequent calls read the following lines until the entire file has been read. When Read-line reaches the end of the file, it returns nil.

EXAMPLES

Given the following:

```
(setq f2 (open "f2" "w"))
(prin1 'ABC f2)
(print 'CDF f2)
(close f2)
(setq f2 (open "f2" "r"))
```

the upcoming function uses Read-line within a repeating loop, ending the loop when the Read-line function returns nil:

```
(while (setq x (read-line f2))
        (prin1 x)
        (princ (chr 32))
)
```

This function displays "ABC" "CDF " in the Command-prompt area and returns " ".

REDRAW

Redraws the display screen. This function can also redraw, remove (but not erase), or highlight individual drawing entities. The Redraw function always returns nil.

REQUIRED ARGUMENTS

None, but Redraw may be supplied with an entity name. If an entity name is supplied, this function may also be supplied with an integer indicating a particular *redraw mode,* as explained in the Usage section below.

USAGE

When this function is called without arguments, it redraws the entire screen, mimicking the Redraw command. In Release 10 and later, if multiple viewports are active, it redraws the current viewport.

If Redraw is called with an entity-name argument, it redraws that particular entity. This is helpful if the entity needs to be refreshed individually; for example, after another entity crossing it was erased. Refer to Chapter 19 for details regarding entity names.

As a further option, after the entity name you may supply an integer from 1 to 4, which will affect the display of the entity as follows:

1   Redraw the entity normally (same as no integer argument)

2   Blank out the entity (entity is not erased, but simply is not displayed until the next redraw)

3   Highlight the entity (if the display device supports highlighting)

4   Display the entity normally (turn off highlighting)

If the entity used as the argument to Redraw is a block with attributes, the block and its attributes will be operated on by the Redraw function if the integer argument is positive. If the integer argument is negative, only the block is operated on.

EXAMPLES

Assume that an entity name has been retrieved and stored in memory variable *x* with the following function:

(setq x (entlast))

The following sample series of redraws will have the given effects:

(grclear)	Blanks out the screen
(redraw x)	Redraws entity *x* only
(redraw x 2)	Blanks out entity *x* only
(redraw x 3)	Highlights entity *x* (it reappears)
(redraw x 4)	Displays entity (same as (redraw x))

REM

Returns the modulus (remainder) of the division of two numbers.

REQUIRED ARGUMENTS

Two numbers, which may be integers or real numbers. If a real number is used, a real number is returned. If both numbers are integers, an integer is returned.

USAGE

Two arguments, both numbers, must be supplied, and the first is always divided by the second. Only the remainder is returned.

EXAMPLES

(rem 24 3)	Returns 0
(rem 25 3)	Returns 1
(rem 26 3.0)	Returns 2.0
(rem 27 3.0)	Returns 0.0

REPEAT

Repeats each expression in a series a given number of times, and returns the result of the last expression in the series.

REQUIRED ARGUMENTS

An integer indicating the number of repetitions to be performed, and an Auto-LISP expression that will be evaluated the indicated number of times. A series of AutoLISP expressions is also accepted by this function; the series need not be a list; that is, it need not be enclosed within parentheses.

USAGE

If a series of expressions is present, each will be evaluated the indicated number of times before the next in the series is evaluated. If you intend that the entire series be evaluated the indicated number of times, enclose the series in the Progn function.

EXAMPLES

The lines

```
(repeat 3
  (prompt "\nExpression 1")
```

```
        (prompt "\nExpression 2")
    )
```

repeat the series of expressions 3 times, and return nil.

REVERSE

Returns a list supplied as its argument with the members in reverse order.

REQUIRED ARGUMENTS

A single list only.

USAGE

The Reverse function is useful in settings where you would like the members of a list to be evaluated from last to first. Other lists within the list are not reversed.

EXAMPLES

(reverse '((0 0 0) (5 5 5) (10 10 10)))   Returns
((10 10 10) (5 5 5) (0 0 0))

RTOS

Returns a real number converted to a string. The string may represent the number in any of AutoCAD's standard units formats, depending on optional arguments that are supplied.

REQUIRED ARGUMENTS

A number. If the number supplied is an integer, it is interpreted as a real whole number. If no other arguments are supplied, the number is converted to a string and returned in the current numeric-units format and decimal precision as set with the Units command.

Following the number, two optional arguments are allowed. The first argument, an integer in the range from 1 to 5, determines the numeric format of the string, as follows:

ARGUMENT	NUMERIC FORMAT	EXAMPLE
1	Scientific units	1.5 = 1.5E +00
2	Decimal units	1.5 = 1.5

ARGUMENT	NUMERIC FORMAT	EXAMPLE
3	Engineering units	1.5 = 1.5"
4	Architectural units	1.5 = 1 1/2"
5	Fractional units	1.5 = 1 1/2

The second optional argument, also an integer, determines the number of decimal (or fractional) places of accuracy. The range of precision is from zero to as high as you like. The practical maximum precision depends on the units format selected, as follows:

FORMAT INTEGER	MAXIMUM PRECISION INTEGER	DISPLAYED PRECISION
1	18	(18 decimal places)
2	22	(22 decimal places)
3	21	(21 decimal places)
4	10	($1/1024$)
5	10	($1/1024$)

USAGE

The string returned by this expression is controlled by the system variables LUNITS, LUPREC, and DIMZIN. Unless the optional arguments are explicitly used, the units format of the string is determined by the settings of LUNITS and LUPREC; that is, by the default setting of AutoCAD's units format using the Units command.

The setting of DIMZIN controls whether zero units are to be included in the string if the number is less than zero in the current format. Refer to Chapter 13 for details regarding DIMZIN.

In Release 11 and later, the output of Rtos is controlled by the UNITMODE system variable. If UNITMODE is zero, the string returned by Rtos will be in AutoCAD's standard output format. If UNITMODE is 1, the string returned by Rtos will be in AutoCAD's input format. Refer to the examples and to the discussion of UNITMODE in Chapter 13 for details.

EXAMPLES

The following examples convert π to a string, using the maximum number of decimal places of precision for each format:

    (rtos pi 1 18)   Returns " 3.141592653589793116E +00 "
    (rtos pi 2 22)   Returns " 3.1415926535897931159979 "

(rtos pi 3 21)	Returns " 3.141592653589793115997" "
(rtos pi 4 10)	Returns " 3 145/1024" "
(rtos pi 5 10)	Returns " 3 145/1024"when UNITMODE = 0
(rtos pi 5 10)	Returns " 3-145/1024 when UNITMODE = 1

SET

Binds a memory-variable name to a value, and returns the value.

REQUIRED ARGUMENTS

A memory-variable name and a value.

USAGE

The Set function requires that the memory-variable name be nested within a Quote function, or that the symbol used as the first argument be bound to a memory-variable name, as shown in the examples ahead. The value used as the second argument can be a number, string, list, entity name, file descriptor, or selection set—either quoted, returned by a function, or represented by a symbol. Once a memory-variable name has been bound to a value, it may be used as an argument to functions requiring its value. If the Set function is nested within another function, the memory variable may be set and the values passed as an argument at the same time.

If a Set function is used within a Defun function to bind a value to a symbol indicated by Defun to be a local variable, the value bound by Set to that variable is bound only while that function is operating. When the function has completed processing, any previous value bound to the variable is returned to the variable. If the variable did not exist previously, it is bound to nil.

In all other circumstances, the memory variable bound to a value using Set is considered global; that is, the variable will remain bound to that value until another Set or Setq function explicitly binds a new value (or nil) to that variable. Refer to the Defun function for more details regarding local and global variables.

When using Set, be careful that you do not use a predefined function name or constant as a memory-variable name. Names like *log, angle, length, nil, t,* and *pi* all have specific meanings to AutoLISP. If you like, one way to guarantee unique memory-variable names is to begin each one with the letter *j* (*jangle, jlength, jnil, jt, jpi,* etc.). No predefined symbols begin with that letter.

EXAMPLES

(set 'a 'b)	Returns B and binds A to that value.
(set 'd 1)	Returns 1 and binds D to 1.
(set a 6)	Returns 6 and binds B to 6. (A is not quoted; therefore, it is evaluated to return the symbol *B*. Thus B is the symbol bound to the value, not A. Compare with the Setq function.)
(set 'e a)	Returns 6 (the value bound to A) and sets E to that value.

SETQ

Binds a memory-variable name to a value, and returns the value.

REQUIRED ARGUMENTS

A memory-variable name and a value. Additional pairs of arguments may be supplied as alternating memory-variable names and the values to which they are bound.

USAGE

Setq, unlike the Set function, assumes that the first argument is a quoted symbol name. Therefore, Setq always assigns the value of its second argument to the memory-variable name supplied as its first argument. Setq is generally less confusing to use than Set. Any AutoLISP expression or symbol can supply the value.

Once a memory-variable name has been bound to a value, it may be used as an argument to functions requiring its value. If the Setq function is nested within another function, the memory variable may be set and the values passed as an argument at the same time.

If names and values are alternated arguments to the function, a single Setq function may be used to bind several memory-variable names to values. Refer to the examples ahead.

If a Setq function is used within a Defun function to bind a value to a symbol indicated by Defun to be a local variable, the value bound by Setq to that variable is bound only while that function is operating. When the function has completed its processing, any previous value bound to that variable is returned to the variable. If the variable did not exist previously, it is bound to nil.

In all other circumstances, the memory variable bound to a value using Setq is considered global; that is, the variable will remain bound to that value until another Setq or Set function explicitly binds a new value (or nil) to that variable. Refer to the Defun function for more details regarding local and global variables.

Warning: When using Setq, be careful that you do not use a predefined function name or constant as a memory-variable name. Names like *log, angle, length, nil, t,* and *pi* all have specific meanings to AutoLISP. One way to guarantee unique memory-variable names is to begin each one with the letter *j,* (producing *jangle, jlength, jnil, jt, jpi,* etc.). No predefined symbols begin with that letter.

EXAMPLES

(setq a '(0 0))	Returns (0 0) and binds A to that value.
(setq d 1)	Returns 1 and binds D to 1.
(set a 6)	Returns 6 and binds A to 6. A is no longer bound to (0 0).
(set e a)	Returns 6 (the value bound to A) and sets E to that value.
(setq A 1 B 2 C 3 D 4 E 5)	Returns 5 and binds A to 1, B to 2, C to 3, D to 4, and E to 5.

SETVAR

Changes the value of any system variable not specified as read-only, and returns the value.

REQUIRED ARGUMENTS

The name of a system variable and a value for that variable.

USAGE

The system variable must not be a read-only variable, and the value for that variable must be a value the system variable can accept. For example, real numbers should not be passed to system variables that accept only integers or strings.

Many read-only system variables can be changed by invoking AutoCAD commands using the Command function. For example, the CECOLOR system variable can be changed by invoking the Color command. You can store the value of this variable in a memory variable using the Getvar function, invoke the Color command to change the value of CECOLOR, and later invoke the command again, using the memory variable that served as an argument to return to the original color.

EXAMPLES

(setvar "CMDECHO" 0)	Returns 0 and changes the value of CMDECHO to zero.
(setvar "BLIPMODE" 0)	Returns 0 and changes the value of BLIPMODE to zero.

The following multiline example uses the Command function to change the value of the read-only system variable CECOLOR to green, and back again to its original state after drawing a green line. This work-around is a substitute for Setvar with read-only variables that can be changed via AutoCAD commands:

(setq x (getvar "CECOLOR"))	Returns the current value of CECOLOR and stores the value to memory variable *x*.
(command "color" "green")	Returns nil and changes the entity color.
(command "line" "0,0" "5,5" "")	Returns nil and draws a line in the new entity color.
(command "color" x)	Returns nil and restores the original entity color.

SIN

Returns the sine of its argument, assumed to be an angle.

REQUIRED ARGUMENTS

A single argument, which should be an angle expressed in radians. Integers are acceptable if they express the desired angle in radians. This function always returns a real number.

USAGE

Sin is the general sine solving function for trigonometric problems. Angles expressed in degrees must be converted to radians before being passed to this function. The first example below includes a nested function that converts 45 degrees to radians; you may use this formula when such conversion is needed.

EXAMPLES

(sin (* pi (/ 45 180.0)))	Returns 0.707107
(sin 6.2)	Returns −0.0830894
(sin 5)	Returns −0.958924

SQRT

Returns the square root of a number.

REQUIRED ARGUMENTS

One number, either integer or real. A real number is always returned.

USAGE

The usage of Sqrt is simple and straightforward. Supply a number as its argument, or a function that returns a number; the square root is calculated and returned.

EXAMPLES

(sqrt 25)	Returns 5
(sqrt 17.5)	Returns 4.1833

STRCASE

Converts all the characters in a string to either uppercase or lowercase.

REQUIRED ARGUMENTS

The string to be converted. As a second, optional argument, you may include any AutoLISP expression that can be evaluated to either nil or a non-nil value.

USAGE

If the second argument is present and is not nil, all characters in the first argument will be converted to lowercase. If the second argument is omitted or nil, the characters in the string will be converted to uppercase. Numbers and punctuation marks are ignored; that is, they are not converted to anything else.

This function is useful in comparing strings in which the case is unimportant as a factor in the comparison. Refer to the last example below.

EXAMPLES

(strcase "Convert This")	Returns "CONVERT THIS"
(strcase "Convert This" nil)	Returns "CONVERT THIS"
(strcase "Convert This" T)	Returns "convert this"
(setq yn (strcase	Returns whatever string the
(getstring	user enters, converted to
"\nPress Y for yes:"	uppercase
)	
)	
)	

STRCAT

Concatenates (connects) two or more strings, and returns the new string.

REQUIRED ARGUMENTS

A series of strings or functions returning strings.

USAGE

Strcat is useful in linking disparate pieces of information into an intelligible whole for displaying to the user, converting to AutoCAD text, or writing to a file.

This function will only concatenate string data. It cannot be used to concatenate numeric data, nor can it connect string data with numeric data. If you wish to concatenate strings with numbers, first use other functions such as Itoa or Rtos, to convert numeric data to string data.

EXAMPLES

The line

    (strcat "Number 12 in current Units format: " (rtos 12))

returns the integer 12 in the current units format.

Given that W = 5.5, L = 37.25, and H = 48,

```
(strcat "Width: " (rtos W 3 2)
        " - Length: " (rtos L 3 2)
        " - Height: " (rtos H 3 2)
)
```

returns "Width: 5.50" - Length: 3'-1.25" - Height: 4' ", regardless of the current units setting (because the Rtos function forces feet and decimal inches).

STRLEN

Returns the length strings.

REQUIRED ARGUMENTS

A string or series of strings..

USAGE

Strlen simply counts the number of characters in strings and returns that total as an integer. It is useful in a wide variety of situations involving strings—for example, when locating characters in a string.

EXAMPLES

(strlen "ABCDE")	Returns 5
(strlen "A B C D E")	Returns 9
(strlen "ABC" "DE")	Returns 5

SUBST

Searches a list for a specified member, replaces every occurrence of that member with a specified replacement atom, and returns the list with the member replaced. If no member to replace is found, the original list is returned.

REQUIRED ARGUMENTS

The replacement member for a list, the current member of a list, and a list to be searched.

USAGE

Subst can be used to replace members in any list, but it is most often used to replace members of entity-association lists. The example below demonstrates how this is done.

EXAMPLES

Assume the following association list, which is stored in memory variable *x*:

```
( (−1 . <Entity name: 60000018>)
  (0 . "LINE")
  (8 . "WALLS")
  (62 . 3)
  (10 2.0 3.75 0.0)
  (11 4.0 5.5 0.0)
  (210 0.0 0.0 1.0)
)
```

The Subst function can change the entity's layer as follows:

```
(setq x
  (subst
    (cons '8 "NEWLAYER")
    (assoc '8 x)
    x
  )
)
```

This returns the updated association list:

```
( (−1 . <Entity name: 60000018>)
  (0 . "LINE")
  (8 . "NEWLAYER")
  (62 . 3)
  (10 2.0 3.75 0.0)
  (11 4.0 5.5 0.0)
  (210 0.0 0.0 1.0)
)
```

Note that, although the association list in the memory variable is updated, AutoCAD's drawing database is not yet updated. To incorporate this sample association list into the drawing database, use the following function:

```
(entmod x)
```

SUBSTR

Returns a substring (portion) of a string.

REQUIRED ARGUMENTS

Two arguments in the following order:

1. A string.
2. A starting position within that string, expressed with an integer.

A third optional argument, another integer indicating the length of the substring, may be provided.

USAGE

The first character of a string is number 1. Thus, to return a substring starting with the first character of the string argument, specify 1 as the second argument. To start with the second character in the string, specify 2 as the second argument, and so on. If the third argument is not present, the function will return a string beginning with the given position and continuing to the end of the original string. If the optional third argument is present, Subst will return a string of the indicated length, beginning with the specified position. The examples ahead demonstrate this.

EXAMPLES

Given the string

```
(setq x "123456789")
```

in memory variable *x,* the following functions are valid:

(substr x 3)	Returns "3456789"
(substr x 3 3)	Returns "345"
(substr x 9 1)	Returns "9"
(substr x 6 22)	Returns "6789"
(substr x 22 6)	Returns "" (a null string)

TERPRI

Prints a line feed in the Command-prompt area and returns nil.

REQUIRED ARGUMENTS

None.

USAGE

Terpri is useful in displaying nonstring information separated by line feeds in the Command-prompt area. It cannot be used to write line feeds to files; to print line feeds in a file, use the Print function.

EXAMPLES

Assume the following user-defined function:

```
(defun lftest( )
    (princ 12)
    (terpri)
    (princ 13)
    (princ)
)
```

Entering

```
(lftest)
```

returns

```
12
13
```

TEXTPAGE

Displays the text screen (in single-screen systems), and clears it.

REQUIRED ARGUMENTS

None.

USAGE

Textpage is especially useful when displaying messages for the operator. In single-screen systems, it will switch to the text screen and clear it of previous AutoCAD command echoes or prompts and other possibly distracting text. Textpage is available in Release 11 and later.

EXAMPLES

The following command sequence displays and clears the text screen:

```
Command: Graphscr
Command: (defun C:CLS( ) (textpage) (princ))
Command: CLS
```

TEXTSCR

Forces the display of the text screen on single-screen systems, and returns nil.

REQUIRED ARGUMENTS

None.

USAGE

Textscr, along with Graphscr, allows you to control the single-screen display from within AutoLISP routines. It is functionally the same as the Textscr command.

EXAMPLES

(textscr)   Changes the display to the text screen. If the text screen is already displayed, this function has no effect other than to return nil.

TRACE

Sets a trace flag for named functions.

REQUIRED ARGUMENTS

The names of previously defined functions. Any number of functions may be used as arguments.

USAGE

The Trace function is an aid to debugging functions, and can be used in situations where your defined functions are working well enough to avoid causing AutoLISP error messages, but you would like to test whether they are returning the results you want.

When the trace flag is set, each time the function is called, AutoLISP will display the message

Entering *function:*

in the Command-prompt area, where *function* is the name of a function for which the trace flag has been set. AutoLISP will display this message indented by a number of spaces corresponding to the depth to which the function has been nested. Thus, if the traced function is nested within two other functions, Auto-LISP will display the message indented two spaces. This is helpful if the function is called several times, or if the function is nested within control functions such as If, in which case it might be bypassed. The indentation helps indicate the point in the processing at which the function is being performed each time the trace message is displayed.

AutoLISP also displays the arguments that are passed to the function. If the arguments are expressions, the results of the expressions are displayed. When the function has completed processing, the result returned by the function is displayed, and the AutoLISP routine continues normally.

EXAMPLES

Consider the following AutoLISP routine, which in its present form does not work correctly:

```
(defun rtd(a)
    (* (/ a pi) 180.0)
)
(defun C:RD( )
    (setq x (getreal "\nEnter radians: "))
    (rtd x)
    (prompt "\nDegrees: ")
    (princ x)
    (princ)
)
```

If you were to load the above routine (see Chapter 16) and invoke the Rd command, AutoCAD would prompt:

Enter radians:

Enter **1.570796**. AutoCAD responds:

Degrees: 1.5708

Since the expected response is 90 degrees, this is not correct. At first, you might guess that the Rtd function is not returning correct results. Set a trace flag on the Rtd function by entering

    (trace rtd)

which returns RTD. Now, reinvoke the Rd command and enter **1.570796** again. AutoCAD responds:

    Entering RTD: 1.5708
    Result: 90.0
    Degrees: 1.5708

The trace flag indicates that the Rtd function is receiving the correct input and returning the correct result! The problem must be elsewhere. Using this information, you can look further and realize that the Rtd function does not update the memory variable x. Therefore, replace the line

    (rtd x)

with this line:

    (setq x (rtd x))

Reload the routine, and the command will work correctly. Now you can remove the trace flag using the Untrace function.

TRANS

Translates a point from one coordinate system to another, and returns the point after translation.

REQUIRED ARGUMENTS

Three arguments in the following order:

1. A 3-D coordinate point list, indicating the point to be translated.

2. An integer code or entity name, indicating the current coordinate system of the point expressed in the first argument.

3. An integer code or entity name indicating the coordinate system of the point to be returned by the function.

An additional fourth argument may be used. If this argument is present, the 3-D point argument is interpreted as a *displacement*—i.e., an amount of increment along each axis, translated from one coordinate system to another.

USAGE

Coordinate systems may be expressed by means of an integer code or an entity name. The allowable integer codes are as follows:

0   The world coordinate system

1   The current user coordinate system

2   The display coordinate system

3   The paper space coordinate system (Release 11 and later)

The world coordinate system and current user coordinate system are those standard coordinate systems that can be made current using the UCS command. Refer to Chapters 6 and 11 for details regarding these coordinate systems.

The display coordinate system is interpolated internally from the viewing angle. When viewing the display screen, you are always in plan view to this coordinate system. The positive z-axis is measured from the target point to the viewing angle—the TARGET to VIEWDIR system variables, respectively. The positive x-axis is always horizontal and to the right, perpendicular to the z-axis, and the y-axis is always perpendicular to both the z-axis and the x-axis. Thus, if the current UCS is in plan view, both the current user coordinate system and the display coordinate system would be the same.

In Release 11 and later, the Trans function permits transformation of points between the model-space DCS (code 2) and the paper-space DCS (code 3). Although you can change the current user coordinate system in paper space, the paper-space DCS never changes. Thus, translation between model-space and paper-space DCs changes only the x and y coordinates and will not be affected by the rotation of the paper-space UCS.

In addition, the coordinate system of an individual entity may be referenced by supplying that entity's name in place of an integer code. Entities that retain coordinate systems of their own include 2-D polylines, arcs, blocks, circles, solids, shapes, traces, and text.

In the case of some common entities, it is not necessary to supply their names to indicate their coordinate system, because it is always the same as the world coordinate system. These entities include 3-D faces, lines, meshes, and polylines, plus 2-D lines and points, and all dimension entities.

Trans is needed because all coordinate point values returned by AutoLISP are relative to the current user coordinate system. Thus, if a point is retrieved and stored to a memory variable while in one user coordinate system, and the user coordinate system is subsequently changed, the coordinate point in that variable will reference a completely different point in 3-D space. The Trans function therefore provides the means for "updating" point variables when moving between coordinate systems.

In addition, point data for entities that maintain their own entity coordinate systems must be translated to the current user coordinate system to be referenced and modified accurately by AutoLISP.

EXAMPLES

Assume that the current user coordinate system has been set by rotating the x-axis of the world coordinate system 45 degrees counterclockwise, and a 2-D polyline is drawn in that coordinate system from point 2,2 to point 5,5. The following functions would then return the indicated results:

(trans '(5 5 0) 1 0)	Returns (5.0 3.53553 3.53553)
(trans '(5 5 0) 0 1)	Returns (5.0 3.53553 −3.53553)
(trans (cdr (assoc '10 (entget (entnext (entlast)))))) (entlast) 0)	Returns (2.0 1.41421 1.41421), which is the starting endpoint of the polyline translated into the world coordinate system
(trans '(10 10 10) 0 (entlast))	Returns (10.0 14.1421 −3.33067e-15), which is world point 10,10,10 translated into the entity coordinate system of the 2-D polyline

TYPE

Returns the data type of its argument as an uppercase string.

REQUIRED ARGUMENTS

A single argument.

USAGE

The Type function is useful in situations where a choice between different processes needs to be made, depending on the data type contained in a variable. It is a good way to keep AutoLISP errors from ending the routine prematurely; refer to the example ahead.

Type returns one of the following strings (always in uppercase), depending on the data type of the argument:

ENAME	Entity name
EXSUBR	External subroutine loaded via Xload
FILE	File descriptor

INT	Integer
LIST	List, including a user-defined function
PAGETB	Function paging table (when virtual memory is enabled)
PICKSET	Selection set
REAL	Real number
STR	String
SUBR	AutoLISP predefined function
SYM	Symbol

Type may also return nil if a null argument (such as an unknown symbol name) is supplied.

EXAMPLES

The following function, named Pull-x, requires one argument, and evaluates it. If the argument is a list of at least two numbers, real or integer, it returns the first number of the list, calling it an x coordinate. Otherwise, it displays a message indicating what was wrong, and returns nil. Notice how the data types LIST, INT, and REAL are quoted, to avoid having them evaluated as symbols. This function could be used to return either an x coordinate or nil in situations where a variable may or may not be a valid coordinate list.

```
(defun pull-x (x)
   (if ( = (type x) 'LIST)
      (if ( >= (length x) 2)
         (if (and (/= (type (car x)) 'INT)
                  ( = (type (car x)) 'REAL) )
            (prompt "\nNot an x-coordinate.")
            (car x)
         ) ; end if not a number
         (prompt "\nList not long enough.")
      ); end if long enough
      (prompt "\nNot a coordinate list")
   ); end if a list
); end defun pull-x
```

UNTRACE

Removes the trace flag from functions, and returns the name of the last function in the series.

REQUIRED ARGUMENTS

The names of valid functions.

USAGE

Untrace is used to remove the trace flag when the debugging process is complete. (Refer to the Trace command for details regarding trace flags.) If no trace flag exists, nothing happens, but the function name is returned. If a trace flag is set for any function, it is removed from that function.

EXAMPLES

(untrace rtd)   Returns RTD and removes the trace flag from the function

VER

Returns a string containing the AutoLISP version number.

REQUIRED ARGUMENTS

None.

USAGE

Ver is useful when routines may be shared among different versions of Auto-LISP. It allows for alternate processing based on which version is being used. In Release 11, Ver returns a string indicating whether extended memory is being used to store AutoLISP functions.

EXAMPLES

In AutoCAD Release 11:

(ver)   Returns "AutoLISP Release 11.0" or a similar message

VPORTS

Returns a list of viewport identification numbers and corner coordinates for the current viewport configuration.

REQUIRED ARGUMENTS

None.

USAGE

The Vports function is available in AutoCAD Release 10 and later.

The list returned by Vports is a list of sublists. Each sublist contains the following members, in the following order:

1. The viewport identification number, which is always an integer.
2. The lower-left corner of the viewport, expressed as a 2-D coordinate point list.
3. The upper-right corner of the viewport, also a 2-D coordinate point list.

The currently active viewport is always the first viewport sublist in the list returned by Vports.

In Release 11 model space, the values in the coordinate point list are always in the range of 0.0 to 1.0, representing the minimum and maximum values for both x and y coordinates. All viewport coordinates fall within this range. In paper space, coordinnates may exceed this range.

In Release 11 and later, the Vports function returns the viewport configuration in model space if the system variable TILEMODE is set to 1. If TILE-MODE is set to zero, the function returns the viewport configuration in paper space.

In paper space, viewport 1 is the paper-space area on display when TILE-MODE is first set to zero, and if there is a currently active viewport, it is listed first.

EXAMPLES

Assuming that the current model space display shows a screen split vertically into two viewports, and the viewport on the left is the current viewport,

    (vports)

returns a list similar to the following (with indentation added to better present the sublists involved):

    (
      (3 (0.0 0.0) (0.5 1.0))
      (2 (0.5 0.0) (1.0 1.0))
)

Here are some additional examples:

(car (vports)	Returns the currently active viewport sublist: (3 (0.0 0.0) (0.5 1.0))
(car (car (vports)))	Returns the identification number of the currently active viewport: 3

WCMATCH

Matches a character string to a control string, usually containing wild-card characters, and returns T (true) if a successful match is made.

REQUIRED ARGUMENTS

Wcmatch requires a character string, called a *test string*, followed by a second string, called a *control string*. If the two strings match, the function returns T.

The control string may include one or more groups of wild-card characters. Wild-card characters allow the function to return T even if the match is not exact.

You may use more than one control string. To do this, place a comma between the control strings and use only one set of quotation marks to surround the entire group.

USAGE

The Wcmatch function, available in Release 11 and later, allows for a sophisticated level of comparisons involving character strings. Each argument may contain up to 500 characters; if a string is longer than this, the excess characters are ignored. The function will return T when a match is made to the following special wild-card characters:

~   If you place a tilde at the beginning of the control pattern, Wcmatch returns T if a match is *not* made. For example:

(wcmatch "XYZ" "~ABC")	Returns T
(wcmatch "ABC" "~ABC")	Returns nil

*   The asterisk will match any substring, including no string, anywhere in the test string. For example:

(wcmatch "WXYZ" "W*Z")	Returns T
(wcmatch "WZ" "W*Z")	Returns T

(wcmatch "WXYZ" "*Z")	Returns T
(wcmatch "WXYZ" "X*")	Returns nil

? The question mark will match a single alphanumeric character anywhere in the pattern. For example:

(wcmatch "WXY" "W?Y")	Returns T
(wcmatch "WXYZ" "W?Z")	Returns nil
(wcmatch "13" "1?3")	Returns nil
(wcmatch "1234" "???4")	Returns T
(wcmatch "WXYZ" "X??")	Returns nil

@ The "at" symbol will match any single alphabetic letter anywhere in the pattern. For example:

(wcmatch "WXY" "W@Y")	Returns T
(wcmatch "WY" "W@Y")	Returns nil
(wcmatch "XYZ" "X@@Z")	Returns nil
(wcmatch "123Z" "@@@Z")	Returns nil

The "pound" symbol will match any single numeric character anywhere in the pattern. For example:

(wcmatch "123" "1#3")	Returns T
(wcmatch "13" "1#3")	Returns nil
(wcmatch "1234" "1#4")	Returns nil
(wcmatch "123Z" "###Z")	Returns T

. The period will match any single non-alphanumeric character, including no character, anywhere in the test string. For example:

(wcmatch "123" "1.3")	Returns nil
(wcmatch "1\n3" "1.3")	Returns T

(Blank Space) A space in the control pattern will match one or more spaces in the test string. For example:

(wcmatch "A F" "A F")	Returns T
(wcmatch "AF" "A F")	Returns nil

[]   Wcmatch will return T if any one of the characters within brackets in the control pattern matches the test string. For example:

(wcmatch "XYZ" "X[AY]Z")	Returns T
(wcmatch "XAZ" "X[AY]Z")	Returns T
(wcmatch "XBZ" "X[AY]Z")	Returns nil

If a tilde (˜) is the first character within brackets, Wcmatch will return true if the test string does *not* match any of the control pattern characters within the brackets. For example:

(wcmatch "XYZ" "X[˜ AY]Z")	Returns nil
(wcmatch "XAZ" "X[˜ AY]Z")	Returns nil
(wcmatch "XBZ" "X[˜ AY]Z")	Returns T

You may specify a consecutive range of single characters within brackets by separating the beginning and end of the range with a hyphen (-). Note that this works only for a range of single characters; characters not separated by a hyphen are treated individually. For example:

(wcmatch "X2Z" "X[1-5]Z")	Returns T
(wcmatch "X8Z" "X[1-5]Z")	Returns nil
(wcmatch "X8Z" "X[1-59]Z")	Returns nil

,   The comma allows you to separate groups of wild-card characters in the control pattern, thus allowing you to compare a series of control patterns. For example:

(wcmatch "WXYZ" "W@@Z,W##Z")	Returns T
(wcmatch "WXYZ" "A@@,???X")	Returns nil

'   The back-quote character allows you to read wild-card characters literally, instead of as control characters. For example:

(wcmatch "XYZ" "'*")	Returns nil
(wcmatch "XYZ" "*")	Returns T

AutoLISP generally interprets the backslash character (\) as a control character whenever it appears in any string; to represent a literal backslash character anywhere in AutoLISP, use two backslashes (\\). If you want to represent a single literal backslash in a control pattern for Wcmatch, use the back-quote character and two backslashes. For example:

(wcmatch "X\\Z" "?'\\?")   Returns T

All characters within brackets are interpreted literally; for example, an asterisk appearing in "[X*Z]" is not interpreted as a wild-card character, but rather as an asterisk. There are exceptions to this rule, however: a hyphen within brackets (see above) is considered a control character, signifying a range. However, if the hyphen appears first, such as in "[-XYZ]" or last, such as in "[XYZ-]", or follows a leading tilde, such as in "[˜ -XYZ]", it will be considered a literal character. A leading tilde following an opening bracket is interpreted as a control character, reversing the bracketed match criterion. For example:

(wcmatch "XYZ" "X[˜ 1-8]Z")   Returns T

If a pair of empty brackets appears in the control pattern, the opening bracket is considered the control character, but the closing bracket will be interpreted as a literal character. This necessitates adding a second closing bracket to the control pattern. For example:

(wcmatch "X]Z" "X[ ]1-8]Z")   Returns T

Character tests by Wcmatch are case-sensitive; thus, "abc" will not match "A*". However, all symbol names (e.g., names of layers) are converted to upper case by AutoLISP; therefore, you should use upper-case control patterns to match them.

The wild-card characters described above may be used in any AutoLISP functions that compare string data, such as Ssget, described in detail in Chapter 19.

EXAMPLES

The following AutoLISP routine will search the drawing database's layer-name listing and change the default layer color to red everywhere "RED" appears in the layer name:

```
; Turn off command line echo:
(setvar "CMDECHO" 0)
; Get first layer:
(setq currlyr (tblnext "layer" T))
; Start command:
(command "layer")
; Loop while layers are found:
(while currlyr
; If a layer's name contains "RED" anywhere:
```

```
(if (wcmatch (cdr (assoc 2 currlyr)) "*RED*")
; change its default color to red:
    (command "c" "red" (cdr (assoc 2 currlyr)))
) ; End If
; Get next layer
(setq currlyr (tblnext "layer"))
) ; End While
; End command:
(command "")
```

WHILE

Evaluates a series of one or more AutoLISP expressions based on whether an initial test expression is evaluated to nil or a non-nil value; returns the value of the last evaluated expression.

REQUIRED ARGUMENTS

At least two AutoLISP expressions. The first expression is the test expression. The following expressions will be evaluated repeatedly in sequence as long as the test expression does not return nil.

USAGE

The While function is an extremely flexible "looping" function that can be used in a wide variety of situations where repetition or decision making is involved. When the While function contains only two argument expressions, it will repeatedly evaluate the second expression based on the results of evaluating the first test expression; thus, the While function may be used to repeat a Get function until the user enters valid data. The test expression would be evaluated to nil when valid data was entered. Still, any processing series may be used inside a looping function, provided that the processing affects the test expression, causing it to return nil at some point. If the test expression is never evaluated to nil, the repeated tasks continue indefinitely. This situation is referred to as an *endless loop*. If you accidentally write an endless loop, the program may appear to be doing nothing, or the same messages may be displayed on the screen over and over. In such a situation, you must cancel the AutoLISP routine by pressing Ctrl-C.

EXAMPLES

In the following example, the While function is used to test the value of the data entered by the user. Notice how the Initget function effectively disallows null, zero, and negative data entry, but cannot prevent the user from entering a value greater than five. The While function will do that. The first argument to While tests to see if the value of *x* is greater than 5 (as it is at the start of the function) and repeats the prompt as long as the user enters data out of range.

```
(initget (+ 1 2 4))
(while (> (setq x (getreal "\nEnter a value between 1 and 5: ")) 5)
    (initget (+ 1 2 4))
)
```

WRITE-CHAR

Writes a single character to either the Command-prompt area or a file; returns the ASCII character code for the character written.

REQUIRED ARGUMENTS

An ASCII code for the character being written. ASCII code 0 (null character) is not allowed. If the character is to be written to a file, a memory variable containing a file descriptor of a file open for either writing or appending must be supplied after the ASCII character code.

USAGE

When a series of characters is written to the screen or to a file with Write-char, each character must be explicitly written by a Write-char function. This includes spaces (code 32) and line-feed sequences (10). Thus, in many cases a series of characters will be more easily written using the Write-line function.

EXAMPLES

Given

```
(setq c 65)
```

the following uses the Write-char function within a repeating loop, ending the loop when five characters have been displayed:

```
(while (< c 70)
        (write-char c)
        (write-char 32)
        (setq c (1+ c))
)
```

This function displays "A B C D E " in the Command-prompt area and returns 70 (the value returned by the last expression).

WRITE-LINE

Writes a string of characters in the Command-prompt area or to a file, and returns the string.

REQUIRED ARGUMENTS

A character string. If the string is to be written to a file, a memory variable containing a file descriptor for a file open for writing must be supplied.

USAGE

When you use Write-line to write a string of characters to a file, the string is written in the file without surrounding quotes, but is displayed on the screen with quotes added. Refer to the example ahead.

Like the Print function, Write-line automatically writes subsequent lines to new lines in the file, but unlike the Print function, does not add a trailing space.

EXAMPLES

Given

(setq f2 (open "f2" "w"))

the following Write-line functions write the indicated character strings to the file named F2:

(write-line "Line number 1" f2)	Returns "Line number 1"
(write-line "Line number 2" f2)	Returns "Line number 2"
(close f 2)	

XLOAD

Loads a compiled program developed with AutoCAD's Advanced Development System (ADS)

REQUIRED ARGUMENTS

A string containing the file name of the compiled ADS program. The file extension (EXE, or EXP in AutoCAD 386) is not required.

USAGE

The syntax of the Xload function is similar to that of the Load function, described in Chapter 16. The Xload function will load only ADS programs into memory. If AutoCAD cannot find the named ADS function on its file search path, or if it lacks sufficient memory to store the program, or if some other condition prevents loading of the complete program, AutoCAD will display an error message indicating the problem and abort the function.

If you attempt to load an ADS program that has already been loaded, Auto-CAD displays an error message but does not abort. Refer to Chapter 21 for an overview of the Advanced Development System.

EXAMPLE

The following example loads the sample ADS program GRAVITY.EXE, which can be found on AutoCAD's Bonus/Samples Disk:

```
(xload "ads\\gravity")
```

XUNLOAD

Removes an ADS program from memory, freeing up space in RAM.

REQUIRED ARGUMENTS

A string containing the name of an ADS program that was previously loaded into memory using the Xload function.

USAGE

If AutoCAD cannot find the named ADS program in memory, or if some other condition prevents unloading of the program, AutoCAD displays an error message indicating the problem and aborts the function. If you are not sure which ADS programs have been loaded into memory, use the Ads function to generate a list of all loaded ADS programs. Refer to Chapter 21 for an overview of the Advanced Development System.

EXAMPLES

The following example unloads the sample ADS program GRAVITY.EXE, which is assumed to have been previously loaded:

```
(xunload "ads\\gravity")
```

The following short routine will unload all currently loaded ADS programs from memory:

```
; Unload first file returned by Ads function:
(xunload (car (setq x (ads))))
; Unload subsequent programs:
(while (setq x (member (cadr x) x))
    (xunload (car x)))
(princ)
```

ZEROP

Tests to determine if a number is zero. Returns T if the number is exactly zero, or nil otherwise.

REQUIRED ARGUMENTS

A number, either real or integer.

USAGE

Zerop is used in situations where the form of processing that takes place depends on whether a variable is zero or not. Notice that numbers less than zero will be evaluated nil; only zero returns T. Depending on how a number is calculated, it may appear to be zero while it is actually a very small value. In such a case, Zerop will return nil.

EXAMPLES

(zerop −1)	Returns nil
(zerop 0.000)	Returns T
(setq x 0.0001)	Returns 0.0001
(rtos x 2 3)	Returns "0.000"
(zerop x)	Returns nil

PART **VII**

CONTROLLING THE DRAWING DATABASE

AutoCAD does more than provide a set of software drafting tools and the environment in which to use them. AutoCAD can also store, retrieve, and export the associated information—such as materials specifications, dimensions, areas, and costs—that is represented by the graphic information in your drawing. By maintaining a database of this type of information and allowing you to access it quickly and easily, AutoCAD becomes more than just a drafting toolbox; it becomes a management tool as well. AutoCAD also has the power to export graphic information in formats that can be read and used by other graphics programs, and to import graphic information from many other graphics programs, thus allowing nonusers to benefit from AutoCAD drawings. Chapter 18 introduces block attributes, the basic means for storing, retrieving, and exporting entity-related information. Chapter 19 presents entity-association lists, the means by which AutoLISP may directly read and modify AutoCAD's underlying database. Chapter 20 describes the format of Drawing Interchange files, which allow other graphics programs to use AutoCAD drawing data.

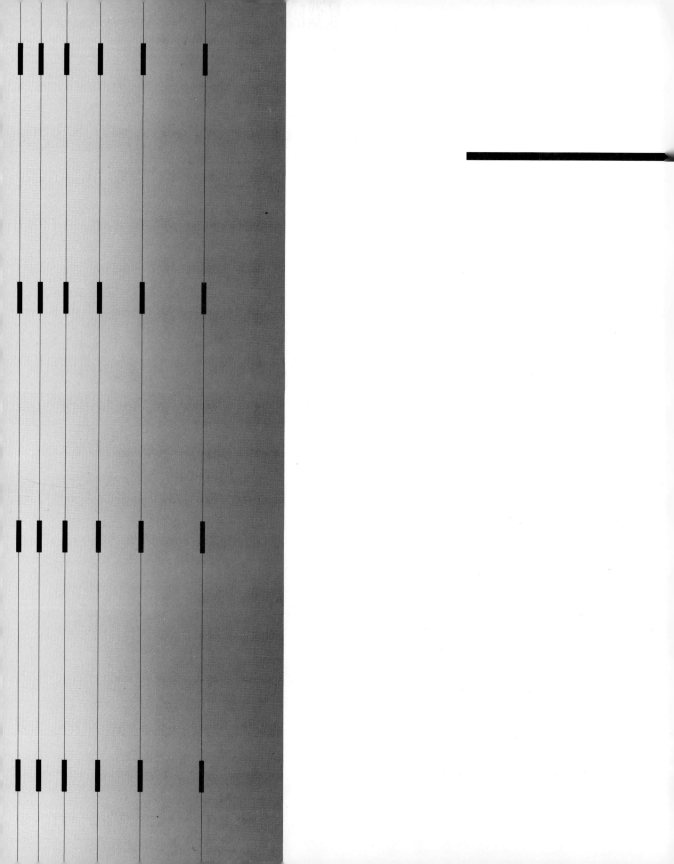

Manipulating Block Attributes

Manipulating Block Attributes

An attribute is a special entity that stores text-based information in the drawing. Any type of information that can be expressed using alphanumeric characters can be stored in an attribute and thus made part of your AutoCAD drawing. Attributes are commonly used to store such information as materials specifications, part numbers, sizes, manufacturer's names, and costs.

The information stored in attributes may be extracted from the drawing file into a separate ASCII file for further processing outside of AutoCAD—using a database, spreadsheet, word processor, other third-party software, or a custom program.

The attribute feature makes it easy to manage related information associated with a drawing. For example, you may use attributes to assemble the data used in a report, such as a bill of materials, while you are drawing.

Functionally, attributes share features of both blocks and memory variables. Like blocks, attributes may be inserted anywhere in a drawing using the Insert command. They may also be written to disk and inserted in different drawings. Like ordinary blocks, they may be rotated, scaled, copied, moved, erased, and so forth. Like memory variables, attributes consist of an attribute name, or *tag*, which will remain constant throughout multiple insertions, and a *value* attached to the tag, which you may or may not change with each insertion of the attribute, as you wish.

Attribute tags—along with associated information such as the attribute's visibility, size, prompts for values, and default values—are created in the drawing editor using the Attdef command, as explained later in this chapter. Once created, one or more attributes may be gathered into a block using the Block command (see Chapter 9). An attribute block may be a standard block including both drawing entities and attributes, or it may consist of only a block name, the attributes, and an insertion point.

Defining Attributes

Each attribute must be defined before it can be gathered into a block and used in a drawing. To define an attribute, you must indicate to AutoCAD the following:

- Whether the attribute will be a visible or invisible part of the drawing.

- Whether the attribute will have a *constant* value (always the same) or a *variable* value (with a prompt for a new value upon each insertion—the value can be edited later if necessary).
- Whether you would prefer to verify each entry of the attribute's value.
- Whether you would prefer that an attribute with a variable value be inserted automatically with its default value, without prompting for a new value.
- The attribute tag.
- A prompt to the user when entering new values for attributes with variable values.
- The default value of a variable attribute, or the constant value if the attribute is defined as constant.
- The location of the attribute tag.
- The alignment of the attribute tag.
- The text style used for the attribute tag.
- The text height for the attribute tag.
- The text rotation angle for the attribute tag.

Although this may seem like a long list of attribute parameters, AutoCAD simplifies the process by means of the Attdef command. Following is a summary of Attdef.

ATTDEF

Defines new attributes.

VERSIONS

All.

COMMAND OPTIONS

The options available for attribute definition are displayed through a series of prompts. The first prompt that appears when you invoke the Attdef command is:

Invisible: Constant: Verify: Preset:

Each of these words represents a mode, and is followed by either *N* or *Y,* indicating that the individual mode is either active (Y, for "Yes") or inactive (N, for "No") for the attribute being defined. You may toggle the indicated mode between the Y and N values by pressing the first letter of the attribute mode in response to the prompt. For example, enter **I** to toggle Invisible mode from its present value to the opposite value.

Each time you enter a mode letter, the prompt is redisplayed, showing the current values for all four modes. You may continue to enter letters until all modes are set as you like. The meaning of each mode value is explained below:

Invisible   If Y, the attribute value will not appear in the drawing, although it is saved in the drawing file and you may extract its value for analysis and processing by other software. If N, the attribute's value will be a visible part of the drawing when it is inserted.

If you wish, you can force the display of all attributes or make all attributes invisible at any time by invoking the Attdisp command, described in detail later in this chapter.

Constant   If Y, the attribute's value is the same each time it is inserted into a drawing. This can be useful when an attribute is used as a label for a block—for example, Door, Desk, Valve, or Gear. If N, AutoCAD will prompt you for new data each time the attribute is inserted (except if the attribute is defined as preset).

Verify   If Y, AutoCAD will supply the prompt

Verify attribute value

and will repeat the verifiable attributes' prompts with the new value as the default value, after all attribute values have been entered. You may then confirm the entry you just made by pressing Enter, or you may enter a new value. (AutoCAD does not ask you to verify the changed values.) If N, AutoCAD assumes all new values are correct, and does not include confirming prompts.

Preset   If Y, a variable attribute will be automatically inserted along with its default data (which you will define shortly). This is useful when the attribute's value changes rarely, and you do not want to be bothered with a prompt each time it is inserted. Unlike the constant attribute, you can edit the preset attribute's value later if you wish. If N, the attribute's default value is not preset, and AutoCAD will prompt for new data with each insertion.

Once the attribute modes are set as you like, press Enter in response to the prompt. AutoCAD responds:

Attribute tag:

Enter the tag for this attribute. The tag is used to identify the attribute to AutoCAD each time it is inserted into the drawing. You may use any sequence of keyboard characters except spaces. After you have entered the tag, AutoCAD prompts:

Attribute prompt:

Enter the message you would like AutoCAD to display when prompted for a value for this attribute. If the attribute is constant, you will not be asked to supply a prompt, as none is necessary. However, preset attributes still require a prompt string. If you like, you may press Enter, indicating no special prompt. AutoCAD will then use the attribute tag as the prompt.

AutoCAD always supplies a colon (:) after the prompt string; therefore, do not supply a trailing colon or other punctuation mark unless it is your desire to display that mark along with AutoCAD's trailing colon character.

After you enter the prompt string or press Enter, AutoCAD prompts:

Default attribute values

Enter the value for the attribute that you would like as the default. AutoCAD will assign this value to the attribute if the user presses Enter in response to the prompt string when the attribute is being inserted. By pressing Enter now, you may elect to provide no default value.

After you enter the default attribute value, AutoCAD prompts you to indicate the location and orientation of the attribute tag in the drawing. (This following sequence will appear even if the attribute is invisible, since you must be able to see the tag in order to make it part of a block definition using the Block command later.)

AutoCAD handles attribute tags the way it handles text entities; therefore, the next prompt is:

Start point or Align/Center/Fit/Middle/Right/Style:

The Align and Style options for this prompt are the same as they are for the Text command (see Chapter 9). You may align the attribute tag and select its style (and thus indicate the same settings for visible attribute values) in relation to other entities and attributes in the drawing, as you wish. After you select the alignment and style, AutoCAD prompts:

Height:

As with the Text command, you may enter a height from the keyboard, "show" AutoCAD the height by picking a point in relation to the indicated starting point, or press Enter to accept the default height displayed. If the text style you have chosen includes a fixed height, or if you have indicated the Align or Fit option, this prompt will not appear. AutoCAD finally prompts:

Rotation angle:

Again, you may enter an angle from the keyboard, pick a point in relation to the previously selected starting point, or press Enter to accept the default offered. At this point, the attribute tag appears on the screen.

If you intend to define other attributes, press Enter; the sequence then repeats itself. The previously entered settings are recalled as defaults, so that in cases where you do not need to change them, you can speed through the process by pressing Enter. However, you will need to supply new tag names, new prompt strings, and new default values for all attributes. As with the Text command, if you press Enter in response to the prompt to align the tag, the new tag will be placed directly under the first.

Once the attributes are defined in the drawing, you are ready to include them in a block definition. Use the Block command (Chapter 9) to create a new block (or define an old one) and include the attributes as entities within the block. After you indicate all the entities you intend to include, AutoCAD erases the attributes from the screen and includes them in the block. From now on, whenever you insert that block using the Insert command, AutoCAD will prompt you first for the usual insertion point, scale, and rotation angle for the block, and then for the values to apply to the attributes you have included in the block definition.

USAGE

When you insert blocks with attributes, the order in which AutoCAD prompts you for attribute values depends on the order in which the attributes were originally gathered into the block, as well as the version of AutoCAD you are using. In Release 10 and later, you will be prompted to enter attribute values in the same order as the attributes were selected when first gathered into the block. In versions prior to Release 10, you will be prompted in the reverse of this order.

This being the case, you may find it preferable to select attributes one by one when gathering them into a block, rather than selecting them by window or crossing mechanisms, so as to retain control over the prompting order. Remember to select them in the order in which you would like AutoCAD to prompt you in Release 10 and later, and in reverse order in Release 9 and earlier.

The setting for Invisible, Constant, Verify, and Preset should be considered permanent. They cannot be changed using Attedit or Change, which do allow you to change the other properties of attributes. If you intend to change these properties, you must redefine the attribute block, affecting existing blocks in varying ways:

- Updated constant attributes will be lost.
- New constant attributes will be added.
- Variable attributes will not be changed.
- New variable attributes will not be added.

You cannot verify preset attributes. Verify and Preset have no meaning for a constant attribute.

If you indicate no default value for an attribute, it will be possible for the user to enter a null value for this attribute at insertion time, creating a *null attribute*. It is more difficult to edit null attributes (refer to the Attedit command, described later in this chapter); therefore, it is recommended that you supply a default value, even if it is just a space or a zero, whenever possible.

You need not include other drawing entities in your block definition. It is entirely permissible to use a block that consists of nothing except attributes. You are free to insert such attribute-only blocks anywhere in your drawing. Thus, a single block can be associated with different sets of attributes within the drawing file. When you extract such attributes, however, it may be difficult to keep track of which drawing-entity block is associated with which attributes-only block. Possible solutions include inserting the attributes at the same insertion point as the drawing block, or storing the name of the nearby block as one of the attributes.

RELATED COMMANDS

Block, Insert.

RELATED SYSTEM VARIABLES

AFLAGS (stores the Invisible, Constant, Verify, and Preset mode defaults for attributes, and may be set using the Setvar command). You may find changing the system variable a little more convenient than setting these modes with the Attdef command. Also, ATTMODE (controls attribute visibility); ATTDIA (controls editing of attributes via dialog boxes). Refer to Chapter 13 for details.

SAMPLE DIALOG

The following dialog creates a set of three invisible attributes that will store dimensions and materials specs for a Window block.

```
Command: Attdef
Attribute modes -- Invisible:N Constant:N Verify:N Preset:N
Enter (ICVP) to change, RETURN when done: I
Enter (ICVP) to change, RETURN when done: (press Enter)
Attribute tag: Height
Attribute prompt: (press Enter)
Default attribute value: 48"
<Start point> justify/style: (pick a point)
Height <0'-0 3/16">: 6"
Rotation angle <0.00>: (press Enter)
```

```
Command: (press Enter)
ATTDEF
Attribute modes -- Invisible:Y Constant:N Verify:N Preset:N
Enter (ICVP) to change, RETURN when done: (press Enter)
Attribute tag: Width
Attribute prompt: (press Enter)
Default attribute value: 48"
<Start point> justify/style: (press Enter)
Command: (press Enter)
ATTDEF
Attribute modes -- Invisible:Y Constant:N Verify:N Preset:N
Enter (ICVP) to change, RETURN when done: (press Enter)
Attribute tag: Specs
Attribute prompt: Material Specs
Default attribute value: Stand. Alum.
<Start point> justify/style: (press Enter)
Command: Block
Block name (or ?) Window
Insertion base point: (pick a point)
Select objects w
First corner: Second corner: (window the attributes plus the window symbol)
Command: Insert
Block (or ?): Window
Insertion point: (pick a point)
X-Scale Factor: (press Enter)
Y-scale factor (default = x): (press Enter)
Rotation angle: (enter 0)
Material specs <Stand. Alum. >: Double Hung Oak.
Width <48"> 36
Height <48"> 36
```

MUTING ATTRIBUTE PROMPTS

If you wish, you may cause all prompts for attributes to be suppressed when you insert attribute blocks. This is useful in situations where attribute values are constant or preset, or you are willing to accept default values for all variable attributes. Under such circumstances, prompting for attribute value would be unnecessary.

To mute all attribute prompts when inserting blocks, set the ATTREQ system variable to 0. To resume normal prompting for attributes, set this variable to 1. Refer to Chapter 13 for details regarding system variables and how to reset their values.

The setting of this system variable does not affect your ability to edit attribute values after they have been inserted. Refer to the next section, "Editing Attributes," for details.

EDITING ATTRIBUTES

After you have created your attributes, gathered them into blocks, and inserted them into drawings, you may sometimes find it necessary to change them. The attribute mode settings (Invisible, Constant, Verify, and Preset) can only be changed by recreating the attribute and redefining the block, in accordance with the instructions given earlier, but all other attribute settings and values can be changed using the Attedit command described below.

ATTEDIT

The Attedit command allows for two types of attribute editing:

- *Individual editing* allows you to step through selected attributes and individually change their value, position, height, angle, style, layer, or color. Only attributes that are visible on the screen may be edited in this fashion.

- *Global editing* works only on attribute values, and allows you to indicate a single change that is to be applied globally to a specified set of attributes, whether visible on the screen or not.

When you invoke the Attedit command, you are first asked to choose between the two types of editing with the following prompt:

Edit attributes one at a time? <Y>

If you respond by entering **Y,** you are choosing individual editing. If you respond with **N,** you are choosing global editing.

Specifying the Attribute Set

Regardless of the type of editing you intend to perform, AutoCAD will ask you for specifications, if any, for the attributes you intend to edit. You can edit attributes that share block names, tag names, values, or any combination. AutoCAD prompts for these specifications as follows:

Block name specifications <*>:

This prompt asks you if you intend to edit attributes that have a specific block name in common. You may use standard *wild-card characters* in the block-name specification , so as to include more than one block name with certain characters in common. For example, the asterisk (*) indicates that any character in the block name is valid, starting at the position of the asterisk. The question mark (?) indicates that any single character in a given position in the block name is valid. In Release 11 and later, AutoCAD provides additional wild-card characters that allow you to narrow your selection of block names to a sophisticated level of inclusion. Refer to Chapter 21 for details about valid wild-card characters.

The next prompt asks you to restrict attribute tags in a similar manner:

Attribute tag specification < * >:

Again, using the same wild-card character rules, you may restrict the attributes you wish to edit to those that have certain tag characters in common.

Lastly, AutoCAD prompts:

Attribute value specification < * >:

Using the same wild-card rules, you may restrict attributes to those that have certain characters in their value specification in common.

Editing Null Attributes

Null attributes are never visible on the screen, and thus may never be edited individually unless you use the special AutoLISP routine in Figure 18.1. However, you may edit the values of null attributes globally with the Attedit command. If you have indicated global editing and wish to edit null attributes, enter a backslash in response to the "Attribute value specification" prompt.

```
(defun C:EDITATT( / valid valid2 blk attr ndata alist)
  (setq valid nil)
  (while (= valid nil)
    (setq blk (car (entsel "\nPick block: ")))
    (if (= blk nil)
      (prompt "\nNo entity found.")
      (if (not (equal (cdr (assoc '0 (entget blk))) "INSERT"))
        (prompt "\nNot a block.")
        (progn
          (setq alist (entnext blk))
          (if (or (= alist nil)
                  (not (equal (cdr (assoc '0 (entget alist)))
                              "ATTRIB"
                  )
              )
          )
```

FIGURE 18.1: EDITATT.LSP. This AutoLISP routine creates the AutoCAD command Editatt, which simplifies the process of changing individual attribute values in a chosen block. To use Editatt, enter the command, and pick the block using the pointing device. Then enter the tag name and the new value. The block will be updated with the new attribute value. You may continue to enter other tags and values for the chosen block. When finished, press Enter.

```
                              )
                              (prompt "\nNo attributes found.")
                              (setq valid T)
                          ) ; end if alist nil or not "ATTRIB"
                     ) ; end progn ("else" - block was found)
                ) ; end if not "INSERT"
           ) ; end if blk nil (no entity found)
      ) ; end while (no block found)
      (setq valid nil
            valid2 nil
      )
      (while (= valid2 nil)
         (while (= valid nil)
            (setq attr
               (getstring "\nAttribute tag to change (RETURN=exit): ")
            )
            (if (or (equal attr nil) (equal attr ""))
               (setq valid T
                     valid2 T
               )
               (progn
                  (prompt "\nLooking...")
                  (while
                     (and
                        (equal (cdr (assoc '0 (entget alist))) "ATTRIB")
                        (not (equal (cdr (assoc '2 (entget alist)))
                                    (strcase attr)
                             )
                        )
                     )
                     (setq alist (entnext alist))
                  ) ; end while (seeking named tag)
                  (if (or
                        (not (equal (cdr (assoc '0 (entget alist)))
                                    "ATTRIB"
                             )
                        )
                        (not (equal (cdr (assoc '2 (entget alist)))
                                    (strcase attr)
                             )
                        )
                     )
                     (progn
                        (prompt (strcat "\nTag " (strcase attr)
                                        " not found."
                                )
                        )
                        (setq alist (entnext blk))
                     ) ; end progn ("then" - tag not found)
                     (progn
                        (setq valid2 nil
                              ndata (getstring T
                                       "found.\nNew attribute value: "
                                    )
                        )
                        (entmod (subst (cons 1 ndata)
                                       (assoc '1 (entget alist))
                                       (entget alist)
                                )
                        )
                        (entupd blk)
                        (setq alist (entnext blk))
                     ) ; end progn ("else" - update attribute)
                  ) ;end if (tag not found - else)
               ) ; end progn (tag was entered)
            ) ; end if (tag or RETURN entered)
         ) ; end loop (get additional tags)
      ) ; end loop (get tag)
      (princ)
   ) ; end DEFUN
; EOF EDATT.LSP   86 lines
```

FIGURE 18.1: EDITATT.LSP (continued).

Individual Editing

Once you have indicated the block name, tag, and value specifications for attributes to edit, if you have selected individual editing, AutoCAD next prompts:

Select attributes:

You may select attributes by picking them individually using the pointing device, or by windowing them with either standard or crossing window selection. When windowing attributes, AutoCAD disregards any nonattribute entities that it finds, as well as any attributes that do not fit the previous criteria you have entered.

After you have selected attributes, an *X* will appear at the text insertion point of the first attribute AutoCAD finds in the selection set, and the following option prompt appears in the Command-prompt area:

Value/Position/Height/Angle/Style/Layer/Color/Next <N>:

Each of these options will change a property of the attribute currently marked with an *X*. No other attributes will be affected by the changes that you make to the currently marked attribute. Especially note that those attributes of the same name in multiple insertions of the same block are not affected by the changes made to one.

After you have changed a property of the currently marked attribute, the options repeat, allowing you to change as many different properties as you wish for the currently marked attribute, before moving on to the next one in the selection set.

Each option is explained below:

Value Enter **V** to edit the attribute value. AutoCAD responds:

Change or Replace? <R>:

Enter **C** to make a change to part of the attribute value. AutoCAD responds:

String to change:

Enter the character string that you intend to change. For example, if the value of the attribute was 21.95 and you wanted to change it to 41.95, you would enter **2.** AutoCAD responds:

New string:

Enter the new string. Continuing with the above example, you would enter **4,** and AutoCAD would replace the first occurrence of *2* that it finds in the attribute value with *4.*

To replace the entire attribute value, enter **R** in response to the "Change or Replace" prompt. AutoCAD responds:

New attribute value:

Enter the new attribute value, and AutoCAD replaces the old value with the new. After changing the values, AutoCAD repeats the options.

Position   Enter **P** to change the position of the attribute in the drawing. Auto-CAD prompts:

Enter text insertion point:

A preview image of the attribute will follow the crosshairs as you move the pointing device. You may pick a new point for the attribute or enter new coordinates from the keyboard.

Height   Enter **H** to change the height of the attribute. AutoCAD responds:

New height:

A rubberband line appears, extending from the text insertion point of the attribute to the intersection of the crosshairs; a preview image of the new height of the attribute will expand and contract as you move the pointing device. You may pick a new height for the attribute or enter a new height from the keyboard.

Angle   Enter **A** to change the angle of orientation of the attribute. AutoCAD responds:

New rotation angle:

A rubberband line appears, extending from the text insertion point of the attribute to the intersection of the crosshairs; a preview image of the attribute will follow the crosshairs as you move the pointing device. You may pick a new orientation angle for the attribute or enter an angle value from the keyboard.

Style   Enter **S** to change the text style of the attribute value that appears on the screen. AutoCAD responds:

Text style: *current style*
New style or RETURN for no change:

Enter the name of a currently defined text style. AutoCAD rewrites the attribute value using the new style.

Layer   Enter **L** to change the layer on which the attribute is drawn. AutoCAD responds:

> New layer:

Enter the name of a new layer to which the attribute is to be moved. The layer you select must already exist. Unlike with other commands, AutoCAD will not create a new layer if it cannot find the layer you specify. Rather, it will display a message to that effect and keep the attribute on its current layer.

Color   Enter **C** to change the color of the attribute. AutoCAD responds:

> New color:

Enter a color number that is supported by your display device. (Refer to Chapter 3 for details regarding color numbers.) You may also enter any of AutoCAD's standard color names (red, white, blue, etc.) or one of the special default color designations, Bylayer or Byblock.

Next   Enter **N** or press Enter to move the X marker to the next attribute in the selection set. The options repeat for this attribute.

You may select each attribute in sequence using this method, but notice that you cannot move backward through the selection set. Once you have moved the X marker through the selection set completely, the Attedit command concludes. You may terminate the command early at any time by pressing Ctrl-C.

Global Editing

If you have selected global editing, AutoCAD next prompts:

> Edit only attributes visible on the screen? <Y>

Enter **Y** or press Enter if you intend to make changes only to visible attributes. Enter **N** if you intend to make a global change to all specified attributes, whether visible on the screen or not. If you are globally editing null attributes, enter **N** in response to this prompt. AutoCAD then prompts for the block name, tag, and value specifications, as described in the previous section.

Visible Attributes

If you have indicated global editing of visible attributes, AutoCAD prompts:

> Select attributes:

You may select attributes by picking them individually using the pointing device, or by windowing them with either standard or crossing window selection. When windowing attributes, AutoCAD disregards any nonattribute entities that it finds, as well as any attributes that do not fit the previous criteria you have entered. AutoCAD highlights the selected attributes.

If you have indicated global editing of all specified attributes, not just visible ones, AutoCAD switches to the text screen (on single-screen systems, if not already there).

AutoCAD then prompts:

> String to change:

Enter the character string that you intend to change. For example, if the value of the selected attribute ended in .95 and you wanted to change it to .98, enter **.95**. Note that wild-card characters are not allowed at this point; you must use literal character strings only.

AutoCAD responds:

> New string:

Enter the new string. Continuing with the example, you would enter **.98** .AutoCAD replaces the first occurrence of .95 that it finds in each selected attribute with .98. If it does not find .95, it leaves the attribute value unchanged.

If you have indicated visible attributes, only the selected attributes are considered. If you have indicated all attributes, AutoCAD searches the entire drawing database for attributes that meet your indicated criteria, and makes the changes when they apply.

DIALOG BOXES FOR ATTRIBUTES

If your configuration supports the Advanced User Interface, you may enter, view, and edit attribute values using a dialog box, by means of the Insert and Ddatte commands, as explained below.

Entering Attributes via Dialog Boxes

The Insert command, described in detail in Chapter 9, will display an attribute-entry dialog box when you are inserting blocks with attributes. To display this dialog box, set the ATTDIA system variable to a value other than zero.

A typical attribute-entry dialog box is shown in Figure 18.2. Default values, if any, will be displayed in the attribute-value boxes. You may use the pointing device to move the arrow icon to one of the attribute-value boxes. You may use the pointing device to move the arrow icon to one of the attribute-value boxes and highlight it. Picking the highlighted box allows you to change its contents, and thus enter the attribute values of the block. When all values have been entered, pick the OK box, and the block is inserted. If you pick the Cancel button instead, the block is not inserted.

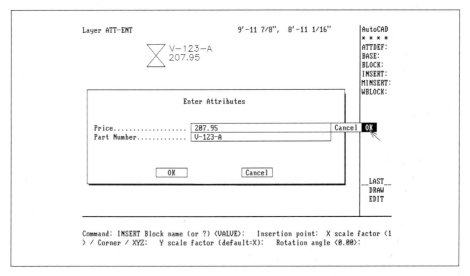

FIGURE 18.2: A typical attribute-entry dialog box. The block named Valve has two attributes, Price and Part Number. Prompts for attributes are displayed to the left; default values are displayed in the attribute-value boxes. In this illustration, the value for Price has been entered as 207.95, and the arrow icon has been moved to the OK box on the right to confirm the entry. After entry of the price, the arrow must be moved to the OK box in the lower left to insert the block with the chosen attribute values.

Note: Verify mode is ignored when using dialog boxes, since the dialog box itself presupposes verification.

Following is a brief summary of the Ddatte command.

Ddatte

Edits attribute values using a dialog box.

VERSIONS

Release 10 and later, with the Advanced User Interface.

COMMAND OPTIONS

Select Block   After you invoke the Ddatte command, AutoCAD prompts you to select a block. You must select a block with attributes.

A typical dialog box for editing attribute values is shown in Figure 18.3. You may use the pointing device to move the arrow icon to one of the attribute-value boxes and highlight it. Picking the highlighted box allows you to change its contents, and thus change the attribute value. When all values have been updated, pick the OK box, and the block is inserted. If you pick the Cancel button instead, the attributes are left unchanged.

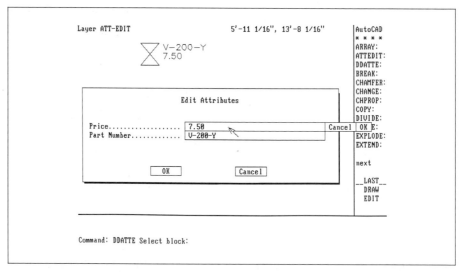

FIGURE 18.3: A typical dialog box for editing attribute values. In this figure, the pointing device has been moved to the Price attribute-value box, and the user has entered the revised price, 7.50. The Cancel and OK verification boxes appear to the right as the new value is entered. After the new value is entered and confirmed, the OK box in the lower left must be selected.

USAGE

In addition to being more interactive and intuitive, the dialog box is a convenient means of viewing the attributes of an inserted block. The dialog box will display all attribute values; you can remove it from the screen by picking either OK or Cancel.

RELATED COMMANDS

Attedit.

Length of Attribute

If you are using a version of AutoCAD earlier than Release 11, only the first 24 characters of an attribute tag are visible in a dialog box. All attribute-tag values are limited to 34 characters total. As of Release 11, you may enter and edit attribute values with a maximum of 255 characters. Any characters that do not fit in the dialog-box window will scroll to the left or right as you move the cursor in the window.

CONTROLLING VISIBILITY

The Attdisp command will control the visibility of attributes at any time during the drawing sessions. Following is a brief summary of the Attdisp command.

Attdisp

Controls the visibility of attributes.

VERSIONS

All.

COMMAND OPTIONS

You are offered three options regarding the visibility of attributes:

Normal   Select **N** if you want attributes to be displayed normally. Attributes with Invisible mode set will not be displayed normally. Attributes with Invisible mode set will not be displayed or plotted. The values of attributes with Visible mode set will be displayed and plotted normally.

ON   Select **ON** if you want all attributes to be visible, regardless of their attribute mode setting. When attributes are made visible using this option, their values (unless null) will appear on the screen, and they will be plotted.

OFF   Select **OFF** if you want all attributes to be invisible, regardless of their attribute mode setting. When attributes are invisible, they will not appear on the screen and they will not be plotted.

USAGE

Attdisp is especially useful when editing attributes with Invisible mode set. If you intend to edit these attributes individually, you must make them visible first. Notice that you do not need to make invisible attributes visible if you are changing values globally and you indicate that invisible attributes are to be included.

The Attdisp command has no effect on null attributes, which are never displayed, since there is no value to display.

RELATED SYSTEM VARIABLES

ATTMODE (controls attribute visibility).

EXTRACTING ATTRIBUTES

After attributes have been created and inserted in your drawing, you may extract them from the drawing and place them into the ASCII files called *extract files* on your hard disk. You have a choice of three possible formats for your extract files; these formats are explained a little later in this section. Extract files can be read by other software programs, such as spreadsheets, word processors, and databases. This allows you to exercise a great deal of analytical power over the attribute data in your drawings.

Briefly summarized, the attribute-extraction process is as follows:

1. Determine which extract-file format is appropriate for your intended use of the attribute data.

2. If necessary, create a *template file* using your word processor. The template file contains special instructions to AutoCAD regarding the type and amount of data you intend to extract.

3. Invoke the Attext command, which will extract the attribute data into a separate ASCII file on disk, according to the parameters you have specified in your template file.

Each of these steps is detailed in the sections that follow.

FILE FORMATS FOR ATTRIBUTE DATA

There are three types of file formats for extracted attribute data: Comma-Delimited (CDF), Standard Data (SDF), and Drawing Interchange (DXF). You may extract attribute data using any of these formats.

Records and Fields

Both CDF and SDF data formats organize attribute data into *records* and *fields,* a common method of organizing data when using microcomputers.

When each block's attribute data is extracted from an AutoCAD drawing, the attribute values for the block will compose a single record. This record will occupy a single line in the CDF or SDF file. Each extracted record will contain fields that correspond to the individual attribute values, plus, if you so desire, some optional information regarding the block itself, such as insertion point, block name, or scaling factors.

Thus, CDF and SDF files are composed of several records, each on its own line, and each record in turn is composed of several fields. The difference between the CDF and SDF formats is the manner in which they distinguish between the fields.

CDF Format

In a CDF (Comma-Delimited Format) file, each character field is surrounded by a special *delimiter,* usually the apostrophe character, and followed by a comma, which separates it from the other fields, as in the following example:

```
'Valve','V-123-A',207.95
'Valve','V-200-Y',7.50
'Gear','G-432',16.95
'Plate','P-670-1C',0.85
'Gear','G-444',12.95
'Plate','P-671-8W',1.75
```

This example contains six records, and each record has three fields. These fields might correspond to the block name, plus attributes tagged Part-Number and Price.

Notice how each field is enclosed within apostrophe characters and followed by a comma, except for the last field, the Price field. The Price field need not be enclosed in apostrophe characters because it is *numeric data,* meaning that, unlike the other fields, the Price field contains data that can be used mathematically (sums, averages, low-high comparisons, and so forth). The other fields, although they may contain numbers, cannot be analyzed mathematically, and are thus referred to as *character data,* and surrounded by apostrophe characters.

The Price field need not be followed by a comma because it is the last field in the record. Since the end of the line signals the end of the record, it signals the end of the field as well.

This type of extract file can be read by many common software packages.

SDF Format

In an SDF or Standard Data Format file, the fields would not require the apostrophes or commas, and would thus look a little different, as follows:

Valve	V-123-A	207.95
Valve	V-200-Y	7.50
Gear	G-432	16.95
Plate	P-670-1C	0.85
Gear	G-444	12.95
Plate	P-671-8W	.75

In this example, the same three records are arranged so that each field occupies the same number of spaces in the line, regardless of the number of characters in the field. Thus, all block names are allotted nine spaces, part numbers are allotted eleven spaces, and all prices are allotted seven spaces, including two decimal places. This format is usually easier to read because all fields are lined up in equal columns. It can be read by many microcomputer database packages, because they work with fields of fixed length.

DXF Format

DXF, or Drawing Interchange Format, uses a different structure that more closely follows the structure of AutoCAD's underlying database. In DXF format, block and attribute data are each listed on a separate line in the field, and are preceded by a unique identifying *group code,* also on its own line. This type of file format can easily become many lines long. A listing of the first sample record in such a file is shown in Figure 18.4.

A detailed explanation of DXF is presented in Chapter 20.

TEMPLATE FILES

If you have determined that the CDF or SDF file format will best suit your needs, your next step is to create a *template file.* A template file is a separate ASCII file; you may give it any name you choose, but it always has the extension TXT. Using a text editor, you must prepare the template file before you attempt to extract attribute data in CDF or SDF format. The purpose of the template file is to show AutoCAD, in outline form, the structure of a single record, which AutoCAD will then follow when creating all the records in the extract file.

```
        0
    INSERT
        8
    0
       66
            1
        2
    VALVE
       10
    96.0
       20
    138.0
       30
    0.0
        0
    ATTRIB
        8
    0
        1
    V-123-A
        2
    PART-NUMBER
       70
            1
        0
    ATTRIB
        8
    0
        1
    207.95
        2
    PRICE
       70
            0
        0
    SEQEND
        8
    0
        0
```

FIGURE 18.4: A single record from a DXF attribute file. The first heading, INSERT, indicates a block, and is followed by group codes indicating the layer, the presence of attributes, the block name, and the insertion point. The ATTRIB headings are followed by similar group codes for layer, value, tag, and visibility. The SEQEND heading indicates the end of fields for this record.

Specifically, the template file will contain the following information for each attribute tag whose data you intend to include in the extract file's records:

- The tag name.
- A code letter (*C* or *N*) indicating whether the values associated with the tag name are character or numeric data.
- The maximum number of spaces allowed for the field in the extract file.
- The number of decimal places, if the values associated with the tag name are numbers.

For example, following is the template file that was used to create the sample CDF and SDF extract files:

```
BL:NAME          C       009 000
PART-NUMBER      C       011 000
PRICE            N       007 002
```

This three-line template file illustrates the structure for all template files. Each line in the template file corresponds to a field in the extract file. The entire template file displays the structure of a single record.

The first entry on each line of the template file is the name of the field. This may be an attribute tag or one of several predefined names for block characteristics, as outlined ahead. In the example just given, the first entry on the first line is the predefined field name for the name of the block. On subsequent lines, the corresponding entries are the attribute tags used in the example: Part-Number and Price.

The field name must be followed by at least one space, to distinguish it from the additional data that follows. If you choose, you may add any number of additional spaces in order to line up all the information that follows into even columns. These extra spaces will be ignored. However, if you choose to line up the data in even columns, use spaces only; do not use the tab character.

To indicate whether the data is character data or numeric data, the code letter *C* or *N* follows the field name. Since the block-name and part-number fields do not contain values that can be manipulated mathematically, they are given the code letter *C*, for character data. The price field, however, does contain data that may be manipulated mathematically, so it is given the code letter *N*, for numeric data. Following the code letter is an optional space, added for the sake of clarity only.

The next three digits represent the maximum size of the field. In the example, the block-name field is given a maximum size of nine character spaces. The field size is always expressed with three digits—in this case, 009. Again for the sake of clarity, another optional space follows.

Lastly, three more digits indicate the number of decimal places. For character data, this is always 000. For numeric data, any number of decimal places may be expressed, but it must be at least two numbers fewer than the field size. This is because at least one space will always precede the decimal point, and another will be used by the decimal point itself. In the current example, the Price tag is given a field size of seven, including two decimal places.

The order of the field names in the template file is important, since the order of the fields in the extract file will match the order of the field name in the template file.

Attribute values will be extracted from the drawing when their attribute tags match a field names in the template file. The match is not case-sensitive; that is, all characters are converted to uppercase during the extraction process.

A template file must contain at least one attribute tag. Any number of additional tags may be included. If a block in the drawing does not contain any of the attribute tags listed in the template file, the block will not be included in the extract file. If a block includes only some of the attribute tags in the template file, it will be included, showing blank spaces (for character data) or zeros (for numeric data) for those attributes that do not apply to that block.

Block Characteristics in Template Files

Template files may also include predefined field names that correspond to characteristics of the blocks in the drawing. If you have included at least one attribute tag, you may also include any combination of these field names, in any order. They are listed in Table 18.1.

BLOCK CHARACTERISTIC	FIELD NAME	DATA TYPE	SAMPLE WIDTH	SAMPLE DECIMAL PLACES
Entity handle	BL:HANDLE	C	016	000
Layer	BL:LAYER	C	031	000
Nesting level	BL:LEVEL	N	005	000
Name	BL:NAME	C	031	000
Number	BL:NUMBER	N	005	000
Rotation angle	BL:ORIENT	N	012	008
X insertion point	BL:X	N	017	008
Y insertion point	BL:Y	N	017	008
Z insertion point	BL:Z	N	017	008
X coordinate, 3-D orientation	BL:XEXTRUDE	N	017	008
Y coordinate, 3-D orientation	BL:YEXTRUDE	N	017	008
Z coordinate, 3-D orientation	BL:ZEXTRUDE	N	017	008
X scale factor	BL:XSCALE	N	017	008
Y scale factor	BL:YSCALE	N	017	008
Z scale factor	BL:ZSCALE	N	017	008

TABLE 18.1: Block Characteristics and Predefined Field Names

While the field name and data type for each of these characteristics is fixed, you may adjust the width of each field as you wish, in order to suit your needs and conserve space in the extract file. The sample figures given in Table 18.1 are based on standard maximum sizes (31 spaces for layer and block names, 8 decimal places of precision for coordinates and angles, 16 significant digits).

As mentioned previously, the number of decimal places for character data (block handle, layer, and name) is always zero. The number of decimal places for the nesting-level and block-number fields should be zero as well, since these numbers are always integers.

The coordinate points that express a block's 3-D orientation are available in Release 10 and later. The coordinate points that reflect the block's insertion point, scale factor, rotation angle, and 3-D orientation are expressed relative to the world coordinate system only; they bear no relationship to the user coordinate system that was in effect at the time the block was inserted.

When data is extracted from nested blocks in any version of AutoCAD, the insertion point, scale factor, rotation angle, and 3-D orientation are expressed in coordinates that reflect the nested block's actual orientation and size relative to AutoCAD's standard x-, y-, and z-axes (the world coordinate system). In other words, these coordinates are not expressed relative to the host block's orientation.

In Release 10 and later, there is the remote possibility that a deeply nested block with different XYZ scale factors and 3-D orientation may not be accurately represented in the extract file using just a single set of world coordinates and one rotation angle. In such cases, scale factors and rotation angle will be set to zero.

Changing the Delimiters

Finally, note that in the case of CDF files, you may substitute a different character for the default apostrophe that surrounds character-data fields, as well as the default comma that separates fields. For example, suppose your third-party software program reads a CDF file in which the fields are surrounded by quotation marks and separated by semicolons. In such a case, you may include two special lines in your template file, as follows:

```
C:QUOTE "
C:DELIM ;
```

These special field names must be followed by at least one space and the character you wish to substitute for the default character. The character following the C:QUOTE field name will replace the default apostrophe, and the character following the C:DELIM field name will replace the default comma character. No data-type code letter, field size, or decimal-place numbers are required or even permitted.

Following is a brief description of the Attext command.

ATTEXT

Extracts attribute data into an ASCII extract file of a chosen format, according to the parameters set up in a predefined template file.

VERSIONS

All.

COMMAND OPTIONS

After you invoke the Attext command, the following prompt appears:

CDF, SDF, DXF Attribute extract (or Entities)?

The options available at this prompt are as follows:

CDF Enter **C** if you intend that the extract file be in Comma-Delimited Format. This format requires that you have previously set up a template file.

SDF Enter **S** if you intend that the extract file be in Standard Data Format. This format requires that you have previously set up a template file.

DXF Enter **D** if you intend that the extract file be in AutoCAD's Drawing Interchange File format. This format does not require a template file.

Entities Enter **E** if you would like to select the set of blocks whose attributes are to be extracted. If you select this option, AutoCAD responds:

Select objects:

You may select the blocks whose attributes you intend to extract by using any of AutoCAD's standard entity-selection methods (see Chapter 5). After you have selected the blocks to include, press Enter, and AutoCAD repeats the format prompt. You may then select the format for the extract file.

The purpose of this option is to allow you the choice of excluding certain blocks when producing an extract file in the DXF format (which would otherwise extract all the attributes in the drawing). Also, in the case of CDF and SDF formats, blocks you have excluded from your selection set will not have their attribute data extracted, even if they contain tag names found in the template file.

After you choose the entities (if desired), AutoCAD prompts for a template file name, if you have chosen either the CDF or SDF formats, and an extract file name. If you are using Release 11 or later, and the FILEDIA system variable is set to 1, and your display supports the Advanced User Interface, then you can designate these entities as entries by means of a dialog box. This dialog box allows you to select the name of the file you intend to use (as well as its drive and subdirectory location) from a list of files. If you attempt to overwrite an existing file, AutoCAD will display a warning message and allow you to confirm the overwrite or select another file name. Refer to Chapter 5 for details regarding dialog boxes. If you cannot use the dialog box, AutoCAD prompts:

Template file:

Enter the name of a template file you have prepared. The file extension TXT is assumed, therefore do not include an extension. You may include a drive letter and subdirectory path name if you wish. You will not see this prompt if you have chosen the DXF file format.

After you have selected your template file, AutoCAD prompts for an extract file:

Extract file name:

Enter the name of the extract file that AutoCAD is to produce. Again, the extension TXT is assumed if you have indicated CDF or SDF format; the extension DXX is used if you have selected DXF format (to distinguish the file from Auto-CAD's standard DXF file—refer to Chapter 20 for details). Therefore, do not supply an extension, although you may supply a drive letter and subdirectory path name to have AutoCAD place the file there.

After you have specified the extract-file name, AutoCAD creates the extract file. You may then process the extract file using another software program.

USAGE

Once you have set up your template file (if necessary), the Attext command provides a quick means of extracting attribute values into an external ASCII file. Template files require only a little practice, after which you will find them easy to set up using your text editor.

Warning: Beware when specifying extract-file If you are using a version of Auto-CAD prior to Release 11, or if dialog boxes are not enabled via the FILEDIA system variable, AutoCAD provides no warning when overwriting existing files of the same name on disk. If you intend to keep previous extract files, make certain that you are entering a unique name for the current one. And, since both the template files and CDF/SDF extract files have the same file extension, TXT, don't name the extract file after the template file, or you will lose your template file!

SAMPLE DIALOG

The following dialog assumes that you have created a template like the sample file shown in this chapter, and have named it SAMPLE.TXT. You will produce an SDF extract file called TEST.TXT.

```
Command: Attext
CDF, SDF, DXF Attribute extract (or Entities)? <C> S
Template file: Sample
Extract file name: Test
6 entities in extract file
```

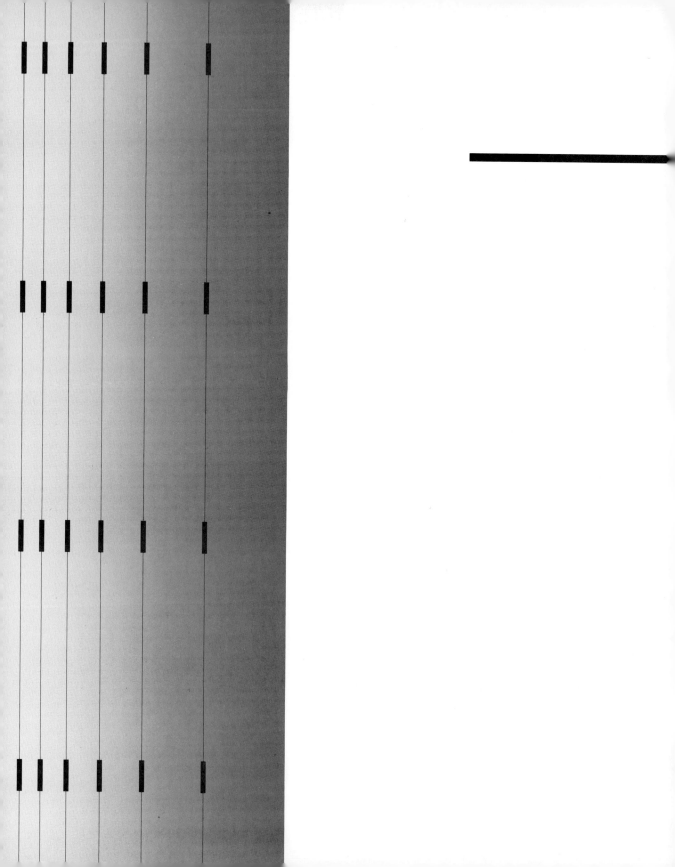

CHAPTER 19

ENTITY-ASSOCIATION LISTS

Entity-Association Lists

All of the entities in an AutoCAD drawing are stored in a specialized entity database. AutoCAD Versions 2.5 and later include several powerful AutoLISP functions that allow you direct access and modification of AutoCAD's entity database, selecting items to be modified either individually or in groups. This can speed up your work by reducing the time spent in the selection process, or free you to do other work while AutoCAD performs complex selection and editing routines for you.

If necessary, review Chapters 16 and 17 to familiarize yourself with the fundamentals of AutoLISP before reading this chapter.

Entity Names and Handles

Each entity in the database is automatically assigned a unique *entity name* during a drawing session. The entity name is actually an eight-digit number in hexadecimal notation. The internal structure of entity names and their assignment to entities is completely transparent to the user.

An entity name is actually a unique AutoLISP data type. When an entity name is retrieved from the underlying database by means of various predefined functions, it will be displayed in the format

<Entity name: *nnnnnnnn*>

where *nnnnnnnn* represents the numbers that make up the entity name. Several functions accept an entity name as an argument, but it must be bound to a memory variable first; or, if it is not necessary to store the entity name in memory, you may use a function that returns an entity name as an argument to a function that accepts one.

Linked to each entity name is the information required to produce that entity on the screen or plotting device. For example, a new line drawn in AutoCAD would automatically be given a unique entity name, and associated with that name would be the type of entity it is ("LINE"), the layer it is on; the linetype (if not the default for the layer), the starting point, the endpoint; the elevation (if any), the thickness (if any), and the color (if not the default for the layer).

In Release 11 and later, drawing entities may also include additional data to be used by external applications developed with AutoLISP or the Advanced Development System. Refer to the section on Extended Entity Data further ahead for details.

Entity handles, available in Release 10 and later, are another means of identifying entities. While an entity name may change from editing session to editing session, an entity handle is permanently associated with a particular entity for as long as it exists in the drawing. Entity handles are alphanumeric strings that are assigned to entities when they are created. Entity handles are useful when creating AutoLISP functions that must automatically access the same set of entities in a drawing across many editing sessions. To use entity handles, you must explicitly instruct AutoCAD to assign them, by means of the Handles command (Chapter 5). Because entity handles can significantly increase the size of AutoCAD's underlying drawing database, their use is optional.

ASSOCIATION LISTS

Using special functions in AutoLISP, the properties of each entity in the database can be extracted and returned in the form of an *association list.* An association list is a list of other lists, called *sublists,* that contain the data necessary to produce the entity.

The first member of each sublist is a special integer called a *group code,* which identifies one particular property of the entity. For example, the first sublist in any association list is the entity name itself. The entity name always has a group code of −1. Given an entity name of 60000014, the sublist for that entity name would look like the following:

(−1 . <Entity name: 60000014>)

As a further example, the group code for the layer location of any entity is 8. Therefore, if the entity existed on layer 0, the sublist for the layer location would appear as follows:

(8 . "0")

The use of group codes allows AutoCAD to identify any particular sublist, regardless of the order in which it appears within the association list. A complete list of sublist group codes associated with AutoCAD entities can be found inside the cover of this book.

Most sublists contain only two members: the group code and the specific item of drawing information associated with that group code. When the sublist contains only two members, it will be displayed showing the members separated by a space, a period, and another space, as in the examples just shown. Such sublists are called *dotted pairs.* Association lists use dotted pairs because they occupy less memory than ordinary lists.

Sublists that contain coordinate point information cannot be dotted pairs, because they contain either three or four members: the group code, the x coordinate, the y coordinate, and often the z coordinate. A dotted pair will not work in this case, so these sublists appear as ordinary data lists. The groups codes for coordinate point information are 10 through 16. Such coordinate point sublists appear as in the following example, which shows a point at 12.5,12.5,0:

```
(10 12.500000 12.500000 0.000000)
```

Finally, following is a complete association list for a green line that begins at point 0,0,0 and ends at point 20,20,12. It is located on layer Lines, and it has a thickness of 2 drawing units and an elevation of 0. Notice how the sublists are aligned in sequence, nested within the set of parentheses that defines the association list:

```
(
    (-1 . <Entity name: 60000014>)
    ( 0 . "LINE")
    ( 8 . "LINES")
    (10 0.000000 0.000000 0.000000)
    (11 20.000000 20.000000 12.000000)
    (39 . 2.000000)
    (62 . 3)
)
```

EXTENDED ENTITY DATA

AutoCAD Release 11 and later allow you to attach additional data to the association lists of individual entities. This data is referred to as *extended data*. Although AutoCAD stores and maintains this information, it does not use it, except in the case of viewport entities in paper space. Extended data is reserved for use by custom applications developed with either AutoLISP or the Advanced Development System.

Each set of extended entity data is grouped into a list and each list must begin with a character string specifying the name of the external application that will use it.

As with AutoCAD's standard entity-association lists, extended data is stored in lists of other lists containing group codes and their associated data. Group codes for extended data are four-digit integers. An individual entity may include several extended-data lists, with a limit of 16383 bytes or just under 16K.

AutoLISP includes all extended-data lists (which begin with a -3 group code) consecutively within a large overall list. An example of this arrangement appears in the following example section.

Following are the group codes used for extended entity data, along with their meanings. They are all optional, depending on the requirements of their associated application:

1000   General descriptive string. Maximum length is 255 bytes. This string may contain character-based information, comments, or whatever you like.

1001   The external application name associated with this data. You must include an application name with any extended-data list you want to append to a standard entity-association list. Furthermore, you must include the application name associated with this group code in AutoCAD's APPID symbol table, which you can do with AutoLISP's Regapp function. Even if you fail to update the APPID symbol table, AutoCAD will maintain the data, but if you attempt to access it, AutoCAD will terminate the drawing session.

The maximum length of this string is 31 characters. Letters and numbers are valid, but spaces are not. It is not case sensitive—all characters are converted to uppercase.

Only one 1001 group code sublist should appear within an extended entity data list. Exceptions to this rule are noted ahead.

The 1001 group code is not returned when you access extended entity data with AutoLISP. AutoLISP simply places the string at the start of the extended-data list. However, the 1001 group code is returned when you access the data with ADS applications. The code is also returned in DXF output files. Refer to Chapter 20 for details on the DXF file format.

When you are processing extended entity data using AutoLISP, the application name must be the first member in any list of extended entity data. If AutoLISP finds a 1001 group code within the list, it will treat the data as a string, not an application name.

Likewise, if you are processing the data using an ADS application, a 1001 group will signify a string if it appears within *control strings,* which are marked using group code 1002.

1002   Indicates a control string for grouping related sublists. As of Release 11, the only characters allowed for grouping are curly brackets ({}). Their purpose is to clarify the organization of the extended entity data list. Because both brackets are paired with group code 1002, the order in which they appear is extremely important. Each opening bracket must be balanced with a closing bracket somewhere further along within the data list. Brackets may be nested to any reasonable level but they must be balanced, the same way parentheses must be balanced within AutoLISP functions.

1003   A string containing the name of a layer where the extended entity data may reside.

1004   General data stored in binary format for use by an ADS external application. Maximum field size is 127 bytes.

1005   An entity handle associated with the extended entity-data list.

1010   Three real numbers. Often this group code will signal point information, but it can be used to store any numeric data.

1011   Three real numbers representing a point location in the world coordinate system. These numbers will change if the drawing entity is moved, scaled, or otherwise updated in a way that moves it in the drawing.

1012   Three real numbers representing a displacement point in the WCS. This point will be updated when an entity is scaled, mirrored, copied, or rotated. It is not updated when the entity is stretched or moved.

1013   Three real numbers that are updated in the same way as the numbers in 1012 sublists. These two lists can be used together to represent an orientation in the WCS.

1040   Indicates a real number.

1041   A real number indicating a distance value. It will be updated if the drawing entity is scaled.

1042   A second real number, often used to represent a scaling factor. It will also be updated if the drawing entity is scaled.

1070   Indicates a 16-bit (short) integer value, for use by both AutoLISP and ADS applications.

1071   Indicates a 32-bit (long) integer value, for use by ADS applications. AutoLISP does not recognize long integers.

The following example shows the extended entity-data list that might be returned by AutoLISP for a paper-space viewport entity, in addition to its standard association list. (Refer to the Entget function later in this chapter for details on extracting extended entity data lists in AutoLISP.)

(-3	Group code indicates the start of extended entity data. Used only in AutoLISP; not used in ADS
("ACAD"	Application name for viewport data
(1000 . "MVIEW")	Data string identifying viewport entity
(1002 . "{")	Start of overall data group
(1070 . 16)	Viewport ID Number
(1010 0.0 0.0 0.0)	View-angle target point
(1010 0.0 0.0 1.0)	View-angle direction vector
(1040 . 0.0)	View twist angle
(1040 . 15.25)	View display height
(1040 . 7.625)	View center
(1040 . 5.52247)	View aspect ratio
(1040 . 50.0)	View lens length
(1040 . 0.0)	Front-clip plane z value
(1040 . 0.0)	Back-clip plane z value
(1070 . 0)	View mode bit-code flag
(1070 . 100)	Circle zoom percentage
(1070 . 1)	Fast zooming enabled
(1070 . 0)	UCSICON setting
(1070 . 1)	Snap on/off switch
(1070 . 1)	Grid on/off switch
(1070 . 0)	Snap style flag
(1070 . 0)	Snap isopair setting
(1040 . 0.0)	Snap angle
(1040 . 0.0)	Snap base
(1040 . 0.25)	Snap X spacing
(1040 . 0.25)	Snap Y spacing
(1040 . 0.0)	Grid X spacing
(1040 . 0.0)	Grid Y spacing
(1070 . 0)	Flag for hidden when plotting
(1002 . "{")	Begin nested data group

(1002 . "}")	End of nested data group
(1002 . "}")	End of overall data group
)	End of "ACAD" application extended data
)	End of -3 group code list

In the above example, notice that the extended data for the viewport entity is contained in a list where the first member is the name of an associated application, in this case, ACAD. This list is nested entirely within another list where the first member is the -3 group code. The list beginning with -3 can store any number of extended entity data lists, each beginning with the name of an associated application.

ENTITY-ACCESS FUNCTIONS

Since association lists are structured as lists of sublists, all enclosed within matched sets of parentheses, they can be used and modified by AutoLISP functions. Some functions have been predefined to act exclusively upon association lists. Predefined AutoLISP functions that act on entity-association lists begin with *Ent*.

Retrieving and acting upon entity-association lists is a three-step process:

1. The entity name is retrieved from the drawing database.
2. Sublists associated with that entity name are retrieved and modified by referencing the appropriate group code.
3. The entire association list is updated in the drawing database to include the changed entities.

Following is a list of functions that act upon entity-association lists.

Entdel

Deletes an entity from the database. If the entity was previously deleted during the current editing session, Entdel will restore it to the drawing database.

REQUIRED ARGUMENTS

An entity name.

USAGE

Entdel acts as a toggle between deleting and restoring entities during the current editing session. Once an editing session has been ended using the End command, deleted entities are discarded permanently.

Certain entities, such as polyline vertices and block attributes, are linked to main entities and cannot be deleted or restored using Entdel. Only the main entities (e.g., "POLYLINE" and "INSERT") can be deleted and restored using this function.

Entget

Returns a list of all the sublists in an entity's association list.

REQUIRED ARGUMENTS

An entity name, either stored in a memory variable or returned by a nested function. In Release 11, a second optional argument, consisting of a list of one or more external application names, may be supplied in order to return extended entity data.

USAGE

Entget is the function to use when you wish to extract the association list for a given entity name.

To extract extended entity data, you may supply the names of external applications in the form of a quoted list of strings. You must supply this argument as a list, even if the list contains only one application name. All application names you use must be in the APPID symbol table. Refer to the Regapp function later in this chapter for details on adding external application names to this table.

Following is an example using the entget function to extract the standard data-association list along with any extended-data list associated with external applications named "Prog-1" and "Prog-2",

```
(entget <entity name> '("PROG-1" "PROG-2"))
```

If extended data exists for the referenced applications, it will be returned. Otherwise, the function simply returns the standard entity-association list.

EXAMPLES

Assume that you have just drawn a line from point 1,1 to point 3,3 on layer 0 using AutoCAD Release 10 and later. The following function then becomes valid:

(setq alist (entget (entlast)))

This function returns an association list similar to the following, and stores it it memory variable *alist*:

```
( ( −1 . <Entity name: 60000030 >)
  (0 . "LINE")
  (8 . "0")
  (10 1.0 1.0 0.0)
  (11 3.0 3.0 0.0)
  (210 0.0 0.0 1.0)
)
```

The following example will prompt you to select an entity and return its association list. If you select a paper-space viewport (that is, one created using the Mview command), the function will include the extended entity data for that viewport:

(entget (car (entsel)) '("ACAD"))

Entlast

Returns the name of the last entity in the drawing database. This has the same effect as selecting the Last option of AutoCAD's "Select objects:" prompt.

REQUIRED ARGUMENTS

None.

USAGE

This function is often used to select and store an entity that has just been created by a previous command or function. Usually an entity name returned by this function has a memory variable bound to it, as in the upcoming example.

If the last entity is a complex entity, such as a Polyline or Block, AutoLISP will return the main entity. If you wish to access the sub-entities, use the Entnext function, described later in this section, to loop through them.

EXAMPLES

In this example, memory variable *x* would be bound to the name of the last entity in the database, and this variable can be passed as an argument to other

AutoLISP functions that expect entities:

(setq x (entlast))   Returns the entity name.

Entmake

Adds a new entity to the drawing database.

REQUIRED ARGUMENTS

A valid entity-association list (such as the Entget function might return) containing the necessary sublists to produce the desired entity. If you call Entmake without arguments, it cancels any complex entity currently under construction.

USAGE

The Entmake function is available in Release 11 and later. Prior releases of AutoLISP produced new entities using the Command function, described in Chapter 17. Entmake is more efficient than the Command function, because it can add new entities without calling upon a dialog with AutoCAD's command processor. However, it requires greater programming overhead, and therefore is more likely to be useful in cases where AutoLISP calculates new entity data, assembles it into an association list, and creates new entities often enough to make the additional programming effort worthwhile.

AutoLISP does not require that the association list passed to it contain every possible sublist for the new entities. At a minimum, the association list must contain the entity type in a dotted pair with a zero group code; for example, **(0."LINE")** or **(0 . "ARC")**, along with the necessary geometry to describe the entity. Optional sublists can include those that indicate layer, linetype, color, thickness, elevation, and so forth. When optional sublists are not supplied, default values (for example, the current layer) are supplied by Entmake.

A common usage of Entmake is to extract the association list of a given entity, modify it in some fashion, and supply the modified list to Entmake, thereby creating a second entity.

An association list's sublists may be in any order, except for the entity type (group code zero). This must be the first sublist in the association list, unless it is preceded by an entity name (group code -1). If the association list passed to Entmake contains an entity-name sublist, the entity name is ignored and a new one is substituted.

The block-definition association list is an exception to the above. This list should contain group-code sublists in the following order: 0, the "BLOCK" entity type; 2, block name; other optional sublists, such as layer or color; 70, block type flag, usually either 0 (unreferenced) or 64 (referenced); and 10, block insertion point (usually 0,0,0).

If a layer sublist (group code 8) indicates a layer that is not already part of the drawing, a new layer is created. If you supply a group code 6 sublist (linetype), the linetype must be previously loaded into the drawing.

All other invalid association lists will cause this function to return nil, and no new entity will be created. If the new entity is created, this function returns the association list for the entity, but not the new entity's name. To determine the new name, use the Entlast function immediately after using Entmake.

In the case of a complex entity such as a polyline or block, you must make a minimum of three Entmake calls. The first should define the entity header, the second, any nested entities such as vertices or attributes, and the last should be the Seqend entity, to indicate that all the sub-entities have been added. A complex entity will not be added to the drawing database or displayed on the screen until a Seqend entity is declared. An example of this process appears below.

If you create a block using Entmake, it will overwrite any existing block definition with the same name. You can use the Tblsearch function to check the Block symbol table for possible duplicate names.

Table 19.1 describes the *minimum* information required by AutoLISP's Entmake function to process new entities. Additional group code sublists may be added to make entity definitions more complete. For additional sublists, follow the format as illustrated in Table 19.1.

Warning: Some third-party ADI display drivers, if not written specifically for Release 11, may have trouble displaying entities created with Entmake. If your display driver has trouble in this regard, you must upgrade to a Release-11 driver.

EXAMPLES

Both of the following functions create simple line entities. The first allows for default information, the second supplies specific information for layer, color, and linetype:

```
(entmake (list (cons 0 "LINE")
               '(10 0 0 0)
               '(11 5 5 0)
        ))
(entmake (list (cons 0 "LINE")
               '(10 0 5 0)
               '(11 5 0 0)
```

Entity	Entmake Function Requires
Point	(entmake (list (cons 0 ''POINT'') '(10 *point*)))
Line	(entmake (list (cons 0 ''LINE'') '(10 *start point*) '(11 *end point*)))
Arc	(entmake (list (cons 0 ''ARC'') '(10 *center point*) (cons 40 *bulge factor*) (cons 50 *start angle*) (cons 51 *end angle*)))
Circle	(entmake (list (cons 0 ''CIRCLE'') '(10 *center point*) (cons 40 *radius*)))
Trace	(entmake (list (cons 0 ''TRACE'') '(10 *1st corner point*) '(11 *2nd corner point*) '(12 *3rd corner point*) '(13 *4th corner point*)))
Shape	(entmake (list (cons 0 ''SHAPE'') (cons 2 ''*shape name*'') '(10 *insert point*)))
Solid*	(entmake (list (cons 0 ''SOLID'') '(10 *1st corner point*) '(11 *2nd corner point*) '(12 *3rd corner point*) '(13 *4th corner point*)))
3D Face*	(entmake (list (cons 0 ''3DFACE'') '(10 *1st corner point*) '(11 *2nd corner point*) '(12 *3rd corner point*)

Table 19.1: Minimum Information for AutoLISP's Entmake Functions

Entity	Entmake Function Requires
	'(13 *4th corner point*)))
Text	(entmake (list (cons 0 "TEXT") (cons 1 *"Text String"*) '(10 *start point*) '(cons 40 *text height*)))
Block Definition	(entmake (list (cons 0 "BLOCK") (cons 2 *"block name"*) (cons 70 *integer block flag*) '(10 *insertion point*)))
Attribute Definition	(entmake (list (cons 0 "ATTDEF") (cons 1 *"Default Value"*) (cons 2 *"Attribute Tag"*) (cons 3 *"Prompt"*) '(10 *insert point*) (cons 40 *text height*) (cons 70 *attribute flag*)))
Block End of Definition	(entmake (list (cons 0 "ENDBLK")))
Normal Block Insertion	(entmake (list (cons 0 "INSERT") (cons 2 *block name*) '(10 *insert point*)) (
Insert with Attributes	(entmake (list (cons 0 "INSERT") (cons 2 *block name*) '(10 *insert point*) (cons 66 1)) (
Insert Block Attribute	(entmake (list (cons 0 "ATTRIB") (cons 1 *"Attribute Value"*) (cons 2 *"Attribute Tag"*) '(10 *insert point*) (cons 40 *text height*) (cons 70 *integer attribute flag*)))

Table 19.1: Minimum Information for AutoLISP's Entmake Functions (continued)

Entity	Entmake Function Requires
2-D Polyline Header	(entmake (list (cons 0 "POLYLINE")))

2-D Polyline Vertex	(entmake (list (cons 0 "VERTEX")
	    '(10 *point*)
	    )
	)

3-D Polyline Header	(entmake (list (cons 0 "POLYLINE")
	    (cons 70 8)
	    )
	)

3-D Polyline Vertex	(entmake (list (cons 0 "VERTEX")
	    '(10 *point*)
	    (cons 70 32)
	    )
	)

End-of-Sequence	(entmake (list (cons 0 "SEQEND")))

NOTES: *Italics* indicate values you must supply, such as strings, points, or angles. String values are indicated by quotes (""). Numeric values are real numbers, except where specifically indicated as integers. Angles are expressed in radians. Observe the Quote function where noted for point lists. Refer to the inside cover for more information regarding the meaning of specific group codes.

* If the figure is three-sided, two adjacent points must be the same point.
† Group code sublists for Block Definition should be supplied in this order: 0, 2, 70, 10.

Table 19.1: Minimum Information for AutoLISP's Entmake Functions (continued)

(cons 6 "DOT")	Linetype
(cons 8 "LINES")	Layer
(cons 62 4)	Color: Cyan
))	

Entmod

Updates entity-association list information in the drawing database.

REQUIRED ARGUMENTS

A single argument: an entity-association list with an entity name that is present in the drawing database.

USAGE

Entmod will replace the sublists in the drawing database with the corresponding sublists referenced in its argument. If Entmod is given an argument that is not a valid association list, or if the entity name found in the argument list does not match an entity name in the drawing database, Entmod does nothing and returns nil.

In addition, Entmod will not allow changes to an entity's handle, type (such as "CIRCLE" or "LINE"), paper-space viewports, or entity name.

In Release 11 it is possible to modify an entity that is part of a block definition. If you do so, all references to that block in the drawing will be changed to reflect the changes you have made to the member entity. However, changes made to block entities may not become visible until you regenerate the drawing.

EXAMPLES

Assume that a line in a drawing is represented by an association list, which has been stored in a memory variable named *alist* by means of the function

```
(setq alist (entlast))
```

The function returns an association list:

```
( ( −1 . <Entity name: 60000030>)
  (0 . "LINE")
  (8 . "0")
  (10 1.0 1.0 0.0)
  (11 3.0 3.0 0.0)
  (210 0.0 0.0 1.0))
```

The following function will change the layer (group code 8) from layer 0 to layer Lines. It uses the Subst and Cons functions to substitute a new layer sublist for the old layer sublist, store the revised association list back to the original memory variable, and update the drawing database:

```
(entmod (setq alist (subst (cons '8 "LINES") (cons '8 "0") alist)))
```

Notice that the dotted pairs used as arguments for the above Subst function are referenced by means of the Cons function, rather than simply being referenced using parentheses and a period. In other words, the following functions would not work, and would cause an error message to appear instead:

```
(entmod (setq alist (subst (8 . "LINES") (8 . "0") alist)))
```

Dotted pairs have a special structure that must be recognized by the Auto-LISP interpreter. To make that structure known to the AutoLISP interpreter, you must reference dotted pairs either by having memory variables bound to dotted pairs returned by functions, or by referencing the Cons function with appropriate arguments, rather than simply by enclosing the data in parentheses with a period in between.

Entnext

Returns an entity name. The exact entity name returned depends on the function argument.

REQUIRED ARGUMENTS

None required. When used without arguments, Entnext returns the first entity name in the drawing database. Entnext may be supplied an entity name as an argument, and it will return the entity name that follows the argument name.

USAGE

The Entnext function is AutoLISP's fundamental retrieving function for entity names. By repeatedly selecting the next entity and storing the entity name to a memory variable, you can go through the entire drawing database one entity name at a time. When Entnext reaches the end of the drawing database, it returns nil.

EXAMPLES

Assume that a drawing database contains three entities. It would be possible to call each one sequentially and store it to a memory variable with the following series of functions:

(setq first (entnext))	Returns the first entity name in the database.
(setq second (entnext first))	Returns the second entity name in the same format.
(setq third (entnext second))	Returns the third entity name in the same format.
(setq fourth (entnext third))	Returns nil.

Entsel

Pauses processing and allows for interactive selection of a single entity that is visible on the screen; returns a list of the entity name as well as the point used to select the entity. If the selected entity is nested within a complex "parent" entity, such as a polyline or block, the "parent" entity is returned.

REQUIRED ARGUMENTS

None required, but an optional prompt argument may be supplied, similar to the prompt arguments used in the Get functions described in Chapter 17.

USAGE

The selection of an entity using Entsel must be by picking a point with the pointing device; Window and Crossing options are not allowed. Entsel is often nested with a Setq function to allow for picking and storing it at the same time, as shown in the examples.

EXAMPLES

Assume that a line segment exists from point 0,0 to point 5,5. The valid function

```
(setq ename (car (setq ent (entsel "Pick line: "))))
```

displays "Pick line:" and pauses. In response to the prompt, the user could either enter a point on the line using the keyboard, or pick the line with the pointing device. If the user picked the endpoint of the line, the Entsel function would return

```
(<Entity name: nnnnnnnn> (5.000000 5.000000))
```

where *nnnnnnnn* represents the numbers that make up the entity name. This list would be passed as an argument to the Setq function, which would store the list in memory variable *ent*. The Setq function would in turn pass the list to the Car function, which would then return:

```
<Entity name: nnnnnnnn>
```

This entity name would be passed as an argument to the Setq function, which would store it in memory variable *ename*.

Memory variable *ent* may be used as a response to any AutoCAD command prompt that expects entity selection. The list will be interpreted by AutoCAD as a selection of the entity by picking the specified point. Memory variable *ename* may be used as a response to AutoLISP functions such as Entnext that expect an entity name as an argument.

The coordinate point sublist may also be extracted from the list returned by Entsel by means of the Cadr function, and operated upon by commands or functions that require coordinate point information.

Handent

Returns an entity name for an entity handle.

REQUIRED ARGUMENTS

A valid entity handle, including any that belong to an entity that was deleted during the current editing session.

USAGE

Handent is available in AutoCAD Release 10 and later. Since entity-access functions require entity names rather than handles, this function is used as the argument when the entity handle is known but the entity name is not.

EXAMPLES

Assume the following entity-association list, with entity handles enabled:

```
( ( −1 . <Entity name: 60000030>)
  (0 . "LINE")
  (8 . "LINES")
  (5 . "2")
  (10 1.0 1.0 0.0)
  (11 3.0 3.0 0.0)
  (210 0.0 0.0 1.0)
)
```

Group code 5 indicates the entity handle, "2"; thus, the function

```
(handent "2")
```

is valid, and returns:

```
<Entity name: 60000030>
```

Nentsel

Pauses processing and allows for interactive selection of a single entity that is visible on the screen. This function is similar to the Entsel function; however, if the selected entity is nested within a complex "parent" entity, such as a polyline or block, the nested member entity, not the "parent" entity, is returned.

REQUIRED ARGUMENTS

None; however, an optional prompt string is accepted as an argument and displayed in the Command prompt area when the function pauses for input.

USAGE

You can use Nentsel whenever you want to select individual member entities of complex entities such as blocks, including hatch patterns, polylines, or meshes.

Nentsel is flexible. If you pick an entity not nested within a complex entity, Nentsel returns a list identical to the one returned by Entsel.

When you select a nested entity, Nentsel returns a list containing four members: the nested entity's name, the pick point, a list of four coordinate points, and a list containing the name of the parent entity. If the parent entity is a block containing other nested blocks, the parent entity list may contain more than one entity name, starting with the most deeply nested block and continuing to the outermost block.

You cannot pass entity names of nested entities to AutoCAD editing commands, such as Erase, Copy, or Move. However, you can pass the name of the outermost parent entity. The following function will return the name of the outermost parent entity:

```
(setq parent (last (last (nentsel))))
```

In an association list of an entity nested inside a block definition, the geometric construction points are relative to the block's insertion point. They are not indicative of the entity's location in the world coordinate system. The third member of the list returned by Nentsel is a list of coordinate points that can be applied as a matrix to the coordinate points of the nested entity, transforming them into coordinate locations in the WCS. An example of how to do this is shown in the following section.

EXAMPLES

This example assumes that a block is defined in the drawing, which contains a circle. The insertion point of the block is the circle's center. Assume further that the block is inserted in the drawing at point 4,4,0. The following function is then valid:

```
(setq nlist (nentsel))
```

Picking a point on the circle will return a list similar to the following:

(<Entity name: 400004d9>	Entity name of the circle
(5.25 4.0 0.0)	Pick point in WCS
((1.0 0.0 0.0)	Point transformation
(0.0 1.0 0.0)	Matrix list
(0.0 0.0 1.0)	
(4.0 4.0 0.0))	
(<Entity name: 6000016c>)	Entity name of parent
)	block

This will be stored in the memory variable Nlist.

The following function will return the circle's association list:

```
(setq alcirc (entget (car (nlist))))
```

The returned association list will be similar to the following:

(-1 . <Entity name: 400004d9>)	
(0 . "CIRCLE")	
(8 . "0")	
(6 . "CONTINUOUS")	
(10 0.0 0.0 0.0)	Circle center point
(40 . 1)	
(210 0.0 0.0 1.0))	

This will be stored in the memory variable Alcirc.

Notice that the center of the circle is shown as 0,0,0 instead of its true location in the drawing, 4,4,0. This is to be expected, as the center of the circle is also the block insertion point. However, if you want AutoLISP to know the location of the circle in the drawing, you must calculate the center point in the world coordinate system. The following function, Wcs_pt, contains a formula that will work:

```
(defun wcs_pt(al_pt mat)
        (list ( + (* (car (nth 0 mat)) (cadr al_pt))
                  (* (car (nth 1 mat)) (caddr al_pt))
                  (* (car (nth 2 mat)) (cadddr al_pt))
                  (car (nth 3 mat))
```

```
          )
          ( + (* (cadr (nth 0 mat)) (cadr al_pt))
                (* (cadr (nth 1 mat)) (caddr al_pt))
                (* (cadr (nth 2 mat)) (cadddr al_pt))
                (cadr (nth 3 mat))
          )
          ( + (* (caddr (nth 0 mat)) (cadr al_pt))
                (* (caddr (nth 1 mat)) (caddr al_pt))
                (* (caddr (nth 2 mat)) (cadddr al_pt))
                (caddr (nth 3 mat))
          )
      ) ; end List
   ) ; end Defun
```

After you have loaded this function into AutoCAD, you can use it by first extracting the point matrix from the list returned by Nentsel:

```
(setq matrix (caddr nlist))
```

This returns:

```
(   (1.0 0.0 0.0)
    (0.0 1.0 0.0)
    (0.0 0.0 1.0)
    (4.0 4.0 0.0)   )
```

This will be stored in the memory variable Matrix. Next, extract the circle's center point from its association list:

```
(setq pt (assoc 10 alcirc))
```

This returns:

```
(10 0.0 0.0 0.0)
```

This will be stored in the memory variable Pt. Now use the list stored in Matrix and the point stored in Pt as arguments for the function Wcs_pt:

```
(wcs_pt pt matrix)
```

This returns:

```
(4.0 4.0 0.0)
```

If all this looks complicated at first, bear in mind that the Wcs_pt function, once defined and loaded, will vastly simplify the process of converting points in a block entity's association list to their correct location in the world coordinate system. Try experimenting with the Wsc_pt function by inserting various blocks and calculating the WCS coordinates of various nested entities. Remember that the Wcs_pt function requires two lists: a group code sublist containing a point (beginning with group code 10, 11, 12, or 13), and the correct point-matrix list, extracted from the list returned by Nentsel.

As an example of how these principles can be applied, the following Release 11 AutoLISP routine will change the radius of a circle. If the selected circle is within a block definition, it will modify all the drawing's references to the block; however, you may have to regenerate the drawing to display the changes.

If a block reference was chosen, the routine offers an option to regenerate. If the circle is not part of a block reference, AutoCAD will update it immediately.

If you have acquired some experience with AutoLISP, you may find the routine in Figure 19.1 useful for in-depth analysis and study, because it demonstrates some sophisticated techniques for validating operator input before making direct modifications to the drawing database. Also, this routine makes good use of the Wcs_pt function to locate the correct coordinate point within a block definition.

```
; Define function Wcs_pt:

    (defun wcs_pt(al_pt mat)

        (list (+ (* (car (nth 0 mat)) (cadr al_pt))
                 (* (car (nth 1 mat)) (caddr al_pt))
                 (* (car (nth 2 mat)) (cadddr al_pt))
                 (car (nth 3 mat))
              )
              (+ (* (cadr (nth 0 mat)) (cadr al_pt))
                 (* (cadr (nth 1 mat)) (caddr al_pt))
                 (* (cadr (nth 2 mat)) (cadddr al_pt))
                 (cadr (nth 3 mat))
              )
              (+ (* (caddr (nth 0 mat)) (cadr al_pt))
                 (* (caddr (nth 1 mat)) (caddr al_pt))
                 (* (caddr (nth 2 mat)) (cadddr al_pt))
                 (caddr (nth 3 mat))
              )
        ) ; end List

    ) ; end Defun

; Define Command NEWCIRC:

(defun C:NEWCIRC(/ a c etype newrad)

; Repeat loop until a circle is picked:

    (while (or (not a)
               (/= "CIRCLE"
                   (setq etype (cdr (assoc '0 (setq c (entget (car a)))))

; Analyze input:

            (cond
```

FIGURE 19.1: This Release 11 routine prompts the operator to select a circle (rejecting other input), and prompts for a new radius. This routine will work whether or not the circle is part of a block, but will not work in earlier versions of AutoCAD.

```
    ; Condition: First time through loop, or nothing picked:

              ( (not a)
                  (while (not (setq a (nentsel "\nPick circle to update:
                  ) ; end While
              )
    ; Condition: A circle was not picked:

              ( (/= "CIRCLE" etype)
                  (princ (strcat "\n" etype " not a circle."))
                  (setq a nil)
              )

                  ) ; end Cond

        ) ; end While
    ; (caddr a) tests for a nested circle:

        (if (caddr a)
    ; If true, process for actual location using Wcs_pt function:

            (setq cpt (wcs_pt (assoc 10 c) (caddr a)))
    ; Else, process as normal entity:

            (setq cpt (cdr (assoc 10 c))))
    ; Enter a new radius:

        (while (<= (setq newrad (getdist cpt "\nNew Radius: ")) 0)

        ) ; end While
    ; Update circle:

        (entmod (subst (cons 40 newrad) (assoc 40 c) c))
    ; Prompt for optional drawing regeneration if nested circle was picked:

        (initget "Yes No")
        (if (and (caddr a)
                 (eq (getkword "\nRegenerate drawing <N>? ") "Yes"))
            (command "regen")

        ) ; end If
    ; Process complete:

        (princ)

    ) ; end Defun
```

FIGURE 19.1: This Release 11 routine prompts the operator to select a circle (rejecting other input), and prompts for a new radius. This routine will work whether or not the circle is part of a block, but will not work in earlier versions of AutoCAD (continued).

Xdroom

Returns an integer value indicating the amount of memory space available, in bytes, for extended data on a particular drawing entity.

REQUIRED ARGUMENTS

A valid entity name or a function that returns an entity name.

USAGE

For details on extended entity data, refer to the section earlier in this chapter. The Xdroom function serves as a test function within AutoLISP applications to determine if sufficient space exists to hold additional extended entity data on a particular entity. Each drawing entity can hold a maximum of 16383 bytes of extended data. A normal paper-space viewport, for example, includes about 200 bytes of extended data. A dotted pair containing an integer uses 3 bytes, a dotted pair containing a real number 9 bytes, a dotted pair containing a string approximately 2 bytes, plus the length of the string, and a list containing a 3-D coordinate point 25 bytes.

EXAMPLES

The following function will return the amount of available extended entity data on a selected entity. Try using it to select both a paper-space viewport and a drawing entity in model space, and compare the results.

```
(xdroom (car (entsel)))
```

Xdsize

Returns an integer value indicating the amount of space, in bytes, currently occupied by an entity's extended data.

REQUIRED ARGUMENTS

A valid extended data-association list, such as might be returned by the Entget function when the external application argument is included. Refer to the discussion of the Entget function earlier in this chapter, as well as the following section, for details on how to retrieve extended-data lists.

USAGE

The Xdsize function is a testing function within AutoLISP applications that determines how much space the extended data occupies. The function requires a valid extended-data list, otherwise an error message is returned. Such a list must begin with a string containing an external-application name, which can be found in the APPID symbol table. Any group of these lists, even if there is only one, must be enclosed within a separate set of parentheses. For example, the following is a valid extended-data list, assuming that "PROGRAM" is a registered external application name:

```
'("PROGRAM" (1000 . "Sample") (1002 . "{") (1070 . 1)
    (1010 0.0 0.0 0.0) (1040 . 0.0) (1002 . "}")
)
```

However, this list would not be accepted by Xdsize unless it were enclosed in another set of parentheses:

```
'(  ("PROGRAM" (1000 . "Sample") (1002 . "{") (1070 . 1)
    (1010 0.0 0.0 0.0) (1040 . 0.0) (1002 . "}")  )
)
```

This extra set of parentheses is required for those cases where you have more than one external-application list. The extra enclosing set of parentheses helps AutoLISP determine the size of the entire group.

EXAMPLES

The following function retrieves extended data for all external applications associated with a selected entity:

```
(assoc -3 (entget
            (car (entsel)) '("*")
        )
)
```

Notice the special syntax for the Entget function: (car (entsel)) returns the entity name, and the asterisk enclosed in the quoted list causes Entget to return extended data (if any) for all external applications. The Assoc function isolates and returns the -3 group code list, which will contain the extended data lists for the selected entity. If no lists exist, the function returns nil.

Before trying to figure the size of extended data, you should test to see if any extended data exists, using a function like the one above. Once you have determined the existence of extended data, you can use the Xdsize argument to determine how much space it occupies.

In the following example, the function will pause for the operator's selection of an entity, then test the selected entity for extended data and return the size of the extended data if any is found. If no extended data is found, the function returns nil:

```
(if (setq xlist (assoc -3 (entget (car (entsel)) '("*"))))
    (xdsize xlist)
)
```

FUNCTIONS FOR CHANGING SUBLISTS

The following are general AutoLISP functions that can be used any time, but are especially handy for retrieving and modifying sublist information.

Assoc

Searches a list that is composed of other sublists for a specified key item, supplied as the first argument of one of the sublists; returns the list containing the key item.

REQUIRED ARGUMENTS

Two arguments: the key item for which to search the sublists, such as a group code, and a list of sublists, such as an entity-association list.

USAGE

Assoc is the first function to use when extracting sublists in order to make changes. Although Assoc can make no changes, it delivers the sublist to functions that can—for example, the Cons function (see Chapter 17). Note that Assoc can only return whole sublists based on the first member in each sublist.

EXAMPLES

Consider the following association list:

```
( ( −1 . <Entity name: 60000030>)
  (0 . "LINE")
  (8 . "LINES")
  (10 1.0 1.0 0.0)
  (11 3.0 3.0 0.0)
  (210 0.0 0.0 1.0)
)
```

Assume that this association list is stored in a memory variable named *x*. The following function will then return the sublist containing the starting point of the line:

```
(assoc 10 x)
```

This function returns:

```
(10 1.0 1.0 0.0)
```

Since the coordinate information is the second item found in the sublist, you may use the Cdr function to extract it from the sublist, as in the following example:

(setq start (cdr (assoc 10 x)))

Here, the Assoc function is nested with the Cdr function, extracting the starting point from the association list stored in memory variable x. Both these functions are nested within a Setq function that automatically stores the starting point returned by Cdr to the memory variable *start*. This function returns:

(1.0 1.0 0.0)

The same technique of Assoc combined with Cdr will extract the data information in any sublist of an association list.

Cdr

Reads a list and returns a list of all members except the first.

REQUIRED ARGUMENTS

A list containing at least two members.

USAGE

Cdr is frequently used to isolate the second element in a dotted pair, such as might be found in an entity-association list. However, it may be used on a list of any number of members, where you intend to remove the first member.

EXAMPLES

The following example applies the Cdr function to a list of integers:

(cdr '(1 2 3))

In this case, the Cdr function returns a list:

(2 3)

The following example creates a dotted pair and stores it in memory variable *dp*:

(setq dp (cons '0 "LINE"))

This returns the dotted pair:

(0 . "LINE")

Then, applying the Cdr function,

(cdr dp)

returns

"LINE"

Refer also to another illustrative example of the Cdr function used in the section on the Assoc function earlier in this chapter.

SELECTION-SET FUNCTIONS

A *selection set* is a group of entity names that is given a name of its own. Once named as a selection set, the group of entities can be acted upon as a whole. This process is similar to the windowing mechanism used in response to AutoCAD's "Select objects:" prompt.

A selection set is actually a unique AutoLISP data type. When a selection set is retrieved from the underlying database by means of various predefined functions, it will be displayed in the format

<Selection set: *n*>

where *n* represents an integer that identifies the selection set. A number of functions accept a selection set as an argument, but it must be bound to a memory variable first; or, if it is not necessary to store the selection set in memory, you may use a function that returns a selection set as an argument to a function that accepts one.

The following AutoLISP functions have been predefined to work specifically with selection sets.

Ssadd

Adds an entity to a selection set, and returns the updated selection set.

REQUIRED ARGUMENTS

None required. If Ssadd is called without arguments, the function will create a new selection set, but it will contain no members. (Members can be added later.) More often, Ssadd is called with two arguments: an entity name followed by a selection set. The function adds the entity name referenced as its first argument to the selection set referenced as the second argument.

USAGE

Once a selection set has been bound to a memory variable, the Ssadd function may be used to add entities to it, one at a time. It is not necessary to rebind the selection set to the memory-variable name after it has been updated; refer to the examples ahead.

If the referenced entity is already a member of the selection set, the function does not add it again. Instead, it simply returns the selection set with nothing added.

EXAMPLES

Assume that a drawing contains at least two entities. The following functions would be valid:

(setq ent1 (entnext))	Returns the entity name of the first entity.
(setq ent2 (entnext ent1))	Returns the entity name of the second entity.
(setq ss1 (ssadd))	Returns a selection set with no members.
(ssadd ent1 ss1)	Returns the selection set bound to memory variable *ss1,* now containing the first entity.
(ssadd ent2 ss1)	Returns the selection set bound to memory variable *ss1,* now containing both the first and second entities.

Ssdel

Deletes a referenced entity name from a referenced selection set, and returns the selection set.

REQUIRED ARGUMENTS

Two arguments: an entity name followed by a selection set. The function deletes the entity name referenced as its first argument from the selection set referenced as the second argument. If the referenced entity name is not found in the selection set, this function returns nil.

USAGE

Ssdel is the functional opposite of Ssadd. After a selection set has been created and bound to a memory variable, the Ssdel function may be used to selectively delete specific entities from it, one at a time. It is not necessary to rebind the selection set to the memory-variable name after it has been updated; refer to the examples below.

EXAMPLES

Assume that the selection set bound to memory variable *ss1* contains two entities, which have been bound to memory variables *ent1* and *ent2*. A third entity, bound to memory variable *ent3,* is not a member of the selection set. The following functions become valid:

(ssdel ent1 ss1)	Returns the selection set stored in *ss1,* with *ent1* deleted from it.
(ssdel ent3 ss1)	Returns nil, because *ent3* is not a member of *ss1.*

Ssget

Pauses processing and allows the user to select a group of one or more entities. Returns a selection set containing those entities.

REQUIRED ARGUMENTS

None required, but Ssget may be supplied with one of the sets of arguments described below.

If Ssget is called without arguments, it is interactive. AutoLISP will display AutoCAD's "Select objects:" prompt, and the user is free to use the normal syntax of Window, Crossing, Add, and Remove options at will, in order to build a selection set.

If Ssget is called with an optional selection-mode argument, it is no longer interactive and will automatically select entities based on the particular mode used. The mode arguments are as follows:

(ssget "C" '(point1) '(point1))	Selects entities crossing a window with opposite corners at *point1* and *point2.*
(ssget "L")	Selects the last entity in the underlying database.
(ssget "P")	Selects the previously selected set.
(ssget "W" '(point1) '(point1))	Selects entities contained within a window with opposite corners at *point1* and *point2.*

(ssget "X" *(group-code criteria list)*)	Searches the entire database for entities containing sublists that match the sublists in the group-code criteria list. Refer to the Usage and Examples sections ahead for details.
(ssget '*(point)*)	Selects the entity passing through the quoted coordinate point.

USAGE

When arguments are supplied to the Ssget function, they mimic the responses a user would make to AutoCAD's "Select objects:" prompt. However, block attributes and polyline vertices are not included in selection sets created using this function. Their main entities are included, however. If you intend to work with attributes and vertices from entities in selection sets, you may do so by extracting the main entity from the selection set (using other selection-set functions) and passing it as an argument to the Entnext function. If doing so, remember that the last attribute or vertex entity is always followed by a "SEQEND" entity. Refer to the Entnext function earlier in this chapter for more details.

The X selection-mode argument is available in Release 9 and later. When this selection-mode argument is passed to Ssget, the function also requires a list that includes one or more entity group-code sublists. All entities with sublists that match the sublists in the list will be included in the selection set.

Group codes accepted by Ssget are:

0	Entity type
2	Block names (or entities with group code 2 are ignored)
6	Linetype
7	Style name for text entities, including attributes
8	Layer
38	Elevation
39	Thickness
62	Color number (color names are not permitted)
66	Attribute block flag
210	Extrusion direction (Release 10 and later)

Notice that when you use any number of these group-code sublists as an argument to Ssget X, they must themselves be enclosed in a data list. This is true even if you are specifying only one group-code sublist. Refer to the "Examples" section below to see how these group-code sublists are used with the X selection mode.

In Release 11 and later, group code sublists that accept string data (that is, groups codes 0 through 8) will accept wild-card characters as part of the string. Also in Release 11 and later, you may include multiple strings (for example, two or more entity types in a group code 0 string), separated by a comma in the string. Refer to the "Examples" section just ahead for details.

When you use group codes 38 and 39 (elevation and thickness), the amount of elevation and thickness should be indicated using the real number that represents drawing units. Integers are not allowed.

When you use group code 62 (color), only color numbers are permitted. Do not use color names—or any string for that matter. If you wish to reference Bylayer as the color to select, use 0. If you wish to reference Byblock, use 256.

Use the Ssget function with the single point argument only in situations where other entities are not very close by. When you use this option, AutoLISP will sometimes select the incorrect entity if more than one entity is very close to the selection point.

An AutoCAD command that uses the "Select objects:" selection mechanism will accept a memory variable that contains a selection set gathered using this function, when selection by Last is also valid at the time.

AutoLISP allows a maximum of six selection sets to be active at one time. To deactivate a selection set, bind its memory-variable name to nil. If you have used all six available selection sets and you subsequently bind one or more to nil, you may need to call the following function before AutoLISP will allow you to create more selection sets:

(gc)

This function will inform the AutoLISP interpreter that node space used by deactivated selection sets is again available for additional selection sets.

EXAMPLES

(setq ss1 (ssget "X" (list (cons '8 "LINES"))))	Returns a selection set stored in memory variable *ss1,* containing all the entities on the Lines layer.
(setq ss2 (ssget "X" (list (cons '8 "LINES") (cons '62 '3))))	Returns a selection set stored in memory variable *ss2,* containing all the green entities on the Lines layer.

(setq ss3 (ssget))	Pauses processing and prompts you to "Select objects:". You may employ any standard entity-selection mechanism. When finished, press Enter to store the selected entities in a selection set bound to memory variable *ss3*.
(setq ss4 (ssget "C" '(0,0) '(20,20)))	Returns a selection set stored in memory variable *ss4*, containing all the entities found by a "crossing" window with opposite corners at points 0,0 and 20,20.

The following examples will work only in Release 11 and later:

(setq ss5 (ssget "X" (list (cons '0 "ARC,CIRCLE"))))	Returns a selection set stored in memory variable *ss5*, containing arcs and circles.
(setq ss6 (ssget "X" (list (cons '62 '3) (cons '8 "G*") (cons '0 "ARC,CIRCLE"))))	Returns a selection set stored in memory variable *ss6*, containing only green arcs and circles and residing on layers whose names begin with the letter "G".

Sslength

Returns an integer equal to the number of entities in the selection set.

REQUIRED ARGUMENTS

A selection set.

USAGE

Sslength is useful in situations where you intend to loop through the entities in a selection set, and you need to determine how many there are, to avoid error messages that might arise if you exhaust the selection set but AutoLISP attempts to continue processing. Refer to the While and Foreach functions in Chapter 17 for details regarding controlled looping functions.

EXAMPLES

Assuming a drawing with at least one entity, the following function will return a selection set and bind it to memory variable *x*:

```
(setq x (ssget "L"))
```

The following function will be valid:

```
(sslength x)
```

It returns 1.

Ssmemb

Determines whether a referenced entity name is a member of a referenced selection set. If so, the function returns the referenced entity name. If not, the function returns nil.

REQUIRED ARGUMENTS

An entity name and a selection set, in that order.

USAGE

Ssmemb allows you to test for the presence of members in a selection set prior to invoking commands or calling functions that use the selection set. This is helpful when a command or function might otherwise produce an error condition, in circumstances where the exact contents of a selection set are not known. Since the function returns the entity name if it finds the name in the selection set, Ssmemb may also be used to extract entities from selection sets.

EXAMPLES

Assume that the selection set bound to memory variable *ss1* contains two entities, which have been bound to memory variables *ent1* and *ent2*. A third entity, bound to memory variable *ent3*, is not a member of the selection set. The following functions become valid:

(ssmemb ent1 ss1)	Returns the entity name bound to *ent1*.
(ssmemb ent3 ss1)	Returns nil, because *ent3* is not a member of ss1.

Ssname

Extracts entity names from a selection set.

REQUIRED ARGUMENTS

A selection set and an integer number, in that order. The integer number must correspond to a number assigned by AutoLISP to an entity in the selection set. Refer to the Usage section ahead for details.

USAGE

Entity names in selection sets are numbered with integers, starting with integer 0. The first argument of Ssname is the name of the selection set being queried. The second argument is the number of the entity within the selection set. If the number is out of range, this function returns nil.

EXAMPLES

(ssname ss1 0)	Returns the first entity in the selection set *ss1*.
(ssname ss1 1)	Returns the second entity in the selection set *ss1*.
(ssname ss1 2)	Returns the third entity in the selection set *ss1*.

SYMBOL-TABLE FUNCTIONS

AutoCAD's *symbol tables* are used to store default data for the drawing environment in association-list format. Symbol tables store named entities and definition data under predefined *table names,* as follows:

TABLE NAME	DATA
Apdid	External applications to extended entity data
Block	Block names and definitions

TABLE NAME	DATA
Dimstyle	Named dimensioning styles
Layer	Layer names and defaults
Ltype	Linetype names and definitions
Style	Text-style names and definitions
Ucs	Names and orientations of user coordinate systems
View	Viewing-angle names and configurations
Vport	Viewport names and configurations

The symbol-table data is read-only; that is, you may use AutoLISP to access the definition and default data and store it in memory variables, which you may then use as arguments to functions or command responses, but you may not update the symbol tables directly.

Two functions are provided for access to the data in AutoCAD's symbol table. They are described ahead. Samples of the association lists returned by symbol-table access functions are shown inside the cover of this book.

In Release 10, these symbol-table access functions return 3-D coordinate points in sublists that begin with group code 10. In prior versions of AutoCAD that support 3-D points (or in Release 10 with the FLATLAND system variable not zero), these functions will return 2-D points in the code 10 sublist; when a z coordinate is required, it is returned in a separate sublist with group code 30.

Regapp

Stores the name of an external application in the APPID symbol table.

REQUIRED ARGUMENTS

A string containing the name of an external application that will make use of extended entity data. The application name may have up to 31 characters. The name may include alphanumeric characters, such as "ABC" or "123," and the special punctuation marks $ (dollar sign), _ (underscore), or - (hyphen). Other characters, including those recognized by AutoCAD as wild-card characters, are not allowed.

USAGE

Refer to the section earlier in this chapter for details on extended entity data. Since AutoCAD does not make direct use of extended entity data, all extended entity data must be associated with the particular external application that will use it. There may be several applications that use extended entity data in a particular drawing. You should associate each set of extended entity data with its own external application so AutoCAD can keep track of which set corresponds to which application.

Each external application must be identified by a unique name. This name is stored in the APPID symbol table. Applications are stored in this symbol table by "registering" them with AutoCAD using this function. The string supplied by this function must be unique (not previously added).

If you wish to delete a registered application name, you may do so only by using the Undo command during the drawing session in which the name was created.

External application names are not saved with the drawing, and must be re-registered at the start of each new drawing session. This is often done with Auto-LISP functions.

EXAMPLES

The following function registers the external application "PROGRAM":

```
(regapp "PROGRAM")
```

It returns: "PROGRAM."

To view the currently registered applications, enter:

```
(tblnext "APPID" T)
```

This returns the symbol table association list:

```
((0 . "APPID") (2 . "ACAD") (70 . 64))
```

Subsequent calls to the symbol table appears as follows:

```
(tblnext "APPID")
```

These return additional external applications, if any. For example, if you loaded "PROGRAM" with the Regapp function, the above function would return:

```
((0 . "APPID") (2 . "PROGRAM") (70 . 0))
```

The group code 70 sublist is set from 0 to 64 when AutoCAD detects the presence of extended entity data that references the named application.

Tblnext

Returns the association list for entries in the referenced symbol table.

REQUIRED ARGUMENTS

The table name for the symbol table you wish to read. If a second argument is provided and is not evaluated to nil, the function will return the first entry in the table.

USAGE

When an entry from the referenced symbol table was previously selected by this function, Tblnext returns the next table entry for this symbol table. When it reaches the end of the symbol table, the function returns nil.

By supplying a second non-nil argument, usually T, you will force the function to return the first entry in the symbol table, and begin referencing additional entries after that.

EXAMPLES

(tblnext "LAYER" T)	Returns the association list for the first entry in the Layer symbol table.
(tblnext "LAYER")	Returns the association list for the next entry in the Layer symbol table.

Tblsearch

Returns an association list for a referenced entry in the referenced symbol table.

REQUIRED ARGUMENTS

At least two arguments: the symbol table to search, and the symbol name to search for. (The symbol name is always found in the sublist with group code 2.) A third optional argument, if supplied and not nil, will set up the next entry following the found entry—if an entry was found and another entry exists following it—for immediate access using the Tblnext function.

USAGE

Tblsearch provides a direct means to extract the symbol's association list when the symbol name is known.

If the third argument is not supplied or is nil, the Tblsearch function will have no effect on the order of entries returned by the Tblnext function. But if a non-nil third argument is supplied to Tblsearch, The Tblnext function will return the entry following that returned by Tblsearch, if such an entry exists.

If Tblsearch cannot find the referenced symbol name, it returns nil.

EXAMPLES

(tblsearch "LAYER" "0")	Returns the symbol-table association list for layer 0.
(tblsearch "LAYER" "0" T)	Returns the symbol-table association list for layer 0, and sets up the Tblnext function to return the layer immediately following the found layer.

SAMPLE ENTITY-MODIFICATION ROUTINES

The routine listed in Figure 19.2 demonstrates several of the database-access functions described in this chapter. It creates a new AutoCAD command called Picklyr, which prompts the user to select a single entity and displays the layer on which that entity is located. Next, the user is prompted to build a selection set of various other entities (which may include the original entity). After the selection set is chosen, all its members are moved to the layer of the originally picked entity. The user may end the command early by pressing Enter without building a selection set.

```
(defun C:PICKLYR( / base ssno ss1 alist)
   (setq base
         (cdr (assoc '8 (entget (car (entsel "\Pick base entity: ")))))
   )
   (Prompt (strcat "\nEntity layer: " base))
   (setq ssno 0
         ss1 (ssget)
   )
   (if (and (/= ss1 nil)
            (> (setq sslen (sslength ss1)) 0)
       )
       (while (< ssno sslen)
              (entmod
                      (subst (cons '8 base)
                             (assoc '8 (entget (ssname ss1 ssno)))
                             (entget (ssname ss1 ssno))
                      )
              )
              (setq ssno (1+ ssno))
       )
   )
   (princ)
)
; EOF PICKLYR.LSP    24 lines
```

FIGURE 19.2: PICKLYR.LSP. This short AutoLISP routine demonstrates a practical application of functions that directly access AutoCAD's underlying database. The routine creates a new command, Picklyr. When invoked, the command prompts the user to select an entity, and then displays the layer upon which that entity is located. Next, the user is prompted to create a selection set, and when the selection set is complete, all the chosen entities are transferred to the displayed layer.

This routine may be easily changed to use other common entity properties, such as color, linetype, or elevation. Figure 19.3 lists the same basic routine, called Pickth, that will make global changes to entity thicknesses based on a picked entity. Notice how, in this version, AutoLISP tests to see if the sublist for thickness (group code 39) already exists in each entity-association list before choosing the correct processing functions.

```
(defun C:PICKTH( / base bth ssno ss1 alist)
   (setq base (entget (car (entsel "\Pick base entity: "))))
   (prompt "\nThickness: ")
   (if (= (assoc '39 base) nil)
       (princ (setq bth 0))
       (princ (setq bth (cdr (assoc '39 base)))))
   )
   (setq ssno 0
         ss1 (ssget)
   )
   (if (and (/= ss1 nil)
            (> (setq sslen (sslength ss1)) 0)
       )
       (while (< ssno sslen)
              (setq alist (entget (ssname ss1 ssno)))
              (if (= (assoc '39 alist) nil)
                  (entmod
                          (cons
                                (cons '39 bth)
                                alist
                          )
                  )
                  (entmod
                          (subst (cons '39 bth)
                                 (assoc '39 alist)
                                 alist
                          )
                  )
              )
              (if (= (cdr (assoc '0 alist)) "INSERT")
                  (prompt "\nBlock found. Thickness unchanged.")
              )
              (setq ssno (1+ ssno))
       )
   )
   (princ)
)
; EOF PICKTH.LSP    38 lines
```

FIGURE 19.3: PICKTH.LSP. A variation on the routine shown in Figure 19.2, this AutoLISP routine changes the thickness of entities to that of a selected entity. In this case, a few extra steps are involved, since the AutoLISP interpreter must first evaluate each entity to determine if it already has a group-code sublist for thickness (which must be modified) or if it does not have such a sublist (in which case one must be added). This function will not work on blocks; however, each time a block entity is found in the selection set, the command will display a message to that effect.

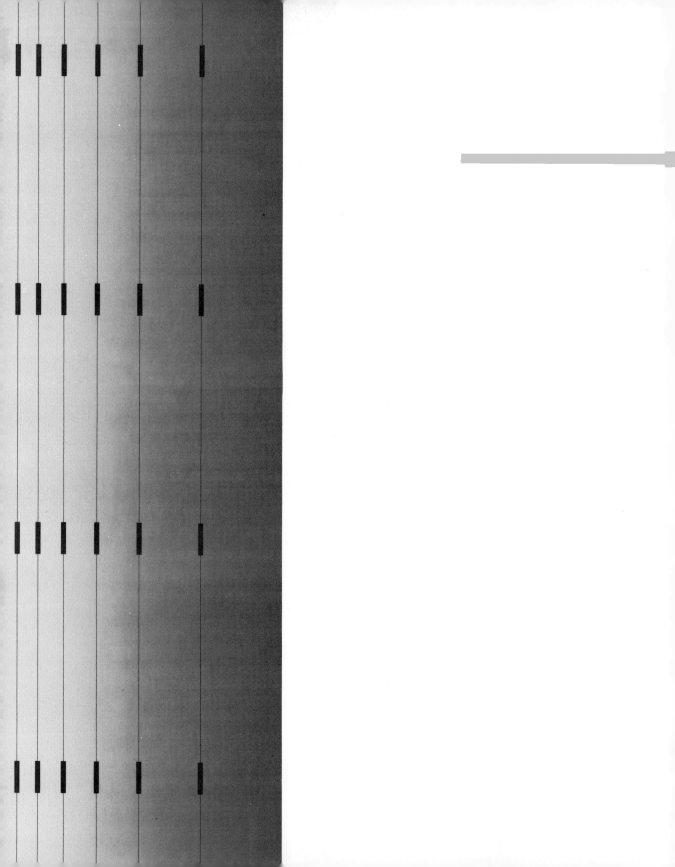

CHAPTER 20

COMMUNICATING WITH OTHER SOFTWARE

COMMUNICATING WITH OTHER SOFTWARE

One of the advantages of CAD is the speed and ease with which drawings on computer disks can be transported between drafters. There are many different CAD systems on the market, however, and each has its own format for storing graphic data. If drafters are using different CAD systems, each with its own special strengths, it does no good to send disks back and forth unless the other drafter's CAD program can read the foreign format.

It is impractical to expect every CAD software manufacturer to provide a means of translating its own format into the various formats of all the others. Instead, intermediate standard formats known as "neutral" formats have been attempted—most notably IGES (Initial Graphics Exchange Specification). The IGES format allows each CAD software manufacturer to write only two translators instead of many: one to translate the manufacturer's format into IGES, and the other to translate IGES back into the manufacturer's format.

AutoCAD provides such an IGES translator, as well as a special intermediate format called the DXF (Drawing Interchange File) format. This format is particularly useful for translating AutoCAD drawing information into a format usable by third-party or add-on software that was written to make use of it. As of Auto-CAD Release 10, this file format is also available in a binary version, for faster loading and more efficient disk storage.

In AutoCAD Version 2.6 and later, a special intermediate binary format called DXB (Binary Drawing Interchange) was introduced. This format is normally created by software outside of AutoCAD to input simple graphic information, but AutoCAD can generate DXB format if you have specially configured it to do so.

This chapter examines the structure of the DXF file format, its binary-file variations, and its possibilities for moving certain drawing data between different versions of AutoCAD. Also, this chapter presents an overview of the DXB and IGES formats.

IGES FORMAT

The IGES format was developed in 1979 under the auspices of the National Bureau of Standards to solve the problem of translating computerized graphic information between a proliferating number of database formats. Simply put, an

IGES file is an ASCII file describing the various entities that should go into a database. CAD software developers are responsible for writing a translator that reads the entity types from the IGES file and fits them into the developer's own format, and that writes files from the developer's format into IGES.

An IGES file is divided into five sections. Each section contains records that relate to a specific data type. The records are numbered at the rightmost position on each line of the file. Following are the IGES file sections:

Start This is a readable header line indicating that the file is an IGES file and naming the source of the file. Record numbers in this section begin with the letter *S*.

Global This section contains such general data as the name of the file, the name of the source file, the AutoCAD version used to produce the drawing, the version of the IGES translation software, the numeric units, the precision, and so forth. Its record numbers begin with the letter *G*.

Directory Entries This section lists the general data types found in the file, the block definitions, and the viewing angles. Its record numbers begin with the letter *D*.

Parameter Data This section contains specific entity information, such as coordinate locations and direction vectors. For each entity in the drawing database, there will be two lines in the Directory Entries section and one or more lines in the Parameter Data section.

Terminate This is a single line at the end of the file, indicating the number of records in each section.

The standard IGES format can define and recognize about 50 different entity types, which in turn can be combined into more complex entities called *structures* (similar to AutoCAD's blocks). The entity types supported by IGES range from simple line entities that are normally combined into wire-frame models, to complex surfaces that can be used for such tasks as architectural design, circuit-board design, electrical engineering, finite-element analysis, piping, and flow modeling.

Ideally, IGES should allow any user to translate graphic data into the IGES format and pass the neutral file to another drafter using a different format; the recipient should then be able to translate the neutral file into the native format with perfect accuracy. In reality, however, the transfer often achieves less than perfect results. The variations in accuracy are the result of the varying abilities of different IGES translators to handle the wide variety of entity types that can be defined in IGES files, as well as the varying ability of different systems to read and understand different entity types from other, possibly unrelated, systems.

For example, two architectural systems should have better success than a circuit-board design system and a solid-modeling system.

In particular, AutoCAD seems to have trouble with certain 2-D entities—such as arcs, circles, and 2-D polylines, with or without extruded thicknesses—that have been drawn in user coordinate systems defined separately from the world coordinate system. Entities of this type are stored in the database using coordinate points that are entirely different from their equivalent points in the world coordinate system, and are subject to misinterpretation when transferred via IGES.

Before attempting to transfer complex drawings, you may find it helpful to experiment with a test drawing, as illustrated in Figure 20.1. In a test drawing, the fundamental entity types subject to transfer are isolated in sections of the drawing, and then transferred and plotted. A look at the plotted output will indicate clearly what data has been transferred successfully. Also, listing the data in the two drawings (with AutoCAD's List command) will show how data was recognized and whether it remained in place.

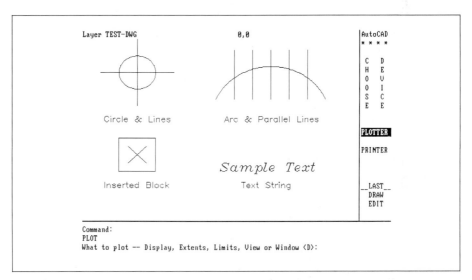

FIGURE 20.1: The types of entities that are useful when testing IGES file transfers to foreign CAD systems. Clockwise from the upper left: lines of equal length intersect at the center point of a circle; parallel lines of equal length and spacing intersect an arc; a string of text; a block consisting of a square with diagonal lines of equal length intersecting in the center. This drawing was made with the snap value set to 1 drawing unit, making all coordinate locations and line lengths easy to test.

The following sections summarize the AutoCAD commands that read and write IGES files.

Igesin

Reads an external IGES file and translates it into a standard AutoCAD drawing.

VERSIONS

Version 2.5 and later.

COMMAND OPTIONS

File name   Enter the name of the IGES file to be loaded into the current drawing. The default is the name of the current drawing. File extensions are not allowed; the extension IGS is assumed. You may include subdirectory names and a drive letter if necessary.

USAGE

The operation of the Igesin command is automatic. However, you may only read an IGES file into a new drawing—that is, a drawing in which no entities currently exist. Many prototype drawings contain entity types, perhaps in the form of block definitions or title blocks. If you intend to load an IGES file, you may be assured of having a new drawing by selecting option 1 from the Main Menu and entering the name of a new drawing followed by an equal sign. Refer to the sample dialog for the Dxbin command later in this chapter for an example of how this is done.

RELATED COMMANDS

Dxbin, Dxfin.

SAMPLE DIALOG

The following dialog loads an IGES file named NEWIGES.IGS into the current drawing:

```
Command: Igesin
File name <NEWIGES>: Newiges
Regenerating drawing
Command:
```

Igesout

Writes the current underlying database into an external IGES file.

VERSIONS

Version 2.5 and later.

COMMAND OPTIONS

File name   Enter the name of the IGES file you wish to create. The default is the name of the current file. File extensions are not allowed; the extension IGS is assumed. However, you may include a drive letter and subdirectory names to have the IGES file written on a drive or directory other than the one currently logged.

USAGE

The operation of the Igesout command is automatic.

Warning: If an IGES file with the same name you enter already exists on disk, it will be overwritten by the new file. No warning is issued; therefore, be certain to manage IGS files very carefully, making frequent backups and moving them to another location on the hard disk if you intend to keep them.

Note: AutoCAD sometimes has trouble translating 2-D entities drawn in user coordinate systems. Whenever you can, make IGES transfers of the following entities drawn only in the world coordinate system: 2-D polylines (including doughnuts, ellipses, and polygons), arcs, blocks, circles, shapes, text, and traces.

RELATED COMMANDS

Dxfout.

SAMPLE DIALOG

The following dialog creates an IGES file containing blocks and lines. Since the creation of IGES files of complex drawings can be time-consuming, Auto-CAD provides a file-creation "progress report":

```
Command: Igesout
File name <NEWIGES>: (Press Enter)
Writing Start section
Writing Global section
Writing view 1 (VIEWANGLE)
```

```
Scanning AutoCAD block 1 (BLOCK_NAME)
Writing subfigure definition 1 (BLOCK_NAME)
**No output for entity type ATTRIBUTE DEFINITION
Translating AutoCAD entity 1 (LINE)
Translating AutoCAD entity 37 (BLOCK REFERENCE)
Writing External Reference File List
Copying DE data record(s)
Copying Parameter data record(s)
Writing Terminate section
Command:
```

STRUCTURE OF DXF FILES

A DXF file is an ASCII file, with the extension DXF, that represents the information found in AutoCAD's underlying database. The primary purpose of the DXF file is to create a standard format for other software to read and process AutoCAD's entity information.

DXF files contain many lines, and each line contains one specific data item. These items include *file-section labels, group codes,* and data associated with each group code. These data items will be explained shortly.

Because they are ASCII files, DXF files can be processed by a text editor, although such manual editing of DXF files requires a great deal of care and patience. One reason for manipulating DXF files with a text editor is to provide *downward compatibility* between different versions of AutoCAD. Normally, AutoCAD files are not downwardly compatible; that is, drawings created on later versions cannot be used on earlier versions. Obviously, this is a significant drawback if two AutoCAD users with different versions would like to share drawing files.

The following discussion of the structure of DXF files is a primer for those interested in creating programs that read DXF files, and for those interested in manipulating DXF files as a means to make drawings downwardly compatible.

DXF File Sections

A DXF file is divided into four major sections, each with its own section label. These sections are:

- HEADER, containing general information on the drawing environment.
- TABLES, containing definitions of named entities such as text styles, viewing angles, viewport configurations, user coordinate systems, layers, and linetypes.

- BLOCKS, containing block definitions.
- ENTITIES, containing the coordinate and entity-property information required to produce the drawing in AutoCAD.

Each section of the DXF file contains successive pairs of lines that are meaningful to AutoCAD. The first line of each pair contains a group-code integer, which is always right-justified in a field of three spaces. The line following the group-code integer will be a particular unit of information, whose meaning is derived from both the group code and its location within the section.

Figure 20.2 illustrates the beginning of a typical DXF file and the start of the HEADER section. In any given drawing, the data will be different, but the header variables (those preceded by dollar signs) will be the same. Notice that this DXF file begins as all such files do, with group code zero followed by the label SECTION, indicating that one section of the file is about to begin:

```
  0
SECTION
```

Following the label SECTION is group code 2, followed by the name of the section that is beginning—in this case, the HEADER section:

```
  2
HEADER
```

After the section has been named, the data in the section is listed. The first item in the sample HEADER section is group code 9 indicating a variable name, followed by the variable name, followed by group code 1 indicating a value for the variable, followed by the value. In this case, the value for the variable $ACADVER is AC1009 (for Release 11). The value for Release 10 is AC1006, and for Release 9 it is AC1004:

```
  9
$ACADVER
  1
AC1009
```

Following the lines indicating the AutoCAD version, the group code for a variable is repeated, followed by the variable name, followed by group codes for the data in the variable name. In this case, the variable $INSBASE contains a 3-D coordinate point, whose x coordinate is identified by group code 10, y coordinate by group code 20, and z coordinate by group code 30. This variable contains the insertion base point of the drawing (0,0,0):

```
  9
$INSBASE
 10
```

```
       0
    SECTION
       2
    HEADER
       9
   $ACADVER
       1
    AC1009
       9
   $INSBASE
      10
      0.0
      20
      0.0
      30
      0.0
       9
   $EXTMIN
      10
    1.232738
      20
    2.15493
      30
      0.0
       9
   $EXTMAX
      10
    8.03206
      20
    5.545775
      30
      0.0
       9
   $LIMMIN
      10
      0.0
      20
      0.0
       9
   $LIMMAX
      10
      8.5
      20
      11.0
       9
   $ORTHOMODE
      70
           0
       9
   $REGENMODE
      70
           1
       9
   $FILLMODE
      70
           1
```

FIGURE 20.2: A typical HEADER section in a Release 11 DXF file. Notice how the file utilizes a repeating pattern or group code, followed by a variable, followed by data, followed by the next group code, and so on. The data following $ACADVER indicates that this is a Release 11 file, as does the presence of a z coordinate (group code 30) following the $EXTMIN variable. Other variable names correspond to AutoCAD system variables (although not all AutoCAD system variables will be found in the DXF file).

```
0.0
20
0.0
30
0.0
```

Other variables follow, each preceded by 9 and followed by the values that it contains; each value is indicated by the correct group code. For example, the following lines indicate the x-y coordinate drawing limits, stored in the variables $LIMMIN and $LIMMAX:

```
9
$LIMMIN
10
0.0
20
0.0
9
$LIMMAX
10
8.5
20
11.0
```

The following variable stores the current status of orthogonal mode. Group code 70 followed by zero indicates that orthogonal mode is currently off:

```
9
$ORTHOMODE
70
0
```

The HEADER section contains many variable names and associated values, which correspond to AutoCAD's system variables and their values. Not all of AutoCAD's systems variables have counterparts that appear in the HEADER section of a DXF file; for example, the AFLAGS system variable does not appear in the HEADER section.

All DXF sections end with the following pair of lines, which indicate the end of the section:

```
0
ENDSEC
```

The TABLES section contains different tables, each with its own initial heading and ending lines. Tables that appear in this section are:

APPID	Registered external application names
DIMSTYLE	Defining named dimension format styles
DWGMGR	Not used (Release 10 only)
LAYER	Defining named layer specifications
LTYPE	Defining named linetype specifications
STYLE	Defining named text styles
UCS	Defining named user coordinate systems (Release 10 +)
VIEW	Defining named viewing angles
VPORT	Defining named viewport configurations (Release 10 +)

A portion of the TABLES section is illustrated in Figure 20.3, which shows the LTYPE table and the LAYER table. Like all sections, the TABLES section begins with group code zero, followed by a SECTION label, followed by group code 2 indicating the section name, TABLES:

```
    0
SECTION
    2
TABLES
```

Each table begins with group code zero, followed by the label TABLE. It in turn is followed by group code 2, followed by the table identifier. (In the example in Figure 20.3, the table identifier is LTYPE.) The table identifier is followed by group code 70 and an integer indicating the number of definitions in the table:

```
    0
TABLE
    2
LTYPE
   70
        1
```

All of the tables in the TABLES section are introduced using this sequence of lines. (Compare these with the lines that indicate the start of the LAYER table.) The following lines form the rest of the LTYPE table, indicating:

- That an individual linetype definition follows:

```
    0
LTYPE
```

```
           0
        SECTION
           2
        TABLES
           0
         TABLE
           2
         LTYPE
          70
               1
           0
         LTYPE
           2
      CONTINUOUS
          70
              64
           3
       Solid line
          72
              65
          73
               0
          40
         0.0
           0
        ENDTAB
           0
         TABLE
           2
         LAYER
          70
               1
           0
         LAYER
           2
           0
          70
              64
          62
               7
           6
      CONTINUOUS
           0
        ENDTAB
```

FIGURE 20.3: A portion of the TABLES section of a DXF file, showing the LTYPE and LAYER tables. Notice how the section is identified by the variable TABLES, and each table within the section is identified with the variable TABLE. The LTYPE table contains only one linetype, Continuous, and the LAYER table contains at least two layers, 0 and Hidden. All tables end with an ENDTAB variable following a zero group code, and the entire TABLES section will end with an ENDSEC variable following a zero group code.

- That the linetype name is "continuous":

  ```
      2
  CONTINUOUS
  ```

- That this linetype is referenced in the drawing (and cannot be purged):

  ```
     70
         64
  ```

- That the linetype's descriptive text is "Solid line":

    3
    Solid line

- That the number of dash-length items in the linetype is zero:

    73
        0

- That the total pattern length is also zero:

      40
    0.0

- Finally, that the LTYPE table is ending:

      0
    ENDTAB

Other tables follow, all using the same essential structure. You can understand the meanings of the various group codes by studying the entity-association list codes that appear on the inside of this book's cover. The lines

      0
    ENDSEC

indicate the end of the TABLES section.

The BLOCKS section of the DXF file contains the block definitions for the drawing. (In the BLOCKS section, unlike the LAYER and LTYPE sections, there is no group code 70 indicating the number of block definitions.) It begins with the following sequence of lines:

      0
    SECTION
      2
    BLOCKS

Each block definition begins with the following sequence of lines:

- An indicator of the start of a block definition:

      0
    BLOCK

- The insertion layer of the block:

      8
      0

- The block name:

      2
      BLOCK-NAME

- Whether the block is referenced in the drawing (and cannot be purged):

      70
        64

- The block's base point, in x-y-z coordinates:

       10
       0.0
       20
       0.0
       30
       0.0
       0

- Repeating the block name for use with drawing audit and recovery procedures:

        3
      block_name

The lines that follow the base point are the group codes for each entity in the block. They are identical to the group codes for entities in the ENTITIES section of the DXF file. The group codes for each entity are outlined in the summary of entity-association lists on the inside cover of this book.

When each block definition is complete, the following indicator appears, signaling both the end of the block and the block's definition layer, before beginning a new block definition:

        0
      ENDBLK
        8
      0

The ENTITIES section contains all the various drawing entities. In a complex drawing, this section can easily become thousands of lines long. It always begins with the sequence

        0
      SECTION
        2
      ENTITIES

and ends with the standard section-end sequence:

0
ENDSEC

Figure 20.4 illustrates a listing of the ENTITIES section from a drawing of a single blue line on a layer named Walls, using a dashed linetype, from point 1,1,0 to point 10,10,10.

```
                  0
                SECTION
                  2
               ENTITIES
                  0
                 LINE
                  8
                WALLS
                  6
                DASHED
                 62
                       5
                 10
                1.0
                 20
                1.0
                 30
                0.0
                 11
                10.0
                 21
                10.0
                 31
                10.0
                  0
                ENDSEC
```

FIGURE 20.4: The entire ENTITIES section of a drawing that contains a single line, drawn on the Walls layer, using a Dashed linetype, color Blue (5), starting point 1,1,0 (group codes 10, 20, and 30), and ending point 10,10,10 (group codes 11, 21, and 31). After the line has been described, a zero group code followed by an ENDSEC variable ends the ENTITIES section. Most drawings will generate DXF files with ENTITIES sections a bit longer than this.

The end of the DXF file is indicated by the following sequence:

0
EOF

Following is a summary of the commands that translate files to and from DXB and DXF formats.

Dxbin

Reads an external DXB file and translates it into a standard AutoCAD drawing.

VERSIONS

Version 2.6 and later.

COMMAND OPTIONS

DXB file   Enter the name of the DXB file to be loaded into the current drawing. The default is the name of the current drawing. File extensions are not allowed; the extension DXB is assumed. You may include subdirectory names and a drive letter if necessary. The DXB file format is different from the DXF and binary DXF file formats, discussed in the Dxfin and Dxfout command sections.

USAGE

The operation of the Dxbin command is automatic. However, notice that there is no special command to create DXB files in AutoCAD. DXB files are normally created by other software, such as AutoShade, to input graphic information to AutoCAD.

You can configure AutoCAD to create DXB files by installing the ADI plotter driver and selecting the DXB option. (Refer to Chapter 3 for details on installation and configuration, and to Chapter 12 for details on plotting options.) Thereafter, you can create a DXB file from an AutoCAD drawing by plotting all or a portion of the drawing to a file using this configuration.

Once you have created the DXB file, you may start a brand-new drawing and use the Dxbin command to load the DXB file back into AutoCAD. When the DXB file is loaded back in, all entities will have been translated into individual line entities. This includes curved entities, blocks, and text, all of which will now be composed of extremely short line segments. Color information is also lost, but you can edit it back in.

This special DXB creation technique can be useful if you need to perform special operations that AutoCAD does not normally allow. Such operations include exploding blocks with different x and y scale factors, creating a separate presentation drawing from a hidden-line display, and converting text to individual line segments for purposes of special editing or even hatching.

RELATED COMMANDS

Dxfin, Igesin.

SAMPLE DIALOG

The following dialog loads ASHADE.DXB into the current drawing:

```
Command: Dxbin
File name <ASHADE>: Ashade
Regenerating drawing
Command:
```

Dxfin

Reads an external DXF file; translates it into a standard AutoCAD drawing.

VERSIONS

All.

COMMAND OPTIONS

File name   Enter the name of the DXF file to be loaded into the current drawing. The default is the name of the current drawing. File extensions are not allowed; the extension DXF is assumed. You may include subdirectory names and a drive letter if necessary.

USAGE

The operation of the Dxfin command is automatic. However, a few special circumstances determine how the file is loaded:

- If you are loading a DXF file into a drawing in which entities are already present, only the ENTITIES section of the DXF file is loaded. (Refer back to "Structure of DXF Files" for details.)
- If you wish to load the other sections of the DXF file as well, you must begin with a new drawing in which no entities are present.
- If your prototype drawing contains entities such as title blocks or drawing boundaries, you can initialize a new drawing without such entities by selecting option 1 from the Main Menu and entering a new drawing followed by an equal sign. Refer to Chapter 3 for details on prototype drawings and new drawings.

If AutoCAD detects trouble with the DXF file, a message similar to the following may appear:

Error *N* in drawing header on line *nn*.
Invalid or incomplete DXF input -- drawing discarded.
Press RETURN to continue:

N is an indication of the type of error that has occurred, and *nn* is the line number at which the problem was detected in the file. This message is often seen after a mistake was made in editing the DXF file. Common problems include wrong or unknown group codes for the data being processed, misspelled string data and variable names, and wrong data types. Refer back to "Structure of DXF Files" for more details on group codes and their accompanying data.

When you receive such an error message, make a note of the line where the error occurred, and then press Enter. AutoCAD will return you to the Main Menu. You must edit the DXF file and correct the problem before trying again.

RELATED COMMANDS

Dxbin, Igesin.

SAMPLE DIALOG

The following dialog starts from the Enter Selection prompt in AutoCAD's Main Menu, begins a new drawing named NEWFILE—note how the use of the equal sign will bypass the prototype drawing—and loads a DXF file named NEWFILE.DXF into a new drawing:

Enter selection: **1**
Enter NAME of drawing: **NEWFILE =**
Drawing editor.
Loaded menu ACAD.mnx
Command: Dxfin
File name <NEWFILE>: **Newfile**
Regenerating drawing
Command:

Dxfout

Writes the current underlying database into an external DXF file.

VERSIONS

All. Version 2.5 and later allow you to create a DXF file of drawing entities only (bypassing header and table information). Release 10 and later allow for a new, more compact binary format of the DXF file information.

COMMAND OPTIONS

File name   Enter the name of the DXF file you wish to create. The default is the name of the current file. File extensions are not allowed; the extension DXF is assumed. However, you may include a drive letter and subdirectory names to have the DXF file written on a drive or directory other than the one currently logged.

Enter decimal places of accuracy (0 to 16)   Enter an integer from 0 to 16 representing the degree of decimal precision for floating-point numbers in the DXF file. The larger the number, the greater the precision; however, a file with greater precision will be larger and will take more time to write and load. The default, 6, is a good number to start with. After you have entered the number of decimal places of accuracy, AutoCAD begins writing the DXF file, in ASCII format. If you intend to select the Entities option, you must do so before entering the decimal places of accuracy.

Entities   Enter **E** if you intend to create a DXF file containing only certain selected entities in the current drawing. AutoCAD responds:

Select objects:

Select the entities you wish to include in the DXF file and press Enter. AutoCAD then repeats the prompt for decimal places of accuracy in the file.

Binary   Enter **B** if you intend to produce a special binary version of the DXF file. The binary DXF file is smaller and loads faster than the normal ASCII file, but cannot be edited as easily. If you select the Binary option, you need not specify decimal places of accuracy; the maximum decimal precision is assumed. After you select this option, AutoCAD begins to write the file.

USAGE

The operation of the Dxfout command is automatic.

ASCII and binary DXF files have the same extension, DXF. Do not confuse the binary DXF file created by this command with the DXB file created using the ADI drawing driver.

Warning: If you are using an earlier version than Release 11, or when the FILEDIA system variable is set to zero, a DXF file already on disk with the same name you enter will be overwritten by the new file. No warning is issued, so be certain to manage DXF files very carefully, making frequent backups and moving them to another location on the hard disk after they have been used.

When using the Entities option, you should not include blocks in your selection set of entities unless you are sure that definitions for those blocks will already be present in the drawing into which you intend to load the DXF file. The only way to include block definitions is to write the entire drawing to a DXF file.

RELATED COMMANDS

Igesout.

SAMPLE DIALOG

The following dialog creates an ASCII DXF file containing selected drawing entities—with six decimal places of accuracy—and places the file on a separate subdirectory:

> Command: **Dxfout**
> File name: **c:\dxffiles\newfile**
> Enter decimal places of accuracy (0 to 16)/Entities/Binary <6>: **E**
> Select objects: **W (window the selected entities)**
> Enter decimal places of accuracy (0 to 16)/Entities/Binary <6>: **6**

DOWNWARD COMPATIBILITY

AutoCAD drawing files are upwardly compatible. This means that drawing files created in earlier versions may be edited using later versions, without special conversion or translation. However, the reverse is not true; a drawing file created in Release 10 cannot be edited using Release 9.

Still, if the situation warrants and you have perseverance, you can use DXF files—after some editing—to create downward compatibility, moving a drawing from a later version to an earlier one. To succeed, this process virtually requires a full-screen text editor with global searching and editing capabilities, as well as macro features. Examples of such text editors are WordStar 4.0 and later in non-document mode, and WordPerfect in DOS Text File mode. In the case of certain drawings that may be too difficult to do over and must be transferred to earlier versions, it may be worth the effort. The following are some guidelines.

Release 11 to Release 10

Before invoking the Dxfout command, make the following changes to the Release 11 drawing. These steps will insure compatibility between entities in the two versions and save you a lot of time when you edit the DXF file:

- Explode all polyface meshes, converting them to 3-D faces. Other meshes may remain as they are.
- Bind all external reference drawings into the current drawing.
- Delete all paper-space entities and viewports.

Create the DXF file using the Dxfout command and edit it as follows, using a text editor:

- Change the value of the $ACADVER variable to AC1006.
- Remove group code 30 and its associated data from the $EXTMIN and $EXTMAX variables.
- You may delete the following Release 11 variables. If you choose not to delete them, Release 10 AutoCAD will still import the DXF file, ignoring them and displaying a message to that effect: $DIMCLRD, $DIMCLRE, $DIMCLRT, $DIMGAP, $DIMSTYLE, $DIMTFAC, $MAXACTVP, $PELEVATION, $PEXTMAX, $PEXTMIN, $PINSBASE, $PLIMCHECK, $PLIMMAX, $PLIMMIN, $PUCSNAME, $PUCSORG, $PUCSXDIR, $PUCSYDIR, $SHADEDGE, $SHADEDIF, $TILEMODE, $UNITMODE, $VISRETAIN.
- You may delete the APPID and DIMSTYLE symbol tables. If you choose not to delete them, Release 10 AutoCAD will still import the DXF file; it will ignore these symbol tables and display a message to that effect.

Make the following changes in the BLOCKS section:

- Remove group code 3 and its associated block name from all block definitions. Do *not* delete group code 3 from the attribute definitions, however.
- Remove group code 73 and its associated data from all block definitions.
- If you did not bind external reference drawings before creating the DXF file, you must delete all block definitions that apply to them. (External reference drawings can be identified by the group code 1, which includes data that begins with XREF.)

Make the following changes in the ENTITIES section:

- Delete all Insert entities that reference the names of any external drawings you deleted from the BLOCKS section.

- If you did not explode polyface meshes before creating the DXF file, delete all POLYLINE entities with group code 70 set to 64 or higher. Be sure to delete all VERTEX entities following the Polyline, up to and including the closing SEQEND entity.
- If you did not delete paper-space viewports before creating the DXF file, delete all VIEWPORT entities.
- Delete all entities that contain group code 67, which indicates that they reside in paper space.
- Delete all group codes and data for extended entity data. These group codes are four-digit integers, starting with 1000.

Save the DXF file, and bring it into Release 10 using the Dxfin command.

Releases 10 and 11 to Release 9

This is by far the most complicated DXF editing job, and probably the most common, as a number of Release 9 users have been slow to upgrade, not certain that the 3-D features in Release 10 and later are right for them. If you want to send a file you have created in Release 10 or 11 to a Release 9 user, the steps presented here will help you make the transition.

The best type of drawing for conversion into Release 9 is a mostly 2-D drawing done in the world coordinate system. Many Release 10 or 11 drawings can satisfy these criteria, but many others cannot. The method shown here, however, will allow you to convert any Release 10 or 11 DXF file to a format that can be read by Release 9, while leaving as many entities as possible with their original entity properties.

You may be able to save yourself some trouble editing the DXF file if you begin by editing the entities in the current drawing editor, matching them to Release 9 drawing entities whenever you can. Here are some tips:

- Explode all polygon meshes and ruled surfaces, thereby turning them into 3-D faces, which are compatible with Release 9.
- Explode all 3-D polylines, turning them into line segments.
- Explode any blocks containing these 3-D entities as well, and then explode any complex entities that emerge from the exploded blocks.
- Use world coordinates when possible to draw over any 2-D line entities that were originally drawn in user coordinate systems. You can do this using 3-D line segments and Osnap. If you are editing in Release 10, use the 3Dline command to draw these revision lines. If you are editing in Release 11, you must draw Line entities and use your text editor to convert them to 3Dline entities in the DXF file. Then erase the 2-D entities.

You can leave entities in user coordinate systems if you want, but some of these 2-D entities (2-D polylines, blocks, arcs, attributes, circles, shapes, solids, and traces) may become distorted or relocated after the transition to Release 9, which has no way of supporting user coordinate systems.

Don't worry if you can't perform all these steps, although these preliminaries will help the two drawings look as much alike as possible after the transition. You may still use the Dxfout command on any Release 10 or 11 entities and continue the editing process on the DXF file using your text editor, but be prepared for possible distortions and subsequent editing in Release 9 afterward.

When you have made your current drawing look as much like a Release 9 drawing as possible, invoke the Dxfout command. If possible, use the DXF Entities option to avoid the necessity of editing the HEADER, TABLES, and BLOCKS sections of the DXF file. But if your drawing contains needed block definitions, layer names, and so forth, you will have to create a DXF file for the entire drawing.

Next, enter your text editor in order to edit the DXF file. Be very careful to make only the changes to be described. Remember that the overall structure of all the elements in the DXF file is the group-code number (right-justified, three digits maximum), followed by the group code's data (strings and floating-point numbers left-justified, integers right-justified).

Tip: If you are a programmer experienced in BASIC or another high-level programming language that can read DXF files, you may consider writing a program that reads the DXF file and makes the changes for you.

If you have produced the file using Release 11, make all the changes to the DXF file as described in the previous section on converting to Release 10. When converting to Release 9, you must delete all Release 11 variables and the APPID and DIMSTYLE symbol tables.

Make the following changes in the HEADER section:

1. Change the value of the $ACADVER variable to AC1004.

2. Check the value for the $INSBASE variable. If it contains a z coordinate (group code 30), delete the 30 and the z coordinate that follows—often it's zero.

3. Check the group code 70 value for the $DIMZIN variable. If it is 4, change it to 3.

4. Delete the following variables: $DIMBLK1, $DIMBLK2, $DIM-SOXD, $DIMSAH, $DIMTIX, $DIMTOFL, $DIMTVP, $FLAT-LAND, $HANDLING, $HANDSEED, $MIRRTEXT, $SPLINETYPE, $SURFTAB1, $SURFTAB2, $SURFTYPE, $SURFU, $SURFV, $UCSNAME, $UCSORG, $UCSXDIR,

$UCSYDIR, $USERI1 through $USERI5, $USERR1 through $USERR5, and $WORLDVIEW. Be sure to delete the preceding group code 9, the variable name, and the data that follows (usually 2–4 lines), up to the next group code 9, or to the 0-ENDSEC entry that ends the HEADER section.

Be certain that the HEADER section ends as follows:

```
      0
    ENDSEC
```

Also, check to be certain that the next section begins:

```
      0
    SECTION
```

Next, in the TABLES section:

1. Delete the following tables in their entirety: DWGMGR, UCS, and VPORT.

2. In the VIEW table, delete the following group codes and their associated data: 12, 22, 32, 42, 43, 44, 50, and 71.

Several changes must be made to the entities listed in the BLOCKS and ENTITIES sections. Some of these changes may not apply to your particular DXF file, but check for them all anyway, just to be certain. Make the following changes:

1. Delete all group codes 210, 220, and 230, and their associated data.

2. All LINE entities in a Release 10 and later DXF file include z coordinate group codes (30–37). Change the entity name (group code 2) to 3DLINE. If your text editor supports macros or a search-and-replace feature, you will find it useful when performing this step. Alternatively, if the z coordinates for the line endpoints (group codes 30 and 31) are both zero, you may prefer to delete these group codes rather than change the entity type. This will reserve any line type information, which is ignored by Release 9's 3-D lines.

3. Delete group code 70 and associated data in all 3DFACE entities.

4. Delete the following group codes and their associated data if they are found in any POLYLINE entities: 10, 20, 30, and 71–75. In VERTEX entities, delete group code 30, but do not alter the 2-D coordinate information—group codes 10–19 and 20–29.

5. Delete all remaining group codes 30 through 37 and associated data in all 2-D entities (ARC, ATTRIB, CIRCLE, DIMENSION, INSERT, POINT, SHAPE, SOLID, TEXT, TRACE).

Save the DXF file, and bring it into Release 9 using the Dxfin command.

As can be seen from the above, the process of converting 10 to Release 9 can be somewhat painstaking. However, the process may be worthwhile in situations where starting over in Release 9 is impractical and the entities in the current drawing are capable of being displayed in a Release 9 drawing (thus requiring as little editing of the BLOCKS and ENTITIES sections as possible).

Release 9 to Version 2.6

The conversion from Release 9 to Version 2.6 is quite simple. Prepare the DXF file in Release 9 by invoking the Dxfout command, and use your text editor to delete the following variables and their values from the HEADER section: $ATTDIA, $ATTREQ, $SPLFRAME, and $SPLINESEGS. Change the value of the $ACADVER variable from AC1004 to AC1003.

Version 2.6 to Version 2.5

Before creating the DXF file, delete all 3-D faces and explode associative dimension entities. Use the Dxfout command in Version 2.6 to prepare the DXF file. Alternatively, you may create the DXF file and delete all the 3-D face and dimension entities using the text editor.

To project 3-D lines onto the X-Y construction plane, use the text editor to eliminate all 30 and 31 group codes, and change the entity name (group code 2) from 3DLINE to LINE.

Delete these dimension variables from the HEADER section: $DIMALT, $DIMALTD, $DIMALTF, $DIMAPOST, $DIMASO, $DIMLFAC, $DIM-POST, and $DIMSHO.

Version 2.5 to Version 2.1

Prepare the DXF file in version 2.5, and edit it in the text editor as follows:

1. Delete these variables from the HEADER section: $ANGBASE, $ANGDIR, $CECOLOR, $CELTYPE, $CLAYER, $COORDS, $DIMBLK, $DIMDLE, $DIMRND, $DIMZIN, $PDMODE, $PDSIZE, $PLINEWID, $SKPOLY, $TDCREATE, $TDINDWG, $TDUPDATE, $TDUSRTIMER, $TEXTSTYLE, and $USRTIMER.

2. Delete group code 4 and its following data line from all styles in the STYLE table.

3. Delete group codes 6 and 62 from all the entities in the BLOCKS and ENTITIES sections.

SPECIAL FEATURES AND ADD-ON SOFTWARE

AutoCAD provides a number of special software tools that enhance its features and complete its CAD toolbox. In addition, many software manufacturers have contributed to a growing library of add-on software that can be used to enhance AutoCAD's power in numerous specialized applications. Some of this add-on software is produced by Autodesk, but most is produced by independent developers who have capitalized on the ability of AutoCAD to be so thoroughly customized and to communicate with outside programs. Chapter 21 describes custom linetypes and hatch patterns, automatic associative dimensioning, access to external applications from within AutoCAD, script files, display slides, freehand sketching, and special data-inquiry commands and convenience options. Chapter 22 focuses on one add-on program, AutoShade, which is of special interest to users of the 3-D features found in AutoCAD Release 10; this chapter also includes a sampling of some of the different kinds of add-on software.

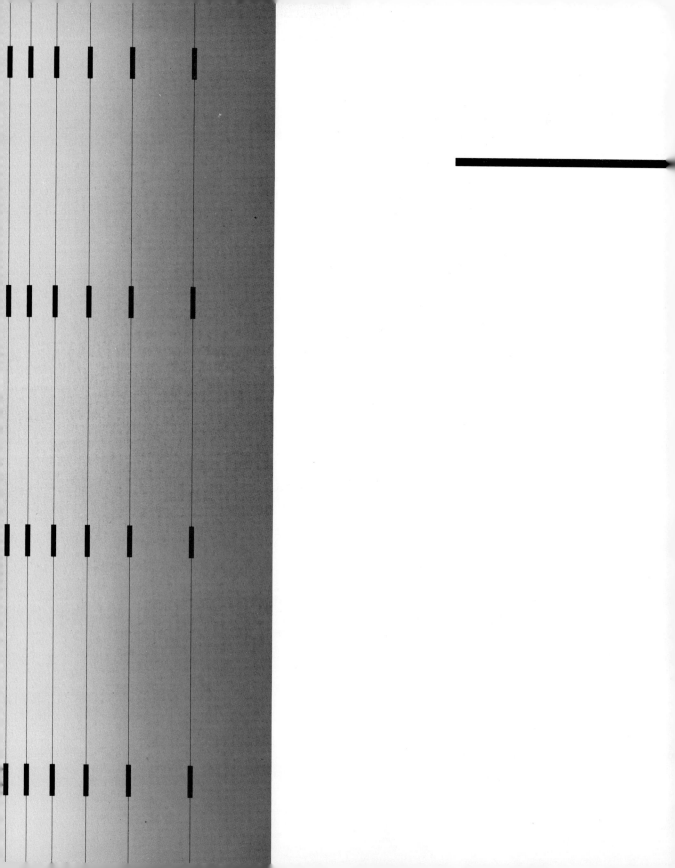

SPECIAL FEATURES

Special Features

This chapter deals with AutoCAD's more specialized tools. Included are task-specific tools (automatic and associative dimensioning, hatching, and sketching); tools to enhance AutoCAD's abilities as a presentation device (scripts and slides); special commands for extracting statistical information (Area, Dist, List, etc.); and convenience tools (external programs, external reference drawings, command modification, and wild-card characters).

Automatic Dimensioning

AutoCAD's automatic dimensioning feature makes it easy to add dimension information to your drawing. Using this feature, you can choose construction points in the drawing—for example, the endpoints of a line—and AutoCAD will automatically measure the line and draw a dimension line, extension or "witness" lines, tick mards or "arrowheads," and the dimension text.

Four basic types of dimensioning are offered: linear, angular, diameter, and radius. Each of these dimension types is discussed separately in this chapter.

Automatic dimensioning looks like a separate program within AutoCAD, with its own prompt that replaces AutoCAD's Command prompt, and special commands and options. You access it by invoking the Dim or Dim1 command. The same subcommands and options are valid for both commands. The difference is that the Dim command allows you to create dimensions for a series of entities before you return to the Command prompt, whereas Dim1 allows you to create a single dimension and then automatically returns you to the Command prompt. In all other respects the commands are the same.

After you invoke the Dim or Dim1 command, the following prompt appears:

    Dim:

If you invoke Dim or Dim1 from the screen menu, you will see AutoCAD's Dimensioning menu appear, as in Figure 21.1.

Controlling Dimension-Entity Appearance

The appearance of the dimension entities drawn by AutoCAD is controlled entirely by system variables. The system variables that affect dimensioning all begin with *DIM*—and variables that begin with these letters affect dimensioning only, nothing else. They are described in detail in Chapter 13.

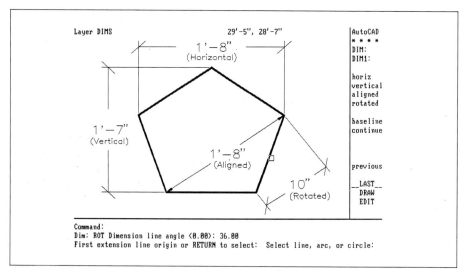

FIGURE 21.1: AutoCAD's linear dimensioning options. AutoCAD's Dimensioning menu lists four linear dimensioning options: Horizontal, Vertical, Aligned, and Rotated. The pentagon in this figure has been dimensioned using each of these options. The angle of the rotated dimension in the lower right, 36 degrees, was taken from the line opposite its starting intersection. Rotating the dimension by this amount allows you to measure the half-width of the pentagon from its lower-right corner.

You may change the values of these system variables in one of three ways:

- By entering the variable name at the Dim prompt, followed by its new value.

- By selecting the *dim vars* option from the Dimensioning screen menu, selecting the variable name from the list that is presented, and then entering the new value.

- By invoking the Setvar command at the AutoCAD Command prompt, followed by the variable name and the new value.

- In Release 11 and later, by invoking the dimension variable name at the Command prompt, followed by the new value.

DIMENSION STYLES

Starting with Release 11, AutoCAD allows you to save various combinations of dimension-variable settings as *dimension styles,* once you have set up the variables to your liking. You may store any number of these dimension styles as part of the drawing. Alternatively, you may store a variety of dimension styles in your prototype drawing for use with new drawings you create.

New dimension styles are created from the current settings of the dimension variables. To save a new dimension style, enter **SAVE** at the Dim: or Dim1: prompt. AutoCAD prompts:

?/Name for new dimension style:

Enter the new name under which AutoCAD will store the current dimension-variable settings. If you enter the name of an existing dimension style, AutoCAD will warn you that the style name already exists, prompting you to confirm your choice before it overwrites the old settings with the new settings.

Once you have created a dimension style, all subsequent dimensions will be drawn using that style, until you either change one of the dimensioning variables or restore a different named style.

To restore a previously saved dimension style, enter **RESTORE** at the Dim: or Dim1: prompt. AutoCAD prompts:

Current dimension style: *Current style name, if any*
?/Enter dimension style name or RETURN to select dimension:

Respond to this prompt by entering your chosen dimension style name from the keyboard or by picking a dimension with the desired properties in the drawing. If the dimension was created when a named dimension style was current, that dimension style now becomes the current style.

You may also enter a question mark at this prompt to see a listing of all named dimension styles in the drawing.

If you enter a dimension-style name preceded by a tilde (˜), AutoCAD will display the values of any dimension variables in the current and named style that differ.

You may change a variable setting without naming a new style. If you do so, AutoCAD will draw the dimensions using the new settings, but will not attach any named style to the dimension entity. This feature allows for some interesting manipulation of dimension appearance. For example, if you draw an associative dimension with a current named style and later update it, it will retain the properties of the dimension style that was current at the time it was drawn, even if you have changed dimension styles or variables in the meantime. This is convenient if you have several dimension styles in the drawing.

On the other hand, if you choose to draw a new associative dimension when a named style is not current, and then update it later, the dimension will adopt the properties of whatever dimension style is current at the time the update is made. Using this feature, you can draw several dimensions in one style for editing, and then change to a fancier dimension style just before you plot the drawing.

LINEAR DIMENSIONING

Linear dimensioning is used to indicate the distance between two points. As illustrated in Figure 21.1, there are four varieties of linear dimensioning in Auto-CAD: horizontal, vertical, aligned, and rotated.

Horizontal   To invoke horizontal dimensioning, enter **HOR** from the keyboard at the Dim command prompt, or select LINEAR followed by *horiz* from the screen menu, or select HORIZ from the standard tablet menu. When you use horizontal dimensioning, AutoCAD will measure only the horizontal distance between the points you subsequently choose, regardless of their orientation.

Vertical   To invoke vertical dimensioning, enter **VER** from the keyboard, or select LINEAR followed by *vertical* from the screen menu, or select VERT from the standard tablet menu. When you use vertical dimensioning, AutoCAD will measure only the vertical distance between the points you subsequently choose, regardless of their actual orientation in the drawing.

Aligned   To invoke aligned dimensioning, enter **ALI** from the keyboard, or select LINEAR followed by *aligned* from the screen menu, or select ALIGNED from the standard tablet menu. When you use aligned dimensioning, AutoCAD will measure the actual straight-line distance between the points you subsequently choose, thus reflecting their orientation in the drawing as well.

Rotated   To invoke rotated dimensioning, enter **ROT** from the keyboard, or select LINEAR followed by *rotated* from the screen menu, or select ROTATED from the standard tablet menu. When you use rotated dimensioning, AutoCAD will measure the distance between the points you subsequently choose, at a specific chosen angle of orientation, regardless of the actual orientation of the line in the drawing. This is helpful in dimensioning irregular objects, as illustrated in Figure 21.1.

Only if you have indicated that you are entering a rotated linear dimension, AutoCAD prompts for the angle of rotation:

Dimension line angle:

Enter the angle of rotation for the dimension line. The angle entered is relative to AutoCAD's angle zero. The rotated dimension angle in Figure 21.1 is 36 degrees.

Regardless of the variation you choose, the remainder of the prompt sequence for linear dimensions is the same. AutoCAD begins by prompting you to select an extension-line origin:

First extension line origin or Return to select:

You may respond to this prompt either by picking the first construction point of the line being dimensioned—for example, an endpoint, or perhaps an intersection with another line—or by pressing Enter.

If you pick a construction point for the first extension-line origin, AutoCAD responds:

Second extension line origin:

Respond to this prompt by picking the second construction point. AutoCAD will measure the distance between the two points, based on the variation of linear dimensioning you have originally chosen.

If you press Enter instead of picking the first construction point, AutoCAD responds:

Select line, arc, or circle:

You may respond to this prompt by picking a point on the entity you intend to dimension. If you pick a line, AutoCAD will measure the endpoints of the line. If you pick an arc, AutoCAD measures the endpoints of the arc. If you pick a circle, AutoCAD measures the diameter of the circle. In each case, the actual orientation of the dimension—and in the case or arcs and lines, the distance between the endpoints—will be affected by the type of linear dimension you have chosen: vertical, horizontal, aligned, or rotated. Figure 21.2 illustrates how the Vertical, Horizontal, and Aligned options measure the same line differently.

Notice as well that AutoCAD will determine the first and second extension-line origin points based on the point used to select the entity. In the case of lines and arcs, the endpoint farthest from the selection point becomes the first extension-line origin point, and the point closest to the selection point becomes the second extension-line origin point.

Whether you have picked two points or selected the entity outright, AutoCAD next prompts:

Dimension line location:

Respond by picking a point near the line being dimensioned. AutoCAD will draw the dimension line so that it intersects this point. AutoCAD next prompts:

Dimension text <*distance*>:

With this prompt, AutoCAD indicates the distance that it has measured between the extension-line origin points, based on your previous input and the type of linear dimensioning you have chosen. If you press Enter in response to this prompt, AutoCAD draws the dimension entity using the default text. If you want, you can enter your own dimension text in response to this prompt, and AutoCAD will use that dimension text instead.

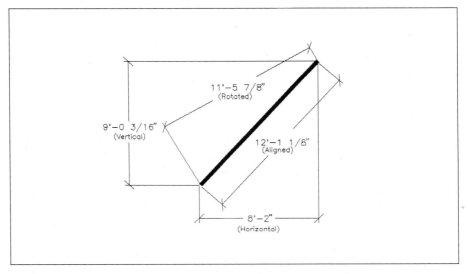

FIGURE 21.2: Linear dimensioning options applied to the same entity. This figure illustrates the differences between linear dimensioning options by applying each one to the same diagonal line. Notice that the horizontal and vertical dimensions are absolute in their orientation, always measuring a horizontal or vertical distance regardless of the angle of the line. The aligned dimension gives the line's true length, while the rotated dimension measures the line as it would be projected into its user-defined angle of orientation (in this case, 30 degrees).

If you want to include the default text in a longer string of your own, you may indicate the placement of the default information in the longer string by entering a less-than/greater-than symbol in your alternate text string. For example, suppose that the default dimension text was *6"*, and you wanted the dimension text to say *Approx. 6"*. You would then respond to the dimension-text prompt by entering:

    Approx. < >

After you have entered the dimension text (or accepted the default), AutoCAD draws the dimension.

If you originally invoked the Dim command, AutoCAD repeats the Dim prompt, allowing you to dimension another entity. If you invoked Dim1, Auto-CAD returns you to the Command prompt.

Dimension Text in Linear Dimensions

AutoCAD normally tries to center the dimension text within the extension lines. When text does not fit between the extension lines, AutoCAD will place it outside the extension lines, always close to the first extension line. Thus, in a situation where you know that text will be outside the extension lines, the order in which you select the origin points or the selection point for the entity becomes important; it will have a direct bearing on the location of the outside-the-lines dimension text.

Baseline Option

From time to time, you may want to show incremental linear dimensions, as illustrated in Figure 21.3. AutoCAD simplifies this process by means of the Baseline option.

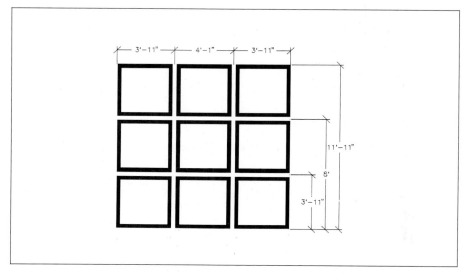

FIGURE 21.3: The Baseline and Continue options. You can instruct AutoCAD to share extension lines when entering a series of linear dimensions. In this figure, the horizontal dimensions were drawn using the Continue option; the second extension line of the previous dimension is used as the first extension line of the subsequent dimension. The vertical dimensions were drawn using the Baseline option; the first extension line of the previous dimension is used as the first extension line of the subsequent dimension.

To use this option, invoke the Dim command and enter your first linear dimension normally, as described earlier. After AutoCAD has drawn the first dimension entity, invoke the Baseline option, either by selecting it from the Linear Dimension screen menu, selecting BASELINE from the standard tablet menu, or entering **BAS** from the keyboard.

AutoCAD responds by skipping the prompts for the first extension-line origin. Instead, it uses the previously selected first extension-line origin, and now prompts only for the second extension-line origin, followed by the normal prompt sequence for linear dimension text.

The dimension lines for incremental dimension entities will be offset from each previous entity; the amount of offset is controlled by the DIMDLI system variable (see Chapter 13).

Continue Option

You may use the Continue option when you intend for a second dimension entity to begin where the previous dimension entity left off, as illustrated in Figure 21.3.

As with the Baseline option, AutoCAD responds by skipping the prompt for the first extension-line origin. Instead, it uses the previously selected second extension-line origin, and now prompts only for the current second extension-line origin, followed by the normal prompt sequence for linear dimension text. This new dimension entity will continue from the previous second extension line to the new second dimension line, using the same orientation.

ANGULAR DIMENSIONING

Angular dimensioning draws a dimension entity that indicates the angle formed by two lines in the drawing, as illustrated in Figure 21.4.

To invoke angular dimensioning, enter **ANG** from the keyboard, or select *angular* from the screen menu, or select ANGULAR from the standard tablet menu. AutoCAD responds:

Select arc, circle, line, or RETURN:

This prompt indicates various means by which you can indicate the angle you intend to measure:

- If you select an arc, AutoCAD assumes that you intend to measure the included angle of the arc.
- If you select a circle, AutoCAD assumes that you intend to measure an angle within the circle, starting with the selection point. You will then see this prompt:

Second angle endpoint:

In response, enter a second point on the circle. If you do not pick a point, the point on the circle nearest to the point you picked will be used.
- If you press Return, AutoCAD assumes that you intend to measure an angle formed by three points, starting with the angle vertex point; thus, it

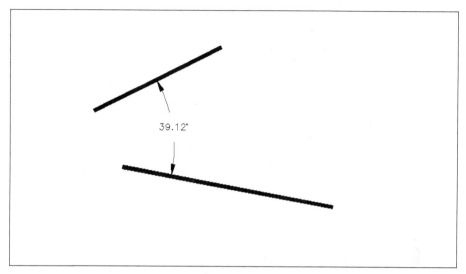

FIGURE 21.4: Angular dimensions. The angle formed by any two nonparallel lines is computed by finding the difference between the lines' relationship to the x-axis of the plane in which they reside. You may select the lines at any point without affecting the appearance of the angle dimension. You are always prompted to pick a point to be intersected by the dimension arc, and a specific point for placement of the angular dimension text. This figure illustrates its default position.

prompts:

    Angle vertex:

Select a point that you intend to use as the vertex of the angle you are measuring. AutoCAD prompts:

    First angle endpoint:
    Second angle endpoint:

Respond to both of these prompts by selecting a point. The two points must be different, although if necessary, one may be the same as the angle vertex point.

   In each of the above cases, AutoCAD will measure the major or minor angle formed by your selections, based on the location you specify for the *dimension-line arc,* described just ahead.

- If you select a line (or segment of a polyline), AutoCAD assumes that you intend to measure the angle formed by two non-parallel lines (or polyline segments), and prompts:

    Second line:

Pick the second line or polyline segment that you intend to measure.

The order in which you select the lines is important, because AutoCAD will measure the angle according to the angle increment direction for which it has been configured—the default is counterclockwise. The first line is always the starting line for measuring the angle.

Once you have determined the angle you intend to measure, AutoCAD prompts:

Enter dimension line arc location:

Respond by picking a point, and AutoCAD will measure the angle using a dimension arc drawn through the selected point. If you have indicated the angle by selecting an arc, a circle, or three points, the location of the dimension-line arc will determine whether the major or minor angle will be measured.

AutoCAD's next prompt is:

Dimension text <*angle*>:

With this prompt, AutoCAD indicates the angle that it has measured, based on the current default for angular units as set with the Units command (see Chapter 6). You may press Enter or type alternate text as described for linear dimensioning.

AutoCAD then prompts:

Enter text location:

Pick an insertion point for the dimension text. The text will be left-justified from this point.

If you originally invoked the Dim command, AutoCAD repeats the Dim prompt, allowing you to dimension another entity. If you invoked Dim1, Auto-CAD returns you to the Command prompt.

DIAMETER AND RADIUS DIMENSIONING

Diameter and radius dimensioning use the same essential sequence of prompts on the same entity types. The difference between them is the dimension type that results—either a diameter or a radius.

The appearance of the diameter or radius is controlled by the DIMTIX and DIMTOFL variables, as illustrated in Figure 21.5. Refer to Chapter 13 for more information on system variables.

To invoke diameter dimensioning, enter **DIA** from the keyboard, or select *diameter* from the screen menu, or select DIAMETER from the standard tablet menu. To invoke radius dimensioning, enter **RAD** from the keyboard, or select *radius* from the screen menu, or select RADIUS from the standard tablet menu.

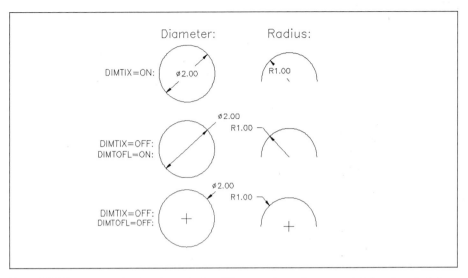

Figure 21.5: Diameter and radius dimensioning. When you dimension arcs and circles, the orientation of the dimension line is determined by the point used to pick the entity. In Release 11, the location of the radius and diameter dimension text is controlled by the dimension variable DIMTIX. If DIMTIX is set to off (or zero), inclusion of the center point symbol is controlled by the dimension variable DIMTOFL, as illustrated here.

AutoCAD responds:

> Select arc or circle:

Pick the arc or circle you intend to measure. The point you use to select the arc or circle will be the point used as the endpoint of the dimension line.

After you select the arc or circle, AutoCAD prompts:

> Dimension text <*distance*>:

With this prompt, AutoCAD indicates the diameter or radius of the circle. You may press Enter or type alternate text as described for linear dimensioning.

In Release 10 and earlier, AutoCAD would draw the diameter dimension, placing the text inside the circle. If the text did not fit, AutoCAD would display a message to that effect and prompt for a leader line from the entity-selection point, placing the text outside the circle. Release 11 controls the location of diameter and radius dimension text by means of the DIMTIX and DIMTOFL variables, as illustrated in Figure 21.5. Refer to Chapter 13 for more information on system variables.

After you enter the dimension text, if the text is to be placed outside the circle or arc, AutoCAD prompts:

> Enter leader length for text

A rubberband line appears, extending from the point used to pick the circle or arc. You may indicate the length of the line by picking a point or entering a length from the keyboard. You may also press Enter, and AutoCAD will use the default leader length, which is always double the arrow or tick-mark size. (If you enter a leader length shorter than the default, the default is used instead.)

In the case of diameter dimensioning, the leader line is always an extension of the diameter dimension line, starting from the point used to select the entity. If you are dimensioning a radius, the leader line will be an extension of the radius line, also starting from the point used to select the entity, unless you indicate the leader length by picking a point on the opposite side of the center point. In that case, AutoCAD draws the leader line as an extension of the radius line, starting from the center of the arc or circle.

AutoCAD then prompts for dimension text as previously described for linear dimensioning.

ORDINATE DIMENSIONING

The Ordinate dimensioning option allows you to use the dimensioning feature to insert call-outs of X- and Y-coordinate locations for selected points in your drawing. When you select this option, AutoCAD prompts:

Select feature:

Respond to this prompt by indicating a point in the drawing. You may use any standard point selection mechanism including object snap to specify the point. After you enter a point, AutoCAD responds:

Leader endpoint (Xdatum/Ydatum):

Respond to this prompt by entering a second point, which indicates the endpoint of the ordinate-dimension leader line. As you move the crosshairs to select a new point, a rubberband line will extend from the selected point to the crosshairs.

Once you select a second point, AutoCAD will determine whether to supply the X or Y coordinate, based on the length and orientation of the indicated leader line. If the X distance (parallel to the x-axis) between the points is greater than the Y distance (parallel to the y-axis), the Y coordinate is given. If it is the reverse, the X coordinate is given. If the distances are equal, the Y coordinate is given.

AutoCAD then draws the leader line from the feature point to the leader endpoint. Unlike the rubberband line, which might have been diagonal, the ordinate leader line is composed of a series of horizontal and vertical line segments.

Depending on the relationship between the two selected points, the starting point of the leader line may be offset slightly from the first selected point. To prevent this offset, toggle Orthogonal mode on before using the Ordinate dimensioning option.

If your intended leader line will cause AutoCAD to supply an incorrect coordinate value, you can force AutoCAD to supply either the X or Y coordinate by entering **X** or **Y** in response to the "Leader endpoint" prompt. If you respond in this manner, AutoCAD repeats the "Leader endpoint" prompt, and you may then pick the ordinate leader endpoint as you would normally. AutoCAD will supply the requested X- or Y-coordinate value.

CENTER DIMENSIONING

To invoke center dimensioning, enter **CEN** from the keyboard, or select *center* from the screen menu, or select CENTER from the standard tablet menu. Auto-CAD prompts:

   Select arc or circle:

Pick the arc or circle you intend to measure. AutoCAD then places center lines or a small cross in the center of the arc or circle. The entity drawn is controlled by the setting of the DIMCEN system variable (see Chapter 13).

LEADER DIMENSIONING

The Leader dimensioning option allows you to draw an arrow along with a single line of accompanying text. To invoke leader dimensioning, enter **LEA** from the keyboard, or select *leader* from the screen menu, or select LEADER from the standard tablet menu. AutoCAD prompts:

   Leader start:

Enter the starting point for the leader line. This point will also be the location of the arrowhead. AutoCAD responds:

   To point:

Pick an endpoint for the leader line.

Each time you pick a point, AutoCAD repeats the "To point:" prompt, allowing you to enter a leader line composed of many segments. When you have finished drawing the leader line, press Enter. AutoCAD then prompts for dimension text, as described for linear dimensioning.

If you intend to draw a leader without text, enter a space in response to the dimension-text prompt, thereby overwriting the default.

OTHER DIMENSIONING COMMANDS

The following commands are also available to you while the Dim prompt is displayed in the Command-prompt area. Except for the Exit command, these commands work only with associative dimensions. They will not work on dimension entities created when the value of DIMASO is OFF. If you select a non-associative dimension entity, you will see the following message:

Entity is not a dimension

If you wish to use the following commands to edit such a dimension, you must erase it and re-create it.

Exit   When the Dim prompt is displayed, you may return to the AutoCAD Command prompt by entering **EXIT** (or pressing Ctrl-C).

Hometext   If you have relocated the dimension text to somewhere other than its default location—using the Stretch command, for example—you may invoke this command to return the dimension text to its default location. AutoCAD prompts:

Select objects:

Select the dimension entities whose text you intend to return to its default position. You may use any of AutoCAD's standard entity-selection methods. Non-associative dimension entities will be ignored.

Newtext   You may use this command to change the dimension text for one or more associative dimension entities. AutoCAD prompts:

Enter new dimension text:

Enter the new dimension text string. If you press Enter instead of entering a text string, the chosen dimension entities will be given the actual measurement as their text. If you enter a string and select several dimension entities, the change will be made globally for all selected dimension entities. You may use empty angle brackets, as described for linear dimensioning, to include the measurement in any string you provide.

For example, to replace all dimension text in the drawing with the dimension measurement plus the string " +/−2.5", enter the following in response to the prompt for new text:

<> +/−2.5

After you enter the new text, AutoCAD prompts:

Select objects:

Select one or more dimension entities whose text you intend to change. You may use any of AutoCAD's standard entity-selection methods. AutoCAD changes the dimension text styles for those entities; nonassociative dimension entities will be ignored.

Oblique You may use this command to change the orientation of an associative dimension's extension lines. Normally the extension lines are drawn perpendicular to the dimension line. If your drawing is crowded with other dimensions or entities that make the dimensions hard to read, you may offset the dimension lines by means of this command. AutoCAD prompts:

Select objects:

Select the dimension entities you wish to offset and press Return. AutoCAD prompts:

Enter obliquing angle (or RETURN for none):

If you press Return, the default perpendicular orientation is used. Otherwise enter an angle value. AutoCAD responds by changing the angle of the extension lines to the angle specified and moving the dimension line accordingly.

Override Enter this command to make temporary, one-time changes to associative-dimension variables. AutoCAD prompts:

Dimension variable to override:

Enter the name of the variable whose value you wish to change. AutoCAD prompts:

Current value <*value*> New Value:

Enter a new value for the variable. AutoCAD then repeats this prompt sequence allowing you to select other variables until you press Return. AutoCAD then prompts:

Select objects:

Select the dimension entities you wish to update with these temporary settings. AutoCAD will update the dimension entities and restore the original settings to the variables.

However, if you select a dimension entity that is associated with a named dimension style, AutoCAD prompts:

Modify dimension style <*name*>? <N>:

If you respond **Y** to this prompt, AutoCAD updates the dimension entity and the named style at the same time. If other dimension entities reference this style, they will be updated as well. If you respond with **N**, AutoCAD will update the selected dimension entity, but will not change the dimension style or update other dimension entities referencing this style.

Redraw   This is the same as AutoCAD's Redraw command.

Status   This command will list all the dimensioning system variables and their current settings for your review.

Style   Enter **Style** to change the style of the dimension text. Dimension text defaults to the current text style. This command simply allows you to make a new style current, as would AutoCAD's standard Style command.

Tedit   You may use this command to change the position and orientation of associative-dimension text relative to its dimension line. When you invoke this command, AutoCAD prompts:

Select dimension:

Select only one dimension entity. AutoCAD then prompts:

Enter Text location (Left/Right/Home/Angle):

You may respond to this prompt by entering a point. AutoCAD will move the center point of the dimension text to the point you choose. Alternatively, you may enter one of the four responses indicated in the prompt. If you enter **Left**, AutoCAD left-aligns the dimension text along the dimension line. If you enter **Right**, AutoCAD right-aligns the text along the dimension line. If you enter **Home**, AutoCAD returns the text to its normal default position and angle. If you enter **Angle**, AutoCAD prompts:

Text angle:

Enter an angle value and AutoCAD will re-orient the text at the angle you specify. Angle information is retained independently of text location. You may change both the location and the angle by repeating the Tedit command. If you change the location of the text after entering the angle, the angle orientation is retained.

Trotate   You may use this command to change the orientation angle of dimension text. It works just like the Angle option of the Tedit command, with one exception: you may select several dimension entities and change their text angles simultaneously. Refer to the previous discussion of the Tedit command for details.

Undo   This command will undo the previous dimension entity. If you use the Undo command repeatedly, you can step back through the dimension entities you have drawn during the current dimensioning session. This is different from AutoCAD's standard Undo command. If you exit the dimensioning session and invoke the Undo command, you will undo all of the dimension entities created during that session.

Update   If you have changed any of the dimensioning parameters—such as the scale factor or the dimension text style—you can invoke this command, and AutoCAD will redraw selected associative dimension entities to reflect those changes. After you invoke the Update command, AutoCAD prompts:

Select objects:

Select one or more dimension entities that you intend to update. You may use any of AutoCAD's standard entity-selection methods. AutoCAD redraws the selected entities; nonassociative dimension entities will be ignored.

Variable   Enter this command to list the dimension variable settings associated with a particular dimension style. AutoCAD prompts:

Current dimension style: <Style name, if current>
?/Enter dimension style name or RETURN to select dimension:

You may enter the name of any saved dimension style or enter a question mark to display a list of saved dimension styles. The prompt repeats after the list is displayed.

Alternatively, you may press Return to select a dimension entity on the screen. If you press Return, AutoCAD prompts:

Select dimension:

Select the desired dimension with the pointing device. The style associated with the selected dimension will be used. If the selected dimension is not associated with a named dimension style, the current dimension style is used instead. If there is no current dimension style, a default dimension style named *UNNAMED is used instead.

AutoCAD then lists the values of all dimension variables associated with the selected dimension style.

ASSOCIATIVE DIMENSIONS

Starting with AutoCAD Version 2.6, dimensions are treated as a single entity, in a manner similar to blocks. Associative dimensions differ from ordinary dimension types in their ability to be updated automatically when you edit the entities to which they are associated. Refer to Figure 21.6 for an illustration of associative dimensioning. All linear dimensions, plus the angular, radius, and diameter dimensions (including center marks and lines), are associative. The center and leader dimensions are not.

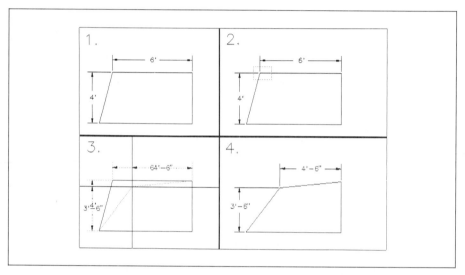

FIGURE 21.6: Associative dimensioning. Step 1: The figure before editing begins using the Stretch command. Step 2: A crossing window selects the lines to be changed, plus a definition point for both of the dimension entities. Step 3: The lines and dimension entities are stretched. Step 4: The resulting entity appears, with updated dimensions. The key to automatic updating of associative dimensions is your ability to select the dimension's definition points, along with the entities to be changed.

The key to accurate, automatic updating of associative dimensions is to select the dimension's *definition point* as part of the selection set being edited. If you do not select the definition point, the drawing entity will be updated, but the dimension will not.

The dimension's definition points are stored on a special layer named Defpoints. This layer operates a bit differently than other AutoCAD layers. Defpoints defaults to an ''off'' state, but the definition points of any particular dimension entity will always be visible if the dimension entity itself is visible. This makes it easier to pick the points when editing dimension entities. The points on the Defpoints layer are not plotted, however, unless you first turn the Defpoints layer on using the Layer On Defpoints command.

Definition points for each dimension entity are illustrated in Figure 21.7.

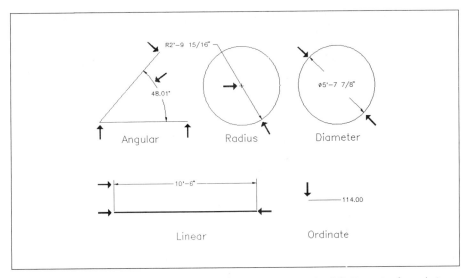

FIGURE 21.7: The five basic types of dimensions, with arrows pointing to the definition points for each. In angular dimensions, the definition points are the endpoints of the lines used to indicate the dimension, plus the point used to locate the dimension arc. In radius dimensions, definition points are the point used to select the circle and the center point. In diameter dimensions, they are the point used to select the circle and the point opposite the selection point. In all variations of linear dimensioning, the definition points are the points used to specify the dimension extension lines, and the intersection of the first extension line and the dimension line. In ordinate dimensions, the definition point is the coordinate datum point.

The easiest means of selecting definition points is to include that part of the dimension entity in a ''crossing'' window when selecting the entity to be changed. The following editing commands will update a dimension entity:

- Array (when rotated in a polar array; rectangular arrays merely copy the included dimension)
- Extend (for linear dimensions only)
- Mirror (MIRRTEXT set to 0)
- Rotate (dimension extension lines follow the original entity dimension points)
- Scale (dimensions remain relative to original selection points at the new scale)
- Stretch (for angular and linear dimensions)
- Trim (for linear dimensions only)

The performance of associative dimension entities depends on the settings for the following system variables (details for which may be found in Chapter 13):

DIMASO Controls the creation of associative dimensions. When DIMASO is set to a value of 1 or "On" (the default), dimensions are associative; otherwise, they are generated as separate entities, without the ability to be updated automatically.

DIMSHO Controls the display of associative dimensions during editing. If DIMSHO is set to a value of 1 or "On," associative dimensions, including their text, will be updated on the screen as they are dragged. If DIMSHO is set to 0 or "Off", the original entity is dragged in its original state, and only updated after the new point or scale is selected.

> *Note:* AutoCAD bases its update of associative dimensions on an imaginary line that connects the definition points of the extension lines. This works well in most cases, but may produce inaccurate results if you use the Trim or Extend command on dimensions whose extension lines are not equal in length (as often happens with horizontal, rotated, or vertical dimensions). If you get inaccurate results using the Trim or Extend command, undo the edit and try using the Stretch command instead. If neither of the commands works, your only recourse is to erase or explode that particular dimension entity and redimension the drawing entity; in other words, treat it as if it were a nonassociative dimension. Still, in the vast majority of cases, associative dimensioning works quite well.

EXTERNAL COMMANDS

AutoCAD provides a means to access other software programs while inside the drawing editor. This feature can be a great convenience, allowing you to switch from the drawing editor to spreadsheets, databases, text editors, or other programs, and back into your drawing without exiting and reloading AutoCAD.

You can configure AutoCAD to recognize external programs by editing the ASCII file ACAD.PGP with your text editor. A portion of the Release 11 version of ACAD.PGP is shown in Figure 21.8.

ACAD.PGP contains a list of DOS commands. Each command occupies its own line in the file. Each line contains five separate elements of information, separated by commas. These items are:

- The command, if any, to be issued while within the drawing editor.
- The actual command AutoCAD passes to DOS when the drawing-editor command is issued. This can include a batch file that changes subdirectories or sets up other environmental requirements before loading the external program.
- The amount of memory required to execute the command.

```
CATALOG,DIR /W,30000,*Files: ,0
DEL,DEL,30000,File to delete: ,0
DIR,DIR,30000,File specification: ,0
EDIT,EDLIN,42000,File to edit: ,0
SH,,30000,*DOS Command: ,0
SHELL,,127000,*DOS Command: ,0
TYPE,TYPE,30000,File to list: ,0
```

FIGURE 21.8: ACAD.PGP contains a list of external commands available while inside AutoCAD's drawing editor. Each line of the file must specify the AutoCAD external command, the corresponding DOS command, the amount of memory required, a prompt to the user to supply additional information if necessary, and finally a code that indicates whether AutoCAD is to return to the graphics or text screen at the conclusion of the command. Thus, the Catalog command actually invokes DIR /W, requires 30K, allows for a filtering list of file names if desired, and returns with the screen in text mode.

- A prompt offered to the user for any additional information needed.
- A special number code used by AutoCAD when it returns to the drawing editor.

Note: Do not invoke any terminate-and-stay-resident programs (such as Side-Kick) by this means. The memory they continue to occupy could conflict with AutoCAD when you return to the drawing editor, causing AutoCAD to crash. Instead, invoke these programs before entering AutoCAD.

For example, assume that you intend to access your text editor as an external program while inside the drawing editor, as an aid in developing AutoLISP routines and custom menus. You would need to know the following before editing ACAD.PGP:

- The command you would like to use to call up the external program while inside AutoCAD. Often, this will be the same as the command used to initialize the program at the DOS prompt. But, if you find that the actual command you need to use is long—for example, if it includes a long string of subdirectory names—you can use an abbreviation while inside AutoCAD.
- The command that will be used to initialize the external program from the DOS prompt, from within the subdirectory that is logged while the AutoCAD drawing editor is active. Often, the simplest means of doing this is to include the text editor's subdirectory as part of the operating system's search path. Refer to the SET PATH command in Chapter 4 for details on this.

   Another possible method (provided that your text editor's program files are small and you have the disk space to spare) is to copy the program files to the same subdirectory as AutoCAD's system files.

   In any event, some experimentation may be required for you to determine exactly how the operating system finds any outside program you intend to initialize while inside the drawing editor.

- The amount of random-access memory the external program requires. (You should have at least 4K more than your program requires.) This information can be found in the documentation for your program. If not, you may have to inquire from the dealer, the manufacturer, another user, or a consultant. As a stopgap measure, if the program is contained in a single file with the extension EXE, you can use the file size as a good approximation of the memory required, or you can repeatedly edit ACAD.PGP, experimenting with different memory sizes until you find a size that works.

When you have this information handy, enter your text editor and edit ACAD.PGP. In this example, assume the following:

- The text-editor subdirectory is included in the operating system's search path, and may be called from any subdirectory using the command ED; optionally, the ED command may be followed by the name of a file that will be opened when the text editor is loaded.
- The text editor requires 45 kilobytes of RAM.
- The command to be used inside AutoCAD's drawing editor will also be ED.

Given the above, you can add the following line to ACAD.PGP:

    ED,ED,45000,File: ,4

This line, like the other lines in ACAD.PGP, contains five items separated by commas. In order, they indicate the following:

ED, This item indicates the command to be used while inside the drawing editor.

ED, The second item indicates the DOS command that will be issued when the first command is invoked.

45000, The third item indicates the amount of memory required by the external program. Notice that abbreviations such as *45k* are not allowed, nor are commas separating thousands from hundreds. You must indicate the literal number of bytes of RAM required. In this case, the amount is forty-five thousand bytes, or 45K. The maximum amount of RAM you can use will vary from system to system. Some systems allow you to use as much as 512K, but 256K is a more commonly allowed maximum. The minimum is 24K.

File: , Since the text editor in this example allows for an optional file name on the DOS command line, the fourth item indicates a prompt that AutoCAD will display when the ED command is invoked. The response you give to this prompt will be included as part of the command that AutoCAD passes to DOS. Notice the space after the colon in the prompt. This will cause a space to appear between the prompt and the name of the file that you enter on the screen, thus improving readability.

4 The fifth item is either 0 or 4. The item must be present, but it affects only single-screen systems, which flip between text mode and graphics mode. If this code is 0, AutoCAD will remain in text mode when it returns to the drawing editor. If this code is 4, AutoCAD will flip back to graphics mode upon its return. In the example, the return code is 4, so AutoCAD will flip back to graphics mode automatically.

Be sure to include a carriage return at the end of this line.

Note: AutoCAD normally responds in the same way to a press of the space bar or the Enter key. This also applies to responses to the optional prompts in ACAD.PGP. If you choose to make further edits to ACAD.PGP and spaces may be required in a response to the optional prompt, precede the optional prompt with an asterisk (*). When the optional prompt is preceded by an asterisk, only the Enter key will enter your response. Refer back to the example of ACAD.PGP in Figure 21.8 to see examples of this feature.

Take a moment now to study the other lines in the file shown in Figure 21.8. Notice how they all have the same basic structure. Notice also that some do not call for a special prompt, but that a comma must be included just the same, so that five "items" are marked with commas on each line.

Command Aliasing in Release 11 ACAD.PGP

Starting with Release 11, ACAD.PGP may include syntax for *command aliasing.* Command aliasing is a means of simplifying command input with the keyboard. It allows you to substitute alternate keystrokes of your choice for standard AutoCAD commands. For example, if you enter the Fillet command frequently, you may use this technique to shorten it to F instead, turning six keystrokes into one.

The ACAD.PGP line format for command aliasing is quite simple: type the new keystrokes (usually just one or two letters) followed by a comma, an asterisk, and the actual AutoCAD command name. For example, to shorten the Fillet command to F, add the following line to ACAD.PGP:

```
F,*FILLET
```

You may not include command options when using the aliasing technique. You may provide aliases only for the command name.

Beginning with Release 11, you may include comment lines in ACAD.PGP. Refer to the discussion of comment lines later in this chapter for details.

ACAD.LIN: AUTOCAD'S LINETYPE DEFINITION FILE

The Linetype command provides a convenient means of creating and storing new linetype definitions while inside AutoCAD. If you prefer, you may enter new linetype definitions by editing the file ACAD.LIN with your text editor. A portion of the Release 11 version of ACAD.LIN appears in Figure 21.9.

```
*DASHED,__ _ _ _ _ _ _ _ _ _ _ _ _ _ _
A,.5,-.25
*HIDDEN,__ _ _ _ _ _ _ _ _ _ _ _ _ _ _ _
A,.25,-.125
*CENTER,____ _ ____ _ ____ _ ____ _ ____ _
A,1.25,-.25,.25,-.25
*PHANTOM,____ _ _ ____ _ _ ____ _ _
A,1.25,-.25,.25,-.25,.25,-.25
*DOT,.............................................
A,0,-.25
*DASHDOT,__ . __ . __ . __ . __ . __ . __ . __
A,.5,-.25,0,-.25
*BORDER,__ __ . __ __ . __ __ . __ __ .
A,.5,-.25,.5,-.25,0,-.25
*DIVIDE,__ . . __ . . __ . . __ . . __
A,.5,-.25,0,-.25,0,-.25
```

FIGURE 21.9: ACAD.LIN. This file contains the definition codes for AutoCAD's eight standard linetypes, and can be modified using a text editor or the Linetype command. The Release 11 ACAD.LIN file contains two additional versions of each linetype, one at 2x scale and the other at 0.5x scale. This file contains alternating header and definition lines. The dots and dashes in the header lines are for the convenience of the user only. The actual dashes and dots are generated using the numbers below the header lines. A positive number generates a dash, negative a space, and zero a dot. Numbers are always decimal, and represent drawing units.

Every linetype definition in ACAD.LIN uses the same fundamental two-line structure, as the following example illustrates:

```
*DASHDOT,__ . __ . __ . __ . __ . __ . __ . __
A,.5,-.25,0,-.25
```

The first line, called the *header line,* always contains three items:

- An *asterisk* (*), indicating the start of a header line.
- The *linetype name,* which must be in uppercase letters following the asterisk, and which is followed by a comma.
- A *linetype description,* which is a representation of the linetype using ASCII characters, usually underline characters, spaces, and periods.

The total length of the header line should be no more than 47 characters.

The second line, called the *definition line,* always begins with an uppercase *A,* which is followed by a comma and a series of as many as 12 but no fewer than 2 numbers (called *elements*) separated by commas. These numbers represent the movements that an imaginary "pen" must make to produce the dashes, dots, and spaces that make up the linetype, according to the following rules:

- Decimal numbers, representing drawing units, are used.
- Positive numbers indicate a dash length (or "pen-down" movement) of the given number of units.
- Negative numbers indicate a space length (or "pen-up" movement) of the given absolute value.
- Zeros indicate dots.
- The linetype definition may begin with a dot or a dash, but must not begin with a space.
- The linetype definition line must contain no more than 80 characters.

Given the above DASHDOT linetype example, then, the definition-line elements indicate the following:

- .5 is a dash segment, 1/2 drawing unit long.
- -.25 is a space segment, 1/4 drawing unit long.
- 0 is a dot.
- -.25 is a space segment, 1/4 drawing unit long.

A line segment drawn using this linetype will repeat this pattern throughout its length.

Refer to the Linetype command in Chapter 6 for an example of a custom linetype.

Beginning with Release 11, you may include comment lines in ACAD.LIN. Refer to the discussion of comment lines later in this chapter for details.

ACAD.PAT: AUTOCAD'S HATCH-PATTERN DEFINITION FILE

ACAD.PAT is AutoCAD's hatch-pattern definition file. AutoCAD only recognizes this file as containing hatch patterns; no other file name or extension is allowed. Thus, if you intend to add new hatch patterns, you must add them to this file.

Like the linetype descriptions in ACAD.LIN, each hatch-pattern description in ACAD.PAT contains a header line, followed by definitions of linetypes—a series of decimal numbers that represent dashes, dots, and spaces. Unlike a linetype definition, however, a hatch-pattern definition may contain any number of different linetypes, each on its own text line in the file.

When a hatch pattern is constructed, AutoCAD first draws a linetype, and then copies the line parallel to itself at a distance specified in the linetype definition. It continues to copy parallel lines, filling an area chosen during the Hatch command (described in detail ahead).

A single hatch-pattern description may comprise any number of linetype definitions. Each linetype in a hatch pattern is drawn and then copied parallel to itself, until all linetypes defined in the pattern are drawn.

As was the case with custom linetypes, you tell AutoCAD how to move an imaginary pen by means of a series of numbers that are separated by commas. However, with hatch patterns, you have to supply some extra information for each line:

- The angle at which the line is drawn and copied.
- A starting point for each line.
- The distance between the parallel copies of the line.
- The degree of offset (if any) for each copy of the line.

What ultimately creates a virtually limitless number of possible patterns is the combination of the angles at which the linetypes are drawn, their starting position, their distance from each other, and the degree of offset, along with their pattern of dashes, dots, and spaces.

A list of custom hatch-pattern descriptions is shown in Figure 21.10 for your study. The patterns produced by these descriptions are illustrated in Figure 21.11.

```
*altbr,Alternating brick squares
0,     1,1,   1,1,.9,-.1,.4,-.1,.4,-.1
0,   1,1.9,   1,1,.9,-.1,.4,-.1,.4,-.1
90,    1,1,   1,1,.4,-.1,.4,-.1,.9,-.1
90,  1.9,1,   1,1,.4,-.1,.4,-.1,.9,-.1
0,   1,1.4,   1,1,.9,-1.1
0,   1,1.5,   1,1,.9,-1.1
90,  2.4,1,   1,1,.9,-1.1
90,  2.5,1,   1,1,.9,-1.1
*mbrick, mortar bricks
0,      0,0,  .5,.4,.95,-.05
0,    0,.35,  .5,.4,.95,-.05
90,     0,0,  .4,.5,.35,-.45
90, -.05,0,   .4,.5,.35,-.45
*parquet,floor pattern
45,   0,0,  .25,.25, 1.25,-.75
135, 0,0,  .25,-.25, 1,-.75,.25
*tile, tiles
0,      0,0,   0,1,.9,-.1
0,    0,.9,   0,1,.9,-.1
90,     0,0,   0,1,.9,-.1
90,  .9,0,   0,1,.9,-.1
*weave,weave pattern
0,    0,0,     .6,.2, .8,-.2
90,  0,-.2,  .6,.2, .8,-.2
```

FIGURE 21.10: The definitions for the hatch patterns illustrated in Figure 21.11. You may use your text editor to copy these hatch-pattern definitions into your copy of ACAD.PAT if any appeal to you. Comparing these line definitions to the actual appearance of the patterns is a useful exercise.

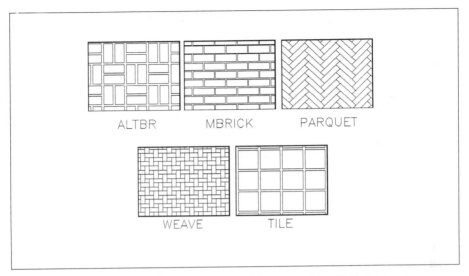

FIGURE 21.11: The hatch patterns generated from the definitions in Figure 21.10. Hatch patterns can look more complicated than they actually are. The Weave pattern, for example, requires only two definition lines, while the Tile pattern requires four. The key to developing hatch patterns is to draw the original pattern in AutoCAD and analyze the relationships between the lines.

Each hatch-pattern description begins with a header line. The header line begins with an asterisk (*) followed by the name of the pattern. The pattern name is followed by a comma, and the comma is followed by a short text description of the hatch pattern. This name and text description will appear in the listing of hatch patterns invoked by AutoCAD's Hatch ? command. The description is optional but recommended. If you choose not to supply a description, then do not supply the comma after the pattern name, either.

The line or lines that follow the header line contain the numbers that describe the various linetypes used to construct the hatch pattern. Each line definition adheres to a rigid structure. The first five numbers are required. As many as six additional numbers follow. The additional numbers describe noncontinuous linetypes and are optional. All numbers are separated by commas. Each numerical line description ends with a carriage return.

The first five elements always indicate the following, in the given order:

- The angle at which the line is to be drawn, relative to AutoCAD's default zero angle.
- The x coordinate of the line's starting point.
- The y coordinate of the line's starting point.
- The degree of offset for each parallel copy of the line.
- The distance between the parallel copies of the line.

The remaining elements (as many as six) describe up-and-down pen motions according to the rules outlined in the previous section on linetype descriptions. For example, following is the hatch-pattern description called Parquet:

```
*parquet,floor pattern
45, 0,0, .25,.25, 1.25,-.75
135, 0,0, .25,-.25, 1,-.75,.25
```

The elements in the first linetype definition line indicate the following:

45,	The line is drawn at a 45-degree angle.
0,0,	The x-y starting point is 0,0.
.25,	Each dashed line is offset from the previous by ¼ drawing unit. (This creates the "straight-stacked" effect of the angled lines, as seen in Figure 21.12.)
.25,	The distance between the parallel copies is ¼ drawing unit.
1.25,	The line begins with a dash segment 1¼ drawing units long.
-.75	The dash segment is followed by a space segment ¾ drawing unit long.

The elements in the second linetype definition line indicate the following:

135,	The line is drawn at a 135-degree angle.
0,0,	The x-y starting point is 0,0.
.25,	Each dashed line is offset from the previous by ¼ drawing unit (again creating the "straight-stacked" effect of the angled lines, as seen in Figure 21.12).
-.25,	The distance between the parallel copies is − ¼ drawing unit. (Since these lines are drawn at the opposite angle, the negative number causes the parallel copies to be made in the opposite direction of previous lines, important in having them drawn in correct relationship to each other.)
1,	The line begins with a dash segment 1 drawing unit long.
-.75	The dash segment is followed by a space segment ¾ drawing unit long.
.25	The space segment is followed by another dash segment ¼ drawing unit long.

Figure 21.12 illustrates how these lines combine to form a complex pattern.

When developing custom hatch patterns, use AutoCAD to create the preliminary design and to measure distances and offsets. With its array of copying, editing, and analysis tools, AutoCAD is perfect for this sort of process.

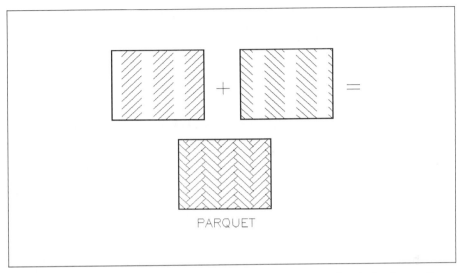

FIGURE 21.12: The two line definitions that form the Parquet hatch pattern described in the text. The key to this pattern is each line's offset element. Each time a parallel dashed line is copied, the dashes are moved ¼ drawing unit farther along the line's angle of orientation, producing the "stacked" effect that you see here in these dashes.

Beginning with Release 11, you may include comment lines in ACAD.PAT. Refer to the discussion of comment lines later in this chapter for details.

Following is a brief discussion of the Hatch command.

Hatch

Fills a selected area of the drawing with a chosen hatch pattern.

VERSIONS

All.

COMMAND OPTIONS

Pattern   Respond to this prompt by entering the name of the hatch pattern you intend to use. Alternatively, you may select one of the following suboptions:

?   Enter a question mark to display the pattern names found in ACAD.PAT.

U   Enter **U** to define a simple pattern of parallel lines at designated angles and spacing. AutoCAD responds:

Angle for crosshatch lines:

Enter the angle at which you would like the crosshatch lines to be drawn, relative to angle zero in the current user coordinate system. AutoCAD then prompts:

Spacing between lines:

Enter the distance, in drawing units, between the hatch lines. Next, AutoCAD prompts:

Double hatch area?

Enter **Y** or **N**. If you answer **Y**, a second set of parallel lines will be drawn perpendicular to the first set of parallel lines. If you answer **N**, only a single set of parallel lines is drawn.

If you enter either a pattern name or **U**, you may follow it with a command and one of three letters indicating the style of hatching. Three hatching styles are allowed, as illustrated in Figure 21.13.

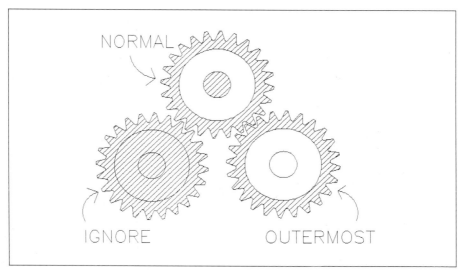

FIGURE 21.13: AutoCAD's three hatching styles. In Normal style (top), the hatch pattern toggles on and off each time it intersects one of the entities chosen to hatch, resulting in the alternating effect that you see here. In the Ignore style (lower left), the outermost boundary is hatched, and the inner entities are ignored. In the Outermost style (lower right), the hatch pattern toggles off the first time it intersects an entity, but ignores other entities it finds that would normally toggle the pattern back on; thus, only the outer areas of the hatch entity are filled.

Normal Enter **N** for Normal hatching style.

Outermost Enter **O** to hatch only the outermost area.

Ignore Enter **I** to ignore all inner areas.

If you have selected a pattern name from ACAD.PAT, you will first receive the following prompt:

> Scale for pattern:

The predefined hatch patterns in ACAD.PAT have been defined so as to appear clearly visible at 1-to-1 scale. If you are drawing at a different scale, the lines in the hatch pattern may be drawn too close together, appearing almost as a solid, or too far apart, showing little if any of the overall pattern. For example, if you are drawing at ¼" = 1', the hatch pattern will appear small, especially when you are viewing a large portion of your drawing on the screen. However, you can enter **48** (1 foot divided by ¼ inch) in response to the above prompt, and redo the Hatch command to make the hatch pattern appear more reasonable in size.

AutoCAD then prompts:

> Angle for pattern:

Hatch patterns default to a base angle of zero, and all lines in the drawing are drawn at an angle relative to that angle zero. If you choose, you may cause Auto-CAD to "tilt" the hatch pattern and hatch at a specified angle. The angle you enter becomes that hatch pattern's "zero" angle, and all lines in the pattern are drawn relative to it instead.

Once the hatch-pattern parameters have been set up, you may select the areas to hatch. AutoCAD prompts:

> Select objects:

If you do not include an entity in the selection set, AutoCAD will completely ignore it during hatching. After you have selected the entities to hatch, Auto-CAD begins the process, and fills the entity areas according to your parameters.

USAGE

Boundary lines for hatching should meet at their endpoints; intersections between lines at points other than their endpoints may lead to incorrect area fills. If necessary, edit your drawing before hatching; break, fillet, and trim lines so that the endpoints of the boundaries are all intersecting.

Hatch patterns are formed relative to the drawing's base point (normally 0,0,0). If necessary, you can align hatch patterns precisely within their boundaries by changing the base point with the Base command (see Chapter 6). Changing the base point back after the hatch pattern is drawn will not affect the alignment of the pattern.

If you are experimenting with different patterns, erasing one and creating another repeatedly, you will enlarge your drawing file considerably with unreferenced hatch-pattern blocks, even though the hatch patterns are not being used. The Purge command (Chapter 6) does not delete unreferenced hatch-pattern blocks. To delete unreferenced hatch patterns, copy the drawing to disk under a new name using the Wblock command (Chapter 9), and then erase the original.

Generally speaking, hatch patterns should be created when the default linetype is Continuous; unpredictable results occur when a noncontinuous linetype is set. If the hatch pattern appears different than expected, check the default linetype.

Text, attributes, and shapes cannot be hatched to their entity edges; if you hatch using these entities, a blank margin will appear around them. This is helpful with text, because it ensures that the text remains readable, but it may lead to undesired effects with shapes. The only work-around is to overdraw the shape using standard line entities, and then erase it. This problem does not occur with blocks, as they are hatched correctly.

RELATED COMMANDS

None.

RELATED SYSTEM VARIABLES

None.

SAMPLE DIALOG

The following dialog selects AutoCAD's standard Grate hatch pattern, hatching outermost entities only at a scale of ¼ inch to 1 foot, and an angle of 45 degrees:

```
Command: Hatch
Pattern (? or name/U,style): GRATE
Scale for pattern <1>: 48
Angle for pattern: 45
Select objects: (select desired entities)
```

COMMENT LINES IN RELEASE 11 ASCII FILES

A *comment line* is a line in an AutoCAD ASCII file that will be ignored by AutoCAD when it uses the file. They are useful for explanations or clarification in the file for other readers or even to refresh your memory if you haven't looked at the file in a long time.

Most of Release 11's ASCII files may include comment lines: ACAD.PGP, ACAD.LIN, ACAD.PAT, and all files with the extensions LSP and SHP. Script files are a notable exception; they may not include comment lines. Release 11 menu files, such as ACAD.MNU, may contain comments, but their format differs from that specified here. Refer to Chapter 14 for details on menu files.

Comment lines must adhere to these rules:

- The comment line must begin with a semicolon.
- Everything on the same line following the semicolon will be ignored by AutoCAD.
- You can include a comment on a line that contains AutoCAD instructions provided that you place a semicolon before it. However, everything on that line following the semicolon will be ignored.

The following file fragment from ACAD.PGP is an example of how comment lines can clarify the meaning of an example command:

```
; The following ACAD.PGP command executes the ED text editor.
; ED.EXE must be available on the operating system's search path:
ED,ED,45000,*File: ,4      ; Calls ED.EXE editor, 45k required
```

WILD-CARD CHARACTERS

Release 11 AutoCAD commands that list named entities and symbols, such as Layer ?, Block ?, and Setvar ?, will accept wild-card character patterns in response to the prompt:

Named entity type to list < * >:

The default response is the asterisk, which indicates that all named entities should be included. You may limit the set of included entities by using various combinations of wild-card characters, as outlined in Table 21.1.

Wild-card characters may be combined. For example:

#*WALL*

would match any string beginning with a number and containing the word WALL.

*#*WALL*

would match any string containing a number followed by the word WALL. Finally:

*#*WALL*, *WALL*#*

Character	Meaning	Example
˜ (tilde)	If first character in pattern, negates the entire test; otherwise, it is treated as a literal character.	˜EXAMPLE = Matches any name except EXAMPLE.
* (asterisk)	Matches any string, including the null string. Can appear anywhere in the pattern.	*XAMPL* = Matches any string that contains XAMPL.
? (question mark)	Matches any single character.	E?AMPLE = Matches any 7-character string that begins with E and ends AMPLE. The second character may be a letter, number, or punctuation mark.
@ (AT symbol)	Matches any single alphabetic letter.	E@AMPLE = Matches any 7-character string that begins with E and ends AMPLE, provided that the second character is a letter.
# (Pound Sign)	Matches any single numeric digit.	E#AMPLE = Matches any 7-character string that begins with E and ends AMPLE, provided that the second character is a number.
. (period)	Matches any single non-alphanumeric character.	E.AMPLE = Matches any 7-character string that begins with E and ends AMPLE, provided that the second character is not a letter, number, or standard punctuation mark.
(blank space)	Matches one or more spaces.	EX* * = Matches any string that begins EX and contains a space.
[ ] (brackets)	Matches any one of the enclosed literal characters.	E[XYZ]AMPLE = Matches EXAMPLE, EYAMPLE, and EZAMPLE.

Table 21.1: AutoCAD's Wild-Card Characters

Character	Meaning	Example
[˜] (brackets with leading tilde enclosed)	Matches any character NOT enclosed in the brackets. If the tilde is not the first character within the brackets, it is treated as a literal character.	E[˜X]AMPLE = Matches any 7-character string that begins with E and ends AMPLE, except EXAMPLE.
[-] (brackets including hyphen)	Used within brackets to indicate a valid range of characters. If the hyphen is the first or last character within the brackets, it is treated as a literal character.	EXAMPLE[1-4] = Matches EXAMPLE1, EXAMPLE2, EXAMPLE3, and EXAMPLE4.
, (comma)	Multi-pattern separator (logical OR).	EXAMPLE,SAMPLE,X* = Matches EXAMPLE, SAMPLE, and any string that begins with X.
' (back quote)	Escape (treat the next character literally).	E'?AMPLE = Matches E?AMPLE only; does not treat the question mark like a wild-card character.

Table 21.1: AutoCAD's Wild-Card Characters (continued)

would match any string containing a number and the word WALL, regardless of their position in the string.

AutoCAD commands that accept wild cards deal mostly with named entities. Since all named entities are uppercase, user input to these prompts is automatically converted to uppercase. The AutoLISP wild-card function, Wcmatch, and its AutoCAD Development System counterpart, ads_wcmatch, are case-sensitive, however.

EXTERNAL REFERENCE DRAWINGS

Release 11 introduces *external reference drawings*, a feature that allows you to incorporate drawings on disk (external references) into individual master drawings without actually adding the referenced entities to the master drawing database. AutoCAD will, however, display and plot external references that are incorporated into master drawings.

Externally referenced drawings cannot be edited from within the master drawing, but they can be edited separately as normal drawings from AutoCAD's Main Menu. A master drawing will always reflect an external reference drawing's most recent changes.

This feature offers several advantages. Many drawings can share a single external reference drawing, thus saving disk space. If a change is made to the external reference drawing, all master drawings that reference it will automatically reflect the changes, thus saving time.

On a network, external reference drawings are locked when the master drawing is being edited. This prevents changes to the external reference drawing during the editing session. AutoCAD will permit another operator on the network to unlock the external reference drawing and edit it; however, changes made to the external reference drawing will not appear in the master drawing until either it is saved and re-loaded or the current operator invokes the Xref Reload command.

If you choose, you may bring the entities in an external reference drawing into the master drawing's database. This is called *binding*. Once its entities are bound into the master drawing, the external drawing is no longer referenced, and the added entities may be edited like any other entity in the master drawing. The process of binding an external reference drawing is analogous to the process that takes place during the Insert command, where external-drawing entities in DWG files are imported directly into the master drawing's database.

Certain named entities in an external drawing, such as styles, layers, and blocks, are renamed when the drawing is referenced in the master drawing. This renaming procedure prevents conflicts that might occur if entities in the master drawing had the same name as those in the external drawing.

For example, imagine you are working on a drawing named MASTER.DWG, which references an external drawing named XREF. Both drawings have a layer named DIMENSION. The DIMENSION layer in XREF is renamed XREF | DIMENSION. The renamed entities might also include the subdirectory location of the referenced drawing file, to further distinguish it from drawings having the same name in other subdirectories.

If you bind XREF's entities into MASTER.DWG, the vertical bars in entity names are replaced by "n", where n is a number that is automatically incremented until there are no duplicate names in the file. This allows you to bind several copies of the same Xref file without name conflicts. If AutoCAD cannot rename the named entities without exceeding the 31-character limit for entity names, it will not permit you to bind the external reference drawing.

In cases where named entities in external reference drawings will exceed 31 characters, you may rename the external reference file at the time you attach it to the master drawing. Refer to the discussion of the Xref command in this chapter for details.

Also, you can bind single blocks (or layers or styles) from an Xref, rather than binding the entire drawing. Refer to the discussion of the Xbind command in this chapter for details.

Attributes in External Reference Drawings

External reference drawings are similar to block insertions. However, there are some important differences with regard to attribute definitions. Constant attributes are brought in with an external reference drawing and output by the Attext command (if the appropriate field is defined in the template file). Attributes that are included as part of block definitions in the external reference drawing also come in without problems. However, variable attribute definitions are not brought in with an external reference, nor are they created when the external reference drawing is bound into the master drawing.

Variable attributes are left out to protect against the operator attempting to change their values. Since the variable attributes in the external reference drawing are not part of the master drawing's database, the changes would be lost at the end of the editing session. The next time the operator loaded the master drawing, the attributes would contain their default values. This could lead to considerable confusion!

If you want to attach variable attributes to an external reference drawing, you can do so by creating a block definition in the master drawing that includes the external reference drawing, along with your desired attributes. The block definition and its associated attributes are, of course, part of the master drawing, thus any changes to the attributes would be saved with it, while the entities in the external reference drawing would still be incorporated into the master drawing by reference only.

Following is a description of the Xref and Xbind commands, which manage external reference drawings.

XREF

Controls externally referenced drawings in the master drawing.

VERSIONS

Release 11

COMMAND OPTIONS

? Enter a question mark to display a list of external reference drawings. Auto-CAD prompts:

Xref(s) to list < * >:

Enter the names of the external reference drawings you would like to list. Wild-card characters are allowed. Refer to the section on wild-card characters earlier in this chapter for details.

Bind Enter **B** to bind the external reference entities into the master drawing. Once this is done, the external reference is deleted and it becomes a block entity in your drawing. AutoCAD prompts:

Xref(s) to bind:

Enter the names of the external reference drawings you would like bound into the master drawing. Wild-card characters are allowed if you would like to bind several at once. Refer to the section on wild-card characters earlier in this chapter for details.

Detach Enter **D** to remove external drawing references from the master draw-ing. AutoCAD prompts:

Xref(s) to detach:

Enter the names of the external reference drawings you would like removed from the master drawing. Wild-card characters are allowed if you would like to remove several at once.

The Detach option is global in nature. If you do not intend to remove all occurrences of an external reference drawing that has been inserted several times, use the Erase command to erase the selected occurrences.

Path Enter **P** to change the name or subdirectory location of the external refer-ence file that AutoCAD has stored in the drawing database. Use this option when an external reference drawing has been renamed or moved since you first attached it to the master drawing. AutoCAD prompts:

Edit path for which Xref(s):

Enter the external references you would like to rename. Wild-card characters are allowed if you would like to rename several at once. After you specify the name or names of the external reference drawings to remove, AutoCAD prompts for each one:

Old path *current drive:\path\name*
New path:

Enter the new path for the indicated external reference drawing. To leave the displayed path unchanged, press Return. If you change the path or name, AutoCAD will verify the existence of the drawing file before accepting the change.

   AutoCAD repeats the prompt until all changes have been made, then updates the external references, using the new path and file names.

Reload   Enter **R** to reload external reference drawings. This option repeats the process that occurs when you load the master drawing. It is useful in situations where an external reference drawing was changed on the network during your current editing session, because it eliminates the need to exit and re-enter the drawing editor or reload every external reference in the master drawing. AutoCAD prompts:

Xref(s) to reload:

Enter the external references you would like to reload. Wild-card characters are allowed if you would like to reload several at once.

Attach   Enter **A** or press Return to attach an external reference drawing to the master drawing. AutoCAD prompts:

Xref to attach:

If an external reference drawing was attached previously during the editing session, its name is presented as the default. You may press Return to select it again; this simplifies attaching several copies of the same external drawing. Alternatively, you may enter the name of a new external reference drawing to attach. You may also respond to this prompt by entering a *tilde* (˜), which will display a dialog box with the names of drawing files on the default subdirectory.

   After you indicate the drawing name to attach, AutoCAD prompts:

Insertion point:

As when inserting a block, select a point to specify the origin of the external reference drawing. The external reference drawing's entities will be displayed relative to this point. AutoCAD then prompts for an X and Y scale factor and rotation angle. If necessary, refer to the discussion of the Insert command in Chapter 9 for details and examples.

USAGE

If your master drawing contains the layer DEFPOINTS, then the DEFPOINTS layer in the external reference drawing (if it exists) is not referenced. If your master drawing does not contain the layer DEFPOINTS and the external reference drawing does, a new DEFPOINTS layer is created in the master drawing.

Properties of layer 0 in the master drawing override properties of layer 0 in the external reference drawing. Properties associated with the Continuous linetype override those of the Continuous linetype in the external reference drawing.

Renaming external references If named entities in the external reference drawing are so long that referencing them exceeds the 31-character limit, you can create more space by renaming the external reference file when you attach it. To do this, enter the new name, an equals sign, and the original drawing name in response to the "Xref to attach:" prompt. For example:

    Xref to attach: x = oldname

would insert the OLDNAME.DWG under the name X.

Nested references It is permissible to attach external reference drawings that in turn contain external reference drawings of their own. You may nest external references to as many levels as you like, up to the limit imposed by available hard-disk space. You must not create circular references, however. For example, a circular reference occurs when you attempt to attach an external reference drawing which in turn references the master drawing. When AutoCAD detects a circular reference, it will not permit you to reference the drawing.

Xref log files AutoCAD maintains an ASCII file that records the actions taken by the Xref command. Each time you invoke the Xref command and take some action, AutoCAD records the actions in a special log file. This file has the same name as the drawing, with the extension XLG. If AutoCAD cannot find an existing log file, it creates one. Otherwise, it adds to the contents of the log file. This file is for your convenience only; you may erase it if it takes up too much space on your hard disk.

RELATED COMMANDS

Insert

SAMPLE DIALOG

The following sample dialog will reference a drawing named PART.DWG into a master drawing:

```
Command: XREF
?/Bind/Detach/Path/Reload/<Attach>: Press Return
Xref to Attach: PART
Attach Xref PART: part
Duplicate DEFPOINTS layer entry ignored.
PART loaded.
Insertion point: 0,0
X scale factor <1> / Corner / XYZ: Press Return
Y scale factor (default=X): Press Return
Rotation angle <0>: Press Return
Command:
```

XBIND

Adds entity definitions from an external reference drawing to the master drawing database, making them a permanent part of it.

VERSIONS

Release 11

COMMAND OPTIONS

Block	Enter **B** to bind block names.
Dimstyle	Enter **D** to bind dimension style names.
LAyer	Enter **LA** to bind layer names.
LType	Enter **LT** to bind Linetype definition names.
Style	Enter **S** to bind text style names.

In each case, AutoCAD prompts:

Dependent *definition* name:

where *definition* is your chosen option. Respond by indicating the externally referenced definition that you wish to bind into the master drawing. Wild-card characters are permitted if you wish to bind several definitions at once. Refer to the discussion of wild-card characters earlier in this chapter for details.

For example, suppose you wish to bind several blocks whose names begin with PIN followed by a number and that are in an external reference drawing named PART. After you invoke Xbind B, AutoCAD prompts:

Dependent block name(s):

To bind all the PIN* blocks, enter the dependent block name as PART | PIN*. Notice that you must indicate the name of the external reference file as part of the block name, separated from the block name by the vertical bar (|) symbol. This syntax tells AutoCAD where to look for the PIN* blocks.

After each block definition is bound into the master drawing, its name becomes PART0PIN, plus a number. This name change will distinguish each new block from other blocks with the same name already in the master drawing. If, after the name update, any block with the same name still exists in the master drawing, AutoCAD increments the number between the dollar signs until the name becomes unique.

The original PIN* blocks in the external reference drawing are left unchanged, and if the original block definitions in PART.DWG are updated, the change will be reflected the next time the master drawing loads the external reference to PART. The block references that were bound into the master drawing are included in the master drawing database and remain unchanged.

The general rules described here apply to whatever externally referenced definitions you choose to bind into a master drawing.

USAGE

The Xbind command is useful when you would like to add an externally referenced definition to your master drawing without the added overhead of binding the entire drawing. If you want to bind an entire drawing, use the Xref Bind command.

If you bind a block definition into your master drawing, any of the block's associated layers, linetypes, text styles, as well as any nested block definitions, are bound in at the same time.

RELATED COMMANDS

Xref Bind

SAMPLE DIALOG

The following sample dialog binds into the current drawing a layer named PART-TABLE from an external reference drawing named PART:

Command: **XBIND**
Block/Dimstyle/LAyer/LType/Style: **LA**

Dependent Layer name(s): **PART | PART_TABLE**
Scanning. . .
1 Layer(s) bound.
Command:

SCRIPTS

A *script file* is an ASCII file containing a series of AutoCAD commands and responses that will be rigorously executed in sequence when loaded by means of the Script command. It is somewhat analogous to a player piano: AutoCAD commands and responses are invoked without an operator at the keyboard. Script files are frequently used as a presentation tool along with a series of slide files, displaying AutoCAD slides in sequence one after another.

Script files are composed using a text editor. As in a custom menu, all spaces and carriage returns in a script file will be read and interpreted. They always have the extension SCR. A sample script file is shown in Figure 21.14.

```
1
x=
PLINE
3,2 3,8 9,8 9,2 C
TEXT
4.25,4.25 2

yo!
ROTATE L
3,2

6,5 90
ROTATE P

6,5 90
ROTATE P

6,5 90
ROTATE P

6,5 90
QUIT Y
```

FIGURE 21.14: A script file. This file demonstrates how a script can begin from AutoCAD's Main Menu, if legal Main Menu options are included. This script file must be invoked from the DOS command line. Once started, it will repeat until you interrupt it with Ctrl-C or Backspace. In order for script files of this type to repeat automatically, they must end with commands that return to the Main Menu—in this example, the Quit Y command.

The following commands control script files.

Delay

Causes a delay of a specified number of milliseconds before moving to the next command in the script file.

VERSIONS

All.

COMMAND OPTIONS

The Delay command is followed by an integer indicating the length of the pause. Of course, a delay of 1000 milliseconds should equal 1 second; however, if you have a system with speed-up options attached, you may find that you need to adjust the delay amounts.

USAGE

The purpose of the Delay command is to allow a script file to pause long enough for the viewer to assimilate the information on the screen, in cases where the continuing script file would otherwise cause the display to change too rapidly (for example, when displaying a series of slides).

The Delay command may be invoked from the Command prompt, but it's hard to imagine a reason for doing so, as it will only prompt for the length of the delay, and then do nothing for the indicated amount of time.

RELATED COMMANDS

None.

RELATED SYSTEM VARIABLES

None.

SAMPLE DIALOG

The following lines, which could appear in an AutoCAD script file, will display three slides named Slide1, Slide2, and Slide3 in sequence, delaying about 3 seconds between each. (If copying this format into a slide file of your own, be sure to include a carriage return at the end of the last line in the file.)

```
Vslide Slide1
Delay 3000
Vslide Slide2
Delay 3000
Vslide Slide3
Delay 3000
Quit Y
```

Resume

Restarts an interrupted script file from the point following the interruption.

VERSIONS

All.

COMMAND OPTIONS

None. However, Resume may be invoked transparently if the script file was interrupted in the middle of a command sequence.

USAGE

Script files can be interrupted by any of the following:

Ctrl-C   Enter the cancel sequence to interrupt a script from the keyboard.

Backspace   Pressing the Backspace key has the same effect as pressing Ctrl-C.

Error condition   If any command or response in the script file causes an Auto-CAD error condition, the file will be interrupted and the Command prompt will reappear. Erroneous responses that do not force AutoCAD error messages will not interrupt the script file, although they could cause unintended results. In such a case, press Backspace or Ctrl-C, and reedit the script file.

To restart a script file from the beginning, invoke the Script command.

RELATED COMMANDS

Script.

RELATED SYSTEM VARIABLES

None.

SAMPLE DIALOG

The following dialog starts a script file named SLIDESHO.SCR, interrupts it, and starts it up again where it left off.

```
Command: Script
Script file: SLIDESHO
VSLIDE SLIDE1
DELAY Delay time in milliseconds: 3000
VSLIDE SLIDE2
DELAY Delay time in milliseconds: 3000 (press Ctrl-C)
Command: Resume
VSLIDE SLIDE3
Command:
```

Rscript

Repeats a script file while inside the drawing editor.

VERSIONS

All.

COMMAND OPTIONS

None.

USAGE

Rscript can be invoked from the Command prompt to repeat a script that has completed, or it can be used in a script file to cause the file to repeat continuously until interrupted by a Backspace or Ctrl-C.

RELATED COMMANDS

Script.

RELATED SYSTEM VARIABLES

None.

SAMPLE DIALOG

The following script file, which displays three slide files, will repeat continuously while inside the drawing editor:

```
VSLIDE SLIDE1
DELAY 3000
VSLIDE SLIDE2
DELAY 3000
VSLIDE SLIDE3
DELAY 3000
RSCRIPT
```

Script

Executes a script file.

VERSIONS

All.

COMMAND OPTIONS

Script file   Enter the name of the script file that AutoCAD is to read.

USAGE

The name of the current drawing file is offered as a default response to this command. If your script file has the same name as your drawing, you may invoke it by pressing Enter. The file extension SCR is assumed, and should not be entered.

You may invoke another script file as one of the commands in a script file. If you do so, the other script file is executed, but you will not return to the original script file at its conclusion.

You may execute a script file automatically when AutoCAD has been loaded, by placing the file's name on the command line. The command structure at the DOS prompt is

ACAD *DRAWING SCRIPT*

where *ACAD* is the command to initialize AutoCAD, *DRAWING* is a drawing name, and *SCRIPT* is the name of a script file. When AutoCAD is opened using this syntax, the script file is called immediately after display of the Main Menu.

Therefore, if the drawing named on the DOS command line is a new drawing, the first two lines in the script file should consist of the number 1 followed by a pair of carriage returns, as in

```
1<
<
```

where < indicates the carriage return, not a less-than character. This script file will invoke Main Menu option number 1, and accept the default drawing, as indicated in the DOS command line.

If the drawing indicated in the DOS command line is an existing drawing, the script file should begin with the number 2, as follows:

```
2<
<
```

Additional AutoCAD commands of your choice could follow these opening lines.

If you prefer, you can name the drawing in the script file. For example, a script file could load an existing drawing file named COLUMBIA.DWG as follows:

```
2<
COLUMBIA
```

If you choose to name a drawing in the script file, you must indicate a "dummy" drawing name in the DOS command line, so that AutoCAD can find and use the desired script file. For example,

```
ACAD X SCRIPT
```

would load AutoCAD with a default drawing name of X, and execute the SCRIPT.SCR file, which in turn loads another drawing to use instead of X.

There are two ways to invoke a script file repeatedly. One is by means of the Rscript command, which repeats a script file that is called using the Script command inside the drawing editor. The other way applies only to script files that are called from the DOS command line, as described earlier. If these files terminate with the End command or Quit Y, AutoCAD returns to the Main Menu and starts them over again automatically.

You can terminate a script file at any time by pressing the Backspace key or Ctrl-C. To end the drawing and the script at the same time, use End or Quit Y and 0 to exit the Main Menu.

Note: One way to help make the writing of script files easier is to execute the commands you intend to place in a script file while the printer echo is turned on. Press Ctrl-Q to toggle the printer echo on while inside the drawing editor; press it a second time to turn the printer echo off. (Be sure the printer is turned on and on-line before doing this.) Refer to the resulting printout of commands and AutoCAD prompts to ensure a more accurate script file the first time.

RELATED COMMANDS

Rscript.

RELATED SYSTEM VARIABLES

None.

SAMPLE DIALOG

The script illustrated in Figure 21.14 demonstrates the principle behind repeating script files. It starts a new drawing named X, draws a rectangle, rotates it in place, quits, and starts all over again. To execute this script file, place the lines in an ASCII file named X.SCR using your text editor. Copy the file to the AutoCAD system subdirectory if necessary, and enter the following at the DOS prompt:

    ACAD X X

To end the repeating script file, press the Backspace key or Ctrl-C.

SLIDES

Slide files enable you to use AutoCAD as a presentation device by displaying complex drawings in the drawing editor without time-consuming drawing regenerations. Slide files are also required if you are creating your own icon menus for displays that support the Advanced User Interface.

Two commands control slide files: Mslide, which creates them, and Vslide, which displays them. Slide files are not ASCII files, but rather are binary bit maps of the current screen.

This section focuses on the mechanics of creating and displaying slide files in the drawing editor. Refer to Chapter 14 for details on creating icon menus and slide libraries.

Mslide

Creates a slide file from the current display.

VERSIONS

All.

COMMAND OPTIONS

Slide file: Enter the name of the slide file you intend to create. The name of the current drawing is supplied as a default response. To create a slide file with the same name as the drawing, press Enter; otherwise, enter a file name. Do not enter a file extension; the extension SLD is assumed. You may include a drive letter and subdirectory names as part of the file name if you intend to store your slides on a subdirectory or drive other than the one currently logged.

USAGE

Once you have entered the name of the slide file, the process of creating the file is fully automatic, and takes only a few seconds.

Warning: If the slide file you name already exists, it is overwritten. No warning is given regarding this, so be certain that you name your slide files carefully to avoid accidental erasure.

RELATED COMMANDS

Vslide.

RELATED SYSTEM VARIABLES

None.

SAMPLE DIALOG

The following dialog will create a slide file of the current display and name it SLIDE1.SLD:

```
Command: Mslide
Slide file <DRAWING>: SLIDE1
Command:
```

Vslide

Displays a slide file in the drawing editor.

VERSIONS

All.

COMMAND OPTIONS

Slide file: Enter the name of the slide file you wish to display. The name of the current drawing is supplied as a default response. To display a slide file with the same name as the drawing, press Enter; otherwise, enter a file name. Do not enter a file extension; the extension SLD is assumed. You may include a drive letter and subdirectory names as part of the file name if you have stored your slides on a subdirectory or drive other than the one currently logged. You may also include a slide library name if your slide files have been gathered into a library. To indicate a slide that is part of a library, enter the library name, followed immediately by the name of the slide file, within parentheses. Do not use spaces. For example, in the line

LIBNAME(SLIDE)

LIBNAME is the name of the slide library file, and SLIDE is the name of the slide file contained in the library.

You may load a slide file into memory but not display it at the same time. Although slides tend to display themselves pretty quickly on most systems, this technique can be a timesaving device when you are loading a series of slides and you want successive slides to appear as quickly as possible. To load a slide into memory only, place an asterisk (*) in front of the slide file's name. Then, when ready to display the slide, invoke the normal Vslide syntax. The preloaded file name will be offered as the default, which you may select by pressing Enter. This is especially useful in script files, as shown in Figure 21.15.

USAGE

Once you have entered the slide file's name in response to the prompt, the process of displaying the file is fully automatic, and takes only a few seconds. Whatever is current in the display is temporarily cleared for the display of the slide file. It is not erased, however; you may quickly restore it by invoking the Redraw command.

Slide files on display may not be edited, but you may add lines to the display by drawing them using standard AutoCAD commands. The lines you add in this fashion are included in AutoCAD's underlying database, not in the slide file.

```
VSLIDE ACAD(EARTH)
VSLIDE *ACAD(FLEX)
DELAY 1000
VSLIDE
VSLIDE *ACAD(HONEY)
DELAY 1000
VSLIDE
VSLIDE *ACAD(HEX)
DELAY 1000
VSLIDE
VSLIDE *ACAD(STARS)
DELAY 1000
VSLIDE
VSLIDE *ACAD(ZIGZAG)
DELAY 1000
VSLIDE
DELAY 1000
RSCRIPT
```

FIGURE 21.15: The presentation of a series of AutoCAD slides. To speed up the display of slides, the next slide is loaded into memory (using an asterisk before the slide name) while the current slide is displayed. A single Vslide command called without a file name will display the preloaded slide quickly, and another slide file will then be loaded into memory. Since this script file is called from within the drawing editor, an Rscript command is added at the end to repeat the command series from the beginning.

They will remain behind in the drawing editor when you clear the slide file using the Redraw command.

RELATED COMMANDS

Mslide.

RELATED SYSTEM VARIABLES

None.

SAMPLE DIALOG

The script file shown in Figure 21.15 displays some AutoCAD hatch patterns found in the slide library file ACAD.SLB. Using your text editor, create a file called HATCHES.SCR, containing the illustrated lines. Provided that this script file and the file ACAD.SLB can be found on AutoCAD's search path, you can execute this script by invoking the Script Hatches command. To cancel the script file, press the Backspace key or Ctrl-C.

SKETCHING

The Sketch command is AutoCAD's tool for entering special irregular lines that are only practical to enter in a freehand style—for example, such entities as a signature, a tree trunk, a pile of earth, or a boulder. Following is a summary of the Sketch command.

Sketch

Draws a freehand line as the pointing device is moved. This line, called a *sketch line,* is actually a series of very small line segments whose length is controlled by the SKETCHINC system variable.

VERSIONS

All.

COMMAND OPTIONS

Record increment   Enter the amount of pointing-device movement required to add a new line segment to the sketch line. This amount is stored in the SKETCHINC system variable.

Pen   The Pen option determines whether a sketch line is being produced. To produce a line, type **P** or press the pointing device's pick button. This action toggles an imaginary "sketch pen" to the down position, meaning that the sketch line is produced on the screen as the pointing device is moved. To move the pointing device without producing a sketch line, type **P** or press the pick button again. This toggles the sketch pen into the up position, and a line is not generated as the pointing device is moved.

You may toggle the pen up and down as many different times as you like, producing any number of sketch lines.

.   Press the period key to generate a straight line from the last endpoint of a sketch line to the current location of the crosshairs. This works only when the pen is in the up position; otherwise, a sketch line is being drawn anyway. The line is produced, but the pen remains in the up position.

Record   Type **R** to place the sketch lines produced so far into AutoCAD's drawing database, where they may be edited using standard AutoCAD commands.

eXit   Type **X** to record all the sketch lines produced so far in AutoCAD's drawing database, and return to the Command prompt as well.

Quit   Type **Q** to discard the sketch lines drawn since the last Record or eXit command, and return to AutoCAD's Command prompt.

Erase   Type **E** to enter Erase mode. AutoCAD prompts:

> Select end of delete.

The pen is automatically placed in the up position, and you may move the cross-hairs to the point where you would like the erasure to begin. If you move the pointing device quickly, the crosshairs may disappear from the screen for a short time. AutoCAD calculates and temporarily removes all portions of the sketch lines that were drawn after the point closest to the intersections of the crosshairs. The crosshairs will reappear on the screen when the calculation is complete.

If you move the crosshairs slowly toward the location of the current endpoint of the sketch line, the erased portion of the sketch line will reappear. When the correct portion of the sketch line is gone from the display, type **P** or press the pick button to have that portion of the sketch line deleted. Pressing **P** or the pick button in this context does not lower the pen. If you want to lower the pen now, type **P** or press the pick button again. If you want to cancel the Erase option before anything is actually erased, type **E** again, and the removed portion of the sketch line will reappear.

Connect   Type **C** to begin drawing the sketch line where the last line left off. You can only invoke this command with the pen up. After you type **C**, AutoCAD prompts:

> Move to endpoint of line.

Move the crosshairs to the endpoint of the last sketch line entered. When the crosshairs are within a single record increment of the line's endpoint, the pen is automatically lowered, and the sketch line continues from that endpoint.

If you want to cancel the Connect option, type **C** again.

USAGE

The Sketch command can easily produce thousands of tiny, individual line segments, adding greatly to the size of your drawing. Therefore, use Sketch sparingly.

The command options available during the sketching process may all be invoked by pressing a letter key at the keyboard. Unlike with other AutoCAD command options, do not press Enter after pressing the letter key.

If snap mode is on, do not set the record increment to less than the snap value, as AutoCAD will snap the crosshairs to snap points before drawing portions of the sketch lines.

If tablet mode is on, you may use the digitizer to trace drawings with the Sketch command. If you invoke the Sketch command with tablet mode on, you may not toggle it off. Likewise, if you invoke the Sketch command with tablet mode off, you may not toggle it on.

It is advisable to trace lines as slowly as you can using the Sketch command, as AutoCAD is making a considerable number of calculations and repeatedly checking the position of the crosshairs. This is even more important if you are sketching with tablet mode on. By entering the record increment as a negative number, you may set a special alarm that will sound a beep if you are moving the pointing device too fast. Entering a negative number does not affect the absolute value of the record increment, which is what AutoCAD uses, but AutoCAD will sound a beep if the pen moves more than twice the record increment before a line segment can be drawn. This helps you maintain the correct pen speed.

If AutoCAD begins to run low on RAM while you are using the Sketch command, it sounds a continuous tone and displays the following message:

Please raise the pen!

When you see this message, stop moving the pointing device and type **P** or press the pick button to raise the pen. You need not stop moving it immediately, but do so as soon as you can. The continuous tone will not stop until you raise the pen. When the pen is in the up position, AutoCAD writes some of the data in RAM out to disk, freeing RAM space for additional sketching, and prompts:

Thank you. Lower the pen and continue.

Type **P** or **C**, or press the pick button, and resume sketching.

You may move between viewports while sketching, but you must raise the pen first. After you have moved into the new viewport, you may use the Connect option to resume from the point where you left off.

If you attempt to use the Sketch command with orthogonal mode enabled, the sketch line will be composed of horizontal and vertical lines only, producing a zigzag effect if the record increment is very large.

RELATED COMMANDS

None.

RELATED SYSTEM VARIABLES

SKETCHINC (stores the value of the record increment for the Sketch command); SKPOLY (when set to a nonzero value, replaces sketch lines with polylines rather than line segments).

SAMPLE DIALOG

The following dialog sets the value of SKPOLY to 1, and draws a small sketch line:

```
Command: SKPOLY
new value for skpoly < 0 >: 1
Command: Sketch
Record increment <0>: 0.01
Sketch. Pen eXit Quit Record Erase Connect. (press P)
<Pen down> (move the pointing device, generating a sketch line) (press P)
<Pen up>
Sketch. Pen eXit Quit Record Erase Connect. (press X)
1 polyline with 62 edges recorded.
```

DATA-MANAGEMENT COMMANDS

AutoCAD comes equipped with commands that allow you to gather statistical information regarding the relationships between the different drawing entities.

Area

Computes the area enclosed by three or more selected points, or by a selected entity.

VERSIONS

All.

COMMAND OPTIONS

Point   Enter a series of points to define the boundary corners of a closed 2-D region, either by using the pointing device or by entering coordinates from the keyboard. After each point is entered, AutoCAD prompts:

Next point:

All selected points must fall within a plane parallel to the current user coordinate system. You may enter as many points as necessary to define the area you intend to calculate. When all points have been selected, press Enter. AutoCAD then displays the area and perimeter formed by the selected points. The calculated area is stored in the AREA system variable, from which it can be extracted and used by AutoLISP programs.

Entity　　Enter **E** to select a single polyline or circle, rather than a series of points. AutoCAD responds:

> Select circle or polyline:

Pick a single circle or polyline. AutoCAD displays the area and circumference of a circle, or the area and perimeter of a closed polyline, or the area and length of an open polyline. If the polyline is open, AutoCAD calculates the area as if a straight line segment connected the endpoints.

In Release 10 and later, you cannot select a 3-D polyline unless all of its vertices are parallel to the current construction plane. If necessary, align the UCS with the polyline before invoking the Area command. Refer to Chapter 6 for details on the UCS command.

Add　　Enter **A** to compute a cumulative total of several areas to be entered in sequence. AutoCAD will repeat the Area command automatically, allowing you to identify and calculate several areas by picking either entities or points (as described for the previous options). Each calculated area is displayed, along with the cumulative total, in the Command-prompt area. The cumulative total is also maintained in the AREA system variable.

Subtract　　Enter **S** to subtract calculated areas from the amount stored in the AREA system variable. AutoCAD will repeat the Area command automatically, allowing you to identify and calculate several areas by picking either entities or points (as described for the previous options). Each calculated area is displayed, subtracted from the value stored in the AREA system variable; the remainder is displayed in the Command-prompt area. The AREA system variable is also updated to reflect the new remainder.

USAGE

The Area command is quite flexible. You may toggle between adding and subtracting areas as necessary to compute the required area of any 2-D region of the drawing.

Each time you invoke the Area command and compute the first area, the value of the AREA system variable is reset. Thereafter, the value of the variable changes depending on whether the Add or Subtract option has been selected.

RELATED SYSTEM VARIABLES

AREA (stores the last computed area, or the cumulative total of areas); PERIMETER (stores the last computed perimeter, circumference, or length).

SAMPLE DIALOG

The following dialog computes the area represented by the shaded portion of the drawing in Figure 21.16:

```
Command: Area
<First point>/Entity/Add/Subtract: A
<First point>/Entity/Subtract: E
(ADD mode) Select circle or polyline: (pick outer perimeter)
Area = 187200.00 square in. (1300.00 square ft.), Perimeter = 210'-0"
Total area = 187200.00 square in. (1300.00 square ft.)
(ADD mode) Select circle or polyline: (press Enter)
<First point>/Entity/Add/Subtract: S
<First point>/Entity/Subtract: E
(SUBTRACT mode) Select circle or polyline: (pick inner perimeter)
Area = 14400.00 square in. (100.00 square ft.), Perimeter = 40'-0"
Total area = 172800.00 square in. (1200.00 square ft.)
(SUBTRACT mode) Select circle or polyline: (pick inner perimeter)
Area = 14400.00 square in. (100.00 square ft.), Perimeter = 40'-0"
Total area = 158400.00 square in. (1100.00 square ft.)
(SUBTRACT mode) Select circle or polyline: (press Enter)
<First point>/Entity/Add: (press Enter)
Command: Setvar
Variable name or ?: Area
AREA = 158400.00 (read only)
Command:
```

Dblist

Displays a list of entity properties for all entities in the drawing.

VERSIONS

All.

COMMAND OPTIONS

If a drawing is even of modest size, the display of listed entities can be quite long and time-consuming. On many DOS-based systems, you can control the screen display by means of control keys:

Ctrl-C Pressing Ctrl-C cancels the listing and returns you to the Command prompt.

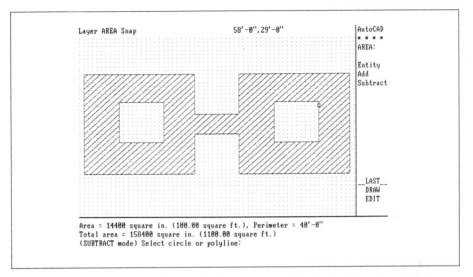

FIGURE 21.16: Computing a complex area. The area represented by the shaded portion of this drawing can be quickly calculated using AutoCAD. First, the Add option is invoked and the outer polyline is selected. AutoCAD stores the total area to memory. Next, the subtract option is invoked and the two inner polylines are selected. The area of these polylines is subtracted from the total, and the final result is displayed in the Command-prompt area and stored in the AREA system variable.

Ctrl-Q   Pressing Ctrl-Q toggles on the *printer echo,* which directs the display on the screen to the printer as well. When the list has finished printing, press Ctrl-Q again to turn the printer echo off.

Ctrl-S   Pressing Ctrl-S temporarily pauses the scrolling of the list on the monitor screen. Pressing the space bar resumes the scrolling process. You may repeat this sequence as often as necessary while reading the display on the screen.

USAGE

The Dblist command produces the following information regarding entities in the drawing:

All Entities   The entity name, layer, and coordinate position relative to the current UCS; extrusion thickness if not zero; color and linetype if not Bylayer; extrusion direction if not parallel to the current z-axis; handle if handles are enabled; In Release 11 and later, the location of the entity in model or paper space.

Line   Starting and ending points; length as projected onto the current construction plane; length in 3-D space; angle of orientation in the current construction plane; angle of orientation in the X-Y plane; x, y, and z coordinate increments from starting to ending points.

2-D Polyline   Area; length if open, perimeter if closed; extrusion direction relative to current UCS.

3-D polyline   Area, plus length if open or perimeter if closed (provided all vertices are coplanar); if mesh, N and M size; if closed mesh, in which direction.

Attribute   Block name, insertion points, scale factors, and rotation angle; text style; font file; starting point; height; obliquing angle.

Arc   Center point; radius; starting and ending angle; if not parallel to the current UCS, total angle.

Block   Name; insertion point; scale factors; rotation angle.

Circle   Center point; radius; area; circumference.

Dimension   Dimension type; extension point; dimension-line point; text position; default text.

Point   x, y, and z coordinate location.

Shape   Name; source file; insertion point.

Solid   Starting and ending corner points.

3-D Face   Four corner points.

Text   Style; font file; orientation; height; width factor; obliquing angle; generation (upside down, backward, normal); text.

Trace   Starting corner points; ending corner points.

Vertex   x, y, and z coordinates; tangent direction; starting width; ending width; if curve-fit, identified as spline control point or point inserted by curve-fitting; if 3-D polyline vertex, identified by Space label; if mesh vertex, identified by Mesh label and coordinate location only.

The last computed area displayed by the Dblist command is stored in the AREA system variable. The last computed circumference, perimeter, or length is stored in the PERIMETER system variable.

RELATED COMMANDS

List.

RELATED SYSTEM VARIABLES

AREA (last computed area); PERIMETER (last computed perimeter, circumference, or length).

SAMPLE DIALOG

Figure 21.17 shows a list of the entities in a very small drawing. You can display such a list by simply invoking the Dblist command from the Command prompt.

```
               CIRCLE    Layer: 0
                         Space: Model space
           center point, X=   3.0000  Y=   6.0000  Z=   0.0000
          radius      3.0000
     circumference   18.8496
           area      28.2743
                TRACE    Layer: 0
                         Space: Model space
            from point, X=   6.9776  Y=   3.0112  Z=   0.0000
             and point, X=   7.0224  Y=   2.9888  Z=   0.0000
              to point, X=   9.9776  Y=   9.0112  Z=   0.0000
             and point, X=  10.0224  Y=   8.9888  Z=   0.0000

                LINE     Layer: 0
                         Space: Model space
            from point, X=  11.0000  Y=   9.0000  Z=   0.0000
              to point, X=  14.0000  Y=   3.0000  Z=   0.0000
        Length =   6.7082,  Angle in X-Y Plane =    297
              Delta X =   3.0000, Delta Y =   -6.0000, Delta Z =   0.0000
```

FIGURE 21.17: The display that results after the Dblist command is invoked in a drawing containing only three entities: a circle, a trace, and a line. Note the additional information provided for each entity: the center point, area, and circumference of the circle are listed; the corner points of the trace are listed (treating the wide line segment as if it were a rectangular solid); and the endpoints, length, angle, and XYZ displacement of the line are displayed, along with the location of each entity in either model or paper space.

Dist

Displays the distance between two selected points, or translates a decimal number into the current units format.

VERSIONS

All.

COMMAND OPTIONS

First point: Enter the first of the pair of points to be entered. Use object snap when calculating distances between selected construction points. Alternatively, you may enter a decimal number in response to this prompt, and AutoCAD will return the number in the current units format.

Second point: If you have entered a point in response to the previous prompt, AutoCAD prompts for a second point. Enter the second point of the pair. Auto-CAD responds by displaying the distance between the two points, plus other information as appropriate. See the Usage section below for details.

USAGE

The distance information returned by the Dist command is always displayed in the current units format. Some additional information will be displayed:

- The angle in the current X-Y plane, relative to the current x-axis.
- The angle of elevation from the current X-Y plane, relative to the X-Y plane.
- The distance, in terms of x and y coordinates, between the starting and ending points of the line, when projected on the x-, y-, and z-axes (called delta X, delta Y, and delta Z).

As of Release 10, there is no provision for computing cumulative distances, such as there is with the Area command.

RELATED COMMANDS

Dim (all linear variations). Refer to the discussion of the Dim command in this chapter for more details.

RELATED SYSTEM VARIABLES

DISTANCE (stores the most recently computed distance information as returned by the Dist command).

SAMPLE DIALOG

The following dialog computes two distances: one between points 1,1 and 7,7, and the other between points 1,1,1 and 7,7,7:

```
Command: Dist
First point: 1,1
Second point: 7,7
Distance = 0'-8 1/2", Angle in X-Y Plane = 45.00,
Angle from X-Y Plane = 0.00
Delta X = 0'-6", Delta Y = 0'-6", Delta Z = 0'-0"
Command: Dist
First point: 1,1,1
Second point: 7,7,7
Distance = 0'-10 3/8", Angle in X-Y Plane = 45.00,
Angle from X-Y Plane = 35.26
Delta X = 0'-6", Delta Y = 0'-6", Delta Z = 0'-6"
Command:
```

Id

Displays the coordinate points of a selected point, or places a blip in the drawing at selected coordinate points.

VERSIONS

All.

COMMAND OPTIONS

Point: Using the pointing device, pick a point whose coordinate location you would like to identify. AutoCAD responds by displaying the coordinate points, as per the sample dialog ahead.

USAGE

In addition to returning coordinate points, the Id command can be used to place blip markers in the drawing at specified points, provided that the BLIPMODE system variable is not set to zero. Thus, if you are interested in displaying the location of point 64.256,512.640, you may enter these coordinates at the keyboard in response to the Point prompt, and AutoCAD will place a blip there (as long as the point is on the screen).

This command will return a 3-D point if you use object snap to locate a 3-D construction point in the drawing. Otherwise, the current elevation is used as the z coordinate when picking points.

The point returned by this command is stored in the LASTPOINT system variable.

RELATED COMMANDS

Point.

RELATED SYSTEM VARIABLES

LASTPOINT.

SAMPLE DIALOG

The following dialog returns a coordinate location found by using object snap on the endpoint of a 3-D line:

```
Command: Id
Point: end of (pick endpoint)
X = 1'-0 5/8" ˜ ISY = 0'-9 1/16" ˜ ISZ = 1'-11 5/8"
Command:
```

List

Displays a list of entity properties for selected entities in the drawing.

VERSIONS

All.

COMMAND OPTIONS

Select objects: Using any of AutoCAD's standard entity-selection methods, select the entities you intend to include in the property list. When all entities are selected, press Enter to generate the list.

USAGE

The List command is the same as the Dblist command, except that List operates on selected entities only. Refer back to the Dblist command for further details on controlling the display of the list, and for the properties that are displayed for each entity type.

RELATED COMMANDS

Dblist.

RELATED SYSTEM VARIABLES

AREA (last computed area); PERIMETER (last computed perimeter, circumference, or length).

SAMPLE DIALOG

The following dialog produces a list of a single line entity in a drawing:

```
Command: List
Select objects: (select a line segment)
Select objects: (press Enter)
     LINE   Layer: 0
  from point, X = 0'-1 5/8" Y = 0'-5 3/4" Z = 0'-0"
    to point, X = 0'-11 3/8" Y = 0'-5 3/4" Z = 0'-0"
 Length = 0'-9 11/16", Angle in X-Y Plane = 0.00
     Delta X = 0'-9 11/16", Delta Y = -0'-0", Delta Z = 0'-0"
Command:
```

Rename

Changes the names of AutoCAD's named entities.

VERSIONS

All.

COMMAND OPTIONS

Block   Enter **B** to change the name of a block.

Dimstyle   Enter **D** to change the name of a dimension style.

LAyer   Enter **LA** to change the name of a layer.

LType   Enter **LT** to change the name of a linetype.

Style   Enter **S** to change the name of a text style.

Ucs   Enter **U** to change the name of a user coordinate system.

VIew   Enter **VI** to change the name of a named viewing angle.

VPort   Enter **VP** to change the name of a viewport configuration.
After you select one of these options, AutoCAD prompts

> Old *nnnnnnn* name:

where *nnnnnnn* is the named entity you intend to change. Enter the current name for the entity. AutoCAD responds:

> New *nnnnnnn* name:

Enter the new name for the indicated entity. AutoCAD updates the database to reflect the new name.

USAGE

The Rename command is the only way to make changes to the names of defined AutoCAD entities that normally reside on the read-only symbol table. They cannot be renamed using AutoLISP, except by routines that call this command.

Layer 0, the Continuous linetype, and loaded shapes cannot be renamed with the Rename command. To rename a shape, you must edit the shape file and recompile it. Refer to Chapter 15 for details.

RELATED COMMANDS

None.

RELATED SYSTEM VARIABLES

None.

SAMPLE DIALOG

The following dialog renames layer Green to layer Blue:

```
Command: Rename
Block/LAyer/LType/Style/Ucs/VIew/VPort: LA
Old layer name: Green
New layer name: Blue
Command:
```

COMMANDS THAT MODIFY OTHER COMMANDS

In AutoCAD Releases 9 and later, you can invoke commands that affect the behavior of AutoCAD's standard commands. You can cause a command to repeat until Ctrl-C is pressed, or you can disable a command altogether, usually to replace it with a custom command of the same name, developed in AutoLISP. Following are brief discussions of the commands that modify other commands.

Multiple

Causes the next command invoked to repeat automatically until Ctrl-C is pressed.

VERSIONS

Release 9 and later.

COMMAND OPTIONS

None. The Multiple command displays no prompt, but simply waits for the command name to be entered. When the command name is entered, this command will be repeated.

USAGE

The Multiple command saves you time when a series of repeated actions is to be performed, as in the sample dialog ahead.

RELATED COMMANDS

This command is the functional equivalent of the "^C^C*" syntax that may be used in custom menus. Refer to Chapter 14 for details.

RELATED SYSTEM VARIABLES

None.

SAMPLE DIALOG

The following dialog will draw a series of points:

Command: **Multiple Point**
Point: **(pick location)**
POINT Point: **(pick location)**
POINT Point: **(pick location)**
POINT Point: **(pick location)**
POINT Point: **(press Ctrl-C)**
Command:

Redefine

Redefines a previously deactivated AutoCAD command.

VERSIONS

Release 9 and later.

COMMAND OPTIONS

Command name: Enter the name of a deactivated AutoCAD command. If the command you enter is currently active, this command will have no effect.

USAGE

Once redefined, an AutoCAD command will resume normal functioning, and will override any custom command of the same name. The custom command remains in AutoLISP memory, however, and can be accessed in one of two ways:

- Deactivate the standard AutoCAD command again.
- Invoke the custom command by entering it within parentheses and preceding it with "C:". For example, assume that you have loaded a custom command named Erase. If the standard Erase command is active, you can still access your custom command by entering:

    (C:ERASE)

RELATED COMMANDS

Undefine.

RELATED SYSTEM VARIABLES

None.

SAMPLE DIALOG

The following dialog deactivates the Erase command and then redefines it:

```
Command: Undefine
Command name: Erase
Command: Erase
Unknown command. Type ? for list of commands.
Command: Redefine
Command name: Erase
Command: Erase
Select objects:
```

Undefine

Deactivates a selected AutoCAD command.

VERSIONS

Release 9 and later.

COMMAND OPTIONS

Command name: Enter the standard AutoCAD command that you intend to deactivate. Commands not invoked from the Command prompt and individual command options cannot be deactivated.

USAGE

Once a command is deactivated, AutoCAD will not recognize it when it is invoked normally. However, you may continue to invoke a deactivated command if you precede the command name with a period.

For example, assume that you have deactivated the Erase command. The following produces an error message:

```
Command: Erase
Unknown command. Type ? for list of commands.
```

However, adding the period before the command enables it to function normally:

Command: **.Erase**
Select objects:

If you develop an AutoLISP routine that creates a custom command with the same name as an AutoCAD command, you normally cannot invoke the custom command from the Command prompt. However, if you have deactivated the command using the Undefine command, AutoCAD will find the custom command you have created. You may define the custom command before or after deactivating the standard command.

Figure 21.18 demonstrates this concept with an AutoLISP routine that redefines the Erase command to always ignore entities on a particular layer. Notice how the standard Erase command is called from within the custom command by means of the preceding period.

```
(command "UNDEFINE" "ERASE")
(defun C:ERASE(/ spare ss1 ssno len memb oldcmd)
  (setq spare (getstring "\Bypass which layer? "))
  (setq ss1 (ssget) ssno 0 len (sslength ss1) oldcmd (getvar "CMDECHO"))
  (setvar "CMDECHO" 0)
  (prompt "\nChecking for allowable objects. One moment...")
  (if (and (/= spare nil) (/= spare ""))
      (while (and (/= len 0) (< ssno len))
             (setq memb (ssname ss1 ssno))
             (if (= (strcase spare) (cdr (assoc '8 (entget memb))))
                 (progn  (ssdel memb ss1)
                         (setq len (sslength ss1))
                 )
                 (setq ssno (1+ ssno))
             )
      )
  )
  (if (<= len 0)
      (prompt "\nNo erasable entities found.")
      (progn  (prompt "\nErasing...")
              (command ".ERASE" ss1 "")
      )
  )
  (setvar "CMDECHO" oldcmd)   (princ)
)
```

FIGURE 21.18: Redefining AutoCAD commands. This AutoLISP routine demonstrates how AutoCAD commands can be deactivated and replaced with custom versions of your own. When loaded, this routine automatically deactivates the Erase command, and then creates a new Erase command that will erase chosen objects as before, but will allow the user to indicate a "bypass" layer; entities on this layer will be considered "safe" and will not be erased, even if included in the selection set. Although this routine prompts the user for a layer name, it could easily be modified to bypass specific layers each time, thus creating "unerasable" layers in your drawing.

The Undefine command's effects are not permanent; the command must be reinvoked at the beginning of each drawing session. You can achieve some degree of permanent command deactivation by placing an Undefine command call within ACAD.LSP. Selected commands will then be undefined automatically.

Note: If you intend to develop AutoLISP applications for a variety of systems, always place the period in front of AutoCAD commands called from within your routines. This ensures that you will be invoking AutoCAD's standard command, and not a custom command or a deactivated command on a particular system.

RELATED COMMANDS

Redefine.

RELATED SYSTEM VARIABLES

None.

SAMPLE DIALOG

The following dialog deactivates the Erase command:

```
Command: Undefine
Command name: Erase
Command: Erase
Unknown command. Type ? for list of commands.
Command:
```

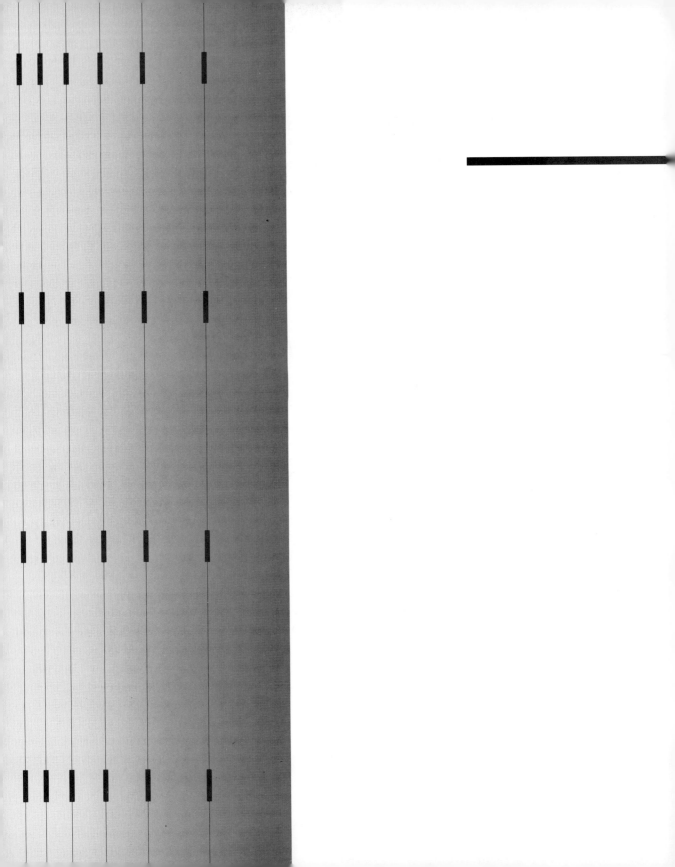

CHAPTER 22

OTHER ADD-ON SOFTWARE

OTHER ADD-ON SOFTWARE

AutoCAD's enormous power, flexibility, and open architecture have led to the development of a wide range of third-party and add-on products designed to increase drawing productivity in a variety of different applications. This chapter presents a brief sampling of the types of products that are available, although it is by no means a complete list.

To learn more about add-on and third-party software, consult your AutoCAD dealer or *The AutoCAD Sourcebook, Autodesk's Official Guide to AutoCAD Applications*, published by Autodesk, 3220 Marinship Way, Sausalito, California 94965.

USING THE ADVANCED MODELING EXTENSION (AME)

The *Advanced Modeling Extension*, or AME, is additional software that can be purchased with AutoCAD. It gives you the ability to create models of solid 3-D entities. Three-dimensional entities generated with AME differ from those created with standard AutoCAD chiefly in that they can be analyzed for their solid properties, such as mass, surface area, moment of inertia, and center of gravity. The AME software also provides several unique commands that allow you to create complex solid entities from simpler solids, called *primitives*, which function as sophisticated building blocks. Primitives can be created using variable parameters, and then added to or subtracted from one another to create sophisticated constructions.

Once you have constructed a solid entity, you may change and analyze its structural and material properties and extract 2-D representations of it at various viewing angles, including cross sections.

AME was developed using the Advanced Development System, AutoCAD's C language interface, and as such is an example of the kinds of sophisticated third-party programs that can be created with this system.

A special version of AME, called AMELITE, is included with AutoCAD Release 11. AMELITE is a selected subset of the full AME command structure that allows you to try out and evaluate the software.

AME is available for AutoCAD 386, OS/2 Presentation Manager 1.1, Xenix, Apollo, DEC 3100, and Sun workstations. It is not available for DOS 80286 platforms, DEC VAX, or OS/2 Presentation Manager 1.2.

Installing and Loading AME

The AME software comes on diskettes and you must install it using Release 11's standard installation procedure. Refer to Chapter 3 for details regarding Release 11 installation.

Once you have installed the AME software, you can load it into your drawing by picking the Solids pull-down menu and selecting the "Load AME" option, or you may enter the following at the Command prompt:

Command: **(xload "AME")**

You can load AMELITE from the same pull-down menu, or by using a similar command:

Command: **(xload "AMELITE")**

The first time you load AME in memory, you are prompted to enter an authorization code. (AMELITE does not require this code.) Each copy of AME has a unique authorization code, which is supplied with the software. Contact your dealer if you do not know your authorization code. AutoCAD prompts as follows:

AutoCAD serial number is *nnn-nnnnnnnn*

where *nnn-nnnnnnnn* is your product serial number. AutoCAD continues:

Enter the maximum number of AME users for this package <1>:
Enter AME authorization code:

Respond by indicating the number of users for whom you purchased AME, followed by the authorization code. AME is now loaded and ready to run. It will remain in memory until you exit AutoCAD.

AME Primitives

An AME *primitive* is a fundamental 3-D entity that represents a basic geometrical shape. It can be created by entering a small set of parameters. AME primitives are illustrated in Figure 22.1.

In addition to the basic primitives, AME allows you to create solid entities from closed AutoCAD polylines. Refer to the section in this chapter on AME commands for detailed information on the parameters necessary to create them.

Composite Solids

Composite solids are combinations of primitive solids that either touch or overlap. Primitives may be combined in three ways: *union, intersection,* and *subtraction.* These combinations are illustrated in Figure 22.2.

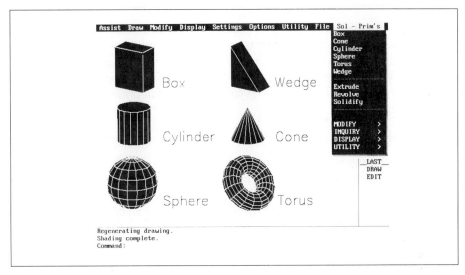

FIGURE 22.1: AME primitives. These fundamental shapes are used as the building blocks of complex solid entities.

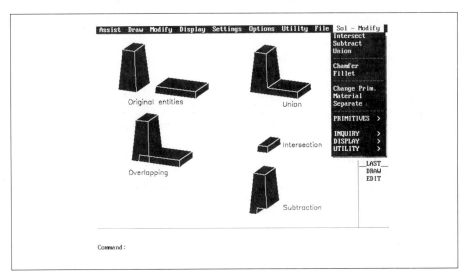

FIGURE 22.2: Union, intersection, and subtraction. AME derives its power from the ability to combine primitive solids easily and intuitively. These solids were created using the Solunion, Solint, and Solsub commands.

A union combines two solids into a single solid equal to the enclosed volume. An intersection combines two solids into a single solid equal to the volume of the overlapping portions. Subtraction deletes the overlapping portion from one of the original solids.

Primitive solids are always combined in pairs. However, you may combine multiple primitives with a single command. When you select multiple primitives, Auto-CAD automatically constructs the composite solid in pairs, keeping track of all construction steps. This makes it possible to reverse the process step by step.

You may, if you wish, combine primitive with composite solids, although this method is usually not as fast as combining several primitives at once.

AME COMMANDS

Following is a quick reference to the Advanced Modeling Extension commands. All of AutoCAD's normal data-entry mechanisms may be used to enter points and parameters. Refer to Chapter 5, if necessary, to review AutoCAD's data-entry tools.

All commands begin with the letters **Sol**. They can be entered as shown from the command prompt or selected from the screen or pull-down menu. The names of the commands are sometimes abbreviated to fit into the screen menu; however, command names may be completely different in the pull-down menu. Therefore, pull-down menu instructions are included in the description of each command.

CREATING PRIMITIVES

These commands are used to construct the primitive solids that form the basis of more complex solid entities.

Solbox

Creates a 3-D rectangular solid.

COMMAND REQUIREMENTS AND OPTIONS

Corner of box   Begin creating a rectangular solid by picking a point to use for one corner of the resulting solid.

Other corner   This is the default option once you have anchored the box in space by picking the first corner. You now select a second point, which becomes the opposite corner for one face of the solid. This face will be located in the current construction plane. A rubberband box appears, allowing you to visualize the dimensions. When you have selected the point, AutoCAD prompts:

Height:

Enter a non-zero value. If you enter a positive value, AutoCAD constructs the solid by creating a second face parallel to the first, at the given distance, or height, along the positive z-axis of the current construction plane. If you enter a negative value, AutoCAD uses the negative z-axis.

You may also "show" AutoCAD a positive z-axis distance by entering two points. The distance between the points (as measured in the current construction plane) is supplied to the prompt as the height. It is always positive.

Cube   Enter **C** to construct a solid with sides of equal length. AutoCAD prompts:

> Length:

Enter the length of the sides. If the value is positive, AutoCAD uses the positive x-, y-, and z-axes of the current construction plane. If you enter a negative value, AutoCAD uses the negative axes. If you indicate the length with two points, the value is considered positive.

Length   Enter **L** to indicate the length, width, and height individually. AutoCAD prompts:

> Length:
> Width:
> Height:

Respond to each of these prompts by entering a value or picking two points. The length value corresponds to the dimensions along the x-axis. Width indicates the dimension along the y-axis, and height, along the z-axis. Use positive and negative values to control whether the box is constructed along the positive or negative axis for each dimension.

PULL-DOWN MENU SEQUENCE

From the Primitives menu, select Box.

Solcone

Creates a 3-D conical solid.

COMMAND REQUIREMENTS AND OPTIONS

Center point   Enter the point you want to be the center of the base of the cone in the current construction plane. AutoCAD prompts:

> Diameter/<Radius>:

Enter a value for the radius of the cone, or indicate the radius by picking a second point relative to the center point. Alternatively, you may enter **D**, and AutoCAD prompts:

Diameter:

Enter a value for the diameter of the cone base or indicate the diameter by showing a distance.

Elliptical Enter **E** to indicate an elliptical base for the cone. AutoCAD prompts:

<Axis endpoint 1>/Center:

Enter a point to be used as the endpoint of the first axis of the ellipse base. AutoCAD prompts:

Axis endpoint 2:

Enter another point indicating the opposite endpoint of the first axis. AutoCAD prompts:

Other axis distance:

Enter the radius of the second axis, which will be perpendicular to the first. To help you visualize the second axis, a rubberband line extends from the midpoint of the first axis.

If you prefer, you may use an alternate means of entering an elliptical base. Instead of entering the first axis endpoint, begin by entering **C**, for center. AutoCAD prompts:

Center of ellipse:

Pick a center point for the cone's base. AutoCAD prompts:

Axis endpoint:

Enter the endpoint of the first axis. This point will be used to measure the radius and orientation of the first axis, starting from the center point. AutoCAD prompts:

Other axis distance:

Enter a value that corresponds to the radius of the second axis, which will always be perpendicular to the first. You may enter the value from the keyboard or indicate the value by picking two points. Since the orientation of this axis is predetermined, the value you enter must be positive.

Once you have defined the properties of the cone's base, AutoCAD prompts for its height:

Height of cone:

Enter a value for the height or indicate the height by picking two points. If you enter a positive value or pick two points, AutoCAD measures the distance along the positive z-axis. If you enter a negative value, AutoCAD measures the distance along the negative z-axis.

USAGE

The option of creating elliptical bases is not available when using AMELITE. Extremely distorted cones may not display properly, and they may not calculate correctly for composite solid purposes. Examples of such distorted cones include those with very large bases and near-zero height, extremely tall cones with near-zero bases, or elliptical cones with extreme differences in the radii of the base axes.

PULL-DOWN MENU SEQUENCE

From the Primitives menu, pick Cone.

Solcyl

Creates a 3-D solid cylinder.

COMMAND REQUIREMENTS AND OPTIONS

The command option sequence is identical to that of the cone, described just previously. The difference here is that instead of tapering the solid to a point, the height value is measured straight up from the base, creating a cylinder instead of a cone.

USAGE

The option of creating elliptical cylinders is not available when using AME-LITE.

Extremely distorted cylinders may not display properly, and may not calculate correctly for composite solid purposes. Examples of such distorted cylinders are extremely tall cylinders with near-zero bases or elliptical cylinders with extreme differences in the radii of the base axes.

PULL-DOWN MENU SEQUENCE

From the Primitives menu, pick Cylinder.

Solsphere

Creates a 3-D solid sphere.

COMMAND REQUIREMENTS AND OPTIONS

Center point　You begin creating a sphere by specifying a center point. This point will not be the exact center of the sphere but the point in the current construction plane upon which the resulting sphere will be positioned. In other words, the sphere is created tangent to the construction plane, not through it, much like a ball resting on a floor.

After you have entered the center point, AutoCAD prompts:

Diameter/<radius>:

Enter a positive value for the radius of the sphere or indicate the radius by picking a second point relative to the center point. Alternatively, you may enter **D**, and AutoCAD prompts:

Diameter:

Enter a positive value for the diameter of the sphere or indicate the diameter by picking two points.

PULL-DOWN MENU SEQUENCE

From the Primitives menu, pick Sphere.

Soltorus

Creates a solid 3-D torus, or donut.

COMMAND REQUIREMENTS AND OPTIONS

Center of torus　Begin constructing a torus by entering its center point. Once you have indicated the center point, you must then supply two values: the first for the overall size of the torus, the second for the size of its "tube," or cylindrical revolution around the center point. AutoCAD prompts:

Diameter/<radius> of torus:

Enter a value for the radius of the torus, or indicate the radius by picking a second point relative to the center point. The radius of the torus is the distance from the center point to a point on the circle indicating the center of its tube. Alternatively, you may enter **D**, and AutoCAD prompts:

Diameter:

Enter a value for the diameter of the torus. This value is the diameter of the circle that forms the center of the torus's tube.

Once you have indicated the overall size of the torus, AutoCAD prompts:

Diameter/<radius> of tube:

Use the method described above to enter the radius or diameter of the torus's tube. AutoCAD then constructs the torus according to the values you have entered.

USAGE

You may enter either a positive or negative value for the radius and diameter of the torus. A negative value results in a "self-intersecting" torus, that is, one pulled in upon itself. If you use a negative value for the torus radius, you must use a value greater than its absolute value for the tube radius. This requirement prevents you from creating an impossible torus or one without a volume.

PULL-DOWN MENU SEQUENCE

From the Primitives menu, pick Torus.

Solwedge

Creates a 3-D solid composed of three rectangular and two triangular faces, tapering to one edge.

COMMAND REQUIREMENTS AND OPTIONS

The command options for the Solwedge command are the same as those for the Solbox command—with the exception of the Cube option, which has no meaning here. The resulting solid looks like a box that has been cut in half along its diagonal.

The base of the wedge is always rectangular and drawn in the current construction plane. A rectangular vertical face of the wedge is coincident with the starting corner point and the base y-axis. The wedge tapers along the x-axis from the indicated height to zero.

PULL-DOWN MENU SEQUENCE

From the Primitives menu, pick Wedge.

Solext

Extrudes a 3-D solid by stretching a third dimension from a closed polyline or circle.

COMMAND REQUIREMENTS AND OPTIONS

Select objects You may extrude solids from circles and the following forms of closed polyline: 2-D and 3-D polylines, donuts, polygons, and ellipses. If the polyline has width, this information is lost when extruding the solid. The Solext command uses the centerline of a wide polyline for its calculations.

The polyline must contain at least three vertices and be closed. If you select a polyline that is not closed, AutoCAD will close it by joining the two endpoints in a straight line if they do not create any intersecting lines.

You cannot extrude polylines that have any intersecting lines or more than 500 vertices. This limitation on the number of vertices applies to all polylines, including those that have been curve or spline fit. To create such solids, break the polylines into smaller closed polylines and combine them into composite solids. After you have selected the polylines you want to extrude, AutoCAD prompts:

Height of extrusion:

Enter a value for the extrusion height or indicate the height by picking two points. If you enter a positive value or pick two points, AutoCAD measures the distance along the positive z-axis. If you enter a negative value, AutoCAD measures the distance along the negative z-axis. AutoCAD then prompts:

Extrusion taper angle from Z <0>:

The default angle, zero, will indicate no tapering, and AutoCAD will extrude the solid parallel to the z-axis. Angles greater than zero will cause tapering, with higher values causing more extreme tapering. Because of this, you cannot enter a tapering angle of 90 degrees or greater. Figure 22.3 illustrates tapering of extruded solids.

USAGE

The option of tapering extrusions is not available if you are using AMELITE.

You can only taper an entity in, not out. The area of the tapered end of the extruded entity will always be smaller than that of the base polyline. If the indicated

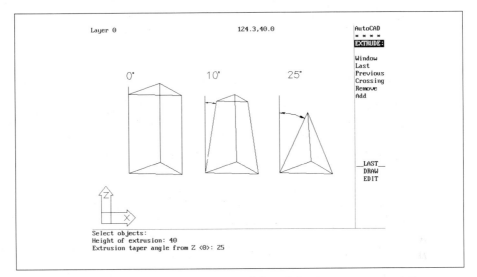

FIGURE 22.3: Extruded solids. Polylines may be extruded parallel to the x-axis or tapered. The greater the angle, the more severe the tapering effect. If the tapering causes the extruded sides to intersect, the extrusion height may be less.

angle of tapering causes the vertical sides to intersect, the volume above the intersection point will be lost and the overall height of the solid may be lower than you specified.

PULL-DOWN MENU SEQUENCE

From the Primitives menu, pick Extrude.

Solrev

Creates 3-D solids by rotating a polyline around a selected axis.

COMMAND REQUIREMENTS AND OPTIONS

Select objects   You may create rotated solids from circles, 2-D and 3-D polylines, donuts, polygons, and ellipses. If the polyline has width, this information is lost when creating the rotated solid. The Solrev command uses the centerline of a wide polyline for its calculations.

The polyline must have at least three vertices but no more than 500. This limitation applies to all polylines, including those that have been curve or spline fit. You may revolve only one polyline at a time.

After you have selected the polyline to revolve, AutoCAD prompts you for the axis of revolution:

Axis of revolution - Entity/X/Y/ <start point of axis >:

The default response allows you to enter a point that will serve as the starting point of the rotation axis. AutoCAD then prompts:

End point on axis:

Enter a second point to fix the rotation axis.

AutoCAD uses the start and end points of the axis to help determine the direction of rotation. AutoCAD calculates the direction of rotation to that it will appear counterclockwise when viewed at an angle from the end point of the axis toward the starting point.

Entity Alternatively, you may enter **E** to pick a line or single-segment polyline to use as the rotation axis. The endpoint of the line closest to the pick point will be considered the axis starting point for purposes of calculating the direction of the rotation angle.

X Enter **X** to use the x-axis of the current UCS as the rotation axis. The UCS origin point is the axis starting point.

Y Enter **Y** to use the y-axis of the current UCS as the rotation axis. As mentioned just above, in this case the origin is used as the start point.

After you have made your selection from these options, AutoCAD prompts:

Included angle <full circle >

Enter the angle of revolution, or press return to accept the full-circle default.

The polyline and axis may not fully inersect each other at any point, but they may touch.

PULL-DOWN MENU SEQUENCE

From the Primitives menu, pick Rotate.

Solidify

Creates solids from AutoCAD entities having a thickness.

COMMAND REQUIREMENTS AND OPTIONS

Select objects Pick the entities that you would like converted into solids using the Solidify command. These entities can be converted, provided that have a thickness other than zero: 2-D and 3-D polylines, as well as 2-D traces, which adhere to the rules specified under the Extrude command; also circles, donuts, ellipses, polygons, and 2-D filled solids created with AutoCAD's Solid command.

PULL-DOWN MENU SEQUENCE

From the Primitives menu, pick Solidify.

COMPOSITE SOLID COMMANDS

These commands are used to create complex solids by exploiting the properties of simpler ones.

Solint

Creates a solid that includes only the overlapping portion of two solids.

COMMAND REQUIREMENTS AND OPTIONS

Select objects Select the overlapping solids you intend to use to calculate an intersection. When you are finished selecting, press Return.

USAGE

All selected solids must overlap. Attempting to create an intersection from non-overlapping solids results in a *null solid,* a solid that has no volume. Auto-CAD aborts all commands that create null solids.

PULL-DOWN MENU SEQUENCE

From the Modify menu, pick Intersect.

Solunion

Creates a solid that includes the combined overall volume of two or more solids.

COMMAND REQUIREMENTS AND OPTIONS

Select objects   Select the overlapping solids you intend to use to create a union. When you are finished selecting, press Return.

PULL-DOWN MENU SEQUENCE

From the Modify menu, pick Union.

Solsub

Creates a solid that consists of the volume of one solid less the overlapping portion of another solid.

COMMAND REQUIREMENTS AND OPTIONS

Source objects   First, select the *source solids,* from which other overlapping solids are to be subtracted. When you are finished selecting, press Return.

Objects to subtract from them   Next, select the overlapping solids that are to be subtracted. When you are finished selecting these solids, press Return.

USAGE

In complex operations involving many solids, it is possible to subtract to an extent that a *null solid,* a solid having no volume, is created—for example, if two equal solids overlap exactly and you attempt to subtract one from the other, a null solid results. If you attempt to create a null solid, the operation is aborted.

If you attempt to subtract nearly all of the volume from a solid, for example when subtracting very nearly equal, overlapping solids, you may create a *thin shell.* This type of solid may be so close to zero that it will not compute correctly for display or for creating other composite solids. Thin solids are possible, but problems develop when this is taken to extremes.

Solsep

Reverses the effects of the Solunion, Solsub, and Solint commands, thereby separating composite solids into the solids from which they were made.

COMMAND REQUIREMENTS AND OPTIONS

Select objects   Select the composite solids that you intend to process. You may operate on more than one composite solid at a time.

USAGE

If you have created a composite solid using multiple invocations of the Solunion, Solsep, and Solint commands, you must invoke the Solsep command separately to reverse the effects of each construction command. For example, if you have created a union from six primitives, you may separate the composite back to the six primitives by invoking Solsep once; but if you have created the composite and then subsequently invoked the Solsub command to subtract some volume from the composite, you must then invoke Solsep twice: once to reverse the Solsub command and a second time to restore the primitives.

PULL-DOWN MENU SEQUENCE

From the Modify menu, pick Separate.

SOLID EDITING COMMANDS

These commands are used to change the appearance of solids or primitives in cases where they cannot be constructed as composite solids.

Solcham

Performs a chamfer on one or more edges of a solid. Refer to the discussion of the Chamfer command in Chapter 10 for details regarding chamfer processing.

COMMAND REQUIREMENTS AND OPTIONS

Select base surface   Pick a point on the edge of the surface that you intend to use. The first chamfer distance will be applied to the base surface.

Since two surfaces share the same selected edge, AutoCAD highlights one of them based on the solid's construction information and prompts:

    <OK>/Next:

If the correct surface is highlighted, press Return. Otherwise, enter **N** to high-light the other surface, then press Return to accept it. AutoCAD prompts:

Select edges to be chamfered:

Pick the edges of the first surface that you want to chamfer. When finished, press Return. AutoCAD prompts:

Enter distance along first surface:

Enter the distance from the edge that you intend to chamfer from the first sur-face. You may enter a value from the keyboard or enter two points. If a default distance is displayed, you may accept it by pressing Return. The value you enter must be positive and non-zero. AutoCAD prompts:

Enter the distance along the second surface:

Enter the distance from the edge that you intend to chamfer from the adjoin-ing surfaces. As before, you may enter a value from the keyboard, enter two points, or accept a default if one is present. The value you enter must be positive and greater than zero. AutoCAD then performs the chamfer.

USAGE

If you want to chamfer a corner, you must chamfer both edges in the same operation. If you make a mistake, you can recover using the Undo command. Entering chamfer distances greater than a face will taper a solid along that face.

PULL-DOWN MENU SEQUENCE

From the Modify menu, pick Chamfer.

Solfill

Performs a fillet along one or more edges of a solid, thereby rounding the edges. Refer to the discussion of the Fillet command in Chapter 10 for details regarding fillet processing.

COMMAND REQUIREMENTS AND OPTIONS

Select edges to be filleted   Select one or more edges of a solid that you intend to fillet. When done selecting, press Return. AutoCAD prompts:

Diameter/<Radius> of fillet:

You may respond to this prompt by entering the radius value used to round the selected edges. You may also indicate the radius by picking two points. The value you enter must be greater than zero. If a default distance is displayed, you may accept it by pressing Return.

Alternatively, enter **D** to indicate a diameter rather than a radius for the fillet. AutoCAD prompts:

> Diameter:

Respond to this prompt by entering a diameter value to be used to round the selected edges. AutoCAD will use this value as the fillet radius. You may also indicate the diameter by picking two points or accepting a default if there is one. In all cases, the value you enter must be greater than zero.

USAGE

If you want to fillet a corner, you must fillet both edges in the same operation. If you make a mistake, you can recover using the Undo command. Entering fillet radii longer than a face may create a *null solid*, a solid with no volume. In this case, AutoCAD will abort the Solfill command.

PULL-DOWN MENU SEQUENCE

From the Modify menu, pick Fillet.

Solchp

Changes the properties of primitives, including those within a composite solid.

COMMAND REQUIREMENTS AND OPTIONS

Select solid   Pick the composite solid containing the primitive you intend to edit or pick a stand-alone primitive. You cannot select these solids using the Last option. If you select a composite solid, AutoCAD prompts:

> Select primitive:

Pick a point on the composite solid that is uniquely coincident with the primitive you intend to edit.

Color   Enter **C** to change the color of the primitive. AutoCAD prompts:

> New color:

Enter a color number or name that is valid for your display device. Refer to Chapter 5 for details regarding colors.

Delete Enter **D** to delete the primitive. If you selected a stand-alone primitive, AutoCAD erases it. If the primitive is part of a composite solid, AutoCAD prompts:

    Retain detached primitive <N>?

If you enter **N** or press Return, AutoCAD erases the primitive. If you enter **Y**, AutoCAD detaches the primitive from the composite solid and retains it in the database.

Evaluate Enter **E** to recombine the composite solid. This can result in more efficient processing of the operations needed to construct a highly complex, frequently edited composite solid.

Instance Enter **I** to create a copy of the primitive without separating the original from the composite. AutoCAD creates the copy in the same position as the original, so you may want to follow this option with AutoCAD's Move Last command.

Move Enter **M** to move the primitive. AutoCAD prompts for points of displacement similar to the standard Move command. Refer to the discussion of this command in Chapter 10 for details. After moving the primitive, AutoCAD recalculates the composite solid.

Next Enter **N** or press Return to select another primitive within a composite solid. This is useful if the desired primitive is difficult to select. AutoCAD will loop though each primitive in the composite until the desired one is highlighted.

Pick Enter **P** to pick another primitive in a composite solid using point selection. AutoCAD prompts:

    Select Primitive:

Respond by picking another point on the solid coincident with your desired primitive.

Replace Enter **R** to replace the selected primitive with another. You may replace the selected primitive with either a stand-alone primitive or one from another composite solid that is accessible by point pick. AutoCAD prompts:

    Select solid to replace primitive:

Pick the replacement solid. AutoCAD replaces the selected primitive and prompts:

Retain detached primitive <N>?

If you enter **N** or press Return, AutoCAD erases the original primitive. If you enter **Y**, AutoCAD detaches the original primitive from the composite solid and retains it in the drawing database.

Size   Enter **S** to change the dimensions of the selected primitive. AutoCAD responds with prompts based on the type of primitive selected.

- For a box or wedge, you are prompted for new x, y and z dimensions.
- For a cone or cylinder, you are prompted for a new x and y base radius, and a new height.
- For a sphere, you are prompted only for a new radius.
- For a torus, you are prompted for a new overall radius and a new tube radius.
- For an extrusion, AutoCAD prompts:

    Change shape?

    If you answer **Y**, AutoCAD produces a 2-D profile of the extrusion. You may then exit the Solchp command and use AutoCAD commands such as Stretch and Pedit to change the profile. Then use the Solext command to create a new solid with extrusion values. Finally, re-enter the Solchp command and use the Replace option to replace the original primitive with the newly edited one. This process applies only to extrusions that are part of composite solids. If editing a stand-alone primitive, you may edit the solid directly using standard AutoCAD commands.

    If you answer **N**, AutoCAD prompts you for new Height and extrusion taper values.

- For a revolution that is part of a composite solid, AutoCAD prompts:

    <Angle>/AXis/Shape:

Angle   Enter **A** or press Return to specify a new angle of revolution. AutoCAD prompts:

Specify angle:

Enter a new angle of revolution, or press Return to accept the current angle, shown as a default.

AXis/Shape   Enter AX or S to change the axis of revolution or shape of the original polyline. AutoCAD produces a 2-D profile of the original polyline and an axis of revolution. You may then exit the Solchp command and use AutoCAD commands such as Stretch and Pedit to change the profile. Next, use the Solext command to create a new revolution solid. Finally, re-enter the Solchp command and use the Replace option to replace the original primitive with the newly edited one. This process applies only to revolution solids that are part of composite solids. If editing a stand-alone primitive, you may edit the solid directly using standard AutoCAD commands.

USAGE

Because this command can encompass any number of complex editing procedures, it can be quite time consuming. For relatively simple composite solids, you might find it easier and more intuitive to use the Solsep command to separate the primitives. Then edit them using standard AutoCAD commands and re-assemble the composite solid.

It is possible to create a *null solid,* a solid without volume, using this command. If AutoCAD detects a null solid, it aborts the command.

PULL-DOWN MENU SEQUENCE

From the Modify menu, pick Change Prim.

Solmove

Relocates solid entities in the drawing.

COMMAND REQUIREMENTS AND OPTIONS

Select objects   Pick the solid entities you intend to move. When finished selecting, press Return.

After you select the entities a special icon appears, indicating an orientation of x-, y-, and z-axes relative to the selected objects. These axes do not have to be the same as the current UCS. These special x-, y-, and z-axes are called the Motion Coordinate System, or MCS. You may enter a variety of *motion description codes* that permit you to move the solid, or re-orient the current setting of the MCS. The MCS consists of a tripod of three lines. The line representing the x-axis ends in a single arrowhead; the line representing the y-axis, a double arrowhead, and the line representing the z-axis, a triple arrowhead. AutoCAD prompts:

<Motion description>/?:

Enter **?** to display a list of motion description codes and their meanings.

The following motion description codes are available in response to this prompt:

AE   Aligns and links the MCS with an edge of one of the solids.

AF   Aligns and links the MCS with a face of one of the solids. To select a face, select one of its edges. If the edge is shared by two faces, AutoCAD highlights one and prompts:

> <OK>/Next:

If the highlighted face is the correct one, press Return; otherwise enter **N** to highlight the other face, then press Return.

AU   Aligns and links the MCS and solids with the current UCS.

AW   Aligns and links the MCS and solids with the world coordinate system.

The following commands relocate the selected solids. If the MCS is aligned and linked with a solid, it will relocate as well.

RX*nn*   Rotates the solids around the x-axis of the MCS, where *nn* indicates the number of degrees of rotation.

RY*nn*   Rotates the solids around the y-axis of the MCS, where *nn* indicates the number of degrees of rotation.

RZ*nn*   Rotates the solids around the x-axis of the MCS, where *nn* indicates the number of degrees of rotation.

TX*nn*   Moves the solid along the x-axis of the MCS, where *nn* indicates the distance to move.

TY*nn*   Moves the solid along the y-axis of the MCS, where *nn* indicates the distance to move.

TZ*nn*   Moves the solid along the z-axis of the MCS, where *nn* indicates the distance to move.

E   Aligns the MCS with a selected edge of one of the selected solids, but does not link it to the solid.

F Aligns the MCS with a selected face of one of the selected solids, but does not link it to the solid. The prompts for this option follow the rules outlined in the AF option described earlier.

U Aligns but does not link the MCS with the current UCS.

W Aligns but does not link the MCS with the world coordinate system.

O Returns the MCS and solids to their original location at the start of the command.

USAGE

You can combine as many motion description codes in a single line as you like, separating them with commas. For example:

<Motion description>/?: **RX-90,RY-90,TX3,TZ-5**

rotates the selected solids 90 degrees clockwise around the MCS x-axis, 90 degrees around the y-axis, and moves them three units along the positive x-axis and five units along the negative z-axis.

PULL-DOWN MENU SEQUENCE

From the Utility menu, pick Solmove.

SOLID INQUIRY COMMANDS

These commands display information about the solids in the drawing.

Sollist

Lists geometric information used to define a solid.

COMMAND REQUIREMENTS AND OPTIONS

Pick solid Press Return to receive a prompt to pick the solid entity to list. Listed information can include the following:

- The entity handles of the component primitives
- The component type or process used to generate it, if a composite solid
- The area if previously computed using the Solarea or Solmesh commands

- Material properties of the solid
- Whether the solid is displayed as a mesh or a wire-frame model
- And the amount and degree of motion and scaling that has been applied to the solid

Edge   Enter **E** for a prompt to select an edge of the solid for which you desire information.

Face   Enter **F** for a prompt to select the face of the solid for which you desire information. To select a face, select one of its edges. If the edge is shared by two faces, AutoCAD highlights one and prompts:

<OK>/Next:

If the highlighted face is the correct one, press Return; otherwise enter **N** to highlight the other face, then press Return.

Tree   Enter **T** to list the definition information of each primitive in a composite solid, and the processes by which they were combined, in order.

USAGE

All solid values are displayed in decimal units, regardless of the current setting of AutoCAD's Units command.

PULL-DOWN MENU SEQUENCE

From the Inquiry menu, pick List Solid.

Solmassp

Calculates and lists the mass properties of selected solids.

COMMAND REQUIREMENTS AND OPTIONS

Select objects   Select the solids to calculate and display mass properties. Auto-CAD displays the total mass; volume; bounding box (the smallest rectangular solid encompassing the entire existing solid; centroid; moment of inertia; product of inertia; radii of gyration; and principal moments and XYZ direction about the centroid. After listing the information, AutoCAD prompts:

Write to file<N>?

Enter **Y** if you would like to create a file on disk containing the information. Otherwise, enter **N** or press Return. If you enter **Y,** AutoCAD prompts you for the name of the file, offering the drawing name as the default. These files have the extension MPR.

PULL-DOWN MENU SEQUENCE

From the Inquiry menu, pick Mass Property.

Solarea

Calculates and displays the surface area of selected solids.

COMMAND REQUIREMENTS AND OPTIONS

Select objects   Select the solids to calculate and display the total surface area. AutoCAD displays the total area.

USAGE

When calculating the area of curved surfaces, you can improve the accuracy of the calculations by increasing the wire-mesh density. Refer to the discussion of the SOLWDENS variable just ahead for details on increasing wire-mesh densities.

PULL-DOWN MENU SEQUENCE

From the Inquiry menu, pick Solid Area.

SOLID DISPLAY COMMANDS

These commands affect the way in which solids are displayed in your drawing.

Solmesh

Displays solids as a mesh. Allows shading and hidden line removal.

COMMAND REQUIREMENTS AND OPTIONS

Select objects   Select the solids you intend to display as a mesh. AutoCAD recalculates and displays the solids.

USAGE

Mesh display allows hidden line removal and shading. It helps you avoid working with curved surfaces, as lines are replaced with straight edges and flat faces. You may also display the mesh-wire frame by setting the SPLFRAME system variable to 1. Refer to Chapter 13 for more information regarding this system variable.

PULL-DOWN MENU SEQUENCE

From the Display menu, pick Mesh.

Solwire

Displays solids as wire-frame models. Allows display of curved lines.

COMMAND REQUIREMENTS AND OPTIONS

Select objects   Select the solids you intend to display as wire-frame models. AutoCAD recalculates and displays the solids.

USAGE

Wire frame display allows you to work with curved lines in your solid display. You cannot, however, remove hidden lines or shade. You may display the mesh frame by setting the SPLFRAME system variable to 1. Refer to Chapter 13 for more information regarding this system variable.

PULL-DOWN MENU SEQUENCE

From the Display menu, pick Wireframe.

2-D DRAFTING COMMANDS

You can use these commands with solid entities to create 2-D representations for more efficient plotting and display of solids.

Solfeat

Creates a 2-D entity from an edge or face of a solid.

COMMAND REQUIREMENTS AND OPTIONS

The command creates a block in the drawing at the location of the selected entity. This block may be moved, edited, and displayed like any 2-D entity.

Edge   Enter **E** to select an edge from a solid entity. When you pick the edge, AutoCAD creates a block containing the desired edge.

Face   The Face option is the default. Select a face by selecting an edge of a solid in the drawing. If the edge is shared by two faces, AutoCAD highlights one and prompts:

<OK>/Next:

If the highlighted face is the correct one, press Return; otherwise enter **N** to highlight the other face, then press Return.

USAGE

The block created by this command may not be re-inserted in the drawing by block name, but it may be edited using standard AutoCAD commands.

PULL-DOWN MENU SEQUENCE

From the Display menu, pick Copy Feature.

Solsect

Displays a cross section of the selected solid.

COMMAND REQUIREMENTS AND OPTIONS

Before running this command, position the UCS so that the X-Y plane intersects the solid at the point of your desired cross section. Then invoke Solsect. AutoCAD prompts:

Select objects

Select the solids to display cross sections. AutoCAD recalculates and displays the cross sections. These cross sections are 2-D entities, created as blocks in the drawing at the location of the computed cross section. This block may be moved, edited, and displayed like any 2-D entity.

USAGE

The block created by this command may not be re-inserted in the drawing by block name, but it may be edited using standard AutoCAD commands, for example Move Last.

The block might be automatically crosshatched, depending on the setting of the SOLHPAT, SOLHANGLE, and SOLHSIZE variables. Refer to the discussion of these variables just ahead for details.

PULL-DOWN MENU SEQUENCE

From the Display menu, pick Cut Section.

Solprof

Produces a 2-D image of the current view of the solid.

COMMAND REQUIREMENTS AND OPTIONS

Before entering this command, set the TILEMODE system variable to zero. Refer to Chapter 13 if you need further information regarding this variable. When TILEMODE is set to zero, create a viewport using Mview (if necessary), and switch to model space, then display the solid at the desired viewing angle. Finally, invoke Solprof. AutoCAD prompts:

> Select objects:

Select the solids to create profile views. AutoCAD prompts:

> Display hidden profile lines on separate layer? <N>:

If you want a hidden-line profile drawing, enter **Y**. Otherwise, the profile is generated without hidden lines.

USAGE

AutoCAD creates the profile as a block, placing it on a specially named layer at the same location as the original solid. To see the profile drawing, turn off only the layer containing the solid. The layer containing the profile block is named according to the following naming convention:

> *Solid's layer*-PV-*current viewport number*

For example, if the original solid were located on a layer named PART, and the profile generated in viewport number 2, the profile would be placed on layer PART-PV-2. If the layer does not already exist, AutoCAD creates it.

Once the profile is generated, you may edit it using standard AutoCAD editing commands.

If AutoCAD calculates hidden lines, it places them on a separate layer. This layer follows the same naming convention, except that the letters PV are replaced by PH. Thus, if you created a hidden-line profile using the above parameters, a second block containing the hidden lines would be placed on layer PART-PH-2. To view the profile with hidden lines removed, turn off both the layer containing the solid and the layer containing the hidden-line block.

PULL-DOWN MENU SEQUENCE

From the Display menu, pick Profile.

AME UTILITY COMMANDS

These commands perform miscellaneous operations affecting the analysis, display, and properties of solids.

Solmat

Manages the material properties of solids.

COMMAND REQUIREMENTS AND OPTIONS

Several definitions for standard material properties of solids are stored in a text file named ACAD.MAT. The Solmat command accesses this file to manage material property definitions and assign material properties to solids.

Change Enter **C** to change the material properties of solids. AutoCAD prompts you to select the solids whose material properties you intend to change. AutoCAD then prompts:

New material:

The current material is offered as the default option. If you enter **?** , AutoCAD will display a list of currently loaded material definitions. You may list the definitions in the ACAD.MAT file or a custom file you have created for this purpose.

After you enter the name of the new material, AutoCAD updates the solid.

Edit Enter **E** to edit the definition of a material. To edit a material definition, you must load it into the current drawing, either using the Load option of this command or by assigning the material to a solid. AutoCAD prompts:

Material name:

Enter the name of the material definition you intend to edit. AutoCAD displays a numbered list of various properties for the named material. These properties are described in the discussion of the New option of this command. Select the number of the property whose value you intend to change, then enter the new value or zero to exit.

After you have edited the definition, AutoCAD prompts you to save the changed specifications in an external file, as described in the discussion of the New option of this command. If the definition already exists in the external file, you are prompted to confirm that you want to overwrite it.

LIst Enter **LI** to list the current values associated with a material definition. AutoCAD prompts:

Material to list:

Enter the name of a material in the drawing or the ACAD.MAT file. If the named material is not found, AutoCAD prompts for the name of another file where it can be found.

LOad Enter **LO** to load a material definition into the drawing from the ACAD.MAT file or another file containing valid material definitions. Materials assigned to solids are loaded into the drawing at assignment time; it is not necessary to explicitly load them first. A definition must be loaded before you can edit it, however.

New Enter **N** to define a new material. AutoCAD prompts:

Material name:

Enter the name of a material not already loaded in the drawing. AutoCAD prompts:

Material description:

Enter a line of text further describing the material definition that you are creating. After you enter the descriptive text, AutoCAD prompts for the following values in turn:

1. Density
2. Young's modulus
3. Poisson's ratio

4. Yield strength

5. Ultimate strength

6. Thermal conductivity

7. Linear expansion coefficient

8. Specific heat

To change any of the values after entering them all, enter the number of the value to change. When you have completed input of the correct values, enter 0. AutoCAD then prompts:

> Save the material to a file <N>

If you would like to save the definition in an external file, enter **Y**. Otherwise, enter **N**. If you enter **Y**, AutoCAD prompts:

> File name <acad>:

Press Return to accept the default file name, or enter a file name of your own. If the material definition is found in the named file, AutoCAD prompts:

> Material is already defined in file.
> Overwrite definition in file <N> ?

If you intend to overwrite the old definition with the new one, enter **Y**. Otherwise, enter N.

Remove   Enter **R** to remove a material definition from the drawing. AutoCAD prompts:

> Material to remove:

Enter the name of the material definition to remove, or enter **?** to see a list of defined materials.

SAve   Enter **SA** to save a material definition in an external file. AutoCAD prompts:

> Material to save:

Enter the name of the material definition to save, or enter **?** to see a list of defined materials. After entering a material name, AutoCAD prompts for an external file name as described in the discussion of the New option of this command.

SEt   Enter **SE** to set the new default material property for newly created solids in your drawing. AutoCAD prompts:

> New default material:

Enter the name of the new default material. If the material you enter is not loaded in the drawing, but can be found in the file ACAD.MAT, it is loaded in the drawing and made default. Otherwise, AutoCAD prompts:

    Set material from file <acad>:

Enter the name of the file containing the material definition.

　　After AutoCAD sets the new default material, it repeats the "New default material" prompt, showing the material name you entered as the new default response. If this is correct, press Return.

eXit　　When you have completed all your changes to material specifications, enter **X** or press Return to exit the Solmat command.

PULL-DOWN MENU SEQUENCE

From the Modify menu, pick Material.

Solucs

Aligns the User Coordinate System (UCS) with the face or edge of a selected solid.

COMMAND REQUIREMENTS AND OPTIONS

Edge　　Enter **E** to select the edge of a solid. AutoCAD aligns the UCS with the selected edge.

Face　　This is the default option. Enter **F** or press return to align the UCS with the face of a solid. AutoCAD prompts:

    Select a face:

Select a face by selecting an edge of a solid in the drawing. If the edge is shared by two faces, AutoCAD highlights one and prompts:

    <OK>/Next:

If the highlighted face is the correct one, press Return; otherwise enter **N** to highlight the other face, then press Return. Once the correct face is selected Auto-CAD realigns the UCS.

PULL-DOWN MENU SEQUENCE

From the Utility menu, pick SolUCS.

Solin

Imports a file from AutoSolid.

COMMAND REQUIREMENTS AND OPTIONS

File name Enter the name of the external AutoSolid file to be imported into the drawing. AutoCAD places the imported solids into the current drawing relative to the origin point.

USAGE

The Solin command allows you to exchange solid data with the AutoSolid program (version 3.1). It is not necessary to use this command to transfer solid data between AutoCAD drawings; AutoCAD's standard Block and Insert commands will serve this purpose.

PULL-DOWN MENU SEQUENCE

From the Utility menu, pick Sol in .asm.

Solout

Exports all solid data in a drawing to a file for use by AutoSolid version 3.1.

COMMAND REQUIREMENTS AND OPTIONS

File name Enter the name of the external AutoSolid file to be created. Auto-CAD places all solid data from the current drawing in this file, giving it the extension ASM.

USAGE

As discussed in the previous section, Solout allows you to exchange solid data with the AutoSolid program (version 3.1). If you intend to export solid data for use by other AutoCAD drawings, use the Block and Wblock commands instead.

PULL-DOWN MENU SEQUENCE

From the Utility menu, pick Sol out .asm.

Solpurge

Manages memory used by the AME program.

COMMAND REQUIREMENTS AND OPTIONS

Memory   Enter **M** to free memory occupied by solid data, if you are through processing solids and would like AutoCAD to use the memory for other types of processing. AutoCAD prompts:

All/<Select>:

Enter **A** if you would like to release all solids data from memory. AutoCAD continues to store solids data in the drawing database. If you return to processing solids, AutoCAD will reload any required data into memory based on your selection of solids for additional processing.

Alternatively, you may select individual solids, and if their data is currently in memory, the memory is released for other processing.

Bfile   Enter **B** to release a solid's link to its *boundary file,* or *bfile* for short. The boundary file contains information about a solid's edges and faces, and is stored using at least two block insertions located on a special frozen layer named AME-FRZ. The data in these blocks is linked to the solid's extended entity data. If you are no longer making modifications to the solid, the boundary file is not required. Releasing links to the bfile can reduce the size of the drawing database. If you later decide to modify the solid, the bfile is rebuilt.

Pmesh   Enter **P** to release a solid's mesh definition. When a solid is meshed, the wire frame definition is stored as a block on the AME_FRZ layer, and the main entity is updated as a mesh definition. Certain processing requires a wire frame definition, and the solid's extended entity data forms a link between the two definitions, calling on the appropriate definition as necessary. If you no longer need mesh definitions in your drawing, use this option to erase them on a selective basis. The wire frame definitions of solids are required and cannot be purged. You can re-create the mesh definition at a later time using the Solmesh command.

Erased   This is the default option. Enter **E** to purge secondary blocks associated with erased solids. When you erase a solid using AutoCAD's Erase command, only the main entity is actually deleted. The secondary blocks (mesh definitions and bfiles) remain. This option locates these "orphaned" blocks and deletes them, thereby reducing the size of your drawing. In large drawings, this operation can take a considerable amount of time.

USAGE

Solid data is loaded into memory when a solid is created or selected for editing or analysis. The solid data remains in memory until the drawing session is ended, AME is unloaded, or the memory is explicitly released. If your memory is constrained, you can improve performance by releasing memory when you are finished processing individual solids. Likewise, removing unneeded secondary blocks from the drawing database can reduce loading and saving time.

PULL-DOWN MENU SEQUENCE

From the Utility menu, pick Purge Solids.

AME SYSTEM VARIABLES

There are a number of special system variables that apply to solids processing. Their broad purpose is similar to that of AutoCAD's system variables; that is, they affect the environment within which AME modifies and analyzes solids. You may change their values at AutoCAD's command prompt like AutoCAD's system variables or by using the Solvar command described just ahead. However, they cannot be changed using AutoCAD's standard Setvar command. Only two are read-only: SOLAMVER (AME version number) and SOLMATCURR (current default material property). Table 22.1 lists current AME variables, a description of their values, data type, and default.

Name	Description	Integer	Options	Default
SOLAMEVER	AME version number (read-only)	Integer	None	N/A
SOLAREAU	Unit of measure for area calculations	String	Any unit of area measure defined in the ACAD.UNT file	Sq cm (square centimeters)
SOLAXCOL	Color of the Motion Coordinate System icon	Integer	Any valid AutoCAD color number	3 (green)

Table 22.1: AME System Variables

Name	Description	Integer	Options	Default
SOLDECOMP	Mass properties decomposition direction axis	String	X, Y, or Z	X (decomposition along the x-axis)
SOLDELENT	Deletes original entity after extrusion or revolution	Integer	1 = never delete; 2 = prompt before deleting; 3 = always delete	(always delete)
SOLDISPLAY	Determines default solid display, either wireframe or mesh	String	Wire or mesh	Wire (displays as wireframe)
SOLHANGLE	Angle of hatch pattern used in cross-section generation	Real Number	0.000000 to 359.999999	0.000000
SOLHPAT	Name of hatch pattern used in cross-section generation	String	Any hatch pattern name defined in the ACAD.PAT file, or NONE	NONE (hatch pattern not used)
SOLHSIZE	Scale factor of hatch pattern used in cross-section generation	Real Number	Any positive, non-zero number	1.00000 (defined pattern scale times 1)
SOLLENGTH	Unit of measure for length calculations	String	Any unit of distance measure defined in the ACAD.UNT file	Cm (centimeters)
SOLMASS	Unit of measure for mass calculations	String	Any unit of mass measure defined in the ACAD.UNT file	Gm(grams)
SOLMATCURR	Default material properties definition	String	Any material properties name defined in the ACAD.MAT file	MILD_STEEL

Table 22.1: AME System Variables (continued)

Name	Description	Integer	Options	Default
SOLPAGELEN	Page length for text messages displayed by AME commands	Integer	0 or above	25
SOLRENDER	Defines use of colors for shading composite solids	String	CSG = shade with colors of primitives; UNIFORM = Shade in color of top-level composite solid	CSG
SOLSERVMSG	Manages AME message display	Integer	0 = No messages; 1 = Display only error messages; 2 = Display Error messages, plus notify at start and end of computations; 3 = Display all messages	3 (display all messages)
SOLSOLIDIFY	Manages automatic conversion of 2-D entities into solids when encountered during processing	Integer	1 = Never attempt to convert; 2 = Prompt before attempting to convert; 3 = Always attempt to convert	2 (prompt before attempting to convert)
SOLSUBDIV	Subdivision level for mass properties calculation	Integer	1–8 levels	3 (subdivide to three levels)
SOLVOLUME	Unit of measure for volume calculations	String	Any unit of volume measure defined in the ACAD.UNT file	Cu cm (cubic centimeters)
SOLWDENS	Wire frame mesh density	Integer	1 (minimum density) to 8 (maximum density)	4 (moderate density)

Table 22.1: AME System Variables (continued)

Solavar

Changes the values of AME solid-processing variables.

COMMAND REQUIREMENTS AND OPTIONS

Variable name   Enter the name of the AME variable whose value you intend to change. AutoCAD responds by prompting for the new value, displaying the current value as the default response. Enter the new value or press Return to leave the variable unchanged.

Enter a question mark (?) to display a list of AME variables and their current values.

PULL-DOWN MENU SEQUENCE

From the Utility menu, pick Solvars.

NOTES ON USING AME

The following suggestions will help you optimize use of the AME program:

AME_FRZ layer   AutoCAD manages secondary data for solids on a special frozen layer named AME_FRZ. Do not attempt to modify any information on this layer. All entities on this layer are processed by the AME program.

Color shading   AME manages color shading by means of the SOLRENDER variable. Refer to Table 22.1 for details on this variable. If you make changes to this variable, current solids will not be affected unless you updated their mesh properties using Solmesh or Solwire.

Dimensions and text   Maintain dimension entities or text associated with solids on a separate layer, and save the viewing angle using the View Save command. When viewing solids from different angles, dimension and text entities may appear seriously misaligned or floating in space. It helps to turn off or freeze the layers containing these entities and display them at the viewing angle in which they were created.

Filleting   If you are creating a solid by extruding a polyline, apply editing commands such as fillet, chamfer, or curve fitting before the extrusion. This is usually much simpler than editing the solid afterward.

Handles   AME uses entity handles extensively. Handles are enabled when AME is loaded. Do not destroy handles in an AME drawing.

IGES file transfer   Solid entity data is not supported by IGES.

Surface density and accuracy   You can increase the accuracy of your solids analysis by increasing the wire-frame and mesh density of your models. Refer to the discussion of the SOLWDENS variable for details. A denser wire frame will calculate to a denser mesh as well. However, increasing the accuracy will decrease the speed of calculations and increase the size of the drawing file, requiring additional memory.

When a solid is meshed, curved lines are represented as straight line segments. If a composite solid contains primitives that are quite close together, false intersections can occur when density is set too low. In some cases, a higher density may be required to accurately display the mesh of a composite solid with cramped primitives.

The AutoCAD Development System

The *AutoCAD Development System,* or *ADS,* is a library of predefined code values, function declarations, and data types for the C programming language. It is intended to be used as a platform for development of high-level applications that may be difficult or impossible to program with AutoLISP. In the case of applications that are also possible with AutoLISP, ADS can increase performance speed and handle memory with greater enough efficiency to justify its more complicated development cycle.

ADS is a tool for the professional developer with a thorough understanding of the C programming language. ADS is not intended for the everyday drafter or casual programmer; these operators should find AutoLISP adequate for their processing and customization needs. ADS is *not* intended as a replacement for AutoLISP; Autodesk has consistently maintained its ongoing support and improvement of the AutoLISP environment.

Additional Software Requirements for Using ADS

To develop an application using ADS, you must purchase compiling and linking software for the C language that is compatible with the AutoCAD platform for which you are developing applications. AutoCAD currently supports ADS on the following platforms with the indicated C compilers and linkers. Many of these products can be obtained together as development kits for general purpose C programming.

Other C compilers not listed may be used provided that they are 100-percent compatible with the function-calling and library conventions used by Auto-CAD's ADS environment.

AutoCAD 386

Compilers: MetaWare High C 386 or WATCOM C 386

Assembler: Phar Lap 386 ASM

Linker: Phar Lap 386 LINK

Debugger (optional): Phar Lap 386 DEBUG

Virtual Memory Manager (optional): Phar Lap 386 VMM

AutoCAD 640K DOS for 80286

Compiler: Microsoft C (version 5.0 or greater) or MetaWare High C Version 1.6 (for 16-bit systems)

Linker: Microsoft Overlay Linker

Debugger: Rational Systems Instant-D

Build Environment: Rational Systems DOS/16M

Build Utility: Microsoft Program Maintenance Utility

AutoCAD OS/2

Compiler: Microsoft C (version 5.1 or greater)

Linker: Microsoft Overlay Linker

Debugger: Microsoft CodeView

Build Utility: Microsoft Program Maintenance Utility

AutoCAD UNIX (Sun and Apollo) or XENIX

Compiler: C compiler supplied with operating system

Linker: Link editor supplied with operating system

Debugger: dbx (for Sun); dde (for Apollo); dbxtool (optional for Sun)

Build Utility: Source-file maintenance utility supplied with operating system

AutoCAD Macintosh

Compiler: Macintosh Programmer's Workbench (version 3.0 or later), or ThinkC. Includes linker, debugger, and build utility

THE ADS ENVIRONMENT

ADS program development requires experience with and understanding of the C programming language, as well as compiling, linking, building, and debugging executable files. A description of the C language is beyond the scope of this book. However, this section describes the ADS development cycle in general terms.

ADS Programs and AutoCAD

A fully functional ADS application consists of an *executable file* (machine-readable instruction code) that is loaded into memory using the AutoLISP Xload function, described in Chapter 17. Once in memory, AutoCAD sets up special links with the ADS application to access its functions and carry out commands. The ADS application receives instructions from AutoCAD to begin processing, processes data based on the instruction codes it receives, and reports on the success or failure of the operation.

Source Code

ADS development begins by composing source code in C using a text editor. ADS programs make use of a number of predefined C functions that process data in a way similar to AutoLISP functions. There are some important exceptions to this similarity, however, based on differences between fundamental language constructs of C and LISP.

Compiling and Linking

Once the source code is written, it is compiled into *object code*, which is in turn *linked* to a library of machine-specific instructions that combine with the object code into machine-recognizable commands to process data. This file is called the *executable file*. It is then loaded into memory, where its instructions can be carried out.

ADS Applications in Memory

When the ADS application is loaded into memory, it sets up communications links with the part of AutoCAD that handles AutoLISP instructions. If the communications links are joined successfully, the application sends a special code to AutoCAD informing it is now ready to to define the functions it contains. Auto-CAD returns a *request code* to the ADS application instructing it to define its functions. This is similar to what occurs when the AutoLISP Defun function is invoked.

Once the ADS application functions are defined, the application waits for a request code from AutoCAD to execute some form of data processing. This request code may be triggered by operator input or other functions that force an evaluation of a defined ADS function.

An ADS function may interact with the operator, process data internally, or even unload itself from memory. At the conclusion of processing, if the ADS application is still in memory, it passes a code to AutoCAD indicating whether the process was successful and awaits another request code from AutoCAD.

While AutoCAD is processing, the ADS application waits for AutoCAD. When the ADS application is processing data, AutoCAD waits for the ADS application to return a code indicating that processing is finished, either through successful completion or termination as the result of some error.

The C language is very powerful and allows the programmer to access every part of the computer's memory, potentially with disturbing and unintended results. It is the programmer's responsibility to write ADS code that will manage and understand every detail of the communication link it sets up with AutoCAD, and that will not create memory conflicts that damage data or crash AutoCAD.

OTHER RESOURCES

The AutoCAD *ADS Programmer's Reference*, supplied as part of your program documentation, contains detailed descriptions of all ADS predefined functions.

If you are interested in learning C or using ADS to develop more powerful AutoCAD applications, the following books may be helpful:

Bolan, Craig, *Mastering C*, SYBEX Books

Hunter, Bruce H., *Understanding C*, SYBEX Books

Kernighan, Brian W., and Dennis M. Ritchie, *The C Programming Language, 2nd ed.*, Prentice Hall

Lafore, Robert, *Microsoft C Programming for the PC*, Howard Sams & Co.

Using AutoShade

AutoShade is a software program developed by Autodesk and designed for use with AutoCAD 3-D drawings.

AutoShade produces a display and/or hard-copy rendering of an AutoCAD 3-D wire-frame drawing with surface shading, for a viewing effect that is far more realistic than is possible using AutoCAD alone. Figures 22.4, 22.5, and 22.6 illustrate the differences between an AutoCAD wire-frame display, a hidden-line display, and an AutoShade rendering of the same drawing.

Shaded renderings are easier to visualize than wire-frame images, and are useful in the design process, which benefits from the most accurate possible images of projected designs.

Creating Scenes in AutoCAD

The first steps toward creating an AutoShade rendering take place in AutoCAD. You must first create an AutoCAD 3-D drawing, which may include any combination of the following entities: circles, solids, wide polylines (including doughnuts), traces, 2-D entities that have been given extruded thicknesses, 3-D faces, and polygon meshes.

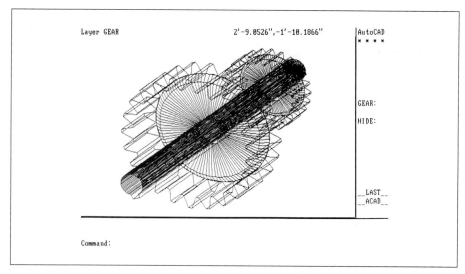

FIGURE 22.4: An AutoCAD 3-D drawing created for rendering in AutoShade. In this wire-frame drawing of a gear and shaft assembly, the dozens of lines make the object difficult to visualize. Compare this figure to the hidden-line display in Figure 22.5 and the AutoShade rendering in Figure 22.6.

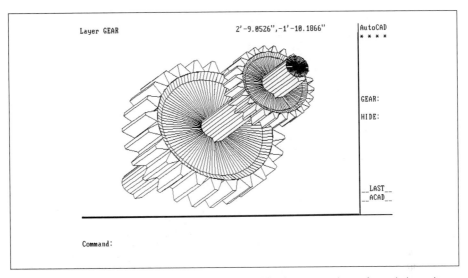

FIGURE 22.5: An AutoCAD hidden-line display. After a hidden-line removal is performed, the outline of the gear display is much easier to visualize. While the hidden-line display is an improvement, the AutoShade rendering in Figure 22.6 goes a step beyond this.

FIGURE 22.6: An AutoShade rendering of the gear assembly. This AutoShade rendering helps to visualize the relationships between the objects. AutoShade allows you to create credible 3-D design representations from AutoCAD wire-frame drawings.

The colors of the entities are important, as AutoShade will use the entity colors you assign in AutoCAD as the basis for assigning colors to the same entities in the shaded rendering.

Once you have created your 3-D drawing in AutoCAD, the next step is to insert special blocks, which will represent at least one light source and a viewing angle. AutoShade uses the locations of light sources and the viewing angle as the basis for computing the shaded rendering of the object.

Loading ASHADE.LSP

After you create a 3-D drawing in AutoCAD, you must load the file ASHADE.LSP in order to prepare the drawing for processing by AutoShade. This file, which is supplied on both the AutoCAD and AutoShade master disks, defines special commands that assist you in the preparation. ASHADE.LSP should be copied to your AutoCAD system subdirectory. You may load the file in one of two ways:

- Enter the following at the AutoCAD Command prompt:

    (load "Ashade")

- Select the Ashade command from AutoCAD's screen menu, or the Lights, Camera, or Action box on AutoCAD's standard tablet menu.

If you select the Ashade command from the screen menu, AutoCAD will display a submenu of AutoShade commands after ASHADE.LSP is loaded. If you select one of the AutoShade commands from the tablet menu, the selected command will be invoked immediately after ASHADE.LSP is loaded. In either case, AutoCAD only loads ASHADE.LSP the first time these commands are picked; reselecting the commands does not reload the file.

In order to produce the shaded rendering, AutoShade will require both a *viewing angle* and a *light source*. These parameters are represented in the drawing by special blocks, which are supplied to you in the form of drawing files that can be found on disk with the Insert command. These drawing files should be copied onto your AutoCAD system subdirectory when AutoShade is installed.

Adjusting the Camera Position

The block that represents the viewing angle is called the *camera,* and it is entered in the drawing with the Camera command. The Camera command first prompts for a camera name, which may be any combination of up to 31 alphanumeric characters, except spaces. After you have entered the camera name, AutoCAD prompts for a target point and a camera-location point. You may use any of AutoCAD's standard point-entry methods to enter these points. The placing of target points and camera-location points is similar to the Points option of the Dview command (Chapter 11), where a camera/target metaphor is also used to create a particular viewing angle on the entities in the drawing. As with Dview, the viewing angle is parallel to an imaginary line segment that extends from the selected camera point to the selected target point. The portion of the drawing that will be visible at the particular viewing angle is based on the distance between the camera and the target; the greater the distance between the two, the more entities will be visible, and the smaller they will appear to be.

You may include any number of cameras in your drawing, and thus have the possibility of producing any number of different AutoShade views.

In AutoCAD Release 10 and later, you can check the resulting view from the current camera/target position by invoking the Camview command and picking the camera whose viewing angle you would like to check. If the viewing angle is not correct, erase the camera and reinsert it. Alternatively, you can move the camera block using the Move command. AutoCAD will compute the new relationship between the camera and the target, but will not automatically rotate the display of the camera block on the screen. This may result in a misleading display of the true camera angle. You would then have to use the Rotate command so that the visual display of the block reflects the new viewing angle. In most cases, it will probably be easier to erase and reinsert the camera. Figure 22.7 illustrates the gear drawing with the camera block inserted.

The AutoShade program will also permit you to adjust the viewing angle by changing the position of the camera. This technique is discussed in the section ''Moving the Camera.''

Adjusting the Lights

AutoShade also bases its shaded renderings on the position of *light sources* with respect to the entities being viewed. These light sources are also represented by blocks, which you enter in the AutoCAD drawing using the Light command.

There are two types of light source: *pointed* and *directed.* Pointed light extends in all directions, like a light bulb hanging from the ceiling of a room. It is used to provide general illumination of the drawing. Directed light is more focused, extending in a single direction, like a spotlight. It is used to highlight and emphasize specific parts of the drawing.

You may include as many light sources of each type as you require to produce the desired AutoShade rendering. All other things being equal, fewer light sources and more directed light will generally produce more contrasts in the shaded rendering, while a greater number of light sources and less directed light will produce less contrast in the shaded rendering.

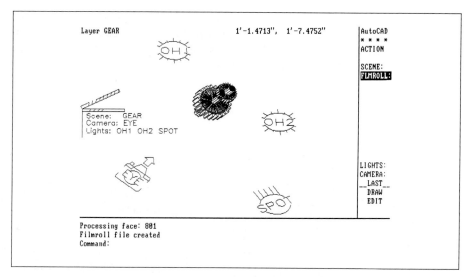

FIGURE 22.7: A 3-D view of the AutoCAD drawing, showing the locations of the camera block (lower left) and the light-source blocks (named OH1, OH2, and SPOT) that will be used by AutoShade to create the rendered drawing in Figure 22.6. To the left is the clapper-board block, which is inserted into the drawing when the camera and lights are grouped together into a scene for inclusion in an AutoShade filmroll file.

You enter a light source using the Light command. AutoCAD prompts you for the name of the light, whether it is pointed or directed, and its location in the drawing. You may use any of AutoCAD's standard point-entry methods to enter the light source's location point.

The positions of the light sources are determined by you in AutoCAD, and there is no way to change those positions in AutoShade. However, AutoShade will permit you to adjust the relative intensity of the various light sources, along with the degree of reflective ability of the surfaces being viewed. This allows for a great deal of flexibility in the appearance of the final shaded rendering. Refer back to Figure 22.7, which shows the gear drawing with camera and lights inserted.

Forming a Scene

The next step in preparing an AutoCAD drawing for rendering in AutoShade is grouping the camera and lights together into a *scene*. Each scene includes one camera and any number of previously inserted lights. You may have any number of scenes in a particular drawing, allowing you to create as many different viewing angles and lighting combinations as you like.

To create a scene, invoke the Scene command. Enter the scene name and pick the camera, followed by the lights that will be included in the scene. Then pick the scene location. For additional scenes, repeat the command as many times as necessary, using a different scene name each time.

Creating a Filmroll File

The final step in AutoCAD is to create a *filmroll file,* which is the file that will be read by AutoShade to produce shaded renderings. You create filmroll files by invoking AutoCAD's Filmroll command. AutoCAD prompts you for a file name, offering the name of the current drawing file as the default. After you enter a file name, the filmroll file is created. It is always given the extension FLM. A single filmroll file contains all the scenes that you have created for the AutoCAD drawing.

Once you have created the filmroll file, end the drawing session, exit AutoCAD, and initialize AutoShade by entering the command **SHADE** at the operating-system prompt.

PRODUCING A SHADED DRAWING IN AUTOSHADE

At its most fundamental level, the process of producing a shaded image with AutoShade can be almost wholly automatic. Most simply, using AutoShade requires only that you load the filmroll file, select a scene, and invoke the command to display the rendered image. However, AutoShade comes equipped with a number of options that allow you a considerable amount of control over the final result. Space permits only a brief introduction to the most frequently used features; for a more in-depth presentation of AutoShade's features, consult the user guide provided with the AutoShade program.

The Program Interface

AutoShade commands can be accessed by means of pull-down menus, as illustrated in Figure 22.8. To access a pull-down menu, use the pointing device to move the screen's arrow pointer until it highlights one of the keywords that appear in the top line of the display. Pressing the pick button on the pointing device will reveal the menu. You may then move the pointing device until the desired command is highlighted, and press the pick button to invoke the highlighted command. You may also use cursor keys to move the arrow pointer, and press the Insert (or Ins) key to select the highlighted item.

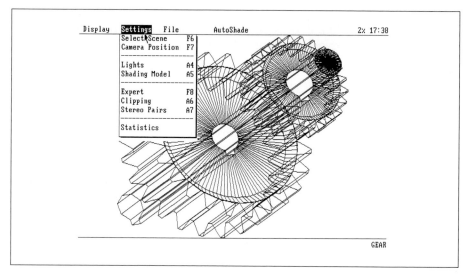

FIGURE 22.8: The Settings pull-down menu along with the wire-frame version of the AutoCAD gear drawing, as displayed by AutoShade. The user moved the small arrow pointer until it highlighted the Settings keyword in the top line of the display. Then, by pressing the pick button or the keyboard's Ins key, the user displayed the Settings pull-down menu. The Settings menu offers various options that will modify the shaded rendering.

Many of the more frequently used commands may be invoked by pressing a keyboard function key. If a command is activated by a function key, the key number appears to the right of the command in the pull-down menu display, preceded by the letter *F*.

You can invoke certain commands by pressing a function key while holding down the Alt key on the keyboard. When a command can be invoked in this fashion, the key number appears to the right of the command name in the pull-down menu, preceded by the letter *A*.

Loading the Filmroll File

The first step after entering AutoShade is to open and load a filmroll file. To do so, press the F10 function key, or select the File pull-down menu followed by the Open option. AutoShade prompts you for the name of the filmroll file to open from a list of files that it finds. Use the arrow pointer to highlight the small box to the left of the file name, and press the pick button to select it. After selecting the file name, move the arrow pointer out of the small box, and either pick the OK box near the bottom of the file list, or press Enter.

AutoShade then reads the entire filmroll file, and when complete, prompts you to select a scene from a list of scene names that it finds in the filmroll file. Use the same technique for selecting the scene name as you used to select the file name.

Displaying the Wire-Frame Image

After you have selected the scene, you may produce a wire-frame image in AutoShade that is similar to the image produced in AutoCAD. You can use this image to be certain that the viewing angle is correct. To produce an AutoShade wire-frame image, pick the Display menu followed by the Wire Frame option, or press the F2 function key. AutoShade takes some time to process the scene (depending on the complexity of the drawing), and then displays the wire-frame image.

Moving the Camera

If the viewing angle in AutoShade is not exactly correct, you can adjust the position of the camera. To do so, pick the Settings menu followed by the Camera Position option, or press the F7 function key. You will see a dialog box that allows you to change the orientation of the camera.

The Camera Position options (Angle from X in X-Y plane, Angle up from X-Y plane, Distance, and Twist degrees) are analogous to the Camera, Distance, and Twist options of AutoCAD's Dview command (see Chapter 11). Unfortunately, there is no feature in AutoShade that allows you to rotate a preview image on the screen to see the final result, as you can using Dview.

To change the camera position in AutoShade, highlight the current angle values with the arrow pointer, and enter the new values for the relative position of the camera. The "Angle from X in X-Y plane" option rotates the camera around the target point, parallel to the X-Y plane. The "Angle up from X-Y plane" option rotates the camera around the target point, perpendicular to the X-Y plane.

The Distance option indicates the distance in drawing units between the camera's location point and target point. The "Twist degrees" option rotates the display, using the line between the camera and the target as the axis of rotation.

The "Lens length" option is analogous to AutoCAD's Dview Zoom option, allowing you to display the drawing closer (showing fewer entities) or farther away (including more entities) while in perspective view. The description of the Dview command in Chapter 11 offers a more detailed explanation of how these options affect the display of 3-D entities.

Adjusting the Lights

You can effect a considerable degree of difference in the relative shading of various surfaces in the drawing by changing the intensity of the different light sources relative to each other. To change the light intensity, pick the Settings menu followed by the Lights option, or hold down the Alt key and press the F4 function key.

AutoShade will display a menu of the various lights available in the current scene and the relative intensity of each. The intensity value normally defaults to 1, indicating that they are all shining at equal intensity.

Bear in mind that the light values are relative only to each other. You can increase or decrease the intensity of light sources only in relation to the intensity of the other light sources in the scene. In other words, setting a light intensity to 100 will not make it 100 times brighter, but only 100 times brighter than those lights with an intensity value of 1. Setting one light to 100 and the other lights to 50 would have the same effect as setting the light intensity to 2 while the others remained at 1.

Testing the Results

Shaded renderings take time to produce—anywhere from several minutes to an hour or more, depending on the complexity of the drawing and your hardware configuration. However, AutoShade provides a means to preview the shaded drawing, albeit in an inexact form, before starting the actual full shading process: Fast Shade. You may invoke it by picking the Display menu followed by the Fast Shade option, or by pressing the F3 function key. AutoShade then computes a quick version of the final shaded drawing. You may use this version to be certain that light intensities and camera positions are correct before creating the final full shaded rendering.

Producing the Shaded Image

Once you are sure that all the settings for the current scene are as you desire, you may produce the final shaded image. You may choose to have the image displayed on the screen, directed to your hard-copy output device, or directed to a file on disk for faster redisplay later.

To produce the shaded image on the display screen, pick the Display menu and select the Full Shade option, or press the F4 function key. AutoShade begins processing the scene, and when complete, displays the final shaded image.

To produce the shaded image on a hard-copy output device, pick the Display menu followed by the Hard Copy option (or hold down the Alt key and press the F2 function key), and then invoke the Full Shade command (or press the F4 function key).

To produce the shaded image in a disk file (called a *rendering file*), pick the Display menu followed by the Record option (or hold down the Alt key and press the F3 function key). When you next invoke a full or fast shade, AutoShade will prompt you for a file name. (Be careful when entering file names. If a file of the same name already exists on the disk, AutoShade will overwrite it without warning.) When finished, turn the Record command off. You may redisplay the shaded image recorded on a disk file by using the Replay command. This command prompts you for a file name and replays the shaded rendering stored in the file.

To end an AutoShade session, pick the File menu and select the Quit option, and you will be returned to the operating-system prompt.

Summary of Other Command Options

AutoShade provides a number of other options. Depending on your application and needs, several of these may be useful to you; others you may never use. They are summarized in this section.

THE DISPLAY MENU

In addition to the options already mentioned, the following options are available from the Display pull-down menu:

Plan View (F5 Function Key)   Displays a plan view of the scene, similar to the plan view you might see in an AutoCAD drawing. Also displayed are the camera location, light locations (unless the light source has an intensity factor of zero or less), field of view as determined by the lens length (omitted if perspective mode is disabled), and direction of the viewing angle parallel to the X-Y plane.

Replay All   Replays all the rendering files in a particular directory, pausing for a specified number of seconds between each.

Make Slide   Creates an AutoCAD slide file of the wire-frame representation. The slide file can be viewed in AutoCAD Release 9 and later.

Make DXB   Writes a special binary-format Drawing Interchange (DXB) file, which can be imported into AutoCAD. The drawing stored in a DXB file is composed of simple line entities only, regardless of the original AutoCAD entities used to produce the drawing. One possible application of this feature is to explode blocks with different x and y scale factors and text. To use this feature:

1. Create the AutoShade scene and filmroll file in AutoCAD.
2. Load it into AutoShade and make the DXB file.
3. Return to AutoCAD.
4. Use the Dxbin command to load the drawing, now translated into individual line segments, back into the drawing editor.

THE SETTINGS MENU

The following options are available from the Settings pull-down menu:

Select Scene (F6 Function Key) Displays a list of scenes in the current filmroll file. You may choose a desired scene by highlighting it and pressing the pick button.

Shading Model (Alt-F5 Function Key) Displays a dialog box that controls the following factors:

- Ambient light factor: Increasing the value of this factor brightens all the objects equally.
- Diffuse factor: Increasing the value of this factor increases the amount of light reflected by surfaces, relative to the angle between the surface and the light source.
- Specular factor: This factor increases the amount of light that will be reflected in a narrow beam—that is, the way light from a single source is reflected on a mirrored or shiny reflective surface. The larger the specular factor, the brighter the mirrored light will be.

  Note: The combined total of the ambient, diffuse, and specular factors should be no more than 1.

- Specular exponent: Increasing this factor will cause the mirrored reflection of light to become narrower; in other words, the higher this number, the "shinier" the surface. However, as the surface becomes shinier, less light is reflected from the light sources positioned at an angle to it. If this figure is set too high, the surface may appear to vanish or turn to black, because no light at all is reflected from it.

- Inverse square: Setting this figure to a nonzero value will cause the light intensity to decrease as the square of the distance between the light source and the center of the surface.

- Linear lighting: Setting this figure to a nonzero value will also cause the light to decrease in intensity as the light source becomes farther from the center of the surface. In the case of linear lighting, the factor of decrease is an equal function of the distance, as opposed to the inverse square, in which light intensity decreases more rapidly as distance become greater.

- Inverse constant: This factor affects the amount of decrease in light intensity as a function of distance from the surface, when linear lighting has been set to a nonzero value. The higher this figure, the less contrast will be produced between shaded surfaces as the distance between the surfaces and the light source becomes greater.

- Background color: Selecting this option displays a list of optional background colors for fast-shaded and full-shaded renderings, from which you may select one.

- Stretch contrast: Selecting this option causes AutoShade to adjust the amount of contrast between the different surfaces in the drawing, so that they are displayed across the widest possible range of relative brightness. The dimmest surfaces in the drawing are displayed at the dimmest setting possible, the brightest surfaces are displayed at the brightest setting possible, and other surfaces are balanced out to degrees of brightness in between.

- Z shading: This option adjusts the degree of brightness of the light reflected from all surfaces as a function of their relative distance from the camera. The farther away the surface is from the light source, the less light is reflected. Z shading automatically uses an ambient light setting of 1, and ignores all other light settings.

- Black and white: Selecting this option causes the colors of the shaded rendering to be represented by a gray scale.

- Red, Green, and Blue component: Selecting these options turns on the indicated color component in color shadings. The default for all three is on. When these colors are off (not selected), the color component is shaded as black. To produce a single color separation, set only one component on and set the background color to black.

- B&W separations: You select this option when producing color separations using gray scales instead of actual hues, for later projection through a color filter.

Expert (F8 Function Key) Displays a dialog box that controls the following factors:

- Target X, Y, and Z: Use these boxes to enter specific x, y, and z coordinate locations for the viewing angle's target point. This is the only means by which you may change the target point in AutoShade.

- Camera X, Y, and Z: Use these boxes to enter specific x, y, and z coordinate locations for the viewing angle's camera location. This option is useful if you are sure of the exact coordinate location of the camera. Relative locations can be entered using the Camera Position option.

- Film diagonal: This option adjusts the diagonal length of the rectangle used as the current viewing plane in perspective views. Increasing or decreasing the size of the diagonal affects the angle of the line of sight around the edges of the drawing; this in turn may affect which entities become visible.

- mm/dwg unit: This option controls the ratio of AutoShade millimeters to AutoCAD drawing units. The default is 25.4, or 25.4 millimeters to 1 AutoCAD inch. If the value of integer 1 does not equal 1 inch in your units setting of AutoCAD, you may have to adjust this figure to indicate the number of millimeters equal to 1 AutoCAD drawing unit.

- Screen percent: This option sets the percentage of the screen display AutoShade uses to produce renderings. If it is set to 100, AutoShade automatically fills the screen. If it is less than 100, AutoShade fills the indicated percentage of the screen. If it is zero or less, AutoShade fills the screen as a function of the distance between the target and camera points.

- Sort roundoff: With this option, you set the minimum distance by which two surfaces must be separated before AutoShade computes which is behind the other in the current viewing angle. A larger number may speed up the shading process, but at a potential loss of accuracy. Conversely, a smaller figure will slow the process, but may be required for finely rendered drawings. Although there are no upper and lower limits that you can enter, setting values lower than 0.00000001 will have no effect, since AutoShade recognizes a maximum of eight decimal places of precision.

- Chop roundoff: This option sets the minimum value by which two surfaces must intersect before they are chopped (i.e., processed as nonintersecting triangular planes). The figure is only used when intersection mode is enabled. Lower figures will increase rendering accuracy but will also significantly increase rendering time.

- Discard back faces: When selected, this option instructs AutoShade to eliminate back faces in rendering the drawing. AutoShade will process all surfaces whose vertices are entered in a clockwise order as back faces, and surfaces whose vertices are entered in the opposite direction as front faces. Therefore, in order for AutoShade to use this setting, all faces in the drawing must be created in a consistent manner. Discarding back faces saves rendering time, but requires manual entry of all surfaces in the drawing. Surfaces created by extrusion, wide polylines, meshes, and other automated generation commands are not created in a consistent manner, and drawings using these entities may not be processed properly if this option is selected.

- Back face is negative: When set, this option reverses the order in which the vertices of a surface are read in order for that surface to be considered a back face. (Refer to the "Discard back faces" option for details.)

- Intersection: When selected, this option sets intersection mode on. When intersection mode is active, if two surfaces intersect (pass through) each other, they are recalculated as separate surfaces that touch. This produces a more accurate rendered drawing. This also adds to the amount of time required to produce the AutoShade image, and thus should only be selected if your drawing contains intersecting faces. (Faces that merely touch are not intersecting faces, and setting this option has no effect on them.) As an alternative, you may consider reediting the AutoCAD drawing to eliminate faces that pass through one another.

- Perspective: When selected, this option activates perspective mode. This is the default state. Perspective mode simulates how objects are viewed in the real world; that is, those that are closer to the camera appear larger, and those farther from the camera appear smaller. When perspective mode is off, 3-D objects are rendered using parallel projection, the way AutoCAD normally displays 3-D drawings.

Clipping (Alt-F6 Function Key)   Displays a dialog box that controls various clipping options. Clipping controls the amount of the drawing that will be visible in perspective views. AutoShade automatically calculates various clipping values based on the distance between target and camera, and on the lens length of the camera in millimeters. If you like, you can adjust one or more *clipping planes* to hide portions of the drawing in perspective views. Following are the available options for clipping:

- Left clip: Activates the left clipping plane, which is parallel to the viewing angle on the left side, as viewed from the camera.

- Left clip X: Indicates the relative distance of the left clipping plane from the viewing-angle line. Decreasing this value will bring the left clipping plane closer to the viewing-angle line, cutting off portions of the drawing on the left side. This figure is not used unless the "Left clip" option is selected.
- Right clip: Activates the right clipping plane, which is parallel to the viewing angle on the right side, as viewed from the camera.
- Right clip X: Indicates the relative position of the right clipping plane to the viewing angle. As with the left clipping plane, decreasing this value will bring the plane closer to the viewing angle, cutting off portions of the drawing on the right side. This figure is not used unless the "Right clip" option is selected.
- Top clip: Activates the top clipping plane, which is parallel to and above the viewing angle, as viewed from the camera.
- Top clip Y: Indicates the relative position of the top clipping plane. Decreasing this value lowers the vertical position of this plane, cutting off the upper portions of the drawing. This figure is not used unless the "Top clip" option is selected.
- Bottom clip: Activates the bottom clipping plane, which is parallel to and below the viewing angle, as viewed from the camera.
- Bottom clip Y: Indicates the relative position of the bottom clipping plane. Decreasing the value raises the vertical position of this plane, cutting off the lower portions of the drawing. This figure is not used unless the "Bottom clip" option is selected.
- Front clip: Activates the front clipping plane, which is perpendicular to the viewing angle between the target point and the camera.
- Front clip Z: Indicates the relative position of the front clipping plane. Decreasing this value moves the clipping plane closer to the target point, cutting off the portions of the drawing between the camera and the plane. This figure is not used unless the "Front clip" option is selected, or if the Clip at Camera option is selected.

  Tip: If portions of the drawing are located behind the camera-location point, it is possible to increase the front clip Z value to a point where it is positioned behind the camera-location point, at which time portions of the drawing behind the camera will become visible. Since this is a physical impossibility, the resulting renderings are likely to be peculiar. Therefore, if the camera is positioned within the entities of a drawing, do not set the front clipping plane to a value greater than the distance, unless strange results are your intention.

- Back clip: Activates the back clipping plane, which is perpendicular to the viewing angle between the target point and that portion of the drawing farthest from the camera.
- Back clip Z: Indicates the relative position of the back clipping plane. Decreasing this value moves the clipping plane closer to the target, cutting off the back portions of the drawing, and leaving visible those portions between the clipping plane and the target point. This figure is not used unless the "Back clip" option is selected.
- Clip at camera: Keeps the front clipping plane at the camera point at all times. The plane will follow the camera when its position is changed. When this option is active, the "Front clip" option is automatically disabled.

Stereo Pairs (Alt-F7 Function Key)   Displays a dialog box for rendering images that can be displayed or viewed stereoptically. The following options are given:

- Left view: Renders the left-eye half of a stereo pair.
- Right view: Renders the right-eye half of a stereo pair. If you select both left view and right view, the two images are rendered side by side.
- Stereoscope: Renders images suitable for viewing with a stereoscope.
- Crossed eye: Renders images that can be viewed by cross-eye fusion technique.
- Interocular angle: Controls the angle of stereo spacing between the two images. A larger value will exaggerate the stereo effect, but too large a value will cause double images, and the stereo effect will be lost. The default is four, which is the normal angle required to visualize the third dimension at a distance of 1 meter.

Statistics   Displays a dialog box showing the number of separate surfaces, triangles used in the rendering process, overlapping faces, and triangles chopped (if intersection mode was on), as well as the drawing extents. The number of triangles is important because AutoShade can render a maximum of 65534 triangles. This statistic will allow you to make a rough estimate of the amount of additional detail you will be able to include in your drawing, or whether you should edit out some detail and reduce the drawing's size. The drawing extents can help you determine the correct placement for clipping planes, the camera distance, and the target point.

THE FILE MENU

The following additional option is available from the File pull-down menu:

Script   Loads and executes a script file, which is an ASCII file containing AutoShade commands. Script files are constructed as follows:

- Each AutoShade command occupies its own line in the file, with no line longer that 60 characters.
- Each command must begin at the leftmost column of the line.
- Commands are not case-sensitive. They may be entered with either uppercase or lowercase characters.
- AutoShade reads the file line by line and executes the commands in sequence. Blank lines are ignored.
- You can include comment lines in AutoShade script files by placing them on a separate line starting with a period (.) or a space.

The following commands are valid within a script file:

CAMERA   Moves the camera to a new position. This command is followed by a 3-D coordinate point expressed as three numbers separated by commas. Example:

    CAMERA 23,23,5.5

moves the target to point 23,23,5.5

DELAY   Causes AutoShade to pause for the number of seconds indicated. Example:

    DELAY 5

pauses 5 seconds.

DISTANCE   Changes the distance between the camera and the target point. Example:

    DISTANCE 25.75

changes the distance to 25.75 drawing units.

DXB   Creates an AutoCAD DXB file of the wire-frame image, using the specified file name. Example:

    DXB WIREFILE

creates a DXB file named WIREFILE.DXB on the currently logged subdirectory.

FASTSHADE Performs a fast shade. If the Hardcopy or Record command has been issued, an optional file name may be supplied after this command. If no file name is supplied, AutoShade will display a dialog box and wait for you to enter a file name before continuing. Example:

FASTSHADE C:\ACAD\RENDFILE

produces a rendering file named RENDFILE.RND on the ACAD subdirectory.

FULLSHADE Performs a full shade. The syntax rules are the same as for the FASTSHADE command.

LENS Changes the size of the camera lens. Example:

LENS 35

changes to a 35-millimeter camera lens.

OPEN Loads a new filmroll file. Example:

OPEN GEAR

loads a file named GEAR.FLM.

PERSPECTIVE Enables/disables perspective view mode. Example:

PERSPECTIVE ON

enables perspective viewing.

QUIT Ends the AutoShade session.

RECORD Enables/disables recording mode for creating a rendering file on disk. (The file name is specified as part of the Fastshade or Fullshade command.) Example:

RECORD ON

enables recording.

REPLAY Replays a previously recorded rendering file. Example:

REPLAY GEAR

replays a file named GEAR.RND.

REWIND Causes AutoShade to repeat the script file from the beginning.

SCENE Selects a scene name from the current filmroll file.

SCONTRAST Enables/disables stretch contrast mode. Example:

SCONTRAST ON

enables stretch contrast mode.

SLIDE Creates an AutoCAD slide file with a given file name. Example:

SLIDE GEAR

creates a slide file named GEAR.SLD.

SPERCENT Changes the value of the screen percent figure. Example:

SPERCENT 90

changes the amount of the screen used by AutoShade to 90 percent.

TARGET Moves the target to a new position. This command is followed by a 3-D coordinate point expressed as three numbers separated by commas. Example:

TARGET 0,0,0

moves the target point to 0,0,0.

TWIST Changes the twist angle of the camera, specified in degrees. Example:

TWIST 45

changes the twist angle to 45 degrees.

A SAMPLE SCRIPT FILE

The following is an example of a script file that loads the filmroll file GEAR.FLM, adjusts the camera position, turns off perspective mode, and performs a fast shade:

OPEN GEAR
SCENE GEAR
PERSPECTIVE OFF
CAMERA 45,45,16
TARGET 23,23,1.75
FASTSHADE

OTHER ADD-ON SOFTWARE

The following list will give you an idea of the different kinds of add-on software that are available for use with AutoCAD. Space does not permit inclusion of all of the hundreds of add-on software products that are available, nor is inclusion on this list intended as an endorsement of the product. For further information, or to determine the suitability of any product for your particular purposes, consult the manufacturer or your dealer.

Animation

Animator
3-D Studio
Autodesk, Inc.
Multimedia Division
2320 Marinship Way
Sausalito, CA 94965
800/445-5415

Animator is a software package that allows you to create objects and produce images from them—including such features as surface shading, fore- and background motion, tweening, lighting, and other animate properties—all in an intuitive and inexpensive environment.

3-D Studio is a sophisticated 3-D modeling, rendering, materials editing, and animation package for 80386- and 80486-based desktop computers. The package includes closed links to AutoCAD and Animator.

Architecture

Auto-Architect
Cadcraft, Inc.
323 Boston Post Road
Old Saybrook, CT 06475

Auto-Architect is a set of custom tablet and screen menus, symbol libraries, and AutoLISP programs that allow the user to create electrical plans, site plans, plumbing layouts, and reflected ceilings. It also includes bidirectional 2-D/3-D symbol conversion, elevations, and section views, along with a schedule generator, calculator, and text editor.

Cadplus Architectural Clipart
Cadplus Products
P.O. Box 30167
Albuquerque, NM 87190-0167

Cadplus Clipart is a library of ready-to-use finishing details, such as trees, vehicles, and people for adding realism to your plan and elevation drawings.

Civil Engineering

CivilCAD
Civilsoft, Inc.
1592 N. Batavia Street, #1A
Orange, CA   92667

CivilCAD is a design program for civil engineers and surveyors. It includes COGO commands for mapping, street and highway geometrics, 2-D and 3-D contour maps, and automatic computation and display of cross-sections and alignments across terrain.

DCA Engineering Software
P.O. Box 955
Henniker, NH   03242

DCA Engineering Software provides a complete set of modular custom AutoCAD interfaces for contour generation, terrain modeling, site development, and surveying applications, among others. Modules are designed to work together, all accessible from within AutoCAD.

Facilities Management

Archibus Facilities & Space Management
Jung/Brannen Research & Development Corp.
177 Milk Street
Boston, MA 02109

Archibus FM Space Management is a software package than enables the AutoCAD operator to optimize use of interior space. It includes tools for managing inventory, forecasting, planning, and layout.

Ecat LAN Documentation
Cable Technology Group
5 Chapel Street
Newton, MA 02160

Ecat LAN software documents local-area network cabling. The program includes a library of data communication symbols and tools for charting a LAN in AutoCAD.

Mechanical Engineering

ANSYS-PC Products
Swanson Analysis Systems, Inc.
P.O. Box 65
Houston, PA 15342-0065

ANSYS-PC is a finite-element analysis program for structural, thermal, magnetic, and fluid applications.

Mechanical Engineering Workbench
ICONNEX Corp.
1501 Reedsdale Street
Pittsburgh, PA 15233

MEW is modeling software that enables the AutoCAD operator to design and analyze mechanical prototypes.

Fasteners and Holes
VEC-Metrics
P.O. Box 387
Mound, MN 55364

Fasteners and Holes is a set of tools to draw both 2-D profile and 3-D wireframe models of screws, nuts, washers, and holes in ANSI and metric sizes.

EZ-CAM
Bridgeport Machines, Inc.
500 Lindley Street
Bridgeport, CT 06606

EZ-CAM creates NC Part programs for MILL/machining centers, TURN turning centers, and EDM wire electrical discharges machines, among others.

Electrical Engineering

AutoPCB
Cadisys Corporation
624 E. Evelyn Avenue
Sunnyvale, CA   94086

AutoPCB is a design system for printed circuit boards. It features automatic routing, interactive part placement and route editing, and a large component-part library.

Electrical Layout
APPA Business Computers
5864 Interface Drive
Ann Arbor, MI   48103

Electrical Layout is a customized digitizing-tablet template integrated with a custom menu, an extensive symbol library, and AutoLISP routines for electrical-layout design.

Piping

CADPIPE
Endeco Engineering, Ltd.
200 Carnegie Drive
St. Albert, Alberta, Canada T8N 5A7

CADPIPE is a modular, interactive piping-design system with custom menus for producing both single- and double-line drawings and hydraulic calculations.

Symbol Libraries

Digital Maps
American Digital Cartography
1000 W. Parkway Boulevard
Appleton, WI   54914

Digital Maps are AutoCAD-compatible aerial map drawings of the United States based on United States Geological Survey data.

CAD Technology Corporation
P.O. Box 4089
Indialantic, FL   32903

CAD Technology Corporation supplies a number of different symbol libraries, including mechanical parts, geometric tolerancing, and welding symbology.

Letterease
CAD Lettering Systems, Inc.
P.O. Box 832
Oldsmar, FL   34677

Letterease is a lettering system that uses blocks and AutoLISP to produce complex, precision fonts and lettering arrangements for logos and special effects. Custom letter and logo transfer into AutoCAD is available as well.

Utilities

Block Librarian
SoftSource
301 W. Holly
Bellingham, WA   98225

Block Librarian is a screen-based storage and retrieval system that helps you organize large numbers of AutoCAD blocks by displaying them and allowing you to select them from a graphic menu while inside AutoCAD's drawing editor.

Concurrent Plot
Digital Control Systems
5 Cabot Place
Stoughton, MA   02072

Concurrent Plot transmits AutoCAD plot files to the plotter as a background process while another program continues to function in the foreground.

Plotmanager
John Intorcio
4B Beacon Village
Burlington, MA 01803

Plotmanager is a plotting utility that enables the AutoCAD operator to view plots on screen, plot sections of drawings, convert PLT to DXF files, and perform screen dumps of plot files to printers.

Zoomit:2
Palisades Research
869 Via De La Paz
Pacific Palisades, CA   90272

Zoomit:2 simplifies management of AutoCAD's virtual-screen feature to allow zooms and pans while avoiding most regenerations of the drawing. A custom menu and tablet template of special zoom and pan commands is included.

APPENDICES

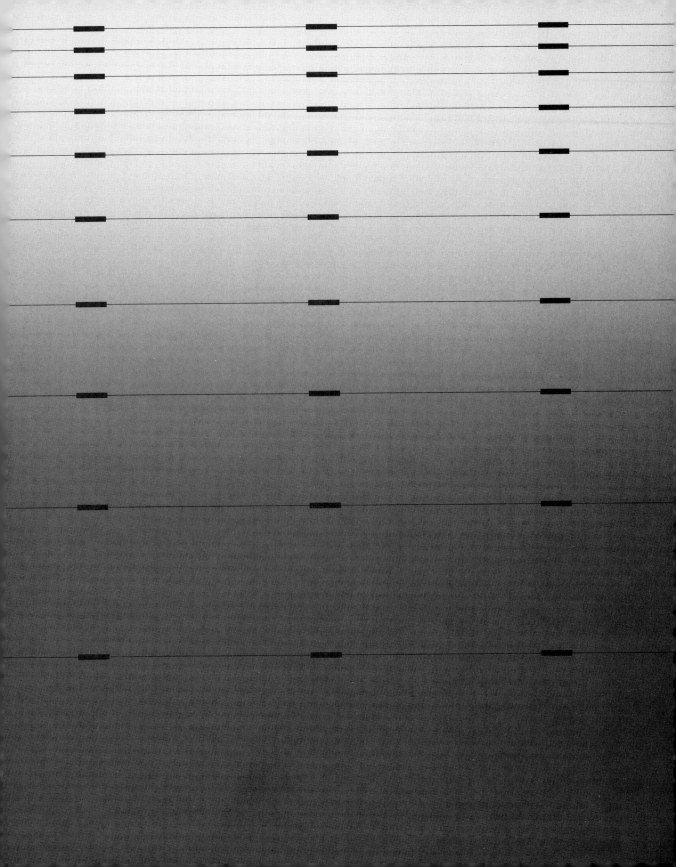

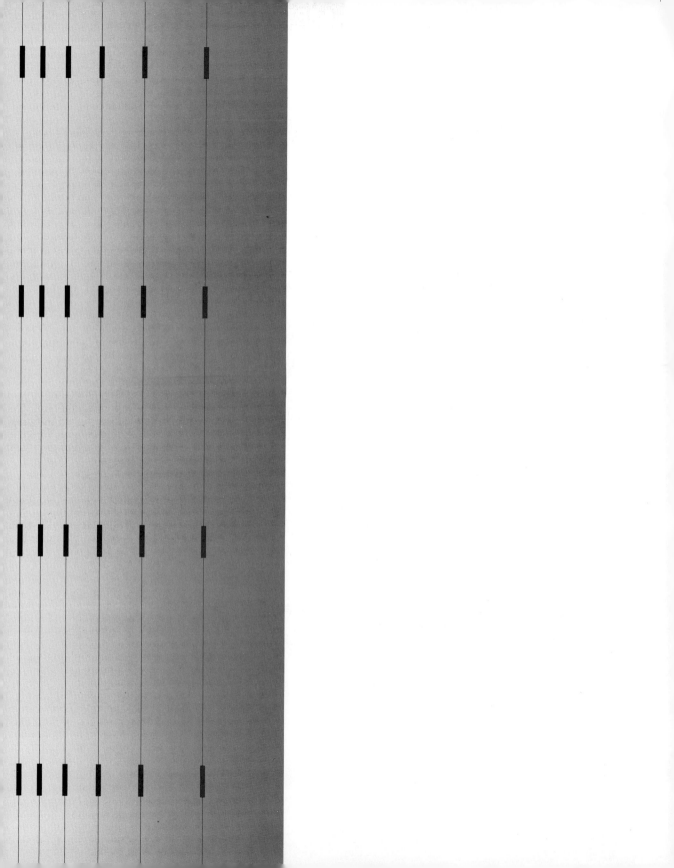

GLOSSARY OF AUTOCAD TERMS

Absolute coordinates   Coordinate points entered from the keyboard and preceded by an asterisk (*)

Access time   A measurement of the time required to pass data to and from the hard disk

ADI device interface   A generic device driver used by manufacturers of peripheral devices to make their hardware compatible with AutoCAD

Advanced User Interface   A special feature of some graphics drivers that allows for the display of pull-down menus, icon menus, and dialog boxes

Alphanumeric characters   The letters, numbers, and punctuation marks represented by ASCII codes

Aperture   A small rectangle surrounding the intersection of the crosshairs, used in finding entities by means of object snap

Arguments   The members of an AutoLISP function that the function operator processes

ASCII code   American Standard Code for Information Interchange, a standard set of numeric codes representing alphanumeric characters

ASCII file   A disk file (also known as a text file) containing only characters represented by ASCII code

Association list   A representation of AutoCAD's underlying database, containing a series of sublists, each consisting of a group code and its associated data

Atom list   The list of AutoLISP functions and symbols

Attributes   Special AutoCAD entities containing text-based information, contained in blocks

Audit trail   The list of AutoCAD commands and responses executed during a drawing session, used by AutoCAD to undo the effects of commands

AutoLISP file   ASCII file containing a sequence of AutoLISP functions that can be loaded into memory and executed by the AutoLISP interpreter

AutoLISP interpreter   An AutoCAD feature that reads and interprets functions written in AutoCAD's internal programming language

Bank switching   The process of assigning pointers in RAM to overlay files on disk, enabling software to run in smaller amounts of RAM than might otherwise be required

Base point   A point relative to which other points are assigned coordinate values and entities may be assigned locations

Bit-code   A special integer value that derives its meaning from the sum of valid integers to which it is found to be equal

Block   A set of drawing entities that may be treated as a single entity

Boundary edge   A line entity used as the outermost boundary to which another entity may be extended

Branching   An AutoLISP control structure used to make either/or decisions regarding which sequence of AutoLISP functions is to be evaluated, based on the results of evaluation of a special conditional expression

Buffer   A predefined amount of memory that is reserved to store data as it is sent from the computer to a peripheral device, usually a plotter or printer

Bulge arc   An arc calculated by applying a value of curvature to a straight line; used in shape-file definitions

Bulge factor   The amount of curvature, expressed as an integer from -127 to $+127$, applied to a straight line to produce an arc

Byte   A group of 8 data bits

Calibration   The process of factoring the x and y scales of a graphics input or output device to produce accurate representations of entities

Camera   The metaphorical term used to describe the source point of a viewing angle

Cartesian coordinate system A standard system of two or three infinitely long axes originating from the same point, which are subdivided into equally spaced segments and used to define coordinate locations of points in space

Central processing unit The microprocessor, RAM, and accompanying circuitry used to perform computerized processes

Character data A data type defined by its inability to serve as part of mathematical processes, used to represent information and concepts to the user

Chord The straight line, perpendicular to the line joining an arc's center and midpoint, that connects the arc's endpoints

Clipping planes Two special 3-D planes, perpendicular to the current construction plane, used to hide portions of a 3-D entity from view

Closed polyline A polyline whose endpoints are the same coordinate point

Command prompt The expression "Command:" displayed in the Command-prompt area, indicating AutoCAD's readiness to receive instructions

Command-prompt area The portion of the display screen that is used to display AutoCAD commands, prompts, and responses

Command sequence A series of commands, command options, or responses, treated as a whole

Comment lines Lines of text in AutoLISP files, preceded by a semicolon and thus ignored by the AutoLISP interpreter

Compiling The translation of ASCII code into code that can be processed by the microprocessor

Complex entity An AutoCAD drawing entity that, while composed of more than one fundamental drawing entity, can be selected and modified as if it were a single unit of graphic information

Concatenation The process of combining more than one string of character data into a single string

Conditional expression An AutoLISP expression whose result will determine the evaluation sequence of functions in an AutoLISP file

Constant   A memory variable whose value never changes

Construction plane   A 2-D plane, oriented in 3-D space, upon which AutoCAD entities are created

Control characters   Special character sequences that are meaningful to Auto-CAD as instructions

Control structures   AutoLISP functions that control the order, sequence, and frequency with which other AutoLISP functions are evaluated

Coordinate   A real number representing a point's relationship to an axis

CPU   *See* Central processing unit

Data bit   The smallest unit of information a computer can process

Data list   An AutoLISP expression consisting of a list of members that does not include a function operator

Debugging   The process of eliminating problems that interfere with an Auto-LISP routine's ability to achieve its intended results

Delimiter   A punctuation mark used to separate the fields in a single record in a database

Device driver   Special software used to make communication possible between AutoCAD and a peripheral device

Dialog box   A special display of command prompts, options, and defaults that appears in the graphics screen

Digitizer   A data-entry device, used as a substitute for the keyboard, that will point to AutoCAD commands as well as coordinate locations on the screen

Digitizing tablet   A flat, electrically sensitive surface that can be configured to respond as a command-entry and coordinate-selection device

Dimension variables   System variables that control the appearance and performance of dimension entities

Direction vector   An imaginary line in 3-D space that describes the relative location of two points

Disk   A magnetic, revolving surface used to store computerized data

Displacement   The amount of increment along each axis in a coordinate system; determines the relative distance and angle in space between two points

Displacement points   The two points used to define a displacement

Display device   A peripheral device consisting of a monitor and a graphics card, used to display graphic information to the user

Documentation   The instruction manuals and other printed explanatory material for hardware and software devices

DOS environment variable   A small portion of RAM that is set aside and given a specific name; a value of some sort, either a number or a character string, is associated with that name and thereby stored in RAM

Dotted pair   A special type of AutoLISP list containing two members and displayed with the members separated by a period

Downward compatibility   The ability of earlier versions of software to use data files created by later versions; for all intents and purposes, AutoCAD is not downwardly compatible

DPI   Dots per inch, a measure of the degree of resolution in dot-matrix and laser printers

Drawing Interchange file   A special file used to transfer AutoCAD's drawing-database information from one software program to another

Drawing unit   The fundamental length of a line segment that will be expressed in AutoCAD by the whole number 1

DXB   A special binary format for Drawing Interchange files; the file-name extension of disk files that use this format

DXF   An ASCII (or optional binary) format for Drawing Interchange files; the file-name extension of disk files that use this format

Elevation The degree to which an entity is positioned along the z-axis relative to the current construction plane

Endless loop A type of AutoLISP control structure in which a sequence of functions will repeat endlessly because a conditional expression cannot be evaluated to nil

Entity A fundamental unit of graphic information

Entity-association list *See* Association list

Entity handles Character-string representations of hexadecimal notation that are permanently associated with an individual drawing entity

Entity name A special data type consisting of an eight-digit number in hexadecimal notation, associated with a single drawing entity throughout an editing session

Entity reference point A special coordinate point that controls the behavior of an entity during the Stretch command

Environment variable *See* DOS environment variable

Expanded memory A form of random-access DOS memory that resides beside 640K and can be addressed by software, such as AutoCAD, that is programmed to recognize it

Extended AutoLISP A version of AutoLISP, available in AutoCAD Release 10, written to use DOS extended memory

Extended memory A form of random-access DOS memory that resides above 1024K and can be addressed by software, such as AutoCAD, that is programmed to recognize it

Extents The size of the drawing based on the entities it contains, rather than on any predefined limits of the drawing area

Extract files The disk files created by the Attext command

Field A fundamental unit of data stored within a record in a database file

File descriptor   An entity type that acts as a pointer to a disk file, keeping track of its physical location on the disk for data storage and access

Floating-point mathematics   Computer math that expresses numbers with any number of decimal places, up to a given limit, needed to express the number accurately

Fragmentation   A condition wherein disk files are broken apart and stored in discrete locations on the storage disk

Function   A list of data items that can be understood by AutoLISP as an instruction to perform a specific type of process and return the result of that process

Function operator   A symbol that appears as the first member of a function list, representing a command to evaluate the remaining data in some specific way

Fuzz factor   A real number that indicates the maximum allowable difference between the two arguments in order for them to be considered equal

Global variable   A memory variable whose value may be transferred between AutoLISP functions

Graphics card   An electronic device that controls the flow of data to and from the monitor

Group code   An integer that identifies the nature of data items stored in Auto-CAD's underlying database and displayed in DXF files and association lists

Handles   *See* Entity handles

Hard Disk   *See* Disk

Header line   The part of a shape, linetype, or hatch-pattern definition that contains information such as the name, size, and text-based description

Heap space   A preallocated portion of memory used to store the intermediate processing results of AutoLISP functions

Hexadecimal numbers   Numbers based on a counting system that cycles in groups of 16, as opposed to decimal numbers, which cycle in groups of 10

Icon   A standard graphic symbol that appears in the display but is not part of the drawing database

Icon menu   A display menu offering choices represented by drawings rather than text

IGES   Initial Graphics Exchange Standard, a standard format for exchanges of graphic information between different graphics programs, developed in 1979 under the direction of the National Bureau of Standards

Integers   Whole numbers within the range -32768 to $+32767$ on 16-bit workstations and $-2,147,483,648$ to $+2,147,483,647$ on 32-bit workstations

Interrupt   A code, sent to the CPU, that interrupts the currently executing task, performs a function, and returns control

I/O port   The part of the central processing unit to which a cable is attached, connecting it to a peripheral device

IPS   Inches per second, a means of measuring the pen speed of a pen plotter

Isoplane   A special configuration of snap points used as a tool for creating isometric drawings

Julian format   A special date format used to perform date mathematics in computers

Keyword   A special character string that is understood by AutoLISP as a particular instruction for optional processing

Kilobyte   1,024 bytes

Limits   A predefined portion of the drawing environment, indicating the area in which drawing entities may be placed. Limits are defined by opposite corners of a rectangle in the X-Y plane of the world coordinate system.

Limits-checking   An AutoCAD feature that prevents the placement of most drawing entities outside of the predefined drawing limits

Linetype   A repeating sequence of dashes, dots, and spaces, used to generate lines. AutoCAD defaults to the "continuous" linetype, a special type that consists of a single unbroken vector.

Linetype definition   A series of numbers used to represent the dashes, dots, and spaces in a linetype

Linetype library file   An ASCII file used to store linetype definitions

List   In AutoLISP, a series of data items enclosed within a set of parentheses

Loading   The process of transferring the data stored in files on disk into the computer's random-access memory

Local variables   Memory variables that retain data only while within a function that binds them to that data

Looping   A control structure that repeats a sequence of AutoLISP functions until a given condition is met

Macro   A sequence of commands, options, and responses that can be executed as a single command

Master disks   The original disks upon which a software program is shipped; used only to transfer the program to a computer

Megabyte   1,024,000 bytes

Member   An individual item of data within an AutoLISP data list

Memory node   A unit of RAM space used to hold AutoLISP data

Memory variable   A portion of RAM set aside under a predefined name, used for the temporary storage of data during processing

Menu bar   A special menu available on display devices that support the Advanced User Interface; overwrites the status line and becomes the source for pull-down menus

Menu processor   The part of the AutoCAD software that reads, compiles, displays, and executes AutoCAD menus

Menu section   A portion of the menu that contains generally related command sequences

Microprocessor A silicon chip containing electronic circuitry, used to perform computer processes

Millisecond One-thousandth of a second

Mirror line A temporary scratch line, not part of the drawing, that AutoCAD will use to determine the location and orientation of a reverse-image entity copy

Mouse An input device, consisting of a hand-held puck (along with a special underlying surface on some models), that, when moved on the desktop, causes movement of the cursor and the crosshairs on the display monitor

Named entity An entity that is accessible by means of a unique name, as opposed to coordinate point picks

Nested blocks Blocks that are included within other blocks

Nested functions AutoLISP functions whose results are used as arguments for other AutoLISP functions

Nil A symbol representing no data (null value, nothing at all)

Null attribute A block attribute that contains no data

Numeric coprocessor A special supplementary microprocessor that is used for floating-point mathematics

Numeric data A data type characterized by its ability to serve as part of a mathematical expression

Object snap A selection tool that permits you to find specific entity construction points quickly

Octant angle One of eight standard angles used in shape files, 45 degrees apart, beginning with angle zero

Octant arc A 45-degree arc used as a standard arc measurement in shape files

Offset arc A nonstandard arc in shape files, defined by its relationship to a standard octant arc

Open polyline A polyline whose endpoints are not closed with the Polyline Close option

Operating system The underlying software system used to manage the flow of data within the central processing unit

Origin The starting point for the axes in a Cartesian coordinate system, identified in AutoCAD as point 0,0,0

Ortho mode An AutoCAD feature that forces all lines to be drawn and entities moved parallel or perpendicular to the current orientation of the crosshairs

Osnap override An AutoCAD feature that forces a single point pick to the nearest user-specified entity construction point

Overwriting The process of replacing data on disk or in RAM with new data

Parallel communication A form of data transfer in which data is moved in groups of 8, 16, or 32 data bits, depending on the system

Path curve A polyline used to define the shape of a ruled surface or polygon mesh generated with the Revsurf or Tabsurf command

Pen-motion optimization An internal process that reduces unnecessary pen motion between entities when the pen is in the "up" position

Pen plotter A device for producing hard-copy output by moving a pen across a flat surface

Peripheral device Any external device connected to and controlled by the central processing unit

Pickbox A small rectangle that replaces the crosshairs on the screen and is used to select entities for editing

Pixel The smallest unit of visual information that the graphic device is capable of displaying

Plan view The viewing angle oriented parallel to the z-axis from a point above the X-Y plane

Plot   As a noun, any form of hard-copy output; as a verb, the process of producing hard-copy output

Plot file   Plotting instructions contained in a file on disk, created as an option using the Plot or Prplot command

Plot origin   The point used by the plotter as a base point, relative to which it will locate drawing entities

Plotter   *See* Pen plotter

Point filter   An optional response to coordinate-point entry prompts that limits picked points to specific x, y, and/or z coordinates, after which the remaining coordinates are supplied separately

Polar coordinates   Coordinate points identified by their relationship to other points, as a function of angle and distance in space

Polygon mesh   A matrix of crisscrossing lines that define a surface

Polyline   A special line composed of one or more straight and/or curved line segments that are treated as a single drawing entity

Printer plotter   A printing device capable of graphic output

Prompt   A message from AutoCAD suggesting responses or commands

Protected mode   A special state that allows the 80286 and 80386 microprocessors to access RAM found between 1 megabyte and 16 megabytes

Prototype drawing   A collection of drawing defaults stored as a drawing file and used by AutoCAD as the starting configuration for new drawings

Pseudocode   A plain-English version of an AutoLISP function sequence, used as a design and debugging tool

Pull-down menu   A special menu available under graphics displays that support the Advanced User Interface; displays temporary menus of AutoCAD commands that appear within the graphics screen

Radians   A system of angle measurements based on the value of pi, used as the angle-measurement system in AutoLISP

RAM   *See* Random-access memory

RAM disk   A portion of random-access memory that is set aside and configured so as to appear to the operating system as a data-storage disk

Random-access memory   The part of the central processing unit where data is temporarily stored and changed during processing

Read-only   A state in which data may not be overwritten, but may be transferred to other areas of the central processing unit

Real number   A number whose expression includes a decimal portion

Record   A collection of individual data fields that is treated as a unit within a database

Regeneration   The process of scanning the entire drawing database and calculating the correct screen display for the current viewport

Resolution   The measurement of the accuracy with which output and display devices produce drawing entities

Result   The data that is returned to the AutoLISP interpreter by a function at the completion of its processing

Result Bit   A data bit, part of a single data byte, that is set to a value of either 0 or 1 depending on a Boolean evaluation of other bits that occupy the same position in other bytes

Root directory   The subdirectory that contains the first level of files on a disk, including the operating-system files and other subdirectories, and onto which the computer logs when it is booted

Scale factor   A number used as a multiplier in producing entities such as dimensions and linetypes

Screen menu   A menu of AutoCAD commands and responses that appears on the monitor throughout the drawing session

Script file   An ASCII file containing a series of AutoCAD commands and responses that will be executed in sequence when loaded in memory using the Script command

Search path   A list of subdirectories used by AutoCAD to locate needed program and data files

Section label   A unique alphanumeric character string used by AutoCAD to identify menu sections in menu files

Selection set   A group of entities, selected by the user or by AutoLISP programs, that can be acted upon as a whole during processing

Serial communication   A form of data transfer in which data is sent bit by bit

Shape definition   A sequence of real numbers used by AutoCAD to define the lines, arcs, and circles that compose a shape or a text font

Shape   An AutoCAD entity inserted into a drawing, based on drawing instructions contained within a shape definition loaded into the drawing

Shape file   A series of shape descriptions in either ASCII or binary format

Signal elements   Special numbers in a shape definition that change the meaning of the numbers that follow

Simple entity   An AutoCAD drawing entity that is itself an irreducible unit of graphic information

Sketch line   A series of very small line or polyline segments generated using the Sketch command

Slide file   A bit-mapped image of the graphics area of the screen, which will be displayed faster than an AutoCAD drawing, but which cannot be edited

Slide library   A collection of slide files within a single disk file

Slider   A special AutoCAD entry device used during the Dview command to enter relative values

Stack space   A predefined portion of memory used to store AutoLISP memory variables and their values, user-defined functions, and character strings

Status line   The top line of the drawing display, containing information such as the current drawing layer and the coordinate location of the crosshairs

Storage capacity The maximum amount of data, measured in bytes, that a disk can hold

String A sequence of alphanumeric characters, surrounded by quotation marks, that are treated as a unit of data during processing

Subdirectory A name under which selected data files on the disk can be grouped together

Sublist A nested AutoLISP data list used as a member of another data list

Submenu A smaller portion of an AutoCAD menu section, headed by a sub-menu label, and containing a list of command sequences that can replace other command sequences in the area of the menu controlled by that menu section

Subshape A shape description nested within another shape description

Symbol A general term used to describe a string of alphanumeric characters that stands for something else

Symbol table The part of the underlying drawing database used to store drawing-environment default data

Syntax The rules for arranging functions into a working sequence

System variables Special memory variables that determine environment parameters inside the AutoCAD drawing editor

Tag The unchanging block-attribute name to which attribute values are bound

Target The metaphorical term that describes the point toward which a viewing angle is directed

Template file An ASCII file used to delineate the fields found in each record of block attributes output to an extract file

Temporary work files Temporary files on disk that store intermediate data used by AutoCAD during an editing session

Text display The part of the screen display that shows text-based information

Text-font files   Special shape files that contain shape definitions of alphanumeric characters, used to draw text

Thickness   The degree of extrusion, parallel to the z-axis, that is applied to a drawing entity

Transparent command   A command that is capable of temporarily interrupting another command, and returning to that command at the point of interruption when it has completed its processing

UCS   *See* User coordinate system

Upward compatibility   The ability of later versions of software to use data files created by earlier versions; AutoCAD is an upwardly compatible program

User coordinate system (UCS)   A plane that can be oriented at any location within the world coordinate system; once a UCS is established, drawing entities may be created based on coordinate points found within that UCS

User coordinate system icon   A symbol that appears in the graphics display area, indicating the orientation of the current user coordinate system

Value   Data that is bound to a variable name

Variable name   An unchanging alphanumeric sequence that can be bound to different values during processing

Vectors   Point locations defined as relative to other point locations within a coordinate system

Vertex marker   A small *x* symbol that appears at a vertex of a polyline or mesh, indicating that the vertex may be edited individually using one of the displayed options

Viewing angle   A direction vector defined by a camera and target point, along which an AutoCAD drawing may be displayed

Viewport   A combination of viewing angle and magnification, resulting in a display using all or a portion of the graphics screen area

Virtual memory   A portion of a hard disk or RAM disk used as temporary storage of currently unneeded parts of the software program in use

Virtual screen   A set of coordinate points that define an area of the drawing capable of being redrawn using integer mathematics, thus avoiding a more time-consuming regeneration

WCS   *See* World coordinate system

Wire frame   A representation of 3-D drawing entities formed from outlines only, resulting in a transparent effect

World coordinate system   The fundamental, unchanging coordinate system formed by fixed Cartesian x-, y-, and z-axes, relative to which all other coordinate systems are oriented

X-axis   The axis that, when displayed in plan view, increments coordinates horizontally and to the right

X-Y plane   The drawing plane formed by the x- and y-axes

X-Z plane   The drawing plane formed by the x- and z-axes

Y-axis   The axis that, when displayed in plan view, increments coordinates vertically and toward the top of the display

Y-Z plane   The drawing plane formed by the y- and z-axes

Z-axis   The axis that, when displayed in plan view, increments coordinates from the origin point outward toward the user

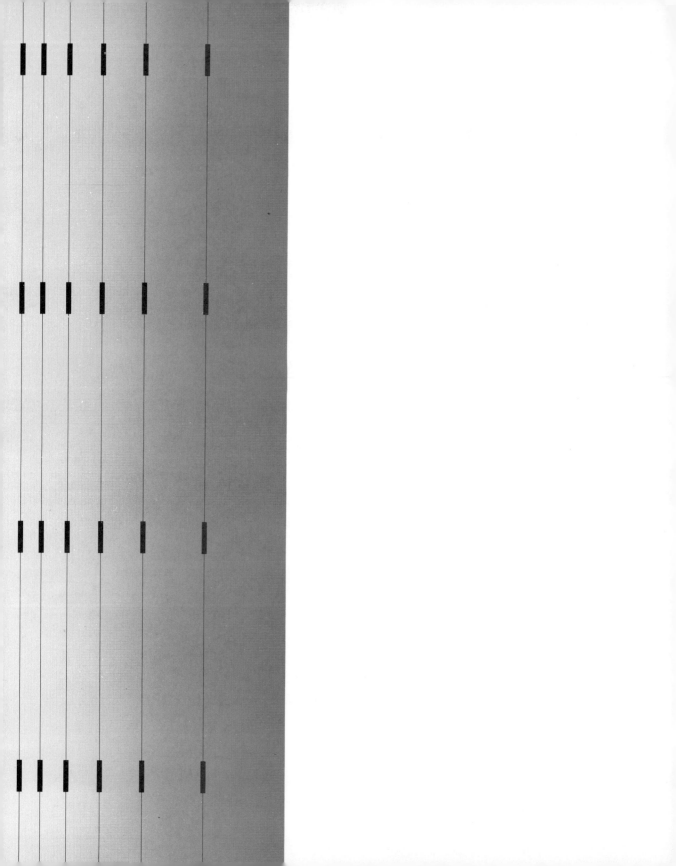

ERRORS AND TROUBLESHOOTING

The following is a list of error messages that can appear in the AutoCAD drawing editor, and responses you may make to them. Many of these error messages will appear in a variety of commands. Where the error message or response references a particular command, the number of the chapter in this text covering the command is given.

ACAD cannot be run as a child process of itself   You have attempted to initialize AutoCAD from the Shell. Type EXIT at the command prompt to return to AutoCAD (Chapter 7).

A color number or standard color name is required.   AutoCAD expects a standard color name (Red, White, Blue, etc.) or a color number in the range 0 to 255 (Chapter 5).

All segments already undone.   Within the PLine or 3Dpoly command, you have undone all the previous line segments entered since the currently active command was invoked (Chapter 9).

Ambiguous response, please clarify...   You have selected a command-option letter that applies to more than one available command option. Reenter the option letter followed by one or more additional letters, which will identify the correct option keyword.

Angle must be in range   Within the Dview command, you have attempted to enter a rotation angle that is out of the required range. Reenter a rotation angle within the indicated range (Chapter 11).

Array expansion terminated.   The Array command was canceled while the array was being generated. The remaining elements in the array are lost. Erase the existing portion of the array and start over (Chapter 10).

Bad control string/nesting/type code in extended entity data.   You have attempted to add extended entity data with unbalanced group codes 1002, which contain opening and closing curled braces ({}) or have included invalid data in the extended data association list. Re-edit the association list (Chapter 19).

Beware, Z insertion base is not zero.   You are creating a block with an insertion point that is not located on the construction plane. This is legal, but subsequent insertions may be inaccurate, misleading, or difficult (Chapter 9).

Block not found   AutoCAD could not find the specified block name in the drawing or on disk. Check that the block name was entered correctly; also check the configuration of AutoCAD's search path (Chapter 5).

Cancel   Ctrl-C was pressed, or a command was selected from a standard menu while within another command. Double-check your input; if it is from a custom tablet menu, command boxes may be misaligned.

Cannot close until two or more segments drawn.   You have selected the Close option with only a single line or polyline segment on the screen. Draw another segment before closing (Chapters 8 and 9).

Cannot find block.   Within the Divide command, AutoCAD cannot locate the requested block. Check the spelling of the block name using the Insert ? command. First reference the desired block in the drawing by inserting and erasing it before invoking Divide.

Cannot modify an externally referenced layer.   You have attempted to edit an external reference drawing. All such edits are illegal (Chapter 21).

Can't open file. Enter another file name (or RETURN for none):   AutoCAD could not find the specified file name along its search path. Check that the file name was entered correctly. Also, check the current configuration of AutoCAD's search path (Chapter 5).

Command has been completely undone.   Within the Dim command, you have undone all the previous commands entered this session (Chapter 21). If attempting to undo a dimensioning command from a previous dimensioning session, you must exit to the AutoCAD Command prompt, and either continue with AutoCAD's standard Undo command (Chapter 6), or erase the dimensioning entities (Chapter 10).

Cannot find layer.   AutoCAD could not locate the layer requested for freezing or thawing, or for changing a default property. Use the Layer ? command to list current layers.

Cannot find UCS.   AutoCAD could not find the specified UCS in the drawing file. Check that the UCS name was entered correctly; also invoke the UCS ? command to check valid named user coordinate systems (Chapter 11).

Cannot find view.   AutoCAD could not find the specified view in the drawing file. Check that the view name was entered correctly; also invoke the View ? command to check valid view names (Chapter 11).

Cannot fillet polyline segments with non-polyline segments.   One of the two entities selected to fillet is a polyline. Use the Explode command (Chapter 10) to change the polyline to a line before attempting to fillet it.

Cannot freeze layer. It is the CURRENT layer.   You have chosen the current layer as one of the layers to freeze. Using the Layer Set command, set a different, thawed layer as current first.

Device (or digitizer) not responding.   AutoCAD cannot send or receive a signal from a peripheral hardware device. Check the cable connection, the settings for any DIP switches on the device, and the software configuration, especially for the correct communication port.

Duplicate Xdata Registered Application Id.   You have attempted to append extended entity data to an entity by using an application ID that is already appended. Change the application ID or modify the association list to merge the new data within the existing ID (Chapter 21).

Edge does not touch another edge.   Within the Edgesurf command, you have selected defining edges that do not intersect. Check the 3-D viewing angle to be certain that the chosen lines are capable of intersecting (Chapter 10). Use the Fillet command (with a radius of zero) or the Extend command to create intersections of the chosen lines (Chapter 11).

Entity does not intersect an edge.   Within the Trim command, the entity chosen to trim does not intersect any of the entities chosen as cutting edges. This often happens because of distortions produced by 3-D viewing angles. Adjust the 3-D viewing angle to gain a better perspective on the relative locations of the selected entities (Chapter 11).

Entity not usable to define ruled surface.   Within the Rulesurf command, you have attempted to select a path curve that is not a line or polyline. Only lines and polylines are allowed to define ruled surface path curves (Chapter 9).

Entity not usable to define surface patch.   Within the Edgesurf command, you have attempted to select a defining edge that is not a line or polyline. Only lines and polylines are allowed to define the edges of a surface patch (Chapter 9).

Entity selected is not a polyline. Do you want to turn it into one? <Y>   Within the PEdit command, AutoCAD has found a line entity rather than a polyline. If you answer **Y,** AutoCAD changes the entity to a polyline; if you answer **N,** Auto-CAD cancels the PEdit command (Chapter 11).

Everything has been undone.   Within the Dview command, AutoCAD indicates that all command options have been reversed, back until the time the command was invoked. If you are attempting to undo a command from a previous Dview session, you must exit to the AutoCAD Command prompt or cancel with Ctrl-C, and then either continue with AutoCAD's standard Undo command (Chapter 6) or edit the entities (Chapter 10).

FATAL ERROR   A variety of internal conditions can produce this error message; a disk-full condition is one common source. Most of the time, this message is followed by a short description of the problem, and this additional message:

> AutoCAD cannot continue, but any changes to your drawing made up to the start of the last command can be saved. Do you want to save your changes? <Y>

Answer **Y** if you want to save your changes, and AutoCAD will return you to the DOS prompt.

In most cases when this error occurs, AutoCAD also produces a file named ACAD.ERR on AutoCAD's system subdirectory, showing the problem that occurred, the date and time, and the name of the drawing that was active when the error occurred.

If the condition producing the error is not clear to you, contact your dealer. Include a copy or printout of ACAD.ERR if the file exists. Your dealer may then contact Autodesk Technical Support for assistance on your behalf.

Fillet requires 2 lines, arcs, or circles.   An entity was not found at one of the selection points used in the Fillet command, or two different types of entities were selected (Chapter 10). Reselect the entities. If necessary, adjust the 3-D viewing angle to plan view in order to choose the entities (Chapter 11).

Grid aspect ratio too ridiculous to display.   You have set the grid or snap aspects to extremely disproportionate values (for example, 100,000 to 0). Reset the aspect (Chapter 7).

Grid too dense to display   The current display will force the grid points to appear too close together, and thus will wash out portions of the drawing. Reset the grid or snap value to a lesser number (Chapter 6).

IGES input may be done only in a new drawing.   You have invoked the IGESIN command in a drawing containing drawing entities or nondefault environment variables. Instead, start a new drawing from the Main Menu, and include an equal sign (=) after the drawing-file name (Chapter 20).

Insufficient memory for command.   AutoCAD does not have enough free RAM to run the invoked command. Increase the value of the ACADFREERAM variable (Chapter 4).

INTERNAL ERROR   *See* FATAL ERROR.

Invalid   Input was unrecognizable to AutoCAD—for example, point or character-string input instead of numeric input, or entity names that include invalid characters such as semicolons, periods, or asterisks. This message is often accompanied by another error message. If not, review the input procedures for the command in question, or invoke the Help command followed by the command name.

Invalid anonymous block.   AutoCAD cannot create or insert an internal block entity required for processing. End the drawing session, re-enter the editor, and invoke the Purge command (Chapter 6).

Invalid block name.   A block name containing invalid characters was entered. If attempting to insert a block, use the Insert ? command to list currently referenced block names (Chapter 10).

Invalid file name   Invalid characters were used when inputting a disk-file name for a shape file, linetype file, file for saving the drawing, etc. Do not use the following when inputting file names: tilde (˜), caret (^), equal sign (=), plus sign (+), greater-than sign (>), less-than sign (<), semicolon (;), open square bracket ([), close square bracket (]), quotation mark (''), question mark (?), comma (,), or period (except to separate the file name from the extension).

Invalid layer name.   A wild = card chartacter was included in the layer name. Reenter the layer name, or invoke the Layer ? command to display a list of current layer names.

Invalid limits. The same point was entered for the minimum and maximum drawing limits, or 3-D points were used. Reenter two different 2-D points.

Invalid linetype name The requested linetype definition was not found in the indicated linetype file. Use the Linetype ? command to list the linetypes in the file, or enter a different file name (Chapter 6).

Invalid object snap modes. An unknown object-snap mode was entered. Use the Help Osnap command to display a list of valid object-snap overrides.

Invalid option keyword. AutoCAD has displayed a prompt indicating optional keyword responses, but has received a response not included among the valid options. Check the capitalized letters within the prompt (flipping to the text screen if necessary) and enter a valid response.

Invalid point. AutoCAD expected a coordinate point but received information that does not conform to a standard point-entry method. (See Chapter 5 for valid methods, or the individual command discussions for exceptions to the standard methods.) Also, this message may appear if a 3-D point was entered when Auto-CAD expected a 2-D point. Check your input and try again.

Invalid selection An incorrect response was given to the "Select objects:" prompt. AutoCAD expects a point, or one of the selection-option keywords (Chapter 5).

Invalid 2D point. AutoCAD was not able to recognize the point entry that was made. Check the input against the settings for the drawing units, and check whether a 3-D point rather than a 2-D point was input for circles, arcs, etc. To draw 2-D entities in three dimensions, first change the UCS (Chapter 8).

Invalid view name. You have entered a named view containing invalid characters. Check the view name using the VIEW ? command and try again (Chapter 6).

Invalid viewport configuration name. AutoCAD could not find the specified named viewport configuration in the drawing file. Check that the viewport name was entered correctly; also invoke the Vports ? command to check currently valid viewport-configuration names (Chapter 11). Listed viewport names beginning with an asterisk cannot be entered in response to the "Viewport Name:" prompt.

Invalid window specification.   AutoCAD expected a coordinate point for a corner of a selection window, but received information that does not conform to a standard point-entry method (Chapter 5). Check your input and try again.

*Linetype not found. Use **LINETYPE** command to load it.*   You have entered a linetype that AutoCAD cannot find either loaded in the drawing or in the file ACAD.LIN. Use the Linetype command to indicate to AutoCAD the file to search for the requested linetype.

Lines to be joined must be coplanar with polyline.   Within the PEdit Join command, you have attempted to join polylines that do not reside on the same construction plane. Adjust the 3-D viewing angle (Chapter 11), and redraw the polylines if necessary (Chapter 10).

Nil   This is sometimes returned by an AutoLISP expression used to respond to a Command prompt (Chapter 16). It is also returned when the exclamation point is entered at the Command prompt.

No changeable entity selected.   You have selected a block or other complex entity that cannot be edited with the Change command. Select a different entity (Chapter 10).

No driver is installed at interrupt vector.   You have not invoked the commands necessary to load your third-party peripheral driver prior to initializing Auto-CAD. Consult your driver documentation for the necessary loading command sequence.

No edge in that direction.   You have attempted to extend an entity, but Auto-CAD cannot find the selected boundary edge, possibly because the line and edge do not exist in the same plane in 3-D space. Adjust the viewing angle if necessary or select or draw a different boundary edge. (Chapter 10).

No line or arc to continue.   You have pressed Enter in response to the starting point for a line or arc entity, and AutoCAD cannot find a previously entered line or arc. Enter a starting point instead.

No object found.   At the "Select objects:" prompt, where a single entity was expected, no entity was located at the indicated point. Check the 3-D viewing angle; then try again from another angle, or from plan view.

Not a block reference, polyline, mesh or dimension. The entity you have selected with the Explode command is not an explodable entity. Select a different entity, or cancel the command.

Not a new drawing—only ENTITIES section will be input. You have invoked the DXFIN command in a drawing containing drawing entities or nondefault environment variables. If you intend for the HEADER, TABLE, and BLOCK sections of the DXF file to be input, start a new drawing from the Main Menu, and include an equal sign (=) after the drawing-file name (Chapter 20).

Not a polyline. AutoCAD requires that the chosen entity be a polyline. Cancel the command, and convert the entity using the PEdit command (Chapter 11), or redraw it as a polyline (Chapter 10).

Nothing recorded. Within the Sketch command, no sketch lines were on the screen when the Exit option was selected. Reinvoke the command and start over (Chapter 21).

Object isn't that long. Within the Measure command, you have entered a segment value longer than the length, circumference, or perimeter of the selected entity. Enter a smaller value.

One-element array, nothing to do. You have indicated a rectangular array with both a single row and a single column. You must specify a value greater than 1 for at least the number of rows or the number of columns.

Out of disk space for swap file. The hard disk is full; AutoCAD cannot enlarge the temporary storage file for use as virtual memory. Erase some files on disk to increase available space or check for the presence of lost clusters with the DOS Chkdsk command.

Please correct adapter/configuration inconsistency. AutoCAD has attempted to load a peripheral-driver file that is different from the one for which it was configured. Check the setting of the ACADCFG variable (Chapter 4); reboot the computer if necessary.

Plotting area exceeds plotter maximum The scale entered for the plot will cause the plotted output to exceed the maximum plot size available. Only a portion of the drawing will be plotted. Cancel the plot with Ctrl-C and enter different scale factors.

Plotter not responding. *See* Device (or digitizer) not responding.

Point or option keyword required.   Invalid input has been made to a prompt for point information that also includes optional keywords. Refer to Chapter 5 for details on standard methods for coordinate point entry, or to the discussion of the individual command for exceptions to standard input methods. Check the uppercase letters in the prompt for valid keyword responses.

Radius is too large   The fillet radius is currently set for too large a value to fillet the chosen lines. Invoke the Fillet Radius command to adjust the value (Chapter 10).

Requires a distance, numberX, or option keyword.   An invalid response was entered for the Grid, Snap, or Axis command. Check your entry against the prompt and try again. Refer to the command discussions for details on valid input.

Requires an integer value.   A command requires a whole number in the range from − 32767 to + 32768 on 16-bit systems, or from − 2,147,483,648 to + 2,147,483,647 on 32-bit systems. Do not attempt to enter points, strings, decimal numbers, keywords, or other noninteger data.

Requires an integer value or an option keyword.   The command requires either a whole number or a special keyword listed as part of the prompt. Do not attempt to enter points, strings, decimal numbers, or other noninteger data.

Requires numeric angle or point.   AutoCAD has paused for angular information, but has received input that it cannot process as an angle. Enter an angle using any of AutoCAD's standard formats for angle data (Chapter 5).

Requires numeric radius, point on circumference, or "D".   Invalid radius information was entered for a center-radius circle. Reenter the radius, or if entering the diameter instead, enter **D.**

Requires numeric distance or second point (or two points).   A distance prompt is expecting a numeric distance, and unrecognizable data was entered. Check the data that was entered against the valid formats set with the Units command (Chapter 6), and if necessary, reinvoke the command and show AutoCAD the correct distance using the pointing device.

Requires numeric distance, second point, or option keyword.   A prompt is expecting a numeric distance or optional keyword, and unrecognizable data was entered. Check the keyword that was entered against the uppercase letters in the prompt. If a numeric distance was entered, check the format that was used against allowable formats under the current Units setting (Chapter 6). If necessary, reinvoke the command and show AutoCAD the distance by picking two points.

Selected entity is not a dimension. You have selected a non-associative dimension for processing with a command that requires an associative dimension. Redo the dimension as an associative type. Check the setting of the DIMASO system variable (Chapter 13).

The file '3d.lsp' was not found in your search path directories. Check installation of the Support Files and try again. You have attempted to draw a 3-D object while the file 3D.LSP could not be found. Check the location of the 3D.LSP file on your hard disk. Copy it to the same subdirectory as the AutoCAD system files. If it is not currently on your hard disk, you may copy it from the Support Files master disk.

The PURGE command cannot be used now. Prior to Release 10, this means that you have invoked the Purge command after another command has been invoked. As of Release 10, it means you have invoked the Purge command after the drawing database has been changed. In either case, invoke the End or Quit command, thus ending the drawing session, and then return and reinvoke the Purge command.

This will undo everything. OK? < Y > You have selected the Undo Back command, and AutoCAD is warning you that the command will undo all processing back to the start of the current drawing session. If this is what you want, enter **Y** (Chapter 6).

2D point or option keyword required. You have attempted to enter a 3-D point in response to a prompt that requires a 2-D point, or you have invoked a subcommand keyword that is not recognizable to AutoCAD from the current prompt. The original prompt will repeat. Enter a 2-D point instead of a 3-D point, or reread the prompt to determine what subcommand keywords are currently valid. If necessary, review the command descriptions in this book to determine how to enter the required keyword.

Type EXIT to return to AutoCAD. Within the Shell or SH command, AutoCAD is indicating that you are now in DOS. (You pressed Enter in response to the "DOS command:" prompt.) To return to the drawing editor, enter **Exit.**

Type EXIT to return to COMMAND prompt.   Within the Dim command, you have entered a command (perhaps a standard AutoCAD command) not recognizable during dimensioning. If the command was a standard AutoCAD command, enter **Exit** at the "Dim:" prompt and try the command again from the AutoCAD Command prompt (Chapter 21).

Unknown command.   AutoCAD expected input of a command name, but could not recognize the command that was entered. Type **?** or **Help,** and press Enter again for a list of valid commands. If you are attempting to enter a custom command, check the spelling, or reload the AutoLISP file (Chapter 16).

Unknown pattern name.   AutoCAD could not find the requested hatch pattern in ACAD.PAT. Check the spelling of the pattern name, or list the available patterns using the Hatch ? command (Chapter 21).

Unknown text style name. Use main STYLE command to create it.   Within the Dim, Text, or Dtext command, AutoCAD was not able to find the named text style—perhaps the style name was different from the font-file name. Check the name for correct spelling, using the Style ? command (Chapter 15).

Unknown variable name. Type SETVAR ? for a list of variables.   You have entered a system-variable name that AutoCAD does not recognize. Check the spelling or enter the Setvar ? command as suggested (Chapter 13).

Value must be positive.   You have entered a negative number or a hyphen. Reenter a positive number or zero.

Value must be positive and nonzero.   You have entered a negative number, a hyphen, or zero. Reenter a positive number.

View is not plan to UCS. Command results may not be obvious.   The current viewing angle is perpendicular (or nearly so) to the current construction plane, making point selection difficult to visualize; adjust the viewing angle or change the orientation of the UCS (Chapter 11).

Warning: negative plot origin   You have invoked the Plot or Prplot commands while specifying an origin point that will not fit onto the plotting surface. If necessary, cancel the command and change the plot parameters to reflect the desired result.

Yes or No, please.   AutoCAD accepts only **Y** or **N** as a response to the currently displayed prompt.

You must personalize AutoCAD before execution.   AutoCAD has lost its password and user ID records. Restore the software from backup; if necessary, reinstall AutoCAD.

INDEX

Selections from The SYBEX Library

CAD

The ABC's of AutoCAD (Second Edition)
Alan R. Miller
375pp. Ref. 584-0

This brief but effective introduction to AutoCAD quickly gets users drafting and designing with this complex CADD package. The essential operations and capabilities of AutoCAD are neatly detailed, using a proven, step-by-step method that is tailored to the results-oriented beginner.

The ABC's of AutoLISP
George Omura
300pp. Ref. 620-0

This book is for users who want to unleash the full power of AutoCAD through the AutoLISP programming language. In non-technical terms, the reader is shown how to store point locations, create new commands, and manipulate coordinates and text. Packed with tips on common coding errors.

The ABC's of Generic CADD
Alan R. Miller
278pp. Ref. 608-1

This outstanding guide to computer-aided design and drafting with Generic CADD assumes no previous experience with computers or CADD. This book will have users doing useful CADD work in record time, including basic drawing with the keyboard or a mouse, erasing and unerasing, making a copy of drawings on your printer, adding text and organizing your drawings using layers.

Advanced Techniques in AutoCAD (Second Edition)
Robert M. Thomas
425pp. Ref. 593-X

Develop custom applications using screen menus, command macros, and AutoLISP programming—no prior programming experience required. Topics include customizing the AutoCAD environment, advanced data extraction techniques, and much more.

AutoCAD Desktop Companion SYBEX Ready Reference Series
Robert M. Thomas
1094pp. Ref. 590-5

This is a complete reference work covering all the features, commands, and user options available under AutoCAD Release 10, including drawing basic and complex entities, editing, displaying, printing, plotting, and customizing drawings, manipulating the drawing database, and AutoLISP programming. Through Release 10.

AutoCAD Instant Reference SYBEX Prompter Series
George Omura
390pp. Ref. 548-4, 4 3/4" × 8"

This pocket-sized reference is a quick guide to all AutoCAD features. Designed for easy use, all commands are organized with exact syntax, a brief description, options, tips, and references. Through Release 10.

Mastering AutoCAD (Third Edition)
George Omura
825pp. Ref. 574-3

Now in its third edition, this tutorial guide to computer-aided design and drafting with AutoCAD is perfect for newcomers to CADD, as well as AutoCAD users seeking greater proficiency. An architectural project serves as an example throughout. For Release 10.

Mastering VersaCAD
David Bassett-Parkins
450pp. Ref. 617-0

For every level of VCAD user, this comprehensive tutorial treats each phase of project design including drawing, modifying, grouping, and filing. The reader will also learn VCAD project management and many tips, tricks, and shortcuts. Version 5.4.

OPERATING SYSTEMS

The ABC's of DOS 4
Alan R. Miller
275pp. Ref. 583-2
This step-by-step introduction to using DOS 4 is written especially for beginners. Filled with simple examples, *The ABC's of DOS 4* covers the basics of hardware, software, disks, the system editor EDLIN, DOS commands, and more.

ABC's of MS-DOS
(Second Edition)
Alan R. Miller
233pp. Ref. 493-3
This handy guide to MS-DOS is all many PC users need to manage their computer files, organize floppy and hard disks, use EDLIN, and keep their computers organized. Additional information is given about utilities like Sidekick, and there is a DOS command and program summary. The second edition is fully updated for Version 3.3.

DOS Assembly Language Programming
Alan R. Miller
365pp. 487-9
This book covers PC-DOS through 3.3, and gives clear explanations of how to assemble, link, and debug 8086, 8088, 80286, and 80386 programs. The example assembly language routines are valuable for students and programmers alike.

DOS Instant Reference
SYBEX Prompter Series
Greg Harvey
Kay Yarborough Nelson
220pp. Ref. 477-1, 4 ¾" × 8"
A complete fingertip reference for fast, easy on-line help:command summaries, syntax, usage and error messages. Organized by function—system commands, file commands, disk management, directories, batch files, I/O, networking, programming, and more. Through Version 3.3.

DOS User's Desktop Companion
SYBEX Ready Reference Series
Judd Robbins
969pp. Ref. 505-0
This comprehensive reference covers DOS commands, batch files, memory enhancements, printing, communications and more information on optimizing each user's DOS environment. Written with step-by-step instructions and plenty of examples, this volume covers all versions through 3.3.

Encyclopedia DOS
Judd Robbins
1030pp. Ref. 699-5
A comprehensive reference and user's guide to all versions of DOS through 4.0. Offers complete information on every DOS command, with all possible switches and parameters -- plus examples of effective usage. An invaluable tool.

Essential OS/2
(Second Edition)
Judd Robbins
445pp. Ref. 609-X
Written by an OS/2 expert, this is the guide to the powerful new resources of the OS/2 operating system standard edition 1.1 with presentation manager. Robbins introduces the standard edition, and details multitasking under OS/2, and the range of commands for installing, starting up, configuring, and running applications. For Version 1.1 Standard Edition.

Essential PC-DOS
(Second Edition)
Myril Clement Shaw
Susan Soltis Shaw
332pp. Ref. 413-5
An authoritative guide to PC-DOS, including version 3.2. Designed to make experts out of beginners, it explores everything from disk management to batch file programming. Includes an 85-page command summary. Through Version 3.2.

Graphics Programming Under Windows

Brian Myers
Chris Doner
646pp. Ref. 448-8

Straightforward discussion, abundant examples, and a concise reference guide to graphics commands make this book a must for Windows programmers. Topics range from how Windows works to programming for business, animation, CAD, and desktop publishing. For Version 2.

Hard Disk Instant Reference SYBEX Prompter Series

Judd Robbins
256pp. Ref. 587-5, 4 ¾" × 8"

Compact yet comprehensive, this pocket-sized reference presents the essential information on DOS commands used in managing directories and files, and in optimizing disk configuration. Includes a survey of third-party utility capabilities. Through DOS 4.0.

The IBM PC-DOS Handbook (Third Edition)

Richard Allen King
359pp. Ref. 512-3

A guide to the inner workings of PC-DOS 3.2, for intermediate to advanced users and programmers of the IBM PC series. Topics include disk, screen and port control, batch files, networks, compatibility, and more. Through Version 3.3.

Inside DOS: A Programmer's Guide

Michael J. Young
490pp. Ref. 710-X

A collection of practical techniques (with source code listings) designed to help you take advantage of the rich resources intrinsic to MS-DOS machines. Designed for the experienced programmer with a basic understanding of C and 8086 assembly language, and DOS fundamentals.

Mastering DOS (Second Edition)

Judd Robbins
722pp. Ref. 555-7

"The most useful DOS book." This seven-part, in-depth tutorial addresses the needs of users at all levels. Topics range from running applications, to managing files and directories, configuring the system, batch file programming, and techniques for system developers. Through Version 4.

MS-DOS Advanced Programming

Michael J. Young
490pp. Ref. 578-6

Practical techniques for maximizing performance in MS-DOS software by making best use of system resources. Topics include functions, interrupts, devices, multitasking, memory residency and more, with examples in C and assembler. Through Version 3.3.

MS-DOS Handbook (Third Edition)

Richard Allen King
362pp. Ref. 492-5

This classic has been fully expanded and revised to include the latest features of MS-DOS Version 3.3. Two reference books in one, this title has separate sections for programmer and user. Multi-DOS partitons, 3 ½-inch disk format, batch file call and return feature, and comprehensive coverage of MS-DOS commands are included. Through Version 3.3.

MS-DOS Power User's Guide, Volume I (Second Edition)

Jonathan Kamin
482pp. Ref. 473-9

A fully revised, expanded edition of our best-selling guide to high-performance DOS techniques and utilities—with details on Version 3.3. Configuration, I/O, directory structures, hard disks, RAM disks, batch file programming, the ANSI.SYS device driver, more. Through Version 3.3.

Programmers Guide to the OS/2 Presentation Manager

Michael J. Young
683pp. Ref. 569-7

This is the definitive tutorial guide to writing programs for the OS/2 Presentation

Manager. Young starts with basic architecture, and explores every important feature including scroll bars, keyboard and mouse interface, menus and accelerators, dialogue boxes, clipboards, multitasking, and much more.

Programmer's Guide to Windows (Second Edition)
David Durant
Geta Carlson
Paul Yao
704pp. Ref. 496-8

The first edition of this programmer's guide was hailed as a classic. This new edition covers Windows 2 and Windows/386 in depth. Special emphasis is given to over fifty new routines to the Windows interface, and to preparation for OS/2 Presentation Manager compatibility.

Understanding DOS 3.3
Judd Robbins
678pp. Ref. 648-0

This best selling, in-depth tutorial addresses the needs of users at all levels with many examples and hands-on exercises. Robbins discusses the fundamentals of DOS, then covers manipulating files and directories, using the DOS editor, printing, communicating, and finishes with a full section on batch files.

Understanding Hard Disk Management on the PC
Jonathan Kamin
500pp. Ref. 561-1

This title is a key productivity tool for all hard disk users who want efficient, error-free file management and organization. Includes details on the best ways to conserve hard disk space when using several memory-guzzling programs. Through DOS 4.

Up & Running with Your Hard Disk
Klaus M Rubsam
140pp. Ref. 666-9

A far-sighted, compact introduction to hard disk installation and basic DOS use. Perfect for PC users who want the practical essentials in the shortest possible time.

In 20 basic steps, learn to choose your hard disk, work with accessories, back up data, use DOS utilities to save time, and more.

Up & Running with Windows 286/386
Gabriele Wentges
132pp. Ref. 691-X

This handy 20-step overview gives PC users all the essentials of using Windows - - whether for evaluating the software, or getting a fast start. Each self-contained lesson takes just 15 minutes to one hour to complete.

DATABASES

The ABC's of dBASE III PLUS
Robert Cowart
264pp. Ref. 379-1

The most efficient way to get beginners up and running with dBASE. Every 'how' and 'why' of database management is demonstrated through tutorials and practical dBASE III PLUS applications.

The ABC's of dBASE IV
Robert Cowart
338pp. Ref. 531-X

This superb tutorial introduces beginners to the concept of databases and practical dBASE IV applications featuring the new menu-driven interface, the new report writer, and Query by Example.

The ABC's of Paradox
Charles Siegel
300pp. Ref. 573-5

Easy to understand and use, this introduction is written so that the computer novice can create, edit, and manage complex Paradox databases. This primer is filled with examples of the Paradox 3.0 menu structure.

Advanced Techniques in dBASE III PLUS
Alan Simpson
454pp. Ref. 369-4

A full course in database design and

structured programming, with routines for inventory control, accounts receivable, system management, and integrated databases.

dBASE Instant Reference
SYBEX Prompter Series
Alan Simpson
471pp. Ref. 484-4; 4 3/4" × 8"
Comprehensive information at a glance: a brief explanation of syntax and usage for every dBASE command, with step-by-step instructions and exact keystroke sequences. Commands are grouped by function in twenty precise categories.

dBASE III PLUS Programmer's
Reference Guide
SYBEX Ready Reference Series
Alan Simpson
1056pp. Ref. 508-5
Programmers will save untold hours and effort using this comprehensive, well-organized dBASE encyclopedia. Complete technical details on commands and functions, plus scores of often-needed algorithms.

dBASE IV Programmer's
Instant Reference
SYBEX Prompter Series
Alan Simpson
544pp. Ref. 538-7, 4 3/4" × 8"
This comprehensive reference to every dBASE command and function has everything for the dBASE programmer in a compact, pocket-sized book. Fast and easy access to adding data, sorting, performing calculations, managing multiple databases, memory variables and arrays, windows and menus, networking, and much more. Version 1.1.

dBASE IV User's
Desktop Companion
SYBEX Ready Reference Series
Alan Simpson
950pp. Ref. 523-9
This easy-to-use reference provides an exhaustive resource guide to taking full advantage of the powerful non-programming features of the dBASE IV Control Center. This book discusses query by example, custom reports and data entry screens, macros, the application generator, and the dBASE command and programming language.

dBASE IV User's
Instant Reference
SYBEX Prompter Series
Alan Simpson
349pp. Ref. 605-7, 4 3/4" × 8"
This handy pocket-sized reference book gives every new dBASE IV user fast and easy access to any dBASE command. Arranged alphabetically and by function, each entry includes a description, exact syntax, an example, and special tips from Alan Simpson.

Mastering dBASE III PLUS:
A Structured Approach
Carl Townsend
342pp. Ref. 372-4
In-depth treatment of structured programming for custom dBASE solutions. An ideal study and reference guide for applications developers, new and experienced users with an interest in efficient programming.

Mastering dBASE IV
Programming
Carl Townsend
496pp. Ref. 540-9
This task-oriented book introduces structured dBASE IV programming and commands by setting up a general ledger system, an invoice system, and a quotation management system. The author carefully explores the unique character of dBASE IV based on his in-depth understanding of the program.

Mastering FoxPro
Charles Seigel
639pp. Ref. 671-5
This guide to the powerful FoxPro DBMS offers a tutorial on database basics, then enables the reader to master new skills and features as needed -- with many examples from business. An in-depth tutorial guides users through the development of a complete mailing list system.

Mastering Paradox
(Fourth Edition)
Alan Simpson

636pp. Ref. 612-X

Best selling author Alan Simpson simplifies all aspects of Paradox for the beginning to intermediate user. The book starts with database basics, covers multiple tables, graphics, custom applications with PAL, and the Personal Programmer. For Version 3.0.

Mastering Q & A
(Second Edition)
Greg Harvey

540pp. Ref. 452-6

This hands-on tutorial explores the Q & A Write, File, and Report modules, and the Intelligent Assistant. English-language command processor, macro creation, interfacing with other software, and more, using practical business examples.

Power User's Guide to R:BASE
Alan Simpson
Cheryl Currid
Craig Gillett

446pp. Ref. 354-6

Supercharge your R:BASE applications with this straightforward tutorial that covers system design, structured programming, managing multiple data tables, and more. Sample applications include ready-to-run mailing, inventory and accounts receivable systems. Through Version 2.11.

Quick Guide to dBASE:
The Visual Approach
David Kolodney

382pp. Ref. 596-4

This illustrated tutorial provides the beginner with a working knowledge of all the basic functions of dBASE IV. Images of each successive dBASE screen tell how to create and modify a database, add, edit, sort and select records, and print custom labels and reports.

Understanding dBASE III
Alan Simpson

300pp. Ref. 267-1

dBASE commands and concepts are illustrated throughout with practical, business oriented examples—for mailing list handling, accounts receivable, and inventory design. Contains scores of tips and techniques for maximizing efficiency and meeting special needs.

Understanding dBASE III PLUS
Alan Simpson

415pp. Ref. 349-X

A solid sourcebook of training and ongoing support. Everything from creating a first database to command file programming is presented in working examples, with tips and techniques you won't find anywhere else.

Understanding dBASE IV
(Special Edition)
Alan Simpson

880pp. Ref. 509-3

This Special Edition is the best introduction to dBASE IV, written by 1 million-reader-strong dBASE expert Alan Simpson. First it gives basic skills for creating and manipulating efficient databases. Then the author explains how to make reports, manage multiple databases, and build applications. Includes Fast Track speed notes.

SYBEX

TO JOIN THE SYBEX MAILING LIST OR ORDER BOOKS
PLEASE COMPLETE THIS FORM

NAME _____ COMPANY _____

STREET _____ CITY _____

STATE _____ ZIP _____

☐ PLEASE MAIL ME MORE INFORMATION ABOUT **SYBEX** TITLES

ORDER FORM (There is no obligation to order)

PLEASE SEND ME THE FOLLOWING:

TITLE	QTY	PRICE
_____	____	____
_____	____	____
_____	____	____
_____	____	____

TOTAL BOOK ORDER   ____ $____

SHIPPING AND HANDLING PLEASE ADD $2.00 PER BOOK VIA UPS   ____

FOR OVERSEAS SURFACE ADD $5.25 PER BOOK PLUS $4.40 REGISTRATION FEE   ____

FOR OVERSEAS AIRMAIL ADD $18.25 PER BOOK PLUS $4.40 REGISTRATION FEE   ____

CALIFORNIA RESIDENTS PLEASE ADD APPLICABLE SALES TAX   ____ __

TOTAL AMOUNT PAYABLE   ____

☐ CHECK ENCLOSED   ☐ VISA
☐ MASTERCARD   ☐ AMERICAN EXPRESS

ACCOUNT NUMBER _____

EXPIR. DATE _____ DAYTIME PHONE _____

CUSTOMER SIGNATURE _____

CHECK AREA OF COMPUTER INTEREST:

☐ BUSINESS SOFTWARE

☐ TECHNICAL PROGRAMMING

☐ OTHER: _____

THE FACTOR THAT WAS MOST IMPORTANT IN YOUR SELECTION:

☐ THE SYBEX NAME

☐ QUALITY

☐ PRICE

☐ EXTRA FEATURES

☐ COMPREHENSIVENESS

☐ CLEAR WRITING

☐ OTHER _____

OTHER COMPUTER TITLES YOU WOULD LIKE TO SEE IN PRINT:

_____

_____

OCCUPATION

☐ PROGRAMMER   ☐ TEACHER

☐ SENIOR EXECUTIVE   ☐ HOMEMAKER

☐ COMPUTER CONSULTANT   ☐ RETIRED

☐ SUPERVISOR   ☐ STUDENT

☐ MIDDLE MANAGEMENT   ☐ OTHER:

☐ ENGINEER/TECHNICAL   _____

☐ CLERICAL/SERVICE

☐ BUSINESS OWNER/SELF EMPLOYED

CHECK YOUR LEVEL OF COMPUTER USE

☐ NEW TO COMPUTERS

☐ INFREQUENT COMPUTER USER

☐ FREQUENT USER OF ONE SOFTWARE

   PACKAGE:

   NAME _____

☐ FREQUENT USER OF MANY SOFTWARE

   PACKAGES

☐ PROFESSIONAL PROGRAMMER

OTHER COMMENTS:

_____

_____

_____

_____

_____

_____

_____

PLEASE FOLD, SEAL, AND MAIL TO SYBEX

– –

SYBEX, INC.
2021 CHALLENGER DR. #100
ALAMEDA, CALIFORNIA USA
94501

SYBEX

SEAL

AutoCAD's Entity Association Sublists (Release 11)

(ENTITIES IN THE UNDERLYING DATABASE)

ADDITIONAL GROUP CODES FOR INDIVIDUAL ENTITY SUBLISTS ARE AS FOLLOWS:

42 . Bulge (if curve-fit)	1000 . Viewport Data Indicator String ("MVIEW" in Release 11)	1070 . Snap Mode Flag (0 = off, 1 = on)
50 . Tangent (if curve-fit)	1001 . Application Name ("ACAD")	1070 . Grid Mode (0 = off, 1 = on)
70 . Vertex Flag (1 = vertex by curve-fit, 2 = curve-fit tangent, 8 = spline vertex, 16 = spline frame control point, 32 = 3D polyline vertex, 64 = 3D polygon mesh vertex, 128 = polyface mesh vertex)	1002 . Start Viewport Data Control String "{"	1070 . Snap Style Flag (0 = standard, 1 = isometric)
	1070 . Version Number ("16" in Release 11)	1070 . Snap Isoplane Flag (0 = left, 1 = top, 2 = right)
	1010 . View Target Point	1040 . Snap Rotation Angle (in radians)
71 . Polyface Mesh Vertex Number (first face)	1011 . View Direction Vector	1040 . Snap Origin Point X Coordinate
	1040 . View Twist Angle	1040 . Snap Origin Point Y Coordinate
72 . Polyface Mesh Vertex Number (second face)	1040 . View Center X Coordinate	1040 . Snap spacing X Coordinate
	1040 . View Center Y Coordinate	1040 . Snap spacing Y Coordinate
73 . Polyface Mesh Vertex Number (third face)	1040 . Lens Length	1040 . Grid spacing X Coordinate
	1040 . Front Clipping Plane (Z-offset from center)	1040 . Grid spacing Y Coordinate
74 . Polyface Mesh Vertex Number (fourth face)	1040 . Back Clipping Plane (Z-offset from center)	1070 . Plot Flag (0 = plot, 1 = Hide in plot)
0 . "VIEWPORT"	1070 . Mode Bit-Code Flag (1 = perspective On, 2 = front clip on, 4 = back clip on, 8 = UCS follow code 1, 16 = front plane not at eye.)	1002 . Start Frozen Layer List Control String ("{")
10 . Center point (in paper space)		1003 . Frozen Layer Name (may repeat for additional layers)
40 . Width (in paper space units)		
41 . Height (in paper space units)		1002 . End Frozen Layer List Control String ("}")
68 . Viewport Status Code (−1 = not active because MAXACTVP value is exceeded, or else off-screen; 0 = off; 1 = active; 2 & Up = not active but visible)	1070 . Circle Zoom Percent	1002 . End Viewport Data Control String ("}")
	1070 . Fast Zoom Mode Flag (0 = off, 1 = on)	
	1070 . UCS Icon Bit-Code Flag (0 = off, 1 = on, 2 = origin)	
69 . Viewport ID Number		

AutoCAD's Symbol Table Sublists

(READ-ONLY)

0 . "APPID"	2 . STYLENAME (Includes settings for some or all of the following:)	46 . DIMDLE
2 . Registered Application Name		47 . DIMTP
0 . "BLOCK"		48 . DIMTM
−2 . Starting Entity Name	3 . DIMPOST	71 . DIMTOL
1 . Xref path name	4 . DIMAPOST	72 . DIMLIM
2 . Block Name	5 . DIMBLK	73 . DIMTIH
10 . Insertion Point	6 . DIMBLK1	74 . DIMTOH
70 . Block Type Flag (1 = pseudo-block, 2 = attributes present, 4 = Xref block, 16 = external dependencies exist, 32 = dependent of external reference, 64 = referenced in drawing)	7 . DIMBLK2	75 . DIMSE1
	40 . DIMSCALE	76 . DIMSE2
	41 . DIMASZ	77 . DIMTAD
	42 . DIMEXO	78 . DIMZIN
	43 . DIMDLI	140 . DIMTXT
	44 . DIMEXE	141 . DIMCEN
	45 . DIMRND	142 . DIMTSZ